The NEW STRONG'S
GUIDE TO
BIBLE WORDS

An English Index to
Hebrew and Greek Words

KEYED TO STRONG'S
NUMBERING SYSTEM

JAMES STRONG, LL.D., S.T.D.

THOMAS NELSON PUBLISHERS
Nashville • Atlanta • London • Vancouver

Published in Nashville, Tennessee, by Thomas Nelson, Inc. Distributed in Canada by Nelson/Word Inc.

The publisher wishes to acknowledge the editorial and composition services of John R. Kohlenberger III and Multnomah Graphics.

Library of Congress Cataloging-in-Publication Data

Strong, James, 1822–1894.
    The new Strong's guide to Bible words / James Strong.
      p. cm.
    ISBN 0-7852-1197-7
    1. Bible—Concordances, English. 2. Hebrew language—Dictionaries—English. 3. Aramaic language—Dictionaries—English. 4. Greek language, Biblical—Dictionaries—English. 5. Bible. O.T.—Dictionaries—Hebrew. 6. Bible. O.T.—Dictionaries—Aramaic. 7. Bible. N.T.—Dictionaries—Greek. I. Strong, James, 1822–1894. New exhaustive concordance of the Bible. II. Strong, James, 1822–1894. New Strong's complete dictionary of Bible words. III. Strong, James, 1822–1894. New Strong's Hebrew and Aramaic dictionary. IV. Strong, James, 1822–1894. New Strong's Greek dictionary. V. Title.
BS425.S85 1997
220.5′2033—dc20
                                                  96–36197
                                                      CIP

Printed in the United States of America
1 2 3 4 5 6 7 8 9 10 — 01 00 99 98 97 96

How to Use the English Index to Hebrew and Greek Words

What the Index Is

The English Index to Hebrew and Greek words contains every major word in the *KJV* with a list of every Hebrew, Aramaic, and Greek word that each English word translates. Words that are omitted from this list include words that appear in the Appendix of Articles in the original *Strong's Exhaustive Concordance* (such as "a," "and," and "the") and words that do not directly translate a Hebrew, Aramaic, or Greek word (such as "aileth," "letting," and "shouldest"). English words are listed in alphabetical order, exactly as they are spelled in the *KJV.*

Under each English entry is a listing of every Hebrew, Aramaic, and Greek word that the English word translates. These lists are organized in alphabetical order (which is also *Strong's* number order): Old Testament words first, then New Testament words. Each line has four elements: (1) *Strong's* number, (2) the original language word in transliteration, (3) the total number of times the word is so translated, and (4) a brief definition. (See the example on the following page.)

(1) If *Strong's* number is not italicized, it refers to an original word in the *Hebrew and Aramaic Dictionary.* If Strong's number and the transliterated word are ***italicized,*** it refers to an original word in the *Greek Dictionary.*

(2) Words are transliterated exactly as in the *Dictionaries.* If more than one Strong's number is listed on an entry line (**4672 + 1767** under "able," for example), in the interest of saving space, only the first word is transliterated. The additional word(s) are transliterated in the *Dictionaries.*

(3) The total number of occurrences is given to show patterns of *KJV* usage and in case you wish to study the original language words in the order of their frequency. For example, Greek word *25 (agapaō)* is translated "love" 70 times in the *KJV* and may be a more significant or interesting word than *2309 (thelō)*, which is translated as "love" only once.

(4) The brief definition summarizes *Strong's* fuller dictionary entries. These definitions actually function as a dictionary to the vocabulary of the *KJV*, informing you that a "habergeon" is a "coat of mail" or that "unction" is a "special endowment of the Holy Spirit." Sometimes these definitions update the scholarship of the *KJV*, as in the case of "unicorn," which is defined as "wild bull." As is the case of the occurrences statistics, the definition may also point out a key Hebrew, Aramaic, or Greek word that you may want to study in more detail by referring to the *Dictionaries.*

Using the Index with *The New Strong's™ Exhaustive Concordance*

The English Index provides a quick and easily used summary of the hundreds of thousands of contexts in *The New Strong's™ Exhaustive Concordance*, while the *Concordance* lists every context for every word of the *KJV*. This allows you to study the use of the word in the Bible itself, which is the most important way to understand how a specific word is used in a specific context. Although *Strong's Hebrew and Aramaic* and *Greek Dictionaries* offer definitions for each word of the original languages, these words do not have the sum total of every definition in every context. Greek word *26 (agapē)*, for example, cannot mean "affection" *and* "love-feast" every time it occurs. It means "affection" in such contexts as Philemon 7 and "love-feast" in Jude 12. Similarly, the historical or etymological materials that *Strong's Dictionaries* often present at the beginning of an entry may show something of the origin of a word, but are not necessarily its *definition* in every biblical context. For example, when Greek word *314 (anaginōskō)* is used in the New Testament, it means "to read," rather than "to know again," as *Strong's Dictionary* describes its origin.

Because the Index lists every Hebrew, Aramaic, and Greek word that is translated by any English word of the *KJV,* it functions as a concise dictionary and thesaurus of the biblical languages. Quickly scanning the entry for the word "love" shows that the word is used of general positive affection, deep compassion, fraternal affection, love for husbands, love for children, and greedy love of money. Reading the appropriate *Dictionary* entries will enlarge on these definitions. Again, if a *Strong's* number is not italicized (e.g., **157**), consult the *Hebrew and Aramaic Dictionary.* If a *Strong's* number is italicized (e.g., *26*), consult the *Greek Dictionary.* Each entry in the *Dictionaries* also provides a complete list of *KJV* words that translate the original language word, following the :— symbol. Greek word *26 (agapē)*, for example, lists four English words: charitably, charity, dear, and love. This shows the range of meaning the *KJV* translators assigned to *agapē.* By returning to the Index and looking up each of these English words, you find even more original language words to study.

In short, the wealth of materials contained in *The New Strong's™ Guide to Bible Words* is truly maximized in conjunction with *The New Strong's™ Exhaustive Concordance* when carefully applied to the study of God's Word.

An Example
from the English Index

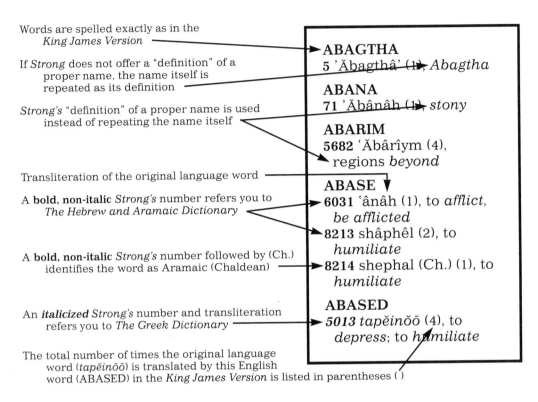

Words are spelled exactly as in the *King James Version*

ABAGTHA
5 'Ăbagthâ' (1), *Abagtha*

If *Strong* does not offer a "definition" of a proper name, the name itself is repeated as its definition

ABANA
71 'Ăbânâh (1), *stony*

Strong's "definition" of a proper name is used instead of repeating the name itself

ABARIM
5682 'Ăbârîym (4), regions *beyond*

Transliteration of the original language word

ABASE
A **bold, non-italic** Strong's number refers you to *The Hebrew and Aramaic Dictionary*

6031 'ânâh (1), to *afflict, be afflicted*
8213 shâphêl (2), to *humiliate*

A **bold, non-italic** Strong's number followed by (Ch.) identifies the word as Aramaic (Chaldean)

8214 shephal (Ch.) (1), to *humiliate*

ABASED
An *italicized* Strong's number and transliteration refers you to *The Greek Dictionary*

5013 tapĕinŏō (4), to *depress*; to *humiliate*

The total number of times the original language word (*tapĕinŏō*) is translated by this English word (ABASED) in the *King James Version* is listed in parentheses ( )

Words Omitted from the English Index

a
about
agone
ailed
aileth
also
am
amounting
an
and
apace
appertained
appertaineth
are
art
as
battering
be
became
becamest
become
becometh
been
belongest
belonging
bestead
busied
but
by
caring
cases
causest
causing
closer

coloured
condition
counting
cunningly
dealer
dealers
dealing
deals
dearly
deputed
description
deserve
deserveth
determine
direction
dost
doth
drewest
duties
easily
ed
employment
entreateth
estates
exploits
extendeth
folks
for
from
guiding
guilt
hadst
he
her

hers
herself
him
himself
his
hurling
I
in
into
infallible
inflicted
its
itself
is
it
karnaim
letting
liers
lign
masteries
me
meanest
mightest
mine
mixt
my
myself
no
none
nor
not
O
of
on

one's
onward
or
our
ours
ourselves
out
parties
pertain
playedst
playeth
practices
provokedst
purposing
quantity
ragged
rests
rovers
sap
seatward
self
selfsame
selves
shall
shalt
she
so
soever
shouldest
slave
soundeth
strongly
such
suits

sunder
surely
taker
tapestry
tend
tendeth
than
that
the
thee
thee-ward
their
theirs
them
themselves
then
thence
thenceforth
therefrom
these
they
thine
things'
this
those
thou
though
thus
thy
thyself
titles
to
too
toward

unperfect
unweighed
unto
up
upon
us
venomous
was
waxen
we
weighing
were
what
whatsoever
which
who
whom
whom
whomsoever
whose
whoso
whosoever
with
witty
ye
you
your
yours
yourselves
you-ward

ENGLISH INDEX TO THE BIBLICAL LANGUAGES

AARON
175 'Ahărôwn (315),
Aharon
2 Aarōn (4), Aaron

AARON'S
175 'Ahărôwn (30),
Aharon
2 Aarōn (1), Aaron

AARONITES
175 'Ahărôwn (2),
Aharon

ABADDON
3 Abaddōn (1),
destroying angel

ABAGTHA
5 'Ăbagthâ' (1), Abagtha

ABANA
71 'Ăbânâh (1), stony

ABARIM
5682 'Ăbârîym (4),
regions beyond

ABASE
6031 'ânâh (1), to afflict,
be afflicted
8213 shâphêl (2), to
humiliate
8214 shephal (Ch.) (1), to
humiliate

ABASED
5013 tapĕinŏō (4), to
depress; to humiliate

ABASING
5013 tapĕinŏō (1), to
depress; to humiliate

ABATED
1639 gâra' (1), to
remove, lessen,
withhold
2637 châçêr (1), to lack;
to fail, want, make less
5127 nûwç (1), to vanish
away, flee
7043 qâlal (2), to be,
make light
7503 râphâh (1), to
slacken

ABBA
5 Abba (3), father

ABDA
5653 'Abdâ' (2), work

ABDEEL
5655 'Abde'êl (1), serving
God

ABDI
5660 'Abdîy (3),
serviceable

ABDIEL
5661 'Abdîy'êl (1),
servant of God

ABDON
5658 'Abdôwn (8),
servitude

ABED-NEGO
5664 'Ăbêd Negôw (1),
servant of -Nego
5665 'Ăbêd Negôw' (Ch.)
(14), servant of -Nego

ABEL
59 'Âbêl (2), meadow

62 'Âbêl Bêyth-Mă'akâh
(2), meadow of
Beth-Maakah
1893 Hebel (8),
emptiness or vanity
6 Abĕl (4), emptiness or
vanity

ABEL-BETH-MAACHAH
62 'Âbêl Bêyth-Mă'akâh
(2), meadow of
Beth-Maakah

ABEL-MAIM
66 'Âbêl Mayim (1),
meadow of water

ABEL-MEHOLAH
65 'Âbêl Mechôwlâh (3),
meadow of dancing

ABEL-MIZRAIM
67 'Âbêl Mitsrayim (1),
meadow of Egypt

ABEL-SHITTIM
63 'Âbêl hash-Shiṭṭîym
(1), meadow of the
acacias

ABEZ
77 'Ebets (1), Ebets

ABHOR
887 bâ'ash (1), to be a
moral stench
1602 gâ'al (4), to detest;
to reject; to fail
2194 zâ'am (1), to be
enraged
3988 mâ'aç (1), to spurn;
to disappear
5006 nâ'ats (1), to scorn
8374 tâ'ab (1), to loathe
8581 tâ'ab (9), to loathe,
i.e. detest
655 apŏstugĕō (1), to
detest utterly, hate

ABHORRED
887 bâ'ash (2), to be a
moral stench
973 bâchal (1), to loathe,
detest
1602 gâ'al (1), to detest;
to reject; to fail
2194 zâ'am (1), to be
enraged
3988 mâ'aç (2), to spurn;
to disappear
5006 nâ'ats (2), to scorn
5010 nâ'ar (1), to reject
6973 qûwts (2), to be,
make disgusted
8262 shâqats (1), to
loathe, pollute
8581 tâ'ab (3), to loathe,
i.e. detest

ABHORREST
6973 qûwts (1), to be,
make disgusted
948 bdĕlussō (1), to
detest, abhor

ABHORRETH
2092 zâham (1), to
loathe, make loatheful
3988 mâ'aç (1), to spurn;
to disappear
5006 nâ'ats (1), to scorn

8581 tâ'ab (2), to loathe,
i.e. detest

ABHORRING
1860 derâ'ôwn (1),
aversion, loathing

ABI
21 'Ăbîy (1), fatherly

ABI-ALBON
45 'Ăbîy-'albôwn (1),
valiant, strong

ABI-EZER
44 'Ăbîy'ezer (2), helpful

ABI-EZRITE
33 'Abîy hâ-'Ezrîy (1),
father of the Ezrite

ABI-EZRITES
33 'Abîy hâ-'Ezrîy (2),
father of the Ezrite

ABIA
29 'Ăbîyâh (1),
worshipper of Jehovah
7 Abia (3), knowing

ABIAH
29 'Ăbîyâh (4),
worshipper of Jehovah

ABIASAPH
23 'Ăbîy'âçâph (1),
gatherer

ABIATHAR
54 'Ebyâthâr (29),
· abundant, liberal
8 Abiathar (1),
abundant, liberal

ABIATHAR'S
54 'Ebyâthâr (1),
abundant, liberal

ABIB
24 'âbîyb (6), head of
grain; month of Abib

ABIDA
28 'Ăbîydâ' (1), knowing

ABIDAH
28 'Ăbîydâ' (1), knowing

ABIDAN
27 'Ăbîydân (5), judge

ABIDE
935 bôw' (1), to go or
come
1481 gûwr (2), to sojourn,
live as an alien
1692 dâbaq (1), to cling
or adhere
2342 chûwl (1), to wait
2583 chânâh (1), to
encamp for abode
3427 yâshab (31), to
dwell, remain; to settle
3557 kûwl (3), to keep in;
to maintain
3867 lâvâh (1), to unite;
to remain
3885 lûwn (5), to be
obstinate
5975 'âmad (2), to stand
6965 qûwm (1), to rise
7937 shâkar (1), to
become tipsy, to satiate
1961 ĕpimĕnō (3), to
remain; to persevere

3306 mĕnō (27), to stay,
remain
3887 paramĕnō (1), to be
permanent, persevere
4357 prŏsmĕnō (1), to
remain; to adhere to

ABIDETH
935 bôw' (1), to go or
come
3427 yâshab (4), to dwell,
to remain; to settle
3885 lûwn (3), to be
obstinate
5975 'âmad (2), to stand
3306 mĕnō (20), to stay,
remain

ABIDING
3427 yâshab (2), to dwell,
to remain; to settle
4723 miqveh (1),
confidence; collection
5596 çâphach (1), to
associate; be united
7931 shâkan (1), to reside
63 agraulĕō (1), to camp
out, live outdoors
1304 diatribō (1), to
remain, stay
3306 mĕnō (2), to stay,
remain

ABIEL
22 'Ăbîy'êl (3), possessor
of God

ABIEZER
44 'Ăbîy'ezer (5), helpful

ABIGAIL
26 'Ăbîygayil (17), source
of joy

ABIHAIL
32 'Ăbîyhayil (6),
possessor of might

ABIHU
30 'Ăbîyhûw' (12),
worshipper of Him

ABIHUD
31 'Ăbîyhûwd (1),
possessor of renown

ABIJAH
29 'Ăbîyâh (20),
worshipper of Jehovah

ABIJAM
38 'Ăbîyâm (5), seaman

ABILENE
9 Abilēnē (1), Abilene

ABILITY
1767 day (1), enough,
sufficient
3581 kôach (2), force,
might; strength
5381 nâsag (1), to reach
1411 dunamis (1), force,
power, miracle
2141 ĕupŏrĕō (1), to have
means, have ability
2479 ischus (1),
forcefulness, power

ABIMAEL
39 'Ăbîymâ'êl (2), father
of Mael

ABIMELECH
40 'Ăbîymelek (65),
father of the king

ABIMELECH'S
40 'Ăbîymelek (2), father
of the king

ABINADAB
41 'Ăbîynâdâb (13),
generous, i.e. liberal

ABINOAM
42 'Ăbîynô'am (4),
gracious

ABIRAM
48 'Ăbîyrâm (11), lofty,
high

ABISHAG
49 'Ăbîyshag (5),
blundering

ABISHAI
52 'Ăbîyshay (25), (poss.)
generous

ABISHALOM
53 'Ăbîyshâlôwm (2),
friendly

ABISHUA
50 'Ăbîyshûwa' (5),
prosperous

ABISHUR
51 'Ăbîyshûwr (2), (poss.)
mason

ABITAL
37 'Ăbîyṭal (2), fresh

ABITUB
36 'Ăbîyṭûwb (1), good

ABIUD
10 Abioŭd (2), possessor
of renown

ABJECTS
5222 nêkeh (1), smiter;
attacker

ABLE
2296 châgar (1), to gird
on a belt; put on armor
2428 chayil (4), army;
wealth; virtue; strength
3201 yâkôl (44), to be able
3202 yᵉkêl (Ch.) (4), to be
able
3318 yâtsâ' (15), to go,
bring out
3320 yâtsab (3), to
station, offer, continue
3546 kᵉhal (Ch.) (2), to be
able
3581 kôach (1), force,
might; strength
4672+1767 mâtsâ' (2), to
find or acquire
4979+3027 mâttânâh (1),
present; offering; bribe
4991+3027 mattâth (2),
present
5060+1767 nâga' (1), to
strike
5375 nâsâ' (2), to lift up
5381 nâsag (6), to reach
5975 'âmad (1), to stand
6113 'âtsar (1), to hold
back; to maintain
6113+3581 'âtsar (2), to
hold back; to maintain
7272 regel (1), foot; step
1410 dunamai (41), to be
able or possible

1415 dunatŏs (10),
powerful or capable
1840 ĕxischuŏ (1), to be
entirely competent
2192 ĕchō (1), to have;
hold; keep
2425 hikanŏs (1), ample;
fit
2427 hikanŏō (1), to
make competent
2480 ischuō (6), to have
or exercise force

ABNER
74 'Abnêr (62),
enlightening

ABNER'S
74 'Abnêr (1),
enlightening

ABOARD
1910 ĕpibainō (1), to
mount, embark, arrive

ABODE
1961 hâyâh (2), to exist,
i.e. be or become
2583 chânâh (3), to
encamp
3427 yâshab (33), to
dwell, remain; to settle
5975 'âmad (1), to stand
7931 shâkan (6), to reside
390 anastrĕphō (1), to
remain, to live
835 aulizŏmai (1), to
pass the night
1304 diatribō (4), to
remain, stay
1961 ĕpimĕnō (1), to
remain; to persevere
2476 histēmi (1), to
stand, establish
2650 katamĕnō (1), to
reside, stay, live
3306 mĕnō (12), to stay,
remain
3438 mŏnē (1), residence,
dwelling place
4160 pŏiĕō (1), to make
or do
5278 hupŏmĕnō (1), to
undergo (trials)

ABODEST
3427 yâshab (1), to dwell,
to remain; to settle

ABOLISH
2498 châlaph (1), to
hasten away

ABOLISHED
2865 châthath (1), to
break down
4229 mâchâh (1), to erase
2673 katargĕō (3), to be,
render entirely useless

ABOMINABLE
2194 zâ'am (1), to be
enraged
6292 piggûwl (3),
unclean, fetid
8251 shiqqûwts (2),
disgusting idol
8262 shâqats (2), to
loathe, pollute
8263 sheqets (2), filthy
idolatrous object
8441 tôw'êbâh (4),
something disgusting
8581 tâ'ab (6), to loathe

111 athĕmitŏs (1),
illegal; detestable
947 bdĕluktŏs (1),
detestable, abominable
948 bdĕlussō (1), to
detest, abhor

ABOMINABLY
8581 tâ'ab (1), to loathe

ABOMINATION
887 bâ'ash (1), to be a
moral stench
6292 piggûwl (1),
unclean, fetid
8251 shiqqûwts (7),
disgusting idol
8262 shâqats (2), to
loathe, pollute
8263 sheqets (9), filthy
idolatrous object
8441 tôw'êbâh (52),
something disgusting
946 bdĕlugma (4),
detestable, abominable

ABOMINATIONS
8251 shiqqûwts (13),
disgusting idol
8441 tôw'êbâh (61),
something disgusting
946 bdĕlugma (2),
detestable, abominable

ABOUND
7227 rab (1), great
4052 pĕrissĕuō (12), to
superabound
4121 plĕŏnazō (4), to
superabound
4129 plēthunō (1), to
increase in numbers
5248 hupĕrpĕrissĕuō (1),
to superabound

ABOUNDED
4052 pĕrissĕuō (4), to
superabound
4121 plĕŏnazō (1), to
superabound

ABOUNDETH
7227 rab (1), great
4052 pĕrissĕuō (1), to
superabound
4121 plĕŏnazō (1), to
superabound

ABOUNDING
3513 kâbad (1), to be
rich, glorious
4052 pĕrissĕuō (2), to
superabound

ABOVE
4480 min (2), from, out of
4605 ma'al (55), upward,
above, overhead
4791 mârôwm (7),
elevation; elation
5921 'al (67), above, over,
upon, or against
5922 'al (Ch.) (1), above,
over, upon, or against
507 anō (5), upward or
on the top, heavenward
509 anōthĕn (5), from
above; from the first
511 anōtĕrŏs (1), upper
part; former part
1883 ĕpanō (2), over or on
1909 ĕpi (5), on, upon
3844 para (4), from; with;
besides; on account of

4012 pĕri (1), about;
around
4117 plĕgma (1), plait or
braid of hair
4253 prŏ (4), before in
time or space
5228 hupĕr (13), over;
above; beyond
5231 hupĕranō (2),
above, upward

ABRAHAM
85 'Abrâhâm (160),
father of a multitude
11 Abraam (68), father of
a multitude

ABRAHAM'S
85 'Abrâhâm (14), father
of a multitude
11 Abraam (5), father of
a multitude

ABRAM
87 'Abrâm (54), high
father

ABRAM'S
87 'Abrâm (7), high
father

ABROAD
1980 hâlak (1), to walk;
live a certain way
2351 chûwts (21),
outside, outdoors
3318 yâtsâ' (1), to go,
bring out
5074 nâdad (1), to rove,
flee; to drive away
5203 nâtash (1), to
disperse; to thrust off
5310 nâphats (1), to dash
to pieces; to scatter
6327 pûwts (4), to dash
in pieces; to disperse
6340 pâzar (1), to scatter
6504 pârad (1), to spread
6524 pârach (1), to break
forth; to bloom
6527 pâraṭ (5), to scatter
words, i.e. prate
6555 pârats (3), to break
out
6566 pâras (5), to break
apart, disperse, scatter
6581 pâsâh (3), to spread
6584 pâshaṭ (1), to strip
7350 râchôwq (1),
remote, far
7554 râqa' (2), to pound
7849 shâṭach (1), to
expand
864 aphiknĕŏmai (1), to
go forth by rumor
1096+5456 ginŏmai (1),
to be, become
1232 diagnōrizō (1), to
tell abroad
1255 dialalĕō (1), to
converse, discuss
1287 diaskŏrpizō (2), to
scatter; to squander
1289 diaspĕirō (3), to
scatter like seed
1290 diaspŏra (1),
dispersion
1310 diaphēmizō (2), to
spread news
1330 diĕrchŏmai (1), to
traverse, travel through

1519+1096 ĕis (1), *to or into*
1519+5318 ĕis (2), *to or into*
1632 ĕkchĕō (1), *to pour forth; to bestow*
1831 ĕxĕrchŏmai (4), *to issue; to leave*
4496 rhiptō (1), *to fling, toss; to lay out*
4650 skŏrpizō (2), *to dissipate, be liberal*

ABSALOM
53 'Ăbîyshâlôwm (102), *friendly*

ABSALOM'S
53 'Ăbîyshâlôwm (5), *friendly*

ABSENCE
666 apŏusia (1), *being away, absence*
817 atĕr (1), *apart from, without*

ABSENT
5641 çâthar (1), *to hide by covering*
548 apĕimi (7), *to be away, be absent*
553 apĕkdĕchŏmai (3), *to expect fully, await*

ABSTAIN
567 apĕchŏmai (6), *to hold oneself off*

ABSTINENCE
776 asitia (1), state of food *fasting*

ABUNDANCE
369+4557 'ayin (1), *there is no, none*
1995 hâmôwn (3), *noise, tumult; many, crowd*
2123 zîyz (1), *fulness of* the breast
3502 yithrâh (1), *wealth, abundance*
4342 makbîyr (1), *plenty*
6109 'otsmâh (1), *numerousness*
6283 'âthereth (1), *copiousness*
7227 rab (1), *great*
7230 rôb (35), *abundance*
7235 râbâh (2), *to increase*
7647 sâbâ' (1), *copiousness*
7962 shalvâh (1), *security, ease*
8228 shepha' (1), *abundance*
8229 shiph'âh (3), *copiousness*
8317 shârats (1), *to swarm, or abound*
100 hadrŏtēs (1), *liberality*
1411 dunamis (1), *force, power, miracle*
4050 pĕrissĕia (2), *superabundance*
4051 pĕrissĕuma (4), *superabundance*
4052 pĕrissĕuō (5), *to superabound*
5236 hupĕrbŏlē (1), *supereminence*

ABUNDANT
1419 gâdôwl (1), *great*
7227 rab (2), *great*
4052 pĕrissĕuō (2), *to superabound*
4055 pĕrissŏtĕrŏs (3), *more superabundant*
4056 pĕrissŏtĕrŏs (2), *more superabundantly*
4121 plĕŏnazō (1), o *superabound*
4183 pŏlus (1), *much*
5250 hupĕrplĕŏnazō (1), *to superabound*

ABUNDANTLY
1288 bârak (1), *to bless*
3381 yârad (1), *to descend*
5042 nâba' (1), *to gush* forth; *to utter*
6524 pârach (1), *to break* forth; *to flourish*
7227 rab (2), *great*
7230 rôb (4), *abundance*
7235 râbâh (1), *to increase*
7301 râvâh (2), *to slake* thirst or appetites
7937 shâkar (1), *to become tipsy; to satiate*
8317 shârats (6), *to swarm, or abound*
1519+4050 ĕis (1), *to or into*
1537+4053 ĕk (1), *out of*
4053 pĕrissŏs (1), *superabundant*
4054 pĕrissŏtĕrŏn (2), *superabundant way*
4056 pĕrissŏtĕrŏs (4), *more superabundantly*
4146 plŏusiōs (2), *copiously, abundantly*

ABUSE
5953 'âlal (2), *to glean; to* overdo
2710 katachraŏmai (1), *to overuse*

ABUSED
5953 'âlal (1), *to glean; to* overdo

ABUSERS
733 arsĕnŏkŏitēs (1), *sodomite*

ABUSING
2710 katachraŏmai (1), *to overuse*

ACCAD
390 'Akkad (1), *Accad*

ACCEPT
1878 dâshên (1), *to be* fat, thrive; *to satisfy*
3947 lâqach (1), *to take*
5375 nâsâ' (8), *to lift up*
7306 rûwach (1), *to smell* or *perceive*
7521 râtsâh (13), *to be pleased with; to satisfy*
588 apŏdĕchŏmai (1), *welcome* persons

ACCEPTABLE
977 bâchar (1), *select, chose, prefer*
2656 chêphets (1), *pleasure; desire*
7522 râtsôwn (9), *delight*

8232 sheᵉphar (Ch.) (1), *to* be beautiful
587 apŏdĕktŏs (2), *agreeable, pleasant*
1184 dĕktŏs (2), *approved, favorable*
2101 ĕuarĕstŏs (4), *fully agreeable, pleasing*
2144 ĕuprŏsdĕktŏs (2), *approved, favorable*
5285 hupŏpnĕō (1), *to breathe gently*

ACCEPTABLY
2102 ĕuarĕstōs (1), *quite agreeably*

ACCEPTANCE
7522 râtsôwn (1), *delight*

ACCEPTATION
594 apŏdŏchē (2), *acceptance, approval*

ACCEPTED
3190 yâṭab (2), *to be, make well*
5307 nâphal (2), *to fall*
5375 nâsâ' (3), *to lift up*
7521 râtsâh (7), *to be pleased with; to satisfy*
7522 râtsôwn (4), *delight*
7613 seᵉêth (1), *elevation;* swelling leprous scab
1184 dĕktŏs (3), *approved, favorable*
1209 dĕchŏmai (2), *to receive, welcome*
2101 ĕuarĕstŏs (1), *fully agreeable, pleasing*
2144 ĕuprŏsdĕktŏs (3), *approved, favorable*
5487 charitŏō (1), *one highly favored*

ACCEPTEST
2983 lambanō (1), *to take, receive*

ACCEPTETH
5375 nâsâ' (1), *to lift up*
7521 râtsâh (2), *to be pleased with; to satisfy*
2983 lambanō (1), *to take, receive*

ACCEPTING
4327 prŏsdĕchŏmai (1), *to receive; to await for*

ACCESS
4318 prŏsagōgē (3), *admission, access*

ACCHO
5910 'Akkôw (1), *to hem in*

ACCOMPANIED
2064+4862 ĕrchŏmai (1), *to go or come*
4311 prŏpĕmpō (1), *to escort or aid in travel*
4902 sunĕpŏmai (1), *to travel in company with*
4905 sunĕrchŏmai (1), *to go with*

ACCOMPANY
2192 ĕchō (1), *to have; hold; keep*

ACCOMPANYING
5973 'îm (1), *with*

ACCOMPLISH
3615 kâlâh (5), *to complete, prepare*

4390 mâlê' (1), *to fill*
6213 'âsâh (2), *to do or make*
6381 pâlâ' (1), *to be, make great, difficult*
6965 qûwm (1), *to rise*
7521 râtsâh (1), *to be pleased with; to satisfy*
8552 tâmam (1), *to complete, finish*
4137 plĕrŏō (1), *to fill, make complete*

ACCOMPLISHED
1961 hâyâh (1), *to exist,* i.e. be or become
3615 kâlâh (7), *to complete, prepare*
4390 mâlê' (6), *to fill*
8552 tâmam (1), *to complete, finish*
1822 ĕxartizō (1), *to finish out; to equip fully*
2005 ĕpitĕlĕō (1), *to terminate; to undergo*
4130 plēthō (4), *to fulfill, complete*
5055 tĕlĕō (4), *to end,* i.e. *complete, execute*

ACCOMPLISHING
2005 ĕpitĕlĕō (1), *to terminate; to undergo*

ACCOMPLISHMENT
1604 ĕkplērōsis (1), *completion, end*

ACCORD
5599 çâphîyach (1), *self-sown* crop; *freshet*
6310 peh (1), *mouth; opening*
830 authairĕtŏs (1), *self-chosen*
844 autŏmatŏs (1), *spontaneous, by itself*
3661 hŏmŏthumadŏn (11), *in togetherness*
4861 sumpsuchŏs (1), *united in spirit*

ACCORDING
413 'êl (2), *to, toward*
834 'âsher (1), *because, in order that*
1767 day (1), *enough, sufficient*
3605 kôl (1), *all, any*
3644 keᵉmôw (2), *like, as*
3651 kên (1), *just; right, correct*
4481 min (Ch.) (1), *from* or *out of*
5921 'al (39), *above, over, upon, or against*
6310 peh (21), *mouth; opening*
6903 qeᵉbêl (Ch.) (1), *on account of, so as, since*
7272 regel (1), *foot; step*
2526 kathŏ (2), *precisely as, in proportion as*
2530 kathŏti (1), *as far* or *inasmuch as*
2531 kathōs (5), *just* or *inasmuch as, that*
2596 kata (109), *down; according to*
4314 prŏs (3), *for; on, at; to, toward; against*
5613 hōs (2), *which, how*

ACCORDINGLY
5922 'al (Ch.) (1), *above, over, upon*, or *against*

ACCOUNT
2803 châshab (1), to *think, regard*; to *value*
2808 cheshbôwn (1), *contrivance; plan*
4557 miçpâr (1), *number*
6030 'ânâh (1), to *respond, answer*
6486 pᵉquddâh (1), *visitation; punishment*
1677 ĕllŏgĕō (1), to *charge to one's account*
2233 hēgĕŏmai (1), to *deem,* i.e. *consider*
3049 lŏgizŏmai (1), to *credit;* to *think, regard*
3056 lŏgŏs (8), *word, matter, thing; Word*

ACCOUNTED
2803 châshab (5), to *think, regard;* to *value*
5608 çâphar (1), to *enumerate;* to *recount*
1380 dŏkĕō (2), to *think, regard, seem* good
2661 kataxiŏō (2), to *deem entirely deserving*
3049 lŏgizŏmai (2), to *credit;* to *think, regard*

ACCOUNTING
3049 lŏgizŏmai (1), to *credit;* to *think, regard*

ACCOUNTS
2941 ṭa'am (Ch.) (1), *sentence, command*

ACCURSED
2763 charam (1), to *devote* to destruction
2764 chêrem (13), *doomed* object
7043 qâlal (1), to *be easy, trifling, vile*
7045 qᵉlâlâh (1), *vilification*
331 anathĕma (4), *excommunicated*

ACCUSATION
7855 siṭnâh (1), *opposition*
156 aitia (3), *logical reason; legal crime*
2724 katēgŏria (3), *legal criminal charge*
2920 krisis (2), *decision; tribunal; justice*
4811 sukŏphantĕō (1), to *exact unlawfully, extort*

ACCUSE
3960 lâshan (1), to *calumniate, malign*
1908 ĕpĕrĕazō (1), to *insult, slander*
2722 katĕchō (11), to *hold down fast*
2723 katēgŏrĕō (2), to *bring a charge*
4811 sukŏphantĕō (1), to *exact unlawfully, extort*

ACCUSED
399+7170 'ăkal (Ch.) (2), to *eat*
1225 diaballō (1), to *malign by accusation*

1458 ĕgkalĕō (4), to *charge, criminate*
1722+2724 ĕn (1), *in; during; because of*
2722 katĕchō (4), to *hold down fast*
2723 katēgŏrĕō (2), to *bring a charge*

ACCUSER
2723 katēgŏrĕō (1), to *bring a charge*

ACCUSERS
1228 diabŏlŏs (2), *traducer,* i.e. *Satan*
2723 katēgŏrĕō (6), to *bring a charge*

ACCUSETH
2723 katēgŏrĕō (1), to *bring a charge*

ACCUSING
2722 katĕchō (1), to *hold down fast*

ACCUSTOMED
3928 limmûwd (1), *instructed* one

ACELDAMA
184 Akeldama (1), *field of blood*

ACHAIA
882 Achaïa (11), *Greece*

ACHAICUS
883 Achaïkŏs (1), *Achaïan*

ACHAN
5912 'Âkân (6), *troublesome*

ACHAR
5917 'Âkâr (1), *troublesome*

ACHAZ
881 Achaz (2), *possessor*

ACHBOR
5907 'Akbôwr (7), *Akbor*

ACHIM
885 Achĕim (2), cf. *Jehovah will raise*

ACHISH
397 'Âkîysh (21), *Akish*

ACHMETHA
307 'Achmᵉthâ' (1), *Ecbatana*

ACHOR
5911 'Âlôwr (5), *troubled*

ACHSA
5915 'Akçâh (1), *anklet*

ACHSAH
5915 'Akçâh (2), *anklet*
5919 'akshûwb (2), *asp, coiling* serpent

ACHSHAPH
407 'Akshâph (3), *fascination*

ACHZIB
392 'Akzîyb (4), *deceitful*

ACKNOWLEDGE
3045 yâda' (5), to *know*
5234 nâkar (6), to *acknowledge*
1921 ĕpiginŏskō (4), to *acknowledge*

ACKNOWLEDGED
3045 yâda' (1), to *know*

5234 nâkar (1), to *acknowledge*
1922 ĕpignōsis (1), *acknowledgement*

ACKNOWLEDGEMENT
1922 ĕpignōsis (1), *acknowledgement*

ACKNOWLEDGING
1922 ĕpignōsis (3), *acknowledgement*

ACQUAINT
5532 çâkan (1), to *be familiar* with

ACQUAINTANCE
3045 yâda' (6), to *know*
4378 makkâr (2), *acquaintance*
1110 gnōstŏs (2), *well-known*
2398 idiŏs (1), *private* or *separate*

ACQUAINTED
3045 yâda' (1), to *know*
5532 çâkan (1), to *be familiar* with

ACQUAINTING
5090 nâhag (1), to *drive forth;* to *lead*

ACQUIT
5352 nâqâh (2), to *be, make clean*

ACRE
4618 ma'ănâh (1), *furrow, plow path*

ACRES
6776 tsemed (1), *acre* (i.e. a day's plowing)

ACT
5556 çol'âm (1), *destructive locust* kind
6467 pô'al (1), *act* or *work, deed*
1888 ĕpautŏphōrō̧ (1), *in actual crime*

ACTIONS
5949 'ălîylâh (1), *opportunity, action*

ACTIVITY
2428 chayil (1), *wealth; virtue; valor; strength*

ACTS
1697 dâbâr (51), *word; matter; thing*
4640 Ma'say (4), *operative*
5949 'ălîylâh (1), *opportunity, action*
6467 pô'al (2), *act* or *work, deed*

ADADAH
5735 'Ăd'ădâh (1), *festival*

ADAH
5711 'Âdâh (8), *ornament*

ADAIAH
5718 'Ădâyâh (9), *Jehovah has adorned*

ADALIA
118 'Ădalyâ' (1), *Adalja*

ADAM
120 'âdâm (14), *human being; mankind*
121 'Âdâm (8), *Adam*

76 Adam (8), *first man*

ADAM'S
76 Adam (1), *first man*

ADAMAH
128 'Ădâmâh (1), *soil; land*

ADAMANT
8068 shâmîyr (2), *thorn;* (poss.) *diamond*

ADAMI
129 'Ădâmîy (1), *earthy*

ADAR
143 'Ădâr (8), (poss.) *fire; Adar*
144 'Ădâr (Ch.) (1), (poss.) *fire; Adar*
146 'Addâr (1), *ample*

ADBEEL
110 'Adbᵉ'êl (2), *chastised of God*

ADD
3254 yâçaph (22), to *add* or *augment*
5414 nâthan (2), to *give*
5595 çâphâh (3), to *accumulate;* to *remove*
2007 ĕpitithēmi (2), to *impose*
2018 ĕpiphĕrō (1), to *inflict, bring upon*
2023 ĕpichŏrēgĕō (1), to *fully supply*
4369 prŏstithēmi (2), to *lay beside, annex*

ADDAN
135 'Addân (1), *firm*

ADDAR
146 'Addâr (1), *ample*

ADDED
3254 yâçaph (4), to *add* or *augment*
3255 yᵉçaph (Ch.) (1), to *add* or *augment*
4323 prŏsanatithēmi (1), to *add;* to *impart*
4369 prŏstithēmi (9), to *lay beside, annex, repeat*

ADDER
6620 pethen (2), *asp*
6848 tsepha' (1), *viper*
8207 shᵉphîyphôn (1), *cerastes* or *adder*

ADDERS'
5919 'akshûwb (1), *asp, coiling* serpent

ADDETH
3254 yâçaph (3), to *add* or *augment*
1928 ĕpidiatassŏmai (1), to *supplement*

ADDI
78 Addi (1), *finery*

ADDICTED
5021 tassō (1), to *arrange*

ADDITION
3914 lôyâh (1), *wreath*

ADDITIONS
3914 lôyâh (2), *wreath*

ADDON
114 'Addôwn (1), *powerful*

ADER
5738 'Eder (1), arrangement

ADIEL
5717 'Ădîy'êl (3), ornament of God

ADIN
5720 'Ādîyn (4), voluptuous

ADINA
5721 'Ădîynâ' (1), effeminacy

ADINO
5722 'ădîynôw (1), his spear

ADITHAIM
5723 'Ădîythayim (1), double prey

ADJURE
7650 shâba' (2), to swear
1844 ĕxŏrkizō (1), to charge under oath
3726 hŏrkizō (2), to solemnly enjoin

ADJURED
422 'âlâh (1), imprecate, utter a curse
7650 shâba' (1), to swear

ADLAI
5724 'Adlay (1), Adlai

ADMAH
126 'Admâh (5), earthy

ADMATHA
133 'Admâthâ' (1), Admatha

ADMINISTERED
1247 diakŏnĕō (2), to act as a deacon

ADMINISTRATION
1248 diakŏnia (1), attendance, aid, service

ADMINISTRATIONS
1248 diakŏnia (1), attendance, aid, service

ADMIRATION
2295 thauma (1), wonder, marvel
2296 thaumazō (1), to wonder; to admire

ADMIRED
2296 thaumazō (1), to wonder; to admire

ADMONISH
3560 nŏuthĕtĕō (3), to caution or reprove

ADMONISHED
2094 zâhar (2), to enlighten
5749 'ûwd (1), to protest, testify; to restore
3867 parainĕō (1), to recommend or advise
5537 chrēmatizō (1), to utter an oracle

ADMONISHING
3560 nŏuthĕtĕō (1), to caution or reprove

ADMONITION
3559 nŏuthĕsia (3), mild rebuke or warning

ADNA
5733 'Adnâ' (2), pleasure

ADNAH
5734 'Adnâh (2), pleasure

ADO
2350 thŏrubĕō (1), to disturb; clamor

ADONI-BEZEK
137 'Ădônîy-Bezeq (3), lord of Bezek

ADONI-ZEDEK
139 'Ădônîy-Tsedeq (2), lord of justice

ADONIJAH
138 'Ădônîyâh (25), worshipper of Jehovah

ADONIKAM
140 'Ădônîyqâm (3), high, lofty

ADONIRAM
141 'Ădônîyrâm (2), lord of height

ADOPTION
5206 huiŏthĕsia (5), adoption

ADORAIM
115 'Ădôwrayim (1), double mound

ADORAM
151 'Ădôrâm (2), Adoram

ADORN
2885 kŏsmĕō (2), to decorate; to snuff

ADORNED
5710 'âdâh (1), to remove; to bedeck
2885 kŏsmĕō (3), to decorate; to snuff

ADORNETH
5710 'âdâh (1), to remove; to bedeck

ADORNING
2889 kŏsmŏs (2), world

ADRAMMELECH
152 'Adrammelek (3), splendor of (the) king

ADRAMYTTIUM
98 Adramuttēnŏs (1), Adramyttene

ADRIA
99 Adrias (1), Adriatic Sea

ADRIEL
5741 'Adrîy'êl (2), flock of God

ADULLAM
5725 'Ădullâm (8), Adullam

ADULLAMITE
5726 'Ădullâmîy (3), Adullamite

ADULTERER
5003 nâ'aph (3), to commit adultery

ADULTERERS
5003 nâ'aph (5), to commit adultery
3432 mŏichŏs (4), male paramour

ADULTERESS
802+376 'ishshâh (1), woman, wife
5003 nâ'aph (2), to commit adultery

ADNAH
3428 mŏichalis (2), adulteress

ADULTERESSES
5003 nâ'aph (2), to commit adultery
3428 mŏichalis (1), adulteress

ADULTERIES
5004 nî'ûph (2), adultery
5005 na'ăphûwph (1), adultery
3430 mŏichĕia (2), adultery

ADULTEROUS
5003 nâ'aph (1), to commit adultery
3428 mŏichalis (3), adulteress

ADULTERY
5003 nâ'aph (17), to commit adultery
3428 mŏichalis (1), adulteress
3429 mŏichaō (6), to commit adultery
3430 mŏichĕia (2), adultery
3431 mŏichĕuō (14), to commit adultery

ADUMMIM
131 'Ădummîym (2), red spots

ADVANCED
1431 gâdal (1), to be great, make great
5375 nâsâ' (2), to lift up
6213 'âsâh (1), to do or make

ADVANTAGE
5532 çâkan (1), to be serviceable to
4053 pĕrissŏs (1), superabundant
4122 plĕŏnĕktĕō (1), to be covetous
5622 ŏphĕlĕia (1), value, advantage

ADVANTAGED
5623 ŏphĕlĕō (1), to benefit, be of use

ADVANTAGETH
3786 ŏphĕlŏs (1), accumulate or benefit

ADVENTURE
5254 nâçâh (1), to test, attempt
1325 didōmi (1), to give

ADVENTURED
7993 shâlak (1), to throw out, down or away

ADVERSARIES
6696 tsûwr (1), to cramp, i.e. confine; to harass
6862 tsar (21), trouble; opponent
6887 tsârar (2), to cramp
7378 rîyb (1), to hold a controversy; to defend
7853 sâtan (5), to attack by accusation
7854 sâtân (1), opponent
480 antikĕimai (4), be adverse to
5227 hupĕnantiŏs (1), opposed; opponent

ADVERSARY
376+7379 'îysh (1), man; male; someone
1166+4941 bâ'al (1), to be master; to marry
6862 tsar (6), trouble; opponent
6869 tsârâh (1), trouble; rival-wife
6887 tsârar (1), to cramp
7854 sâtân (6), opponent
476 antidikŏs (5), opponent
480 antikĕimai (1), be adverse to

ADVERSITIES
6869 tsârâh (1), trouble; rival-wife
7451 ra' (1), bad; evil

ADVERSITY
6761 tsela' (1), limping
6862 tsar (1), trouble; opponent
6869 tsârâh (4), trouble; rival-wife
7451 ra' (3), bad; evil
2558 kakŏuchĕō (1), to maltreat; to torment

ADVERTISE
1540+241 gâlâh (1), to denude; to reveal
3289 yâ'ats (1), to advise

ADVICE
1697 dâbâr (2), word; matter; thing
2940 ţa'am (1), intelligence; mandate
3289 yâ'ats (2), to advise
5779 'ûwts (1), to consult
6098 'êtsâh (1), advice; plan; prudence
8458 tachbûlâh (2), guidance; plan
1106 gnōmē (1), cognition, opinion

ADVISE
3045 yâda' (1), to know
3289 yâ'ats (1), to advise
7200 râ'âh (1), to see

ADVISED
3289 yâ'ats (1), to advise
1012+5087 bŏulē (1), purpose, plan, decision

ADVISEMENT
6098 'êtsâh (1), advice; plan; prudence

ADVOCATE
3875 paraklētŏs (1), intercessor, consoler

AENEAS
132 Ainĕas (2), (poss.) praise

AENON
137 Ainōn (1), springs

AFAR
4801 merchâq (3), distant place; from afar
7350 râchôwq (29), remote, far
7368 râchaq (1), to recede; remove
3112 makran (2), at a distance, far away
3113 makrŏthĕn (13), from a distance or afar

3467 muôpazô (1), to *see indistinctly, be myopic*
4207 pŏrrhôthĕn (2), *distantly, at a distance*

AFFAIRS
1697 dâbâr (2), *word; matter; thing*
5673 'ăbîydâh (Ch.) (2), *labor or business*
2596 kata (1), *down; according to*
4012 pĕri (2), *about; around*
4230 pragmatĕia (1), *transaction*

AFFECT
2206 zēlŏŏ (2), to *have warmth of feeling for*

AFFECTED
2206 zēlŏŏ (1), to *have warmth of feeling for*
2559 kakŏŏ (1), to *injure; to oppress; to embitter*

AFFECTETH
5953 'âlal (1), to *glean; to overdo*

AFFECTION
7521 râtsâh (1), to *be pleased with; to satisfy*
794 astörgŏs (2), *hard-hearted*
3806 pathŏs (1), *passion, concupiscence*
4698 splagchnŏn (1), *intestine; affection, pity*
5426 phrŏnĕŏ (1), to *be mentally disposed*

AFFECTIONATELY
2442 himĕirŏmai (1), to *long for, desire*

AFFECTIONED
5387 philŏstŏrgŏs (1), *lovingly devoted*

AFFECTIONS
3804 pathēma (1), *passion; suffering*
3806 pathŏs (1), *passion, concupiscence*

AFFINITY
2859 châthan (3), to *become related*

AFFIRM
1226 diabĕbaiŏŏmai (2), to *confirm thoroughly*
5346 phēmi (1), to *speak or say*

AFFIRMED
1340 diïschurizŏmai (2), to *asseverate*
5335 phaskō (1), to *assert a claim*

AFFLICT
3013 yâgâh (1), to *grieve; to torment*
3513 kâbad (1), to *be heavy, severe, dull*
3905 lâchats (1), to *press; to distress*
6031 'ânâh (28), to *afflict, be afflicted*
6887 tsârar (2), to *cramp*
7489 râ'a' (2), to *break to pieces*

AFFLICTED
1790 dak (1), *injured, oppressed*
3013 yâgâh (3), to *grieve; to torment*
4523 mâç (1), *disconsolate*
6031 'ânâh (21), to *afflict, be afflicted*
6040 'ŏnîy (1), *depression, i.e. misery*
6041 'ânîy (15), *depressed*
6862 tsar (1), *trouble; opponent*
6887 tsârar (2), to *cramp*
7043 qâlal (1), to *be easy, trifling, vile*
7489 râ'a' (3), to *break to pieces*
2346 thlibō (3), to *crowd, press, trouble*
2347 thlipsis (1), *pressure, trouble*
2553 kakŏpathĕō (1), to *undergo hardship*
5003 talaipōrĕō (1), to *be wretched*

AFFLICTEST
6031 'ânâh (1), to *afflict, be afflicted*

AFFLICTION
205 'âven (3), *trouble, vanity, wickedness*
3905 lâchats (3), to *press; to distress*
4157 mûw'âqâh (1), *pressure; distress*
6039 'ênûwth (1), *affliction*
6040 'ŏnîy (33), *depression, i.e. misery*
6862 tsar (3), *trouble; opponent*
6869 tsârâh (7), *trouble; rival-wife*
6887 tsârar (1), to *cramp*
7451 ra' (1), *bad; evil*
7667 sheber (2), *fracture; ruin*
2347 thlipsis (11), *pressure, trouble*
2552 kakŏpathĕia (1), *hardship, suffering*
2561 kakōsis (1), *maltreatment*
4797 sugchĕō (1), to *throw into disorder*

AFFLICTIONS
6031 'ânâh (1), to *afflict, be afflicted*
7451 ra' (1), *bad; evil*
2347 thlipsis (6), *pressure, trouble*
2553 kakŏpathĕō (1), to *undergo hardship*
3804 pathēma (3), *passion; suffering*
4777 sugkakŏpathĕō (1), to *suffer hardship*

AFFORDING
6329 pûwq (1), to *issue; to furnish; to secure*

AFFRIGHT
3372 yârê' (1), to *fear; to revere*

AFFRIGHTED
270+8178 'âchaz (1), to *seize, grasp; possess*
926 bâhal (1), to *tremble; be, make agitated*
1204 bâ'ath (1), to *fear*
2865 châthath (1), to *break down*
6206 'ârats (1), to *awe; to dread; to harass*
1568 ĕkthambĕō (2), to *astonish utterly*
1719 ĕmphŏbŏs (2), *alarmed, terrified*

AFOOT
3978 pĕzĕuō (1), to *travel by land, i.e. on foot*
3979 pĕzȩ̄ (1), *on foot*

AFORE
3808 lô' (1), *no, not*
6440 pânîym (2), *face; front*
6924 qedem (1), *before, anciently*
4270 prŏgraphō (1), to *write previously*
4279 prŏĕpaggĕllŏmai (1), to *promise from before*
4282 prŏĕtŏimazō (1), to *fit up in advance*

AFOREHAND
4301 prŏlambanō (1), to *take before*

AFORETIME
4481+6928+1836 min (Ch.) (1), *from or out of*
6440 pânîym (2), *face; front*
6924 qedem (1), *before, anciently*
7223 rî'shôwn (1), *first, in place, time or rank*
4218 pŏtĕ (1), *at some time, ever*
4270 prŏgraphō (1), to *write previously*

AFRAID
926 bâhal (3), to *tremble; be, make agitated; hasten, hurry anxiously*
1204 bâ'ath (10), to *fear*
1481 gûwr (6), to *sojourn, live as an alien*
1672 dâ'ag (3), *be anxious, be afraid*
1763 d°chal (Ch.) (1), to *fear; be formidable*
2119 zâchal (1), to *crawl; glide*
2296 châgar (1), to *gird on a belt; put on armor*
2342 chûwl (1), to *dance, whirl; to writhe*
2727 chârag (1), to *be dismayed, tremble*
2729 chârad (20), to *shudder with terror*
2730 chârêd (1), *fearful*
2865 châthath (6), to *break down, either by violence, or by fear*
3025 yâgôr (5), to *fear*
3372 yârê' (78), to *fear; to revere*
3373 yârê' (3), *fearing; reverent*

AFTER
167 'âhal (1), to *pitch a tent*
310 'achar (492), *after*
311 'achar (Ch.) (3), *after*
314 'achărôwn (5), *late or last; behind; western*
413 'êl (4), *to, toward*
834 'âsher (2), *because, in order that*
870 'âthar (Ch.) (3), *after*
1767 day (2), *enough, sufficient*
1863 dardar (1), *thorn*
3602 kâkâh (4), *just so*
4480 min (1), *from, out of*
4481 min (Ch.) (1), *from or out of*
5921 'al (18), *above, over, upon, or against*
6256 'êth (1), *time*
6310 peh (1), *mouth; opening*
7093 qêts (10), *extremity; after*
7097 qâtseh (1), *extremity*
7272 regel (4), *foot; step*
516 axiōs (1), *appropriately, suitable*
1207 dĕutĕrŏprōtŏs (1), *second-first*
1223 dia (3), *through, by means of; because of*
1230 diaginŏmai (1), to *have time elapse*
1377 diōkō (1), to *pursue; to persecute*
1534 ĕita (3), *then, moreover*
1567 ĕkzētĕō (2), to *seek out*
1722 ĕn (1), *in; during; because of*
1836 hĕxēs (1), *successive, next*
1872 ĕpakŏlŏuthĕō (1), to *accompany, follow*
1887 ĕpauriŏn (1), *to-morrow*
1894 ĕpĕidē (1), *when, whereas*
1899 ĕpĕita (3), *thereafter, afterward*
1905 ĕpĕrōtaō (1), to *inquire, seek*

1909 ĕpi (3), *on, upon*
1934 ĕpizētĕō (4), *to search (inquire) for*
1938 ĕpithumētēs (1), *craver*
1971 ĕpipŏthĕō (3), *intensely crave*
2089 ĕti (1), *yet, still*
2517 kathĕxēs (1), *in a sequence*
2569 kalŏpŏiĕō (3), *to do well*
2596 kata (58), *down; according to*
2614 katadiōkō (1), *to search for, look for*
2628 katakŏlŏuthĕō (2), *to accompany closely*
3195 mĕllō (2), *to intend,* i.e. *be about* to be
3326 mĕta (96), *with, among; after, later*
3693 ŏpisthĕn (2), *at the back; after*
3694 ŏpisō (22), *behind, after, following*
3753 hŏtĕ (3), *when; as*
3765 ŏukĕti (1), *not yet, no longer*
3779 hŏutō (2), *in this way; likewise*
4023 pĕriĕchō (1), *to clasp; to encircle*
4137 plērŏō (1), *to fill, make complete*
4329 prŏsdŏkia (1), *apprehension*
4459 pŏs (1), *in what way?; how?; how* much!
5225 huparchō (1), *to come into existence*
5613 hŏs (3), *which, how,* i.e. *in that manner*
5615 hōsautōs (1), *in the same way*
5618 hōspĕr (1), *exactly like*

AFTERNOON
5186+3117 nâţâh (1), *to stretch* or spread out

AFTERWARD
310 'achar (21), *after*
314 'achărôwn (2), *late* or *last; behind; western*
1208 dĕutĕrŏs (1), *second; secondly*
1534 ĕita (1), *then, moreover*
1899 ĕpeita (2), *thereafter, afterward*
2517 kathĕxēs (1), *in a sequence*
2547 kakĕithĕn (1), *from that place* (or *time*)
3347 mĕtĕpĕita (1), *thereafter*
5305 hustĕrŏn (7), *more lately,* i.e. *eventually*

AFTERWARDS
268 'âchôwr (1), *behind, backward; west*
310 'achar (5), *after*
310+3651 'achar (2), *after*
314 'achărôwn (1), *late* or *last; behind; western*
1899 ĕpeita (1), *thereafter, afterward*

5305 hustĕrŏn (1), *more lately,* i.e. *eventually*

AGABUS
13 Agabŏs (2), *locust*

AGAG
90 'Ăgag (8), *flame*

AGAGITE
91 'Ăgâgîy (5), *Agagite*

AGAIN
310 'achar (1), *after*
322 'ăchôranniyth (1), *by turning around*
1571 gam (2), *also; even*
1906 hêd (1), *shout of joy*
1946 hûwk* (Ch.) (1), *to go, come*
3138 yôwreh (2), *autumn rain* showers
3254 yâçaph (49), *to add* or *augment*
3284 ya'ănâh (1), *ostrich*
5437 çâbab (1), *to surround*
5750 'ôwd (51), *again; repeatedly; still; more*
7725 shûwb (246), *to turn back; to return*
7999 shâlam (3), *to reciprocate*
8138 shânâh (1), *to fold; to transmute*
8145 shênîy (7), *second; again*
8579 tinyânûwth* (Ch.) (1), *second time*
313 anagĕnnaō (2), *to beget or bear again*
321 anagō (2), *to lead up; to bring out*
326 anazaō (3), *to recover life, live again*
330 anathallō (1), *to flourish; to revive*
344 anakamptō (1), *to turn back, come back*
364 anamnēsis (1), *recollection*
375 anapĕmpō (2), *to send up or back*
386 anastasis (2), *resurrection* from death
450 anistēmi (15), *to come back to life*
456 anŏikŏdŏmĕō (2), *to rebuild*
467 antapŏdidōmi (2), *to requite* good or evil
470 antapŏkrinŏmai (1), *to contradict or dispute*
479 antikalĕō (1), *to reciprocate*
483 antilĕgō (1), *to dispute, refuse*
486 antilŏidŏrĕō (1), *to rail in reply, retaliate*
488 antimĕtrĕō (2), *to measure in return*
509 anōthĕn (2), *from the first; anew*
518 apaggĕllō (2), *to announce, proclaim*
523 apaitĕō (1), *to demand back*
560 apĕlpizō (1), *to fully expect* in return
591 apŏdidōmi (2), *to give away*

600 apŏkathistēmi (1), *to reconstitute*
618 apŏlambanō (1), *to receive; be repaid*
654 apŏstrĕphō (2), *to turn away or back*
1208 dĕutĕrŏs (3), *second; secondly*
1364 dis (2), *twice*
1453 ĕgĕirō (8), *to waken,* i.e. *rouse*
1458 ĕgkalĕō (1), *to charge*
1515 ĕirēnē (1), *peace; health; prosperity*
1880 ĕpanĕrchŏmai (1), *return home*
1994 ĕpistrĕphō (5), *to revert, turn back to*
3326 mĕta (1), *with, among; after, later*
3825 palin (141), *anew,* i.e. *back; once more*
4388 prŏtithĕmai (2), *to place before*
4762 strĕphō (2), *to turn around or reverse*
5290 hupŏstrĕphō (6), *to return*

AGAINST
413 'êl (144), *to, toward*
431 'ălûw* (Ch.) (1), *lo!*
834 'ăsher (1), *because, in order that*
4136 mûwl (19), *in front of, opposite*
4775 mârad (1), *to rebel*
5048 neged (33), *over against or before*
5227 nôkach (11), *opposite, in front of*
5704 'ad (3), *as far (long) as; during; while; until*
5921 'al (525), *above, over, upon,* or *against*
5922 'al* (Ch.) (7), *above, over, upon,* or *against*
5971 'am (1), *people; tribe; troops*
5973 'îm (35), *with*
5978 'immâd (1), *along with*
5980 'ummâh (26), *near, beside, along with*
6440 pânîym (11), *face; front*
6640 tsᵉbûw* (Ch.) (1), *affair; matter of determination*
6655 tsad* (Ch.) (1), *at or upon the side of; against*
6903 qᵉbêl* (Ch.) (1), *in front of, before*
6965 qûwm (1), *to rise*
7125 qîr'âh (41), *to encounter, to happen*
210 akŏn (1), *unwilling*
368 anantirrhētŏs (1), *indisputable*
470 antapŏkrinŏmai (1), *to contradict or dispute*
471 antĕpō (1), *to refute*
481 antikru (1), *opposite*
483 antilĕgō (5), *to dispute, refuse*
495 antipĕran (1), *on the opposite side*

497 antistratĕuŏmai (1), *to wage war against*
561 apĕnanti (2), *before or against*
1519 ĕis (24), *to or into*
1690 ĕmbrimaŏmai (1), *to blame, warn sternly*
1693 ĕmmainŏmai (1), *to rage at*
1715 ĕmprŏsthĕn (1), *in front of*
1722 ĕn (1), *in; during*
1727 ĕnantiŏs (1), *opposite*
1909 ĕpi (38), *on, upon*
2018 ĕpiphĕrō (1), *to inflict, bring upon*
2019 ĕpiphōnĕō (1), *to exclaim, shout*
2596 kata (59), *down; according to*
2620 katakauchaŏmai (2), *to exult against*
2649 katamarturĕō (1), *to testify against*
2691 katastrēniaō (1), *to be voluptuous against*
2702 kataphĕrō (1), *to bear down*
2713 katĕnanti (4), *directly opposite*
2729 katischuŏ (1), *to overpower, prevail*
3326 mĕta (4), *with, among; after, later*
3844 para (2), *from; with; besides; on account of*
4012 pĕri (2), *around*
4314 prŏs (23), *for; on, at; to, toward; against*
4366 prŏsrēgnumi (1), *to burst upon*
5396 phluarĕō (1), *to berate*

AGAR
28 Agar (2), *Hagar*

AGATE
3539 kadkôd (1), (poss.) *sparkling* ruby
7618 shᵉbûw (2), *agate*

AGATES
3539 kadkôd (1), (poss.) *sparkling* ruby

AGE
582 'ĕnôwsh (1), *man; person, human*
1121 bên (3), *son, descendant; people*
1755 dôwr (2), *dwelling*
2207 zôqen (1), *old age*
2209 ziqnâh (1), *old age*
2465 cheled (2), *fleeting* time; this *world*
3117 yôwm (6), *day; time period*
3485 Yissâ°kâr (1), *he will bring a reward*
3624 kelach (2), *maturity*
7869 sêyb (1), *old age*
7872 sêybâh (6), *old age*
2244 hēlikia (4), *maturity*
2250 hēmĕra (1), *day; period of time*
5046 tĕlĕiŏs (1), *complete; mature*
5230 hupĕrakmŏs (1), *past the prime* of youth

AGED
2204 zâqên (1), to *be old*
2205 zâqên (4), *old*
3453 yâshîysh (1), *old man*
4246 prĕsbutēs (2), *old man*
4247 prĕsbutis (1), *old woman*

AGEE
89 'Âgê' (1), *Agee*

AGES
165 aiōn (2), *perpetuity, ever; world*
1074 gĕnĕa (2), *generation; age*

AGO
3117 yôwm (1), *day; time period*
6928 qadmâh (Ch.) (1), *former time; formerly*
7350 râchôwq (3), *remote, far*
575 apŏ (4), *from, away*
3819 palai (2), *formerly; sometime since*
4253 prŏ (1), *before in time or space*

AGONY
74 agōnia (1), *anguish, anxiety*

AGREE
1526 ĕisi (1), they are
2132 ĕunŏĕŏ (1), to *reconcile*
2470 isŏs (1), *similar*
4160+3391+1106 pŏiĕō (1), to *make or do*
4856 sumphōnĕŏ (3), to *be harmonious*

AGREED
3259 yâ'ad (1), to *meet; to summon; to direct*
800 asumphōnŏs (1), *disagreeable*
2470 isŏs (1), *similar*
3982 pĕithō (1), to *pacify or conciliate*
4856 sumphōnĕŏ (2), to *be harmonious*
4934 suntithĕmai (2), to *consent, concur, agree*

AGREEMENT
2374 chôzeh (1), *beholder in vision*
2380 châzûwth (1), *revelation; compact*
4339 mêyshâr (1), *straightness; rectitude*
4783 sugkatathĕsis (1), *accord* with

AGREETH
3662 hŏmŏiazō (1), to *resemble, be like*
4856 sumphōnĕŏ (1), to *be harmonious*

AGRIPPA
67 Agrippas (12), *wild-horse* tamer

AGROUND
2027 ĕpŏkĕllō (1), to *beach* a ship vessel

AGUE
6920 qaddachath (1), *inflammation*

AGUR
94 'Âgûwr (1), *one received*

AH
162 'ăhâhh (8), *Oh!, Alas!, Woe!*
253 'âch (2), *Oh!; Alas!*
1945 hôwy (7), *oh!, woe!*
3758 ŏua (1), *ah!; so!*

AHA
253 'âch (7), *Oh!; Alas!*

AHAB
256 'Ach'âb (90), *friend of* (his) *father*

AHAB'S
256 'Ach'âb (2), *friend of* (his) *father*

AHARAH
315 'Acharach (1), *after* (his) *brother*

AHARHEL
316 'Ăcharchêl (1), *safe*

AHASAI
273 'Achzay (1), *seizer*

AHASBAI
308 'Ăchaçbay (1), *Achasbai*

AHASUERUS
325 'Ăchashvêrôwsh (30), *Xerxes*

AHASUERUS'
325 'Ăchashvêrôwsh (1), *Xerxes*

AHAVA
163 'Ahăvâ' (3), *Ahava*

AHAZ
271 'Âchâz (41), *possessor*

AHAZIAH
274 'Ăchazyâh (37), *Jehovah has seized*

AHBAN
257 'Achbân (1), *one who understands*

AHER
313 'Achêr (1), *Acher*

AHI
277 'Ăchîy (2), *brotherly*

AHIAH
281 'Ăchîyâh (4), *worshipper of Jehovah*

AHIAM
279 'Ăchîy'âm (2), *uncle*

AHIAN
291 'Achyân (1), *brotherly*

AHIEZER
295 'Ăchîy'ezer (6), *brother of help*

AHIHUD
282 'Ăchîyhûwd (1), *possessor of renown*
284 'Ăchîychûd (1), *mysterious*

AHIJAH
281 'Ăchiyâh (20), *worshipper of Jehovah*

AHIKAM
296 'Ăchîyqâm (20), *high, exalted*

AHILUD
286 'Ăchîylûwd (5), *brother of one born*

AHIMAAZ
290 'Ăchîyma'ats (15), *brother of anger*

AHIMAN
289 'Ăchîyman (4), *gift*

AHIMELECH
288 'Ăchîymelek (16), *brother of* (the) *king*

AHIMELECH'S
288 'Ăchîymelek (1), *brother of* (the) *king*

AHIMOTH
287 'Ăchîymôwth (1), *brother of death*

AHINADAB
292 'Ăchîynâdâb (1), *brother of liberality*

AHINOAM
293 'Ăchîynô'am (7), *brother of pleasantness*

AHIO
283 'Achyôw (6), *brotherly*

AHIRA
299 'Ăchîyra' (5), *brother of wrong*

AHIRAM
297 'Ăchîyrâm (1), *high, exalted*

AHIRAMITES
298 'Ăchîyrâmîy (1), *Achiramite*

AHISAMACH
294 'Ăchîyçâmâk (3), *brother of support*

AHISHAHAR
300 'Achîyshachar (1), *brother of* (the) *dawn*

AHISHAR
301 'Ăchîyshâr (1), *brother of* (the) *singer*

AHITHOPHEL
302 'Ăchîythôphel (20), *brother of folly*

AHITUB
285 'Ăchîytûwb (15), *brother of goodness*

AHLAB
303 'Achlâb (1), *fertile*

AHLAI
304 'Achlay (2), *wishful*

AHOAH
265 'Ăchôwach (1), *brotherly*

AHOHITE
266 'Ăchôwchîy (4), *Achochite*
1121+266 bên (1), *son, descendant; people*

AHOLAH
170 'Ohŏlâh (5), *her tent* (idolatrous *sanctuary*)

AHOLIAB
171 'Ohŏlîy'âb (5), *tent of* (his) *father*

AHOLIBAH
172 'Ohŏlîybâh (6), *my tent* (is) *in her*

AHOLIBAMAH
173 'Ohŏlîybâmâh (8), *tent of* (the) *height*

AHUMAI
267 'Ăchûwmay (1), *neighbor of water*

AHUZAM
275 'Ăchuzzâm (1), *seizure*

AHUZZATH
276 'Ăchuzzath (1), *possession*

AI
5857 'Ay (34), *ruin*
5892 'îyr (1), *city, town,* unwalled-*village*

AIAH
345 'Ayâh (5), *hawk*

AIATH
5857 'Ay (1), *ruin*

AIDED
2388+3027 châzaq (1), to *be strong; courageous*

AIJA
5857 'Ay (1), *ruin*

AIJALON
357 'Ayâlôwn (7), *deer-field*

AIJELETH
365 'ayeleth (1), *doe* deer

AIN
5871 'Ayin (5), *fountain*

AIR
7307 rûwach (1), *breath; wind;* life-*spirit*
8064 shâmayim (21), *sky; unseen celestial places*
109 aēr (7), *air, sky*
3772 ŏuranŏs (10), *sky; air; heaven*

AJAH
345 'Ayâh (1), *hawk*

AJALON
357 'Ayâlôwn (3), *deer-field*

AKAN
6130 'Ăqân (1), *crooked*

AKKUB
6126 'Aqqûwb (8), *insidious*

AKRABBIM
6137 'aqrâb (2), *scorpion*

ALABASTER
211 alabastrŏn (3), *alabaster*

ALAMETH
5964 'Âlemeth (1), *covering*

ALAMMELECH
487 'Allammelek (1), *oak of* (the) *king*

ALAMOTH
5961 'Âlâmôwth (2), *soprano*

ALARM
7321 rûwa' (4), to *shout* for alarm or joy
8643 t⁵rûw'âh (6), *battle-cry; clangor*

ALAS
160 'ahăbâh (7), affection, love
188 'ôwy (1), Oh!, Woe!
253 'âch (1), Oh!; Alas!
994 bîy (1), Oh that!
1930 hôw (1), oh! ah!
1945 hôwy (2), oh!, woe!
3758 ŏua (5), ah!; so!

ALBEIT
2443 hina (1), in order that

ALEMETH
5964 'Ălemeth (3), covering

ALEXANDER
223 Alĕxandrŏs (5), man-defender

ALEXANDRIA
221 Alĕxandrĕus (3), of Alexandria

ALEXANDRIANS
221 Alĕxandrĕus (1), of Alexandria

ALGUM
418 'algûwmmîym (3), Algum-wood

ALIAH
5933 'Alvâh (1), moral perverseness

ALIAN
5935 'Alvân (1), lofty

ALIEN
1616 gêr (1), foreigner
5236 nêkâr (1), foreigner
5237 nokrîy (3), foreign; non-relative

ALIENATE
5674 'âbar (1), to cross over; to transition

ALIENATED
3363 yâqa' (2), to be dislocated
5361 nâqa' (3), to feel aversion
526 apallŏtriŏō (2), to be excluded

ALIENS
5237 nokrîy (1), foreign; non-relative
245 allŏtriŏs (1), not one's own
526 apallŏtriŏō (1), to be excluded

ALIKE
259 'echâd (1), first
834 'âsher (1), who, which, what, that
1571 gam (1), also; even
3162 yachad (5), unitedly
7737 shâvâh (1), to equalize; to resemble

ALIVE
2416 chay (30), alive; raw; fresh; life
2418 chăyâ' (Ch.) (1), to live
2421 châyâh (34), to live; to revive
8300 sârîyd (1), survivor; remainder
326 anazaō (2), to recover life, live again
2198 zaō (15), to live

2227 zōŏpŏiĕō (1), to (re-) vitalize, give life

ALL
622 'âçaph (1), to gather, collect
1571 gam (1), also; even
3162 yachad (1), unitedly
3605 kôl (4194), all, any
3606 kôl (Ch.) (50), all, any or every
3632 kâlîyl (2), whole, entire; complete; whole
3885 lûwn (14), to be obstinate with
4393 mᵉlô' (9), fulness
4557 miçpâr (3), number
5973 'îm (2), with
7230 rôb (1), abundance
8552 tâmam (2), to complete, finish
537 hapas (39), all, every one, whole
1273 dianuktĕrĕuō (1), to pass, spend the night
2178 ĕphapax (1), once for all
2527 kathŏlŏu (1), entirely, completely
3122 malista (1), in the greatest degree
3364 ŏu mē (7), not at all, absolutely not
3367 mēdĕis (1), not even one
3650 hŏlŏs (62), whole or all, i.e. complete
3654 hŏlōs (2), completely
3745 hŏsŏs (6), as much as
3762 ŏudĕis (4), none, nobody, nothing
3779 hŏutō (1), in this way; likewise
3829 pandŏchĕiŏn (1), public lodging-place
3832 panŏiki (1), with the whole family
3833 panŏplia (1), full armor
3837 pantachŏu (1), universally, everywhere
3843 pantōs (2), entirely; at all events
3956 pas (947), all, any, every, whole
4219 pŏtĕ (1), at what time?
4561 sarx (1), flesh

ALLEGING
3908 paratithēmi (1), to present something

ALLEGORY
238 allēgŏrĕō (1), to allegorize

ALLELUIA
239 allēlŏuïa (4), praise Jehovah!

ALLIED
7138 qârôwb (1), near, close

ALLON
438 'Allôwn (2), oak

ALLON-BACHUTH
439 'Allôwn Băkûwth (1), oak of weeping

ALLOW
1097 ginōskō (1), to know
4327 prŏsdĕchŏmai (1), to receive; to await for
4909 sunĕudŏkĕō (1), to assent to, feel gratified

ALLOWANCE
737 'ărûchâh (1), ration, portion of food

ALLOWED
1381 dŏkimazō (1), to test; to approve

ALLOWETH
1381 dŏkimazō (1), to test; to approve

ALLURE
6601 pâthâh (1), to be, make simple; to delude
1185 dĕlĕazō (1), to delude, seduce

ALMIGHTY
7706 Shadday (48), the Almighty God
3841 pantŏkratōr (9), Absolute sovereign

ALMODAD
486 'Almôwdâd (2), Almodad

ALMON
5960 'Almôwn (1), hidden

ALMON-DIBLATHAIM
5963 'Almôn Diblâthâyᵉmâh (2), Almon toward Diblathajim

ALMOND
8247 shâqêd (2), almond tree or nut

ALMONDS
8246 shâqad (6), to be, almond-shaped
8247 shâqêd (2), almond tree or nut

ALMOST
4592 mᵉ'aṭ (5), little or few
3195 mĕllō (1), to intend, i.e. be about to be
4975 schĕdŏn (3), nigh, i.e. nearly

ALMS
1654 ĕlĕēmŏsunē (13), benefaction

ALMSDEEDS
1654 ĕlĕēmŏsunē (1), benefaction

ALMUG
484 'almuggiym (3), Almug-wood

ALOES
174 'ăhâlîym (4), aloe-wood sticks
250 alŏē (1), aloes

ALONE
259 'echâd (4), first
905 bad (42), apart, only, besides
909 bâdad (9), to be solitary, be alone
2308 chădal (2), to desist, stop; be fat
4422 mâlaṭ (1), to escape as if by slipperiness

7503 râphâh (4), to slacken
7662 shᵉbaq (Ch.) (1), to allow to remain
7896 shîyth (1), to place, put
863 aphiēmi (6), to leave; to pardon, forgive
1439 ĕaō (3), to let be, i.e. permit or leave alone
2651 katamŏnas (2), separately, alone
3440 mŏnŏn (3), merely, just
3441 mŏnŏs (21), single, only; by oneself

ALONG
1980 hâlak (3), to walk; live a certain way

ALOOF
5048 neged (1), over against or before

ALOTH
1175 Bᵉ'âlôwth (1), mistresses

ALOUD
1419+3605 gâdôwl (1), great
1627 gârôwn (1), throat
1993 hâmâh (1), to be in great commotion
2429 chayil (Ch.) (3), strength; loud sound
5414+854+6963 nâthan (1), to give
6670 tsâhal (2), to be cheerful; to sound
6963+1419 qôwl (1), voice or sound
7311+1419 rûwm (1), to be high; to rise or raise
7321 rûwa' (1), to shout for alarm or joy
7442 rânan (5), to shout for joy
7452 rêa' (1), crash; noise; shout
7768 shâva' (1), to halloo, call for help
310 anabŏaō (1), to cry out

ALPHA
1 A (4), first

ALPHAEUS
256 Alphaiŏs (5), Alphæus

ALREADY
3528 kᵉbâr (5), long ago, formerly, hitherto
2235 ēdē (18), even now
4258 prŏamartanō (1), to sin previously
5348 phthanō (1), to be beforehand

ALTAR
741 'ărî'êyl (3), altar
4056 madbach (Ch.) (1), sacrificial altar
4196 mizbêach (347), altar
1041 bōmŏs (1), altar
2379 thusiastēriŏn (21), altar

ALTARS
4196 mizbêach (52), altar

2379 thusiastērion (1),
altar

ALTASCHITH
516 'Al tashchêth (4),
"Thou must not
destroy"

ALTER
2498 châlaph (1), to
hasten away; to pass
8133 sheⁿâ' (Ch.) (2), to
alter, change
8138 shânâh (1), to
transmute

ALTERED
5674 'âbar (1), to cross
over; to transition
1096+2087 ginōmai (1),
to be, become

ALTERETH
5709 'ădâ' (Ch.) (2), to
pass on or continue

ALTHOUGH
272 'ăchuzzâh (2),
possession
3588 kîy (7), for, that
because
2543 kaitŏi (1),
nevertheless

ALTOGETHER
259 'echâd (1), first
1571 gam (1), also; even
3162 yachad (5), unitedly
3605 kôl (4), all, any
3617 kâlâh (3), complete
destruction
3650 hŏlŏs (1), whole or
all, i.e. complete
3843 pantōs (2), entirely;
at all events

ALUSH
442 'Âlûwsh (2), Alush

ALVAH
5933 'Alvâh (1), moral
perverseness

ALVAN
5935 'Alvân (1), lofty

ALWAY
3605+3117 kôl (4), all,
any or every
5331 netsach (1),
splendor; lasting
5769 'ôwlâm (2), eternity;
ancient; always
8548 tâmîyd (4),
constantly, regularly
104 aĕi (8), ever, always
1275 diapantŏs (2),
constantly, continually
3842 pantŏtĕ (1), at all
times
3956+2250 pas (1), all,
any, every, whole

ALWAYS
3605+3117 kôl (4), all,
any or every
3605+6256 kôl (4), all,
any or every
5331 netsach (2),
splendor; lasting
5769 'ôwlâm (3), eternity;
ancient; always
8548 tâmîyd (6),
constantly, regularly
104 aĕi (3), ever, always

1223+3956 dia (3),
through, by means of
1275 diapantŏs (3),
constantly, continually
1539 hĕkastŏtĕ (1), at
every time
1722+3956+2540 ĕn (2),
in; during; because of
3839 pantĕ (1), wholly
3842 pantŏtĕ (29), at all
times

AMAD
6008 'Am'âd (1), people
of time

AMAL
6000 'Âmâl (1), wearing
effort; worry

AMALEK
6002 'Ămâlêq (24),
Amalek

AMALEKITE
6003 'Ămâlêqîy (3),
Amalekite

AMALEKITES
6003 'Ămâlêqîy (24),
Amalekite

AMAM
538 'Ămâm (1),
gathering-spot

AMANA
549 'Ămânâh (1),
covenant

AMARIAH
568 'Ămaryâh (14),
Jehovah has promised

AMASA
6021 'Ămâsâ' (16),
burden

AMASAI
6022 'Ămâsay (5),
burdensome

AMASHAI
6023 'Ămashçay (1),
burdensome

AMASIAH
6007 'Ămaçyâh (1),
Jehovah has loaded

AMAZED
926 bâhal (2), to tremble;
be, make agitated
2865 châthath (1), to
break down
8074 shâmêm (1), to
devastate; to stupefy
8539 tâmahh (1), to be
astounded
1096+2285 ginōmai (1),
to be, become
1568 ĕkthambĕō (2), to
astonish utterly
1605 ĕkplēssō (3), to
astonish
1611 ĕkstasis (1),
astonishment
1611+2983 ĕkstasis (1),
astonishment
1839 ĕxistēmi (6), to
become astounded
2284 thambĕō (2), to
astound, be amazed

AMAZEMENT
1611 ĕkstasis (1),
astonishment

4423 ptŏēsis (1),
something alarm

AMAZIAH
558 'Ămatsyâh (40),
strength of Jehovah

AMBASSADOR
6735 tsîyr (3), hinge;
herald or errand-doer
4243 prĕsbĕuō (1), to act
as a representative

AMBASSADORS
3887 lûwts (1), to scoff; to
interpret; to intercede
4397 mal'âk (4),
messenger
6735 tsîyr (2), hinge;
herald or errand-doer
4243 prĕsbĕuō (1), to act
as a representative

AMBASSAGE
4242 prĕsbĕia (1),
ambassadors

AMBER
2830 chashmal (3),
bronze

AMBUSH
693 'ârab (7), to ambush,
lie in wait

AMBUSHES
693 'ârab (1), to ambush,
lie in wait

AMBUSHMENT
3993 ma'ărâb (2),
ambuscade, ambush

AMBUSHMENTS
693 'ârab (1), to ambush,
lie in wait

AMEN
543 'âmên (22), truly,
"may it be so!"
281 amĕn (51), surely; so
be it

AMEND
2388 châzaq (1), to
fasten upon; to seize
3190 yâṭab (4), to be,
make well
2192+2866 ĕchō (1), to
have; hold; keep

AMENDS
7999 shâlam (1), to be
friendly; to reciprocate

AMERCE
6064 'ânash (1), to inflict
a penalty, to fine

AMETHYST
306 'achlâmâh (2),
amethyst
271 amĕthustŏs (1),
amethyst

AMI
532 'Âmîy (1), skilled
craftsman

AMIABLE
3039 yedîyd (1), loved

AMINADAB
284 Aminadab (3),
people of liberality

AMISS
5753 'âvâh (1), to be
crooked
7955 shâlâh (Ch.) (1),
wrong

824 atŏpŏs (1), improper;
injurious; wicked
2560 kakŏs (1), badly;
wrongly; ill

AMITTAI
573 'Ămittay (2),
veracious

AMMAH
522 'Ammâh (1), cubit

AMMI
5971 'am (1), people

AMMI-NADIB
5993 'Ammîy Nâdîyb (1),
my people (are) liberal

AMMIEL
5988 'Ammîy'êl (6),
people of God

AMMIHUD
5989 'Ammîyhûwd (10),
people of splendor

AMMINADAB
5992 'Ammîynâdâb (13),
people of liberality

AMMISHADDAI
5996 'Ammîyshadday
(5), people of (the)
Almighty

AMMIZABAD
5990 'Ammîyzâbâd (1),
people of endowment

AMMON
5983 'Ammôwn (91),
inbred

AMMONITE
5984 'Ammôwnîy (9),
Ammonite

AMMONITES
1121+5984 bên (7), son,
descendant; people
5984 'Ammôwnîy (16),
Ammonite

AMMONITESS
5984 'Ammôwnîy (4),
Ammonite

AMNON
550 'Amnôwn (25),
faithful

AMNON'S
550 'Amnôwn (3), faithful

AMOK
5987 'Âmôwq (2), deep

AMON
526 'Âmôwn (17), skilled
craftsman
300 Amōn (2), skilled
craftsman

AMONG
413 'êl (7), to, toward
854 'êth (8), with; among
996 bêyn (33), between
997 bêyn (Ch.) (1),
between; "either...or"
1460 gêv (1), middle,
inside, in, on, etc.
1767 day (1), enough,
sufficient
4480 min (4), from, out of
5921 'al (7), above, over,
upon, or against
5973 'îm (8), with
7130 qereb (74), nearest
part, i.e. the center

7310 rᵉvâyâh (1),
satisfaction
8432 tâvek (142), center,
middle
575 apŏ (1), from, away
1223 dia (1), through, by
means of; because of
1519 ĕis (18), to or into
1537 ĕk (5), out, out of
1722 ĕn (115), in; during;
because of
1909 ĕpi (4), on, upon
2596 kata (2), down;
according to
3319 mĕsŏs (7), middle
3326 mĕta (5), with,
among; after, later
3844 para (2), from; with;
besides; on account of
4045 pĕripiptŏ (1), to fall
into the hands of
4314 prŏs (19), for; on, at;
to, toward; against
4315 prŏsabbatŏn (1),
Sabbath-eve
5259 hupŏ (1), under; by
means of; at

AMONGST
8432 tâvek (2), center,
middle

AMORITE
567 'Ĕmôrîy (14),
mountaineer

AMORITES
567 'Ĕmôrîy (73),
mountaineer

AMOS
5986 'Âmôwç (7),
burdensome
301 Amŏs (1), strong

AMOZ
531 'Âmôwts (13), strong

AMPHIPOLIS
295 Amphipŏlis (1), city
surrounded by a river

AMPLIAS
291 Amplias (1), enlarged

AMRAM
2566 Chamrân (1), red
6019 'Amrâm (13), high
people

AMRAM'S
6019 'Amrâm (1), high
people

AMRAMITES
6020 'Amrâmîy (2),
Amramite

AMRAPHEL
569 'Amrâphel (2),
Amraphel

AMZI
557 'Amtsîy (2), strong

ANAB
6024 'Ănâb (2), fruit

ANAH
6034 'Ănâh (12), answer

ANAHARATH
588 'Ănâchărâth (1),
gorge or narrow pass

ANAIAH
6043 'Ănâyâh (2),
Jehovah has answered

ANAK
6061 'Ânâq (9), necklace
chain

ANAKIMS
6062 'Ănâqîy (9), Anakite

ANAMIM
6047 'Ănâmîm (2),
Anamim

ANAMMELECH
6048 'Ănammelek (1),
Anammelek

ANAN
6052 'Ânân (1), cloud

ANANI
6054 'Ănânîy (1), cloudy

ANANIAH
6055 'Ănanyâh (2),
Jehovah has covered

ANANIAS
367 Ananias (11),
Jehovah has favored

ANATH
6067 'Ănâth (2), answer

ANATHEMA
331 anathĕma (1),
excommunicated

ANATHOTH
6068 'Ănâthôwth (16),
answers

ANCESTORS
7223 rî'shôwn (1), first, in
place, time or rank

ANCHOR
45 agkura (1), anchor

ANCHORS
45 agkura (2), anchor

ANCIENT
2204 zâqên (6), to be old,
venerated
3453 yâshîysh (1), old
man
5769 'ôwlâm (6), eternity;
ancient; always
6267 'attîyq (1), weaned;
antique
6268 'attîyq (Ch.) (3),
venerable, old
6917 qâdûwm (1),
pristine hero
6924 qedem (8), East,
eastern; antiquity;
before, anciently

ANCIENTS
2204 zâqên (9), to be old,
venerated
6931 qadmôwnîy (1),
anterior time; oriental

ANCLE
4974 sphurŏn (1), ankle

ANCLES
657 epheç (1), end; no
further

ANDREW
406 Andrĕas (13), manly

ANDRONICUS
408 Andrŏnikŏs (1), man
of victory

ANEM
6046 'Ănêm (1), two
fountains

ANER
6063 'Ânêr (3), Aner

ANETHOTHITE
6069 'Anthôthîy (1),
Antothite

ANETOTHITE
6069 'Anthôthîy (1),
Antothite

ANGEL
4397 mal'âk (100),
messenger
4398 mal'ak (Ch.) (2),
messenger
32 aggĕlŏs (95),
messenger; angel

ANGEL'S
32 aggĕlŏs (2),
messenger; angel

ANGELS
430 'ĕlôhîym (1), the true
God; gods; great ones
4397 mal'âk (10),
messenger
8136 shin'ân (1), change,
i.e. repetition
32 aggĕlŏs (80),
messenger; angel
2465 isaggĕlŏs (1),
angelic, like an angel

ANGELS'
47 'abbîyr (1), mighty

ANGER
639 'aph (173), nose or
nostril; face; person
2195 za'am (1), fury,
anger
2534 chêmâh (1), heat;
anger; poison
3707 kâ'aç (42), to grieve,
rage, be indignant
3708 ka'aç (2), vexation,
grief
5006 nâ'ats (1), to scorn
5674 'âbar (1), to cross
over; to transition
5678 'ebrâh (1), outburst
of passion
6440 pânîym (3), face;
front
7307 rûwach (1), breath;
wind; life-spirit
3709 ŏrgē (3), ire;
punishment
3949 parŏrgizŏ (1), to
enrage, exasperate

ANGERED
7107 qâtsaph (1), to burst
out in rage

ANGLE
2443 chakkâh (2), fish
hook

ANGRY
599 'ânaph (13), be
enraged, be angry
639 'aph (4), nose or
nostril; face; person
1149 bᵉnaç (Ch.) (1), to
be enraged, be angry
2194 zâ'am (2), to be
enraged
2734 chârâh (10), to
blaze up
3707 kâ'aç (2), to grieve,
rage, be indignant
3708 ka'aç (1), vexation,
grief
4751+5315 mar (1), bitter;
bitterness; bitterly

6225 'âshan (1), to
envelope in smoke
7107 qâtsaph (2), to burst
out in rage
3710 ŏrgizŏ (5), to
become exasperated,
enraged
3711 ŏrgilŏs (1),
irascible, hot-tempered
5520 chŏlaŏ (1), irritable,
enraged

ANGUISH
2342 chûwl (1), to dance,
whirl; to writhe in pain
4689 mâtsôwq (1),
confinement; disability
4691 mᵉtsûwqâh (1),
trouble, anguish
6695 tsôwq (3), distress
6862 tsar (1), trouble;
opponent
6869 tsârâh (5), trouble;
rival-wife
7115 qôtser (1),
shortness (of spirit)
7661 shâbâts (1),
intanglement
2347 thlipsis (1),
pressure, trouble
4730 stĕnŏchôria (1),
calamity, distress
4928 sunŏchē (1),
anxiety, distress

ANIAM
593 'Ănîy'âm (1),
groaning of (the) people

ANIM
6044 'Ănîym (1),
fountains

ANISE
432 anēthŏn (1), dill
seed for seasoning

ANNA
451 Anna (1), favored

ANNAS
452 Annas (4), Jehovah
has favored

ANOINT
4886 mâshach (25), to
rub or smear
5480 çûwk (5), to smear
218 alĕiphŏ (3), to oil
with perfume, anoint
1472 ĕgchriŏ (1), to
besmear, anoint
3462 murizŏ (1), to apply
perfumed unguent to

ANOINTED
1101 bâlal (1), to mix
1121+3323 bên (1), son,
descendant; people
4473 mimshach (1), with
outstretched wings
4886 mâshach (43), to
rub or smear with oil
4888 mishchâh (1),
unction; gift
4899 mâshîyach (37),
consecrated person;
Messiah
5480 çûwk (2), to smear
218 alĕiphŏ (5), to oil
with perfume, anoint
2025 ĕpichriŏ (1), to
smear over, anoint

2025+1909 ĕpichriō (1), to *smear over, anoint*
5548 chriō (5), to *smear or rub* with oil

ANOINTEDST
4886 mâshach (1), to *rub or smear* with oil

ANOINTEST
1878 dâshên (1), to *anoint; to satisfy*

ANOINTING
4888 mishchâh (24), *unction; gift*
8081 shemen (1), *olive*
218 alĕiphō (1), to *oil with perfume, anoint*
5545 chrisma (2), special *endowment*

ANON
2112 ĕuthĕōs (1), *at once or soon*
2117 ĕuthus (1), *at once, immediately*

ANOTHER
250 'Ezrâchîy (22), *Ezrachite*
251 'âch (1), *brother; relative*
259 'echâd (35), *first*
269 'achôwth (6), *sister*
312 'achêr (58), *other, another, different; next*
317 'ochŏrîy (Ch.) (5), *other, another*
321 'ochŏrân (Ch.) (1), *other, another*
376 'îysh (5), *man; male; someone*
1668 dâ' (Ch.) (2), *this*
1836 dên (Ch.) (1), *this*
2088 zeh (10), *this or that*
2090 zôh (1), *this or that*
2114 zûwr (3), to *be foreign, strange*
3671 kânâph (1), *edge or extremity; wing*
5234 nâkar (2), to *treat as a foreigner*
5997 'âmîyth (2), *comrade or kindred*
7453 rêa' (20), *associate*
7468 rᵉ'ûwth (2), *female associate*
8145 shênîy (7), *second; again*
8264 shâqaq (1), to *seek greedily*
240 allēlōn (70), *one another*
243 allŏs (60), *different, other*
245 allŏtriŏs (4), *not one's own*
246 allŏphulŏs (1), *Gentile, foreigner*
1438 hĕautŏu (7), *himself, herself, itself*
1520 hĕis (2), *one*
2087 hĕtĕrŏs (44), *other or different*
3588 hŏ (1), *"the," i.e. the definite article*
3739 hŏs (6), *who, which*
4299 prŏkrima (1), *prejudgment*
4835 sumpathēs (1), *commiserative*

ANOTHER'S
7453 rêa' (2), *associate; one close*
240 allēlōn (2), *one another*
2087 hĕtĕrŏs (1), *other or different*

ANSWER
559 'âmar (9), to *say, speak*
1696 dâbar (1), to *speak, say; to subdue*
1697 dâbâr (7), *word; matter; thing*
3045 yâda' (1), to *know*
4405 millâh (1), *word; discourse; speech*
4617 ma'ăneh (7), *reply, answer*
6030 'ânâh (60), to *respond, answer;*
6600 pithgâm (Ch.) (2), *decree; report*
7725 shûwb (12), to *turn back; to return*
8421 tûwb (Ch.) (2), to *reply, answer*
470 antapŏkrinŏmai (1), to *contradict or dispute*
611 apŏkrinŏmai (12), to *respond*
612 apŏkrisis (3), *response*
626 apŏlŏgĕŏmai (4), to *give an account of self*
627 apŏlŏgia (4), *plea or verbal defense*
1906 ĕpĕrōtēma (1), *inquiry*
2036 ĕpō (1), to *speak*
5538 chrēmatismŏs (1), *divine response*

ANSWERABLE
5980 'ummâh (1), *near, beside, along with*

ANSWERED
559 'âmar (90), to *say, speak*
1697 dâbâr (4), *word; matter; thing*
6030 'ânâh (175), to *respond, answer*
6032 'ânâh (Ch.) (16), to *respond, answer*
6039 'ĕnûwth (1), *affliction*
7725 shûwb (2), to *turn back; to return*
8421 tûwb (Ch.) (1), to *reply, answer*
611 apŏkrinŏmai (201), to *respond*
626 apŏlŏgĕŏmai (2), to *give an account of self*

ANSWEREDST
6030 'ânâh (2), to *respond, answer*

ANSWEREST
6030 'ânâh (2), to *respond, answer*
611 apŏkrinŏmai (4), to *respond*

ANSWERETH
6030 'ânâh (6), to *respond, answer*
7725 shûwb (1), to *turn back; to return*

611 apŏkrinŏmai (4), to *respond*
4960 sustŏichĕō (1), to *correspond to*

ANSWERING
488 antimĕtrĕō (1), to *measure in return*
611 apŏkrinŏmai (29), to *respond*
5274 hupŏlambanō (1), to *take up, i.e. continue*

ANSWERS
8666 tᵉshûwbâh (2), *reply*
612 apŏkrisis (1), *response*

ANT
5244 nᵉmâlâh (1), *ant*

ANTICHRIST
500 antichristŏs (4), *opponent of Messiah*

ANTICHRISTS
500 antichristŏs (1), *opponent of Messiah*

ANTIOCH
490 Antiŏchĕia (18), *Antiochia*
491 Antiŏchĕus (1), *inhabitant of Antiochia*

ANTIPAS
493 Antipas (1), *instead of father*

ANTIPATRIS
494 Antipatris (1), *Antipatris*

ANTIQUITY
6927 qadmâh (1), *priority in time; before; past*

ANTOTHIJAH
6070 'Anthôthîyâh (1), *answers of Jehovah*

ANTOTHITE
6069 'Anthôthîy (2), *Antothite*

ANTS
5244 nᵉmâlâh (1), *ant*

ANUB
6036 'Ânûwb (1), *borne*

ANVIL
6471 pa'am (1), *time; step; occurence*

ANY
259 'echâd (18), *first*
376 'îysh (25), *man*
1697 dâbâr (2), *thing*
1991 hêm (1), *wealth*
3254 yâçaph (2), to *add*
3605 kôl (175), *all, any*
3606 kôl (Ch.) (8), *all, any or every*
3792 kᵉthâb (Ch.) (1), *writing, record or book*
3972 mᵉ'ûwmâh (12), *something; anything*
4310 mîy (1), *who?*
5315 nephesh (3), *life; breath; soul; wind*
5750 'ôwd (9), *again; repeatedly; still; more*
5769 'ôwlâm (1), *eternity; ancient; always*
1520 hĕis (2), *one*
1535 ĕitĕ (1), *if too*
1536 ĕi tis (52), *if any*
1538 hĕkastŏs (1), *each*

APHSES
2089 ĕti (10), *yet, still*
3361 mē (1), *not; lest*
3362 ĕan mē (2), *if not*
3364 ŏu mē (2), *not at all*
3367 mēdĕis (5), *not even one*
3370 Mēdŏs (2), *inhabitant of Media*
3379 mēpŏtĕ (7), *not ever; if, or lest ever*
3381 mēpōs (4), *lest somehow*
3387 mētis (6), *whether any*
3588 hŏ (1), *"the," i.e. the definite article*
3762 ŏudĕis (12), *none, nobody, nothing*
3763 ŏudĕpŏtĕ (2), *never at all*
3765 ŏukĕti (4), *not yet, no longer*
3956 pas (9), *all, any, every, whole*
4218 pŏtĕ (4), *at some time, ever*
4455 pōpŏtĕ (3), *at no time*
4458 -pōs (4), *particle used in composition*
5100 tis (122), *some or any person or object*
5150 trimĕnŏn (1), *three months' space*

APART
905 bad (6), *apart, only, besides*
5079 niddâh (3), *time of menstrual impurity*
5674 'âbar (1), to *cross over; to transition*
6395 pâlâh (1), to *distinguish*
659 apŏtithēmi (1), to *put away; get rid of*
2596 kata (7), *down; according to*

APELLES
559 Apĕllēs (1), *Apelles*

APES
6971 qôwph (2), *ape or monkey*

APHARSACHITES
671 'Ăpharçᵉkay (Ch.) (2), *Apharsekite*

APHARSATHCHITES
671 'Ăpharçᵉkay (Ch.) (1), *Apharsekite*

APHARSITES
670 'Ăphârᵉçay (Ch.) (1), *Apharesite*

APHEK
663 'Ăphêq (8), *fortress*

APHEKAH
664 'Ăphêqâh (1), *fortress*

APHIAH
647 'Ăphîyach (1), *breeze*

APHIK
663 'Ăphêq (1), *fortress*

APHRAH
1036 Bêyth lᵉ-'Aphrâh (1), *house of dust*

APHSES
6483 Pitstsêts (1), *dispersive*

APIECE
259 'echâd (1), *first*
5982+259 'ammûwd (1), *column, pillar*
303 ana (2), *each; in turn; among*

APOLLONIA
624 Apŏllōnia (1), *sun*

APOLLOS
625 Apŏllōs (10), *sun*

APOLLYON
623 Apŏlluŏn (1), *Destroyer*

APOSTLE
652 apŏstŏlŏs (19), *commissioner* of Christ

APOSTLES
652 apŏstŏlŏs (53), *commissioner* of Christ
5570 psĕudapŏstŏlŏs (1), *pretended preacher*

APOSTLES'
652 apŏstŏlŏs (5), *commissioner* of Christ

APOSTLESHIP
651 apŏstŏlē (4), office of *apostle*

APOTHECARIES
7543 râqach (1), to *perfume, blend spice*

APOTHECARIES'
4842 mirqachath (1), *unguent; unguent-pot*

APOTHECARY
7543 râqach (4), to *perfume, blend spice*

APPAIM
649 'Appayim (2), *two nostrils*

APPAREL
899 beged (4), *clothing; treachery or pillage*
1264 bᵉrôwm (1), *damask*
3830 lᵉbûwsh (8), *garment; wife*
3847 lâbash (1), to *clothe*
4254 machălâtsâh (1), *mantle, garment*
4403 malbûwsh (4), *garment, clothing*
8071 simlâh (2), *dress, mantle*
2066 ĕsthēs (3), to *clothe; dress*
2440 himation (1), to *put on clothes*
2441 himatismŏs (1), *clothing*
2689 katastŏlē (1), *costume or apparel*

APPARELLED
3847 lâbash (1), to *clothe*
2441 himatismŏs (1), *clothing*

APPARENTLY
4758 mar'eh (1), *appearance; vision*

APPEAL
1941 ĕpikalĕŏmai (2), to *invoke*

APPEALED
1941 ĕpikalĕŏmai (4), to *invoke*

APPEAR
1540 gâlâh (1), to *denude; uncover*
1570 gâlash (2), to *caper*
4286 machsôph (1), *peeling, baring*
6524 pârach (1), to *break forth; to bloom; to fly*
7200 râ'âh (24), to *see*
82 adēlŏs (1), *indistinct, not clear*
398 anaphainō (1), to *appear*
1718 ĕmphanizō (1), to *show forth*
2064 ĕrchŏmai (1), to *go or come*
3700 ŏptanŏmai (2), to *appear*
5316 phainō (9), to *show; to appear, be visible*
5318+5600 phanĕrŏs (1), *apparent, visible, clear*
5319 phanĕrŏō (9), to *render apparent*

APPEARANCE
4758 mar'eh (30), *appearance; vision*
5869 'ayin (1), *eye; sight; fountain*
1491 ĕidŏs (1), *form, appearance, sight*
3799 ŏpsis (1), *face; appearance*
4383 prŏsōpŏn (2), *face, presence*

APPEARANCES
4758 mar'eh (2), *appearance; vision*

APPEARED
1540 gâlâh (1), to *denude; uncover*
3318 yâtsâ' (1), to *go, bring out*
6437 pânâh (1), to *turn, to face*
7200 râ'âh (39), to *see*
1718 ĕmphanizō (1), to *show forth*
2014 ĕpiphainō (3), to *become visible*
3700 ŏptanŏmai (15), to *appear*
5316 phainō (5), to *show; to appear, be visible*
5319 phanĕrŏō (3), to *render apparent*

APPEARETH
1540 gâlâh (1), to *denude; uncover*
4758 mar'eh (1), *appearance; vision*
7200 râ'âh (3), to *see*
8259 shâqaph (1), to *peep or gaze*
5316 phainō (3), to *show; to appear, be visible*

APPEARING
602 apŏkalupsis (1), *disclosure, revelation*
2015 ĕpiphanĕia (5), *manisfestation*

APPEASE
3722+6440 kâphar (1), to *cover; to expiate*

APPEASED
7918 shâkak (1), to *lay a trap; to allay*
2687 katastĕllō (1), to *quell, quiet*

APPEASETH
8252 shâqaṭ (1), to *repose*

APPERTAIN
2969 yâ'âh (1), to *be suitable, proper*

APPETITE
2416 chay (1), *alive; raw; fresh; life*
5315 nephesh (2), *life; breath; soul; wind*
8264 shâqaq (1), to *seek greedily*

APPHIA
682 Apphia (1), *Apphia*

APPII
675 'Appiŏs (1), *Appius*

APPLE
380 'îyshôwn (2), *pupil, eyeball*
380+1323 'îyshôwn (1), *pupil, eyeball*
892 bâbâh (1), *pupil of the eye*
1323 bath (1), *daughter, descendant, woman*
8598 tappûwach (3), *apple*

APPLES
8598 tappûwach (3), *apple*

APPLIED
5414 nâthan (2), to *give*
5437 çâbab (1), to *surround*

APPLY
935 bôw' (2), to *go, come*
5186 nâṭâh (1), to *stretch or spread out*
7896 shîyth (1), to *place, put*

APPOINT
559 'âmar (1), to *say, speak*
977 bâchar (1), *select, chose, prefer*
3259 yâ'ad (2), to *meet; to summon; to direct*
5344 nâqab (1), to *specify, designate, libel*
5414 nâthan (4), to *give*
5975 'âmad (2), to *stand*
6485 pâqad (10), to *visit, care for, count*
6680 tsâvâh (1), to *constitute, enjoin*
7136 qârâh (1), to *bring about; to impose*
7760 sûwm (11), to *put*
7896 shîyth (2), to *place*
7971 shâlach (1), to *send away*
1303 diatithĕmai (1), to *put apart, i.e. dispose*
2525 kathistēmi (1), to *designate, constitute*
5087 tithēmi (2), to *place, put*

APPOINTED
559 'âmar (2), to *say*

561 'ēmer (1), *something said*
1121 bēn (3), *son, people* of a class or kind
1696 dâbar (1), to *speak, say; to subdue*
2163 zâman (3), to *fix a time*
2296 châgar (3), to *gird on a belt; put on armor*
2706 chôq (1), *appointment; allotment*
2708 chuqqâh (1), to *delineate*
2710 châqaq (1), to *enact laws; to prescribe*
2764 chêrem (1), *doomed object*
3045 yâda' (1), to *know*
3198 yâkach (2), to *decide, justify*
3245 yâçad (1), *settle, consult, establish*
3259 yâ'ad (3), to *meet; to summon; to direct*
3677 keçe' (2), *full moon*
4150 môw'êd (20), *assembly, congregation*
4151 môw'âd (1), *ranking of troop*
4152 mûw'âdâh (1), *appointed place*
4487 mânâh (4), to *allot; to enumerate or enroll*
4662 miphqâd (1), *designated spot; census*
5324 nâtsab (1), to *station*
5414 nâthan (7), to *give*
5567 çâman (1), to *designate*
5975 'âmad (10), to *stand*
6213 'âsâh (2), to *do or make*
6485 pâqad (4), to *visit, care for, count*
6635 tsâbâ' (3), *army, military host*
6680 tsâvâh (4), to *constitute, enjoin*
6942 qâdâsh (1), to *be, make clean*
7760 sûwm (8), to *put*
7896 shîyth (1), to *place*
322 anadĕiknumi (1), to *indicate, appoint*
606 apŏkĕimai (1), to *be reserved; to await*
1299 diatassō (4), to *institute, prescribe*
1303 diatithĕmai (1), to *put apart, i.e. dispose*
1476 hĕdraiŏs (1), *immovable; steadfast*
1935 ĕpithanatiŏs (1), *doomed to death*
2476 histēmi (1), to *stand, establish*
2749 kĕimai (1), to *lie outstretched*
4160 pŏiĕō (1), to *do*
4287 prŏthĕsmiŏs (1), *designated day or time*
4384 prŏtassō (1), to *prescribe beforehand*
4929 suntassō (2), to *direct, instruct*
5021 tassō (3), to *assign or dispose*

5081 tĕlaugōs (1), in a far-shining manner
5087 tithēmi (3), to *put*

APPOINTETH
6966 qûwm (Ch.) (1), to *rise*

APPOINTMENT
3259 yâ'ad (1), to *meet;* to *summon;* to *direct*
3883 lûwl (1), *spiral* step
6310 peh (2), *mouth; opening*

APPREHEND
2638 katalambanō (1), to *seize;* to *understand*
4084 piazō (1), to *seize, arrest,* or *capture*

APPREHENDED
2638 katalambanō (2), to *seize;* to *possess;* to *understand*
4084 piazō (1), to *seize, arrest,* or *capture*

APPROACH
5066 nâgash (5), to *be, come, bring near*
7126 qârab (12), to *approach, bring near*
7138 qârôwb (1), *near, close*
676 aprŏsitŏs (1), *unapproachable*

APPROACHED
5066 nâgash (1), to *be, come, bring near*
7126 qârab (1), to *approach, bring near*

APPROACHETH
1448 ĕggizō (1), to *approach*

APPROACHING
7132 qᵉrâbâh (1), *approach*
1448 ĕggizō (1), to *approach*

APPROVE
7520 râtsad (1), to *look askant;* to *be jealous*
1381 dŏkimazō (2), to *test;* to *approve*

APPROVED
584 apŏdĕiknumi (1), to *accredit*
1384 dŏkimŏs (6), *acceptable, approved*
4921 sunistaō (1), to *introduce* (favorably)

APPROVEST
1381 dŏkimazō (1), to *test;* to *approve*

APPROVETH
7200 râ'âh (1), to *see*

APPROVING
4921 sunistaō (1), to *introduce* (favorably)

APRONS
2290 châgôwr (1), *belt* for the waist
4612 simikinthiŏn (1), narrow *apron*

APT
6213 'âsâh (1), to *do*
1317 didaktikŏs (2), *instructive*

AQUILA
207 Akulas (6), *eagle*

AR
6144 'Âr (6), *city*

ARA
690 'Ărâ' (1), *lion*

ARAB
694 'Ărâb (1), *ambush*

ARABAH
6160 'ărâbâh (2), *desert, wasteland*

ARABIA
6152 'Ărâb (6), *Arabia*
688 Arabia (2), *Arabia*

ARABIAN
6153 'ereb (1), *dusk*
6163 'Ărâbîy (3), *Arabian*

ARABIANS
6163 'Ărâbîy (5), *Arabian*
690 'Araps (1), *native of Arabia*

ARAD
6166 'Ărâd (5), *fugitive*

ARAH
733 'Ărach (4), *way-faring*

ARAM
758 'Ărâm (7), *highland*
689 Aram (3), *high*

ARAM-NAHARAIM
763 'Ăram Nahărayim (1), *Aram of* (the) *two rivers*

ARAM-ZOBAH
760 'Ăram Tsôwbâh (1), *Aram of* Coele-Syria

ARAMITESS
761 'Ărammîy (1), *Aramite*

ARAN
765 'Ărân (2), *stridulous*

ARARAT
780 'Ărâraṭ (2), *Ararat*

ARAUNAH
728 'Ăravnâh (9), *Aravnah* or *Ornah*

ARBA
704 'Arba' (2), *four*

ARBAH
704 'Arba' (1), *four*

ARBATHITE
6164 'Arbâthîy (2), *Arbathite*

ARBITE
701 'Arbîy (1), *Arbite*

ARCHANGEL
743 archaggĕlŏs (2), *chief angel*

ARCHELAUS
745 Archĕlaŏs (1), *people-ruling*

ARCHER
1869 dârak (1), to *walk, lead;* to *string* a bow
7198 qesheth (1), *bow; rainbow*

ARCHERS
1167+2671 ba'al (1), *master; husband*
1869+7198 dârak (1), to *walk;* to *string* a bow

ARCHES
361 'êylâm (15), *portico, porch*

ARCHEVITES
756 'Arkᵉvay (Ch.) (1), *Arkevite*

ARCHI
757 'Arkîy (1), *Arkite*

ARCHIPPUS
751 Archippŏs (2), *horse-ruler*

ARCHITE
757 'Arkîy (5), *Arkite*

ARCTURUS
5906 'Ayish (2), Great *Bear* constellation

ARD
714 'Ard (3), *fugitive*

ARDITES
716 'Ardîy (1), *Ardite*

ARDON
715 'Ardôwn (1), *roaming*

ARELI
692 'Ar'êlîy (2), *heroic*

ARELITES
692 'Ar'êlîy (1), *heroic*

AREOPAGITE
698 Arĕŏpagitēs (1), *Areopagite*

AREOPAGUS
697 Arĕiŏs Pagŏs (1), *rock of Ares*

ARETAS
702 Arĕtas (1), *Aretas*

ARGOB
709 'Argôb (5), *stony*

ARGUING
3198 yâkach (1), to *be correct;* to *argue*

ARGUMENTS
8433 tôwkêchâh (1), *correction, refutation*

ARIDAI
742 'Ărîyday (1), *Aridai*

ARIDATHA
743 'Ărîydâthâ' (1), *Aridatha*

ARIEH
745 'Aryêh (1), *lion*

ARIEL
740 'Ări'êl (5), *Lion of God*

ARIGHT
3190 yâṭab (1), to *be, make well*
3559 kûwn (1), to *render sure, proper*
3651 kên (1), *just; right, correct*

ARIMATHAEA
707 Arimathaia (4), *height*

ARIOCH
746 'Ăryôwk (7), *Arjok*

ARISAI
747 'Ăriyçay (1), *Arisai*

ARISE
2224 zârach (3), to *rise;* to *be bright*
5782 'ûwr (1), to *awake*
5927 'âlâh (2), to *ascend, be high, mount*
5975 'âmad (1), to *stand*
6965 qûwm (106), to *rise*
6966 qûwm (Ch.) (3), to *rise*
6974 qûwts (1), to *awake*
7721 sôw' (1), *rising*
305 anabainō (1), to *go up, rise*
393 anatĕllō (1), to *cause to arise*
450 anistēmi (14), to *stand up;* to *come back to life*
1453 ĕgĕirō (13), to *waken,* i.e. *rouse*

ARISETH
2224 zârach (4), to *rise;* to *be bright*
5927 'âlâh (1), to *ascend, be high, mount*
6965 qûwm (2), to *rise*
450 anistēmi (1), to *stand up;* to *come back to life*
1096 ginŏmai (2), to *be, become*
1453 ĕgĕirō (1), to *waken,* i.e. *rouse*

ARISING
6965 qûwm (1), to *rise*

ARISTARCHUS
708 Aristarchŏs (5), *best ruling*

ARISTOBULUS'
711 Aristŏbŏulŏs (1), *best counselling*

ARK
727 'ârôwn (194), *box*
8392 têbâh (28), *box, basket*
2787 kibôtŏs (6), *ark; chest* or *box*

ARKITE
6208 'Arqîy (2), *tush*

ARM
248 'ezrôwa' (2), *arm*
2220 zᵉrôwa' (59), *arm; foreleg; force, power*
2502 châlats (1), to *depart;* to *equip*
3802 kâthêph (1), *side-piece*
1023 brachiōn (3), *arm*
3695 hŏplizō (1), to *equip*

ARMAGEDDON
717 Armagĕddōn (1), *hill* of the *rendezvous*

ARMED
2502 châlats (16), to *equip;* to *present*

2571 châmûsh (3), able-bodied *soldiers*
3847 lâbash (3), to *clothe*
4043 mâgên (2), small *shield (buckler)*
5401 nâshaq (3), to *kiss*; to *equip* with weapons
5402 nesheq (1), military *arms, arsenal*
7324 rûwq (1), to *pour out*, i.e. *empty*
2528 kathŏplizō (1), to *equip fully* with armor

ARMENIA
780 'Ărârat̲ (2), *Ararat*

ARMHOLES
679+3027 'atstsîyl (2), *joint* of the hand

ARMIES
1416 gᵉdûwd (1), *band of soldiers*
2428 chayil (4), *army; wealth; virtue; valor*
4264 machăneh (4), *encampment*
4630 ma'ărâh (1), *open spot*
4634 ma'ărâkâh (6), *row; pile*; military *array*
6635 tsâbâ' (22), *army, military host*
3925 parĕmbŏlē (1), *battle-array*
4753 stratĕuma (3), body of *troops*
4760 stratŏpĕdŏn (1), body of *troops*

ARMONI
764 'Armônîy (1), *palatial*

ARMOUR
2185 zônôwth (1), *harlots*
2290 chăgôwr (1), *belt for the waist*
2488 chălîytsâh (1), *spoil, booty of the dead*
3627 kᵉlîy (11), *implement, thing*
4055 mad (2), *vesture, garment; carpet*
5402 nesheq (3), military *arms, arsenal*
3696 hŏplŏn (2), *implement, or utensil or tool*
3833 panŏplia (3), *full armor*

ARMOURBEARER
5375+3627 nâsâ' (18), *lift up*

ARMOURY
214 'ôwtsâr (1), *depository*
5402 nesheq (1), military *arms, arsenal*
8530 talpîyâh (1), *something tall*

ARMS
1672 dâ'ag (1), *be anxious, be afraid*
2220 zᵉrôwa' (24), *arm; foreleg; force, power*
2684 chôtsen (1), *bosom*
43 agkalē (1), *arm*
1723 ĕnagkalizŏmai (2), to *take into one's arms*

ARMY
1416 gᵉdûwd (4), *band of soldiers*
2426 chêyl (1), *rampart, battlement*
2426+6635 chêyl (1), *rampart, battlement*
2428 chayil (52), *army; wealth; virtue; valor*
2429 chayil (Ch.) (2), *army; strength*
2502 châlats (1), to *deliver, equip*
4634 ma'ărâkâh (7), *row; pile*; military *array*
4675 matstsâbâh (1), military *guard*
6635 tsâbâ' (7), *army, military host*
4753 stratĕuma (3), body of *troops*

ARNAN
770 'Arnân (1), *noisy*

ARNON
769 'Arnôwn (25), *brawling stream*

AROD
720 'Ărôwd (1), *fugitive*

ARODI
722 'Ărôwdîy (1), *Arodite*

ARODITES
722 'Ărôwdîy (1), *Arodite*

AROER
6177 'Ărô'êr (16), *nudity* of situation

AROERITE
6200 'Ărô'êrîy (1), *Aroërite*

AROSE
2224 zârach (2), to *rise*; to *be bright*
5927 'âlâh (2), to *ascend, be high, mount*
5975 'âmad (1), to *stand*
6965 qûwm (107), to *rise*
6966 qûwm (Ch.) (1), to *rise*
7925 shâkam (7), to *start early* in the morning
305 anabainō (1), to *go up, rise*
450 anistēmi (24), to *stand up*; to *come back to life*
906 ballō (1), to *throw*
1096 ginŏmai (11), to *be, become*
1326 diĕgĕirō (2), to *arouse, stimulate*
1453 ĕgĕirō (13), to *waken*, i.e. *rouse*
1525 ĕisĕrchŏmai (1), to *enter*

ARPAD
774 'Arpâd (4), *spread out*

ARPHAD
774 'Arpâd (2), *spread out*

ARPHAXAD
775 'Arpakshad (9), *Arpakshad*
742 Arphaxad (1), *Arphaxad*

ARRAY
631 'âçar (1), to *fasten*; to *join* battle
3847 lâbash (2), to *clothe*
5844 'âṭâh (1), to *wrap*, i.e. *cover, veil, clothe*
6186 'ârak (26), to set in a *row*, i.e. *arrange*
7896 shîyth (1), to *place*
2441 himatismŏs (1), *clothing*

ARRAYED
3847 lâbash (4), to *clothe*
1746 ĕnduō (1), to *invest* with clothing
4016 pĕriballō (6), to *wrap around, clothe*

ARRIVED
2668 kataplĕō (1), to *sail down*
3846 paraballō (1), to *reach* a place; to *liken*

ARROGANCY
1347 gâ'ôwn (3), *ascending; majesty*
6277 'âthâq (1), *impudent*

ARROW
1121+7198 bên (1), *people* of a class or kind
2671 chêts (11), *arrow; shaft* of a spear
2678 chitstsîy (4), *arrow*

ARROWS
1121 bên (1), *people* of a class or kind
2671 chêts (36), *arrow; wound; shaft* of a spear
2678 chitstsîy (1), *arrow*
2687 châtsâts (1), *gravel, grit*
7565 resheph (1), *flame*

ARTAXERXES
783 'Artachshastâ' (Ch.) (14), *Artaxerxes*

ARTAXERXES'
783 'Artachshastâ' (Ch.) (1), *Artaxerxes*

ARTEMAS
734 Artĕmas (1), *gift of Artemis*

ARTIFICER
2794 chôrêsh (1), skilled *fabricator* worker
2796 chârâsh (1), skilled *fabricator* or worker

ARTIFICERS
2796 chârâsh (2), skilled *fabricator* or worker

ARTILLERY
3627 kᵉlîy (1), *implement, thing*

ARTS
4021 pĕriĕrgŏs (1), *magic, sorcery*

ARUBOTH
700 'Ărubbôwth (1), *Arubboth*

ARUMAH
725 'Ărûwmâh (1), *height*

ARVAD
719 'Arvad (2), *refuge for the roving*

ARVADITE
721 'Arvâdîy (2), *Arvadite*

ARZA
777 'artsâ' (1), *earthiness*

ASA
609 'Âçâ' (57), *Asa*
760 Asa (2), *Asa*

ASA'S
609 'Âçâ' (1), *Asa*

ASAHEL
760 'Ăram Tsôwbâh (1), *Aram of* Coele-Syria
6214 'Ăsâh'êl (17), *God has made*

ASAHIAH
6222 'Ăsâyâh (2), *Jehovah has made*

ASAIAH
6222 'Ăsâyâh (6), *Jehovah has made*

ASAPH
623 'Âçâph (44), *collector*

ASAPH'S
623 'Âçâph (1), *collector*

ASAREEL
840 'Ăsar'êl (1), *right of God*

ASARELAH
841 'Ăsar'êlâh (1), *right toward God*

ASCEND
5927 'âlâh (9), to *ascend, be high, mount*
305 anabainō (4), to *go up, rise*

ASCENDED
5927 'âlâh (10), to *ascend, be high, mount*
305 anabainō (9), to *go up, rise*

ASCENDETH
305 anabainō (2), to *go up, rise*

ASCENDING
5927 'âlâh (2), to *ascend, be high, mount*
305 anabainō (3), to *go up, rise*

ASCENT
4608 ma'ăleh (2), *elevation; platform*
5930 'ôlâh (1), *sacrifice wholly consumed in fire*
5944 'ălîyâh (1), *upper things; second-story*

ASCRIBE
3051 yâhab (1), to *give*
5414 nâthan (2), to *give*

ASCRIBED
5414 nâthan (2), to *give*

ASENATH
621 'Âçᵉnath (3), *Asenath*

ASER
768 Asēr (2), *happy*

ASH
766 'ôren (1), *ash tree*

ASHAMED
954 bûwsh (79), to be *ashamed; disappointed*
1322 bôsheth (1), *shame*
2659 châphêr (4), to be *ashamed, disappointed*
3637 kâlam (12), to *taunt or insult*

153 aischunŏmai (5), *to feel shame for oneself*
422 anĕpaischuntŏs (1), *unashamed*
1788 ĕntrĕpō (2), *to respect; to confound*
1870 ĕpaischunŏmai (11), *to feel shame*
2617 kataischunō (7), *to disgrace or shame*

ASHAN
6228 'Âshân (4), *smoke*

ASHBEA
791 'Ashbêa' (1), *adjurer*

ASHBEL
788 'Ashbêl (3), *flowing*

ASHBELITES
789 'Ashbêlîy (1), *Ashbelite*

ASHCHENAZ
813 'Ashkᵉnaz (2), *Ashkenaz*

ASHDOD
795 'Ashdôwd (21), *ravager*

ASHDODITES
796 'Ashdôwdîy (1), *Ashdodite*

ASHDOTH-PISGAH
798+6449 'Ashdôwth hap-Piçgâh (3), *ravines of the Pisgah*

ASHDOTHITES
796 'Ashdôwdîy (1), *Ashdodite*

ASHER
836 'Âshêr (42), *happy*

ASHERITES
843 'Âshêrîy (1), *Asherite*

ASHES
665 'êpher (24), *ashes*
1878 dâshên (2), *to be fat, thrive; to fatten*
1880 deshen (8), *fat; fatness, ashes*
6083 'âphâr (2), *dust, earth, mud; clay,*
6368 pîyach (2), *powder dust or ashes*
4700 spôdŏs (3), *ashes*
5077 tĕphrŏō (1), *to incinerate*

ASHIMA
807 'Ăshîymâ' (1), *Ashima*

ASHKELON
831 'Ashqᵉlôwn (9), *Ashkelon*

ASHKENAZ
813 'Ashkᵉnaz (1), *Ashkenaz*

ASHNAH
823 'Ashnâh (2), *Ashnah*

ASHPENAZ
828 'Ashpᵉnaz (1), *Ashpenaz*

ASHRIEL
845 'Asrî'êlîy (1), *Asrielite*

ASHTAROTH
6252 'Ashtârôwth (11), *increases*

ASHTERATHITE
6254 'Ashtᵉrâthîy (1), *Ashterathite*

ASHTEROTH
6255 'Ashtᵉrôth Qarnayim (1), *Ashtaroth of (the) double horns*

ASHTORETH
6252 'Ashtârôwth (3), *increases*

ASHUR
804 'Ashshûwr (2), *successful*

ASHURITES
843 'Âshêrîy (2), *Asherite*

ASHVATH
6220 'Ashvâth (1), *bright*

ASIA
773 Asia (20), *Asia Minor*
775 Asiarchēs (1), *ruler in Asia*

ASIDE
2015 hâphak (1), *to turn about or over*
3943 lâphath (1), *to clasp; to turn aside*
5186 nâṭâh (16), *to stretch or spread out*
5265 nâça' (1), *start on a journey*
5437 çâbab (2), *to surround*
5493 çûwr (4), *to turn off*
5844 'âṭâh (5), *to wrap, i.e. cover, veil, clothe*
6437 pânâh (1), *to turn, to face*
7750 sûwṭ (1), *become derelict*
7847 sâṭâh (5), *to deviate from duty, go astray*
402 anachōrĕō (3), *to retire, withdraw*
565 apĕrchŏmai (1), *to go off, i.e. depart*
659 apŏtithēmi (2), *to put away; get rid of*
863 aphiēmi (1), *to leave; to pardon, forgive*
1824 ĕxautēs (2), *instantly, at once*
2596 kata (1), *down; according to*
5087 tithēmi (1), *to place, put*
5298 hupŏchōrĕō (1), *to vacate down, i.e. retire*

ASIEL
6221 'Ăsîy'êl (1), *made of God*

ASK
1156 bᵉ'â' (Ch.) (2), *to seek or ask*
1245 bâqash (1), *to search out*
1875 dârash (1), *to pursue or search*
7592 shâ'al (41), *to ask*
154 aitĕō (38), *to ask for*
523 apaitĕō (1), *to demand back*
1833 ĕxĕtazō (1), *to ascertain or interrogate*
1905 ĕpĕrōtaō (8), *to inquire, seek*

2065 ĕrōtaō (11), *to interrogate; to request*
4441 punthanŏmai (2), *to ask for information*

ASKED
1156 bᵉ'â' (Ch.) (1), *to seek or ask*
1245 bâqash (1), *to search out*
7592 shâ'al (49), *to ask*
7593 shᵉ'êl (Ch.) (3), *to ask*
154 aitĕō (4), *to ask for*
1905 ĕpĕrōtaō (45), *to inquire, seek*
2065 ĕrōtaō (11), *to interrogate; to request*
3004 lĕgō (1), *to say*
4441 punthanŏmai (4), *to ask for information*

ASKELON
831 'Ashqᵉlôwn (3), *Ashkelon*

ASKEST
7592 shâ'al (1), *to ask*
154 aitĕō (1), *to ask for*
1905 ĕpĕrōtaō (1), *to inquire, seek*

ASKETH
7592 shâ'al (5), *to ask*
154 aitĕō (5), *to ask for*
2065 ĕrōtaō (1), *to interrogate; to request*

ASKING
7592 shâ'al (3), *to ask*
350 anakrinō (2), *to interrogate, determine*
1905 ĕpĕrōtaō (1), *to inquire, seek*
2065 ĕrōtaō (1), *to interrogate; to request*

ASLEEP
3463 yâshên (2), *sleepy*
7290 râdam (2), *to stupefy*
879 aphupnŏō (1), *to drop (off) in slumber*
2518 kathĕudō (5), *to fall asleep*
2837 kŏimaō (6), *to slumber; to decease*

ASNAH
619 'Açnâh (1), *Asnah*

ASNAPPER
620 'Oçnappar (Ch.) (1), *Osnappar*

ASP
6620 pethen (1), *asp*

ASPATHA
630 'Açpâthâ' (1), *Aspatha*

ASPS
6620 pethen (3), *asp*
785 aspis (1), *serpent, (poss.) asp*

ASRIEL
844 'Asrîy'êl (2), *right of God*

ASRIELITES
845 'Asrî'êlîy (1), *Asrielite*

ASS
860 'âthôwn (16), *female donkey, ass*

2543 chămôwr (55), *male donkey or ass*
5601 çappîyr (1), *sapphire*
5895 'ayîr (2), *young robust donkey or ass*
6171 'ârôwd (1), *onager or wild donkey*
6501 pere' (3), *onager, wild donkey*
3678 ŏnariŏn (1), *little donkey*
3688 ŏnŏs (5), *donkey*
5268 hupŏzugiŏn (2), *donkey*

ASS'S
860 'âthôwn (1), *female donkey, ass*
2543 chămôwr (1), *male donkey or ass*
6501 pere' (1), *onager, wild donkey*
3688 ŏnŏs (1), *donkey*

ASSAULT
6696 tsûwr (1), *to cramp, i.e. confine; to harass*
3730 hŏrmē (1), *violent impulse, i.e. onset*

ASSAULTED
2186 ĕphistēmi (1), *to be present; to approach*

ASSAY
5254 nâçâh (1), *to test, attempt*

ASSAYED
2974 yâ'al (1), *to assent; to undertake, begin*
5254 nâçâh (1), *to test, attempt*
3985 pĕirazō (1), *to endeavor, scrutinize, entice, discipline*
3987 pĕiraō (1), *to attempt, try*

ASSAYING
3984+2983 pĕira (1), *attempt, experience*

ASSEMBLE
622 'âçaph (10), *to gather, collect*
1481 gûwr (1), *to sojourn, live as an alien*
2199 zâ'aq (2), *to call out, convene publicly*
3259 yâ'ad (1), *to meet; to summon; to direct*
5789 'ûwsh (1), *to hasten*
6908 qâbats (5), *to collect, assemble*

ASSEMBLED
622 'âçaph (4), *to gather, collect*
662 'âphaq (1), *to abstain*
1413 gâdad (1), *to gash, slash oneself*
2199 zâ'aq (1), *to call out, convene publicly*
3259 yâ'ad (3), *to meet; to summon; to direct*
6633 tsâbâ' (1), *to mass an army or servants*
6638 tsâbâh (1), *to array an army against*
6908 qâbats (1), *to collect, assemble*

ASSEMBLIES
6950 qâhal (11), to convoke, gather
7284 rᵉgash (Ch.) (3), to gather tumultuously
1096 ginŏmai (1), to be, become
4863 sunagō (6), to gather together
4871 sunalizō (1), to accumulate
4905 sunĕrchŏmai (1), to gather together

ASSEMBLIES
627 'ăçuppâh (1), collection of sayings
4150 môw'êd (1), assembly, congregation
4744 miqrâ' (2), public meeting
5712 'êdâh (1), assemblage; family
6116 'ătsârâh (1), assembly

ASSEMBLING
6633 tsâbâ' (1), to mass an army or servants
1997 ĕpisunagōgē (1), meeting, gathering

ASSEMBLY
4150 môw'êd (3), assembly, congregation
4186 môwshâb (1), seat; site; abode
5475 çôwd (5), intimacy; consultation; secret
5712 'êdâh (8), assemblage; family
6116 'ătsârâh (9), assembly
6951 qâhâl (17), assemblage
6952 qᵉhillâh (1), assemblage
1577 ĕkklēsia (3), congregation
3831 panēguris (1), mass-meeting
4864 sunagōgē (1), assemblage

ASSENT
6310 peh (1), mouth; opening

ASSENTED
4934 suntithĕmai (1), to place jointly

ASSES
860 'âthôwn (17), female donkey, ass
2543 chămôwr (40), male donkey or ass
5895 'ayîr (2), young robust donkey or ass
6167 'ărâd (Ch.) (1), onager or wild donkey
6501 pere' (4), onager, wild donkey

ASSHUR
804 'Ashshûwr (8), successful

ASSHURIM
805 'Ăshûwrîy (1), Ashurite

ASSIGNED
5414 nâthan (2), to give

ASSIR
617 'Aççîyr (5), prisoner

ASSIST
3936 paristēmi (1), to stand beside, present

ASSOCIATE
7489 râ'a' (1), to break to pieces; to make

ASSOS
789 Assŏs (2), Assus

ASSUR
804 'Ashshûwr (2), successful

ASSURANCE
539 'âman (1), to be firm, faithful, true; to trust
983 beţach (1), safety, security, trust
4102 pistis (1), faithfulness; faith, belief
4136 plērŏphŏria (4), full assurance

ASSURE
3983 pĕinaō (1), to famish; to crave

ASSURED
571 'emeth (1), certainty, truth, trustworthiness
6966 qûwm (Ch.) (1), to rise
4104 pistŏō (1), to assure

ASSUREDLY
571 'emeth (1), certainty, truth, trustworthiness
3045 yâda' (1), to know
3318 yâtsâ' (1), to go, bring out
3588 kîy (3), for, that because
8354 shâthâh (1), to drink, imbibe
806 asphalōs (1), securely
4822 sumbibazō (1), to unite; to infer, show

ASSWAGE
2820 châsak (1), to refuse, spare, preserve

ASSWAGED
2820 châsak (1), to refuse, spare, preserve
7918 shâkak (1), to lay a trap; to allay

ASSYRIA
804 'Ashshûwr (118), successful

ASSYRIAN
804 'Ashshûwr (13), successful

ASSYRIANS
804 'Ashshûwr (10), successful

ASTAROTH
6252 'Ashtârôwth (1), increases

ASTONIED
1724 dâham (1), to be astounded
7672 shᵉbash (Ch.) (1), to perplex, be baffled
8074 shâmêm (6), to devastate; to stupefy
8075 shᵉmam (Ch.) (1), to devastate; to stupefy
8429 tᵉvahh (Ch.) (1), to amaze, take alarm

ASTONISHED
8074 shâmêm (14), to devastate; to stupefy
8539 tâmahh (1), to be astounded
1605 ĕkplēssō (10), to astonish
1839 ĕxistēmi (6), to become astounded
2284 thambĕō (2), to astound, be amazed
4023+2285 pĕriĕchō (1), to clasp; to encircle

ASTONISHMENT
8047 shammâh (14), ruin; consternation
8074 shâmêm (1), to devastate; to stupefy
8078 shimmâmôwn (2), stupefaction, despair
8541 timmâhôwn (2), consternation, panic
8653 tar'êlâh (1), reeling, staggering
1611 ĕkstasis (1), bewilderment, ecstasy, astonishment

ASTRAY
5080 nâdach (1), to push off, scattered
7683 shâgag (1), to stray
7686 shâgâh (2), to stray
8582 tâ'âh (13), to vacillate, stray
4105 planaō (5), to roam, wander from safety

ASTROLOGER
826 'ashshâph (Ch.) (1), conjurer, enchanter

ASTROLOGERS
825 'ashshâph (2), conjurer, enchanter
826 'ashshâph (Ch.) (5), conjurer, enchanter
1895+8064 hâbar (1), to be a horoscopist

ASUNDER
996 bêyn (1), between
673 apŏchōrizō (1), to rend apart; to separate
1288 diaspaō (1), to sever or dismember
1371 dichŏtŏmĕō (1), to flog severely
2997 laschō (1), to crack open
4249 prizō (1), to saw in two
5563 chōrizō (2), to place room between

ASUPPIM
624 'âçûph (2), stores of goods

ASYNCRITUS
799 Asugkritŏs (1), incomparable

ATAD
329 'âţâd (2), buckthorn tree

ATARAH
5851 'Ăţârâh (1), crown

ATAROTH
5852 'Ăţârôwth (5), crowns

ATAROTH-ADAR
5853 'Ăţrôwth 'Addâr (1), crowns of Addar

ATAROTH-ADDAR
5853 'Ăţrôwth 'Addâr (1), crowns of Addar

ATE
398 'âkal (2), to eat
2719 katĕsthiō (1), to devour

ATER
333 'Âţêr (5), maimed

ATHACH
6269 'Ăthâk (1), lodging

ATHAIAH
6265 'Ăthâyâh (1), Jehovah has helped

ATHALIAH
6271 'Ăthalyâh (17), Jehovah has constrained

ATHENIANS
117 Athēnaiŏs (1), inhabitant of Athenæ

ATHENS
116 Athēnai (6), city Athenæ
117 Athēnaiŏs (1), inhabitant of Athenæ

ATHIRST
6770 tsâmê' (2), to thirst
1372 dipsaō (3), to thirst for

ATHLAI
6270 'Athlay (1), compressed

ATONEMENT
3722 kâphar (73), to cover; to expiate
3725 kippûr (7), expiation
2643 katallagē (1), restoration

ATONEMENTS
3725 kippûr (1), expiation

ATROTH
5855 'Ăţrôwth Shôwphân (1), crowns of Shophan

ATTAI
6262 'Attay (4), timely

ATTAIN
3201 yâkôl (1), to be able
5381 nâsag (1), to reach
7069 qânâh (1), to create; to procure
2658 katantaō (2), to attain or reach

ATTAINED
935 bôw' (4), to go or come
5381 nâsag (1), to reach
2638 katalambanō (1), to seize; to possess
2983 lambanō (1), to take, receive
3877 parakŏlŏuthĕō (1), to attend; trace out
5348 phthanō (2), to anticipate or precede

ATTALIA
825 Attalĕia (1), Attaleia

ATTEND
6440 pânîym (1), *face; front*
7181 qâshab (9), to *prick up* the ears
2145 ĕuprŏsĕdrŏs (1), *diligent service*

ATTENDANCE
4612 ma'ămâd (2), *position; attendant*
4337 prŏsĕchŏ (2), to *pay attention to*

ATTENDED
995 bîyn (1), to *understand; discern*
7181 qâshab (1), to *prick up* the ears
4337 prŏsĕchŏ (1), to *pay attention to*

ATTENDING
4343 prŏskartĕrĕsis (1), *persistency*

ATTENT
7183 qashshâb (2), *hearkening*

ATTENTIVE
7183 qashshâb (3), *hearkening*
1582 ĕkkrĕmamai (1), to *listen closely*

ATTENTIVELY
8085 shâma' (1), to *hear* intelligently

ATTIRE
2871 ţâbûwl (1), *turban*
7196 qishshûr (1), *girdle* or *sash* for women
7897 shîyth (1), *garment*

ATTIRED
6801 tsânaph (1), to *wrap*, i.e. *roll* or *dress*

AUDIENCE
241 'ôzen (7), *ear*
189 akŏē (1), *hearing; thing heard*
191 akŏuŏ (4), to *hear; obey*

AUGMENT
5595 çâphâh (1), to *scrape*; to *accumulate*

AUGUSTUS
828 Augŏustŏs (3), *revered one*

AUGUSTUS'
828 Augŏustŏs (1), *revered one*

AUL
4836 martsêa' (2), *awl* for *piercing*

AUNT
1733 dôwdâh (1), *aunt*

AUSTERE
840 austĕrŏs (2), *severe, harsh; exacting*

AUTHOR
159 aitiŏs (1), *causer*
747 archēgŏs (1), *chief leader; founder*

AUTHORITIES
1849 ĕxŏusia (1), *authority, power, right*

AUTHORITY
7235 râbâh (1), to *increase*
8633 tôqeph (1), *might*
831 authĕntĕŏ (1), to *have authority*
1413 dunastēs (1), *ruler* or *officer*
1849 ĕxŏusia (28), *authority, power, right*
1850 ĕxŏusiazŏ (1), to *control, master another*
2003 ĕpitagē (1), *injunction* or *decree*
2715 katĕxŏusiazŏ (2), to *wield full privilege over*
5247 hupĕrŏchē (1), *superiority*

AVA
5755 'Ivvâh (1), *overthrow, ruin*

AVAILETH
7737 shâvâh (1), to *level*; to *resemble*; to *adjust*
2480 ischuŏ (3), to *have* or *exercise force*

AVEN
206 'Âven (3), *idolatry*

AVENGE
5358 nâqam (8), to *avenge* or *punish*
5358+5360 nâqam (1), to *avenge* or *punish*
5414+5360 nâthan (1), to *give*
6485 pâqad (1), to *visit, care for, count*
1556 ĕkdikĕŏ (4), to *vindicate; retaliate*
4160+3588+1557 pŏiĕŏ (2), to *make* or *do*

AVENGED
3467 yâsha' (1), to *make safe, free*
5358 nâqam (9), to *avenge* or *punish*
5414+5360 nâthan (1), to *give*
8199 shâphaţ (2), to *judge*
1556 ĕkdikĕŏ (1), to *vindicate; retaliate*
2919+3588+2917 krinŏ (1), to *decide*; to *try*

AVENGER
1350 gâ'al (6), to *redeem*; to *be the next of kin*
5358 nâqam (2), to *avenge* or *punish*
1558 ĕkdikŏs (1), *punisher, avenger*

AVENGETH
5414+5360 nâthan (2), to *give*

AVENGING
3467 yâsha' (2), to *make safe, free*
6544+6546 pâra' (1), to *absolve, begin*

AVERSE
7725 shûwb (1), to *turn back*; to *return*

AVIM
5761 'Avvîym (1), *Avvim*

AVIMS
5757 'Avvîy (1), *Avvite*

AVITES
5757 'Avvîy (2), *Avvite*

AVITH
5762 'Ăvîyth (2), *ruin*

AVOID
6544 pâra' (1), to *loosen*; to *expose, dismiss*
1223 dia (1), *through*, by means of; *because of*
1578 ĕkklinŏ (1), to *shun*; to *decline*
3868 paraitĕŏmai (1), to *deprecate, decline*
4026 pĕriistēmi (1), to *stand around*; to *avoid*

AVOIDED
5437 çâbab (1), to *surround*

AVOIDING
1624 ĕktrĕpŏ (1), to *turn away*
4724 stĕllŏ (1), to *repress, abstain* from

AVOUCHED
559 'âmar (2), to *say, speak*

AWAIT
1917 ĕpibŏulē (1), *plot, plan*

AWAKE
5782 'ûwr (20), to *awake*
6974 qûwts (11), to *awake*
1235 diagrēgŏrĕŏ (1), to *waken thoroughly*
1326 diĕgĕirŏ (1), to *arouse, stimulate*
1453 ĕgĕirŏ (2), to *waken*, i.e. *rouse*
1594 ĕknēphŏ (1), to *rouse* (oneself) *out*
1852 ĕxupnizŏ (1), to *waken, rouse*

AWAKED
3364 yâqats (4), to *awake*
6974 qûwts (4), to *awake*

AWAKEST
5782 'ûwr (1), to *awake*
6974 qûwts (1), to *awake*

AWAKETH
6974 qûwts (3), to *awake*

AWAKING
1096+1853 ginŏmai (1), to *be, become*

AWARE
3045 yâda' (2), to *know*
1097 ginŏskŏ (2), to *know*
1492 ĕidŏ (1), to *know*

AWAY
310 'achar (1), *after*
1197 bâ'ar (16), to *be brutish, be senseless*
1272 bârach (1), to *flee suddenly*
1473 gôwlâh (7), *exile; captive*
1497 gâzal (4), to *rob*
1540 gâlâh (17), to *denude; uncover*
1541 gᵉlâh (Ch.) (1), to *reveal mysteries*
1546 gâlûwth (4), *captivity; exiles*
1589 gânab (1), to *thieve*; to *deceive*
1639 gâra' (1), to *shave, remove, lessen*
1870 derek (1), *road; course* of life
1898 hâgâh (2), to *remove, expel*
1920 hâdaph (1), to *push away* or *down*; *drive out*
2219 zârâh (1), to *toss about*; to *diffuse*
2763 charam (1), to *devote* to destruction
2846 châthâh (1), to *lay hold* of; to *take away*
2862 châthaph (1), to *clutch, snatch*
3212 yâlak (4), to *walk*; to *live*; to *carry*
3318 yâtsâ' (4), to *go, bring out*
3988 mâ'aç (1), to *spurn*; to *disappear*
4422 mâlaţ (1), to *escape* as if by *slipperiness*
5074 nâdad (1), to *rove, flee*; to *drive away*
5077 nâdâh (1), to *exclude*, i.e. *banish*
5111 nûwd (Ch.) (1), to *flee*
5186 nâţâh (1), to *stretch* or *spread out*
5265 nâça' (3), *start* on a journey
5493 çûwr (70), to *turn off*
5496 çûwth (1), to *stimulate*; to *seduce*
5674 'âbar (7), to *cross over*; to *transition*
5709 'ădâ' (Ch.) (3), to *remove*; to *bedeck*
5710 'âdâh (1), to *pass on* or *continue*; to *remove*
7311 rûwm (2), to *be high*; to *rise* or *raise*
7368 râchaq (3), to *recede; remove*
7617 shâbâh (7), to *transport* into captivity
7628 shᵉbîy (1), *exile; booty*
7673 shâbath (1), to *repose; to desist* from
7726 shôwbâb (1), *apostate*, i.e. *idolatrous*
7953 shâlâh (1), to *draw out* or *off*, i.e. *remove*
115 athĕtēsis (1), *cancellation*
142 airŏ (12), to *lift*, to *take up*
337 anairĕŏ (1), to *take away*, i.e. *abolish*
343 anakaluptŏ (1), to *unveil*
520 apagŏ (12), to *take away*
522 apairŏ (1), to *remove, take away*
565 apĕrchŏmai (15), to *go off*, i.e. *depart*
577 apŏballŏ (2), to *throw off*; fig. to *lose*
580 apŏbŏlē (1), *rejection, loss*
595 apŏthĕsis (1), *laying aside*
617 apŏkuliŏ (3), to *roll away, roll back*

B

AWE
628 apŏlŏuō (1), to *wash fully*
630 apŏluō (27), to *relieve, release*
645 apŏspaō (1), to *withdraw* with force
646 apŏstasia (1), *defection* from truth
649 apŏstĕllō (4), to *send out* on a mission
654 apŏstrĕphō (6), to *turn away* or *back*
657 apŏtassŏmai (1), to *say adieu*; to *renounce*
659 apŏtithēmi (1), to *put away*; *get rid of*
665 apŏtrĕpō (1), to *deflect, avoid*
667 apŏhĕrŏ (3), to *bear off, carry away*
683 apŏthĕŏmai (4), to *push off*; to *reject*
726 harpazŏ (2), to *seize*
851 aphairĕŏ (8), to *remove, cut off*
863 aphiēmi (4), to *leave*; to *pardon, forgive*
868 aphistēmi (2), *instigate* to revolt
1294 diastrĕphō (1), to *distort*
1544 ĕkballō (1), to *throw out*
1593 ĕknĕuō (1), to *quietly withdraw*
1599 ĕkpĕmpŏ (1), to *despatch, send out*
1601 ĕkpiptŏ (1), to *drop away*
1602 ĕkplĕŏ (1), to *depart* by ship
1808 ĕxairŏ (1), to *remove, drive away*
1813 ĕxalĕiphŏ (2), to *obliterate*
1821 ĕxapŏstĕllō (4), to *despatch, or* to *dismiss*
1831 ĕxĕrchŏmai (1), to *issue*; to *leave*
1854 ĕxŏ (1), *out, outside*
2210 zēmiŏŏ (1), to *experience detriment*
2673 katargĕŏ (6), to *be, render entirely useless*
3179 mĕthistĕmi (1), to *move*
3334 mĕtakinĕŏ (1), to *be removed, shifted from*
3350 mĕtŏikĕsia (3), *expatriation, exile*
3351 mĕtŏikizŏ (1), to *transfer* as a *settler* or *captive*
3895 parapiptŏ (1), to *apostatize, fall away*
3911 paraphĕrō (1), to *carry off*; to *avert*
3928 parĕrchŏmai (5), to *go by*; to *perish*
4014 pĕriairĕŏ (3), to *cast off* anchor; to *expiate*
4879 sunapagō (2), to *take off together*
5217 hupagō (3), to *withdraw* or *retire*

AWE
1481 gûwr (1), to *sojourn, live as an alien*
6342 pâchad (1), to *be startled*; to *fear*
7264 râgaz (1), to *quiver*

AWOKE
3364 yâqats (6), to *awake*
1326 diĕgĕirō (1), to *arouse, stimulate*
1453 ĕgĕirō (1), to *waken*, i.e. *rouse*

AX
1270 barzel (1), *iron; iron implement*
1631 garzen (2), *axe*
4601 Ma'ăkâh (1), *depression*
4621 ma'ătsâd (1), *axe*
7134 qardôm (1), *axe*
513 axinē (1), *axe*

AXE
1631 garzen (2), *axe*
7134 qardôm (1), *axe*
513 axinē (1), *axe*

AXES
2719 chereb (1), *knife, sword*
3781 kashshîyl (1), *axe*
4037 magzêrâh (1), *cutting blade, ax*
4050 mᵉgêrâh (1), stone cutting *saw*
7134 qardôm (3), *axe*

AXLETREES
3027 yâd (2), *hand; power*

AZAL
682 'Âtsêl (1), *noble*

AZALIAH
683 'Ătsalyâhûw (2), *Jehovah has reserved*

AZANIAH
245 'Ăzanyâh (1), *heard by Jehovah*

AZARAEL
5832 'Ăzar'êl (1), *God has helped*

AZAREEL
5832 'Ăzar'êl (5), *God has helped*

AZARIAH
5838 'Ăzaryâh (47), *Jehovah has helped*
5839 'Ăzaryâh (Ch.) (1), *Jehovah has helped*

AZAZ
5811 'Âzâz (1), *strong*

AZAZIAH
5812 'Ăzazyâhûw (3), *Jehovah has strengthened*

AZBUK
5802 'Azbûwq (1), *stern depopulator*

AZEKAH
5825 'Ăzêqâh (7), *tilled*

AZEL
682 'Âtsêl (6), *noble*

AZEM
6107 'Etsem (2), *bone*

AZGAD
5803 'Azgâd (4), *stern troop*

AZIEL
5815 'Ăzîy'êl (1), *strengthened of God*

AZIZA
5819 'Ăzîyzâ' (1), *strengthfulness*

AZMAVETH
5820 'Azmâveth (8), *strong* (one) *of death*

AZMON
6111 'Atsmôwn (3), *bone-like*

AZNOTH-TABOR
243 'Aznôwth Tâbôwr (1), *flats of Tabor*

AZOR
107 Azōr (2), *helpful*

AZOTUS
108 Azōtŏs (1), *Azotus*, i.e. *Ashdod*

AZRIEL
5837 'Azrîy'êl (3), *help of God*

AZRIKAM
5840 'Azrîyqâm (6), *help of an enemy*

AZUBAH
5806 'Ăzûwbâh (4), *forsaking*

AZUR
5809 'Azzûwr (2), *helpful*

AZZAH
5804 'Azzâh (3), *strong*

AZZAN
5821 'Azzân (1), *strong one*

AZZUR
5809 'Azzûwr (1), *helpful*

BAAL
1168 Ba'al (61), *master*
896 Baal (1), *master*

BAAL'S
1168 Ba'al (1), *master*

BAAL-BERITH
1170 Ba'al Bᵉrîyth (2), *Baal of* (the) *covenant*

BAAL-GAD
1171 Ba'al Gâd (3), *Baal of Fortune*

BAAL-HAMON
1174 Ba'al Hâmôwn (1), *possessor of a multitude*

BAAL-HANAN
1177 Ba'al Chânân (5), *possessor of grace*

BAAL-HAZOR
1178 Ba'al Châtsôwr (1), *possessor of a village*

BAAL-HERMON
1179 Ba'al Chermôwn (2), *possessor of Hermon*

BAAL-MEON
1186 Ba'al Mᵉ'ôwn (3), *Baal of* (the) *habitation*

BAAL-PEOR
1187 Ba'al Pᵉ'ôwr (6), *Baal of Peor*

BAAL-PERAZIM
1188 Ba'al Pᵉ'râtsîym (4), *possessor of breaches*

BAAL-SHALISHA
1190 Ba'al Shâlîshâh (1), *Baal of Shalishah*

BAAL-TAMAR
1193 Ba'al Tâmâr (1), *possessor of* (the) *palm-tree*

BAAL-ZEBUB
1176 Ba'al Zᵉbûwb (4), *Baal of* (the) *Fly*

BAAL-ZEPHON
1189 Ba'al Tsᵉphôwn (3), *Baal of winter*

BAALAH
1173 Ba'ălâh (5), *mistress*

BAALATH
1191 Ba'ălâth (3), office of *mistress*

BAALATH-BEER
1192 Ba'ălath Bᵉ'êr (1), *mistress of a well*

BAALE
1184 Ba'ăley Yᵉhûwdâh (1), *masters of Judah*

BAALI
1180 Ba'ălîy (1), *my master*

BAALIM
1168 Ba'al (18), *master*

BAALIS
1185 Ba'ălîç (1), *in exultation*

BAANA
1195 Ba'ănâ' (2), *in affliction*

BAANAH
1195 Ba'ănâ' (10), *in affliction*

BAARA
1199 Bâ'ărâ' (1), *brutish*

BAASEIAH
1202 Ba'ăsêyâh (1), *in* (the) *work of Jehovah*

BAASHA
1201 Ba'shâ' (28), *offensiveness*

BABBLER
1167+3956 ba'al (1), *master; husband*
4691 spĕrmŏlŏgŏs (1), *gossip* or *trifler* in talk

BABBLING
7879 sîyach (1), uttered *contemplation*

BABBLINGS
2757 kĕnŏphōnia (2), *fruitless discussion*

BABE
5288 na'ar (1), male *child; servant*
1025 brĕphŏs (4), *infant*
3516 nēpiŏs (1), *infant; simple-minded* person

BABEL
894 Bâbel (2), *confusion*

BABES
5768 'ôwlêl (2), *suckling child*
8586 ta'ălûwl (1), *caprice* (as a fit *coming on*)
1025 brĕphŏs (1), *infant*

3516 nĕpiŏs (5), *infant; simple-minded* person

BABYLON
894 Bâbel (247), *confusion*
895 Bâbel (Ch.) (25), *confusion*
897 Babulōn (12), *Babylon*

BABYLON'S
894 Bâbel (8), *confusion*

BABYLONIANS
896 Bablîy (Ch.) (1), *Babylonian*
1121+894 bên (3), *people of a class or kind*

BABYLONISH
8152 Shin'âr (1), *Shinar*

BACA
1056 Bâkâ' (1), *Baca*

BACHRITES
1076 Bakrîy (1), *Bakrite*

BACK
268 'âchôwr (16), *behind, backward; west*
310 'achar (1), *after*
322 'ăchôrannîyth (1), *backwardly, by turning*
1354 gab (1), *mounded or rounded: top or rim*
1355 gab (Ch.) (1), *back*
1458 gav (7), *back*
1639 gâra' (1), *to shave, remove, lessen*
1973 hâlᵉâh (1), *far away; thus far*
2015 hâphak (2), *to turn about or over*
2820 châsak (4), *to restrain or refrain*
3607 kâlâ' (1), *to hold back or in; to prohibit*
4185 mûwsh (1), *to withdraw*
4513 mâna' (4), *to deny, refuse*
5253 nâçag (1), *to retreat*
5437 çâbab (1), *to surround*
5472 çûwg (3), *to go back, to retreat*
5493 çûwr (2), *to turn off*
5637 çârar (1), *to be refractory, stubborn*
6203 'ôreph (4), *nape or back of the neck*
6437 pânâh (6), *to turn, to face*
6544 pâra' (1), *to loosen; to expose, dismiss*
7725 shûwb (70), *to turn back; to return*
7926 shᵉkem (2), *neck; spur of a hill*
617 apŏkuliō (2), *to roll away, roll back*
650 apŏstĕrĕō (1), *to deprive; to despoil*
3557 nŏsphizŏmai (2), *to sequestrate*
3577 nōtŏs (1), *back*
3694 ŏpisō (5), *behind, after, following*
4762 strĕphō (1), *to turn quite around or reverse*
5288 hupŏstĕllō (2), *to cower or shrink*

5289 hupŏstŏlē (1), *shrinkage, timidity*
5290 hupŏstrĕphō (3), *to turn under, behind*

BACKBITERS
2637 katalalŏs (1), *slanderer*

BACKBITETH
7270 râgal (1), *to reconnoiter; to slander*

BACKBITING
5643 çêther (1), *cover, shelter*

BACKBITINGS
2636 katalalia (1), *defamation, slander*

BACKBONE
6096 'âtseh (1), *spine*

BACKS
268 'âchôwr (1), *behind, backward; west*
1354 gab (1), *mounded or rounded: top or rim*
1458 gav (1), *back*
6203 'ôreph (4), *nape of the neck*

BACKSIDE
268 'âchôwr (1), *behind, backward; west*
310 'achar (1), *after*
3693 ŏpisthĕn (1), *at the back; after*

BACKSLIDER
5472 çûwg (1), *to go back, to apostatize*

BACKSLIDING
4878 mᵉshûwbâh (7), *apostasy*
5637 çârar (1), *to be refractory, stubborn*
7726 shôwbâb (2), *apostate, i.e. idolatrous*
7728 shôwbêb (2), *apostate, heathenish*

BACKSLIDINGS
4878 mᵉshûwbâh (4), *apostasy*

BACKWARD
268 'âchôwr (11), *behind, backward; west*
322 'ăchôrannîyth (6), *backwardly, by turning*
1519+3588+3694 ĕis (1), *to or into*

BAD
873 bî'ûwsh (Ch.) (1), *wicked, evil*
7451 ra' (13), *bad; evil*
2556 kakŏs (1), *bad, evil*
4190 pŏnērŏs (1), *malice, wicked, bad; crime*
4550 saprŏs (1), *rotten, i.e. worthless*

BADE
559 'âmar (6), *to say, speak*
1696 dâbar (1), *to speak, say; to subdue*
6680 tsâvâh (3), *to constitute, enjoin*
657 apŏtassŏmai (1), *to say adieu; to renounce*
2036 ĕpō (3), *to speak*
2564 kalĕō (4), *to call*

BADEST
1696 dâbar (1), *to speak, say; to subdue*

BADGERS'
8476 tachash (14), (poss.) *antelope*

BADNESS
7455 rôa' (1), *badness*

BAG
3599 kîyç (4), *cup; utility bag*
3627 kᵉlîy (2), *implement, thing*
6872 tsᵉrôwr (3), *parcel; kernel or particle*
1101 glōssŏkŏmŏn (2), *money purse*

BAGS
2754 chârîyṭ (1), *pocket*
6696 tsûwr (1), *to cramp, i.e. confine; to harass*
905 balantiŏn (1), *money pouch*

BAHARUMITE
978 Bachărûwmîy (1), *Bacharumite*

BAHURIM
980 Bachûrîym (5), *young men*

BAJITH
1006 Bayith (1), *house; temple; family, tribe*

BAKBAKKAR
1230 Baqbaqqar (1), *searcher*

BAKBUK
1227 Baqbûwq (2), *bottle*

BAKBUKIAH
1229 Baqbuqyâh (3), *wasting of Jehovah*

BAKE
644 'âphâh (6), *to bake*
1310 bâshal (1), *to boil up, cook; to ripen*
5746 'ûwg (1), *to bake*

BAKED
644 'âphâh (2), *to bake*
1310 bâshal (1), *to boil up, cook; to ripen*

BAKEMEATS
3978+4639+644 ma'ăkâl (1), *food*

BAKEN
644 'âphâh (4), *to bake*
7246 râbak (1), *to soak bread in oil*
8601 tûphîyn (1), *baked cake*

BAKER
644 'âphâh (8), *to bake*

BAKERS
644 'âphâh (2), *to bake*

BAKERS'
644 'âphâh (1), *to bake*

BAKETH
644 'âphâh (1), *to bake*

BALAAM
1109 Bil'âm (57), *foreigner*
903 Balaam (3), *foreigner*

BALAAM'S
1109 Bil'âm (3), *foreigner*

BALAC
904 Balak (1), *waster*

BALADAN
1081 Bal'ădân (2), *Bel (is his) lord*

BALAH
1088 Bâlâh (1), *failure*

BALAK
1111 Bâlâq (42), *waster*

BALAK'S
1111 Bâlâq (1), *waster*

BALANCE
3976 mô'zên (7), *pair of balance scales*
7070 qâneh (1), *reed*

BALANCES
3976 mô'zên (8), *pair of balance scales*
3977 mô'zên (Ch.) (1), *pair of balance scales*

BALANCINGS
4657 miphlâs (1), *poising*

BALD
1371 gibbêach (1), *bald forehead*
1372 gabbachath (3), *baldness on forehead*
5556 çol'âm (1), *destructive locust kind*
7139 qârach (1), *to depilate, shave*
7142 qêrêach (3), *bald on the back of the head*
7144 qorchâh (1), *baldness*
7146 qârachath (1), *bald spot; threadbare spot*

BALDNESS
7144 qorchâh (9), *baldness*

BALL
1754 dûwr (1), *circle; ball*

BALM
6875 tsᵉrîy (6), *balsam*

BAMAH
1117 Bâmâh (1), *elevation, high place*

BAMOTH
1120 Bâmôwth (2), *heights*

BAMOTH-BAAL
1120 Bâmôwth (1), *heights of Baal*

BAND
613 'ĕçûwr (Ch.) (2), *manacles, chains*
1416 gᵉdûwd (5), *band of soldiers*
2428 chayil (2), *army; wealth; virtue; valor*
5688 'ăbôth (1), *entwined things: a string, wreath*
8193 sâphâh (1), *lip, language, speech*
4686 spĕira (7), *tenth of a Roman Legion*

BANDED
4160+4963 pŏiĕō (1), *to make or do*

BANDS
102 'aggâph (7), *crowds of troops*

B

612 'êçûwr (2),
manacles, chains
631 'âçar (1), to *fasten;* to
join battle
1416 gᵉdûwd (8), *band of
soldiers*
2256 chebel (3),
company, band
2683 chêtsen (1), *bosom*
2784 chartsubbâh (2),
fetter; pain
4133 môwṭâh (2), *pole;
ox-bow; yoke*
4147 môwçêr (6), *halter;
restraint*
4189 môwshᵉkâh (1),
cord, band
4264 machăneh (2),
encampment
5688 'âbôth (3), *entwined
things: a string, wreath*
7218 rô'sh (2), *head*
1199 dĕsmŏn (3),
shackle; impediment
2202 zĕuktēria (1),
tiller-rope, band
4886 sundĕsmŏs (1),
ligament; control

BANI
1137 Bânîy (15), *built*

BANISHED
5080 nâdach (2), to *push
off, scattered*

BANISHMENT
4065 maddûwach (1),
seduction, misleading
8331 sharshâh (1), *chain*

BANK
5550 çôlᵉlâh (3), siege
mound, i.e. *rampart*
8193 sâphâh (10), *lip;
edge, margin*
5132 trapĕza (1), *table* or
stool

BANKS
1415 gâdâh (3), *border,
bank* of a river
1428 gidyâh (1), *border,
bank* of a river

BANNER
1714 degel (1), *flag,
standard, banner*
5251 nêç (2), *flag; signal;
token*

BANNERS
1713 dâgal (3), to *be
conspicuous*

BANQUET
3738 kârâh (1), to *dig;* to
plot; to *bore, hew*
4797 mirzach (1), *cry of
joy; revel* or *feast*
4960 mishteh (10), *drink;
banquet* or feast
4961 mishteh (Ch.) (1),
drink; banquet or feast
8354 shâthâh (1), to
drink, imbibe

BANQUETING
3196 yayin (1), *wine;
intoxication*

BANQUETINGS
4224 pŏtŏs (1),
drinking-bout

BAPTISM
908 baptisma (22),
baptism

BAPTISMS
909 baptismŏs (1),
baptism

BAPTIST
907 baptizō (1), *baptize*
910 Baptistēs (13),
baptizer

BAPTIST'S
910 Baptistēs (1),
baptizer

BAPTIZE
907 baptizō (9), *baptize*

BAPTIZED
907 baptizō (57), *baptize*

BAPTIZEST
907 baptizō (1), *baptize*

BAPTIZETH
907 baptizō (2), *baptize*

BAPTIZING
907 baptizō (4), *baptize*

BAR
270 'âchaz (1), to *seize,
grasp; possess*
1280 bᵉrîyach (4), *bolt;
cross-bar* of a door
4132 môwṭ (2), *pole; yoke*

BAR-JESUS
919 Bariēsŏus (1), *son of
Joshua*

BAR-JONA
920 Bariōnas (1), *son of
Jonah*

BARABBAS
912 Barabbas (11), *son of
Abba*

BARACHEL
1292 Bârak'êl (2), *God
has blessed*

BARACHIAS
914 Barachias (1),
blessing of Jehovah

BARAK
1301 Bârâq (13), *(flash
of) lightning*
913 Barak (1), *(flash of)
lightning*

BARBARIAN
915 barbarŏs (3),
foreigner, non-Greek

BARBARIANS
915 barbarŏs (2),
foreigner, non-Greek

BARBAROUS
915 barbarŏs (1),
foreigner, non-Greek

BARBED
7905 sukkâh (1), *dart,
harpoon*

BARBER'S
1532 gallâb (1), *barber*

BARE
2029 hârâh (1), to
conceive, be pregnant
2308 châdal (1), to *desist,
stop; be fat*
2342 chûwl (1), to *dance,
whirl;* to *writhe* in pain
2554 châmaç (1), to *be
violent;* to *maltreat*

BARE-FOOT
2834 châsaph (4), to
drain away or *bail* up
3205 yâlad (110), to *bear
young;* to *father a child*
4910 mâshal (1), to *rule*
5190 nâṭal (1), to *lift;* to
impose
5375 nâsâ' (34), to *lift up*
6181 'eryâh (4), *nudity*
6209 'ârar (1), to *bare;* to
demolish
6544 pâra' (1), to *loosen;*
to *expose, dismiss*
7146 qârachath (1), *bald
spot; threadbare* spot
7287 râdâh (1), to
subjugate; to *crumble*
7980 shâlaṭ (1), to
dominate, i.e. *govern*
399 anaphĕrō (1), to *take
up;* to *lead up*
941 bastazō (4), to *lift,
bear*
1080 gĕnnaō (1), to
procreate, regenerate
1131 gumnŏs (1), *nude
or not well clothed*
3140 marturĕō (9), to
testify; to *commend*
4160 pŏiĕō (2), to *make
or do*
5342 phĕrō (1), to *bear or
carry*
5576 psĕudŏmarturĕō
(2), to *offer false
evidence*

BAREFOOT
3182 yâchêph (4), *not
wearing sandals*

BAREST
4910 mâshal (1), to *rule*
5375 nâsâ' (1), to *lift up*
3140 marturĕō (1), to
testify; to *commend*

BARHUMITE
1273 Barchûmîy (1),
Barchumite

BARIAH
1282 Bârîyach (1),
Bariach

BARK
5024 nâbach (1), to *bark*

BARKED
7111 qᵉtsâphâh (1),
fragment

BARKOS
1302 Barqôwç (2), *Barkos*

BARLEY
8184 sᵉ'ôrâh (33), *barley*
2915 krithē (1), *barley*
2916 krithinŏs (2),
consisting of barley

BARN
1637 gōren (1), open *area*
4035 mᵉgûwrâh (1),
fright; granary
596 apŏthēkē (2),
granary, grain barn

BARNABAS
921 Barnabas (29), *son of
prophecy*

BARNFLOOR
1637 gōren (1), open *area*

BARNS
618 'âçâm (1), *barn*

BARN
4460 mammᵉgûrâh (1),
granary, grain pit
596 apŏthēkē (2),
granary, grain barn

BARREL
3537 kad (3), *jar, pitcher*

BARRELS
3537 kad (1), *jar, pitcher*

BARREN
4420 mᵉlêchâh (1),
salted land, i.e. a *desert*
6115 'ôtser (1), *closure;
constraint*
6135 'âqâr (11), *sterile,
barren*
6723 tsîyâh (1), *arid
desert*
7909 shakkuwl (2),
bereaved
7921 shâkôl (2), to
miscarry
692 argŏs (1), *lazy;
useless*
4722 stĕgō (4), to *endure*
patiently

BARRENNESS
4420 mᵉlêchâh (1),
salted land, i.e. a *desert*

BARS
905 bad (1), *limb,
member; bar; chief*
1280 bᵉrîyach (35), *bolt;
cross-bar* of a door
4800 merchâb (1), *open
space; liberty*

BARSABAS
923 Barsabas (2), *son of
Sabas*

BARTHOLOMEW
918 Barthŏlŏmaiŏs (4),
son of Tolmai

BARTIMAEUS
924 Bartimaiŏs (1), *son
of the unclean*

BARUCH
1263 Bârûwk (26),
blessed

BARZILLAI
1271 Barzillay (12),
iron-hearted

BASE
1097+8034 bᵉlîy (1),
without, not yet
3653 kên (2), *pedestal* or
station of a basin
4350 mᵉkôwnâh (7),
pedestal; spot or *place*
4369 mᵉkûnâh (1), *spot*
7034 qâlâh (1), to *be light*
8217 shâphâl (4),
depressed, low
36 agĕnēs (1), *ignoble,
lowly*
5011 tapĕinŏs (1),
humiliated, lowly

BASER
60 agŏraiŏs (1), people
of the *market place*

BASES
4350 mᵉkôwnâh (13),
pedestal; spot or *place*
4369 mᵉkûnâh (1), *spot*

BASEST
8215 sh^ephal (Ch.) (1), *low*
8217 shâphâl (1), *depressed, low*

BASHAN
1316 Bâshân (59), *Bashan*

BASHAN-HAVOTH-JAIR
1316+2334 Bâshân (1), *Bashan*

BASHEMATH
1315 Bosmath (6), *fragrance*

BASKET
1731 dûwd (2), *pot, kettle; basket*
2935 ṭene' (4), *basket*
3619 k^elûwb (2), *bird-trap; basket*
5536 çal (12), *basket*
4553 sarganê (1), *wicker basket*
4711 spuris (1), *hamper or lunch-receptacle*

BASKETS
1731 dûwd (1), *pot, kettle; basket*
1736 dûwday (1), *basket*
5536 çal (2), *basket*
5552 çalçillâh (1), *twig*
2894 kŏphînŏs (6), *small basket*
4711 spuris (4), *hamper or lunch-receptacle*

BASMATH
1315 Bosmath (1), *fragrance*

BASON
3713 k^ephôwr (2), *bowl; white frost*
5592 çaph (2), *dish*
3537 niptēr (1), *basin for washing*

BASONS
101 'aggân (1), *bowl*
3713 k^ephôwr (3), *bowl; white frost*
4219 mîzrâq (11), *bowl for sprinkling*
5592 çaph (2), *dish*

BASTARD
4464 mamzêr (2), *mongrel*

BASTARDS
3541 nŏthŏs (1), *spurious or illegitimate son*

BAT
5847 'ăṭallêph (2), *mammal, bat*

BATH
1324 bath (6), *liquid measure*

BATH-RABBIM
1337 Bath Rabbîym (1), *city of Rabbah*

BATH-SHEBA
1339 Bath-Sheba' (11), *daughter of an oath*

BATH-SHUA
1340 Bath-Shûwa' (1), *daughter of wealth*

BATHE
7364 râchats (18), to *lave, bathe*

BATHED
7301 râvâh (1), to *slake thirst or appetites*

BATHS
1324 bath (8), *liquid measure*
1325 bath (Ch.) (1), *liquid measure*

BATS
5847 'ăṭallêph (1), *bat*

BATTERED
7843 shâchath (1), to *decay; to ruin*

BATTLE
3593 kîydôwr (1), (poss.) *tumult, battle*
4221 môach (1), *bone marrow*
4264 machăneh (1), *encampment*
4421 milchâmâh (143), *battle; war; fighting*
4661 mappêts (1), *war-club*
5402 nesheq (1), *military arms, arsenal*
5430 ç^e'ôwn (1), *military boot*
6635 tsâbâ' (5), *army, military host*
6635+4421 tsâbâ' (1), *army, military host*
7128 q^erâb (5), *hostile encounter*
4171 pŏlĕmŏs (5), *warfare; battle; fight*

BATTLEMENT
4624 ma'ăqeh (1), *parapet*

BATTLEMENTS
5189 n^eṭîyshâh (1), *tendril plant shoot*

BATTLES
4421 milchâmâh (6), *battle; war; fighting*

BAVAI
942 Bavvay (1), *Bavvai*

BAY
249 'ezrâch (1), *native born*
554 'âmôts (2), *red*
3956 lâshôwn (3), *tongue; tongue-shaped*

BAZLITH
1213 Batslûwth (1), *peeling*

BAZLUTH
1213 Batslûwth (1), *peeling*

BDELLIUM
916 b^edôlach (2), *bdellium, amber; pearl*

BEACON
8650 tôren (1), *mast pole; flag-staff pole*

BEALIAH
1183 B^e'alyâh (1), *Jehovah (is) master*

BEALOTH
1175 B^e'âlôwth (1), *mistresses*

BEAM
708 'ereg (1), *weaving; braid; also shuttle*

3714 kâphîyç (1), *girder, beam*
4500 mânôwr (4), *frame of a loom*
5646 'âb (1), *architrave*
6982 qôwrâh (2), *rafter; roof*
1385 dŏkŏs (6), *stick or plank*

BEAMS
1356 gêb (1), *well, cistern*
3773 kârûthâh (3), *hewn timber beams*
6763 tsêlâ' (1), *side of a person or thing*
6982 qôwrâh (2), *rafter; roof*
7136 qârâh (4), to *bring about; to impose*

BEANS
6321 pôwl (2), *beans*

BEAR
1319 bâsar (4), to *announce* (good news)
1677 dôb (10), *bear*
1678 dôb (Ch.) (1), *bear*
2398 châṭâ' (2), to *sin*
3205 yâlad (16), to *bear young; to father a child*
3212 yâlak (1), to *walk; to live; to carry*
3318 yâtsâ' (1), to *go, bring out*
3557 kûwl (1), to *keep in; to measure*
4910 mâshal (1), to *rule*
5187 n^eṭîyl (1), *laden*
5201 nâṭar (1), to *guard; to cherish anger*
5375 nâsâ' (100), to *lift up*
5445 çâbal (3), to *carry*
5749 'ûwd (1), to *protest, testify; to encompass*
6030 'ânâh (2), to *respond, answer*
6213 'âsâh (4), to *do*
7287 râdâh (1), to *subjugate; to crumble*
7981 sh^elêṭ (Ch.) (1), to *dominate, i.e. govern*
8323 sârar (1), to *have, exercise, get dominion*
8382 tâ'am (1), to *be twinned, i.e. duplicate*
8505 tâkan (1), to *balance, i.e. measure*
142 airō (4), to *lift, to take up*
399 anaphèrō (1), to *take up; to lead up*
430 anĕchŏmai (4), *put up with, endure*
503 antŏphthalmĕō (1), to *face into the wind*
715 arktŏs (1), *bear* (animal)
941 bastazō (11), to *lift, bear*
1080 gĕnnaō (1), to *procreate, regenerate*
3114 makrŏthumĕō (1), to *be forbearing, patient*
3140 marturĕō (21), to *testify; to commend*
4160 pŏiĕō (1), to *do*
5041 tĕknŏgŏnĕō (1), to *be a child bearer*

5297 hupŏphĕrō (1), to *bear from underneath*
5342 phĕrō (4), to *bear*
5409 phŏrĕō (1), to *wear*
5576 psĕudŏmarturĕō (4), to *offer falsehood in evidence*

BEARD
2206 zâqân (14), *beard*
8222 sâphâm (1), *beard*

BEARDS
2206 zâqân (4), *beard*

BEARERS
5449 çabbâl (3), *porter, carrier*

BEAREST
3205 yâlad (1), to *bear young; to father a child*
941 bastazō (1), to *lift, bear*
3140 marturĕō (1), to *testify; to commend*
5088 tiktō (1), to *produce from seed*

BEARETH
3205 yâlad (2), to *bear young; to father a child*
4910 mâshal (1), to *rule*
5375 nâsâ' (7), to *lift up*
6030 'ânâh (2), to *respond, answer*
6509 pârâh (1), to *bear fruit*
6779 tsâmach (1), to *sprout*
8382 tâ'am (1), to *be twinned, i.e. duplicate*
1627 ĕkphĕrō (1), to *bear out; to produce*
2592 karpŏphŏrĕō (1), to *be fertile*
3140 marturĕō (3), to *testify; to commend*
4722 stĕgō (1), to *endure patiently*
4828 summarturĕō (1), to *testify jointly*
5342 phĕrō (2), to *bear or carry*
5409 phŏrĕō (1), to *wear*

BEARING
2232 zâra' (1), to *sow seed; to disseminate*
3205 yâlad (3), to *bear young; to father a child*
5375 nâsâ' (10), to *lift up*
941 bastazō (3), to *lift, bear*
4064 pĕriphĕrō (1), to *transport*
4828 summarturĕō (2), to *testify jointly*
4901 sunĕpimarturĕō (1), to *testify further jointly*
5342 phĕrō (1), to *bear or carry*

BEARS
1677 dôb (2), *bear*

BEAST
929 b^ehêmâh (83), *animal, beast*
1165 b^e'îyr (1), *cattle, livestock*
2123 zîyz (1), *moving creature*

B

2416 chay (34), *alive; raw; fresh; life*
2423 chêyvâ' (Ch.) (6), wild *animal; monster*
5038 nᵉbêlâh (1), *carcase* or *carrion*
5315 nephesh (1), *life; breath; soul; wind*
5315+929 nephesh (1), *life; breath; soul; wind*
7409 rekesh (1), *relay of* animals
2226 zôôn (7), *living animal*
2342 thêriŏn (40), *dangerous animal*
2934 ktēnŏs (1), domestic *animal*

BEAST'S
2423 chêyvâ' (Ch.) (1), wild *animal; monster*

BEASTS
338 'îy (3), solitary wild creature that *howls*
929 bᵉhêmâh (51), *animal, beast*
1165 bᵉ'îyr (3), *cattle, livestock*
2123 zîyz (1), *moving creature*
2416 chay (42), *alive; raw; fresh; life*
2423 chêyvâ' (Ch.) (13), wild *animal; monster*
2874 ṭebach (1), *butchery*
2966 ṭᵉrêphâh (5), *torn prey*
3753 karkârâh (1), cow-*camel*
4806 mᵉrîy' (2), *stall-fed* animal
6728 tsîyîy (3), wild *beast*
2226 zôôn (16), *living animal*
2341 thêriŏmachêŏ (1), to *be a beast fighter*
2342 thêriŏn (6), *dangerous animal*
2934 ktēnŏs (3), domestic *animal*
4968 sphagiŏn (1), *offering for slaughter*
5074 tĕtrapŏus (2), *quadruped* animal

BEAT
1743 dûwk (1), to *pulverize* in a mortar
1792 dâkâ' (1), to *pulverize; be contrite*
1849 dâphaq (1), to *knock; to press severely*
1854 dâqaq (2), to *crush*
2040 hâraç (1), to *pull* down; *break, destroy*
2251 châbaṭ (2), to *knock* out or off, *thresh* a tree
3807 kâthath (4), to *bruise or strike, beat*
5221 nâkâh (4), to *strike, kill*
5422 nâthats (3), to *tear* down
7554 râqaʻ (1), to *pound*
7833 shâchaq (3), to *grind or wear away*
1194 dĕrō (5), to *flay*, i.e. to *scourge or thrash*

1911 ĕpiballō (1), to *throw upon*
4350 prŏskŏptō (1), to *trip up; to strike*
4363 prŏspiptō (1), to *beat or strike*
4366 prŏsrēgnumi (2), to *burst upon*
4463 rhabdizō (1), to *strike with a stick*
5180 tuptō (2), to *strike, beat, wound*

BEATEN
1643 geres (2), *grain*
1851 daq (1), *crushed; small* or *thin*
1986 hâlam (1), to *strike, beat, stamp, conquer*
2251 châbaṭ (1), to *knock* out or off, *thresh* a tree
2865 châthath (1), to *break* down
3795 kâthîyth (4), pure oil from *beaten* olives
3807 kâthath (3), to *bruise or strike, beat*
4347 makkâh (1), *blow; wound; pestilence*
4749 miqshâh (8), work molded by *hammering*
5060 nâgaʻ (1), to *strike*
5062 nâgaph (1), to *strike*
5221 nâkâh (4), to *strike, kill*
5310 nâphats (1), to *dash* to pieces; to *scatter*
7820 shâchaṭ (1), to *hammer* out
1194 dĕrō (5), to *flay*, i.e. to *scourge or thrash*
4463 rhabdizō (1), to *strike with a stick*

BEATEST
2251 châbaṭ (1), to *knock* out or off, *thresh* a tree
5221 nâkâh (1), to *strike, kill*

BEATETH
1194 dĕrō (1), to *flay*, i.e. to *scourge or thrash*

BEATING
1986 hâlam (1), to *strike, beat, stamp, conquer*
1194 dĕrō (1), to *flay*, i.e. to *scourge or thrash*
5180 tuptō (1), to *strike, beat, wound*

BEAUTIES
1926 hâdâr (1), *magnificence*

BEAUTIFUL
2896 ṭôwb (1), *good; well*
2896+4758 ṭôwb (1), *good; well*
3303 yâpheh (7), *beautiful; handsome*
3303+8389 yâpheh (2), *beautiful; handsome*
4998 nâ'âh (1), to be *pleasant*, i.e. *beautiful*
6643 tsᵉbîy (2), *conspicuous* splendor
8597 tiph'ârâh (6), *ornament*
5611 hōraiŏs (4), *flourishing, beauteous*

BEAUTIFY
6286 pâ'ar (3), to *shake a* tree

BEAUTY
1926 hâdâr (3), *magnificence*
1927 hădârâh (4), *decoration, ornament*
1935 hôwd (1), *grandeur, majesty*
2530 châmad (1), to *delight* in; *lust for*
3308 yŏphîy (20), *beauty*
4758 mar'eh (1), *appearance; vision*
5276 nâ'êm (1), to be *agreeable*
5278 no'am (4), *delight, suitableness*
6287 pᵉ'êr (1), fancy *head-dress*
6643 tsᵉbîy (2), *conspicuous* splendor
6736 tsîyr (1), *carved* idolatrous *image*
8597 tiph'ârâh (10), *ornament*

BEBAI
893 Bêbay (6), *Bebai*

BECAUSE
413 'êl (3), *to, toward*
834 'ăsher (42), *because, in order that*
1115 biltîy (3), *except, without, unless, besides*
1558 gâlal (4), on *account of, because of*
1697 dâbâr (1), *word; matter; thing*
1768 dîy (Ch.) (2), *that; of*
1870 derek (1), *road; course* of life
3027 yâd (2), *hand; power*
3282 ya'an (59), *because, for this reason*
3588 kîy (455), *for, that because*
3605 kôl (1), *all, any*
4480 min (2), *from, out of*
4481 min (Ch.) (1), *from* or *out of*
4616 ma'an (11), *on account of*
5668 'âbûwr (7), on *account of*
5921 'al (45), *above, over, upon, or against*
6118 'êqeb (1), *unto the end; for ever*
6119 'âqêb (1), *track, footprint*
6440 pânîym (67), *face; front*
6448 pâçag (1), to *contemplate*
8478 tachath (1), *bottom; underneath; in lieu of*
575 apŏ (1), *from, away*
1063 gar (5), *for, indeed, but, because*
1223 dia (54), *through, by means of; because of*
1360 diŏti (13), *on the very account that*
1537 ĕk (2), *out, out of*
1722 ĕn (3), *in; during; because of*
1893 ĕpĕi (7), *since*

1894 ĕpĕidē (2), *when, whereas*
1909 ĕpi (1), *on, upon*
2443 hina (1), *in order that*
2530 kathŏti (2), *as far* or *inasmuch as*
3704 hŏpōs (1), *in the manner that*
3754 hŏti (184), *that; because; since*
4314 prŏs (2), *for; on, at; to, toward; against*
5484 charin (2), *on account* of, *because* of

BECHER
1071 Beker (5), young bull *camel*

BECHORATH
1064 Bᵉkôwrath (1), *primogeniture*

BECKONED
1269 dianĕuō (1), to *nod* or *express* by signs
2656 katanĕuō (1), to *make a sign or signal*
2678 katasĕiō (2), to *motion a signal* or *sign*
3506 nĕuō (2), *nod*, i.e. *signal*

BECKONING
2678 katasĕiō (1), to *motion a signal or sign*

BED
3326 yâtsûwaʻ (3), *bed; wing or lean-to*
3331 yâtsaʻ (1), to *strew*
4296 miṭṭâh (23), *bed; sofa, litter or bier*
4702 matstsâʻ (1), *couch*
4903 mishkab (Ch.) (6), *bed*
4904 mishkâb (29), *bed; sleep; intercourse*
6170 'ărûwgâh (1), *parterre*, kind of *garden*
6210 'eres (4), *canopy couch*
6210+3326 'eres (1), *canopy couch*
2825 klinē (8), *couch*
2845 kŏitē (2), *couch; conception*
2895 krabbatŏs (10), *sleeping mat*
4766 strōnnumi (1), to *spread a couch*

BED'S
4296 miṭṭâh (1), *bed; sofa, litter or bier*

BEDAD
911 Bᵉdad (2), *separation*

BEDAN
917 Bᵉdân (2), *servile*

BEDCHAMBER
2315+4296 cheder (3), *apartment, chamber*
2315+4904 cheder (3), *apartment, chamber*

BEDEIAH
912 Bêdᵉyâh (1), *servant of Jehovah*

BEDS
4296 miṭṭâh (2), *bed; sofa, litter or bier*

4904 mishkâb (5), *bed; sleep; intercourse*
6170 'ărûwgâh (1), *parterre, kind of garden*
2825 klinē (1), *couch*
2895 krabbatŏs (1), *sleeping mat*

BEDSTEAD
6210 'eres (1), *canopy couch*

BEE
1682 dᵉbôwrâh (1), *bee*

BEELIADA
1182 Bᵉʿelyâdâʿ (1), *Baal has known*

BEELZEBUB
954 Bĕĕlzĕbŏul (7), *dung-god*

BEER
876 Bᵉʾêr (2), *well, cistern*

BEER-ELIM
879 Bᵉʾêr 'Êlîym (1), *well of heroes*

BEER-LAHAI-ROI
883 Bᵉʾêr la-Chay Rôʾîy (1), *well of a living (One) my seer*

BEER-SHEBA
884 Bᵉʾêr Sheba' (34), *well of an oath*

BEERA
878 Bᵉʾêrâʾ (1), *well*

BEERAH
880 Bᵉʾêrâh (1), *well*

BEERI
882 Bᵉʾêrîy (2), *fountain*

BEEROTH
881 Bᵉʾêrôwth (6), *wells*

BEEROTHITE
886 Bᵉʾêrôthîy (4), *Beërothite*

BEEROTHITES
886 Bᵉʾêrôthîy (1), *Beërothite*

BEES
1682 dᵉbôwrâh (3), *bee*

BEESH-TERAH
1203 Bᵉʾeshtᵉrâh (1), *with Ashtoreth*

BEETLE
2728 chargôl (1), *leaping insect*

BEEVES
1241 bâqâr (7), *plowing ox; herd*

BEFALL
579 'ânâh (1), *to meet, to happen*
4672 mâtsâʾ (1), *to find or acquire; to occur, meet or be present*
7122 qârâʾ (4), *to encounter, to happen*
7136 qârâh (2), *to bring about; to impose*
4876 sunantaō (1), *meet with; to occur*

BEFALLEN
4672 mâtsâʾ (3), *to find or acquire; to occur*
4745 miqreh (1), *accident or fortune*

BEFALLETH
4745 miqreh (2), *accident or fortune*

BEFELL
935 bôwʾ (1), *to go, come*
4672 mâtsâʾ (1), *to find or acquire; to occur*
7136 qârâh (1), *to bring about; to impose*
1096 ginŏmai (1), *to be, become*
4819 sumbainō (1), *to concur, happen*

BEFORE
413 'êl (8), *to, toward*
639 'aph (2), *nose or nostril; face; person*
854 'êth (4), *with; by; at*
865 'ethmôwl (1), *heretofore, formerly*
2958 tᵉrôwm (1), *not yet, before*
2962 ṭerem (41), *not yet or before*
3808 lôʾ (2), *no, not*
3942 liphnay (1), *anterior, in front of*
4136 mûwl (1), *in front of, opposite*
4551 maççâʾ (1), stone *quarry; projectile*
4608 maʿăleh (1), *elevation; platform*
5048 neged (70), *over against or before*
5084 nâdân (1), *sheath*
5226 nêkach (1), *opposite*
5227 nôkach (9), *opposite, in front of*
5703 'ad (1), *perpetuity; ancient*
5704 'ad (1), *as far (long) as; during; while; until*
5869 'ayin (8), *eye; sight; fountain*
5921 'al (12), *above, over, upon, or against*
5973 'îm (5), *with*
6440 pânîym (1110), *face; front*
6471 paʿam (1), *time; step; occurence*
6903 qᵉbêl (Ch.) (3), *in front of, before*
6905 qâbâl (1), *in front of*
6924 qedem (10), *before, anciently*
6925 qŏdâm (Ch.) (29), *before*
6931 qadmôwnîy (1), *anterior time*
7130 qereb (1), *nearest part, i.e. the center*
7223 riʾshôwn (3), *first, in place, time or rank*
561 apᵉnanti (2), *opposite, before*
575 apŏ (2), *from, away*
1519 eis (3), *to or into*
1715 ĕmprŏsthĕn (41), *in front of*

1722 ĕn (1), *in; during; because of*
1725 ĕnanti (1), *before, in presence of*
1726 ĕnantiŏn (4), *in the presence of*
1773 ĕnnuchŏn (1), *by night*
1799 ĕnōpiŏn (63), *in the face of, before*
1909 ĕpi (17), *on, upon*
2596 kata (2), *down; according to*
2713 katĕnanti (1), *directly opposite*
2714 katĕnōpiŏn (3), *directly in front of*
3319 mĕsŏs (1), *middle*
3764 ŏudĕpō (1), *not even yet*
3844 para (3), *from; with; besides; on account of*
3908 paratithēmi (9), *to present something*
3936 paristēmi (2), *to stand beside, present*
4250 prin (7), *prior, sooner, before*
4253 prŏ (43), *before in time or space*
4254 prŏagō (15), *to lead forward; to precede*
4256 prŏaitiaŏmai (1), *to previously charge*
4257 prŏakŏuō (1), *to hear beforehand*
4264 prŏbibazō (1), *to bring to the front*
4267 prŏginōskō (1), *to know beforehand*
4270 prŏgraphō (1), *to write previously*
4275 prŏĕidō (1), *to foresee*
4277 prŏĕpō (1), *to say already, to predict*
4278 prŏĕnarchŏmai (1), *to commence already*
4280 prŏĕrĕō (8), *to say already, predict*
4281 prŏĕrchŏmai (4), *to go onward, precede*
4282 prŏĕtŏimazō (1), *to fit up in advance*
4283 prŏĕuaggĕlizŏmai (1), *to announce in advance*
4293 prŏkataggĕllō (3), *to predict, promise, foretell*
4295 prŏkĕimai (3), *to be present to the mind*
4296 prŏkērussō (1), *to proclaim in advance*
4299 prŏkrima (1), *prejudgment*
4300 prŏkurŏō (1), *to ratify previously*
4301 prŏlambanō (1), *to take before*
4302 prŏlĕgō (2), *to predict, forewarn*
4304 prŏmĕlĕtaō (1), *to premeditate*
4308 prŏŏraō (1), *to notice previously*
4309 prŏŏrizō (1), *to predetermine*

4310 prŏpaschō (1), *to undergo previously*
4313 prŏpŏrĕuŏmai (1), *to precede as guide*
4314 prŏs (2), *for; on, at; to, toward; against*
4315 prŏsabbatŏn (1), *Sabbath-eve*
4363 prŏspiptō (5), *to prostrate oneself*
4384 prŏtassō (1), *to prescribe beforehand*
4386 prŏtĕrŏn (4), *previously*
4391 prŏüparchō (1), *to be or do previously*
4401 prŏchĕirŏtŏnĕō (1), *to elect in advance*
4412 prōtŏn (1), *firstly*
4413 prōtŏs (2), *foremost*

BEFOREHAND
4271 prŏdēlŏs (2), *obvious, evident*
4294 prŏkatartizō (1), *to prepare in advance*
4303 prŏmarturŏmai (1), *to witness beforehand*
4305 prŏmĕrimnaō (1), *to care in advance*

BEFORETIME
865+832 'ethmôwl (1), *heretofore, formerly*
6440 pânîym (5), *face; front*
7223 riʾshôwn (1), *first, in place, time or rank*
8543+8032 tᵉmôwl (2), *yesterday*
4391 prŏüparchō (1), *to be or do previously*

BEG
7592 shâʾal (2), *to ask*
1871 ĕpaitĕō (1), *to ask for, beg*

BEGAN
2490 châlal (34), *to profane, defile*
2974 yâʾal (1), *to assent; to undertake, begin*
3246 yᵉçûd (1), *foundation; beginning)*
5927 'âlâh (1), *to ascend, be high, mount*
6751 tsâlal (1), *to shade; to grow dark*
8271 shᵉrêʾ (Ch.) (1), *to unravel, commence*
756 archŏmai (64), *to begin*
2020 ĕpiphōskō (1), *to grow light*
2192 ĕchō (1), *to have; hold; keep*

BEGAT
3205 yâlad (176), *to bear young; to father a child*
616 apŏkuĕō (1), *to generate, bring to being*
1080 gĕnnaō (43), *to procreate, regenerate*

BEGET
3205 yâlad (10), *to bear young; to father a child*

BEGETTEST
3205 yâlad (2), *to bear young; to father a child*

B

BEGETTETH
3205 yâlad (3), to *bear
young; to father a child*

BEGGAR
34 'ebyôwn (1), *destitute;
poor*
4434 ptōchŏs (2), *pauper,
beggar*

BEGGARLY
4434 ptōchŏs (1), *pauper,
beggar*

BEGGED
154 aitĕō (2), *to ask for*
4319 prŏsaitĕō (1), *to
solicit, beg*

BEGGING
1245 bâqash (1), *to
search; to strive after*
4319 prŏsaitĕō (2), *to
solicit, beg*

BEGIN
2490 châlal (12), *to
profane, defile*
8462 tᵉchillâh (1),
original; originally
756 archŏmai (11), *to
begin*
3195 mĕllō (1), *to intend,
i.e. be about to be*

BEGINNEST
2490 châlal (1), *to
profane, defile*

BEGINNING
227 'âz (3), *at that time
or place; therefore*
1931 hûw' (2), *he, she, it;
this or that*
5769 'ôwlâm (1), *eternity;
ancient; always*
7218 rô'sh (12), *head*
7223 rî'shôwn (4), *first*
7225 rê'shîyth (18), *first*
8462 tᵉchillâh (14),
original; originally
509 anōthĕn (1), *from
above; from the first*
746 archē (39), *first in
rank; first in time*
756 archŏmai (8), *to
begin*
4412 prōtŏn (1), *firstly*
4413 prōtŏs (1), *foremost*

BEGINNINGS
7218 rô'sh (2), *head*
7221 rî'shâh (1),
beginning
746 archē (1), *first*

BEGOTTEN
3205 yâlad (7), *to bear
young; to father a child*
3318 yâtsâ' (1), *to go,
bring out*
4138 môwledeth (1),
lineage, offspring
313 anagĕnnaō (1), *to
beget or bear again*
1080 gĕnnaō (7), *to
procreate, regenerate*
3439 mŏnŏgĕnēs (6),
sole, one and only
4416 prōtŏtŏkŏs (1),
first-born

BEGUILE
2603 katabrabĕuō (1), *to
award a price against*

BEGUILED
5230 nâkal (1), *to act
treacherously*
5377 nâshâ' (1), *to lead
astray, to delude*
7411 râmâh (2), *to hurl;
to shoot; to delude*
1818 ĕxapataō (1), *to
seduce wholly, deceive*

BEGUILING
1185 dĕlĕazō (1), *to
delude, seduce*

BEGUN
2490 châlal (6), *to
profane, defile*
756 archŏmai (1), *to
begin*
1728 ĕnarchŏmai (2), *to
commence on, begin*
2691 katastrēniaō (1), *to
be voluptuous against*
4278 prŏĕnarchŏmai (2),
to commence already

BEHALF
854 'êth (1), *with; by; at*
5973 'îm (1), *with*
8478 tachath (1), *bottom;
underneath; in lieu of*
1909 ĕpi (1), *on, upon*
3313 mĕrŏs (2), *division
or share*
4012 pĕri (1), *about;
around*
5228 hupĕr (4), *over; in
behalf of*

BEHAVE
2388 châzaq (1), *to
fasten upon; to seize*
5234 nâkar (1), *to care
for, respect, revere*
7292 râhab (1), *to urge
severely*
7919 sâkal (1), *to be
circumspect*
390 anastrĕphō (1), *to
remain, to live*
807 aschēmŏnĕō (1), *to
be, act unbecoming*

BEHAVED
1980 hâlak (1), *to walk;
live a certain way*
7489 râ'a' (1), *to be good
for nothing*
7737 shâvâh (1), *to level,
i.e. equalize*
7919 sâkal (4), *to be
circumspect*
812 ataktĕō (1), *to be,
act irregular*
1096 ginŏmai (1), *to be,
become*

BEHAVETH
807 aschēmŏnĕō (1), *to
be, act unbecoming*

BEHAVIOUR
2940 ṭa'am (2), *taste;
perception*
2688 katastēma (1),
demeanor
2887 kŏsmiŏs (1), *orderly*

BEHEADED
5493+7218 çûwr (1), *to
turn off*

BEGUILED / (third column)

3884 paralŏgizŏmai (1),
to delude, deceive

BEGUILED
5230 nâkal (1), *to act
treacherously*

BEHELD
2370+944 chăzâ' (Ch.)
(6), *to gaze upon*
5027 nâbaṭ (2), *to scan;
to regard with favor*
7200 râ'âh (23), *to see*
333 anathĕōrĕō (1), *to
look again*
991 blĕpō (2), *to look at*
1492 ĕidō (10), *to know*
1689 ĕmblĕpō (3), *to
observe; to discern*
2300 thĕaŏmai (2), *to
look closely at*
2334 thĕōrĕō (4), *to see;
to discern*

BEHEMOTH
930 bᵉhêmôwth (1),
hippopotamus

BEHIND
268 'âchôwr (5), *behind,
backward; west*
310 'achar (49), *after*
3498 yâthar (1), *to
remain or be left*
5975 'âmad (1), *to stand*
2641 katalĕipō (1), *to
abandon*
3693 ŏpisthĕn (4), *at the
back; after*
3694 ŏpisō (6), *behind,
after, following*
5278 hupŏmĕnō (1), *to
undergo (trials)*
5302 hustĕrĕō (4), *to be
inferior; to fall short*

BEHOLD
431 'ălûw (Ch.) (5), *lo!*
718 'ărûw (Ch.) (4), *lo!,
behold!*
1887 hê' (1), *Lo!, Look!*
2005 hên (237), *lo!; if!*
2009 hinnêh (770), *lo!;
Look!*
2205 zâqên (2), *old,
venerated*
2209 ziqnâh (1), *old age*
2372 châzâh (7), *to gaze
at; to perceive*
5027 nâbaṭ (9), *to scan;
to regard with favor*
6822 tsâphâh (1), *to peer
into the distance*
7200 râ'âh (58), *to see*
7789 shûwr (5), *to spy
out, survey*
7891 shîyr (1), *to sing*
816 atĕnizō (1), *to gaze
intently*
991 blĕpō (3), *to look at*
1492 ĕidō (5), *to know*
1689 ĕmblĕpō (1), *to
observe; to discern*
1896 ĕpĕidŏn (1), *to
regard*
2029 ĕpŏptĕuō (2), *to
watch, observe*
2334 thĕōrĕō (3), *to see;
to discern*
2396 idĕ (24), *surprise!,
lo!, look!*

2400 idŏu (180), *lo!,
note!, see!*
2657 katanŏĕō (2), *to
observe fully*

BEHOLDEST
5027 nâbaṭ (1), *to scan;
to regard with favor*
991 blĕpō (3), *to look at*

BEHOLDETH
6437 pânâh (1), *to turn,
to face*
7200 râ'âh (2), *to see*
2657 katanŏĕō (1), *to
observe fully*

BEHOLDING
6822 tsâphâh (1), *to peer;
to observe, await*
7200 râ'âh (2), *to see*
816 atĕnizō (2), *to gaze
intently*
991 blĕpō (2), *to look at*
1689 ĕmblĕpō (1), *to
observe; to discern*
2334 thĕōrĕō (4), *to see;
to discern*
2657 katanŏĕō (1), *to
observe fully*
2734 katŏptrizŏmai (1),
to see reflected
3708 hŏraō (1), *to stare,
see clearly*

BEHOVED
1163 dĕi (1), *it is (was)
necessary*
3784 ŏphĕilō (1), *to owe;
to be under obligation*

BEING
1961 hâyâh (4), *to exist,
i.e. be or become*
5750 'ôwd (2), *again;
repeatedly; still; more*
1096 ginŏmai (5), *to be,
become*
1909 ĕpi (1), *on, upon*
2070 ĕsmĕn (1), *we are*
2192 ĕchō (1), *to have;
hold; keep*
5225 huparchō (13), *to
come into existence*
5605 ōdinō (1), *to
experience labor pains*
5607 ŏn (35), *being,
existence*

BEKAH
1235 beqa' (1), *half
shekel*

BEL
1078 Bêl (3), *Bel (Baal)*

BELA
1106 Bela' (13), *gulp;
destruction*

BELAH
1106 Bela' (1), *gulp;
destruction*

BELAITES
1108 Bal'îy (1), *Belaite*

BELCH
5042 nâba' (1), *to gush
forth; emit a foul odor*

BELIAL
1100 bᵉlîya'al (16),
wickedness, trouble
955 Bĕlial (1),
worthlessness

BELIED
3584 kâchash (1), to *lie, disown; to disappoint*

BELIEF
4102 pistis (1), *faith, belief; conviction*

BELIEVE
539 'âman (19), to *be firm, faithful, true*
544 apĕithĕō (1), to *disbelieve*
569 apistĕō (2), to *disbelieve, disobey*
571 apistŏs (4), *without faith; untrustworthy*
4100 pistĕuō (109), to *have faith, i.e. credit; to entrust*
4100+1722 pistĕuō (1), to *have faith, i.e. credit*
4100+1909 pistĕuō (1), to *have faith, i.e. credit*
4102 pistis (1), *faith, belief; conviction*
4103 pistŏs (2), *trustful; reliable*

BELIEVED
539 'âman (21), to *be firm, faithful, true*
540 'âman (Ch.) (1), to *be firm, faithful, true*
544 apĕithĕō (6), to *disbelieve*
569 apistĕō (3), to *disbelieve, disobey*
569+4100 apistĕō (1), to *disbelieve, disobey*
3982 pĕithō (3), to *rely by inward certainty*
4100 pistĕuō (76), to *have faith, i.e. credit*
4103 pistŏs (2), *trustworthy; reliable*
4135 plērŏphŏrĕō (1), to *assure or convince*

BELIEVERS
4100 pistĕuō (1), to *have faith, i.e. credit*
4103 pistŏs (1), *trustworthy; reliable*

BELIEVEST
4100 pistĕuō (8), to *have faith, i.e. credit*

BELIEVETH
539 'âman (4), to *be firm, faithful, true; to trust*
544 apĕithĕō (1), to *disbelieve*
569 apistĕō (1), to *disbelieve, disobey*
571 apistŏs (3), *without faith; untrustworthy*
1537+4102 ĕk (1), *out of*
4100 pistĕuō (33), to *have faith, i.e. credit*
4103 pistŏs (2), *trustworthy; reliable*

BELIEVING
4100 pistĕuō (6), to *have faith, i.e. credit*
4103 pistŏs (2), *trustworthy; reliable*

BELL
6472 pa'ămôn (3), *bell*

BELLIES
1064 gastēr (1), *stomach; womb; gourmand*

BELLOW
6670 tsâhal (1), to *be cheerful; to sound*

BELLOWS
4647 mappûach (1), *bellows*

BELLS
4698 mᵉtsillâh (1), *small bell*
6472 pa'ămôn (3), *bell*

BELLY
990 beṭen (30), *belly; womb; body*
1512 gâchôwn (2), *belly*
3770 kᵉrês (1), *paunch*
4577 mᵉ'âh (Ch.) (1), *bowels, belly*
4578 mê'âh (3), *viscera; anguish, tenderness*
6897 qôbâh (1), *abdomen*
2836 kŏilia (10), *abdomen, womb, heart*

BELONG
1510 ĕimi (1), I *exist, I am*

BELONGED
4490 mânâh (1), *ration; lot or portion*
1510 ĕimi (1), I *exist, I am*

BELONGETH
1510 ĕimi (1), I *exist, I am*

BELOVED
157 'âhab (6), to *have affection, love*
1730 dôwd (29), *beloved, friend; relative*
2530 châmad (3), to *delight in; lust for*
3033 yᵉdîdûwth (1), *darling object*
3039 yᵉdîyd (5), *loved*
4261 machmâd (1), *object of affection or desire*
25 agapaŏ (5), to *love*
27 agapētŏs (57), *beloved*

BELOVED'S
1730 dôwd (2), *beloved, friend; relative*

BELSHAZZAR
1113 Bêlsha'tstsar (Ch.) (8), *Belshatstsar*

BELTESHAZZAR
1095 Bêlṭᵉsha'tstsar (2), *Belteshatstsar*
1096 Bêlṭᵉsha'tstsar (Ch.) (8), *Belteshatstsar*

BEMOAN
5110 nûwd (5), to *deplore; to taunt*

BEMOANED
5110 nûwd (1), to *deplore; to taunt*

BEMOANING
5110 nûwd (1), to *deplore; to taunt*

BEN
1122 Bên (1), *son*

BEN-AMMI
1151 Ben-'Ammîy (1), *son of my people*

BEN-HADAD
1130 Ben-Hădad (18), *son of Hadad*
1131 Binnûwy (7), *built*

BEN-HAIL
1134 Ben-Chayil (1), *son of might*

BEN-HANAN
1135 Ben-Chânân (1), *son of Chanan*

BEN-ONI
1126 Ben-'Ôwnîy (1), *son of my sorrow*

BEN-ZOHETH
1132 Ben-Zôwchêth (1), *son of Zocheth*

BENAIAH
1141 Bᵉnâyâh (42), *Jehovah has built*

BENCHES
7175 qeresh (1), *slab or plank; deck of a ship*

BEND
1869 dârak (7), to *tread, trample; to string a bow*
3719 kâphan (1), to *bend*

BENDETH
1869 dârak (2), to *walk, lead; to string a bow*

BENDING
7817 shâchach (1), to *sink or depress*

BENE-BERAK
1138 Bunnîy (1), *built*

BENE-JAAKAN
1142 Bᵉnêy Ya'ăqân (2), *sons of Yaakan*

BENEATH
4295 maṭṭâh (7), *below or beneath*
8478 tachath (17), *bottom; underneath*
2736 katō (3), *downwards*

BENEFACTORS
2110 ĕuĕrgĕtēs (1), *philanthropist*

BENEFIT
1576 gᵉmûwl (1), *act; service; reward*
3190 yâṭab (1), to *be, make well*
18 agathŏs (1), *good*
2108 ĕuĕrgĕsia (1), *beneficence*
5485 charis (1), *gratitude; benefit given*

BENEFITS
1576 gᵉmûwl (1), *act; service; reward*
8408 tagmûwl (1), *bestowment*

BENEVOLENCE
2133 ĕunŏia (1), *eagerly, with a whole heart*

BENINU
1148 Bᵉnîynûw (1), *our son*

BENJAMIN
1144 Binyâmîyn (158), *son of (the) right hand*
953 bᵉbĕlŏō (4), to *desecrate, profane*

BENJAMIN'S
1144 Binyâmîyn (4), *son of (the) right hand*

BENJAMITE
1145 Ben-yᵉmîynîy (9), *son of (the) right hand*

BENJAMITES
1145 Ben-yᵉmîynîy (8), *son of (the) right hand*

BENO
1121 bên (2), *son, descendant; people*

BENT
1869 dârak (7), to *walk, lead; to string a bow*
8511 tâlâ' (1), to *suspend; to be uncertain*

BEON
1194 Bᵉ'ôn (1), *Beon*

BEOR
1160 Bᵉ'ôwr (10), *lamp*

BERA
1298 Bera' (1), *Bera*

BERACHAH
1294 Bᵉrâkâh (3), *benediction, blessing*

BERACHIAH
1296 Berekyâh (1), *blessing of Jehovah*

BERAIAH
1256 Bᵉrâ'yâh (1), *Jehovah has created*

BEREA
960 Bĕrŏia (3), *region beyond the coast-line*

BEREAVE
2637 châçêr (1), to *lack; to fail, want, make less*
3782+(7921) kâshal (1), to *totter, waver; to falter*
7921 shâkôl (4), to *miscarry*

BEREAVED
7909 shakkuwl (2), *bereaved*
7921 shâkôl (3), to *miscarry*

BEREAVETH
7921 shâkôl (1), to *miscarry*

BERECHIAH
1296 Berekyâh (10), *blessing of Jehovah*

BERED
1260 Bered (2), *hail*

BERI
1275 Bêrîy (1), *Beri*

BERIAH
1283 Bᵉrîy'âh (11), *in trouble*

BERIITES
1284 Bᵉrîy'îy (1), *Beriite*

BERITES
1276 Bêrîy (1), *Berites*

BERITH
1286 Bᵉrîyth (1), *Berith*

BERNICE
959 Bĕrnikē (3), *victorious*

BERODACH-BALADAN
1255 Bᵉrô'dak Bal'ădăn (1), *Berodak-Baladan*

BEROTHAH
1268 Bêrôwthâh (1), *cypress-like*

BEROTHAI
1268 Bêrôwthâh (1), *cypress-like*

BEROTHITE
1307 Bêrôthîy (1), *Berothite*

BERRIES
1620 gargar (1), *berry*
1636 ĕlaia (1), *olive*

BERYL
8658 tarshîysh (7), (poss.) *topaz*
969 bĕrullŏs (1), *beryl*

BESAI
1153 Bᵉçay (2), *domineering*

BESEECH
577 'ânnâ' (8), *I ask you!*
2470+6440 châlâh (1), *to be weak, sick, afflicted*
4994 nâ' (26), *I pray!, please!, I beg you!*
1189 dĕŏmai (6), *to beg, petition, ask*
2065 ĕrōtaō (4), *to interrogate; to request*
3870 parakalĕō (20), *to call, invite*

BESEECHING
2065 ĕrōtaō (1), *to interrogate; to request*
3870 parakalĕō (2), *to call, invite*

BESET
3803 kâthar (1), *to enclose, besiege; to wait*
5437 çâbab (3), *to surround*
6696 tsûwr (1), *to cramp, i.e. confine; to harass*
2139 ĕupĕristatŏs (1), *entangling, obstructing*

BESIDE
310 'achar (1), *after*
413 'êl (2), *to, toward*
657 'epheç (3), *end; no further*
681 'êtsel (12), *side; near*
854 'êth (2), *with; by; at; among*
905 bad (45), *apart, only, besides*
1107 bil'ădêy (7), *except, without, besides*
1115 biltîy (3), *except, without, unless, besides*
2108 zûwlâh (6), *except; apart from; besides*
3027 yâd (1), *hand; power*
5921 'al (17), *above, over, upon, or against*
5973 'îm (4), *with*
5980 'ummâh (2), *near, beside, along with*
6654 tsad (3), *side; adversary*
846 autŏs (1), *he, she, it*
1839 ĕxistēmi (2), *to astound*
1909 ĕpi (3), *on, upon*

BESIDES
905 bad (1), *apart, only, besides*
2108 zûwlâh (1), *except; apart from; besides*
5750 'ôwd (4), *again; repeatedly; still; more*
5921 'al (1), *above, over, upon, or against*
3063 lŏipŏn (1), *something remaining; finally*
4359 prŏsŏphĕilō (1), *to be indebted*

BESIEGE
6696 tsûwr (8), *to cramp, i.e. confine; to harass*
6887 tsârar (3), *to cramp*

BESIEGED
935+4692 bôw' (3), *to go or come*
4692 mâtsôwr (1), *siege-mound; distress*
4693 mâtsôwr (2), *limit, border*
5341 nâtsar (2), *to guard, protect, maintain*
5437 çâbab (1), *to surround*
6696 tsûwr (14), *to cramp, i.e. confine*

BESODEIAH
1152 Bᵉçôwdᵉyâh (1), *in (the) counsel of Jehovah*

BESOM
4292 maṭ'ăṭê' (1), *broom*

BESOR
1308 Bᵉsôwr (3), *cheerful*

BESOUGHT
1245 bâqash (2), *to search out*
2470 châlâh (5), *to be weak, sick, afflicted*
2603 chânan (4), *to implore*
1189 dĕŏmai (3), *to beg, petition, ask*
2065 ĕrōtaō (9), *to interrogate; to request*
3870 parakalĕō (21), *to call, invite*

BEST
2173 zimrâh (1), *choice*
2459 cheleb (5), *fat; choice part*
2896 ṭôwb (8), *good; well*
3190 yâṭab (1), *to be, make well*
4315 mêyṭab (6), *best*
5324 nâtsab (1), *to station*
6338 pâzaz (1), *to refine gold*
2909 krĕittōn (1), *stronger, i.e. nobler*
4413 prōtŏs (1), *foremost*

BESTIR
2782 chârats (1), *to be alert; to decide*

BESTOW
5414 nâthan (2), *to give*

BESTOWED
1580 gâmal (2), *to benefit or requite; to wean*
3240 yânach (2), *to allow to stay*
5414 nâthan (2), *to give*
6485 pâqad (1), *to visit, care for, count*
1325 didōmi (2), *to give*
2872 kŏpiaō (3), *to feel fatigue; to work hard*

BETAH
984 Beṭach (1), *safety, security, trust*

BETEN
991 Beṭen (1), *belly; womb; body*

BETH-ANATH
1043 Bêyth 'Ănâth (3), *house of replies*

BETH-ANOTH
1042 Bêyth 'Ănôwth (1), *house of replies*

BETH-ARABAH
1026 Bêyth hâ-'Ărâbâh (3), *house of the desert*

BETH-ARAM
1027 Bêyth hâ-Râm (1), *house of the height*

BETH-ARBEL
1009 Bêyth 'Arbê'l (1), *house of God's ambush*

BETH-AVEN
1007 Bêyth 'Âven (7), *house of vanity*

BETH-AZMAVETH
1041 Bêyth 'Azmâveth (1), *house of Azmaveth*

BETH-BAAL-MEON
1010 Bêyth Ba'al Mᵉ'ôwn (1), *house of Baal of (the) habitation*

BETH-BARAH
1012 Bêyth Bârâh (2), *house of (the) river ford*

BETH-BIREI
1011 Bêyth Bir'îy (1), *house of a creative one*

BETH-CAR
1033 Bêyth Kar (1), *house of pasture*

BETH-DAGON
1016 Bêyth-Dâgôwn (2), *house of Dagon*

BETH-DIBLATHAIM
1015 Bêyth Diblâthayim (1), *house of (the) two figcakes*

BETH-EL
1008 Bêyth-'Êl (66), *house of God*

BETH-ELITE
1017 Bêyth hâ-'Ĕlîy (1), *Beth-elite*

BETH-EMEK
1025 Bêyth hâ-'Êmeq (1), *house of the valley*

BETH-EZEL
1018 Bêyth hâ-'Êtsel (1), *house of the side*

BETH-GADER
1013 Bêyth-Gâdêr (1), *house of (the) wall*

BETH-GAMUL
1014 Bêyth Gâmûwl (1), *house of (the) weaned*

BETH-HACCEREM
1021 Bêyth hak-Kerem (2), *house of the vineyard*

BETH-HARAN
1028 Bêyth hâ-Rân (1), *house of the height*

BETH-HOGLA
1031 Bêyth Choglâh (1), *house of a partridge*

BETH-HOGLAH
1031 Bêyth Choglâh (2), *house of a partridge*

BETH-HORON
1032 Bêyth Chôwrôwn (14), *house of hollowness*

BETH-JESHIMOTH
1020 Bêyth ha-Yᵉshîy-môwth (3), *house of the deserts*

BETH-JESIMOTH
1020 Bêyth ha-Yᵉshîy-môwth (1), *house of the deserts*

BETH-LEBAOTH
1034 Bêyth Lᵉbâ'ôwth (1), *house of lionesses*

BETH-LEHEM
1035 Bêyth Lechem (30), *house of bread*

BETH-LEHEM-JUDAH
1035 Bêyth Lechem (10), *house of bread*

BETH-LEHEMITE
1022 Bêyth hal-Lachmîy (4), *Beth-lechemite*

BETH-MAACHAH
1038 Bêyth Ma'ăkâh (2), *house of Maakah*

BETH-MARCABOTH
1024 Bêyth ham-Markâbôwth (2), *place of (the) chariots*

BETH-MEON
1010 Bêyth Ba'al Mᵉ'ôwn (1), *house of Baal of (the) habitation*

BETH-NIMRAH
1039 Bêyth Nimrâh (2), *house of (the) leopard*

BETH-PALET
1046 Bêyth Peleṭ (1), *house of escape*

BETH-PAZZEZ
1048 Bêyth Patstsêts (1), *house of dispersion*

BETH-PEOR
1047 Bêyth Pᵉʻôwr (4), house of Peor

BETH-PHELET
1046 Bêyth Peleṭ (1), house of escape

BETH-RAPHA
1051 Bêyth Râphâ' (1), house of (the) giant

BETH-REHOB
1050 Bêyth Rᵉchôwb (2), house of (the) street

BETH-SHAN
1052 Bêyth Shᵉ'ân (3), house of ease

BETH-SHEAN
1052 Bêyth Shᵉ'ân (6), house of ease

BETH-SHEMESH
1053 Bêyth Shemesh (21), house of (the) sun

BETH-SHEMITE
1030 Bêyth hash-Shimshîy (2), Beth-shimshite

BETH-SHITTAH
1029 Bêyth hash-Shiṭṭâh (1), house of the acacia

BETH-TAPPUAH
1054 Bêyth Tappûwach (1), house of (the) apple

BETH-ZUR
1049 Bêyth Tsûwr (4), house of (the) rock

BETHABARA
962 Bēthabara (1), ferry-house

BETHANY
963 Bēthania (11), date-house

BETHER
1336 Bether (1), section

BETHESDA
964 Bēthĕsda (1), house of kindness

BETHINK
7725+413+3820 shûwb (2), to turn back

BETHLEHEM
1035 Bêyth Lechem (1), house of bread
965 Bēthlĕĕm (8), house of bread

BETHPHAGE
967 Bēthphagē (3), fig-house

BETHSAIDA
966 Bēthsaida (7), fishing-house

BETHUEL
1328 Bᵉthûw'êl (10), destroyed of God

BETHUL
1329 Bᵉthûwl (1), Bethuel

BETIMES
7836 shâchar (3), to search for
7925 shâkam (2), to load up, i.e. to start early

BETONIM
993 Bᵉṭônîym (1), hollows

BETRAY
7411 râmâh (1), to hurl; to shoot; to delude
3860 paradidōmi (17), to hand over

BETRAYED
3860 paradidōmi (18), to hand over

BETRAYERS
4273 prŏdŏtēs (1), betraying

BETRAYEST
3860 paradidōmi (1), to hand over

BETRAYETH
3860 paradidōmi (3), to hand over

BETROTH
781 'âras (4), to engage for matrimony, betroth

BETROTHED
781 'âras (6), to engage for matrimony, betroth
2778 châraph (1), to spend the winter
3259 yâʻad (2), to engage for marriage

BETTER
2896 ṭôwb (75), good; well
3027 yâd (1), hand; power
3148 yôwthêr (1), moreover; rest; gain
3190 yâṭab (4), to be, make well
3504 yithrôwn (1), preeminence, gain
1308 diaphĕrō (3), to differ; to surpass
2570 kalŏs (5), good; beautiful; valuable
2573 kalŏs (1), well
2909 krĕittōn (18), stronger, i.e. nobler
3081 lusitĕlĕi (1), it is advantageous
4052 pĕrissĕuō (1), to superabound
4284 prŏĕchŏmai (1), to excel
4851 sumphĕrō (1), collect; advantage
5242 hupĕrĕchō (1), to excel; superior
5543 chrēstŏs (1), employed, i.e. useful

BETTERED
5623 ōphĕlĕō (1), to benefit, be of use

BETWEEN
996 bêyn (190), between
997 bêyn (Ch.) (1), between; "either...or"
5921 'al (1), upon, against
5973 'îm (2), with
8432 tâvek (3), center, middle
1722 ĕn (1), in; during; because of
3307 mĕrizō (1), to apportion, bestow
3342 mĕtaxu (6), betwixt
4314 prŏs (2), for; on, at; to, toward; against

BETWIXT
996 bêyn (13), between
6293 pâgaʻ (1), to impinge

1537 ĕk (1), out, out of

BEULAH
1166 bâʻal (1), to be master; to marry

BEWAIL
1058 bâkâh (4), to weep, moan
2799 klaiō (1), to sob, wail
3996 pĕnthĕō (1), to grieve

BEWAILED
1058 bâkâh (1), to weep, moan
2875 kŏptō (2), to beat the breast

BEWAILETH
3306 yâphach (1), to breathe hard, gasp

BEWARE
6191 'âram (1), to be cunning; be prudent
8104 shâmar (9), to watch
991 blĕpō (6), to look at
4337 prŏsĕchō (7), to pay attention to
5442 phulassō (2), to watch, i.e. be on guard

BEWITCHED
940 baskainō (1), to fascinate, bewitch
1839 ĕxistēmi (2), to astound; to be insane

BEWRAY
1540 gâlâh (1), to denude; uncover

BEWRAYETH
5046 nâgad (1), to announce
7121 qârâ' (1), to call out
1212+4160 dēlŏs (1), clear, plain, evident

BEYOND
1973 hâlĕ'âh (5), far away; thus far
5674 'âbar (4), to cross over; to transition
5675 'âbar (Ch.) (7), region across
5676 'êber (21), opposite side; east
5921 'al (2), above, over
1900 ĕpĕkĕina (1), on the further side of, beyond
4008 pĕran (7), across, beyond
5228 hupĕr (1), over; above; beyond
5233 hupĕrbainō (1), to transcend
5238 hupĕrĕkĕina (1), beyond, still farther
5239 hupĕrĕktĕinō (1), to overreach
5249 hupĕrpĕrissōs (1), exceedingly

BEZAI
1209 Bêtsay (3), Betsai

BEZALEEL
1212 Bᵉtsal'êl (9), in (the) protection of God

BEZEK
966 Bezeq (3), lightning

BEZER
1221 Betser (5), inaccessible spot

BICHRI
1075 Bikrîy (8), youthful

BID
559 'âmar (6), to say
1696 dâbar (2), to speak, say; to subdue
6942 qâdâsh (1), to be, make clean
479 antikalĕō (1), to invite in return
657 apŏtassŏmai (1), to say adieu; to renounce
2036 ĕpō (2), to speak
2564 kalĕō (2), to call
2753 kĕlĕuō (1), to order
3004 lĕgō (1), to say

BIDDEN
559 'âmar (1), to say
7121 qârâ' (2), to call out
2564 kalĕō (10), to call
4367 prŏstassō (1), to arrange towards

BIDDETH
3004 lĕgō (1), to say

BIDDING
4928 mishma'ath (1), royal court; obedience

BIDKAR
920 Bidqar (1), stabbing assassin

BIER
4296 miṭṭâh (1), bed; sofa, litter or bier
4673 sŏrŏs (1), funeral bier

BIGTHA
903 Bigthâ' (1), Bigtha

BIGTHAN
904 Bigthân (1), Bigthan

BIGTHANA
904 Bigthân (1), Bigthana

BIGVAI
902 Bigvay (6), Bigvai

BILDAD
1085 Bildad (5), Bildad

BILEAM
1109 Bil'âm (1), foreigner

BILGAH
1083 Bilgâh (3), desistance

BILGAI
1084 Bilgay (1), desistant

BILHAH
1090 Bilhâh (11), timid

BILHAN
1092 Bilhân (4), timid

BILL
5612 çêpher (4), writing
975 bibliŏn (1), scroll; certificate
1121 gramma (2), writing; education

BILLOWS
1530 gal (1), heap; ruins
4867 mishbâr (1), breaker

BILSHAN
1114 Bilshân (2), Bilshan

B

BIMHAL
1118 Bimhâl (1), *with pruning*

BIND
631 'âçar (13), to *fasten; to join* battle
2280 châbash (6), to *wrap* firmly, *bind*
3729 kᵉphath (Ch.) (1), to *fetter, bind*
6029 'ânad (1), to *lace fast, bind*
6887 tsârar (3), to *cramp*
7164 qâraç (1), to *hunch*
7194 qâshar (10), to *tie, bind*
7405 râkaç (2), to *tie, bind*
7573 râtham (1), to *yoke*
1195 dĕsmĕuō (1), to *enchain, tie on*
1210 dĕō (9), to *bind*
5265 hupŏdĕō (1), to *put on* shoes or sandals

BINDETH
247 'âçar (1), to *belt*
631 'âçar (1), to *fasten; to join* battle
2280 châbash (4), to *wrap* firmly, *bind*
6014 'âmar (1), to *gather* grain into sheaves
6887 tsârar (2), to *cramp*

BINDING
481 'âlam (1), to be *tongue-tied, be silent*
632 'ĕçâr (1), *obligation, vow, pledge*
681 'êtsel (1), *side; near edge, margin*
8193 sâphâh (1), *lip, edge, margin*
1195 dĕsmĕuō (1), to *enchain, tie on*

BINEA
1150 Bin'â' (2), *Bina*

BINNUI
1131 Binnûwy (7), *built*

BIRD
1167+3671 ba'al (1), *master; owner; citizen*
5775 'ôwph (3), *bird*
5861 'ayiṭ (2), bird of prey (poss.) *hawk*
6833 tsippôwr (21), little *hopping bird*
3732 ŏrnĕŏn (3), *bird*

BIRD'S
6833 tsippôwr (1), little *hopping bird*

BIRDS
5775 'ôwph (6), winged *bird*
5861 'ayiṭ (1), bird of prey (poss.) *hawk*
6833 tsippôwr (10), little *hopping bird*
4071 pĕṭeinŏn (5), *bird which flies*
4421 ptēnŏn (1), *bird*

BIRDS'
6853 tsᵉphar (Ch.) (1), *bird*

BIRSHA
1306 Birsha' (1), *with wickedness*

BIRTH
3205 yâlad (2), to *bear young; to father a child*
4351 mᵉkûwrâh (1), *origin*
4866 mishbêr (2), vaginal *opening*
5309 nephel (3), *abortive miscarriage*
7665 shâbar (1), to *burst*
8435 tôwlᵉdâh (1), family *descent*, family *record*
1079 gĕnĕtē (1), *birth*
1083 gĕnĕsis (2), *nativity*
5605 ōdinō (2), to *experience labor pains*

BIRTHDAY
3117+3205 yôwm (1), *day; time period*
1077 gĕnĕsia (2), *birthday* ceremonies

BIRTHRIGHT
1062 bᵉkôwrâh (9), *state of, rights of first born*
4415 prōtŏtŏkia (1), *primogeniture rights*

BIRZAVITH
1269 Birzôwth (1), *holes*

BISHLAM
1312 Bishlâm (1), *Bishlam*

BISHOP
1984 ĕpiskŏpē (1), *episcopate*
1985 ĕpiskŏpŏs (5), *overseer, supervisor*

BISHOPRICK
1984 ĕpiskŏpē (1), *episcopate*

BISHOPS
1985 ĕpiskŏpŏs (1), *overseer, supervisor*

BIT
4964 metheg (1), *bit*
5391 nâshak (2), to *strike; to oppress*

BITE
5391 nâshak (6), to *strike; to oppress*
1143 daknō (1), to *bite*

BITETH
5391 nâshak (2), to *strike; to oppress*

BITHIAH
1332 Bithyâh (1), *worshipper of Jehovah*

BITHRON
1338 Bithrôwn (1), *craggy spot*

BITHYNIA
978 Bithunia (2), *Bithynia*

BITS
5469 chalinŏs (1), *curb* or *head-stall*, i.e. *bit*

BITTEN
5391 nâshak (2), to *strike; to oppress*

BITTER
4751 mar (20), *bitter; bitterness; bitterly*
4784 mârâh (1), to *rebel* or *resist; to provoke*

BITTERLY
779 'ârar (1), to *execrate, place a curse*
4751 mar (3), *bitter; bitterness; bitterly*
4843 mârar (2), to *be, make bitter*
8563 tamrûwr (1), *bitterness*
4090 pikrōs (2), *bitterly*, i.e. *violently*

BITTERN
7090 qippôwd (3), *bittern*

BITTERNESS
4470 memer (1), *sorrow*
4472 mamrôr (1), *bitterness, misery*
4751 mar (10), *bitter; bitterness; bitterly*
4814 mᵉrîyrûwth (1), *bitterness*
4843 mârar (4), to *be, make bitter*
4844 mᵉrôr (1), *bitter herb*
4088 pikria (4), *acridity, bitterness*

BIZJOTHJAH
964 bizyôwthᵉyâh (1), *contempts of Jehovah*

BIZTHA
968 Bizthâ' (1), *Biztha*

BLACK
380 'îyshôwn (1), *pupil, eyeball; middle*
3648 kâmar (1), to *shrivel* with heat
5508 çôchereth (1), (poss.) black *tile*
6937 qâdar (4), to *be dark-colored*
7835 shâchar (1), to *be dim or dark in color*
7838 shâchôr (6), *dusky, jet black*
7840 shᵉcharchôreth (1), *swarthy, dark*
3189 mĕlas (3), *black*

BLACKER
2821 châshak (1), to *be dark; to darken*

BLACKISH
6937 qâdar (1), to *be dark-colored*

BLACKNESS
3650 kimrîyr (1), *obscuration, eclipse*
6289 pâ'rûwr (2), *flush* of anxiety

4805 mᵉrîy (1), *rebellion, rebellious*
4815 mᵉrîyrîy (1), *bitter*, i.e. *poisonous*
4843 mârar (2), to *be, make bitter*
4844 mᵉrôr (2), *bitter herb*
4846 mᵉrôrâh (2), bitter *bile; venom* of a serpent
8563 tamrûwr (2), *bitterness*
4087 pikrainō (4), to *embitter, turn sour*
4089 pikrŏs (2), *sharp, pungent*, i.e. *bitter*

BLADE
3851 lahab (2), *flame* of fire; *flash* of a *blade*
7929 shikmâh (1), *shoulder-bone*
5528 chŏrtŏs (2), *pasture, herbage* or *vegetation*

BLAINS
76 'ăba'bû'âh (2), *pustule, skin eruption*

BLAME
2398 châṭâ' (2), to *sin*
299 amōmŏs (1), *unblemished, blameless*
3469 mōmaŏmai (1), to *carp at*, i.e. to *censure*

BLAMED
2607 kataginōskō (1), to *find fault with*
3469 mōmaŏmai (1), to *carp at*, i.e. to *censure*

BLAMELESS
5352 nâqâh (1), to *be, make clean; to be bare*
5355 nâqîy (2), *innocent*
273 amĕmptŏs (3), *irreproachable*
274 amĕmptōs (1), *faultlessly*
298 amōmĕtŏs (1), *unblamable*
338 anaitiŏs (1), *innocent*
410 anĕgklētŏs (4), *irreproachable*
423 anĕpilēptŏs (2), *not open to blame*

BLASPHEME
1288 bârak (2), to *bless*
5006 nâ'ats (2), to *scorn*
987 blasphēmĕō (6), to *speak impiously*

BLASPHEMED
1442 gâdaph (5), to *revile, blaspheme*
2778 châraph (2), to *spend the winter*
5006 nâ'ats (2), to *scorn*
5344 nâqab (1), to *specify, designate, libel*
987 blasphēmĕō (7), to *speak impiously*

BLASPHEMER
989 blasphēmŏs (1), *slanderous*

BLASPHEMERS
987 blasphēmĕō (1), to *speak impiously*
989 blasphēmŏs (1), *slanderous*

BLASPHEMEST
987 blasphēmĕō (1), to *speak impiously*

BLASPHEMETH
1442 gâdaph (1), to *revile, blaspheme*
5344 nâqab (2), to *specify, designate, libel*
987 blasphēmĕō (2), to *speak impiously*

6940 qadrûwth (1), *duskiness*
1105 gnŏphŏs (1), *gloom* as of a storm, *darkness*
2217 zŏphŏs (1), *gloom*

BLASPHEMIES
5007 nᵉ'âtsâh (1), *scorn; to bloom*
988 blasphēmia (5), impious speech

BLASPHEMING
987 blasphēmĕō (1), to speak impiously

BLASPHEMOUS
989 blasphēmŏs (2), slanderous

BLASPHEMOUSLY
987 blasphēmĕō (1), to speak impiously

BLASPHEMY
5007 nᵉ'âtsâh (2), *scorn; to bloom*
987 blasphēmĕō (1), to speak impiously
988 blasphēmia (11), impious speech

BLAST
5397 nᵉshâmâh (3), *breath, life*
7307 rûwach (4), *breath; wind; life-spirit*

BLASTED
7709 shᵉdêmâh (1), *cultivated field*
7710 shâdaph (3), to *scorch*
7711 shᵉdêphâh (1), *blight; scorching*

BLASTING
7711 shᵉdêphâh (5), *blight; scorching*

BLASTUS
986 Blastŏs (1), (poss.) to yield fruit

BLAZE
1310 diaphēmizō (1), to spread news

BLEATING
6963 qôwl (1), *voice or sound*

BLEATINGS
8292 shᵉrûwqâh (1), *whistling; scorn*

BLEMISH
3971 m'ûwm (15), *blemish; fault*
8400 tᵉballûl (1), *cataract in the eye*
8549 tâmîym (44), *entire, complete; integrity*
299 amōmŏs (2), unblemished, blameless

BLEMISHES
3971 m'ûwm (1), *blemish; fault*
3470 mōmŏs (1), *flaw or blot*

BLESS
1288 bârak (115), to *bless*
2127 ĕulŏgĕō (10), to invoke a benediction

BLESSED
833 'âshar (7), to be *honest, prosper*
835 'esher (27), *how happy!*
1288 bârak (175), to *bless*
1289 bᵉrak (Ch.) (4), to *bless*

1293 bᵉrâkâh (3), *benediction, blessing*
1757 ĕnĕulŏgĕō (2), to confer a benefit, bless
2127 ĕulŏgĕō (30), to invoke a benediction
2128 ĕulŏgētŏs (8), adorable, praised
3106 makarizō (1), to pronounce fortunate
3107 makariŏs (43), fortunate, well off

BLESSEDNESS
3108 makarismŏs (3), fortunate

BLESSEST
1288 bârak (3), to *bless*

BLESSETH
1288 bârak (8), to *bless*

BLESSING
1288 bârak (1), to *bless*
1293 bᵉrâkâh (51), *benediction, blessing*
2127 ĕulŏgĕō (1), to invoke a benediction
2129 ĕulŏgia (12), benediction

BLESSINGS
1293 bᵉrâkâh (11), *benediction, blessing*
2129 ĕulŏgia (1), benediction

BLEW
8628 tâqa' (18), to *clatter, slap, drive, clasp*
1920 ĕpiginŏmai (1), to come up, happen
4154 pnĕō (3), to breeze
5285 hupŏpnĕō (1), to breathe gently

BLIND
5786 'âvar (1), to *blind*
5787 'ivvêr (26), *blind*
5788 'ivvârôwn (1), *blindness*
5956 'âlam (1), to *veil from sight, i.e. conceal*
5185 tuphlŏs (52), blindness; blind person

BLINDED
4456 pōrŏō (2), to render stupid or callous
5186 tuphlŏō (3), to cause blindness

BLINDETH
5786 'âvar (1), to *blind*

BLINDFOLDED
4028 pĕrikaluptō (1), to cover eyes

BLINDNESS
5575 çanvêr (3), *blindness*
5788 'ivvârôwn (2), *blindness*
4457 pōrōsis (2), stupidity or callousness

BLOOD
1818 dâm (337), *blood; juice; life*
5332 nêtsach (1), blood (as if *red juice*)
129 haima (97), blood
130 haimatĕkchusia (1), pouring of blood

131 haimŏrrhĕō (1), to have a hemorrhage

BLOODGUILTINESS
1818 dâm (1), *blood; juice; life*

BLOODTHIRSTY
582+1818 'ĕnôwsh (1), *man; person, human*

BLOODY
1818 dâm (15), *blood; juice; life*
1420 dusĕntĕria (1), dysentery

BLOOMED
6692 tsûwts (1), to *blossom, flourish*

BLOSSOM
6524 pârach (4), to *bloom; to fly; to flourish*
6525 perach (1), *calyx flower; bloom*
6692 tsûwts (1), to *blossom, flourish*

BLOSSOMED
6692 tsûwts (1), to *blossom, flourish*

BLOSSOMS
5322 nêts (1), *flower*
6731 tsîyts (1), burnished *plate; bright flower*

BLOT
3971 m'ûwm (2), *blemish; fault*
4229 mâchâh (10), to *erase; to grease*
1813 ĕxalĕiphō (1), to obliterate

BLOTTED
4229 mâchâh (5), to *erase; to grease*
1813 ĕxalĕiphō (1), to obliterate

BLOTTETH
4229 mâchâh (1), to *erase; to grease*

BLOTTING
1813 ĕxalĕiphō (1), to obliterate

BLOW
2690 châtsar (1), to blow *the trumpet*
4347 makkâh (1), *blow; wound; pestilence*
5265 nâça' (1), *start on a journey*
5301 nâphach (3), to *inflate, blow hard*
5380 nâshab (1), to *blow; to disperse*
5398 nâshaph (2), to *breeze as the wind*
6315 pûwach (2), to *blow, to fan, kindle; to utter*
7321 rûwa' (1), to *shout*
8409 tigrâh (1), *strife, i.e. infliction*
8628 tâqa' (23), to *clatter, slap, drive, clasp*
8643 tᵉrûw'âh (1), *battle-cry; clangor*
4154 pnĕō (2), to breeze

BLOWETH
5301 nâphach (1), to *inflate, blow hard*

5380 nâshab (1), to *blow; to disperse*
8628 tâqa' (1), to *clatter, slap, drive, clasp*
4154 pnĕō (1), to breeze

BLOWING
8628 tâqa' (2), to *clatter, slap, drive, clasp*
8643 tᵉrûw'âh (2), *battle-cry; clangor*

BLOWN
5301 nâphach (1), to *inflate, blow hard*
8628 tâqa' (3), to *clatter, slap, drive, clasp*

BLUE
8504 tᵉkêleth (50), color *violet*

BLUENESS
2250 chabbûwrâh (1), *weal, bruise*

BLUNT
6949 qâhâh (1), to be *dull; be blunt*

BLUSH
3637 kâlam (3), to *taunt or insult*

BOANERGES
993 Bŏanĕrgĕs (1), sons of commotion

BOAR
2386 chăzîyr (1), *hog, boar*

BOARD
7175 qeresh (17), *slab or plank; deck of a ship*

BOARDS
3871 lûwach (4), *tablet*
6763 tsêlâ' (2), *side*
7175 qeresh (33), *slab*
7713 sᵉdêrâh (1), *row, i.e. rank of soldiers*
4548 sanis (1), planked timber, board

BOAST
559 'âmar (1), to *say*
1984 hâlal (6), to *boast*
3235 yâmar (1), to *exchange*
3513 kâbad (1), to be *heavy, severe, dull*
6286 pâ'ar (1), to *shake a tree*
2620 katakauchaŏmai (1), to exult against
2744 kauchaŏmai (8), to glory in; to boast

BOASTED
1431 gâdal (1), to be *great, make great*
2744 kauchaŏmai (1), to glory in; to boast

BOASTERS
213 alazōn (2), braggart

BOASTEST
1984 hâlal (1), to *boast*

BOASTETH
1984 hâlal (3), to *boast*
3166 mĕgalauchĕō (1), to be arrogant, egotistic

BOASTING
2744 kauchaŏmai (1), to glory in; to boast

B

2745 kauchēma (1), boast; brag
2746 kauchēsis (6), boasting; bragging
3004 lĕgō (1), to say

BOASTINGS
212 alazŏnĕia (1), boasting

BOAT
5679 'âbârâh (1), crossing-place
4142 plŏiariŏn (2), small boat
4627 skaphē (3), skiff or yawl, i.e. life boat

BOATS
4142 plŏiariŏn (1), small boat

BOAZ
1162 Bô'az (24), Boaz

BOCHERU
1074 Bôk⁸rûw (2), first-born

BOCHIM
1066 Bôkîym (2), weepers

BODIES
1354 gab (1), mounded or rounded: top or rim
1472 g⁸vîyâh (7), dead body
1480 gûwphâh (1), corpse
1655 geshem (Ch.) (2), body
5038 n⁸bêlâh (2), carcase or carrion
6297 peger (6), carcase; corpse
4430 ptōma (3), corpse, carrion
4983 sōma (11), body

BODILY
4983 sōma (1), body
4984 sōmatikŏs (2), corporeal or physical
4985 sōmatikōs (1), corporeally

BODY
990 beṭen (8), belly; womb; body
1320 bâsâr (2), flesh; body; person
1460 gêv (1), middle, inside, in, on, etc.
1465 'âchôr (1), back
1472 g⁸vîyâh (3), dead body
1480 gûwphâh (1), corpse
1655 geshem (Ch.) (3), body
3409 yârêk (1), leg or shank; side
5038 n⁸bêlâh (4), carcase or carrion
5085 nidneh (Ch.) (1), sheath; body
5315 nephesh (9), life; breath; soul; wind
6106 'etsem (2), bone; body; substance
7607 she'êr (1), flesh, meat; kindred by blood
4954 sussŏmŏs (1), fellow-member
4983 sōma (131), body
5559 chrōs (1), skin

BODY'S
4983 sōma (1), body

BOHAN
932 Bôhan (2), thumb

BOIL
1158 bâ'âh (1), to ask; be bulging, swelling
1310 bâshal (4), to boil up, cook; to ripen
7570 râthach (2), to boil, churn
7822 she chîyn (9), inflammation, ulcer

BOILED
1310 bâshal (2), to boil
7570 râthach (1), to boil, churn

BOILING
4018 m⁸bashshelâh (1), cooking hearth

BOILS
7822 she chîyn (2), inflammation, ulcer

BOISTEROUS
2478 ischurŏs (1), forcible, powerful

BOLD
982 bâṭach (1), to trust, be confident or sure
662 apŏtŏlmaō (1), to bring forth boldly
2292 tharrhĕō (2), to be bold
3954 parrhēsia (1), frankness, boldness
3955 parrhēsiazŏmai (2), to be frank, confident
5111 tŏlmaō (4), to be bold, courageous

BOLDLY
983 beṭach (1), safety, security, trust
2292 tharrhĕō (1), to be bold
3954 parrhēsia (3), frankness, boldness
3955 parrhēsiazŏmai (6), to be frank, confident
5111 tŏlmaō (1), to be bold, courageous
5112 tŏlmērŏtĕrŏn (1), with greater confidence

BOLDNESS
5797 'ôz (1), strength
3954 parrhēsia (9), frankness, boldness

BOLLED
1392 gib'ôl (1), calyx

BOLSTER
4763 m⁸ra'ăshâh (6), headpiece; head-rest

BOLT
5274 nâ'al (1), to fasten up, lock

BOLTED
5274 nâ'al (1), to fasten up, lock

BOND
632 'ĕçâr (7), obligation, vow, pledge
4148 mûwçâr (1), reproof, warning
4562 mâçôreth (1), band

1199 dĕsmŏn (1), shackle; impediment
1401 dŏulŏs (6), slave, servant
4886 sundĕsmŏs (3), ligament; control

BONDAGE
3533 kâbash (2), to conquer, subjugate
5647 'âbad (1), to do, work, serve
5650 'ebed (10), servant
5656 'ăbôdâh (8), work
5659 'abdûwth (3), servitude
1397 dŏulĕia (5), slavery, bondage
1398 dŏulĕuō (4), to serve as a slave
1402 dŏulŏō (4), to enslave
2615 katadŏulŏō (2), to enslave utterly

BONDMAID
8198 shiphchâh (1), household female slave
3814 paidiskē (1), female slave or servant

BONDMAIDS
519 'âmâh (2), female servant or slave

BONDMAN
5650 'ebed (5), servant
1401 dŏulŏs (1), slave, servant

BONDMEN
5647 'âbad (1), to do, work, serve
5650 'ebed (16), servant

BONDS
632 'ĕçâr (3), obligation, vow, pledge
4147 môwçêr (5), halter; restraint
254 halusis (1), fetter or manacle
1198 dĕsmiŏs (2), bound captive; one arrested
1199 dĕsmŏn (14), shackle; impediment or disability
1210 dĕō (1), to bind

BONDSERVANT
5656+5650 'ăbôdâh (1), work of any kind

BONDSERVICE
5647 'âbad (1), to do, work, serve

BONDWOMAN
519 'âmâh (4), maid-servant or female slave
3814 paidiskē (4), female slave or servant

BONDWOMEN
8198 shiphchâh (3), household female slave

BONE
1634 gerem (1), bone; self
6106 'etsem (14), bone; body; substance
7070 qâneh (1), reed
3747 ŏstĕŏn (1), bone

BONES
1633 gâram (1), to crunch the bones
1634 gerem (2), bone; self
1635 gerem (Ch.) (1), bone
6106 'etsem (89), bone; body; substance
3747 ŏstĕŏn (4), bone
4974 sphurŏn (1), ankle

BONNETS
4021 migbâ'âh (4), cap wrapped around head
6287 pe'êr (2), fancy head-dress

BOOK
1697 dâbâr (7), word; matter; thing
5609 çephar (Ch.) (3), book
5612 çêpher (136), writing
974 bibliaridiŏn (4), little scroll
975 bibliŏn (23), scroll; certificate
976 biblŏs (15), scroll

BOOKS
5609 çephar (Ch.) (1), book
5612 çêpher (2), writing
975 bibliŏn (4), scroll; certificate
976 biblŏs (1), scroll of writing

BOOTH
5521 çukkâh (2), tabernacle; shelter

BOOTHS
5521 çukkâh (8), tabernacle; shelter

BOOTIES
4933 m⁸shiççâh (1), plunder

BOOTY
957 baz (1), plunder, loot
4455 malqôwach (1), spoil, plunder
4953 mashrôwqîy (Ch.) (1), musical pipe

BOOZ
1003 Bŏŏz (3), Boŏz

BORDER
1366 g⁸bûwl (136), boundary, border
1379 gâbal (2), to set a boundary line, limit
3027 yâd (1), hand; power
3411 ye rêkâh (1), recesses, far away
4526 miçgereth (6), margin; stronghold
7093 qêts (2), extremity; after
7097 qâtseh (2), extremity; edge, margin
8193 sâphâh (3), lip; edge, margin
2899 kraspĕdŏn (2), margin

BORDERS
1366 g⁸bûwl (20), boundary, border
1367 g⁸bûwlâh (1), boundary marker
1552 g⁸lîylâh (3), circuit or region

3027 yâd (1), *hand; power*
3671 kânâph (2), *edge or extremity; wing*
4526 miçgereth (7), *margin; stronghold*
5299 náphâh (1), *height*
7093 qêts (1), *extremity*
7097 qâtseh (1), *extremity*
8444 tôwtsâ'âh (1), *exit, i.e. boundary*
8447 tôwr (1), *succession, order*
2899 kraspĕdŏn (1), *margin*
3181 mĕthŏriŏs (1), *frontier* region
3725 hŏriŏn (1), *region, area, vicinity*

BORE
5344 nâqab (1), *to puncture, perforate*
7527 râtsa' (1), *to pierce*

BORED
5344 nâqab (1), *to puncture, perforate*

BORN
249 'ezrâch (11), *native born*
990 beţen (1), *belly; womb; body*
1121 bên (2), *son, descendant*
3205 yâlad (80), *to bear young; to father a child*
3209 yillôwd (4), *born*
3211 yâlîyd (6), *born; descendants*
4138 môwledeth (2), *offspring, family*
313 anagĕnnaŏ (1), *to beget or bear again*
1080 gĕnnaŏ (39), *to procreate, regenerate*
1084 gĕnnētŏs (2), *pertaining to birth*
1085 gĕnŏs (2), *kin, offspring in kind*
1626 ĕktrŏma (1), *untimely birth*
5088 tiktŏ (3), *to produce from seed*

BORNE
3205 yâlad (3), *to bear young; to father a child*
5190 nâţal (1), *to lift; to impose*
5375 nâsâ' (14), *to lift up*
5445 çâbal (1), *to carry*
5564 çâmak (1), *to lean upon; take hold of*
6006 'âmaç (1), *to impose a burden*
142 airō (1), *to lift, to take up*
941 bastazō (4), *to lift, bear*
1418 dus- (2), *hard, i.e. with difficulty*
5409 phŏrĕō (1), *to wear*

BORROW
3867 lâvâh (1), *to borrow; to lend*
5670 'âbaţ (1), *to pawn; to lend; to entangle*
7592 shâ'al (4), *to ask*
1155 danĕizō (1), *to loan on interest; to borrow*

BORROWED
3867 lâvâh (1), *to borrow; to lend*
7592 shâ'al (2), *to ask*

BORROWER
3867 lâvâh (2), *to borrow; to lend*

BORROWETH
3867 lâvâh (1), *to borrow; to lend*

BOSCATH
1218 Botsqath (1), *swell of ground*

BOSOM
2243 chôb (1), *bosom*
2436 chêyq (32), *bosom, heart*
2683 chêtsen (1), *bosom*
6747 tsallachath (2), *bosom*
2859 kŏlpŏs (5), *lap area*

BOSOR
1007 Bŏsŏr (1), *lamp*

BOSSES
1354 gab (1), *mounded or rounded: top or rim*

BOTCH
7822 shᵉchîyn (2), *inflammation, ulcer*

BOTH
413 'êl (1), *to, toward*
1571 gam (30), *also; even; "both...and"*
3162 yachad (1), *unitedly*
8147 shᵉnayim (78), *two-fold*
8174 Sha'aph (2), *fluctuation*
297 amphŏtĕrŏs (14), *both*
1417 duŏ (2), *two*
1538 hĕkastŏs (1), *each or every*
2532 kai (45), *and; or; even; also*
5037 tĕ (39), *both or also*

BOTTLE
1228 baqbûk (2), *bottle*
2573 chêmeth (4), *skin bottle*
4997 nô'd (4), *skin bag*
5035 nebel (5), *skin bag*

BOTTLES
178 'ôwb (1), *wineskin; necromancer, medium*
2573 chêmeth (1), *skin bottle*
4997 nô'd (2), *skin bag*
5035 nebel (3), *skin bag*
779 askŏs (12), *leather bottle or bag*

BOTTOM
773 'ar'îyth (Ch.) (1), *bottom, dirt floor*
2436 chêyq (2), *bosom, heart*
3247 yᵉçôwd (10), *foundation*
4688 mᵉtsôwlâh (1), *deep place*
4699 mᵉtsullâh (1), *shade, deep*
7172 qarqa' (1), *floor*
7507 rᵉphîydâh (1), *railing*

8328 sheresh (1), *root*
2736 katō (2), *downwards*

BOTTOMLESS
12 abussŏs (7), *deep place, abyss*

BOTTOMS
7095 qetseb (1), *shape; base*

BOUGH
534 'âmîyr (1), *top*
1121 bên (2), *son, descendant; people*
2793 chôresh (1), *wooded forest*
6288 pᵉ'ôrâh (1), *foliage, branches*
7754 sôwk (2), *branch*

BOUGHS
5577 çançin (1), *twig*
5589 çᵉ'appâh (2), *twig*
5634 çar'appâh (1), *twig*
5688 'ăbôth (3), *entwined things: foliage*
6056 'ănaph (Ch.) (1), *bough, branch*
6057 'ânâph (3), *twig*
6288 pᵉ'ôrâh (2), *foliage, branches*
6529 pᵉrîy (1), *fruit*
6528 qâtsîyr (3), *harvest; limb of a tree*
7730 sôwbek (1), *thicket*

BOUGHT
3739 kârâh (1), *to purchase by bargaining*
4736 miqnâh (1), *acquisition*
7069 qânâh (21), *to create; to procure*
7666 shâbar (1), *to deal in cereal grain*
59 agŏrazŏ (13), *to purchase; to redeem*
5608 ōnĕŏmai (1), *purchase, buy*

BOUND
615 'âçîyr (2), *captive, prisoner*
631 'âçar (33), *to fasten; to join battle*
640 'âphad (1), *to fasten; gird*
1366 gᵉbûwl (4), *boundary, border*
2280 châbash (4), *to wrap firmly, bind*
3256 yâçar (1), *to chastise; to instruct*
3729 kᵉphath (Ch.) (3), *to fetter, bind*
4205 mâzôwr (1), *sore needing a bandage*
6123 'âqad (1), *to tie the feet with thongs*
6616 pâthîyl (1), *twine, cord*
6887 tsârar (7), *to cramp*
7194 qâshar (4), *to tie, bind*
7576 râthaq (1), *to fasten, bind*
8244 sâqad (1), *to fasten, bind*
8379 ta'ăvâh (1), *limit, i.e. full extent*
332 anathĕmatizō (3), *to declare or vow an oath*

1196 dĕsmĕō (1), *shackle; bind*
1210 dĕō (28), *to bind*
2611 katadĕō (1), *to bandage a wound*
3784 ŏphĕilō (2), *to owe; to be under obligation*
4019 pĕridĕō (1), *to wrap around*
4029 pĕrikĕimai (1), *to enclose, encircle*
4385 prŏtĕinō (1), *to tie prostrate for scourging*
4887 sundĕō (1), *to be a fellow-prisoner*

BOUNDS
1366 gᵉbûwl (1), *boundary, border*
1367 gᵉbûwlâh (2), *boundary marker*
1379 gâbal (2), *to set a boundary*
2706 chôq (2), *appointment; allotment*
3734 hŏrŏthĕsia (1), *boundary-line*

BOUNTIFUL
2896 ţôwb (1), *good; well*
7771 shôwa' (1), *noble, i.e. liberal; opulent*

BOUNTIFULLY
1580 gâmal (4), *to benefit or requite; to wean*
2129 ĕulŏgia (1), *benediction*

BOUNTIFULNESS
572 haplŏtēs (1), *sincerity; generosity*

BOUNTY
3027 yâd (1), *hand; power*
2129 ĕulŏgia (2), *benediction*

BOW
86 'abrêk (1), *kneel*
3721 kâphaph (2), *to curve, bow*
3766 kâra' (9), *to prostrate*
5186 nâţâh (6), *to stretch or spread out*
5791 'âvath (1), *to wrest, twist*
7198 qesheth (55), *bow, rainbow*
7812 shâchâh (17), *to prostrate in homage*
7817 shâchach (2), *to sink or depress*
2578 kamptō (3), *to bend*
4781 sugkamptō (1), *to afflict*
5115 tŏxŏn (1), *bow*

BOWED
3721 kâphaph (3), *to curve, bow*
3766 kâra' (11), *to prostrate; to make miserable*
5186 nâţâh (5), *to stretch or spread out*
5791 'âvath (1), *to wrest, twist*
6915 qâdad (13), *to bend*
7743 shûwach (1), *to sink*
7812 shâchâh (35), *prostrate in homage*

B

7817 shâchach (4), *to sink* or *depress*
1120 gŏnupĕtĕō (1), *to fall on the knee, kneel*
2578 kamptō (1), *to bend*
2827 klinō (2), *to slant* or *slope*
4794 sugkuptō (1), *to be completely overcome*

BOWELS
4578 mê'âh (26), *viscera; anguish, tenderness*
7130 qereb (1), *nearest part*, i.e. the *center*
7358 rechem (2), *womb*
4698 splagchnŏn (9), *intestine; affection, pity*

BOWETH
3766 kâra' (2), *to prostrate*
7817 shâchach (1), *to sink* or *depress*

BOWING
5186 nâţâh (2), *to stretch* or *spread out*
5087 tithēmi (1), *to put*

BOWL
1543 gullâh (3), *fountain; bowl* or *globe*
4219 mîzrâq (13), *bowl for sprinkling*
5602 çêphel (1), *basin, bowl*

BOWLS
1375 gᵉbîya' (8), *goblet; bowl*
1543 gullâh (3), *fountain; bowl* or *globe*
4219 mîzrâq (8), *bowl for sprinkling*
4518 mᵉnaqqîyth (3), *sacrificial basin*
5592 çaph (2), *dish*

BOWMEN
7411+7198 râmâh (1), *to hurl; to shoot*

BOWS
7198 qesheth (13), *bow, rainbow*

BOWSHOT
2909+7198 ţâchâh (1), *to stretch* a bow

BOX
6378 pak (2), *flask, jug*
8391 tᵉ'ashshûwr (2), *cedar*
211 alabastrŏn (4), *alabaster, vase*

BOY
3206 yeled (1), *young male*

BOYS
3206 yeled (1), *young male*
5288 na'ar (1), *male child; servant*

BOZEZ
949 Bôwtsêts (1), *shining*

BOZKATH
1218 Botsqath (1), *swell of ground*

BOZRAH
1224 Botsrâh (9), *sheep-fold, animal pen*

BRACELET
685 'ets'âdâh (1), *bracelet*

BRACELETS
2397 châch (1), *ring for the nose or lips*
6616 pâthîyl (2), *twine, cord*
6781 tsâmîyd (6), *bracelet; lid*
8285 shêrâh (1), *wrist-band*

BRAKE
1234 bâqa' (3), *to cleave, break, tear open*
1518 gîyach (1), *to issue forth; to burst forth*
1855 dᵉqaq (Ch.) (5), *to crumble; crush*
1961 hâyâh (1), *to exist*, i.e. *be* or *become*
3807 kâthath (1), *to bruise* or *strike, beat*
5310 nâphats (1), *to dash to pieces; to scatter*
5422 nâthats (12), *to tear down*
5423 nâthaq (3), *to tear off*
6555 pârats (4), *to break out*
6561 pâraq (1), *to break off* or *crunch; to deliver*
6565 pârar (2), *to break up; to violate, frustrate*
7323 rûwts (1), *to run*
7533 râtsats (1), *to crack in pieces, smash*
7665 shâbar (20), *to burst*
1284 diarrhēssō (2), *to tear asunder*
2608 katagnumi (2), *to crack apart*
2622 kataklaō (2), *to divide in pieces*
2806 klaō (9), *to break bread*
4937 suntribō (1), *to crush completely*

BRAKEST
7533 râtsats (1), *to crack in pieces, smash*
7665 shâbar (4), *to burst*

BRAMBLE
329 'âţâd (3), *buckthorn*
942 batŏs (1), *brier*

BRAMBLES
2336 chôwach (1), *thorn; hook; ring* for the nose

BRANCH
534 'âmîyr (1), *top*
1121 bên (1), *son, descendant; people*
2156 zᵉmôwrâh (3), *twig, vine branch*
2158 zâmîyr (1), *song*
3127 yôwneqeth (1), *sprout, new shoot*
3712 kippâh (3), *leaf*
5342 nêtser (4), *shoot* of a plant; *descendant*
5929 'âleh (1), *leaf; foliage*
6057 'ânâph (1), *twig*
6780 tsemach (5), *sprout, branch*
6788 tsammereth (2), *foliage*

7070 qâneh (5), *reed*
7105 qâtsîyr (2), *harvest; limb* of a tree
2798 kladŏs (2), *twig* or *bough*
2814 klēma (3), *limb* or *shoot*

BRANCHES
905 bad (3), *limb, member; bar; chief*
1121 bên (1), *son, descendant; people*
1808 dâlîyâh (8), *bough, branch*
2156 zᵉmôwrâh (1), *pruned twig, branch*
3127 yôwneqeth (3), *sprout, new shoot*
3709 kaph (1), *hollow of hand; paw; sole*
5189 nᵉţîyshâh (1), *tendril plant shoot*
5585 çâ'îyph (2), *fissure* of rocks; *bough*
5688 'ǎbôth (1), *entwined things: string or foliage*
5929 'âleh (3), *leaf; foliage*
6056 'ǎnaph (Ch.) (3), *bough, branch*
6057 'ânâph (3), *twig*
6058 'ânêph (1), *branching*
6073 'ŏphe' (1), *bough*
6288 pᵉ'ôrâh (4), *foliage, branches*
7070 qâneh (19), *reed*
7641 shibbôl (1), *stream; ear* of grain
7976 shilluchâh (1), *shoot* of a vine
8299 sârîyg (3), *entwining tendril*
902 baiŏn (1), *palm twig*
2798 kladŏs (9), *twig* or *bough*
2814 klēma (1), *limb* or *shoot*
4746 stŏibas (1), *bough* of a tree so employed

BRAND
181 'ûwd (1), *poker stick* for a fire

BRANDISH
5774 'ûwph (1), *to cover, to fly; to faint*

BRANDS
3940 lappîyd (1), *flaming torch, lamp* or *flame*

BRASEN
5178 nᵉchôsheth (27), *copper; bronze*
5473 chalkiŏn (1), *copper dish* or *kettle*

BRASS
5153 nâchûwsh (1), *coppery*, i.e. hard
5154 nᵉchûwshâh (7), *copper; bronze*
5174 nᵉchâsh (Ch.) (9), *copper*
5178 nᵉchôsheth (102), *copper; bronze*
5470 chalkĕŏs (1), *copper*
5474 chalkŏlibanŏn (2), *burnished copper*
5475 chalkŏs (3), *copper*

BRAVERY
8597 tiph'ârâh (1), *ornament*

BRAWLER
269 amachŏs (1), *not quarrelsome*

BRAWLERS
269 amachŏs (1), *not quarrelsome*

BRAWLING
4090 mᵉdân (2), *contest* or *quarrel*

BRAY
3806 kâthash (1), *to pound* in a mortar
5101 nâhaq (1), *to bray; to scream* from hunger

BRAYED
5101 nâhaq (1), *to bray; to scream* from hunger

BREACH
919 bedeq (1), *gap*
1234 bâqa' (2), *to cleave, break, tear open*
6555 pârats (1), *to break out*
6556 perets (10), *break, gap*
7667 sheber (5), *fracture; ruin*
8569 tᵉnûw'âh (1), *enmity*

BREACHES
919 bedeq (7), *gap*
1233 bᵉqîya' (1), *fissure, breach*
4664 miphrâts (1), *haven, cove*
6555 pârats (1), *to break out*
6556 perets (3), *break, gap*
7447 râçîyç (1), *ruin; dew-drop*
7667 sheber (1), *fracture; ruin*

BREAD
3899 lechem (236), *food, bread*
740 artos (72), *loaf of bread*

BREADTH
2947 ţêphach (1), *palm-breadth*
2948 ţôphach (3), *palm-breadth*
4800 merchâb (1), *open space; liberty*
6613 pᵉthay (Ch.) (2), *width*
7338 rachab (1), *width, expanse*
7341 rôchab (75), *width*
4114 platŏs (4), *width*

BREAK
215 'ôwr (1), *to be luminous*
1234 bâqa' (3), *to cleave, break, tear open*
1633 gâram (2), *to crunch* the bones
1758 dûwsh (1), *to trample* or *thresh*
1792 dâkâ' (3), *to pulverize; be contrite*
1854 dâqaq (3), *to crush; crumble*

1986 hâlam (1), to *strike, beat, stamp, conquer*
2000 hâmam (1), to *disturb, drive, destroy*
2040 hâraç (7), to *pull down; break, destroy*
2490 châlal (3), to *profane, defile*
3318 yâtsâ' (1), to *go, bring out*
5003 nâ'aph (1), to *commit adultery*
5106 nûw' (1), to *refuse, forbid, dissuade*
5214 nîyr (2), to *till the soil*
5310 nâphats (10), to *dash to pieces*
5422 nâthats (6), to *tear down*
5423 nâthaq (2), to *tear off*
5670 'âbaṭ (1), to *pawn;* to *lend;* to *entangle*
6202 'âraph (3), to *break the neck,* to *destroy*
6206 'ârats (1), to *awe;* to *dread;* to *harass*
6315 pûwach (2), to *blow,* to *fan, kindle;* to *utter*
6476 pâtsach (6), to *break out in sound*
6524 pârach (2), to *break forth;* to *bloom;* to *fly*
6555 pârats (7), to *break out*
6561 pâraq (3), to *break off* or *crunch;* to *deliver*
6562 pᵉraq (Ch.) (1), to *discontinue, stop*
6565 pârar (14), to *break up;* to *violate, frustrate*
6605 pâthach (1), to *open wide;* to *loosen, begin*
6743 tsâlach (1), to *push forward*
6746 tsᵉlôchîyth (1), *vial* or *salt-cellar*
7489 râ'a' (3), to *break to pieces*
7533 râtsats (1), to *crack in pieces, smash*
7665 shâbar (33), to *burst*
7702 sâdad (2), to *break ground*
827 augē (1), *radiance, dawn*
1358 diörussō (2), to *penetrate* burglariously
2608 katagnumi (1), to *crack apart*
2806 klaō (2), to *break bread*
3089 luō (1), to *loosen*
4486 rhēgnumi (2), to *break, burst forth*
4919 sunthruptō (1), to *crush together*

BREAKER
6555 pârats (1), to *break out*
3848 parabatēs (1), *violator, lawbreaker*

BREAKEST
7665 shâbar (1), to *burst*

BREAKETH
1234 bâqa' (1), to *cleave, break, tear open*

1638 gâraç (1), to *crush, break;* to *dissolve*
1855 dᵉqaq (Ch.) (1), to *crumble; crush*
2040 hâraç (1), to *pull down; break, destroy*
5927 'âlâh (1), to *ascend, be high, mount*
6327 pûwts (1), to *dash in pieces;* to *disperse*
6555 pârats (3), to *break out*
6566 pâras (1), to *break apart, disperse, scatter*
7665 shâbar (5), to *burst*
7779 shûwph (1), to *gape,* i.e. *snap* at
7940 Sâkar (1), *recompense*

BREAKING
4290 machtereth (1), *burglary*
4866 mishbêr (1), vaginal *opening*
5927 'âlâh (1), to *ascend, be high, mount*
6524 pârach (2), to *break forth;* to *bloom;* to *fly*
6556 perets (3), *break, gap*
6565 pârar (2), to *break up;* to *violate, frustrate*
6979 qûwr (1), to *throw forth;* to *wall up*
7667 sheber (2), *fracture; ruin*
7670 shibrôwn (1), *ruin*
2800 klasis (2), *fracturing*
2806 klaō (1), to *break bread*
3847 parabasis (1), *violation, breaking*

BREAKINGS
7667 sheber (1), *fracture; ruin*

BREAST
2306 chădîy (Ch.) (1), *breast*
2373 châzeh (11), animal *breast meat*
7699 shad (3), female *breast*
4738 stēthŏs (3), area of the human *chest*

BREASTPLATE
2833 chôshen (25), *gorget*
8302 shiryôwn (1), *corslet, coat of mail*
2382 thōrax (2), *corslet, chest*

BREASTPLATES
2382 thōrax (3), *corslet, chest*

BREASTS
1717 dad (2), female *breast or bosom*
2373 châzeh (2), animal *breast meat*
3824 lêbâb (1), *heart*
5845 'ăṭîyn (1), *receptacle* for milk
7699 shad (19), female *breast*
4738 stēthŏs (2), area of the human *chest*

BREATH
5315 nephesh (1), *life; breath; soul; wind*
5396 nishmâ' (Ch.) (1), *breath, life*
5397 nᵉshâmâh (12), *breath, life*
7307 rûwach (27), *breath; wind; life-spirit*
4157 pnŏē (1), *breeze; breath*

BREATHE
3307 yâphêach (1), *puffing; breathing out*
5301 nâphach (1), to *inflate, blow hard*
5397 nᵉshâmâh (2), *breath, life*
1720 ĕmphusaō (1), to *blow at* or *on*

BREATHED
5301 nâphach (1), to *inflate, blow hard*
5397 nᵉshâmâh (2), *breath, life*

BREATHETH
5397 nᵉshâmâh (1), *breath, life*

BREATHING
7309 rᵉvâchâh (1), *relief*
1709 ĕmpnĕō (1), to *be animated by*

BRED
7311 rûwm (1), to *be high;* to *rise or raise*

BREECHES
4370 miknâç (5), *drawers concealing* the privates

BREED
1121 bên (1), *people* of a class or kind
8317 shârats (1), to *swarm,* or *abound*

BREEDING
4476 mimshâq (1), *possession*

BRETHREN
251 'âch (329), *brother; relative; member*
252 'ach (Ch.) (1), *brother; relative*
80 adĕlphŏs (225), *brother*
81 adĕlphŏtēs (1), *fraternity, brotherhood*
5360 philadĕlphia (1), *fraternal affection*
5361 philadĕlphŏs (1), *fraternal*
5569 psĕudadĕlphŏs (2), *pretended associate*

BRETHREN'S
251 'âch (1), *brother; relative; member*

BRIBE
3724 kôpher (2), *redemption-price*

BRIBERY
7810 shachad (1), to *bribe; gift*

BRIBES
7810 shachad (3), to *bribe; gift*

BRICK
3835 lâban (3), to *make bricks*
3843 lᵉbênâh (4), *brick*

BRICKKILN
4404 malbên (3), *brick-kiln*

BRICKS
3843 lᵉbênâh (4), *brick*

BRIDE
3618 kallâh (9), *bride; son's wife*
3565 numphē (5), young *married* woman

BRIDECHAMBER
3567 numphōn (3), *bridal room*

BRIDEGROOM
2860 châthân (8), *bridegroom*
3566 numphiŏs (15), *bridegroom*

BRIDEGROOM'S
3566 numphiŏs (1), *bridegroom*

BRIDLE
4269 machçôwm (1), *muzzle*
4964 metheg (3), *bit*
7448 reçen (4), *jaw restraint* of a horse
5469 chalinŏs (1), *bit* or *bridle*

BRIDLES
5469 chalinŏs (1), *bit* or *bridle*

BRIDLETH
5468 chalinagōgĕō (1), to *curb, hold in check*

BRIEFLY
346 anakĕphalaiŏmai (1), to *sum up*
1223+3641 dia (1), *through,* by means of

BRIER
2312 chêdeq (1), *prickly* plant
5544 çillôwn (1), *prickle*
5636 çarpâd (1), *stinging nettle*

BRIERS
1303 barqân (2), *thorn, biers*
5621 çârâb (1), *thistle*
8068 shâmîyr (8), *thorn;* (poss.) *diamond*
5146 tribŏlŏs (1), *thorny caltrop* plant

BRIGANDINE
5630 çiyrôn (1), coat of *mail,* scale armor

BRIGANDINES
5630 çiyrôn (1), coat of *mail,* scale armor

BRIGHT
216 'ôwr (1), *luminary; lightning; happiness*
925 bâhîyr (1), *shining, bright*
934 bôhereth (11), *whitish, bright* spot
1300 bârâq (1), *lightning; flash of lightning*

B

1305 bârar (1), to *brighten; purify*
2385 chăzîyz (1), *flash* of lightning
3851 lahab (1), *flame* of fire; *flash* of a *blade*
3974 mâ'ôwr (1), *luminary, light source*
4803 mâraṭ (1), to *polish; to make bald*
4838 mâraq (1), to *polish; to sharpen; to rinse*
5051 nôgahh (1), *brilliancy*
6219 'âshôwth (1), *polished*
6247 'esheth (1), *fabric*
7043 qâlal (1), to *be, make light*
796 astrapē (1), *lightning; light's glare*
2986 lamprŏs (2), *radiant; clear*
5460 phōtĕinŏs (1), *well-illuminated*

BRIGHTNESS
2096 zôhar (2), *brilliancy, shining*
2122 zîyv (Ch.) (2), *cheerfulness*
3314 yiph'âh (2), *splendor, beauty*
3368 yâqâr (1), *valuable*
5051 nôgahh (11), *brilliancy*
5054 nᵉgôhâh (1), *splendor, luster*
541 apaugasma (1), *effulgence, radiance*
2015 ĕpiphanĕia (1), *manisfestation*
2987 lamprŏtēs (1), *brilliancy*

BRIM
7097 qâtseh (1), *extremity*
8193 sâphâh (7), *lip; edge, margin*
507 anō (1), *upward* or *on the top, heavenward*

BRIMSTONE
1614 gophrîyth (7), *sulphur*
2303 thĕiŏn (7), *sulphur*
2306 thĕiōdēs (1), *sulphurous* yellow

BRING
338 'îy (1), solitary wild creature that *howls*
503 'âlaph (1), *increase by thousands*
622 'âçaph (2), to *gather, collect*
858 'âthâh (Ch.) (2), to *arrive; go*
935 bôw' (248), to *go* or *come*
1069 bâkar (1), to *give the birthright*
1431 gâdal (1), to *be great, make great*
1518 gîyach (1), to *issue forth; to burst forth*
1876 dâshâ' (1), to *sprout new plants*
1980 hâlak (1), to *walk; live a certain way*
2142 zâkar (2), to *remember; to mention*

2342 chûwl (1), to *dance, whirl; to writhe* in pain
2381 Chăzîy'êl (1), *seen of God*
2986 yâbal (5), to *bring*
3051 yâhab (2), to *give*
3205 yâlad (17), to *bear young; to father a child*
3212 yâlak (3), to *walk; to live; to carry*
3254 yâçaph (1), to *add* or *augment*
3318 yâtsâ' (73), to *go, bring out*
3381 yârad (24), to *descend*
3513 kâbad (1), to *be heavy, severe, dull*
3533 kâbash (1), to *conquer, subjugate*
3665 kâna' (3), to *humiliate, vanquish*
3947 lâqach (17), to *take*
4608 ma'âleh (1), *elevation; platform*
4672 mâtsâ' (2), to *find* or *acquire; to occur*
5060 nâga' (3), to *strike*
5066 nâgash (14), to *be, come, bring near*
5080 nâdach (1), to *push off, scattered*
5107 nûwb (1), to (*make*) *flourish; to utter*
5375 nâsâ' (10), to *lift up*
5381 nâsag (1), to *reach*
5414 nâthan (11), to *give*
5437 çâbab (2), to *surround*
5647 'âbad (1), to *do, work, serve*
5674 'âbar (1), to *cross over; to transition*
5924 'êllâ' (Ch.) (3), *above*
5927 'âlâh (35), to *ascend, be high, mount*
6049 'ânan (1), to *cover, becloud; to act covertly*
6213 'âsâh (9), to *do* or *make*
6315 pûwach (1), to *blow, to fan, kindle; to utter*
6398 pâlach (1), to *slice; to break open; to pierce*
6509 pârâh (2), to *bear fruit*
6779 tsâmach (1), to *sprout*
6805 tsâ'ad (1), to *pace, step regularly*
7034 qâlâh (1), to *hold in contempt*
7126 qârab (36), to *approach, bring near*
7311 rûwm (1), to *be high; to rise* or *raise*
7392 râkab (1), to *ride*
7665 shâbar (1), to *burst*
7725 shûwb (72), to *turn back; to return*
7760 sûwm (1), to *put, place*
7817 shâchach (1), to *sink* or *depress*
7896 shîyth (1), to *place*
7971 shâlach (1), to *send away*
8045 shâmad (1), to *desolate*

8074 shâmêm (2), to *devastate; to stupefy*
8213 shâphêl (4), to *humiliate*
8317 shârats (3), to *wriggle, swarm*
71 agō (14), to *lead; to bring, drive; to weigh*
114 athĕtĕō (1), to *disesteem, neutralize*
321 anagō (2), to *lead up; to bring out; to sail*
363 anamimnēskō (1), to *remind; to recollect*
518 apaggĕllō (2), to *announce, proclaim*
520 apagō (1), to *take away*
667 apŏhĕrō (1), to *bear off, carry away*
1295 diasōzō (1), to *cure, preserve, rescue*
1396 dŏulagōgĕō (1), to *enslave, subdue*
1402 dŏulŏō (1), to *enslave*
1521 ĕisagō (1), to *lead into*
1533 ĕisphĕrō (2), to *carry inward*
1625 ĕktrĕphō (1), to *cherish* or *train*
1627 ĕkphĕrō (1), to *bear out; to produce*
1863 ĕpagō (2), *inflict; charge*
2018 ĕpiphĕrō (1), to *inflict, bring upon*
2036 ĕpō (1), to *speak* or *say*
2097 ĕuaggĕlizō (2), to *announce good news*
2592 karpŏphŏrĕō (4), to *be fertile*
2609 katagō (3), to *lead down; to moor a vessel*
2615 katadŏulŏō (2), to *enslave utterly*
2673 katargĕō (1), to *be, render entirely useless*
3919 parĕisagō (1), to *lead in aside*
4160 pŏiĕō (6), to *do*
4311 prŏpĕmpō (3), to *send forward*
4317 prŏsagō (2), to *bring near*
4374 prŏsphĕrō (2), to *present to; to treat as*
5062 tĕssarakŏnta (1), *forty*
5088 tiktō (3), to *produce from seed*
5179 tupŏs (1), *shape*, i.e. *statue* or *resemblance*
5342 phĕrō (17), to *bear* or *carry*
5461 phōtizō (1), to *shine* or to *brighten* up

BRINGERS
539 'âman (1), to *be firm, faithful, true; to trust*

BRINGEST
935 bôw' (1), to *go, come*
1319 bâsar (3), to *announce* (good news)
1533 ĕisphĕrō (1), to *carry inward*

BRINGETH
935 bôw' (6), to *go* or *come*
1069 bâkar (1), to *give the birthright*
1319 bâsar (5), to *announce* (good news)
2142 zâkar (1), to *remember*
2659 châphêr (1), to *shame, reproach*
3318 yâtsâ' (18), to *go, bring out*
3381 yârad (2), to *descend*
3615 kâlâh (1), to *complete, prepare*
5060 nâga' (1), to *strike*
5107 nûwb (1), to (*make*) *flourish; to utter*
5148 nâchâh (1), to *guide*
5414 nâthan (3), to *give*
5927 'âlâh (3), to *ascend, be high, mount*
6213 'âsâh (1), to *do* or *make*
6331 pûwr (1), to *crush*
6445 pânaq (1), to *enervate, reduce vigor*
6779 tsâmach (1), to *sprout*
7725 shûwb (3), to *turn back; to return*
7737 shâvâh (1), to *level, equalize; to resemble*
7817 shâchach (1), to *sink* or *depress*
8213 shâphêl (1), to *humiliate*
399 anaphĕrō (1), to *take up; to lead up*
616 apŏkuĕō (1), to *bring into being*
1521 ĕisagō (1), to *lead into*
1544 ĕkballō (3), to *throw out*
2592 karpŏphŏrĕō (2), to *be fertile*
4160 pŏiĕō (7), to *do*
4393 prŏphĕrō (2), to *bear forward*
4992 sōtēriŏn (1), *defender* or *defence*
5088 tiktō (2), to *produce from seed*
5342 phĕrō (2), to *bear* or *carry*

BRINGING
935 bôw' (6), to *go, come*
2142 zâkar (1), to *remember; to mention*
3318 yâtsâ' (3), to *go, bring out*
5375 nâsâ' (3), to *lift up*
7725 shûwb (2), to *turn back; to return*
71 agō (1), to *lead; to bring, drive; to weigh*
163 aichmalōtizō (2), to *make captive*
1863 ĕpagō (1), *inflict; charge*
1898 ĕpĕisagōgē (1), *introduction*
4160 pŏiĕō (1), to *do*
5342 phĕrō (3), to *bear* or *carry*

BRINK
7097 qâtseh (1), *extremity*
8193 sâphâh (5), *lip;
edge, margin*

BROAD
7338 rachab (1), *width,
expanse*
7338+3027 rachab (1),
width, expanse
7339 rᵉchôb (3), *myriad*
7341 rôchab (21), *width*
7342 râchâb (5), *roomy,
spacious*
7554 râqa' (1), *to pound*
7555 riqqûa' (1), *thin*
metallic *plate*
2149 ĕuruchôrŏs (1),
spacious, wide
4115 platunō (1), *to
widen*

BROADER
7342 râchâb (1), *roomy,
spacious*

BROIDED
4117 plĕgma (1), *plait* or
braid of hair

BROIDERED
7553 riqmâh (7),
embroidery
8665 tashbêts (1),
checkered stuff

BROILED
3702 ŏptŏs (1), *roasted,
broiled*

BROKEN
6 'âbad (1), *perish;
destroy*
1234 bâqa' (6), *to cleave,
break, tear open*
1638 gâraç (1), *to crush,
break; to dissolve*
1792 dâkâ' (3), *to
pulverize;* be *contrite*
1794 dâkâh (3), *to
collapse; contrite*
1854 dâqaq (1), *to crush;
crumble*
1986 hâlam (2), *to strike,
beat, stamp, conquer*
2040 hâraç (4), *to pull
down; break, destroy*
2490 châlal (1), *to
profane, defile*
2844 chath (6), *terror*
2865 châthath (6), *to
break down*
3807 kâthath (1), *to
bruise* or *strike*
4535 maççâch (1),
cordon; barrier; in turn
4790 mᵉrôwach (1),
bruised, pounded
5181 nâchath (2), *to sink,
descend; to press*
5218 nâkê' (3), *smitten;
afflicted*
5310 nâphats (1), *to dash*
to pieces; *to scatter*
5421 nâtha' (1), *to tear
out*
5422 nâthats (5), *to tear
down*
5423 nâthaq (7), *to tear
off*
5927 'âlâh (1), *to ascend,
be high, mount*

6105 'âtsam (1), *to be,
make powerful*
6209 'ârar (1), *to bare;* to
demolish
6331 pûwr (1), *to crush*
6480 pâtsam (1), *to rend,
tear* by earthquake
6524 pârach (2), *to break
forth; to bloom*
6531 perek (1), *severity*
6555 pârats (12), *to
break out*
6565 pârar (9), *to break
up;* to *violate, frustrate*
7280 râga' (1), *to stir up*
7462 râ'âh (1), *to tend* a
flock, i.e. *pasture* it
7465 rô'âh (1), *breakage*
7489 râ'a' (2), *to break* to
pieces
7533 râtsats (4), *to crack*
in pieces, *smash*
7616 shâbâb (1),
fragment, i.e. *ruin*
7665 shâbar (65), *to burst*
8406 tᵉbar (Ch.) (1), *to be
fragile*
1358 diŏrussō (2), *to
penetrate* burglariously
1575 ĕkklaō (3), *to
exscind, cut off*
1846 ĕxŏrussō (1), *to dig
out*
2608 katagnumi (1), *to
crack apart*
2801 klasma (2), *piece,
bit*
2806 klaō (3), *to break*
bread
3089 luō (6), *to loosen*
4917 sunthlaō (2), *to
dash together, shatter*
4937 suntribō (3), *to
crush completely*
4977 schizō (1), *to split
or sever*

BROKENFOOTED
7667+7272 sheber (1),
fracture; ruin

BROKENHANDED
7667+3027 sheber (1),
fracture; ruin

BROKENHEARTED
7665+3820 shâbar (1), *to
burst*
4937+2588 suntribō (1),
to crush completely

BROOD
3555 nŏssia (1), hen's
brood

BROOK
4323 mîykâl (1), *brook*
5158 nachal (37), *valley,
ravine;* mine *shaft*
5493 chĕimarrhŏs (1),
winter-torrent

BROOKS
650 'âphîyq (1), *valley;
stream; mighty, strong*
2975 yᵉ'ôr (4), Nile *River;*
Tigris *River*
5158 nachal (9), *valley,
ravine;* mine *shaft*

BROTH
4839 mârâq (2),
soup-broth

6564 pârâq (1),
fragments in soup

BROTHER
251 'âch (244), *brother;
relative; member*
1730 dôwd (1), *beloved,
friend; relative*
2992 yâbam (2), *to marry*
a brother's widow
2993 yâbâm (2),
husband's brother
7453 rêa' (1), *associate;*
one *close*
80 adĕlphŏs (109),
brother

BROTHER'S
251 'âch (25), *brother;
relative; member*
2994 yᵉbêmeth (3), dead
brother's widow, i.e.
sister-in-law
80 adĕlphŏs (7), *brother*

BROTHERHOOD
264 'achăvâh (1),
fraternity; brotherhood
81 adĕlphŏtēs (1),
fraternity, brotherhood

BROTHERLY
251 'âch (1), *brother;
relative; member*
5360 philadĕlphia (5),
fraternal affection

BROTHERS'
1730 dôwd (1), *beloved,
friend; relative*

BROUGHT
539 'âman (5), *to be firm,
faithful, true; to trust*
622 'âçaph (3), *to gather,
collect*
656 'âphêç (1), *to cease*
857 'âthâh (1), *to arrive;
go*
858 'âthâh (Ch.) (7), *to
arrive; go*
935 bôw' (264), *to go* or
come
1197 bâ'ar (1), *to be
brutish, be senseless*
1310 bâshal (1), *to boil
up, cook; to ripen*
1319 bâsar (2), *to
announce* (good news)
1431 gâdal (6), *to be
great, make great*
1468 gûwz (1), *to pass*
rapidly
1540 gâlâh (1), *to
denude; uncover*
1541 gᵉlâh (Ch.) (1), *to
reveal mysteries*
1589 gânab (1), *to thieve;
to deceive*
1809 dâlal (3), *to
slacken, dangle*
1820 dâmâh (2), *to be
silent; to fail, cease*
1946 hûwk (Ch.) (1), *to
go, come*
1961 hâyâh (2), *to exist,*
i.e. *be* or *become*
2254 châbal (2), *to bind*
by a *pledge;* to *pervert*
2342 chûwl (3), *to dance,
whirl; to writhe* in pain
2659 châphêr (3), *to be
ashamed, disappointed*

2986 yâbal (7), *to bring*
2987 yᵉbal (Ch.) (2), *to
bring*
3205 yâlad (12), *to bear
young; to father a child*
3212 yâlak (8), *to walk;
to live; to carry*
3218 yekeq (1), *young
locust*
3318 yâtsâ' (127), *to go,
bring out*
3381 yârad (17), *to
descend*
3467 yâsha' (2), *to make
safe, free*
3474 yâshar (1), *to be
straight; to make right*
3533 kâbash (3), *to
conquer, subjugate*
3665 kâna' (4), *to
humiliate, vanquish*
3766 kâra' (2), *to make
miserable*
3947 lâqach (8), *to take*
4161 môwtsâ' (2), *going
forth*
4355 mâkak (2), *to
tumble; to perish*
4551 maççâ' (1), stone
quarry; projectile
5060 nâga' (1), *to strike*
5066 nâgash (13), *to be,
come, bring near*
5090 nâhag (4), *to drive*
forth; *to carry away*
5148 nâchâh (2), *to guide*
5265 nâça' (3), *start* on a
journey
5375 nâsâ' (13), *to lift up*
5414 nâthan (3), *to give*
5437 çâbab (1), *to
surround*
5493 çûwr (1), *to turn* off
5674 'âbar (6), *to cross
over; to transition*
5927 'âlâh (65), *to
ascend, be high, mount*
5954 'ălal (Ch.) (4), *to go
in; to lead in*
6030 'ânâh (1), *to
respond, answer*
6213 'âsâh (3), *to do or
make*
6565 pârar (1), *to break
up;* to *violate, frustrate*
6819 tsâ'ar (1), *to be
small; be trivial*
6908 qâbats (1), *to
collect, assemble*
7126 qârab (27), *to
approach, bring near*
7127 qᵉrêb (Ch.) (1), *to
approach, bring near*
7136 qârâh (1), *to bring
about; to impose*
7235 râbâh (1), *to
increase*
7311 rûwm (1), *to be
high; to rise or raise*
7323 rûwts (1), *to run*
7392 râkab (1), *to ride*
7617 shâbâh (1), *to
transport* into captivity
7725 shûwb (39), *to turn
back; to return*
7760 sûwm (4), *to put,
place*
7817 shâchach (3), *to
sink or depress*

BROUGHTEST

7971 shâlach (1), to *send away*
8213 shâphêl (3), to *humiliate*
8239 shâphath (1), to *place or put*
8317 shârats (2), to *swarm, or abound*
71 agō (32), to *lead; to bring, drive; to weigh*
321 anagō (4), to *lead up; to bring out; to sail*
397 anatrĕphō (1), to *rear, care for*
654 apŏstrĕphō (1), to *turn away or back*
985 blastanō (1), to *yield fruit*
1080 gĕnnaō (1), to *procreate, regenerate*
1096 ginŏmai (2), to *be, become*
1325 didōmi (1), to *give*
1402 dŏulŏō (1), to *enslave*
1521 ĕisagō (7), to *lead into*
1533 ĕisphĕrō (2), to *carry inward*
1627 ĕkphĕrō (1), to *bear out; to produce*
1806 ĕxagō (6), to *lead forth, escort*
1850 ĕxŏusiazō (1), to *control, master another*
2018 ĕpiphĕrō (2), to *inflict, bring upon*
2049 ĕrēmŏō (2), to *lay waste*
2064 ĕrchŏmai (1), to *go*
2097 ĕuaggĕlizō (1), to *announce good news*
2164 ĕuphŏrĕō (1), to *be fertile, produce a crop*
2476 histēmi (1), to *stand, establish*
2601 katabibazō (1), to *cause to bring down*
2609 katagō (4), to *lead down; to moor a vessel*
2865 kŏmizō (1), to *provide for*
2989 lampō (1), to *radiate brilliancy*
3350 mĕtŏikĕsia (1), *exile, deportation*
3860 paradidōmi (1), to *hand over*
3920 parĕisaktŏs (1), *smuggled in, infiltrated*
3930 parĕchō (2), to *hold near, i.e. to present*
3936 paristēmi (2), to *stand beside, present*
4160 pŏiĕō (1), to *make*
4254 prŏagō (3), to *lead forward; to precede*
4311 prŏpĕmpō (4), to *send forward*
4317 prŏsagō (1), to *bring near*
4374 prŏsphĕrō (15), to *present to; to treat as*
4851 sumphĕrō (1), to *collect; to conduce*
4939 suntrŏphŏs (1), one *brought up with*
5013 tapĕinŏō (1), to *depress; to humiliate*

5044 tĕknŏtrŏphĕō (1), to *be a child-rearer*
5088 tiktō (4), to *produce from seed*
5142 trĕphō (1), to *nurse, feed, care for*
5342 phĕrō (17), to *bear or carry*
5461 phōtizō (1), to *shine or to brighten* up

BROUGHTEST

935 bôw' (4), to *go or come*
3318 yâtsâ' (7), to *go, bring out*
5927 'âlâh (2), to *ascend, be high, mount*

BROW

4696 mêtsach (1), *forehead*
3790 ŏphrus (1), eye-*brow*

BROWN

2345 chûwm (4), *sunburnt or swarthy*

BRUISE

1792 dâkâ' (1), to *pulverize; be contrite*
1854 dâqaq (1), to *crush; crumble*
7490 rᵉ'a' (Ch.) (1), to *shatter, dash to pieces*
7667 sheber (2), *fracture; ruin*
7779 shûwph (2), to *gape, i.e. snap at*
4937 suntribō (1), to *crush completely*

BRUISED'

1792 dâkâ' (1), to *pulverize; be contrite*
1854 dâqaq (1), to *crush; crumble*
4600 mâ'ak (1), to *press, to pierce, emasculate*
6213 'âsâh (2), to *do or make*
7533 râtsats (2), to *crack in pieces, smash*
2352 thrauō (1), to *crush*
4937 suntribō (1), to *crush completely*

BRUISES

2250 chabbûwrâh (1), *weal, bruise*

BRUISING

6213 'âsâh (1), to *do or make*
4937 suntribō (1), to *crush completely*

BRUIT

8052 shᵉmûw'âh (1), *announcement*
8088 shêma' (1), *something heard*

BRUTE

249 alŏgŏs (2), *irrational, not reasonable*

BRUTISH

1197 bâ'ar (11), to *be brutish, be senseless*

BUCKET

1805 dᵉlîy (1), *pail, bucket*

BUCKETS

1805 dᵉlîy (1), *pail, bucket*

BUCKLER

4043 mâgên (6), small *shield (buckler); skin*
5507 çôchêrâh (1), *surrounding shield*
6793 tsinnâh (3), large *shield; piercing cold*
7420 rômach (1), iron *pointed spear*

BUCKLERS

4043 mâgên (3), small *shield (buckler); skin*
6793 tsinnâh (2), large *shield; piercing cold*

BUD

4161 môwtsâ' (1), *going forth*
5132 nûwts (1), to *fly away, leave*
6524 pârach (2), to *break forth; to bloom*
6525 perach (1), *calyx flower; bloom*
6779 tsâmach (6), to *sprout*

BUDDED

5132 nûwts (1), to *fly away, leave*
6524 pârach (3), to *break forth; to bloom*
985 blastanō (1), to *yield fruit*

BUDS

6525 perach (1), *calyx flower; bloom*

BUFFET

2852 kŏlaphizō (2), to *strike*

BUFFETED

2852 kŏlaphizō (3), to *strike*

BUILD

1124 bᵉnâ' (Ch.) (6), to *build*
1129 bânâh (140), to *build; to establish*
456 anŏikŏdŏmĕō (2), to *rebuild*
2026 ĕpŏikŏdŏmĕō (2), to *rear up, build up*
3618 ŏikŏdŏmĕō (12), *construct; edification*

BUILDED

1124 bᵉnâ' (Ch.) (10), to *build*
1129 bânâh (36), to *build; to establish*
2680 kataskĕuazō (2), to *construct; to arrange*
3618 ŏikŏdŏmĕō (1), *construct; edification*
4925 sunŏikŏdŏmĕō (1), to *construct*

BUILDEDST

1129 bânâh (1), to *build; to establish*

BUILDER

5079 tĕchnitēs (1), *artisan, craftsman*

BUILDERS

1129 bânâh (9), to *build; to establish*
3618 ŏikŏdŏmĕō (5), *construct; edification*

BUILDEST

1129 bânâh (3), to *build; to establish*
3618 ŏikŏdŏmĕō (2), *construct; edification*

BUILDETH

1129 bânâh (7), to *build; to establish*
2026 ĕpŏikŏdŏmĕō (2), to *rear up, build up*

BUILDING

1124 bᵉnâ' (Ch.) (3), to *build*
1129 bânâh (15), to *build; to establish*
1140 binyâh (1), *structure*
1146 binyân (7), *edifice, building*
1147 binyân (Ch.) (1), *edifice, building*
4746 mᵉqâreh (1), *frame of timbers*
1739 ĕndōmēsis (1), *structure*
2026 ĕpŏikŏdŏmĕō (1), to *rear up, build up*
2937 ktisis (1), *formation*
3618 ŏikŏdŏmĕō (1), *construct; edification*
3619 ŏikŏdŏmē (3), *structure; edification*

BUILDINGS

3619 ŏikŏdŏmē (3), *structure; edification*

BUILT

1124 bᵉnâ' (Ch.) (1), to *build*
1129 bânâh (155), to *build; to establish*
2026 ĕpŏikŏdŏmĕō (3), to *rear up, build up*
2680 kataskĕuazō (1), to *construct; to arrange*
3618 ŏikŏdŏmĕō (10), *construct; edification*

BUKKI

1231 Buqqîy (5), *wasteful*

BUKKIAH

1232 Buqqîyâh (2), *wasting of Jehovah*

BUL

945 Bûwl (1), *rain*

BULL

7794 shôwr (1), *bullock*
8377 tᵉ'ôw (1), *antelope*

BULLOCK

1121+1241 bên (3), *son, descendant*
1241 bâqâr (1), *plowing ox; herd*
5695 'êgel (1), bull-*calf*
6499 par (89), *bullock*
7794 shôwr (10), *bullock*

BULLOCK'S

6499 par (3), *bullock*

BULLOCKS

1241 bâqâr (4), *plowing ox; herd*
5695 'êgel (1), bull-*calf*
6499 par (36), *bullock*
7794 shôwr (1), *bullock*
8450 tôwr (Ch.) (3), *bull*

BULLS

47 'abbîyr (4), *mighty*

1241 bâqâr (1), *plowing
ox; herd*
6499 par (2), *bullock*
5022 taurŏs (2), *bullock,
ox*

BULRUSH
100 'agmôwn (1), *rush;
rope of rushes*

BULRUSHES
1573 gŏme' (2), *papyrus
plant*

BULWARKS
2426 chêyl (1),
entrenchment, rampart
2430 chêylâh (1),
entrenchment, rampart
4685 mâtsôwd (1), *net or
snare; besieging tower*
4692 mâtsôwr (1),
siege-mound; distress
6438 pinnâh (1),
pinnacle; chieftain

BUNAH
946 Bûwnâh (1),
discretion

BUNCH
92 'ăguddâh (1), *band;
bundle; knot; arch*

BUNCHES
1707 dabbesheth (1),
hump of a camel
6778 tsammûwq (2),
lump of dried grapes

BUNDLE
6872 tseᵉrôwr (3), *parcel;
kernel or particle*
4128 plêthŏs (1), *large
number, throng*

BUNDLES
6872 tseᵉrôwr (1), *parcel;
kernel or particle*
1197 děsmē (1), *bundle*

BUNNI
1137 Bânîy (3), *built*

BURDEN
3053 yeᵉhâb (1), *lot given*
4853 massâ' (52), *burden,
utterance*
4858 massâ'âh (1),
*conflagration from the
rising of smoke*
4864 mas'êth (1), *raising;
beacon; present*
5445 çâbal (1), to *carry*
5448 çôbel (3), *load,
burden*
5449 çabbâl (1), *porter,
carrier*
6006 'âmaç (1), to *impose
a burden*
922 barŏs (3), *load,
abundance, authority*
1117 gŏmŏs (1), *cargo,
wares or freight*
2599 katabarěŏ (1), to *be
a burden*
5413 phŏrtiŏn (2),
burden, task or service

BURDENED
916 barěŏ (1), to *weigh
down, cause pressure*
2347 thlipsis (1),
pressure, trouble

BURDENS
92 'ăguddâh (1), *band;
bundle; knot; arch*
4853 massâ' (5), *burden,
utterance*
4864 mas'êth (2), *raising;
beacon; present*
4942 mishpâth (1), *pair
of stalls for cattle*
5447 çêbel (1), *load;
forced labor*
5449 çabbâl (5), *porter,
carrier*
5450 çeᵉbâlâh (6),
porterage; forced labor
922 barŏs (1), *load,
abundance, authority*
5413 phŏrtiŏn (3),
burden, task or service

BURDENSOME
4614 ma'ămâçâh (1),
burdensomeness
4 abarēs (1), *not
burdensome*
1722+922 ĕn (1), *in;
during; because of*
2655 katanarkaŏ (2), to
be a burden

BURIAL
6900 qeᵉbûwrâh (4),
sepulchre
1779 ĕntaphiazŏ (1), to
enswathe for burial

BURIED
6912 qâbar (96), to *inter,
pile up*
2290 thaptō (7), to
celebrate funeral rites
4916 sunthaptō (2), to *be
buried with*

BURIERS
6912 qâbar (1), to *inter,
pile up*

BURN
1197 bâ'ar (19), to *be
brutish, be senseless*
1754 dûwr (1), *circle;
ball; pile*
2734 chârâh (1), to *blaze*
2787 chârar (1), to *melt,
burn, dry up*
3344 yâqad (3), to *burn*
3857 lâhaṭ (1), to *blaze*
4729 miqṭâr (1), *hearth*
5400 nâsaq (1), to *catch
fire*
5927 'âlâh (2), to *ascend,
be high, mount*
6702 tsûwth (1), to *blaze,
set on fire*
6999 qâṭar (59), to *turn
into fragrance by fire*
8313 sâraph (40), to *be,
set on fire*
2370 thumiaŏ (1), to
offer aromatic fumes
2545 kaiŏ (1), to *set on
fire*
2618 katakaiŏ (4), to
*consume wholly by
burning*
4448 purŏŏ (2), to *be
ignited, glow; inflamed*

BURNED
1197 bâ'ar (8), to *be
brutish, be senseless*

2787 chârar (7), to *melt,
burn, dry up*
3341 yâtsath (9), to *burn
or set on fire*
3554 kâvâh (2), to *blister,
be scorched*
3857 lâhaṭ (2), to *blaze*
5375 nâsâ' (2), to *lift up*
6866 tsârab (1), to *burn*
6999 qâṭar (19), to *turn
into fragrance by fire*
8313 sâraph (33), to *be,
set on fire*
8314 sârâph (1),
poisonous serpent
8316 seᵉrêphâh (1),
cremation
1572 ĕkkaiŏ (1), to
inflame deeply
1714 ĕmprēthō (1), to
burn, set on fire
2545 kaiŏ (3), to *set on
fire*
2618 katakaiŏ (6), to
*consume wholly by
burning*
2740 kausis (1), *act of
burning*
4448 purŏŏ (1), to *be
ignited, glow; inflamed*

BURNETH
1197 bâ'ar (4), to *be
brutish, be senseless*
2142 zâkar (1), to
remember; to mention
3344 yâqad (1), to *burn*
3857 lâhaṭ (2), to *blaze*
4348 mikvâh (1), *burn*
5635 çâraph (1), to
cremate
6919 qâdach (1), to
inflame
6999 qâṭar (2), to *turn
into fragrance by fire*
8313 sâraph (4), to *be,
set on fire*
2545 kaiŏ (1), to *set on
fire*

BURNING
784 'êsh (3), *fire*
1197 bâ'ar (6), to *be
brutish, be senseless*
1513 gechel (1), *ember,
hot coal*
1814 dâlaq (1), to *flame;
to pursue*
1815 deᵉlaq (Ch.) (1), to
flame, burn
2746 charchûr (1), *hot
fever*
3344 yâqad (3), to *burn*
3345 yeᵉqad (Ch.) (10), to
burn
3346 yeᵉqêdâ' (Ch.) (1),
consuming fire
3350 yeᵉqôwd (1),
burning, blazing
3555 keᵉvîyâh (1),
branding, scar
3587 kîy (1), *brand or
scar*
3940 lappîyd (1), *flaming
torch, lamp or flame*
4169 môwqeᵉdâh (1), *fuel*
4348 mikvâh (4), *burn*
6867 tsârebeth (2),
conflagration
6920 qaddachath (1),
inflammation

6999 qâṭar (1), to *turn
into fragrance by fire*
7565 resheph (1), *flame*
8316 seᵉrêphâh (9),
cremation
2545 kaiŏ (6), to *set on
fire*
2742 kausōn (1), *burning
heat, hot day*
4451 purōsis (2), *ignition;
conflagration, calamity*

BURNINGS
4168 môwqêd (1),
conflagration, burning
4955 misrâphâh (2),
cremation

BURNISHED
7044 qâlâl (1),
brightened, polished

BURNT
398 'âkal (1), to *eat*
1197 bâ'ar (6), to *be
brutish, be senseless*
3632 kâlîyl (1), *whole,
entire; complete; whole*
4198 mâzeh (1),
exhausted, empty
5927 'âlâh (1), to *ascend,
be high, mount*
5928 'ălâh (Ch.) (1),
wholly consumed in fire
5930 'ôlâh (284), *sacrifice
wholly consumed in fire*
6999 qâṭar (24), to *turn
into fragrance by fire*
8313 sâraph (36), to *be,
set on fire*
8316 seᵉrêphâh (2),
cremation
2618 katakaiŏ (2), to
*consume wholly by
burning*
3646 hŏlŏkautōma (3),
wholly-consumed

BURST
1234 bâqa' (1), to *cleave,
break, tear open*
5423 nâthaq (4), to *tear
off*
6555 pârats (1), to *break
out*
2997 laschō (1), to *crack
open*
4486 rhēgnumi (2), to
break, burst forth

BURSTING
4386 meᵉkittâh (1),
fracture

BURY
6912 qâbar (33), to *inter,
pile up*
1779 ĕntaphiazŏ (1), to
enswathe for burial
2290 thaptō (4), to
celebrate funeral rites
5027 taphē (1), *burial*

BURYING
6912 qâbar (2), to *inter,
pile up*
1780 ĕntaphiasmŏs (2),
preparation for burial

BURYINGPLACE
6913 qeber (7), *sepulchre*

BUSH
5572 çeᵉneh (6), *bramble*
942 batŏs (5), *brier*

BUSHEL
3426 mŏdiŏs (3), *dry measure* of *volume*

BUSHES
5097 nahălôl (1), *pasture*
7880 sîyach (2), *shrubbery*

BUSHY
8534 taltal (1), *wavy*

BUSINESS
1697 dâbâr (8), *word; matter; thing*
4399 mᵉlâ'kâh (12), *work; property*
4639 ma'ăseh (1), *action; labor*
6045 'inyân (2), *employment, labor*
2398 idiŏs (1), *private* or *separate*
4229 pragma (1), *matter, deed, affair*
4710 spŏudĕ (1), *despatch; eagerness*
5532 chrĕia (1), *affair; occasion, demand*

BUSY
6213 'âsâh (1), to *do* or *make*

BUSYBODIES
4020 pĕriĕrgazŏmai (1), to *meddle*
4021 pĕriĕrgŏs (1), *busybody; magic*

BUSYBODY
244 allotriĕpiskŏpŏs (1), *meddler, busybody*

BUTLER
4945 mashqeh (8), *butler; drink; well-watered*

BUTLERS
4945 mashqeh (1), *butler; drink; well-watered*

BUTLERSHIP
4945 mashqeh (1), *butler; drink; well-watered*

BUTTER
2529 chem'âh (10), *curds, milk* or *cheese*
4260 machămâ'âh (1), *buttery; flattery*

BUTTOCKS
4667 miphsâ'âh (1), *crotch* area
8357 shêthâh (2), *seat* i.e. buttock

BUY
3739 kârâh (1), to *purchase* by bargaining
3947 lâqach (2), to *take*
7066 qᵉnâ' (Ch.) (1), to *purchase*
7069 qânâh (24), to *create; to procure*
7666 shâbar (14), to *deal* in cereal grain
59 agŏrazŏ (13), to *purchase; to redeem*
1710 ĕmpŏrĕuŏmai (1), to *trade, do business*

BUYER
7069 qânâh (3), to *create; to procure*

BUYEST
7069 qânâh (2), to *create; to procure*

BUYETH
3947 lâqach (1), to *take*
59 agŏrazŏ (2), to *purchase; to redeem*

BUZ
938 Bûwz (3), *disrespect, scorn*

BUZI
941 Bûwzîy (1), *Buzi*

BUZITE
940 Bûwzîy (2), *Buzite*

BYWAYS
734+6128 'ôrach (1), *well-traveled road*

BYWORD
4405 millâh (1), *word; discourse; speech*
4912 mâshâl (1), *pithy maxim; taunt*
4914 mᵉshôl (1), *satire*
8148 shᵉnîynâh (3), *gibe, verbal taunt*

CAB
6894 qab (1), *dry measure* of *volume*

CABBON
3522 Kabbôwn (1), *hilly*

CABINS
2588 chânûwth (1), *vault* or *cell*

CABUL
3521 Kâbûwl (2), *sterile*

CAESAR
2541 Kaisar (21), *Cæsar*

CAESAR'S
2541 Kaisar (9), *Cæsar*

CAESAREA
2542 Kaisarĕia (17), of *Cæsar*

CAGE
3619 kᵉlûwb (1), *bird-trap; basket*
5438 phulakĕ (1), *guarding* or *guard*

CAIAPHAS
2533 Kaïaphas (9), *dell*

CAIN
7014 Qayin (17), *lance*
2535 Kaïn (3), *lance*

CAINAN
7018 Qêynân (5), *fixed*
2536 Kaïnan (2), fixed

CAKE
1690 dᵉbêlâh (1), *cake* of *pressed figs*
2471 challâh (7), *cake shaped as a ring*
4580 mâ'ôwg (1), *cake* of *bread, provision*
5692 'uggâh (3), *round-cake*
6742 tsᵉlûwl (1), *round* or *flattened cake*

CAKES
1690 dᵉbêlâh (2), *cake* of *pressed figs*
2471 challâh (8), *cake shaped as a ring*
3561 kavvân (2), *sacrificial wafer*

3823 lâbab (1), to *make cakes*
3834 lâbîybâh (3), *fried* or *turned cake*
4682 matstsâh (4), *unfermented cake*
5692 'uggâh (4), *round-cake*
7550 râqîyq (1), *thin cake, wafer*

CALAH
3625 Kelach (2), *maturity*

CALAMITIES
343 'êyd (1), *misfortune, ruin, disaster*
1942 havvâh (1), *desire; craving*
7451 ra' (1), *bad; evil*

CALAMITY
343 'êyd (16), *misfortune, ruin, disaster*
1942 havvâh (3), *desire; craving*

CALAMUS
7070 qâneh (3), *reed*

CALCOL
3633 Kalkôl (1), *sustenance*

CALDRON
100 'agmôwn (1), *rush; rope of rushes*
5518 çîyr (3), *thorn; hook*
7037 qallachath (2), *kettle*

CALDRONS
1731 dûwd (1), *pot, kettle; basket*
5518 çîyr (2), *thorn; hook*

CALEB
3612 Kâlêb (32), *forcible*

CALEB'S
3612 Kâlêb (4), *forcible*

CALEB-EPHRATAH
3613 Kâlêb 'Ephrâthâh (1), *Caleb-Ephrathah*

CALF
1121+1241 bên (2), *son, descendant*
5695 'êgel (21), *calf*
3447 mŏschŏpŏiĕō (1), to *fabricate a bullock-idol*
3448 mŏschŏs (4), *young bullock*

CALF'S
5695 'êgel (1), *calf*

CALKERS
2388+919 châzaq (2), to *fasten* upon; to *seize*

CALL
559 'âmar (2), to *say, speak*
833 'âshar (5), to *go forward; guide*
2142 zâkar (3), to *remember; to mention*
5493 çûwr (1), to *turn off*
5749 'ûwd (3), to *duplicate* or *repeat*
7121 qârâ' (131), to *call out*
7725 shûwb (1), to *turn back; to return*
8085 shâma' (2), to *hear intelligently*

363 *anamimnēskŏ* (1), to *remind; to recollect*
1941 *ĕpikalĕŏmai* (9), to *invoke*
2564 *kalĕō* (17), to *call*
2840 *kŏinŏō* (2), to *make profane*
2983 *lambanō* (1), to *take, receive*
3004 *lĕgō* (4), to *say*
3106 *makarizō* (1), to *pronounce fortunate*
3333 *mĕtakalĕō* (2), to *summon for, call for*
3343 *mĕtapĕmpō* (2), to *summon* or *invite*
3687 *ŏnŏmazō* (1), to *give a name*
4341 *prŏskalĕŏmai* (2), to *call toward oneself*
4779 *sugkalĕō* (1), to *convoke, call together*
5455 *phōnĕō* (4), to *emit a sound*

CALLED
559 'âmar (4), to *say, speak*
935 bôw' (1), to *go* or *come*
2199 zâ'aq (3), to *call out, announce*
6817 tsâ'aq (2), to *shriek; to proclaim*
7121 qârâ' (380), to *call out*
7123 qᵉrâ' (Ch.) (1), to *call out*
7760 sûwm (1), to *put, place*
8085 shâma' (1), to *hear intelligently*
154 aitĕō (1), to *ask* for
363 anamimnēskŏ (1), to *remind; to recollect*
1458 ĕgkalĕō (1), to *charge, criminate*
1528 ĕiskalĕō (1), to *invite in*
1941 ĕpikalĕŏmai (4), to *invoke*
1951 ĕpilĕgŏmai (1), to *surname, select*
2028 ĕpŏnŏmazō (1), to *be called, denominate*
2036 ĕpō (1), to *speak*
2046 ĕrĕō (1), to *utter*
2564 kalĕō (103), to *call*
2822 klētŏs (11), *appointed, invited*
2919 krinō (2), to *decide; to try, condemn, punish*
3004 lĕgō (36), to *say*
3044 Linŏs (1), (poss.) *flax linen*
3333 mĕtakalĕō (2), to *summon for, call for*
3686 ŏnŏma (4), *name*
3687 ŏnŏmazō (1), to *give a name*
3739+2076 hŏs (1), *who, which, what, that*
3870 parakalĕō (1), to *call, invite*
4316 prŏsagŏrĕuŏ (1), to *designate a name*
4341 prŏskalĕŏmai (25), to *call toward oneself*
4377 prŏsphōnĕō (2), to *address, exclaim*

4779 sugkalĕō (5), to *convoke, call together*
4867 sunathrŏizō (1), to *convene*
5455 phōnéō (16), to *emit a sound*
5537 chrēmatizō (2), to *utter an oracle*
5581 psĕudōnumŏs (1), *untruly named*

CALLEDST
6485 pâqad (1), to *visit, care for, count*
7121 qârâ' (3), to *call out*

CALLEST
3004 lĕgō (3), to *say*

CALLETH
7121 qârâ' (13), to *call out*
2564 kalĕō (6), to *call*
3004 lĕgō (4), to *say*
4341 prŏskalĕŏmai (1), to *call toward oneself*
4779 sugkalĕō (2), to *convoke, call together*
5455 phōnéō (4), to *emit a sound*

CALLING
2142 zâkar (1), to *remember; to mention*
4744 miqrâ' (1), *public meeting*
7121 qârâ' (3), to *call out*
363 anamimnĕskō (1), to *remind; to recollect*
1941 ĕpikalĕŏmai (2), to *invoke*
2564 kalĕō (1), to *call*
2821 klēsis (10), *invitation; station in life*
4341 prŏskalĕŏmai (2), to *call toward oneself*
4377 prŏsphōnéō (2), to *address, exclaim*
5455 phōnéō (1), to *emit a sound*

CALM
1827 dᵉmâmâh (1), *quiet*
8367 shâthaq (2), to *subside*
1055 galēnē (3), *tranquillity, calm*

CALNEH
3641 Kalneh (2), *Calneh or Calno*

CALNO
3641 Kalneh (1), *Calneh or Calno*

CALVARY
2898 kraniŏn (1), *skull*

CALVE
2342 chûwl (2), to *dance, whirl; to writhe* in pain

CALVED
3205 yâlad (1), to *bear young; to father a child*

CALVES
1121 bên (2), *son, descendant*
1121+1241 bên (1), *son, descendant*
5695 'êgel (10), bull *calf*
5697 'eglâh (2), cow *calf*
6499 par (1), *bullock*

3448 mŏschŏs (2), *young bullock*

CALVETH
6403 pâlaṭ (1), to *slip out, i.e. escape; to deliver*

CAME
857 'âthâh (4), to *arrive; go*
858 'âthâh (Ch.) (3), to *arrive; go*
935 bôw' (668), to *go or come*
1061 bikkûwr (1), *first-fruits* of the crop
1518 gîyach (1), to *issue forth; to burst forth*
1691 Diblayim (1), *two cakes*
1916 hădôm (2), *foot-stool*
1946 hûwk (Ch.) (1), to *go, come*
1961 hâyâh (527), to *exist, i.e. be or become*
1980 hâlak (7), to *walk; live a certain way*
2015 hâphak (1), to *turn about or over*
3212 yâlak (6), to *walk; to live; to carry*
3318 yâtsâ' (106), to *go, bring out*
3329 yâtsîy (1), *issue forth, i.e. offspring*
3381 yârad (42), to *descend*
3847 lâbash (3), to *clothe*
3996 mâbôw' (1), *entrance; sunset; west*
4161 môwtsâ' (1), *going forth*
4291 mᵉṭâ' (Ch.) (4), to *arrive, to extend*
4672 mâtsâ' (2), to *find or acquire; to occur*
5060 nâga' (5), to *strike*
5066 nâgash (27), to *be, come, bring near*
5182 nᵉchath (Ch.) (1), to *descend; to depose*
5312 nᵉphaq (Ch.) (3), to *issue forth; to bring out*
5437 çâbab (1), to *surround*
5559 çᵉlîq (Ch.) (5), to *ascend, go up*
5674 'âbar (4), to *cross over; to transition*
5927 'âlâh (82), to *ascend, be high, mount*
5954 'ălal (Ch.) (4), to *go in; to lead in*
5957 'âlam (Ch.) (1), *forever*
6293 pâga' (1), to *impinge*
6473 pâ'ar (1), to *open wide*
6555 pârats (1), to *break out*
6743 tsâlach (5), to *push forward*
7122 qârâ' (1), to *encounter, to happen*
7126 qârab (20), to *approach, bring near*
7127 qᵉrêb (Ch.) (5), to *approach, bring near*
7131 qârêb (1), *near*

7725 shûwb (16), to *turn back; to return*
191 akŏuō (1), to *hear; obey*
305 anabainō (3), to *go up, rise*
565 apĕrchŏmai (1), to *go off, i.e. depart*
1096 ginŏmai (88), to *be, become*
1237 diadĕchŏmai (1), *succeed, receive in turn*
1448 ĕggizō (3), to *approach*
1525 ĕisĕrchŏmai (10), to *enter*
1531 ĕispŏrĕuŏmai (1), to *enter*
1607 ĕkpŏrĕuŏmai (1), to *depart, be discharged*
1831 ĕxĕrchŏmai (38), to *issue; to leave*
1904 ĕpĕrchŏmai (1), to *supervene*
1910 ĕpibainō (1), to *mount, ascend*
1994 ĕpistrĕphō (1), to *revert, turn back to*
1998 ĕpisuntrĕchō (1), to *hasten together upon*
2064 ĕrchŏmai (199), to *go or come*
2113 ĕuthudrŏmĕō (1), to *sail direct*
2186 ĕphistēmi (7), to *be present; to approach*
2240 hēkō (3), to *arrive, i.e. be present*
2597 katabainō (16), to *descend*
2658 katantaō (8), to *arrive at; to attain*
2718 katĕrchŏmai (6), to *go, come down*
2944 kuklŏō (1), to *surround, encircle*
2983 lambanō (1), to *take, receive*
3415 mnaŏmai (1), to *bear in mind*
3719 ŏrthrizō (1), to *get up early in the morning*
3854 paraginŏmai (16), to *arrive; to appear*
3918 parĕimi (1), to *be present; to have come*
3922 parĕisĕrchŏmai (1), to *supervene*
3928 parĕrchŏmai (1), to *go by; to perish*
4130 plēthō (1), to *fulfill, complete*
4334 prŏsĕrchŏmai (65), to *come near, visit*
4370 prŏstrĕchō (1), to *hasten by running*
4836 sumparaginŏmai (1), to *convene*
4863 sunagō (6), to *gather together*
4872 sunanabainō (2), to *ascend in company*
4905 sunĕrchŏmai (8), to *gather together*
5342 phĕrō (3), to *bear or carry*

CAMEL
1581 gâmâl (5), *camel*
2574 kamēlŏs (4), *camel*

CAMEL'S
1581 gâmâl (1), *camel*
2574 kamēlŏs (2), *camel*

CAMELS
327 'ăchastârân (2), *mule*
1581 gâmâl (44), *camel*

CAMELS'
1581 gâmâl (3), *camel*

CAMEST
935 bôw' (8), to *go, come*
1518 gîyach (1), to *issue forth; to burst forth*
1980 hâlak (3), to *walk; live a certain way*
3318 yâtsâ' (7), to *go, bring out*
3381 yârad (3), to *descend*
7126 qârab (1), to *approach, bring near*
7725 shûwb (1), to *turn back; to return*
1096 ginŏmai (1), to *be, become*
1525 ĕisĕrchŏmai (1), to *enter*
1831 ĕxĕrchŏmai (1), to *issue; to leave*
2064 ĕrchŏmai (1), to *go or come*

CAMON
7056 Qâmôwn (1), *elevation*

CAMP
2583 chânâh (3), to *encamp*
4264 machăneh (127), *encampment*
8466 tachănâh (1), *encampment*
3925 parĕmbŏlē (3), *encampment*

CAMPED
2583 chânâh (1), to *encamp*

CAMPHIRE
3724 kôpher (2), *village; bitumen; henna*

CAMPS
4264 machăneh (7), *encampment*

CAN
3045 yâda' (1), to *know*
3201 yâkôl (18), to *be able*
3202 yᵉkêl (Ch.) (2), to *be able*
1097 ginōskō (1), to *know*
1410 dunamai (65), to *be able or possible*
1492 ĕidō (2), to *know*
2480 ischuō (1), to *have or exercise force*

CANA
2580 Kana (4), *Cana*

CANAAN
3667 Kᵉna'an (90), *humiliated*
5478 Chanaanaiŏs (1), *Kenaanite*

CANAANITE
3669 Kᵉna'ăniy (12), *Kenaanite; merchant*
2581 Kananitēs (2), *zealous*

CANAANITES
3669 Kᵉna'ăniy (55), *Kenaanite; merchant*

CANAANITESS
3669 Kᵉna'ăniy (1), *Kenaanite; merchant*

CANAANITISH
3669 Kᵉna'ăniy (2), *Kenaanite; merchant*

CANDACE
2582 Kandakē (1), *Candacë*

CANDLE
5216 nîyr (8), *lamp; lamplight*
3088 luchnŏs (8), *portable lamp*

CANDLES
5216 nîyr (1), *lamp; lamplight*

CANDLESTICK
4501 mᵉnôwrâh (34), *chandelier, lamp-stand*
5043 nebrᵉshâ' (Ch.) (1), *lamp-stand*
3087 luchnia (6), *lamp-stand*

CANDLESTICKS
4501 mᵉnôwrâh (6), *chandelier, lamp-stand*
3087 luchnia (6), *lamp-stand*

CANE
7070 qâneh (2), *reed*

CANKER
1044 gaggraina (1), *ulcer*, i.e. *gangrene*

CANKERED
2728 katiŏō (1), to *corrode, tarnish*

CANKERWORM
3218 yekeq (6), *young locust*

CANNEH
3656 Kanneh (1), *Canneh*

CANNOT
369 'ayin (1), *there is no*, i.e., *not exist, none*
408 'al (2), *not; nothing*
518 'îm (1), *whether?; if, although; Oh that!*
1077 bal (2), *nothing; not at all; lest*
1097 bᵉlîy (1), *without, not yet; lacking;*
1115 biltîy (1), *not, except, without, unless*
3201 yâkôl (3), to *be able*
3308 yŏphîy (2), *beauty*
3808 lô' (57), *no, not*
176 akatagnōstŏs (1), *unblamable*
180 akatapaustŏs (1), *unrefraining, unceasing*
215 alalētŏs (1), *unspeakable*
368 anantirrhētŏs (1), *indisputable*
551 apĕirastŏs (1), *not temptable*
761 asalĕutŏs (1), *immovable, fixed*
893 apsĕudēs (1), *veracious, free of deceit*
1492 ĕidō (2), to *know*

CANST
3201 yâkôl (6), to *be able*
3202 yᵉkêl (Ch.) (2), to *be able*
1097 ginōskō (1), to *know*
1410 dunamai (9), to *be able* or *possible*
1492 ĕidō (1), to *know*

CAPERNAUM
2584 Kapĕrnaŏum (16), *walled village which is comfortable*

CAPHTHORIM
3732 Kaphtôrîy (1), *Caphtorite*

CAPHTOR
3731 Kaphtôr (3), *wreath-shaped island*

CAPHTORIM
3732 Kaphtôrîy (1), *Caphtorite*

CAPHTORIMS
3732 Kaphtôrîy (1), *Caphtorite*

CAPPADOCIA
2587 Kappadŏkia (2), *Cappadocia*

CAPTAIN
1167 ba'al (1), *master; husband; owner; citizen*
2951 ţiphçar (1), *military governor*
5057 nâgîyd (5), *commander, official*
5387 nâsîy' (12), *leader; rising mist, fog*
5921 'al (1), *above, over, upon, or against*
6346 pechâh (2), *prefect, officer*
7101 qâtsîyn (2), *magistrate*
7218 rô'sh (4), *head*
7227 rab (23), *great*
7229 rab (Ch.) (1), *great*
7990 shallîyţ (Ch.) (1), *premier, sovereign*
7991 shâlîysh (2), *officer; of the third rank*
8269 sar (51), *head person, ruler*
747 archĕgŏs (1), *chief leader; founder*
4755 stratēgŏs (3), *military governor*
4759 stratŏpĕdarchēs (1), *military commander*
5506 chiliarchŏs (18), *colonel*

CAPTAINS
441 'allûwph (1), *friend, one familiar; chieftain*
2951 ţiphçar (1), *military governor*
3733 kar (1), *ram sheep; battering ram*
3746 kârîy (2), *life-guardsman*
5057 nâgîyd (1), *commander, official*
6346 pechâh (7), *prefect, officer*

CAPTIVE
1473 gôwlâh (4), *exile; captive*
1540 gâlâh (24), to *denude; uncover*
1546 gâlûwth (2), *captivity; exiles*
6808 tsâ'âh (1), to *depopulate; imprison*
7617 shâbâh (21), to *transport* into *captivity*
7628 shᵉbîy (3), *exile; booty*
162 aichmalōtĕuō (2), to *capture*
163 aichmalōtizō (1), to *make captive*
2221 zōgrĕō (1), to *capture* or *ensnare*

CAPTIVES
1123+1547 bên (Ch.) (1), *son*
1473 gôwlâh (3), *exile; captive*
1540 gâlâh (3), to *denude; uncover*
1546 gâlûwth (3), *captivity; exiles*
7617 shâbâh (16), to *transport* into *captivity*
7628 shᵉbîy (8), *exile; booty*
7633 shibyâh (8), *exile; captive*
164 aichmalōtŏs (1), *captive*

CAPTIVITY
1473 gôwlâh (28), *exile; captive*
1540 gâlâh (9), to *denude; uncover*
1546 gâlûwth (11), *captivity; exiles*
1547 gâlûwth (Ch.) (3), *captivity; exiles*
2925 ţaltêlâh (1), *overthrow* or *rejection*
7622 shᵉbûwth (31), *exile; prisoners*
7628 shᵉbîy (30), *exile; booty*
7633 shibyâh (6), *exile; captive*
161 aichmalōsia (2), *captivity*
163 aichmalōtizō (2), to *make captive*

CARBUNCLE
1304 bârᵉqath (3), *flashing gem* (poss.) *emerald*

CARBUNCLES
68+688 'eben (1), *stone*

CARCAS
3752 Karkaç (1), *Karkas*

CARCASE
1472 gᵉvîyâh (2), *dead body*
4658 mappeleth (1), *down-fall; ruin; carcase*
5038 nᵉbêlâh (29), *carcase* or *carrion*
6297 peger (1), *carcase; corpse*
4430 ptōma (1), *corpse, carrion*

CARCASES
5038 nᵉbêlâh (7), *carcase* or *carrion*
6297 peger (13), *carcase; corpse*
2966 kōlŏn (1), *corpse*

CARCHEMISH
3751 Karkᵉmîysh (2), *Karkemish*

CARE
983 beţach (1), *safety, security, trust*
1674 dᵉ'âgâh (1), *anxiety*
1697 dâbâr (1), *word; matter; thing*
2731 chărâdâh (1), *fear, anxiety*
7760+3820 sûwm (2), to *put, place*
1959 ĕpimĕlĕŏmai (3), to *care for*
3199 mĕlō (3), *it is a care* or *concern*
3308 mĕrimna (3), *solicitude; worry*
3309 mĕrimnaō (2), to *be anxious about*
4710 spŏudē (2), *despatch; eagerness*
5426 phrŏnĕō (1), to *be mentally disposed*

CAREAH
7143 Qârêach (1), *bald*

CARED
1875 dârash (1), to *pursue* or *search*
3199 mĕlō (2), *it is a care* or *concern*

CAREFUL
1672 dâ'ag (1), *be anxious, be afraid*
2729 chârad (1), to *hasten with anxiety*
2818 chăshach (Ch.) (1), to *need*
3309 mĕrimnaō (2), to *be anxious about*
5426 phrŏnĕō (1), to *be mentally disposed*
5431 phrŏntizō (1), *be anxious; to be careful*

CAREFULLY
2470 châlâh (1), to *be weak, sick, afflicted*
8085 shâma' (1), to *hear intelligently*
1567 ĕkzētĕō (1), to *seek out*
4708 spŏudaiŏtĕrōs (1), *more speedily*

CAREFULNESS
1674 dᵉ'âgâh (2), *anxiety*

275 amĕrimnŏs (1), *not anxious, free of care*
4710 spŏudē (1), *despatch; eagerness*

CARELESS
982 bâṭach (3), *to trust, be confident* or *sure*
983 beṭach (2), *safety, security, trust*

CARELESSLY
983 beṭach (3), *safety, security, trust*

CARES
3303 mĕn (3), *not translated*

CAREST
3199 mĕlō (3), *it is a care* or *concern*

CARETH
1875 dârash (1), *to pursue* or *search*
3199 mĕlō (2), *it is a care* or *concern*
3309 mĕrimnaō (4), *to be anxious about*

CARMEL
3760 Karmel (26), *planted field; garden*

CARMELITE
3761 Karmᵉlîy (5), *Karmelite*

CARMELITESS
3762 Karmᵉlîyth (2), *Karmelitess*

CARMI
3756 Karmîy (8), *gardener*

CARMITES
3757 Karmîy (1), *Karmite*

CARNAL
4559 sarkikŏs (9), *pertaining to flesh*
4561 sarx (2), *flesh*

CARNALLY
7902+2233 shᵉkâbâh (2), *lying down*
7903+2233 shᵉkôbeth (1), *sexual lying down with*
4561 sarx (1), *flesh*

CARPENTER
2796 chârâsh (1), *skilled fabricator* or *worker*
2796+6086 chârâsh (1), *skilled fabricator*
5045 tĕktōn (1), *craftsman in wood*

CARPENTER'S
5045 tĕktōn (1), *craftsman in wood*

CARPENTERS
2796 chârâsh (6), *skilled fabricator* or *worker*
2796+6086 chârâsh (2), *skilled fabricator*
6086 'êts (1), *wood, things made of wood*

CARPUS
2591 Karpŏs (1), *(poss.) fruit*

CARRIAGE
3520 kᵉbûwddâh (1), *magnificence, wealth*

3627 kᵉlîy (2), *implement, thing*

CARRIAGES
3627 kᵉlîy (1), *implement, thing*
5385 nᵉsûw'âh (1), *load, burden*
643 apŏskĕuazō (1), *to pack up baggage*

CARRIED
935 bôw' (10), *to go, come*
1473 gôwlâh (10), *exile; captive*
1540 gâlâh (35), *to denude; uncover*
1541 gᵉlâh (Ch.) (1), *to reveal mysteries*
1546 gâlûwth (3), *captivity; exiles*
1980 hâlak (1), *to walk; live a certain way*
2986 yâbal (3), *to bring*
3212 yâlak (1), *to walk; to live; to carry*
3318 yâtsâ' (3), *to go, bring out*
3947 lâqach (3), *to take*
4116 mâhar (1), *to hurry; promptly*
4131 môwṭ (1), *to slip, shake, fall*
5090 nâhag (3), *to drive; to lead, carry away*
5095 nâhal (1), *to conduct; to protect*
5186 nâṭâh (2), *to stretch or spread out*
5375 nâsâ' (15), *to lift up*
5376 nᵉsâ' (Ch.) (1), *to lift up*
5437 çâbab (3), *to surround*
5445 çâbal (1), *to carry*
5674 'âbar (1), *to cross over; to transition*
5927 'âlâh (3), *to ascend, be high, mount*
7392 râkab (3), *to ride*
7617 shâbâh (18), *to transport into captivity*
7725 shûwb (2), *to turn back; to return*
71 agō (1), *to lead; to bring, drive; to weigh*
339 anakathizō (1), *to sit up*
520 apagō (1), *to take away*
667 apŏhĕrō (4), *to bear off, carry away*
941 bastazō (1), *to lift, bear*
1580 ĕkkŏmizō (1), *to bear forth to burial*
1627 ĕkphĕrō (1), *to bear out; to produce*
1643 ĕlaunō (1), *to push*
3346 mĕtatithēmi (1), *to transport; to exchange*
3350 mĕtŏikĕsia (1), *exile, deportation*
4064 pĕriphĕrō (3), *to transport*
4216 pŏtamŏphŏrētŏs (1), *overwhelmed by a stream*
4792 sugkŏmizō (1), *to convey together*

4879 sunapagō (1), *to take off together*

CARRIEST
2229 zâram (1), *to gush water, pour forth*

CARRIETH
1589 gânab (1), *to thieve; to deceive*
5375 nâsâ' (1), *to lift up*
941 bastazō (1), *to lift, bear*

CARRY
935 bôw' (7), *to go or come*
1319 bâsar (1), *to announce* (good news)
1540 gâlâh (5), *to denude; uncover*
1980 hâlak (1), *to walk; live a certain way*
2904 ṭûwl (1), *to cast down or out, hurl*
2986 yâbal (1), *to bring*
2987 yᵉbal (Ch.) (1), *to bring*
3212 yâlak (3), *to walk; to live; to carry*
3318 yâtsâ' (18), *to go, bring out*
3381 yârad (2), *to descend*
3947 lâqach (2), *to take*
4853 massâ' (1), *burden, utterance*
5182 nᵉchath (Ch.) (1), *to descend; to depose*
5375 nâsâ' (18), *to lift up*
5445 çâbal (3), *to carry*
5674 'âbar (2), *to cross over; to transition*
5927 'âlâh (4), *to ascend, be high, mount*
6403 pâlaṭ (1), *to slip out, i.e. escape; to deliver*
7400 râkîyl (1), *scandal-monger*
7617 shâbâh (5), *to transport into captivity*
7725 shûwb (4), *to turn back; to return*
142 airō (1), *to lift, to take up*
941 bastazō (1), *to lift, bear*
1308 diaphĕrō (1), *to bear, carry; to differ*
1627 ĕkphĕrō (2), *to bear out; to produce*
3351 mĕtŏikizō (1), *to transfer as a captive*
4046 pĕripŏiĕŏmai (1), *to acquire; to gain*
5342 phĕrō (1), *to bear or carry*

CARRYING
1540 gâlâh (1), *to denude; uncover*
5375 nâsâ' (1), *to lift up*
7411 râmâh (1), *to hurl; to shoot; to delude*
1627 ĕkphĕrō (1), *to bear out; to produce*
3350 mĕtŏikĕsia (2), *exile, deportation*

CARSHENA
3771 Karshᵉnâ' (1), *Karshena*

CART
5699 'ăgâlâh (15), *wheeled vehicle*

CARVED
2405 chăṭûbâh (1), *tapestry*
2707 châqah (1), *to carve; to delineate*
4734 miqla'ath (1), *bas-relief sculpture*
6456 pᵉçîyl (3), *idol*
6459 peçel (2), *idol*
6603 pittûwach (2), *sculpture; engraving*
7049 qâla' (3), *to sling a stone; to carve*

CARVING
2799 chărôsheth (2), *skilled work*

CARVINGS
4734 miqla'ath (1), *bas-relief sculpture*

CASE
1697 dâbâr (1), *word; matter; thing*
3602 kâkâh (1), *just so*
7725 shûwb (2), *to turn back; to return*
156 aitia (1), *logical reason; legal crime*
3364 ŏu mē (1), *not at all, absolutely not*

CASEMENT
822 'eshnâb (1), *latticed window*

CASIPHIA
3703 Kâçiphyâ' (2), *silvery*

CASLUHIM
3695 Kaçlûchîym (2), *Casluchim*

CASSIA
6916 qiddâh (2), *cassia*
7102 qᵉtsîy'âh (1), *cassia*

CAST
1299 bâraq (1), *to flash lightning*
1457 gâhar (1), *to prostrate oneself*
1602 gâ'al (1), *to detest; to reject; to fail*
1644 gârash (9), *to drive out; to expatriate*
1740 dûwach (1), *to rinse clean, wash*
1760 dâchâh (1), *to push down; to totter*
1920 hâdaph (2), *to push away or down; drive out*
1972 hâlâ' (1), *to remove or be remote*
2186 zânach (17), *to reject, forsake, fail*
2219 zârah (1), *to toss about; to diffuse*
2490 châlal (1), *to profane, defile*
2904 ṭûwl (12), *to cast down or out, hurl*
3032 yâdad (3), *to throw lots*
3034 yâdâh (2), *to throw; to revere* or *worship*
3240 yânach (1), *to allow to stay*

3332 yâtsaq (10), to *pour out*

3333 yᵉtsûqâh (1), *poured* out into a mold

3381 yârad (3), to *descend*

3384 yârâh (4), to *throw, shoot* an arrow

3423 yârash (10), to *inherit; to impoverish*

3766 kâra' (1), to *prostrate*

3782 kâshal (3), to *totter, waver; to falter*

3874 lûwṭ (1), to *wrap* up

3988 mâ'aç (10), to *spurn; to disappear*

4048 mâgar (1), to *yield up, be thrown*

4054 migrâsh (1), *open country*

4131 môwṭ (1), to *slip, shake, fall*

4166 mûwtsâqâh (1), *casting* of metal; *tube*

4788 mârûwd (1), *outcast; destitution*

5060 nâga' (1), to *strike*

5077 nâdâh (1), to *exclude*, i.e. *banish*

5080 nâdach (4), to *push off, scattered*

5203 nâṭash (1), to *disperse; to thrust* off

5221 nâkâh (1), to *strike, kill*

5307 nâphal (24), to *fall*

5375 nâsâ' (1), to *lift up*

5390 nᵉshîyqâh (1), *kiss*

5394 nâshal (1), to *divest, eject, or drop*

5414 nâthan (5), to *give*

5422 nâthats (3), to *tear down*

5437 çâbab (1), to *surround*

5499 çᵉchâbâh (2), *rag*

5549 çâlal (4), to *mound* up; to *exalt;* to *oppose*

5619 çâqal (1), to *throw large stones*

5927 'âlâh (2), to *ascend, be high, mount*

6080 'âphar (1), to be *dust*

6327 pûwts (2), to *dash* in pieces; to *disperse*

6437 pânâh (1), to *turn, to face*

6696 tsûwr (1), to *cramp,* i.e. *confine; to harass*

7290 râdam (1), to *stupefy*

7324 rûwq (1), to *pour* out, i.e. *empty*

7368 râchaq (1), to *recede; remove*

7412 rᵉmâh (Ch.) (11), to *throw; to set; to assess*

7760 sûwm (1), to *put, place*

7817 shâchach (4), to *sink* or *depress*

7843 shâchath (1), to *decay; to ruin*

7921 shâkôl (3), to *miscarry*

7933 sheken (4), *residence*

7971 shâlach (14), to *send* away

7993 shâlak (113), to *throw* out, down

7995 shalleketh (1), *felling* of trees

7998 shâlâl (1), *booty*

8210 shâphak (8), to *spill* forth; to *expend*

8213 shâphêl (1), to *humiliate*

8628 tâqa' (1), to *clatter, slap, drive, clasp*

114 athĕtĕō (1), to *disesteem, neutralize*

577 apŏballō (1), to *throw off;* fig. to *lose*

641 apŏrrhiptō (1), to *throw oneself into*

656 apŏsunagōgŏs (1), *excommunicated*

683 apōthĕŏmai (2), to *push off; to reject*

906 ballō (81), to *throw*

1000 bŏlē (1), *throw* as a measure

1260 dialŏgizŏmai (1), to *deliberate*

1544 ĕkballō (51), to *throw out*

1601 ĕkpiptō (1), to *drop away*

1614 ĕktĕinō (1), to *stretch*

1620 ĕktithēmi (1), to *expose; to declare*

1685 ĕmballō (1), to *throw in*

1911 ĕpiballō (2), to *throw upon*

1977 ĕpirrhiptō (1), to *throw upon*

2210 zēmiŏō (1), to *experience detriment*

2598 kataballō (2), to *throw down*

2630 katakrĕmnizō (1), to *precipitate down*

2975 lagchanō (1), to *determine* by lot

3036 lithŏbŏlĕō (1), to *throw stones*

3679 ŏnĕidizō (1), to *rail at, chide, taunt*

3860 paradidōmi (1), to *hand over*

4016 pĕriballō (3), to *wrap around, clothe*

4406 prŏïmŏs (1), *autumnal showering*

4496 rhiptō (5), to *fling, toss;* to *lay out*

5011 tapĕinŏs (1), *humiliated, lowly*

5020 tartarŏō (1), to *incarcerate* in Tartaros

CASTAWAY

96 adŏkimŏs (1), *failing the test, worthless*

CASTEDST

5307 nâphal (1), to *fall*

CASTEST

2186 zânach (1), to *reject, forsake, fail*

6565 pârar (1), to *break* up; to *violate, frustrate*

7993 shâlak (1), to *throw* out, down or away

CASTETH

1920 hâdaph (1), to *push* away or down; *drive* out

3381 yârad (1), to *descend*

3384 yârâh (1), to *throw, shoot* an arrow

5307 nâphal (1), to *fall*

6884 tsâraph (1), to *fuse* metal; to *refine*

6979 qûwr (2), to *throw* forth; to *wall up*

7921 shâkôl (1), to *miscarry*

7993 shâlak (1), to *throw* out, down or away

8213 shâphêl (1), to *humiliate*

906 ballō (2), to *throw*

1544 ĕkballō (4), to *throw out*

CASTING

2866 chăthath (1), *dismay*

3445 yeshach (1), *hunger*

4165 mûwtsâq (1), *casting* of metal

5307 nâphal (1), to *fall*

7901 shâkab (1), to *lie down*

8210 shâphak (1), to *spill* forth; to *expend*

577 apŏballō (1), to *throw off;* fig. to *lose*

580 apŏbŏlē (1), *rejection, loss*

906 ballō (6), to *throw*

1544 ĕkballō (3), to *throw out*

1977 ĕpirrhiptō (1), to *throw upon*

2507 kathairĕō (1), to *lower,* or *demolish*

CASTLE

759 'armôwn (1), *citadel, high fortress*

4679 mᵉtsad (1), *stronghold*

4686 mâtsûwd (1), *net* or *capture; fastness*

3925 parĕmbŏlē (6), *encampment*

CASTLES

1003 bîyrânîyth (2), *fortress, citadel*

2918 ṭîyrâh (3), *fortress; hamlet*

4026 migdâl (1), *tower; rostrum*

CASTOR

1359 Diŏskŏurŏi (1), *twins of Zeus*

CATCH

1641 gârar (1), to *drag* off roughly

2414 châṭaph (3), to *seize* as a prisoner

2480 châlaṭ (1), to *snatch* at, *seizing*

2963 ṭâraph (2), to *pluck* off or *pull* to pieces

3920 lâkad (2), to *catch;* to *capture*

4672 mâtsâ' (1), to *find* or *acquire;* to *occur*

5367 nâqash (1), to *entrap* with a noose

8610 tâphas (1), to *manipulate,* i.e. *seize*

64 agrĕuō (1), to *entrap, catch*

2221 zōgrĕō (1), to *capture* or *ensnare*

2340 thĕrĕuō (1), to *carp* at

CATCHETH

6679 tsûwd (1), to *lie* in wait; to *catch*

726 harpazō (2), to *seize*

CATERPILLER

2625 chaçîyl (5), *locust*

CATERPILLERS

2625 chaçîyl (1), *locust*

3218 yekeq (3), *young locust*

CATTLE

926 bâhal (1), to *tremble; be, make agitated*

929 bᵉhêmâh (56), *animal, beast*

1165 bᵉ'îyr (2), *cattle, livestock*

1241 bâqâr (1), *plowing ox; herd*

4399 mᵉlâ'kâh (1), *work; property*

4734 miqla'ath (1), *bas-relief sculpture*

4735 miqneh (57), *live-stock*

4806 mᵉrîy' (3), *stall-fed animal*

6629 tsô'n (13), *flock* of sheep or goats

7069 qânâh (1), to *create; to procure*

7716 seh (7), *sheep* or *goat*

2353 thrĕmma (1), *stock*

4165 pŏimainō (1), to *tend* as a shepherd

CAUGHT

270 'âchaz (4), to *seize, grasp; possess*

962 bâzaz (1), to *plunder, take booty*

1497 gâzal (1), to *rob*

2388 châzaq (8), to *fasten upon; to seize*

3920 lâkad (3), to *catch;* to *capture*

8610 tâphas (3), to *manipulate,* i.e. *seize*

726 harpazō (5), to *seize*

1949 ĕpilambanŏmai (2), to *seize*

2983 lambanō (3), to *take, receive*

4084 piazō (2), to *seize, arrest, or capture*

4815 sullambanō (1), to *seize (arrest, capture)*

4884 sunarpazō (4), to *snatch together*

CAUL

3508 yôthereth (11), *lobe* or *flap* of the liver

5458 çᵉgôwr (1), *breast*

CAULS

7636 shâbîyç (1), *netting*

CAUSE

657 'epheç (1), *end; no further*

834 'âsher (1), *because, in order that*
1697 dâbâr (6), *word; matter; thing*
1700 dibrâh (1), *because, on account of*
1779 dîyn (7), *judge; judgment; law suit*
1961 hâyâh (1), *to exist, i.e. be or become*
2600 chinnâm (15), *gratis, free*
3651 kên (1), *just; right, correct*
4616 ma'an (1), *on account of*
4941 mishpâṭ (12), *verdict; formal decree*
5252 n°çibbâh (1), *turn of affairs*
5414 nâthan (5), *to give*
5438 çibbâh (1), *turn of affairs*
5668 'âbûwr (1), *on account of*
7379 rîyb (23), *contest, personal or legal*
7387 rêyqâm (2), *emptily; ineffectually*
7945 shel (1), *on account of; whatsoever*
8267 sheqer (1), *untruth; sham*
156 aitia (9), *logical reason; legal crime*
158 aitiŏn (2), *reason, basis; crime*
846 autŏs (1), *he, she, it*
873 aphŏrizō (1), *to limit, exclude, appoint*
1223 dia (13), *because of, for the sake of*
1352 diŏ (2), *consequently, therefore*
1432 dōrĕan (1), *gratuitously, freely*
1500 ĕikē (1), *idly, i.e. without reason or effect*
1752 hĕnĕka (4), *on account of*
2289 thanatŏō (3), *to kill*
3056 lŏgŏs (1), *word, matter, thing*
4160 pŏiĕō (3), *to do*
5484 charin (3), *on account of, because of*

CAUSED
1961 hâyâh (1), *to exist, i.e. be or become*
5414 nâthan (7), *to give*
3076 lupĕō (1), *to distress; to be sad*
4160 pŏiĕō (2), *to do*

CAUSELESS
2600 chinnâm (2), *gratis, free*

CAUSES
182 'ôwdôwth (1), *on account of; because*
1697 dâbâr (2), *word; matter; thing*
7379 rîyb (1), *contest, personal or legal*
1752 hĕnĕka (1), *on account of*

CAUSETH
5414 nâthan (1), *to give*

2358 thriambĕuō (1), *to lead in triumphal procession*
2716 katĕrgazŏmai (1), *to finish; to accomplish*
4160 pŏiĕō (3), *to do*

CAUSEWAY
4546 m°çillâh (2), *main thoroughfare; viaduct*

CAVE
4631 m°'ârâh (32), *dark cavern*
4693 spēlaiŏn (1), *cavern; hiding-place*

CAVE'S
4631 m°'ârâh (1), *dark cavern*

CAVES
2356 chôwr (1), *cavity, socket, den*
4247 m°chillâh (1), *cavern, hole*
4631 m°'ârâh (3), *dark cavern*
3692 ŏpē (1), *hole, i.e. cavern; spring of water*

CEASE
988 bâṭêl (1), *to desist from labor, cease*
989 b°ṭêl (Ch.) (3), *to stop*
1820 dâmâh (1), *to be silent; to fail, cease*
1826 dâmam (1), *to stop, cease; to perish*
2308 châdal (12), *to desist, stop; be fat*
2790 chârash (1), *to be silent; to be deaf*
3254 yâçaph (1), *to add or augment*
3615 kâlâh (1), *to complete, consume*
4185 mûwsh (1), *to withdraw*
6565 pârar (1), *to break up; to violate, frustrate*
7503 râphâh (1), *to slacken*
7647 sâbâ' (1), *copiousness*
7673 shâbath (37), *to repose; to desist*
7725 shûwb (1), *to turn back; to return*
7918 shâkak (1), *to lay a trap; to allay*
8552 tâmam (1), *to complete, finish*
180 akatapaustŏs (1), *unrefraining, unceasing*
3973 pauō (4), *to stop, i.e. restrain, quit*

CEASED
989 b°ṭêl (Ch.) (1), *to stop*
1826 dâmam (1), *to stop, cease; to perish*
1934+989 hăvâ' (Ch.) (1), *to be, to exist*
2308 châdal (6), *to desist, stop; be fat*
5117 nûwach (1), *to rest; to settle down*
5307 nâphal (1), *to fall*
5975 'âmad (1), *to stand*
6313 pûwg (1), *to be sluggish; be numb*

7673 shâbath (6), *to repose; to desist*
1257 dialĕipō (1), *to intermit, stop*
2270 hēsuchazō (1), *to refrain*
2664 katapauō (1), *to cause to desist*
2673 katargĕō (1), *to be, render entirely useless*
2869 kŏpazō (3), *to tire, i.e. to relax*
3973 pauō (7), *to stop, i.e. restrain, quit*

CEASETH
1584 gâmar (1), *to end; to complete; to fail*
1820 dâmâh (1), *to be silent; to fail, cease*
2308 châdal (1), *to desist, stop; be fat*
3615 kâlâh (1), *to cease, be finished, perish*
7673 shâbath (4), *to repose; to desist*
8367 shâthaq (1), *to subside*
3973 pauō (1), *to stop, i.e. restrain, quit*

CEASING
2308 châdal (1), *to desist, stop; be fat*
83 adĕlŏtēs (1), *uncertainty*
89 adialĕiptŏs (4), *without omission*
1618 ĕktĕnēs (1), *intent, earnest*

CEDAR
729 'âraz (1), *of cedar*
730 'erez (49), *cedar tree*
731 'arzâh (1), *cedar paneling*

CEDARS
730 'erez (24), *cedar tree*

CEDRON
2748 Kĕdrōn (1), *dusky place*

CELEBRATE
1984 hâlal (1), *to speak words of thankfulness*
2278 chăbereth (1), *consort, companion*
7673 shâbath (1), *to repose*

CELESTIAL
2032 ĕpŏuraniŏs (2), *above the sky, celestial*

CELLARS
214 'ôwtsâr (2), *depository*

CENCHREA
2747 Kĕgchrĕai (2), *millet*

CENSER
4289 machtâh (7), *pan for live coals*
4730 miqṭereth (2), *incense coal-pan*
2369 thumiastēriŏn (1), *altar of incense*
3031 libanōtŏs (2), *censer for incense*

CENSERS
4289 machtâh (8), *pan for live coals*

CENTURION
1543 hĕkatŏntarchēs (17), *captain of a hundred*
2760 kĕnturiōn (3), *captain of a hundred*

CENTURION'S
1543 hĕkatŏntarchēs (1), *captain of a hundred*

CENTURIONS
1543 hĕkatŏntarchēs (3), *captain of a hundred*

CEPHAS
2786 Kēphas (6), *rock*

CEREMONIES
4941 mishpâṭ (1), *verdict; formal decree; justice*

CERTAIN
259 'echâd (9), *first*
376 'îysh (4), *man; male; someone*
582 'ĕnôwsh (8), *man; person, human*
592 'ănîyâh (2), *groaning*
1400 g°bar (Ch.) (2), *person; someone*
1697 dâbâr (2), *word; matter; thing*
3045 yâda' (3), *to know*
3330 yatstsîyb (Ch.) (1), *fixed, sure*
3559 kûwn (2), *to render sure, proper*
6256 'êth (1), *time*
6422 palmŏwnîy (1), *a certain one*
444 anthrōpŏs (2), *human being; mankind*
444+5100 anthrōpŏs (1), *human being; mankind*
790 astatĕō (1), *homeless, vagabond*
804 asphalēs (1), *secure; certain*
1212 dēlŏs (1), *clear, plain, evident*
1520 hĕis (5), *one*
4225 pŏu (2), *somewhere, i.e. nearly*
5100 tis (112), *some or any person or object*

CERTAINLY
389 'ak (1), *surely; only, however*
403 'âkên (1), *surely!, truly!; but*
3588 kîy (1), *for, that because*
3689 ŏntōs (1), *really, certainly*

CERTAINTY
3330 yatstsîyb (Ch.) (1), *fixed, sure*
3559 kûwn (1), *to render sure, proper*
7189 qôsheṭ (1), *reality*
803 asphalĕia (1), *security; certainty*
804 asphalēs (2), *secure; certain*

CERTIFIED
559 'âmar (1), *to say*
3064 Y°hûwdîy (1), *Jehudite*

C

CERTIFY
3046 yᵉda' (Ch.) (3), to
know
5046 nâgad (1), to
announce
1107 gnŏrizō (1), to
make known, reveal

CHAFED
4751 mar (1), bitter;
bitterness; bitterly

CHAFF
2842 châshash (2), dry
grass, chaff
4671 môts (8), chaff
5784 'ûwr (Ch.) (1), chaff
8401 teben (1), threshed
stalks of cereal grain
892 achurŏn (2), chaff of
grain

CHAIN
2002 hamnîyk (Ch.) (3),
necklace
5178 nᵉchôsheth (1),
copper; bronze
6059 'ânaq (1), to collar;
to fit out
6060 'ânâq (1), necklace
chain
7242 râbîyd (2), collar
spread around the neck
7659 shib'âthayim (1),
seven-fold
8333 sharshᵉrâh (1),
chain
254 halusis (3), fetter or
manacle

CHAINS
246 'âziqqîym (2),
manacles, chains
685 'ets'âdâh (1), bracelet
2131 zîyqâh (3), burning
arrow; bond, fetter
2397 châch (2), ring for
the nose or lips
2737 chârûwz (1), strung
beads
3574 kôwshârâh (1),
prosperity
5178 nᵉchôsheth (2),
copper; bronze
5188 nᵉṭîyphâh (1),
pendant for the ears
5688 'ăbôth (3), entwined
things: string, wreath
6060 'ânâq (2), necklace
chain
7569 rattôwq (2), chain
8333 sharshᵉrâh (6),
chain
8337 shêsh (1), six; sixth
254 halusis (7), fetter or
manacle
1199 dĕsmŏn (1),
shackle; impediment
4577 sĕira (1), chain, as
binding or drawing

CHALCEDONY
5472 chalkēdōn (1),
copper-like, chalcedony

CHALCOL
3633 Kalkôl (1),
sustenance

CHALDAEANS
5466 Chaldaiŏs (1),
native or the region of
the lower Euphrates

CHALDEA
3778 Kasdîy (7),
astrologer

CHALDEAN
3777 Kesed (2), Kesed

CHALDEANS
3778 Kasdîy (48),
astrologer
3779 Kasday (Ch.) (17),
magian or astrologer

CHALDEANS'
3778 Kasdîy (1),
astrologer

CHALDEES
3778 Kasdîy (13),
astrologer

CHALDEES'
3778 Kasdîy (1),
astrologer

CHALKSTONES
68+1615 'eben (1), stone

CHALLENGETH
559 'âmar (1), to say

CHAMBER
2315 cheder (15),
apartment, chamber
2646 chuppâh (1), canopy
3326 yâtsûwa' (1), bed;
wing or lean-to
3957 lishkâh (14), room
5393 nishkâh (2), room,
cell
5944 'ălîyâh (6),
second-story room
5952 'allîyth (Ch.) (1),
second-story room
6763 tsêlâ' (3), side of a
person or thing
8372 tâ' (4), room
5253 hupĕrǭŏn (3), third
story apartment

CHAMBERING
2845 kŏitē (1), couch;
conception

CHAMBERLAIN
5631 çârîyç (4), eunuch;
official of state
1909+3588+2846 ĕpi (1),
on, upon
3623 ŏikŏnŏmŏs (1),
overseer, manager

CHAMBERLAINS
5631 çârîyç (9), eunuch;
official of state

CHAMBERS
2315 cheder (8),
apartment, chamber
3326 yâtsûwa' (2), bed;
wing or lean-to of a
building
3957 lishkâh (31), room
in a building
5393 nishkâh (1), room,
cell
5944 'ălîyâh (6), upper
things; second-story
room
6763 tsêlâ' (8), side of a
person or thing
8372 tâ' (4), room
5009 tamĕiŏn (1), room

CHAMELEON
3581 kôach (1), large
lizard

CHAMOIS
2169 zemer (1), gazelle

CHAMPAIGN
6160 'ărâbâh (1), desert,
wasteland

CHAMPION
376+1143 'îysh (2), man;
male; someone
1368 gibbôwr (1),
powerful; great warrior

CHANAAN
5477 Chanaan (2),
humiliated

CHANCE
4745 miqreh (1),
accident or fortune
6294 pega' (1), casual
impact
7122 qârâ' (2), to
encounter, to happen
4795 sugkuria (1),
chance occurrence
5177 tugchanō (1), to
happen; perhaps

CHANCELLOR
1169+2942 bᵉ'êl (Ch.) (3),
master

CHANCETH
4745 miqreh (1),
accident or fortune

CHANGE
2015 hâphak (1), to
change, overturn
2487 chălîyphâh (4),
alternation, change
2498 châlaph (4), to
pierce; to change
4171 mûwr (5), to alter;
to barter, to dispose of
4254 machălâtsâh (1),
mantle, garment
7760 sûwm (1), to put,
place
8133 shᵉnâ' (Ch.) (1), to
alter, change
8138 shânâh (3), to fold,
i.e. duplicate; to
transmute
8545 tᵉmûwrâh (1),
barter, compensation
236 allassō (2), to make
different, change
3331 mĕtathĕsis (1),
transferral,
disestablishment
3337 mĕtallassō (1), to
exchange
3345 mĕtaschĕmatizō
(1), to transfigure or
disguise; to apply

CHANGEABLE
4254 machălâtsâh (1),
mantle, garment

CHANGED
2015 hâphak (2), to
change, overturn
2498 châlaph (6), to pass
on; to change
2664 châphas (1), to
seek; to mask
4171 mûwr (6), to alter;
to barter, to dispose of
5437 çâbab (2), to
surround
8132 shânâ' (3), to alter,
change

8133 shᵉnâ' (Ch.) (12), to
alter, change
8138 shânâh (3), to fold,
to transmute
236 allassō (4), to make
different, change
3328 mĕtaballō (1), to
turn about in opinion
3337 mĕtallassō (1), to
exchange
3339 mĕtamŏrphŏō (1),
to transform, i.e.
metamorphose
3346 mĕtatithĕmi (1), to
transport; to exchange

CHANGERS
2773 kĕrmatistēs (1),
money-broker

CHANGERS'
2855 kŏllubistēs (1),
coin-dealer

CHANGES
2487 chălîyphâh (7),
alternation, change

CHANGEST
8138 shânâh (1), to fold,
to transmute

CHANGETH
4171 mûwr (1), to alter;
to barter, to dispose of
8133 shᵉnâ' (Ch.) (1), to
alter, change

CHANGING
8545 tᵉmûwrâh (1),
barter, compensation

CHANNEL
7641 shibbôl (1), stream;
ear of grain

CHANNELS
650 'âphîyq (3), valley;
stream; mighty, strong

CHANT
6527 pâraṭ (1), to scatter
words, i.e. prate

CHAPEL
4720 miqdâsh (1),
sanctuary of deity

CHAPITER
3805 kôthereth (12),
capital of a column
6858 tsepheth (1),
capital of a column

CHAPITERS
3805 kôthereth (12),
capital of a column
7218 rô'sh (4), head

CHAPMEN
582+8846 'ĕnôwsh (1),
man; person, human

CHAPT
2865 châthath (1), to
break down

CHARASHIM
2798 Chărâshîym (1),
skilled worker

CHARCHEMISH
3751 Karkᵉmîysh (1),
Karkemish

CHARGE
3027 yâd (1), hand; power
4931 mishmereth (46),
watch, sentry, post

4941 mishpâṭ (1), *verdict; formal decree; justice*
5414 nâthan (1), *to give*
5447 çêbel (1), *load; forced labor*
5749 'ûwd (1), *to protest, testify*
5921 'al (3), *above, over, upon, or against*
6213 'âsâh (1), *to do or make*
6485 pâqad (1), *to visit, care for, count*
6486 pᵉquddâh (2), *visitation; punishment*
6496 pâqîyd (1), *superintendent, officer*
6680 tsâvâh (16), *to constitute, enjoin*
7130 qereb (1), *nearest part, i.e. the center*
7592 shâ'al (1), *to ask*
7650 shâba' (7), *to swear*
77 adapanŏs (1), *free of charge*
1263 diamarturŏmai (2), *to attest or protest*
1458+2596 ĕgkalĕō (1), *to charge, criminate*
1462 ĕgklēma (1), *accusation*
1781 ĕntĕllŏmai (2), *to enjoin, give orders*
1909 ĕpi (1), *on, upon*
2004 ĕpitassŏ (1), *to order, command*
2476 histēmi (1), *to stand, establish*
3049 lŏgizŏmai (1), *to take an inventory*
3726 hŏrkizō (1), *to solemnly enjoin*
3852 paraggĕlia (2), *mandate, order*
3853 paraggĕllō (4), *to enjoin; to instruct*

CHARGEABLE
3513 kâbad (2), *to be rich, glorious*
1912 ĕpibarĕō (2), *to be severe toward*
2655 katanarkaō (1), *to be a burden*

CHARGED
559 'âmar (1), *to say*
5414 nâthan (1), *to give*
5674+5921 'âbar (1), *to cross over; to transition*
6485 pâqad (3), *to visit, care for, count*
6680 tsâvâh (23), *to constitute, enjoin*
7650 shâba' (2), *to swear*
7760 sûwm (1), *to put, place*
916 barĕŏ (1), *to weigh down, cause pressure*
1291 diastĕllŏmai (6), *to distinguish*
1690 ĕmbrimaŏmai (2), *to blame, warn sternly*
1781 ĕntĕllŏmai (1), *to enjoin, give orders*
2008 ĕpitimaō (5), *to rebuke, warn, forbid*
3146 mastigŏō (1), *to punish by flogging*
3853 paraggĕllō (3), *to enjoin; to instruct*

CHARGEDST
5749 'ûwd (1), *to protest, testify; to encompass*

CHARGER
7086 qᵉ'ârâh (13), *bowl*
4094 pinax (4), *plate, platter, dish*

CHARGERS
105 'ăgarṭâl (2), *basin*
7086 qᵉ'ârâh (1), *bowl*

CHARGES
4931 mishmereth (4), *watch, sentry, post*
1159 dapanaō (1), *to incur cost; to waste*
3800 ŏpsōniŏn (1), *rations, stipend or pay*

CHARGEST
6485 pâqad (1), *to visit, care for, count*

CHARGING
1263 diamarturŏmai (1), *to attest or protest*
3853 paraggĕllō (1), *to enjoin; to instruct*

CHARIOT
668 'appiryôwn (1), *palanquin, carriage*
4818 merkâbâh (23), *chariot*
5699 'ăgâlâh (1), *wheeled vehicle*
7393 rekeb (28), *vehicle for riding*
7395 rakkâb (2), *charioteer*
7398 rᵉkûwb (1), *vehicle ridden on*
716 harma (3), *chariot, carriage*

CHARIOTS
2021 hôtsen (1), *weapon*
4817 merkâb (1), *chariot; seat in chariot*
4818 merkâbâh (20), *chariot*
7393 rekeb (87), *vehicle for riding*
7396 rikbâh (1), *chariot*
716 harma (1), *chariot, carriage*
4480 rhĕda (1), *wagon for riding*

CHARITABLY
2596+26 kata (1), *down; according to*

CHARITY
26 agapē (28), *love; love-feast*

CHARMED
3908 lachash (1), *incantation; amulet*

CHARMER
2266+2267 châbar (1), *to fascinate by spells*

CHARMERS
328 'aṭ (1), *gently, softly*
3907 lâchash (1), *to whisper a magic spell*

CHARMING
2266+2267 châbar (1), *to fascinate by spells*

CHARRAN
5488 Charrhan (2), *parched*

CHASE
1760 dâchâh (1), *to push down; to totter*
7291 râdaph (5), *to run after with hostility*

CHASED
1272 bârach (1), *to flee suddenly*
5074 nâdad (2), *to rove, flee; to drive away*
5080 nâdach (1), *to push off, scattered*
6679 tsûwd (1), *to lie in wait; to catch*
7291 râdaph (8), *to run after with hostility*

CHASETH
1272 bârach (1), *to flee suddenly*

CHASING
1814 dâlaq (1), *to flame; to pursue*

CHASTE
53 hagnŏs (3), *innocent, modest, perfect, pure*

CHASTEN
3198 yâkach (1), *to decide, justify, convict*
3256 yâçar (3), *to chastise; to instruct*
6031 'ânâh (1), *to afflict, be afflicted*
3811 paidĕuō (1), *to educate or discipline*

CHASTENED
3198 yâkach (1), *to decide, justify, convict*
3256 yâçar (1), *to chastise; to instruct*
8433 tôwkêchâh (1), *chastisement*
3811 paidĕuō (3), *to educate or discipline*

CHASTENEST
3256 yâçar (1), *to chastise; to instruct*

CHASTENETH
3256 yâçar (2), *to chastise; to instruct*
4148 mûwçâr (1), *reproof, warning*
3811 paidĕuō (2), *to educate or discipline*

CHASTENING
4148 mûwçâr (3), *reproof, warning*
3809 paidĕia (3), *disciplinary correction*

CHASTISE
3256 yâçar (6), *to chastise; to instruct*
3811 paidĕuō (2), *to educate or discipline*

CHASTISED
3256 yâçar (5), *to chastise; to instruct*

CHASTISEMENT
4148 mûwçâr (3), *reproof, warning*
3809 paidĕia (1), *disciplinary correction*

CHASTISETH
3256 yâçar (1), *to chastise; to instruct*

CHATTER
6850 tsâphaph (1), *to coo or chirp as a bird*

CHEBAR
3529 Kᵉbâr (8), *length*

CHECK
4148 mûwçâr (1), *reproof, warning*

CHECKER
7639 sᵉbâkâh (1), *net-work balustrade*

CHEDORLAOMER
3540 Kᵉdorlâ'ômer (5), *Kedorlaomer*

CHEEK
3895 lᵉchîy (6), *jaw; area of the jaw*
4973 mᵉthalle'âh (1), *tooth*
4600 siagōn (2), *cheek*

CHEEKS
3895 lᵉchîy (5), *jaw; area of the jaw*

CHEER
3190 yâṭab (1), *to be, make well*
8055 sâmach (1), *to be, make gleesome*
2114 ĕuthumĕō (3), *to be cheerful*
2293 tharsĕō (5), *to have courage; take heart!*

CHEERETH
8055 sâmach (1), *to be, make gleesome*

CHEERFUL
2896 ṭôwb (1), *good; well*
3190 yâṭab (1), *to be, make well*
5107 nûwb (1), *to (make) flourish; to utter*
2431 hilarŏs (1), *prompt or willing*

CHEERFULLY
2115 ĕuthumŏs (1), *cheerful, encouraged*

CHEERFULNESS
2432 hilarŏtēs (1), *cheerful readiness*

CHEESE
1385 gᵉbînah (1), *curdled milk*
8194 shâphâh (1), *cheese*

CHEESES
2757+2461 chârîyts (1), *slice, portion*

CHELAL
3636 Kᵉlâl (1), *complete*

CHELLUH
3622 Kᵉlûwhay (1), *completed*

CHELUB
3620 Kᵉlûwb (2), *bird-trap; basket*

CHELUBAI
3621 Kᵉlûwbay (1), *forcible*

CHEMARIMS
3649 kâmâr (1), *pagan priest*

C

CHINNERETH
3672 Kinnᵉrôwth (4), (poss.) *harp*-shaped

CHINNEROTH
3672 Kinnᵉrôwth (2), (poss.) *harp*-shaped

CHIOS
5508 Chiŏs (1), *Chios*

CHISLEU
3691 Kiçlêv (2), *Hebrew month*

CHISLON
3692 Kiçlôwn (1), *hopeful*

CHISLOTH-TABOR
3696 Kiçlôth Tâbôr (1), *flanks of Tabor*

CHITTIM
3794 Kittîy (6), *islander*

CHIUN
3594 Kîyûwn (1), *deity* (poss.) *Priapus or Baal-peor*

CHLOE
5514 Chlŏē (1), *green*

CHODE
7378 rîyb (2), to *hold a controversy*; to *defend*

CHOICE
970 bâchûwr (3), *male youth; bridegroom*
977 bâchar (4), *select, chose, prefer*
1249 bar (1), *beloved; pure; empty*
1305 bârar (2), to *examine; select*
4005 mibchâr (9), *select*
8321 sôrêq (1), *choice vine* stock
1586 ĕklĕgŏmai (1), to *select, choose, pick out*

CHOICEST
4055 mad (1), *vesture, garment; carpet*
8321 sôrêq (1), *choice vine* stock

CHOKE
4846 sumpnigō (2), to *drown*; to *crowd*

CHOKED
638 apŏpnigō (3), to *stifle or choke*
4155 pnigō (1), to *throttle or strangle*; to *drown*
4846 sumpnigō (2), to *drown*; to *crowd*

CHOLER
4843 mârar (2), to *be, make bitter*

CHOOSE
972 bâchîyr (1), *selected one*
977 bâchar (53), *select, chose, prefer*
1254 bârâ' (2), to *create; fashion*
1262 bârâh (1), to *feed*
6901 qâbal (1), to *take*
138 hairĕŏmai (1), to *prefer, choose*

CHOOSEST
977 bâchar (2), *select, chose, prefer*

CHOOSETH
977 bâchar (3), *select, chose, prefer*

CHOOSING
138 hairĕŏmai (1), to *prefer, choose*

CHOP
6566 pâras (1), to *break apart, disperse, scatter*

CHOR-ASHAN
3565 Kôwr 'Âshân (1), *furnace of smoke*

CHORAZIN
5523 Chŏrazin (2), *Chorazin*

CHOSE
977 bâchar (24), *select, chose, prefer*
1586 ĕklĕgŏmai (4), to *select, choose, pick out*
1951 ĕpilĕgŏmai (1), to *surname, select*

CHOSEN
970 bâchûwr (21), *male youth; bridegroom*
972 bâchîyr (8), *selected one*
977 bâchar (58), *select, chose, prefer*
1305 bârar (2), to *examine; select*
4005 mibchâr (4), *select*
138 hairĕŏmai (1), to *prefer, choose*
140 hairĕtizō (1), to *make a choice*
1586 ĕklĕgŏmai (15), to *select, choose, pick out*
1588 ĕklĕktŏs (7), *selected; chosen*
1589 ĕklŏgē (1), *selection, choice*
4400 prŏchĕirizŏmai (1), to *purpose*
4401 prŏchĕirŏtŏnĕō (1), to *elect in advance*
4758 stratŏlŏgĕō (1), to *enlist in the army*
5500 chĕirŏtŏnĕō (1), to *select or appoint*

CHOZEBA
3578 Kôzᵉbâ' (1), *fallacious*

CHRIST
5477 Chanaan (1), *humiliated*
5547 Christŏs (551), *Anointed One*

CHRIST'S
5547 Christŏs (15), *Anointed One*

CHRISTIAN
5546 Christianŏs (2), *follower of Christ*

CHRISTIANS
5546 Christianŏs (1), *follower of Christ*

CHRISTS
5580 psĕudŏchristŏs (2), *spurious Messiah*

CHRONICLES
1697+3117 dâbâr (38), *word; matter; thing*

CHRYSOLITE
5555 chrusŏlithŏs (1), *yellow chrysolite*

CHRYSOPRASUS
5556 chrusŏprasŏs (1), *greenish-yellow chrysoprase*

CHUB
3552 Kûwb (1), *Kub*

CHUN
3560 Kûwn (1), *established*

CHURCH
1577 ĕkklĕsia (80), *congregation*

CHURCHES
1577 ĕkklĕsia (36), *congregation*
2417 hiĕrŏsulŏs (1), *temple-despoiler*

CHURL
3596 kîylay (2), *begrudging*

CHURLISH
7186 qâsheh (1), *severe*

CHURNING
4330 mîyts (1), *pressure*

CHUSHAN-RISHATHAIM
3573 Kûwshan Rish'âthâyim (4), *Cushan of double wickedness*

CHUZA
5529 Chŏuzas (1), *Chuzas*

CIELED
2645 châphâh (1), to *cover; to veil, to encase*
5603 çâphan (2), to *hide by covering; to roof*
7824 shâchîyph (1), *board, panel*

CIELING
5604 çippûn (1), *wainscot, paneling*

CILICIA
2791 Kilikia (8), *Cilicia*

CINNAMON
7076 qinnâmôwn (3), *cinnamon spice*
2792 kinamōmŏn (1), *cinnamon*

CINNEROTH
3672 Kinnᵉrôwth (1), (poss.) *harp*-shaped

CIRCLE
2329 chûwg (1), *circle*

CIRCUIT
2329 chûwg (1), *circle*
5437 çâbab (1), to *surround*
8622 tᵉqûwphâh (1), *revolution, course*

CIRCUITS
5439 çâbîyb (1), *circle; neighbor; environs*

CIRCUMCISE
4135 mûwl (5), to *circumcise*
5243 nâmal (1), to *be circumcised*
4059 pĕritĕmnō (4), to *circumcise*

CIRCUMCISED
4135 mûwl (23), to *circumcise*
203 akrŏbustia (1), *uncircumcised*
4059 pĕritĕmnō (13), to *circumcise*
4061 pĕritŏmē (1), *circumcision; Jews*

CIRCUMCISING
4135 mûwl (1), to *circumcise*
4059 pĕritĕmnō (1), to *circumcise*

CIRCUMCISION
4139 mûwlâh (1), *circumcision*
4061 pĕritŏmē (35), *circumcision; Jews*

CIRCUMSPECT
8104 shâmar (1), to *watch*

CIRCUMSPECTLY
199 akribōs (1), *exactly, carefully*

CIS
2797 Kis (1), *bow*

CISTERN
953 bôwr (4), *pit hole, cistern, well*

CISTERNS
877 bô'r (1), *well, cistern*

CITIES
5892 'îyr (419), *city, town, unwalled-village*
7141 Qôrach (1), *ice*
8179 sha'ar (2), *opening, i.e. door or gate*
4172 pŏlis (19), *town*

CITIZEN
4177 pŏlitēs (2), *citizen*

CITIZENS
4177 pŏlitēs (1), *citizen*

CITY
4062 madhêbâh (1), *gold making*
5892 'îyr (650), *city, town, unwalled-village*
5982 'ammûwd (1), *column, pillar*
7149 qiryâ' (Ch.) (6), *city*
7151 qiryâh (32), *city*
7176 qereth (5), *city*
7179 qash (1), *dry straw*
8179 sha'ar (2), *opening, i.e. door or gate*
3390 mētrŏpŏlis (1), *main city*
4172 pŏlis (143), *town*
4173 pŏlitarchēs (2), *magistrate, city official*

CLAD
3680 kâçâh (1), to *cover*
5844 'âṭâh (1), to *wrap, i.e. cover, veil, clothe*

CLAMOROUS
1993 hâmâh (1), to *be in great commotion*

CLAMOUR
2906 kraugē (1), *outcry*

CLAP
4222 mâchâ' (2), to *strike the hands together*

5606 çâphaq (2), to *clap*
the hands
8628 tâqa' (2), to *clatter,*
slap, drive, clasp

CLAPPED
4222 mâchâ' (1), to *strike*
the hands together
5221 nâkâh (1), to *strike,*
kill

CLAPPETH
5606 çâphaq (1), to *clap*
the hands

CLAUDA
2802 *Klaudē* (1), *Claude*

CLAUDIA
2803 *Klaudia* (1), *Claudia*

CLAUDIUS
2804 *Klaudiŏs* (3),
Claudius

CLAVE
1234 bâqa' (6), to *cleave,*
break, tear open
1692 dâbaq (6), to *cling*
or *adhere*
2388 châzaq (1), to
fasten upon; to seize; to
be strong; courageous
2853 *kŏllaō* (1), to *glue*
together

CLAWS
6541 parçâh (2), split
hoof

CLAY
2563 chômer (11), *clay;*
dry measure
2635 chăçaph (Ch.) (9),
clay
2916 tîyt (3), *mud* or *clay*
4423 meleṭ (1), smooth
clay *cement floor*
4568 ma'ăbeh (2),
compact part of soil
5671 'abṭîyt (1),
something *pledged,* i.e.
(collect.) *pawned* goods
4081 *pēlŏs* (6), lump of
clay

CLEAN
656 'âphêç (1), to *cease*
1249 bar (3), *beloved;*
pure; empty
1305 bârar (1), to
brighten; purify
2134 zak (2), *pure; clear*
2135 zâkâh (4), to *be*
translucent
2141 zâkak (2), to *be*
transparent; clean, pure
2548 châmîyts (1), *salted*
provender or fodder
2889 ṭâhôwr (49), *pure,*
clean, flawless
2891 ṭâhêr (41), to *be*
pure, unadulterated
5355 nâqîy (1), *innocent*
6565 pârar (1), to *break*
up; to *violate, frustrate*
8552 tâmam (3), to
complete, finish
2511 *katharizō* (5), to
cleanse
2513 *katharŏs* (10),
clean, pure
2889 *kŏsmŏs* (3), *world*
3689 *ŏntōs* (1), *really,*
certainly

CLEANNESS
1252 bôr (4), *purity,*
cleanness
5356 niqqâyôwn (1),
clearness; cleanness

CLEANSE
1305 bârar (1), to
brighten; purify
2135 zâkâh (1), to *be*
translucent
2398 châṭâ' (7), to *sin*
2891 ṭâhêr (15), to *be*
pure, unadulterated
5352 nâqâh (3), to *be,*
make clean; to be bare
2511 *katharizō* (6), to
cleanse

CLEANSED
2135 zâkâh (1), to *be*
translucent
2891 ṭâhêr (23), to *be*
pure, unadulterated
2893 ṭohŏrâh (1),
purification; purity
3722 kâphar (1), to
cover; to expiate
5352 nâqâh (1), to *be,*
make clean; to be bare
6663 tsâdaq (1), to *be,*
make right
2511 *katharizō* (9), to
cleanse

CLEANSETH
2891 ṭâhêr (1), to *be*
pure, unadulterated
8562 tamrûwq (1),
scouring, i.e. *soap*
2511 *katharizō* (1), to
cleanse

CLEANSING
2893 ṭohŏrâh (8),
purification; purity
2512 *katharismŏs* (2),
ablution; expiation

CLEAR
216 'ôwr (1), *luminary;*
lightning; happiness
1249 bar (1), *beloved;*
pure; empty
2135 zâkâh (1), to *be*
translucent
3368 yâqâr (1), *valuable*
5352 nâqâh (3), to *be,*
make clean; to be bare
5355 nâqîy (1), *innocent*
6663 tsâdaq (1), to *be,*
make right
6703 tsach (1), *dazzling,*
i.e. *sunny, bright*
53 hagnŏs (1), *innocent,*
modest, perfect, pure
2513 *katharŏs* (1), *clean,*
pure
2929 *krustallizō* (1), to
appear as ice
2986 *lamprŏs* (1),
radiant; clear

CLEARER
6965 qûwm (1), to *rise*

CLEARING
5352 nâqâh (1), to *be,*
make clean; to be bare
627 *apŏlŏgia* (1), *plea* or
verbal defense

CLEARLY
1305 bârar (1), to
brighten; purify
1227 diablĕpō (2), *see*
clearly
2529 *kathŏraō* (1), to
distinctly apprehend
5081 *tēlaugōs* (1), *plainly*

CLEARNESS
2892 ṭôhar (1),
brightness; purification

CLEAVE
1234 bâqa' (3), to *cleave,*
break, tear open
1692 dâbaq (18), to *cling*
or *adhere; to catch*
1693 dᵉbaq (Ch.) (1), to
stick; to be united
1695 dâbêq (1),
adhering, sticking to
3867 lâvâh (1), to *unite*
5596 çâphach (1), to
associate; be united
8156 shâça' (1), to *split*
or *tear; to upbraid*
2853 *kŏllaō* (1), to *glue*
together
4347 *prŏskŏllaō* (3), to
glue to, i.e. to *adhere*

CLEAVED
1692 dâbaq (3), to *cling*
or *adhere; to catch*

CLEAVETH
1234 bâqa' (2), to *cleave,*
break, tear open
1692 dâbaq (6), to *cling*
or *adhere; to catch*
3332 yâtsaq (1), to *pour*
out
6398 pâlach (1), to *slice;*
to *break open; to pierce*
6821 tsâphad (1), to
adhere, join
8157 sheça' (1), *fissure,*
split
2853 *kŏllaō* (1), to *glue*
together

CLEFT
1234 bâqa' (1), to *cleave,*
break, tear open
8156 shâça' (1), to *split*
or *tear; to upbraid*

CLEFTS
1233 bᵉqîya' (1), *fissure,*
breach
2288 chăgâv (3), *rift, cleft*
in rocks
5366 nᵉqârâh (1), *fissure*

CLEMENCY
1932 *ĕpiĕikĕia* (1),
mildness, gentleness

CLEMENT
2815 *Klēmēs* (1), *merciful*

CLEOPAS
2810 *Klĕŏpas* (1), *renown*
father

CLEOPHAS
2832 *Klōpas* (1), cf. *friend*
of (his) *father*

CLIFF
4608 ma'ăleh (1),
elevation; platform

CLIFFS
6178 'ârûwts (1), *feared;*
horrible place or *chasm*

CLIFT
5366 nᵉqârâh (1), *fissure*

CLIFTS
5585 çâ'îyph (1), *fissure*
of rocks; *bough*

CLIMB
5927 'âlâh (4), to *ascend,*
be high, mount

CLIMBED
5927 'âlâh (1), to *ascend,*
be high, mount
305 anabainō (1), to *go*
up, rise

CLIMBETH
305 anabainō (1), to *go*
up, rise

CLIPPED
1639 gâra' (1), to *shave,*
remove, lessen

CLODS
1487 gûwsh (1), *mass* of
earth, dirt *clod*
4053 migrâphâh (1), *clod*
of cultivated dirt
7263 regeb (2), *lump* of
clay
7702 sâdad (2), to
harrow a field

CLOKE
4598 mᵉ'îyl (1), outer
garment or *robe*
1942 ĕpikaluma (1),
pretext, covering
2440 himatiŏn (2), to *put*
on clothes
4392 prŏphasis (2),
pretext, excuse
5341 phĕlŏnēs (1), outer
garment, mantle, cloak

CLOSE
681 'êtsel (1), *side; near*
1443 gâdar (1), to *build a*
stone wall
1692 dâbaq (1), to *cling*
or *adhere; to catch*
4526 miçgereth (2),
margin; stronghold
5641 çâthar (1), to *hide*
by covering
5956 'âlam (1), to *veil*
from sight, i.e. *conceal*
6113 'âtsar (1), to *hold*
back; to maintain
6862 tsar (1), *trouble;*
opponent
788 assŏn (1), *more*
nearly, i.e. *very near*
4601 sigaō (1), to *keep*
silent

CLOSED
2115 zûwr (1), to *press*
together, tighten
3680 kâçâh (1), to *cover*
5437 çâbab (1), to
surround
5462 çâgar (2), to *shut*
up; to *surrender*
5640 çâtham (1), to *stop*
up; to *keep secret*
6105 'âtsam (1), to *be,*
make powerful
6113 'âtsar (1), to *hold*
back; to maintain
2576 kammuō (2), to
close or *shut* the eyes

4428 ptussō (1), to *fold*, i.e. *furl* or *roll* a scroll

CLOSEST
8474 tachârâh (1), to *vie* with a rival

CLOSET
2646 chuppâh (1), *canopy*
5009 tameïŏn (1), *room*

CLOSETS
5009 tameïŏn (1), *room*

CLOTH
899 beged (9), *clothing; treachery* or *pillage*
4346 makbâr (1), *netted-cloth*
8071 simlâh (2), *dress, mantle*
4470 rhakŏs (2), *piece* of cloth
4616 sindōn (3), *byssos*, i.e. bleached *linen*

CLOTHE
3847 lâbash (12), to *clothe*
294 amphiĕnnumi (2), to *enrobe, clothe*

CLOTHED
3680 kâçâh (1), to *cover*
3736 karbêl (1), to *gird* or *clothe*
3830 lebûwsh (1), *garment; wife*
3847 lâbash (39), to *clothe*
3848 lebash (Ch.) (3), to *clothe*
294 amphiĕnnumi (2), to *enrobe, clothe*
1463 ĕgkŏmbŏōmai (1), to *wear, be clothed*
1737 ĕndiduskō (1), to *clothe*
1746 ĕnduō (6), to *invest* with clothing, i.e. to *dress*
1902 ĕpĕnduŏmai (2), to *clothe*
2439 himatizō (2), to *dress, clothe*
4016 pĕriballō (14), to *wrap around, clothe*

CLOTHES
899 beged (69), *clothing; treachery* or *pillage*
1545 gelôwm (1), *clothing, fabric*
4055 mad (1), *vesture, garment; carpet*
5497 çûwth (1), *clothing*
8008 salmâh (3), *clothing*
8071 simlâh (6), *dress, mantle*
2440 himatiŏn (12), to put on *clothes*
3608 ŏthŏniŏn (5), strips of linen *bandage*
4683 sparganŏō (2), to *wrap* with cloth
5509 chitōn (1), *tunic* or *shirt*

CLOTHEST
3847 lâbash (1), to *clothe*

CLOTHING
899 beged (1), *clothing; treachery* or *pillage*

3830 lebûwsh (9), *garment; wife*
4374 mekaççeh (1), *covering*
8071 simlâh (2), *dress, mantle*
8516 talbôsheth (1), *garment*
1742 ĕnduma (1), *apparel*, outer *robe*
2066 ĕsthēs (2), to *clothe*
4749 stŏlē (1), *long-fitting gown*

CLOTHS
899 beged (4), *clothing; treachery* or *pillage*

CLOUD
5645 'âb (9), *thick clouds; thicket*
5743 'ûwb (1), to darkly *becloud*
6051 'ânân (75), *nimbus cloud*
6053 'ânânâh (1), *cloudiness*
6205 'arâphel (1), *gloom, darkness*
3507 nĕphĕlē (18), *cloud*
3509 nĕphŏs (1), *cloud*

CLOUDS
2385 chăzîyz (1), *flash* of lightning
3709 kaph (1), hollow of *hand; paw; sole* of foot
5387 nâsîy' (1), *leader; rising mist, fog*
5645 'âb (20), *thick clouds; thicket*
6050 'ănan (Ch.) (1), *nimbus cloud*
6051 'ânân (5), *nimbus cloud*
6053 'ânânâh (1), *cloudiness*
7834 shachaq (11), *firmament, clouds*
3507 nĕphĕlē (8), *cloud*

CLOUDY
6051 'ânân (6), *nimbus cloud*

CLOUTED
2921 țâlâ' (1), to be *spotted* or *variegated*

CLOUTS
5499 çechâbâh (2), *rag*

CLOVEN
8156 shâça' (1), to *split* or *tear*; to *upbraid*
1266 diamĕrizō (1), to *distribute*

CLOVENFOOTED
8156+8157 shâça' (1), to *split* or *tear*; to *upbraid*
8156+8157+6541 shâça' (2), to *split* or *tear*

CLUSTER
811 'eshkôwl (5), *bunch* of grapes

CLUSTERS
811 'eshkôwl (4), *bunch* of grapes
6778 tsammûwq (2), lump of *dried* grapes
1009 bŏtrus (1), *bunch, cluster* of grapes

CNIDUS
2834 Knidŏs (1), *Cnidus*

COAL
1513 gechel (2), *ember, hot coal*
7531 ritspâh (1), hot *stone; pavement*
7815 shechôwr (1), *soot*

COALS
1513 gechel (16), *ember, hot coal*
6352 pechâm (3), *black coal, charcoal*
7529 retseph (1), *red-hot stone* for baking
7565 resheph (2), *flame*
439 anthrakia (2), fire bed of burning *coals*
440 anthrax (1), live *coal*

COAST
1366 gebûwl (47), *boundary, border*
2256 chebel (4), *company, band*
2348 chôwph (1), *cove, sheltered* bay
3027 yâd (5), *hand; power*
5299 nâphâh (1), *height; sieve*
7097 qâtseh (1), *extremity*
3864 parathalassiŏs (1), *by the lake*
3882 paraliŏs (1), *maritime; seacoast*

COASTS
1366 gebûwl (23), *boundary, border*
1367 gebûwlâh (5), *region*
1552 gelîylâh (1), *circuit* or *region*
2348 chôwph (1), *cove, sheltered* bay
3027 yâd (1), *hand; power*
3411 yerêkâh (3), *far away places*
7097 qâtseh (2), *extremity*
7098 qâtsâh (1), *termination; fringe*
3313 mĕrŏs (3), *division* or *share*
3725 hŏriŏn (10), *region, area, vicinity*
5117 tŏpŏs (1), *place*
5561 chōra (1), *territory*

COAT
3801 kethôneth (16), *garment that covers*
4598 me'îyl (1), *outer garment or robe*
8302 shiryôwn (3), *corslet, coat of mail*
1903 ĕpĕndutēs (1), *outer garment, coat*
5509 chitōn (4), *tunic or shirt*

COATS
3801 kethôneth (7), *garment that covers*
5622 çarbal (Ch.) (2), *cloak*
5509 chitōn (5), *tunic or shirt*

COCK
220 alĕktōr (12), *rooster*

COCKATRICE
6848 tsepha' (1), *hissing viper*

COCKATRICES
6848 tsepha' (1), *hissing viper*

COCKCROWING
219 alektŏrŏphōnia (1), *rooster-crowing*

COCKLE
890 bo'shâh (1), *weed*

COFFER
712 'argâz (3), *box, chest*

COFFIN
727 'ârôwn (1), *box*

COGITATIONS
7476 ra'yôwn (Ch.) (1), *mental conception*

COLD
2779 chôreph (1), *autumn* (and winter)
6793 tsinnâh (1), *large shield; piercing cold*
7119 qar (2), *cool; quiet; cool-headed*
7120 qôr (1), *cold*
7135 qârâh (5), *coolness, cold*
5592 psuchŏs (3), *coolness, cold*
5593 psuchrŏs (4), *chilly, cold*
5594 psuchō (1), to *chill, grow cold*

COLHOZEH
3626 Kol-Chôzeh (2), *every seer*

COLLAR
6310 peh (1), *mouth; opening*

COLLARS
5188 netîyphâh (1), *pendant* for the ears

COLLECTION
4864 mas'êth (2), *raising; beacon; present*
3048 lŏgia (1), *contribution, collection*

COLLEGE
4932 mishneh (2), *duplicate copy; double*

COLLOPS
6371 pîymâh (1), *obesity*

COLONY
2862 kŏlōnia (1), *colony*

COLORS
6320 pûwk (1), *stibium*

COLOSSE
2857 Kŏlŏssai (1), *colossal*

COLOSSIANS
2858 Kŏlŏssaĕus (1), *inhabitant of Colossæ*

COLOUR
5869 'ayin (11), *eye; sight; fountain*
4392 prŏphasis (1), *pretext, excuse*

COLOURS
2921 țâlâ' (1), to be *spotted* or *variegated*
6446 paç (5), *long-sleeved* tunic

C

COLT

6648 tseba' (3), *dye*

7553 riqmâh (2),
variegation of color

COLT

1121 bên (1), *son,
descendant*

5895 'ayîr (2), *young
robust donkey* or *ass*

4454 pôlŏs (12), *young
donkey*

COLTS

1121 bên (1), *son,
descendant*

5895 'ayîr (2), *young
robust donkey* or *ass*

COME

270 'âchaz (1), to *seize,
grasp; possess*

314 'achărôwn (8), *late*
or *last; behind; western*

635 'Eçtêr (1), *Esther*

835 'esher (3), *how
happy!*

857 'âthâh (12), to *arrive*

858 'âthâh (Ch.) (3), to
arrive; go

935 bôw' (681), to *go,
come*

1869 dârak (1), to *walk,
lead;* to *string* a bow

1934 hăvâ' (Ch.) (3), to
be, to *exist*

1961 hâyâh (131), to
exist, i.e. *be* or *become*

1980 hâlak (7), to *walk;
live a certain way*

3045 yâda' (3), to *know*

3051 yâhab (1), to *give*

3205 yâlad (1), to *bear
young;* to *father a child*

3212 yâlak (72), to *walk;*
to *live;* to *carry*

3318 yâtsâ' (84), to *go,
bring out*

3381 yârad (57), to
descend

4279 mâchar (8),
tomorrow; hereafter

4291 mᵉṭâ' (Ch.) (1), to
arrive, to *extend*

4609 ma'ălâh (1),
thought arising

4672 mâtsâ' (8), to *find*
or *acquire;* to *occur*

5060 nâga' (13), to *strike*

5066 nâgash (28), to *be,
come, bring near*

5181 nâchath (2), to *sink,
descend*

5185 nâchêth (1),
descending

5312 nᵉphaq (Ch.) (1), to
issue forth; to *bring out*

5506 çᵉchôrâh (1), *traffic*

5674 'âbar (14), to *cross
over;* to *transition*

5927 'âlâh (104), to
ascend, be high, mount

6213 'âsâh (1), to *do* or
make

6264 'âthîyd (1),
prepared; treasure

6631 tse'ĕtsâ' (1),
produce, children

6743 tsâlach (1), to *push
forward*

6923 qâdam (5), to
anticipate, hasten

7122 qârâ' (4), to
encounter, to *happen*

7125 qîr'âh (1), to
encounter, to *happen*

7126 qârab (33), to
approach, bring near

7131 qârêb (2), *near*

7136 qârâh (2), to *bring
about;* to *impose*

7138 qârôwb (1), *near,
close*

7725 shûwb (30), to *turn
back;* to *return*

8175 sâ'ar (1), to *storm;*
to *shiver,* i.e. *fear*

8622 tᵉqûwphâh (1),
revolution, course

191 akŏuō (1), to *hear;
obey*

305 anabainō (7), to *go
up, rise*

565 apérchŏmai (3), to
go off, i.e. *depart*

576 apŏbainō (1), to
eventuate, become

864 aphiknĕŏmai (1), to
go forth by rumor

1096 ginŏmai (43), to *be,
become*

1204 dĕurŏ (8), *hither!;
hitherto*

1205 dĕutĕ (12), *come
hither!*

1224 diabainō (1), to
pass by, over, across

1330 diérchŏmai (1), to
traverse, travel through

1448 ĕggizō (9), to
approach

1511 ĕinai (8), to *exist*

1525 ĕisérchŏmai (18), to
enter

1531 ĕispŏrĕuŏmai (1), to
enter

1607 ĕkpŏrĕuŏmai (3), to
depart, be discharged

1684 ĕmbainō (2), to
embark; to *reach*

1764 ĕnistēmi (1), to *be
present*

1831 ĕxérchŏmai (24), to
issue; to *leave*

1834 ĕxēgĕŏmai (1), to
tell, relate again

1880 ĕpanérchŏmai (1),
return home

1904 ĕpérchŏmai (8), to
supervene

1910 ĕpibainō (1), to
ascend, embark, arrive

1975 ĕpipŏrĕuŏmai (1),
to *go, come* to

2049 ĕrēmŏō (1), to *lay
waste*

2064 ĕrchŏmai (290), to
go or *come*

2186 ĕphistēmi (2), to *be
present;* to *approach*

2240 hēkō (24), to *arrive,*
i.e. *be present*

2597 katabainō (20), to
descend

2638 katalambanō (1), to
seize; to *possess*

2647 kataluō (1), to *halt*
for the night

2658 katantaō (3), to
arrive at; to *attain*

2673 katargĕō (1), to *be,
render entirely useless*

2718 katérchŏmai (2), to
go, come down

3195 mĕllō (16), to
intend, i.e. *be about* to

3854 paraginŏmai (15),
to *arrive;* to *appear*

3918 parĕimi (6), to *be
present;* to *have come*

3928 parérchŏmai (1), to
go by; to *perish*

3936 paristēmi (1), to
stand beside, present

4137 plērŏō (1), to *fill,
make complete*

4301 prŏlambanō (1) to
take before

4331 prŏsĕggizō (1), to
approach near

4334 prŏsérchŏmai (6),
to *come near, visit*

4365 prŏspŏrĕuŏmai (1),
to *come towards*

4845 sumplērŏō (2), to *be
complete, fulfill*

4905 sunérchŏmai (14),
to *go with*

4940 suntugchanō (1), to
come together

5290 hupŏstrĕphō (1), to
turn under, behind

5302 hustĕrĕō (3), to *be
inferior; to fall short*

5348 phthanō (4), to
anticipate or *precede*

5562 chōrĕō (1), to *pass,
enter;* to *hold, admit*

COMELINESS

1926 hâdâr (3),
magnificence

1935 hôwd (1), *grandeur,
majesty*

2157 ĕuschēmŏsunē (1),
decorousness

COMELY

2433 chîyn (1), *graceful
beauty*

3190 yâṭab (1), to *be,
make well*

3303 yâpheh (1),
beautiful; handsome

4998 nâ'âh (1), to *be
pleasant* or *suitable*

5000 nâ'veh (7), *suitable
or beautiful*

8389 tô'ar (1), *outline,
figure* or *appearance*

8597 tiph'ârâh (1),
ornament

2158 ĕuschēmōn (2),
decorous, proper; noble

4241 prĕpō (1), to *be
suitable* or *proper*

COMERS

4334 prŏsérchŏmai (1),
to *come near, visit*

COMEST

935 bôw' (22), to *go* or
come

2199 zâ'aq (1), to *call
out, announce*

7126 qârab (2), to
approach, bring near

2064 ĕrchŏmai (3), to *go
or come*

COMETH

857 'âthâh (3), to *arrive*

935 bôw' (89), to *go, come*

1961 hâyâh (1), to *exist,*
i.e. *be* or *become*

1980 hâlak (2), to *walk;
live a certain way*

3318 yâtsâ' (19), to *go,
bring out*

3381 yârad (1), to
descend

4672 mâtsâ' (1), to *occur,
meet* or *be present*

5034 nâbêl (1), to *wilt;* to
fall away

5060 nâga' (1), to *strike*

5414 nâthan (1), to *give*

5674 'âbar (1), to *cross
over;* to *transition*

5927 'âlâh (10), to
ascend, be high, mount

6293 pâga' (1), to *impinge*

6437 pânâh (1), to *turn,
to face*

6627 tsâ'âh (2), human
excrement

6631 tse'ĕtsâ' (1),
produce, children

7131 qârêb (5), *near*

7698 sheger (1), *what
comes forth*

7725 shûwb (3), to *turn
back;* to *return*

305 anabainō (1), to *go
up, rise*

1096 ginŏmai (2), to *be,
become*

1511 ĕinai (1), to *exist*

1607 ĕkpŏrĕuŏmai (2), to
depart, be discharged

1831 ĕxérchŏmai (1), to
issue; to *leave*

1999 ĕpisustasis (1),
insurrection

2064 ĕrchŏmai (97), to *go
or come*

2186 ĕphistēmi (1), to *be
present;* to *approach*

2591 Karpŏs (1), (poss.)
fruit

2597 katabainō (3), to
descend

3854 paraginŏmai (3), to
arrive; to *appear*

4334 prŏsérchŏmai (1),
to *come near, visit*

4905 sunérchŏmai (1), to
gather together

COMFORT

1082 bâlag (2), to *be
comforted*

4010 mablîygîyth (1),
desolation

5162 nâcham (33), to *be
sorry;* to *pity, console*

5165 nechâmâh (1),
consolation

5582 çâ'ad (3), to *support*

7502 râphad (1), to
spread a bed; to *refresh*

2174 ĕupsuchĕō (1), to
feel encouraged

2293 tharsĕō (3), to *have
courage; take heart!*

3870 parakalĕō (9), to
call, invite

3874 paraklēsis (6),
imploring, exhortation

3888 paramuthĕŏmai (2), to *console*
3889 paramuthia (1), *consolation*
3890 paramuthiŏn (1), *consolation*
3931 parēgŏria (1), *consolation, comfort*

COMFORTABLE
4496 mᵉnûwchâh (1), *peacefully; consolation*
5150 nichûwm (1), *consoled; solace*

COMFORTABLY
5921+3820 ʾal (4), *above, over, upon, or against*
5921+3824 ʾal (1), *above, over, upon, or against*

COMFORTED
5162 nâcham (20), to *be sorry; to pity, console*
3870 parakalĕŏ (13), to *call, invite*
3888 paramuthĕŏmai (2), to *console*
4837 sumparakalĕŏ (1), to *console jointly*

COMFORTEDST
5162 nâcham (1), to *be sorry; to pity, console*

COMFORTER
5162 nâcham (3), to *be sorry; to pity, console*
3875 paraklētŏs (4), *intercessor, consoler*

COMFORTERS
5162 nâcham (5), to *be sorry; to pity, console*

COMFORTETH
5162 nâcham (3), to *be sorry; to pity, console*
3870 parakalĕŏ (2), to *call, invite*

COMFORTLESS
3737 ŏrphanŏs (1), *parentless, orphaned*

COMFORTS
5150 nichûwm (1), *consoled; solace*
8575 tanchûwm (1), *compassion, solace*

COMING
857 ʾâthâh (1), to *arrive*
935 bôwʾ (19), to *go, come*
1980 hâlak (1), to *walk; live a certain way*
3318 yâtsâʾ (2), to *go, bring out*
3381 yârad (2), to *descend*
3996 mâbôwʾ (1), *entrance; sunset; west*
4126 môwbâʾ (1), *entrance*
5182 nᵉchath (Ch.) (1), to *descend; to depose*
5674 ʾâbar (1), to *cross over; to transition*
7122 qârâʾ (1), to *encounter, to happen*
7272 regel (1), *foot; step*
305 anabainŏ (2), to *go up, rise*
602 apŏkalupsis (1), *disclosure, revelation*

1525 ĕisĕrchŏmai (3), to *enter*
1529 ĕisŏdŏs (1), *entrance*
1531 ĕispŏrĕuŏmai (1), to *enter*
1660 ĕlĕusis (1), *advent, coming*
1831 ĕxĕrchŏmai (1), to *issue; to leave*
1904 ĕpĕrchŏmai (1), to *supervene*
2064 ĕrchŏmai (27), to *go or come*
2186 ĕphistēmi (1), to *be present; to approach*
2597 katabainŏ (1), to *descend*
3854 paraginŏmai (1), to *arrive; to appear*
3952 parŏusia (22), *advent, coming*
4334 prŏsĕrchŏmai (3), to *come near, visit*

COMINGS
4126 môwbâʾ (1), *entrance*

COMMAND
559 ʾâmar (2), to *say*
6310 peh (1), *mouth; opening*
6680 tsâvâh (84), to *constitute, enjoin*
1781 ĕntĕllŏmai (4), to *enjoin, give orders*
2004 ĕpitassŏ (1), to *order, command*
2036 ĕpŏ (3), to *speak*
2753 kĕlĕuŏ (1), to *order, direct*
3853 paraggĕllŏ (8), to *enjoin; to instruct*

COMMANDED
559 ʾâmar (25), to *say*
560 ʾâmar (Ch.) (12), to *say, speak*
1696 dâbar (4), to *speak, say; to subdue*
4480+2941 min (1), *from or out of*
4687 mitsvâh (2), *command*
6680 tsâvâh (333), to *constitute, enjoin*
7761+2942 sûwm (Ch.) (3), to *put, place*
1291 diastĕllŏmai (1), to *enjoin*
1299 diatassŏ (6), to *institute, prescribe*
1781 ĕntĕllŏmai (6), to *enjoin, give orders*
2004 ĕpitassŏ (4), to *order, command*
2036 ĕpŏ (5), to *speak*
2750 kĕiria (1), *swathe of cloth*
2753 kĕlĕuŏ (20), to *order, direct*
3853 paraggĕllŏ (11), to *enjoin; to give instruction*
4367 prŏstassŏ (6), to *enjoin*
4483 rhĕŏ (1), to *utter, i.e. speak or say*

COMMANDEDST
6680 tsâvâh (4), to *constitute, enjoin*

COMMANDER
6680 tsâvâh (1), to *constitute, enjoin*

COMMANDEST
6680 tsâvâh (2), to *constitute, enjoin*
2753 kĕlĕuŏ (1), to *order, direct*

COMMANDETH
559 ʾâmar (3), to *say, speak*
6680 tsâvâh (6), to *constitute, enjoin*
2004 ĕpitassŏ (3), to *order, command*
3853 paraggĕllŏ (1), to *enjoin; to instruct*

COMMANDING
6680 tsâvâh (1), to *constitute, enjoin*
1299 diatassŏ (1), to *institute, prescribe*
2753 kĕlĕuŏ (1), to *order, direct*

COMMANDMENT
559 ʾâmar (2), to *say*
565 ʾimrâh (1), *something said*
1697 dâbâr (15), *word; matter; thing*
1881 dâth (2), royal *edict or statute*
2941 ṭaʾam (Ch.) (2), *sentence, command*
2942 ṭᵉʾêm (Ch.) (2), *judgment; account*
3318 yâtsâʾ (1), to *go, bring out*
3982 maʾămar (2), *edict, command*
4406 millâh (Ch.) (1), *word, command*
4662 miphqâd (1), *appointment*
4687 mitsvâh (43), *command*
6310 peh (37), *mouth; opening*
6673 tsav (1), *injunction*
6680 tsâvâh (9), to *constitute, enjoin*
1291 diastĕllŏmai (1), to *enjoin*
1297 diatagma (1), *authoritative edict*
1781 ĕntĕllŏmai (2), to *enjoin, give orders*
1785 ĕntŏlē (42), *prescription, regulation*
2003 ĕpitagē (6), *injunction or decree*
2753 kĕlĕuŏ (1), to *order, direct*
3852 paraggĕlia (1), *mandate, order*
3853 paraggĕllŏ (1), to *enjoin; to instruct*

COMMANDMENTS
1697 dâbâr (5), *word; matter; thing*
2706 chôq (1), *appointment; allotment*
4687 mitsvâh (130), *command*

COMMANDEDST
6680 tsâvâh (4), to *constitute, enjoin*

COMMANDER
6680 tsâvâh (1), to *constitute, enjoin*

COMMANDEST
6680 tsâvâh (2), to *constitute, enjoin*
2753 kĕlĕuŏ (1), to *order, direct*

COMMANDETH
559 ʾâmar (3), to *say, speak*
6680 tsâvâh (6), to *constitute, enjoin*
2004 ĕpitassŏ (3), to *order, command*
3853 paraggĕllŏ (1), to *enjoin; to instruct*

COMMANDING
6680 tsâvâh (1), to *constitute, enjoin*
1299 diatassŏ (1), to *institute, prescribe*
2753 kĕlĕuŏ (1), to *order, direct*

COMMANDMENT
(see above)

COMMANDMENTS
(see above)

6490 piqqûwd (2), *mandate of God, Law*
1778 ĕntalma (3), *precept, command*
1781 ĕntĕllŏmai (1), to *enjoin, give orders*
1785 ĕntŏlē (27), *prescription, regulation*
3852 paraggĕlia (1), *mandate, order*

COMMEND
3908 paratithēmi (2), to *present something*
4921 sunistaŏ (5), to *set together*

COMMENDATION
4956 sustatikŏs (2), *recommendatory*

COMMENDED
1984 hâlal (2), to *speak words of thankfulness*
7623 shâbach (1), to *address in a loud tone*
1867 ĕpainĕŏ (1), to *applaud, commend*
3908 paratithēmi (1), to *present something*
4921 sunistaŏ (1), to *set together*

COMMENDETH
3936 paristēmi (1), to *stand beside, present*
4921 sunistaŏ (3), to *set together*

COMMENDING
4921 sunistaŏ (1), to *set together*

COMMISSION
2011 ĕpitrŏpē (1), *permission*

COMMISSIONS
1881 dâth (1), royal *edict or statute*

COMMIT
1556 gâlal (2), to *roll; to commit*
2181 zânâh (11), to *commit adultery*
4560 mâçar (1), to *set apart; apostatize*
4603 mâʾal (4), to *act treacherously*
5003 nâʾaph (6), to *commit adultery*
5414 nâthan (1), to *give*
5753 ʾâvâh (2), to *be crooked*
6213 ʾâsâh (14), to *do or make*
6313 pûwg (1), to *be sluggish; be numb*
6466 pâʾal (1), to *do, make or practice*
6485 pâqad (2), to *visit, care for, count*
7760 sûwm (1), to *put, place*
2038 ĕrgazŏmai (1), to *toil*
2416 hiĕrŏsulĕŏ (1), to *be a temple-robber*
3429 mŏichaŏ (2), to *commit adultery*
3431 mŏichĕuŏ (10), to *commit adultery*

COMMITTED
3908 paratithēmi (3), *to present something*
4100 pisteúō (2), *to have faith, to entrust*
4160 pŏiĕō (2), *to make*
4203 pŏrnĕuō (3), *to indulge unlawful lust*
4238 prassō (2), *to execute, accomplish*

COMMITTED
1961 hâyâh (2), *to exist, i.e. be or become*
2181 zânâh (5), *to commit adultery*
2398 châṭâ' (6), *to sin*
4600 mâ'ak (6), *to pierce, emasculate, handle*
5003 nâ'aph (5), *to commit adultery*
5414 nâthan (5), *to give*
5753 'âvâh (2), *to be crooked*
6213 'âsâh (28), *to do or make*
6485 pâqad (4), *to visit, care for, count*
7561 râsha' (1), *to be, do, declare wrong*
8581 tâ'ab (1), *to loathe, i.e. detest*
764 asĕbĕŏ (1), *to be, act impious or wicked*
1325 didōmi (1), *to give*
1439 ĕaō (1), *to let be, i.e. permit or leave alone*
3431 mŏichĕuō (1), *to commit adultery*
3860 paradidōmi (2), *to hand over*
3866 parathēkē (1), *trust, deposit entrusted*
3872 parakatathēkē (2), *deposit, trust*
3908 paratithēmi (1), *to present something*
4100 pisteúō (5), *to have faith; to entrust*
4160 pŏiĕō (4), *to make*
4203 pŏrnĕuō (4), *to indulge unlawful lust*
4238 prassō (3), *to execute, accomplish*
5087 tithēmi (1), *to place*

COMMITTEST
2181 zânâh (1), *to commit adultery*

COMMITTETH
5003 nâ'aph (4), *to commit adultery*
5800 'âzab (1), *to loosen; relinquish; permit*
6213 'âsâh (4), *to do or make*
3429 mŏichaō (4), *to commit adultery*
3431 mŏichĕuō (2), *to commit adultery*
4160 pŏiĕō (3), *to make or do*
4203 pŏrnĕuō (1), *to indulge unlawful lust*

COMMITTING
5003 nâ'aph (1), *to commit adultery*
6213 'âsâh (1), *to do or make*

COMMODIOUS
428 anĕuthĕtŏs (1), *inconvenient*

COMMON
776 'erets (1), *earth, land, soil; country*
1121 bên (1), *people* of a class or kind
2455 chôl (2), *profane, common, not holy*
2490 châlal (1), *to profane, defile*
7227 rab (1), *great*
7230 rôb (1), *abundance*
442 anthrōpinŏs (1), *human*
1219 dēmŏsiŏs (1), *public; in public*
2839 kŏinŏs (8), *common,* i.e. *profane*
2840 kŏinŏō (1), *to make profane*
4183 pŏlus (1), *much, many*
4232 praitōriŏn (1), *governor's court-room*

COMMONLY
1310 diaphēmizō (1), *to spread news*
3654 hŏlōs (1), *altogether*

COMMONWEALTH
4174 pŏlitĕia (1), *citizenship*

COMMOTION
7494 ra'ash (1), *bounding, uproar*

COMMOTIONS
181 akatastasia (1), *disorder, riot*

COMMUNE
559 'âmar (1), *to say*
1696 dâbar (4), *to speak, say; to subdue*
1697 dâbâr (1), *word; matter; thing*
5608 çâphar (1), *to enumerate; to recount*
7878 sîyach (1), *to ponder, muse aloud*

COMMUNED
1696 dâbar (14), *to speak, say; to subdue*
1255 dialalĕō (1), *to converse, discuss*
3656 hŏmilĕō (2), *to converse, talk*
4814 sullalĕō (1), *to talk together,* i.e. *converse*

COMMUNICATE
2841 kŏinōnĕō (1), *to share or participate*
2842 kŏinōnia (1), *benefaction; sharing*
2843 kŏinōnikŏs (1), *liberal*
4790 sugkŏinōnĕō (1), *to co-participate in*

COMMUNICATED
394 anatithĕmai (1), *propound, set forth*
2841 kŏinōnĕō (1), *to share or participate*

COMMUNICATION
1697 dâbâr (1), *word; matter; thing*

COMMODIOUS cont.
7879 sîyach (1), *uttered contemplation*
148 aischrŏlŏgia (1), *vile conversation*
2842 kŏinōnia (1), *benefaction; sharing*
3056 lŏgŏs (2), *word, matter, thing; Word*

COMMUNICATIONS
3056 lŏgŏs (1), *word, matter, thing*
3657 hŏmilia (1), *associations*

COMMUNING
1696 dâbar (2), *to speak, say; to subdue*

COMMUNION
2842 kŏinōnia (4), *benefaction; sharing*

COMPACT
2266 châbar (1), *to fascinate by spells*

COMPACTED
4822 sumbibazō (1), *to drive together*

COMPANIED
4905 sunĕrchŏmai (1), *to gather together*

COMPANIES
736 'ôr^echâh (1), *caravan*
1416 g^edûwd (1), *band of soldiers*
1979 hălîykâh (1), *walking; procession*
4256 machălôqeth (1), *section or division*
4264 machăneh (1), *encampment*
6951 qâhâl (1), *assemblage*
7218 rô'sh (7), *head*
4849 sumpŏsiŏn (1), *group*

COMPANION
2270 châbêr (2), *associate, friend*
2278 chăbereth (1), *consort, companion*
4828 mêrêa' (3), *close friend*
7453 rêa' (3), *associate; one close*
7462 râ'âh (2), *to associate as a friend*
4791 sugkŏinōnŏs (1), *co-participant*
4904 sunĕrgŏs (1), *fellow-worker*

COMPANIONS
2269 châbar (Ch.) (1), *associate, friend*
2270 châbêr (5), *associate, friend*
2271 chabbâr (1), *partner*
3675 k^enâth (Ch.) (8), *colleague*
4828 mêrêa' (1), *close friend*
7453 rêa' (1), *associate; one close*
7464 rê'âh (2), *female associate*
2844 kŏinōnŏs (1), *associate, partner*
4898 sunĕkdēmŏs (1), *fellow-traveller*

COMPANIONS'
7453 rêa' (1), *associate; one close*

COMPANY
736 'ôr^echâh (1), *caravan*
1323 bath (1), *daughter, descendant, woman*
1416 g^edûwd (3), *band of soldiers*
1995 hâmôwn (1), *noise, tumult; many, crowd*
2199 zâ'aq (1), *to convene publicly*
2256 chebel (2), *company, band*
2267 cheber (1), *society, group; magic spell;*
2274 chebrâh (1), *association*
2416 chay (1), *alive; raw; fresh; life*
2428 chayil (1), *army; wealth; virtue; valor; strength*
3862 lahăqâh (1), *assembly*
4246 m^echôwlâh (1), *round-dance*
4264 machăneh (5), *encampment*
5712 'êdâh (13), *assemblage; crowd*
6635 tsâbâ' (1), *army, military host*
6951 qâhâl (16), *assemblage*
7218 rô'sh (5), *head*
7285 regesh (1), *tumultuous crowd*
7462 râ'âh (1), *associate as a friend*
8229 shiph'âh (2), *copiousness*
2398 idiŏs (1), *private or separate*
2828 klisia (1), *party or group*
2853 kŏllaō (1), *to glue together*
3461 murias (1), *ten-thousand*
3588+4012 hŏ (1), *"the"*
3658 hŏmilŏs (1), *multitude*
3792 ŏchlŏpŏiĕō (1), *to raise a disturbance*
3793 ŏchlŏs (7), *throng*
4012 pĕri (1), *about; around*
4128 plēthŏs (1), *large number, throng*
4874 sunanamignumi (3), *to associate with*
4923 sunŏdia (1), *traveling company*

COMPARABLE
5577 çançin (1), *twig*

COMPARE
4911 mâshal (1), *to use figurative language*
6186 'ârak (1), *to set in a row,* i.e. *arrange,*
3846 paraballō (1), *to reach a place; to liken*
4793 sugkrinō (1), *to combine*

COMPARED
1819 dâmâh (1), to resemble, liken
6186 'ârak (1), to set in a row, i.e. arrange,
7737 shâvâh (2), to resemble; to adjust

COMPARING
4793 sugkrinō (2), to combine

COMPARISON
3644 kᵉmôw (1), like, as; for; with
3850 parabŏlē (1), fictitious narrative

COMPASS
247 'âzar (1), to belt
2329 chûwg (1), circle
3749 karkôb (2), rim, ledge, or top margin
3803 kâthar (2), to enclose, besiege; to wait
4230 mᵉchûwgâh (1), compass
4524 mêçab (1), around, surround
5362 nâqaph (3), to surround or circulate
5437 çâbab (22), to surround
5439 çâbîyb (2), circle; environs; around
5849 'âṭar (1), to encircle, enclose in; to crown
4013 pĕriagō (1), to walk around
4022 pĕriĕrchŏmai (1), to stroll, vacillate, veer
4033 pĕrikuklŏō (1), to blockade completely

COMPASSED
661 'âphaph (5), to surround
2328 chûwg (1), to describe a circle
5362 nâqaph (4), to surround or circulate
5437 çâbab (28), to surround
5849 'âṭar (1), to encircle, enclose in; to crown
2944 kukloō (3), to surround, encircle
4029 pĕrikĕimai (2), to enclose, encircle

COMPASSEST
2219 zârâh (1), to toss about; to diffuse

COMPASSETH
5437 çâbab (4), to surround
6059 'ânaq (1), to collar; to fit out

COMPASSING
5362 nâqaph (2), to surround or circulate
5437 çâbab (1), to surround

COMPASSION
2550 châmal (5), to spare, have pity on
7349 rachûwm (5), compassionate
7355 râcham (8), to be compassionate

7356 racham (2), compassion; womb
1653 ĕlĕĕŏ (3), to give out compassion
3356 mĕtriŏpathĕō (1), to deal gently
3627 ŏiktĕirō (1), to exercise pity
4697 splagchnizŏmai (12), to feel sympathy
4834 sumpathĕō (1), to commiserate
4835 sumpathēs (1), commiserative

COMPASSIONS
7355 râcham (1), to be compassionate
7356 racham (1), compassion; womb

COMPEL
597 'ânaç (1), to insist, compel
5647 'âbad (1), to do, work, serve
29 aggarĕuō (2), to press into public service
315 anagkazō (1), to necessitate, compel

COMPELLED
5080 nâdach (1), to push off, scattered
6555 pârats (1), to break out
29 aggarĕuō (1), to press into public service
315 anagkazō (3), to necessitate, compel

COMPELLEST
315 anagkazō (1), to necessitate, compel

COMPLAIN
596 'ânan (1), complain
1058 bâkâh (1), to weep, moan
7378 rîyb (1), to hold a controversy; to defend
7878 sîyach (1), to ponder, muse aloud

COMPLAINED
596 'ânan (1), complain
7878 sîyach (1), to ponder, muse aloud

COMPLAINERS
3202 mĕmpsimŏirŏs (1), discontented

COMPLAINING
6682 tsᵉvâchâh (1), screech of anguish

COMPLAINT
7878 sîyach (9), to ponder, muse aloud

COMPLAINTS
157 aitiama (1), thing charged

COMPLETE
8549 tâmîym (1), entire, complete; integrity
4137 plērŏō (2), to fill, make complete

COMPOSITION
4971 mathkôneth (2), proportion

COMPOUND
4842 mirqachath (1), unguent; unguent-pot

COMPOUNDETH
7543 râqach (1), to perfume, blend spice

COMPREHEND
3045 yâda' (1), to know
2638 katalambanō (1), to possess; to understand

COMPREHENDED
3557 kûwl (1), to measure; to maintain
346 anakĕphalaiŏmai (1), to sum up
2638 katalambanō (1), to possess; to understand

CONANIAH
3562 Kôwnanyâhûw (1), Jehovah has sustained

CONCEAL
2790 chârash (1), to be silent; to be deaf
3582 kâchad (2), to destroy; to hide
3680 kâçâh (2), to cover
5641 çâthar (1), to hide

CONCEALED
3582 kâchad (2), to destroy; to hide

CONCEALETH
3680 kâçâh (2), to cover

CONCEIT
4906 maskîyth (1), carved figure
5869 'ayin (4), eye; sight; fountain

CONCEITS
3844+1438 para (2), from; with; besides

CONCEIVE
2029 hârâh (3), to conceive, be pregnant
2030 hâreh (4), pregnant
2232 zâra' (1), to sow seed; to disseminate
3179 yâcham (4), to conceive
2602 katabŏlē (1), conception, beginning
4815 sullambanō (1), to conceive; to aid

CONCEIVED
2029 hârâh (1), to conceive, be pregnant
2030 hâreh (33), pregnant
2232 zâra' (1), to sow seed; to disseminate
2803 châshab (1), to plot; to think, regard
3179 yâcham (2), to conceive
3254 yâçaph (1), to add or augment
1080 gĕnnaō (1), to procreate, regenerate
2845+2192 kŏitē (1), couch; conception
4815 sullambanō (4), to conceive; to aid
5087 tithēmi (1), to place

CONCEIVING
2030 hâreh (1), pregnant

CONCEPTION
2032 hêrôwn (3), pregnancy

CONCERN
4012 pĕri (2), about; around

CONCERNETH
1157 bᵉ'ad (1), at, beside, among, behind, for

CONCERNING
413 'êl (15), to, toward
854 'êth (1), with; by; at; among
5921 'al (78), above, over, upon, or against
5922 'al (Ch.) (6), above, over, upon, or against
6655 tsad (Ch.) (1), at the side of; against
1519 ĕis (5), to or into
2596 kata (5), down; according to
3754 hŏti (1), that; because; since
4012 pĕri (44), about; around
4314 prŏs (1), for; on, at; to, toward; against
5228 hupĕr (1), over; above; beyond

CONCISION
2699 katatŏmē (1), mutilation, cutting

CONCLUDE
3049 lŏgizŏmai (1), to credit; to think, regard

CONCLUDED
2919 krinō (1), to decide; to try, condemn, punish
4788 sugklĕiō (2), to net fish; to lock up persons

CONCLUSION
5490 çôwph (1), termination; end

CONCORD
4857 sumphōnēsis (1), accordance, agreement

CONCOURSE
1993 hâmâh (1), to be in great commotion
4963 sustrŏphē (1), riotous crowd

CONCUBINE
6370 pîylegesh (22), concubine

CONCUBINES
3904 lᵉchênâh (Ch.) (3), concubine
6370 pîylegesh (14), concubine

CONCUPISCENCE
1939 ĕpithumia (3), longing

CONDEMN
7561 râsha' (11), to be, do, declare wrong
8199 shâphaṭ (1), to judge
2607 kataginōskō (2), to condemn
2618 katakaiō (1), to consume wholly by burning
2632 katakrinō (7), to judge against
2633 katakrisis (1), act of sentencing adversely
2919 krinō (1), to decide; to try, condemn, punish

CONDEMNATION
2631 *katakrima* (3), adverse sentence
2633 *katakrisis* (1), act of sentencing adversely
2917 *krima* (5), decision
2920 *krisis* (2), decision; tribunal; justice
5272 *hupŏkrisis* (1), deceit, hypocrisy

CONDEMNED
3318+7563 *yâtsâ'* (1), to go, bring out
6064 *'ânash* (2), to inflict a penalty, to fine
7561 *râsha'* (1), to be, do, declare wrong
176 *akatagnōstŏs* (1), unblamable
843 *autŏkatakritŏs* (1), self-condemned
1519+2917 *ĕis* (1), to or into
2613 *katadikazō* (4), to condemn
2632 *katakrinō* (8), to judge against
2919 *krinō* (2), to decide; to try, condemn, punish

CONDEMNEST
2632 *katakrinō* (1), to judge against

CONDEMNETH
7561 *râsha'* (2), to be, do, declare wrong
2632 *katakrinō* (1), to judge against
4314 *prŏs* (1), for; on, at; to, toward; against

CONDEMNING
7561 *râsha'* (1), to be, do, declare wrong
2919 *krinō* (1), to decide; to try, condemn, punish

CONDESCEND
4879 *sunapagō* (1), to take off together

CONDITIONS
4314 *prŏs* (1), for; on, at; to, toward; against

CONDUCT
5674 *'âbar* (1), to cross over; to transition
7971 *shâlach* (1), to send away
4311 *prŏpĕmpō* (1), to send forward

CONDUCTED
5674 *'âbar* (1), to cross over; to transition
2525 *kathistēmi* (1), to designate, constitute

CONDUIT
8585 *tᵉ'âlâh* (4), irrigation channel; bandage or plaster

CONEY
8227 *shâphân* (2), rock-rabbit, (poss.) hyrax

CONFECTION
7545 *rôqach* (1), aromatic, fragrance

CONFECTIONARIES
7543 *râqach* (1), to perfume, blend spice

CONFEDERACY
1285 *bᵉrîyth* (1), compact, agreement
7195 *qesher* (2), unlawful alliance

CONFEDERATE
1167+1285 *ba'al* (1), master; owner; citizen
1285+3772 *bᵉrîyth* (1), compact, agreement
5117 *nûwach* (1), to rest; to settle down

CONFERENCE
4323 *prŏsanatithēmi* (1), to add; to consult

CONFERRED
1961+1697 *hâyâh* (1), to exist, i.e. be or become
4323 *prŏsanatithēmi* (1), to add; to consult
4814 *sullalĕō* (1), to talk together, i.e. converse
4820 *sumballō* (1), to converse, consult

CONFESS
3034 *yâdâh* (11), to revere or worship
1843 *ĕxŏmŏlŏgĕō* (5), to acknowledge or agree
3670 *hŏmŏlŏgĕō* (12), to acknowledge, agree

CONFESSED
3034 *yâdâh* (3), to throw; to revere or worship
1843 *ĕxŏmŏlŏgĕō* (1), to acknowledge or agree
3670 *hŏmŏlŏgĕō* (3), to acknowledge, agree

CONFESSETH
3034 *yâdâh* (1), to throw; to revere or worship
3670 *hŏmŏlŏgĕō* (2), to acknowledge, agree

CONFESSING
3034 *yâdâh* (1), to throw; to revere or worship
1843 *ĕxŏmŏlŏgĕō* (2), to acknowledge or agree

CONFESSION
3034 *yâdâh* (2), to throw; to revere or worship
8426 *tôwdâh* (2), expressions of thanks
3670 *hŏmŏlŏgĕō* (1), to acknowledge, agree
3671 *hŏmŏlŏgia* (1), confession

CONFIDENCE
982 *bâṭach* (4), to trust, be confident or sure
983 *beṭach* (1), safety, security, trust
985 *biṭchâh* (1), trust
986 *biṭṭâchôwn* (2), trust
3689 *keçel* (1), loin; back; viscera; trust
3690 *kiçlâh* (1), trust
4009 *mibṭâch* (8), security; assurance
2292 *tharrhĕō* (1), exercise courage
3954 *parrhēsia* (6), frankness, boldness
3982 *pĕithō* (6), to rely
4006 *pĕpŏithēsis* (5), reliance, trust

CONFEDERACY (col. 3)
5287 *hupŏstasis* (2), essence; assurance

CONFIDENCES
4009 *mibṭâch* (1), security; assurance

CONFIDENT
982 *bâṭach* (2), to trust, be confident or sure
2292 *tharrhĕō* (2), to exercise courage
3982 *pĕithō* (3), to rely
5287 *hupŏstasis* (1), essence; assurance

CONFIDENTLY
1340 *diïschurizŏmai* (1), to asseverate

CONFIRM
553 *'âmats* (1), to be strong; be courageous
1396 *gâbar* (1), to be strong; to prevail
2388 *châzaq* (2), to bind, restrain, conquer
3559 *kûwn* (1), to set up: establish, fix, prepare
4390 *mâlê'* (1), to fill; be full
6965 *qûwm* (4), to rise
950 *bĕbaiŏō* (2), to stabilitate, keep strong
2964 *kurŏō* (1), to ratify, validate a treaty

CONFIRMATION
951 *bĕbaiōsis* (2), confirmation

CONFIRMED
2388 *châzaq* (1), to bind, restrain, conquer
3559 *kûwn* (2), to render sure, proper or prosperous
5975 *'âmad* (2), to stand
6965 *qûwm* (2), to rise
950 *bĕbaiŏō* (2), to stabilitate, keep strong
1991 *ĕpistērizō* (1), to re-establish, strengthen
2964 *kurŏō* (1), to ratify, validate a treaty
3315 *mĕsitĕuō* (1), to ratify as surety, confirm
4300 *prŏkurŏō* (1), to ratify previously

CONFIRMETH
6965 *qûwm* (3), to rise

CONFIRMING
950 *bĕbaiŏō* (1), to stabilitate, keep strong
1991 *ĕpistērizō* (2), to re-establish, strengthen

CONFISCATION
6065 *'ănash* (Ch.) (1), fine, penalty, mulct

CONFLICT
73 *agōn* (2), contest, struggle

CONFORMABLE
4832 *summŏrphŏs* (1), similar, conformed to

CONFORMED
4832 *summŏrphŏs* (1), similar, conformed to
4964 *suschēmatizō* (1), to conform

CONFOUND
1101 *bâlal* (2), to mix; confuse
2865 *châthath* (1), to break down
2617 *kataischunō* (2), to disgrace or shame

CONFOUNDED
954 *bûwsh* (21), be ashamed; disappointed
2659 *châphêr* (6), to be ashamed, disappointed
3001 *yâbêsh* (9), to dry up; to wither
3637 *kâlam* (11), to taunt or insult
2617 *kataischunō* (2), to disgrace or shame
4797 *sugchĕō* (2), to throw into disorder

CONFUSED
7494 *ra'ash* (1), bounding, uproar
4797 *sugchĕō* (1), to throw into disorder

CONFUSION
954 *bûwsh* (1), be ashamed, disappointed
1322 *bôsheth* (7), shame
2659 *châphêr* (2), to be ashamed, disappointed
3637 *kâlam* (1), to taunt or insult
3639 *kᵉlimmâh* (6), disgrace, scorn
7036 *qâlôwn* (1), disgrace
8397 *tebel* (2), confused mixture
8414 *tôhûw* (3), waste, desolation, formless
181 *akatastasia* (2), disorder, riot
4799 *sugchusis* (1), riotous disturbance

CONGEALED
7087 *qâphâ'* (1), to thicken, congeal

CONGRATULATE
1288 *bârak* (1), to bless

CONGREGATION
482 *'êlem* (1), silence
2416 *chay* (2), alive; raw; fresh; life
4150 *môw'êd* (147), assembly, congregation
5712 *'êdâh* (123), assemblage; crowd
6951 *qâhâl* (85), assemblage
6952 *qᵉhillâh* (1), assemblage
4865 *sunagōnizŏmai* (1), to be a partner

CONGREGATIONS
4150 *môw'êd* (1), assembly, congregation
4721 *maqhêl* (2), assembly

CONIAH
3659 *Konyâhûw* (3), Jehovah will establish

CONIES
8226 *sâphan* (2), to conceal

CONONIAH
3562 Kôwnanyâhûw (2),
Jehovah has sustained

CONQUER
3528 nikaō (1), to
subdue, conquer

CONQUERING
3528 nikaō (1), to
subdue, conquer

CONQUERORS
5245 hupĕrnikaō (1), to
gain a decisive *victory*

CONSCIENCE
4893 sunĕidēsis (31),
moral *consciousness*

CONSCIENCES
4893 sunĕidēsis (1),
moral *consciousness*

CONSECRATE
2763 charam (1), to
devote to destruction
4390+3027 mâlê' (10), to
fill; be full
5144 nâzar (1), to *devote*
6942 qâdâsh (2), to *be,
make clean*

CONSECRATED
4390+3027 mâlê' (7), to
fill; be full
6942 qâdâsh (4), to *be,
make clean*
6944 qôdesh (1), *sacred*
place or thing
1457 ĕgkainizō (1), to
inaugurate
5048 tĕlĕiŏō (1), to
perfect, complete

CONSECRATION
4394 millû' (7), *fulfilling;
setting; consecration*
5145 nezer (2), *set apart;
dedication*

CONSECRATIONS
4394 millû' (4), *fulfilling;
setting; consecration*

CONSENT
14 'âbâh (4), to *be
acquiescent*
225 'ûwth (3), to *assent*
376 'îysh (1), *man; male*
3820 lêb (1), *heart*
7926 shᵉkem (2), *neck;
spur* of a hill
4334 prŏsĕrchŏmai (1),
to *assent to*
4852 sumphēmi (1), to
assent to
4859 sumphōnŏs (1),
agreeing; agreement

CONSENTED
225 'ûwth (1), to *assent;
agree*
8085 shâma' (1), to *hear*
1962 ĕpinĕuō (1), to
assent, give consent
4784 sugkatatithēmai
(1), to *accord* with

CONSENTEDST
7521 râtsâh (1), to *be
pleased with; to satisfy*

CONSENTING
4909 sunĕudŏkĕō (2), to
assent to, *feel gratified*

CONSIDER
559 'âmar (1), to *say*
995 bîyn (20), to
understand; discern
3045 yâda' (4), to *know*
5027 nâbaṭ (5), to *scan;
to regard* with favor
6448 pâçag (1), to
contemplate
7200 râ'âh (15), to *see*
7725 shûwb (1), to *turn
back; to return*
7760 sûwm (2), to *put*
7760+3820 sûwm (4), to
put, place
7760+3820+5921 sûwm
(2), to *put, place*
7919 sâkal (2), to *be* or
act circumspect
357 analŏgizŏmai (1), to
contemplate
1260 dialŏgizŏmai (1), to
deliberate
1492 ĕidō (1), to *know*
2334 thĕōrĕō (1), to *see;
to discern*
2648 katamanthanō (1),
to *note carefully*
2657 katanŏĕō (4), to
observe fully
3539 nŏiĕō (1), to
exercise the *mind*

CONSIDERED
995 bîyn (1), to
understand; discern
2803 châshab (1), to
think, regard; to value
5414 nâthan (1), to *give*
7200 râ'âh (4), to *see*
7760+3820 sûwm (2), to
put, place
7896+3820 shîyth (1), to
place, put
7920 sᵉkal (Ch.) (1), to *be
or act circumspect*
8085 shâma' (1), to *hear*
2657 katanŏĕō (2), to
observe fully
4894 sunĕidō (1), to
understand
4920 suniēmi (1), to
comprehend

CONSIDEREST
7200 râ'âh (1), to *see*
2657 katanŏĕō (1), to
observe fully

CONSIDERETH
995 bîyn (1), to
understand; discern
2161 zâmam (1), to *plan*
3045 yâda' (2), to *know*
7200 râ'âh (2), to *see*
7725 shûwb (1), to *turn
back; to return*
7919 sâkal (2), to *be or
act circumspect*

CONSIDERING
995 bîyn (2), to
understand; discern
333 anathĕōrĕō (1), to
look again
4648 skŏpĕō (1), to *watch
out for,* i.e. to *regard*

CONSIST
4921 sunistaō (1), to *set
together*

CONSISTETH
2076 ĕsti (1), he (she or
it) *is;* they *are*

CONSOLATION
8575 tanchûwm (1),
compassion, solace
3874 paraklēsis (14),
imploring, solace

CONSOLATIONS
8575 tanchûwm (3),
compassion, solace

CONSORTED
4845 sumplērŏō (1), to *be
complete, fulfill*

CONSPIRACY
7195 qesher (9), *unlawful
alliance*
4945 sunōmŏsia (1), *plot,
conspiracy*

CONSPIRATORS
7194 qâshar (1), to *tie,
bind*

CONSPIRED
5320 Naphtûchîym (1),
Naphtuchim
7194 qâshar (18), to *tie,
bind*

CONSTANT
2388 châzaq (1), to
fasten upon; to seize

CONSTANTLY
5331 netsach (1),
splendor; lasting
1226 diabĕbaiŏŏmai (1),
to *confirm thoroughly*
1340 diïschurizŏmai (1),
to *asseverate*

CONSTELLATIONS
3685 Kᵉçîyl (1),
constellation Orion

CONSTRAIN
315 anagkazō (1), to
necessitate, compel

CONSTRAINED
2388 châzaq (1), to
fasten upon; to seize
315 anagkazō (3), to
necessitate, compel
3849 parabiazŏmai (2),
to *compel by entreaty*

CONSTRAINETH
6693 tsûwq (1), to
oppress, distress
4912 sunĕchō (1), to *hold
together*

CONSTRAINT
317 anagkastōs (1),
compulsorily

CONSULT
3289 yâ'ats (1), to *advise*

CONSULTATION
4824 sumbŏuliŏn (1),
advisement

CONSULTED
3272 yᵉ'aṭ (Ch.) (1), to
counsel
3289 yâ'ats (8), to *advise*
4427 mâlak (1), to *reign
as king*
7592 shâ'al (1), to *ask*
1011 bŏulĕuō (1), to
deliberate; to resolve
4823 sumbŏulĕuō (1), to
recommend, deliberate

CONSULTER
7592 shâ'al (1), to *ask*

CONSULTETH
1011 bŏulĕuō (1), to
deliberate; to resolve

CONSUME
398 'âkal (9), to *eat*
402 'oklâh (1), *food*
1086 bâlâh (1), to *wear
out, decay; consume*
1497 gâzal (1), to *rob*
2000 hâmam (1), to
disturb, drive, destroy
2628 châçal (1), to *eat
off, consume*
3423 yârash (1), to
inherit; to impoverish
3615 kâlâh (23), to
complete, consume
4529 mâçâh (1), to
dissolve, melt
4743 mâqaq (4), to *melt;
to flow, dwindle, vanish*
5486 çûwph (4), to
terminate
5487 çûwph (Ch.) (1), to
come to an end
5595 çâphâh (1), to
scrape; to accumulate
8046 shᵉmad (Ch.) (1), to
desolate
8552 tâmam (2), to
complete, finish
355 analiskō (2), *destroy*
1159 dapanaō (1), to
incur cost; to waste

CONSUMED
398 'âkal (21), to *eat*
622 'âçaph (1), to *gather*
1846 dâ'ak (1), to *be
extinguished; to expire*
3615 kâlâh (37), to
complete, consume
4127 mûwg (1), to *soften,
flow down, disappear*
5486 çûwph (1), to
terminate
5595 çâphâh (5), to
scrape; to accumulate
6244 'âshêsh (3), to *fail*
6789 tsâmath (1), to
extirpate, root out
8552 tâmam (24), to
complete, finish
355 analiskō (1), *destroy*

CONSUMETH
398 'âkal (2), to *eat*
1086 bâlâh (1), to *wear
out, decay; consume*
7503 râphâh (1), to
slacken

CONSUMING
398 'âkal (2), to *eat*
2654 katanaliskō (1), to
consume utterly

CONSUMMATION
3617 kâlâh (1), *complete
destruction*

CONSUMPTION
3617 kâlâh (2), *complete
destruction*
3631 killâyôwn (1),
pining, destruction
7829 shachepheth (2),
wasting disease

433 anēkō (2), *be proper, fitting*
2119 ĕukairēō (1), to *have opportunity*
2121 ĕukairŏs (1), *opportune, suitable*
2520 kathēkō (1), *becoming, proper*
2540 kairŏs (1), *occasion, set* or *proper*

CONVENIENTLY
2122 ĕukairŏs (1), *opportunely*

CONVERSANT
1980 hâlak (2), to *walk; live a certain way*

CONVERSATION
1870 derek (2), *road; course* of life
390 anastrĕphō (2), to *remain, to live*
391 anastrŏphē (13), *behavior*
4175 pŏlitĕuma (1), *citizenship*
4176 pŏlitĕuŏmai (1), to *behave as a citizen*
5158 trŏpŏs (1), *deportment, character*

CONVERSION
1995 ĕpistrŏphē (1), *moral revolution*

CONVERT
7725 shûwb (1), to *turn back; to return*
1994 ĕpistrĕphō (1), to *revert, turn back to*

CONVERTED
2015 hâphak (1), to *turn about or over*
7725 shûwb (1), to *turn back; to return*
1994 ĕpistrĕphō (6), to *revert, turn back to*
4762 strĕphō (1), to *turn around or reverse*

CONVERTETH
1994 ĕpistrĕphō (1), to *revert, turn back to*

CONVERTING
7725 shûwb (1), to *turn back; to return*

CONVERTS
7725 shûwb (1), to *turn back; to return*

CONVEY
5674 'âbar (1), to *cross over; to transition*
7760 sûwm (1), to *put*

CONVEYED
1593 ĕknĕuō (1), to quietly *withdraw*

CONVICTED
1651 ĕlĕgchō (1), to *confute, admonish*

CONVINCE
1651 ĕlĕgchō (1), to *confute, admonish*
1827 ĕxĕlĕgchō (1), to *punish*

CONVINCED
3198 yâkach (1), to *be correct; to argue*

1246 diakatĕlĕgchŏmai (1), to *prove downright*
1651 ĕlĕgchō (2), to *confute, admonish, rebuke*

CONVINCETH
1651 ĕlĕgchō (1), to *confute, admonish*

CONVOCATION
4744 miqrâ' (15), public *meeting*

CONVOCATIONS
4744 miqrâ' (3), public *meeting*

COOK
2876 ṭabbâch (2), *butcher, cook*

COOKS
2876 ṭabbâch (1), *butcher, cook*

COOL
7307 rûwach (1), *breath; wind; life*-spirit
2711 katapsuchō (1), to *refresh, cool off*

COOS
2972 Kōs (1), *Cos*

COPIED
6275 'âthaq (1), to *grow old;* to *transcribe*

COPING
2947 ṭêphach (1), *palm-breadth*

COPPER
5178 nᵉchôsheth (1), *copper; bronze*

COPPERSMITH
5471 chalkĕus (1), *copper-worker*

COPULATION
7902 shᵉkâbâh (3), *lying down*

COPY
4932 mishneh (2), *duplicate copy; double*
6572 parshegen (3), *transcript*
6573 parshegen (Ch.) (4), *transcript*

COR
3734 kôr (1), dry *measure*

CORAL
7215 râ'mâh (2), *high* in value, (poss.) *coral*

CORBAN
2878 kŏrban (1), *votive offering or gift*

CORD
2256 chebel (4), *company, band*
2339 chûwṭ (1), *string; measuring tape; line*
3499 yether (1), *remainder;* small *rope*

CORDS
2256 chebel (12), *company, band*
4340 mêythâr (8), *tent-cord; bow-string*
5688 'ăbôth (5), *entwined things*
4979 schŏiniŏn (1), *rushlet, i.e. grass-withe*

CORE
2879 Kŏrĕ (1), *ice*

CORIANDER
1407 gad (2), *coriander*

CORINTH
2882 Kŏrinthŏs (6), *Corinthus*

CORINTHIANS
2881 Kŏrinthiŏs (4), *inhabitant of Corinth*

CORINTHUS
2882 Kŏrinthŏs (1), *Corinthus*

CORMORANT
6893 qâ'ath (2), *pelican*
7994 shâlâk (2), *bird of prey* (poss.) *pelican*

CORN
1098 bᵉlîyl (1), *feed, fodder*
1121 bên (1), *son, descendant*
1250 bâr (9), cereal *grain*
1637 gŏren (1), open *area*
1643 geres (2), *grain*
1715 dâgân (37), *grain*
3759 karmel (1), *planted field; garden produce*
5669 'âbûwr (2), *kept over; stored* grain
6194 'ârêm (1), *heap, mound; sheaf*
7054 qâmâh (7), *stalk of cereal grain*
7383 rîyphâh (1), *grits cereal*
7668 sheber (7), *grain*
7688 shâgach (1), to *glance sharply at*
2848 kŏkkŏs (1), *kernel*
4621 sitŏs (2), *grain, especially wheat*
4702 spŏrimŏs (1), *field planted with seed*
4719 stachus (3), *head of grain*

CORNELIUS
2883 Kŏrnēliŏs (10), *Cornelius*

CORNER
2106 zâvîyth (1), *angle, corner* (as *projecting*)
3671 kânâph (1), *edge or extremity; wing*
3802 kâthêph (2), *shoulder-piece; wall*
4742 mᵉquts'âh (1), *angle*
6285 pê'âh (5), *direction; region; extremity*
6434 pên (1), *angle*
6437 pânâh (1), to *turn, to face*
6438 pinnâh (17), *pinnacle; chieftain*
204 akrŏgōniaiŏs (2), *corner, cornerstone*
1137 gōnia (1), *angle; cornerstone*

CORNERS
2106 zâvîyth (1), *angle, corner* (as *projecting*)
3671 kânâph (2), *edge or extremity; wing*
4740 maqtsôwa' (1), *angle*
4742 mᵉquts'âh (6), *angle*

CORE
6284 pâ'âh (1), to *blow away*
6285 pê'âh (11), *region; extremity*
6438 pinnâh (6), *pinnacle; chieftain*
6471 pa'am (3), *time; step; occurence*
6763 tsêlâ' (2), *side*
7098 qâtsâh (1), *termination; fringe*
7106 qâtsa' (1), to *strip off, i.e.* (partially) *scrape*
746 archē (2), *first in rank; first in time*
1137 gōnia (2), *angle; cornerstone*

CORNET
7162 qeren (Ch.) (4), *horn*
7782 shôwphâr (3), curved *ram's horn*

CORNETS
4517 mᵉna'na' (1), *rattling* instrument
7782 shôwphâr (1), curved *ram's horn*

CORNFLOOR
1637+1715 gŏren (1), open *area*

CORPSE
4430 ptōma (1), *corpse, carrion*

CORPSES
1472 gᵉvîyâh (2), dead *body*
6297 peger (2), *carcase; corpse*

CORRECT
3198 yâkach (1), to *be correct; to argue*
3256 yâçar (6), to *chastise; to instruct*

CORRECTED
3256 yâçar (1), to *chastise; to instruct*
3810 paidĕutēs (1), *teacher or discipliner*

CORRECTETH
3198 yâkach (2), to *be correct; to argue*

CORRECTION
3198 yâkach (1), to *be correct; to argue*
4148 mûwçâr (8), *reproof, warning*
7626 shêbeṭ (1), *stick; clan, family*
8433 tôwkêchâh (1), *correction*
1882 ĕpanŏrthōsis (1), *rectification, correction*

CORRUPT
1605 gâ'ar (1), to *chide, reprimand*
2254 châbal (1), to *bind* by a *pledge; to pervert*
2610 chânêph (1), to *soil, be defiled*
4167 mûwq (1), to *blaspheme, scoff*
4743 mâqaq (1), to *melt; to flow, dwindle, vanish*
7843 shâchath (11), to *decay; to ruin*
7844 shᵉchath (Ch.) (1), to *decay; to ruin*

CORRUPTED
853 aphanizō (2), to consume (becloud)
1311 diaphthĕirō (1), to ruin, to pervert
2585 kapēlĕuō (1), to retail, i.e. to adulterate
2704 kataphthĕirō (1), to spoil entirely
4550 saprŏs (6), rotten, i.e. worthless
5351 phthĕirō (4), to spoil; to deprave

CORRUPTED
7843 shâchath (11), to decay; to ruin
4595 sēpō (1), to putrefy, rot
5351 phthĕirō (2), to spoil; to deprave

CORRUPTERS
7843 shâchath (2), to decay; to ruin

CORRUPTETH
1311 diaphthĕirō (1), to ruin, to pervert

CORRUPTIBLE
862 aphthartŏs (1), undecaying, immortal
5349 phthartŏs (6), perishable, not lasting

CORRUPTING
7843 shâchath (1), to decay; to ruin

CORRUPTION
1097 bᵉlîy (1), without, not yet; lacking;
4889 mashchîyth (2), destruction; corruption
4893 mishchâth (1), disfigurement
7845 shachath (4), pit; destruction
1312 diaphthŏra (6), decay, corruption
5356 phthŏra (7), ruin; depravity, corruption

CORRUPTLY
2254 châbal (1), to bind by a pledge; to pervert
7843 shâchath (1), to decay; to ruin

COSAM
2973 Kōsam (1), Cosam

COST
2600 chinnâm (2), free
1160 dapanē (1), expense, cost

COSTLINESS
5094 timiŏtēs (1), expensiveness

COSTLY
3368 yâqâr (4), valuable
4185 pŏlutĕlēs (1), extremely expensive
4186 pŏlutimŏs (1), extremely valuable

COTES
220 'ăvêrâh (1), stall, pen

COTTAGE
4412 mᵉlûwnâh (1), hut
5521 çukkâh (1), tabernacle; shelter

COTTAGES
3741 kârâh (1), meadow

COUCH
3326 yâtsûwa' (1), bed; wing or lean-to
4904 mishkâb (1), bed; sleep
6210 'eres (2), canopy couch
7742 sûwach (1), to muse pensively
2826 klinidiŏn (2), pallet or little couch

COUCHED
3766 kâra' (1), to prostrate
7257 râbats (1), to recline, repose, brood

COUCHES
6210 'eres (1), canopy couch
2895 krabbatŏs (1), sleeping mat

COUCHETH
7257 râbats (1), to recline, repose, brood

COUCHING
7257 râbats (1), to recline, repose, brood

COUCHINGPLACE
4769 marbêts (1), resting place

COULD
3045 yâda' (2), to know
3201 yâkôl (46), to be able
3202 yᵉkêl (Ch.) (1), to be able
3546 kᵉhal (Ch.) (1), to be able
5074 nâdad (1), to rove, flee; to drive away
5234 nâkar (1), to acknowledge
5346 Neqeb (1), dell
102 adunatŏs (1), weak; impossible
1410 dunamai (29), to be able or possible
1415 dunatŏs (1), powerful or capable
2192 ĕchō (3), to have; hold; keep
2480 ischuō (7), to have or exercise force
2489 Iōanna (1), Jehovah-favored
5342 phĕrō (1), to bear or carry

COULDEST
3201 yâkôl (1), to be able
2480 ischuō (1), to have or exercise force

COULDST
3202 yᵉkêl (Ch.) (1), to be able

COULTER
855 'êth (1), digging implement

COULTERS
855 'êth (1), digging implement

COUNCIL
7277 rigmâh (1), throng
4824 sumbŏuliŏn (2), deliberative body
4892 sunĕdriŏn (20), tribunal

COUNCILS
4891 sunĕgĕirō (2), to raise up with

COUNSEL
1697 dâbâr (1), word; matter; thing
3245 yâçad (2), settle, consult
3289 yâ'ats (21), to advise
4431 mᵉlak (Ch.) (1), counsel, advice
5475 çôwd (6), intimacy; consultation; secret
5843 'êṭâ (Ch.) (1), prudence
6098 'êtsâh (80), advice; plan; prudence
8458 tachbûlâh (2), guidance; plan
1011 bŏulĕuō (1), to deliberate; to resolve
1012 bŏulē (9), purpose, plan, decision
4823 sumbŏulĕuō (4), to recommend, deliberate
4824 sumbŏuliŏn (5), deliberative body

COUNSELED
3289 yâ'ats (1), to advise

COUNSELLED
3289 yâ'ats (3), to advise

COUNSELLOR
3289 yâ'ats (10), to advise
6098 'êtsâh (1), advice; plan; prudence
1010 bŏulĕutēs (2), adviser, councillor
4825 sumbŏulŏs (1), adviser

COUNSELLORS
1884 dᵉthâbâr (Ch.) (2), skilled in law; judge
1907 haddâbâr (Ch.) (4), vizier, high official
3272 yᵉ'aṭ (Ch.) (2), to counsel
3289 yâ'ats (12), to advise
6098 'êtsâh (1), advice; plan; prudence

COUNSELS
4156 môw'êtsâh (6), purpose, plan
6098 'êtsâh (2), advice; plan; prudence
8458 tachbûlâh (3), guidance; plan
1012 bŏulē (1), purpose, plan, decision

COUNT
1961 hâyâh (1), to exist, i.e. be or become
2803 châshab (3), to think; to compute
3699 kâçaç (1), to estimate, determine
4487 mânâh (1), to allot; to enumerate or enroll
5414 nâthan (1), to give
5608 çâphar (4), to inscribe; to enumerate
515 axiŏō (1), to deem entitled or fit, worthy
2192 ĕchō (2), to have; hold; keep
2233 hēgĕŏmai (7), to deem, i.e. consider

COUNTED
2803 châshab (18), to think; to compute
5608 çâphar (2), to inscribe; to enumerate
6485 pâqad (3), to visit, care for, count
515 axiŏō (2), to deem entitled or fit, worthy
1075 gĕnĕalŏgĕō (1), trace in genealogy
2192 ĕchō (2), to have; hold; keep
2233 hēgĕŏmai (3), to deem, i.e. consider
2661 kataxiŏō (2), to deem entirely deserving
3049 lŏgizŏmai (3), to credit; to think, regard
4860 sumpsēphizō (1), to compute jointly

COUNTENANCE
639 'aph (1), nose or nostril; face; person
1921 hâdar (1), to favor or honor; to be proud
2122 zîyv (Ch.) (4), cheerfulness
4758 mar'eh (8), appearance; vision
5869 'ayin (1), eye; sight; fountain
6440 pânîym (30), face
8389 tô'ar (1), outline, figure or appearance
2397 idĕa (1), sight
3799 ŏpsis (1), face; appearance
4383 prŏsōpŏn (3), face, presence
4659 skuthrōpŏs (1), gloomy or mournful

COUNTENANCES
4758 mar'eh (2), appearance; vision

COUNTERVAIL
7737 shâvâh (1), to resemble; to adjust

COUNTETH
2803 châshab (2), to think; to compute
5585 psēphizō (1), to compute, estimate

COUNTRIES
776 'erets (48), earth, land, soil; country
5316 nepheth (1), height
5561 chōra (1), space of territory

COUNTRY
127 'ădâmâh (1), soil; land
249 'ezrâch (5), native born
339 'îy (1), dry land; coast; island
776 'erets (91), earth, land, soil; country
1552 gᵉlîylâh (1), circuit or region

2256 chebel (1),
company, band
4725 mâqôwm (1),
general *locality, place*
6521 pᵉrâzîy (1), *rustic*
7704 sâdeh (17), *field*
68 *agrŏs* (8), *farm*land,
countryside
589 *apŏdēmĕŏ* (4), *visit a
foreign land*
1085 *gĕnŏs* (1), *kin,
offspring in kind*
1093 *gē* (2), *soil, region,
whole earth*
3968 *patris* (8),
hometown
4066 *pĕrichŏrŏs* (4),
surrounding country
5561 *chōra* (15), *space of
territory*

COUNTRYMEN
1085 *gĕnŏs* (1), *kin,
offspring in kind*
4853 *sumphulĕtēs* (1), *of
the same country*

COUPLE
2266 châbar (5), *to
fascinate* by spells
6776 tsemed (4), *paired
yoke*
8147 shᵉnayim (1),
two-fold

COUPLED
2266 châbar (7), *to
fascinate* by spells
8382 tâ'am (2), *to be
twinned*, i.e. *duplicate*
8535 tâm (2), *morally
pious; gentle, dear*

COUPLETH
2279 chôbereth (2), *joint*

COUPLING
2279 chôbereth (2), *joint*
4225 machbereth (8),
junction

COUPLINGS
4226 mᵉchabbᵉrâh (1),
joiner

COURAGE
553 'âmats (9), *to be
strong; be courageous*
2388 châzaq (8), *to be
strong; courageous*
3824 lêbâb (1), *heart*
7307 rûwach (1), *breath;
wind; life*-spirit
2294 *tharsŏs* (1),
boldness, courage

COURAGEOUS
533+3820 'ammîyts (1),
strong; mighty; brave
553 'âmats (2), *to be
strong; be courageous*
2388 châzaq (2), *to be
strong; courageous*

COURAGEOUSLY
2388 châzaq (1), *to be
strong; courageous*

COURSE
4131 môwṭ (1), *to slip,
shake, fall*
4256 machălôqeth (19),
section or division
4794 mᵉrûwtsâh (2), *race*
165 *aiōn* (1), *perpetuity,
ever; world*

1408 drŏmŏs (3), *career,
course of life*
2113 *ĕuthudrŏmĕŏ* (1), *to
sail direct*
2183 *ĕphēmĕria* (2),
rotation or class
3313 *mĕrŏs* (1), *division
or share*
4144 *plŏŏs* (2),
navigation, voyage
5143 *trĕchō* (1), *to run or
walk hastily; to strive*
5164 *trŏchŏs* (1), *wheel;
circuitous course of life*

COURSES
2487 chălîyphâh (1),
alternation, change
2988 yâbâl (1), *stream*
4255 machlᵉqâh (Ch.) (1),
section or division
4256 machălôqeth (14),
section or division
4546 mᵉçillâh (1), *main
thoroughfare; viaduct*

COURT
1004 bayith (1), *house;
temple; family, tribe*
2681 châtsîyr (1), *court
or abode*
2691 châtsêr (114),
enclosed yard
5835 'ăzârâh (2),
enclosure; border
5892 'îyr (1), *city, town,
unwalled-village*
833 aulē (1), *palace;
house; courtyard*

COURTEOUS
5391 *philŏphrōn* (1),
kind, well-disposed

COURTEOUSLY
5364 *philanthrōpŏs* (1),
fondly to mankind
5390 *philŏphrŏnŏs* (1),
friendliness of mind

COURTS
2691 châtsêr (24),
enclosed yard

COUSIN
4773 suggĕnēs (1),
relative; countryman

COUSINS
4773 suggĕnēs (1),
relative; countryman

COVENANT
1285 bᵉrîyth (264),
compact, agreement
1242 diathēkē (17),
contract; devisory will

COVENANTBREAKERS
802 asunthĕtŏs (1),
untrustworthy

COVENANTED
3772 kârath (2), *to make
an agreement*
2476 histēmi (1), *to
stand, establish*
4934 suntithĕmai (1), *to
consent, concur, agree*

COVENANTS
1242 diathēkē (3),
contract; devisory will

COVER
2645 châphâh (1), *to
cover; to veil, to encase*

3680 kâçâh (50), *to cover*
4374 mᵉkaçceh (1),
covering
5258 nâçak (4), *to pour a
libation; to anoint*
5526 çâkak (5), *to fence
in; cover over; protect*
5844 'âṭâh (5), *to wrap,
i.e. cover, veil, clothe*
7159 qâram (1), *to cover*
7779 shûwph (1), *to
gape, to overwhelm*
2572 kaluptŏ (2), *to cover*
2619 katakaluptō (1),
cover with a veil
4028 pĕrikaluptŏ (1), *to
cover eyes*

COVERED
1104 bâla' (1), *to
swallow; to destroy*
2645 châphâh (7), *to
cover; to veil, to encase*
2926 ṭâlal (1), *to cover,
roof*
3271 yâ'aṭ (1), *to clothe,
cover*
3680 kâçâh (61), *to cover*
3728 kâphash (1), *to
tread down*
3780 kâsâh (1), *to grow
fat*
3813 lâ'aṭ (1), *to muffle,
cover*
4374 mᵉkaçceh (1),
covering
5526 çâkak (8), *to fence
in; cover over; protect*
5603 çâphan (3), *to hide
by covering; to roof*
5743 'ûwb (1), *to darkly
becloud*
5844 'âṭâh (3), *to wrap,
i.e. cover, veil, clothe*
5848 'âṭaph (1), *to
shroud, clothe*
6632 tsâb (1), *covered
cart*
6823 tsâphâh (5), *to
sheet over with metal*
7159 qâram (1), *to cover*
1943 ĕpikaluptŏ (1), *to
forgive*
2572 kaluptŏ (2), *to cover*
2596 kata (1), *down*
2619 katakaluptō (2),
cover with a veil
4780 sugkaluptō (1), *to
conceal altogether*

COVEREDST
3680 kâçâh (1), *to cover*

COVEREST
3680 kâçâh (1), *to cover*
5844 'âṭâh (1), *to wrap,
i.e. cover, veil, clothe*

COVERETH
3680 kâçâh (20), *to cover*
4374 mᵉkaçceh (2),
covering
5526 çâkak (2), *to fence
in; cover over; protect*
5844 'âṭâh (1), *to wrap,
i.e. cover, veil, clothe*
5848 'âṭaph (1), *to
shroud, i.e. clothe*
2572 kaluptō (1), *to cover*

COVERING
168 'ôhel (1), *tent*

3680 kâçâh (2), *to cover*
3681 kâçûwy (2), *covering*
3682 kᵉçûwth (6), *cover;
veiling*
3875 lôwṭ (1), *veil*
4372 mikçeh (16),
covering
4539 mâçâk (7), *veil;
shield*
4540 mᵉçukkâh (1),
covering
4541 maççêkâh (2), *cast
image); woven coverlet*
4817 merkâb (1), *chariot,
seat in chariot*
5526 çâkak (2), *to fence
in; cover over; protect*
5643 çêther (1), *cover,
shelter*
5844 'âṭâh (1), *to wrap,
i.e. cover, veil, clothe*
6781 tsâmîyd (1),
bracelet; lid
6826 tsippûwy (3),
encasement with metal
4018 pĕribŏlaiŏn (1),
mantle, veil

COVERINGS
4765 marbad (2),
coverlet, covering

COVERS
7184 qâsâh (3), *jug*

COVERT
4329 mêyçâk (1),
covered portico
4563 miçtôwr (1), *refuge,
hiding place*
5520 çôk (1), *hut of
entwined boughs; lair*
5521 çukkâh (1),
tabernacle; shelter
5643 çêther (5), *cover,
shelter*

COVET
183 'âvâh (1), *to wish for,
desire*
2530 châmad (3), *to
delight in; lust for*
1937 ĕpithumĕŏ (2), *to
long for*
2206 zēlŏŏ (2), *to have
warmth of feeling for*

COVETED
2530 châmad (1), *to
delight in; lust for*
1937 ĕpithumĕŏ (1), *to
long for*
3713 ŏrĕgŏmai (1), *to
reach out after, long for*

COVETETH
183 'âvâh (1), *to wish for,
desire*
1214 bâtsa' (1), *to
plunder; to finish*

COVETOUS
1214 bâtsa' (1), *to
plunder; to finish*
866 aphilargurŏs (1), *not
greedy*
4123 plĕŏnĕktēs (4),
eager for gain, greedy
4124 plĕŏnĕxia (1),
fraudulence, extortion
5366 philargurŏs (2),
avaricious

C

COVETOUSNESS
1215 betsa' (10), *plunder; unjust gain*
866 aphilargurŏs (1), *not greedy*
4124 plĕŏnĕxia (8), *fraudulence, avarice*

COVOCATION
4744 miqrâ' (1), *public meeting*

COW
5697 'eglâh (1), *cow calf*
6510 pârâh (2), *heifer*
7794 shôwr (2), *bullock*

COW'S
1241 bâqâr (1), *plowing ox; herd*

COZ
6976 Qôwts (1), *thorns*

COZBI
3579 Kozbîy (2), *false*

CRACKLING
6963 qôwl (1), *voice or sound*

CRACKNELS
5350 niqqud (1), *crumb, morsel; biscuit*

CRAFT
4820 mirmâh (1), *fraud*
1388 dŏlŏs (1), *wile, deceit, trickery*
2039 ĕrgasia (1), *occupation; profit*
3313 mĕrŏs (1), *division or share*
3673 hŏmŏtĕchnŏs (1), *fellow-artificer*
5078 tĕchnē (1), *trade, craft; skill*

CRAFTINESS
6193 'ôrem (1), *stratagem, craftiness*
3834 panŏurgia (4), *trickery or sophistry*

CRAFTSMAN
2976 yâ'ash (1), *to despond, despair*
5079 tĕchnitēs (1), *skilled craftsman*

CRAFTSMEN
2796 chârâsh (5), *skilled fabricator or worker*
5079 tĕchnitēs (2), *skilled craftsman*

CRAFTY
6175 'ârûwm (2), *cunning; clever*
6191 'âram (1), *to be cunning; be prudent*
3835 panŏurgŏs (1), *shrewd, clever*

CRAG
8127 shên (1), *tooth; ivory; cliff*

CRANE
5483 çûwç (2), *horse; bird swallow*

CRASHING
7667 sheber (1), *fracture; ruin*

CRAVED
154 aitĕō (1), *to ask for*

CRAVETH
404 'âkaph (1), *to urge*

CREATE
1254 bârâ' (8), *to create; fashion*

CREATED
1254 bârâ' (33), *to create; fashion*
2936 ktizō (12), *to fabricate, create*

CREATETH
1254 bârâ' (1), *to create; fashion*

CREATION
2937 ktisis (6), *formation*

CREATOR
1254 bârâ' (3), *to create; fashion*
2936 ktizō (1), *to fabricate, create*
2939 ktistēs (1), *founder*

CREATURE
2416 chay (6), *alive; raw; fresh; life*
5315 nephesh (9), *life; breath; soul; wind*
8318 sherets (1), *swarm, teeming mass*
2937 ktisis (11), *formation*
2938 ktisma (2), *created product*

CREATURES
255 'ôach (1), *creature that howls;*
2416 chay (9), *alive; raw; fresh; life*
2938 ktisma (2), *created product*

CREDITOR
1167+4874+3027 ba'al (1), *master; owner; citizen*
5383 nâshâh (1), *to lend or borrow*
1157 danĕistēs (1), *money lender*

CREDITORS
5383 nâshâh (1), *to lend or borrow*

CREEK
2859 kŏlpŏs (1), *lap area; bay*

CREEP
7430 râmas (2), *to glide swiftly, i.e. crawl*
8317 shârats (2), *to wriggle, swarm*
8318 sherets (2), *swarm, teeming mass*
1744+1519 ĕndunō (1), *to sneak in, creep in*

CREEPETH
7430 râmas (9), *to glide swiftly, i.e. crawl*
7431 remes (1), *any rapidly moving animal*
8317 shârats (4), *to wriggle, swarm*

CREEPING
7431 remes (15), *any rapidly moving animal*
8318 sherets (11), *swarm, teeming mass*
2062 hĕrpĕtŏn (3), *reptile*

CREPT
3921 parĕisdunō (1), *to slip in secretly*

CRESCENS
2913 Krēskēs (1), *growing*

CRETE
2914 Krētē (5), *Cretë*

CRETES
2912 Krēs (1), *inhabitant of Crete*

CRETIANS
2912 Krēs (2), *inhabitant of Crete*

CREW
5455 phōnĕō (5), *to emit a sound*

CRIB
18 'êbûwç (3), *manger or stall*

CRIED
2199 zâ'aq (31), *to call out, announce*
2200 ze'îq (Ch.) (1), *to make an outcry, shout*
2980 yâbab (1), *to bawl, cry out*
5414 nâthan (1), *to give*
6817 tsâ'aq (29), *to shriek; to proclaim*
7121 qârâ' (54), *to call out*
7123 qerâ' (Ch.) (3), *to call out*
7321 rûwa' (2), *to shout for alarm or joy*
7768 shâva' (10), *to halloo, call for help*
310 anabŏaō (2), *to cry out*
349 anakrazō (5), *to scream aloud*
863 aphiēmi (1), *to leave; to pardon, forgive*
994 bŏaō (3), *to shout for help*
2019 ĕpiphōnĕō (2), *to exclaim, shout*
2896 krazō (43), *to call aloud*
2905 kraugazō (6), *to clamor, shout*
5455 phōnĕō (5), *to emit a sound*

CRIES
995 bŏē (1), *to call for aid*

CRIEST
2199 zâ'aq (2), *to call out, announce*
6817 tsâ'aq (1), *to shriek; to proclaim*
7121 qârâ' (2), *to call out*

CRIETH
2199 zâ'aq (1), *to call out, announce*
5414+6963 nâthan (1), *to give*
6817 tsâ'aq (2), *to shriek; to proclaim*
7121 qârâ' (4), *to call out*
7442 rânan (3), *to shout for joy*
7768 shâva' (2), *to halloo, call for help*
2896 krazō (4), *to call aloud*

CRIME
2154 zimmâh (1), *bad plan*
1462 ĕgklēma (1), *accusation*

CRIMES
4941 mishpâṭ (1), *verdict; formal decree; justice*
156 aitia (1), *logical reason; legal crime*

CRIMSON
3758 karmîyl (3), *carmine, deep red*
8144 shânîy (1), *crimson dyed stuffs*
8438 tôwlâ' (1), *maggot worm; crimson-grub*

CRIPPLE
5560 chōlŏs (1), *limping, crippled*

CRISPING
2754 chârîyṭ (1), *pocket*

CRISPUS
2921 Krispŏs (2), *crisp*

CROOKBACKT
1384 gibbên (1), *hunch-backed*

CROOKED
1281 bârîyach (1), *fleeing, gliding serpent*
1921 hâdar (1), *to favor or honor; to be high*
4625 ma'ăqâsh (1), *crook in a road*
5753 'âvâh (1), *to be crooked*
5791 'âvath (2), *to wrest, twist*
6121 'âqôb (1), *fraudulent; tracked*
6128 'ăqalqal (1), *crooked*
6129 'ăqallâthôwn (1), *crooked*
6140 'âqash (1), *to knot or distort; to pervert*
6141 'iqqêsh (1), *distorted, warped, false*
6618 pethaltôl (1), *tortuous, perverse*
4646 skŏliŏs (2), *crooked; perverse*

CROP
4760 mur'âh (1), *craw or crop of a bird*
6998 qâṭaph (1), *to strip off, pick off*

CROPPED
6998 qâṭaph (1), *to strip off, pick off*

CROSS
4716 staurŏs (28), *pole or cross*

CROSSWAY
6563 pereq (1), *rapine; fork in roads*

CROUCH
7812 shâchâh (1), *to prostrate in homage*

CROUCHETH
1794 dâkâh (1), *to collapse; contrite*

CROW
5455 phōnĕō (7), *to emit a sound*

CROWN
2213 zêr (10), border molding on a building
3804 kether (3), royal headdress
5145 nezer (11), royal chaplet
5850 'ăṭârâh (20), crown
6936 qodqôd (7), crown of the head
4735 stĕphanŏs (15), chaplet, wreath

CROWNED
3803 kâthar (1), to enclose, besiege; to wait
4502 minnᵉzâr (1), prince
5849 'âṭar (2), to encircle, enclose in; to crown
4737 stephanŏŏ (2), to adorn with a wreath

CROWNEDST
4737 stephanŏŏ (1), to adorn with a wreath

CROWNEST
5849 'âṭar (1), to encircle, enclose in; to crown

CROWNETH
5849 'âṭar (1), to encircle, enclose in; to crown

CROWNING
5849 'âṭar (1), to encircle, enclose in; to crown

CROWNS
5850 'ăṭârâh (3), crown
1238 diadēma (3), crown or diadem
4735 stĕphanŏs (3), chaplet, wreath

CRUCIFIED
4362 prŏspēgnumi (1), to fasten to a cross
4717 staurŏŏ (31), to crucify
4957 sustaurŏŏ (5), to crucify with

CRUCIFY
388 anastaurŏŏ (1), to re-crucify
4717 staurŏŏ (13), to crucify

CRUEL
393 'akzâr (3), violent, deadly; brave
394 'akzârîy (8), terrible, cruel
395 'akzᵉrîyûwth (1), fierceness, cruelty
2555 châmâç (1), violence; malice
2556 châmêts (1), to be fermented; be soured
7185 qâshâh (2), to be tough or severe
7186 qâsheh (1), severe

CRUELLY
6233 'ôsheq (1), injury; fraud; distress

CRUELTY
2555 châmâç (4), violence; malice
6531 perek (1), severity

CRUMBS
5589 psichiŏn (3), little bit or morsel

CRUSE
1228 baqbûk (1), bottle
6746 tsᵉlôchîyth (1), vial or salt-cellar
6835 tsappachath (7), flat saucer

CRUSH
1792 dâkâ' (1), to pulverize; be contrite
2115 zûwr (1), to press together, tighten
7533 râtsats (1), to crack in pieces, smash
7665 shâbar (1), to burst

CRUSHED
1792 dâkâ' (2), to pulverize; be contrite
2000 hâmam (1), to disturb, drive, destroy
2116 zûwreh (1), trodden on
3807 kâthath (1), to bruise, strike, beat
3905 lâchats (1), to press; to distress
7533 râtsats (1), to crack in pieces, smash

CRY
602 'ânaq (3), to shriek, cry out in groaning
1993 hâmâh (1), to be in great commotion
2199 zâ'aq (25), to call out, announce
2201 za'aq (18), shriek, outcry, lament
5414+6963 nâthan (1), to give
6030 'ânâh (2), to respond, answer
6165 'ârag (1), to long for, pant for
6463 pâ'âh (1), to scream in childbirth
6670 tsâhal (3), to be cheerful; to sound
6682 tsᵉvâchâh (2), screech of anguish
6817 tsâ'aq (15), to shriek; to proclaim
6818 tsa'ăqâh (19), shriek, wail
6873 tsârach (1), to whoop
6963 qôwl (1), voice or sound
7121 qârâ' (37), to call out
7321 rûwa' (5), to shout for alarm or joy
7440 rinnâh (12), shout
7442 rânan (1), to shout for joy
7768 shâva' (8), to call for help
7769 shûwa' (1), call
7773 sheva' (1), call
7775 shav'âh (11), call
8173 shâ'a' (1), to fondle, please or amuse (self)
994 bŏaŏ (2), to shout for help
2896 krazŏ (3), to call
2905 kraugazŏ (1), to clamor, shout
2906 kraugē (3), outcry

CRYING
603 'ănâqâh (1), shrieking, groaning
2201 za'aq (2), shriek, outcry, lament
4191 mûwth (1), to die; to kill
6682 tsᵉvâchâh (1), screech of anguish
6818 tsa'ăqâh (2), shriek, wail
7121 qârâ' (1), to call out
7771 shôwa' (1), call
8663 tᵉshû'âh (1), crashing or clamor
310 anabŏaŏ (1), to cry out
994 bŏaŏ (6), to shout for help
1916 ĕpibŏaŏ (1), to cry out loudly
2896 krazŏ (9), to call
2906 kraugē (2), outcry

CRYSTAL
2137 zᵉkûwkîyth (1), transparent glass
7140 qerach (1), ice; hail; rock crystal
2929 krustallizŏ (1), to appear as ice
2930 krustallŏs (2), rock crystal

CUBIT
520 'ammâh (35), cubit
1574 gômed (1), measurement of length
4083 pēchus (2), measure of time or length

CUBITS
520 'ammâh (197), cubit
521 'ammâh (Ch.) (4), cubit
4088 pikria (2), acridity, bitterness

CUCKOW
7828 shachaph (2), gull

CUCUMBERS
4750 miqshâh (1), cucumber field
7180 qishshu' (1), cucumber

CUD
1625 gêrâh (11), cud

CUMBERED
4049 pĕrispaŏ (1), to be distracted

CUMBERETH
2673 katargĕŏ (1), to be, render entirely useless

CUMBRANCE
2960 ṭôrach (1), burden

CUMI
2891 kŏumi (1), rise!

CUMMIN
3646 kammôn (3), cummin
2951 kuminŏn (1), dill or fennel

CUNNING
542 'âmân (1), expert artisan, craftsman
995 bîyn (1), to understand; discern
1847 da'ath (1), understanding

CUP
1375 gᵉbîya (4), goblet; bowl
3563 kôwç (29), cup; (poss.) owl
3599 kîyç (1), cup; utility bag
5592 çaph (1), dish
4221 pŏtēriŏn (31), drinking-vessel

CUPBEARER
4945 mashqeh (1), butler; drink; well-watered

CUPBEARERS
4945 mashqeh (2), butler; drink; well-watered

CUPS
101 'aggân (1), bowl
3563 kôwç (1), cup
4518 mᵉnaqqîyth (1), sacrificial basin
7184 qâsâh (1), jug
4221 pŏtēriŏn (2), drinking-vessel

CURDLED
7087 qâphâ' (1), to thicken, congeal

CURE
1455 gâhâh (1), to heal
7495 râphâ' (1), to cure, heal
2323 thĕrapĕuŏ (2), to relieve disease

CURED
8585 tᵉ'âlâh (1), bandage or plaster
2323 thĕrapĕuŏ (3), to relieve disease

CURES
2392 iasis (1), curing

CURIOUS
4284 machăshâbâh (1), contrivance; plan
4021 pĕriĕrgŏs (1), meddlesome, busybody

CURIOUSLY
7551 râqam (1), variegation; embroider

CURRENT
5674 'âbar (1), to cross over; to transition

CURSE
423 'âlâh (9), imprecation: curse
779 'ârar (15), to execrate, place a curse
1288 bârak (3), to bless
2764 chêrem (4), doomed object
3994 mᵉ'êrâh (4), execration, curse
5344 nâqab (4), to specify, designate, libel
6895 qâbab (7), to stab with words
7043 qâlal (17), to be easy, trifling, vile

CROWN
2450 châkâm (10), wise, intelligent, skillful
2803 châshab (11), to plot; to think, regard
3045 yâda' (4), to know
4284 machăshâbâh (3), contrivance; plan

CURSED

7045 qᵉlâlâh (24),
vilification
7621 shᵉbûw'âh (1),
sworn oath
8381 ta'ălâh (1),
imprecation
332 anathĕmatizō (3), to
declare or *vow an oath*
2652 katanathĕma (1),
imprecation
2653 katanathĕmatizō
(1), to *imprecate*
2671 katara (3),
imprecation, execration
2672 kataraŏmai (4), to
execrate, curse

CURSED

779 'ârar (44), to
execrate, place a curse
1288 bârak (1), to *bless*
2764 chêrem (3),
doomed object
5344 nâqab (1), to
specify, designate, libel
6895 qâbab (1), to *stab
with words*
7043 qâlal (17), to *be
easy, trifling, vile*
1944 ĕpikataratŏs (3),
execrable, cursed
2671 katara (1),
imprecation, execration
2672 kataraŏmai (1), to
execrate, curse

CURSEDST

422 'âlâh (1), *imprecate,
utter a curse*
2672 kataraŏmai (1), to
execrate, curse

CURSES

423 'âlâh (5),
imprecation: curse
7045 qᵉlâlâh (3),
vilification

CURSEST

779 'ârar (1), to *execrate,
place a curse*

CURSETH

779 'ârar (2), to *execrate,
place a curse*
7043 qâlal (6), to *be easy,
trifling, vile*
2551 kakŏlŏgĕō (2), to
revile, curse

CURSING

423 'âlâh (4),
imprecation: curse
3994 mᵉ'êrâh (1),
execration, curse
7045 qᵉlâlâh (4),
vilification
685 ara (1), *imprecation,
curse*
2671 katara (2),
imprecation, execration

CURSINGS

7045 qᵉlâlâh (1),
vilification

CURTAIN

1852 dôq (1), *fine, thin*
cloth
3407 yᵉrîy'âh (23),
drapery
4539 mâçâk (1), *veil;
shield*

CURTAINS

3407 yᵉrîy'âh (31),
drapery

CUSH

3568 Kûwsh (8), *Cush*

CUSHAN

3572 Kûwshân (1),
Cushan

CUSHI

3569 Kûwshîy (10),
Cushite

CUSTODY

3027 yâd (4), *hand; power*
6486 pᵉquddâh (1),
visitation; punishment

CUSTOM

1870 derek (1), *road;
mode of action*
1983 hălâk (Ch.) (3), *toll,
duty on goods at a road*
2706 chôq (2),
appointment; allotment
4941 mishpâṭ (2), *verdict;
formal decree; justice*
1480 ĕthizō (1),
customary, required
1485 ĕthŏs (2), *usage*
3588+1486 hŏ (1), *"the"*
i.e. the definite article
4914 sunētheia (2),
usage, custom
5056 tĕlŏs (2), *conclusion*
of an act or state
5058 tĕlōniŏn (3),
tax-gatherer's booth

CUSTOMS

2708 chuqqâh (2), to
delineate
1485 ĕthŏs (5), *usage*

CUT

1214 bâtsa' (3), to
plunder; to finish
1219 bâtsar (1), to *be
inaccessible*
1254 bârâ' (2), to *create;
fashion*
1413 gâdad (5), to *gash,
slash oneself*
1438 gâda' (21), to *fell a
tree; to destroy*
1494 gâzaz (2), to *shear;
shave; destroy*
1504 gâzar (8), to *cut
down; to destroy*
1505 gᵉzar (Ch.) (2), to
quarry rock
1629 gâraz (1), to *cut off*
1820 dâmâh (5), to *be
silent; to fail, cease*
1826 dâmam (5), to *stop,
cease; to perish*
2404 châṭab (1), to *chop
or carve wood*
2498 châlaph (1), to
pierce; to change
2672 châtsab (1), to *cut
stone or carve wood*
2686 châtsats (1), to
curtail
3582 kâchad (10), to
destroy; to hide
3683 kâçach (2), to *cut off*
3772 kârath (175), to *cut
(off, down or asunder)*
4135 mûwl (2), to
circumcise

5243 nâmal (4), to *be
circumcised*
5352 nâqâh (2), to *be,
make clean; to be bare*
5362 nâqaph (1), to
strike; to surround
5408 nâthach (7), to
dismember, cut up
5648 'âbad (Ch.) (2), to
do, work, serve
5927 'âlâh (1), to *ascend,
be high, mount*
6780 tsemach (1), *sprout,
branch*
6789 tsâmath (7), to
extirpate, destroy
6990 qâṭaṭ (1), to *destroy*
6998 qâṭaph (2), to *strip
off, pick off*
7059 qâmaṭ (1), to *pluck,
i.e. destroy*
7082 qâçaç (1), to *lop off*
7088 qâphad (1), to *roll
together*
7094 qâtsab (1), to *clip,
or chop*
7096 qâtsâh (1), to *cut
off; to destroy*
7112 qâtsats (10), to *chop
off; to separate*
7113 qᵉtsats (Ch.) (1), to
chop off, lop off
7167 qâra' (1), to *rend*
7787 sûwr (1), to *saw*
8295 sâraṭ (1), to *gash
oneself*
8456 tâzaz (1), to *lop off*
581 apŏgĕnŏmĕnŏs (1),
deceased
609 apŏkŏptō (6),
mutilate the genitals
851 aphairĕō (1), to
remove, cut off
1282 diapriō (2), to *be
furious*
1371 dichŏtŏmĕō (2), to
flog severely
1581 ĕkkŏptō (7), to *cut
off; to frustrate*
2875 kŏptō (2), to *beat
the breast*
4932 suntĕmnō (1), to *cut
short, i.e. do speedily*

CUTH

3575 Kûwth (1), *Cuth or
Cuthah*

CUTHAH

3575 Kûwth (1), *Cuth or
Cuthah*

CUTTEST

7114 qâtsar (1), to
curtail, cut short

CUTTETH

1234 bâqa' (1), to *cleave,
break, tear open*
3772 kârath (1), to *cut
(off, down or asunder)*
6398 pâlach (1), to *slice;
to break open; to pierce*
7096 qâtsâh (1), to *cut
off; to destroy*
7112 qâtsats (1), to *chop
off; to separate*
7167 qâra' (1), to *rend*

CUTTING

1824 dᵉmîy (1), *quiet,
peacefulness*

2799 chărôsheth (2),
skilled work
7096 qâtsâh (1), to *cut
off; to destroy*
2629 katakŏptō (1), to
mangle, cut up

CUTTINGS

1417 gᵉdûwd (1), *furrow
ridge*
8296 sereṭ (2), *incision*

CYMBAL

2950 kumbalŏn (1),
cymbal

CYMBALS

4700 mᵉtsêleth (13), *pair
of cymbals*
6767 tsᵉlâtsal (3),
whirring

CYPRESS

8645 tirzâh (1), (poss.)
cypress

CYPRUS

2954 Kuprŏs (8), *Cyprus*

CYRENE

2957 Kurēnē (4), *Cyrenë*

CYRENIAN

2956 Kurēnaiŏs (2),
inhabitant of Cyrene

CYRENIANS

2956 Kurēnaiŏs (1),
inhabitant of Cyrene

CYRENIUS

2958 Kurēniŏs (1),
Quirinus

CYRUS

3566 Kôwresh (15),
Koresh
3567 Kôwresh (Ch.) (8),
Koresh

DABAREH

1705 Dâbᵉrath (1),
Daberath

DABBASHETH

1708 Dabbesheth (1),
hump of a camel

DABERATH

1705 Dâbᵉrath (2),
Daberath

DAGGER

2719 chereb (3), *knife,
sword*

DAGON

1712 Dâgôwn (11),
fish-god

DAGON'S

1712 Dâgôwn (1),
fish-god

DAILY

3117 yôwm (20), *day;
time period*
3117+259 yôwm (1), *day;
time period*
3119 yôwmâm (2), *daily*
3605+3117 kôl (11), *all,
any or every*
8548 tâmîyd (7),
constantly, regularly
1967 ĕpiŏusiŏs (2), *for
subsistence, i.e. needful*
2184 ĕphēmĕrŏs (1),
diurnal, i.e. daily
2522 kathēmĕrinŏs (1),
quotidian, i.e. daily

2596+1538+2250 kata (1),
down; according to
2596+2250 kata (15),
down; according to
2596+3956+2250 kata (1),
down; according to
3956+2250 pas (1), all,
any, every, whole

DAINTIES
4303 mat'am (1), delicacy
4516 man'am (1),
delicacy eaten
4574 ma'ădân (1),
delicacy; pleasure

DAINTY
4303 mat'am (1), delicacy
8378 ta'ăvâh (1), longing;
delight
3045 liparŏs (1), costly,
rich

DALAIAH
1806 Dᵉlâyâh (1),
Jehovah has delivered

DALE
6010 'êmeq (2), broad
depression or valley

DALMANUTHA
1148 Dalmanŏutha (1),
Dalmanutha

DALMATIA
1149 Dalmatia (1),
Dalmatia

DALPHON
1813 Dalphôwn (1),
dripping

DAM
517 'êm (5), mother

DAMAGE
2257 chăbal (Ch.) (1),
harm, wound
2555 châmâç (1),
violence; malice
5142 nᵉzaq (Ch.) (1), to
suffer, inflict loss
5143 nêzeq (1), injure,
loss
2209 zēmia (1),
detriment; loss
2210 zēmiŏō (1), to
experience detriment

DAMARIS
1152 Damaris (1), gentle

DAMASCENES
1159 dapanaŏ (1), to
incur cost; to waste

DAMASCUS
1833 dᵉmesheq (1),
damask fabric
1834 Dammeseq (44),
Damascus
1154 Damaskŏs (15),
Damascus

DAMNABLE
684 apŏlĕia (1), ruin or
loss

DAMNATION
684 apŏlĕia (1), ruin or
loss
2917 krima (7), decision
2920 krisis (3), decision;
tribunal; justice

DAMNED
2632 katakrinŏ (2), to
judge against

2919 krinō (1), to decide;
to try, condemn, punish

DAMSEL
3207 yaldâh (1), young
female
5291 na'ărâh (24),
female child; servant
7356 racham (1), womb;
maiden
2877 kŏrasiŏn (6), little
girl
3813 paidiŏn (4), child:
boy or girl; immature
3814 paidiskē (4), female
slave or servant

DAMSEL'S
5291 na'ărâh (8), female
child; servant

DAMSELS
5291 na'ărâh (2), female
child; servant
5959 'almâh (1), lass,
young woman

DAN
1835 Dân (71), judge

DAN-JAAN
1842 Dân Ya'an (1),
judge of purpose

DANCE
2342 chûwl (1), to dance,
whirl; to writhe
4234 mâchôwl (4),
(round) dance
7540 râqad (3), to spring
about wildly or for joy

DANCED
2342 chûwl (1), to dance,
whirl; to writhe in pain;
to wait; to pervert
3769 kârar (1), to dance
in whirling motion
3738 ŏrchĕŏmai (4), to
dance

DANCES
4246 mᵉchôwlâh (5),
round-dance

DANCING
2287 châgag (1), to
observe a festival
3769 kârar (1), to dance
in whirling motion
4234 mâchôwl (1),
(round) dance
4246 mᵉchôwlâh (2),
round-dance
7540 râqad (1), to spring
about wildly or for joy
5525 chŏrŏs (1), round
dance; dancing

DANDLED
8173 shâ'a' (1), to fondle,
please or amuse (self)

DANGER
1777 ĕnŏchŏs (5), liable
2793 kindunĕuŏ (2), to
undergo peril

DANGEROUS
2000 ĕpisphalēs (1),
insecure, unsafe

DANIEL
1840 Dânîyê'l (29), judge
of God
1841 Dânîyê'l (Ch.) (50),
judge of God

1158 Daniēl (2), judge of
God

DANITES
1839 Dâniy (4), Danite

DANNAH
1837 Dannâh (1), Dannah

DARA
1873 Dâra' (1), Dara

DARDA
1862 Darda' (1), pearl of
knowledge

DARE
5111 tŏlmaŏ (4), to be
bold; to dare

DARIUS
1867 Dârᵉyâvêsh (10),
Darejavesh
1868 Dârᵉyâvêsh (Ch.)
(15), Darejavesh

DARK
651 'âphêl (1), dusky,
dark
653 'ăphêlâh (1),
duskiness, darkness
2420 chîydâh (5), puzzle;
conundrum; maxim
2821 châshak (5), to be
dark; to darken
2822 chôshek (7),
darkness; misery
2824 cheshkâh (1),
darkness, dark
2841 chashrâh (1),
gathering of clouds
3544 kêheh (5), feeble;
obscure
4285 machshâk (3),
darkness; dark place
5399 nesheph (1), dusk,
dawn
5939 'ălâtâh (1), dusk
6205 'ărâphel (2), gloom,
darkness
6751 tsâlal (1), to shade;
to grow dark
6937 qâdar (4), to be
dark-colored
7087 qâphâ' (1), to
thicken, congeal
850 auchmĕrŏs (1),
obscure, dark
4652 skŏtĕinŏs (1), dark,
very dark
4653 skŏtia (2), dimness

DARKEN
2821 châshak (1), to be
dark; to darken

DARKENED
2821 châshak (7), to be
dark; to darken
3543 kâhâh (1), to grow
dull, fade; to be faint
6150 'ârab (1), to grow
dusky at sundown
6272 'âtham (1), be
desolated by scorching
6937 qâdar (1), to be
dark-colored
4654 skŏtizŏ (8), to be,
become dark

DARKENETH
2821 châshak (1), to be
dark; to darken

DARKISH
3544 kêheh (1), feeble;
obscure

DARKLY
1722+135 ĕn (1), in;
during; because of

DARKNESS
652 'ôphel (6), dusk,
darkness
653 'ăphêlâh (6),
duskiness, darkness
2816 chăshôwk (Ch.) (1),
dark, darkness
2821 châshak (1), to be
dark; to darken
2822 chôshek (69),
darkness; misery
2825 chăshêkâh (5),
darkness; misery
3990 ma'ăphêl (1),
opaque, dark
3991 ma'phêlᵉyâh (1),
opaqueness, darkness
4285 machshâk (4),
darkness; dark place
5890 'êyphâh (2),
covering of darkness
6205 'ărâphel (13),
gloom, darkness
2217 zŏphŏs (2), gloom
4652 skŏtĕinŏs (2), dark,
very dark
4653 skŏtia (13), dimness
4655 skŏtŏs (31),
darkness
4656 skŏtŏō (1), to make
dark, i.e. blind

DARKON
1874 Darqôwn (2),
Darkon

DARLING
3173 yâchîyd (2), only
son; alone; beloved

DART
2671 chêts (1), arrow;
wound; shaft of a spear
4551 maççâ' (1), stone
quarry; projectile
1002 bŏlis (1), javelin,
projectile

DARTS
7626 shêbet (1), stick;
clan, family
7973 shelach (1), spear;
shoot of growth
8455 tôwthâch (1), stout
club
956 bĕlŏs (1), spear or
arrow

DASH
5062 nâgaph (1), to strike
5310 nâphats (2), to dash
to pieces; to scatter
7376 râtash (2), to dash
down
4350 prŏskŏptō (2), to
trip up; to strike

DASHED
7376 râtash (4), to dash
down
7492 râ'ats (1), to break
in pieces; to harass

DASHETH
5310 nâphats (1), to dash
to pieces; to scatter

6327 pûwts (1), to *dash in pieces*; to *disperse*

DATHAN
1885 Dâthân (10), *Dathan*

DAUB
2902 tûwach (1), to *whitewash*

DAUBED
2560 châmar (1), to *glow*; to *smear*
2902 tûwach (6), to *whitewash*

DAUBING
2915 tîyach (1), *plaster, whitewash coating*

DAUGHTER
1004 bayith (1), *house; temple; family, tribe*
1121 bên (1), *son, descendant*
1323 bath (270), *daughter, descendant*
3618 kallâh (13), *bride; son's wife*
2364 thugatĕr (24), *female child*
2365 thugatriŏn (2), *little daughter*
3565 numphē (3), *young married woman*

DAUGHTER'S
1323 bath (3), *daughter, descendant, woman*

DAUGHTERS
1121 bên (244), *son, descendant*
3618 kallâh (3), *bride*
2364 thugatĕr (5), *female child,* or *descendant*
5043 tĕknŏn (1), *child*

DAVID
1732 Dâvîd (1019), *loving*
1138 Dabid (58), *loving*

DAVID'S
1732 Dâvîd (53), *loving*
1138 Dabid (1), *loving*

DAWN
1306 diaugazŏ (1), to *dawn, shine through*
2020 ĕpiphŏskŏ (1), to *grow light*

DAWNING
5399 nesheph (2), *dusk, dawn*
5927 'âlâh (1), to *ascend, be high, mount*
6079 'aph'aph (1), *morning ray*
6437 pânâh (1), to *turn, to face*

DAY
215 'ôwr (1), to *be luminous*
216 'ôwr (1), *luminary; lightning; happiness*
1242 bôqer (4), *morning*
3117 yôwm (1250), *day; time period*
3118 yôwm (Ch.) (4), *day; time period*
3119 yôwmâm (53), *daily*
4283 mochŏrâth (2), *tomorrow, next day*
5399 nesheph (1), *dusk, dawn*

7837 shachar (6), *dawn*
737 arti (1), *just now; at once*
827 augē (1), *radiance, dawn*
839 auriŏn (1), *to-morrow*
1773 ĕnnuchŏn (1), *by night*
1887 ĕpauriŏn (8), *to-morrow*
2250 hēmera (200), *day; period of time*
3574 nuchthēmĕrŏn (1), *full day*
3588+2596+2250 hŏ (2), *"the,"* definite article
4594 sēmĕrŏn (38), *this day, today, now*
4594+2250 sēmĕrŏn (1), *this day, today, now*
4595 sēpŏ (1), to *putrefy, rot*
5459 phŏsphŏrŏs (1), *morning-star*
5610 hōra (1), *hour,* i.e. a *unit of time*

DAY'S
3117 yôwm (6), *day; time period*
2250 hēmera (1), *day; period of time*
4594 sēmĕrŏn (1), *this day, today, now*

DAYS
3117 yôwm (665), *day; time period*
3118 yôwm (Ch.) (9), *day; time period*
8543 tĕmôwl (1), (day before) *yesterday*
1909 ĕpi (2), *on, upon*
2250 hēmera (154), *day; period of time*
5066 tĕtartaiŏs (1), *of the fourth day*

DAYS'
3117 yôwm (13), *day; time period*

DAYSMAN
3198 yâkach (1), to *decide, justify, convict*

DAYSPRING
7837 shachar (1), *dawn*
395 anatŏlē (1), *dawn of sun; east*

DAYTIME
3119 yôwmâm (8), *daily*

DEACON
1247 diakŏnĕŏ (2), to *act as a deacon*

DEACONS
1249 diakŏnŏs (3), *attendant, deacon(-ess)*

DEAD
1472 gᵉvîyâh (1), *dead body*
1478 gâva' (1), to *expire, die*
4191 mûwth (136), to *die; to kill*
4194 mâveth (7), *death; dead*
5038 nᵉbêlâh (7), *carcase or carrion*
5315 nephesh (8), *life; breath; soul; wind*

6297 peger (6), *carcase; corpse*
7496 râphâ' (7), *dead*
7703 shâdad (1), to *ravage*
581 apŏgĕnŏmĕnŏs (1), *deceased*
599 apŏthnēskŏ (29), to *die off*
2258 ēn (1), I *was*
2289 thanatŏŏ (1), to *kill*
2348 thnēskŏ (12), to *die, be dead*
2837 kŏimaŏ (1), to *slumber; to decease*
3498 nĕkrŏs (130), *corpse; dead*
3499 nĕkrŏŏ (2), to *deaden,* i.e. to *subdue*
4430 ptōma (3), *corpse, carrion*
4880 sunapŏthnēskŏ (1), to *decease with*
5053 tĕlĕutaŏ (3), to *finish life,* i.e. *expire*

DEADLY
4194 mâveth (1), *death; dead*
5315 nephesh (1), *life; breath; soul; wind*
2286 thanasimŏs (1), *poisonous, deadly*
2287 thanatēphŏrŏs (1), *fatal,* i.e. *bringing death*
2288 thanatŏs (2), *death*

DEADNESS
3500 nĕkrŏsis (1), *death, deadness*

DEAF
2790 chârash (1), to *be silent; to be deaf*
2795 chêrêsh (9), *deaf*
2974 kōphŏs (5), *deaf* or *silent*

DEAL
1580 gâmal (2), to *benefit or requite; to wean*
6213 'âsâh (26), to *do*
6536 pâraç (1), to *split, distribute*
4054 pĕrissŏtĕrŏn (1), *more superabundantly*

DEALEST
6213 'âsâh (1), to *do*

DEALETH
6213 'âsâh (7), to *do*
4374 prŏsphĕrŏ (1), to *present to; to treat as*

DEALINGS
1697 dâbâr (1), *word; matter; thing*
4798 sugchraŏmai (1), to *have dealings with*

DEALT
1580 gâmal (2), to *benefit or requite; to wean*
2505 châlaq (2), to *be smooth; be slippery*
6213 'âsâh (18), to *do* or *make*
1793 ĕntugchanŏ (1), to *entreat, petition*
2686 katasŏphizŏmai (1), to *be crafty against*
3307 mĕrizŏ (1), to *apportion, bestow*

4160 pŏiĕŏ (2), to *do*

DEAR
3357 yaqqîyr (1), *precious*
26 agapē (1), *love*
27 agapētŏs (3), *beloved*
1784 ĕntimŏs (1), *valued, considered precious*
5093 timiŏs (1), *honored, esteemed,* or *beloved*

DEARTH
1226 batstsŏreth (1), *drought*
7458 râ'âb (5), *hunger*
3042 limŏs (2), *scarcity, famine*

DEATH
4191 mûwth (82), to *die; to kill*
4192 Mûwth (1), *"To die for the son"*
4193 môwth (Ch.) (1), *death*
4194 mâveth (126), *death; dead*
6757 tsalmâveth (18), *shade of death*
7523 râtsach (1), to *murder*
8546 tᵉmûwthâh (1), *execution, death*
336 anairĕsis (5), *act of killing*
337 anairĕŏ (2), to *take away,* i.e. to *abolish, murder*
520 apagŏ (1), to *take away*
599 apŏthnēskŏ (1), to *die off*
615 apŏktĕinŏ (6), to *kill outright; to destroy*
1935 ĕpithanatiŏs (1), *doomed to death*
2079 ĕschatŏs (1), *finally,* i.e. *at the extremity*
2288 thanatŏs (113), *death*
2289 thanatŏŏ (7), to *kill*
5054 tĕlĕutē (1), *deceasedness, death*

DEATHS
4194 mâveth (1), *death; dead*
4463 mâmôwth (2), *mortal disease, death*
2288 thanatŏs (1), *death*

DEBASE
8213 shâphêl (1), to *humiliate*

DEBATE
4683 matstsâh (1), *quarrel*
7378 rîyb (2), to *hold a controversy; to defend*
2054 ĕris (1), *quarrel,* i.e. *wrangling*

DEBATES
2054 ĕris (1), *quarrel,* i.e. *wrangling*

DEBIR
1688 Dᵉbîyr (14), *inmost part of the sanctuary*

DEBORAH
1683 Dᵉbôwrâh (10), *bee*

DEBT
3027 yâd (1), *hand; power*

5378 nâshâ' (1), to *lend
on interest*
5386 nᵉshîy (1), *debt*
1156 danĕiŏn (1), *loan;
debt*
3782 ŏphĕilē (1), *sum
owed; obligation*
3783 ŏphĕilēma (1), *due;
moral fault*
3784 ŏphĕilō (1), to *owe;
to be under obligation*

DEBTOR
2326 chôwb (1), *debt*
3781 ŏphĕilĕtēs (2),
person indebted
3784 ŏphĕilō (1), to *owe;
to be under obligation*

DEBTORS
3781 ŏphĕilĕtēs (3),
person indebted
5533 chrĕŏphĕilĕtēs (2),
indebted person

DEBTS
4859 mashshâ'âh (1),
secured loan
3783 ŏphĕilēma (1), *due;
moral fault*

DECAPOLIS
1179 Dĕkapŏlis (3),
ten-city region

DECAY
4131 môwṭ (1), to *slip,
shake, fall*

DECAYED
2723 chorbâh (1),
desolation, dry desert
3782 kâshal (1), to *totter,
waver; to falter*

DECAYETH
2717 chârab (1), to
parch; desolate, destroy
4355 mâkak (1), to
tumble in ruins
3822 palaiŏō (1), to
become worn out

DECEASE
1841 ĕxŏdŏs (2), *exit*, i.e.
death

DECEASED
7496 râphâ' (1), *dead*
5053 tĕlĕutaō (1), to
finish life, i.e. *expire*

DECEIT
4820 mirmâh (19), *fraud*
4860 mashshâ'ôwn (1),
dissimulation
7423 rᵉmîyâh (2),
remissness; treachery
8267 sheqer (1), *untruth*
8496 tôk (2), *oppression*
8649 tormâh (4), *fraud*
539 apatē (1), *delusion*
1387 dŏliŏō (1), to
practice deceit
1388 dŏlŏs (2), *wile,
deceit, trickery*
4106 planē (1),
fraudulence; straying

DECEITFUL
3577 kâzâb (1),
falsehood; idol
4820 mirmâh (8), *fraud*
6121 'âqôb (1),
fraudulent; tracked

6280 'âthar (1), to *be,
make abundant*
7423 rᵉmîyâh (4),
remissness; treachery
8267 sheqer (2), *untruth;
sham*
8501 tâkâk (1), to
dissever, i.e. *crush*
8649 tormâh (1), *fraud*
539 apatē (1), *delusion*
1386 dŏliŏs (1), *guileful,
tricky*

DECEITFULLY
898 bâgad (2), to *act
covertly*
2048 hâthal (1), to
deride, mock
4820 mirmâh (3), *fraud*
6231 'âshaq (1), to
oppress; to defraud
7423 rᵉmîyâh (3),
remissness; treachery
1389 dŏlŏō (1), to
adulterate, falsify

DECEITFULNESS
539 apatē (3), *delusion*

DECEITS
4123 mahăthallâh (1),
delusion
4820 mirmâh (1), *fraud*

DECEIVABLENESS
539 apatē (1), *delusion*

DECEIVE
2048 hâthal (1), to
deride, mock
3884 lûwlê' (1), *if not*
5377 nâshâ' (7), to *lead
astray, to delude*
6601 pâthâh (2), to *be,
make simple; to delude*
7952 shâlah (1), to
mislead
538 apataō (1), to *cheat,
delude*
1818 ĕxapataō (3), to
seduce wholly, deceive
4105 planaō (10), to
wander; to deceive
4106 planē (1),
fraudulence; straying

DECEIVED
2048 hâthal (2), to
deride, mock
5377 nâshâ' (5), to *lead
astray, to delude*
6231 'âshaq (1), to
oppress; to defraud
6601 pâthâh (6), to *be,
make simple; to delude*
7411 râmâh (4), to *hurl;
to shoot; to delude*
7683 shâgag (1), to *stray;
to sin*
7686 shâgâh (1), to *stray,
wander; to transgress*
8582 tâ'âh (1), to
vacillate, reel or stray
538 apataō (2), to *cheat,
delude*
1818 ĕxapataō (1), to
seduce wholly, deceive
4105 planaō (10), to
wander; to deceive

DECEIVER
5230 nâkal (1), to *act
treacherously*

7686 shâgâh (1), to *stray,
wander; to transgress*
8591 tâ'a' (1), to *cheat; to
maltreat*
4108 planŏs (2), *roving;
impostor or misleader*

DECEIVERS
4108 planŏs (2), *roving;
impostor or misleader*
5423 phrĕnapatēs (1),
seducer, misleader

DECEIVETH
7411 râmâh (1), to *hurl;
to shoot; to delude*
538 apataō (1), to *cheat,
delude*
4105 planaō (3), to *roam,
wander; to deceive*
5422 phrĕnapataō (1), to
delude, deceive

DECEIVING
3884 paralŏgizŏmai (1),
to *delude, deceive*
4105 planaō (1), to *roam,
wander; to deceive*

DECEIVINGS
539 apatē (1), *delusion*

DECENTLY
2156 ĕuschēmŏnōs (1),
fittingly, properly

DECIDED
2782 chârats (1), to *be
alert, to decide*

DECISION
2742 chârûwts (2),
diligent, earnest

DECK
3302 yâphâh (1), to *be
beautiful*
5710 'âdâh (1), to
remove; to bedeck

DECKED
5710 'âdâh (3), to
remove; to bedeck
7234 râbad (1), to *spread*
5558 chrusŏō (2), to
guild, bespangle

DECKEDST
5710 'âdâh (1), to
remove; to bedeck
6213 'âsâh (1), to *do*

DECKEST
5710 'âdâh (1), to
remove; to bedeck

DECKETH
3547 kâhan (1), to
officiate as a priest

DECLARATION
262 'achvâh (1),
utterance
6575 pârâshâh (1),
exposition
1335 diēgĕsis (1), *recital,
written account*

DECLARE
560 'ămar (Ch.) (1), to
say, speak
874 bâ'ar (1), to *explain*
952 bûwr (1), to *examine*
1696 dâbar (1), to *speak,
say; to subdue*
3045 yâda' (3), to *know*
5046 nâgad (46), to
announce

5608 çâphar (20), to
enumerate; to recount
7878 sîyach (1), to
ponder, muse aloud
8085 shâma' (1), to *hear
intelligently*
312 anaggĕllō (2), to
announce, report
518 apaggĕllō (2), to
announce, proclaim
1107 gnōrizō (3), to
make known, reveal
1213 dēlŏō (1), to *make
plain by words*
1334 diēgĕŏmai (1), to
relate fully, describe
1555 ĕkdiēgĕŏmai (1), to
narrate through wholly
1718 ĕmphanizō (1), to
show forth
1732 ĕndĕixis (2),
demonstration
2097 ĕuaggĕlizō (1), to
announce good news
2605 kataggĕllō (1), to
proclaim, promulgate
3853 paraggĕllō (1), to
enjoin; to instruct
5419 phrazō (2), to
indicate, to expound

DECLARED
559 'âmar (1), to *say,
speak*
1696 dâbar (1), to *speak,
say; to subdue*
3045 yâda' (3), to *know*
5046 nâgad (13), to
announce
5608 çâphar (4), to
enumerate; to recount
6567 pârash (1), to
separate; to specify
8085 shâma' (1), to *hear*
312 anaggĕllō (1), to
announce, report
394 anatithĕmai (1), to
set forth a declaration
518 apaggĕllō (1), to
announce, proclaim
1107 gnōrizō (1), to
make known, reveal
1213 dēlŏō (2), to *make
plain by words*
1229 diaggĕllō (1), to
herald thoroughly
1334 diēgĕŏmai (2), to
relate fully, describe
1834 ĕxēgĕŏmai (4), to
tell, relate again
2097 ĕuaggĕlizō (1), to
announce good news
3724 hŏrizō (1), to
appoint, decree, specify
5319 phanĕrŏō (1), to
render apparent

DECLARETH
5046 nâgad (4), to
announce

DECLARING
5046 nâgad (1), to
announce
1555 ĕkdiēgĕŏmai (1), to
narrate through wholly
1834 ĕxēgĕŏmai (1), to
tell, relate again
2605 kataggĕllō (1), to
proclaim, promulgate

DECLINE
5186 nâṭâh (3), to *stretch* or *spread out*
5493 çûwr (1), to *turn off*
7847 sâṭâh (1), to *deviate* from duty, *go astray*

DECLINED
5186 nâṭâh (3), to *stretch* or *spread out*
5493 çûwr (1), to *turn off*

DECLINETH
5186 nâṭâh (2), to *stretch* or *spread out*

DECREASE
4591 mâ'aṭ (1), to *be, make small* or *few*
1642 ĕlattŏō (1), to *lessen*

DECREASED
2637 châçêr (1), to *lack;* to *fail, want, make less*

DECREE
633 'ĕçâr (Ch.) (7), *edict, decree*
1504 gâzar (1), to *exclude; decide*
1510 gᵉzêrâh (Ch.) (2), *decree, decision*
1697 dâbâr (1), *word; matter; thing*
1881 dâth (9), *royal edict* or *statute*
1882 dâth (Ch.) (3), *Law; royal edict* or *statute*
2706 chôq (7), *appointment; allotment*
2710 châqaq (2), to *engrave;* to *enact laws*
2940 ṭa'am (1), *taste; intelligence; mandate*
2942 ṭᵉ'êm (Ch.) (13), *judgment; account*
3982 ma'ămar (1), *edict, command*
6599 pithgam (1), judicial *sentence; edict*
1378 dŏgma (1), *law*

DECREED
1504 gâzar (1), to *destroy, exclude; decide*
2706 chôq (1), *appointment; allotment*
2782 chârats (1), to *be alert,* to *decide*
6965 qûwm (1), to *rise*
2919 krinō (1), to *decide;* to *try, condemn, punish*

DECREES
2711 chêqeq (1), *enactment, resolution*
1378 dŏgma (2), *law*

DEDAN
1719 Dᵉdân (11), *Dedan*

DEDANIM
1720 Dᵉdânîym (1), *Dedanites*

DEDICATE
2596 chânak (1), to *initiate* or *discipline*
6942 qâdâsh (3), to *be, make clean*

DEDICATED
2596 chânak (3), to *initiate* or *discipline*
2764 chêrem (1), *doomed object*

DEDICATING
2598 chănukkâh (2), *dedication*

DEDICATION
2597 chănukkâ' (Ch.) (4), *dedication*
2598 chănukkâh (6), *dedication*
1456 ĕgkainia (1), *Feast of Dedication*

DEED
199 'ûwlâm (2), *however* or *on the contrary*
1697 dâbâr (3), *word; matter; thing*
3559 kûwn (1), to *set up: establish, fix, prepare*
4639 ma'ăseh (1), *action; labor*
2041 ĕrgŏn (6), *work*
2108 ĕuĕrgĕsia (1), *beneficence*
4162 pŏïēsis (1), *action,* i.e. *performance*
4334 prŏsĕrchŏmai (1), to *come near, visit*

DEEDS
1578 gᵉmûwlâh (1), *act; service; reward*
1697 dâbâr (2), *word; matter; thing*
4639 ma'ăseh (2), *action; labor*
5949 'ălîylâh (2), *opportunity, action*
6467 pô'al (2), *act or work, deed*
1411 dunamis (1), *force, power, miracle*
2041 ĕrgŏn (16), *work*
2735 katŏrthōma (1), *made fully upright*
3739+4238 hŏs (1), *who, which, what, that*
4234 praxis (3), *act; function*

DEEMED
5282 hupŏnŏĕō (1), to *think;* to *expect*

DEEP
4113 mahămôrâh (1), (poss.) *abyss, pits*
4278 mechqâr (1), *recess, unexplored* place
4615 ma'ămâq (2), *deep place*
4688 mᵉtsôwlâh (5), *deep place*
4950 mishqâ' (1), *clear pond with settled water*
5994 'ămîyq (Ch.) (1), *profound, unsearchable*
6009 'âmaq (5), to *be, make deep*
6013 'âmôq (8), *deep, profound*
6683 tsûwlâh (1), *watery abyss*
7290 râdam (2), to *stupefy*

DEEPER
6012 'âmêq (1), *deep, obscure*
6013 'âmôq (8), *deep, profound*

DEEPLY
6009 'âmaq (2), to *be, make deep*
389 anastĕnazō (1), to *sigh deeply*

DEEPNESS
899 bathŏs (1), *extent; mystery,* i.e. *deep*

DEEPS
4688 mᵉtsôwlâh (3), *deep place*
8415 tᵉhôwm (1), *abyss of the sea,* i.e. the *deep*

DEER
3180 yachmûwr (1), *deer*

DEFAMED
987 blasphēmĕō (1), to *speak impiously*

DEFAMING
1681 dibbâh (1), *slander, bad report*

DEFEAT
6565 pârar (2), to *break up;* to *violate, frustrate*

DEFENCE
1220 betser (1), *gold*
2646 chuppâh (1), *canopy*
4043 mâgên (2), *small shield (buckler); animal skin*
4686 mâtsûwd (1), *net or capture; fastness*
4692 mâtsôwr (2), *siege-mound; distress*
4869 misgâb (7), *refuge*
5526 çâkak (1), to *fence in; cover over; protect*
6738 tsêl (3), *shade; protection*
626 apŏlŏgĕŏmai (1), to *give an account*
627 apŏlŏgia (3), *plea or verbal defense*

DEFENCED
1219 bâtsar (5), to *be inaccessible*
4013 mibtsâr (4), *fortification; defender*

DEFEND
1598 gânan (7), to *protect*
3467 yâsha' (1), to *make safe, free*
7682 sâgab (2), to *be, make lofty; be safe*

DEEP
8257 shâqa' (1), to *be overflowed;* to *cease*
8328 sheresh (1), *root*
8415 tᵉhôwm (20), *abyss of the sea,* i.e. the *deep*
8639 tardêmâh (7), *trance, deep sleep*
12 abussŏs (2), *deep place, abyss*
899 bathŏs (3), *extent; mystery,* i.e. *deep*
901 bathus (2), *deep, profound*
1037 buthŏs (1), *deep sea*
2532+900 kai (1), *and; or; even; also*

DEEPER
6012 'âmêq (1), *deep, obscure*
6013 'âmôq (8), *deep, profound*

DEFENDED
5337 nâtsal (1), to *deliver*
292 amunŏmai (1), to *protect, help*

DEFENDEST
5526 çâkak (1), to *fence in; cover over; protect*

DEFENDING
1598 gânan (1), to *protect*

DEFER
309 'âchar (2), to *remain;* to *delay*
748 'ârak (1), to *be, make long*

DEFERRED
309 'âchar (2), to *remain;* to *delay*
4900 mâshak (1), to *draw out;* to *be tall*
306 anaballŏmai (1), to *put off, adjourn*

DEFERRETH
748 'ârak (1), to *be, make long*

DEFIED
2194 zâ'am (1), to *be enraged*
2778 châraph (5), to *spend the winter*

DEFILE
1351 gâ'al (2), to *soil, stain; desecrate*
2490 châlal (2), to *profane, defile*
2930 ṭâmê' (25), to *be morally contaminated*
2936 ṭânaph (1), to *soil, make dirty*
733 arsĕnŏkŏitēs (1), *sodomite*
2840 kŏinŏō (6), to *make profane*
3392 miainō (1), to *contaminate*
5351 phthĕirō (1), to *spoil, ruin;* to *deprave*

DEFILED
1351 gâ'al (2), to *soil, stain; desecrate*
2490 châlal (5), to *profane, defile*
2610 chânêph (3), to *soil, be defiled*
2930 ṭâmê' (44), to *be morally contaminated*
2931 ṭâmê' (5), *foul; ceremonially impure*
2933 ṭâmâh (1), to *be ceremonially impure*
5953 'âlal (1), to *glean;* to *overdo*
6031 'ânâh (1), to *afflict, be afflicted*
6942 qâdâsh (1), to *be, make clean*
2839 kŏinŏs (1), *common,* i.e. *profane*
3392 miainō (4), to *contaminate*
3435 mŏlunō (3), to *soil, make impure*

DEFILEDST
2490 châlal (1), to *profane, defile*

D

DEFILETH
2490 châlal (1), to
profane, defile
2610 chânêph (1), to *soil,
be defiled*
2930 țâmê' (1), to *be foul;
be morally
contaminated*
2840 kôinôō (5), to *make
profane*
4695 spilŏō (1), to *stain
or soil*

DEFRAUD
6231 'âshaq (1), to
oppress; to defraud
650 apŏstĕrĕō (3), to
despoil or defraud
4122 plĕŏnĕktĕō (1), to
be covetous

DEFRAUDED
6231 'âshaq (2), to
oppress; to defraud
650 apŏstĕrĕō (1), to
despoil or defraud
4122 plĕŏnĕktĕō (1), to
be covetous

DEFY
2194 zâ'am (2), to *be
enraged*
2778 châraph (3), to
spend the winter

DEGENERATE
5494 çûwr (1), *turned off;
deteriorated*

DEGREE
898 bathmŏs (1), *grade*
of dignity
5011 tapĕinŏs (2),
humiliated, lowly

DEGREES
4609 ma'ălâh (24),
thought arising

DEHAVITES
1723 Dahăvâ' (Ch.) (1),
Dahava

DEKAR
1857 Deqer (1), *stab*

DELAIAH
1806 Dᵉlâyâh (6),
Jehovah has delivered

DELAY
309 'âchar (1), to *remain;
to delay; to
procrastinate*
311 anabŏlē (1), *putting
off, delay*
3635 ŏknĕō (1), to *be
slow, delay*

DELAYED
954 bûwsh (1), to *be
disappointed; delayed*
4102 mâhahh (1), to *be
reluctant*

DELAYETH
5549 chrŏnizō (2), to
take time, i.e. linger

DELECTABLE
2530 châmad (1), to
delight in; lust for

DELICACIES
4764 strēnŏs (1), *luxury,
sensuality*

DELICATE
6026 'ânag (1), to *be soft
or pliable*
6028 'ânôg (3), *luxurious*
8588 ta'ănûwg (1),
luxury; delight

DELICATELY
4574 ma'ădân (2),
delicacy; pleasure
6445 pânaq (1), to
enervate, reduce vigor
5172 truphē (1), *luxury
or debauchery*

DELICATENESS
6026 'ânag (1), to *be soft
or pliable*

DELICATES
5730 'êden (1), *pleasure*

DELICIOUSLY
4763 strēniaō (2), to *be
luxurious, live sensually*

DELIGHT
1523 gîyl (1), *rejoice*
2530 châmad (1), to
delight in; lust for
2531 chemed (1), *delight*
2654 châphêts (17), to *be
pleased with, desire*
2655 châphêts (1),
pleased with
2656 chêphets (3),
pleasure; desire
2836 châshaq (1), to *join;
to love, delight*
4574 ma'ădân (1),
delicacy; pleasure
5276 nâ'êm (1), to *be
agreeable*
6026 'ânag (6), to *be soft
or pliable*
6027 'ôneg (1), *luxury*
7521 râtsâh (2), to *be
pleased with*
7522 râtsôwn (5), *delight*
8173 shâ'a' (4), to *fondle,
please or amuse* (self)
dismay, i.e. stare
8191 sha'shûa' (4),
enjoyment
8588 ta'ănûwg (1),
luxury; delight
4913 sunēdŏmai (1), to
rejoice in with oneself

DELIGHTED
2654 châphêts (10), to *be
pleased with, desire*
5727 'âdan (1), to *be soft
or pleasant*
6026 'ânag (1), to *be soft
or pliable*

DELIGHTEST
7521 râtsâh (1), to *be
pleased with*

DELIGHTETH
2654 châphêts (12), to *be
pleased with, desire*
7521 râtsâh (2), to *be
pleased with*

DELIGHTS
5730 'êden (1), *pleasure*
8191 sha'shûa' (3),
enjoyment
8588 ta'ănûwg (2),
luxury; delight

DELIGHTSOME
2656 chêphets (1),
pleasure; desire

DELILAH
1807 Dᵉlîylâh (6),
languishing

DELIVER
579 'ânâh (1), to *meet, to
happen*
1350 gâ'al (1), to *redeem;
to be the next of kin*
2502 châlats (5), to
depart; to deliver
3467 yâsha' (3), to *make
safe, free*
4042 mâgan (2), to
rescue, to surrender
4422 mâlaț (17), to *be
delivered; be smooth*
4672 mâtsâ' (1), to *find
or acquire; to occur*
5186 nâțâh (1), to *stretch
or spread out*
5337 nâtsal (115), to
deliver
5338 nᵉtsal (Ch.) (2), to
extricate, deliver
5414 nâthan (78), to *give*
5462 çâgar (10), to *shut
up; to surrender*
6299 pâdâh (3), to
ransom; to release
6308 pâda' (1), to *retrieve*
6403 pâlaț (11), to
escape; to deliver
6561 pâraq (1), to *break
off or crunch; to deliver*
7725 shûwb (5), to *turn
back; to return*
7804 shᵉzab (Ch.) (6), to
leave; to free
8000 shᵉlam (Ch.) (1), to
restore; be safe
8199 shâphaț (1), to *judge*
525 apallassō (1), to
release; be reconciled
1325 didōmi (1), to *give*
1807 ĕxairĕō (2), to *tear
out; to select; to release*
3860 paradidōmi (15), to
hand over
4506 rhuŏmai (8), to
rescue
5483 charizŏmai (2), to
grant as a favor, rescue

DELIVERANCE
2020 hatstsâlâh (1),
rescue, deliverance
3444 yᵉshûw'âh (2),
deliverance; aid
6405 pallêț (1), *escape*
6413 pᵉlêyțâh (5),
escaped portion
8668 tᵉshûw'âh (5),
rescue, deliverance
629 apŏlutrōsis (1),
ransom in full
859 aphĕsis (1), *pardon,
freedom*

DELIVERANCES
3444 yᵉshûw'âh (1),
deliverance; aid

DELIVERED
2502 châlats (9), to
depart; to deliver
3052 yᵉhab (Ch.) (1), to
give

3205 yâlad (6), to *bear
young; to father a child*
3467 yâsha' (8), to *make
safe, free*
4042 mâgan (1), to
rescue, to surrender
4422 mâlaț (16), to *be
delivered; be smooth*
4560 mâçar (1), to *set
apart; apostatize*
4672 mâtsâ' (1), to *find
or acquire; to occur*
5234 nâkar (1), to
acknowledge, care for
5337 nâtsal (58), to
deliver
5414 nâthan (98), to *give*
5462 çâgar (6), to *shut
up; to surrender*
5674 'âbar (1), to *cross
over; to transition*
6299 pâdâh (2), to
ransom; to release
6403 pâlaț (3), to *slip out,
i.e. escape; to deliver*
6487 piqqâdôwn (2),
deposit
7804 shᵉzab (Ch.) (2), to
leave; to free
325 anadidōmi (1), to
hand over, deliver
525 apallassō (1), to
release; be reconciled
591 apŏdidōmi (2), to
give away
1080 gĕnnaō (1), to
procreate, regenerate
1325 didōmi (2), to *give*
1560 ĕkdŏtŏs (1),
surrendered
1659 ĕlĕuthĕrŏō (1), to
exempt, liberate
1807 ĕxairĕō (2), to *tear
out; to select; to release*
1825 ĕxĕgĕirō (1), to
resuscitate; release
1929 ĕpididōmi (2), to
give over
2673 katargĕō (1), to *be,
render entirely useless*
3860 paradidōmi (44), to
hand over
4506 rhuŏmai (9), to
rescue
5088 tiktō (5), to *produce
from seed*

DELIVEREDST
5414 nâthan (1), to *give*
3860 paradidōmi (2), to
hand over

DELIVERER
3467 yâsha' (2), to *make
safe, free*
5337 nâtsal (1), to *deliver*
6403 pâlaț (5), to *slip out,
i.e. escape; to deliver*
3086 lutrōtēs (1),
redeemer, deliverer
4506 rhuŏmai (1), to
rescue

DELIVEREST
5337 nâtsal (1), to *deliver*
6403 pâlaț (1), to *slip out,
i.e. escape; to deliver*

DELIVERETH
2502 châlats (2), to
depart; to deliver
5337 nâtsal (7), to *deliver*

DELIVERING

5414 nâthan (1), to *give*
6403 pâlaṭ (1), to *slip* out,
i.e. *escape; to deliver*
6475 pâtsâh (1), to *rend*,
i.e. *open*
7804 sheᶻab (Ch.) (1), to
leave; to free

DELIVERING

1807 ĕxaireō (1), to *tear
out; to select; to release*
3860 paradidōmi (2), to
hand over

DELIVERY

3205 yâlad (1), to *bear
young; to father a child*

DELUSION

4106 plánē (1),
fraudulence; straying

DELUSIONS

8586 ta'ălûwl (1), *caprice*
(as a fit *coming on*)

DEMAND

7592 shâ'al (3), to *ask*
7595 sheᵉêlâ' (Ch.) (1),
judicial *decision*

DEMANDED

559 'âmar (1), to *say*
7592 shâ'al (1), to *ask*
7593 sheᵉêl (Ch.) (1), to
ask
1905 ĕpĕrōtaō (2), to
inquire, seek
4441 punthanŏmai (2), to
ask for information

DEMAS

1214 Dēmas (3), *Demas*

DEMETRIUS

1216 Dēmētriŏs (3),
Demetrius

DEMONSTRATION

585 apŏdĕixis (1),
manifestation, proof

DEN

1358 gôb (Ch.) (10), lion
pit
3975 meᵉûwrâh (1),
serpent's *hole* or *den*
4583 mâ'ôwn (2), *retreat
or asylum dwelling*
4585 meᵉôwnâh (1), *abode*
4631 meᵉârâh (1), *dark
cavern*
5520 çôk (1), *hut of
entwined boughs*
4693 spēlaiŏn (3),
cavern; hiding-place

DENIED

3584 kâchash (2), to *lie,
disown; to disappoint*
4513 mâna' (1), to *deny,
refuse*
533 aparnĕŏmai (2),
disown, deny
720 arnĕŏmai (14), to
disavow, reject

DENIETH

720 arnĕŏmai (4), to
disavow, reject

DENOUNCE

5046 nâgad (1), to
announce

DENS

695 'ereb (1), *hiding
place; lair*

4492 minhârâh (1),
cavern, fissure
4585 meᵉôwnâh (4), *abode*
4631 meᵉârâh (1), *dark
cavern*
4693 spēlaiŏn (2),
cavern; hiding-place

DENY

3584 kâchash (3), to *lie,
disown; to disappoint,
cringe*
4513 mâna' (1), to *deny,
refuse*
7725 shûwb (1), to *turn
back; to return*
483 antilĕgō (1), to
dispute, refuse
533 aparnĕŏmai (11),
disown, deny
720 arnĕŏmai (7), to
disavow, reject

DENYING

720 arnĕŏmai (4), to
disavow, reject

DEPART

1540 gâlâh (1), to
denude; uncover
1980 hâlak (3), to *walk;
live a certain way*
3212 yâlak (15), to *walk;
to live; to carry*
3249 yâçûwr (1),
departing
3318 yâtsâ' (3), to *go,
bring out*
3363 yâqa' (1), to *be
dislocated*
3868 lûwz (2), to *depart;
to be perverse*
4185 mûwsh (8), to
withdraw
5493 çûwr (42), to *turn off*
5927 'âlâh (2), to *ascend,
be high, mount*
6852 tsâphar (1), to
return
7971 shâlach (4), to *send
away*
8159 shâ'âh (1), to *be
nonplussed, bewildered*
321 anagō (1), to *lead
up; to bring out; to sail*
360 analuō (1), to *depart*
565 apĕrchŏmai (4), to
go off, i.e. *depart*
630 apŏluō (2), to *relieve,
release*
672 apŏchōrĕō (1), to *go
away, leave*
868 aphistēmi (4), to
desist, desert
1607 ĕkpŏrĕuŏmai (2), to
depart, be discharged
1633 ĕkchōrĕō (1), to
depart, go away
1826 ĕxĕimi (1), *leave;
escape*
1831 ĕxĕrchŏmai (7), to
issue; to leave
3327 mĕtabainō (3), to
depart, move from
4198 pŏrĕuŏmai (5), to
go, come; to travel
5217 hupagō (1), to
withdraw or retire
5562 chōrĕō (6), to *pass,
enter; to hold, admit*

DEPARTED

935 bôw' (1), to *go, come*
1540 gâlâh (3), to
denude; uncover
1980 hâlak (3), to *walk;
live a certain way*
3212 yâlak (47), to *walk;
to live; to carry*
3318 yâtsâ' (10), to *go,
bring out*
4185 mûwsh (2), to
withdraw
5074 nâdad (1), to *rove,
flee; to drive away*
5265 nâça' (30), *start* on
a journey
5493 çûwr (31), to *turn off*
5709 'ădâ' (Ch.) (1), to
pass on or continue
5927 'âlâh (1), to *ascend,
be high, mount*
321 anagō (2), to *lead
up; to bring out; to sail*
402 anachōrĕō (8), to
retire, withdraw
525 apallassō (1), to
release; be reconciled
565 apĕrchŏmai (24), to
go off, i.e. *depart*
630 apŏluō (1), to *relieve,
release; to let die,
pardon or divorce*
673 apŏchōrizō (2), to
rend apart; to separate
868 aphistēmi (6), to
desist, desert
1316 diachōrizŏmai (1),
to *remove* (oneself)
1330 diĕrchŏmai (1), to
traverse, travel through
1607 ĕkpŏrĕuŏmai (1), to
depart, be discharged
1826 ĕxĕimi (1), *leave;
escape*
1831 ĕxĕrchŏmai (22), to
issue; to leave
2718 katĕrchŏmai (1), to
go, come down
3327 mĕtabainō (3), to
depart, move from
3332 mĕtairō (2), to
move on, leave
3855 paragō (1), to *go
along or away*
4198 pŏrĕuŏmai (6), to
go, come; to travel
5562 chōrĕō (1), to *pass,
enter; to hold, admit*
5563 chōrizō (1), to *part;
to go away*

DEPARTETH

3212 yâlak (2), to *walk;
to live; to carry*
4185 mûwsh (1), to
withdraw
5493 çûwr (3), to *turn off*
672 apŏchōrĕō (1), to *go
away, leave*

DEPARTING

3318 yâtsâ' (2), to *go,
bring out*
5253 nâçag (1), to *retreat*
5493 çûwr (2), to *turn off*
672 apŏchōrĕō (1), to *go
away, leave*
867 aphixis (1),
departure, leaving
868 aphistēmi (1), to
desist, desert

1831 ĕxĕrchŏmai (1), to
issue; to leave
1841 ĕxŏdŏs (1), *exit*, i.e.
death
5217 hupagō (1), to
withdraw or retire

DEPARTURE

3318 yâtsâ' (1), to *go,
bring out*
359 analusis (1),
departure

DEPOSED

5182 neᶜchath (Ch.) (1), to
descend; to depose

DEPRIVED

5382 nâshâh (1), to *forget*
6485 pâqad (1), to *visit,
care for, count*
7921 shâkôl (1), to
miscarry

DEPTH

6009 'âmaq (1), to *be,
make deep*
6012 'âmêq (1), *deep,
obscure*
8415 teʰhôwm (5), *abyss
of the sea*, i.e. the *deep*
899 bathŏs (4), *extent;
mystery*, i.e. *deep*
3989 pĕlagŏs (1), deep or
open sea

DEPTHS

4615 ma'ămâq (3), *deep
place*
4688 metsôwlâh (2), *deep
place*
6010 'êmeq (1), broad
depression or valley
8415 teʰhôwm (10), *abyss
of the sea*, i.e. the *deep*
899 bathŏs (1), *extent;
mystery*, i.e. *deep*

DEPUTIES

6346 pechâh (2), *prefect,
officer*
446 anthupatŏs (1),
Roman *proconsul*

DEPUTY

5324 nâtsab (1), to *station*
446 anthupatŏs (4),
Roman *proconsul*

DERBE

1191 Dĕrbē (4), *Derbe*

DERIDE

7832 sâchaq (1), to
laugh; to scorn; to play

DERIDED

1592 ĕkmuktĕrizō (2), to
sneer at, ridicule

DERISION

3887 lûwts (1), to *scoff; to
interpret; to intercede*
3932 lâ'ag (5), to *deride;
to speak unintelligibly*
7047 qeleç (3),
laughing-stock
7814 seᶜchôwq (5),
laughter; scorn
7832 sâchaq (1), to
laugh; to scorn; to play

DESCEND

3381 yârad (6), to
descend
2597 katabainō (4), to
descend

DESCENDED
3381 yârad (12), to descend
2597 katabainō (7), to descend

DESCENDETH
2718 katĕrchŏmai (1), to go, come down

DESCENDING
3381 yârad (1), to descend
2597 katabainō (7), to descend

DESCENT
35 agĕnĕalŏgĕtŏs (1), unregistered as to birth
1075 gĕnĕalŏgĕō (1), trace in genealogy
2600 katabasis (1), declivity, slope

DESCRIBE
3789 kâthab (4), to write

DESCRIBED
3789 kâthab (2), to write

DESCRIBETH
1125 graphō (1), to write
3004 lĕgō (1), to say

DESCRY
8446 tûwr (1), to wander, meander for trade

DESERT
1576 gᵉmûwl (1), act; service; reward
2723 chorbâh (1), desolation, dry desert
3452 yᵉshîymôwn (4), desolation
4057 midbâr (13), desert; also speech; mouth
6160 'ărâbâh (8), desert, wasteland
6728 tsîyîy (3), desert-dweller; beast
2048 ĕrēmŏs (12), remote place, deserted place

DESERTS
2723 chorbâh (2), desolation, dry desert
4941 mishpât (1), verdict; formal decree; justice
6160 'ărâbâh (1), desert, wasteland
2047 ĕrēmia (1), place of solitude, remoteness
2048 ĕrēmŏs (1), remote place, deserted place

DESERVING
1576 gᵉmûwl (1), act; service; reward

DESIRABLE
2531 chemed (3), delight

DESIRE
15 'âbeh (1), longing
35 'ăbîyôwnâh (1), caper-berry
183 'âvâh (7), to wish for, desire
1156 bᵉ'â' (Ch.) (1), to seek or ask
1245 bâqash (1), to search out; to strive
2530 châmad (4), to delight in; lust for
2532 chemdâh (3), delight

2654 châphêts (6), to be pleased with, desire
2655 châphêts (2), pleased with
2656 chêphets (9), pleasure; desire
2836 châshaq (1), to join; to love, delight
2837 chêsheq (1), delight, desired thing
3700 kâçaph (1), to pine after; to fear
4261 machmâd (3), object of desire
5315 nephesh (3), life; breath; soul; wind
5375+5315 nâsâ' (2), to lift up
7522 râtsôwn (3), delight
7592 shâ'al (3), to ask
7602 shâ'aph (1), to be angry; to hasten
8378 ta'ăvâh (14), longing; delight
8420 tâv (1), mark, signature
8669 tᵉshûwqâh (3), longing
154 aitĕō (5), to ask for
515 axiŏō (1), to deem entitled or fit, worthy
1934 ĕpizĕtĕō (2), to demand, to crave
1937 ĕpithumĕō (4), to long for
1939 ĕpithumia (3), longing
1971 ĕpipŏthĕō (1), intensely crave
1972 ĕpipŏthēsis (2), longing for
1974 ĕpipŏthia (1), intense longing
2065 ĕrōtaō (1), to interrogate; to request
2107 ĕudŏkia (1), delight, kindness, wish
2206 zēlŏō (2), to have warmth of feeling for
2309 thĕlō (9), to will; to desire; to choose
3713 ŏrĕgŏmai (2), to reach out after, long for

DESIRED
183 'âvâh (5), to wish for, desire
559 'âmar (1), to say, speak
1156 bᵉ'â' (Ch.) (1), to seek or ask
2530 châmad (5), to delight in; lust for
2532 chemdâh (1), delight
2654 châphêts (1), to be pleased with, desire
2656 chêphets (2), pleasure; desire
2836 châshaq (2), to join; to love, delight
3700 kâçaph (1), to pine after; to fear
7592 shâ'al (4), to ask
154 aitĕō (10), to ask for
1809 ĕxaitĕŏmai (1), to demand
1905 ĕpĕrōtaō (1), to inquire, seek

1934 ĕpizĕtĕō (1), to demand, to crave
1937 ĕpithumĕō (1), to long for
1939 ĕpithumia (1), longing
2065 ĕrōtaō (4), to interrogate; to request
2212 zētĕō (1), to seek
2309 thĕlō (1), to will; to desire; to choose
3870 parakalĕō (5), to call, invite

DESIREDST
7592 shâ'al (1), to ask
3870 parakalĕō (1), to call, invite

DESIRES
3970 ma'ăvay (1), desire
4862 mish'âlâh (1), request
2307 thĕlēma (1), purpose; inclination

DESIREST
2654 châphêts (2), to be pleased with, desire

DESIRETH
183 'âvâh (4), to wish for, desire
559 'âmar (1), to say, speak
2530 châmad (2), to delight in; lust for
2655 châphêts (1), pleased with
2656 chêphets (1), pleasure; desire
7592 shâ'al (1), to ask
7602 shâ'aph (1), to be angry; to hasten
8378 ta'ăvâh (3), longing; delight
1937 ĕpithumĕō (1), to long for
2065 ĕrōtaō (1), to interrogate; to request
2309 thĕlō (1), to will; to desire; to choose

DESIRING
154 aitĕō (2), to ask for
1937 ĕpithumĕō (1), to long for
1971 ĕpipŏthĕō (3), intensely crave
2212 zētĕō (2), to seek
2309 thĕlō (2), to will; to desire; to choose
3870 parakalĕō (2), to call, invite

DESIROUS
183 'âvâh (1), to wish for, desire
2309 thĕlō (3), to will; to desire; to choose
2442 himĕirŏmai (1), to long for, desire
2755 kĕnŏdŏxŏs (1), self-conceited

DESOLATE
490 'almânâh (2), widow
816 'âsham (6), to be guilty; to be punished
820 'ashmân (1), uninhabited places
910 bâdâd (1), separate, alone

1327 battâh (1), area of desolation
1565 galmûwd (2), sterile, barren, desolate
2717 chârab (5), to parch through drought; desolate, destroy
2723 chorbâh (7), desolation, dry desert
3173 yâchîyd (1), only son; alone; beloved
3341 yâtsath (1), to burn or set on fire
3456 yâsham (4), to lie waste
3582 kâchad (1), to destroy; to hide
4923 mᵉshammâh (2), waste; object of horror
5352 nâqâh (1), to be, make clean; to be bare
7722 shôw' (2), tempest; devastation
8047 shammâh (11), ruin; consternation
8074 shâmêm (43), to devastate; to stupefy
8076 shâmêm (8), ruined, deserted
8077 shᵉmâmâh (42), devastation
2048 ĕrēmŏs (4), remote place, deserted place
2049 ĕrēmŏō (2), to lay waste
3443 mŏnŏō (1), to isolate, i.e. bereave

DESOLATION
2721 chôreb (1), ruined; desolate
2723 chorbâh (5), desolation, dry desert
4875 mᵉshôw'âh (1), ruin
7584 sha'ăvâh (1), rushing tempest
7612 shê'th (1), devastation
7701 shôd (2), violence, ravage, destruction
7722 shôw' (4), tempest; devastation
8047 shammâh (12), ruin; consternation
8074 shâmêm (3), to devastate; to stupefy
8077 shᵉmâmâh (11), devastation
2049 ĕrēmŏō (2), to lay waste
2050 ĕrēmōsis (3), despoliation, desolation

DESOLATIONS
2723 chorbâh (3), desolation, dry desert
4876 mashshûw'âh (1), ruin
8047 shammâh (1), ruin; consternation
8074 shâmêm (4), to devastate; to stupefy
8077 shᵉmâmâh (2), devastation

DESPAIR
2976 yâ'ash (2), to despond, despair
1820 ĕxapŏrĕŏmai (1), to be utterly at a loss

DESPAIRED
1820 ĕxapŏrĕŏmai (1), to be utterly at a loss

DESPERATE
605 'ânash (1), to *be frail, feeble*
2976 yâ'ash (1), to *despond, despair*

DESPERATELY
605 'ânash (1), to *be frail, feeble*

DESPISE
936 bûwz (4), to *disrespect, scorn*
959 bâzâh (6), to *ridicule, scorn*
2107 zûwl (1), to *treat lightly*
3988 mâ'aç (9), to *spurn; to disappear*
5006 nâ'ats (1), to *scorn*
7043 qâlal (1), to *be easy, trifling, vile*
7590 shâ't (2), *reject by maligning*
114 athĕtĕō (1), to *disesteem, neutralize*
1848 ĕxŏuthĕnĕō (3), to *treat with contempt*
2706 kataphrŏnĕō (7), to *disesteem, despise*
3643 ŏligŏrĕō (1), to *disesteem, despise*
4065 pĕriphrŏnĕō (1), to *depreciate, contemn*

DESPISED
937 bûwz (4), *disrespect, scorn*
939 bûwzâh (1), *something scorned*
959 bâzâh (26), to *ridicule, scorn*
3988 mâ'aç (12), to *spurn; to disappear*
5006 nâ'ats (6), to *scorn*
7034 qâlâh (1), to *be, hold in contempt*
7043 qâlal (2), to *be easy, trifling, vile*
7590 shâ't (1), *reject by maligning*
114 athĕtĕō (1), to *disesteem, set aside*
818 atimazŏ (1), to *maltreat, dishonor*
820 atimŏs (1), *without honor*
1519+3762+3049 ĕis (1), *to or into*
1848 ĕxŏuthĕnĕō (3), to *treat with contempt*

DESPISERS
865 aphilagathŏs (1), *hostile to virtue*
2707 kataphrŏntēs (1), *contemner, scoffer*

DESPISEST
2706 kataphrŏnĕō (1), to *disesteem, despise*

DESPISETH
936 bûwz (4), to *disrespect, scorn*
959 bâzâh (4), to *ridicule, scorn*
960 bâzôh (1), *scorned*
3988 mâ'aç (3), to *spurn; to disappear*

DESPISING
2706 kataphrŏnĕō (1), to *disesteem, despise*

DESPITE
7589 she'âṭ (1), *contempt*
1796 ĕnubrizŏ (1), to *insult*

DESPITEFUL
7589 she'âṭ (2), *contempt*
5197 hubristēs (1), *maltreater*

DESPITEFULLY
1908 ĕpērĕazŏ (2), to *insult, slander*
5195 hubrizŏ (1), to *exercise violence*

DESTITUTE
2638 châçêr (1), *lacking*
5800 'âzab (1), to *loosen; relinquish; permit*
6168 'ârâh (1), to *empty, pour out; demolish*
6199 'ar'âr (1), *naked; poor*
8047 shammâh (1), *ruin; consternation*
650 apŏstĕrĕō (1), to *deprive; to despoil*
3007 lĕipŏ (1), to *fail or be absent*
5302 hustĕrĕō (1), to *be inferior; to fall short*

DESTROY
6 'âbad (38), *perish; destroy*
7 'ăbad (Ch.) (4), *perish; destroy*
9 'ăbêdâh (1), *destruction*
622 'âçaph (1), to *gather, collect*
816 'âsham (1), to *be guilty; to be punished*
1104 bâla' (7), to *swallow; to destroy*
1641 gârar (1), to *ruminate; to saw*
1792 dâkâ' (1), to *be contrite, be humbled*
1820 dâmâh (1), to *be silent; to fail, cease*
1949 hûwm (1), to *make an uproar; agitate*
2000 hâmam (3), to *disturb, drive, destroy*
2040 hâraç (1), to *pull down; break, destroy*
2254 châbal (5), to *pervert, destroy*
2255 châbal (Ch.) (2), to *ruin, destroy*
2763 charam (14), to *devote to destruction*
3238 yânâh (1), to *rage or be violent*
3423 yârash (1), to *inherit; to impoverish*
3615 kâlâh (1), to *complete, consume*
3772 kârath (2), to *cut (off, down or asunder)*
4049 meʿgar (Ch.) (1), to *overthrow, depose*
4135 mûwl (3), to *circumcise*

4191 mûwth (1), to *die; to kill*
4229 mâchâh (2), to *erase; to grease*
4889 mashchîyth (4), *destruction; corruption*
5255 nâçach (1), to *tear away*
5362 nâqaph (1), to *strike; to surround*
5395 nâsham (1), to *destroy*
5422 nâthats (4), to *tear down*
5595 çâphâh (3), to *scrape; to remove*
6789 tsâmath (4), to *extirpate, destroy*
6979 qûwr (1), to *throw forth; to wall up*
7665 shâbar (2), to *burst*
7703 shâdad (1), to *ravage*
7722 shŏw' (1), *tempest; devastation*
7843 shâchath (68), to *decay; to ruin*
7921 shâkôl (1), to *miscarry*
8045 shâmad (40), to *desolate*
8074 shâmêm (2), to *devastate; to stupefy*
622 apŏllumi (19), to *destroy fully; to perish*
1311 diaphthĕirŏ (1), to *ruin, to decay*
2647 kataluō (6), to *demolish; to halt*
2673 katargĕō (3), to *be, render entirely useless*
3089 luō (2), to *loosen*
5351 phthĕirŏ (1), to *spoil, ruin; to deprave*

DESTROYED
6 'âbad (17), *perish; destroy*
7 'ăbad (Ch.) (1), *perish; destroy*
1104 bâla' (1), to *swallow; to destroy*
1696 dâbar (1), to *speak, say; to subdue*
1792 dâkâ' (1), to *pulverize; be contrite*
1820 dâmâh (1), to *be silent; to fail, cease*
1822 dummâh (1), *desolation*
2026 hârag (1), to *kill, slaughter*
2040 hâraç (3), to *pull down; break, destroy*
2254 châbal (2), to *pervert, destroy*
2255 châbal (Ch.) (3), to *ruin, destroy*
2717 chârab (1), to *desolate, destroy*
2718 chărab (Ch.) (1), to *demolish*
2763 charam (23), to *devote to destruction*
2764 chêrem (1), *extermination*
3615 kâlâh (1), to *cease, be finished, perish*
3772 kârath (2), to *cut (off, down or asunder)*

3807 kâthath (3), to *bruise, strike, beat*
4229 mâchâh (3), to *erase; to grease*
5422 nâthats (1), to *tear down*
5428 nâthash (1), to *tear away, be uprooted*
5595 çâphâh (2), to *scrape; to remove*
5642 çeʿthar (Ch.) (1), to *demolish*
6658 tsâdâh (1), to *desolate*
6789 tsâmath (1), to *extirpate, destroy*
7321 rûwa' (1), to *shout*
7665 shâbar (7), to *burst*
7703 shâdad (1), to *ravage*
7843 shâchath (21), to *decay; to ruin*
8045 shâmad (43), to *desolate*
8074 shâmêm (1), to *devastate; to stupefy*
622 apŏllumi (7), to *destroy fully; to perish*
1311 diaphthĕirŏ (1), to *ruin, to pervert*
1842 ĕxŏlŏthrĕuŏ (1), to *extirpate*
2507 kathairĕō (2), to *lower, or demolish*
2647 kataluō (2), to *demolish; to halt*
2673 katargĕō (2), to *be, render entirely useless*
3645 ŏlŏthrĕuŏ (1), to *slay, destroy*
4199 pŏrthĕō (1), to *ravage, pillage*
5356 phthŏra (1), *ruin; depravity, corruption*

DESTROYER
2717 chârab (1), to *desolate, destroy*
6530 peʿrîyts (1), *violent, i.e. a tyrant*
7703 shâdad (1), to *ravage*
7843 shâchath (3), to *decay; to ruin*
3644 ŏlŏthrĕutēs (1), *serpent which destroys*

DESTROYERS
2040 hâraç (1), to *pull down; break, destroy*
4191 mûwth (1), to *die; to kill*
7843 shâchath (3), to *decay; to ruin*
8154 shâçâh (1), to *plunder*

DESTROYEST
6 'âbad (1), *perish; destroy*
7843 shâchath (1), to *decay; to ruin*
2647 kataluō (2), to *demolish; to halt*

DESTROYETH
6 'âbad (4), *perish; destroy*
3615 kâlâh (1), to *complete, consume*
4229 mâchâh (1), to *erase; to grease*

7843 shâchath (2), to *decay*; to *ruin*

DESTROYING
1104 bâla' (1), to *swallow*; to *destroy*
2763 charam (5), to *devote* to destruction
4889 mashchîyth (1), *destruction; corruption*
4892 mashchêth (1), *destruction*
6986 qeṭeb (1), *ruin*
7843 shâchath (5), to *decay*; to *ruin*

DESTRUCTION
6 'âbad (1), *perish; destroy*
10 'ăbaddôh (1), *perishing*
11 'ăbaddôwn (5), *perishing*
12 'abdân (1), *perishing*
13 'obdân (1), *perishing*
343 'êyd (7), *misfortune, ruin, disaster*
1793 dakkâ' (1), *crushed, destroyed; contrite*
2035 hărîyçûwth (1), *demolition, destruction*
2041 hereç (1), *demolition, destruction*
2256 chebel (1), *company, band*
2475 chălôwph (1), destitute *orphans*
2764 chêrem (2), *extermination*
3589 kîyd (1), *calamity, destruction*
4103 mᵉhûwmâh (3), *confusion or uproar*
4288 mᵉchittâh (7), *ruin; consternation*
4876 mashshûw'âh (1), *ruin*
4889 mashchîyth (2), *destruction; corruption*
6365 pîyd (2), *misfortune*
6986 qeṭeb (2), *ruin*
6987 qôṭeb (1), *extermination*
7089 qᵉphâdâh (1), *terror*
7171 qerets (1), *extirpation*
7591 shᵉ'îyâh (1), *desolation*
7667 sheber (20), *fracture; ruin*
7670 shibrôwn (1), *ruin*
7701 shôd (7), *violence, ravage, destruction*
7722 shôw' (2), *tempest; devastation*
7843 shâchath (1), to *decay*; to *ruin*
7845 shachath (2), *pit; destruction*
8045 shâmad (1), to *desolate*
8395 tᵉbûwçâh (1), *ruin*
8399 tablîyth (1), *consumption*
684 apōlĕia (5), *ruin or loss*
2506 kathairĕsis (2), *demolition*
3639 ŏlĕthrŏs (4), *death, punishment*

4938 suntrimma (1), complete *ruin*

DESTRUCTIONS
2723 chorbâh (1), *desolation, dry* desert
7722 shôw' (1), *tempest; devastation*
7825 shᵉchîyth (1), *pit-fall*

DETAIN
6113 'âtsar (2), to *hold back*; to *maintain*

DETAINED
6113 'âtsar (1), to *hold back*; to *maintain*

DETERMINATE
3724 hŏrizō (1), to *appoint, decree, specify*

DETERMINATION
4941 mishpâṭ (1), *verdict; formal decree; justice*

DETERMINED
559 'âmar (1), to *say*
2782 chârats (6), to *be alert*, to *decide*
2852 châthak (1), to *decree*
3289 yâ'ats (2), to *advise*
3615 kâlâh (5), to *cease, be finished, perish*
7760 sûwm (1), to *put, place*
1011 bŏulĕuō (1), to *deliberate*; to *resolve*
1956 ĕpiluō (1), to *explain*; to *decide*
2919 krinō (7), to *decide; to try, condemn, punish*
3724 hŏrizō (3), to *appoint, decree, specify*
4309 prŏŏrizō (1), to *predetermine*
5021 tassō (1), to *assign or dispose*

DETEST
8262 shâqats (1), to *loathe, pollute*

DETESTABLE
8251 shiqqûwts (6), *disgusting idol*

DEUEL
1845 Dᵉ'ûw'êl (4), *known of God*

DEVICE
1902 higgâyôwn (1), *musical notation*
2808 cheshbôwn (1), *contrivance; plan*
4209 mᵉzimmâh (1), *plan; sagacity*
4284 machăshâbâh (4), *contrivance; plan*
1761 ĕnthumēsis (1), *deliberation; idea*

DEVICES
2154 zimmâh (1), bad *plan*
4156 môw'êtsâh (1), *purpose, plan*
4209 mᵉzimmâh (5), *plan; sagacity*
4284 machăshâbâh (8), *contrivance; plan*
3540 nŏēma (1), *perception, purpose*

DEVIL
1139 daimŏnizŏmai (7), to *be demonized*
1140 daimŏniŏn (18), *demonic being*
1142 daimōn (1), *evil supernatural spirit*
1228 diabŏlŏs (35), *traducer*, i.e. *Satan*

DEVILISH
1141 daimŏniŏdēs (1), *demon-like, of the devil*

DEVILS
7700 shêd (2), *demon*
8163 sâ'îyr (2), *shaggy; he-goat; goat idol*
1139 daimŏnizŏmai (6), to *be demonized*
1140 daimŏniŏn (40), *demonic being*
1142 daimōn (4), *evil supernatural spirit*

DEVISE
2790 chârash (3), to *engrave; to plow*
2803 châshab (13), to *weave, fabricate*

DEVISED
908 bâdâ' (1), to *invent; to choose*
1819 dâmâh (1), to *resemble, liken*
2161 zâmam (3), to *plan*
2803 châshab (5), to *plot; to think, regard*
4284 machăshâbâh (1), *contrivance; plan*
4679 sŏphizō (1), to *make wise*

DEVISETH
2790 chârash (2), to *engrave; to plow*
2803 châshab (4), to *plot; to think, regard*
3289 yâ'ats (2), to *advise*

DEVOTE
2763 charam (1), to *devote* to destruction

DEVOTED
2763 charam (1), to *devote* to destruction
2764 chêrem (5), *doomed object*

DEVOTIONS
4574 sĕbasma (1), *object of worship*

DEVOUR
398 'âkal (57), to *eat*
399 'ăkal (Ch.) (2), to *eat*
402 'oklâh (2), *food*
7462 râ'âh (1), to *tend a flock*, i.e. *pasture* it
7602 shâ'aph (1), to *be angry; to hasten*
2068 ĕsthiō (1), to *eat*
2666 katapinō (1), to *devour by swallowing*
2719 katĕsthiō (6), to *devour*

DEVOURED
398 'âkal (42), to *eat*
399 'ăkal (Ch.) (2), to *eat*
402 'oklâh (1), *food*
1104 bâla' (2), to *swallow*; to *destroy*

3898 lâcham (1), to *fight* a *battle*, i.e. *consume*
2719 katĕsthiō (5), to *devour*

DEVOURER
398 'âkal (1), to *eat*

DEVOUREST
398 'âkal (1), to *eat*

DEVOURETH
398 'âkal (6), to *eat*
1104 bâla' (2), to *swallow*; to *destroy*
3216 yâla' (1), to *blurt* or *utter inconsiderately*
2719 katĕsthiō (1), to *devour*

DEVOURING
398 'âkal (5), to *eat*
1105 bela' (1), *gulp; destruction*

DEVOUT
2126 ĕulabēs (3), *circumspect, pious*
2152 ĕusĕbēs (3), *pious*
4576 sĕbŏmai (3), to *revere*, i.e. *adore*

DEW
2919 ṭal (30), *dew, morning mist*
2920 ṭal (Ch.) (5), *dew, morning mist*

DIADEM
4701 mitsnepheth (1), *turban*
6797 tsânîyph (2), *head-dress, turban*
6843 tsᵉphîyrâh (1), *encircling crown*

DIAL
4609 ma'ălâh (2), *thought* arising

DIAMOND
3095 yahălôm (3), (poss.) *onyx*
8068 shâmîyr (1), *thorn*; (poss.) *diamond*

DIANA
735 Artĕmis (5), *prompt*

DIBLAIM
1691 Diblayim (1), *two cakes*

DIBLATH
1689 Diblâh (1), *Diblah*

DIBON
1769 Dîybôwn (9), *pining*

DIBON-GAD
1769 Dîybôwn (2), *pining*

DIBRI
1704 Dibrîy (1), *wordy*

DID
1580 gâmal (2), to *benefit* or *requite*; to *wean*
1961 hâyâh (1), to *exist*, i.e. *be* or *become*
2052 Vâhêb (1), *Vaheb*
5648 'ăbad (Ch.) (1), to *do, work, serve*
6213 'âsâh (327), to *do* or *make*
6313 pûwg (1), to *be sluggish; be numb*
7965 shâlôwm (2), *safe; well; health, prosperity*

D

15 agathŏpŏiĕŏ (1), to be
a well-doer
91 adikĕŏ (1), to do
wrong
1731 ĕndĕiknumi (1), to
show, display
3000 latrĕuŏ (1), to
minister to God
4160 pŏiĕŏ (54), to make
or do
4238 prassŏ (1), to
execute, accomplish

DIDDEST
387 anastatŏŏ (1), to
disturb, cause trouble

DIDST
6213 'âsâh (14), to do or
make
6466 pâ'al (1), to do,
make or practice

DIDYMUS
1324 Didumŏs (3), twin

DIE
1478 gâva' (8), to expire,
die
4191 mûwth (255), to die;
to kill
4194 mâveth (7), death;
dead
8546 tᵉmûwthâh (1),
execution, death
599 apŏthnēskŏ (40), to
die off
622 apŏllumi (1), to
destroy fully; to perish
684 apŏlĕia (1), ruin or
loss
4880 sunapŏthnēskŏ (2),
to decease with
5053 tĕlĕutaŏ (3), to
finish life, i.e. expire

DIED
1478 gâva' (3), to expire,
die
4191 mûwth (154), to die;
to kill
4194 mâveth (7), death;
dead
5038 nᵉbêlâh (1), carcase
or carrion
5307 nâphal (1), to fall
599 apŏthnēskŏ (32), to
die off
5053 tĕlĕutaŏ (2), to
finish life, i.e. expire

DIEST
4191 mûwth (1), to die; to
kill

DIET
737 'ărûchâh (2), ration,
portion of food

DIETH
4191 mûwth (16), to die;
to kill
4194 mâveth (4), death;
dead
5038 nᵉbêlâh (4), carcase
or carrion
599 apŏthnēskŏ (2), to
die off
5053 tĕlĕutaŏ (3), to
finish life, i.e. expire

DIFFER
1252 diakrinŏ (1), to
decide; to hesitate

DIFFERENCE
914 bâdal (3), to divide,
separate, distinguish
6395 pâlâh (1), to
distinguish
1252 diakrinŏ (2), to
decide; to hesitate
1293 diastŏlē (2),
variation, distinction
3307 mĕrizŏ (1), to
disunite, differ

DIFFERENCES
1243 diairēsis (1),
distinction or variety

DIFFERETH
1308 diaphĕrŏ (2), to
bear, carry; to differ

DIFFERING
1313 diaphŏrŏs (1),
varying; surpassing

DIG
2658 châphar (3), to
delve, to explore
2672 châtsab (1), to cut
stone or carve wood
2864 châthar (5), to
break or dig into
3738 kârâh (2), to dig; to
plot; to bore, hew
4626 skaptŏ (2), to dig

DIGGED
2658 châphar (13), to
delve, to explore
2672 châtsab (3), to cut
stone or carve wood
2864 châthar (2), to
break or dig into
3738 kârâh (8), to dig; to
plot; to bore, hew
5365 nâqar (3), to bore;
to gouge
5737 'âdar (2), to hoe a
vineyard
6131 'âqar (1), to pluck
up; to hamstring
2679 kataskaptŏ (1), to
destroy, be ruined
3736 ŏrussŏ (3), to
burrow, to dig out
4626 skaptŏ (1), to dig

DIGGEDST
2672 châtsab (1), to cut
stone or carve wood

DIGGETH
2658 châphar (1), to
delve, to explore
3738 kârâh (2), to dig; to
plot; to bore, hew

DIGNITIES
1891 Ĕpaphrŏditŏs (2),
devoted to Venus

DIGNITY
1420 gᵉdûwlâh (1),
greatness, grandeur
4791 mârôwm (1),
elevation; haughtiness
7613 sᵉ'êth (2), elevation;
swelling scab

DIKLAH
1853 Diqlâh (2), Diklah

DILEAN
1810 Dil'ân (1), Dilan

DILIGENCE
4929 mishmâr (1), guard,
deposit; usage; example

2039 ĕrgasia (1),
occupation; profit
4704 spŏudazŏ (2), to
make effort
4710 spŏudē (6),
despatch; eagerness

DILIGENT
2742 chârûwts (5),
diligent, earnest
3190 yâṭab (1), to be,
make well
3966 mᵉ'ôd (1), very,
utterly
4106 mâhîyr (1), skillful
4704 spŏudazŏ (2), to
make effort
4705 spŏudaiŏs (1),
prompt, energetic
4707 spŏudaiŏtĕrŏs (1),
more earnest

DILIGENTLY
149 'adrazdâ' (Ch.) (1),
carefully, diligently
995 bîyn (1), to
understand; discern
3190 yâṭab (2), to be,
make well
3966 mᵉ'ôd (4), very,
utterly
5172 nâchash (1), to
prognosticate
7182 qesheb (1),
hearkening
7836 shâchar (2), to
search for
8150 shânan (1), to
pierce; to inculcate
199 akribōs (2), exactly,
carefully
1567 ĕkzētĕŏ (1), to seek
out
1960 ĕpimĕlōs (1),
carefully, diligently
4706 spŏudaiŏtĕrŏn (1),
more earnestly
4709 spŏudaiŏs (1),
earnestly, promptly

DIM
2821 châshak (1), to be
dark; to darken
3513 kâbad (1), to be
heavy, severe, dull
3543 kâhâh (3), to grow
dull, fade; to be faint
3544 kêheh (1), feeble;
obscure
6004 'âmam (1), to
overshadow
6965 qûwm (1), to rise
8159 shâ'âh (1), to
inspect, consider

DIMINISH
1639 gâra' (6), to shave,
remove, lessen
4591 mâ'aṭ (2), to be,
make small or few

DIMINISHED
1639 gâra' (2), to shave,
remove, lessen
4591 mâ'aṭ (3), to be,
make small or few

DIMINISHING
2275 hēttēma (1), failure
or loss

DIMNAH
1829 Dimnâh (1),
dung-heap

DIMNESS
4155 mûw'âph (1),
obscurity; distress
4588 mâ'ûwph (1),
darkness, gloom

DIMON
1775 Dîymôwn (2),
Dimon

DIMONAH
1776 Dîymôwnâh (1),
Dimonah

DINAH
1783 Dîynâh (7), justice

DINAH'S
1783 Dîynâh (1), justice

DINAITES
1784 Dîynay (Ch.) (1),
Dinaite

DINE
398 'âkal (1), to eat
709 aristaŏ (2), to eat a
meal

DINED
709 aristaŏ (1), to eat a
meal

DINHABAH
1838 Dinhâbâh (2),
Dinhabah

DINNER
737 'ărûchâh (1), ration,
portion of food
712 aristŏn (3), breakfast
or lunch; feast

DIONYSIUS
1354 Diŏnusiŏs (1),
reveller

DIOTREPHES
1361 Diŏtrĕphēs (1),
Zeus-nourished

DIP
2881 ṭâbal (9), to dip
911 baptŏ (1), to
overwhelm, cover

DIPPED
2881 ṭâbal (6), to dip
4272 mâchats (1), to
crush; to subdue
911 baptŏ (2), to
overwhelm, cover
1686 ĕmbaptŏ (1), to wet

DIPPETH
1686 ĕmbaptŏ (2), to wet

DIRECT
3384 yârâh (1), to point;
to teach
3474 yâshar (3), to be
straight; to make right
3559 kûwn (1), to set up:
establish, fix, prepare
3787 kâshêr (1), to be
straight or right
5414 nâthan (1), to give
6186 'ârak (1), to set in a
row, i.e. arrange,
2720 katĕuthunŏ (2), to
direct, lead, direct

DIRECTED
3559 kûwn (1), to set up:
establish, fix, prepare
6186 'ârak (1), to set in a
row, i.e. arrange,
8505 tâkan (1), to
balance, i.e. measure

DIRECTETH
3474 yâshar (1), to be straight; to make right
3559 kûwn (2), to set up: establish, fix, prepare

DIRECTLY
413+5227 'êl (1), to, toward
1903 hâgîyn (1), (poss.) suitable or turning

DIRT
2916 ţîyţ (2), mud or clay
6574 parsh°dôn (1), crotch or anus

DISALLOW
5106 nûw' (1), to refuse, forbid, dissuade

DISALLOWED
5106 nûw' (3), to refuse, forbid, dissuade
593 apŏdŏkimazō (2), to repudiate, reject

DISANNUL
6565 pârar (2), to break up; to violate, frustrate
208 akurŏō (1), to invalidate, nullify

DISANNULLED
3722 kâphar (1), to placate or cancel

DISANNULLETH
114 athĕtĕō (1), to neutralize or set aside

DISANNULLING
115 athĕtēsis (1), cancellation

DISAPPOINT
6923 qâdam (1), to anticipate, hasten

DISAPPOINTED
6565 pârar (1), to break up; to violate, frustrate

DISAPPOINTETH
6565 pârar (1), to break up; to violate, frustrate

DISCERN
995 bîyn (2), to understand; discern
3045 yâda' (3), to know
5234 nâkar (4), to acknowledge
7200 râ'âh (1), to see
8085 shâma' (2), to hear intelligently
1252 diakrinō (1), to decide; to hesitate
1253 diakrisis (1), estimation
1381 dŏkimazō (1), to test; to approve

DISCERNED
995 bîyn (1), to understand; discern
5234 nâkar (2), to acknowledge
350 anakrinō (1), to interrogate, determine

DISCERNER
2924 kritikŏs (1), discriminative

DISCERNETH
3045 yâda' (1), to know

DISCERNING
1252 diakrinō (1), to decide; to hesitate
1253 diakrisis (1), estimation

DISCHARGE
4917 mishlachath (1), mission; release; army

DISCHARGED
5310 nâphats (1), to dash to pieces; to scatter

DISCIPLE
3100 mathētĕuō (1), to become a student
3101 mathētēs (27), pupil, student
3102 mathētria (1), female pupil, student

DISCIPLES
3928 limmûwd (1), instructed one
3101 mathētēs (240), pupil, student

DISCIPLES'
3101 mathētēs (1), pupil, student

DISCIPLINE
4148 mûwçâr (1), reproof, warning

DISCLOSE
1540 gâlâh (1), to denude; uncover

DISCOMFITED
1949 hûwm (3), to make an uproar; agitate
2000 hâmam (2), to put in commotion
2522 châlash (1), to prostrate, lay low
2729 chârad (1), to shudder with terror
3807 kâthath (1), to bruise, strike, beat
4522 maç (1), forced labor

DISCOMFITURE
4103 m°hûwmâh (1), confusion or uproar

DISCONTENTED
4751+5315 mar (1), bitter; bitterness; bitterly

DISCONTINUE
8058 shâmaţ (1), to let alone, desist, remit

DISCORD
4066 mâdôwn (1), contest or quarrel
4090 m°dân (1), contest or quarrel

DISCOURAGE
5106 nûw' (1), to refuse, forbid, dissuade

DISCOURAGED
2865 châthath (1), to break down
4549 mâçaç (1), to waste; to faint
5106 nûw' (1), to refuse, forbid, dissuade
7114 qâtsar (1), to curtail, cut short
7533 râtsats (1), to crack in pieces, smash

DISCERNING
1252 diakrinō (1), to decide; to hesitate
1253 diakrisis (1), estimation

DISCOVER
1540 gâlâh (10), to denude; uncover
2834 châsaph (1), to drain away or bail up
6168 'ârâh (1), to be, make bare; to empty

DISCOVERED
1540 gâlâh (18), to denude; uncover
3045 yâda' (1), to know
6168 'ârâh (1), to be, make bare; to empty
398 anaphainō (1), to appear
2657 katanŏĕō (1), to observe fully

DISCOVERETH
1540 gâlâh (1), to denude; uncover
2834 châsaph (1), to drain away or bail up

DISCOVERING
6168 'ârâh (1), to be, make bare; to empty

DISCREET
995 bîyn (2), to understand; discern
4998 sōphrōn (1), self-controlled

DISCREETLY
3562 nŏunĕchōs (1), prudently

DISCRETION
2940 ţa'am (1), taste; intelligence; mandate
4209 m°zimmâh (4), plan; sagacity
4941 mishpâţ (2), verdict; formal decree; justice
7922 sekel (1), intelligence; success
8394 tâbûwn (1), intelligence; argument

DISDAINED
959 bâzâh (1), to ridicule, scorn
3988 mâ'aç (1), to spurn; to disappear

DISEASE
1697 dâbâr (1), word; matter; thing
2483 chŏlîy (7), malady; anxiety; calamity
4245 machâleh (1), sickness
3119 malakia (3), enervation, debility
3553 nŏsēma (1), ailment, disease

DISEASED
2456 châlâ' (2), to be sick
2470 châlâh (2), to be weak, sick, afflicted
770 asthĕnĕō (1), to be feeble
2560+2192 kakōs (2), badly; wrongly; ill

DISEASES
4064 madveh (2), sickness
4245 machâleh (1), sickness

120 athumĕō (1), to be disheartened

DISCOVER
1540 gâlâh (10), to denude; uncover
2834 châsaph (1), to drain away or bail up
6168 'ârâh (1), to be, make bare; to empty

DISCOVERED
1540 gâlâh (18), to denude; uncover
3045 yâda' (1), to know
6168 'ârâh (1), to be, make bare; to empty
398 anaphainō (1), to appear
2657 katanŏĕō (1), to observe fully

DISFIGURE
853 aphanizō (1), to consume (becloud)

DISGRACE
5034 nâbêl (1), to be foolish or wicked

DISGUISE
2664 châphas (2), to let be sought; to mask
8138 shânâh (1), to transmute

DISGUISED
2664 châphas (5), to let be sought; to mask

DISGUISETH
5643 çêther (1), cover, shelter

DISH
5602 çêphel (1), basin, bowl
6747 tsallachath (1), bowl
5165 trubliŏn (2), bowl

DISHAN
1789 Dîyshân (5), antelope

DISHES
7086 q°'ârâh (3), bowl

DISHON
1788 dîyshôn (7), antelope

DISHONEST
1215 betsa' (2), plunder; unjust gain

DISHONESTY
152 aischunē (1), shame or disgrace

DISHONOUR
3639 k°limmâh (3), disgrace, scorn
6173 'arvâh (Ch.) (1), nakedness
7036 qâlôwn (1), disgrace
818 atimazō (2), to maltreat, dishonor
819 atimia (4), disgrace

DISHONOUREST
818 atimazō (1), to maltreat, dishonor

DISHONOURETH
5034 nâbêl (1), to wilt; to be foolish or wicked
2617 kataischunō (2), to disgrace or shame

DISINHERIT
3423 yârash (1), to inherit; to impoverish

DISMAYED
926 bâhal (1), to tremble; hurry anxiously
2844 chath (1), terror
2865 châthath (26), to break down
8159 shâ'âh (2), to be bewildered

DISEASE
1697 dâbâr (1), word; matter; thing
4251 machlûy (1), disease
8463 tachălûw' (2), malady, disease
769 asthĕnĕia (1), feebleness of body
3554 nŏsŏs (6), malady, disease

DISMAYING
4288 mᵉchittâh (1), *ruin; consternation*

DISMISSED
6362 pâṭar (1), to *burst through; to emit*
630 apŏluŏ (2), to *relieve, release; to divorce*

DISOBEDIENCE
543 apĕithĕia (3), *disbelief*
3876 parakŏē (3), *disobedience*

DISOBEDIENT
4784 mârâh (2), to *rebel or resist; to provoke*
506 anupŏtaktŏs (1), *insubordinate*
544 apĕithĕō (4), to *disbelieve*
545 apĕithēs (6), *willful disobedience*

DISOBEYED
4784 mârâh (1), to *rebel or resist; to provoke*

DISORDERLY
812 ataktĕō (1), to *be, act irregular*
814 ataktŏs (2), *morally irregularly*

DISPATCH
1254 bârâ' (1), to *create; fashion*

DISPENSATION
3622 ŏikŏnŏmia (4), *administration*

DISPERSE
2219 zârâh (7), to *toss about; to diffuse*
6327 pûwts (1), to *dash in pieces; to disperse*

DISPERSED
2219 zârâh (1), to *toss about; to diffuse*
5310 nâphats (1), to *dash to pieces; to scatter*
6327 pûwts (2), to *dash in pieces; to disperse*
6340 pâzar (1), to *scatter*
6504 pârad (1), to *spread or separate*
6555 pârats (1), to *break out*
1287 diaskŏrpizŏ (1), to *scatter; to squander*
1290 diaspŏra (1), *dispersion*
4650 skŏrpizŏ (1), to *dissipate*

DISPERSIONS
8600 tᵉphôwtsâh (1), *dispersal*

DISPLAYED
5127 nûwç (1), to *vanish away, flee*

DISPLEASE
2734 chârâh (1), to *blaze up*
6213+7451+5869 'âsâh (1), to *do or make*
7489+5869 râ'a' (3), to *be good for nothing*

DISPLEASED
599 'ânaph (1), *be enraged, be angry*

888 bᵉ'êsh (Ch.) (1), to *be displeased*
2198 zâ'ĕph (2), *angry, raging*
2734 chârâh (3), to *blaze up*
3415+5869 yâra' (1), to *fear*
6087 'âtsab (1), to *worry, have pain* or *anger*
7107 qâtsaph (3), to *burst out in rage*
7451+241 ra' (1), *bad; evil*
7489+5869 râ'a' (7), to *be good for nothing*
23 aganaktĕō (3), to *be indignant*
2371 thumŏmachĕō (1), to *be exasperated*

DISPLEASURE
2534 chêmâh (3), *heat; anger; poison*
2740 chârôwn (1), *burning of anger*
7451 ra' (1), *bad; evil*

DISPOSED
7760 sûwm (2), to *put, place*
1014 bŏulŏmai (1), to *be willing, desire*
2309 thĕlō (1), to *will; to desire; to choose*

DISPOSING
4941 mishpâṭ (1), *verdict; formal decree; justice*

DISPOSITION
1296 diatagē (1), *putting into effect*

DISPOSSESS
3423 yârash (2), to *inherit; to impoverish*

DISPOSSESSED
3423 yârash (2), to *inherit; to impoverish*

DISPUTATION
4803 suzētēsis (1), *discussion, dispute*

DISPUTATIONS
1253 diakrisis (1), *estimation*

DISPUTE
3198 yâkach (1), to *be correct; to argue*

DISPUTED
1256 dialĕgŏmai (3), to *discuss*
1260 dialŏgizŏmai (1), to *deliberate*
4802 suzētĕō (1), to *discuss, controvert*

DISPUTER
4804 suzētētēs (1), *sophist*

DISPUTING
1256 dialĕgŏmai (3), to *discuss*
4802 suzētĕō (1), to *discuss, controvert*
4803 suzētēsis (1), *discussion, dispute*

DISPUTINGS
1261 dialŏgismŏs (1), *consideration; debate*
3859 paradiatribē (1), *meddlesomeness*

DISQUIET
7264 râgaz (1), to *quiver*

DISQUIETED
1993 hâmâh (4), to *be in great commotion*
7264 râgaz (2), to *quiver*

DISQUIETNESS
5100 nᵉhâmâh (1), *snarling, growling*

DISSEMBLED
3584 kâchash (1), to *lie, disown; to disappoint*
8582 tâ'âh (1), to *vacillate, reel* or *stray*
4942 sunupŏkrinŏmai (1), to *act hypocritically*

DISSEMBLERS
5956 'âlam (1), to *veil from sight, i.e. conceal*

DISSEMBLETH
5234 nâkar (1), to *treat as a foreigner*

DISSENSION
4714 stasis (3), one *leading an uprising*

DISSIMULATION
505 anupŏkritŏs (1), *sincere, genuine*
5272 hupŏkrisis (1), *deceit, hypocrisy*

DISSOLVE
8271 shᵉrê' (Ch.) (1), to *unravel, commence*

DISSOLVED
4127 mûwg (3), to *soften, flow down, disappear*
4743 mâqaq (1), to *melt; to flow, dwindle, vanish*
6565 pârar (1), to *break up; to violate, frustrate*
2647 kataluŏ (1), to *demolish; to halt*
3089 luŏ (2), to *loosen*

DISSOLVEST
4127 mûwg (1), to *soften, flow down, disappear*

DISSOLVING
8271 shᵉrê' (Ch.) (1), to *free, separate*

DISTAFF
6418 pelek (1), *spindle-whorl; crutch*

DISTANT
7947 shâlab (1), to *make equidistant*

DISTIL
5140 nâzal (1), to *drip, or shed by trickling*
7491 râ'aph (1), to *drip*

DISTINCTION
1293 diastŏlē (1), *variation, distinction*

DISTINCTLY
6567 pârash (1), to *separate; to specify*

DISTRACTED
6323 pûwn (1), to *be perplexed*

DISTRACTION
563 apĕrispastŏs (1), *undistractedly*

DISTRESS
4689 mâtsôwq (1), *confinement; disability*
4691 mᵉtsûwqâh (1), *trouble, anguish*
4712 mêtsar (1), *trouble*
6693 tsûwq (5), to *oppress, distress*
6696 tsûwr (2), to *cramp, i.e. confine; to harass*
6862 tsar (4), *trouble; opponent*
6869 tsârâh (8), *trouble; rival-wife*
6887 tsârar (5), to *cramp*
7451 ra' (1), *bad; evil*
318 anagkē (3), *constraint; distress*
4730 stĕnŏchôria (1), *calamity, distress*
4928 sunŏchē (1), *anxiety, distress*

DISTRESSED
3334 yâtsar (4), to *be in distress*
5065 nâgas (2), to *exploit; to tax, harass*
6696 tsûwr (1), to *cramp, i.e. confine; to harass*
6887 tsârar (2), to *cramp*
6973 qûwts (1), to *be, make disgusted*
4729 stĕnŏchōrĕō (1), to *hem in closely*

DISTRESSES
4691 mᵉtsûwqâh (5), *trouble, anguish*
6862 tsar (1), *trouble; opponent*
4730 stĕnŏchôria (2), *calamity, distress*

DISTRIBUTE
2505 châlaq (1), to *be smooth; be slippery*
5157 nâchal (1), to *inherit*
5414 nâthan (1), to *give*
1239 diadidōmi (1), to *divide up, distribute*
2130 ĕumĕtadŏtŏs (1), *liberal, generous*

DISTRIBUTED
2505 châlaq (2), to *be smooth; be slippery*
5157 nâchal (1), to *inherit*
1239 diadidōmi (1), to *divide up, distribute*
3307 mĕrizō (2), to *apportion, bestow*

DISTRIBUTETH
2505 châlaq (1), to *be smooth; be slippery*

DISTRIBUTING
2841 kŏinōnĕō (1), to *share* or *participate*

DISTRIBUTION
1239 diadidōmi (1), to *divide up, distribute*
2842 kŏinōnia (1), *benefaction; sharing*

DITCH
4724 miqvâh (1), *water reservoir*
7745 shûwchâh (1), *chasm*
7845 shachath (2), *pit; destruction*

999 bŏthunŏs (2), *cistern, pit-hole*

DITCHES
1356 gêb (1), *well, cistern; pit*

DIVERS
582 'ĕnôwsh (1), *man; person, human*
2921 tâlâ' (1), *to be spotted or variegated*
3610 kil'ayim (1), *two different kinds of thing*
6446 paç (2), *long -sleeved tunic*
6648 tseba' (3), *dye*
7553 riqmâh (2), *variegation of color*
8162 sha'aṭnêz (1), *linen and woolen*
1313 diaphŏrŏs (1), *varying; surpassing*
4164 pŏikilŏs (8), *various in character or kind*
4187 pŏlutrŏpŏs (1), *in many ways*
5100 tis (2), *some or any*

DIVERSE
3610 kil'ayim (1), *two different kinds of thing*
8133 shᵉnâ' (Ch.) (5), *to alter, change*
8138 shânâh (2), *to duplicate; to transmute*

DIVERSITIES
1085 gĕnŏs (1), *kin, offspring in kind*
1243 diairĕsis (2), *distinction or variety*

DIVIDE
914 bâdal (5), *to divide, separate, distinguish*
1234 bâqa' (2), *to cleave, break, tear open*
1504 gâzar (2), *to destroy, divide*
2505 châlaq (17), *to be smooth; be slippery*
2673 châtsâh (3), *to cut or split in two; to halve*
5157 nâchal (3), *to inherit*
5307 nâphal (4), *to fall*
5312 nᵉphaq (Ch.) (2), *to issue forth; to bring out*
6385 pâlag (1), *to split*
6536 pâraç (4), *to break in pieces; to split*
6565 pârar (1), *to break up; to violate, frustrate*
1266 diamĕrizō (1), *distribute*
3307 mĕrizō (1), *to apportion, bestow*

DIVIDED
914 bâdal (2), *to divide, separate, distinguish*
1234 bâqa' (2), *to cleave, break, tear open*
1334 bâthar (2), *to chop up, cut up*
1504 gâzar (1), *to destroy, divide*
2505 châlaq (21), *to be smooth; be slippery*
2673 châtsâh (8), *to cut or split in two; to halve*
5307 nâphal (1), *to fall*

5408 nâthach (1), *to dismember, cut up*
5504 çachar (1), *profit from trade*
6385 pâlag (3), *to split*
6386 pᵉlag (Ch.) (1), *dis-united*
6504 pârad (2), *to spread or separate*
6537 pᵉraç (Ch.) (1), *to split up*
7280 râga' (1), *to settle, to stir up*
7323 rûwts (1), *to run*
1096 ginŏmai (1), *to be, become*
1244 diairĕō (1), *distribute, apportion*
1266 diamĕrizō (4), *to distribute*
2624 kataklĕrŏdŏtĕō (1), *to apportion an estate*
3307 mĕrizō (8), *to apportion, bestow*
4977 schizō (2), *to split or sever*

DIVIDER
3312 mĕristēs (1), *apportioner*

DIVIDETH
2672 châtsab (1), *to cut stone or carve wood*
6536 pâraç (5), *to break; to split, distribute*
7280 râga' (2), *to settle, to stir up*
873 aphŏrizō (1), *to limit, exclude, appoint*
1239 diadidōmi (1), *to divide up, distribute*

DIVIDING
1234 bâqa' (1), *to cleave, break, tear open*
2505 châlaq (1), *to be smooth; be slippery*
6387 pᵉlag (Ch.) (1), *half-time unit*
1244 diairĕō (1), *distribute, apportion*
3311 mĕrismŏs (1), *separation, distribution*
3718 ŏrthŏtŏmĕō (1), *to expound correctly*

DIVINATION
4738 miqçâm (2), *augury, divination*
7080 qâçam (1), *to divine magic*
7081 qeçem (8), *divination*
4436 Puthōn (1), *inspiration in soothsaying*

DIVINATIONS
7081 qeçem (1), *divination*

DIVINE
5172 nâchash (1), *to prognosticate*
7080 qâçam (5), *to divine magic*
7081 qeçem (1), *divination*
7181 qâshab (1), *to prick up the ears*
2304 thĕiŏs (2), *divinity*
2999 latrĕia (1), *worship, ministry service*

DIVINERS
7080 qâçam (7), *to divine magic*

DIVINETH
5172 nâchash (1), *to prognosticate*

DIVINING
7080 qâçam (1), *to divine magic*

DIVISION
2515 chăluqqâh (1), *distribution, portion*
6304 pᵉdûwth (1), *distinction; deliverance*
1267 diamĕrismŏs (1), *disunion*
4978 schisma (3), *dissension, i.e. schism*

DIVISIONS
4256 machălôqeth (8), *section or division*
4653 miphlaggâh (1), *classification, division*
6391 pᵉluggâh (3), *section*
6392 pᵉluggâh (Ch.) (1), *section*
1370 dichŏstasia (2), *dissension*
4978 schisma (2), *dissension, i.e. schism*

DIVORCE
3748 kᵉrîythûwth (1), *divorce*

DIVORCED
1644 gârash (3), *to drive out; to divorce*
630 apŏluō (1), *to relieve, release; to divorce*

DIVORCEMENT
3748 kᵉrîythûwth (3), *divorce*
647 apŏstasiŏn (3), *marriage divorce*

DIZAHAB
1774 Dîy zâhâb (1), *of gold*

DO
1167 ba'al (1), *master; husband; owner; citizen*
1580 gâmal (1), *to benefit or requite; to wean*
3190 yâṭab (2), *to be, make well*
3318 yâtsâ' (1), *to go, bring out*
4640 Ma'say (1), *operative*
5647 'âbad (17), *to do, work, serve*
5648 'ăbad (Ch.) (5), *to do, work, serve*
5674 'âbar (1), *to cross over; to transition*
5953 'âlal (2), *to glean; to overdo*
6213 'âsâh (617), *to do*
6466 pâ'al (6), *to do*
6467 pô'al (1), *act or work, deed*
14 agathŏĕrgĕō (1), *to do good work*
15 agathŏpŏiĕō (6), *to be a well-doer*
17 agathŏpŏiŏs (1), *virtuous one*

91 adikĕō (2), *to do wrong*
1107 gnōrizō (1), *to make known, reveal*
1286 diasĕiō (1), *to intimidate*
1398 dŏulĕuō (1), *to serve as a slave*
1754 ĕnĕrgĕō (1), *to be active, efficient, work*
2005 ĕpitĕlĕō (1), *to terminate; to undergo*
2038 ĕrgazŏmai (2), *to toil*
2140 ĕupŏiïa (1), *beneficence, doing good*
2192 ĕchō (2), *to have; hold; keep*
2480 ischuō (1), *to have or exercise force*
2554 kakŏpŏiĕō (2), *to injure; to sin, do wrong*
2698 katatithēmi (1), *to place down*
2716 katĕrgazŏmai (3), *to finish; to accomplish*
3930 parĕchō (1), *to hold near, i.e. to present*
4160 pŏiĕō (199), *to do*
4238 prassō (15), *to execute, accomplish*
4704 spŏudazō (2), *to make effort*
4982 sōzō (1), *to deliver; to protect*

DOCTOR
3547 nŏmŏdidaskalŏs (1), *Rabbi*

DOCTORS
1320 didaskalŏs (1), *instructor*
3547 nŏmŏdidaskalŏs (1), *Rabbi*

DOCTRINE
3948 leqach (4), *instruction*
4148 mûwçâr (1), *reproof, warning*
8052 shᵉmûw'âh (1), *announcement*
1319 didaskalia (15), *instruction*
1322 didachē (28), *instruction*
3056 lŏgŏs (1), *word, matter, thing*

DOCTRINES
1319 didaskalia (4), *instruction*
1322 didachē (1), *instruction*

DODAI
1739 dâveh (1), *menstrual; fainting*

DODANIM
1721 Dôdânîym (2), *Dodanites*

DODAVAH
1735 Dôwdâvâhûw (1), *love of Jehovah*

DODO
1734 Dôwdôw (5), *loving*

DOEG
1673 Dô'êg (6), *anxious*

DOER
6218 'âsôwr (3), group of ten
2557 kakŏurgŏs (1), criminal, evildoer
4163 pŏiētēs (3), performer; poet

DOERS
6213 'âsâh (2), to do or make
6466 pâ'al (1), to do, make or practice
4163 pŏiētēs (2), performer; poet

DOEST
5648 'âbad (Ch.) (1), to do, work, serve
6213 'âsâh (18), to do or make
6466 pâ'al (1), to do, make or practice
7965 shâlôwm (1), safe; well; health, prosperity
4160 pŏiĕō (14), to do
4238 prassō (1), to execute, accomplish

DOETH
1580 gâmal (1), to benefit or requite; to wean
5648 'âbad (Ch.) (1), to do, work, serve
6213 'âsâh (44), to do
7760 sûwm (1), to put, place
15 agathŏpŏiĕō (1), to be a well-doer
91 adikĕō (1), to do wrong
2554 kakŏpŏiĕō (1), to injure; to sin, do wrong
4160 pŏiĕō (34), to do
4238 prassō (3), to execute, accomplish
4374 prŏsphĕrō (1), to present to; to treat as

DOG
3611 keleb (14), dog; male prostitute
2965 kuōn (1), dog

DOG'S
3611 keleb (2), dog; male prostitute

DOGS
3611 keleb (16), dog; male prostitute
2952 kunariŏn (4), small dog
2965 kuōn (4), dog

DOING
854 'êth (1), with; by; at; among
4640 Ma'say (1), operative
5949 'ăliylâh (1), opportunity, action
6213 'âsâh (14), to do or make
15 agathŏpŏiĕō (2), to be a well-doer
16 agathŏpŏiïa (1), virtue, doing good
92 adikēma (1), wrong done
1096 ginŏmai (2), to be, become
1398 dŏulĕuō (1), to serve as a slave

2041 ĕrgŏn (1), work
2109 ĕuĕrgĕtĕō (1), to be philanthropic
2554 kakŏpŏiĕō (1), to injure; to sin, do wrong
2569 kalŏpŏiĕō (1), to do well
4160 pŏiĕō (8), to do

DOINGS
4611 ma'ălâl (35), act, deed
4640 Ma'say (3), operative
5949 'ăliylâh (13), opportunity, action

DOLEFUL
255 'ôach (1), creature that howls;
5093 nihyâh (1), lamentation

DOMINION
1166 bâ'al (1), to be master; to marry
1196 Ba'ănâh (1), in affliction
3027 yâd (2), hand; power
4474 mimshâl (2), ruler; dominion, rule
4475 memshâlâh (10), rule; realm or a ruler
4896 mishţâr (1), jurisdiction, rule
4910 mâshal (7), to rule
4915 môshel (2), empire; parallel
7287 râdâh (9), to subjugate
7300 rûwd (1), to ramble free or disconsolate
7980 shâlaţ (1), to dominate, i.e. govern
7985 sholţân (Ch.) (11), official
2634 katakuriĕuō (1), to control, subjugate
2904 kratŏs (4), vigor, strength
2961 kuriĕuō (4), to rule, be master of
2963 kuriŏtēs (2), rulers, masters

DOMINIONS
7985 sholţân (Ch.) (1), official
2963 kuriŏtēs (1), rulers, masters

DONE
466 'Ĕlîyphelêhûw (1), God of his distinction
1254 bârâ' (1), to create; fashion
1580 gâmal (1), to benefit or requite; to wean
1639 gâra' (1), to shave, remove, lessen
1697 dâbâr (1), word; matter; thing
1961 hâyâh (2), to exist, i.e. be or become
3254 yâçaph (1), to add or augment
3615 kâlâh (9), to complete, prepare
5414 nâthan (1), to give
5647 'âbad (1), to do, work, serve

5648 'âbad (Ch.) (4), to do, work, serve
5953 'âlal (3), to glean; to overdo
6213 'âsâh (318), to do or make
6466 pâ'al (21), to do, make or practice
7760 sûwm (1), to put, place
8552 tâmam (2), to complete, finish
91 adikĕō (3), to do wrong
1096 ginŏmai (61), to be, become
1796 ĕnubrizō (1), to insult
2673 katargĕō (4), to be, render entirely useless
2716 katĕrgazŏmai (2), to finish; to accomplish
4160 pŏiĕō (52), to do
4238 prassō (6), to execute, accomplish

DOOR
1004 bayith (1), house; temple; family, tribe
1817 deleth (21), door; gate
4201 mezûwzâh (2), door-post
4947 mashqôwph (1), lintel
5592 çaph (11), dish
6607 pethach (114), opening; door
6907 qubba'ath (2), goblet, cup
8179 sha'ar (1), opening, i.e. door or gate
2374 thura (28), entrance, i.e. door, gate
2377 thurōrŏs (2), doorkeeper

DOORKEEPER
5605 çâphaph (1), to wait at (the) threshold

DOORKEEPERS
7778 shôw'êr (2), janitor, door-keeper

DOORS
1817 deleth (48), door; gate
5592 çaph (2), dish
6607 pethach (11), opening; door
8179 sha'ar (1), opening, i.e. door or gate
2374 thura (1), entrance, i.e. door, gate

DOPHKAH
1850 Dophqâh (2), knock

DOR
1756 Dôwr (6), dwelling

DORCAS
1393 Dŏrkas (2), gazelle

DOTE
2973 yâ'al (1), to be or act foolish

DOTED
5689 'âgab (6), to lust sensually

DOTHAN
1886 Dôthân (3), Dothan

DOTING
3552 nŏsĕō (1), to be sick, be ill

DOUBLE
3717 kâphal (2), to fold together; to repeat
3718 kephel (3), duplicate, double
4932 mishneh (8), duplicate copy; double
8147 shenayim (5), two-fold
1362 diplŏus (2), two-fold
1374 dipsuchŏs (2), vacillating
3588+1362 hŏ (1), "the," i.e. the definite article

DOUBLED
3717 kâphal (3), to fold together; to repeat
8138 shânâh (1), to fold, i.e. duplicate

DOUBLETONGUED
1351 dilŏgŏs (1), insincere

DOUBT
551 'omnâm (1), verily, indeed, truly
142+5590 airō (1), to lift, to take up
639 apŏrĕō (1), be at a mental loss, be puzzled
686 ara (1), then, so, therefore
1063 gar (1), for, indeed, but, because
1252 diakrinō (2), to decide; to hesitate
1280 diapŏrĕō (1), to be thoroughly puzzled
1365 distazō (1), to waver in opinion
3843 pantōs (1), at all events; in no event

DOUBTED
639 apŏrĕō (1), be at a mental loss, be puzzled
1280 diapŏrĕō (2), to be thoroughly puzzled
1365 distazō (1), to waver in opinion

DOUBTETH
1252 diakrinō (1), to decide; to hesitate

DOUBTFUL
1261 dialŏgismŏs (1), consideration; debate
3349 mĕtĕōrizō (1), to be anxious

DOUBTING
639 apŏrĕō (1), be at a mental loss, be puzzled
1252 diakrinō (2), to decide; to hesitate
1261 dialŏgismŏs (1), consideration; debate

DOUBTLESS
518 'îm (1), whether?; if, although; Oh that!
3588 kîy (1), for, that because
1065 gĕ (1), particle of emphasis
1211 dē (1), now, then; indeed, therefore

3304 mĕnŏungĕ (1), *so then at least*

DOUBTS
7001 q^{e}ṭar (Ch.) (2), *riddle*

DOUGH
1217 bâtsêq (4), *fermenting dough*
6182 'ăriyçâh (4), *ground-up meal*

DOVE
3123 yôwnâh (14), *dove*
4058 pĕristĕra (4), *pigeon, dove*

DOVE'S
1686 dibyôwn (1), (poss.) *vegetable or root*

DOVES
3123 yôwnâh (5), *dove*
4058 pĕristĕra (5), *pigeon, dove*

DOVES'
3123 yôwnâh (2), *dove*

DOWN
935 bôw' (11), *to go or come*
1288 bârak (1), *to bless*
1438 gâda' (9), *to fell a tree; to destroy*
1457 gâhar (1), *to prostrate, bow down*
1760 dâchâh (1), *to push down; to totter*
2040 hâraç (22), *to pull down; break, destroy*
2904 ṭûwl (2), *to cast down or out, hurl*
3212 yâlak (1), *to walk; to live; to carry*
3281 Ya'lâm (1), *occult*
3332 yâtsaq (1), *to pour out*
3381 yârad (339), *to descend*
3665 kâna' (3), *to humiliate, vanquish*
3766 kâra' (9), *to prostrate*
3782 kâshal (4), *to totter, waver, stumble*
3996 mâbôw' (2), *entrance; sunset; west; towards*
4174 môwrâd (3), *descent, slope*
4295 maṭṭâh (1), *below or beneath*
4535 maççâch (1), *cordon; military barrier*
4606 mê'al (Ch.) (1), *setting of the sun*
4769 marbêts (2), *resting place*
5117 nûwach (1), *to rest; to settle down*
5128 nûwa' (1), *to waver*
5181 nâchath (4), *to sink, descend; to lead down*
5182 n^{e}chath (Ch.) (2), *to descend; to depose*
5183 nachath (1), *descent; quiet*
5186 nâṭâh (8), *to stretch or spread out*
5242 N^{e}mûw'êliy (2), *Nemuelite*

5243 nâmal (1), *to be circumcised*
5307 nâphal (9), *to fall*
5422 nâthats (29), *to tear down*
5456 çâgad (4), *to prostrate oneself*
5493 çûwr (1), *to turn off*
6131 'âqar (1), *to pluck up; to hamstring*
6201 'âraph (1), *to drip*
6915 qâdad (5), *to bend*
7250 râba' (2), *to lay down*
7252 reba' (1), *prostration for sleep*
7257 râbats (13), *to recline, repose, brood*
7323 rûwts (1), *to run*
7491 râ'aph (1), *to drip*
7503 râphâh (2), *to slacken*
7665 shâbar (1), *to burst*
7673 shâbath (1), *to repose; to desist*
7743 shûwach (1), *to sink*
7812 shâchâh (20), *to prostrate in homage*
7817 shâchach (12), *to sink or depress*
7821 sh^{e}chîyṭâh (1), *slaughter*
7901 shâkab (40), *to lie down*
7971 shâlach (2), *to send away*
8045 shâmad (2), *to desolate*
8058 shâmaṭ (2), *to jostle; to let alone*
8213 shâphêl (7), *to humiliate*
8214 sh^{e}phal (Ch.) (1), *to humiliate*
8231 shâphar (1), *to be, make fair*
8257 shâqa' (1), *to be overflowed; to cease*
8497 tâkâh (1), *to strew, i.e. encamp*
345 anakĕimai (2), *to recline at a meal*
347 anaklinō (7), *to lean back, recline*
377 anapiptō (10), *lie down, lean back*
387 anastatŏō (1), *to disturb, cause trouble*
1308 diaphĕrō (1), *to bear, carry; to differ*
1581 ĕkkŏptō (5), *to cut off; to frustrate*
1931 ĕpiduō (1), *to set*
2504 kagō (1), *and also*
2506 kathairĕsis (1), *demolition*
2507 kathairĕō (6), *to lower, or demolish*
2521 kathēmai (4), *to sit down; to remain, reside*
2523 kathizō (14), *to seat down, dwell*
2524 kathiēmi (4), *to lower, let down*
2596 kata (3), *down; according to*
2597 katabainō (64), *to descend*

2598 kataballō (2), *to throw down*
2601 katabibazō (2), *to cause to bring down*
2609 katagō (5), *to lead down; to moor a vessel*
2621 katakĕimai (1), *to lie down; to recline*
2625 kataklinō (2), *to take a place at table*
2630 katakrēmnizō (1), *to precipitate down*
2647 kataluō (3), *to halt for the night*
2662 katapatĕō (1), *to trample down; to reject*
2667 katapiptō (1), *to fall down*
2673 katargĕō (1), *to be, render entirely useless*
2679 kataskaptō (1), *to destroy, be ruined*
2701 katatrĕchō (1), *to hasten, run*
2718 katĕrchŏmai (6), *to go, come down*
2736 katō (5), *downwards*
2778 kēnsŏs (1), *enrollment*
2875 kŏptō (2), *to beat the breast*
3879 parakuptō (3), *to lean over*
3935 pariēmi (1), *to neglect; to be weakened*
4098 piptō (2), *to fall*
4496 rhiptō (2), *to fling, toss; to lay out*
4776 sugkathizō (1), *to give, take a seat with*
4781 sugkamptō (1), *to afflict*
4782 sugkatabainō (1), *to descend with*
5011 tapĕinŏs (1), *humiliated, lowly*
5294 hupŏtithēmi (1), *to hazard; to suggest*
5465 chalaō (5), *to lower as into a void*

DOWNSITTING
3427 yâshab (1), *to dwell, to remain; to settle*

DOWNWARD
4295 maṭṭâh (5), *below or beneath*

DOWRY
2065 zebed (1), *gift*
4119 môhar (3), *wife-price*

DRAG
4365 mikmereth (2), *fishing-net*

DRAGGING
4951 surō (1), *to trail, drag, sweep*

DRAGON
8577 tannîyn (6), *sea-serpent; jackal*
1404 *drakōn* (13), *fabulous kind of serpent*

DRAGONS
8568 tannâh (1), female *jackal*
8577 tannîyn (15), *sea-serpent; jackal*

DRAMS
150 'ădarkôn (2), *daric*
1871 dark^{e}môwn (4), *coin*

DRANK
4960 mishteh (2), *drink; banquet or feast*
8354 shâthâh (8), *to drink, imbibe*
8355 sh^{e}thâh (Ch.) (3), *to drink, imbibe*
4095 pinō (5), *to imbibe, drink*

DRAUGHT
4280 machărâ'âh (1), *privy sink, latrine*
61 agra (2), *haul of fish in a net*
856 aphĕdrōn (2), *privy or latrine*

DRAVE
1644 gârash (3), *to drive out; to expatriate*
3423 yârash (2), *to impoverish; to ruin*
5071 n^{e}dâbâh (1), *abundant gift*
5090 nâhag (4), *to drive forth; to lead*
5394 nâshal (1), *to divest, eject, or drop*
556 apĕlaunō (1), *to dismiss, eject*
1856 ĕxōthĕō (1), *to expel; to propel*

DRAW
748 'ârak (1), *to be, make long*
1518 gîyach (1), *to issue forth; to burst forth*
1802 dâlâh (1), *to draw out water); to deliver*
2502 châlats (1), *to pull off; to strip; to depart*
2834 châsaph (1), *to drain away or bail up*
3318 yâtsâ' (1), *to go, bring out*
4900 mâshak (11), *to draw out; to be tall*
5423 nâthaq (1), *to tear off*
5498 çâchab (3), *to trail along*
6329 pûwq (1), *to issue; to furnish; to secure*
7324 rûwq (8), *to pour out, i.e. empty*
7579 shâ'ab (9), *to bale up water*
8025 shâlaph (4), *to pull out, up or off*
501 antlĕō (3), *dip water*
502 antlēma (1), *bucket for drawing water*
645 apŏspaō (1), *unsheathe a sword*
1670 hĕlkuō (4), *to drag, draw, pull in*
4334 prŏsĕrchŏmai (1), *to come near, visit*
5288 hupŏstĕllō (1), *to cower or shrink*
5289 hupŏstŏlē (1), *shrinkage, timidity*

DRAWER
7579 shâ'ab (1), *to bale up water*

D

DRAWERS
7579 shâ'ab (3), to *bale up water*

DRAWETH
4900 mâshak (2), to *draw out; to be tall*
7503 râphâh (1), to *slacken*

DRAWING
4857 mash'âb (1), water *trough for cattle*
1096 ginômai (1), to *be, become*

DRAWN
3318 yâtsâ' (1), to *go, bring out*
3947 lâqach (1), to *take*
4900 mâshak (2), to *draw out; to be tall*
5080 nâdach (1), to *push off, scattered*
5203 nâṭash (1), to *disperse; to thrust* off
5423 nâthaq (3), to *tear* off
5498 çâchab (1), to *trail along*
6267 'attîyq (1), *weaned; antique*
6605 pâthach (2), to *open wide; to loosen, begin*
6609 peᵗhîchâh (1), *drawn sword*
7579 shâ'ab (1), to *bale up water*
7725 shûwb (1), to *turn back; to return*
8025 shâlaph (5), to *pull out, up or* off
8388 tâ'ar (5), to *delineate; to extend*
385 anaspaō (1), to *take up or extricate*
1828 *exelkō (1), to *drag away*, i.e. *entice*

DREAD
367 'êymâh (1), *fright*
2844 chath (1), *terror*
3372 yârê' (1), to *fear; to revere*
4172 môwrâ' (1), *fearful*
6206 'ârats (2), to *awe to; to dread; to harass*
6343 pachad (1), *sudden alarm, fear*

DREADFUL
1763 deᶜchal (Ch.) (2), to *fear; be formidable, awesome*
3372 yârê' (5), to *fear; to revere*
3374 yir'âh (1), *fear; reverence*
6343 pachad (1), *sudden alarm, fear*

DREAM
2472 chălôwm (44), *dream; dreamer*
2492 châlam (1), to *dream*
2493 chêlem (Ch.) (21), *dream*
1798 ĕnupniŏn (1), *dream, vision*
3677 ŏnar (6), *dream*

DREAMED
2492 châlam (19), to *dream*

DREAMER
1167+2472 ba'al (1), *master; owner; citizen*
2492 châlam (3), to *dream*

DREAMERS
2492 châlam (1), to *dream*
1797 ĕnupniazŏmai (1), to *dream*

DREAMETH
2492 châlam (2), to *dream*

DREAMS
2472 chălôwm (19), *dream; dreamer*
2493 chêlem (Ch.) (1), *dream*
1797 ĕnupniazŏmai (1), to *dream*

DREGS
6907 qubba'ath (2), *goblet, cup*
8105 shemer (1), *settlings of wine, dregs*

DRESS
5647 'âbad (2), to *do, work, serve*
6213 'âsâh (7), to *do or make*

DRESSED
6213 'âsâh (6), to *do or make*
1090 gĕōrgĕō (1), to *till the soil*

DRESSER
289 ampĕlŏurgŏs (1), *vineyard caretaker*

DRESSERS
3755 kôrêm (1), *vinedresser*

DRESSETH
3190 yâṭab (1), to *be, make well*

DREW
748 'ârak (2), to *be, make long*
1802 dâlâh (2), to *draw out water; to deliver*
1869 dârak (1), to *walk, lead; to string a bow*
3318 yâtsâ' (1), to *go, bring out*
4871 mâshâh (3), to *pull out*
4900 mâshak (6), to *draw out; to be tall*
7579 shâ'ab (4), to *bale up water*
7725 shûwb (2), to *turn back; to return*
8025 shâlaph (15), to *pull out, up or* off
307 anabibazō (1), *haul up a net*
501 antlĕō (1), *dip water*
645 apŏspaō (1), *unsheathe a sword*
868 aphistēmi (1), *desist, desert*
1670 hĕlkuō (4), to *drag, draw, pull in*

DRIED
1809 dâlal (1), to *slacken, dangle*
2717 chârab (9), to *parch; desolate, destroy*
2787 chârar (1), to *melt, burn, dry up*
3001 yâbêsh (22), to *dry up; to wither*
3002 yâbêsh (1), *dry*
6704 tsîcheh (1), *parched*
7033 qâlâh (1), to *toast, scorch*
3583 xērainō (3), to *shrivel, to mature*

DRIEDST
3001 yâbêsh (1), to *dry up; to wither*

DRIETH
3001 yâbêsh (3), to *dry up; to wither*

DRINK
1572 gâmâ' (1), to *swallow*
4469 mamçâk (1), *mixed*-wine
4945 mashqeh (2), *butler; drink; well-watered*
4960 mishteh (3), *drink; banquet or feast*
5257 neᶜçîyk (1), *libation; molten image; prince*
5261 neᶜçak (Ch.) (1), *libation*
5262 neçek (59), *libation; cast idol*
5435 çôbe' (1), *wine*
7937 shâkar (2), to *become tipsy, to satiate*
7941 shêkâr (21), *liquor*
8248 shâqâh (42), to *quaff*, i.e. *irrigate*
8249 shiqqûv (1), *draught, drink*
8250 shiqqûwy (1), *beverage; refreshment*
8353 shêth (Ch.) (1), *six; sixth*
8354 shâthâh (161), to *drink, imbibe*
8355 sheᵗhâh (Ch.) (1), to *drink, imbibe*
4095 pinō (50), to *imbibe, drink*
4188 pŏma (1), *beverage, drink*
4213 pŏsis (3), *draught, drink*
4222 pŏtizō (9), to *furnish drink, irrigate*
4608 sikĕra (1), *intoxicant*
4844 sumpinō (1), to *partake a beverage*

DRINK (col 4)
5202 hudrŏpŏtĕō (1), to *drink water exclusively*

DRINKERS
8354 shâthâh (1), to *drink, imbibe*

DRINKETH
6231 'âshaq (1), to *overflow*
8354 shâthâh (8), to *drink, imbibe*
4095 pinō (7), to *imbibe, drink*

DRINKING
4945 mashqeh (2), *butler; drink; well-watered*
8354 shâthâh (12), to *drink, imbibe*
8360 sheᵗhîyâh (1), *manner of drinking*
4095 pinō (6), to *imbibe, drink*

DRINKS
4188 pŏma (1), *beverage, drink*

DRIVE
1644 gârash (12), to *drive out; to divorce*
1920 hâdaph (2), to *push away or down; drive out*
2957 ṭerad (Ch.) (2), to *expel, drive on*
3423 yârash (30), to *impoverish; to ruin*
5080 nâdach (5), to *push off, scattered*
5086 nâdaph (1), to *disperse, be windblown*
5090 nâhag (2), to *drive forth; to carry away*
6327 pûwts (1), to *dash in pieces; to disperse*
1929 ĕpididōmi (1), to *give over*

DRIVEN
1644 gârash (5), to *drive out; to divorce*
1760 dâchâh (2), to *push down; to totter*
1920 hâdaph (1), to *push away or down; drive out*
2957 ṭerad (Ch.) (2), to *expel, drive on*
3423 yârash (2), to *impoverish; to ruin*
5080 nâdach (23), to *push off, scattered*
5086 nâdaph (4), to *disperse, be windblown*
5437 çâbab (2), to *surround*
5472 çûwg (1), to *go back, to retreat*
5590 çâ'ar (1), to *rush upon; to toss about*
7617 shâbâh (1), to *transport into captivity*
416 anemizō (1), to *toss with the wind*
1308 diaphĕrō (1), to *bear, carry; to differ*
1643 ĕlaunō (2), to *push*
5342 phĕrō (1), to *bear or carry*

DRIVER
5065 nâgas (1), to *exploit; to tax, harass*

7395 rakkâb (1),
charioteer

DRIVETH
2342 chûwl (1), to *dance,
whirl;* to *writhe*
5086 nâdaph (1), to
disperse, be windblown
5090 nâhag (1), to *drive
forth;* to *carry away*
1544 ĕkballō (1), to
throw out

DRIVING
1644 gârash (1), to *drive
out;* to *divorce*
3423 yârash (1), to
impoverish; to *ruin*
4491 minhâg (2),
chariot-*driving*

DROMEDARIES
1070 beker (1), young
bull *camel*
7409 rekesh (1), *relay* of
animals on a post-route
7424 rammâk (1), brood
mare

DROMEDARY
1072 bikrâh (1), young
she-*camel*

DROP
4752 mar (1), *drop* in a
bucket
5140 nâzal (1), to *drip,* or
shed by trickling
5197 nâṭaph (7), to *fall in
drops*
6201 'âraph (2), to *drip*
7491 râ'aph (4), to *drip*

DROPPED
1982 hêlek (1), *wayfarer,
visitor; flowing*
5197 nâṭaph (5), to *fall in
drops*
5413 nâthak (1), to *flow
forth, pour* out

DROPPETH
1811 dâlaph (1), to *drip*

DROPPING
1812 deleph (2), *dripping*
5197 nâṭaph (1), to *fall in
drops*

DROPS
96 'egel (1), *reservoir*
5197 nâṭaph (1), to *fall in
drops*
7447 râçîyç (1), *ruin;*
dew-*drop*
2361 thrŏmbŏs (1), *clot* of
blood

DROPSY
5203 hudrōpikŏs (1), to
suffer edema

DROSS
5509 çîyg (8), *refuse,
scoria*

DROUGHT
1226 batstsôreth (1),
drought
2721 chôreb (3),
parched; ruined
2725 chărâbôwn (1),
parching *heat*
6710 tsachtsâchâh (1),
dry desert place
6723 tsîyâh (2), arid
desert

6774 tsimmâ'ôwn (1),
desert
8514 tal'ûwbâh (1),
dehydration

DROVE
1272 bârach (1), to *flee*
suddenly
1644 gârash (3), to *drive*
out; to *divorce*
3423 yârash (2), to
impoverish; to *ruin*
4264 machăneh (1),
encampment
5380 nâshab (1), to *blow;*
to *disperse*
5425 nâthar (1), to *jump;*
to *terrify; shake* off
5739 'êder (3), *muster,
flock*
1544 ĕkballō (1), to
throw out

DROVES
5739 'êder (1), *muster,
flock*

DROWN
7857 shâṭaph (1), to
gush; to *inundate*
1036 buthizō (1), to *sink;*
to *plunge*

DROWNED
2823 châshôk (1), *obscure*
8248 shâqâh (2), to *quaff,*
i.e. to *irrigate*
2666 katapinō (1), to
devour by swallowing
2670 katapŏntizō (1), to
submerge, be drowned

DROWSINESS
5124 nûwmâh (1),
sleepiness

DRUNK
7301 râvâh (1), to *slake*
thirst or appetites
7910 shikkôwr (2),
intoxicated
7937 shâkar (4), to
become tipsy, to *satiate*
8354 shâthâh (15), to
drink, imbibe
8355 shᵉthâh (Ch.) (1), to
drink, imbibe
3182 mĕthuskō (2), to
become drunk
3184 mĕthuō (1), to *get
drunk*
4095 pinō (2), to *imbibe,
drink*

DRUNKARD
5435 çôbe' (2), *wine*
7910 shikkôwr (2),
intoxicated
3183 mĕthusŏs (1),
drunkard

DRUNKARDS
5435 çôbe' (1), *wine*
7910 shikkôwr (3),
intoxicated
8354+7941 shâthâh (1), to
drink, imbibe
3183 mĕthusŏs (1),
drunkard

DRUNKEN
5435 çôbe' (1), *wine*
7301 râvâh (1), to *slake*
thirst or appetites

7910 shikkôwr (6),
intoxicated
7937 shâkar (13), to
become tipsy, to *satiate*
7943 shikkârôwn (2),
intoxication
8354 shâthâh (3), to
drink, imbibe
3182 mĕthuskō (1), to
become drunk
3184 mĕthuō (5), to *get
drunk*
4095 pinō (1), to *imbibe,
drink*

DRUNKENNESS
7302 râveh (1), *sated, full*
with drink
7943 shikkârôwn (2),
intoxication
8358 shᵉthîy (1),
intoxication
3178 mĕthē (3),
intoxication

DRUSILLA
1409 Drŏusilla (1),
Drusilla

DRY
954 bûwsh (1), be
ashamed; disappointed
2717 chârab (3), to
parch, desolate, destroy
2720 chârêb (3),
parched; ruined
2721 chôreb (3),
parched; ruined
2724 chârâbâh (8),
desert, dry land
3001 yâbêsh (9), to *dry*
up; to *wither*
3002 yâbêsh (7), *dry*
3004 yabbâshâh (14), *dry*
ground
3006 yabbesheth (2), *dry*
ground
5424 netheq (1), *scurf,*
i.e. diseased skin
6703 tsach (1), *dazzling,*
i.e. *sunny, bright*
6707 tsᵉchîychâh (1),
parched desert region
6723 tsîyâh (10), arid
desert
6724 tsîyôwn (2), *desert*
6774 tsimmâ'ôwn (1),
desert
6784 tsâmaq (1), to *dry*
up, *shrivel* up
504 anudrŏs (2), *dry, arid*
3584 xērŏs (2), *scorched;
arid; withered*

DRYSHOD
5275 na'al (1), *sandal*

DUE
1167 ba'al (1), *master;
husband; owner; citizen*
1697 dâbâr (1), *word;
matter; thing*
2706 chôq (2),
appointment; allotment
4941 mishpâṭ (1), *verdict;
formal decree; justice*
514 axiŏs (1), *deserving,
comparable* or *suitable*
2398 idiŏs (3), *private* or
separate
3784 ŏphĕilō (2), to *owe;*
to *be under obligation*

DUES
3782 ŏphĕilē (1), *sum
owed; obligation*

DUKE
441 'allûwph (20), *friend,*
one *familiar; chieftain*

DUKES
441 'allûwph (13), *friend,*
one *familiar; chieftain*
5257 nᵉçîyk (1), *libation;*
molten *image; prince*

DULCIMER
5481 çûwmpôwnᵉyâh
(Ch.) (3), *bagpipe*

DULL
917 barĕōs (2), *heavily,
with difficulty*
3576 nōthrŏs (1), *lazy;
stupid*

DUMAH
1746 Dûwmâh (4),
silence; death

DUMB
481 'âlam (7), to be
tongue-tied, be silent
483 'illêm (6), *speechless*
1748 dûwmâm (1),
silently
216 alalŏs (3), *mute, not
able to speak*
880 aphōnŏs (3), *mute,
silent; unmeaning*
2974 kōphŏs (8), *deaf* or
silent
4623 siōpaō (1), to *be
quiet*

DUNG
830 'ashpôth (4), heap of
rubbish; Dung gate
1557 gâlâl (1), *dung*
pellets
1561 gêlel (4), *dung;
dung* pellets
1828 dômen (6), *manure,
dung*
2716+(6675) chere' (2),
excrement
2755 chărêy-yôwnîym
(1), *excrements of
doves* or a vegetable
6569 peresh (7),
excrement
6832 tsᵉphûwa' (1),
excrement
906+2874 ballō (1), to
throw
4657 skubalŏn (1), what
is *thrown* to the dogs

DUNGEON
953 bôwr (13), pit *hole,
cistern, well; prison*

DUNGHILL
830 'ashpôth (2), heap of
rubbish; Dung gate
4087 madmênâh (1),
dunghill
5122 nᵉvâlûw (Ch.) (3), to
be foul; sink
2874 kŏpria (1), *manure*
or *rubbish* pile

DUNGHILLS
830 'ashpôth (1), heap of
rubbish; Dung gate

DURA
1757 Dûwrâ' (Ch.) (1), circle or dwelling

DURABLE
6266 'âthîyq (1), venerable or splendid
6276 'âthêq (1), enduring value

DURETH
2076 ĕsti (1), he (she or it) is; they are

DURST
3372 yârê' (1), to fear; to revere
5111 tŏlmaŏ (7), to be bold; to dare

DUST
80 'âbâq (5), fine dust; cosmetic powder
1854 dâqaq (1), to crush; crumble
6083 'âphâr (91), dust, earth, mud; clay,
7834 shachaq (1), firmament, clouds
2868 kŏniŏrtŏs (5), blown dust
5522 chŏŏs (2), loose dirt

DUTY
1697 dâbâr (2), word; matter; thing
3784 ŏphĕilŏ (2), to owe; to fail in duty

DWARF
1851 daq (1), crushed; small or thin

DWELL
1481 gûwr (11), to sojourn, live as an alien
1752 dûwr (1), remain
1753 dûwr (Ch.) (3), to reside, live in
2073 zᵉbûwl (1), residence, dwelling
2082 zâbal (1), to reside
3427 yâshab (210), to dwell, to remain
3488 yᵉthîb (Ch.) (1), to sit or dwell
3885 lûwn (1), to be obstinate
4186 môwshâb (1), seat; site; abode
5975 'âmad (1), to stand
7931 shâkan (69), to reside
7932 shᵉkan (Ch.) (1), to reside
1774 ĕnŏikĕŏ (2), to inhabit, live with
2521 kathēmai (1), to sit down; to remain, reside
2730 katŏikĕŏ (19), to reside, live in
3306 mĕnō (2), to stay, remain
3611 ŏikĕŏ (4), to reside, inhabit, remain
4637 skēnŏŏ (4), to occupy; to reside
4924 sunŏikĕŏ (1), to reside together as a family

DWELLED
3427 yâshab (6), to dwell, to remain; to settle

DWELLERS
7931 shâkan (1), to reside
2730 katŏikĕŏ (2), to reside, live in

DWELLEST
3427 yâshab (14), to dwell, to remain
7931 shâkan (3), to reside
2730 katŏikĕŏ (1), to reside, live in
3306 mĕnō (1), to stay, remain

DWELLETH
1481 gûwr (1), to sojourn, live as an alien
3427 yâshab (20), to dwell, to remain
4908 mishkân (1), residence
7931 shâkan (9), to reside
8271 shᵉrê' (Ch.) (1), to free, separate; to reside
1774 ĕnŏikĕŏ (2), to inhabit, live with
2730 katŏikĕŏ (7), to reside, live in
3306 mĕnō (9), to stay, remain
3611 ŏikĕŏ (4), to reside, inhabit, remain

DWELLING
168 'ôhel (3), tent
2073 zᵉbûwl (1), residence, dwelling
3427 yâshab (17), to dwell, to remain
4070 mᵉdôwr (Ch.) (4), dwelling
4186 môwshâb (5), seat; site; abode
4349 mâkôwn (2), basis; place
4583 mâ'ôwn (6), retreat or asylum dwelling
4585 mᵉ'ôwnâh (1), abode
4908 mishkân (4), residence
5116 nâveh (3), at home; lovely; home
7931 shâkan (1), to reside
1460 ĕgkatŏikĕŏ (1), reside, live among
2730 katŏikĕŏ (3), to reside, live in
2731 katŏikēsis (1), residence
3611 ŏikĕŏ (1), to reside, inhabit, remain

DWELLINGPLACE
4186 môwshâb (1), seat; site; abode
790 astatĕŏ (1), homeless, vagabond

DWELLINGPLACES
4186 môwshâb (2), seat; site; abode
4908 mishkân (3), residence

DWELLINGS
4033 mâgôwr (2), abode
4186 môwshâb (8), seat; site; abode
4908 mishkân (6), residence
5116 nâveh (1), at home; lovely; home

DWELT
1753 dûwr (Ch.) (2), to reside, live in
2583 chânâh (2), to encamp
3427 yâshab (189), to dwell, to remain
4186 môwshâb (2), seat; site; abode
7931 shâkan (11), to reside
1774 ĕnŏikĕŏ (1), to inhabit, live with
2730 katŏikĕŏ (12), to reside, live in
3306 mĕnō (2), to stay, remain
3940 parŏikia (1), foreign residence
4039 pĕriŏikĕŏ (1), to be a neighbor
4637 skēnŏŏ (1), to occupy; to reside

DYED
2556 châmêts (1), to be fermented; be soured
2871 ţâbûwl (1), turban

DYING
1478 gâva' (1), to expire, die
599 apŏthnēskŏ (4), to die off
3500 nĕkrōsis (1), death, deadness

EACH
259 'echâd (10), first
376 'îysh (5), man; male; someone
802 'ishshâh (2), woman, wife; women, wives
905 bad (1), limb, member; bar; chief
240 allēlōn (2), one another
303 ana (1), each; in turn; among
1538 hĕkastŏs (2), each or every

EAGLE
5404 nesher (19), large bird of prey
7360 râchâm (2), kind of vulture
105 aĕtŏs (2), eagle, vulture

EAGLE'S
5403 nᵉshar (Ch.) (1), large bird of prey
5404 nesher (1), large bird of prey

EAGLES
5404 nesher (5), large bird of prey
105 aĕtŏs (2), eagle, vulture

EAGLES'
5403 nᵉshar (Ch.) (1), large bird of prey
5404 nesher (1), large bird of prey

EAR
24 'âbîyb (1), head of grain; month of Abib
238 'âzan (33), to listen
241 'ôzen (63), ear

DWELL (cont.)
2790 chârash (1), to be silent; to be deaf
5647 'âbad (1), to do, work, serve
8085 shâma' (1), to hear intelligently
3775 ŏus (13), ear; listening
4719 stachus (2), head of grain
5621 ōtiŏn (5), earlet, ear (-lobe)

EARED
5647 'âbad (1), to do, work, serve

EARING
2758 chârîysh (2), plowing; plowing season

EARLY
1242 bôqer (3), morning
6852 tsâphar (1), to return
7836 shâchar (6), to search for
7837 shachar (2), dawn
7925 shâkam (62), to start early
8238 shᵉpharphar (Ch.) (1), dawn
260+4404 hama (1), at the same time, together
3719 ŏrthrizō (1), to get up early in the morning
3721 ŏrthriŏs (1), up at day-break
3722 ŏrthrŏs (3), dawn, daybreak
4404 prōï (3), at dawn; day-break watch
4405 prōïa (1), day-dawn, early morn
4406 prōïmŏs (1), autumnal showering

EARNEST
603 apŏkaradŏkia (2), intense anticipation
728 arrhabōn (3), pledge, security
1972 ĕpipŏthēsis (1), longing for
4056 pĕrissŏtĕrōs (1), more superabundantly
4710 spŏudē (1), eagerness, earnestness

EARNESTLY
2734 chârâh (1), to blaze up
3190 yâţab (1), to be, make well
816 atĕnizō (3), to gaze intently
1617 ĕktĕnĕstĕrŏn (1), more earnest
1864 ĕpagōnizŏmai (1), to struggle for, fight for
1971 ĕpipŏthĕŏ (1), intensely crave
2206 zēlŏŏ (1), to have warmth of feeling for
4335 prŏsĕuchē (1), prayer; prayer chapel

EARNETH
7936 sâkar (1), to hire

EARRING
5141 nezem (5), nose-ring

EARRINGS
3908 lachash (1),
incantation; amulet
5141 nezem (9),
nose-ring
5694 'âgîyl (2), ear-*ring*

EARS
24 'âbîyb (1), *head of
grain;* month of *Abib*
241 'ôzen (100), *ear*
3759 karmel (3), *planted
field;* garden *produce*
4425 mᵉlîylâh (1), *cut*-off
head of cereal grain
7641 shibbôl (13),
stream; ear of grain
189 akŏē (4), *hearing;
thing heard*
191 akŏuō (1), to *hear;
obey*
3775 ŏus (24), *ear;
listening*
4719 stachus (3), *head* of
grain

EARTH
127 'ădâmâh (52), *soil;
land*
772 'ăra' (Ch.) (20),
earth, ground, land
776 'erets (710), *earth,
land, soil; country*
778 'ăraq (Ch.) (1), *earth*
2789 cheres (1), piece of
earthenware *pottery*
3007 yabbesheth (Ch.)
(1), *dry* land
6083 'âphâr (7), *dust,
earth, mud; clay,*
1093 gē (186), *soil,
region,* whole *earth*
1919 ĕpigĕiŏs (1),
worldly, earthly
2709 katachthŏniŏs (1),
infernal
3625 ŏikŏumĕnē (1),
Roman empire
3749 ŏstrakinŏs (1),
made of clay

EARTHEN
2789 cheres (8), piece of
earthenware *pottery*
3335 yâtsar (1), to *form;
potter;* to *determine*
3749 ŏstrakinŏs (1),
made of clay

EARTHLY
1537+3588+1093 ĕk (1),
out, out of
1919 ĕpigĕiŏs (4),
worldly, earthly

EARTHQUAKE
7494 ra'ash (6),
vibration, uproar
4578 sĕismŏs (10), *gale
storm; earthquake*

EARTHQUAKES
4578 sĕismŏs (3), *gale
storm; earthquake*

EARTHY
5517 chŏïkŏs (4), *dusty,
dirty,* i.e. *terrene*

EASE
2896 tôwb (1), *good; well*
3427 yâshab (1), to *dwell,*
to *remain;* to *settle*

4496 mᵉnûwchâh (1),
peacefully; consolation
5162 nâcham (1), to *be
sorry;* to *pity, console*
5375 nâsâ' (1), to *lift up*
7043 qâlal (2), to *be easy,
trifling, vile*
7280 râga' (1), to *settle,*
i.e. *quiet;* to *wink*
7599 shâ'an (2), to *loll,*
i.e. *be peaceful*
7600 sha'ănân (6),
secure; haughty
7946 shal'ănân (1),
tranquil
7961 shâlêv (2), *carefree;
security, at ease*
373 anapauō (1), to
repose; to *refresh*

EASED
1980 hâlak (1), to *walk;
live a certain way*
425 anĕsis (1),
relaxation; relief

EASIER
7043 qâlal (1), to *be easy,
trifling, vile*
2123 ĕukŏpŏtĕrŏs (7),
better for toil

EAST
2777 charçûwth (1),
pottery
4161 môwtsâ' (1), *going
forth*
4217 mizrâch (33), place
of *sunrise; east*
4217+8121 mizrâch (2),
place of *sunrise; east*
6921 qâdîym (61), *east;
eastward; east wind*
6924 qedem (42), *east,
eastern; antiquity*
6926 qidmâh (3), *east;* on
the *east, in front*
6930 qadmôwn (1),
eastern
6931 qadmôwnîy (4),
oriental, eastern
395 anatŏlē (9), *dawn* of
sun; *east*

EASTER
3957 pascha (1),
Passover events

EASTWARD
1870+6921 derek (1),
road; course of life
4217 mizrâch (19), place
of *sunrise; east*
4217+8121 mizrâch (1),
place of *sunrise; east*
6921 qâdîym (7), *East;
eastward; east wind*
6924 qedem (11), *east,
eastern; antiquity*
6926 qidmâh (1), *east;* on
the *east, in front*

EASY
7043 qâlal (1), to *be easy,
trifling, vile*
2138 ĕupĕithēs (1),
compliant, submissive
2154 ĕusēmŏs (1),
significant
5543 chrēstŏs (1),
employed, i.e. *useful*

EAT
398 'âkal (497), to *eat*

399 'ăkal (Ch.) (1), to *eat*
402 'ŏklâh (2), *food*
1262 bârâh (4), to *feed*
2490 châlal (1), to
profane, defile
2939 ṭᵉ'am (Ch.) (2), to
feed
3898 lâcham (5), to *fight*
a *battle,* i.e. *consume*
3899 lechem (1), *food,
bread*
6310 peh (1), *mouth;
opening*
7462 râ'âh (2), to *tend* a
flock, i.e. *pasture* it
1089 gĕuŏmai (1), to
taste; to *eat*
2068 ĕsthiō (39), to *eat*
2719 katĕsthiō (1), to
devour
3335 mĕtalambanō (1),
to *participate*
3542+2192 nŏmē (1),
pasture, feeding
4906 sunĕsthiō (4), to
take food with
5315 phagō (88), to *eat*

EATEN
398 'âkal (86), to *eat*
935+413+7130 bôw' (2), to
go or come
1197 bâ'ar (2), to *be
brutish, be senseless*
2490 châlal (1), to
profane, defile
7462 râ'âh (1), to *tend* a
flock, i.e. *pasture* it
977 bibrōskō (1), to *eat*
1089 gĕuŏmai (2), to
taste; to *eat*
2068 ĕsthiō (1), to *eat*
2719 katĕsthiō (1), to
devour
2880 kŏrĕnnumi (1), to
cram, i.e. *glut or sate*
4662 skōlĕkŏbrōtŏs (1),
diseased with maggots
5315 phagō (5), to *eat*

EATER
398 'âkal (3), to *eat*

EATERS
2151 zâlal (1), to *be loose
morally, worthless*

EATEST
398 'âkal (3), to *eat*

EATETH
398 'âkal (31), to *eat*
1104 bâla' (1), to
swallow; to *destroy*
2068 ĕsthiō (13), to *eat*
4906 sunĕsthiō (1), to
take food with
5176 trōgō (5), to *gnaw
or chew,* i.e. to *eat*

EATING
398 'âkal (13), to *eat*
400 'ôkel (4), *food*
3894 lâchûwm (1), *flesh*
as food
1035 brōsis (1), *food;
rusting corrosion*
2068 ĕsthiō (6), to *eat*
5176 trōgō (1), to *gnaw
or chew,* i.e. to *eat*
5315 phagō (1), to *eat*

EBAL
5858 'Êybâl (8), *bare, bald*

EBED
5651 'Ebed (6), *servant*

EBED-MELECH
5663 'Ebed Melek (6),
servant of a king

EBEN-EZER
72 'Eben hâ-'êzer (3),
stone of the help

EBER
5677 'Êber (13), *regions
beyond*

EBIASAPH
43 'Ebyâçâph (3),
Ebjasaph

EBONY
1894 hôben (1), *ebony*

EBRONAH
5684 'Ebrônâh (2),
Ebronah

EDAR
5740 'Êder (1), *flock*

EDEN
5731 'Êden (20), *pleasure*

EDER
5740 'Êder (3), *flock*

EDGE
5310 nâphats (1), to *dash
to pieces;* to *scatter*
6310 peh (34), *mouth;
opening*
6440 pânîym (1), *face;
front*
6697 tsûwr (1), *rock*
6949 qâhâh (3), to *be
dull; be blunt*
7097 qâtseh (8), *extremity*
8193 sâphâh (5), *lip;
edge, margin*
4750 stŏma (2), *mouth;
edge*

EDGES
6366 pêyâh (1), *edge*
7098 qâtsâh (1),
termination; fringe
7099 qetsev (1), *limit,
borders*
1366 distŏmŏs (1),
double-edged

EDIFICATION
3619 ŏikŏdŏmē (4),
edification

EDIFIED
3618 ŏikŏdŏmĕō (2), to
construct, edify

EDIFIETH
3618 ŏikŏdŏmĕō (3), to
construct, edify

EDIFY
3618 ŏikŏdŏmĕō (2), to
construct, edify
3619 ŏikŏdŏmē (1),
edification

EDIFYING
3618 ŏikŏdŏmĕō (1), to
construct, edify
3619 ŏikŏdŏmē (7),
edification

EDOM
123 'Êdôm (87), *red*

EDOMITE
130 'Êdômîy (6), *Edomite*

EDOMITES
130 'Ĕdômîy (12),
Edomite

EDREI
154 'edre'îy (8), *mighty*

EFFECT
1697 dâbâr (1), *word;*
matter; thing
5106 nûw' (1), to *refuse,*
forbid, dissuade
5656 'âbôdâh (1), *work of*
any kind
6213 'âsâh (1), to *do or*
make
6565 pârar (1), to *break*
up; to violate, frustrate
208 akurŏŏ (2), to
invalidate, nullify
1601 ĕkpiptŏ (1), to *drop*
away
2673 katargĕŏ (4), to *be,*
render entirely useless
2758 kĕnŏŏ (1), to *make*
empty

EFFECTED
6743 tsâlach (1), to *push*
forward

EFFECTUAL
1753 ĕnĕrgĕia (2),
efficiency, energy
1754 ĕnĕrgĕŏ (2), to *be*
active, efficient, work
1756 ĕnĕrgĕs (2), *active,*
operative

EFFECTUALLY
1754 ĕnĕrgĕŏ (2). to *be*
active, efficient, work

EFFEMINATE
3120 malakŏs (1), *soft;*
catamite homosexual

EGG
2495 challâmûwth (1),
(poss.) *purslain* plant
5609 ŏŏn (1), *egg*

EGGS
1000 bêytsâh (6), *egg*

EGLAH
5698 'Eglâh (2), *heifer*

EGLAIM
97 'Eglayim (1), *double*
pond

EGLON
5700 'Eglôwn (13),
vituline

EGYPT
4713 Mitsrîy (1), *Mitsrite*
4714 Mitsrayim (585),
double *border*
125 Aiguptŏs (24),
Ægyptus

EGYPTIAN
4713 Mitsrîy (18), *Mitsrite*
4714 Mitsrayim (2),
double *border*
124 Aiguptiŏs (3),
inhabitant of Ægyptus

EGYPTIAN'S
4713 Mitsrîy (4), *Mitsrite*

EGYPTIANS
4713 Mitsrîy (7), *Mitsrite*
4714 Mitsrayim (88),
double *border*
124 Aiguptiŏs (2),
inhabitant of Ægyptus

EHI
278 'Êchîy (1), *Echi*

EHUD
261 'Êchûwd (10), *united*

EIGHT
8083 sheмôneh (74),
eight; eighth
3638 ŏktŏ (6), *eight*

EIGHTEEN
7239+8083 ribbôw (1),
myriad
8083+6240 sheмôneh
(18), *eight; eighth*
1176+2532+3638 dĕka (3),
ten

EIGHTEENTH
8083+6240 sheмôneh
(11), *eight; eighth*

EIGHTH
8066 sheмîynîy (28),
eight, eighth
8083 sheмôneh (4),
eight; eighth
3590 ŏgdŏŏs (5), *eighth*
3637 ŏktaĕмĕrŏs (1),
eighth-day

EIGHTIETH
'084 sheмônîym (1),
eighty; eightieth

EIGHTY
8084 sheмônîym (3),
eighty; eightieth

EITHER
176 'ôw (7), *or, whether;*
desire
376 'îysh (3), *man; male;*
someone
518 'îm (1), *whether?; if,*
although; Oh that!
1571 gam (1), *also; even;*
"both...and"
3588 kîy (1), *for, that*
because
8145 shênîy (1), *second;*
again
2228 ĕ (9), *or; than*

EKER
6134 'Êqer (1),
naturalized citizen

EKRON
6138 'Eqrôwn (22),
eradication

EKRONITES
6139 'Eqrôwnîy (2),
Ekronite

EL-BETH-EL
416 'Êl Bêyth-'Êl (1), *God*
of Bethel

EL-ELOHE-ISRAEL
415 'Êl 'ĕlôhêy Yisrâ'êl
(1), *mighty God of Israel*

EL-PARAN
364 'Êyl Pâ'rân (1), *oak*
of Paran

ELADAH
497 'El'âdâh (1), *God has*
decked

ELAH
425 'Êlâh (17), *oak*

ELAM
5867 'Êylâm (28), *distant*

ELAMITES
5962 'Almîy (Ch.) (1),
Elamite
1639 Ĕlamîtēs (1),
distant ones

ELASAH
501 'El'âsâh (2), *God has*
made

ELATH
359 'Êylôwth (5), *grove*
(of palms)

ELDAAH
420 'Eldâ'âh (2), *God of*
knowledge

ELDAD
419 'Eldâd (2), *God has*
loved

ELDER
1419 gâdôwl (8), *great*
2205+3117 zâqên (1), *old,*
venerated
7227 rab (1), *great*
3187 мĕizŏn (1), *larger,*
greater
4245 prĕsbutĕrŏs (7),
elderly; older; presbyter
4850 sumprĕsbutĕrŏs (1),
co-presbyter

ELDERS
2205 zâqên (113), *old,*
venerated
7868 sîyb (Ch.) (5), to
become aged
4244 prĕsbutĕriŏn (2),
order of elders
4245 prĕsbutĕrŏs (58),
elderly; older; presbyter

ELDEST
1060 bekôwr (5),
firstborn, i.e. oldest son
1419 gâdôwl (6), *great*
2205 zâqên (1), *old,*
venerated
7223 rî'shôwn (1), *first,* in
place, time or rank
4245 prĕsbutĕrŏs (1),
elderly; older; presbyter

ELEAD
496 'El'âd (1), *God has*
testified

ELEALEH
500 'El'âlê' (5), *God (is)*
going up

ELEASAH
501 'El'âsâh (4), *God has*
made

ELEAZAR
499 'El'âzâr (71), *God (is)*
helper
1648 Ĕlĕazar (2), *God (is)*
helper

ELECT
972 bâchîyr (4), *selected*
one
1588 ĕklĕktŏs (13),
selected; chosen

ELECT'S
1588 ĕklĕktŏs (3),
selected; chosen

ELECTED
4899 sunĕklĕktŏs (1),
co-elected

ELECTION
1589 ĕklŏgē (6),
selection, choice

ELEMENTS
4747 stŏichĕiŏn (4),
elements, elementary

ELEPH
507 'Eleph (1), *thousand*

ELEVEN
259+6240 'echâd (9), *first*
505+3967 'eleph (3),
thousand
6249+6240 'ashtêy (6),
eleven; eleventh
1733 hĕndĕka (6), *eleven*

ELEVENTH
259+6240 'echâd (4), *first*
6249+6240 'ashtêy (12),
eleven; eleventh
1734 hĕndĕkatŏs (3),
eleventh

ELHANAN
445 'Elchânân (4), *God*
(is) *gracious*

ELI
5941 'Êlîy (32), *lofty*
2241 ĕli (1), *my God*

ELI'S
5941 'Êlîy (1), *lofty*

ELIAB
446 'Ĕlîy'âb (20), *God of*
(his) *father*

ELIAB'S
446 'Ĕlîy'âb (1), *God of*
(his) *father*

ELIADA
450 'Elyâdâ' (3), *God (is)*
knowing

ELIADAH
450 'Elyâdâ' (1), *God (is)*
knowing

ELIAH
452 'Êlîyâh (2), *God of*
Jehovah

ELIAHBA
455 'Elyachbâ' (2), *God*
will hide

ELIAKIM
471 'Elyâqîym (12), *God*
of raising
1662 Ĕliakĕim (3), *God of*
raising

ELIAM
463 'Ĕlîy'âm (2), *God of*
(the) *people*

ELIAS
2243 Hēlias (30), *God of*
Jehovah

ELIASAPH
460 'Ĕlyâçâph (6), *God*
(is) *gatherer*

ELIASHIB
475 'Elyâshîyb (17), *God*
will restore

ELIATHAH
448 'Ĕlîy'âthâh (2), *God*
of (his) *consent*

ELIDAD
449 'Ĕlîydâd (1), *God of*
(his) *love*

ELIEL
447 'Ĕlîy'êl (10), God of
(his) God

ELIENAI
462 'Ĕlîy'êynay (1),
Elienai

ELIEZER
461 'Ĕlîy'ezer (14), God
of help
1663 Ĕliĕzĕr (1), God of
help

ELIHOENAI
454 'Ely^ehôw'êynay (1),
toward Jehovah (are)
my eyes

ELIHOREPH
456 'Ĕlîychôreph (1),
God of autumn

ELIHU
453 'Ĕlîyhûw (11), God of
him

ELIJAH
452 'Ĕlîyâh (69), God of
Jehovah

ELIKA
470 'Ĕlîyqâ' (1), God of
rejection

ELIM
362 'Êylîm (6), palm-trees

ELIMELECH
458 'Ĕlîymelek (4), God
of (the) king

ELIMELECH'S
458 'Ĕlîymelek (2), God
of (the) king

ELIOENAI
454 'Ely^ehôw'êynay (8),
toward Jehovah (are)
my eyes

ELIPHAL
465 'Ĕlîyphâl (1), God of
judgment

ELIPHALET
467 'Ĕlîypheleţ (2), God
of deliverance

ELIPHAZ
464 'Ĕlîyphaz (15), God
of gold

ELIPHELEH
466 'Ĕlîyph^elêhûw (2),
God of his distinction

ELIPHELET
467 'Ĕlîypheleţ (6), God
of deliverance

ELISABETH
1665 Ĕlisabĕt (8), God of
(the) oath

ELISABETH'S
1665 Ĕlisabĕt (1), God of
(the) oath

ELISEUS
1666 Ĕlissaiŏs (1), Elisha

ELISHA
477 'Ĕlîyshâ' (58), Elisha

ELISHAH
473 'Ĕlîyshâh (3), Elishah

ELISHAMA
476 'Ĕlîyshâmâ' (17), God
of hearing

ELISHAPHAT
478 'Ĕlîyshâphâţ (1), God
of judgment

ELISHEBA
472 'Ĕlîysheba' (1), God
of (the) oath

ELISHUA
474 'Ĕlîyshûwa' (2), God
of supplication (or of
riches)

ELIUD
1664 Ĕliŏud (2), God of
majesty

ELIZAPHAN
469 'Ĕlîytsâphân (4), God
of treasure

ELIZUR
468 'Ĕlîytsûwr (5), God of
(the) rock

ELKANAH
511 'Elqânâh (20), God
has obtained

ELKOSHITE
512 'Elqôshîy (1),
Elkoshite

ELLASAR
495 'Ellâçâr (2), Ellasar

ELMODAM
1678 Ĕlmōdam (1),
Elmodam

ELMS
424 'êlâh (1), oak

ELNAAM
493 'Elna'am (1), God (is
his) delight

ELNATHAN
494 'Elnâthân (7), God (is
the) giver

ELOI
1682 ĕlōï (1), my God

ELON
356 'Êylôwn (7),
oak-grove

ELON-BETH-HANAN
358 'Êylôwn Bêyth
Chânân (1), oak-grove
of (the) house of favor

ELONITES
440 'Êlôwnîy (1), Elonite

ELOQUENT
376+1697 'îysh (1), man;
male; someone
995 bîyn (1), to
understand; discern
3052 lŏgiŏs (1), fluent,
i.e. an orator

ELOTH
359 'Êylôwth (3), grove
(of palms)

ELPAAL
508 'Elpa'al (3), God (is)
act

ELPALET
467 'Ĕlîypheleţ (1), God
of deliverance

ELSE
369 'ayin (1), there is no,
i.e., not exist, none
518 'îm (1), whether?; if,
although; Oh that!
3588 kîy (3), for, that
because

ELSHAPHAT
5750 'ôwd (13), again;
repeatedly; still; more
1490 ĕi dĕ mē(gĕ) (8), but
if not
1893 ĕpĕi (2), since
2087 hĕtĕrŏs (1), other or
different
2532 kai (1), and; or;
even; also

ELTEKEH
514 'Elt^eqê' (2), Eltekeh

ELTEKON
515 'Elt^eqôn (1), God (is)
straight

ELTOLAD
513 'Eltôwlad (2), God
(is) generator

ELUL
435 'Ĕlûwl (1), Elul

ELUZAI
498 'El'ûwzay (1), God
(is) defensive

ELYMAS
1681 Ĕlumas (1), Elymas

ELZABAD
443 'Elzâbâd (2), God
has bestowed

ELZAPHAN
469 'Ĕlîytsâphân (2), God
of treasure

EMBALM
2590 chânaţ (1), to
embalm; to ripen

EMBALMED
2590 chânaţ (3), to
embalm; to ripen

EMBOLDENED
3618 ŏikŏdŏmĕō (1), to
construct, edify

EMBOLDENETH
4834 mârats (1), to be
pungent or vehement

EMBRACE
2263 châbaq (8), to clasp
the hands, embrace

EMBRACED
2263 châbaq (3), to clasp
the hands, embrace
782 aspazŏmai (2), to
salute, welcome

EMBRACING
2263 châbaq (1), to clasp
the hands, embrace
4843 sumpĕrilambanō
(1), to embrace

EMBROIDER
7660 shâbats (1), to
interweave

EMBROIDERER
7551 râqam (2),
variegation; embroider

EMERALD
5306 nôphek (3), (poss.)
garnet
4664 smaragdinŏs (1), of
emerald
4665 smaragdŏs (1),
green emerald

EMERALDS
5306 nôphek (1), (poss.)
garnet

EMERODS
2914 ţ^echôr (2), piles,
tumor
6076 'ôphel (6), tumor;
fortress

EMIMS
368 'Êymîym (3), terrors

EMINENT
1354 gab (3), mounded
or rounded: top or rim
8524 tâlal (1), to elevate

EMMANUEL
1694 Ĕmmanŏuĕl (1),
God with us

EMMAUS
1695 Ĕmmaŏus (1),
Emmaüs

EMMOR
1697 Ĕmmŏr (1), male
donkey or ass

EMPIRE
4438 malkûwth (1), rule;
dominion

EMPLOY
935+6440 bôw' (1), to go
or come

EMPLOYED
5921 'al (1), above, over,
upon, or against
5975 'âmad (1), to stand

EMPTIED
1238 bâqaq (2), to
depopulate, ruin
1809 dâlal (1), to
slacken, dangle
6168 'ârâh (2), to be,
make bare; to empty
7324 rûwq (2), to pour
out, i.e. empty
7386 rêyq (1), empty;
worthless

EMPTIERS
1238 bâqaq (1), to
depopulate, ruin

EMPTINESS
922 bôhûw (1), ruin,
desolation

EMPTY
950 bûwqâh (1), empty,
pillaged
1238 bâqaq (3), to
depopulate, ruin
6437 pânâh (1), to turn,
to face
6485 pâqad (3), to visit,
care for, count
7324 rûwq (5), to pour
out, i.e. empty
7385 rîyq (5), emptiness;
worthless thing; in vain
7386 rêyq (2), empty;
worthless
7387 rêyqâm (12),
emptily; ineffectually
8414 tôhûw (1), waste,
desolation, formless
2756 kĕnŏs (4), empty;
vain; useless
4980 schŏlazō (1), to
take a holiday

EMULATION
3863 parazēlŏō (1), to
excite to rivalry

EMULATIONS
2205 zēlŏs (1), *zeal, ardor; jealousy, malice*

EN-DOR
5874 'Êyn-Dô'r (3), *fountain of dwelling*

EN-EGLAIM
5882 'Êyn 'Eglayim (1), *fountain of two calves*

EN-GANNIM
5873 'Êyn Gannîym (3), *fountain of gardens*

EN-GEDI
5872 'Êyn Gedîy (6), *fountain of a kid*

EN-HADDAH
5876 'Êyn Chaddâh (1), *fountain of sharpness*

EN-HAKKORE
5875 'Êyn haq-Qôwrê' (1), *fountain of One calling*

EN-HAZOR
5877 'Êyn Châtsôwr (1), *fountain of a village*

EN-MISHPAT
5880 'Êyn Mishpâṭ (1), *fountain of judgment*

EN-RIMMON
5884 'Êyn Rimmôwn (1), *fountain of a pomegranate*

EN-ROGEL
5883 'Êyn Rôgêl (4), *fountain of a traveller*

EN-SHEMESH
5885 'Êyn Shemesh (2), *fountain of (the) sun*

EN-TAPPUAH
5887 'Êyn Tappûwach (1), *fountain of an apple tree*

ENABLED
1743 ĕndunamŏō (1), to *empower, strengthen*

ENAM
5879 'Êynayim (1), *double fountain*

ENAN
5881 'Êynân (5), *having eyes*

ENCAMP
2583 chânâh (11), to *encamp for abode or siege*

ENCAMPED
2583 chânâh (33), to *encamp*

ENCAMPETH
2583 chânâh (2), to *encamp*

ENCAMPING
2583 chânâh (1), to *encamp*

ENCHANTER
5172 nâchash (1), to *prognosticate*

ENCHANTERS
6049 'ânan (1), to *cover, becloud; to act covertly*

ENCHANTMENT
3908 lachash (1), *incantation; amulet*
5172 nâchash (2), to *prognosticate*

ENCHANTMENTS
2267 cheber (2), *society, group; magic spell*
3858 lahaṭ (1), *blaze; magic*
3909 lâṭ (3), *incantation; secrecy; covertly*
5172 nâchash (4), to *prognosticate*

ENCOUNTERED
4820 sumballō (1), to *consider; to aid; to join*

ENCOURAGE
2388 châzaq (4), to *be strong; courageousd, restrain, conquer*

ENCOURAGED
2388 châzaq (5), to *be strong; courageous*

END
319 'achărîyth (21), *future; posterity*
657 'epheç (1), *end; no further*
1104 bâla' (1), to *swallow; to destroy*
1584 gâmar (1), to *end; to complete; to fail*
1700 dibrâh (1), *reason, suit or style; because*
2583 chânâh (1), to *encamp*
2856 châtham (1), to *close up; to affix a seal*
3318 yâtsâ' (1), to *go, bring out*
3615 kâlâh (56), to *complete, prepare*
4390 mâlê' (1), to *fill; be full*
4616 ma'an (8), *in order that*
5239 nâlâh (1), to *complete, attain*
5331 netsach (2), *splendor; lasting*
5486 çûwph (1), to *terminate*
5490 çôwph (3), *termination; end*
5491 çôwph (Ch.) (5), *end*
5704+5769+5703 'ad (1), *during; while; until*
6118 'êqeb (2), *on account of*
6285 pê'âh (1), *direction; region; extremity*
6310 peh (3), *mouth; opening*
7078 qenets (1), *perversion*
7093 qêts (51), *extremity; after*
7097 qâtseh (48), *extremity*
7098 qâtsâh (4), *termination; fringe*
7117 qᵉtsâth (3), *termination; portion*
7118 qᵉtsâth (Ch.) (2), *termination; portion*

7999 shâlam (2), to *be safe; complete*
8503 taklîyth (2), *extremity*
8537 tôm (1), *completeness*
8552 tâmam (2), to *complete, finish*
8622 tᵉqûwphâh (2), *revolution, course*
165+3588+165 aiōn (1), *perpetuity, ever; world*
206 akrŏn (1), *extremity: end, top*
1519 ĕis (4), *to or into*
1545 ĕkbasis (1), *exit, way out*
2078 ĕschatŏs (1), *farthest, final*
3796 ŏpsĕ (1), *late in the day*
4009 pĕras (1), *extremity, end, limit*
4930 suntĕlĕia (6), *entire completion*
5049 tĕlĕiŏs (1), *completely*
5055 tĕlĕō (1), to *end, i.e. complete, conclude*
5056 tĕlŏs (34), *conclusion*

ENDAMAGE
5142 nᵉzaq (Ch.) (1), to *suffer, inflict loss*

ENDANGER
2325 chûwb (1), to *tie, to owe, to forfeit*

ENDANGERED
5533 çâkan (1), to *damage; to grow*

ENDEAVOUR
4704 spŏudazō (1), to *make effort*

ENDEAVOURED
2212 zētĕō (1), to *seek*
4704 spŏudazō (1), to *make effort*

ENDEAVOURING
4704 spŏudazō (1), to *make effort*

ENDEAVOURS
4611 ma'ălâl (1), *act, deed*

ENDED
3615 kâlâh (7), to *cease, be finished, perish*
7999 shâlam (2), to *be safe; be complete*
8552 tâmam (5), to *complete, finish*
1096 ginŏmai (1), to *be, become*
4137 plērŏō (2), to *fill, make complete*
4931 suntĕlĕō (4), to *complete entirely*

ENDETH
2308 châdal (1), to *desist, stop; be fat*

ENDING
5056 tĕlŏs (1), *conclusion of an act or state*

ENDLESS
179 akatalutŏs (1), *permanent*

562 apĕrantŏs (1), *without a finish*

ENDOW
4117 mâhar (1), to *wed a wife by bargaining*

ENDS
657 'epheç (13), *end; no further*
1383 gablûth (2), *twisted chain or lace*
3671 kânâph (2), *edge or extremity; wing*
4020 migbâlâh (1), *border on garb*
7097 qâtseh (7), *extremity*
7098 qâtsâh (17), *termination; fringe*
7099 qetsev (4), *limit, borders*
7218 rô'sh (2), *head*
2078 ĕschatŏs (1), *farthest, final*
4009 pĕras (1), *extremity, end, limit*
5056 tĕlŏs (1), *conclusion of an act or state*

ENDUED
2064 zâbad (1), to *confer, bestow a gift*
3045 yâda' (2), to *know*
1746 ĕnduō (1), to *dress*
1990 ĕpistēmōn (1), *intelligent, learned*

ENDURE
1961 hâyâh (3), to *exist, i.e. be or become*
3201 yâkôl (2), to *be able*
3427 yâshab (2), to *dwell, to remain; to settle*
3885 lûwn (1), to *be obstinate*
5975 'âmad (3), to *stand*
6440 pânîym (1), *face; front*
6965 qûwm (1), to *rise*
7272 regel (1), *foot; step*
430 anĕchŏmai (2), *put up with, endure*
2076 ĕsti (1), *he (she or it) is; they are*
2553 kakŏpathĕō (2), to *undergo hardship*
5278 hupŏmĕnō (5), to *undergo (trials)*
5297 hupŏphĕrō (1), to *undergo hardship*
5342 phĕrō (1), to *bear or carry*

ENDURED
1961 hâyâh (1), to *exist, i.e. be or become*
2594 kartĕrĕō (1), to *be steadfast or patient*
3114 makrŏthumĕō (1), to *be forbearing, patient*
5278 hupŏmĕnō (3), to *undergo (trials)*
5297 hupŏphĕrō (1), to *undergo hardship*
5342 phĕrō (1), to *bear or carry*

ENDURETH
1097 bᵉlîy (1), *without, not yet; lacking*
5975 'âmad (4), to *stand*
3306 mĕnō (2), to *stay, remain*

ENDURING
5278 hupŏmĕnō (3), to undergo (trials)

ENDURING
5975 'âmad (1), to stand
3306 mĕnō (1), to stay, remain
5281 hupŏmŏnē (1), endurance, constancy

ENEMIES
341 'ôyêb (199), adversary, enemy
6145 'âr (1), foe
6146 'âr (Ch.) (1), foe
6862 tsar (26), trouble; opponent
6887 tsârar (9), to cramp
6965 qûwm (1), to rise
7790 shûwr (1), foe as lying in wait
8130 sânê' (3), to hate
8324 shârar (5), opponent
2190 ĕchthrŏs (19), adversary

ENEMIES'
341 'ôyêb (3), adversary, enemy

ENEMY
340 'âyab (1), to be hostile, be an enemy
341 'ôyêb (78), adversary, enemy
6145 'âr (1), foe
6862 tsar (9), trouble; opponent
6887 tsârar (5), to cramp
8130 sânê' (2), to hate
2190 ĕchthrŏs (11), adversary

ENEMY'S
341 'ôyêb (1), adversary, enemy
6862 tsar (2), trouble; opponent

ENFLAMING
2552 châmam (1), to be hot; to be in a rage

ENGAGED
6148 'ârab (1), to intermix

ENGINES
2810 chishshâbôwn (1), machination, scheme
4239 mᵉchîy (1), stroke of a battering-ram

ENGRAFTED
1721 ĕmphutŏs (1), implanted

ENGRAVE
6605 pâthach (2), to open wide; to plow, carve

ENGRAVEN
1795 ĕntupŏō (1), to engrave, carve

ENGRAVER
2796 chârâsh (3), skilled fabricator or worker

ENGRAVINGS
6603 pittûwach (5), sculpture; engraving

ENJOIN
2004 ĕpitassō (1), to order, command

ENJOINED
6485 pâqad (1), to visit, care for, count

ENGRAFTED
6965 qûwm (1), to rise
1781 ĕntĕllŏmai (1), to enjoin, give orders

ENJOY
1086 bâlâh (1), to wear out; consume, spend
1961 hâyâh (1), to exist, i.e. be or become
3423 yârash (2), to inherit; to impoverish
7200 râ'âh (4), to see
7521 râtsâh (3), to be pleased with; to satisfy
619 apŏlausis (1), full enjoyment, pleasure
2192+619 ĕchō (2), to have; hold; keep
5177 tugchanō (1), to take part in; to obtain

ENJOYED
7521 râtsâh (1), to be pleased with; to satisfy

ENLARGE
6601 pâthâh (1), to be, make simple; to delude
7235 râbâh (1), to increase
7337 râchab (7), to broaden
3170 mĕgalunō (1), to increase or extol

ENLARGED
7337 râchab (8), to broaden
3170 mĕgalunō (1), to increase or extol
4115 platunō (2), to widen

ENLARGEMENT
7305 revach (1), room; deliverance

ENLARGETH
7337 râchab (2), to broaden
7849 shâṭach (1), to expand

ENLARGING
7337 râchab (1), to broaden

ENLIGHTEN
5050 nâgahh (1), to illuminate

ENLIGHTENED
215 'ôwr (4), to be luminous
5461 phōtizō (2), to shine or to brighten up

ENLIGHTENING
215 'ôwr (1), to be luminous

ENMITY
342 'êybâh (2), hostility
2189 ĕchthra (5), hostility; opposition

ENOCH
2585 Chănôwk (9), initiated
1802 Ĕnōch (3), initiated

ENOS
583 'Ĕnôwsh (6), man; person, human
1800 Ĕnōs (1), man

ENOSH
583 'Ĕnôwsh (1), man; person, human

ENOUGH
1767 day (6), enough, sufficient
1952 hôwn (2), wealth
3027 yâd (1), hand; power
3605 kôl (1), all, any or every
4672 mâtsâ' (1), to find or acquire; to occur
7227 rab (7), great
7654 sob'âh (2), satiety
566 apĕchĕi (1), it is sufficient
713 arkĕtŏs (1), satisfactory, enough
714 arkĕō (1), to avail; be satisfactory
2425 hikanŏs (1), ample; fit
2880 kŏrĕnnumi (1), to cram, i.e. glut or sate
4052 pĕrissĕuō (1), to superabound

ENQUIRE
1158 bâ'âh (2), to ask; be bulging, swelling
1239 bâqar (2), to inspect, admire, care for, consider
1240 bᵉqar (Ch.) (1), to inspect, admire, care for, consider
1875 dârash (32), to pursue or search; to seek or ask; to worship
7592 shâ'al (7), to ask
1231 diaginŏskō (1), to ascertain exactly
1833 ĕxĕtazō (1), to ascertain or interrogate
1934 ĕpizētĕō (1), to search (inquire) for
2212 zētĕō (2), to seek
4441 punthanŏmai (1), to ask for information
4802 suzētĕō (1), to discuss, controvert

ENQUIRED
1245 bâqash (2), to search; to strive after
1875 dârash (10), to pursue or search
7592 shâ'al (15), to ask
7836 shâchar (1), to search for
198 akribŏō (2), to ascertain, find out
1567 ĕkzētĕō (1), to seek
4441 punthanŏmai (1), to ask for information

ENQUIREST
1245 bâqash (1), to search; to strive after

ENQUIRY
1239 bâqar (1), to inspect, admire, care
1331 diĕrōtaō (1), to question throughout

ENRICH
6238 'âshar (2), to grow, make rich

ENRICHED
4148 plŏutizō (2), to make wealthy

ENRICHEST
6238 'âshar (1), to grow, make rich

ENSAMPLE
5179 tupŏs (1), shape or resemblance; "type"
5262 hupŏdĕigma (1), exhibit, specimen

ENSAMPLES
5179 tupŏs (3), shape or resemblance; "type"

ENSIGN
226 'ôwth (1), signal, sign
5251 nêç (6), flag; signal
5264 nâçaç (1), to gleam; to flutter a flag

ENSIGNS
226 'ôwth (1), signal, sign

ENSNARED
4170 môwqêsh (1), noose for catching animals

ENSUE
1377 diōkō (1), to pursue; to persecute

ENTANGLE
3802 pagidĕuō (1), to ensnare, entrap

ENTANGLED
943 bûwk (1), to be confused
1707 ĕmplĕkō (1), to involve with
1758 ĕnĕchō (1), to keep a grudge

ENTANGLETH
1707 ĕmplĕkō (1), to involve with

ENTER
935 bôw' (81), to go or come
1980 hâlak (1), to walk; live a certain way
5674 'âbar (1), to cross over; to transition
1525 ĕisĕrchŏmai (63), to enter
1529 ĕisŏdŏs (1), entrance
1531 ĕispŏrĕuŏmai (1), to enter

ENTERED
935 bôw' (38), to go or come
305 anabainō (2), to go up, rise
1524 ĕisĕimi (1), to enter
1525 ĕisĕrchŏmai (53), to enter
1531 ĕispŏrĕuŏmai (3), to enter
1684 ĕmbainō (7), to embark; to reach
2064 ĕrchŏmai (2), to go or come
3922 parĕisĕrchŏmai (1), to supervene

ENTERETH
935 bôw' (9), to go or come
5181 nâchath (1), to sink, descend; to press down
1531 ĕispŏrĕuŏmai (5), to enter
1535 ĕitĕ (4), if too

ENTERING
935 bôw' (15), to *go, come*
3996 mâbôw' (3), *entrance; sunset; west*
6607 pethach (17), *opening; entrance* way
1525 ĕisĕrchŏmai (4), to *enter*
1529 ĕisŏdŏs (1), *entrance*
1531 ĕispŏrĕuŏmai (4), to *enter*
1684 ĕmbainō (1), to *embark; to reach*
1910 ĕpibainō (1), to *mount, arrive*

ENTERPRISE
8454 tûwshîyâh (1), *ability, undertaking*

ENTERTAIN
5381 philŏnĕxia (1), *hospitableness*

ENTERTAINED
3579 xĕnizō (1), to *be a host; to be a guest*

ENTICE
5496 çûwth (1), to *stimulate; to seduce*
6601 pâthâh (7), to *be, make simple; to delude*

ENTICED
6601 pâthâh (2), to *be, make simple; to delude*
1185 dĕlĕazō (1), to *delude, seduce*

ENTICETH
6601 pâthâh (1), to *be, make simple; to delude*

ENTICING
3981 pĕithŏs (1), *persuasive*
4086 pithanŏlŏgia (1), *persuasive language*

ENTIRE
3648 hŏlŏklĕrŏs (1), *entirely sound* in body

ENTRANCE
935 bôw' (2), to *go or come*
2978 yeʻîthôwn (1), *entry*
3996 mâbôw' (3), *entrance; sunset; west*
6607 pethach (2), *opening; entrance* way
6608 pêthach (1), *opening*
1529 ĕisŏdŏs (2), *entrance*

ENTRANCES
6607 pethach (1), *opening; entrance* way

ENTREAT
6293 pâga' (1), to *impinge*
2559 kakŏō (1), to *injure; to oppress; to embitter*

ENTREATED
818 atimazō (1), to *maltreat, dishonor*
2559 kakŏō (1), to *injure; to oppress; to embitter*
5195 hubrizō (3), to *exercise violence*
5530 chraŏmai (1), to *employ* or to *act toward*

ENTRIES
6607 pethach (1), *opening; entrance* way

ENTRY
872 beʻâh (1), *entrance*
3996 mâbôw' (6), *entrance; sunset; west*
6310 peh (1), *mouth; opening*
6607 pethach (7), *opening; entrance* way

ENVIED
7065 qânâ' (5), to *be, make jealous, envious*
7068 qin'âh (1), *jealousy or envy*

ENVIES
5355 phthŏnŏs (1), spiteful *jealousy, envy*

ENVIEST
7065 qânâ' (1), to *be, make jealous, envious*

ENVIETH
2206 zēlŏō (1), to *have warmth* of feeling for

ENVIOUS
7065 qânâ' (4), to *be, make jealous, envious*

ENVIRON
5437 çâbab (1), to *surround*

ENVY
7065 qânâ' (3), to *be, make zealous, jealous or envious*
7068 qin'âh (7), *jealousy or envy*
2205 zēlŏs (1), *zeal, ardor; jealousy, malice*
2206 zēlŏō (2), to *have warmth* of feeling for
5355 phthŏnŏs (7), spiteful *jealousy, envy*

ENVYING
2205 zēlŏs (4), *zeal, ardor; jealousy, malice*
5354 phthŏnĕō (1), to *be jealous* of

ENVYINGS
2205 zēlŏs (1), *zeal, ardor; jealousy, malice*
5355 phthŏnŏs (1), spiteful *jealousy, envy*

EPAENETUS
1866 Ĕpainĕtŏs (1), *praised*

EPAPHRAS
1889 Ĕpaphras (3), *devoted to Venus*

EPAPHRODITUS
1891 Ĕpaphrŏditŏs (3), *devoted to Venus*

EPHAH
374 'êyphâh (34), dry grain *measure*
5891 'Êyphâh (5), *obscurity*

EPHAI
5778 'Ôwphay (1), *birdlike*

EPHER
6081 'Êpher (4), *gazelle*

EPHES-DAMMIM
658 'Epheç Dammîym (1), *boundary of blood*

EPHESIAN
2180 Ĕphĕsiŏs (1), *Ephesian*

EPHESIANS
2180 Ĕphĕsiŏs (5), *Ephesian*

EPHESUS
2181 Ĕphĕsŏs (17), *Ephesus*

EPHLAL
654 'Ephlâl (2), *judge*

EPHOD
641 'Êphôd (1), *Ephod*
642 'êphuddâh (2), *plating*
646 'êphôwd (49), *ephod*

EPHPHATHA
2188 ĕphphatha (1), *be opened!*

EPHRAIM
669 'Ephrayim (171), *double fruit*
2187 Ĕphraïm (1), *double fruit*

EPHRAIM'S
669 'Ephrayim (4), *double fruit*

EPHRAIMITE
673 'Ephrâthîy (1), *Ephrathite or Ephraimite*

EPHRAIMITES
669 'Ephrayim (5), *double fruit*

EPHRAIN
6085 'Ephrôwn (1), *fawn-like*

EPHRATAH
672 'Ephrâth (5), *fruitfulness*

EPHRATH
672 'Ephrâth (5), *fruitfulness*

EPHRATHITE
673 'Ephrâthîy (3), *Ephrathite or Ephraimite*

EPHRATHITES
673 'Ephrâthîy (1), *Ephrathite or Ephraimite*

EPHRON
6085 'Ephrôwn (13), *fawn-like*

EPICUREANS
1946 Ĕpikŏurĕiŏs (1), *servant*

EPISTLE
1992 ĕpistŏlē (13), *written message*

EPISTLES
1992 ĕpistŏlē (2), *written message*

EQUAL
1809 dâlal (1), to *slacken, dangle*
4339 mêyshâr (1), *straightness; rectitude*

ERRED
7686 shâgâg (4), to *stray, wander; to transgress*
8582 tâ'âh (14), to *vacillate, i.e. stray*
4105 planaō (6), to *roam, wander; to deceive*

ERRAND
1697 dâbâr (3), *word; matter; thing*

ERRED
7683 shâgag (5), to *stray; to sin*
7686 shâgâh (2), to *stray, wander; to transgress*
8582 tâ'âh (2), to *vacillate, i.e. stray*

6186 'ârak (2), to *set in a row, i.e. arrange,*
6187 'êrek (1), *pile, equipment, estimate*
7737 shâvâh (3), to *level, i.e. equalize*
8505 tâkan (7), to *balance, i.e. measure*
2465 isaggĕlŏs (1), *angelic, like an angel*
2470 isŏs (4), *similar*
2471 isŏtēs (1), *likeness; fairness*

EQUALITY
2471 isŏtēs (2), *likeness; fairness*

EQUALLY
7947 shâlab (1), to *make equidistant*

EQUALS
4915 sunēlikiŏtēs (1), *alike, contemporary*

EQUITY
3476 yôsher (1), *right*
3477 yâshâr (1), *straight*
3788 kishrôwn (1), *success; advantage*
4334 mîyshôwr (2), *plain; justice*
4339 mêyshâr (4), *straightness; rectitude*
5229 nekôchâh (1), *integrity; truth*

ER
6147 'Êr (10), *watchful*
2262 Ēr (1), *watchful*

ERAN
6197 'Êrân (1), *watchful*

ERANITES
6198 'Êrânîy (1), *Eranite*

ERASTUS
2037 Ĕrastŏs (3), *beloved*

ERE
2962 ṭerem (4), *not yet* or *before*
3808 lô' (4), no, *not*
4250 prin (1), *prior, sooner, before*

ERECH
751 'Erek (1), *length*

ERECTED
5324 nâtsab (1), to *station*

ERI
6179 'Êrîy (2), *watchful*

ERITES
6180 'Êrîy (1), *Erite*

ERR
7686 shâgâh (4), to *stray, wander; to transgress*
8582 tâ'âh (14), to *vacillate, i.e. stray*
4105 planaō (6), to *roam, wander; to deceive*

635 apŏplanaō (1), to *lead astray*; to *wander*
795 astŏchĕō (2), *deviate* or *wander* from truth

ERRETH
7686 shágâh (1), to *stray*, *wander*; to *transgress*
8582 tâ'âh (1), to *vacillate*, i.e. *stray*

ERROR
4879 m°shûwgâh (1), *mistake*
7684 sh°gâgâh (2), *mistake*
7944 shal (1), *fault*
7960 shâlûw (Ch.) (1), *fault, error*
8432 tâvek (1), *center, middle*
4106 planē (7), *fraudulence; straying*

ERRORS
7691 sh°gîy'âh (1), moral *mistake*
8595 ta'tûa' (2), *fraud*
51 agnŏēma (1), *sin committed in ignorance*

ESAIAS
2268 Hēsaïas (21), *Jehovah has saved*

ESAR-HADDON
634 'Êçar-Chaddôwn (3), *Esar-chaddon*

ESAU
6215 'Êsâv (84), *rough*
2269 Ēsau (3), *rough*

ESAU'S
6215 'Êsâv (12), *rough*

ESCAPE
3318 yâtsâ' (1), to *go, bring out*
4422 mâlaṭ (22), to *escape*; be *delivered*
4498+6 mânôwç (1), *fleeing*; place of *refuge*
4655 miphlâṭ (1), *escape, shelter*
5337 nâtsal (1), to *deliver*; to be *snatched*
5674 'âbar (1), to *cross over*; to *transition*
6403 pâlaṭ (2), to *slip* out, i.e. *escape*; to *deliver*
6405 pallêṭ (1), *escape*
6412 pâlîyṭ (12), *refugee*
6413 p°lêyṭâh (9), *escaped* portion
1309 diaphĕugō (1), to *escape, flee*
1545 ĕkbasis (1), *exit, way out*
1628 ĕkphĕugō (4), to *flee out, escape*
5343 phĕugō (1), to *run away*; to *vanish*
5343+575 phĕugō (1), to *run away*; to *vanish*

ESCAPED
3318 yâtsâ' (1), to *go, bring out*
4422 mâlaṭ (25), to *escape*; be *delivered*
5337 nâtsal (1), to *deliver*; to be *snatched*
6412 pâlîyṭ (8), *refugee*

6413 p°lêyṭâh (11), *escaped* portion
7611 sh°'êrîyth (1), *remainder* or *residual*
668 apŏphĕugō (3), to *escape* from
1295 diasōzō (3), to *cure, preserve, rescue*
1628 ĕkphĕugō (1), to *flee out, escape*
1831 ĕxĕrchŏmai (1), to *issue*; to *leave*
5343 phĕugō (2), to *run away*; to *vanish*

ESCAPETH
4422 mâlaṭ (3), to *escape*; be *delivered*; be *smooth*
6412 pâlîyṭ (2), *refugee*
6413 p°lêyṭâh (1), *escaped* portion

ESCAPING
6413 p°lêyṭâh (1), *escaped* portion

ESCHEW
1578 ĕkklinō (1), to *shun*; to *decline*

ESCHEWED
5493 çûwr (1), to *turn* off

ESCHEWETH
5493 çûwr (2), to *turn* off

ESEK
6230 'Êseq (1), *strife*

ESH-BAAL
792 'Eshba'al (2), *man of Baal*

ESHBAN
790 'Eshbân (2), *vigorous*

ESHCOL
812 'Eshkôl (6), *bunch of grapes*

ESHEAN
824 'Esh'ân (1), *support*

ESHEK
6232 'Êsheq (1), *oppression*

ESHKALONITES
832 'Eshq°lôwnîy (1), *Ashkelonite*

ESHTAOL
847 'Eshtâ'ôl (7), *entreaty*

ESHTAULITES
848 'Eshtâ'ûlîy (1), *Eshtaolite*

ESHTEMOA
851 'Esht°môa' (5), *Eshtemoa* or *Eshtemoh*

ESHTEMOH
851 'Esht°môa' (1), *Eshtemoa* or *Eshtemoh*

ESHTON
850 'Eshtôwn (2), *restful*

ESLI
2069 Ĕsli (1), *Esli*

ESPECIALLY
3966 m°'ôd (1), *very, utterly*
3122 malista (4), *in the greatest degree*

ESPIED
7200 râ'âh (1), to *see*
8446 tûwr (1), to *wander, meander*

ESPOUSALS
2861 châthunnâh (1), *wedding*
3623 k°lûwlâh (1), *bridehood*

ESPOUSED
781 'âras (1), to *engage* for matrimony, *betroth*
718 harmŏzō (1), to *betroth* for marriage
3423 mnēstĕuō (3), to *betroth*, be *engaged*

ESPY
6822 tsâphâh (1), to *peer*; to *observe, await*
7270 râgal (1), to *reconnoiter*; to *slander*

ESROM
2074 Ĕsrōm (3), *court-yard*

ESTABLISH
3322 yâtsag (1), to *place* permanently
3427 yâshab (1), to *dwell*, to *remain*; to *settle*
3559 kûwn (14), to *set up*: *establish, fix, prepare*
5324 nâtsab (1), to *station*
5582 çâ'ad (1), to *support*
5975 'âmad (3), to *stand*
6965 qûwm (17), to *rise*
6966 qûwm (Ch.) (2), to *rise*
2476 histēmi (3), to *stand, establish*
4741 stĕrizō (1), to *turn resolutely*; to *confirm*

ESTABLISHED
539 'âman (7), to be *firm, faithful, true*; to *trust*
553 'âmats (1), to be *strong*; be *courageous*
2388 châzaq (1), to *fasten upon*; to *seize*
3245 yâçad (2), *settle*, *establish a foundation*
3559 kûwn (44), to *set up*: *establish, fix, prepare*
5564 çâmak (1), to *lean upon*; *take hold* of
5975 'âmad (1), to *stand*
6965 qûwm (9), to *rise*
8627 t°qan (Ch.) (1), to *straighten* up, *confirm*
950 bĕbaiŏō (1), to *stabilitate, keep strong*
2476 histēmi (2), to *stand, establish*
3549 nŏmŏthĕtĕō (1), to be *founded, enacted*
4732 stĕrĕŏō (1), to *be, become strong*
4741 stĕrizō (1), to *turn resolutely*; to *confirm*

ESTABLISHETH
5975 'âmad (1), to *stand*
6965 qûwm (1), to *rise*
6966 qûwm (Ch.) (1), to *rise*

ESTABLISHMENT
571 'emeth (1), *certainty, truth, trustworthiness*

ESTATE
1700 dibrâh (1), *reason, suit* or *style*; *because*

ESPOUSALS *(continued above)*

3653 kên (5), *pedestal* or *station* of a basin
8448 tôwr (1), *manner*
3588+4012 hŏ (1), "*the*," i.e. the definite article

ESTEEM
2803 châshab (1), to *plot*; to *think, regard*
6186 'ârak (1), to set in a row, i.e. *arrange*,
2233 hēgĕŏmai (2), to *deem*, i.e. *consider*

ESTEEMED
2803 châshab (3), to *plot*; to *think, regard*
5034 nâbêl (1), to *wilt*; to *fall away*; to be *foolish*
6845 tsâphan (1), to *deny*; to *protect*; to *lurk*
7043 qâlal (2), to *be, make light*
1848 ĕxŏuthĕnĕō (1), to *treat with contempt*

ESTEEMETH
2803 châshab (1), to *plot*; to *think, regard*
2919 krinō (2), to *decide*; to *try, condemn, punish*
3049 lŏgizŏmai (1), to *credit*; to *think, regard*

ESTEEMING
2233 hēgĕŏmai (1), to *lead*; to *deem, consider*

ESTHER
635 'Eçtêr (52), *Esther*

ESTHER'S
635 'Eçtêr (3), *Esther*

ESTIMATE
6186 'ârak (2), to set in a row, i.e. *arrange*,

ESTIMATION
6187 'êrek (23), *pile, equipment, estimate*

ESTIMATIONS
6187 'êrek (1), *pile, equipment, estimate*

ESTRANGED
2114 zûwr (4), to be *foreign, strange*
5234 nâkar (1), to *treat as a foreigner*

ETAM
5862 'Êyṭâm (5), *hawk-ground*

ETERNAL
5769 'ôwlâm (1), *eternity; ancient; always*
6924 qedem (1), *eastern; antiquity; before*
126 aïdiŏs (1), *everduring, eternal*
165 aiōn (2), *perpetuity, ever; world*
166 aiōniŏs (42), *perpetual, long ago*

ETERNITY
5703 'ad (1), *perpetuity; ancient*

ETHAM
864 'Êthâm (4), *Etham*

ETHAN
387 'Êythân (8), *permanent*

ETHANIM
388 Êythânîym (1), *permanent* brooks

ETHBAAL
856 'Ethba'al (1), *with Baal*

ETHER
6281 'Ether (2), *abundance*

ETHIOPIA
3568 Kûwsh (19), *Cush*
128 Aithiŏps (1), *inhabitant of Æthiop*

ETHIOPIAN
3569 Kûwshîy (8), *Cushite*

ETHIOPIANS
3569 Kûwshîy (12), *Cushite*
128 Aithiŏps (1), *inhabitant of Æthiop*

ETHNAN
869 'Ethnan (1), *gift price of harlotry*

ETHNI
867 'Ethnîy (1), *munificence, lavishness*

EUBULUS
2103 Ĕubŏulŏs (1), *good-willer*

EUNICE
2131 Ĕunikē (1), *victorious*

EUNUCH
5631 çârîyç (2), *eunuch; official* of state
2135 ĕunŏuchŏs (5), *castrated; impotent*

EUNUCHS
5631 çârîyç (15), *eunuch; official* of state
2134 ĕunŏuchizŏ (3), *to castrate*
2135 ĕunŏuchŏs (2), *castrated; impotent*

EUODIAS
2136 Ĕuŏdia (1), *fine travelling*

EUPHRATES
6578 Pᵉrâth (19), *rushing*
2166 Ĕuphratēs (2), *Euphrates*

EUROCLYDON
2148 Ĕurŏkludōn (1), *wind* from the east

EUTYCHUS
2161 Ĕutuchŏs (1), *fortunate*

EVANGELIST
2099 ĕuaggĕlistēs (2), *preacher* of the gospel

EVANGELISTS
2099 ĕuaggĕlistēs (1), *preacher* of the gospel

EVE
2332 Chavvâh (2), *life-giver*
2096 Ĕua (2), *life-giver*

EVEN
227 'âz (1), *at that time* or *place; therefore*
389 'ak (2), *surely; only, however*

518 'îm (1), *whether?; if, although; Oh that!*
637 'aph (7), *also* or *yea; though*
853 'êth (25), *not* translated
1571 gam (50), *also; even; yea; though*
1887 hê' (1), *Lo!, Look!*
3588 kîy (7), *for, that because*
3602 kâkâh (5), *just so*
3651 kên (3), *just; right, correct*
4334 mîyshôwr (1), *plain; justice*
5704 'ad (3), *as far (long) as; during; while; until*
5705 'ad (Ch.) (2), *as far (long) as; during*
6153 'ereb (71), *dusk*
6664 tsedeq (1), *right*
7535 raq (1), *merely; although*
737 arti (1), just *now; at once*
891 achri (1), *until* or *up to*
1063 gar (1), *for, indeed, but, because*
1161 dĕ (3), *but, yet; and then*
2089 ĕti (1), *yet, still*
2193 hĕŏs (2), *until*
2504 kagō (7), *and also, even*
2509 kathapĕr (2), *exactly as*
2531 kathŏs (24), *just* or *inasmuch as, that*
2532 kai (108), *and; or; even; also*
2548 kakĕinŏs (2), *likewise that* or *those*
3303 mĕn (1), *not* translated
3483 nai (4), *yes*
3676 hŏmŏs (1), *at the same* time, *yet still*
3761 ŏudĕ (3), *neither, nor, not even*
3779 hŏutō (3), *in this way; likewise*
3796 ŏpsĕ (2), *late* in the day
3798 ŏpsiŏs (8), *late; early eve; later eve*
5037 tĕ (1), *both* or *also*
5613 hŏs (5), *which, how,* i.e. *in that manner*
5615 hōsautōs (1), *in the same way*
5618 hōspĕr (2), *exactly like*

EVENING
6150 'ârab (2), *to grow dusky* at sundown
6153 'ereb (49), *dusk*
2073 hĕspĕra (2), *evening*
3798 ŏpsiŏs (5), *late; early eve; later eve*

EVENINGS
6160 'ărâbâh (1), *desert, wasteland*

EVENINGTIDE
6256+6153 'êth (2), *time*

EVENT
4745 miqreh (3), *accident* or *fortune*

EVENTIDE
6153 'ereb (1), *dusk*
6256+6153 'êth (2), *time*
2073 hĕspĕra (1), *evening*

EVER
753+3117 'ôrek (2), *length*
3605+3117 kôl (18), *all, any* or *every*
3808 lô' (1), *no, not*
3809 lâ' (Ch.) (1), *as nothing*
5331 netsach (23), *splendor; lasting*
5703 'ad (40), *perpetuity; ancient*
5704+5769 'ad (1), *as far (long) as; during; while*
5750 'ôwd (1), *again; repeatedly; still; more*
5757 'Avvîy (1), *Avvite*
5769 'ôwlâm (266), *ancient; always*
5769+5703 'ôwlâm (1), *ancient; always*
5865 'êylôwm (1), *forever*
5957 'âlam (Ch.) (11), *forever*
6783 tsᵉmîythûth (2), *perpetually*
6924 qedem (1), *eastern; antiquity; before*
8548 tâmîyd (3), *constantly, regularly*
104 aĕi (1), *ever, always*
165 aiōn (49), *perpetuity, ever; world*
166 aiōniŏs (1), *perpetual, long ago*
1336 diēnĕkĕs (2), *perpetually, endless*
2250+165 hēmĕra (1), *day; period of time*
3364 ŏu mē (1), *not* at all, *absolutely not*
3745 hŏsŏs (3), *as much as*
3842 pantŏtĕ (6), *at all times*
3956+165 pas (1), *all, any, every, whole*
4218 pŏtĕ (1), at *some time, ever*
4253 prŏ (1), *before in time* or *space*

EVERLASTING
5703 'ad (2), *perpetuity; ancient*
5769 'ôwlâm (60), *ancient; always*
5957 'âlam (Ch.) (4), *forever*
6924 qedem (1), *eastern; antiquity; before*
126 aïdiŏs (1), *everduring, eternal*
166 aiōniŏs (25), *perpetual, long ago*

EVERMORE
1755 dôwr (1), *dwelling*
3605+3117 kôl (2), *all, any* or *every*
5331 netsach (1), *splendor; lasting*
5703 'ad (1), *perpetuity; ancient*

5769 'ôwlâm (15), *ancient; always*
8548 tâmîyd (1), *constantly, regularly*
3588+165 hŏ (3), *"the,"* i.e. *the definite article*
3842 pantŏtĕ (2), *at all times*

EVERY
259 'echâd (5), *first*
376 'îysh (125), *man; male; someone*
802 'ishshâh (4), *woman, wife; women, wives*
1397 geber (1), *person, man*
3605 kôl (451), *all, any* or *every*
3606 kôl (Ch.) (4), *all, any* or *every*
3632 kâlîyl (1), *whole, entire; complete; whole*
5437 çâbab (26), *to surround*
7218 rô'sh (1), *head*
303 ana (2), *each; in turn; among*
376 anapērŏs (1), *maimed; crippled*
537 hapas (2), *all, every one, whole*
1330 diĕrchŏmai (1), *to traverse, travel through*
1538 hĕkastŏs (73), *each* or *every*
2596 kata (15), *down; according to*
3596 hŏdŏipŏrĕō (2), *to travel*
3650 hŏlŏs (2), *whole* or *all,* i.e. *complete*
3836 pantachŏthĕn (1), *from all directions*
3837 pantachŏu (1), *universally, everywhere*
3840 pantŏthĕn (1), *from, on all sides*
3956 pas (162), *all, any, every, whole*
5100 tis (2), *some* or *any person* or *object*
5101 tis (1), *who?, which?* or *what?*

EVI
189 'Ĕvîy (2), *desirous*

EVIDENCE
5612 çêpher (6), *writing*
1650 ĕlĕgchŏs (1), *proof, conviction*

EVIDENCES
5612 çêpher (2), *writing*

EVIDENT
5921+6440 'al (1), *above, over, upon,* or *against*
1212 dēlŏs (1), *clear, plain, evident*
1732 ĕndĕixis (1), *demonstration*
2612 katadēlŏs (1), *manifest, clear*
4271 prŏdēlŏs (1), *obvious, evident*

EVIDENTLY
4270 prŏgraphō (1), *to announce, prescribe*
5320 phanĕrŏs (1), *plainly,* i.e. *clearly*

EVIL
205 'âven (1), *trouble, vanity, wickedness*
1100 bᵉlîya'al (1), *wickedness, trouble*
1681 dibbâh (1), *slander, bad report*
7451 ra' (434), *bad; evil*
7455 rôa' (11), *badness, evil*
7462 râ'âh (1), *to associate* with
7489 râ'a' (24), *to be good for nothing*
92 adikēma (1), *wrong done*
987 blasphēmĕō (9), *to speak impiously*
988 blasphēmia (1), *impious speech*
1426 dusphēmia (1), *defamation, slander*
2549 kakia (1), *depravity; malignity*
2551 kakŏlŏgĕō (1), *to revile, curse*
2554 kakŏpŏiĕō (4), *to injure; to sin, do wrong*
2556 kakŏs (44), *bad, evil, wrong*
2557 kakŏurgŏs (1), *criminal, evildoer*
2559 kakŏō (3), *to injure; to oppress; to embitter*
2560 kakŏs (2), *badly; wrongly; ill*
2635 katalalĕō (4), *to speak slander*
2636 katalalia (1), *defamation, slander*
4190 pŏnērŏs (49), *malice, wicked, bad*
4190+4487 pŏnērŏs (1), *malice, wicked, bad*
5337 phaulŏs (4), *foul or flawed, i.e. wicked*

EVIL-MERODACH
192 'Ĕvîyl Mᵉrôdak (2), *Evil-Merodak*

EVILDOER
7489 râ'a' (1), *to be good for nothing*
2555 kakŏpŏiŏs (1), *bad-doer; criminal*

EVILDOERS
7489 râ'a' (9), *to be good for nothing*
2555 kakŏpŏiŏs (3), *bad-doer; criminal*

EVILFAVOUREDNESS
1697+7451 dâbâr (1), *word; matter; thing*

EVILS
7451 ra' (8), *bad; evil*
4190 pŏnērŏs (1), *malice, wicked, bad; crime*

EWE
3535 kibsâh (6), *ewe sheep*
7716 seh (1), *sheep or goat*

EWES
5763 'ûwl (1), *to suckle, i.e. give milk*
7353 râchêl (2), *ewe*

EXACT
5065 nâgas (3), *to exploit; to tax, harass*
5378 nâshâ' (2), *to lend on interest*
5383 nâshâh (2), *to lend or borrow*
4238 prassō (1), *to execute, accomplish*

EXACTED
3318 yâtsâ' (1), *to go, bring out*
5065 nâgas (1), *to exploit; to tax, harass*

EXACTETH
5382 nâshâh (1), *to forget*

EXACTION
4855 mashshâ' (1), *loan; interest on a debt*

EXACTIONS
1646 gᵉrûshâh (1), *dispossession*

EXACTORS
5065 nâgas (1), *to exploit; to tax, harass*

EXALT
1361 gâbahh (3), *to be lofty; to be haughty*
5375 nâsâ' (2), *to lift up*
5549 çâlal (1), *to mound up; to exalt; to oppose*
7311 rûwm (17), *to be high; to rise or raise*
1869 ĕpairō (1), *to raise up, look up*
5312 hupsŏō (2), *to elevate; to exalt*

EXALTED
1361 gâbahh (5), *to be lofty; to be haughty*
5375 nâsâ' (8), *to lift up*
5927 'âlâh (2), *to ascend, be high, mount*
7311 rûwm (28), *to be high; to rise or raise*
7426 râmam (1), *to rise*
7682 sâgab (5), *to be, make lofty; be safe*
5229 hupĕrairŏmai (2), *to raise oneself over*
5251 hupĕrupsŏō (1), *to raise to the highest*
5311 hupsŏs (1), *altitude; sky; dignity*
5312 hupsŏō (10), *to elevate; to exalt*

EXALTEST
5549 çâlal (1), *to mound up; to exalt; to oppose*

EXALTETH
1361 gâbahh (1), *to be lofty; to be haughty*
7311 rûwm (3), *to be high; to rise or raise*
7682 sâgab (1), *to be, make lofty; be safe*
1869 ĕpairō (1), *to raise up, look up*
5229 hupĕrairŏmai (1), *to raise oneself over*
5312 hupsŏō (2), *to elevate; to exalt*

EXAMINATION
351 anakrisis (1), *judicial investigation*

EXAMINE
974 bâchan (1), *to test; to investigate*
1875 dârash (1), *to seek or ask; to worship*
350 anakrinō (1), *to interrogate, determine*
1381 dŏkimazō (1), *to test; to approve*
3985 pĕirazō (1), *to endeavor, scrutinize*

EXAMINED
350 anakrinō (4), *to interrogate, determine*
426 anĕtazō (2), *to investigate; to question*

EXAMINING
350 anakrinō (1), *to interrogate, determine*

EXAMPLE
1164 dĕigma (1), *specimen, example*
3856 paradĕigmatizō (1), *to expose to infamy*
5179 tupŏs (1), *shape, resemblance; "type"*
5261 hupŏgrammŏs (1), *copy, example, model*
5262 hupŏdĕigma (4), *exhibit; specimen*

EXAMPLES
5179 tupŏs (1), *shape, resemblance; "type"*

EXCEED
3254 yâçaph (2), *to add or augment*
4052 pĕrissĕuō (2), *to superabound*

EXCEEDED
1396 gâbar (1), *to be strong; to prevail*
1431 gâdal (2), *to be great, make great*

EXCEEDEST
3254 yâçaph (1), *to add or augment*

EXCEEDETH
3254 yâçaph (1), *to add or augment*

EXCEEDING
430 'ĕlôhîym (1), *the true God; gods; great ones*
1419 gâdôwl (1), *great*
2302 châdâh (1), *to rejoice, be glad*
2493 chêlem (Ch.) (1), *dream*
3493 yattîyr (Ch.) (1), *preeminent; very*
3499 yether (1), *remainder; small rope*
3966 mᵉ'ôd (18), *very, utterly*
4605 ma'al (2), *upward, above, overhead*
5628 çârach (1), *to extend even to excess*
7235 râbâh (1), *increase*
7235+3966 râbâh (1), *to increase*
7689 saggîy' (1), *mighty*
8057 simchâh (1), *blithesomeness or glee*
1519+5236 ĕis (1), *to or into*

EXCEEDINGLY
413+1524 'êl (1), *to, toward*
1419 gâdôwl (5), *great*
1419+3966 gâdôwl (1), *great*
3493 yattîyr (Ch.) (1), *preeminent; very*
3966 mᵉ'ôd (9), *very, utterly*
4605 ma'al (4), *upward, above, overhead*
7227 rab (2), *great*
7235 râbâh (1), *to increase*
7235+3966 râbâh (1), *to increase*
8057 simchâh (1), *blithesomeness or glee*
1613 ĕktarassō (1), *to disturb wholly*
1630 ĕkphŏbŏs (1), *frightened out of one's wits*
4056 pĕrissŏtĕrŏs (3), *more superabundantly*
4057 pĕrissŏs (1), *superabundantly*
4970 sphŏdra (1), *vehemently, much*
4971 sphŏdrōs (1), *very much*
5228+1537+4053 hupĕr (1), *over; above; beyond*
5401+3173 phŏbŏs (1), *alarm, or fright*

EXCEL
1368 gibbôwr (1), *powerful; great warrior*
3498 yâthar (1), *to remain or be left*
5329 nâtsach (1), *i.e. to be eminent*
4052 pĕrissĕuō (1), *to superabound*

EXCELLED
7227 rab (1), *great*

EXCELLENCY
1346 ga'ăvâh (3), *arrogance; majesty*
1347 gâ'ôwn (10), *ascending; majesty*
1363 gôbahh (1), *height; grandeur; arrogance*
1926 hâdâr (2), *magnificence*
3499 yether (2), *remainder; small rope*
3504 yithrôwn (1), *preeminence, gain*

EXCELLENCY
2596+5236 kata (1), *down; according to*
3029 lian (5), *very much*
3588+2316 hŏ (1), "*the,*" *i.e. the definite article*
4036 pĕrilupŏs (3), *intensely sad*
4970 sphŏdra (4), *vehemently, much*
5228 hupĕr (1), *over; above; beyond*
5235 hupĕrballō (3), *to surpass*
5248 hupĕrpĕrissĕuō (1), *to superabound*
5250 hupĕrplĕŏnazō (1), *to superabound*

7613 sᵉˈêth (2), *elevation; swelling* scab
7863 sîyˈ (1), *elevation*
5236 hupĕrbŏlē (1), *super-eminence*
5242 hupĕrĕchō (1), to *excel; be superior*
5247 hupĕrŏchē (1), *superiority*

EXCELLENT
117 ˈaddîyr (4), *powerful; majestic*
977 bâchar (1), *select, chose, prefer*
1347 gâˈôwn (1), *ascending; majesty*
1348 gêˈûwth (1), *ascending; majesty*
1420 gᵉdûwlâh (1), *greatness, grandeur*
1431 gâdal (1), to *be great, make great*
3368 yâqâr (1), *valuable*
3493 yattîyr (Ch.) (5), *preeminent; very*
3499 yether (1), *remainder;* small *rope*
5057 nâgîyd (1), *commander, official*
5716 ˈădîy (1), *finery; outfit; headstall*
7119 qar (1), *cool; quiet; cool*-headed
7218 rôˈsh (1), *head*
7230 rôb (1), *abundance*
7682 sâgab (1), to *be, make lofty; be safe*
7689 saggîyˈ (1), *mighty*
7991 shâlîysh (1), *officer; of the third rank*
8446 tûwr (1), to *wander, meander*
1308 diaphĕrō (2), to *differ; to surpass*
1313 diaphŏrŏs (2), *varying; surpassing*
2596+5236 kata (1), *down; according to*
2903 kratistŏs (2), *very honorable*
3169 mĕgalŏprĕpēs (1), *befitting greatness*
4119 plĕîŏn (1), *more*

EXCELLEST
5927 ˈâlâh (1), to *ascend, be high, mount*

EXCELLETH
3504 yithrôwn (2), *preeminence, gain*
5235 hupĕrballō (1), to *surpass*

EXCEPT
369 ˈayin (1), *there is no, i.e., not exist, none*
905 bad (1), *chief; apart, only, besides*
1115 biltîy (3), *not, except, without, unless*
3588 kîy (2), *for, that because*
3861 lâhên (Ch.) (3), *therefore; except*
3884 lûwlê (3), *if not*
7535 raq (1), *merely; although*
1508 ĕi mē (7), *if not*
1509 ĕi mē ti (3), *if not somewhat*

2228 ē (1), *or; than*
3362 ĕan mē (33), *if not, i.e. unless*
3923 parĕisphĕrō (1), to *bear in alongside*
4133 plēn (1), *albeit, save that, rather, yet*

EXCEPTED
1622 ĕktŏs (1), *aside from, besides; except*

EXCESS
192 akrasia (1), *lack of control of self*
401 anachusis (1), *excessively pour out*
810 asōtia (1), *profligacy, debauchery*
3632 ŏinŏphlugia (1), *drunkenness*

EXCHANGE
4171 mûwr (1), to *alter; to barter, to dispose of*
8545 tᵉmûwrâh (2), *barter, compensation*
465 antallagma (2), *equivalent exchange*

EXCHANGERS
5133 trapĕzitēs (1), *money-broker*

EXCLUDE
1576 ĕkklĕiō (1), to *shut out, exclude*

EXCLUDED
1576 ĕkklĕiō (1), to *shut out, exclude*

EXCUSE
379 anapŏlŏgĕtŏs (1), *without excuse*
626 apŏlŏgĕŏmai (1), to *give an account*
3868 paraitĕŏmai (1), to *deprecate, decline*

EXCUSED
3868 paraitĕŏmai (2), to *deprecate, decline*

EXCUSING
626 apŏlŏgĕŏmai (1), to *give an account*

EXECRATION
423 ˈâlâh (2), *curse, oath, public agreement*

EXECUTE
1777 dîyn (1), to *judge;* to *strive or contend for*
5647 ˈâbad (1), to *do, work, serve*
6213 ˈâsâh (25), to *do or make*
8199 shâphaṭ (2), to *judge*
4160 pŏiĕō (2), to *do*

EXECUTED
5648 ˈăbad (Ch.) (1), to *do, work, serve*
6213 ˈâsâh (15), to *do or make*
2407 hiĕratĕuō (1), to *be a priest*

EXECUTEDST
6213 ˈâsâh (1), to *do*

EXECUTEST
6213 ˈâsâh (1), to *do*

EXECUTETH
6213 ˈâsâh (5), to *do*

EXECUTING
6213 ˈâsâh (1), to *do*

EXECUTION
6213 ˈâsâh (1), to *do*

EXECUTIONER
4688 spĕkŏulatōr (1), *life-guardsman*

EXEMPTED
5355 nâqîy (1), *innocent*

EXERCISE
1980 hâlak (1), to *walk; live a certain way*
6213 ˈâsâh (1), to *do or make*
778 askĕō (1), to *strive for one's best*
1128 gumnazō (1), to *train by exercise*
1129 gumnasia (1), *training of the body*
1850 ĕxŏusiazō (1), to *control, master another*
2634 katakuriĕuō (2), to *control, subjugate*
2715 katĕxŏusiazō (2), to *wield full privilege over*
2961 kuriĕuō (1), to *rule, be master of*

EXERCISED
6031 ˈânâh (2), to *afflict, be afflicted*
1128 gumnazō (3), to *train by exercise*

EXERCISETH
4160 pŏiĕō (1), to *do*

EXHORT
3867 parainĕō (1), to *recommend or advise*
3870 parakalĕō (14), to *call, invite*

EXHORTATION
3870 parakalĕō (2), to *call, invite*
3874 paraklēsis (8), *imploring, exhortation*

EXHORTED
3870 parakalĕō (3), to *call, invite*

EXHORTETH
3870 parakalĕō (1), to *call, invite*

EXHORTING
3870 parakalĕō (3), to *call, invite*
4389 prŏtrĕpŏmai (1), to *encourage*

EXILE
1540 gâlâh (1), to *denude; uncover*
6808 tsâˈâh (1), to *tip over; to depopulate*

EXORCISTS
1845 ĕxŏrkistēs (1), *exorcist, i.e. conjurer*

EXPECTATION
4007 mabbâṭ (3), *expectation, hope*
8615 tiqvâh (7), *cord; expectancy*
603 apŏkaradŏkia (2), *intense anticipation*
4328 prŏsdŏkaō (1), to *anticipate; to await*

4329 prŏsdŏkia (1), *apprehension of evil*

EXPECTED
8615 tiqvâh (1), *cord; expectancy*

EXPECTING
1551 ĕkdĕchŏmai (1), to *await, expect*
4328 prŏsdŏkaō (1), to *anticipate; to await*

EXPEDIENT
4851 sumphĕrō (7), to *collect; to conduce*

EXPEL
1644 gârash (1), to *drive out; to expatriate*
1920 hâdaph (1), to *push away or down; drive out*

EXPELLED
3423 yârash (2), to *inherit; to impoverish*
5080 nâdach (1), to *push off, scattered*
1544 ĕkballō (1), to *throw out*

EXPENCES
5313 niphqâˈ (Ch.) (2), *outgo, i.e. expense*

EXPERIENCE
5172 nâchash (1), to *prognosticate*
7200 râˈâh (1), to *see*
1382 dŏkimē (2), *test,* i.e. *trustiness*

EXPERIMENT
1382 dŏkimē (1), *test,* i.e. *trustiness*

EXPERT
3925 lâmad (1), to *teach, train*
6186 ˈârak (3), to *set in a row, i.e. arrange*
7919 sâkal (1), to *be or act circumspect*
1109 gnōstēs (1), *knower, expert*

EXPIRED
3615 kâlâh (1), to *cease, be finished, perish*
4390 mâlê (3), to *fill; be full*
8666 tᵉshûwbâh (3), *recurrence; reply*
4137 plērŏō (1), to *fill, make complete*
5055 tĕlĕō (1), to *end,* i.e. *complete, execute*

EXPOUND
5046 nâgad (1), to *announce*

EXPOUNDED
5046 nâgad (1), to *announce*
1329 diĕrmēnĕuō (1), to *explain thoroughly*
1620 ĕktithēmi (3), to *expose; to declare*
1956 ĕpiluō (1), to *explain; to decide*

EXPRESS
5481 charaktēr (1), *exact copy or representation*

EXPRESSED
5344 nâqab (5), to
specify, designate, libel

EXPRESSLY
559 'âmar (1), to *say*
4490 rhētŏs (1),
out-spoken, distinctly

EXTEND
4900 mâshak (1), to *draw
out; to be tall*
5186 nâṭâh (1), to *stretch
or spread out*

EXTENDED
5186 nâṭâh (2), to *stretch
or spread out*

EXTINCT
1846 dâ'ak (1), to *be
extinguished; to expire*
2193 zâ'ak (1), to
extinguish

EXTOL
5549 çâlal (1), to *mound
up; to exalt; to oppose*
7311 rûwm (2), to *be
high; to rise or raise*
7313 rûwm (Ch.) (1),
elation, arrogance

EXTOLLED
5375 nâsâ' (1), to *lift up*
7318 rôwmâm (1),
exaltation, praise

EXTORTION
6233 ôsheq (1), *fraud;
distress; unjust gain*
724 harpagē (1), *pillage;
greediness; robbery*

EXTORTIONER
4160 mûwts (1), to
oppress
5383 nâshâh (1), to *lend
or borrow*
727 harpax (1),
rapacious; robbing

EXTORTIONERS
727 harpax (3),
rapacious; robbing

EXTREME
2746 charchûr (1), *hot
fever*

EXTREMITY
6580 pash (1), *stupidity
as a result of grossness*

EYE
5869 'ayin (73), *eye;
sight; fountain*
5870 'ayin (Ch.) (1), *eye;
sight*
3442 mŏnŏphthalmŏs
(2), *one-eyed*
3788 ŏphthalmŏs (29),
eye
5168 trumalia (2),
needle's eye
5169 trupēma (1),
needle's eye

EYE'S
5869 'ayin (1), *eye; sight;
fountain*

EYEBROWS
1354+5869 gab (1),
*rounded: top or rim;
arch*

EYED
5770 'âvan (1), to *watch
with jealousy*
5869 'ayin (1), *eye; sight;
fountain*

EYELIDS
6079 'aph'aph (9),
fluttering eyelash

EYES
5869 'ayin (417), *eye;
sight; fountain*
5870 'ayin (Ch.) (5), *eye;
sight*
3659 ŏmma (1), *eye*
3788 ŏphthalmŏs (70),
eye

EYESALVE
2854 kŏllŏuriŏn (1),
poultice

EYESERVICE
3787 ŏphthalmŏdŏulĕia
(2), *service that needs
watching*

EYESIGHT
5869 'ayin (1), *eye; sight;
fountain*

EYEWITNESSES
845 autŏptēs (1),
eyewitness
2030 ĕpŏptēs (1),
looker-on

EZAR
687 'Etser (1), *treasure*

EZBAI
229 'Ezbay (1),
hyssop-like

EZBON
675 'Etsbôwn (2), *Etsbon*

EZEKIAS
1478 Ĕzĕkias (2),
*strengthened of
Jehovah*

EZEKIEL
3168 Yᵉchezqê'l (2), *God
will strengthen*

EZEL
237 'ezel (1), *departure*

EZEM
6107 'Etsem (1), *bone*

EZER
687 'Etser (4), *treasure*
5827 'Ezer (1), *help*
5829 'Êzer (4), *aid*

EZION-GABER
6100 'Etsyôwn (short (4),
backbone-like of a man

EZION-GEBER
6100 'Etsyôwn (short (3),
backbone-like of a man

EZNITE
6112 'Êtsen (1), *spear*

EZRA
5830 'Ezrâ' (26), *aid*

EZRAHITE
250 'Ezrâchîy (3),
Ezrachite

EZRI
5836 'Ezrîy (1), *helpful*

FABLES
3454 muthŏs (5), *tale,
fiction, myth*

FACE
600 'ănaph (Ch.) (1), *face*
639 'aph (19), *nose or
nostril; face; person*
5869 'ayin (9), *eye; sight;
fountain*
6440 pânîym (313), *face;
front*
1799 ĕnôpiŏn (1), *in the
face of, before*
3799 ŏpsis (1), *face;
appearance*
4383 prŏsôpŏn (48), *face,
presence*
4750 stŏma (4), *mouth;
edge*

FACES
639 'aph (3), *nose or
nostril; face; person*
6440 pânîym (62), *face;
front*
4383 prŏsôpŏn (5), *face,
presence*

FADE
5034 nâbêl (5), to *wilt; to
fall away; to be foolish*
3133 marainô (1), to *pass
away, fade away*

FADETH
5034 nâbêl (5), to *wilt; to
fall away; to be foolish*
262 amarantinŏs (1),
fadeless
263 amarantŏs (1),
perpetual, never fading

FADING
5034 nâbêl (2), to *wilt; to
fall away; to be foolish*

FAIL
235 'âzal (1), to *disappear*
656 'âphêç (1), to *cease*
1238 bâqaq (1), to
depopulate, ruin
1584 gâmar (1), to *end;
to complete; to fail*
1809 dâlal (1), to
slacken, dangle
2637 châçêr (3), to *lack;
to fail, want, make less*
2638 châçêr (1), *lacking*
3543 kâhâh (1), to *grow
dull, fade; to be faint*
3576 kâzab (1), to *lie,
deceive*
3584 kâchash (2), to *lie,
disown; to disappoint*
3615 kâlâh (14), to *cease,
be finished, perish*
3772 kârath (6), to *cut
(off, down or asunder)*
3808+539 lô' (1), *no, not*
5307 nâphal (2), to *fall*
5405 nâshath (1), to *dry
up*
5674 'âbar (2), to *cross
over; to transition*
5737 'âdar (1), to
arrange as a battle
5848 'âṭaph (1), to
shroud, to languish
6461 paçaç (1), to
disappear
6565 pârar (1), to *break
up; to violate, frustrate*
7503 râphâh (4), to
slacken

FAIN
7673 shâbath (2), to
repose; to desist
7960 shâlûw (Ch.) (2),
fault, error
8266 shâqar (1), to *cheat,
i.e. be untrue in words*
1587 ĕklĕipô (3), to *die;
to spot*
1952 ĕpilĕipô (1), to *be
insufficient for*
2673 katargĕô (1), to *be,
render entirely useless*
4098 piptô (1), to *fall*
5302 hustĕrĕô (1), to *be
inferior; to fall short*

FAILED
6 'âbad (1), *perish;
destroy*
2308 châdal (1), to *desist,
stop; be fat*
3318 yâtsâ' (2), to *go,
bring out*
3615 kâlâh (1), to *cease,
be finished, perish*
5307 nâphal (4), to *fall*
5405 nâshath (1), to *dry
up*
8552 tâmam (2), to
complete, finish

FAILETH
6 'âbad (1), *perish;
destroy*
369 'ayin (1), *there is no,
i.e., not exist, none*
656 'âphêç (1), to *cease*
1602 gâ'al (1), to *detest;
to reject; to fail*
2638 châçêr (1), *lacking*
3584 kâchash (1), to *lie,
disown; to disappoint*
3615 kâlâh (4), to *cease,
be finished, perish*
3782 kâshal (1), to *totter,
waver; to falter*
5405 nâshath (1), to *dry
up*
5737 'âdar (3), to
arrange as a battle
5800 'âzab (2), to *loosen;
relinquish; permit*
413 anĕklĕiptŏs (1), *not
failing*
1601 ĕkpiptô (1), to *drop
away*

FAILING
3631 killâyôwn (1),
pining, destruction
674 apŏpsuchō (1), to
faint

FAIN
1272 bârach (1), to *flee
suddenly*
1937 ĕpithumĕô (1), to
long for

FAINT
1738 dâvâh (1), to *be in
menstruation cycle*
1739 dâveh (1),
menstrual; fainting
1742 davvây (3), *sick;
troubled, afflicted*
3286 yâ'aph (3), to *tire*
3287 yâ'êph (2),
exhausted
3543 kâhâh (1), to *grow
dull, fade; to be faint*

4127 mûwg (3), to *soften, flow down, disappear*
4549 mâçaç (1), to *waste*; to *faint*
5774 'ûwph (3), to *cover, to fly*; to *faint*
5848 'âṭaph (1), to *shroud, to languish*
5889 'âyêph (6), *languid*
5968 'âlaph (1), to *be languid, faint*
6296 pâgar (2), to *become exhausted*
7401 râkak (2), to *soften*
7503 râphâh (2), to *slacken*
1573 ĕkkakĕō (4), to *be weak, fail*
1590 ĕkluō (5), to *lose heart*

FAINTED
1961 hâyâh (1), to *exist*, i.e. *be or become*
3021 yâga' (1), to *be exhausted, to tire*
3856 lâhahh (1), to *languish*
5848 'âṭaph (2), to *shroud, to languish*
5968 'âlaph (2), to *be languid, faint*
5969 'ulpeh (1), *mourning*
6313 pûwg (1), to *be sluggish; be numb*
1590 ĕkluō (1), to *lose heart*
2577 kamnō (1), to *tire*; to *faint, sicken*

FAINTEST
3811 lâ'âh (1), to *tire*; to *be, make disgusted*

FAINTETH
3286 yâ'aph (1), to *tire*
3615 kâlâh (2), to *cease, be finished, perish*
4549 mâçaç (1), to *waste*; to *faint*

FAINTHEARTED
3824+7401 lêbâb (1), *heart*
4127 mûwg (1), to *soften*; to *fear, faint*
7390+3824 rak (1), *tender; weak*

FAINTNESS
4816 môrek (1), despondent *fear*

FAIR
2091 zâhâb (1), *gold, golden colored*
2603 chânan (1), to *implore*
2889 ṭâhôwr (2), *pure, clean, flawless*
2896 ṭôwb (6), *good; well*
2896+4758 ṭôwb (1), *good; well*
2897+4758 Ṭôwb (1), *good*
2898 ṭûwb (1), *good; goodness; beauty*
3302 yâphâh (12), to *be beautiful*
3303 yâpheh (14), *beautiful; handsome*
3303+8389 yâpheh (1), *beautiful; handsome*

3304 yᵉphêh-phîyâh (1), *very beautiful*
3948 leqach (1), *instruction*
6320 pûwk (1), *stibium*
8209 sappîyr (Ch.) (2), *beautiful*
8597 tiph'ârâh (3), *ornament*
791 astĕiŏs (1), *handsome*
2105 ĕudia (1), *clear sky*, i.e. *fine weather*
2129 ĕulŏgia (1), *benediction*
2146 ĕuprŏsōpĕō (1), to *make a good display*
2568 Kalŏi Limĕnĕs (1), *Good Harbors*

FAIRER
2896 ṭôwb (2), *good; well*
3302 yâphâh (1), to *be beautiful*

FAIREST
3303 yâpheh (3), *beautiful; handsome*

FAIRS
5801 'izzâbôwn (6), *trade, merchandise*

FAITH
529 'êmûwn (1), *trustworthiness; faithful*
530 'ĕmûwnâh (1), *fidelity; steadiness*
1680 ĕlpis (1), *expectation; hope*
3640 ŏligŏpistŏs (5), *lacking full confidence*
4102 pistis (238), *faithfulness; faith, belief*

FAITHFUL
529 'êmûwn (3), *trustworthiness; faithful*
530 'ĕmûwnâh (3), *fidelity; steadiness*
539 'âman (20), to *be firm, faithful, true*
540 'ăman (Ch.) (1), to *be firm, faithful, true*
571 'emeth (1), *certainty, truth, trustworthiness*
4103 pistŏs (53), *trustworthy; reliable*

FAITHFULLY
530 'ĕmûwnâh (5), *fidelity; steadiness*
571 'emeth (2), *certainty, truth, trustworthiness*
4103 pistŏs (1), *trustworthy; reliable*

FAITHFULNESS
530 'ĕmûwnâh (18), *fidelity; steadiness*
3559 kûwn (1), to *render sure, proper*

FAITHLESS
571 apistŏs (4), *without faith; untrustworthy*

FALL
2342 chûwl (1), to *dance, whirl*; to *writhe* in pain
3318 yâtsâ' (1), to *go, bring out*
3381 yârad (1), to *descend*

3782 kâshal (22), to *totter, waver*; to *falter*
3783 kishshâlôwn (1), *ruin*
3832 lâbaṭ (3), to *overthrow; to fall*
3872 Lûwchîyth (1), *floored*
4131 môwṭ (1), to *slip, shake, fall*
4383 mikshôwl (1), *stumbling-block*
4658 mappeleth (7), *down-fall; ruin; carcase*
5034 nâbêl (1), to *wilt*; to *fall away*; to *be foolish*
5064 nâgar (1), to *pour out*; to *deliver over*
5203 nâṭash (1), to *disperse*; to *thrust* off
5307 nâphal (149), to *fall*
5308 nᵉphal (Ch.) (3), to *fall*
5456 çâgad (2), to *prostrate oneself*
6293 pâga' (8), to *impinge*
7264 râgaz (1), to *quiver*
7812 shâchâh (2), to *prostrate in homage*
7997 shâlal (1), to *drop or strip*; to *plunder*
868 aphistēmi (1), to *desist, desert*
1601 ĕkpiptō (4), to *drop away*
1706 ĕmpiptō (3), to *be entrapped by*
3895 parapiptō (1), to *apostatize, fall away*
3900 paraptōma (2), *error; transgression*
4045 pĕripiptō (1), to *fall into the hands of*
4098 piptō (22), to *fall*
4417 ptaiō (1), to *trip up, stumble morally*
4431 ptōsis (2), *downfall, crash*
4625 skandalŏn (1), *snare*

FALLEN
935 bôw' (1), to *go or come*
3782 kâshal (2), to *totter, waver*; to *falter*
4131+3027 môwṭ (1), to *slip, shake, fall*
4803 mâraṭ (2), to *polish*; to *make bald*
5307 nâphal (55), to *fall*
1601 ĕkpiptō (3), to *drop away*
1706 ĕmpiptō (1), to *be entrapped by*
1968 ĕpipiptō (1), to *embrace; to seize*
2064 ĕrchŏmai (1), to *go or come*
2667 katapiptō (2), to *fall down*
2702 kataphĕrō (1), to *bear down*
2837 kŏimaō (1), to *slumber; to decease*
4098 piptō (4), to *fall*

FALLEST
5307 nâphal (1), to *fall*

FALLETH
3918 layish (1), *lion*
5034 nâbêl (1), to *wilt*; to *fall away*; to *be foolish*
5307 nâphal (15), to *fall*
5308 nᵉphal (Ch.) (2), to *fall*
5456 çâgad (2), to *prostrate oneself*
7122 qârâ' (1), to *encounter; to happen*
1601 ĕkpiptō (2), to *drop away*
1911 ĕpiballō (1), to *throw upon*
4098 piptō (3), to *fall*

FALLING
1762 dᵉchîy (2), *stumbling fall*
3782 kâshal (1), to *totter, waver*; to *falter*
4131 môwṭ (1), to *slip, shake, fall*
5034 nâbêl (1), to *wilt*; to *fall away*; to *be foolish*
5307 nâphal (3), to *fall*
646 apŏstasia (1), *defection, rebellion*
679 aptaistŏs (1), *not stumbling, without sin*
2597 katabainō (1), to *descend*
4045 pĕripiptō (1), to *fall into the hands of*
4098 piptō (1), to *fall*
4248+1096 prēnēs (1), *headlong*
4363 prŏspiptō (1), to *prostrate oneself*

FALLOW
3180 yachmûwr (1), kind of *deer*
5215 nîyr (2), freshly *plowed* land

FALLOWDEER
3180 yachmûwr (1), kind of *deer*

FALSE
205 'âven (1), *trouble, vanity, wickedness*
2555 châmâç (2), *violence; malice*
3577 kâzâb (1), *falsehood; idol*
4820 mirmâh (2), *fraud*
7423 rᵉmîyâh (1), *remissness; treachery*
7723 shâv' (5), *ruin; guile; idolatry*
8267 sheqer (20), *untruth; sham*
1228 diabŏlŏs (2), *traducer*, i.e. *Satan*
4811 sukŏphantĕō (1), to *defraud, extort*
5569 psĕudadĕlphŏs (2), *pretended associate*
5570 psĕudapŏstŏlŏs (1), *pretended preacher*
5571 psĕudēs (1), *erroneous, deceitful*
5572 psĕudŏdidaskalŏs (1), *propagator of erroneous doctrine*
5573 psĕudŏlŏgŏs (4), *promulgating erroneous doctrine*

F

5575 pseŭdŏmartur (3), bearer of untrue testimony
5576 pseŭdŏmartureō (6), to offer falsehood
5577 pseŭdŏmarturia (1), untrue testimony
5578 pseŭdŏprŏphētēs (6), pretended foreteller
5580 pseŭdŏchristŏs (2), spurious Messiah

FALSEHOOD
4604 ma'al (1), sinful treachery
8267 sheqer (13), untruth; sham

FALSELY
3584 kâchash (1), to lie, disown; to disappoint
5921+8267 'al (1), above, over, upon, or against
7723 shâv' (1), ruin; guile; idolatry
8266 shâqar (2), to cheat, i.e. be untrue in words
8267 sheqer (12), untruth; sham
5574 pseŭdŏmai (1), to utter an untruth
5581 pseŭdŏnumŏs (1), untruly named

FALSIFYING
5791 'âvath (1), to wrest, twist

FAME
6963 qôwl (1), voice or sound
8034 shêm (4), appellation, i.e. name
8052 shᵉmûw'âh (2), announcement
8088 shêma' (5), something heard
8089 shôma' (4), report; reputation
189 akŏē (3), hearing; thing heard
1310 diaphēmizō (1), to spread news
2279 ēchŏs (1), roar; rumor
3056 lŏgŏs (1), word, matter, thing; Word
5345 phēmē (2), news, report

FAMILIAR
3045 yâda' (1), to know
7965 shâlôwm (1), safe; well; health, prosperity

FAMILIARS
7965 shâlôwm (1), safe; well; health, prosperity

FAMILIES
1004 bayith (2), house; temple; family, tribe
1004+1 bayith (2), house; temple; family, tribe
2945 ṭaph (1), family of children and women
4940 mishpâchâh (169), family, clan, people

FAMILY
504 'eleph (1), ox; cow or cattle
1004 bayith (1), house; temple; family, tribe

4940 mishpâchâh (120), family, clan, people
3965 patria (1), family, race, nation

FAMINE
3720 kâphân (2), hunger
7458 râ'âb (86), hunger
7459 rᵉ'âbôwn (3), famine
3042 limŏs (4), scarcity of food, famine

FAMINES
3042 limŏs (3), scarcity of food, famine

FAMISH
7329 râzâh (1), to make, become thin
7456 râ'êb (1), to hunger

FAMISHED
7456 râ'êb (1), to hunger
7458 râ'âb (1), hunger

FAMOUS
117 'addîyr (2), powerful; majestic
3045 yâda' (1), to know
7121 qârâ' (2), to call out
7148 qârîy' (1), called, i.e. select
8034 shêm (4), appellation, i.e. name

FAN
2219 zârâh (4), to toss about; to winnow
4214 mizreh (1), winnowing shovel
4425 ptuŏn (2), winnowing-fork

FANNERS
2114 zûwr (1), to be foreign, strange

FAR
1419 gâdôwl (1), great
2008 hênnâh (2), from here; from there
2186 zânach (1), to reject, forsake, fail
2486 châlîylâh (9), far be it!, forbid!
3966 mᵉ'ôd (3), very, utterly
4801 merchâq (15), distant place; from afar
5048 neged (3), over against or before
5079 niddâh (1), time of menstrual impurity
7350 râchôwq (59), remote, far
7352 rachîyq (Ch.) (1), far away; aloof
7368 râchaq (39), to recede; remove
7369 râchêq (2), remote, far
891 achri (2), until or up to
1519 ĕis (1), to or into
2193 hĕŏs (4), until
2436 hilĕŏs (1), God be gracious!, far be it!
3112 makran (6), at a distance, far away
3113 makrŏthen (1), from a distance or afar
3117 makrŏs (2), long, in place or time

4054 pĕrissŏtĕrŏn (1), in a superabundant way
4183 pŏlus (3), much, many
4206 pŏrrhō (2), forwards, at a distance
5231 hupĕranō (2), above, upward

FARE
7939 sâkâr (1), payment, salary; compensation
7965 shâlôwm (1), safe; well; health, prosperity
4517 rhŏnnumi (1), to strengthen

FARED
2165 ĕuphrainō (1), to rejoice, be glad

FAREWELL
657 apŏtassŏmai (2), to say adieu; to renounce
4517 rhŏnnumi (1), to strengthen
5463 chairō (1), to be cheerful

FARM
68 agrŏs (1), farmland, countryside

FARTHER
4008 pĕran (1), across, beyond
4260 prŏbainō (1), to advance
4281 prŏĕrchŏmai (1), to go onward, precede

FARTHING
787 assariŏn (1), assarius
2835 kŏdrantēs (2), quadrans

FARTHINGS
787 assariŏn (1), assarius

FASHION
1823 dᵉmûwth (1), resemblance, likeness
3559 kûwn (1), to set up: establish, fix, prepare
4941 mishpâṭ (2), verdict; formal decree; justice
8498 tᵉkûwnâh (1), structure; equipage
1491 ĕidŏs (1), form, appearance, sight
3778 hŏutŏs (1), this or that
4383 prŏsōpŏn (1), face, presence
4976 schēma (2), form or appearance
5179 tupŏs (1), shape, resemblance; "type"

FASHIONED
3335 yâtsar (3), to form; potter; to determine
3559 kûwn (2), to set up: establish, fix, prepare
6213 'âsâh (1), to do or make
4832 summŏrphŏs (1), similar, conformed to

FASHIONETH
3335 yâtsar (3), to form; potter; to determine

FASHIONING
4964 suschēmatizō (1), to conform to the same

FASHIONS
4941 mishpâṭ (1), verdict; formal decree; justice

FAST
629 'oçparnâ' (Ch.) (1), diligently
3966 mᵉ'ôd (1), very, utterly
6684 tsûwm (8), to fast from food
6685 tsôwm (16), fast from food
472 antĕchŏmai (1), to adhere to; to care for
805 asphalizō (1), to render secure
2722 katĕchō (3), to hold down fast
3521 nēstĕia (1), abstinence
3522 nēstĕuō (16), to abstain from food

FASTED
6684 tsûwm (12), to fast from food
3522 nēstĕuō (3), to abstain from food

FASTEN
2388 châzaq (1), to fasten upon; to seize
5414 nâthan (3), to give
8628 tâqa' (1), to clatter, slap, drive, clasp

FASTENED
270 'âchaz (3), to seize, grasp; possess
2388 châzaq (1), to fasten upon; to seize
2883 ṭâba' (1), to sink; to be drowned
3559 kûwn (1), to set up: establish, fix, prepare
5193 nâṭa' (1), to plant
5414 nâthan (2), to give
6775 tsâmad (1), to link, i.e. gird
6795 tsânach (1), to descend, i.e. drive down
8628 tâqa' (4), to clatter, slap, drive, clasp
816 atĕnizō (2), to gaze intently
2510 kathaptō (1), to seize upon

FASTENING
816 atĕnizō (1), to gaze intently

FASTEST
2522 kathēmĕrinŏs (1), quotidian, i.e. daily

FASTING
2908 ṭᵉvâth (Ch.) (1), hunger
6685 tsôwm (8), fast
777 asitŏs (1), without taking food
3521 nēstĕia (4), abstinence
3522 nēstĕuō (1), to abstain from food
3523 nēstis (2), abstinent from food

FASTINGS
6685 tsôwm (1), fast
3521 nēstĕia (3), abstinence

FAT

1254 bârâ' (1), *to create; fashion*
1277 bârîy' (6), *fatted or plump; healthy*
1878 dâshên (7), *to be fat, thrive; to fatten*
1879 dâshên (3), *fat; rich, fertile*
2459 cheleb (79), *fat; choice part*
2502 châlats (1), *to pull off; to strip; to depart*
2954 ṭâphash (1), *to be stupid*
3368 yâqâr (1), *valuable*
4220 mêach (1), *fat; rich*
4770 marbêq (1), *stall*
4806 m⁰rîy' (4), *stall-fed animal*
4924 mashmân (2), *fatness; rich dish; fertile field; robust man*
4945 mashqeh (1), *butler; drink; well-watered*
6309 peder (3), *suet*
6335 pûwsh (1), *to spread; to act proudly*
6371 pîymâh (1), *obesity*
8080 shâman (3), *to be, make oily or gross*
8081 shemen (4), *olive oil, wood, lotions*
8082 shâmên (10), *rich; fertile*

FATFLESHED

1277 bârîy' (2), *fatted or plump; healthy*

FATHER

1 'âb (504), *father*
2 'ab (Ch.) (13), *father*
25 'Ăbîy Gib'ôwn (67), *founder of Gibon*
1121 bên (1), *son, descendant; people*
2524 châm (4), *father-in-law*
2589 channôwth (1), *supplication*
2859 châthan (20), *to become related*
540 apatōr (1), *of unrecorded paternity*
3962 patēr (344), *father*
3995 pĕnthĕrŏs (1), *wife's father*

FATHER'S

1 'âb (126), *father*
1730 dôwd (2), *beloved, friend; relative*
1733 dôwdâh (1), *aunt*
3962 patēr (17), *father*

FATHERLESS

369+1 'ayin (1), *there is no, i.e., not exist, none*
3490 yâthôwm (41), *child alone, fatherless child*
3737 ŏrphanŏs (1), *parentless, orphaned*

FATHERS

1 'âb (475), *father*
2 'ab (Ch.) (3), *father*
3962 patēr (52), *father*
3964 patralŏias (1), *killing of father*
3967 patrikŏs (1), *ancestral, paternal*

3970 patrŏparadŏtŏs (1), *traditionary*
3971 patrŏᵢŏs (3), *from forefathers*

FATHERS'

1 'âb (10), *father*
3962 patēr (1), *father*

FATHOMS

3712 ŏrguia (2), *measure of about six feet*

FATLING

4806 m⁰rîy' (1), *stall-fed animal*

FATLINGS

4220 mêach (1), *fat; rich*
4806 m⁰rîy' (2), *stall-fed animal*
4932 mishneh (1), *duplicate copy; double*
4619 sitistŏs (1), *grained, i.e. fatted*

FATNESS

1880 deshen (7), *fat; fatness, abundance*
2459 cheleb (4), *fat; choice part*
4924 mashmân (3), *fatness; fertile; robust*
8081 shemen (1), *olive oil, wood, lotions*
4096 piŏtēs (1), *oiliness, i.e. nourishing sap*

FATS

3342 yeqeb (2), *wine-vat, wine-press*

FATTED

75 'âbaç (1), *to feed; be fattened with feed*
4770 marbêq (1), *stall*
4618 sitĕutŏs (3), *fattened, i.e. stall-fed*

FATTER

1277 bârîy' (1), *fatted or plump; healthy*

FATTEST

4924 mashmân (2), *fatness; fertile; robust*

FAULT

2398 châṭâ' (1), *to sin*
3972 m⁰'ûwmâh (1), *something; anything*
5771 'âvôn (2), *moral evil*
7564 rish'âh (1), *moral wrong*
7844 sh⁰chath (Ch.) (2), *to decay; to ruin*
156 aitia (3), *logical reason; legal crime*
158 aitiŏn (2), *reason, basis; crime*
299 amōmŏs (1), *unblemished, blameless*
1651 ĕlĕgchŏ (1), *to confute, admonish*
2275 hēttēma (1), *failure or loss*
3201 mĕmphŏmai (3), *to blame*
3900 paraptōma (1), *error; transgression*

FAULTLESS

278 amĕtamĕlētŏs (1), *irrevocable*
299 amōmŏs (1), *unblemished, blameless*

FAULTS

2399 chêṭ' (1), *crime or its penalty*
264 hamartanŏ (1), *to miss the mark, to err*
3900 paraptōma (1), *error; transgression*

FAULTY

816 'âsham (1), *to be guilty; to be punished*
818 'âshêm (1), *bearing guilt, guilty*

FAVOUR

2580 chên (26), *graciousness; beauty*
2594 chănîynâh (1), *graciousness, kindness*
2603 chânan (8), *to implore*
2617 cheçed (3), *kindness, favor*
2655 châphêts (1), *pleased with*
2896 ṭôwb (2), *good; well*
3190 yâṭab (1), *to be, make well*
6440 pânîym (4), *face; front*
7520 râtsad (1), *to look askant; to be jealous*
7522 râtsôwn (15), *delight*
7965 shâlôwm (1), *safe; well; health, prosperity*
8467 t⁰chinnâh (1), *gracious entreaty*
5485 charis (6), *gratitude; benefit given*

FAVOURABLE

2603 chânan (1), *to implore*
7520 râtsad (3), *to look askant; to be jealous*

FAVOURED

2603 chânan (1), *to implore*
4758 mar'eh (7), *appearance; vision*
8389 tô'ar (2), *outline, i.e. figure or appearance*
5487 charitŏŏ (1), *to give special honor; one highly favored*

FAVOUREST

2654 châphêts (1), *to be pleased with, desire*

FAVOURETH

2654 châphêts (1), *to be pleased with, desire*

FEAR

367 'êymâh (5), *fright*
1481 gûwr (2), *to sojourn, live as an alien*
1674 d⁰'âgâh (1), *anxiety*
1763 d⁰chal (Ch.) (1), *to fear; be formidable, awesome*
2342 chûwl (2), *to dance, whirl; to writhe in pain; to wait; to pervert*
2731 chărâdâh (2), *fear, anxiety*
2844 chath (1), *terror*
3025 yâgôr (1), *to fear*
3372 yârê' (148), *to fear; to revere*

3373 yârê' (35), *fearing; reverent*
3374 yir'âh (41), *fear; reverence*
4032 mâgôwr (6), *fright, horror*
4034 m⁰gôwrâh (1), *affright, dread*
4172 môwrâ' (6), *fearful*
6206 'ârats (2), *to awe; to dread; to harass*
6342 pâchad (9), *to be startled; to fear*
6343 pachad (41), *sudden alarm, fear*
6345 pachdâh (1), *awe*
6440 pânîym (8), *face; front*
7267 rôgez (1), *disquiet; anger*
7374 reṭeṭ (1), *terror, panic*
7461 ra'ad (1), *shudder*
820 atimŏs (1), *dishonoured; without honor*
870 aphŏbŏs (3), *fearlessly*
1167 dĕilia (1), *timidity, cowardice*
1630+1510 ĕkphŏbŏs (1), *frightened out of one's wits*
2124 ĕulabĕia (1), *reverence; submission*
2125 ĕulabĕŏmai (1), *to have reverence*
5399 phŏbĕŏ (35), *to fear, be frightened; to revere*
5401 phŏbŏs (40), *alarm, or fright; reverence*
5401+2192 phŏbŏs (1), *fright; reverence*

FEARED

1481 gûwr (1), *to sojourn, live as an alien*
1763 d⁰chal (Ch.) (1), *to fear; be formidable*
3372 yârê' (38), *to fear; to revere*
3373 yârê' (8), *fearing; reverent*
4172 môwrâ' (1), *fearful*
6206 'ârats (1), *to awe; to dread; to harass*
6342 pâchad (3), *to be startled; to fear*
8175 sâ'ar (1), *to storm; to shiver, i.e. fear*
2124 ĕulabĕia (1), *reverence; submission*
5399 phŏbĕŏ (17), *to fear, to be in awe of, revere*
5399+5401 phŏbĕŏ (1), *to fear, be in awe of*

FEAREST

1481 gûwr (1), *to sojourn, live as an alien*
3372 yârê' (1), *to fear; to revere*
3373 yârê' (1), *fearing; reverent*

FEARETH

3372 yârê' (2), *to fear; to revere*
3373 yârê' (13), *fearing; reverent*

6342 pâchad (1), to *be startled; to fear*
5399 phôbĕŏ (4), to *fear, be in awe of, revere*

FEARFUL
3372 yârê' (2), to *fear; to revere*
3373 yârê' (2), *fearing; reverent*
4116 mâhar (1), to *hurry; promptly*
1169 dĕilŏs (3), *timid, i.e. faithless*
5398 phôbĕrŏs (2), *frightful, i.e. formidable*
5400 phôbĕtrŏn (1), *frightening thing*

FEARFULLY
3372 yârê' (1), to *fear; to revere*

FEARFULNESS
3374 yir'âh (1), *fear; reverence*
6427 pallâtsûwth (1), *affright, trembling fear*
7461 ra'ad (1), *shudder*

FEARING
3372 yârê' (1), to *fear; to revere*
2125 ĕulabĕŏmai (1), to *have reverence*
5399 phôbĕŏ (6), to *fear, be in awe of, revere*

FEARS
2849 chathchath (1), *terror, horror*
4035 mᵉgûwrâh (2), *fright; granary*
5401 phôbŏs (1), *alarm, or fright; reverence*

FEAST
2282 chag (53), *solemn festival*
2287 châgag (4), to *observe a festival*
3899 lechem (1), *food, bread*
3900 lᵉchem (Ch.) (1), *food, bread*
4150 môw'êd (3), *assembly, congregation*
4960 mishteh (21), *drink; banquet or feast*
755 architriklinŏs (3), *director of the entertainment*
1408 drŏmŏs (2), *career, course of life*
1456 ĕgkainia (1), *Feast of Dedication*
1858 hĕŏrtazŏ (1), to *observe a festival*
1859 hĕŏrtē (26), *festival*
4910 sunĕuŏchĕŏ (2), to *feast together*

FEASTED
6213+4960 'âsâh (1), to *do or make*

FEASTING
4960 mishteh (7), *drink; banquet or feast*

FEASTS
2282 chag (5), *solemn festival*
4150 môw'êd (19), *assembly, congregation*

4580 mâ'ôwg (1), *cake of bread, provision*
4960 mishteh (2), *drink; banquet or feast*
1173 dĕipnŏn (3), *principal meal*

FEATHERED
3671 kânâph (2), *edge or extremity; wing*

FEATHERS
84 'ebrâh (2), *pinion*
2624 chăçîydâh (1), *stork*
5133 nôwtsâh (3), *plumage*

FED
398 'âkal (5), to *eat*
1277 bârîy' (1), *fatted or plump; healthy*
2109 zûwn (1), to *nourish; feed*
2110 zûwn (Ch.) (1), to *nourish; feed*
2939 ṭᵉ'am (Ch.) (1), to *feed*
3557 kûwl (3), to *keep in; to measure*
4806 mᵉrîy' (1), *stall-fed animal*
5095 nâhal (1), to *flow; to protect, sustain*
7462 râ'âh (10), to *tend a flock, i.e. pasture it*
1006 bŏskŏ (2), to *pasture a flock*
4222 pŏtizŏ (1), to *furnish drink, irrigate*
5142 trĕphŏ (1), to *nurse, feed, care for*
5526 chŏrtazŏ (1), to *supply food*

FEEBLE
535 'âmal (1), to *be weak; to be sick*
537 'ămêlâl (1), *languid, feeble*
2826 châshal (1), to *make unsteady*
3766 kâra' (1), to *make miserable*
3782 kâshal (4), to *totter, waver; to falter*
3808+3524 lô' (1), *no, not*
3808+6099 lô' (1), *no, not*
5848 'âṭaph (1), to *shroud; to languish*
6313 pûwg (1), to *be sluggish; be numb*
7503 râphâh (6), to *slacken*
772 asthĕnēs (1), *strengthless, weak*
3886 paraluŏ (1), to *be paralyzed or enfeebled*

FEEBLEMINDED
3642 ŏligŏpsuchŏs (1), *timid, faint-hearted*

FEEBLENESS
7510 riphyôwn (1), *slackness*

FEEBLER
5848 'âṭaph (1), to *shroud, to languish*

FEED
398 'âkal (8), to *eat*
1197 bâ'ar (1), to *be brutish, be senseless*

2963 ṭâraph (1), to *supply, provide food*
3557 kûwl (3), to *keep in; to measure*
3938 lâ'aṭ (1), to *swallow greedily, gulp*
7462 râ'âh (55), to *tend a flock, i.e. pasture it*
1006 bŏskŏ (3), to *pasture a flock*
4165 pŏimainŏ (4), to *tend as a shepherd*
5142 trĕphŏ (1), to *nurse, feed, care for*
5595 psōmizŏ (2), to *nourish, feed*

FEEDEST
398 'âkal (1), to *eat*
7462 râ'âh (1), to *tend a flock, i.e. pasture it*

FEEDETH
7462 râ'âh (5), to *tend a flock, i.e. pasture it*
4165 pŏimainŏ (1), to *tend as a shepherd*
5142 trĕphŏ (2), to *nurse, feed, care for*

FEEDING
7462 râ'âh (4), to *tend a flock, i.e. pasture it*
1006 bŏskŏ (3), to *pasture a flock*
4165 pŏimainŏ (2), to *tend as a shepherd*

FEEL
995 bîyn (1), to *understand; discern*
3045 yâda' (1), to *know*
4184 mûwsh (2), to *touch, feel*
4959 mâshash (1), to *feel of; to grope*
5584 psēlaphaŏ (1), to *verify by contac*

FEELING
524 apalgĕŏ (1), *become apathetic, callous*
4834 sumpathĕŏ (1), to *commiserate*

FEET
4772 margᵉlâh (5), *at the foot*
6471 pa'am (6), *time; step; occurence*
7166 qarçôl (2), *ankles*
7271 rᵉgal (Ch.) (7), *pair of feet*
7272 regel (151), *foot; step*
939 basis (1), *foot*
4228 pŏus (76), *foot*

FEIGN
5234 nâkar (1), to *treat as a foreigner*
5271 hupŏkrinŏmai (1), to *pretend*

FEIGNED
4820 mirmâh (1), *fraud*
4112 plastŏs (1), *artificial, fabricated*

FEIGNEDLY
8267 sheqer (1), *untruth; sham*

FEIGNEST
908 bâdâ' (1), to *invent; to choose*

FELIX
5344 Phēlix (8), *happy*

FELIX'
5344 Phēlix (1), *happy*

FELL
1961 hâyâh (7), to *exist, i.e. be or become*
3318 yâtsâ' (2), to *go, bring out*
3381 yârad (2), to *descend*
3766 kâra' (2), to *prostrate*
3782 kâshal (2), to *totter, waver; to falter*
5307 nâphal (122), to *fall*
5308 nᵉphal (Ch.) (5), to *fall*
5927 'âlâh (2), to *ascend, be high, mount*
6293 pâga' (4), to *impinge*
6298 pâgash (1), to *come in contact with*
6584 pâshaṭ (2), to *strip, i.e. unclothe, plunder*
7257 râbats (1), to *recline, repose, brood*
7812 shâchâh (2), to *prostrate*
634 apŏpiptŏ (1), to *fall off, drop off*
1096 ginŏmai (1), to *be, become*
1356 diŏpĕtēs (1), *sky-fallen*
1601 ĕkpiptŏ (1), to *drop away*
1706 ĕmpiptŏ (1), to *be entrapped by*
1968 ĕpipiptŏ (10), to *embrace; to seize*
2597 katabainŏ (1), to *descend*
4045 pĕripiptŏ (1), to *fall into the hands of*
4098 piptŏ (56), to *fall*
4363 prŏspiptŏ (6), to *prostrate oneself*

FELLED
5307 nâphal (1), to *fall*

FELLER
3772 kârath (1), to *cut (off, down or asunder)*

FELLEST
5307 nâphal (1), to *fall*

FELLING
5307 nâphal (1), to *fall*

FELLOES
2839 chishshûq (1), *wheel-spoke*

FELLOW
376 'îysh (1), *man; male; someone*
2270 châbêr (1), *associate, friend*
5997 'âmîyth (1), *comrade or kindred*
7453 rêa' (9), *associate; one close*

FELLOW'S
7453 rêa' (1), *associate; one close*

FELLOWCITIZENS
4847 sumpŏlitēs (1), *fellow citizen*

FELLOWDISCIPLES
4827 summathḗtēs (1), co-learner

FELLOWHEIRS
4789 sugklērŏnŏmŏs (1), participant in common

FELLOWHELPER
4904 sunĕrgŏs (1), fellow-worker

FELLOWHELPERS
4904 sunĕrgŏs (1), fellow-worker

FELLOWLABOURER
4904 sunĕrgŏs (2), fellow-worker

FELLOWLABOURERS
4904 sunĕrgŏs (2), fellow-worker

FELLOWPRISONER
4869 sunaichmalŏtŏs (2), co-captive

FELLOWPRISONERS
4869 sunaichmalŏtŏs (1), co-captive

FELLOWS
582 'ĕnŏwsh (1), *man; person, human*
2269 chăbar (Ch.) (2), *associate, friend*
2270 châbêr (3), *associate, friend*
2273 chabrâh (Ch.) (1), *similar, associated*
7453 rêa' (1), *associate; one close*
7464 rê'âh (1), *female associate*
435 anĕr (1), *man; male*
2083 hĕtairŏs (1), comrade, friend
3353 mĕtŏchŏs (1), sharer, associate

FELLOWSERVANT
4889 sundŏulŏs (6), servitor of the same master

FELLOWSERVANTS
4889 sundŏulŏs (4), servitor of the same master

FELLOWSHIP
2266 châbar (1), to *fascinate by spells*
8667+3027 t⁰sûwmeth (1), *deposit, i.e. pledging*
2842 kŏinōnia (12), benefaction; sharing
2844 kŏinōnŏs (1), associate, partner
3352 mĕtŏchē (1), something in common
4790 sugkŏinōnĕō (1), to co-participate

FELLOWSOLDIER
4961 sustratiōtēs (1), soldier together with

FELT
3045 yâda' (1), to *know*
4959 mâshash (2), to *feel of; to grope*
1097 ginōskō (1), to *know*
3958 paschō (1), to experience pain

FEMALE
802 'ishshâh (2), *woman, wife; women, wives*
5347 n⁰qêbâh (19), *female, woman*
2338 thēlus (3), female

FENCE
1447 gâdêr (1), *enclosure, wall or fence*

FENCED
1211 betsel (1), *onion*
1219 bâtsar (15), to *be inaccessible*
1443 gâdar (1), to *build a stone wall*
4013 mibtsâr (12), *fortification; defender*
4390 mâlê' (1), to *fill; be full*
4692 mâtsôwr (1), *siege-mound; distress*
4694 m⁰tsûwrâh (5), *rampart, fortification*
5823 'âzaq (1), to *grub over, dig*
7753 sûwk (1), to *shut in with hedges*

FENS
1207 bitstsâh (1), *swamp, marsh*

FERRET
604 'ănâqâh (1), *gecko*

FERRY
5679 'ăbârâh (1), *crossing-place*

FERVENT
1618 ĕktĕnēs (1), intent, earnest
2204 zĕō (2), to be fervid or earnest
2205 zēlŏs (1), zeal, ardor; jealousy, malice

FERVENTLY
1619 ĕktĕnōs (1), intently, earnestly

FESTUS
5347 Phēstŏs (12), festal

FESTUS'
5347 Phēstŏs (1), festal

FETCH
935 bôw' (1), to *go or come*
3318 yâtsâ' (1), to *go, bring out*
3947 lâqach (20), to *take*
5375 nâsâ' (1), to *lift up*
5437 çâbab (1), to *surround*
5670 'âbaṭ (1), to *pawn; to lend; to entangle*
5927 'âlâh (1), to *ascend, be high, mount*
7725 shûwb (1), to *turn back; to return*
1806 ĕxagō (1), to lead forth, escort

FETCHED
622 'âçaph (1), to *gather, collect*
3318 yâtsâ' (1), to *go, bring out*
3947 lâqach (10), to *take*
5375 nâsâ' (1), to *lift up*
5927 'âlâh (1), to *ascend, be high, mount*

FETCHETH
5080 nâdach (1), to *push off, scattered*

FETCHT
3947 lâqach (1), to *take*

FETTERS
2131 zîyqâh (1), *arrow; bond, fetter*
3525 kebel (2), *fetter, shackles*
5178 n⁰chôsheth (5), *copper; bronze*
3976 pĕdē (3), shackle for the feet

FEVER
6920 qaddachath (1), *inflammation*
4445 purĕssō (2), to burn with a fever
4446 purĕtŏs (6), fever

FEW
259 'echâd (3), *first*
4213 miz'âr (1), *fewness, smallness*
4557 miçpâr (5), *number*
4591 mâ'aṭ (4), to *be, make small or few*
4592 m⁰'aṭ (24), *little or few*
4962 math (4), *men*
7116 qâtsêr (1), *short*
1024 brachus (1), little, short
3641 ŏligŏs (20), puny, small
4935 suntŏmŏs (1), briefly

FEWER
4592 m⁰'aṭ (1), *little or few*

FEWEST
4592 m⁰'aṭ (1), *little or few*

FEWNESS
4591 mâ'aṭ (1), to *be, make small or few*

FIDELITY
4102 pistis (1), faithfulness; faith, belief

FIELD
776 'erets (1), *earth, land, soil; country*
1251 bar (Ch.) (8), *field*
2513 chelqâh (3), *flattery; allotment*
7704 sâdeh (246), *field*
68 agrŏs (22), *farmland, countryside*
5564 chōriŏn (3), spot or plot of ground

FIELDS
2351 chûwts (2), *outside, outdoors; countryside*
3010 yâgêb (1), *plowed field*
7704 sâdeh (46), *field*
7709 sh⁰dêmâh (4), *cultivated field*
8309 sh⁰rêmâh (1), *common*
68 agrŏs (1), *farmland, countryside*
5561 chōra (2), space of territory*

FIERCE
393 'akzâr (1), *violent, deadly; brave*
2300 châdad (1), to *be, make sharp; fierce*
2740 chârôwn (23), *burning of anger*
2750 chŏrîy (3), *burning anger*
3267 yâ'az (1), to *be obstinate, be arrogant*
5794 'az (4), *strong, vehement, harsh*
7826 shachal (3), *lion*
434 anĕmĕrŏs (1), brutal, savage
2001 ĕpischuō (1), to insist stoutly
4642 sklērŏs (1), hard or tough; harsh, severe
5467 chalĕpŏs (1), difficult, furious

FIERCENESS
2740 chârôwn (9), *burning of anger*
7494 ra'ash (1), *bounding, uproar*
2372 thumŏs (2), passion, anger

FIERCER
7185 qâshâh (1), to *be tough or severe*

FIERY
784 'êsh (1), *fire*
799 'eshdâth (1), *fire-law*
5135 nûwr (Ch.) (10), *fire*
8314 sârâph (5), *poisonous serpent*
4442 pur (1), fire
4448 purŏō (1), to be ignited, glow
4451 purōsis (1), ignition, conflagration, calamity

FIFTEEN
2568+6240 châmêsh (16), *five*
6235+2568 'eser (1), *ten*
7657+2568 shib'îym (3), *seventy*
1178 dĕkapĕntĕ (3), fifteen
1440+4002 hĕbdŏ-mēkŏnta (1), seventy

FIFTEENTH
2568+6240 châmêsh (17), *five*
4003 pĕntĕkaidĕkatŏs (1), five and tenth

FIFTH
2549 chămîyshîy (44), *fifth; fifth part*
2567 châmash (1), to *tax a fifth*
2568 châmêsh (6), *five*
2569 chômesh (1), *fifth tax*
2570 chômesh (4), *abdomen, belly*
3991 pĕmptŏs (4), fifth

FIFTIES
2572 chămishshîym (5), *fifty*
4004 pĕntĕkŏnta (2), fifty

FIFTIETH
2572 chămishshîym (4), *fifty*

FIFTY
2572 chămishshîym (148), *fifty*
4002+3461 pĕntĕ (1), *five*
4004 pĕntēkŏnta (5), *fifty*

FIG
8384 tᵉʼên (24), *fig tree or fruit*
4808 sukē (16), *fig-tree*

FIGHT
3898 lâcham (85), to *fight a battle*, i.e. *consume*
4421 milchâmâh (5), *battle; war; fighting*
4634 maʼărâkâh (1), *row; pile*; military *array*
6633 tsâbâʼ (4), to *mass an army or servants*
73 agŏn (1), *contest, struggle*
75 agŏnizŏmai (2), to *struggle; to contend*
119 athlēsis (1), *struggle, contest*
2313 thĕŏmachĕō (1), to *resist deity*
2314 thĕŏmachŏs (1), *opponent of deity*
3164 machŏmai (1), to *war*, i.e. to *quarrel*
4170 pŏlĕmĕō (1), to *battle, make war*
4171 pŏlĕmŏs (1), *warfare; battle; fight*
4438 puktĕō (1), to *box as a sporting event*

FIGHTETH
3898 lâcham (3), to *fight a battle*, i.e. *consume*

FIGHTING
3898 lâcham (2), to *fight a battle*, i.e. *consume*
6213+4421 ʼâsâh (1), to *do or make*

FIGHTINGS
3163 machē (2), *controversy, conflict*

FIGS
6291 pag (1), *unripe fig*
8384 tᵉʼên (15), *fig tree or fruit*
3653 ŏlunthŏs (1), *unripe fig*
4810 sukŏn (4), *fig*

FIGURE
5566 çemel (1), *likeness*
8403 tabnîyth (1), *model, resemblance*
499 antitupŏn (1), *representative*
3345 mĕtaschĕmatizō (1), to *transfigure*
3850 parabŏlē (2), *fictitious narrative*
5179 tupŏs (1), *shape, resemblance; "type"*

FIGURES
4734 miqlaʼath (1), *bas-relief sculpture*
499 antitupŏn (1), *representative*
5179 tupŏs (1), *shape, resemblance; "type"*

FILE
6477+6310 pᵉtsîyrâh (1), *bluntness*

FILL
4390 mâlêʼ (33), to *fill; be full*
4393 mᵉlôʼ (2), *fulness*
5433 çâbâʼ (1), to *quaff to satiety*
7301 râvâh (1), to *slake thirst or appetites*
7646 sâbaʼ (1), *fill to satiety*
7648 sôbaʼ (2), *satisfaction*
466 antanaplērŏō (1), to *fill up*
878 aphrŏn (1), *ignorant; egotistic; unbelieving*
1072 gĕmizō (1), to *fill entirely*
2767 kĕrannumi (1), to *mingle, i.e. to pour*
4137 plērŏō (3), to *fill, make complete*
4138 plērōma (1), what *fills;* what is *filled*
5526 chŏrtazō (1), to *supply food*

FILLED
4390 mâlêʼ (74), to *fill; be full*
4391 mᵉlâʼ (Ch.) (1), to *fill; be full*
7059 qâmaṭ (1), to *pluck, i.e. destroy*
7301 râvâh (1), to *slake thirst or appetites*
7646 sâbaʼ (22), *fill to satiety*
1072 gĕmizō (7), to *fill entirely*
1705 ĕmpiplēmi (3), to *satisfy*
2767 kĕrannumi (1), to *mingle, i.e. to pour*
4130 plēthō (17), to *fulfill, complete*
4137 plērŏō (17), to *fill, make complete*
4138 plērōma (1), what *fills;* what is *filled*
4845 sumplērŏō (1), to be *complete, fulfill*
5055 tĕlĕō (1), to *end, i.e. complete, execute*
5526 chŏrtazō (11), to *supply food*

FILLEDST
4390 mâlêʼ (1), to *fill; be full*
7646 sâbaʼ (1), *fill to satiety*

FILLEST
4390 mâlêʼ (1), to *fill; be full*

FILLET
2339 chûwṭ (1), *string; measuring tape; line*

FILLETED
2836 châshaq (3), to *join; to love, delight*

FILLETH
4390 mâlêʼ (2), to *fill; be full*
5844 ʼâṭâh (1), to *wrap, i.e. cover, veil, clothe*
7646 sâbaʼ (2), *fill to satiety*

FILLETS
2838 châshûq (8), *fence-rail or rod*

FILLING
1705 ĕmpiplēmi (1), to *satisfy*

FILTH
6675 tsôwʼâh (1), *pollution*
4027 pĕrikatharma (1), *refuse, scum*
4509 rhupŏs (1), *dirt*, i.e. *moral depravity*

FILTHINESS
2932 ṭumʼâh (7), *ceremonial impurity*
5079 niddâh (2), *time of menstrual impurity*
5178 nᵉchôsheth (1), *copper; bronze*
6675 tsôwʼâh (2), *pollution*
151 aischrŏtēs (1), *obscenity*
168 akathartēs (1), *state of impurity*
3436 mŏlusmŏs (1), *contamination*
4507 rhuparia (1), *moral dirtiness*

FILTHY
444 ʼâlach (3), to be or *turn morally corrupt*
4754 mârâʼ (1), to *rebel; to lash with whip; flap*
5708 ʼêd (1), *periodical menstrual flux*
6674 tsôwʼ (2), *excrementitious, soiled*
147 aischrŏkĕrdŏs (1), *sordidly, greedily*
148 aischrŏlŏgia (1), *filthy speech*
150 aischrŏs (2), *shameful thing, base*
766 asĕlgĕia (1), *debauchery, lewdness*
4510 rhupŏō (2), to *become morally dirty*

FINALLY
3063 lŏipŏn (5), *finally*
5056 tĕlŏs (1), *conclusion*

FIND
2803 châshab (1), to *think, regard;* to *value*
4672 mâtsâʼ (100), to *find or acquire;* to *occur*
7912 shᵉkach (Ch.) (6), to *discover, find out*
2147 hĕuriskō (46), to *find*

FINDEST
4672 mâtsâʼ (2), to *find or acquire;* to *occur*

FINDETH
4672 mâtsâʼ (11), to *find or acquire;* to *occur*
2147 hĕuriskō (12), to *find*

FINDING
2714 chêqer (1), *examination*
4672 mâtsâʼ (2), to *find or acquire;* to *occur*

FINE
421 anĕxichniastŏs (1), *unsearchable*
429 anĕuriskŏ (1), to *find out*
2147 hĕuriskō (4), to *find*

FINE
2212 zâqaq (1), to *strain, refine; extract, clarify*
2869 ṭâb (Ch.) (1), *good*
2896 ṭôwb (2), *good; well*
6668 tsâhab (1), to be *golden in color*
8305 sᵉrîyqâh (1), *linen cloth*
4585 sĕmidalis (1), *fine wheat flour*

FINER
6884 tsâraph (1), to *fuse metal; to refine*

FINEST
2459 cheleb (2), *fat; choice part*

FINGER
676 ʼetsbaʼ (19), *finger; toe*
1147 daktulŏs (5), *finger*

FINGERS
676 ʼetsbaʼ (11), *finger; toe*
677 ʼetsbaʼ (Ch.) (1), *finger; toe*
1147 daktulŏs (3), *finger*

FINING
4715 mitsrêph (2), *crucible*

FINISH
1214 bâtsaʼ (1), to *plunder; to finish*
3607 kâlâʼ (1), to *hold back or in; to prohibit*
3615 kâlâh (1), to *cease, be finished, perish*
535 apartismŏs (1), *completion*
1615 ĕktĕlĕō (2), to *complete fully, finish*
2005 ĕpitĕlĕō (1), to *terminate; to undergo*
4931 suntĕlĕō (1), to *complete entirely*
5048 tĕlĕiŏō (3), to *perfect, complete*

FINISHED
3319 yᵉtsâʼ (Ch.) (1), to *complete*
3615 kâlâh (19), to *cease, be finished, perish*
3635 kᵉlal (Ch.) (1), to *complete*
7999 shâlam (3), to be *safe; be complete*
8000 shᵉlam (Ch.) (2), to *complete, to restore*
8552 tâmam (4), to *complete, finish*
658 apŏtĕlĕō (1), to *bring to completion*
1096 ginŏmai (1), to be, *become*
1274 dianuō (1), to *accomplish thoroughly*
5048 tĕlĕiŏō (1), to *perfect, complete*
5055 tĕlĕō (8), to *end, complete, conclude*

FINISHER
5047 tĕlĕiōtēs (1),
completeness; maturity

FINS
5579 çᵉnappîyr (5), *fin*

FIR
1265 bᵉrôwsh (20), (poss.)
cypress
1266 bᵉrôwth (1), (poss.)
cypress

FIRE
215 'ôwr (1), to *be
luminous*
217 'ûwr (4), *flame; East*
784 'êsh (375), *fire*
1200 bᵉ'êrâh (1), *burning*
3857 lâhaṭ (4), to *blaze*
5135 nûwr (Ch.) (8), *fire*
4442 pur (73), *fire*
4443 pura (2), *fire*
4447 purinŏs (1), *fiery,*
i.e. *flaming*
4448 purŏō (1), to *be
ignited, glow*
5394 phlŏgizō (2), to
cause a blaze
5457 phōs (2),
luminousness, light

FIREBRAND
181 'ûwd (1), *poker stick
for a fire*
3940 lappîyd (1), *flaming
torch, lamp or flame*

FIREBRANDS
181 'ûwd (1), *poker stick
for a fire*
2131 zîyqâh (1), *flash of
fire*
3940 lappîyd (1), *flaming
torch, lamp or flame*

FIREPANS
4289 machtâh (4), *pan
for live coals*

FIRES
217 'ûwr (1), *flame; East*

FIRKINS
3355 mĕtrētēs (1), liquid
measure: 8-10 gallons

FIRM
1277 bârîy' (1), *fatted or
plump; healthy*
3332 yâtsaq (2), to *pour
out*
3559 kûwn (2), to *set up:
establish, fix, prepare*
8631 tᵉqêph (Ch.) (1), to
become, make mighty
949 bĕbaiŏs (1), *stable,
certain, binding*

FIRMAMENT
7549 râqîya' (17), *expanse*

FIRST
259 'echâd (34), *first*
1061 bikkûwr (1),
first-fruits of the crop
1069 bâkar (1), *bear the
first born*
1073 bakkûrâh (1),
first-ripe fruit of a fig
1121 bên (51), *son,
descendant*
1323 bath (3), *daughter,
descendant, woman*
2298 chad (Ch.) (4), *one;
single; first; at once*

2490 châlal (1), to
profane, defile
3138 yôwreh (1), *autumn
rain showers*
4395 mᵉlê'âh (1),
fulfilled; abundance
6440 pânîym (1), *face;
front*
6933 qadmay (Ch.) (3),
first
7218 rô'sh (6), *head*
7223 rî'shôwn (130), *first,
in place, time or rank*
7224 rî'shônîy (1), *first*
7225 rê'shîyth (11), *first*
8462 tᵉchillâh (7),
original; originally
509 anŏthĕn (1), *from
above; from the first*
746 archē (4), *first in
rank; first in time*
1207 dĕutĕrŏprōtŏs (1),
second-first
1722+4413 ĕn (1), *in;
during; because of*
3391 mia (7), *one or first*
3891 paranŏmĕō (1), to
transgress, violate law
4272 prŏdidōmi (1), to
give before
4276 prŏĕlpizō (1), to
hope in advance of
4295 prŏkĕimai (1), to *be
present to the mind*
4386 prŏtĕrŏn (3),
previously
4412 prōtŏn (58), *firstly*
4413 prōtŏs (84), *foremost*
4416 prōtŏtŏkŏs (1),
first-born

FIRSTBEGOTTEN
4416 prōtŏtŏkŏs (1),
first-born

FIRSTBORN
1060 bᵉkôwr (101),
firstborn
1062 bᵉkôwrâh (1), *state
of, rights of first born*
1067 bᵉkîyrâh (6), *first
born, eldest daughter*
1069 bâkar (1), *bear the
first born*
4416 prōtŏtŏkŏs (7),
first-born

FIRSTFRUIT
7225 rê'shîyth (1), *first*
536 aparchē (1), *first-fruit*

FIRSTFRUITS
1061 bikkûwr (13),
first-fruits of the crop
7225 rê'shîyth (11), *first*
536 aparchē (7), *first-fruit*

FIRSTLING
1060 bᵉkôwr (8),
firstborn, i.e. oldest son
1069 bâkar (1), *bear the
first born*
6363 peṭer (4), *firstling,
first born*

FIRSTLINGS
1060 bᵉkôwr (1),
firstborn, i.e. oldest son
1062 bᵉkôwrâh (5), *state
of, rights of first born*

FIRSTRIPE
1061 bikkûwr (1),
first-fruits of the crop

1063 bikkûwrâh (3),
early fig

FISH
1709 dâg (11), *fish; fishes*
1710 dâgâh (14), *fish;
fishes*
1770 dîyg (1), to catch
fish
5315 nephesh (1), *life;
breath; soul; wind*
2486 ichthus (5), *fish*
3795 ŏpsariŏn (3), *small
fish*

FISH'S
1710 dâgâh (1), *fish;
fishes*

FISHER'S
1903 ĕpĕndutēs (1), *outer
garment, coat*

FISHERMEN
231 haliĕus (1), *one who
fishes for a living*

FISHERS
1728 davvâg (2),
fisherman
1771 dayâg (1), *fisherman*
231 haliĕus (4), *one who
fishes for a living*

FISHES
1709 dâg (8), *fish; fishes*
2485 ichthudiŏn (2), *little
fish*
2486 ichthus (15), *fish*
3795 ŏpsariŏn (2), *small
fish*

FISHHOOKS
5518+1729 çîyr (1), *thorn;
hook*

FISHING
232 haliĕuō (1), to catch
fish

FISHPOOLS
1295 bᵉrêkâh (1),
reservoir, pool

FIST
106 'egrŏph (2), *clenched
hand*

FISTS
2651 chôphen (1), *pair of
fists*

FIT
6257 'âthad (1), to
prepare
6261 'ittîy (1), *timely*
433 anĕkō (1), *be proper,
fitting*
2111 ĕuthĕtŏs (2),
appropriate, suitable
2520 kathĕkō (1),
becoming, proper

FITCHES
3698 kuççemeth (1), *spelt*
7100 qetsach (3),
fennel-flower

FITLY
5921+655 'al (1), *above,
over, upon, or against*
5921+4402 'al (1), *above,
over, upon, or against*
4883 sunarmŏlŏgĕō (2),
to render close-jointed

FITTED
3474 yâshar (1), to *be
straight; to make right*

3559 kûwn (1), to *render
sure, proper*
2675 katartizō (1), to
repair; to prepare

FITTETH
6213 'âsâh (1), to *do or
make*

FIVE
2568 châmêsh (271), *five*
3999 pĕntakis (1), *five
times*
4000 pĕntakischiliŏi (16),
five times a thousand
4001 pĕntakŏsiŏi (2), *five
hundred*
4002 pĕntĕ (25), *five*

FIXED
3559 kûwn (4), to *render
sure, proper*
4741 stĕrizō (1), to *turn
resolutely; to confirm*

FLAG
260 'âchûw (1), *bulrush
or any marshy grass*

FLAGON
809 'âshîyshâh (2), *cake
of raisins*

FLAGONS
809 'âshîyshâh (2), *cake
of raisins*
5035 nebel (1), skin-*bag
for liquids; vase; lyre*

FLAGS
5488 çûwph (3), *papyrus
reed; reed*

FLAKES
4651 mappâl (1), *chaff;
flap or fold of skin*

FLAME
785 'êsh (Ch.) (1), *fire*
3632 kâlîyl (1), *whole,
entire; complete; whole*
3827 labbâh (1), *flame*
3851 lahab (6), *flame of
fire; flash of a blade*
3852 lehâbâh (12), *flame;
flash*
4864 mas'êth (2), *raising;
beacon; present*
7631 sᵉbîyb (Ch.) (2),
flame tongue
7957 shalhebeth (3),
flare, flame of fire
5395 phlŏx (6), *flame;
blaze*

FLAMES
3851 lahab (2), *flame of
fire; flash of a blade*
3852 lehâbâh (1), *flame;
flash*

FLAMING
784 'êsh (1), *fire*
3852 lehâbâh (5), *flame;
flash*
3857 lâhaṭ (1), to *blaze*
3858 lahaṭ (1), *blaze;
magic*
5395 phlŏx (1), *flame;
blaze*

FLANKS
3689 keçel (6), *loin;
back; viscera*

FLASH
965 bâzâq (1), *flash of
lightning*

FLAT
2763 charam (1), to *devote* to destruction
8478 tachath (2), *bottom; underneath;* in *lieu* of

FLATTER
2505 châlaq (1), to *be smooth; be slippery*
6601 pâthâh (1), to *be, make simple;* to *delude*

FLATTERETH
2505 châlaq (5), to *be smooth; be slippery*
6601 pâthâh (1), to *be, make simple;* to *delude*

FLATTERIES
2514 chălaqqâh (1), *smoothness; flattery*
2519 chălaqlaqqâh (2), *smooth; treacherous*

FLATTERING
2506 chêleq (1), *smoothness* of tongue
2509 châlâq (2), *smooth, slippery* of tongue
2513 chelqâh (2), *smoothness; flattery*
3665 kâna' (2), to *humiliate, vanquish*
2850 kŏlakĕia (1), *flattery*

FLATTERY
2506 chêleq (1), *smoothness* of tongue
2513 chelqâh (1), *smoothness; flattery*

FLAX
6593 pishteh (7), linen, made of *carded* thread
6594 pishtâh (3), *flax; flax wick*
3043 linŏn (1), flax *linen*

FLAY
6584 pâshaṭ (3), to *strip,* i.e. *unclothe, flay*

FLAYED
6584 pâshaṭ (1), to *strip,* i.e. *unclothe, flay*

FLEA
6550 par'ôsh (2), *flea*

FLED
1272 bârach (40), to *flee suddenly*
5074 nâdad (8), to *rove, flee;* to *drive away*
5127 nûwç (83), to *vanish away, flee*
5132 nûwts (1), to *fly away, leave*
1628 ĕkphĕugō (2), to *flee out, escape*
2703 kataphĕugō (2), to *flee down*
5343 phĕugō (11), to *run away;* to *shun*

FLEDDEST
1272 bârach (1), to *flee suddenly*
5127 nûwç (1), to *vanish away, flee*

FLEE
1227 Baqbûwq (1), *gurgling bottle*
1272 bârach (14), to *flee suddenly*
3680 kâçâh (1), to *cover*

FLEE
4498 mânôwç (1), *fleeing; place* of *refuge*
5074 nâdad (4), to *rove, flee;* to *drive away*
5110 nûwd (1), to *waver;* to *wander, flee*
5127 nûwç (62), to *vanish away, flee*
5323 nâtsâ' (1), to *go away*
5756 'ûwz (1), to *save* by fleeing
7368 râchaq (1), to *recede; remove*
5343 phĕugō (15), to *run away;* to *shun*

FLEECE
1488 gêz (2), shorn *fleece;* mown *grass*
1492 gazzâh (7), wool *fleece*

FLEEING
4499 mᵉnuwçâh (1), *retreat, fleeing*
5127 nûwç (1), to *vanish away, flee*
6207 'âraq (1), to *gnaw;* a *pain*

FLEETH
1272 bârach (1), to *flee suddenly*
5127 nûwç (4), to *vanish away, flee*
5211 nîyç (1), *fugitive*
5775 'ôwph (1), *bird*
5343 phĕugō (2), to *run away;* to *shun*

FLESH
829 'eshpâr (2), *measured portion*
1320 bâsâr (253), *flesh; body; person*
1321 bᵉsar (Ch.) (3), *flesh; body; person*
2878 ṭibchâh (1), *butchery*
3894 lâchûwm (1), *flesh*
7607 shᵉ'êr (7), *flesh, meat; kindred* by blood
2907 krĕas (2), butcher's *meat*
4561 sarx (143), *flesh*

FLESHHOOK
4207 mazlêg (2), *three-tined meat fork*

FLESHHOOKS
4207 mazlêg (5), *three-tined meat fork*

FLESHLY
4559 sarkikŏs (2), *pertaining to flesh*

FLESHY
4560 sarkinŏs (1), *similar to flesh*

FLEW
5774 'ûwph (1), to *cover,* to *fly;* to *faint*
6213 'âsâh (1), to *do or make*

FLIES
2070 zᵉbûwb (1), stinging *fly*
6157 'ârôb (2), swarming *mosquitoes*

FLIETH
1675 dâ'âh (1), to *fly rapidly, soar*
5774 'ûwph (2), to *cover,* to *fly;* to *faint*
5775 'ôwph (1), *bird*

FLIGHT
1272 bârach (1), to *flee suddenly*
4498 mânôwç (1), *fleeing; place* of *refuge*
4499 mᵉnuwçâh (1), *retreat, fleeing*
5127 nûwç (1), to *vanish away, flee*
7291 râdaph (1), to *run after* with hostility
5437 phugē (2), *escape, flight, fleeing*

FLINT
2496 challâmîysh (3), *flint, flinty rock*
6864 tsôr (2), flint-*stone knife*

FLINTY
2496 challâmîysh (1), *flint, flinty rock*

FLOATS
1702 dôbᵉrâh (1), *raft, collection of logs*

FLOCK
5739 'êder (16), *muster, flock*
6629 tsô'n (83), *flock*
4167 pŏimnē (4), *flock*
4168 pŏimniŏn (5), *flock*

FLOCKS
2835 châsîph (1), small *company, flock*
4735 miqneh (3), *stock*
4830 mir'îyth (1), *pasturage; flock*
5739 'êder (16), *muster, flock*
6251 'ashtᵉrâh (4), *flock of ewes*
6629 tsô'n (54), *flock*

FLOOD
2229 zâram (1), to *gush water, pour forth*
2230 zerem (1), *gush* of *water, flood*
2975 yᵉ'ôr (6), Nile *River;* Tigris *River*
3999 mabbûwl (13), *deluge*
5104 nâhâr (8), *stream;* Nile; Euphrates; Tigris
5158 nachal (3), *valley, ravine;* mine *shaft*
7858 sheṭeph (3), *deluge, torrent*
2627 kataklusmŏs (4), *inundation, flood*
4182 pŏlupŏikilŏs (1), *many-sided*
4215 pŏtamŏs (2), *current, brook*
4216 pŏtamŏphŏrētŏs (1), *overwhelmed by a stream*

FLOODS
5104 nâhâr (10), *stream;* Nile; Euphrates; Tigris
5140 nâzal (3), to *drip,* or *shed* by trickling

FLOOR
1637 gôren (10), open *area*
7136 qârâh (1), to *bring about;* to *impose*
7172 qarqa' (6), *floor* of a building or the sea
257 halôn (2), threshing-*floor*

FLOORS
1637 gôren (1), open *area*

FLOTES
7513 raphçôdâh (1), log *raft*

FLOUR
1217 bâtsêq (1), *fermenting dough*
5560 çôleth (52), *fine flour*
7058 qemach (4), *flour*
4585 sĕmidalis (1), fine wheat *flour*

FLOURISH
5006 nâ'ats (1), to *scorn*
6524 pârach (9), to *break forth;* to *bloom, flourish*
6692 tsûwts (3), to *blossom, flourish*

FLOURISHED
6524 pârach (1), to *break forth;* to *bloom, flourish*
330 anathallō (1), to *flourish;* to *revive*

FLOURISHETH
6692 tsûwts (2), to *blossom, flourish*

FLOURISHING
7487 ra'ânan (Ch.) (1), *prosperous*
7488 ra'ănân (1), *verdant; prosperous*

FLOW
2151 zâlal (1), to *be loose morally, worthless*
3212 yâlak (2), to *walk;* to *live;* to *carry*
5064 nâgar (1), to *pour out;* to *deliver* over
5102 nâhar (5), to *sparkle;* to *flow*
5140 nâzal (3), to *drip,* or *shed* by trickling
4482 rhĕō (1), to *flow water*

FLOWED
2151 zâlal (1), to *be loose morally, worthless*
3212 yâlak (1), to *walk;* to *live;* to *carry*
6687 tsûwph (1), to *overflow*

FLOWER
582 'ĕnôwsh (1), *man; person, human*
5328 nitstsâh (2), *blossom*
6525 perach (5), *calyx flower; bloom*

6731 tsîyts (6), burnished plate; bright *flower*
6733 tsîytsâh (1), *flower*
438 anthŏs (4), flower blossom
5230 hupĕrakmŏs (1), past the *bloom* of youth

FLOWERS
4026 migdâl (1), *tower; rostrum*
5079 niddâh (2), time of menstrual *impurity;* idolatry
5339 nitstsân (1), *blossom*
6525 perach (9), *calyx flower; bloom*
6731 tsîyts (4), burnished plate; bright *flower*

FLOWETH
2100 zûwb (12), to *flow* freely, *gush*

FLOWING
2100 zûwb (9), to *flow* freely, *gush*
5042 nâba' (1), to *gush* forth; to *utter*
5140 nâzal (1), to *drip*, or *shed* by trickling
7857 shâṭaph (1), to *gush;* to *inundate*

FLUTE
4953 mashrôwqîy (Ch.) (4), musical *pipe*

FLUTTERETH
7363 râchaph (1), to *brood;* to *be relaxed*

FLUX
1420 dusĕntĕria (1), *dysentery*

FLY
82 'âbar (1), to *soar*
1675 dâ'âh (3), to *fly* rapidly, *soar*
2070 zᵉbûwb (1), *fly*
3286 yâ'aph (1), to *tire*
5774 'ûwph (13), to *cover,* to *fly;* to *faint*
5860 'îyṭ (1), to *swoop* down upon; to *insult*
6524 pârach (2), to *break* forth; to *bloom;* to *fly*
4072 pĕtŏmai (3), to *fly*

FLYING
3671 kânâph (1), *edge* or *extremity; wing*
5774 'ûwph (6), to *cover,* to *fly;* to *faint*
5775 'ôwph (2), *bird*
4072 pĕtŏmai (2), to *fly*

FOAL
1121 bên (1), *son, descendant*
5895 'ayîr (1), young donkey or *ass*
5207 huiŏs (1), *son*

FOALS
5895 'ayîr (1), young donkey or *ass*

FOAM
7110 qetseph (1), *rage* or *strife*

FOAMETH
875 aphrizō (1), to *froth* at the mouth

876 aphrŏs (1), *froth, foam*

FOAMING
875 aphrizō (1), to *froth* at the mouth
1890 ĕpaphrizō (1), to *foam upon*

FODDER
1098 bᵉlîyl (1), *feed, fodder*

FOES
341 'ôyêb (2), *adversary, enemy*
6862 tsar (2), *trouble; opponent*
8130 sânê' (1), to *hate*
2190 ĕchthrŏs (2), *adversary*

FOLD
1699 dôber (1), grazing *pasture*
4356 miklâ'âh (1), sheep or goat *pen*
5116 nâveh (3), *at home; lovely; home*
7257 râbats (1), to *recline, repose, brood*
833 aulē (1), *palace; house; sheepfold*
1667 hĕlissō (1), to *coil, roll up, or wrap*
4167 pŏimnē (1), *flock*

FOLDEN
5440 çâbak (1), to *entwine*

FOLDETH
2263 châbaq (1), to *clasp* the hands, *embrace*

FOLDING
1550 gâlîyl (2), *valve* of a folding door
2264 chibbûq (2), *folding*

FOLDS
1448 gᵉdêrâh (3), *enclosure* for flocks
4356 miklâ'âh (1), sheep or goat *pen*
5116 nâveh (1), *at home; lovely; home*

FOLK
3816 lᵉ'ôm (1), *community, nation*
5971 'am (2), *people; tribe; flock*

FOLLOW
310 'achar (5), *after*
935+310 bôw' (1), to *go or come*
1692 dâbaq (1), to *cling* or *adhere;* to *catch*
1961 hâyâh (3), to *exist,* i.e. *be* or *become*
1961+310 hâyâh (1), to *exist,* i.e. *be* or *become*
1980+310 hâlak (1), to *walk; live a certain way*
1980+7272 hâlak (1), to *walk; live a certain way*
3212+310 yâlak (8), to *walk; to live; to carry*
7272 regel (3), *foot; step*
7291 râdaph (11), to *run after* with hostility
190 akŏlŏuthĕō (30), to *accompany, follow*

1205+3694 dĕutĕ (1), *come hither!*
1377 diōkō (8), to *pursue;* to *persecute*
1811 ĕxakŏlŏuthĕō (1), to *imitate, obey*
1872 ĕpakŏlŏuthĕō (2), to *accompany, follow*
2071 ĕsŏmai (1), *will be*
2517 kathĕxēs (1), *in a sequence*
3326+5023 mĕta (1), *with, among; after, later*
3401 mimĕŏmai (4), to *imitate,* i.e. *model*
3877 parakŏlŏuthĕō (1), to *attend; trace out*
4870 sunakŏlŏuthĕō (1), to *follow, accompany*

FOLLOWED
310 'achar (16), *after*
1692 dâbaq (4), to *cling* or *adhere;* to *catch*
1961+310 hâyâh (2), to *exist,* i.e. *be* or *become*
1980+310 hâlak (7), to *walk; live a certain way*
3112+310 Yôwyâkîyn (1), *Jehovah will establish*
3212+310 yâlak (9), to *walk; to live; to carry*
3318+310 yâtsâ' (1), to *go, bring out*
6213 'âsâh (1), to *do or make*
7272 regel (1), *foot; step*
7291 râdaph (2), to *run after* with hostility
190 akŏlŏuthĕō (53), to *accompany, follow*
1096 ginŏmai (1), to *be, become*
1377 diōkō (2), to *pursue;* to *persecute*
1811 ĕxakŏlŏuthĕō (1), to *imitate, obey*
1872 ĕpakŏlŏuthĕō (2), to *accompany, follow*
2076+3326 ĕsti (1), he (she or it) *is*
2614 katadiōkō (1), to *search for, look for*
2628 katakŏlŏuthĕō (2), to *accompany closely*
4870 sunakŏlŏuthĕō (1), to *follow, accompany*

FOLLOWEDST
3212+310 yâlak (1), to *walk; to live; to carry*

FOLLOWERS
3402 mimētēs (7), *imitator, example*
4831 summimētēs (1), *co-imitator*

FOLLOWETH
310 'achar (1), *after*
935+310 bôw' (2), to *go or come*
1692 dâbaq (1), to *cling* or *adhere;* to *catch*
7291 râdaph (6), to *run after* with hostility
190 akŏlŏuthĕō (5), to *accompany, follow*

FOLLOWING
310 'achar (26), *after*
310+3651 'achar (1), *after*

312 'achêr (1), *other, another, different; next*
314 'achărôwn (1), *late or last; behind; western*
3212+310 yâlak (2), to *walk; to live; to carry*
190 akŏlŏuthĕō (3), to *accompany, follow*
1811 ĕxakŏlŏuthĕō (1), to *imitate, obey*
1836 hĕxēs (1), *successive, next*
1872 ĕpakŏlŏuthĕō (1), to *accompany, follow*
1887 ĕpauriŏn (2), *to-morrow*
1966 ĕpiŏusa (1), *ensuing*
2192 ĕchō (1), to *have; hold; keep*

FOLLY
200 'ivveleth (13), *silliness, foolishness*
3689 keçel (2), *loin; back; viscera; silliness*
3690 kiçlâh (1), *trust; silliness*
5039 nᵉbâlâh (10), *moral wickedness; crime*
5529 çekel (1), *silliness; dolts*
5531 çiklûwth (5), *silliness*
8417 tohŏlâh (1), *bluster, braggadocio,* i.e. *fatuity*
8604 tiphlâh (2), *frivolity, foolishness*
454 anŏia (1), *stupidity; rage*
877 aphrŏsunē (1), *senselessness*

FOOD
398 'âkal (1), to *eat*
400 'ôkel (16), *food*
402 'oklâh (1), *food*
944 bûwl (1), *produce*
3899 lechem (21), *food, bread*
3978 ma'ăkâl (5), *food, something to eat*
4361 makkôleth (1), *nourishment*
6718 tsayid (1), *hunting game; lunch, food*
7607 shᵉ'êr (1), *flesh, meat; kindred* by blood
1035 brōsis (1), *food; rusting corrosion*
1304 diatribō (1), to *remain, stay*
5160 trŏphē (2), *nourishment; rations*

FOOL
191 'ĕvîyl (11), *silly; fool*
3684 kᵉçîyl (34), *stupid or silly*
5030 nâbîy' (1), *prophet; inspired man*
5036 nâbâl (6), *stupid; impious*
5528 çâkal (1), to *be silly*
5530 çâkâl (3), *silly*
5536 çal (1), *basket*
876 aphrŏs (6), *froth, foam*
3474 mōrŏs (2), *heedless, moral blockhead*
3912 paraphrŏnĕō (1), to *be insane*

F

3359 mĕtōpŏn (6),
forehead

FOREIGNER
5237 nokrîy (1), *foreign;
non-relative; different*
8453 tôwshâb (1),
temporary dweller

FOREIGNERS
5237 nokrîy (1), *foreign;
non-relative; different*
3941 parîkŏs (1),
strange; stranger

FOREKNEW
4267 prŏginŏskō (1), *to
know beforehand*

FOREKNOW
4267 prŏginŏskō (1), *to
know beforehand*

FOREKNOWLEDGE
4268 prŏgnōsis (2),
forethought

FOREMOST
7223 rî'shôwn (3), *first*

FOREORDAINED
4267 prŏginŏskō (1), *to
know beforehand*

FOREPART
6440 pânîym (4), *face;
front*
4408 prōra (1), *prow*, i.e.
forward part of a vessel

FORERUNNER
4274 prŏdrŏmŏs (1),
runner ahead

FORESAW
4308 prŏŏraō (1), *to
notice previously*

FORESEEING
4375 prŏsphilēs (1),
acceptable, pleasing

FORESEETH
7200 râ'âh (2), *to see*

FORESHIP
4408 prōra (1), *prow*, i.e.
forward part of a vessel

FORESKIN
6188 'ârêl (1), *to refrain
from using*
6190 'orlâh (8), *prepuce
or penile foreskin*

FORESKINS
6190 'orlâh (5), *prepuce
or penile foreskin*

FOREST
3293 ya'ar (37), *honey* in
the comb
6508 pardêç (1), *park,
cultivated garden area*

FORESTS
2793 chôresh (1),
wooded forest
3293 ya'ar (1), *honey* in
the comb
3295 ya'ărâh (1), *honey*
in *the comb*

FORETELL
4302 prŏlĕgō (1), *to
predict, forewarn*

FORETOLD
4280 prŏĕrĕō (1), *to say
already, predict*
4293 prŏkataggĕllō (1),
to predict, foretell

FOREWARN
5263 hupŏdĕiknumi (1),
to exemplify, instruct

FOREWARNED
4277 prŏĕpō (1), *to say
already*, to predict

FORFEITED
2763 charam (1), *to
devote to destruction*

FORGAT
5382 nâshâh (1), *to forget*
7911 shâkach (7), *to be
oblivious of, forget*

FORGAVE
3722 kâphar (1), *to
cover; to expiate*
863 aphiēmi (2), *to leave;
to pardon, forgive*
5483 charizŏmai (4), *to
grant as a favor, pardon*

FORGAVEST
5375 nâsâ' (2), *to lift up*

FORGED
2950 ţâphal (1), *to
impute falsely*

FORGERS
2950 ţâphal (1), *to
impute falsely*

FORGET
5382 nâshâh (2), *to forget*
7911 shâkach (48), *to be
oblivious of, forget*
7913 shâkêach (2),
oblivious, forgetting
1950 ĕpilanthanŏmai (2),
to lose out of mind

FORGETFUL
1950 ĕpilanthanŏmai (1),
to lose out of mind
1953 ĕpilēsmŏnē (1),
negligence

FORGETFULNESS
5388 nᵉshîyâh (1),
oblivion

FORGETTEST
7911 shâkach (2), *to be
oblivious of, forget*

FORGETTETH
7911 shâkach (2), *to be
oblivious of, forget*
7913 shâkêach (1),
oblivious, forgetting
1950 ĕpilanthanŏmai (1),
to lose out of mind

FORGETTING
1950 ĕpilanthanŏmai (1),
to lose out of mind

FORGIVE
3722 kâphar (1), *to
cover; to expiate*
5375 nâsâ' (8), *to lift up*
5545 çâlach (18), *to
forgive*
5546 çallâch (1),
placable, tolerant
630 apŏluō (1), *to relieve,
release; to pardon*
863 aphiēmi (22), *to
leave; to pardon, forgive*
5483 charizŏmai (3), *to
grant as a favor, pardon*

FORGIVEN
3722 kâphar (1), *to
cover; to expiate*

5375 nâsâ' (4), *to lift up*
5545 çâlach (13), *to
forgive*
630 apŏluō (1), *to relieve,
release; to pardon*
863 aphiēmi (21), *to
leave; to pardon, forgive*
5483 charizŏmai (2), *to
grant as a favor, pardon*

FORGIVENESS
5547 çᵉlîychâh (1),
pardon
859 aphĕsis (6), *pardon,
freedom*

FORGIVENESSES
5547 çᵉlîychâh (1),
pardon

FORGIVETH
5545 çâlach (1), *to forgive*
863 aphiēmi (1), *to leave;
to pardon, forgive*

FORGIVING
5375 nâsâ' (2), *to lift up*
5483 charizŏmai (2), *to
grant as a favor, pardon*

FORGOT
7911 shâkach (1), *to be
oblivious of, forget*

FORGOTTEN
5382 nâshâh (1), *to forget*
7911 shâkach (39), *to be
oblivious of, forget*
7913 shâkêach (2),
oblivious, forgetting
1585 ĕklanthanŏmai (1),
to forget
1950 ĕpilanthanŏmai (3),
to lose out of mind
3024+2983 lēthē (1),
forgetfulness

FORKS
7969+7053 shâlôwsh (1),
three; third; thrice

FORM
3335 yâtsar (1), *to form;
potter; to determine*
4758 mar'eh (1),
appearance; vision
4941 mishpâţ (1), *verdict;
formal decree; justice*
6440 pânîym (1), *face;
front*
6699 tsûwrâh (2), *rock;
form as if pressed out*
6755 tselem (Ch.) (1),
idolatrous figure
7299 rêv (Ch.) (2), *aspect,
appearance*
8389 tô'ar (3), *outline,
i.e. figure, appearance*
8403 tabnîyth (3), *model,
resemblance*
8414 tôhûw (2), *waste,
desolation, formless*
3444 mŏrphē (3), *shape,
form; nature, character*
3446 mŏrphōsis (2),
appearance; semblance
5179 tupŏs (1), *shape
resemblance; "type"*
5296 hupŏtupōsis (1),
example, pattern

FORMED
2342 chûwl (5), *to dance,
whirl; to writhe in pain*

3335 yâtsar (23), *to form;
potter; to determine*
7169 qârats (1), *to bite
the lips, blink the eyes*
3445 mŏrphŏō (1), *to
fashion, take on a form*
4110 plasma (2), *molded,
what is formed*
4111 plassō (1), *to mold,
i.e. shape or fabricate*

FORMER
570 'emesh (1), *last night*
3138 yôwreh (2), *autumn
rain* showers
3335 yâtsar (2), *to form;
potter; to determine*
4175 môwreh (1), *archer;
teaching; early rain*
6440 pânîym (1), *face;
front*
6927 qadmâh (3), *priority
in time; before; past*
6931 qadmôwnîy (2),
anterior time; eastern
7223 rî'shôwn (32), *first*
4386 prŏtĕrŏn (2),
previously
4387 prŏtĕrŏs (1), *prior
or previous*
4413 prōtŏs (2), foremost

FORMETH
3335 yâtsar (2), *to form;
potter; to determine*

FORMS
6699 tsûwrâh (2), *rock;
form as if pressed out*

FORNICATION
2181 zânâh (3), *to
commit adultery*
8457 taznûwth (1),
harlotry
1608 ĕkpŏrnĕuō (1), *to
fornicate*
4202 pŏrnĕia (24), *sexual
immorality*
4203 pŏrnĕuō (7), *to
indulge unlawful lust*

FORNICATIONS
8457 taznûwth (1),
harlotry
4202 pŏrnĕia (2), *sexual
immorality*

FORNICATOR
4205 pŏrnŏs (2), *sexually
immoral person*

FORNICATORS
4205 pŏrnŏs (3), *sexually
immoral person*

FORSAKE
2308 châdal (1), *to desist,
stop; be fat*
5203 nâţash (7), *to
disperse; to abandon*
5800 'âzab (45), *to
loosen; relinquish*
7503 râphâh (2), *to
slacken*
646+575 apŏstasia (1),
defection, rebellion
1459 ĕgkatalĕipō (1), *to
desert, abandon*

FORSAKEN
488 'almân (1),
discarded, forsaken
5203 nâţash (6), *to
disperse; to abandon*

5428 nâthash (1), to *tear
away, be uprooted*
5800 'âzab (60), to
loosen; relinquish
7971 shâlach (1), to *send
away*
*863 aphiĕmi (2), to leave;
to pardon, forgive*
*1459 ĕgkatalĕipō (4), to
desert, abandon*
*2641 katalĕipō (1), to
abandon*

FORSAKETH
5800 'âzab (5), to *loosen;
relinquish; permit*
*657 apŏtassŏmai (1), to
say adieu; to renounce*

FORSAKING
5805 'ăzûwbâh (1),
desertion, forsaking
*1459 ĕgkatalĕipō (1), to
desert, abandon*

FORSOMUCH
*2530 kathŏti (1), as far
or inasmuch as*

FORSOOK
5203 nâṭash (2), to
disperse; to abandon
5800 'âzab (16), to
loosen; relinquish
*863 aphiĕmi (4), to leave;
to pardon, forgive*
*1459 ĕgkatalĕipō (1), to
desert, abandon*
*2641 katalĕipō (1), to
abandon*

FORSOOKEST
5800 'âzab (2), to *loosen;
relinquish; permit*

FORSWEAR
*1964 ĕpiŏrkĕō (1), to
commit perjury*

FORT
1785 dâyêq (3),
battering-tower
4581 mâ'ôwz (1), *fortified*
place; *defense*
4686 mâtsûwd (1), *net or
capture; fastness*
4869 misgâb (1), *high
refuge*

FORTH
935 bôw' (1), to *go or
come*
1310 bâshal (1), to *boil
up, cook; to ripen*
1319 bâsar (1), to
announce (good news)
1518 gîyach (4), to *issue
forth; to burst forth*
1645 geresh (1), *produce,
yield*
1876 dâshâ' (1), to *sprout
new plants*
1921 hâdar (1), to *favor
or honor; to be high*
2254 châbal (2), to *writhe
in labor pain*
2315 cheder (1),
apartment, chamber
2330 chûwd (4), to
propound a riddle
2342 chûwl (4), to *dance,
whirl; to writhe* in pain
2590 chânaṭ (1), to
embalm; to ripen

2904 ṭûwl (3), to *cast
down or out, hurl*
2986 yâbal (1), to *bring*
3205 yâlad (26), to *bear
young; to father a child*
3209 yillôwd (1), *born*
3318 yâtsâ' (403), to *go,
bring out*
3329 yâtsîy' (1), *issue
forth,* i.e. offspring
4161 môwtsâ' (11), *going
forth*
4163 môwtsâ'âh (3),
family *descent*
4866 mishbêr (1), *vaginal
opening*
5066 nâgash (2), to *be,
come, bring near*
5107 nûwb (2), to *(make)
flourish;* to *utter*
5132 nûwts (1), to *fly
away, leave*
5221 nâkâh (1), to *strike,
kill*
5265 nâça' (5), *start* on a
journey
5312 nᵉphaq (Ch.) (7), to
issue forth; to *bring out*
5375 nâsâ' (1), to *lift up*
5414 nâthan (1), to *give*
5608 çâphar (1), to
inscribe; to *enumerate*
5674 'âbar (2), to *cross
over;* to *transition*
5975 'âmad (1), to *stand*
6213 'âsâh (10), to *do or
make*
6398 pâlach (1), to *slice;*
to *break* open; to *pierce*
6440 pânîym (1), *face;
front*
6509 pârâh (1), to *bear
fruit*
6556 perets (1), *break,
gap*
6566 pâras (1), to *break
apart, disperse, scatter*
6605 pâthach (1), to *open
wide;* to *loosen, begin*
6631 tse'ĕtsâ' (1),
produce, children
6779 tsâmach (4), to
sprout
7126 qârab (1), to
approach, bring near
7737 shâvâh (1), to *level,*
i.e. *equalize*
7971 shâlach (27), to
send away
8317 shârats (5), to
swarm, or *abound*
8444 tôwtsâ'âh (2), *exit,
boundary; deliverance*
*321 anagō (3), to lead
up; to bring out; to sail*
*392 anatassŏmai (1), to
arrange*
*584 apŏdĕiknumi (1), to
demonstrate*
*616 apŏkuĕō (1), to bring
into being*
*649 apŏstĕllō (11), to
send out on a mission*
*669 apŏphthĕggŏmai (1),
declare, address*
*985 blastanō (1), to yield
fruit*
*1032 bruō (1), to gush,
pour forth*

*1080 gĕnnaō (1), to
procreate, regenerate*
*1544 ĕkballō (7), to
throw out*
*1554 ĕkdidōmi (2), to
lease, rent*
*1584 ĕklampō (1), to be
resplendent, shine*
*1599 ĕkpĕmpō (1), to
despatch, send out*
*1600 ĕkpĕtannumi (1), to
extend, spread out*
*1607 ĕkpŏrĕuŏmai (4), to
depart, be discharged*
*1614 ĕktĕinō (17), to
stretch*
*1627 ĕkphĕrō (3), to bear
out; to produce*
*1631 ĕkphuō (2), to
sprout up, put forth*
*1632 ĕkchĕō (1), to pour
forth; to bestow*
*1731 ĕndĕiknumi (1), to
show, display*
*1754 ĕnĕrgĕō (2), to be
active, efficient, work*
*1804 ĕxaggĕllō (1), to
declare, proclaim*
*1806 ĕxagō (1), to lead
forth, escort*
*1821 ĕxapŏstĕllō (4), to
despatch, or to dismiss*
*1831 ĕxĕrchŏmai (32), to
issue; to leave*
1854 ĕxō (8), out, outside
*1901 ĕpĕktĕinŏmai (1), to
stretch oneself forward*
*1907 ĕpĕchō (1), to
retain; to detain*
*1911 ĕpiballō (1), to
throw upon*
*2164 ĕuphŏrĕō (1), to be
fertile, produce a crop*
2564 kalĕō (1), to call
*2592 karpŏphŏrĕō (2), to
be fertile*
*2604 kataggĕlĕus (1),
proclaimer*
*2609 katagō (1), to lead
down; to moor a vessel*
3004 lĕgō (1), to say
*3318 Mĕsŏpŏtamia (2),
between the Rivers*
*3855 paragō (1), to go
along or away*
*3860 paradidōmi (1), to
hand over*
*3908 paratithēmi (2), to
present something*
*3928 parĕrchŏmai (1), to
go by; to perish*
4160 pŏiĕō (14), to do
*4198 pŏrĕuŏmai (1), to
go, come; to travel*
*4254 prŏagō (2), to lead
forward; to precede*
*4261 prŏballō (1), to push
to the front, germinate*
*4270 prŏgraphō (1), to
announce, prescribe*
*4295 prŏkĕimai (1), to
stand forth*
*4311 prŏpĕmpō (1), to
send forward*
*4388 prŏtithēmai (1), to
place before, exhibit*
*4393 prŏphĕrō (2), to
bear forward*

*4486 rhēgnumi (1), to
break, burst forth*
5087 tithēmi (1), to place
*5088 tiktō (9), to produce
from seed*
*5319 phanĕrŏō (1), to
render apparent*
*5348 phthanō (1), to be
beforehand, precede*

FORTHWITH
629 'oçparnâ' (Ch.) (1),
with diligence
*2112 ĕuthĕōs (7), at once
or soon*
*2117 ĕuthus (1), at once,
immediately*
*3916 parachrēma (1),
instantly, immediately*

FORTIETH
705 'arbâ'îym (4), *forty*

FORTIFIED
2388 châzaq (2), to
fasten upon; *be strong*
4692 mâtsôwr (1),
siege-mound; distress
5800 'âzab (1), to *loosen;
relinquish; permit*

FORTIFY
553 'âmats (1), to *be
strong; be courageous*
1219 bâtsar (2), to *be
inaccessible*
2388 châzaq (2), to
fasten upon; *be strong*
5800 'âzab (1), to *loosen;
relinquish; permit*
6696 tsûwr (1), to *cramp,*
i.e. *confine;* to *harass*

FORTRESS
4013 mibtsâr (4),
fortification; defender
4581 mâ'ôwz (3), *fortified
place; defense*
4686 mâtsûwd (6), *net or
capture; fastness*
4693 mâtsôwr (2), *limit,
border*

FORTRESSES
4013 mibtsâr (2),
fortification; defender

FORTS
1785 dâyêq (3),
battering-tower
4679 mᵉtsad (1),
stronghold
4694 mᵉtsûwrâh (1),
rampart, fortification
6076 'ôphel (1), *tumor;
fortress*

FORTUNATUS
5415 Phŏrtŏunatŏs (2),
fortunate

FORTY
702+7239 'arba' (2), *four*
705 'arbâ'îym (126), *forty*
5062 tĕssarakŏnta (22),
forty
5063 tĕssarakŏntaĕtēs
(2), *of forty years* of age

FORTY'S
705 'arbâ'îym (1), *forty*

FORUM
675 'Appiŏs (1), *Appius*

FORWARD

1973 hâl^{e}âh (5), *far away; thus far*
1980 hâlak (1), *to walk; live a certain way*
3276 yâ'al (1), *to be valuable*
4605 ma'al (2), *upward, above, overhead*
5265 nâça' (18), *start on a journey*
5921 'al (3), *above, over, upon, or against*
6440 pânîym (4), *face; front*
6584 pâshaṭ (1), *to strip, i.e. unclothe, plunder*
6924 qedem (1), *eastern; antiquity; before*
2309 thĕlō (1), *to will; to desire; to choose*
4261 prŏballō (1), *to push to the front, germinate*
4281 prŏĕrchŏmai (1), *to go onward, precede*
4311 prŏpĕmpō (1), *to send forward*
4704 spŏudazō (1), *to make effort*
4707 spŏudaiŏtĕrŏs (1), *more earnest*

FORWARDNESS

4288 prŏthumia (1), *alacrity, eagerness*
4710 spŏudē (1), *despatch; eagerness*

FOUGHT

3898 lâcham (58), *to fight a battle, i.e. consume*
6633 tsâbâ' (1), *to mass an army or servants*
75 agōnizŏmai (1), *to struggle; to contend*
2341 thēriŏmachĕō (1), *to be a beast fighter*
4170 pŏlĕmĕō (2), *to battle, make war*

FOUL

2560 châmar (1), *to ferment, foam; to glow*
7515 râphas (1), *to trample, i.e. roil water*
169 akathartŏs (2), *impure; evil*
5494 chĕimōn (1), *winter season; stormy weather*

FOULED

4833 mirpâs (1), *muddied water*

FOULEDST

7515 râphas (1), *trample, i.e. roil water*

FOUND

2713 châqar (2), *to examine, search*
4672 mâtsâ' (267), *to find or acquire; to occur*
7912 sh^{e}kach (Ch.) (11), *to discover, find out*
429 anĕuriskō (1), *to find out*
1096 ginŏmai (1), *to be, become*
2147 hĕuriskō (111), *to find*
2638 katalambanō (1), *to seize; to possess*

FOUNDATION

787 'ôsh (Ch.) (1), *foundation*
3245 yâçad (15), *settle, establish a foundation*
3247 y^{e}çôwd (7), *foundation*
3248 y^{e}çûwdâh (5), *foundation*
4143 mûwçâd (2), *foundation*
4527 maççad (1), *foundation*
2310 thĕmĕliŏs (12), *substruction*
2311 thĕmĕliŏō (1), *to erect; to consolidate*
2602 katabŏlē (10), *conception, beginning*

FOUNDATIONS

134 'eden (1), *base, footing*
787 'ôsh (Ch.) (2), *foundation*
803 'ăshûwyâh (1), *foundation*
808 'âshîysh (1), *(ruined) foundation*
3245 yâçad (4), *settle, establish a foundation*
3247 y^{e}çôwd (3), *foundation*
4146 môwçâdâh (13), *foundation*
4328 m^{e}yuççâdâh (1), *foundation*
4349 mâkôwn (1), *basis; place*
8356 shâthâh (1), *basis*
2310 thĕmĕliŏs (4), *substruction*

FOUNDED

3245 yâçad (8), *settle, establish a foundation*
2311 thĕmĕliŏō (2), *to erect; to consolidate*

FOUNDER

6884 tsâraph (5), *to fuse metal; to refine*

FOUNDEST

4672 mâtsâ' (1), *to find or acquire; to occur*

FOUNTAIN

953 bôwr (1), *pit hole, cistern, well*
4002 mabbûwa' (1), *fountain, water spring*
4599 ma'yân (9), *fountain; source*
4726 mâqôwr (11), *flow*
5869 'ayin (7), *eye; sight; fountain*
4077 pēgē (4), *source or supply*

FOUNTAINS

4599 ma'yân (7), *fountain; source*
5869 'ayin (4), *eye; sight; fountain*
4077 pēgē (4), *source or supply*

FOUR

702 'arba' (258), *four*
703 'arba' (Ch.) (8), *four*
5064 tĕssarĕs (43), *four*
5066 tĕtartaiŏs (1), *of the fourth day*

FOUR

5067 tĕtartŏs (1), *fourth*
5070 tĕtrakischiliŏi (5), *four times a thousand*
5071 tĕtrakŏsiŏi (2), *four hundred*
5072 tĕtramēnŏn (1), *four months' time*

FOURFOLD

706 'arba'tayim (1), *fourfold*
5073 tĕtraplŏŏs (1), *quadruple, i.e. four-fold*

FOURFOOTED

5074 tĕtrapŏus (3), *quadruped*

FOURSCORE

8084 sh^{e}mônîym (34), *eighty; eightieth*
3589 ŏgdŏĕkŏnta (2), *ten times eight*

FOURSQUARE

7243 r^{e}bîy'îy (1), *fourth; fourth*
7251 râba' (8), *to be four sided, to be quadrate*
5068 tĕtragōnŏs (1), *four-cornered*

FOURTEEN

702+6240 'arba' (2), *four*
702+6246 'arba' (4), *four*
702+7657 'arba' (3), *four*
1180 dĕkatĕssarĕs (5), *fourteen*

FOURTEENTH

702+6240 'arba' (23), *four*
5065 tĕssarĕskaidĕkatŏs (2), *fourteenth*

FOURTH

702 'arba' (5), *four*
7243 r^{e}bîy'îy (55), *fourth; fourth*
7244 r^{e}bîy'ay (Ch.) (5), *fourth; fourth*
7253 reba' (2), *fourth part or side*
7255 rôba' (2), *quarter*
7256 ribbêa' (4), *fourth; fourth generation*
5067 tĕtartŏs (9), *fourth*

FOWL

1257 barbûr (1), *fowl*
5775 'ôwph (23), *bird*
5776 'ôwph (Ch.) (1), *bird*
5861 'ayiṭ (1), *bird of prey (poss.) hawk*
6833 tsippôwr (5), *little hopping bird*

FOWLER

3353 yâqûwsh (3), *snarer, trapper of fowl*

FOWLERS

3369 yâqôsh (1), *to ensnare, trap*

FOWLS

5775 'ôwph (36), *winged bird*
5776 'ôwph (Ch.) (1), *winged bird*
5861 'ayiṭ (3), *bird of prey (poss.) hawk*
6833 tsippôwr (1), *little hopping bird*
6853 ts^{e}phar (Ch.) (3), *bird*
3732 ŏrnĕŏn (2), *bird*

FOX

7776 shûw'âl (1), *jackal*
258 alōpĕx (1), *fox*

FOXES

7776 shûw'âl (6), *jackal*
258 alōpĕx (2), *fox*

FRAGMENTS

2801 klasma (7), *piece, bit*

FRAIL

2310 châdêl (1), *ceasing or destitute*

FRAME

3335 yâtsar (1), *to form; potter; to determine*
3336 yêtser (1), *form*
3559 kûwn (1), *to set up: establish, fix, prepare*
4011 mibneh (1), *building*
5414 nâthan (1), *to give*

FRAMED

3335 yâtsar (1), *to form; potter; to determine*
3336 yêtser (1), *form*
2675 katartizō (1), *to repair; to prepare*
4883 sunarmŏlŏgĕō (1), *to render close-jointed*

FRAMETH

3335 yâtsar (1), *to form; potter; to determine*
6775 tsâmad (1), *to link, i.e. gird*

FRANKINCENSE

3828 l^{e}bôwnâh (15), *frankincense*
3030 libanŏs (2), *fragrant incense resin or gum*

FRANKLY

5435 Phrugia (1), *Phrygia*

FRAUD

8496 tôk (1), *oppression*
650 apŏstĕrĕō (1), *to deprive; to despoil*

FRAY

2729 chârad (3), *to shudder; to hasten*

FRECKLED

933 bôhaq (1), *white scurf, rash*

FREE

2600 chinnâm (1), *gratis, free*
2666 châphash (1), *to loose; free from slavery*
2670 chophshîy (16), *exempt, free*
5071 n^{e}dâbâh (2), *abundant gift*
5081 nâdîyb (1), *magnanimous*
5082 n^{e}dîybâh (1), *nobility, i.e. reputation*
5352 nâqâh (2), *to be, make clean; to be bare*
5355 nâqîy (1), *innocent*
6362 pâṭar (1), *to burst through; to emit*
6605 pâthach (1), *to open wide; to loosen, begin*
1658 ĕlĕuthĕrŏs (20), *not a slave*

F

1659 ĕlĕuthĕrŏō (6), to *exempt, liberate*
5486 charisma (2), spiritual *endowment*

FREED
3772 kárath (1), to *cut* (off, down or asunder)
1344 dikaiŏō (1), *show* or *regard* as *innocent*

FREEDOM
2668 chuphshâh (1), *liberty* from slavery
4174 pŏlitĕia (1), *citizenship*

FREELY
2600 chinnâm (1), *gratis, free*
5071 nᵉdâbâh (2), *abundant gift*
1432 dōrĕan (6), *gratuitously, freely*
3326+3954 mĕta (1), *with, among; after, later*
3955 parrhēsiazŏmai (1), to *be confident*

FREEMAN
558 apĕlĕuthĕrŏs (1), *freedman*

FREEWILL
5069 nᵉdab (Ch.) (2), *be, give without coercion*
5071 nᵉdâbâh (15), *abundant gift*

FREEWOMAN
1658 ĕlĕuthĕrŏs (2), *not a slave*

FREQUENT
4056 pĕrissŏtĕrōs (1), *more superabundantly*

FRESH
2319 châdâsh (1), *new, recent*
3955 lᵉshad (1), *juice; vigor; sweet or fat cake*
7488 ra'ănân (1), *new; prosperous*
1099 glukus (1), *sweet, fresh*

FRESHER
7375 rûwṭăphash (1), to *be rejuvenated*

FRET
2734 chârâh (4), to *blaze up*
6356 pᵉchetheth (1), *mildewed garment hole*
7107 qâtsaph (1), to *burst out in rage*
7481 râ'am (1), to *crash thunder; to irritate*

FRETTED
7264 râgaz (1), to *quiver*

FRETTETH
2196 zá'aph (1), to *be angry*

FRETTING
3992 mâ'ar (3), to *be painful; destructive*

FRIED
7246 râbak (2), to *soak bread in oil*

FRIEND
157 'âhab (4), to *have affection, love*

7451 ra' (1), *bad; evil*
7453 rêa' (27), *associate; one close*
7462 râ'âh (1), to *associate* as a friend
7463 rê'eh (3), *male advisor*
2083 hĕtairŏs (3), *comrade, friend*
3982 pĕithō (1), to *pacify* or *conciliate*
5384 philŏs (12), *friend; friendly*

FRIENDLY
3820 lêb (2), *heart*
7489 râ'a' (1), to *make, be good for nothing*

FRIENDS
157 'âhab (8), to *have affection, love*
441 'allûwph (2), *friend, one familiar; chieftain*
605+7965 'ânash (1), to *be frail, feeble*
4828 mêrêa' (3), *close friend*
4962 math (1), *men*
7453 rêa' (14), *associate; one close*
3588+3844 hŏ (1), "the," i.e. the definite article
4674 sŏs (1), *things that are yours*
5384 philŏs (17), *friend; friendly*

FRIENDSHIP
7462 râ'âh (1), to *associate* as a friend
5373 philia (1), *fondness*

FRINGE
6734 tsîytsîth (2), *fore-lock of hair; tassel*

FRINGES
1434 gᵉdîl (1), *tassel; festoon*
6734 tsîytsîth (2), *fore-lock of hair; tassel*

FRO
235 'âzal (1), to *disappear*
7725 shûwb (1), to *turn back; to return*
7751 shûwṭ (8), to *travel, roam*
8264 shâqaq (1), to *seek greedily*
2831 kludōnizŏmai (1), to *fluctuate back and forth on the waves*

FROGS
6854 tsᵉphardêa' (13), *frog, leaper*
944 batrachŏs (1), *frog*

FRONT
6440 pânîym (2), *face; front*

FRONTIERS
7097 qâtseh (1), *extremity*

FRONTLETS
2903 ṭôwphâphâh (3), *sign* or *symbolic box*

FROST
2602 chănâmâl (1), *aphis* or *plant-louse*
3713 kᵉphôwr (3), *bowl; white frost*

7140 qerach (3), *ice; hail; rock crystal*

FROWARD
2019 hăphakpak (1), *very perverse, crooked*
3868 lûwz (2), to *depart; to be perverse*
6141 'iqqêsh (6), *distorted, warped, false*
6143 'iqqᵉshûwth (2), *perversity*
6617 pâthal (3), to *struggle; to be tortuous*
8419 tahpûkâh (6), *perversity or fraud*
4646 skŏliŏs (1), *crooked; perverse*

FROWARDLY
7726 shôwbâb (1), *apostate, i.e. idolatrous*

FROWARDNESS
8419 tahpûkâh (3), *perversity or fraud*

FROZEN
3920 lâkad (1), to *catch; to capture*

FRUIT
4 'êb (Ch.) (3), *green plant*
1061 bikkûwr (2), *first-fruits of the crop*
2981 yᵉbûwl (3), *produce, crop; harvest*
3206 yeled (1), *young male*
3899 lechem (1), *food, bread*
3978 ma'ăkâl (1), *food, something to eat*
4395 mᵉlê'âh (1), *fulfilled; abundance*
5107 nûwb (1), to (*make*) *flourish; to utter*
5108 nôwb (2), *agricultural produce*
6509 pârâh (1), to *bear fruit*
6529 pᵉrîy (106), *fruit*
7920 sᵉkal (Ch.) (1), to *be or act circumspect*
8270 shôr (1), *umbilical cord; strength*
8393 tᵉbûw'âh (7), *income, i.e. produce*
8570 tᵉnûwbâh (2), *crop, produce*
175 akarpŏs (1), *barren, unfruitful*
1081 gĕnnēma (3), *offspring; produce*
2590 karpŏs (54), *fruit; crop*
2592 karpŏphŏrĕō (7), to *be fertile*
5052 tĕlĕsphŏrĕō (1), to *ripen fruit*
5352 phthinŏpōrinŏs (1), *autumnal*

FRUITFUL
1121+8081 bên (1), *people of a class or kind*
2233 zera' (1), *seed; fruit, plant, sowing-time*
3759 karmel (7), *planted field; garden produce*
6500 pârâ' (1), to *bear fruit*

7140 qerach (3), *ice; hail;*

6509 pârâh (21), to *bear fruit*
6529 pᵉrîy (2), *fruit*
2592 karpŏphŏrĕō (1), to *be fertile*
2593 karpŏphŏrŏs (1), *fruitbearing*

FRUITS
3 'êb (1), *green* plant
1061 bikkûwr (1), *first-fruits of the crop*
2173 zimrâh (1), *choice fruit*
3581 kôach (1), *force, might; strength*
4395 mᵉlê'âh (1), *fulfilled; abundance*
6529 pᵉrîy (7), *fruit*
8393 tᵉbûw'âh (6), *income, i.e. produce*
8570 tᵉnûwbâh (1), *crop, produce*
1081 gĕnnēma (2), *offspring; produce*
2590 karpŏs (12), *fruit; crop*
3703 ŏpōra (1), *ripe fruit*

FRUSTRATE
656 'âphêç (1), to *cease*
114 athĕtĕō (1), to *disesteem, neutralize*

FRUSTRATETH
6565 pârar (1), to *break up; to violate, frustrate*

FRYING
4802 marchesheth (1), *stew-pan*

FRYINGPAN
4802 marchesheth (1), *stew-pan*

FUEL
402 'oklâh (3), *food*
3980 ma'ăkôleth (2), *fuel for fire*

FUGITIVE
5128 nûwa' (2), to *waver*

FUGITIVES
1280 bᵉrîyach (1), *bolt; cross-bar of a door*
4015 mibrâch (1), *refugee*
5307 nâphal (1), to *fall*
6412 pâlîyṭ (1), *refugee*

FULFIL
3615 kâlâh (1), to *complete, consume*
4390 mâlê' (7), to *fill; be full*
6213 'âsâh (2), to *do or make*
378 anaplērŏō (1), to *complete; to occupy*
4137 plērŏō (6), to *fill, make complete*
4160 pŏiĕō (2), to *make or do*
5055 tĕlĕō (3), to *end, i.e. complete, execute*

FULFILLED
1214 bâtsa' (1), to *finish; to stop*
3615 kâlâh (2), to *complete, consume*
4390 mâlê' (20), to *fill; be full*
5487 çûwph (Ch.) (1), to *come to an end*

6213 'âsâh (1), to *do*
378 anaplērŏŏ (1), to *complete; accomplish*
1096 ginŏmai (3), to *be, become*
1603 ĕkplērŏŏ (1), to *accomplish, fulfill*
4137 plērŏŏ (45), to *fill, make complete*
4931 suntĕlĕŏ (1), to *complete entirely*
5048 tĕlĕiŏŏ (2), to *perfect, complete*
5055 tĕlĕŏ (4), to *end,* i.e. *complete, execute*

FULFILLING
6213 'âsâh (1), to *do or make*
4138 plērŏma (1), what *fills;* what is *filled*
4160 pŏiĕŏ (1), to *do*

FULL
3117 yôwm (10), *day; time period*
3624 kelach (1), *maturity*
3759 karmel (1), *planted field; garden produce*
4390 mâlê' (50), to *fill; be full*
4391 mᵉlâ' (Ch.) (1), to *fill; be full*
4392 mâlê' (58), *full; filling; fulness; fully*
4393 mᵉlô' (11), *fulness*
7227 rab (1), *great*
7235 râbâh (1), to *increase*
7646 sâba' (20), *fill to satiety*
7648 sôba' (3), *satisfaction*
7649 sâbêa' (2), *satiated*
7654 sob'âh (3), *satiety*
7999 shâlam (1), to *be safe; be, make complete*
8003 shâlêm (2), *complete; friendly; safe*
8537 tôm (1), *completeness*
8549 tâmîym (1), *entire, complete; integrity*
8552 tâmam (1), to *complete, finish*
1072 gĕmizŏ (1), to *fill entirely*
1073 gĕmŏ (11), to *swell out,* i.e. *be full*
1705 ĕmpiplĕmi (1), to *satisfy*
2880 kŏrĕnnumi (1), to *cram,* i.e. *glut or sate*
3324 mĕstŏs (8), *replete, full*
3325 mĕstŏŏ (1), to *intoxicate*
4130 plēthŏ (1), to *fulfill, complete*
4134 plērēs (17), *replete, full, complete*
4135 plērŏphŏrĕŏ (1), to *fill completely*
4136 plērŏphŏria (3), *full assurance*
4137 plērŏŏ (9), to *fill, make complete*
4138 plērŏma (1), what *fills;* what is *filled*
5046 tĕlĕiŏs (1), *complete; mature*

5460 phŏtĕinŏs (4), *well-illuminated*
5526 chŏrtazŏ (1), to *supply food until full*

FULLER
1102 gnaphĕus (1), cloth-*dresser*

FULLER'S
3526 kâbaç (3), to *wash*

FULLERS'
3526 kâbaç (1), to *wash*

FULLY
3615 kâlâh (1), to *complete, consume*
4390 mâlê' (3), to *fill; be full*
4392 mâlê' (1), *full; filling; fulness; fully*
5046 nâgad (1), to *announce*
3877 parakŏlŏuthĕŏ (1), to *attend; trace out*
4135 plērŏphŏrĕŏ (3), to *fill completely*
4137 plērŏŏ (1), to *fill, make complete*
4845 sumplērŏŏ (1), to *be complete, fulfill*

FULNESS
4390 mâlê' (1), to *fill; be full*
4393 mᵉlô' (8), *fulness*
4395 mᵉlê'âh (1), *fulfilled; abundance*
7648 sôba' (1), *satisfaction*
7653 sib'âh (1), *satiety*
4138 plērŏma (13), what *fills;* what is *filled*

FURBISH
4838 mâraq (1), to *polish;* to *sharpen;* to *rinse*

FURBISHED
4803 mâraṭ (5), to *polish;* to *sharpen*

FURIOUS
1167+2534 ba'al (1), *master; owner; citizen*
2534 chêmâh (4), *heat; anger; poison*
7108 qᵉtsaph (Ch.) (1), to *become enraged*

FURIOUSLY
2534 chêmâh (1), *heat; anger; poison*
7697 shiggâ'ôwn (1), *craziness*

FURLONGS
4712 stadiŏn (5), *length of about 200 yards*

FURNACE
861 'attûwn (Ch.) (10), fire *furnace*
3536 kibshân (4), smelting *furnace*
3564 kûwr (9), smelting *furnace*
5948 'ălîyl (1), (poss.) *crucible*
8574 tannûwr (2), *fire-pot*
2575 kaminŏs (4), *furnace*

FURNACES
8574 tannûwr (2), *fire-pot*

FURNISH
4390 mâlê' (1), to *fill; be full*
6059 'ânaq (1), to *collar;* to *fit out*
6186 'ârak (1), to *set in a row,* i.e. *arrange,*
6213+3627 'âsâh (1), to *do or make*

FURNISHED
5375 nâsâ' (1), to *lift up*
6186 'ârak (1), to *set in a row,* i.e. *arrange, complete*
1822 ĕxartizŏ (1), to *finish out;* to *equip fully*
4130 plēthŏ (1), to *fulfill, complete*
4766 strŏnnumi (2), *strew, spread* a carpet

FURNITURE
3627 kᵉlîy (7), *implement, thing*
3733 kar (1), *saddle bag*

FURROW
8525 telem (1), *bank or terrace*

FURROWS
1417 gᵉdûwd (1), *furrow ridge*
4618 ma'ănâh (1), *furrow, plow path*
5869 'ayin (1), *eye; sight; fountain*
6170 'ărûwgâh (2), *parterre,* kind of *garden*
8525 telem (3), *bank or terrace*

FURTHER
3148 yôwthêr (1), *moreover; rest; gain*
3254 yâçaph (4), to *add or augment*
5750 'ôwd (2), *again; repeatedly; still; more*
6329 pûwq (1), to *issue; to furnish; to secure*
1339 diïstēmi (1), to *remove, intervene*
2089 ĕti (6), *yet, still*
4206 pŏrrhŏ (1), *forwards, at a distance*

FURTHERANCE
4297 prŏkŏpē (2), *progress, advancement*

FURTHERED
5375 nâsâ' (1), to *lift up*

FURTHERMORE
637 'aph (1), *also or yea; though*
5750 'ôwd (1), *again; repeatedly; still; more*
1161 dĕ (1), *but, yet; and then*
1534 ĕita (1), *succession, then, moreover*
3063 lŏipŏn (1), *remaining; finally*

FURY
2528 chĕmâ' (Ch.) (2), *anger*
2534 chêmâh (67), *heat; anger; poison*
2740 chârôwn (1), *burning* of anger

GAAL
1603 Ga'al (9), *loathing*

GAASH
1608 Ga'ash (4), *quaking*

GABA
1387 Geba' (3), *Geba*

GABBAI
1373 Gabbay (1), *collective*

GABBATHA
1042 gabbatha (1), *knoll*

GABRIEL
1403 Gabrîy'êl (2), *man of God*
1043 Gabriēl (2), *man of God*

GAD
1410 Gâd (71), *Gad*
1045 Gad (1), *Gad*

GADARENES
1046 Gadarēnŏs (3), *inhabitant of Gadara*

GADDEST
235 'âzal (1), to *disappear*

GADDI
1426 Gaddîy (1), *Gaddi*

GADDIEL
1427 Gaddîy'êl (1), *fortune of God*

GADI
1424 Gâdîy (2), *fortunate*

GADITE
1425 Gâdîy (1), *Gadite*

GADITES
1425 Gâdîy (14), *Gadite*

GAHAM
1514 Gacham (1), *flame*

GAHAR
1515 Gachar (2), *lurker*

GAIN
1214 bâtsa' (9), to *plunder;* to *finish;* to *stop*
2084 zᵉban (Ch.) (1), to *acquire* by purchase
4242 mᵉchîyr (1), *price, payment, wages*
8393 tᵉbûw'âh (1), *income,* i.e. *produce*
8636 tarbîyth (1), *percentage or bonus*
2039 ĕrgasia (2), *occupation; profit*
2770 kĕrdainŏ (9), to *gain;* to *spare*
2771 kĕrdŏs (2), *gain, profit*
4122 plĕŏnĕktĕŏ (2), to *be covetous*
4200 pŏrismŏs (2), *money-getting*

GAINED
1214 bâtsa' (2), to *plunder;* to *finish*
1281 diapragmatĕuŏmai (1), to *earn, make gain*
2770 kĕrdainŏ (5), to *gain;* to *spare*
4160 pŏiĕŏ (1), to *make or do*
4333 prŏsĕrgazŏmai (1), to *acquire besides*

GAINS
2039 ĕrgasia (1), *occupation; profit*

G

GAINSAY
471 antĕpō (1), to refute or deny

GAINSAYERS
483 antilĕgō (1), to dispute, refuse

GAINSAYING
369 anantirrhētōs (1), without raising objection
483 antilĕgō (1), to dispute, refuse
485 antilŏgia (1), dispute, disobedience

GAIUS
1050 Gaïŏs (5), Gaïus

GALAL
1559 Gâlâl (3), great

GALATIA
1053 Galatia (4), Galatia
1054 Galatikŏs (2), relating to Galatia

GALATIANS
1052 Galatēs (2), inhabitant of Galatia

GALBANUM
2464 chelbᵉnâh (1), fragrant resin gum

GALEED
1567 Gal'êd (2), heap of testimony

GALILAEAN
1057 Galilaiŏs (3), belonging to Galilæa

GALILAEANS
1057 Galilaiŏs (5), belonging to Galilæa

GALILEE
1551 Gâlîyl (6), circle as a special circuit
1056 Galilaia (66), heathen circle

GALL
4845 mᵉrêrâh (1), bitter bile of the gall bladder
4846 mᵉrôrâh (2), bitter bile; venom of a serpent
7219 rô'sh (9), poisonous plant; poison
5521 chŏlē (2), gall or bile; bitterness

GALLANT
117 'addîyr (1), powerful; majestic

GALLERIES
862 'attûwq (3), ledge or offset
7298 rahaṭ (1), ringlet of hair

GALLERY
862 'attûwq (1), ledge or offset

GALLEY
590 'ŏnîy (1), ship; fleet of ships

GALLIM
1554 Gallîym (2), springs

GALLIO
1058 Galliōn (3), Gallion, i.e. Gallio

GALLOWS
6086 'êts (8), wood, things made of wood

GAMALIEL
1583 Gamliy'êl (5), reward of God
1059 Gamaliēl (2), reward of God

GAMMADIMS
1575 Gammâd (1), warrior

GAMUL
1577 Gâmûwl (1), rewarded

GAP
6556 perets (1), break, gap

GAPED
6473 pâ'ar (1), to open wide
6475 pâtsâh (1), to rend, i.e. open

GAPS
6556 perets (1), break, gap

GARDEN
1588 gan (39), garden
1593 gannâh (3), garden, grove
1594 ginnâh (4), garden, grove
2779 kēpŏs (5), garden, grove

GARDENER
2780 kēpŏurŏs (1), gardener

GARDENS
1588 gan (3), garden
1593 gannâh (9), garden, grove

GAREB
1619 Gârêb (3), scabby

GARLANDS
4725 stĕmma (1), wreath

GARLICK
7762 shûwm (1), garlic

GARMENT
155 'addereth (4), large; splendid
899 beged (36), clothing; treachery or pillage
3801 kᵉthôneth (2), garment that covers
3830 lᵉbûwsh (7), garment; wife
3831 lᵉbûwsh (Ch.) (1), garment
4055 mad (3), vesture, garment; carpet
4594 ma'ăṭeh (1), vestment, garment
7897 shîyth (1), garment
8008 salmâh (4), clothing
8071 simlâh (4), dress, mantle
8162 sha'aṭnêz (1), linen and woolen
8509 takrîyk (1), wrapper or robe
1742 ĕnduma (2), apparel, outer robe
2440 himatiŏn (15), to put on clothes
4158 pŏdērēs (1), robe reaching the ankles
4749 stŏlē (1), long-fitting gown as a mark of dignity

GARMENTS
899 beged (69), clothing; treachery or pillage
3801 kᵉthôneth (3), garment that covers
3830 lᵉbûwsh (2), garment; wife
3831 lᵉbûwsh (Ch.) (1), garment
4055 mad (1), vesture, garment; carpet
4060 middâh (1), portion; vestment; tribute
4063 medev (2), dress, garment
8008 salmâh (4), clothing
8071 simlâh (2), dress, mantle
2067 ĕsthēsis (1), clothing
2440 himatiŏn (15), to put on clothes

GARMITE
1636 Garmîy (1), strong

GARNER
596 apŏthēkē (2), granary, grain barn

GARNERS
214 'ôwtsâr (1), depository
4200 mezev (1), granary

GARNISH
2885 kŏsmĕō (1), to decorate; to snuff

GARNISHED
6823 tsâphâh (1), to sheet over with metal
8235 shiphrâh (1), brightness of skies
2885 kŏsmĕō (3), to decorate; to snuff

GARRISON
4673 matstsâb (7), spot; office; military post
4675 matstsâbâh (1), military guard
5333 nᵉtsîyb (4), military post; statue
5432 phrŏurĕō (1), to post spies at gates

GARRISONS
4676 matstsêbâh (1), column or stone
5333 nᵉtsîyb (5), military post; statue

GASHMU
1654 Geshem (1), rain downpour

GAT
622 'âçaph (1), to gather, collect
935 bôw' (2), to go or come
3212 yâlak (4), to walk; to live; to carry
5927 'âlâh (7), to ascend, be high, mount
6213 'âsâh (2), to do or make
7392 râkab (1), to ride

GATAM
1609 Ga'tâm (3), Gatam

GATE
6607 pethach (4), opening; door; entrance
8179 sha'ar (240), opening, door or gate
8651 tᵉra' (Ch.) (1), door
2374 thura (1), entrance, i.e. door, gate
4439 pulē (8), gate
4440 pulōn (5), gate-way, door-way

GATES
1817 deleth (14), door; gate
5592 çaph (2), dish
6607 pethach (3), opening; door, entrance
8179 sha'ar (112), opening, door or gate
4439 pulē (2), gate
4440 pulōn (11), gate-way, door-way

GATH
1661 Gath (33), wine-press or vat

GATH-HEPHER
1662 Gath-ha-Chêpher (1), wine-press of (the) well

GATH-RIMMON
1667 Gath-Rimmôwn (4), wine-press of (the) pomegranate

GATHER
103 'âgar (1), to harvest
622 'âçaph (36), to gather, collect
1219 bâtsar (2), to gather grapes
1413 gâdad (2), to gash, slash oneself
1481 gûwr (3), to sojourn, live as an alien
1716 dâgar (1), to brood over; to care for young
2490 châlal (1), to profane, defile
3259 yâ'ad (1), to meet; to summon; to direct
3664 kânaç (5), to collect; to enfold
3673 kânash (Ch.) (1), to assemble
3950 lâqaṭ (13), to pick up, gather; to glean
3953 lâqash (1), to gather the after crop
4390 mâlê' (2), to fill; be full
5619 çâqal (1), to throw large stones
5756 'ûwz (3), to strengthen
6908 qâbats (56), to collect, assemble
6910 qᵉbûtsâh (1), hoard, gathering
6950 qâhal (8), to convoke, gather
7197 qâshash (4), to assemble
346 anakĕphalaiŏmai (1), to sum up
1996 ĕpisunagō (2), to collect upon
4816 sullĕgō (6), to collect, gather

GATHERED (cont.)

4863 sunagō (11), to gather together
5166 trugaō (2), to collect the vintage

GATHERED

622 'âçaph (97), to gather, collect
626 'âçêphâh (1), (collect) together
717 'ârâh (1), to pluck, pick fruit
1219 bâtsar (1), to gather grapes
1481 gûwr (2), to sojourn, live as an alien
2199 zâ'aq (4), to call out, announce
3254 yâçaph (1), to add or augment
3259 yâ'ad (3), to meet; to summon; to direct
3664 kânaç (2), to collect; to enfold
3673 kânash (Ch.) (2), to assemble
3950 lâqaṭ (11), to pick up, gather; to glean
4390 mâlê' (1), to fill; be full
5413 nâthak (2), to flow forth, pour out
5596 çâphach (1), to associate; be united
6192 'âram (1), to pile up
6213 'âsâh (1), to do or make
6651 tsâbar (2), to aggregate, gather
6817 tsâ'aq (5), to shriek; to proclaim
6908 qâbats (57), to collect, assemble
6950 qâhal (19), to convoke, gather
6960 qâvâh (2), to collect; to expect
7035 qâlahh (1), to assemble
7197 qâshash (1), to assemble
7408 râkash (1), to lay up, i.e. collect
8085 shâma' (1), to hear intelligently
1865 ĕpathrŏizō (1), to accumulate, increase
1996 ĕpisunagō (4), to collect upon
3792 ŏchlŏpŏiĕō (1), to raise a disturbance
4816 sullĕgō (2), to collect, gather
4863 sunagō (29), to gather together
4867 sunathrŏizō (1), to convene
4896 sunĕimi (1), to assemble, gather
4962 sustrĕphō (1), to collect a bundle, crowd
5166 trugaō (1), to collect the vintage

GATHERER

1103 bâlaç (1), to pinch sycamore figs

GATHEREST

1219 bâtsar (1), to gather grapes

GATHERETH

103 'âgar (2), to harvest
622 'âçaph (4), to gather, collect
3664 kânaç (2), to collect; to enfold
3950 lâqaṭ (1), to pick up, gather; to glean
6908 qâbats (4), to collect, assemble
1996 ĕpisunagō (1), to collect upon
4863 sunagō (3), to gather together

GATHERING

625 'ôçeph (2), fruit harvest collection
962 bâzaz (1), to plunder, take booty
3349 yiqqâhâh (1), obedience
4723 miqveh (1), confidence; collection
7197 qâshash (3), to assemble
1997 ĕpisunagōgē (1), meeting, gathering
4822 sumbibazō (1), to drive together
4863 sunagō (1), to gather together

GATHERINGS

3048 lŏgia (1), contribution, collection

GAVE

935 bôw' (1), to go, come
1696 dâbar (3), to speak, say; to subdue
3052 yᵉhab (Ch.) (4), to give
3254 yâçaph (1), to add or augment
3289 yâ'ats (2), to advise
5414 nâthan (252), to give
5462 çâgar (3), to shut up; to surrender
7121 qârâ' (3), to call out
7311 rûwm (4), to be high; to rise or raise
7725 shûwb (1), to turn back; to return
7760 sûwm (4), to put, place
7971 shâlach (1), to send away
437 anthŏmŏlŏgĕŏmai (1), to give thanks
591 apŏdidōmi (2), to give away
1291 diastĕllŏmai (1), to distinguish
1325 didōmi (77), to give
1433 dōrĕŏmai (1), to bestow gratuitously
1502 ĕikō (1), to be weak, i.e. yield
1781 ĕntĕllŏmai (1), to enjoin, give orders
1788 ĕntrĕpō (1), to respect; to confound
1907 ĕpĕchō (1), to retain; to detain
1929 ĕpididōmi (2), to give over
2010 ĕpitrĕpō (3), allow, permit
2702 kataphĕrō (1), to bear down

GAVEST

2753 kĕlĕuō (1), to order, direct
3140 marturĕō (3), to testify; to commend
3860 paradidōmi (7), to hand over
4160 pŏiĕō (2), to make or do
4222 pŏtizō (5), to furnish drink, irrigate
4337 prŏsĕchō (3), to pay attention to
4823 sumbŏulĕuō (1), to recommend, deliberate
5483 charizŏmai (2), to grant as a favor, pardon

GAVEST

5414 nâthan (21), to give
7760 sûwm (1), to put, place
1325 didōmi (11), to give

GAY

2986 lamprŏs (1), clear; magnificent

GAZA

5804 'Azzâh (18), strong
1048 Gaza (1), strong

GAZATHITES

5841 'Azzâthîy (1), Azzathite

GAZE

7200 râ'âh (1), to see

GAZER

1507 Gezer (2), portion, piece

GAZEZ

1495 Gâzêz (2), shearer

GAZING

1689 ĕmblĕpō (1), to observe; to discern

GAZINGSTOCK

7210 rô'îy (1), sight; spectacle
2301 thĕatrizō (1), to expose as a spectacle

GAZITES

5841 'Azzâthîy (1), Azzathite

GAZZAM

1502 Gazzâm (2), devourer

GEBA

1387 Geba' (12), Geba

GEBAL

1381 Gᵉbâl (2), mountain

GEBER

1398 Geber (2), (valiant) man

GEBIM

1374 Gêbîym (1), cisterns

GEDALIAH

1436 Gᵉdalyâh (32), Jehovah has become great

GEDEON

1066 Gĕdĕōn (1), warrior

GEDER

1445 Geder (1), wall or fence

GEDERAH

1449 Gᵉdêrâh (1), enclosure for flocks

GEDERATHITE

1452 Gᵉdêrâthîy (1), Gederathite

GEDERITE

1451 Gᵉdêrîy (1), Gederite

GEDEROTH

1450 Gᵉdêrôwth (2), walls

GEDEROTHAIM

1453 Gᵉdêrôthayim (1), double wall

GEDOR

1446 Gᵉdôr (7), enclosure

GEHAZI

1522 Gêychăzîy (12), valley of a visionary

G

GELILOTH

1553 Gᵉlîylôwth (1), circles

GEMALLI

1582 Gᵉmalliy (1), camel-driver

GEMARIAH

1587 Gᵉmaryâh (5), Jehovah has perfected

GENDER

7250 râba' (1), to lay down; have sex
1080 gĕnnaō (1), to procreate, regenerate

GENDERED

3205 yâlad (1), to bear young; to father a child

GENDERETH

5674 'âbar (1), to cross over; to transition
1080 gĕnnaō (1), to procreate, regenerate

GENEALOGIES

3187 yâchas (6), to enroll by family list
1076 gĕnĕalŏgia (2), genealogy, lineage

GENEALOGY

3188 yachas (15), family list

GENERAL

8269 sar (1), head person, ruler
3831 panĕguris (1), mass-meeting

GENERALLY

3605 kôl (1), all, any or every

GENERATION

1755 dôwr (50), dwelling
1859 dâr (Ch.) (2), age; generation
1074 gĕnĕa (30), generation; age
1078 genesis (1), nativity, nature
1081 gĕnnēma (4), offspring; produce
1085 gĕnŏs (1), kin, offspring in kind

GENERATIONS

1755 dôwr (73), dwelling
8435 tôwlᵉdâh (39), family descent, family record

GENNESARET
1074 gĕnĕa (6), *generation; age*

GENNESARET
1082 Gĕnnēsarĕt (3), (poss.) *harp*-shaped

GENTILE
1672 Hĕllēn (2), *Greek (-speaking)*

GENTILES
1471 gôwy (30), *foreign nation; Gentiles*
1483 ĕthnikŏs (1), *as a Gentile*
1484 ĕthnŏs (93), *race; tribe; pagan*
1672 Hĕllēn (5), *Greek (-speaking)*

GENTLE
1933 ĕpiĕikēs (3), *mild, gentle*
2261 ēpiŏs (2), *affable, i.e. mild or kind*

GENTLENESS
6031 'ănâh (1), *to afflict, be afflicted*
6038 'ănâvâh (1), *modesty, clemency*
1932 ĕpiĕikĕia (1), *mildness, gentleness*
5544 chrēstŏtēs (1), *moral excellence*

GENTLY
3814 lâ'ṭ (1), *silently*

GENUBATH
1592 Gᵉnûbath (2), *theft*

GERA
1617 Gêrâ' (9), *cereal grain*

GERAHS
1626 gêrâh (5), *measure*

GERAR
1642 Gᵉrâr (10), *rolling country*

GERGESENES
1086 Gĕrgĕsēnŏs (1), *Gergesene*

GERIZIM
1630 Gᵉrîzîym (4), *rocky*

GERSHOM
1648 Gêrᵉshôwn (14), *refugee*

GERSHON
1647 Gêrᵉshôm (17), *refugee*

GERSHONITE
1649 Gerᵉshunnîy (3), *Gereshonite*

GERSHONITES
1649 Gerᵉshunnîy (9), *Gereshonite*

GESHAM
1529 Gêyshân (1), *lumpish*

GESHEM
1654 Geshem (3), *rain downpour*

GESHUR
1650 Gᵉshûwr (8), *bridge*

GESHURI
1651 Gᵉshûwrîy (2), *Geshurite*

GESHURITES
1651 Gᵉshûwrîy (5), *Geshurite*

GET
776 'erets (1), *earth, land, soil; country*
935 bôw' (8), *to go or come*
1214 bâtsa' (1), *to plunder; to finish*
1245 bâqash (1), *to search; to strive after*
1980 hâlak (1), *to walk; live a certain way*
3212 yâlak (17), *to walk; to carry*
3318 yâtsâ' (7), *to go, bring out*
3381 yârad (9), *to descend*
3513 kâbad (1), *to be heavy, severe, dull*
3947 lâqach (5), *to take*
4422 mâlaṭ (1), *to escape as if by slipperiness*
4672 mâtsâ' (2), *to find or acquire; to occur*
5110 nûwd (1), *to waver; to wander, flee*
5111 nûwd (Ch.) (1), *to flee*
5265 nâça' (1), *start on a journey*
5381 nâsag (6), *to reach*
5674 'âbar (1), *to cross over; to transition*
5927 'âlâh (18), *to ascend, be high, mount*
6213 'âsâh (2), *to do or make*
6965 qûwm (1), *to rise*
7069 qânâh (8), *to create; to procure*
7426 râmam (1), *to rise*
7725 shûwb (1), *to turn back; to return*
1684 ĕmbainō (2), *to embark; to reach*
1826 ĕxĕimi (1), *leave; escape*
1831 ĕxĕrchŏmai (3), *to issue; to leave*
2147 hĕuriskō (1), *to find*
2597 katabainō (1), *to descend*
4122 plĕŏnĕktĕō (1), *to be covetous*
5217 hupagō (4), *to withdraw or retire*

GETHER
1666 Gether (2), *Gether*

GETHSEMANE
1068 Gĕthsēmanē (2), *oil-press*

GETTETH
3947 lâqach (1), *to take*
5060 nâga' (1), *to strike*
5927 'âlâh (1), *to ascend, be high, mount*
6213 'âsâh (1), *to do or make*
6329 pûwq (1), *to issue; to furnish; to secure*
7069 qânâh (3), *to create; to procure*

GETTING
6467 pô'al (1), *act or work, deed*
7069 qânâh (1), *to create; to procure*
7075 qinyân (1), *acquisition, purchase*

GEUEL
1345 Gᵉ'ûw'êl (1), *majesty of God*

GEZER
1507 Gezer (13), *portion, piece*

GEZRITES
1511 Gizrîy (1), *Gezerite; Girzite*

GHOST
1478 gâva' (9), *to expire, die*
5315 nephesh (2), *life; breath; soul; wind*
1606 ĕkpnĕō (3), *to expire*
1634 ĕkpsuchō (3), *to expire, die*
4151 pnĕuma (92), *spirit*

GIAH
1520 Gîyach (1), *fountain*

GIANT
1368 gibbôwr (1), *powerful; great warrior*
7497 râphâ' (7), *giant*

GIANTS
1368 gibbôwr (1), *powerful; great warrior*
5303 nᵉphîyl (2), *bully or tyrant*
7497 râphâ' (10), *giant*

GIBBAR
1402 Gibbâr (1), *Gibbar*

GIBBETHON
1405 Gibbᵉthôwn (6), *hilly spot*

GIBEA
1388 Gib'â' (1), *hill*

GIBEAH
1390 Gib'âh (48), *hillock*

GIBEATH
1394 Gib'ath (1), *hilliness*

GIBEATHITE
1395 Gib'âthîy (1), *Gibathite*

GIBEON
1391 Gib'ôwn (35), *hilly*

GIBEONITE
1393 Gib'ônîy (2), *Gibonite*

GIBEONITES
1393 Gib'ônîy (6), *Gibonite*

GIBLITES
1382 Giblîy (1), *Gebalite*

GIDDALTI
1437 Giddaltîy (2), *I have made great*

GIDDEL
1435 Giddêl (4), *stout*

GIDEON
1439 Gîd'ôwn (39), *warrior*

GIDEONI
1441 Gid'ônîy (5), *warlike*

GIDOM
1440 Gid'ôm (1), *desolation*

GIER
7360 râchâm (2), *kind of vulture*

GIFT
4503 minchâh (1), *tribute; offering*
4976 mattân (4), *present, gift*
4979 mâttânâh (5), *present; offering; bribe*
4991 mattâth (3), *present*
5379 nissê'th (1), *present*
7810 shachad (6), *to bribe; gift*
1390 dŏma (1), *present, gift*
1394 dŏsis (1), *gift*
1431 dōrĕa (11), *gratuity, gift*
1434 dōrēma (1), *bestowment, gift*
1435 dōrŏn (10), *sacrificial present*
5485 charis (1), *gratitude; benefit given*
5486 charisma (10), *spiritual endowment*

GIFTS
814 'eshkâr (1), *gratuity, gift; payment*
4503 minchâh (6), *tribute; offering*
4864 mas'êth (1), *tribute; reproach*
4976 mattân (1), *present, gift*
4978 mattᵉnâ' (Ch.) (3), *present, gift*
4979 mâttânâh (11), *present; offering; bribe*
5078 nêdeh (1), *bounty, reward for prostitution*
5083 nâdân (1), *present for prostitution*
7810 shachad (4), *to bribe; gift*
8641 tᵉrûwmâh (1), *tribute, present*
334 anathēma (1), *votive offering to God*
1390 dŏma (2), *present, gift*
1435 dōrŏn (9), *sacrificial present*
3311 mĕrismŏs (1), *distribution*
5486 charisma (7), *spiritual endowment*

GIHON
1521 Gîychôwn (6), *stream*

GILALAI
1562 Gîlălay (1), *dungy*

GILBOA
1533 Gilbôa' (8), *bubbling fountain*

GILEAD
1568 Gil'âd (100), *Gilad*

GILEAD'S
1568 Gil'âd (1), *Gilad*

GILEADITE
1569 Gil'âdîy (9), *Gileadite*

GILEADITES
1569 Gil'âdîy (4), *Giladite*

GILGAL
1537 Gilgâl (39), *wheel*

GILOH
1542 Gîlôh (2), *open*

GILONITE
1526 Gîylônîy (2), *Gilonite*

GIMZO
1579 Gimzôw (1), Gimzo

GIN
4170 môwqêsh (1), *noose*
6341 pach (2), *thin metallic sheet; net*

GINATH
1527 Gîynath (2), *Ginath*

GINNETHO
1599 Ginnᵉthôwn (1), *gardener*

GINNETHON
1599 Ginnᵉthôwn (2), *gardener*

GINS
4170 môwqêsh (2), *noose*

GIRD
247 'âzar (4), to *belt*
640 'âphad (1), to *fasten, gird*
2290 chăgôwr (1), *belt for the waist*
2296 châgar (16), to *gird on a belt; put on armor*
328 anazônnumi (1), to *gird, bind afresh*
2224 zônnumi (2), to *bind about*
4024 pĕrizônnumi (2), to *fasten on one's belt*

GIRDED
247 'âzar (7), to *belt*
631 'âçar (1), to *fasten; to join battle*
2280 châbash (1), to *wrap firmly, bind*
2289 chăgôwr (1), *belted around waist*
2296 châgar (18), to *gird on a belt; put on armor*
8151 shânaç (1), to *compress*
1241 diazônnumi (2), to *gird tightly, wrap*
4024 pĕrizônnumi (2), to *fasten on one's belt*

GIRDEDST
2224 zônnumi (1), to *bind about*

GIRDETH
247 'âzar (1), to *belt*
631 'âçar (1), to *fasten; to join battle*
2296 châgar (2), to *gird on a belt; put on armor*

GIRDING
2296 châgar (1), to *gird on a belt; put on armor*
4228 machăgôreth (1), *girdle of sackcloth*

GIRDLE
73 'abnêṭ (6), *belt*
232 'êzôwr (13), *belt; band around waist*

GIRDLE (cont.)
2290 chăgôwr (5), *belt for the waist*
2805 chêsheb (8), *belt, waistband*
4206 mâzîyach (1), *leather belt*
2223 zônē (5), *belt, sash*

GIRDLES
73 'abnêṭ (3), *belt*
232 'êzôwr (1), *belt; band around waist*
2289 chăgôwr (1), *belted around waist*
2223 zônē (1), *belt, sash*

GIRGASHITE
1622 Girgâshîy (1), *Girgashite*

GIRGASHITES
1622 Girgâshîy (5), *Girgashite*

GIRGASITE
1622 Girgâshîy (1), *Girgashite*

GIRL
3207 yaldâh (1), *young female*

GIRLS
3207 yaldâh (1), *young female*

GIRT
247 'âzar (1), to *belt*
1241 diazônnumi (1), to *gird tightly, wrap*
4024 pĕrizônnumi (2), to *fasten on one's belt*

GISPA
1658 Gishpâ' (1), *Gishpa*

GITTAH-HEPHER
1662 Gath-ha-Chêpher (1), *wine-press of* (the) *well*

GITTAIM
1664 Gittayim (2), *double wine-press*

GITTITE
1663 Gittîy (8), *Gittite*

GITTITES
1663 Gittîy (2), *Gittite*

GITTITH
1665 Gittîyth (3), *harp*

GIVE
1262 bârâh (1), to *feed*
1478 gâva' (3), to *expire, die*
1696 dâbar (1), to *speak, say; to subdue*
1961+413 hâyâh (1), to *exist,* i.e. *be or become*
3051 yâhab (24), to *give*
3052 yᵉhab (Ch.) (2), to *give*
3190 yâṭab (1), to *be, make well*
4900 mâshak (1), to *draw out; to be tall*
4991 mattâth (2), *present*
5066 nâgash (1), to *be, come, bring near*
5414 nâthan (482), to *give*
5415 nᵉthan (Ch.) (2), to *give*
5441 çôbek (1), *copse or thicket*

GIVE (cont.)
5534 çâkar (1), to *shut up; to surrender*
6213 'âsâh (1), to *do or make*
7311 rûwm (1), to *be high; to rise or raise*
7725 shûwb (3), to *turn back; to return or restore*
7760 sûwm (5), to *put, place*
7761 sûwm (Ch.) (1), to *put, place*
7999 shâlam (1), to *be safe; be, make complete*
402 anachôrĕō (1), to *retire, withdraw*
591 apŏdidōmi (8), to *give away*
1096 ginŏmai (1), to *be, become*
1239 diadidōmi (1), to *divide up, distribute*
1325 didōmi (139), to *give*
1929 ĕpididōmi (5), to *give over*
2014 ĕpiphainō (1), to *become known*
2468 isthi (1), *be thou*
3330 mĕtadidōmi (1), to *share, distribute*
3844 para (1), *from; with; besides; on account of*
3860 paradidōmi (1), to *hand over*
3930 parĕchō (1), to *hold near,* i.e. to *present*
3936 paristēmi (1), to *stand beside, present*
4222 pŏtizō (3), to *furnish drink, irrigate*
4342 prŏskartĕrĕō (1), to *attend; to adhere*
4980 schŏlazō (1), to *devote oneself wholly to*
5461 phōtizō (1), to *shine or to brighten up*
5483 charizŏmai (1), to *grant as a favor*

GIVEN
1167 ba'al (2), *master; husband; owner; citizen*
1478 gâva' (1), to *expire, die*
1576 gᵉmûwl (1), *act; reward, recompense*
2505 châlaq (1), to *be smooth; be slippery*
2603 chânan (1), to *implore*
3052 yᵉhab (Ch.) (16), to *give*
3254 yâçaph (1), to *add or augment*
3289 yâ'ats (2), to *advise*
5221 nâkâh (3), to *strike, kill*
5301 nâphach (1), to *inflate, blow, scatter*
5375 nâsâ' (1), to *lift up*
5414 nâthan (253), to *give*
5462 çâgar (1), to *shut up; to surrender*
6213 'âsâh (1), to *do or make*
7760 sûwm (1), to *put, place*
7761 sûwm (Ch.) (1), to *put, place*

GIVEN (cont.)
1325 didōmi (123), to *give*
1377 diōkō (1), to *pursue; to persecute*
1402 dŏulŏō (1), to *enslave*
1433 dōrĕŏmai (2), to *bestow gratuitously*
1547 ĕkgamizō (1), to *marry off a daughter*
2227 zōŏpŏiĕō (1), to (*re-*)*vitalize, give life*
3860 paradidōmi (2), to *hand over*
3930 parĕchō (1), to *present, afford, exhibit*
3943 parŏinŏs (2), *tippling*
4272 prŏdidōmi (1), to *give before*
4337 prŏsĕchō (1), to *pay attention to*
4369 prŏstithēmi (1), to *lay beside, repeat*
5483 charizŏmai (5), to *grant as a favor*

GIVER
1395 dŏtēs (1), *giver*

GIVEST
5414 nâthan (7), to *give*
7971 shâlach (1), to *send away*

GIVETH
1478 gâva' (1), to *expire, die*
3052 yᵉhab (Ch.) (1), to *give*
5414 nâthan (77), to *give*
5415 nᵉthan (Ch.) (3), to *give*
1325 didōmi (13), to *give*
3330 mĕtadidōmi (1), to *share, distribute*
3930 parĕchō (1), to *present, afford, exhibit*
5087 tithēmi (1), to *place*
5524 chŏrēgĕō (1), to *furnish, supply, provide*

GIVING
4646 mappâch (1), *expiring, dying*
5414 nâthan (5), to *give*
632 apŏnĕmō (1), to *bestow, treat with respect*
1325 didōmi (3), to *give*
1394 dŏsis (1), *gift*
3004 lĕgō (1), to *say*
3548 nŏmŏthĕsia (1), *legislation, law*
3923 parĕisphĕrō (1), to *bear in alongside*

GIZONITE
1493 Gizôwnîy (1), *Gizonite*

GLAD
1523 gîyl (6), *rejoice*
1528 gîyr (Ch.) (4), *lime for plaster*
2302 châdâh (1), to *rejoice, be glad*
2868 ṭᵉ'êb (Ch.) (1), to *rejoice, be pleased*
2896 ṭôwb (2), *good; well*
7796 Sôwrêq (2), *vine*
7797 sûws (1), to *be bright,* i.e. *cheerful*
7996 Shalleketh (1), *felling of trees*

G

8056 sâmêach (49),
blithe or *gleeful*
8190 Sha'ashgaz (1),
Shaashgaz
21 *agalliaō* (2), to *exult*
2097 *ĕuaggĕlizō* (4), to
announce good news
2165 *ĕuphrainō* (1), to
rejoice, be glad
5463 *chairō* (14), to be
cheerful

GLADLY
780 *asmĕnōs* (2), *with
pleasure, gladly*
2234 *hēdĕōs* (3), *with
pleasure, with delight*
2236 *hēdista* (2), *with
great pleasure*

GLADNESS
1524 *gîyl* (1), *age, stage
in life*
2304 chedvâh (1),
rejoicing, joy
2898 ṭûwb (1), *good;
goodness; gladness*
7440 rinnâh (1), *shout*
8057 simchâh (34),
blithesomeness or *glee*
8342 sâsôwn (2),
cheerfulness; welcome
20 *agalliasis* (3),
exultation, delight
2167 *ĕuphrŏsunē* (1),
joyfulness, cheerfulness
5479 *chara* (3), *calm
delight, joy*

GLASS
7209 rᵉ'îy (1), *mirror*
2072 *ĕsŏptrŏn* (2), *mirror
for looking into*
2734 *katŏptrizŏmai* (1),
to *see reflected*
5193 *hualinŏs* (3),
pertaining to glass
5194 *hualŏs* (2), *glass,
crystal*

GLASSES
1549 gîllâyôwn (1), *tablet
for writing; mirror*

GLEAN
3950 lâqaṭ (7), to *pick* up,
gather; to *glean*
5953 'âlal (3), to *glean*; to
overdo

GLEANED
3950 lâqaṭ (5), to *pick* up,
gather; to *glean*
5953 'âlal (1), to *glean*; to
overdo

GLEANING
3951 leqeṭ (1), *gleaning
after a harvest*
5955 'ôlêlâh (4),
gleaning; gleaning-time

GLEANINGS
3951 leqeṭ (1), *gleaning*

GLEDE
7201 râ'âh (1), *bird of
prey* (poss. *vulture*)

GLISTERING
6320 pûwk (1), *stibium*
1823 *ĕxastraptō* (1), to *be
radiant*

GLITTER
1300 bârâq (1), *lightning;
flash of lightning*

GLITTERING
1300 bârâq (5), *lightning;
flash of lightning*
3851 lahab (1), *flame of
fire; flash of a blade*

GLOOMINESS
653 'âphêlâh (2),
duskiness, darkness

GLORIEST
1984 hâlal (1), to *shine,
flash, radiate*

GLORIETH
1984 hâlal (1), to *shine,
flash, radiate*
2744 *kauchaŏmai* (2), to
glory in, rejoice in

GLORIFIED
1922 hâdar (Ch.) (1), to
magnify, glorify
3513 kâbad (6), to *be
heavy, severe, dull;* to
be rich, glorious
6286 pâ'ar (6), to *shake a
tree*
1392 *dŏxazō* (34), to
render, esteem glorious
1740 *ĕndŏxazō* (2), to
glorify
4888 *sundŏxazō* (1), to
share glory with

GLORIFIETH
3513 kâbad (1), to *be
rich, glorious*

GLORIFY
3513 kâbad (7), to *be
rich, glorious*
6286 pâ'ar (1), to *shake a
tree*
1392 *dŏxazō* (17), to
render, esteem glorious

GLORIFYING
1392 *dŏxazō* (3), to
render, esteem glorious

GLORIOUS
117 'addîyr (1), *powerful;
majestic*
142 'âdar (2),
magnificent; glorious
215 'ôwr (1), to *be
luminous*
1921 hâdar (1), to *favor
or honor;* to *be high* or
proud
1926 hâdâr (1),
magnificence
1935 hôwd (1), *grandeur,
majesty*
3513 kâbad (5), to *be
rich, glorious*
3519 kâbôwd (11),
splendor, wealth
3520 kᵉbûwddâh (1),
magnificence, wealth
6643 tsᵉbîy (5),
conspicuous splendor
8597 tiph'ârâh (3),
ornament
1223+1391 dia (1),
through, by means of
1391 *dŏxa* (6), *glory;
brilliance*
1392 *dŏxazō* (1), to
render, esteem glorious

1722+1391 ĕn (3), *in;
during; because of*
1741 *ĕndŏxŏs* (2),
splendid; noble

GLORIOUSLY
3519 kâbôwd (1),
splendor, copiousness

GLORY
155 'addereth (1), *large;
splendid*
1925 heder (1), *honor*
1926 hâdâr (7),
magnificence
1935 hôwd (9), *grandeur,
majesty*
1984 hâlal (12), to *shine,
flash, radiate*
2892 ṭôhar (1),
brightness; purification
3367 yᵉqâr (Ch.) (5),
glory, honor
3513 kâbad (1), to *be
rich, glorious*
3519 kâbôwd (155),
splendor, wealth
6286 pâ'ar (1), to *shake a
tree*
6643 tsᵉbîy (7),
conspicuous splendor
7623 shâbach (1), to
address; to pacify
8597 tiph'ârâh (22),
ornament
1391 *dŏxa* (146), *glory;
brilliance*
1392 *dŏxazō* (3), to
render, esteem glorious
2620 katakauchaŏmai
(1), to *exult against*
2744 *kauchaŏmai* (18),
to *glory in, rejoice in*
2745 *kauchēma* (3),
boast; brag
2746 *kauchēsis* (1),
boasting; bragging
2755 *kĕnŏdŏxŏs* (1),
self-conceited
2811 *klĕŏs* (1), *renown,
credited honor*

GLORYING
2744 *kauchaŏmai* (1), to
glory in, rejoice in
2745 *kauchēma* (2),
boast; brag
2746 *kauchēsis* (1),
boasting; bragging

GLUTTON
2151 zâlal (2), to *be loose*
morally, *worthless*

GLUTTONOUS
5314 phagŏs (2), *glutton*

GNASH
2786 châraq (2), to *grate,
grind* the teeth

GNASHED
2786 châraq (1), to *grate,
grind* the teeth
1031 bruchō (1), to *grate,
grind* teeth

GNASHETH
2786 châraq (2), to *grate,
grind* the teeth
5149 trizō (1), to *grate*
the teeth in frenzy

GNASHING
1030 brugmŏs (7),
grinding of teeth

GNAT
2971 kōnōps (1), *stinging
mosquito*

GNAW
1633 gâram (1), to
crunch the bones

GNAWED
3145 massaŏmai (1), to
chew, gnaw

GO
236 'ăzal (Ch.) (1), to
depart
258 'âchad (1), to *unify,*
i.e. *collect*
833 'âshar (2), to *go
forward; guide*
935 bôw' (154), to *go,
come*
1718 dâdâh (1), to *walk
gently; lead*
1869 dârak (2), to *tread,
trample;* to *walk, lead*
1946 hûwk (Ch.) (1), to
go, come
1961 hâyâh (2), to *exist,*
i.e. *be or become*
1980 hâlak (83), to *walk;
live a certain way*
1982 hêlek (1), *wayfarer,
visitor; flowing*
2498 châlaph (1), to
hasten away; to *pass* on
2559 châmaq (1), to
depart, i.e. turn about
3051 yâhab (4), to *give*
3212 yâlak (351), to *walk;
to live; to carry*
3312 Yᵉphunneh (1), *he
will be prepared*
3318 yâtsâ' (185), to *go,
bring out*
3381 yârad (73), to
descend
3518 kâbâh (1), to
extinguish
4161 môwtsâ' (1), *going
forth*
4609 ma'ălâh (1),
thought arising
4994 nâ' (2), *I pray!,
please!, I beg you!*
5066 nâgash (2), to *be,
come, bring near*
5181 nâchath (1), to *sink,
descend;* to *press* down
5186 nâṭâh (1), to *stretch
or spread out*
5265 nâça' (7), *start* on a
journey
5362 nâqaph (2), to
strike; to *surround*
5437 çâbab (7), to
surround
5472 çûwg (1), to *go
back,* to *retreat*
5493 çûwr (4), to *turn off*
5503 çâchar (1), to *travel*
round; to *palpitate*
5674 'âbar (51), to *cross*
over; to *transition*
5927 'âlâh (129), to
ascend, be high, mount
5930 'ôlâh (1), *sacrifice
wholly consumed in fire*
6213 'âsâh (1), to *do*

5562 chōrĕō (1), to *pass,
enter;* to *hold, admit*

GOG
1463 Gôwg (10), *Gog*
1136 Gôg (1), *Gog*

GOING
235 'âzal (1), to *disappear*
838 'âshshûwr (1), *step;
track*
935 bôw' (7), to *go or
come*
1980 hâlak (8), to *walk;
live a certain way*
3212 yâlak (5), to *walk;
to live; to carry*
3318 yâtsâ' (13), to *go,
bring out*
3381 yârad (3), to
descend
3996 mâbôw' (5),
entrance; sunset; west
4161 môwtsâ' (5), *going
forth*
4174 môwrâd (3),
descent, slope
4606 mê'al (Ch.) (1),
setting of the sun
4608 ma'âleh (9),
elevation; platform
5362 nâqaph (1), to
strike; to *surround*
5674 'âbar (2), to *cross
over;* to *transition*
5927 'âlâh (4), to *ascend,
be high, mount*
5944 'ălîyâh (2), *upper
things; second-story*
6807 tse'âdâh (2),
stepping *march*
7751 shûwṭ (2), to *travel,
roam*
8444 tôwtsâ'âh (1), *exit,
boundary; deliverance*
8582 tâ'âh (1), to
vacillate, reel or *stray*
71 agō (1), to *lead;* to
bring, drive; to *weigh*
305 anabainō (2), to *go
up, rise*
565 apérchŏmai (1), to
go off, i.e. *depart*
1330 diĕrchŏmai (1), to
traverse, travel through
1607 ĕkpŏrĕuŏmai (1), to
depart, be discharged
2212 zētĕō (1), to *seek*
2597 katabainō (1), to
descend
4105 planaō (1), to *roam,
wander;* to *deceive*
4108 planŏs (1), *roving,
impostor* or *misleader*
4198 pŏrĕuŏmai (1), to
go/come; to *travel*
4254 prŏagō (2), to *lead
forward;* to *precede*
4260 prŏbainō (1), to
advance
4281 prŏĕrchŏmai (1), to
go onward, precede
5217 hupagō (1), to
withdraw or *retire*

GOINGS
838 'âshshûwr (2), *step;
track*
1979 hălîykâh (2),
walking; procession

4161 môwtsâ' (4), *going
forth*
4163 môwtsâ'âh (1),
family *descent*
4570 ma'gâl (2), *circular
track* or camp *rampart*
4703 mits'âd (1), *step;
companionship*
6471 pa'am (1), *time;
step; occurence*
6806 tsa'ad (1), *pace* or
regular *step*
8444 tôwtsâ'âh (12), *exit,
boundary; deliverance*

GOLAN
1474 Gôwlân (4), *captive*

GOLD
1220 betser (2), *gold*
1222 betsar (1), *gold*
1722 dehab (Ch.) (14),
gold
2091 zâhâb (340), *gold,
golden colored*
2742 chârûwts (6),
mined *gold; trench*
3800 kethem (7), *pure
gold*
5458 çegôwr (1), *breast;
gold*
6337 pâz (9), *pure gold*
5552 chrusĕŏs (3), made
of *gold*
5553 chrusiŏn (9), *golden
thing*
5554 chrusŏdaktuliŏs
(1), *gold-ringed*
5557 chrusŏs (13), *gold;
golden article*

GOLDEN
1722 dehab (Ch.) (9), *gold*
2091 zâhâb (38), *gold,
golden colored*
3800 kethem (1), *pure
gold*
4062 madhêbâh (1), *gold
making*
5552 chrusĕŏs (15), made
of *gold*

GOLDSMITH
6884 tsâraph (3), to *fuse
metal;* to *refine*

GOLDSMITH'S
6885 Tsôrephîy (1), *refiner*

GOLDSMITHS
6884 tsâraph (2), to *fuse
metal;* to *refine*

GOLGOTHA
1115 Golgŏtha (3), *skull
knoll*

GOLIATH
1555 Golyath (6), *exile*

GOMER
1586 Gômer (6),
completion

GOMORRAH
6017 'Ămôrâh (19),
(ruined) *heap*
1116 Gŏmŏrrha (1),
ruined *heap*

GOMORRHA
1116 Gŏmŏrrha (4),
ruined *heap*

GONE
230 'âzad (Ch.) (2), *firm,
assured*

235 'âzal (2), to *disappear*
369 'ayin (4), *there is no,*
i.e., *not exist, none*
656 'âphêç (1), to *cease*
935 bôw' (10), to *go or
come*
1540 gâlâh (1), to
denude; uncover
1961 hâyâh (1), to *exist,*
i.e. *be* or *become*
1980 hâlak (22), to *walk;
live a certain way*
2114 zûwr (1), to *be
foreign, strange*
3212 yâlak (17), to *walk;
to live; to carry*
3318 yâtsâ' (31), to *go,
bring out*
3381 yârad (14), to
descend
4059 middad (1), *flight*
4161 môwtsâ' (2), *going
forth*
4185 mûwsh (1), to
withdraw
5128 nûwa' (1), to *waver*
5186 nâṭâh (1), to *stretch*
or *spread out*
5312 nephaq (Ch.) (1), to
issue forth; to *bring out*
5362 nâqaph (2), to
surround or *circulate*
5437 çâbab (1), to
surround
5472 çùwg (1), to *go
back,* to *retreat*
5493 çûwr (2), to *turn off*
5674 'âbar (6), to *cross
over;* to *transition*
5927 'âlâh (22), to
ascend, be high, mount
6805 tsâ'ad (1), to *pace,
step regularly*
7725 shûwb (2), to *turn
back;* to *return*
7751 shûwṭ (2), to *travel,
roam*
7847 sâṭâh (2), to *deviate*
from duty, *go astray*
8582 tâ'âh (2), to
vacillate, reel or *stray*
305 anabainō (2), to *go
up, rise*
402 anachōrĕō (1), to
retire, withdraw
565 apérchŏmai (4), to
go off, i.e. *depart*
576 apŏbainō (1), to
disembark
1276 diapĕraō (1), to
cross over
1330 diĕrchŏmai (4), to
traverse, travel through
1339 diïstēmi (1), to
remove, intervene
1525 ĕisĕrchŏmai (1), to
enter
1578 ĕkklinō (1), to *shun;*
to *decline*
1607 ĕkpŏrĕuŏmai (1), to
depart, proceed, project
1826 ĕxĕimi (1), *leave;
escape*
1831 ĕxĕrchŏmai (11), to
issue; to *leave*
3985 pĕirazō (1), to
endeavor, scrutinize
4105 planaō (2), to *roam,
wander*

4198 pŏrĕuŏmai (3), to
go, come; to *travel*
4260 prŏbainō (1), to
advance
4570 sbĕnnumi (1), to
extinguish, snuff out
5055 tĕlĕō (1), to *end,* i.e.
complete, execute

GOOD
1319 bâsar (7), to
announce (good news)
1390 Gib'âh (1), *hillock*
1580 gâmal (1), to *benefit*
or *requite;* to *wean*
2492 châlam (1), to *be,
make plump;* to *dream*
2617 cheçed (1),
kindness, favor
2623 châçîyd (1),
religiously *pious, godly*
2869 ṭâb (Ch.) (1), *good*
2895 ṭowb (6), to *be good*
2896 ṭôwb (363), *good;
well*
2898 ṭûwb (11), *good;
goodness; beauty,
gladness, welfare*
3190 yâṭab (20), to *be,
make well*
3191 yeṭab (Ch.) (1), to
be, make well
3276 yâ'al (1), to *be
valuable*
3474 yâshar (1), to *be
straight;* to *make right*
3788 kishrôwn (1),
success; advantage
3966 meôd (3), *very,
utterly*
5750 'ôwd (1), *again;
repeatedly; still; more*
6743 tsâlach (1), to *push
forward*
7368 râchaq (2), to
recede; remove
7522 râtsôwn (2), *delight*
7965 shâlôwm (1), *safe;
well; health, prosperity*
7999 shâlam (6), to *be
safe; be, make complete*
8232 shephar (Ch.) (1), to
be beautiful
14 agathŏĕrgĕō (1), to *do
good work*
15 agathŏpŏiĕō (6), to *be
a well-doer*
18 agathŏs (98), *good*
515 axiŏō (1), to *deem
entitled* or *fit, worthy*
865 aphilagathŏs (1),
hostile to virtue
979 biŏs (1), *livelihood;
property*
2095 ĕu (1), *well*
2097 ĕuaggĕlizō (2), to
announce good news
2106 ĕudŏkĕō (1), to
think well, i.e. *approve*
2107 ĕudŏkia (3),
delight, kindness, wish
2108 ĕuĕrgĕsia (1),
beneficence
2109 ĕuĕrgĕtĕō (1) to *be
philanthropic*
2133 ĕunŏia (1), *eagerly,
with a whole heart*
2140 ĕupŏiïa (1),
beneficence, doing good

2162 ĕuphēmia (1), *good repute*
2163 ĕuphēmŏs (1), *reputable*
2425 hikanŏs (1), *ample; fit*
2480 ischuō (1), *to have or exercise force*
2565 kalliĕlaiŏs (1), *cultivated olive*
2567 kalŏdidaskalŏs (1), *teacher of the right*
2570 kalŏs (78), *good; beautiful; valuable*
2573 kalŏs (3), *well*, i.e. *rightly*
2750 kĕiria (2), *swathe of cloth*
3112 makran (1), *at a distance, far away*
4851 sumphĕrō (1), *to collect; to conduce*
5358 philagathŏs (1), *promoter of virtue*
5542 chrēstŏlŏgia (1), *fair speech, plausibility*
5543 chrēstŏs (1), *employed,* i.e. *useful*
5544 chrēstŏtēs (1), *moral excellence*

GOODLIER
2896 ţôwb (1), *good; well*

GOODLIEST
2896 ţôwb (2), *good; well*

GOODLINESS
2617 cheçĕd (1), *kindness, favor*

GOODLY
117 'addîyr (1), *powerful; majestic*
145 'eder (1), *mantle; splendor*
155 'addereth (1), *large; splendid*
410 'êl (1), *mighty;* the *Almighty*
1926 hâdâr (1), *magnificence*
1935 hôwd (1), *grandeur, majesty*
2530 châmad (1), *to delight* in; *lust for*
2532 chemdâh (1), *delight*
2896 ţôwb (11), *good; well*
4261 machmâd (1), *delightful*
4758 mar'eh (1), *appearance; vision*
6287 pᵉ'êr (1), *fancy head-dress*
6643 tsᵉbîy (1), *conspicuous splendor*
7443 renen (1), *female ostrich*
8231 shâphar (1), *to be, make fair*
8233 shepher (1), *beauty*
2573 kalŏs (2), *well,* i.e. *rightly*
2986 lamprŏs (2), *radiant; magnificent*

GOODMAN
376 'îysh (1), *man; male; someone*
3611 ŏikĕō (5), *to reside, inhabit, remain*

GOODNESS
2617 cheçĕd (12), *kindness, favor*
2896 ţôwb (16), *good; well*
2898 ţûwb (13), *good; goodness; beauty*
19 agathōsunē (4), *virtue or beneficence*
5543 chrēstŏs (1), *employed,* i.e. *useful*
5544 chrēstŏtēs (4), *moral excellence*

GOODNESS'
2898 ţûwb (1), *good; goodness; beauty*

GOODS
202 'ôwn (1), *ability, power; wealth*
2428 chayil (2), *army; wealth; virtue; valor*
2896 ţôwb (2), *good; well*
2898 ţûwb (3), *good; goodness; beauty*
4399 mᵉlâ'kâh (2), *work; property*
5232 nᵉkaç (Ch.) (2), *treasure, riches*
7075 qinyân (2), *purchase, wealth*
7399 rᵉkûwsh (12), *property*
18 agathŏs (2), *good*
3776 ŏusia (1), *wealth, property, possessions*
4147 plŏutĕō (1), *to be, become wealthy*
4632 skĕuŏs (2), *vessel, implement, equipment*
4674 sŏs (1), *things that are yours*
5223 huparxis (1), *property, wealth*
5224 huparchŏnta (7), *property or possessions*

GOPHER
1613 gôpher (1), (poss.) *cypress*

GORE
5055 nâgach (1), *to butt with bull's horns*

GORED
5055 nâgach (2), *to butt with bull's horns*

GORGEOUS
2986 lamprŏs (1), *radiant; magnificent*

GORGEOUSLY
4358 miklôwl (1), *perfection; splendidly*
1741 ĕndŏxŏs (1), *splendid; noble*

GOSHEN
1657 Gôshen (15), *Goshen*

GOSPEL
2097 ĕuaggĕlizō (24), *to announce good news*
2098 ĕuaggĕliŏn (73), *good message*
4283 prŏĕuaggĕlizŏmai (1), *to announce glad news in advance*

GOSPEL'S
2098 ĕuaggĕliŏn (3), *good message*

GOT
3318 yâtsâ' (2), *to go, bring out*
3423 yârash (1), *to inherit; to impoverish*
7069 qânâh (3), *to create; to procure*
7408 râkash (1), *to lay up,* i.e. *collect*

GOTTEN
622 'âçaph (1), *to gather, collect*
3254 yâçaph (1), *to add or augment*
4069 maddûwa' (1), *why?, what?*
4672 mâtsâ' (2), *to find or acquire; to occur*
5414 nâthan (1), *to give*
6213 'âsâh (8), *to do or make*
7069 qânâh (1), *to create; to procure*
7408 râkash (3), *to lay up,* i.e. *collect*
645 apŏspaō (1), *unsheathe; withdraw*

GOURD
7021 qîyqâyôwn (5), *gourd plant*

GOURDS
6498 paqqû'âh (1), *wild cucumber*

GOVERN
2280 châbash (1), *to wrap firmly, bind*
5148 nâchâh (1), *to guide*
6213 'âsâh (1), *to do*

GOVERNMENT
4475 memshâlâh (1), *rule; realm* or a *ruler*
4951 misrâh (2), *empire*
2963 kuriŏtēs (1), *rulers, masters*

GOVERNMENTS
2941 kubĕrnēsis (1), *directorship*

GOVERNOR
441 'allûwph (1), *friend, one familiar; chieftain*
4910 mâshal (3), *to rule*
5057 nâgîyd (3), *commander, official*
5387 nâsîy' (1), *leader; rising mist, fog*
5921 'al (1), *above, over, upon,* or *against*
6346 pechâh (10), *prefect, officer*
6347 pechâh (Ch.) (6), *prefect, officer*
6485 pâqad (5), *to visit, care for, count*
7989 shallîyţ (1), *prince or warrior*
8269 sar (4), *head person, ruler*
755 architriklinŏs (2), *director of* the *entertainment*
1481 ĕthnarchēs (1), *governor of a district*
2116 ĕuthunō (1), *to straighten or level*
2230 hēgĕmŏnĕuō (3), *to act as ruler*

GOT
2232 hēgĕmōn (15), *chief person*
2233 hēgĕŏmai (2), *to lead,* i.e. *command*

GOVERNOR'S
2232 hēgĕmōn (1), *chief person*

GOVERNORS
441 'allûwph (2), *friend, one familiar; chieftain*
2710 châqaq (2), *to engrave; to enact* laws
4910 mâshal (1), *to rule*
5461 çâgân (5), *prfect of a province*
6346 pechâh (7), *prefect, officer*
8269 sar (2), *head person, ruler*
2232 hēgĕmōn (2), *chief person*
3623 ŏikŏnŏmŏs (1), *overseer, manager*

GOZAN
1470 Gôwzân (5), *quarry*

GRACE
2580 chên (37), *graciousness; beauty*
8467 tᵉchinnâh (1), *gracious entreaty, supplication*
2143 ĕuprĕpĕia (1), *gracefulness*
5485 charis (127), *gratitude; benefit given*

GRACIOUS
2580 chên (2), *graciousness; beauty*
2587 channûwn (14), *gracious*
2589 channôwth (1), *supplication*
2603 chânan (11), *to implore*
5485 charis (1), *gratitude; benefit given*
5543 chrēstŏs (1), *employed,* i.e. *useful*

GRACIOUSLY
2603 chânan (3), *to implore*
2896 ţôwb (1), *good; well*

GRAFF
1461 ĕgkĕntrizō (1), *to engraft*

GRAFFED
1461 ĕgkĕntrizō (5), *to engraft*

GRAIN
6872 tsᵉrôwr (1), *parcel; kernel or particle*
2848 kŏkkŏs (6), *kernel*

GRANDMOTHER
3125 mammē (1), *grandmother*

GRANT
5414 nâthan (12), *to give*
7558 rîshyôwn (1), *permit*
1325 didōmi (7), *to give*
2036 ĕpō (1), *to speak or say*

GRANTED
935 bôw' (1), *to go or come*
5414 nâthan (9), *to give*

6213 'âsâh (1), to *do or make*
1325 didŏmi (3), to *give*
5483 charizŏmai (1), to *grant as a favor*

GRAPE
1154 beçer (1), *immature, sour* grapes
1155 bôçer (3), *immature, sour* grapes
5563 çᵉmâdar (2), vine *blossom*
6025 'ênâb (1), *grape* cluster
6528 pereṭ (1), *stray or single* berry

GRAPEGATHERER
1219 bâtsar (1), to *gather* grapes

GRAPEGATHERERS
1219 bâtsar (2), to *gather* grapes

GRAPEGLEANINGS
5955 'ôlêlâh (1), *gleaning; gleaning-time*

GRAPES
891 bᵉ'ûshîym (2), *rotten fruit*
1154 beçer (1), *immature, sour* grapes
5563 çᵉmâdar (1), vine *blossom*
6025 'ênâb (15), *grape* cluster
4718 staphulē (3), *cluster* of grapes

GRASS
1758 dûwsh (1), to *trample* or *thresh*
1877 deshe' (7), *sprout; green grass*
1883 dethe' (Ch.) (2), *sprout; green grass*
2682 châtsîyr (17), *grass; leek* plant
3418 yereq (1), *green* grass or vegetation
6211 'âsh (5), *moth*
6212 'eseb (16), *grass, or any green, tender shoot*
5528 chŏrtŏs (12), *pasture, herbage*

GRASSHOPPER
697 'arbeh (1), *locust*
2284 châgâb (2), *locust*

GRASSHOPPERS
697 'arbeh (3), *locust*
1462 gôwb (2), *locust*
2284 châgâb (2), *locust*

GRATE
4345 makbêr (6), *grate, lattice*

GRAVE
1164 bᵉ'îy (1), *prayer*
6603 pittûwach (1), *sculpture; engraving*
6605 pâthach (3), to *open wide; to loosen, begin*
6900 qᵉbûwrâh (4), *sepulchre*
6913 qeber (19), *sepulchre*
7585 shᵉ'ôwl (30), abode of the *dead*
7845 shachath (1), *pit; destruction*

86 haⱼdēs (1), *Hades,* i.e. place of the dead
3419 mnēmĕiŏn (4), place of *interment*
4586 sĕmnŏs (3), *honorable, noble*

GRAVE'S
7585 shᵉ'ôwl (1), abode of the *dead*

GRAVECLOTHES
2750 kĕiria (1), *swathe of cloth*

GRAVED
6605 pâthach (2), to *loosen, plow, carve*

GRAVEL
2687 châtsâts (2), *gravel, grit*
4579 mê'âh (1), *belly*

GRAVEN
2672 châtsab (1), to *cut* stone or *carve* wood
2710 châqaq (1), to *engrave; to enact laws*
2790 chârash (1), to *engrave; to plow*
2801 chârath (1), to *engrave*
6456 pᵉçîyl (18), *idol*
6458 pâçal (1), to *carve, to chisel*
6459 peçel (29), *idol*
6605 pâthach (2), to *loosen, plow, carve*
5480 charagma (1), *mark, sculptured figure*

GRAVES
6913 qeber (16), *sepulchre*
3418 mnēma (1), *sepulchral monument*
3419 mnēmĕiŏn (4), *place of interment*

GRAVETH
2710 châqaq (1), to *engrave; to enact* laws

GRAVING
2747 chereṭ (1), *chisel; style* for writing
6603 pittûwach (2), *sculpture; engraving*

GRAVINGS
4734 miqla'ath (1), *bas-relief sculpture*

GRAVITY
4587 sĕmnŏtēs (2), *venerableness*

GRAY
7872 sêybâh (5), old *age*

GRAYHEADED
7867 sîyb (2), to *become* aged, i.e. to *grow gray*

GREASE
2459 cheleb (1), *fat; choice* part

GREAT
410 'êl (1), *mighty;* the *Almighty*
417 'elgâbîysh (3), *hail*
430 'ĕlôhîym (2), the true *God; gods; great ones*
679 'atstsîyl (1), *joint of* the hand

1004 bayith (1), *house; temple; family, tribe*
1167 ba'al (1), *master; husband; owner; citizen*
1241 bâqâr (1), *plowing* ox; *herd*
1396 gâbar (2), to *be strong; to prevail; to act insolently*
1419 gâdôwl (413), *great*
1420 gᵉdûwlâh (3), *greatness, grandeur*
1431 gâdal (33), to *be great, make great*
1432 gâdêl (2), *large, powerful*
1462 gôwb (1), *locust*
1560 gᵉlâl (Ch.) (2), *large* stones
2030 hâreh (1), *pregnant*
2342 chûwl (1), to *dance, whirl; to writhe in pain*
2750 chŏrîy (2), *burning* anger
3244 yanshûwph (2), *bird*
3514 kôbed (1), *weight, multitude, vehemence*
3515 kâbêd (8), *numerous; severe*
3699 kâçaç (1), to *estimate, determine*
3833 lâbîy' (3), *lion, lioness*
3966 mᵉ'ôd (11), *very, utterly*
4306 mâṭar (1), *rain, shower of rain*
4459 maltâ'âh (1), *grinder, molar tooth*
4766 marbeh (1), *increasing; greatness*
5006 nâ'ats (1), to *scorn*
6099 'âtsûwm (1), *powerful; numerous*
6105 'âtsam (1), to *be, make powerful*
6343 pachad (1), *sudden alarm, fear*
7091 qippôwz (1), *arrow-snake*
7227 rab (125), *great*
7229 rab (Ch.) (7), *great*
7230 rôb (7), *abundance*
7235 râbâh (9), to *increase*
7236 rᵉbâh (Ch.) (1), to *increase*
7239 ribbôw (1), *myriad, indefinite large number*
7260 rabrab (Ch.) (8), *huge; domineering*
7350 râchôwq (2), *remote, far*
7451 ra' (1), *bad; evil*
7689 saggîy' (1), *mighty*
7690 saggîy' (Ch.) (3), *large*
7991 shâlîysh (2), *officer;* of the *third* rank
8514 tal'ûwbâh (1), *desiccation*
1974 ĕpipŏthia (1), *intense longing*
2245 hēlikŏs (2), *how much, how great*
2425 hikanŏs (2), *ample; fit*
3029 lian (1), *very much*

3112 makran (1), *at a distance, far away*
3123 mallŏn (1), *in a greater degree*
3166 mĕgalauchĕō (1), to *be arrogant, egotistic*
3167 mĕgalĕiŏs (1), *great things, wonderful works*
3170 mĕgalunō (1), to *increase or extol*
3171 mĕgalōs (1), *much, greatly*
3173 mĕgas (149), *great, many*
3175 mĕgistanĕs (2), *great person*
3176 mĕgistŏs (1), *greatest or very great*
3745 hŏsŏs (6), *as much as*
3819 palai (1), *formerly; sometime since*
3827 pampŏlus (1), *full many,* i.e. *immense*
4080 pēlikŏs (1), *how much, how great*
4118 plĕistŏs (1), *largest number or very large*
4183 pŏlus (60), *much, many*
4185 pŏlutĕlēs (2), *extremely expensive*
4186 pŏlutimŏs (1), *extremely valuable*
4214 pŏsŏs (1), *how much?; how much!*
5082 tēlikŏutŏs (3), *so vast*
5118 tŏsŏutŏs (5), *such great*
5246 hupĕrŏgkŏs (2), *insolent, boastful*

GREATER
1419 gâdôwl (20), *great*
1431 gâdal (3), to *be great, make great*
1980 hâlak (1), to *walk; live a certain way*
7227 rab (4), *great*
7235 râbâh (2), to *increase*
3186 mĕizŏtĕrŏs (1), *still larger, greater*
3187 mĕizŏn (34), *larger, greater*
4055 pĕrissŏtĕrŏs (3), *more superabundant*
4119 plĕiŏn (6), *more*

GREATEST
1419 gâdôwl (9), *great*
4768 marbîyth (1), *multitude; offspring*
3173 mĕgas (2), *great, many*
3187 mĕizŏn (9), *larger, greater*

GREATLY
3966 mᵉ'ôd (49), *very, utterly*
7227 rab (3), *great*
7230 rôb (1), *abundance*
7690 saggîy' (Ch.) (1), *large*
1568 ĕkthambĕō (1), to *astonish utterly*
1569 ĕkthambŏs (1), *utterly astounded*

GRISLED
1261 bârôd (4), *spotted, dappled*

GROAN
584 'ânach (1), to *sigh, moan*
602 'ânaq (1), to *shriek, cry out in groaning*
5008 nâ'aq (2), to *groan*
4727 stěnazō (3), to *sigh, murmur, pray* inaudibly

GROANED
1690 ĕmbrimaŏmai (1), to *blame,* to *sigh*

GROANETH
4959 sustēnazō (1), to *moan jointly*

GROANING
585 'ânâchâh (4), *sighing, moaning*
603 'ănâqâh (1), *shrieking, groaning*
5009 nᵉ'âqâh (2), *groaning*
1690 ĕmbrimaŏmai (1), to *blame,* to *sigh*
4726 stěnagmŏs (1), *sigh, groan*

GROANINGS
5009 nᵉ'âqâh (2), *groaning*
4726 stěnagmŏs (1), *sigh, groan*

GROPE
1659 gâshash (2), to *feel about, grope* around
4959 mâshash (3), to *feel of;* to *grope*

GROPETH
4959 mâshash (1), to *feel of;* to *grope*

GROSS
6205 'ărâphel (2), *gloom, darkness*
3975 pachunō (2), to *fatten;* to *render callous*

GROUND
127 'ădâmâh (44), *soil; land*
776 'erets (97), *earth, land, soil; country*
2513 chelqâh (1), *smoothness; allotment*
2758 chârîysh (1), *plowing (season)*
2912 țâchan (3), to *grind flour meal*
6083 'âphâr (1), *dust, earth, mud; clay*
7383 rîyphâh (1), *grits cereal*
7704 sâdeh (4), *field*
68 agrŏs (1), *farmland, countryside*
1093 gē (18), *soil, region, whole earth*
1474 ĕdaphizō (1), to *raze, dash to the ground*
1475 ĕdaphŏs (1), *soil, ground*
1477 hĕdraiōma (1), *basis, foundation*
5476 chamai (2), *toward the ground*
5561 chōra (1), *space of territory*

5564 chōriŏn (1), *spot or plot* of ground

GROUNDED
4145 mûwçâdâh (1), *foundation*
2311 thĕmĕliŏō (2), to *erect;* to *consolidate*

GROVE
815 'êshel (1), *tamarisk tree*
842 'ăshêrâh (16), *happy; Astarte (goddess)*

GROVES
842 'ăshêrâh (24), *happy; Astarte (goddess)*

GROW
1342 gâ'âh (1), to *rise;* to *grow tall; be majestic*
1431 gâdal (2), to *be great, make great*
1711 dâgâh (1), to *become numerous*
3212 yâlak (1), to *walk;* to *live;* to *carry*
3318 yâtsâ' (1), to *go, bring out*
5599 çâphîyach (2), *self-sown crop; freshet*
5927 'âlâh (2), to *ascend, be high, mount*
6335 pûwsh (1), to *spread;* to *act proudly*
6509 pârâh (1), to *bear fruit*
6524 pârach (2), to *break forth;* to *bloom; flourish*
6779 tsâmach (9), to *sprout*
7235 râbâh (1), to *increase*
7680 sᵉgâ' (Ch.) (1), to *increase*
7685 sâgâh (1), to *enlarge, be prosperous*
7735 sûwg (1), to *hedge in, make grow*
7971 shâlach (1), to *send away*
837 auxanō (5), to *grow, i.e. enlarge*
1096 ginŏmai (2), to *be, become*
3373 mēkunō (1), to *enlarge, grow long*
4886 sundĕsmŏs (1), *ligament; control*

GROWETH
2498 châlaph (2), to *spring up;* to *change*
2583 chânâh (1), to *encamp*
3332 yâtsaq (1), to *pour out*
5599 çâphîyach (3), *self-sown crop; freshet*
5927 'âlâh (1), to *ascend, be high, mount*
6524 pârach (1), to *break forth;* to *bloom; flourish*
6779 tsâmach (1), to *sprout*
8025 shâlaph (1), to *pull out, up or off*
305 anabainō (1), to *go up, rise*
837 auxanō (1), to *grow, i.e. enlarge*

5232 hupĕrauxanō (1), to *increase above*

GROWN
648 'âphîyl (1), *unripe*
1431 gâdal (9), to *be great, make great*
5927 'âlâh (1), to *ascend, be high, mount*
6335 pûwsh (1), to *spread;* to *act proudly*
6779 tsâmach (4), to *sprout*
6965 qûwm (2), to *rise*
7236 rᵉbâh (Ch.) (3), to *increase*
837 auxanō (1), to *grow, i.e. enlarge*

GROWTH
3954 leqesh (2), *after crop, second crop*

GRUDGE
3885 lûwn (1), to *be obstinate*
5201 nâțar (1), to *guard;* to *cherish anger*
4727 stěnazō (1), to *sigh, murmur, pray* inaudibly

GRUDGING
1112 gŏggusmŏs (1), *grumbling*

GRUDGINGLY
1537+3077 ĕk (1), *out, out of*

GUARD
2876 țabbâch (29), *king's guard, executioner*
2877 țabbâch (Ch.) (1), *king's guard, executioner*
4928 mishma'ath (2), *royal court; subject*
4929 mishmâr (3), *guard; deposit; usage; example*
7323 rûwts (14), to *run*
4759 stratŏpĕdarchēs (1), *military commander*

GUARD'S
2876 țabbâch (1), *king's guard, executioner*

GUDGODAH
1412 Gudgôdâh (2), *cleft*

GUEST
2647 kataluō (1), to *halt for the night*

GUESTCHAMBER
2646 kataluma (2), *lodging-place*

GUESTS
7121 qârâ' (4), to *call out*
345 anakĕimai (2), to *recline at a meal*

GUIDE
441 'allûwph (4), *friend, one familiar; leader*
833 'âshar (1), to *go forward; guide*
1869 dârak (1), to *tread, trample;* to *walk, lead*
3289 yâ'ats (1), to *advise*
3557 kûwl (1), to *keep in;* to *measure*
5090 nâhag (1), to *drive forth;* to *lead*
5095 nâhal (3), to *flow;* to *conduct;* to *protect*

5148 nâchâh (4), to *guide*
7101 qâtsîyn (1), *magistrate, leader*
2720 katĕuthunō (1), to *direct, lead, direct*
3594 hŏdĕgĕō (2), to *show the way, guide*
3595 hŏdĕgŏs (2), *conductor, guide*
3616 ŏikŏdĕspŏtĕō (1), to *be the head of a family*

GUIDED
5090 nâhag (1), to *drive forth;* to *lead*
5095 nâhal (2), to *flow;* to *conduct;* to *protect*
5148 nâchâh (2), to *guide*

GUIDES
3595 hŏdĕgŏs (2), *conductor, guide*

GUILE
4820 mirmâh (2), *fraud*
6195 'ormâh (1), *trickery; discretion*
7423 rᵉmîyâh (1), *remissness; treachery*
1388 dŏlŏs (7), *wile, deceit, trickery*

GUILTINESS
817 'âshâm (1), *guilt; fault; sin-offering*

GUILTLESS
5352 nâqâh (5), to *be, make clean; to be bare*
5355 nâqîy (4), *innocent*
338 anaitiŏs (1), *innocent*

GUILTY
816 'âsham (16), to *be guilty; to be punished*
7563 râshâ' (1), *morally wrong; bad person*
1777 ĕnŏchŏs (4), *liable*
3784 ŏphĕilō (1), to *owe; to be under obligation*
5267 hupŏdikŏs (1), *under sentence*

GULF
5490 chasma (1), *chasm or vacancy*

GUNI
1476 Gûwnîy (4), *protected*

GUNITES
1477 Gûwnîy (1), *Gunite*

GUR
1483 Gûwr (1), *cub*

GUR-BAAL
1485 Gûwr-Ba'al (1), *dwelling of Baal*

GUSH
5140 nâzal (1), to *drip, or shed by trickling*

GUSHED
2100 zûwb (3), to *flow freely, gush*
8210 shâphak (1), to *spill forth;* to *expend*
1632 ĕkchĕō (1), to *pour forth;* to *bestow*

GUTTER
6794 tsinnûwr (1), *culvert, water-shaft*

GUTTERS
7298 rahaṭ (2), *ringlet of hair*

HA
1889 he'âch (1), *aha!*

HAAHASHTARI
326 'ăchashtârîy (1), *courier*

HABAIAH
2252 Chăbayâh (2), *Jehovah has hidden*

HABAKKUK
2265 Chăbaqqûwq (2), *embrace*

HABAZINIAH
2262 Chăbatstsanyâh (1), *Chabatstsanjah*

HABERGEON
8302 shiryôwn (1), *corslet, coat of mail*
8473 tachărâ' (2), *linen corslet*

HABERGEONS
8302 shiryôwn (2), *corslet, coat of mail*

HABITABLE
8398 têbêl (1), *earth; world; inhabitants*

HABITATION
1628 gêrûwth (1), *(temporary) residence*
2073 zᵉbûwl (3), *residence, dwelling*
2918 ṭîyrâh (1), *fortress; hamlet*
3427 yâshab (3), to *dwell, to remain; to settle*
4186 môwshâb (4), *seat; site; abode*
4349 mâkôwn (2), *basis; place*
4351 mᵉkûwrâh (1), *origin*
4583 mâ'ôwn (9), *retreat or asylum dwelling*
4907 mishkan (Ch.) (1), *residence*
4908 mishkân (3), *residence*
5115 nâvâh (1), to *rest as at home*
5116 nâveh (21), *at home; lovely; home*
7931 shâkan (1), to *reside*
7932 shᵉkan (Ch.) (1), to *reside*
7933 sheken (1), *residence*
1886 ĕpaulis (1), *dwelling,residence*
2732 katŏikētēriŏn (2), *dwelling-place, home*
2733 katŏikia (1), *residence, dwelling*
3613 ŏikētēriŏn (1), *residence, home*

HABITATIONS
4186 môwshâb (8), *seat; site; abode*
4380 mᵉkêrâh (1), *stabbing-sword*
4583 mâ'ôwn (1), *retreat or asylum dwelling*
4585 mᵉ'ôwnâh (1), *abode*
4908 mishkân (2), *residence*

HA

GUTTERS

HADAD

HADAD

4999 nâ'âh (5), *home, dwelling; pasture*
5116 nâveh (1), *at home; lovely; home*
4638 skēnōma (1), *dwelling*: the *Temple*

HABOR
2249 Châbôwr (3), *united*

HACHALIAH
2446 Chăkalyâh (2), *darkness (of) Jehovah*

HACHILAH
2444 Chakîylâh (3), *dark*

HACHMONI
2453 Chakmôwnîy (1), *skillful*

HACHMONITE
2453 Chakmôwnîy (1), *skillful*

HAD
935 bôw' (1), to *go, come*
1961 hâyâh (104), to *exist*, i.e. *be or become*
2370 chăzâ' (Ch.) (1), to *gaze* upon; to *dream*
3426 yêsh (5), *there is*
3884 lûwlê' (1), *if not*
7760 sûwm (1), to *put*
1096 ginŏmai (1), to *be, become*
1510 ĕimi (8), I *exist*, I *am*
1746 ĕnduō (1), to *dress*
2192 ĕchō (106), to *have*
2722 katĕchō (1), to *hold down fast*
2983 lambanō (2), to *take, receive*
3844 para (1), *from; with; besides; on account of*
5607 ŏn (1), *being, existence*

HADAD
1908 Hădad (13), *Hadad*
2301 Chădad (1), *fierce*

HADADEZER
1909 Hădad'ezer (9), *Hadad (is his) help*

HADADRIMMON
1910 Hădadrimmôwn (1), *Hadad-Rimmon*

HADAR
1924 Hădar (2), *magnificence*

HADAREZER
1928 Hădar'ezer (12), *Hadad is his help*

HADASHAH
2322 Chădâshâh (1), *new*

HADASSAH
1919 Hădaççâh (1), *Esther*

HADATTAH
2675 Châtsôwr Chădattâh (1), *new village*

HADID
2307 Châdîyd (3), *peak*

HADLAI
2311 Chadlay (1), *idle*

HADORAM
1913 Hădôwrâm (4), *Hadoram*

HADRACH
2317 Chadrâk (1), *Syrian deity*

HAFT
5325 nitstsâb (1), *handle of a sword or dagger*

HAGAB
2285 Châgâb (1), *locust*

HAGABA
2286 Chăgâbâ' (1), *locust*

HAGABAH
2286 Chăgâbâ' (1), *locust*

HAGAR
1904 Hâgâr (12), *Hagar*

HAGARENES
1905 Hagrîy (1), *Hagrite*

HAGARITES
1905 Hagrîy (3), *Hagrite*

HAGERITE
1905 Hagrîy (1), *Hagrite*

HAGGAI
2292 Chaggay (11), *festive*

HAGGERI
1905 Hagrîy (1), *Hagrite*

HAGGI
2291 Chaggîy (2), *festive*

HAGGIAH
2293 Chaggîyâh (1), *festival of Jehovah*

HAGGITES
2291 Chaggîy (1), *festive*

HAGGITH
2294 Chaggîyîth (5), *festive*

HAI
5857 'Ay (2), *ruin*

HAIL
1258 bârad (1), to *rain hail*
1259 bârâd (26), *hail, hailstones*
5463 chairō (6), *salutation, "be well"*
5464 chalaza (4), *frozen ice crystals*, i.e. *hail*

HAILSTONES
68+417 'eben (3), *stone*
68+1259 'eben (2), *stone*

HAIR
1803 dallâh (1), *loose thread; loose hair*
4748 miqsheh (1), *curl of beautiful tresses*
4803 mâraṭ (2), to *polish; to make bald*
5145 nezer (1), *set apart; royal chaplet*
8177 sᵉ'ar (Ch.) (2), *hair*
8181 sê'âr (23), *tossed hair*
8185 sa'ărâh (5), *hairiness*
2359 thrix (9), *hair; single hair*
2863 kŏmaō (2), to *wear long hair*
2864 kŏmē (1), *long hair*
4117 plĕgma (1), *plait or braid of hair*
5155 trichinŏs (1), *made of hair*

HAIRS
8177 sᵉ'ar (Ch.) (1), *hair*
8181 sê'âr (1), *tossed hair*
8185 sa'ărâh (2), *hairiness*
2359 thrix (5), *hair*

HAIRY
1167+8181 ba'al (1), *master; owner; citizen*
8163 sâ'îyr (2), *shaggy; he-goat; goat idol*
8181 sê'âr (2), *tossed hair*

HAKKATAN
6997 Qâṭân (1), *small*

HAKKOZ
6976 Qôwts (1), *thorns*

HAKUPHA
2709 Chăqûwphâ' (2), to *bend, crooked*

HALAH
2477 Chălach (3), *Chalach*

HALAK
2510 Châlâq (2), *bare*

HALE
2694 katasurō (1), to *arrest* judicially

HALF
1235 beqa' (1), *half shekel*
2673 châtsâh (1), to *cut or split in two; to halve*
2677 chêtsîy (106), *half or middle, midst*
4275 mechĕtsâh (1), *halving, half*
4276 machătsîyth (14), *halving* or the *middle*
8432 tâvek (1), *center, middle*
2253 hēmithanēs (1), *entirely exhausted*
2255 hēmisu (5), *half*
2256 hēmiŏriŏn (1), *half-hour*

HALHUL
2478 Chalchûwl (1), *contorted*

HALI
2482 Chălîy (1), *polished trinket, ornament*

HALING
4951 surō (1), to *trail, drag, sweep*

HALL
833 aulē (2), *palace; house; courtyard*
4232 praitōriŏn (6), *governor's court-room*

HALLOHESH
3873 Lôwchêsh (1), *enchanter*

HALLOW
6942 qâdâsh (15), to *be, make clean*

HALLOWED
4720 miqdâsh (1), *sanctuary of deity*
6942 qâdâsh (10), to *be, make clean*
6944 qôdesh (9), *sacred place or thing*
37 hagiazō (2), to *purify or consecrate*

HALOHESH
3873 Lôwchêsh (1), *enchanter*

HALT
6452 pâcach (1), *to hop, skip over; to hesitate*
6761 tsela' (1), *limping*
5560 chôlôs (4), *limping, crippled*

HALTED
6761 tsela' (2), *limping*

HALTETH
6761 tsela' (2), *limping*

HALTING
6761 tsela' (1), *limping*

HAM
1990 Hâm (1), *Ham*
2526 Châm (16), *hot*

HAMAN
2001 Hâmân (50), *Haman*

HAMAN'S
2001 Hâmân (3), *Haman*

HAMATH
2574 Chămâth (33), *walled*
2579 Chămath Rabbâh (1), *walled of Rabbah*

HAMATH-ZOBAH
2578 Chămath Tsôwbâh (1), *walled of Tsobah*

HAMATHITE
2577 Chămâthîy (2), *Chamathite*

HAMMATH
2575 Chammath (1), *hot springs*

HAMMEDATHA
4099 Mᵉdâthâ (5), *Medatha*

HAMMELECH
4429 Melek (2), *king*

HAMMER
1989 halmûwth (1), *hammer or mallet*
4717 maqqâbâh (1), *hammer*
4718 maqqebeth (1), *hammer*
6360 paṭṭîysh (3), *hammer which pounds*

HAMMERS
3597 kêylaph (1), *club or sledge-hammer*
4717 maqqâbâh (2), *hammer*

HAMMOLEKETH
4447 Môleketh (1), *queen*

HAMMON
2540 Chammôwn (2), *warm spring*

HAMMOTH-DOR
2576 Chammôth Dô'r (1), *hot springs of Dor*

HAMON-GOG
1996 Hămôwn Gôwg (2), *multitude of Gog*

HAMONAH
1997 Hămôwnâh (1), *multitude*

HAMOR
2544 Chămôwr (12), male donkey or *ass*

HAMOR'S
2544 Chămôwr (1), male donkey or *ass*

HAMUEL
2536 Chammûw'êl (1), *anger of God*

HAMUL
2538 Châmûwl (3), *pitied*

HAMULITES
2539 Chămûwlîy (1), *Chamulite*

HAMUTAL
2537 Chămûwṭal (3), *father-in-law of dew*

HANAMEEL
2601 Chănam'êl (4), *God has favored*

HANAN
2605 Chânân (12), *favor*

HANANEEL
2606 Chănan'êl (4), *God has favored*

HANANI
2607 Chănânîy (11), *gracious*

HANANIAH
2608 Chănanyâh (29), *Jehovah has favored*

HAND
405 'ekeph (1), *stroke, blow*
854 'êth (1), *with; by; at; among*
2026 hârag (1), *to kill, slaughter*
2651 chôphen (1), *pair of fists*
2947 ṭephach (1), *palm-breadth*
2948 ṭôphach (4), *palm-breadth*
3027 yâd (1086), *hand; power*
3028 yad (Ch.) (12), *hand; power*
3079 Yᵉhôwyâqîym (2), *Jehovah will raise*
3221 yâm (Ch.) (1), *sea; basin; west*
3225 yâmîyn (87), *right; south*
3227 yᵉmîynîy (1), *right*
3235 yâmar (1), *to exchange*
3325 Yitshârîy (1), *Jitsharite*
3709 kaph (52), hollow of *hand; paw; sole of foot*
4672 mâtsâ' (1), *to find or acquire; to occur*
7126 qârab (4), *to approach, bring near*
7138 qârôwb (5), *near, close*
8040 sᵉmô'wl (14), *north; left hand*
8041 sâma'l (1), *to use the left hand or go left*
8042 sᵉmâ'lîy (2), *on the left side; northern*
1448 ěggizō (9), *to approach*
1451 ěggus (6), *near, close*
1764 ěnistēmi (1), *to be present*

2021 ěpichěirěō (1), *to undertake, try*
2186 ěphistēmi (1), *to be present; to approach*
5495 chěir (87), *hand*
5496 chěiragōgěō (2), *to guide a blind person by the hand*
5497 chěiragōgŏs (1), *conductor* of a blind *person by the hand*

HANDBREADTH
2947 ṭephach (2), *palm-breadth*
2948 ṭôphach (1), *palm-breadth*

HANDED
3027 yâd (1), *hand; power*

HANDFUL
4390+3709 mâlê' (3), *to fill; be full*
4393+7062 mᵉlô' (2), *fulness*
5995 'âmîyr (1), *bunch of cereal new-cut grain*
6451 piççâh (1), *abundance*
7061 qâmats (1), *to grasp a handful*
7062 qômets (1), *handful; abundance*

HANDFULS
4393+2651 mᵉlô' (1), *fulness*
6653 tsebeth (1), *lock of stalks, bundle of grain*
7062 qômets (1), *handful; abundance*
8168 shô'al (2), *palm of hand; handful*

HANDKERCHIEFS
4676 sŏudariŏn (1), *towel*

HANDLE
270 'âchaz (1), *to seize, grasp; possess*
4184 mûwsh (1), *to touch, feel*
4900 mâshak (1), *to draw out; to be tall*
6186 'ârak (1), *to set in a row, i.e. arrange,*
8610 tâphas (5), *to manipulate, i.e. seize*
2345 thigganō (1), *to touch*
5584 psēlaphaō (1), *to manipulate*

HANDLED
8610+3709 tâphas (1), *to manipulate, i.e. seize*
821 atimŏō (1), *to maltreat, disgrace*
5584 psēlaphaō (1), *to manipulate*

HANDLES
3709 kaph (1), hollow of *hand; paw; sole of foot*

HANDLETH
5921 'al (1), *above, over, upon, or against*
8610 tâphas (2), *to manipulate, i.e. seize*

HANDLING
8610 tâphas (1), *to manipulate, i.e. seize*

1389 dŏlŏō (1), *to adulterate, falsify*

HANDMAID
519 'âmâh (22), *female servant or slave*
8198 shiphchâh (22), household *female slave*
1399 dŏulē (1), *female slave*

HANDMAIDEN
1399 dŏulē (1), *female slave*

HANDMAIDENS
8198 shiphchâh (2), household *female slave*
1399 dŏulē (1), *female slave*

HANDMAIDS
519 'âmâh (1), *female servant or slave*
8198 shiphchâh (7), household *female slave*

HANDS
2651 chôphen (3), pair of *fists*
3027 yâd (274), *hand; power*
3028 yad (Ch.) (4), *hand; power*
3709 kaph (67), hollow of *hand; paw; sole of foot*
849 autŏchěir (1), *self-handed, personally*
886 achěirŏpŏiētŏs (3), *unmanufactured*
2902 kratěō (2), *to seize*
4084 piazō (1), *to seize, arrest, or capture*
4475 rhapisma (1), *slap, strike*
5495 chěir (90), *hand*
5499 chěirŏpŏiētŏs (6), *of human construction*

HANDSTAVES
4731+3027 maqqêl (1), *shoot; stick; staff*

HANDWRITING
5498 chěirŏgraphŏn (1), *document or bond*

HANDYWORK
4639+3027 ma'ăseh (1), *action; labor*

HANES
2609 Chânêç (1), *Chanes*

HANG
3363 yâqa' (2), *to be dislocated; to impale*
3381 yârad (1), *to descend*
5414 nâthan (3), *to give*
5628 çârach (2), *to extend even to excess*
8511 tâlâ' (1), *to suspend; to be uncertain*
8518 tâlâh (7), *to suspend, hang*
2910 krěmannumi (2), *to hang*
3935 pariēmi (1), *to neglect; to be weakened*

HANGED
2614 chânaq (1), *choke oneself*
3363 yâqa' (2), *to be dislocated; to impale*

4223 m°châ' (Ch.) (1), to strike; to impale
8511 tâlâ' (1), to suspend; to be uncertain
8518 tâlâh (18), to suspend, hang
519 apagchŏmai (1), to strangle oneself
2910 krĕmannumi (4), to hang
4029 pĕrikĕimai (2), to enclose, encircle

HANGETH
8518 tâlâh (1), to suspend, hang
2910 krĕmannumi (1), to hang

HANGING
4539 mâçâk (17), veil; shield
8518 tâlâh (1), to suspend, hang

HANGINGS
1004 bayith (1), house; temple; family, tribe
7050 qela' (15), slinging weapon; door screen

HANIEL
2592 Chănnîy'êl (1), favor of God

HANNAH
2584 Channâh (13), favored

HANNATHON
2615 Channâthôn (1), favored

HANNIEL
2592 Chănnîy'êl (1), favor of God

HANOCH
2585 Chănôwk (5), initiated

HANOCHITES
2599 Chănôkîy (1), Chanokite

HANUN
2586 Chânûwn (11), favored

HAP
4745 miqreh (1), accident or fortune

HAPHRAIM
2663 Chăphârayîm (1), double pit

HAPLY
3863 lûw' (1), if; would that!
686 ara (2), then, so, therefore
3379 mĕpŏtĕ (2), not ever; if, or lest ever
3381 mĕpôs (1), lest somehow

HAPPEN
579 'ânâh (1), to meet, to happen
7136 qârâh (2), to bring about; to impose
4819 sumbainō (1), to concur, happen

HAPPENED
1961 hâyâh (1), to exist, i.e. be or become

7122 qârâ' (2), to encounter, to happen
7136 qârâh (2), to bring about; to impose
1096 ginŏmai (1), to be, become
4819 sumbainō (5), to concur, happen

HAPPENETH
4745 miqreh (1), accident or fortune
5060 nâga' (2), to strike
7136 qârâh (3), to bring about; to impose

HAPPIER
3107 makariŏs (1), fortunate, well off

HAPPY
833 'âshar (2), to be honest, prosper
835 'esher (16), how happy!
837 'ôsher (1), happiness, blessedness
7951 shâlâh (1), to be tranquil, i.e. secure
3106 makarizō (1), to esteem fortunate
3107 makariŏs (5), fortunate, well off

HARA
2024 Hârâ' (1), mountainousness

HARADAH
2732 Chărâdâh (2), fear, anxiety

HARAN
2039 Hârân (1), mountaineer
2309 chedel (6), state of the dead, deceased
2771 Chârân (12), parched

HARARITE
2043 Hărârîy (5), mountaineer

HARBONA
2726 Charbôwnâ' (1), Charbona, Charbonah

HARBONAH
2726 Charbôwnâ' (1), Charbona, Charbonah

HARD
280 'ăchîydâh (Ch.) (1), enigma
386 'êythân (1), never-failing; eternal
681 'êtsel (1), side; near
1692 dâbaq (4), to cling or adhere; to catch
2420 chîydâh (2), puzzle; conundrum; maxim
3332 yâtsaq (1), to pour out
3515 kâbêd (2), severe, difficult, stupid
5066 nâgash (1), to be, come, bring near
5221 nâkâh (1), to strike, kill
5564 çâmak (1), to lean upon; take hold of
5980 'ummâh (1), near, beside, along with
6277 'âthâq (1), impudent

6381 pâlâ' (5), to be, make great, difficult
7185 qâshâh (5), to be tough or severe
7186 qâsheh (6), severe
1421 dusĕrmĕnĕutŏs (1), difficult to explain
1422 duskŏlŏs (1), impracticable, difficult
1425 dusnŏētŏs (1), difficult of perception
4642 sklērŏs (5), hard or tough; harsh, severe
4927 sunŏmŏrĕō (1), to border together

HARDEN
533 'ammîyts (1), strong; mighty; brave
2388 châzaq (4), to be obstinate; to bind
5513 Çîynîy (1), Sinite
5539 çâlad (1), to leap with joy
7185 qâshâh (2), to be tough or severe
4645 sklērunō (3), to indurate, be stubborn

HARDENED
553 'âmats (1), to be strong; be courageous
2388 châzaq (9), to be obstinate; to bind
3513 kâbad (4), to be heavy, severe, dull
3515 kâbêd (3), severe, difficult, stupid
7185 qâshâh (8), to be tough or severe
7188 qâshach (2), to be, make unfeeling
8631 tᵉqêph (Ch.) (1), to be obstinate
4456 pōrŏō (3), to render stupid or callous
4645 sklērunō (2), to indurate, be stubborn

HARDENETH
5810 'âzaz (1), to be stout; be bold
7185 qâshâh (2), to be tough or severe
4645 sklērunō (1), to indurate, be stubborn

HARDER
2388 châzaq (1), to be obstinate; to bind
2389 châzâq (1), strong; severe, hard, violent

HARDHEARTED
7186+3820 qâsheh (1), severe

HARDLY
6031 'ânâh (1), to afflict, be afflicted
7185 qâshâh (2), to be tough or severe
1423 duskŏlōs (3), impracticably, with difficulty
3425 mŏgis (1), with difficulty
3433 mŏlis (1), with difficulty

HARDNESS
4165 mûwtsâq (1), casting of metal

2553 kakŏpathĕō (1), to undergo hardship
4457 pōrōsis (1), stupidity or callousness
4641 sklērŏkardia (3), hard-heartedness
4643 sklērŏtēs (1), stubbornness

HARE
768 'arnebeth (2), hare, rabbit

HAREPH
2780 Chârêph (1), reproachful

HARETH
2802 Chereth (1), forest

HARHAIAH
2736 Charhăyâh (1), fearing Jehovah

HARHAS
2745 Charchaç (1), sun

HARHUR
2744 Charchûwr (2), inflammation

HARIM
2766 Chârîm (11), snub-nosed

HARIPH
2756 Chârîyph (2), autumnal

HARLOT
2181 zânâh (33), to commit adultery
6948 qᵉdêshâh (3), sacred female prostitute
4204 pŏrnē (4), strumpet, i.e. prostitute; idolater

HARLOT'S
2181 zânâh (2), to commit adultery

HARLOTS
2181 zânâh (2), to commit adultery
6948 qᵉdêshâh (1), sacred female prostitute
4204 pŏrnē (4), strumpet, i.e. prostitute; idolater

HARLOTS'
2181 zânâh (1), to commit adultery

HARM
1697+7451 dâbâr (1), word; matter; thing
2398 châţâ' (1), to sin
3415 yâra' (1), to fear
7451 ra' (4), bad; evil
7489 râ'a' (3), to make, be good for nothing
824 atŏpŏs (1), improper; injurious; wicked
2556 kakŏs (2), bad, evil, wrong
2559 kakŏō (1), to injure; to oppress; to embitter
4190 pŏnērŏs (1), malice, wicked, bad; crime
5196 hubris (1), insult; injury

HARMLESS
172 akakŏs (1), innocent, blameless

185 akĕraiŏs (2), *innocent*

HARNEPHER
2774 Charnepher (1), *Charnepher*

HARNESS
631 'âçar (1), to *fasten*; to *join* battle
5402 nesheq (1), military *arms, arsenal*
8302 shiryôwn (2), *corslet, coat of mail*

HARNESSED
2571 châmûsh (1), able-bodied *soldiers*

HAROD
5878 'Êyn Chărôd (1), *fountain of trembling*

HARODITE
2733 Chărôdîy (1), *Charodite*

HAROEH
7204 Rô'êh (1), *seer*

HARORITE
2033 Hărôwrîy (1), *mountaineer*

HAROSHETH
2800 Chărôsheth (3), skilled *worker*

HARP
3658 kinnôwr (25), *harp*
7030 qîythârôç (Ch.) (4), *lyre*
2788 kithara (1), *lyre*

HARPED
2789 kitharizō (1), to *play a lyre*

HARPERS
2790 kitharōịdŏs (2), one who *plays a lyre*

HARPING
2789 kitharizō (1), to *play a lyre*

HARPS
3658 kinnôwr (17), *harp*
2788 kithara (3), *lyre*

HARROW
7702 sâdad (1), to *harrow* a field

HARROWS
2757 chârîyts (2), *threshing-sledge; slice*

HARSHA
2797 Charshâ' (2), *magician*

HART
354 'ayâl (9), *stag* deer

HARTS
354 'ayâl (2), *stag* deer

HARUM
2037 Hârûm (1), *high, exalted*

HARUMAPH
2739 Chărûwmaph (1), *snub-nosed*

HARUPHITE
2741 Chărûwphîy (1), *Charuphite*

HARUZ
2743 Chârûwts (1), *earnest*

HARVEST
7105 qâtsîyr (47), *harvest; limb* of a tree
2326 thĕrismŏs (13), *harvest, crop*

HARVESTMAN
7105 qâtsîyr (1), *harvest; limb* of a tree
7114 qâtsar (1), to *curtail, cut short*

HASADIAH
2619 Chăçadyâh (1), *Jehovah has favored*

HASENUAH
5574 Çᵉnûw'âh (1), *pointed*

HASHABIAH
2811 Chăshabyâh (15), *Jehovah has regarded*

HASHABNAH
2812 Chăshabnâh (1), *inventiveness*

HASHABNIAH
2813 Chăshabnᵉyâh (2), *thought of Jehovah*

HASHBADANA
2806 Chashbaddânâh (1), *considerate judge*

HASHEM
2044 Hâshêm (1), *wealthy*

HASHMONAH
2832 Chashmônâh (2), *fertile*

HASHUB
2815 Chashshûwb (4), *intelligent*

HASHUBAH
2807 Chăshûbâh (1), *estimation*

HASHUM
2828 Châshûm (5), *enriched*

HASHUPHA
2817 Chăsûwphâ' (1), *nakedness*

HASRAH
2641 Chaçrâh (1), *want*

HASSENAAH
5570 Çᵉnâ'âh (1), *thorny*

HASSHUB
2815 Chashshûwb (1), *intelligent*

HAST
1961 hâyâh (2), to *exist*, i.e. *be* or *become*
3426 yêsh (3), there *is* or *are*
2076 ĕsti (1), he (she or it) *is*; they *are*
2192 ĕchō (28), to *have; hold; keep*
5224 huparchŏnta (1), *property* or *possessions*

HASTE
213 'ûwts (1), to *be close, hurry, withdraw*
924 bᵉhîylûw (Ch.) (1), *hastily, at once*
926 bâhal (1), to *hasten, hurry anxiously*
927 bᵉhal (Ch.) (3), to *terrify; hasten*

1272 bârach (1), to *flee* suddenly
2363 chûwsh (11), to *hurry; to be eager*
2439 chîysh (1), to *hurry, hasten*
2648 châphaz (5), to *hasten away, to fear*
2649 chîppâzôwn (3), *hasty flight*
4116 mâhar (20), to *hurry; promptly*
5169 nâchats (1), to *be urgent*
4692 spĕudō (4), to *urge* on diligently
4710 spŏudē (2), *despatch; eagerness*

HASTED
213 'ûwts (2), to *be close, hurry, withdraw*
926 bâhal (1), to *hasten, hurry anxiously*
1765 dâchaph (2), to *urge; to hasten*
2363 chûwsh (2), to *hurry; to be eager*
2648 châphaz (2), to *hasten away, to fear*
4116 mâhar (14), to *hurry; promptly*
4692 spĕudō (1), to *urge* on diligently

HASTEN
2363 chûwsh (4), to *hurry; to be eager*
4116 mâhar (3), to *hurry; promptly*
8245 shâqad (1), to *be alert*, i.e. *sleepless*

HASTENED
213 'ûwts (2), to *be close, hurry, withdraw*
926 bâhal (1), to *hasten, hurry anxiously*
1765 dâchaph (1), to *urge; to hasten*
4116 mâhar (2), to *hurry; promptly*

HASTENETH
4116 mâhar (1), to *hurry; promptly*

HASTETH
213 'ûwts (1), to *be close, hurry, withdraw*
926 bâhal (1), to *hasten, hurry anxiously*
2363 chûwsh (1), to *hurry; to be eager*
2648 châphaz (1), to *hasten away, to fear*
2907 ṭûws (1), to *pounce* or *swoop upon*
4116 mâhar (3), to *hurry; promptly*
7602 shâ'aph (1), to *be angry; to hasten*

HASTILY
926 bâhal (1), to *hasten, hurry anxiously*
4116 mâhar (2), to *hurry; promptly*
4118 mahêr (2), *in a hurry*
4120 mᵉhêrâh (1), *hurry; promptly*
7323 rûwts (1), to *run*

5030 tachĕōs (1), *speedily, rapidly*

HASTING
4106 mâhîyr (1), *skillful*
4692 spĕudō (1), to *urge* on diligently

HASTY
213 'ûwts (2), to *be close, hurry, withdraw*
926 bâhal (2), to *hasten, hurry anxiously*
1061 bikkûwr (1), *first-fruits* of the crop
2685 chătsaph (Ch.) (1), to *be severe*
4116 mâhar (2), to *hurry; promptly*
7116 qâtsêr (1), *short*

HASUPHA
2817 Chăsûwphâ' (1), *nakedness*

HATACH
2047 Hăthâk (4), *Hathak*

HATCH
1234 bâqa' (2), to *cleave, break, tear open*

HATCHETH
3205 yâlad (1), to *bear young; to father a child*

HATE
7852 sâṭam (2), to *persecute*
8130 sânê' (67), to *hate*
8131 sᵉnê' (Ch.) (1), *enemy*
3404 misĕō (16), to *detest, to love less*

HATED
7852 sâṭam (2), to *persecute*
8130 sânê' (42), to *hate*
8135 sin'âh (2), *hate, malice*
8146 sânîy' (1), *hated*
3404 misĕō (12), to *detest; to love less*

HATEFUL
8130 sânê' (1), to *hate*
3404 misĕō (1), to *detest, persecute; to love less*
4767 stugnĕtŏs (1), *hated*, i.e. *odious*

HATEFULLY
8135 sin'âh (1), *hate, malice*

HATERS
8130 sânê' (1), to *hate*
2319 thĕŏstugĕs (1), *impious, God-hating*

HATEST
8130 sânê' (5), to *hate*
3404 misĕō (1), to *detest, persecute; to love less*

HATETH
7852 sâṭam (1), to *persecute*
8130 sânê' (20), to *hate*
3404 misĕō (9), to *detest; to love less*

HATH
413 'êl (1), *to, toward*
1167 ba'al (3), *master; husband; owner; citizen*

H

1172 ba'ălâh (2),
mistress; female owner
1933 hâvâ' (1), to *be,* to
exist
1961 hâyâh (6), to *exist,*
i.e. *be* or *become*
3426 yêsh (3), there *is* or
are
4672 mâtsâ' (1), to *find*
or *acquire; to occur,*
meet or *be present*
2192 ĕchō (128), to *have;*
hold; keep
5220 hupandrŏs (1),
married woman
5224 huparchŏnta (2),
property or *possessions*

HATHATH
2867 Chăthath (1),
dismay

HATING
8130 sânê' (1), to *hate*
3404 misĕŏ (2), to *detest,*
persecute; to *love less*

HATIPHA
2412 Chăţîyphâ' (2),
robber

HATITA
2410 Chăţîyţa' (2),
explorer

HATRED
342 'êybâh (2), *hostility*
4895 masţêmâh (2),
enmity
8135 sin'âh (13), *hate,*
malice
2189 ĕchthra (1),
hostility; opposition

HATS
3737 karbᵉlâ' (Ch.) (1),
mantle

HATTIL
2411 Chaţţîyl (2),
fluctuating

HATTUSH
2407 Chaţţûwsh (5),
Chattush

HAUGHTILY
7317 rôwmâh (1), *proudly*

HAUGHTINESS
1346 ga'ăvâh (2),
arrogance; majesty
7312 rûwm (3), *elevation;*
elation

HAUGHTY
1361 gâbahh (5), to *be*
lofty; to *be haughty*
1363 gôbahh (1), *height;*
grandeur; arrogance
1364 gâbôahh (1), *high;*
powerful; arrogant
3093 yâhîyr (1), *arrogant*
4791 mârôwm (1),
elevation; haughtiness
7311 rûwm (1), to *be*
high; to *rise* or *raise*

HAUNT
1980 hâlak (1), to *walk;*
live a certain way
3427 yâshab (1), to *dwell,*
to *remain;* to *settle*
7272 regel (1), *foot; step*

HAURAN
2362 Chavrân (2),
cavernous

HAVE
270 'âchaz (1), to *seize,*
grasp; possess
383 'îythay (Ch.) (3),
there *is*
935 bôw' (1), to *go, come*
1167 ba'al (1), *master;*
husband; owner; citizen
1934 hăvâ' (Ch.) (2), to
be, to *exist*
1961 hâyâh (87), to *exist,*
i.e. *be* or *become*
3045 yâda' (2), to *know*
3318 yâtsâ' (3), to *go,*
bring out
3426 yêsh (12), there *is*
3947 lâqach (1), to *take*
4672 mâtsâ' (1), to *find*
or *acquire;* to *occur*
5307 nâphal (1), to *fall*
5375 nâsâ' (1), to *lift up*
5674 'âbar (1), to *cross*
over; to *transition*
5921 'al (1), *above, over,*
upon, or *against*
474 antiballō (1), to
exchange words
568 apĕchō (4), to *be*
distant
1096 ginŏmai (1), to *be,*
become
1099 glukus (1), *sweet,*
fresh
1526 ĕisi (1), they *are*
1699 ĕmŏs (1), *my*
1751 ĕnĕimi (1), to *be*
within
2070 ĕsmĕn (1), we *are*
2071 ĕsŏmai (6), *will be*
2076 ĕsti (11), he (she or
it) *is;* they *are*
2192 ĕchō (266), to *have;*
hold; keep
2701 katatrĕchō (1), to
hasten, run
2983 lambanō (1), to
take, receive
3335 mĕtalambanō (1),
to *accept* and use
3918 parĕimi (1), to *be*
present; to *have come*
5224 huparchŏnta (1),
property or *possessions*
5225 huparchō (1), to
come into existence

HAVEN
2348 chôwph (2), *cove,*
sheltered bay
4231 mâchôwz (1),
harbor
3040 limēn (2), *harbor*

HAVENS
2568 Kalŏi Limĕnĕs (1),
Good Harbors

HAVILAH
2341 Chăvîylâh (7),
circular

HAVING
1167 ba'al (2), *master;*
husband; owner; citizen
5414 nâthan (1), to *give*
1746 ĕnduō (1), to *dress*
2192 ĕchō (85), to *have;*
hold; keep

HAVOCK
3075 lumainŏmai (1), to
insult, maltreat

HAVOTH-JAIR
2334 Chavvôwth Yâ'îyr
(2), *hamlets of Jair*

HAWK
5322 nêts (3), *flower;*
hawk
8464 tachmâç (2),
unclean bird (poss.) *owl*

HAY
2682 châtsîyr (2), *grass;*
leek plant
5528 chŏrtŏs (1), *pasture,*
herbage or *vegetation*

HAZAEL
2371 Chăzâ'êl (23), *God*
has seen

HAZAIAH
2382 Chăzâyâh (1),
Jehovah has seen

HAZAR-ADDAR
2692 Chătsar 'Addâr (1),
village of Addar

HAZAR-ENAN
2703 Chătsar 'Êynôwn
(1), *village of springs*
2704 Chătsar 'Êynân (3),
village of springs

HAZAR-GADDAH
2693 Chătsar Gaddâh
(1), *village of Fortune*

HAZAR-HATTICON
2694 Chătsar
hat-Tîykôwn (1), *village*
of the middle

HAZAR-SHUAL
2705 Chătsar Shûw'âl
(4), *village of* (the) *fox*

HAZAR-SUSAH
2701 Chătsar Çûwçâh
(1), *village of cavalry*

HAZAR-SUSIM
2702 Chătsar Çûwçîym
(1), *village of horses*

HAZARDED
3860 paradidōmi (1), to
hand over

HAZARMAVETH
2700 Chătsarmâveth (2),
village of death

HAZAZON-TAMAR
2688 Chatsᵉtsôwn
Tâmâr (1), *row of* (the)
palm-tree

HAZEL
3869 lûwz (1), *nut-tree,*
(poss.) *almond*

HAZELELPONI
6753 Tsᵉlelpôwnîy (1),
shade-facing

HAZERIM
2699 Chătsêrîym (1),
yards

HAZEROTH
2698 Chătsêrowth (6),
yards

HAZEZON-TAMAR
2688 Chatsᵉtsôwn
Tâmâr (1), *row of* (the)
palm-tree

HAZIEL
2381 Chăzîy'êl (1), *seen*
of God

HAZO
2375 Chăzow (1), *seer*

HAZOR
2674 Châtsôwr (18),
village
2675 Châtsôwr
Chădattâh (1), *new*
village

HEAD
1270 barzel (2), *iron; iron*
implement
1538 gulgôleth (1), *skull*
3852 lehâbâh (1), *flame;*
flash
4763 mᵉra'ăshâh (1),
headpiece; head-rest
6936 qodqôd (8), *crown*
of the head
7217 rê'sh (Ch.) (11),
head
7218 rô'sh (262), *head*
2775 kĕphalaiŏŏ (1), to
strike on the head
2776 kĕphalē (55), *head*

HEADBANDS
7196 qishshûr (1), *girdle*
or *sash for women*

HEADLONG
2630 katakrēmnizō (1),
to *precipitate down*
4248 prēnēs (1), *head*
foremost, headlong

HEADS
7217 rê'sh (Ch.) (1), *head*
7218 rô'sh (83), *head*
2776 kĕphalē (19), *head*

HEADSTONE
68+7222 'eben (1), *stone*

HEADY
4312 prŏpĕtēs (1), *falling*
forward headlong

HEAL
7495 râphâ' (21), to *cure,*
heal
1295 diasōzō (1), to *cure,*
preserve, rescue
2323 thĕrapĕuō (10), to
relieve disease
2390 iaŏmai (6), to *cure,*
heal
2392 iasis (2), *curing*

HEALED
5414+7499 nâthan (1), to
give
7495 râphâ' (31), to *cure,*
heal
2323 thĕrapĕuō (25), to
relieve disease
2390 iaŏmai (18), to *cure,*
heal
4982 sōzō (3), to *deliver;*
to *protect*

HEALER
2280 châbash (1), to
wrap firmly, bind

HEALETH
7495 râphâ' (4), to *cure,*
heal

HEALING
3545 kêhâh (1),
alleviation, i.e. a *cure*
4832 marpê' (3), *cure;*
deliverance; placidity
8585 tᵉ'âlâh (1), *bandage*
or *plaster*

2322 thĕrapĕia (2), cure, healing; domestics
2323 thĕrapĕuō (3), to relieve disease
2386 iama (2), cure
2390 iaŏmai (1), to cure, heal
2392 iasis (1), curing

HEALINGS
2386 iama (1), cure

HEALTH
724 'ărûwkâh (4), wholeness, health
3444 yᵉshûw'âh (2), aid; victory; prosperity
4832 marpê' (5), cure; deliverance; placidity
7500 riph'ûwth (1), cure, healing
7965 shâlôwm (2), safe; well; health, prosperity
4491 rhiza (1), root
5198 hugiainō (1), to have sound health

HEAP
1530 gal (12), heap; ruins
2266 châbar (1), to fascinate by spells
2563 chômer (1), clay; dry measure
2846 châthâh (1), to lay hold of; to pick up fire
3664 kânaç (1), to collect; to enfold
4596 mᵉ'îy (1), pile of rubbish, ruin
5067 nêd (6), mound, heap, dam
5595 çâphâh (1), to scrape; to accumulate
5856 'îy (1), ruin; rubble
6194 'ârêm (3), heap, mound; sheaf
6651 tsâbar (2), to aggregate, gather
7235 râbâh (1), to increase
7760 sûwm (1), to put, place
8510 têl (4), mound
2002 ἐpisōrĕuō (1), to accumulate further
4987 sōrĕuō (1), to pile up, load up

HEAPED
6651 tsâbar (1), to aggregate, gather
2343 thēsaurizō (1), to amass or reserve, store

HEAPETH
6651 tsâbar (1), to aggregate, gather
6908 qâbats (1), to collect, assemble

HEAPS
1530 gal (6), heap; ruins
2563 chômer (1), clay; dry measure
2565 chămôrâh (1), heap
5856 'îy (3), ruin; rubble
6194 'ârêm (6), heap, mound; sheaf
6632 tsâb (1), lizard; covered cart
8564 tamrûwr (1), erection, i.e. pillar

HEAR
238 'âzan (2), to listen
2045 hâshmâ'ûwth (1), communication
6030 'ânâh (28), to respond, answer
7181 qâshab (1), to prick up the ears
8085 shâma' (364), to hear
8086 shᵉma' (Ch.) (4), to hear
191 akŏuō (131), to hear; obey
1251 diakŏuŏmai (1), to patiently listen
1522 ĕisakŏuō (1), to listen to
3878 parakŏuō (2), to disobey

HEARD
6030 'ânâh (11), to respond, answer
7181 qâshab (1), to prick up the ears
8085 shâma' (376), to hear
8086 shᵉma' (Ch.) (4), to hear
189 akŏē (1), hearing; thing heard
191 akŏuō (239), to hear; obey
1522 ĕisakŏuō (4), to listen to
1873 ĕpakŏuō (1), to hearken favorably to
1874 ĕpakrŏaŏmai (1), to listen intently to
4257 prŏakŏuō (1), to hear beforehand

HEARDEST
6030 'ânâh (1), to respond, answer
8085 shâma' (11), to hear

HEARER
202 akrŏatēs (2), hearer

HEARERS
191 akŏuō (2), to hear; obey
202 akrŏatēs (2), hearer

HEAREST
6030 'ânâh (1), to respond, answer
8085 shâma' (6), to hear
191 akŏuō (4), to hear; obey

HEARETH
8085 shâma' (29), to hear
191 akŏuō (22), to hear; obey

HEARING
241 'ôzen (5), ear
4926 mishmâ' (1), report
7182 qesheb (1), hearkening
8085 shâma' (6), to hear
8088 shêma' (1), something heard
189 akŏē (10), hearing; thing heard
191 akŏuō (13), to hear; obey
201 akrŏatēriŏn (1), audience-room

1233 diagnōsis (1), magisterial examination

HEARKEN
238 'âzan (5), to listen
7181 qâshab (21), to prick up the ears
8085 shâma' (119), to hear
191 akŏuō (6), to hear; obey
1801 ĕnōtizŏmai (1), to take in one's ear
5219 hupakŏuō (1), to listen attentively

HEARKENED
238 'âzan (1), to listen
7181 qâshab (5), to prick up the ears
8085 shâma' (74), to hear
3980 pĕitharchĕō (1), to submit to authority

HEARKENEDST
8085 shâma' (1), to hear

HEARKENETH
8085 shâma' (2), to hear

HEARKENING
8085 shâma' (1), to hear

HEART
1079 bâl (Ch.) (1), heart, mind
3820 lêb (479), heart
3821 lêb (Ch.) (1), heart
3823 lâbab (2), to transport with love
3824 lêbâb (207), heart
3825 lᵉbab (Ch.) (7), heart
3826 libbâh (2), heart
4578 mê'âh (1), viscera; anguish, tenderness
5315 nephesh (12), life; breath; soul; wind
7130 qereb (1), nearest part, i.e. the center
7907 sekvîy (1), mind
2588 kardia (101), heart, i.e. thoughts or feelings
4641 sklērŏkardia (2), hard-heartedness
5590 psuchē (1), soul, vitality; heart, mind

HEART'S
3820 lêb (1), heart
5315 nephesh (1), life; breath; soul; wind
2588 kardia (1), heart, i.e. thoughts or feelings

HEARTED
3820 lêb (8), heart

HEARTH
254 'âch (3), fire-pot
3344 yâqad (1), to burn
3595 kîyôwr (1), dish; caldron; washbowl
4168 môwqêd (1), conflagration, burning

HEARTILY
1537+5590 ĕk (1), out, out of

HEARTS
3820 lêb (21), heart
3824 lêbâb (22), heart
3826 libbâh (6), heart
5315 nephesh (2), life; breath; soul; wind

674 apŏpsuchō (1), to faint
2588 kardia (57), heart, i.e. thoughts or feelings
2589 kardiŏgnōstēs (2), heart-knower
4641 sklērŏkardia (1), hard-heartedness

HEARTS'
3820 lêb (1), heart

HEARTY
5315 nephesh (1), life; breath; soul; wind

HEAT
228 'ăzâ (Ch.) (1), to heat
2527 chôm (9), heat
2534 chêmâh (1), heat; anger; poison
2535 chammâh (1), heat of sun
2552 châmam (2), to be hot; to be in a rage
2721 chôreb (6), parched; ruined
2750 chŏrîy (1), burning anger
3179 yâcham (1), to conceive
7565 resheph (1), flame
8273 shârâb (1), glow of the hot air; mirage
2329 thĕrmē (1), warmth, heat
2738 kauma (2), scorching heat
2741 kausŏō (2), to set on fire
2742 kausōn (3), burning heat, hot day

HEATED
228 'ăzâ (Ch.) (1), to heat
1197 bâ'ar (1), to be brutish, be senseless

HEATH
6176 'ărôw'êr (2), juniper bush

HEATHEN
1471 gôwy (143), foreign nation; Gentiles
1482 ĕthnikŏs (2), Gentile
1484 ĕthnŏs (5), race; tribe; pagan

HEAVE
7311 rûwm (1), to be high; to rise or raise
8641 tᵉrûwmâh (28), sacrifice, tribute

HEAVED
7311 rûwm (3), to be high; to rise or raise

HEAVEN
1534 galgal (1), wheel; something round
7834 shachaq (2), firmament, clouds
8064 shâmayim (285), sky; unseen celestial places
8065 shâmayin (Ch.) (35), sky; unseen celestial places
2032 ĕpŏuraniŏs (1), above the sky, celestial
3321 mĕsŏuranēma (3), mid-sky, mid-heaven

HEAVEN'S
3771 ŏuranŏthĕn (2),
from the sky or heaven
3772 ŏuranŏs (248), *sky;
air; heaven*

HEAVEN'S
3772 ŏuranŏs (1), *sky;
air; heaven*

HEAVENLY
1537+3772 ĕk (1), *out, out
of*
2032 ĕpŏuraniŏs (16),
above the sky, celestial
3770 ŏuraniŏs (6),
*belonging to or coming
from the sky or heaven*

HEAVENS
6160 'ărâbâh (1), *desert,
wasteland*
6183 'ârîyph (1), *sky*
8064 shâmayim (107),
*sky; unseen celestial
places*
8065 shâmayin (Ch.) (3),
*sky; unseen celestial
places*
3772 ŏuranŏs (19), *sky;
air; heaven*

HEAVIER
3513 kâbad (3), *to be
heavy, severe, dull*

HEAVILY
3513 kâbad (1), *to be
heavy, severe, dull*
3517 kᵉbêdûth (1),
difficulty
6957 qav (1), *rule for
measuring; rim*

HEAVINESS
1674 dᵉʼâgâh (1), *anxiety*
3544 kêheh (1), *feeble;
obscure*
5136 nûwsh (1), *to be sick*
6440 pânîym (1), *face;
front*
8386 ta'ănîyâh (1),
lamentation
8424 tûwgâh (3),
depression; grief
8589 ta'ănîyth (1),
affliction of self, fasting
85 adēmŏnĕō (1), *to be in
mental distress*
2726 katēphĕia (1),
sadness, dejection
3076 lupĕō (1), *to
distress; to be sad*
3077 lupē (2), *sadness,
grief*

HEAVY
3513 kâbad (16), *to be
heavy, severe, dull*
3514 kôbed (2), *weight,
multitude, vehemence*
3515 kâbêd (8), *severe,
difficult, stupid*
4133 môwṭâh (1), *pole;
ox-bow; yoke*
4751 mar (1), *bitter;
bitterness; bitterly*
5620 çar (2), *peevish,
sullen*
7186 qâsheh (1), *severe*
7451 ra' (1), *bad; evil*
85 adēmŏnĕō (2), *to be in
mental distress*
916 barĕō (3), *to weigh
down, cause pressure*

926 barus (1), *weighty*

HEBER
2268 Cheber (10),
community
5677 'Êber (2), *regions
beyond*
1443 Ēbĕr (1), *regions
beyond*

HEBER'S
2268 Cheber (1),
community

HEBERITES
2277 Chebrîy (1),
Chebrite

HEBREW
5680 'Ibrîy (14), *Eberite
(i.e. Hebrew)*
1444 Hĕbraïkŏs (1),
*Hebraïc or the Jewish
language*
1446 Hĕbraïs (4), *Hebrew
or Jewish language*
1447 Hĕbraïsti (6),
*Hebraistically or in the
Jewish language*

HEBREWESS
5680 'Ibrîy (1), *Eberite
(i.e. Hebrew)*

HEBREWS
5680 'Ibrîy (17), *Eberite
(i.e. Hebrew)*
1445 Hĕbraïŏs (3),
Hebrew or Jew

HEBREWS'
5680 'Ibrîy (1), *Eberite
(i.e. Hebrew)*

HEBRON
2275 Chebrôwn (72),
seat of association

HEBRONITES
2276 Chebrôwnîy (6),
Chebronite

HEDGE
1447 gâdêr (3),
enclosure, wall or fence
4534 mᵉçûwkâh (1),
thorn-hedge
4881 mᵉsûwkâh (2),
thorn hedge
7753 sûwk (2), *to shut in
with hedges*
5418 phragmŏs (1), *fence
or enclosing barrier*

HEDGED
1443 gâdar (1), *to build a
stone wall*
5526 çâkak (1), *to
entwine; to fence in*
5418+4060 phragmŏs (1),
fence or barrier

HEDGES
1447 gâdêr (1),
enclosure, wall or fence
1448 gᵉdêrâh (4),
enclosure for flocks
5418 phragmŏs (1), *fence
or enclosing barrier*

HEED
238 'âzan (1), *to listen*
2095 zᵉhar (Ch.) (1), *be
admonished, be careful*
5414+3820 nâthan (1), *to
give*
5535 çâkath (1), *to be
silent*

7181 qâshab (3), *to prick
up the ears*
7182 qesheb (1),
hearkening
7200 râ'âh (2), *to see*
8104 shâmar (35), *to
watch*
433 anĕkō (1), *be proper,
fitting*
991 blĕpō (14), *to look at*
1907 ĕpĕchō (2), *to
detain; to pay attention*
3708 hŏraō (5), *to stare,
see clearly; to discern*
4337 prŏsĕchō (11), *to
pay attention to*
4648 skŏpĕō (1), *to watch
out for, i.e. to regard*

HEEL
6117 'âqab (1), *to seize by
the heel; to circumvent*
6119 'âqêb (4), *track,
footprint; rear position*
4418 ptĕrna (1), *heel*

HEELS
6119 'âqêb (2), *track,
footprint; rear position*
6120 'âqêb (1), *one who
lies in wait*
8328 sheresh (1), *root*

HEGAI
1896 Hêgê' (3), *Hege or
Hegai*

HEGE
1896 Hêgê' (1), *Hege or
Hegai*

HEIFER
5697 'eglâh (11), *cow calf*
6510 pârâh (6), *heifer*
1151 damalis (1), *heifer*

HEIFER'S
5697 'eglâh (1), *cow calf*

HEIGHT
1361 gâbahh (2), *to be
lofty; to be haughty*
1363 gôbahh (8), *height;
grandeur; arrogance*
1364 gâbôahh (2), *high;
powerful; arrogant*
4791 mârôwm (9),
elevation; elation
6967 qôwmâh (30), *height*
7218 rô'sh (1), *head*
7312 rûwm (2), *elevation;
elation*
7314 rûwm (Ch.) (4),
altitude, tallness
7419 râmûwth (1), *heap
of carcases*
5311 hupsŏs (2), *altitude;
sky; dignity*
5313 hupsōma (1),
altitude; barrier

HEIGHTS
1116 bâmâh (1),
elevation, high place
4791 mârôwm (1),
elevation; elation

HEINOUS
2154 zimmâh (1), *bad
plan*

HEIR
3423 yârash (9), *to
inherit; to impoverish*
2816 klērŏnŏmĕō (1), *to
be an heir to, inherit*

2818 klērŏnŏmŏs (8),
*possessor by
inheritance*

HEIRS
3423 yârash (1), *to
inherit; to impoverish*
2816 klērŏnŏmĕō (1), *to
be an heir to, inherit*
2818 klērŏnŏmŏs (7),
*possessor by
inheritance*
4789 sugklērŏnŏmŏs (2),
participant in common

HELAH
2458 Chel'âh (2), *rust*

HELAM
2431 Chêylâm (2),
fortress

HELBAH
2462 Chelbâh (1), *fertility*

HELBON
2463 Chelbôwn (1),
fruitful

HELD
270 'âchaz (3), *to seize,
grasp; possess*
631 'âçar (1), *to fasten; to
join battle*
1102 bâlam (1), *to
muzzle, control*
1826 dâmam (1), *to be
silent; to be astonished*
2244 châbâ' (1), *to secrete*
2388 châzaq (6), *to
fasten upon; to seize*
2790 chârash (10), *to
engrave; to plow*
2814 châshâh (2), *to
hush or keep quiet*
2820 châsak (1), *to
restrain or refrain*
3447 yâshaṭ (2), *to extend*
3557 kûwl (1), *to keep in;
to measure*
5582 çâ'ad (1), *to support*
6213 'âsâh (1), *to do*
6901 qâbal (1), *to admit;
to take*
7311 rûwm (2), *to be
high; to rise or raise*
8557 temeç (1), *melting
disappearance*
2192 ĕchō (1), *to have;
hold; keep*
2258 ēn (1), *I was*
2270 hēsuchazō (2), *to
refrain*
2722 katĕchō (1), *to hold
down fast*
2902 kratĕō (2), *to seize*
2983 lambanō (1), *to
take, receive*
4160 pŏiĕō (1), *to make*
4601 sigaō (2), *to keep
silent*
4623 siōpaō (4), *to be
quiet*
4912 sunĕchō (1), *to hold
together*

HELDAI
2469 Chelday (2),
worldliness

HELEB
2460 Chêleb (1), *fatness*

HELED
2466 Chêled (1), *fleeting time; this world*

HELEK
2507 Chêleq (2), *portion*

HELEKITES
2516 Chelqîy (1), *Chelkite*

HELEM
2494 Chêlem (2), *dream*

HELEPH
2501 Cheleph (1), *change*

HELEZ
2503 Chelets (5), *strength*

HELI
2242 Hēli (1), *lofty*

HELKAI
2517 Chelqay (1), *apportioned*

HELKATH
2520 Chelqath (2), *smoothness*

HELKATH-HAZZURIM
2521 Chelqath hats-Tsûrîym (1), *smoothness of the rocks*

HELL
7585 she'ôwl (31), *abode of the dead*
86 haįdēs (10), *Hades, i.e. place of the dead*
1067 gĕĕnna (12), *valley of (the son of) Hinnom, fig. hell*
5020 tartaröö (1), *to incarcerate in Tartaros*

HELM
4079 pēdaliŏn (1), *blade of an oar which steers*

HELMET
3553 kôwba' (4), *helmet*
6959 qôwba' (2), *helmet*
4030 pĕrikĕphalaia (2), *helmet*

HELMETS
3553 kôwba' (2), *helmet*

HELON
2497 Chêlôn (5), *strong*

HELP
2388 châzaq (2), *to fasten upon; to seize*
3444 yeshûw'âh (2), *deliverance; aid*
3447 yâshaţ (1), *to extend*
3467 yâsha' (9), *to make safe, free*
5375 nâsâ' (1), *to lift up*
5800 'âzab (2), *to loosen; relinquish; permit*
5826 'âzar (44), *to protect or aid*
5828 'êzer (21), *aid*
5833 'ezrâh (24), *aid*
6965 qûwm (2), *to rise*
7125 qir'âh (1), *to encounter, to happen*
8668 teshûw'âh (5), *rescue, deliverance*
996 bŏĕthĕia (1), *aid*
997 bŏĕthĕō (5), *to aid or relieve*
1947 ĕpikŏuria (1), *assistance, aid*
4815 sullambanō (2), *to conceive; to aid*

HENADAD
2582 Chênâdâd (4), *favor of Hadad*

HENCE
2088 zeh (14), *this or that*
3212 yâlak (1), *to walk; to live; to carry*
3318 yâtsâ' (1), *to go, bring out*
1782 ĕntĕuthĕn (9), *hence, from here*
1821 ĕxapŏstĕllō (1), *to despatch, or to dismiss*
3326+5025 mĕta (1), *with, among; after, later*
5217 hupagō (1), *to withdraw or retire*

HENCEFORTH
3254 yâçaph (5), *to add or augment*
5750 'ôwd (2), *again; repeatedly; still; more*
6258 'attâh (5), *at this time, now*
534 aparti (1), *henceforth, from now*
575+737 apŏ (2), *from, away*
575+3588+3568 apŏ (1), *from, away*
737 arti (1), *just now; at once*
2089 ĕti (1), *yet, still*
3063 lŏipŏn (4), *remaining; finally*
3371 mĕkĕti (4), *no further*
3568 nun (4), *now; the present or immediate*
3765 ŏukĕti (1), *not yet, no longer*

HENCEFORWARD
1973 hâl'êah (1), *far away; thus far*
3371 mĕkĕti (1), *no further*

HENOCH
2585 Chănôwk (2), *initiated*

HEPHER
2660 Chêpher (9), *pit or shame*

HEPHERITES
2662 Chephrîy (1), *Chephrite*

HEPHZI-BAH
2657 Chephtsîy bâhh (2), *my delight (is) in her*

HERALD
3744 kârôwz (Ch.) (1), *herald*

HERB
1877 deshe' (6), *sprout; green grass*
2682 châtsîyr (1), *grass; leek plant*
6212 'eseb (12), *grass, or any green, tender shoot*

HERBS
216 'ôwr (1), *luminary; lightning; happiness*
219 'ôwrâh (2), *luminousness, light*
3419 yârâq (3), *vegetable greens*

HELPED
3467 yâsha' (2), *to make safe, free*
5375 nâsâ' (1), *to lift up*
5826 'âzar (18), *to protect or aid*
5833 'ezrâh (1), *aid*
997 bŏĕthĕō (1), *to aid or relieve*
4820 sumballō (1), *to aid; to join, attack*

HELPER
5826 'âzar (7), *to protect or aid*
998 bŏĕthŏs (1), *succorer, helper*
4904 sunĕrgŏs (1), *fellow-worker*

HELPERS
5826 'âzar (4), *to protect or aid*
5833 'ezrâh (1), *aid*
4904 sunĕrgŏs (2), *fellow-worker*

HELPETH
5826 'âzar (2), *to protect or aid*
4878 sunantilambanŏmai (1), *co-operate, assist*
4903 sunĕrgĕō (1), *to be a fellow-worker*

HELPING
3467 yâsha' (1), *to make safe, free*
5582 çâ'ad (1), *to support*
4943 sunupŏurgĕō (1), *assist, join to help*

HELPS
484 antilēpsis (1), *relief, aid*
996 bŏĕthĕia (1), *aid*

HELVE
6086 'êts (1), *wood, things made of wood*

HEM
7757 shûwl (5), *skirt; bottom edge*
2899 kraspĕdŏn (2), *margin*

HEMAM
1967 Hêymâm (1), *raging*

HEMAN
1968 Hêymân (16), *faithful*

HEMATH
2574 Chămâth (3), *walled*

HEMDAN
2533 Chemdân (1), *pleasant*

HEMLOCK
3939 la'ănâh (1), *poisonous wormwood*
7219 rô'sh (1), *poisonous plant; poison*

HEMS
7757 shûwl (1), *skirt; bottom edge*

HEN
2581 Chên (1), *grace*
3733 ŏrnis (2), *hen*

HENA
2012 Hêna' (3), *Hena*

HERD
1241 bâqâr (14), *plowing ox; herd*
34 agĕlē (8), *drove, herd*

HERDMAN
951 bôwkêr (1), *herder, cattle-tender*

HERDMEN
5349 nôqêd (1), *owner or tender of sheep*
7462 râ'âh (6), *to tend a flock, i.e. pasture it*

HERDS
1241 bâqâr (30), *plowing ox; herd*
4735 miqneh (1), *live-stock*
5739 'êder (2), *muster, flock*

HERE
645 'êphôw (1), *then*
1988 hălôm (2), *hither, to here*
2005 hên (5), *lo!; if!*
2008 hênnâh (2), *from here; from there*
2009 hinnêh (12), *lo!; Look!*
2088 zeh (12), *this or that*
2236 zâraq (1), *to sprinkle, scatter*
3541 kôh (4), *thus*
4672 mâtsâ' (1), *to find or acquire; to occur*
6311 pôh (43), *here or hence*
8033 shâm (2), *where, there*
8552 tâmam (1), *to complete, finish*
848 hautŏu (1), *self*
1759 ĕnthadĕ (3), *here, hither*
3918 parĕimi (2), *to be present; to have come*
3936 paristēmi (1), *to stand beside, present*
4840 sumparĕimi (1), *to be at hand together*
5602 hŏdĕ (44), *here or hither*

HEREAFTER
268 'âchôwr (1), *behind, backward; west*
310 'achar (1), *after*
737 arti (1), *just now; at once*
2089 ĕti (1), *yet, still*
3195 mĕllō (1), *to intend, i.e. be about to*
3370 Mēdŏs (1), *inhabitant of Media*

HEREBY
2063 zô'th (4), *this*
1537+5124 ĕk (1), *out, out of*
1722+5129 ĕn (8), *in; during; because of*

HEREIN
2063 zô'th (1), *this*

5921+2063 'al (1), *above, over, upon, or against*
1722+5129 ĕn (7), *in; during; because of*

HEREOF
3778 hŏutŏs (1), *this or that*
5026 tautē͏ᵢ (1), *(toward or of) this*

HERES
2776 Chereç (1), *shining*

HERESH
2792 Cheresh (1), *magical craft; silence*

HERESIES
139 hairĕsis (3), *party, sect; disunion or heresy*

HERESY
139 hairĕsis (1), *party, sect; disunion or heresy*

HERETICK
141 hairĕtikŏs (1), *schismatic, division*

HERETOFORE
865 'ethmôwl (1), *heretofore, formerly*
8543 tᵉmôwl (6), *yesterday*
4258 prŏamartanō (1), *to sin previously*

HEREUNTO
1519+5124 ĕis (1), *to or into*

HEREWITH
2063 zô'th (2), *this*

HERITAGE
3425 yᵉrushâh (1), *conquest*
4181 môwrâshâh (1), *possession*
5157 nâchal (1), *to inherit*
5159 nachălâh (26), *occupancy*
2819 klērŏs (1), *lot, portion*

HERITAGES
5159 nachălâh (1), *occupancy*

HERMAS
2057 Hĕrmas (1), *born of god Hermes*

HERMES
2060 Hĕrmēs (1), *born of god Hermes*

HERMOGENES
2061 Hĕrmŏgĕnēs (1), *born of god Hermes*

HERMON
2768 Chermôwn (13), *abrupt*

HERMONITES
2769 Chermôwnîym (1), *peaks of Hermon*

HEROD
2264 Hērōdēs (40), *heroic*

HEROD'S
2264 Hērōdēs (4), *heroic*

HERODIANS
2265 Hērōdianŏi (3), *Herodians*

HERODIAS
2266 Hērōdias (4), *heroic*

HERODIAS'
2266 Hērōdias (2), *heroic*

HERODION
2267 Hērōdiōn (1), *heroic*

HERON
601 'ănâphâh (2), *(poss.) parrot*

HESED
2618 Cheçed (1), *favor*

HESHBON
2809 Cheshbôwn (38), *contrivance; plan*

HESHMON
2829 Cheshmôwn (1), *opulent*

HETH
2845 Chêth (14), *terror*

HETHLON
2855 Chethlôn (2), *enswathed*

HEW
1414 gᵉdad (Ch.) (2), *to cut down*
1438 gâda' (1), *to fell a tree; to destroy*
2404 châṭab (1), *to chop or carve wood*
2672 châtsab (2), *to cut stone or carve wood*
3772 kârath (3), *to cut (off, down or asunder)*
6458 pâçal (3), *to carve, to chisel*

HEWED
1496 gâzîyth (5), *dressed stone*
2672 châtsab (3), *to cut stone or carve wood*
4274 machtsêb (1), *quarry stone*
5408 nâthach (1), *to dismember, cut up*
6458 pâçal (2), *to carve, to chisel*
8158 shâçaph (1), *to hack in pieces, i.e. kill*

HEWER
2404 châṭab (1), *to chop or carve wood*

HEWERS
2404 châṭab (5), *to chop or carve wood*
2672 châtsab (4), *to cut stone or carve wood*

HEWETH
2672 châtsab (2), *to cut stone or carve wood*
3772 kârath (1), *to cut (off, down or asunder)*

HEWN
1438 gâda' (1), *to fell a tree; to destroy*
1496 gâzîyth (5), *dressed stone*
2672 châtsab (2), *to cut stone or carve wood*
4274 machtsêb (2), *quarry stone*
7060 qâmal (1), *to wither*
1581 ĕkkŏptō (3), *to cut off; to frustrate*
2991 laxĕutŏs (1), *rock-quarried*
2998 latŏmĕō (2), *to quarry*

HEZEKI
2395 Chizqîy (1), *strong*

HEZEKIAH
2396 Chizqîyâh (128), *strengthened of Jehovah*

HEZION
2383 Chezyôwn (1), *vision*

HEZIR
2387 Chêzîyr (2), *protected*

HEZRAI
2695 Chetsrôw (1), *enclosure*

HEZRO
2695 Chetsrôw (1), *enclosure*

HEZRON
2696 Chetsrôwn (17), *court-yard*

HEZRON'S
2696 Chetsrôwn (1), *court-yard*

HEZRONITES
2697 Chetsrôwnîy (2), *Chetsronite*

HID
2244 châbâ' (25), *to secrete*
2934 ṭâman (16), *to hide*
3582 kâchad (6), *to destroy; to hide*
3680 kâçâh (2), *to cover*
4301 maṭmôwn (2), *secret storehouse*
5641 çâthar (30), *to hide by covering*
5956 'âlam (11), *to veil from sight, i.e. conceal*
6845 tsâphan (8), *to hide; to hoard or reserve*
8587 ta'ălummâh (1), *secret*
613 apŏkruptō (5), *to keep secret, conceal*
614 apŏkruphŏs (2), *secret, hidden things*
1470 ĕgkruptō (2), *incorporate with, mix in*
2572 kaluptō (1), *to cover up*
2927 kruptŏs (3), *private, unseen*
2928 kruptō (10), *to conceal*
2990 lanthanō (2), *to lie hid; unwittingly*
3871 parakaluptō (1), *to veil, be hidden*
4032 pĕrikruptō (1), *to conceal all around*

HIDDAI
1914 Hidday (1), *Hiddai*

HIDDEKEL
2313 Chiddeqel (2), *Tigris river*

HIDDEN
2664 châphas (1), *to seek; to mask*
2934 ṭâman (1), *to hide*
4301 maṭmôwn (1), *secret storehouse*
4710 mitspûn (1), *secret*

5341 nâtsar (1), *to guard; to conceal, hide*
5640 çâtham (1), *to stop up; to keep secret*
5956 'âlam (1), *to veil from sight, i.e. conceal*
6381 pâlâ' (1), *to be, make great, difficult*
6845 tsâphan (3), *to hide; to hoard or reserve*
613 apŏkruptō (1), *to keep secret, conceal*
2927 kruptŏs (3), *private, unseen*
2928 kruptō (1), *to conceal*
2990 lanthanō (1), *to lie hid; unwittingly*

HIDE
2244 châbâ' (6), *to secrete*
2247 châbah (5), *to hide*
2934 ṭâman (5), *to hide*
3582 kâchad (10), *to destroy; to hide*
3680 kâçâh (3), *to cover*
5127 nûwç (1), *to vanish away, flee*
5641 çâthar (33), *to hide by covering*
5785 'ôwr (2), *skin, leather*
5956 'âlam (8), *to veil from sight, i.e. conceal*
6004 'âmam (2), *to overshadow by huddling together*
6845 tsâphan (5), *to hide; to hoard or reserve*
2572 kaluptō (1), *to cover*
2928 kruptō (2), *conceal*

HIDEST
5641 çâthar (5), *to hide by covering*
5956 'âlam (1), *to veil from sight, i.e. conceal*

HIDETH
2244 châbâ' (1), *to secrete*
2821 châshak (1), *to be dark; to darken*
2934 ṭâman (2), *to hide*
3680 kâçâh (1), *to cover*
5641 çâthar (5), *to hide by covering*
5848 'âṭaph (1), *to shroud, i.e. clothe*
5956 'âlam (2), *to veil from sight, i.e. conceal*
6845 tsâphan (1), *to hide; to hoard or reserve*
2928 kruptō (1), *to conceal*

HIDING
2253 chebyôwn (1), *concealment, hiding*
2934 ṭâman (1), *to hide*
4224 machăbê' (1), *refuge, shelter*
5643 çêther (3), *cover, shelter*

HIEL
2419 Chîy'êl (1), *living of God*

HIERAPOLIS
2404 Hiĕrapŏlis (1), *holy city*

HIGGAION
1902 higgâyôwn (1), *musical notation*

HIGH
376 'îysh (2), *man; male; someone*
753 'ôrek (1), *length*
1111 Bâlâq (1), *waster*
1116 bâmâh (99), *elevation, high place*
1361 gâbahh (4), *to be lofty; to be haughty*
1362 gâbâhh (3), *high; lofty*
1363 gôbahh (2), *height; grandeur; arrogance*
1364 gâbôahh (25), *high; powerful; arrogant*
1386 gabnôn (2), *peak of hills*
1419 gâdôwl (22), *great*
1870 derek (1), *road; course of life*
4546 mᵉçillâh (1), *main thoroughfare; viaduct*
4605 ma'al (7), *upward, above, overhead*
4608 ma'ăleh (1), *elevation; platform*
4791 mârôwm (33), *elevation; elation*
4796 Mârôwth (1), *bitter springs*
4869 misgâb (4), high *refuge*
5375 nâsâ' (1), *to lift up*
5920 'al (3), the *Highest God*
5943 'illay (Ch.) (9), the *supreme God*
5945 'elyôwn (37), *loftier, higher; Supreme God*
5946 'elyôwn (Ch.) (4), the *Supreme God*
6381 pâlâ' (1), *to be, make great, difficult*
6877 tsᵉrîyach (1), *citadel*
6967 qôwmâh (5), *height*
7218 rô'sh (3), *head*
7311 rûwm (25), *to be high; to rise or raise*
7312 rûwm (3), *elevation; elation*
7315 rôwm (1), *aloft, on high*
7319 rôwmᵉmâh (1), *exaltation, i.e. praise*
7413 râmâh (4), *height; high seat of idolatry*
7682 sâgab (6), *to be, make lofty; be safe*
8192 shâphâh (1), *to bare*
8203 Shᵉphaṭyâh (2), *Jehovah has judged*
8205 shᵉphîy (7), *bare hill or plain*
8564 tamrûwr (1), *erection, i.e. pillar*
8643 tᵉrûw'âh (1), *battle-cry; clangor*
507 anō (1), *upward or on the top, heavenward*
749 archiĕrĕus (59), *high-priest, chief priest*
2032 ĕpŏuraniŏs (1), *above the sky, celestial*
2409 hiĕrĕus (1), *priest*
3173 mĕgas (2), *great, many*

5308 hupsēlŏs (9), *lofty* in place or character
5310 hupsistŏs (5), the *Supreme God*
5311 hupsŏs (3), *altitude; sky; dignity*
5313 hupsōma (1), *altitude; barrier*

HIGHER
1354 gab (1), *mounded or rounded: top or rim*
1361 gâbahh (4), *to be lofty; to be haughty*
1364 gâbôahh (5), *high; powerful; arrogant*
3201 yâkôl (1), *to be able*
5945 'elyôwn (4), *loftier, higher; Supreme God*
6706 tsᵉchîyach (1), *glaring*
7311 rûwm (2), *to be high; to rise or raise*
511 anōtĕrŏs (1), *upper part; former part*
5242 hupĕrĕchō (1), *to excel; superior*
5308 hupsēlŏs (1), *lofty*

HIGHEST
1364 gâbôahh (1), *high; powerful; arrogant*
4791 mârôwm (1), *elevation; elation*
5945 'elyôwn (3), *loftier, higher; Supreme God*
6788 tsammereth (2), *foliage*
7218 rô'sh (1), *head*
4410 prōtŏkathĕdria (1), *pre-eminence in council*
4411 prōtŏklisia (1), *pre-eminence at meals*
5310 hupsistŏs (8), the *Supreme God*

HIGHLY
1537+4053 ĕk (1), *out of*
2371 thumŏmachĕō (1), *to be exasperated*
5251 hupĕrupsŏō (1), *to raise to the highest*
5252 hupĕrphrŏnĕō (1), *to esteem oneself overmuch*
5308 hupsēlŏs (1), *lofty* in place or character

HIGHMINDED
5187 tuphŏō (1), *to inflate with self-conceit*
5309 hupsēlŏphrŏnĕō (2), *to be lofty in mind*

HIGHNESS
1346 ga'ăvâh (1), *arrogance; majesty*
7613 sᵉ'êth (1), *elevation; swelling leprous scab*

HIGHWAY
4546 mᵉçillâh (13), *main thoroughfare; viaduct*
4547 maçlûwl (1), *main thoroughfare*
3598 hŏdŏs (1), *road*

HIGHWAYS
734 'ôrach (1), *well-traveled road; manner of life*
2351 chûwts (1), *outside, outdoors; open market*

4546 mᵉçillâh (6), *main thoroughfare; viaduct*
1327+3598 diĕxŏdŏs (1), *open square*
3598 hŏdŏs (2), *road*

HILEN
2432 Chîylên (1), *fortress*

HILKIAH
2518 Chilqîyâh (33), *portion (of) Jehovah*

HILKIAH'S
2518 Chilqîyâh (1), *portion (of) Jehovah*

HILL
1389 gib'âh (30), *hillock*
2022 har (34), *mountain or range of hills*
4608 ma'ăleh (1), *elevation; platform*
7161 qeren (1), *horn*
697 Arĕiŏs Pagŏs (1), *rock of Ares*
1015 bŏunŏs (1), small *hill*
3714 ŏrĕinŏs (2), *Highlands of Judæa*
3735 ŏrŏs (3), *hill, mountain*

HILL'S
2022 har (1), *mountain or range of hills*

HILLEL
1985 Hillêl (2), *praising (God)*

HILLS
1389 gib'âh (39), *hillock*
2022 har (23), *mountain or range of hills*
2042 hârâr (2), *mountain*
1015 bŏunŏs (1), small *hill*

HIN
1969 hîyn (22), *liquid measure*

HIND
355 'ayâlâh (1), *doe deer*
365 'ayeleth (2), *doe deer*

HINDER
268 'âchôwr (3), *behind, backward; west*
309 'âchar (1), *to remain; to delay*
310 'achar (1), *after*
314 'achărôwn (1), *late or last; behind; western*
4513 mâna' (1), *to deny, refuse*
5490 çôwph (1), *termination; end*
6213+8442 'âsâh (1), *to do or make*
7725 shûwb (2), *to turn back; to return*
348 anakŏptō (1), *to beat back, i.e. check*
2967 kōluō (1), *to stop*
4403 prumna (2), *stern of a ship*
5100+1464+1325 tis (1), *some or any person*

HINDERED
989 bᵉṭêl (Ch.) (1), *to stop*
1465 ĕgkŏptō (2), *to impede, detain*

1581 ĕkkŏptō (1), *to cut off; to frustrate*
2967 kōluō (1), *to stop*

HINDERETH
2820 châsak (1), *to restrain or refrain*

HINDERMOST
314 'achărôwn (1), *late or last; behind; western*
319 'achărîyth (1), *future; posterity*

HINDMOST
314 'achărôwn (1), *late or last; behind; western*
2179 zânab (2), *militarily attack the rear position*

HINDS
355 'ayâlâh (4), *doe deer*

HINDS'
355 'ayâlâh (3), *doe deer*

HINGES
6596 pôth (1), *hole; hinge; female genitals*
6735 tsîyr (1), *hinge*

HINNOM
2011 Hinnôm (13), *Hinnom*

HIP
7785 shôwq (1), lower *leg*

HIRAH
2437 Chîyrâh (2), *splendor*

HIRAM
2438 Chîyrâm (22), *noble*

HIRAM'S
2438 Chîyrâm (1), *noble*

HIRE
868 'ethnan (7), *gift price of harlotry*
4242 mᵉchîyr (1), *price, payment, wages*
7936 sâkar (2), *to hire*
7939 sâkâr (8), *payment, salary; compensation*
3408 misthŏs (3), *pay for services*
3409 misthŏō (1), *to hire*

HIRED
7916 sâkîyr (11), man at *wages, hired hand*
7917 sᵉkîyrâh (1), *hiring*
7936 sâkar (14), *to hire*
8566 tânâh (2), *to bargain with a harlot*
3407 misthiŏs (2), *hired-worker*
3409 misthŏō (1), *to hire*
3410 misthōma (1), *rented building*
3411 misthōtŏs (1), *wage-worker*

HIRELING
7916 sâkîyr (6), man at *wages, hired hand*
3411 misthōtŏs (2), *wage-worker*

HIRES
868 'ethnan (1), *gift price of harlotry*

HIREST
7806 shâzar (1), *to twist a thread of straw*

H

HISS
8319 shâraq (12), to whistle or *hiss*

HISSING
8292 sh⁽ᵉ⁾rûwqâh (1), *whistling; scorn*
8322 sh⁽ᵉ⁾rêqâh (7), *derision*

HIT
4672 mâtsâ' (2), to *find* or *acquire; to occur*

HITHER
1988 hălôm (6), *hither, to here*
2008 hênnâh (2), *from here; from there*
5066 nâgash (7), to *be, come, bring near*
6311 pôh (1), *here or hence*
1204 dĕurŏ (2), *hither!; hitherto*
1759 ĕnthadĕ (4), *here, hither*
3333 mĕtakalĕŏ (1), to *summon for, call for*
5602 hŏdĕ (14), *here or hither*

HITHERTO
227 'âz (1), *at that time* or *place; therefore*
1973 hâl⁽ᵉ⁾âh (2), *far away; thus far*
1988 hălôm (2), *hither, to here*
5704+2008 'ad (6), *as far (long) as; during*
5704+3541 'ad (2), *as far (long) as; during*
5704+6311 'ad (1), *as far (long) as; during*
5705+3542 'ad (Ch.) (1), *as far (long) as; during*
891+1204 achri (1), *until or up to*
2193+737 hĕōs (2), *until*
3768 ŏupŏ (1), *not yet*

HITTITE
2850 Chittîy (26), *Chittite*

HITTITES
2850 Chittîy (22), *Chittite*

HIVITE
2340 Chivvîy (9), *villager*

HIVITES
2340 Chivvîy (16), *villager*

HIZKIAH
2396 Chizqîyâh (1), *strengthened of Jehovah*

HIZKIJAH
2396 Chizqîyâh (1), *strengthened of Jehovah*

HO
1945 hôwy (3), *oh!, woe!*

HOAR
3713 k⁽ᵉ⁾phôwr (2), *bowl; white frost*
7872 sêybâh (3), *old age*

HOARY
3713 k⁽ᵉ⁾phôwr (1), *bowl; white frost*
7872 sêybâh (3), *old age*

HOBAB
2246 Chôbâb (2), *cherished*

HOBAH
2327 chôwbâh (1), *hiding place*

HOD
1963 hêyk (1), *how?*

HODAIAH
1939 Howday⁽ᵉ⁾vâhûw (1), *majesty of Jehovah*

HODAVIAH
1938 Hôwdavyâh (3), *majesty of Jehovah*

HODESH
2321 Chôdesh (1), *new moon*

HODEVAH
1937 Hôwd⁽ᵉ⁾vâh (1), *majesty of Jehovah*

HODIAH
1940 Hôwdîyâh (1), *Jewess*

HODIJAH
1940 Hôwdîyâh (5), *Jewess*

HOGLAH
2295 Choglâh (4), *partridge*

HOHAM
1944 Hôwhâm (1), *Hoham*

HOISED
1869 ĕpairŏ (1), to *raise up, look up*

HOLD
270 'âchaz (26), to *seize, grasp; possess*
816 'âsham (1), to *be guilty; to be punished*
1225 bitstsârôwn (1), *fortress*
2013 hâçâh (2), to *hush, be quiet*
2388 châzaq (35), to *fasten upon; to seize*
2790 chârash (16), to *engrave; to plow*
2814 châshâh (1), to *hush or keep quiet*
3447 yâshaṭ (1), to *extend*
3557 kûwl (1), to *keep in; to maintain*
3905 lâchats (1), to *press; to distress*
3943 lâphath (1), to *clasp; to turn around*
4013 mibtsâr (2), *fortification; defender*
4581 mâ'ôwz (1), *fortified place; defense*
4672 mâtsâ' (2), to *find or acquire; to occur*
4679 m⁽ᵉ⁾tsad (2), *stronghold*
4686 mâtsûwd (7), *net or capture; fastness*
4692 mâtsôwr (1), *distress; fastness*
5253 nâçag (1), to *retreat*
5375 nâsâ' (1), to *lift up*
5381 nâsag (5), to *reach*
5553 çela' (1), *craggy rock; fortress*
5582 çâ'ad (1), to *support*

HOLDS
4013 mibtsâr (11), *fortification; defender*
4581 mâ'ôwz (1), *fortified place; defense*
4679 m⁽ᵉ⁾tsad (6), *stronghold*
4686 mâtsûwd (1), *net or capture; fastness*
4694 m⁽ᵉ⁾tsûwrâh (1), *rampart, fortification*

HOLE
2356 chôwr (4), *cavity, socket, den*
4718 maqqebeth (1), *hammer*
5357 nâqîyq (1), *cleft, crevice*
6310 peh (6), *mouth; opening*

HOLE'S
6354 pachath (1), *pit*

HOLES
2356 chôwr (4), *cavity, socket, den*
4526 miçgereth (1), *margin; stronghold*
4631 m⁽ᵉ⁾ârâh (1), *dark cavern*
5344 nâqab (1), to *puncture, perforate*
5357 nâqîyq (2), *cleft, crevice*
5454 phôlĕŏs (2), *burrow, den hole*

HOLIER
6942 qâdâsh (1), to *be, make clean*

HOLIEST
39 hagiŏn (3), *sacred thing, place or person*

HOLILY
3743 hŏsiōs (1), *piously*

HOLINESS
6944 qôdesh (30), *sacred place or thing*
38 hagiasmŏs (5), *state of purity*
41 hagiŏtēs (1), *state of holiness*
42 hagiōsunē (3), *quality of holiness*
2150 ĕusĕbĕia (1), *piety, religious*
2412 hiĕrŏprĕpēs (1), *reverent*
3742 hŏsiŏtēs (2), *piety*

HOLLOW
3709 kaph (4), *hollow of hand; paw; sole of foot*
4388 maktêsh (1), *mortar; socket*
5014 nâbab (3), to *be hollow; be foolish*
8168 shô'al (1), *palm of hand; handful*
8258 sh⁽ᵉ⁾qa'rûwrâh (1), *depression*

HOLON
2473 Chôlôwn (3), *sandy*

6076 'ôphel (1), *tumor; fortress*
6877 ts⁽ᵉ⁾rîyach (3), *citadel*
6901 qâbal (1), to *admit; to take*
6965 qûwm (1), to *rise*
8551 tâmak (4), to *obtain, keep fast*
8610 tâphas (7), to *manipulate, i.e. seize*
472 antĕchŏmai (2), to *adhere to; to care for*
1949 ĕpilambanŏmai (5), to *seize*
2192 ĕchō (3), to *have; hold; keep*
2722 katĕchō (5), to *hold down fast*
2902 kratĕō (19), to *seize*
4601 sigaŏ (2), to *keep silent*
4623 siōpaŏ (5), to *be quiet*
5083 tērĕō (1), to *keep, guard, obey*
5084 tērēsis (1), *observance; prison*
5392 phimŏō (2), to *restrain to silence*
5438 phulakē (1), *guarding or guard*

HOLDEN
270 'âchaz (1), to *seize, grasp; possess*
2388 châzaq (1), to *fasten upon; to seize*
2814 châshâh (1), to *hush or keep quiet*
3920 lâkad (1), to *catch; to capture*
5564 çâmak (1), to *lean upon; take hold of*
5582 çâ'ad (1), to *support*
6213 'âsâh (2), to *do or make*
8551 tâmak (1), to *obtain, keep fast*
2902 kratĕō (2), to *seize*

HOLDEST
270 'âchaz (1), to *seize, grasp; possess*
2790 chârash (2), to *engrave; to plow*
2803 châshab (1), to *weave, fabricate*
8610 tâphas (1), to *manipulate, i.e. seize*
2902 kratĕō (1), to *seize*

HOLDETH
270 'âchaz (1), to *seize, grasp; possess*
2388 châzaq (2), to *fasten upon; to seize*
2790 chârash (2), to *engrave; to plow*
7760 sûwm (1), to *put, place*
8551 tâmak (2), to *obtain, keep fast*
2902 kratĕō (1), to *seize*

HOLDING
3557 kûwl (1), to *keep in; to measure*
8551 tâmak (1), to *obtain, keep fast*
472 antĕchŏmai (1), to *adhere to; to care for*

1907 ĕpĕchō (1), to *retain; to pay attention*
2192 ĕchō (2), to *have; hold; keep*
2902 kratĕō (3), to *seize*

HOLPEN
2220 zᵉrôwa' (1), *arm;*
foreleg; force, power
5826 'âzar (3), to *protect*
or aid
482 *antilambanŏmai* (1),
to *come to the aid*

HOLY
2623 châçîyd (5),
religiously *pious, godly*
4720 miqdâsh (3),
sanctuary of deity
6918 qâdôwsh (100),
sacred
6922 qaddîysh (Ch.) (7),
sacred
6942 qâdâsh (7), to *be,
make clean*
6944 qôdesh (297),
sacred place or thing
37 *hagiazŏ* (1), to *purify
or consecrate*
39 *hagiŏn* (3), *sacred*
thing, place or person
40 *hagiŏs* (162), *sacred,
holy*
2413 *hiĕrŏs* (2), *sacred,
set apart for God*
3741 *hŏsiŏs* (6),
hallowed, pious, sacred

HOLYDAY
2287 châgag (1), to
observe a festival
1859 *hĕŏrtĕ* (1), *festival*

HOMAM
1950 Hôwmâm (1), *raging*

HOME
168 'ôhel (1), *tent*
1004 bayith (26), *house;
temple; family, tribe*
4725 mâqôwm (3),
general *locality, place*
5115 nâvâh (1), to *rest* as
at home
7725 shûwb (5), to *turn*
back; to *return*
8432 tâvek (1), *center,
middle*
1438 *hĕautŏu* (1),
himself, herself, itself
1736 *ĕndĕmĕō* (1), to *be
at home*
2398 *idiŏs* (2), *private* or
separate
3614 *ŏikia* (1), *abode;
family*
3624 *ŏikŏs* (4), *dwelling;
family*
3626 *ŏikŏurŏs* (1),
domestically inclined

HOMEBORN
249 'ezrâch (1), *native
born*
1004 bayith (1), *house;
temple; family, tribe*

HOMER
2563 chômer (10), *clay;*
dry *measure*

HOMERS
2563 chômer (1), *clay;*
dry *measure*

HONEST
2570 kalŏs (5), *good;
valuable; virtuous*
4586 *sĕmnŏs* (1),
honorable, noble

HONESTLY
2156 *ĕuschĕmŏnŏs* (2),
fittingly, properly
2573 kalŏs (1), *well,* i.e.
rightly

HONESTY
4587 *sĕmnŏtēs* (1),
venerableness

HONEY
1706 dᵉbash (52), *honey*
3192 *mĕli* (4), *honey*

HONEYCOMB
3293 ya'ar (1), *honey* in
the *comb*
3295+1706 ya'ârâh (1),
honey in the *comb*
5317 nôpheth (4), *honey*
from the comb
5317+6688 nôpheth (1),
honey from the comb
6688+1706 tsûwph (1),
comb of *dripping honey*
3193+2781 *mĕlissiŏs* (1),
honeybee comb

HONOUR
1921 hâdar (2), to *favor*
or *honor;* to *be high*
1922 hâdar (Ch.) (1), to
magnify, glorify
1923 hădar (Ch.) (2),
magnificence, glory
1926 hâdâr (5),
magnificence
1927 hădârâh (1),
ornament; splendor
1935 hôwd (6), *grandeur,
majesty*
3366 yᵉqâr (12), *wealth;
costliness; dignity*
3367 yᵉqâr (Ch.) (2),
glory, honor
3513 kâbad (22), to *be
rich, glorious*
3515 kâbêd (1), *severe,
difficult, stupid*
3519 kâbôwd (32),
splendor, wealth
8597 tiph'ârâh (4),
ornament
820 atimŏs (2),
dishonoured
1391 *dŏxa* (6), *glory;
brilliance*
5091 timaŏ (14), to
revere, honor
5092 timĕ (31), *esteem;
nobility; money*

HONOURABLE
142 'âdar (1),
magnificent; glorious
1935 hôwd (2), *grandeur,
majesty*
3368 yâqâr (1), *valuable*
3513 kâbad (13), to *be
rich, glorious*
3519 kâbôwd (2),
splendor, wealth
5375+6440 nâsâ' (4), to
lift up
820 atimŏs (1),
dishonoured
1741 *ĕndŏxŏs* (1), *noble;
honored*
1784 *ĕntimŏs* (1), *valued,*
considered *precious*
2158 *ĕuschĕmŏn* (3),
decorous, proper; noble

5093 timiŏs (1), *costly;
honored, esteemed*

HONOURED
1921 hâdar (1), to *favor*
or *honor;* to *be high*
1922 hădar (Ch.) (1), to
magnify, glorify
3513 kâbad (5), to *be
rich, glorious*
1392 *dŏxazŏ* (1), to
render, esteem glorious
5092 timĕ (1), *esteem;
nobility; money*

HONOUREST
3513 kâbad (1), to *be
rich, glorious*

HONOURETH
3513 kâbad (4), to *be
rich, glorious*
1392 *dŏxazŏ* (1), to
render, esteem glorious
5091 timaŏ (3), to *revere,
honor, show respect*

HONOURS
5091 timaŏ (1), to *revere,
honor, show respect*

HOODS
6797 tsânîyph (1),
head-dress, turban

HOOF
6541 parçâh (12), *split
hoof*

HOOFS
6536 pâraç (1), to *break
in pieces;* to *split*
6541 parçâh (5), *split
hoof*

HOOK
100 'agmôwn (1), *rush;
rope of rushes*
2397 châch (2), *ring* for
the nose or lips
2443 chakkâh (1), *fish
hook*
44 agkistrŏn (1), *fish
hook*

HOOKS
2053 vâv (13), *hook*
2397 châch (2), *ring* for
the nose or lips
6793 tsinnâh (1), *large
shield; piercing cold*
8240 shâphâth (1),
two-pronged hook

HOPE
982 bâṭach (1), to *trust,
be confident* or *sure*
983 beṭach (1), *safety,
security, trust*
986 biṭṭâchôwn (1), *trust*
2342 chûwl (1), to *dance,
whirl;* to *wait;* to *pervert*
2620 châçâh (1), to *flee
to;* to *confide* in
2976 yâ'ash (3), to
despond, despair
3176 yâchal (19), to *wait;
to be patient, hope*
3689 keçel (3), *loin;
back; viscera; trust*
4009 mibṭâch (1),
security; assurance
4268 machăçeh (2),
shelter; refuge
4723 miqveh (4),
confidence; collection

7663 sâbar (1), to *expect*
with hope
7664 sêber (2),
expectation
8431 tôwcheleth (6),
hope, expectation
8615 tiqvâh (23), *cord;
expectancy*
1679 *ĕlpizō* (7), to *expect*
or *confide, hope for*
1680 *ĕlpis* (51), *hope;
confidence*

HOPE'S
1679 *ĕlpizō* (1), to *expect*
or *confide, hope for*

HOPED
982 bâṭach (1), to *trust,
be confident* or *sure*
3176 yâchal (3), to *wait;
to be patient, hope*
7663 sâbar (2), to *expect*
with hope
1679 *ĕlpizō* (4), to *expect*
or *confide, hope for*

HOPETH
1679 *ĕlpizō* (1), to *expect*
or *confide, hope for*

HOPHNI
2652 Chophnîy (5), *pair
of fists*

HOPING
560 apĕlpizō (1), to *fully
expect* in return
1679 *ĕlpizō* (2), to *expect*
or *confide, hope for*

HOR
2023 Hôr (12), *mountain*

HOR-HAGIDGAD
2735 Chôr hag-Gidgâd
(2), *hole of the cleft*

HORAM
2036 Hôrâm (1), *high,
exalted*

HOREB
2722 Chôrêb (17),
desolate

HOREM
2765 Chŏrêm (1), *devoted*

HORI
2753 Chôrîy (4),
cave-dweller

HORIMS
2752 Chôrîy (2),
cave-dweller

HORITE
2752 Chôrîy (1),
cave-dweller

HORITES
2752 Chôrîy (3),
cave-dweller

HORMAH
2767 Chormâh (9),
devoted

HORN
7161 qeren (28), *horn*
7162 qeren (Ch.) (5), *horn*
2768 kĕras (1), *horn*

HORNET
6880 tsir'âh (2), *wasp*

HORNETS
6880 tsir'âh (1), *wasp*

HORNS
3104 yôwbêl (3), *blast of a ram's horn*
7160 qâran (1), *to protrude out horns*
7161 qeren (46), *horn*
7162 qeren (Ch.) (5), *horn*
2768 kĕras (10), *horn*

HORONAIM
2773 Chôrônayim (4), *double cave-town*

HORONITE
2772 Chôrônîy (3), *Choronite*

HORRIBLE
2152 zal'âphâh (1), *glow; famine*
7588 shâ'ôwn (1), *uproar; destruction*
8186 sha'ărûwrâh (4), something *fearful*

HORRIBLY
8175 sâ'ar (1), *to storm; to shiver,* i.e. *fear*
8178 sa'ar (1), *tempest; terror*

HORROR
367 'êymâh (1), *fright*
2152 zal'âphâh (1), *glow; famine*
6427 pallâtsûwth (2), *affright, trembling fear*

HORSE
5483 çûwç (35), *horse*
2462 hippŏs (8), *horse*

HORSEBACK
5483 çûwç (1), *horse*
7392 râkab (2), *to ride*
7392+5483 râkab (2), *to ride*

HORSEHOOFS
6119+5483 'âqêb (1), *track, footprint*

HORSELEACH
5936 'ălûwqâh (1), *leech*

HORSEMAN
6571 pârâsh (1), *horse; chariot driver*
7395 rakkâb (1), *charioteer*

HORSEMEN
6571 pârâsh (56), *horse; chariot driver*
2460 hippĕus (2), *member of a cavalry*
2461 hippikŏn (1), *cavalry force*

HORSES
5483 çûwç (96), *horse*
5484 çûwçâh (1), *mare*
2462 hippŏs (7), *horse*

HORSES'
5483 çûwç (1), *horse*
2462 hippŏs (1), *horse*

HOSAH
2621 Chôçâh (5), *hopeful*

HOSANNA
5614 hōsanna (6), "oh save!"

HOSEA
1954 Hôwshêä' (3), *deliverer*

HOSEN
6361 paṭṭîysh (Ch.) (1), *garment*

HOSHAIAH
1955 Hôwshi'yâh (3), *Jehovah has saved*

HOSHAMA
1953 Hôwshâmâ' (1), *Jehovah has heard*

HOSHEA
1954 Hôwshêä' (11), *deliverer*

HOSPITALITY
5381 philŏnĕxia (1), *hospitableness*
5382 philŏxĕnŏs (3), *hospitable*

HOST
2426 chêyl (2), *rampart, battlement*
2428 chayil (28), *army; wealth; virtue; valor*
4264 machăneh (54), *encampment*
6635 tsâbâ' (100), *army, military host*
3581 xĕnŏs (1), *alien; guest or host*
3830 pandŏchĕus (1), *innkeeper*
4756 stratia (2), *army; celestial luminaries*

HOSTAGES
1121+8594 bên (2), *son, descendant; people*

HOSTS
2428 chayil (1), *army; wealth; virtue; valor*
4264 machăneh (4), *encampment*
6635 tsâbâ' (293), *army, military host*

HOT
228 'ăzâ' (Ch.) (1), *to heat*
784 'êsh (1), *fire*
2525 châm (1), *hot, sweltering*
2527 chôm (4), *heat*
2534 chêmâh (3), *heat; anger; poison*
2552 châmam (3), *to be hot; to be in a rage*
2734 chârâh (10), *to blaze up*
3179 yâcham (2), *to conceive*
7565 resheph (1), *flame*
2200 zĕstŏs (3), *hot,* i.e. *fervent*
2743 kautēriazō (1), *to brand or cauterize*

HOTHAM
2369 Chôwthâm (1), *seal*

HOTHAN
2369 Chôwthâm (1), *seal*

HOTHIR
1956 Hôwthîyr (2), *he has caused to remain*

HOTLY
1814 dâlaq (1), *to flame; to pursue*

HOTTEST
2389 châzâq (1), *strong; severe, hard, violent*

HOUGH
6131 'âqar (1), *to pluck up roots; to hamstring*

HOUGHED
6131 'âqar (3), *to pluck up roots; to hamstring*

HOUR
8160 shâ'âh (Ch.) (5), *immediately*
734 Artĕmas (1), *gift of Artemis*
2256 hēmiōriŏn (1), *half-hour*
5610 hōra (85), *hour,* i.e. *a unit of time*

HOURS
5610 hōra (3), *hour,* i.e. *a unit of time*

HOUSE
1004 bayith (1745), *house; temple; family*
1005 bayith (Ch.) (41), *house; temple; family*
1008 Bêyth-'Êl (5), *house of God*
1035 Bêyth Lechem (1), *house of bread*
5854 'Aṭrôwth Bêyth Yôw'âb (1), *crowns of* (the) *house of Joäb*
3609 ŏikĕiŏs (1), *of the household*
3613 ŏikētēriŏn (1), *residence, home*
3614 ŏikia (84), *abode; family*
3616 ŏikŏdĕspŏtĕō (1), *to be the head of a family*
3617 ŏikŏdĕspŏtēs (7), *head of a family*
3624 ŏikŏs (96), *dwelling; family*
3832 panŏiki (1), *with the whole family*

HOUSEHOLD
1004 bayith (47), *house; temple; family; tribe*
5657 'ăbuddâh (1), *service*
2322 thĕrapĕia (2), *cure, healing; domestics*
3609 ŏikĕiŏs (2), *of the household*
3610 ŏikĕtēs (1), *menial domestic servant*
3614 ŏikia (1), *abode; family*
3615 ŏikiakŏs (2), *relatives*
3624 ŏikŏs (3), *dwelling; family*

HOUSEHOLDER
3617 ŏikŏdĕspŏtēs (4), *head of a family*

HOUSEHOLDS
1004 bayith (7), *house; temple; family; tribe*

HOUSES
490 'almânâh (1), *widow*
1004 bayith (116), *house; temple; family; tribe*
1005 bayith (Ch.) (2), *house; temple; family*
4999 nâ'âh (1), *home, dwelling; pasture*

HOUSETOP
1406 gâg (2), *roof; top*
1430 dōma (5), *roof, housetop*

HOUSETOPS
1406 gâg (5), *roof; top*
1430 dōma (2), *roof, housetop*

HOW
335 'ay (1), *where?*
346 'ayêh (2), *where?*
349 'êyk (75), *how? or how!; where?*
434 'ĕlûwl (1), *good for nothing*
637 'aph (18), *also or yea; though*
834 'ăsher (26), *how, because, in order that*
1963 hêyk (2), *how?*
3588 kîy (11), *for, that because*
4069 maddûwa' (1), *why?, what?*
4100 mâh (59), *how?, how!; what, whatever*
4101 mâh (Ch.) (3), *how?, how!; what, whatever*
5704 'ad (47), *as far (long) as; during*
2193 hĕōs (6), *until*
2245 hēlikŏs (1), *how much, how great*
2531 kathōs (1), *just or inasmuch as, that*
3386 mētigĕ (1), *not to say (the rather still)*
3704 hŏpōs (4), *in the manner that*
3745 hŏsŏs (7), *as much as*
3754 hŏti (14), *that; because; since*
4012 pĕri (1), *about; around*
4080 pēlikŏs (2), *how much, how great*
4212 pŏsakis (2), *how many times*
4214 pŏsŏs (26), *how much?; how much!*
4219 pŏtĕ (1), *at what time?*
4459 pōs (96), *in what way?; how?; how much!*
4559 sarkikŏs (2), *pertaining to flesh*
5101 tis (11), *who?, which? or what?*
5613 hōs (19), *which, how,* i.e. *in that manner*

HOWBEIT
199 'ûwlâm (1), *however or on the contrary*
389 'ak (1), *surely; only, however*
657 'epheç (1), *end; no further*
3651 kên (1), *just; right; correct*
7535 raq (1), *merely; although*
235 alla (8), *but, yet, except, instead*

1161 dĕ (1), *but, yet*
3305 mĕntŏi (1), *however*

HOWL
3213 yâlal (27), to *howl,*
wail, yell
3649 ŏlŏluzŏ (1), to *howl,*
i.e. *shriek* or *wail*

HOWLED
3213 yâlal (1), to *howl,*
wail, yell

HOWLING
3213 yâlal (5), to *howl,*
wail, yell
3214 yᵉlêl (1), *howl, wail*

HOWLINGS
3213 yâlal (1), to *howl,*
wail, yell

HOWSOEVER
1961+4101 hâyâh (1), to
exist, i.e. *be* or *become*
3605+834 kôl (1), *all, any*
or *every*
7535 raq (1), *merely;*
although

HUGE
7230 rôb (1), *abundance*

HUKKOK
2712 Chuqqôq (1),
appointed

HUKOK
2712 Chuqqôq (1),
appointed

HUL
2343 Chûwl (2), *circle*

HULDAH
2468 Chuldâh (2), *weasel*

HUMBLE
3665 kâna' (2), to
humiliate, vanquish,
subdue
6031 'ânâh (4), to *afflict,*
be afflicted
6041 'ânîy (5), *depressed*
7511 râphaç (1), to
trample; to prostrate
7807+5869 shach (1),
sunk, i.e. *downcast*
8213 shâphêl (2), to
humiliate
8217 shâphâl (3),
depressed, low
5011 tapĕinŏs (2),
humiliated, lowly
5013 tapĕinŏŏ (5), to
depress; to humiliate

HUMBLED
1792 dâkâ' (1), to be
contrite, be humbled
3665 kâna' (13), to
humiliate, vanquish
6031 'ânâh (7), to *afflict,*
be afflicted
7743 shûwach (1), to *sink*
8213 shâphêl (4), to
humiliate
8214 shᵉphal (Ch.) (1), to
humiliate
5013 tapĕinŏŏ (1), to
depress; to humiliate

HUMBLEDST
3665 kâna' (1), to
humiliate, vanquish

HUMBLENESS
5012 tapĕinŏphrŏsunē
(1), *modesty, humility*

HUMBLETH
3665 kâna' (2), to
humiliate, vanquish
7817 shâchach (1), to
sink or *depress*
8213 shâphêl (2), to
humiliate
5013 tapĕinŏŏ (2), to
depress; to humiliate

HUMBLY
6800 tsâna' (1), to
humiliate
7812 shâchâh (1), to
prostrate in homage

HUMILIATION
5014 tapĕinōsis (1),
humbleness, lowliness

HUMILITY
6038 'ănâvâh (3),
condescension
5012 tapĕinŏphrŏsunē
(4), *modesty, humility*

HUMTAH
2457 chel'âh (1), *rust*

HUNDRED
520 'ammâh (1), *cubit*
3967 mê'âh (545),
hundred
3969 mᵉ'âh (Ch.) (7),
hundred
1250 diakŏsiŏi (8), *two*
hundred
1540 hĕkatŏn (14),
hundred
1541 hĕkatŏntaĕtēs (1),
centenarian
3461 murias (1),
ten-thousand
4001 pĕntakŏsiŏi (2), *five*
hundred
5071 tĕtrakŏsiŏi (4), *four*
hundred
5145 triakŏsiŏi (2), *three*
hundred
5516 chi xi stigma (2), 666

HUNDREDFOLD
3967+8180 mê'âh (1),
hundred
1540 hĕkatŏn (2),
hundred
1542 hĕkatŏntaplasiōn
(3), *hundred times*

HUNDREDS
3967 mê'âh (27), *hundred*
1540 hĕkatŏn (1),
hundred

HUNDREDTH
3967 mê'âh (3), *hundred*

HUNGER
7456 râ'êb (5), to *hunger*
7457 râ'êb (8), *hungry*
3042 limŏs (3), *scarcity,*
famine
3983 pĕinaŏ (8), to
famish; to crave

HUNGERBITTEN
7457 râ'êb (1), *hungry*

HUNGERED
3983 pĕinaŏ (2), to
famish; to crave

HUNGRED
3983 pĕinaŏ (9), to
famish; to crave

HUNGRY
7456 râ'êb (25), to *hunger*
3983 pĕinaŏ (4), to
famish; to crave
4361 prŏspĕinŏs (1),
intensely hungry

HUNT
6679 tsûwd (11), to *lie in*
wait; to *catch*
7291 râdaph (1), to *run*
after with hostility

HUNTED
4686 mâtsûwd (1), *net* or
capture; fastness

HUNTER
6718 tsayid (4), *hunting*
game; lunch, food

HUNTERS
6719 tsayâd (1),
huntsman

HUNTEST
6658 tsâdâh (1), to
desolate
6679 tsûwd (1), to *lie in*
wait; to *catch*

HUNTETH
6679 tsûwd (1), to *lie in*
wait; to *catch*

HUNTING
6718 tsayid (2), *hunting*
game; lunch, food

HUPHAM
2349 Chûwphâm (1),
protection

HUPHAMITES
2350 Chûwphâmîy (1),
Chuphamite

HUPPAH
2647 Chuppâh (1),
canopy

HUPPIM
2650 Chuppîym (3),
canopies

HUR
2354 Chûwr (16), *cell* of a
prison or *white* linen

HURAI
2360 Chûwray (1),
linen-worker

HURAM
2361 Chûwrâm (6), *noble*
2438 Chîyrâm (6), *noble*

HURI
2359 Chûwrîy (1),
linen-worker

HURL
7993 shâlak (1), to *throw*
out, down or away

HURLETH
8175 sâ'ar (1), to *storm;*
to *shiver,* i.e. *fear*

HURT
1697 dâbâr (1), *word;*
matter; thing
2248 chăbûwlâh (Ch.)
(1), *crime, wrong*
2250 chabbûwrâh (1),
weal, bruise
2255 chăbal (Ch.) (1), to
ruin, destroy
2257 chăbal (Ch.) (2),
harm, wound
3637 kâlam (2), to *taunt*
or *insult*
5062 nâgaph (2), to
inflict a disease
5142 nᵉzaq (Ch.) (1), to
suffer, inflict loss
6031 'ânâh (1), to *afflict,*
be afflicted
6087 'âtsab (1), to *worry,*
have pain or *anger*
6485 pâqad (1), to *visit,*
care for, count
7451 ra' (20), *bad; evil*
7489 râ'a' (7), to *break to*
pieces
7665 shâbar (3), to *burst*
7667 sheber (4), *fracture;*
ruin
91 adikĕŏ (10), to *do*
wrong
984 blaptŏ (2), to *hinder,*
i.e. *to injure*
2559 kakŏŏ (1), to *injure;*
to *oppress; to embitter*
5196 hubris (1), *insult;*
injury

HURTFUL
5142 nᵉzaq (Ch.) (1), to
suffer, inflict loss
7451 ra' (1), *bad; evil*
983 blabĕrŏs (1),
injurious, harmful

HURTING
7489 râ'a' (1), to *break* to
pieces

HUSBAND
376 'îysh (66), *man;*
male; someone
1167 ba'al (13), *master;*
husband; owner; citizen
2860 châthân (2),
bridegroom
435 anēr (38), *man; male*
5220 hupandrŏs (1),
married woman

HUSBAND'S
376 'îysh (2), *man; male;*
someone
2992 yâbam (2), to *marry*
a dead brother's widow
2993 yâbâm (2),
husband's brother

HUSBANDMAN
376+127 'îysh (1), *man;*
male; someone
406 'ikkâr (2), *farmer*
5647 'âbad (1), to *do,*
work, serve
1092 gĕŏrgŏs (3), *farmer;*
tenant farmer

HUSBANDMEN
406 'ikkâr (3), *farmer*
1461 gûwb (1), to *dig*
3009 yâgab (1), to *dig* or
plow
1092 gĕŏrgŏs (16),
farmer; tenant farmer

HUSBANDRY
127 'ădâmâh (1), *soil;*
land
1091 gĕŏrgiŏn (1),
cultivable, i.e. *farm*

HUSBANDS
376 'îysh (1), *man; male*

582 'ĕnôwsh (3), *man; person, human*
1167 ba'al (2), *master; husband; owner; citizen*
435 anēr (12), *man; male*
5362 philandrŏs (1), *affectionate* as a wife to her *husband*

HUSHAH
2364 Chûwshâh (1), *haste*

HUSHAI
2365 Chûwshay (14), *hasty*

HUSHAM
2367 Chûwshâm (4), *hastily*

HUSHATHITE
2843 Chûshâthîy (5), *Chushathite*

HUSHIM
2366 Chûwshîym (4), those who *hasten*

HUSK
2085 zâg (1), grape *skin*
6861 tsiqlôn (1), tied up *sack*

HUSKS
2769 kĕratiŏn (1), *pod*

HUZ
5780 'Ûwts (1), *consultation*

HUZZAB
5324 nâtsab (1), to *station*

HYMENAEUS
5211 Humĕnaiŏs (2), one *dedicated to the god of weddings*

HYMN
5214 humnĕō (1), to *celebrate* God in song

HYMNS
5215 humnŏs (2), *hymn* or religious *ode*

HYPOCRISIES
5272 hupŏkrisis (1), *deceit, hypocrisy*

HYPOCRISY
2612 chôneph (1), moral *filth*, i.e. *wickedness*
505 anupŏkritŏs (1), *sincere, genuine*
5272 hupŏkrisis (4), *deceit, hypocrisy*

HYPOCRITE
120+2611 'âdâm (1), *human being; mankind*
2611 chânêph (6), *soiled* (i.e. with sin), *impious*
5273 hupŏkritēs (3), *dissembler, hypocrite*

HYPOCRITE'S
2611 chânêph (1), *soiled* (i.e. with sin), *impious*

HYPOCRITES
120+2611 'âdâm (1), *human being; mankind*
2611 chânêph (2), *soiled* (i.e. with sin), *impious*
5273 hupŏkritēs (17), *dissembler, hypocrite*

HYPOCRITICAL
2611 chânêph (2), *soiled* (i.e. with sin), *impious*

HYSSOP
231 'êzôwb (10), *hyssop*
5301 hussōpŏs (2), *hyssop* plant

I-CHABOD
350 Îy-kâbôwd (1), *inglorious*

I-CHABOD'S
350 Îy-kâbôwd (1), *inglorious*

IBHAR
2984 Yibchar (3), *choice*

IBLEAM
2991 Yiblᵉ'âm (3), *devouring people*

IBNEIAH
2997 Yibnᵉyâh (1), *built of Jehovah*

IBNIJAH
2998 Yibnîyâh (1), *building of Jehovah*

IBRI
5681 'Ibrîy (1), *Eberite* (i.e. Hebrew)

IBZAN
78 'Ibtsân (2), *splendid*

ICE
7140 qerach (3), *ice; hail;* rock *crystal*

ICONIUM
2430 Ikŏniŏn (6), *image-like*

IDALAH
3030 Yid'ălâh (1), *Jidalah*

IDBASH
3031 Yidbâsh (1), *honeyed*

IDDO
112 'Iddôw (2), *Iddo*
3035 Yiddôw (1), *praised*
3260 Yᵉ'dîy (1), *appointed*
5714 'Iddôw (10), *timely*

IDLE
7423 rᵉmîyâh (1), *remissness; treachery*
7504 râpheh (2), *slack*
692 argŏs (6), *lazy; useless*
3026 lērŏs (1), *twaddle*, i.e. an *incredible* story

IDLENESS
6104 'atslûwth (1), *indolence*
8220 shiphlûwth (1), *remissness, idleness*
8252 shâqaṭ (1), to *repose*

IDOL
205 'âven (1), *trouble, vanity, wickedness*
457 'ĕlîyl (1), *vain idol*
4656 miphletseth (4), *terror idol*
5566 çemel (2), *likeness*
6089 'etseb (1), earthen *vessel*; painful *toil*
6090 'ôtseb (1), fashioned *idol; pain*
1494 ĕidōlŏthutŏn (1), *idolatrous offering*
1497 ĕidōlŏn (4), *idol*, or the *worship* of such

IDOL'S
1493 ĕidōlĕiŏn (1), *idol temple*

IDOLATER
1496 ĕidōlŏlatrēs (2), *image-worshipper*

IDOLATERS
1496 ĕidōlŏlatrēs (5), *image-worshipper*

IDOLATRIES
1495 ĕidōlŏlatrĕia (1), *image-worship*

IDOLATROUS
3649 kâmâr (1), pagan *priest*

IDOLATRY
8655 tᵉrâphîym (1), *healer*
1495 ĕidōlŏlatrĕia (3), *image-worship*
2712 katĕidōlŏs (1), *utterly idolatrous*

IDOLS
367 'êymâh (1), *fright*
410 'êl (1), *mighty;* the *Almighty*
457 'ĕlîyl (16), *vain idol*
1544 gillûwl (47), *idol*
2553 chammân (1), *sun*-pillar
6091 'âtsâb (16), *image, idol*
6736 tsîyr (1), *carved* idolatrous *image*
8251 shiqqûwts (1), *disgusting; idol*
8655 tᵉrâphîym (1), *healer*
1494 ĕidōlŏthutŏn (9), *idolatrous offering*
1497 ĕidōlŏn (7), *idol*, or the *worship* of such

IDUMAEA
2401 Idŏumaia (1), *Idumæa*, i.e. Edom

IDUMEA
123 'Ĕdôm (4), *red*

IF
176 'ôw (3), *or, whether*
194 'ûwlay (9), *if not*
432 'illûw (1), *if*
518 'îm (557), *whether?; if*
834 'ăsher (19), *who, which, what, that*
2005 hên (3), *lo!; if!*
2006 hên (Ch.) (11), *lo; whether, but, if*
3588 kîy (159), *for, that because*
3808 lô' (1), *no, not*
3863 lûw' (7), *if; would that!*
3883 lûwl (1), *spiral step*
3884 lûwlê' (2), *if not*
6112 'Êtsen (1), *spear*
148 aischrŏlŏgia (3), *vile conversation*
1437 ĕan (216), *in case that, provided*
1477 hĕdraiōma (5), *basis, foundation*
1487 ĕi (305), *if, whether*
1489 ĕigĕ (5), *if indeed*
1490 ĕi dĕ mē(gĕ) (4), *but if not*
1499 ĕi kai (6), *if also*

1512 ĕi pĕr (4), *if perhaps*
1513 ĕi pōs (4), *if somehow*
1535 ĕitĕ (1), *if too*
2579 kan (5), *and if*
3379 mēpŏtĕ (1), *not ever; if*, or *lest ever*

IGAL
3008 Yig'âl (2), *avenger*

IGDALIAH
3012 Yigdalyâhûw (1), *magnified of Jehovah*

IGEAL
3008 Yig'âl (1), *avenger*

IGNOMINY
7036 qâlôwn (1), *disgrace*

IGNORANCE
7684 shᵉgâgâh (12), *mistake, transgression*
7686 shâgâh (1), to *transgress by mistake*
52 agnŏia (4), *ignorance*
56 agnŏsia (1), state of *ignorance*

IGNORANT
3808+3045 lô' (3), no, *not know; not understand*
50 agnŏĕō (10), to *not know; not understand*
2399 idiōtēs (1), *not initiated; untrained*
2990 lanthanō (2), to *lie hid; unwittingly*

IGNORANTLY
1097+1847 bᵉlîy (1), *not yet; lacking*
7683 shâgag (1), to *sin through oversight*
50 agnŏĕō (2), to *not know; not understand*

IIM
5864 'Iyîym (2), *ruins*

IJE-ABARIM
5863 'Iyêy hâ-'Ăbârîym (2), *ruins of the passers*

IJON
5859 'Iyôwn (3), *ruin*

IKKESH
6142 'Iqqêsh (3), *perverse*

ILAI
5866 'Îylay (1), *elevated*

ILL
3415 yâra' (2), to *fear*
6709 tsachănâh (1), *stench*
7451 ra' (8), *bad; evil*
7489 râ'a' (3), to *be good for nothing*
2556 kakŏs (1), *bad, evil, wrong*

ILLUMINATED
5461 phōtizō (1), to *shine* or to *brighten* up

ILLYRICUM
2437 Illurikŏn (1), *Illyricum*

IMAGE
4676 matstsêbâh (3), *column or stone*
4906 maskîyth (1), *carved figure*
5566 çemel (2), *likeness*
6459 peçel (2), *idol*
6676 tsavva'r (Ch.) (1), *back of the neck*

6754 tselem (6), *phantom; idol*
6755 tselem (Ch.) (16), idolatrous *figure*
6816 tsa'tsûa' (1), *sculpture* work
8544 tᵉmûwnâh (1), something *fashioned*
8655 tᵉrâphîym (2), *healer*
1504 ĕikŏn (22), likeness
5481 charaktēr (1), exact copy or representation

IMAGE'S
6755 tselem (Ch.) (1), idolatrous *figure*

IMAGERY
4906 maskîyth (1), carved *figure*

IMAGES
457 'ĕlîyl (1), *vain idol*
1544 gillûwl (1), *idol*
2553 chammân (6), *sun*-pillar
4676 matstsêbâh (14), *column* or *stone*
6091 'âtsâb (1), *image, idol*
6456 pᵉçîyl (2), *idol*
6754 tselem (9), *phantom; idol*
8655 tᵉrâphîym (5), *healer*

IMAGINATION
3336 yêtser (4), *form*
8307 shᵉrîyrûwth (9), *obstinacy*
1271 dianŏia (1), mind or thought

IMAGINATIONS
3336 yêtser (3), *form*
4284 machăshâbâh (3), *contrivance; plan*
1261 dialŏgismŏs (1), consideration; debate
3053 lŏgismŏs (1), reasoning; conscience

IMAGINE
1897 hâgâh (2), to *murmur, ponder*
2050 hâthath (1), to *assail, verbally attack*
2554 châmaç (1), to be *violent; to maltreat*
2790 chârash (1), to be *silent; to be deaf*
2803 châshab (5), to *plot; to think, regard*
3191 mĕlĕtaŏ (1), to *plot, think about*

IMAGINED
2161 zâmam (1), to *plan*
2803 châshab (2), to *plot; to think, regard*

IMAGINETH
2803 châshab (1), to *plot; to think, regard*

IMLA
3229 Yimlâ' (2), *full*

IMLAH
3229 Yimlâ' (2), *full*

IMMANUEL
6005 'Immânûw'êl (2), *with us* (is) *God*

IMMEDIATELY
1824 ĕxautēs (3), instantly, at once
2112 ĕuthĕŏs (35), at once or soon
2117 ĕuthus (3), at once, immediately
3916 parachrēma (13), instantly, immediately

IMMER
564 'Immêr (10), *talkative*

IMMORTAL
862 aphthartŏs (1), undecaying, immortal

IMMORTALITY
110 athanasia (3), deathlessness
861 aphtharsia (2), unending existence

IMMUTABILITY
276 amĕtathĕtŏs (1), unchangeable

IMMUTABLE
276 amĕtathĕtŏs (1), unchangeable

IMNA
3234 Yimnâ' (1), *he will restrain*

IMNAH
3232 Yimnâh (2), *prosperity*

IMPART
3330 mĕtadidōmi (2), to share, distribute

IMPARTED
2505 châlaq (1), to be *smooth; be slippery*
3330 mĕtadidōmi (1), to share, distribute

IMPEDIMENT
3424 mŏgilalŏs (1), hardly talking

IMPENITENT
279 amĕtanŏĕtŏs (1), unrepentant

IMPERIOUS
7986 shalleṭeth (1), dominant woman

IMPLACABLE
786 aspŏndŏs (1), not reconcilable

IMPLEAD
1458 ĕgkalĕō (1), to charge, criminate

IMPORTUNITY
335 anaidĕia (1), importunity, boldness

IMPOSE
7412 rᵉmâh (Ch.) (1), to *throw; to set; to assess*

IMPOSED
1942 ĕpikaluma (1), pretext, covering

IMPOSSIBLE
101 adunatĕō (2), to be impossible
102 adunatŏs (6), weak; impossible
418 anĕndĕktŏs (1), impossible

IMPOTENT
102 adunatŏs (1), weak; impossible
770 asthĕnĕō (2), to be *feeble*
772 asthĕnēs (1), *strengthless, weak*

IMPOVERISH
7567 râshash (1), to *demolish*

IMPOVERISHED
1809 dâlal (1), to be *feeble; to be oppressed*
5533 çâkan (1), to *grow, make poor*
7567 râshash (1), to *demolish*

IMPRISONED
5439 phulakizō (1), to incarcerate, imprison

IMPRISONMENT
613 'ĕçûwr (Ch.) (1), *manacles, chains*
5438 phulakē (1), watch; prison; haunt

IMPRISONMENTS
5438 phulakē (1), watch; prison; haunt

IMPUDENT
2389+4696 châzâq (1), *severe, hard, violent*
5810 'âzaz (1), to be *stout; be bold*
7186+6440 qâsheh (1), *severe*

IMPUTE
2803 châshab (1), to *regard; to compute*
7760 sûwm (1), to *put, place*
3049 lŏgizŏmai (1), to credit; to think, regard

IMPUTED
2803 châshab (2), to *think, regard; compute*
1677 ĕllŏgĕō (1), to charge to one's account
3049 lŏgizŏmai (5), to credit; to think, regard

IMPUTETH
2803 châshab (1), to *think, regard; compute*
3049 lŏgizŏmai (1), to credit; to think, regard

IMPUTING
3049 lŏgizŏmai (1), to credit; to think, regard

IMRAH
3236 Yimrâh (1), *interchange*

IMRI
556 'Imrîy (2), *strength, force*

INASMUCH
1115 biltîy (1), *except, without, unless, besides*
3588 kîy (1), *for, that because*
2526 kathŏ (1), precisely as, in proportion as

INCENSE
3828 lᵉbôwnâh (6), *frankincense*

IMPOTENT 6999 qâṭar (58), *to turn into fragrance* by fire
7002 qiṭṭêr (1), *perfume*
7004 qᵉṭôreth (57), *fumigation*
2368 thumiama (4), incense offering
2370 thumiaŏ (1), to offer aromatic fumes

INCENSED
2734 chârâh (2), to *blaze*

INCLINE
5186 nâṭâh (15), to *stretch* or spread out
7181 qâshab (1), to *prick up* the ears

INCLINED
5186 nâṭâh (13), to *stretch* or spread out

INCLINETH
7743 shûwach (1), to *sink*

INCLOSE
6696 tsûwr (1), to *cramp*, i.e. *confine; to harass*

INCLOSED
1443 gâdar (1), to *build a* stone *wall*
3803 kâthar (1), to *enclose, besiege; to wait*
4142 mûwçabbâh (2), *backside; fold*
5274 nâ'al (1), to *fasten up, lock*
5362 nâqaph (1), to *surround or circulate*
5462 çâgar (1), to *shut up; to surrender*
4788 sugklĕiō (1), to net fish; to lock up persons

INCLOSINGS
4396 millû'âh (2), *setting*

INCONTINENCY
192 akrasia (1), lack of control of self

INCONTINENT
193 akratēs (1), without self-control

INCORRUPTIBLE
862 aphthartŏs (4), undecaying, immortal

INCORRUPTION
861 aphtharsia (4), unending existence

INCREASE
2981 yᵉbûwl (10), *produce, crop; harvest*
3254 yâçaph (6), to *add or augment*
4768 marbîyth (3), *interest* on money
5107 nûwb (1), to (*make*) *flourish; to utter*
6555 pârats (1), to *break out*
7235 râbâh (18), to *increase*
7239 ribbôw (1), *myriad,* indefinite *large number*
7685 sâgâh (2), to *enlarge, be prosperous*
7698 sheger (1), *what comes forth*
8393 tᵉbûw'âh (23), *income,* i.e. *produce*

8570 tᵉnûwbâh (2), *crop, produce*
8635 tarbûwth (6), *progeny, brood*
837 auxanō (4), *to grow, i.e. enlarge*
838 auxēsis (2), *growth, increase*
4052 pĕrissĕuō (1), *to superabound*
4121 plĕŏnazō (1), *to increase; superabound*
4298 prŏkŏptō (1), *to go ahead, advance*
4369 prŏstithēmi (1), *to lay beside, annex*

INCREASED
1431 gâdal (1), *to be great, make great*
3254 yâçaph (5), *to add or augment*
5927 'âlâh (3), *to ascend, be high, mount*
6105 'âtsam (4), *to be, make numerous*
6509 pârâh (3), *to bear fruit*
6555 pârats (4), *to break out*
7227 rab (2), *great*
7230 rôb (1), *abundance*
7231 râbab (3), *to increase; to multiply*
7235 râbâh (15), *to increase*
8317 shârats (1), *to swarm, or abound*
837 auxanō (3), *to grow, i.e. enlarge*
1743 ĕndunamŏō (1), *to empower, strengthen*
4052 pĕrissĕuō (1), *to superabound*
4147 plŏutĕō (1), *to be, become wealthy*
4298 prŏkŏptō (1), *to go ahead, advance*

INCREASEST
7235 râbâh (1), *to increase*

INCREASETH
553 'âmats (1), *to be strong; be courageous*
1342 gâ'âh (1), *to rise; to grow tall; be majestic*
3254 yâçaph (4), *to add or augment*
5927 'âlâh (1), *to ascend, be high, mount*
7235 râbâh (5), *to increase*
7679 sâgâ' (1), *to laud, extol*
837 auxanō (1), *to grow, i.e. enlarge*

INCREASING
837 auxanō (1), *to grow, i.e. enlarge*

INCREDIBLE
571 apistŏs (1), *without faith; incredible*

INCURABLE
369+4832 'ayin (1), *there is no, i.e., not exist*
605 'ânash (5), *to be frail, feeble*

INDEBTED
3784 ŏphĕilō (1), *to owe; to be under obligation*

INDEED
61 'ăbâl (2), *truly, surely; yet, but*
389 'ak (1), *surely; only, however*
546 'omnâh (2), *surely*
551 'omnâm (2), *verily, indeed, truly*
552 'umnâm (3), *verily, indeed, truly*
1571 gam (1), *also; even; yea; though*
230 alēthōs (6), *truly, surely*
235 alla (1), *but, yet, except, instead*
1063 gar (2), *for, indeed, but, because*
2532 kai (2), *and; or; even; also*
3303 mĕn (22), *indeed*
3689 ŏntōs (6), *really, certainly*

INDIA
1912 Hôdûw (2), *India*

INDIGNATION
2194 zâ'am (4), *to be enraged*
2195 za'am (20), *fury, anger*
2197 za'aph (2), *anger, rage*
2534 chêmâh (1), *heat; anger; poison*
3707 kâ'aç (1), *to grieve, rage, be indignant*
3708 ka'aç (1), *vexation, grief*
7110 qetseph (3), *rage or strife*
23 aganaktĕō (4), *to be indignant*
24 aganaktēsis (1), *indignation*
2205 zēlŏs (2), *zeal, ardor; jealousy, malice*
2372 thumŏs (1), *passion, anger*
3709 ŏrgē (1), *ire; punishment*

INDITING
7370 râchash (1), *to gush*

INDUSTRIOUS
6213+4399 'âsâh (1), *to do or make*

INEXCUSABLE
379 anapŏlŏgētŏs (1), *without excuse*

INFAMOUS
2931+8034 țâmê' (1), *foul; ceremonially impure*

INFAMY
1681 dibbâh (2), *slander, bad report*

INFANT
5764 'ûwl (1), *nursing babe*
5768 'ôwlêl (1), *suckling child*

INFANTS
5768 'ôwlêl (2), *suckling child*
1025 brĕphŏs (1), *infant*

INFERIOR
772 'ără' (Ch.) (1), *earth, ground, land; inferior*
5307 nâphal (2), *to fall*
2274 hēttaō (1), *to rate lower, be inferior*

INFIDEL
571 apistŏs (2), *without faith; untrustworthy*

INFINITE
369+4557 'ayin (1), *there is no, i.e., not exist*
369+7093 'ayin (2), *there is no, i.e., not exist*

INFIRMITIES
769 asthĕnĕia (10), *feebleness; malady*
771 asthĕnēma (1), *failing, weakness*
3554 nŏsŏs (1), *malady, disease*

INFIRMITY
1738 dâvâh (1), *to be in menstruation cycle*
2470 châlâh (1), *to be weak, sick, afflicted*
4245 machăleh (1), *sickness*
769 asthĕnĕia (7), *feebleness; malady*

INFLAME
1814 dâlaq (1), *to flame; to pursue*

INFLAMMATION
1816 dalleqeth (1), *burning fever*
6867 tsârebeth (1), *conflagration*

INFLUENCES
4575 ma'ădannâh (1), *bond, i.e. group*

INFOLDING
3947 lâqach (1), *to take*

INFORM
3384 yârâh (1), *to point; to teach*

INFORMED
995 bîyn (1), *to understand; discern*
1718 ĕmphanizō (3), *to show forth*
2727 katēchĕō (2), *to indoctrinate*

INGATHERING
614 'âçîyph (2), *harvest, gathering in of crops*

INHABIT
3427 yâshab (8), *to dwell, to remain; to settle*
7931 shâkan (2), *to reside*

INHABITANT
1481 gûwr (1), *to sojourn, live as an alien*
3427 yâshab (31), *to dwell, to remain*
7934 shâkên (1), *resident; fellow-citizen*

INHABITANTS
1753 dûwr (Ch.) (2), *to reside, live in*
3427 yâshab (190), *to dwell, to remain*
7934 shâkên (2), *resident; fellow-citizen*

8453 tôwshâb (1), *temporary dweller*
2730 katŏikĕō (1), *to reside, live in*

INHABITED
1509 gᵉzêrâh (1), *desert, unfertile place*
3427 yâshab (29), *to dwell, to remain*
4186 môwshâb (1), *seat; site; abode*
7931 shâkan (1), *to reside*

INHABITERS
2730 katŏikĕō (2), *to reside, live in*

INHABITEST
3427 yâshab (1), *to dwell, to remain; to settle*

INHABITETH
3427 yâshab (1), *to dwell, to remain; to settle*
7931 shâkan (1), *to reside*

INHABITING
6728 tsîyîy (1), *desert-dweller; wild beast*

INHERIT
3423 yârash (21), *to inherit; to impoverish*
5157 nâchal (25), *to inherit*
5159 nachălâh (2), *occupancy*
2816 klĕrŏnŏmĕō (14), *to be an heir to, inherit*

INHERITANCE
2490 châlal (1), *to profane, defile*
2506 chêleq (1), *allotment*
3423 yârash (1), *to inherit; to impoverish*
3425 yᵉrushâh (2), *conquest*
4181 môwrâshâh (2), *possession*
5157 nâchal (18), *to inherit*
5159 nachălâh (189), *occupancy*
2817 klĕrŏnŏmia (14), *inherited possession*
2819 klĕrŏs (2), *lot, portion*
2820 klĕrŏō (2), *to allot*

INHERITANCES
5159 nachălâh (1), *occupancy*

INHERITED
3423 yârash (2), *to inherit; to impoverish*
5157 nâchal (3), *to inherit*
2816 klĕrŏnŏmĕō (1), *to be an heir to, inherit*

INHERITETH
5157 nâchal (1), *to inherit*

INHERITOR
3423 yârash (1), *to inherit; to impoverish*

INIQUITIES
1647+5771 Gêrᵉshôm (1), *refugee*
5758 'ivyâ' (Ch.) (1), *perverseness*
5766 'evel (1), *moral evil*
5771 'âvôn (47), *evil*

92 adikēma (1), *wrong done*
458 anŏmia (3), *violation of law, wickedness*
4189 pŏnēria (1), *malice, evil, wickedness*

INIQUITY
205 'âven (47), *trouble, vanity, wickedness*
1942 havvâh (1), *desire; craving*
5753 'âvâh (4), to *be crooked*
5766 'evel (35), *moral evil*
5771 'âvôn (170), *moral evil*
5932 'alvâh (1), *moral perverseness*
5999 'âmâl (1), *wearing effort; worry*
7562 resha' (1), *moral wrong*
93 adikia (6), *wrongfulness*
458 anŏmia (8), *violation of law, wickedness*
3892 paranŏmia (1), *transgression*

INJURED
91 adikĕō (1), to *do wrong*

INJURIOUS
5197 hubristēs (1), *maltreater, violent*

INJUSTICE
2555 châmâç (1), *violence; malice*

INK
1773 dᵉyôw (1), *ink*
3188 mĕlan (3), *black ink*

INKHORN
7083 qeçeth (3), *ink-stand*

INN
4411 mâlôwn (3), *lodgment* for night
2646 kataluma (1), *lodging-place*
3829 pandŏchĕiŏn (1), public *lodging-place*

INNER
2315 cheder (4), *apartment, chamber*
6441 pᵉnîymâh (1), *indoors, inside*
6442 pᵉnîymîy (30), *interior, inner*
2080 ĕsō (1), *inside, inner, in*
2082 ĕsōtĕrŏs (1), *interior, inner*

INNERMOST
2315 cheder (2), *apartment, chamber*

INNOCENCY
2136 zâkûw (Ch.) (1), *purity; justice*
5356 niqqâyôwn (4), *clearness; cleanness*

INNOCENT
2600 chinnâm (1), *gratis, free*
2643 chaph (1), *pure, clean*

5352 nâqâh (5), to *be, make clean;* to *be bare*
5355 nâqîy (29), *innocent*
121 athŏŏs (2), *not guilty*

INNOCENTS
5355 nâqîy (2), *innocent*

INNUMERABLE
369+4557 'ayin (4), *there is no, i.e., not exist*
382 anarithmētŏs (1), *without number*
3461 murias (2), *ten-thousand*

INORDINATE
5691 'ăgâbâh (1), *love, amorousness*
3806 pathŏs (1), *passion, concupiscence*

INQUISITION
1245 bâqash (1), to *search;* to *strive after*
1875 dârash (2), to *pursue or search*

INSCRIPTION
1924 ĕpigraphō (1), to *inscribe, write upon*

INSIDE
1004 bayith (1), *house; temple; family, tribe*

INSOMUCH
1519 ĕis (1), to *or into*
5620 hōstĕ (17), *thus, therefore*

INSPIRATION
5397 nᵉshâmâh (1), *breath, life*
2315 thĕŏpnĕustŏs (1), *divinely breathed in*

INSTANT
6621 petha' (2), *wink, i.e. moment; quickly*
7281 rega' (2), *very short space of time*
1945 ĕpikĕimai (1), to *rest upon; press upon*
2186 ĕphistēmi (1), to *be present;* to *approach*
4342 prŏskartĕrĕō (1), to *attend;* to *adhere*
5610 hōra (1), *hour, i.e. a unit of time*

INSTANTLY
1722+1616 ĕn (1), *in; during; because of*
4705 spŏudaiŏs (1), *prompt, energetic*

INSTEAD
8478 tachath (35), *underneath;* in *lieu of*

INSTRUCT
995 bîyn (1), to *understand; discern*
3250 yiççôwr (1), *reprover, corrector*
3256 yâçar (3), to *chastise;* to *instruct*
3925 lâmad (1), to *teach, train*
7919 sâkal (2), to *be or act circumspect*
4822 sumbibazō (1), to *unite;* to *show, teach*

INSTRUCTED
995 bîyn (2), to *understand; discern*

3045 yâda' (1), to *know*
3245 yâçad (1), to *settle, consult, establish*
3256 yâçar (5), to *chastise;* to *instruct*
3384 yârâh (1), to *point;* to *teach*
3925 lâmad (2), to *teach, train*
7919 sâkal (1), to *be or act circumspect*
2727 katēchĕō (3), to *indoctrinate*
3100 mathētĕuō (1), to *become a student*
3453 muĕō (1), to *initiate*
4264 prŏbibazō (1), to *bring to the front*

INSTRUCTER
3913 lâṭash (1), to *sharpen;* to *pierce*

INSTRUCTERS
3807 paidagōgŏs (1), *tutor, cf. pedagogue*

INSTRUCTING
3811 paidĕuō (1), to *educate or discipline*

INSTRUCTION
4148 mûwçâr (30), *reproof, warning*
4561 môçâr (1), *admonition*
3809 paidĕia (1), *disciplinary correction*

INSTRUCTOR
3810 paidĕutēs (1), *teacher or discipliner*

INSTRUMENT
3627 kᵉlîy (2), *implement, thing*

INSTRUMENTS
1761 dachăvâh (Ch.) (1), musical *instrument*
3627 kᵉlîy (37), *implement, thing*
4482 mên (1), *part;* musical *chord*
7991 shâlîysh (1), *triangle* instrument
3696 hŏplŏn (2), *implement, or utensil*

INSURRECTION
5376 nᵉsâ' (Ch.) (1), to *lift up*
7285 regesh (1), *tumultuous crowd*
2721 katĕphistēmi (1), to *rush upon in an assault*
4714 stasis (1), one *leading an uprising*
4955 sustasiastēs (1), *fellow-insurgent*

INTEGRITY
8537 tôm (11), *prosperity; innocence*
8538 tummâh (5), *innocence*

INTELLIGENCE
995 bîyn (1), to *understand; discern*

INTEND
559 'âmar (2), to *say*
1014 bŏulŏmai (1), to *be willing, desire; choose*

3195 mĕllō (1), to *intend, i.e. be about to*

INTENDED
5186 nâṭâh (1), to *stretch or spread out*

INTENDEST
559 'âmar (1), to *say*

INTENDING
1011 bŏulĕuō (1), to *deliberate;* to *resolve*
2309 thĕlō (1), to *will;* to *desire;* to *choose*
3195 mĕllō (1), to *intend, i.e. be about to*

INTENT
1701 dibrâh (Ch.) (1), *because, on account of*
4616 ma'an (2), *on account of;* in *order*
5668 'ăbûwr (1), *on account of;* in *order*
2443 hina (2), in *order that*
3056 lŏgŏs (1), *word, matter, thing*

INTENTS
4209 mᵉzimmâh (1), *plan; sagacity*
1771 ĕnnŏia (1), *moral understanding*

INTERCESSION
6293 pâga' (4), to *impinge*
1793 ĕntugchanō (4), to *entreat, petition*
5241 hupĕrĕntugchanō (1), to *intercede*

INTERCESSIONS
1783 ĕntĕuxis (1), *intercession*

INTERCESSOR
6293 pâga' (1), to *impinge*

INTERMEDDLE
6148 'ârab (1), to *intermix*

INTERMEDDLETH
1566 gâla' (1), to *be obstinate;* to *burst forth*

INTERMISSION
2014 hăphûgâh (1), *relaxation*

INTERPRET
6622 pâthar (4), to *interpret* a dream
1329 diĕrmēnĕuō (4), to *explain thoroughly*

INTERPRETATION
4426 mᵉlîytsâh (1), *aphorism, saying*
6591 pᵉshar (Ch.) (30), *interpretation*
6592 pêsher (1), *interpretation*
6623 pithrôwn (5), *interpretation*
7667 sheber (1), *solution* of a dream
1329 diĕrmēnĕuō (1), to *explain thoroughly*
1955 ĕpilusis (1), *interpretation*
2058 hĕrmēnĕia (2), *translation*
2059 hĕrmēnĕuō (3), to *translate*
3177 mĕthĕrmēnĕuō (1), to *translate*

INTERPRETATIONS
6591 pᵉshar (Ch.) (1), *interpretation*
6623 pithrôwn (1), *interpretation*

INTERPRETED
6622 pâthar (3), to *interpret* a dream
8638 tirgam (1), to *translate, interpret*
2059 hĕrmēnĕuō (1), to *translate*
3177 mĕthĕrmēnĕuō (6), to *translate*

INTERPRETER
3887 lûwts (2), to *scoff*; to *interpret*; to *intercede*
6622 pâthar (1), to *interpret* a dream
1328 diĕrmēnĕutēs (1), *explainer, translator*

INTERPRETING
6591 pᵉshar (Ch.) (1), *interpretation*

INTREAT
2470 châlâh (3), to be *weak, sick, afflicted*
6279 'âthar (6), *intercede*
6293 pâga' (2), to *impinge*
6419 pâlal (1), to *intercede, pray*
2065 ĕrōtaō (1), to *interrogate*; to *request*
3870 parakaleō (2), to *call, invite*

INTREATED
2470 châlâh (1), to be *weak, sick, afflicted*
2589 channôwth (1), *supplication*
2603 chânan (1), to *implore*
6279 'âthar (12), *intercede* in prayer
2138 ĕupĕithēs (1), *compliant, submissive*
3862 paradōsis (1), *precept; tradition*
3870 parakaleō (1), to *call, invite*

INTREATIES
8469 tachănûwn (1), earnest *prayer, plea*

INTREATY
3874 paraklēsis (1), *imploring, exhortation*

INTRUDING
1687 ĕmbatĕuō (1), to *intrude on*

INVADE
935 bôw' (1), to *go* or *come*
1464 gûwd (1), to *attack*

INVADED
935 bôw' (1), to *go* or *come*
6584 pâshaţ (4), to *strip*, i.e. *unclothe, plunder*

INVASION
6584 pâshaţ (1), to *strip*, i.e. *unclothe, plunder, flay*

INVENT
2803 châshab (1), to *weave, fabricate*

INVENTED
2803 châshab (1), to *weave, fabricate*

INVENTIONS
2810 chishshâbôwn (1), *machination, scheme*
4209 mᵉzimmâh (1), *plan; sagacity*
4611 ma'ălâl (2), *act, deed*
5949 'ălîylâh (1), *opportunity, action*

INVENTORS
2182 ĕphĕurĕtēs (1), *contriver, inventor*

INVISIBLE
517 aŏratŏs (5), *invisible, not seen*

INVITED
7121 qârâ' (3), to *call* out

INWARD
1004 bayith (7), *house; temple; family, tribe*
2315 cheder (2), *apartment, chamber*
2910 ţûwchâh (2), inmost *thought*
5475 côwd (1), *intimacy; consultation; secret*
6441 pᵉnîymâh (2), *indoors, inside*
6442 pᵉnîymîy (1), *interior, inner*
7130 qereb (5), *nearest part*, i.e. the *center*
2080 ĕsō (1), *inside, inner, in*
2081 ĕsōthĕn (2), *from inside; inside*
4698 splagchnŏn (1), *intestine; affection, pity* or *sympathy*

INWARDLY
7130 qereb (1), *nearest part*, i.e. the *center*
1722+2927 ĕn (1), *in; during; because of*
2081 ĕsōthĕn (1), *from inside; inside*

INWARDS
7130 qereb (19), *nearest part*, i.e. the *center*

IPHEDEIAH
3301 Yiphdᵉyâh (1), *Jehovah will liberate*

IR
5893 'Îyr (1), *city, town, unwalled-village*

IR-NAHASH
5904 'Îyr Nâchâsh (1), *city of a serpent*

IR-SHEMESH
5905 'Îyr Shemesh (1), *city of* (the) *sun*

IRA
5896 'Îyrâ' (6), *wakefulness*

IRAD
5897 'Îyrâd (2), *fugitive*

IRAM
5902 'Îyrâm (2), *city-wise*

IRI
5901 'Îyrîy (1), *urbane*

IRIJAH
3376 Yir'îyâyh (2), *fearful of Jehovah*

IRON
1270 barzel (72), *iron; iron implement*
3375 Yir'ôwn (1), *fearfulness*
6523 parzel (Ch.) (19), *iron*
4603 sidērŏs (5), made *of iron*
4604 sidērŏs (1), *iron*

IRONS
7905 sukkâh (1), *dart, harpoon*

IRPEEL
3416 Yirpᵉ'êl (1), *God will heal*

IRU
5902 'Îyrâm (1), *city-wise*

ISAAC
3327 Yitschâq (104), *laughter*
3446 Yischâq (4), *he will laugh*
2464 Isaak (20), *he will laugh*

ISAAC'S
3327 Yitschâq (4), *laughter*

ISAIAH
3470 Yᵉsha'yâh (32), *Jehovah has saved*

ISCAH
3252 Yiçkâh (1), *observant*

ISCARIOT
2469 Iskariōtēs (11), *inhabitant of Kerioth*

ISH-BOSHETH
378 'Îysh-Bôsheth (11), *man of shame*

ISH-TOB
382 'Îysh-Ţôwb (2), *man of Tob*

ISHBAH
3431 Yishbach (1), *he will praise*

ISHBAK
3435 Yishbâq (2), *he will leave*

ISHBI-BENOB
3430 Yishbôw bᵉ-Nôb (1), *his dwelling* (is) *in Nob*

ISHI
376 'îysh (1), *man; male; someone*
3469 Yish'îy (5), *saving*

ISHIAH
3449 Yishshîyâh (1), *Jehovah will lend*

ISHIJAH
3449 Yishshîyâh (1), *Jehovah will lend*

ISHMA
3457 Yishmâ' (1), *desolate*

ISHMAEL
3458 Yishmâ'ê'l (47), *God will hear*

ISHMAEL'S
3458 Yishmâ'ê'l (1), *God will hear*

ISHMAELITE
3458 Yishmâ'ê'l (1), *God will hear*

ISHMAELITES
3459 Yishmâ'ê'lîy (2), *Jishmaëlite*

ISHMAIAH
3460 Yishma'yâh (1), *Jehovah will hear*

ISHMEELITE
3459 Yishmâ'ê'lîy (1), *Jishmaëlite*

ISHMEELITES
3459 Yishmâ'ê'lîy (4), *Jishmaëlite*

ISHMERAI
3461 Yishmᵉray (1), *preservative*

ISHOD
379 'Îyshhôwd (1), *man of renown*

ISHPAN
3473 Yishpân (1), *he will hide*

ISHUAH
3438 Yishvâh (1), *he will level*

ISHUAI
3440 Yishvîy (1), *level*

ISHUI
3440 Yishvîy (1), *level*

ISLAND
336 'îy (1), *not*
338 'îy (1), solitary wild creature that *howls*
3519 nēsiŏn (1), small *island*
3520 nēsŏs (6), *island*

ISLANDS
338 'îy (1), solitary wild creature that *howls*
339 'îy (6), dry *land; coast; island*

ISLE
339 'îy (3), *coast; island*
3520 nēsŏs (3), *island*

ISLES
339 'îy (27), dry *land; coast; island*

ISMACHIAH
3253 Yiçmakyâhûw (1), *Jehovah will sustain*

ISMAIAH
3460 Yishma'yâh (1), *Jehovah will hear*

ISPAH
3472 Yishpâh (1), *he will scratch*

ISRAEL
3478 Yisrâ'êl (2477), *he will rule* (as) *God*
3479 Yisrâ'êl (Ch.) (8), *he will rule* (as) *God*
3481 Yisrᵉ'êlîy (1), *Jisreëlite*
2474 Israēl (70), *he will rule* (as) *God*
2475 Israēlitēs (5), descendants *of Israel*

ISRAEL'S
3478 Yisrâ'êl (10), *he will rule* (as) *God*

ISRAELITE
1121+3478 bên (1), *son, descendant; people*
3481 Yisreʼêlîy (1), *Jisreëlite*
2475 Israēlitēs (2), descendants *of Israel*

ISRAELITES
3478 Yisrâ'êl (16), *he will rule* (as) *God*
2475 Israēlitēs (2), descendants *of Israel*

ISRAELITISH
3482 Yisreʼêlîyth (3), *Jisreëlitess*

ISSACHAR
3485 Yissâˢkâr (43), *he will bring a reward*
2466 Isachar (1), *he will bring a reward*

ISSHIAH
3449 Yishshîyâh (2), *Jehovah will lend*

ISSUE
2100 zûwb (16), *to flow freely, gush*
2101 zôwb (11), *flux or discharge*
2231 zirmâh (1), *emission* of semen
3318 yâtsâ' (3), *to go, bring out*
4138 môwledeth (1), *offspring, family*
4726 mâqôwr (1), *flow*
6849 tsⁿephîʼâh (1), *outcast thing, offshoots*
131 haimŏrrhĕŏ (1), *to have a hemorrhage*
4511 rhusis (3), *flux*
4690 spĕrma (1), *seed, offspring*

ISSUED
3318 yâtsâ' (4), *to go, bring out*
5047 nⁿegad (Ch.) (1), *to flow*
1607 ĕkpŏrĕuŏmai (2), *to depart, be discharged*

ISSUES
8444 tôwtsâ'âh (2), *exit, boundary; source*

ISUAH
3440 Yishvîy (1), *level*

ISUI
3440 Yishvîy (1), *level*

ITALIAN
2483 Italikŏs (1), *belonging to Italia*

ITALY
2482 Italia (4), *Italia*

ITCH
2775 chereç (1), *itch; sun*

ITCHING
2833 knēthō (1), *to tickle, feel an itch*

ITHAI
863 'Ittay (1), *near*

ITHAMAR
385 'Îythâmâr (21), *coast of the palm-tree*

ITHIEL
384 'Îythîy'êl (3), *God has arrived*

ITHMAH
3495 Yithmâh (1), *orphanage*

ITHNAN
3497 Yithnân (1), *extensive*

ITHRA
3501 Yithrâ' (1), *wealth*

ITHRAN
3506 Yithrân (3), *excellent*

ITHREAM
3507 Yithrⁿeʼâm (2), *excellence of people*

ITHRITE
3505 Yithrîy (4), *Jithrite*

ITHRITES
3505 Yithrîy (1), *Jithrite*

ITTAH-KAZIN
6278 'Êth Qâtsîyn (1), *time of a judge*

ITTAI
863 'Ittay (8), *near*

ITURAEA
2434 hilasmŏs (1), *atonement, expiator*

IVAH
5755 'Ivvâh (3), *overthrow, ruin*

IVORY
8127 shên (10), *tooth; ivory; cliff*
8143 shenhabbîym (2), *elephant's ivory tusk*
1661 ĕlĕphantinŏs (1), *of ivory*

IZEHAR
3324 Yitshâr (1), *olive oil; anointing*

IZEHARITES
3325 Yitshârîy (1), *Jitsharite*

IZHAR
3324 Yitshâr (8), *olive oil; anointing*

IZHARITES
3325 Yitshârîy (3), *Jitsharite*

IZRAHIAH
3156 Yizrachyâh (2), *Jehovah will shine*

IZRAHITE
3155 Yizrâch (1), *Ezrachite or Zarchite*

IZRI
3342 yeqeb (1), *wine-vat, wine-press*

JAAKAN
3292 Ya'ăqân (1), *Jaakan*

JAAKOBAH
3291 Ya'ăqôbâh (1), *heel-catcher*

JAALA
3279 Ya'ălâ' (1), *to be valuable*

JAALAH
3279 Ya'ălâ' (1), *to be valuable*

JAALAM
3281 Ya'lâm (4), *occult*

JAANAI
3285 Ya'ănay (1), *responsive*

JAARE-OREGIM
3296 Ya'ărêy 'Orⁿegîym (1), *woods of weavers*

JAASAU
3299 Ya'ăsûw (1), *they will do*

JAASIEL
3300 Ya'ăsîy'êl (1), *made of God*

JAAZANIAH
2970 Ya'ăzanyâh (4), *heard of Jehovah*

JAAZER
3270 Ya'ăzêyr (2), *helpful*

JAAZIAH
3269 Ya'ăzîyâhûw (2), *emboldened of Jehovah*

JAAZIEL
3268 Ya'ăzîy'êl (1), *emboldened of God*

JABAL
2989 Yâbâl (1), *stream*

JABBOK
2999 Yabbôq (7), *pouring forth*

JABESH
3003 Yâbêsh (12), *dry*

JABESH-GILEAD
3003+1568 Yâbêsh (12), *dry*

JABEZ
3258 Ya'bêts (4), *sorrowful*

JABIN
2985 Yâbîyn (7), *intelligent*

JABIN'S
2985 Yâbîyn (1), *intelligent*

JABNEEL
2995 Yabnⁿe'êl (2), *built of God*

JABNEH
2996 Yabneh (1), *building*

JACHAN
3275 Ya'kân (1), *troublesome*

JACHIN
3199 Yâkîyn (8), *he* (or *it*) *will establish*

JACHINITES
3200 Yâkîynîy (1), *Jakinite*

JACINTH
5191 huakinthinŏs (1), *deep blue* color
5192 huakinthŏs (1), *blue gem,* (poss.) *zircon*

JACOB
3290 Ya'ăqôb (331), *heel-catcher*
2384 Iakŏb (26), *heel-catcher*

JACOB'S
3290 Ya'ăqôb (17), *heel-catcher*

2384 Iakŏb (1), *heel-catcher*

JADA
3047 Yâdâ' (2), *knowing*

JADAU
3035 Yiddôw (1), *praised*

JADDUA
3037 Yaddûwa' (3), *knowing*

JADON
3036 Yâdôwn (1), *thankful*

JAEL
3278 Yâ'êl (6), *ibex* animal

JAGUR
3017 Yâgûwr (1), *lodging*

JAH
3050 Yâhh (1), *Jehovah,* (the) *self-Existent* or *Eternal One*

JAHATH
3189 Yachath (8), *unity*

JAHAZ
3096 Yahats (5), *threshing-floor*

JAHAZA
3096 Yahats (1), *threshing-floor*

JAHAZAH
3096 Yahats (2), *threshing-floor*

JAHAZIAH
3167 Yachzⁿeyâh (1), *Jehovah will behold*

JAHAZIEL
3166 Yachăzîy'êl (6), *beheld of God*

JAHDAI
3056 Yehday (1), *Judaistic*

JAHDIEL
3164 Yachdîy'êl (1), *unity of God*

JAHDO
3163 Yachdôw (1), *his unity*

JAHLEEL
3177 Yachlⁿe'êl (2), *expectant of God*

JAHLEELITES
3178 Yachlⁿe'êlîy (1), *Jachleëlite*

JAHMAI
3181 Yachmay (1), *hot*

JAHZAH
3096 Yahats (1), *threshing-floor*

JAHZEEL
3183 Yachtsⁿe'êl (2), *God will allot*

JAHZEELITES
3184 Yachtsⁿe'êlîy (1), *Jachtseëlite*

JAHZERAH
3170 Yachzêrâh (1), *protection*

JAHZIEL
3185 Yachtsîy'êl (1), *allotted of God*

JAILER
1200 dĕsmŏphulax (1),
jailer

JAIR
2971 Yâ'îyr (10),
enlightener

JAIRITE
2972 Yâ'îrîy (1), Jaïrite

JAIRUS
2383 Iaĕirŏs (2),
enlightener

JAKAN
3292 Ya'ăqân (1), Jaakan

JAKEH
3348 Yâqeh (1), obedient

JAKIM
3356 Yâqîym (2), he will
raise

JALON
3210 Yâlôwn (1), lodging

JAMBRES
2387 Iambrēs (1),
Jambres

JAMES
2385 Iakŏbŏs (41),
heel-catcher

JAMIN
3226 Yâmîyn (6), right;
south

JAMINITES
3228 Yᵉmîynîy (1),
Jeminite

JAMLECH
3230 Yamlêk (1), he will
make king

JANGLING
3150 mataiŏlŏgia (1),
babble, meaningless
talk

JANNA
2388 Ianna (1), Janna

JANNES
2389 Iannēs (1), Jannes

JANOAH
3239 Yânôwach (1), quiet

JANOHAH
3239 Yânôwach (2), quiet

JANUM
3241 Yânîym (1), asleep

JAPHETH
3315 Yepheth (11),
expansion

JAPHIA
3309 Yâphîya' (5), bright

JAPHLET
3310 Yaphlêt̬ (3), he will
deliver

JAPHLETI
3311 Yaphlêt̬iy (1),
Japhletite

JAPHO
3305 Yâphôw (1),
beautiful

JARAH
3294 Ya'râh (2), honey in
the comb

JAREB
3377 Yârêb (2), he will
contend

JARED
3382 Yered (5), descent
2391 Iarĕd (1), descent

JARESIAH
3298 Ya'ăreshyâh (1),
Jaareshjah

JARHA
3398 Yarchâ' (2), Jarcha

JARIB
3402 Yârîyb (3),
contentious; adversary

JARMUTH
3412 Yarmûwth (7),
elevation

JAROAH
3386 Yârôwach (1), (born
at the) new moon

JASHEN
3464 Yâshên (1), sleepy

JASHER
3477 yâshâr (2), straight

JASHOBEAM
3434 Yâshob'âm (3),
people will return

JASHUB
3437 Yâshûwb (3), he
will return

JASHUBI-LEHEM
3433 Yâshûbîy Lechem
(1), returner of bread

JASHUBITES
3432 Yâshûbîy (1),
Jashubite

JASIEL
3300 Ya'ăsîy'êl (1), made
of God

JASON
2394 Iasŏn (5), about to
cure

JASPER
3471 yâshᵉphêh (3),
jasper stone
2393 iaspis (4), jasper

JATHNIEL
3496 Yathnîy'êl (1),
continued of God

JATTIR
3492 Yattîyr (4),
redundant

JAVAN
3120 Yâvân (7),
effervescent

JAVELIN
2595 chănîyth (6), lance,
spear
7420 rômach (1), iron
pointed spear

JAW
3895 lᵉchîy (3), jaw;
jaw-bone
4973 mᵉthallᵉ'âh (1),
tooth

JAWBONE
3895 lᵉchîy (3), jaw;
jaw-bone

JAWS
3895 lᵉchîy (4), jaw;
jaw-bone
4455 malqôwach (1),
spoil, plunder
4973 mᵉthallᵉ'âh (1),
tooth

JAZER
3270 Ya'ăzêyr (11),
helpful

JAZIZ
3151 Yâzìyz (1), he will
make prominent

JEALOUS
7065 qânâ' (11), to be,
make zealous, jealous
7067 qannâ' (4), jealous
7072 qannôw' (2), jealous
2206 zēlŏŏ (1), to have
warmth of feeling for

JEALOUSIES
7068 qin'âh (1), jealousy
or envy

JEALOUSY
7065 qânâ' (5), to be,
make zealous, jealous
7068 qin'âh (23), jealousy
7069 qânâh (1), to create;
to procure
2205 zēlŏs (1), zeal,
ardor; jealousy, malice

JEARIM
3297 Yᵉ'ârîym (1), forests

JEATERAI
2979 Yᵉ'âthᵉray (1),
stepping

JEBERECHIAH
3000 Yᵉberekyâhûw (1),
blessed of Jehovah

JEBUS
2982 Yᵉbûwç (4), trodden

JEBUSI
2983 Yᵉbûwçîy (2),
Jebusite

JEBUSITE
2983 Yᵉbûwçîy (14),
Jebusite

JEBUSITES
2983 Yᵉbûwçîy (25),
Jebusite

JECAMIAH
3359 Yᵉqamyâh (1),
Jehovah will rise

JECHOLIAH
3203 Yᵉkolyâh (1),
Jehovah will enable

JECHONIAS
2423 Iĕchŏnias (2),
Jehovah will establish

JECOLIAH
3203 Yᵉkolyâh (1),
Jehovah will enable

JECONIAH
3204 Yᵉkonyâh (7),
Jehovah will establish

JEDAIAH
3042 Yᵉdâyâh (2),
praised of Jehovah
3048 Yᵉda'yâh (11),
Jehovah has known

JEDIAEL
3043 Yᵉdîy'ă'êl (6),
knowing God

JEDIDAH
3040 Yᵉdîydâh (1),
beloved

JEDIDIAH
3041 Yᵉdîydᵉyâh (1),
beloved of Jehovah

JEDUTHUN
3038 Yᵉdûwthûwn (16),
laudatory

JEEZER
372 'Îy'ezer (1), helpless

JEEZERITES
373 'Îy'ezrîy (1), Iezrite

JEGAR-SAHADUTHA
3026 Yᵉgar Sahădûwthâ'
(Ch.) (1), heap of the
testimony

JEHALELEEL
3094 Yᵉhallel'êl (1),
praising God

JEHALELEL
3094 Yᵉhallel'êl (1),
praising God

JEHDEIAH
3165 Yechdîyâhûw (2),
unity of Jehovah

JEHEZEKEL
3168 Yᵉchezqê'l (1), God
will strengthen

JEHIAH
3174 Yᵉchîyâh (1),
Jehovah will live

JEHIEL
3171 Yᵉchîy'êl (14), God
will live
3273 Yᵉ'îy'êl (2), carried
away of God

JEHIELI
3172 Yᵉchîy'êlîy (2),
Jechiëlite

JEHIZKIAH
3169 Yᵉchizqîyâh (1),
strengthened of
Jehovah

JEHOADAH
3085 Yᵉhôw'addâh (2),
Jehovah-adorned

JEHOADDAN
3086 Yᵉhôw'addîyn (2),
Jehovah-pleased

JEHOAHAZ
3059 Yᵉhôw'âchâz (21),
Jehovah-seized
3099 Yôw'âchâz (1),
Jehovah-seized

JEHOASH
3060 Yᵉhôw'âsh (17),
Jehovah-fired

JEHOHANAN
3076 Yᵉhôwchânân (6),
Jehovah-favored

JEHOIACHIN
3078 Yᵉhôwyâkîyn (10),
Jehovah will establish

JEHOIACHIN'S
3112 Yôwyâkîyn (1),
Jehovah will establish

JEHOIADA
3111 Yôwyâdâ' (52),
Jehovah-known

JEHOIAKIM
3079 Yᵉhôwyâqîym (37),
Jehovah will raise

JEHOIARIB
3080 Yᵉhôwyârîyb (2),
Jehovah will contend

J

JEHONADAB
3082 Yᵉhôwnâdâb (3), Jehovah-largessed

JEHONATHAN
3083 Yᵉhôwnâthân (3), Jehovah-given

JEHORAM
3088 Yᵉhôwrâm (23), Jehovah-raised

JEHOSHABEATH
3090 Yᵉhôwshab'ath (2), Jehovah-sworn

JEHOSHAPHAT
3046 Yᵉda' (Ch.) (1), to know
3092 Yᵉhôwshâphâṭ (84), Jehovah-judged

JEHOSHEBA
3089 Yᵉhôwsheba' (1), Jehovah-sworn

JEHOSHUA
3091 Yᵉhôwshûw'a (1), Jehovah-saved

JEHOSHUAH
3091 Yᵉhôwshûw'a (1), Jehovah-saved

JEHOVAH
3068 Yᵉhôvâh (4), (the) self-Existent or Eternal

JEHOVAH-JIREH
3070 Yᵉhôvâh Yir'eh (1), Jehovah will see (to it)

JEHOVAH-NISSI
3071 Yᵉhôvâh Niççîy (1), Jehovah (is) my banner

JEHOVAH-SHALOM
3073 Yᵉhôvâh Shâlôwm (1), Jehovah (is) peace

JEHOZABAD
3075 Yᵉhôwzâbâd (4), Jehovah-endowed

JEHOZADAK
3087 Yᵉhôwtsâdâq (2), Jehovah-righted

JEHU
3058 Yêhûw' (57), Jehovah (is) He

JEHUBBAH
3160 Yᵉchubbâh (1), hidden

JEHUCAL
3081 Yᵉhûwkal (1), potent

JEHUD
3055 Yᵉhûd (1), celebrated

JEHUDI
3065 Yᵉhûwdîy (4), Jehudite

JEHUDIJAH
3057 Yᵉhûdîyâh (1), celebrated

JEHUSH
3266 Yᵉ'ûwsh (1), hasty

JEIEL
3273 Yᵉ'îy'êl (11), carried away of God

JEKABZEEL
3343 Yᵉqabtsᵉ'êl (1), God will gather

JEKAMEAM
3360 Yᵉqam'âm (2), people will rise

JEKAMIAH
3359 Yᵉqamyâh (2), Jehovah will rise

JEKUTHIEL
3354 Yᵉqûwthîy'êl (1), obedience of God

JEMIMA
3224 Yᵉmîymâh (1), dove

JEMUEL
3223 Yᵉmûw'êl (2), day of God

JEOPARDED
2778 châraph (1), to spend the winter

JEOPARDY
2793 kindunĕuō (2), to undergo peril

JEPHTHAE
2422 Iĕphthaĕ (1), he will open

JEPHTHAH
3316 Yiphtâch (29), he will open

JEPHUNNEH
3312 Yᵉphunneh (16), he will be prepared

JERAH
3392 Yerach (2), lunar month

JERAHMEEL
3396 Yᵉrachmᵉ'êl (8), God will be compassionate

JERAHMEELITES
3397 Yᵉrachmᵉ'êlîy (2), Jerachmeëlite

JERED
3382 Yered (2), descent

JEREMAI
3413 Yᵉrêmay (1), elevated

JEREMIAH
3414 Yirmᵉyâh (146), Jehovah will rise

JEREMIAH'S
3414 Yirmᵉyâh (1), Jehovah will rise

JEREMIAS
2408 Hiĕrĕmias (1), Jehovah will rise

JEREMOTH
3406 Yᵉrîymôwth (5), elevations

JEREMY
2408 Hiĕrĕmias (2), Jehovah will rise

JERIAH
3404 Yᵉrîyâh (2), Jehovah will throw

JERIBAI
3403 Yᵉrîybay (1), contentious

JERICHO
3405 Yᵉrîychôw (57), its month, or fragrant
2410 Hiĕrichó (7), its month or fragrant

JERIEL
3400 Yᵉrîy'êl (1), thrown of God

JERIJAH
3404 Yᵉrîyâh (1), Jehovah will throw

JERIMOTH
3406 Yᵉrîymôwth (8), elevations

JERIOTH
3408 Yᵉrîy'ôwth (1), curtains

JEROBOAM
3379 Yârob'âm (102), people will contend

JEROBOAM'S
3379 Yârob'âm (2), people will contend

JEROHAM
3395 Yᵉrôchâm (10), compassionate

JERUBBAAL
3378 Yᵉrubba'al (14), Baal will contend

JERUBBESHETH
3380 Yᵉrubbesheth (1), the idol will contend

JERUEL
3385 Yᵉrûw'êl (1), founded of God

JERUSALEM
3389 Yᵉrûwshâlaim (640), founded peaceful
3390 Yᵉrûwshâlêm (Ch.) (26), founded peaceful
2414 Hiĕrŏsŏluma (61), founded peaceful
2419 Hiĕrŏusalĕm (81), founded peaceful

JERUSALEM'S
3389 Yᵉrûwshâlaim (3), founded peaceful

JERUSHA
3388 Yᵉrûwshâ' (1), possessed

JERUSHAH
3388 Yᵉrûwshâ' (1), possessed

JESAIAH
3470 Yᵉsha'yâh (2), Jehovah has saved

JESHAIAH
3740 kêrâh (5), purchase

JESHANAH
3466 Yᵉshânâh (1), old

JESHARELAH
3480 Yᵉsar'êlâh (1), right towards God

JESHEBEAB
3434 Yâshob'âm (1), people will return

JESHER
3475 Yêsher (1), right

JESHIMON
3452 yᵉshîymôwn (5), desolation

JESHISHAI
3454 Yᵉshîyshay (1), aged

JESHOHAIAH
3439 Yᵉshôwchâyâh (1), Jehovah will empty

JESHUA
3442 Yêshûwa' (28), he will save
3443 Yêshûwa' (Ch.) (2), he will save

JESHURUN
3484 Yᵉshûrûwn (3), upright

JESIAH
3449 Yishshîyâh (2), Jehovah will lend

JESIMIEL
3450 Yᵉsîymâ'êl (1), God will place

JESSE
3448 Yîshay (41), extant
2421 Iĕssai (5), extant

JESTING
2160 ĕutrapĕlia (1), ribaldry

JESUI
3440 Yishvîy (1), level

JESUITES
3441 Yishvîy (1), Jishvite

JESURUN
3484 Yᵉshûrûwn (1), upright

JESUS
846 autŏs (1), he, she, it
2424 Iēsŏus (967), Jehovah-saved

JESUS'
2424 Iēsŏus (10), Jehovah-saved

JETHER
3500 Yether (8), remainder

JETHETH
3509 Yᵉthêyth (2), Jetheth

JETHLAH
3494 Yithlâh (1), be high

JETHRO
3503 Yithrôw (10), his excellence

JETUR
3195 Yᵉṭûwr (3), enclosed

JEUEL
3262 Yᵉ'ûw'êl (1), carried away of God

JEUSH
3266 Yᵉ'ûwsh (8), hasty

JEUZ
3263 Yᵉ'ûwts (1), counselor

JEW
3064 Yᵉhûwdîy (10), Jehudite
2453 Iŏudaiŏs (22), belonging to Jehudah

JEWEL
3627 kᵉlîy (1), implement, thing
5141 nezem (2), nose-ring

JEWELS
2484 chelyâh (2), trinket, ornament
3627 kᵉlîy (18), implement, thing
5141 nezem (1), nose-ring
5459 çᵉgullâh (1), wealth

JEWESS
2453 Iŏudaiŏs (2), belonging to Jehudah

JEWISH
2451 Iŏudaïkŏs (1), resembling a Judæan

JEWRY
3061 Yᵉhûwd (Ch.) (1), celebrated
2449 Iŏudaia (2), Judæan land

JEWS
3054 yâhad (1), to become Jewish
3062 Yᵉhûwdâ'îy (Ch.) (8), Jew
3064 Yᵉhûwdîy (65), Jehudite
2450 Iŏudaïzō (1), to Judaize, live as a Jew
2452 Iŏudaïkŏs (1), in a Judæan manner
2453 Iŏudaiŏs (167), belonging to Jehudah

JEWS'
3064 Yᵉhûwdîy (4), Jehudite
3066 Yᵉhûwdîyth (4), in the Jewish language
2453 Iŏudaiŏs (4), belonging to Jehudah
2454 Iŏudaismŏs (2), Jewish faith

JEZANIAH
3153 Yᵉzanyâh (2), heard of Jehovah

JEZEBEL
348 'Îyzebel (21), chaste
2403 Iĕzabĕl (1), chaste

JEZEBEL'S
348 'Îyzebel (1), chaste

JEZER
3337 Yêtser (3), form

JEZERITES
3339 Yitsrîy (1), formative

JEZIAH
3150 Yizzîyâh (1), sprinkled of Jehovah

JEZIEL
3149 Yᵉzav'êl (1), sprinkled of God

JEZLIAH
3152 Yizlîy'ah (1), he will draw out

JEZOAR
3328 Yitschar (1), he will shine

JEZRAHIAH
3156 Yizrachyâh (1), Jehovah will shine

JEZREEL
3157 Yizrᵉ'ê'l (36), God will sow

JEZREELITE
3158 Yizrᵉ'ê'lîy (8), Jizreëlite

JEZREELITESS
3159 Yizrᵉ'ê'liyth (5), Jezreëlitess

JIBSAM
3005 Yibsâm (1), fragrant

JIDLAPH
3044 Yidlâph (1), tearful

JIMNA
3232 Yimnâh (1), prosperity

JIMNAH
3232 Yimnâh (1), prosperity

JIMNITES
3232 Yimnâh (1), prosperity

JIPHTAH
3316 Yiphtâch (1), he will open

JIPHTHAH-EL
3317 Yiphtach-'êl (2), God will open

JOAB
3097 Yôw'âb (137), Jehovah-fathered
5854 'Atrôwth Bêyth Yôw'âb (1), crowns of (the) house of Joâb

JOAB'S
3097 Yôw'âb (8), Jehovah-fathered

JOAH
3098 Yôw'âch (11), Jehovah-brothered

JOAHAZ
3098 Yôw'âch (1), Jehovah-brothered

JOANNA
2489 Iōanna (3), Jehovah-favored

JOASH
3101 Yôw'âsh (47), Jehovah-fired
3135 Yôw'âsh (2), Jehovah-hastened

JOATHAM
2488 Iōatham (2), Jehovah (is) perfect

JOB
347 'Îyôwb (57), persecuted
3102 Yôwb (1), Job
2492 Iōb (1), persecuted

JOB'S
347 'Îyôwb (1), persecuted

JOBAB
3103 Yôwbâb (9), howler

JOCHEBED
3115 Yôwkebed (2), Jehovah-gloried

JOED
3133 Yôw'êd (1), appointer

JOEL
3100 Yôw'êl (19), Jehovah (is his) God
2493 Iōēl (1), Jehovah (is his) God

JOELAH
3132 Yôw'ê'lâh (1), furthermore

JOEZER
3134 Yôw'ezer (1), Jehovah (is his) help

JOGBEHAH
3011 Yogbᵉhâh (2), hillock

JOGLI
3020 Yoglîy (1), exiled

JOHA
3109 Yôwchá' (2), Jehovah-revived

JOHANAN
3076 Yᵉhôwchânân (3), Jehovah-favored
3110 Yôwchânân (24), Jehovah-favored

JOHN
2491 Iōannēs (131), Jehovah-favored

JOHN'S
2491 Iōannēs (2), Jehovah-favored

JOIADA
3111 Yôwyâdâ' (4), Jehovah-known

JOIAKIM
3113 Yôwyâqîym (4), Jehovah will raise

JOIARIB
3114 Yôwyârîyb (5), Jehovah will contend

JOIN
2266 châbar (2), to fascinate by spells
2859 châthan (1), to become related
3254 yâçaph (1), to add or augment
3867 lâvâh (2), to unite; to remain; to borrow
5060 nâga' (1), to strike
5526 çâkak (1), to entwine; to fence in
7126 qârab (1), to approach, bring near
2853 kŏllaō (3), to glue together

JOINED
977 bâchar (1), select, chose, prefer
1692 dâbaq (2), to cling or adhere; to catch
2266 châbar (8), to fascinate by spells
2302 châdâh (1), to rejoice, be glad
2338 chûwt (Ch.) (1), to repair; lay a foundation
2859 châthan (1), to become related
3161 yâchad (1), to be, become one
3867 lâvâh (8), to unite; to remain; to borrow
5208 nîychôwach (Ch.) (1), pleasure
5595 çâphâh (1), to scrape; to accumulate
6186 'ârak (1), to set in a row, i.e. arrange,
6775 tsâmad (3), to link, i.e. gird
7000 qâtar (1), to enclose
7126 qârab (1), to approach, bring near
7194 qâshar (1), to tie, bind
2675 katartizō (1), to repair; to prepare
2853 kŏllaō (3), to glue together

4347 prŏskŏllaō (2), to glue to, i.e. to adhere
4801 suzĕugnumi (2), to conjoin in marriage
4883 sunarmŏlŏgĕō (1), to render close-jointed
4927 sunŏmŏrĕō (1), to border together

JOINING
1692 dâbaq (1), to cling or adhere; to catch

JOININGS
4226 mᵉchabbᵉrâh (1), joiner, brace or cramp

JOINT
3363 yâqa' (1), to be dislocated
4154 mûw'edeth (1), dislocated
6504 pârad (1), to spread or separate
860 haphê (1), fastening ligament, joint

JOINT-HEIRS
4789 sugklērŏnŏmŏs (1), participant in common

JOINTS
1694 debeq (2), joint
2542 chammûwq (1), wrapping, i.e. drawers
7001 qᵉtar (Ch.) (1), riddle; vertebra
719 harmŏs (1), articulation, body-joint
860 haphê (1), fastening ligament, joint

JOKDEAM
3347 Yoqdᵉ'âm (1), burning of (the) people

JOKIM
3137 Yôwqîym (1), Jehovah will raise

JOKMEAM
3361 Yoqmᵉ'âm (1), people will be raised

JOKNEAM
3362 Yoqnᵉ'âm (4), people will be lamented

JOKSHAN
3370 Yoqshân (4), insidious

JOKTAN
3355 Yoqtân (6), he will be made little

JOKTHEEL
3371 Yoqthᵉ'êl (2), veneration of God

JONA
2495 Iōnas (1), dove

JONADAB
3082 Yᵉhôwnâdâb (4), Jehovah-largessed
3122 Yôwnâdâb (8), Jehovah-largessed

JONAH
3124 Yôwnâh (19), dove

JONAN
2494 Iōnan (1), Jehovah-favored or a dove

JONAS
2495 Iōnas (12), dove

JONATH-ELEM-RECHOKIM
3128 Yôwnath 'êlem rᵉchôqîym (1), *dove of (the) silence*

JONATHAN
3083 Yᵉhôwnâthân (81), *Jehovah-given*
3129 Yôwnâthân (37), *Jehovah-given*

JONATHAN'S
3129 Yôwnâthân (3), *Jehovah-given*

JOPPA
3305 Yâphôw (3), *beautiful*
2445 Iŏppē (10), *beautiful*

JORAH
3139 Yôwrâh (1), *rainy*

JORAI
3140 Yôwray (1), *rainy*

JORAM
3141 Yôwrâm (19), *Jehovah-raised*
3088 Yᵉhôwrâm (7), *Jehovah-raised*
2496 Iōram (2), *Jehovah-raised*

JORDAN
3383 Yardên (182), *descender*
2446 Iŏrdanēs (15), *descender*

JORIM
2497 Iōrĕim (1), (poss.) *Jehovah-raised*

JORKOAM
3421 Yorqᵉ'âm (1), *people will be poured forth*

JOSABAD
3107 Yôwzâbâd (1), *Jehovah-endowed*

JOSAPHAT
2498 Iōsaphat (2), *Jehovah-judged*

JOSE
2499 Iōsē (1), (poss.) *let him add*

JOSEDECH
3087 Yᵉhôwtsâdâq (6), *Jehovah-righted*

JOSEPH
3084 Yᵉhôwçêph (1), *let him add or adding*
3130 Yôwçêph (193), *let him add or adding*
2501 Iōsēph (33), *let him add or adding*

JOSEPH'S
3130 Yôwçêph (20), *let him add or adding*
2501 Iōsēph (2), *let him add or adding*

JOSES
2500 Iōsēs (6), (poss.) *let him add*

JOSHAH
3144 Yôwshâh (1), *Joshah*

JOSHAPHAT
3146 Yôwshâphâṭ (1), *Jehovah-judged*

JOSHAVIAH
3145 Yôwshavyâh (1), *Jehovah-set*

JOSHBEKASHAH
3436 Yoshbᵉqâshâh (2), *hard seat*

JOSHUA
3091 Yᵉhôwshûw'a (215), *Jehovah-saved*

JOSIAH
2977 Yô'shîyâh (53), *founded of Jehovah*

JOSIAS
2502 Iōsias (2), *founded of Jehovah*

JOSIBIAH
3143 Yôwshîbyâh (1), *Jehovah will cause to dwell*

JOSIPHIAH
3131 Yôwçiphyâh (1), *Jehovah (is) adding*

JOT
2503 iōta (1), *iota*

JOTBAH
3192 Yoṭbâh (1), *pleasantness*

JOTBATH
3193 Yoṭbâthâh (1), *pleasantness*

JOTBATHAH
3193 Yoṭbâthâh (2), *pleasantness*

JOTHAM
3147 Yôwthâm (24), *Jehovah (is) perfect*

JOURNEY
1870 derek (23), *road; course* of life; *mode* of action
4109 mahălâk (3), *passage* or a *distance*
4550 maçça' (1), *departure*
5265 nâça' (12), *start* on a journey
5575+7272 çanvêr (1), *blindness*
589 apŏdēmĕō (2), *visit a foreign land*
590 apŏdēmŏs (1), *foreign traveller*
1279 diapŏrĕuŏmai (1), to *travel through*
2137 ĕuŏdŏō (1), to *succeed* in business
3596 hŏdŏipŏrĕō (1), to *travel*
3597 hŏdŏipŏria (1), *traveling*
3598 hŏdŏs (6), *road*
4198 pŏrĕuŏmai (2), to *go, come;* to *travel*

JOURNEYED
5265 nâça' (28), *start* on a journey
6213+1870 'âsâh (1), to *do* or *make*
3593 hŏdĕuŏ (1), to *travel*
4198 pŏrĕuŏmai (2), to *go/come;* to *travel*
4922 sunŏdĕuō (1), to *travel* in company *with*

JOURNEYING
4550 maçça' (1), *departure*
5265 nâça' (1), *start* on a journey
4197+4160 pŏrĕia (1), *journey;* life's *conduct*

JOURNEYINGS
4550 maçça' (1), *departure*
3597 hŏdŏipŏria (1), *traveling*

JOURNEYS
4550 maçça' (9), *departure*

JOY
1523 gîyl (2), *rejoice*
1524 gîyl (3), *age, stage in life*
1525 gîylâh (1), *joy, delight*
2304 chedvâh (1), *rejoicing, joy*
2305 chedvâh (Ch.) (1), *rejoicing, joy*
2898 ṭûwb (1), *good; beauty, gladness*
4885 mâsôws (12), *delight*
7440 rinnâh (3), *shout*
7442 rânan (3), to *shout for joy*
7796 Sôwrêq (1), *vine*
8055 sâmach (4), to *be, make gleesome*
8056 sâmêach (2), *blithe* or *gleeful*
8057 simchâh (43), *blithesomeness* or *glee*
8342 sâsôwn (14), *cheerfulness; welcome*
8643 tᵉrûw'âh (2), *battle-cry; clangor*
20 agalliasis (2), *exultation, delight*
21 agalliaō (1), to *exult*
2167 ĕuphrŏsunē (1), *joyfulness, cheerfulness*
2744 kauchaŏmai (1), to *glory in, rejoice in;* to *boast*
3685 ŏninēmi (1), to *gratify, derive pleasure*
5468 chalinagōgĕō (3), to *curb, hold in check*
5479 chara (51), *calm delight, joy*
5485 charis (1), *gratitude; benefit given*

JOYED
5463 chairō (1), to *be cheerful*

JOYFUL
1523 gîyl (4), *rejoice*
2896 ṭôwb (1), *good; well*
5937 'âlaz (2), to *jump for joy*
5970 'âlats (1), to *jump for joy*
7442 rânan (1), to *shout for joy*
7445 rᵉnânâh (2), *shout for joy*
8055 sâmach (2), to *be, make gleesome*
8056 sâmêach (3), *blithe* or *gleeful*

JOURNEYING (cont.)
8643 tᵉrûw'âh (1), *battle-cry; clangor* of trumpets
5479 chara (1), *calm delight, joy*

JOYFULLY
2416 chay (1), *alive; raw; fresh; life*
3326+5479 mĕta (1), *with, among; after, later*
5463 chairō (1), to *be cheerful*

JOYFULNESS
8057 simchâh (1), *blithesomeness* or *glee*
5479 chara (1), *calm delight, joy*

JOYING
5463 chairō (1), to *be cheerful*

JOYOUS
5947 'allîyz (3), *exultant; reveling*
5479 chara (1), *calm delight, joy*

JOZABAD
3107 Yôwzâbâd (9), *Jehovah-endowed*

JOZACHAR
3108 Yôwzâkâr (1), *Jehovah-remembered*

JOZADAK
3136 Yôwtsâdâq (5), *Jehovah-righted*

JUBAL
3106 Yûwbâl (1), *stream*

JUBILE
3104 yôwbêl (21), *blast of a ram's horn*
8643 tᵉrûw'âh (1), *battle-cry; clangor*

JUCAL
3116 Yûwkal (1), *potent*

JUDA
2448 Iŏuda (1), *celebrated*
2455 Iŏudas (7), *celebrated*

JUDAEA
2449 Iŏudaia (41), *Judæan land*
2453 Iŏudaiŏs (1), *belonging to Jehudah*
2499 Iōsē (1), (poss.) *let him add*

JUDAH
3061 Yᵉhûwd (Ch.) (5), *celebrated*
3063 Yᵉhûwdâh (806), *celebrated*
3064 Yᵉhûwdîy (1), *Jehudite*
2455 Iŏudas (1), *celebrated*

JUDAH'S
3063 Yᵉhûwdâh (4), *celebrated*

JUDAS
2455 Iŏudas (33), *celebrated*

JUDE
2455 Iŏudas (1), *celebrated*

JUDEA
3061 Yᵉhûwd (Ch.) (1), *celebrated*

JUDGE
430 'ĕlôhîym (1), *God; magistrates, judges*
1777 dîyn (14), to *judge; to strive* or *contend for*
1781 dayân (1), *judge; advocate*
1784 Dîynay (Ch.) (1), *Dinaite*
3198 yâkach (1), to *decide, justify, convict*
6416 pᵉlîylîy (1), *judicial*
8199 shâphaṭ (102), to *judge*
350 anakrinō (1), to *interrogate, determine*
1252 diakrinō (3), to *decide; to hesitate*
1348 dikastēs (3), one who *judges*
2919 krinō (45), to *decide; to try*
2922 kritēriŏn (1), *rule; tribunal; lawsuit*
2923 kritēs (13), *judge*

JUDGED
1777 dîyn (2), to *judge; to strive* or *contend for*
4941 mishpâṭ (1), *verdict; formal decree; justice*
5307 nâphal (1), to *fall*
6419 pâlal (1), to *intercede, pray*
8199 shâphaṭ (28), to *judge*
350 anakrinō (3), to *interrogate, determine*
2233 hēgĕŏmai (1), to *deem,* i.e. *consider*
2919 krinō (26), to *decide; to try, condemn, punish*

JUDGES
148 'ădargâzêr (Ch.) (2), *chief diviner*
430 'ĕlôhîym (4), *God; magistrates, judges*
1782 dayân (Ch.) (1), *judge*
6414 pâlîyl (3), *magistrate*
8199 shâphaṭ (38), to *judge*
2923 kritēs (4), *judge*

JUDGEST
8199 shâphaṭ (2), to *judge*
2919 krinō (6), to *decide; to try, condemn, punish*

JUDGETH
1777 dîyn (1), to *judge; to strive* or *contend for*
8199 shâphaṭ (5), to *judge*
350 anakrinō (1), to *interrogate, determine*
2919 krinō (10), to *try, condemn, punish*

JUDGING
8199 shâphaṭ (4), to *judge*
2919 krinō (2), to *decide; to try, condemn, punish*

JUDGMENT
1777 dîyn (1), to *judge; to strive* or *contend for*

1779 dîyn (9), *judge; judgment; law suit*
1780 dîyn (Ch.) (5), *judge; judgment*
2940 ṭa'am (1), *perception; mandate*
4055 mad (1), *vesture, garment; carpet*
4941 mishpâṭ (187), *verdict; decree; justice*
6415 pᵉlîylâh (1), *justice*
6417 pᵉlîylîyâh (1), *judgment*
6419 pâlal (1), to *intercede, pray*
6485 pâqad (2), to *visit, care for, count*
8196 shᵉphôwṭ (2), *sentence, punishment*
8199 shâphaṭ (2), to *judge*
8201 shepheṭ (2), *criminal sentence*
144 aisthēsis (1), *discernment*
968 bēma (10), *tribunal platform; judging place*
1106 gnōmē (3), *cognition, opinion*
1341 dikaiŏkrisia (1), *just sentence*
1345 dikaiōma (1), *statute* or *decision*
1349 dikē (1), *justice*
2250 hēmĕra (1), *day; period of time*
2917 krima (12), *decision*
2920 krisis (39), *decision; tribunal; justice*
2922 kritēriŏn (1), *rule; tribunal; lawsuit*
4232 praitōriŏn (5), *governor's court-room*

JUDGMENTS
4941 mishpâṭ (108), *verdict; decree; justice*
8201 shepheṭ (14), *criminal sentence*
1345 dikaiōma (1), *deed; statute* or *decision*
2917 krima (1), *decision*
2920 krisis (2), *decision; tribunal; justice*
2922 kritēriŏn (1), *rule; tribunal; lawsuit*

JUDITH
3067 Yᵉhûwdîyth (1), *Jewess*

JUICE
6071 'âçîyç (1), *expressed fresh grape-juice*

JULIA
2456 Iŏulia (1), *Julia*

JULIUS
2457 Iŏuliŏs (2), *Julius*

JUMPING
7540 râqad (1), to *spring about wildly* or *for joy*

JUNIA
2458 Iŏunias (1), *Junias*

JUNIPER
7574 rethem (4), *broom tree*

JUPITER
1356 diŏpĕtēs (1), *sky-fallen*

2203 Zĕus (2), *Jupiter* or *Jove*

JURISDICTION
1849 ĕxŏusia (1), *authority, dominion*

JUSHAB-HESED
3142 Yûwshab Cheçed (1), *kindness will be returned*

JUST
3477 yâshâr (1), *straight*
4941 mishpâṭ (1), *verdict; formal decree; justice*
6662 tsaddîyq (42), *just*
6663 tsâdaq (3), to *be, make right*
6664 tsedeq (8), *right*
8003 shâlêm (1), *complete; friendly; safe*
1342 dikaiŏs (33), *equitable, holy*
1738 ĕndikŏs (2), *equitable, deserved, just*

JUSTICE
4941 mishpâṭ (1), *verdict; formal decree; justice*
6663 tsâdaq (2), to *be, make right*
6664 tsedeq (10), *right*
6666 tsᵉdâqâh (15), *rightness*

JUSTIFICATION
1345 dikaiōma (1), *deed; statute* or *decision*
1347 dikaiōsis (2), *acquittal, vindication*

JUSTIFIED
6663 tsâdaq (12), to *be, make right*
1344 dikaiŏō (31), *show* or *regard* as *just*

JUSTIFIER
1344 dikaiŏō (1), *show* or *regard* as *just*

JUSTIFIETH
6663 tsâdaq (2), to *be, make right*
1344 dikaiŏō (2), *show* or *regard* as *just*

JUSTIFY
6663 tsâdaq (7), to *be, make right*
1344 dikaiŏō (4), *show* or *regard* as *just*

JUSTIFYING
6663 tsâdaq (2), to *be, make right*

JUSTLE
8264 shâqaq (1), to *seek greedily*

JUSTLY
4941 mishpâṭ (1), *verdict; formal decree; justice*
1346 dikaiōs (2), *equitably*

JUSTUS
2459 Iŏustŏs (3), *just*

JUTTAH
3194 Yuṭṭâh (2), *extended*

KABZEEL
6909 Qabtsᵉ'êl (3), *God has gathered*

KADESH
6946 Qâdêsh (17), *sanctuary*

KADESH-BARNEA
6947 Qâdêsh Barnêa' (10), Kadesh of (the) *Wilderness of Wandering*

KADMIEL
6934 Qadmîy'êl (8), *presence of God*

KADMONITES
6935 Qadmônîy (1), *ancient*

KALLAI
7040 Qallay (1), *frivolous*

KANAH
7071 Qânâh (3), *reediness*

KAREAH
7143 Qârêach (13), *bald*

KARKAA
7173 Qarqa' (1), *ground-floor*

KARKOR
7174 Qarqôr (1), *foundation*

KARTAH
7177 Qartâh (1), *city*

KARTAN
7178 Qartân (1), *city-plot*

KATTATH
7005 Qaṭṭâth (1), *littleness*

KEDAR
6938 Qêdâr (12), *dusky*

KEDEMAH
6929 Qêdᵉmâh (2), *precedence*

KEDEMOTH
6932 Qᵉdêmôwth (4), *beginnings*

KEDESH
6943 Qedesh (11), *sanctum*

KEDESH-NAPHTALI
6943+5321 Qedesh (1), *sanctum*

KEEP
1692 dâbaq (3), to *cling* or *adhere; to catch*
1961 hâyâh (1), to *exist,* i.e. *be* or *become*
2287 châgag (12), to *observe* a festival
2820 châsak (1), to *refuse, spare, preserve*
3533 kâbash (1), to *conquer, subjugate*
3607 kâlâ' (1), to *hold back* or *in; to prohibit*
4513 mâna' (2), to *deny, refuse*
4931 mishmereth (1), *watch, sentry, post*
5201 nâṭar (3), to *guard; to cherish* anger
5341 nâtsar (26), to *guard, protect*
5647 'âbad (1), to *do, work, serve*
5737 'âdar (2), to *arrange* as a battle

K

6113 'âtsar (1), to *hold back; to maintain, rule*
6213 'âsâh (30), to *do or make*
6485 pâqad (1), to *visit, care for, count*
6942 qâdâsh (1), to *be, make clean*
7069 qânâh (1), to *create; to procure*
7368 râchaq (1), to *recede; remove*
8104 shâmar (186), to *watch*
1301 diatērĕō (1), to *observe* strictly
1314 diaphulassō (1), to *protect, guard carefully*
1858 hĕŏrtazō (1), to *observe a festival*
2722 katĕchō (3), to *hold down fast*
2853 kŏllaō (1), to *glue together*
3557 nŏsphizŏmai (1), to *sequestrate, embezzle*
4160 pŏiĕō (2), to *do*
4238 prassō (1), to *execute, accomplish*
4601 sigaō (2), to *keep silent*
4874 sunanamignumi (1), to *associate with*
4912 sunĕchō (1), to *hold together*
5083 tērĕō (32), to *keep, guard, obey*
5299 hupōpiazō (1), to *beat up; to wear out*
5432 phrŏurĕō (1), to *hem in, protect*
5442 phulassō (13), to *watch, i.e. be on guard*

KEEPER
5201 nâtsar (1), to *guard; to cherish* anger
5341 nâtsar (1), to *guard, protect, maintain*
7462 râ'âh (1), to *tend a flock, i.e. pasture it*
8104 shâmar (13), to *watch*
8269 sar (3), *head person, ruler*
1200 dĕsmŏphulax (2), *jailer*

KEEPERS
5201 nâtsar (1), to *guard; to cherish* anger
8104 shâmar (15), to *watch*
3626 ŏikŏurŏs (1), *domestically inclined*
5083 tērĕō (1), to *keep, guard, obey*
5441 phulax (3), *watcher or sentry*

KEEPEST
8104 shâmar (3), to *watch*
5442 phulassō (1), to *watch, i.e. be on guard*

KEEPETH
2820 châsak (1), to *refuse, spare, preserve*
4513 mâna' (1), to *deny, refuse*
5307 nâphal (1), to *fall*

5341 nâtsar (7), to *guard, protect, maintain*
7462 râ'âh (1), to *tend a flock, i.e. pasture it*
7623 shâbach (1), to *address; to pacify*
8104 shâmar (18), to *watch*
4160 pŏiĕō (1), to *do*
5083 tērĕō (10), to *keep, guard, obey*
5442 phulassō (1), to *watch, i.e. be on guard*

KEEPING
5341 nâtsar (1), to *guard, protect, maintain*
7462 râ'âh (1), to *tend a flock, i.e. pasture it*
8104 shâmar (7), to *watch*
5084 tērĕsis (1), *observance; prison*
5442 phulassō (1), to *watch, i.e. be on guard*

KEHELATHAH
6954 Qᵉhêlâthâh (2), *convocation*

KEILAH
7084 Qᵉʻîylâh (18), *citadel*

KELAIAH
7041 Qêlâyâh (1), *insignificance*

KELITA
7042 Qᵉlîyṭâ' (3), *maiming*

KEMUEL
7055 Qᵉmûw'êl (3), *raised of God*

KENAN
7018 Qêynân (1), *fixed*

KENATH
7079 Qᵉnâth (2), *possession*

KENAZ
7073 Qᵉnaz (11), *hunter*

KENEZITE
7074 Qᵉnizzîy (3), *Kenizzite*

KENITE
7014 Qayin (2), *lance*
7017 Qêynîy (4), *Kenite*

KENITES
7017 Qêynîy (8), *Kenite*

KENIZZITES
7074 Qᵉnizzîy (1), *Kenizzite*

KEPT
631 'âçar (1), to *fasten; to join* battle
680 'âtsal (1), to *select; refuse; narrow*
1639 gâra' (1), to *shave, remove, or withhold*
1692 dâbaq (1), to *cling or adhere; to catch*
2287 châgag (1), to *observe a festival*
2790 chârash (2), to *engrave; to plow*
2820 châtsan (2), to *refuse, spare, preserve*
3607 kâlâ' (1), to *hold back or in; to prohibit*

4513 mâna' (2), to *deny, refuse*
4931 mishmereth (6), *watch, sentry, post*
5201 nâṭar (1), to *guard; to cherish* anger
5202 nᵉṭar (Ch.) (1), to *retain*
5341 nâtsar (4), to *guard, protect, maintain*
5641 çâthar (2), to *hide by covering*
5648 ʻâbad (Ch.) (1), to *do, work, serve*
6113 'âtsar (2), to *hold back; to maintain, rule*
6213 'âsâh (18), to *do or make*
6942 qâdâsh (1), to *be, make clean*
7462 râ'âh (3), to *tend a flock, i.e. pasture it*
7673 shâbath (1), to *repose; to desist*
8104 shâmar (70), to *watch*
71 agō (1), to *lead; to bring, drive; to weigh*
650 apŏstĕrĕō (1), to *deprive; to despoil*
1006 bŏskō (1), to *pasture a flock*
1096 ginŏmai (1), to *be, become*
1301 diatērĕō (1), to *observe* strictly
2192 ĕchō (1), to *have; hold; keep*
2343 thēsaurizō (1), to *amass or reserve, store*
2377 thurōrŏs (2), *doorkeeper*
2621 katakĕimai (1), to *lie down in bed*
2902 kratĕō (1), to *seize*
2967 kōluō (1), to *stop*
3557 nŏsphizŏmai (1), to *sequestrate, embezzle*
3930 parĕchō (1), to *hold near, i.e. to present*
4160 pŏiĕō (1), to *do*
4601 sigaō (2), to *keep silent*
4933 suntērĕō (1), to *protect*
5083 tērĕō (15), to *keep, guard, obey*
5288 hupŏstĕllō (1), to *conceal (reserve)*
5432 phrŏurĕō (3), to *hem in, protect*
5442 phulassō (8), to *watch, i.e. be on guard*

KERCHIEFS
4556 miçpachath (2), *scurf, rash*

KEREN-HAPPUCH
7163 Qeren Hap-pûwk (1), *horn of cosmetic*

KERIOTH
7152 Qᵉrîyôwth (3), *buildings*

KERNELS
2785 chartsan (1), *sour, tart grape*

KEROS
7026 Qêyrôç (2), *ankled*

KETTLE
1731 dûwd (1), *pot, kettle; basket*

KETURAH
6989 Qᵉṭûwrâh (4), *perfumed*

KEY
4668 maphtêach (2), *opening; key*
2807 klĕis (4), *key*

KEYS
2807 klĕis (2), *key*

KEZIA
7103 Qᵉtsîy'âh (1), *cassia*

KEZIZ
7104 Qᵉtsîyts (1), *abrupt*

KIBROTH-HATTAAVAH
6914 Qibrôwth hat-Ta'ăvâh (5), *graves of the longing*

KIBZAIM
6911 Qibtsayim (1), *double heap*

KICK
1163 bâ'aṭ (1), *kick*
2979 laktizō (2), to *recalcitrate, kick back*

KICKED
1163 bâ'aṭ (1), *kick*

KID
1423 gᵉdîy (8), *young male goat*
1423+5795 gᵉdîy (5), *young male goat*
5795 ʻêz (1), *she-goat; goat's hair*
8163 sâ'îyr (26), *shaggy; he-goat; goat idol*
8166 sᵉ'îyrâh (2), *she-goat*
2056 ĕriphŏs (1), *kid or goat*

KIDNEYS
3629 kilyâh (18), *kidney; mind, heart, spirit*

KIDRON
6939 Qidrôwn (11), *dusky place*

KIDS
1423 gᵉdîy (4), *young male goat*
5795 ʻêz (1), *she-goat; goat's hair*
8163 sâ'îyr (2), *shaggy; he-goat; goat idol*

KILL
2026 hârag (17), to *kill, slaughter*
2076 zâbach (3), to *(sacrificially) slaughter*
2491 châlâl (2), *pierced to death, one slain*
2873 ṭâbach (1), to *kill, butcher*
4191 mûwth (24), to *die; to kill*
5221 nâkâh (4), to *strike, kill*
5362 nâqaph (1), to *strike; to surround*
7523 râtsach (4), to *murder*
7819 shâchaṭ (22), to *slaughter; butcher*

KILLED

337 anairĕō (6), to
abolish, *murder*
615 apŏktĕinō (28), to
kill outright; to *destroy*
1315 diachĕirizŏmai (1),
to *lay hands upon*
2380 thuō (3), to *kill*; to
butcher; to *sacrifice*
4969 sphazō (1), to
slaughter or to *maim*
5407 phŏnĕuō (8), to
commit murder

KILLED

2026 hârag (3), to *kill,
slaughter*
2076 zâbach (1), to
(sacrificially) *slaughter*
2873 ṭâbach (3), to *kill,
butcher*
3076 Yᵉhôwchânân (1),
Jehovah-favored
4191 mûwth (6), to *die*; to
kill
5221 nâkâh (3), to *strike,
kill*
7523 râtsach (1), to
murder
7819 shâchaṭ (15), to
slaughter; butcher
337 anairĕō (3), to *take
away, murder*
615 apŏktĕinō (22), to
kill outright; to *destroy*
2289 thanatŏō (2), to *kill*
2380 thuō (5), to *kill*; to
butcher; to *sacrifice*
5407 phŏnĕuō (2), to
commit murder

KILLEDST

2026 hârag (2), to *kill,
slaughter*

KILLEST

615 apŏktĕinō (2), to *kill*
outright; to *destroy*

KILLETH

2026 hârag (1), to *kill,
slaughter*
4191 mûwth (2), to *die*; to
kill
5221 nâkâh (13), to
strike, kill
6991 qâṭal (1), to *put to
death*
7819 shâchaṭ (3), to
slaughter; butcher
615 apŏktĕinō (3), to *kill*
outright; to *destroy*

KILLING

2026 hârag (1), to *kill,
slaughter*
7523 râtsach (1), to
murder
7819 shâchaṭ (1), to
slaughter; butcher
7821 shᵉchîyṭâh (1),
slaughter
615 apŏktĕinō (1), to *kill*
outright; to *destroy*

KIN

1320 bâsâr (2), *flesh;
body; person*
7138 qârôwb (1), *near,
close*
7607 shᵉʾêr (2), *flesh,
meat; kindred by blood*
4773 suggĕnēs (1), *blood
relative; countryman*

KINAH

7016 Qîynâh (1), *dirge*

KIND

2896 ṭôwb (1), *good; well*
4327 mîyn (29), *sort,* i.e.
species
1085 gĕnŏs (3), *kin,*
offspring *in kind*
5100 tis (1), *some* or *any*
person or object
5449 phusis (1), *genus* or
sort
5541 chrēstĕuŏmai (1), to
show oneself useful
5543 chrēstŏs (2),
employed, i.e. *useful*

KINDLE

215 ʾôwr (1), to *be
luminous*
1197 bâʾar (4), to *be
brutish, be senseless*
1814 dâlaq (2), to *flame;*
to *pursue*
2787 chârar (1), to *melt,
burn, dry* up
3341 yâtsath (8), to *burn*
or *set on fire*
3344 yâqad (1), to *burn*
6919 qâdach (1), to
inflame
6999 qâṭar (1), to *turn
into fragrance* by fire

KINDLED

1197 bâʾar (9), to *be
brutish, be senseless*
2734 chârâh (43), to
blaze up
3341 yâtsath (4), to *burn*
or *set on fire*
3648 kâmar (1), to
shrivel with heat
5400 nâsaq (1), to *catch*
fire
6919 qâdach (3), to
inflame
8313 sâraph (1), to *be,
set on fire*
381 anaptō (2), to *kindle,
set on fire*
681 haptō (1), to *set on*
fire

KINDLETH

3857 lâhaṭ (1), to *blaze*
5400 nâsaq (1), to *catch*
fire
381 anaptō (1), to *kindle,
set on fire*

KINDLY

2617 cheçed (5),
kindness, favor
2896 ṭôwb (2), *good; well*
5921+3820 ʾal (2), *above,
over, upon,* or *against*
5387 philŏstŏrgŏs (1),
fraternal, devoted

KINDNESS

2617 cheçed (40),
kindness, favor
2896 ṭôwb (1), *good; well*
5360 philadĕlphia (2),
fraternal affection
5363 philanthrōpia (1),
benevolence
5544 chrēstŏtēs (4),
moral excellence

KINDRED

250 ʾEzrâchîy (1),
Ezrachite
1353 gᵉullâh (1), *blood
relationship*
4130 môwdaʾath (1),
distant relative
4138 môwledeth (11),
lineage, family
4940 mishpâchâh (6),
family, clan, people
1085 gĕnŏs (3), *kin*
4772 suggĕnĕia (3),
relatives; one's people
5443 phulē (2), *race* or
clan

KINDREDS

4940 mishpâchâh (3),
family, clan, people
3965 patria (1), *family,
group, race,* i.e. *nation*
5443 phulē (4), *race* or
clan

KINDS

2177 zan (5), *form* or *sort*
4327 mîyn (1), *sort,* i.e.
species
4940 mishpâchâh (2),
family, clan, people
1085 gĕnŏs (2), *kin,*
offspring *in kind*

KINE

504 ʾeleph (4), *ox; cow* or
cattle
1241 bâqâr (2), *plowing
ox; herd*
6510 pârâh (18), *heifer*

KING

4427 mâlak (43), to *reign
as king*
4428 melek (1957), *king*
4430 melek (Ch.) (140),
king
935 basilĕus (86),
sovereign

KING'S

4410 mᵉlûwkâh (2),
realm, rulership
4428 melek (259), *king*
4430 melek (Ch.) (18),
king
4467 mamlâkâh (1),
royal dominion
935 basilĕus (2),
sovereign
937 basilikŏs (1),
befitting the sovereign

KINGDOM

4410 mᵉlûwkâh (18),
realm, rulership
4437 malkûw (Ch.) (45),
dominion
4438 malkûwth (47),
rule; dominion
4467 mamlâkâh (61),
royal dominion
4468 mamlâkûwth (8),
royal dominion
932 basilĕia (155), *rule;
realm*

KINGDOMS

4437 malkûw (Ch.) (2),
dominion
4438 malkûwth (1), *rule;
dominion*
4467 mamlâkâh (49),
royal dominion

932 basilĕia (5), *rule;
realm*

KINGLY

4437 malkûw (Ch.) (1),
dominion

KINGS

4428 melek (283), *king*
4430 melek (Ch.) (13),
king
935 basilĕus (29),
sovereign
936 basilĕuō (1), to *rule*

KINGS'

4428 melek (3), *king*
933 basilĕiŏn (1), *royal
palace*
935 basilĕus (1),
sovereign

KINSFOLK

7138 qârôwb (1), *near,
close*
4773 suggĕnēs (1), *blood
relative; countryman*

KINSFOLKS

1350 gâʾal (1), to *redeem;
to be the next of kin*
3045 yâdaʾ (1), to *know*
4773 suggĕnēs (1), *blood
relative; countryman*

KINSMAN

1350 gâʾal (12), to *be the
next of kin*
3045 yâdaʾ (1), to *know*
7607 shᵉʾêr (1), *flesh,
meat; kindred by blood*
4773 suggĕnēs (2), *blood
relative; countryman*

KINSMAN'S

1350 gâʾal (1), to *redeem;
to be the next of kin*

KINSMEN

1350 gâʾal (1), to *redeem;
to be the next of kin*
7138 qârôwb (1), *near,
close*
4773 suggĕnēs (5), *blood
relative; countryman*

KINSWOMAN

4129 môwdaʾ (1), *distant
relative*
7607 shᵉʾêr (2), *flesh,
meat; kindred by blood*

KINSWOMEN

7608 shaʾărâh (1), *female
kindred by blood*

KIR

7024 Qîyr (5), *fortress*

KIR-HARASETH

7025 Qîyr Cheres (1),
fortress of earthenware

KIR-HARESETH

7025 Qîyr Cheres (1),
fortress of earthenware

KIR-HARESH

7025 Qîyr Cheres (1),
fortress of earthenware

KIR-HERES

7025 Qîyr Cheres (2),
fortress of earthenware

KIRIATHAIM

7156 Qiryâthayim (3),
double city

7741 Shâvêh Qiryâthayim (1), *plain of a double city*

KIRIOTH
7152 Qᵉrîyôwth (1), *buildings*

KIRJATH
7157 Qiryath Yᵉ'ârîym (1), *city of forests*

KIRJATH-ARBA
7153 Qiryath 'Arba' (6), *city of Arba or of the four* (giants)

KIRJATH-ARIM
7157 Qiryath Yᵉ'ârîym (1), *city of forests or of towns*

KIRJATH-BAAL
7154 Qiryath Ba'al (2), *city of Baal*

KIRJATH-HUZOTH
7155 Qiryath Chûtsôwth (1), *city of streets*

KIRJATH-JEARIM
7157 Qiryath Yᵉ'ârîym (18), *city of forests*

KIRJATH-SANNAH
7158 Qiryath Çannâh (1), *city of branches or of a book*

KIRJATH-SEPHER
7158 Qiryath Çannâh (4), *city of branches or of a book*

KIRJATHAIM
7156 Qiryâthayim (3), *double city*

KISH
7027 Qîysh (20), *bow*

KISHI
7029 Qîyshîy (1), *bowed*

KISHION
7191 Qishôwn (1), *hard ground*

KISHON
7028 Qîyshôwn (5), *winding*
7191 Qishôwn (1), *hard ground*

KISON
7028 Qîyshôwn (1), *winding*

KISS
5401 nâshaq (9), *to kiss*
2705 kataphilĕō (1), *to kiss earnestly*
5368 philĕō (3), *to be a friend, to kiss*
5370 philēma (7), *kiss*

KISSED
5401 nâshaq (21), *to kiss*
2705 kataphilĕō (5), *to kiss earnestly*

KISSES
5390 nᵉshîyqâh (2), *kiss*

KITE
344 'ayâh (2), *hawk*

KITHLISH
3798 Kithlîysh (1), *wall of a man*

KITRON
7003 Qiṭrôwn (1), *fumigative*

KITTIM
3794 Kittîy (2), *islander*

KNEAD
3888 lûwsh (2), *to knead*

KNEADED
3888 lûwsh (3), *to knead*

KNEADINGTROUGHS
4863 mish'ereth (2), *kneading-trough*

KNEE
1290 berek (1), *knee*
1119 gŏnu (3), *knee*

KNEEL
1288 bârak (2), *to bless*

KNEELED
1288 bârak (1), *to bless*
1289 bᵉrak (Ch.) (1), *bless*
1120 gŏnupĕtĕō (1), *to fall on the knee, kneel*
5087+1119 tithēmi (5), *place, put*

KNEELING
3766 kâra' (1), *to prostrate*
1120 gŏnupĕtĕō (2), *to fall on the knee, kneel*

KNEES
755 'arkûbâh (Ch.) (1), *knees*
1290 berek (24), *knee*
1291 berek (Ch.) (1), *knee*
1119 gŏnu (4), *knee joint*

KNEW
1847 da'ath (1), *knowledge*
3045 yâda' (83), *to know*
3046 yᵉda' (Ch.) (2), *to know*
5234 nâkar (9), *to acknowledge*
50 agnŏĕō (1), *to not know; understand*
1097 ginōskō (30), *to know*
1492 ĕidō (27), *to know*
1912 ĕpibarĕō (1), *to be severe toward*
1921 ĕpiginōskō (13), *to acknowledge*
4267 prŏginōskō (1), *to know beforehand*

KNEWEST
3045 yâda' (5), *to know*
3046 yᵉda' (Ch.) (1), *to know*
1097 ginōskō (1), *to know*
1492 ĕidō (3), *to know*

KNIFE
2719 chereb (2), *knife, sword*
3979 ma'ăkeleth (3), *knife*
7915 sakkîyn (1), *knife*

KNIT
2270 châbêr (1), *associate, friend*
3162 yachad (1), *unitedly*
7194 qâshar (1), *to tie, bind*
1210 dĕō (1), *to bind*

4822 sumbibazō (2), *to drive together*

KNIVES
2719 chereb (3), *knife, sword*
3979 ma'ăkeleth (1), *knife*
4252 machălâph (1), *butcher knife*

KNOCK
2925 krŏuō (4), *to rap, knock*

KNOCKED
2925 krŏuō (1), *to rap, knock*

KNOCKETH
1849 dâphaq (1), *to knock; to press severely*
2925 krŏuō (3), *to rap, knock*

KNOCKING
2925 krŏuō (1), *to rap, knock*

KNOP
3730 kaphtôr (10), *capital; button or disk*

KNOPS
3730 kaphtôr (6), *capital; button or disk*
6497 peqa' (3), *ornamental semi-globe*

KNOW
995 bîyn (1), *to understand; discern*
1847 da'ath (4), *knowledge*
3045 yâda' (429), *to know*
3046 yᵉda' (Ch.) (15), *to know*
5234 nâkar (9), *to acknowledge*
50 agnŏĕō (2), *to not know; not understand*
1097 ginōskō (92), *to know*
1110 gnōstŏs (1), *well-known*
1231 diaginōskō (1), *ascertain exactly*
1492 ĕidō (176), *to know*
1921 ĕpiginōskō (8), *to acknowledge*
1987 ĕpistamai (9), *to be acquainted with*
2467 isēmi (2), *to know*
4267 prŏginōskō (1), *to know beforehand*
4892 sunĕdriŏn (1), *head Jewish tribunal*

KNOWEST
1847 da'ath (1), *knowledge*
3045 yâda' (66), *to know*
1097 ginōskō (5), *to know*
1492 ĕidō (15), *to know*
1921 ĕpiginōskō (1), *to acknowledge*
2589 kardiŏgnōstēs (1), *heart-knower*

KNOWETH
854 'êth (1), *with; by; at; among*
3045 yâda' (59), *to know*
3046 yᵉda' (Ch.) (1), *to know*

5234 nâkar (1), *to acknowledge*
1097 ginōskō (16), *to know*
1492 ĕidō (22), *to know*
1921 ĕpiginōskō (2), *to acknowledge*
1987 ĕpistamai (1), *to comprehend*
2589 kardiŏgnōstēs (1), *heart-knower*

KNOWING
3045 yâda' (2), *to know*
50 agnŏĕō (1), *to not know; not understand*
1097 ginōskō (5), *to know*
1492 ĕidō (38), *to know*
1921 ĕpiginōskō (2), *to acknowledge*
1987 ĕpistamai (3), *to comprehend*

KNOWLEDGE
998 bîynâh (3), *understanding*
1843 dêa' (2), *knowledge*
1844 dê'âh (6), *knowledge*
1847 da'ath (82), *knowledge*
3045 yâda' (19), *to know*
4093 maddâ' (4), *intelligence*
5234 nâkar (2), *to treat as a foreigner*
5869 'ayin (1), *eye; sight; fountain*
7922 sekel (1), *intelligence; success*
56 agnōsia (1), *state of ignorance*
1097 ginōskō (1), *to know*
1108 gnōsis (28), *knowledge*
1492 ĕidō (1), *to know*
1921 ĕpiginōskō (3), *to acknowledge*
1922 ĕpignōsis (16), *full discernment*
1990 ĕpistēmōn (1), *intelligent, learned*
4907 sunĕsis (1), *intelligence, intellect*

KNOWN
3045 yâda' (105), *to know*
3046 yᵉda' (Ch.) (24), *to know*
5234 nâkar (2), *to acknowledge*
319 anagnōrizŏmai (1), *to make oneself known*
1097 ginōskō (46), *to know*
1107 gnōrizō (16), *to make known, reveal*
1110 gnōstŏs (11), *well-known*
1232 diagnōrizō (1), *to tell abroad*
1492 ĕidō (6), *to know*
1921 ĕpiginōskō (4), *to acknowledge*
3877 parakŏlŏuthĕō (1), *to attend; trace out*
4135 plērŏphŏrĕō (1), *to assure or convince*
5318 phanĕrŏs (3), *apparent, visible, clear*

KOA
6970 Qôwa' (1),
curtailment

KOHATH
6955 Q^ehâth (32), *allied*

KOHATHITES
6956 Qŏhâthîy (15),
Kohathite

KOLAIAH
6964 Qôwlâyâh (2), *voice of Jehovah*

KORAH
7141 Qôrach (37), *ice*

KORAHITE
7145 Qorchîy (1),
Korchite

KORAHITES
7145 Qorchîy (1),
Korchite

KORATHITES
7145 Qorchîy (1),
Korchite

KORE
6981 Qôwrê' (3), *crier*
7145 Qorchîy (1),
Korchite

KORHITES
7145 Qorchîy (4),
Korchite

KOZ
6976 Qôwts (4), *thorns*

KUSHAIAH
6984 Qûwshâyâhûw (1),
entrapped of Jehovah

LAADAH
3935 La'dâh (1), *Ladah*

LAADAN
3936 La'dân (7), *Ladan*

LABAN
3837 Lâbân (51), *white*

LABAN'S
3837 Lâbân (4), *white*

LABOUR
213 'ûwts (1), *to be close, hurry, withdraw*
1518 gîyach (1), *to issue forth; to burst forth*
3018 y^egîya' (12), *toil, work; produce, property*
3021 yâga' (8), *to be exhausted, to tire,*
3023 yâgêa' (1), *tiresome*
3027 yâd (1), *hand; power*
3205 yâlad (2), *to bear young; to father a child*
4399 m^elâ'kâh (1), *work; property*
4639 ma'ăseh (1), *action; labor*
5445 çâbal (1), *to carry*
5647 'âbad (2), *to do, work, serve*
5656 'ăbôdâh (1), *work of any kind*
5998 'âmal (2), *to work severely, put forth effort*
5999 'âmâl (25), *wearing effort; worry*
6001 'âmêl (1), *toiling; laborer; sorrowful*
6089 'etseb (1), earthen *vessel; painful toil*
6213 'âsâh (2), *to do*

LABOURED
3021 yâga' (4), *to be exhausted, to tire,*
3022 yâgâ' (1), *earnings, i.e. the product of toil*
5998 'âmal (5), *to work severely, put forth effort*
6001 'âmêl (1), *toiling; laborer; sorrowful*
6213 'âsâh (1), *to do or make*
7712 sh^edar (Ch.) (1), *to endeavor, strive*
2872 kŏpiaŏ (5), *to feel fatigue; to work hard*
4866 sunathlĕō (1), *to wrestle with*

LABOURER
2040 ĕrgatēs (2), *toiler, worker*

LABOURERS
2040 ĕrgatēs (8), *toiler, worker*
4904 sunĕrgŏs (1), *fellow-worker*

LABOURETH
5998 'âmal (1), *to work severely, put forth effort*
6001 'âmêl (2), *toiling; laborer; sorrowful*
2872 kŏpiaŏ (1), *to feel fatigue; to work hard*

LABOURING
5647 'âbad (1), *to do, work, serve*
75 agōnizŏmai (1), *to struggle; to contend*
2872 kŏpiaŏ (1), *to feel fatigue; to work hard*
2873 kŏpŏs (1), *toil; pains*

LABOURS
3018 y^egîya' (3), *toil, work; produce, property*
4639 ma'ăseh (3), *action; labor*
6089 'etseb (1), earthen *vessel; painful toil; mental pang*
6092 'âtsêb (1), hired *workman*
2873 kŏpŏs (5), *toil; pains*

LACE
6616 pâthîyl (4), *twine, cord*

LACHISH
3923 Lâchîysh (24),
Lakish

LACK
1097 b^elîy (3), *without, not yet; lacking*
2637 châçêr (4), *to lack; to fail, want, make less*

4270 machçôwr (1),
impoverishment
7326 rûwsh (1), *to be destitute*
1641 ĕlattŏnĕō (1), *to fall short, have too little*
3007 lĕipō (1), *to fail or be absent*
5302 hustĕrĕō (1), *to be inferior; to fall short*
5303 hustĕrēma (1), *deficit; poverty; lacking*
5332 pharmakĕus (1), *magician, sorcerer*

LACKED
2637 châçêr (2), *to lack; to fail, want, make less*
2638 châçêr (1), *lacking*
5737 'âdar (2), *to arrange as a battle*
6485 pâqad (1), *to visit, care for, count*
170 akairĕŏmai (1), *to fail of a proper occasion*
1729 ĕndĕēs (1), *lacking; deficient in; needy*
3361+2192 mē (1), *not; lest*
5302 hustĕrĕō (2), *to be inferior; to fall short*

LACKEST
3007 lĕipō (1), *to fail or be absent*
5302 hustĕrĕō (1), *to be inferior; to fall short*

LACKETH
2638 châçêr (3), *lacking*
6485 pâqad (1), *to visit, care for, count*
3361+3918 mē (1), *not; lest*

LACKING
5737 'âdar (1), *to arrange as a battle*
6485 pâqad (2), *to visit, care for, count*
7038 qâlaṭ (1), *to be maim*
7673 shâbath (1), *to repose; to desist*
5303 hustĕrēma (3), *deficit; poverty; lacking*

LAD
5288 na'ar (32), male *child; servant*
3808 paidariŏn (1), *little boy*

LAD'S
5288 na'ar (1), male *child; servant*

LADDER
5551 çullâm (1),
stair-case

LADE
2943 ṭâ'an (1), *to load a beast*
6006 'âmaç (1), *to impose a burden*
5412 phŏrtizō (1), *to overburden*

LADED
5375 nâsâ' (1), *to lift up*
6006 'âmaç (2), *to impose a burden*
2007 ĕpitithēmi (1), *to impose*

LADEN
3515 kâbêd (1), *severe, difficult, stupid*
5375 nâsâ' (2), *to lift up*
4987 sōrĕuō (1), *to pile up, load up*
5412 phŏrtizō (1), *to overburden*

LADETH
3515 kâbêd (1), *severe, difficult, stupid*

LADIES
8282 sârâh (2), *female noble*

LADING
6006 'âmaç (1), *to impose a burden*
5414 phŏrtŏs (1), *cargo of a ship*

LADS
5288 na'ar (1), male *child; servant*

LADY
1404 g^ebereth (2), *mistress, noblewoman*
2959 Kuria (2), *Lady*

LAEL
3815 Lâ'êl (1), *belonging to God*

LAHAD
3854 lahag (1), *mental application*

LAHAI-ROI
883 B^e'êr la-Chay Rô'îy (2), *well of a living (One) my seer*

LAHMAM
3903 Lachmâç (1),
food-like

LAHMI
3902 Lachmîy (1), *foodful*

LAID
935 bôw' (1), *to go or come*
2470 châlâh (1), *to be weak, sick, afflicted*
2630 châçan (1), *to hoard, store up*
2934 ṭâman (2), *to hide*
3052 y^ehab (Ch.) (1), *to give*
3240 yânach (1), *to allow to stay*
3241 Yânîym (8), *asleep*
3318 yâtsâ' (2), *to go, bring out*
3332 yâtsaq (1), *to pour out*
3369 yâqôsh (1), *to ensnare, trap*
3384 yârâh (1), *to point; to teach*
3515 kâbêd (1), *numerous; severe*
3647 kâmaç (1), *to store away*
5060 nâga' (1), *to strike*
5182 n^echath (Ch.) (1), *to descend; to depose*
5186 nâṭâh (1), *to stretch or spread out*
5324 nâtsab (1), *to station*
5375 nâsâ' (4), *to lift up*
5414 nâthan (13), *to give*

L

5446 çᵉbal (Ch.) (1), to *raise*
5493 çûwr (1), to *turn* off
5564 çâmak (6), to *lean* upon; *take hold of*
5674 ʾâbar (1), to *cross over; to transition*
5927 ʿâlâh (1), to *ascend, be high, mount*
6293 pâgaʿ (1), to *impinge*
6485 pâqad (2), to *visit, care for, count*
6486 pᵉquddâh (1), *visitation; punishment*
6845 tsâphan (3), to *hide; to hoard or reserve; to deny; to protect; to lurk*
7737 shâvâh (3), to *level,* i.e. *equalize*
7760 sûwm (38), to *put, place*
7896 shîyth (8), to *place, put*
7901 shâkab (17), to *lie down*
7971 shâlach (6), to *send away*
8371 shâthath (1), to *place,* i.e. *array; to lie*
8610 tâphas (1), to *manipulate,* i.e. *seize*
347 anaklinō (1), to *lean back, recline*
606 apŏkĕimai (3), to be *reserved; to await*
659 apŏtithēmi (1), to *put away; get rid of*
906 ballō (3), to *throw*
1096 ginŏmai (1), to be, *become*
1462 ĕgklēma (2), *accusation*
1911 ĕpiballō (7), to *throw upon*
1945 ĕpikĕimai (2), to *rest upon; press upon*
2007 ĕpitithēmi (13), to *impose*
2071 ĕsŏmai (1), *will be*
2698 katatithēmi (1), to *place down*
2749 kĕimai (6), to *lie outstretched*
3049 lŏgizŏmai (1), to *credit; to think, regard*
4369 prŏstithēmi (1), to *lay beside, annex*
5087 tithēmi (29), to *place, put*
5294 hupŏtithēmi (1), to *hazard; to suggest*
5342 phĕrō (1), to *bear*

LAIDST
7760 sûwm (1), to *put*

LAIN
3045+4904 yâdaʿ (1), to *know*
5414+7903 nâthan (1), to *give*
7901 shâkab (2), to *lie down*
2749 kĕimai (1), to *lie outstretched*

LAISH
3919 Layish (7), *lion*

LAKE
3041 limnē (10), *pond; lake*

LAKUM
3946 Laqqûwm (1), (poss.) *fortification*

LAMA
2982 lama (2), *why?*

LAMB
2924 ṭâleh (2), *lamb*
3532 kebes (44), *young ram*
3535 kibsâh (5), *ewe sheep*
3733 kar (1), *ram sheep; battering ram*
3775 keseb (3), *young ram sheep*
3776 kisbâh (1), *young ewe sheep*
6629 tsôʾn (1), *flock of sheep or goats*
7716 seh (17), *sheep or goat*
286 amnŏs (4), *lamb*
721 arniŏn (27), *lamb, sheep*

LAMB'S
721 arniŏn (2), *lamb, sheep*

LAMBS
563 ʾimmar (Ch.) (3), *lamb*
1121+6629 bēn (2), *son, descendant; people*
2922 ṭᵉlâʾ (1), *lamb*
3532 kebes (60), *young ram*
3535 kibsâh (3), *ewe sheep*
3733 kar (9), *ram sheep; battering ram*
3775 keseb (1), *young ram sheep*
704 arēn (1), *male lamb*
721 arniŏn (1), *lamb, sheep*

LAME
5223 nâkeh (2), *maimed; dejected*
6452 pâçach (1), to *hop, skip over; to hesitate*
6455 piççêach (14), *lame*
5560 chōlŏs (10), *limping, crippled*

LAMECH
3929 Lemek (11), *Lemek*
2984 Lamĕch (1), *Lemek*

LAMENT
56 ʾâbal (2), to *bewail*
421 ʾâlâh (1), to *bewail, mourn*
578 ʾânâh (1), to *groan, lament*
5091 nâhâh (1), to *bewail; to assemble*
5594 çâphad (9), to *tear the hair, wail*
6969 qûwn (4), to *chant or wail at a funeral*
8567 tânâh (1), to *ascribe praise,* i.e. *celebrate*
2354 thrēnĕō (1), to *bewail, lament*
2875 kŏptō (1), to *beat the breast*

LAMENTABLE
6088 ʿătsab (Ch.) (1), to *afflict; be afflicted*

LAMENTATION
592 ʾănîyâh (1), *groaning*
1058 bâkâh (1), to *weep, moan*
4553 miçpêd (3), *lamentation, howling*
5092 nᵉhîy (3), *elegy*
7015 qîynâh (14), *dirge*
2355 thrēnŏs (1), *wailing, funeral song*
2870 kŏpĕtŏs (1), *mourning*

LAMENTATIONS
7015 qîynâh (3), *dirge*

LAMENTED
56 ʾâbal (1), to *bewail*
5091 nâhâh (1), to *bewail; to assemble*
5594 çâphad (4), to *tear the hair, wail*
6969 qûwn (3), to *chant or wail at a funeral*
2354 thrēnĕō (1), to *bewail, lament*
2875 kŏptō (1), to *beat the breast*

LAMP
3940 lappîyd (3), *flaming torch, lamp or flame*
5216 nîyr (9), *lamp; lamplight*
2985 lampas (1), *lamp, lantern, torch*

LAMPS
3940 lappîyd (5), *flaming torch, lamp or flame*
5216 nîyr (26), *lamp; lamplight*
2985 lampas (6), *lamp, lantern, torch*

LANCE
3591 kîydôwn (1), *dart, javelin*

LANCETS
7420 rômach (1), *iron pointed spear*

LAND
127 ʾădâmâh (123), *soil; land*
249 ʾezrâch (2), *native born*
776 ʾerets (1505), *earth, land, soil; country*
3004 yabbâshâh (1), *dry ground*
7704 sâdeh (7), *field*
68 agrŏs (1), *farmland, countryside*
1093 gē (42), *soil, region, whole earth*
3584 xērŏs (1), *scorched; arid; withered*
5561 chōra (3), *space of territory*
5564 chōriŏn (2), *spot or plot of ground*

LANDED
2609 katagō (1), to *lead down; to moor a vessel*
2718 katĕrchŏmai (1), to *go/come down*

LANDING
2609 katagō (1), to *lead down; to moor a vessel*

LANDMARK
1366 gᵉbûwl (4), *boundary, border*

LANDMARKS
1367 gᵉbûwlâh (1), *boundary marker*

LANDS
127 ʾădâmâh (3), *soil; land*
776 ʾerets (34), *earth, land, soil; country, nation*
7704 sâdeh (4), *field*
68 agrŏs (3), *farmland, countryside*
5564 chōriŏn (1), *spot or plot of ground*

LANES
4505 rhumē (1), *alley or crowded avenue*

LANGUAGE
1697 dâbâr (1), *word; matter; thing*
3937 lâʿaz (1), to *speak in a foreign tongue*
3956 lâshôwn (9), *tongue; tongue*-shaped
3961 lishshân (Ch.) (1), *nation*
8193 sâphâh (7), *lip, language, speech*
1258 dialĕktŏs (1), *known language*

LANGUAGES
3956 lâshôwn (1), *tongue; tongue*-shaped
3961 lishshân (Ch.) (6), *nation*

LANGUISH
535 ʾâmal (5), to be *weak; to be sick*

LANGUISHED
535 ʾâmal (1), to be *weak; to be sick*

LANGUISHETH
535 ʾâmal (8), to be *weak; to be sick*

LANGUISHING
1741 dᵉvay (1), *sickness*

LANTERNS
5322 phanŏs (1), *light; lantern,* i.e. *torch*

LAODICEA
2993 Laŏdikĕia (5), *Laodicea*

LAODICEANS
2994 Laŏdikĕus (2), *inhabitant of Laodicea*

LAP
899 beged (1), *clothing; treachery or pillage*
2436 chêyq (2), *bosom, heart*
2684 chôtsen (1), *bosom*

LAPIDOTH
3941 Lappîydôwth (1), *flaming torch, lamp*

LAPPED
3952 lâqaq (2), to *lick or lap*

LAPPETH
3952 lâqaq (2), to *lick or lap*

LAPWING
1744 dûwkîyphath (2), hoopoe; (poss.) grouse

LARGE
4800 merchâb (5), open space; liberty
7304 râvach (1), to revive; to have ample room
7337 râchab (2), to broaden
7342 râchâb (5), roomy, spacious
2425 hikanŏs (1), ample; fit
3173 mĕgas (2), great, many
4080 pēlikŏs (1), how much, how great
5118 tŏsŏutŏs (1), such great

LARGENESS
7341 rôchab (1), width

LASCIVIOUSNESS
766 asĕlgĕia (6), licentiousness

LASEA
2996 Lasaia (1), Lasæa

LASHA
3962 Lesha' (1), boiling spring

LASHARON
8289 Shârôwn (1), plain

LAST
314 'achărôwn (20), late or last; behind; western
318 'ochôrêyn (Ch.) (1), at last, finally
319 'achărîyth (10), future; posterity
6119 'âqēb (1), track, footprint; rear position
2078 ĕschatŏs (48), farthest, final
4218 pŏtĕ (1), at some time, ever
5305 hustĕrŏn (4), more lately, i.e. eventually

LASTED
1961 hâyâh (1), to exist, i.e. be or become

LASTING
5769 'ôwlâm (1), eternity; ancient; always

LATCHET
8288 sᵉrôwk (1), sandal thong
2438 himas (3), strap; lash

LATE
309 'âchar (1), to delay; to procrastinate
865 'ethmôwl (1), formerly; yesterday
3568 nun (1), now; the present or immediate

LATELY
4373 prŏsphatŏs (1), recently

LATIN
4513 Rhōmaïkŏs (2), Latin

LATTER
314 'achărôwn (8), late or last; behind; western
319 'achărîyth (20), future; posterity
320 'achărîyth (Ch.) (1), later, end
3954 leqesh (2), after crop, second crop
4456 malqôwsh (8), spring rain
2078 ĕschatŏs (1), farthest, final
3797 ŏpsimŏs (1), later, i.e. vernal showering
5305 hustĕrŏn (1), more lately, i.e. eventually

LATTICE
822 'eshnâb (1), latticed window
2762 cherek (1), window lattice
7639 sᵉbâkâh (1), net-work balustrade

LAUD
1867 ĕpainĕō (1), to applaud, commend

LAUGH
3932 lâ'ag (4), to deride; to speak unintelligibly
6711 tsâchaq (3), to laugh; to scorn
6712 tsᵉchôq (1), laughter; scorn
7832 sâchaq (8), to laugh; to scorn; to play
1070 gĕlaō (2), to laugh

LAUGHED
3932 lâ'ag (3), to deride; to speak unintelligibly
6711 tsâchaq (3), to laugh; to scorn
6712 tsᵉchôq (1), laughter; scorn
7832 sâchaq (3), to laugh; to scorn; to play
2606 katagĕlaō (3), to laugh down, i.e. deride

LAUGHETH
7832 sâchaq (1), to laugh; to scorn; to play

LAUGHING
7814 sᵉchôwq (1), laughter; scorn

LAUGHTER
7814 sᵉchôwq (6), laughter; scorn
1071 gĕlōs (1), laughter

LAUNCH
1877 ĕpanagō (1), to put out to sea; to return

LAUNCHED
321 anagō (4), to bring out; to sail away

LAVER
3595 kîyôwr (15), caldron; washbowl

LAVERS
3595 kîyôwr (5), caldron; washbowl

LAVISH
2107 zûwl (1), to treat lightly

LAW
1881 dâth (6), royal edict or statute
1882 dâth (Ch.) (9), Law; royal edict or statute
2524 châm (4), father-in-law
2545 chămôwth (11), mother-in-law
2706 chôq (4), appointment; allotment
2710 châqaq (1), to engrave; to enact laws; to prescribe
2859 châthan (32), to become related
2860 châthân (5), relative by marriage
2994 yᵉbêmeth (2), sister-in-law
3618 kallâh (17), bride; son's wife
4687 mitsvâh (1), command
4941 mishpâṭ (2), verdict; formal decree; justice
8451 tôwrâh (206), precept or statute
60 agŏraiŏs (1), people of the market place
458 anŏmia (1), violation of law, wickedness
459 anŏmŏs (3), without Jewish law
460 anŏmŏs (1), lawlessly
1772 ĕnnŏmŏs (1), legal, or subject to law
2917 krima (1), decision
2919 krinō (2), to decide; to try, condemn, punish
3544 nŏmikŏs (1), expert in the (Mosaic) law
3547 nŏmŏdidaskalŏs (3), a Rabbi
3548 nŏmŏthĕsia (1), legislation, law
3549 nŏmŏthĕtĕō (1), to be given law
3551 nŏmŏs (192), law
3565 numphē (3), young married woman
3891 paranŏmĕō (1), to transgress, violate law
3994 pĕnthĕra (3), wife's mother, mother-in-law
3995 pĕnthĕrŏs (1), wife's father
4160+458 pŏiĕō (1), to make or do

LAWFUL
4941 mishpâṭ (7), verdict; formal decree; justice
6662 tsaddîyq (1), just
7990 shalliyṭ (Ch.) (1), premier, sovereign
1772 ĕnnŏmŏs (1), legal, or subject to law
1832 ĕxĕsti (12), it is right, it is proper
1833 ĕxĕtazō (17), to ascertain or interrogate

LAWFULLY
3545 nŏmimŏs (2), agreeably to the rules

LAWGIVER
2710 châqaq (6), to engrave; to enact laws

3550 nŏmŏthĕtēs (1), legislator, lawgiver

LAWLESS
459 anŏmŏs (1), without Jewish law

LAWS
1881 dâth (3), royal edict or statute
1882 dâth (Ch.) (2), Law; royal edict or statute
8451 tôwrâh (12), precept or codified statute
8541 timmâhôwn (1), consternation, panic
3551 nŏmŏs (2), law

LAWYER
3544 nŏmikŏs (3), expert in the (Mosaic) law

LAWYERS
3544 nŏmikŏs (5), expert in the (Mosaic) law

LAY
3241 Yânîym (10), asleep
3331 yâtsa' (1), to strew as a surface
3885 lûwn (1), to be obstinate
4422 mâlaṭ (1), to be delivered; be smooth
5117 nûwach (1), to rest; to settle down
5186 nâṭâh (1), to stretch or spread out
5307 nâphal (4), to fall
5414 nâthan (20), to give
5493 çûwr (1), to turn off
5564 çâmak (12), to lean upon; take hold of
6651 tsâbar (1), to aggregate, gather
6845 tsâphan (2), to hide; to hoard or reserve
7126 qârab (1), to approach, bring near
7257 râbats (3), to recline, repose, brood
7258 rebets (1), place of repose
7760 sûwm (26), to put, place
7871 shîybâh (1), residence
7896 shîyth (5), to place, put
7901 shâkab (45), to lie down
7902 shᵉkâbâh (2), lying down
7931 shâkan (1), to reside
7971 shâlach (8), to send away
659 apŏtithēmi (2), to put away; get rid of
1458 ĕgkalĕō (1), to charge, criminate
1474 ĕdaphizō (1), to dash to the ground
1911 ĕpiballō (2), to throw upon
1945 ĕpikĕimai (2), to rest upon; press upon
1949 ĕpilambanŏmai (2), to seize
2007 ĕpitithēmi (7), to impose
2343 thēsaurizō (1), to amass or reserve, store

2476 histēmi (1), to stand, establish
2621 katakĕimai (5), to lie down; to recline
2749 kĕimai (1), to lie outstretched
2827 klinō (2), to slant or slope
5087 tithēmi (13), to place

LAYEDST
5087 tithēmi (1), to place

LAYEST
7760 sûwm (1), to put

LAYETH
5381 nâsag (1), to reach
5414 nâthan (1), to give
6845 tsâphan (2), to hide; to hoard or reserve
7760 sûwm (5), to place
7896 shîyth (1), to place
7971 shâlach (1), to send away
2007 ĕpitithēmi (1), to impose

LAYING
2934 ţâman (1), to hide
597 apŏthēsaurizō (1), to store treasure away
659 apŏtithēmi (1), to put away; get rid of
863 aphiēmi (1), to leave; to pardon, forgive
1748 ĕnĕdrĕuō (1), to lurk
1917 ĕpibŏulē (1), plot, plan
1936 ĕpithĕsis (3), imposition
2598 kataballō (1), to throw down
4160 pŏiĕō (1), to make or do

LAZARUS
2976 Lazarŏs (15), God (is) helper

LEAD
833 'âshar (1), to go forward; guide
1869 dârak (2), to tread, trample; to walk, lead
1980 hâlak (1), to walk; live a certain way
2986 yâbal (1), to bring
3212 yâlak (2), to walk; to live; to carry
3318 yâtsâ' (1), to go, bring out
5090 nâhag (9), to drive forth; to lead, carry
5095 nâhal (2), to flow; to conduct; to protect
5148 nâchâh (16), to guide
5777 'ôwphereth (9), mineral lead
7218 rô'sh (1), head
71 agō (1), to lead; to bring, drive; to weigh
162 aichmalōtĕuō (1), to capture
520 apagō (2), to take away
1236 diagō (1), to pass time, conduct one's life
1533 ĕisphĕrō (2), to carry inward
1806 ĕxagō (1), to lead forth, escort

3594 hŏdēgĕō (3), to show the way, i.e. lead
4013 pĕriagō (1), to take around as a companion
5497 chĕiragōgŏs (1), conductor of the blind

LEADER
5057 nâgîyd (3), commander, official

LEADERS
833 'âshar (1), to go forward; guide
5057 nâgîyd (1), commander, official
3595 hŏdēgŏs (1), conductor, guide

LEADEST
5090 nâhag (1), to drive forth; to lead away

LEADETH
1869 dârak (1), to tread, trample; to walk, lead
3212 yâlak (3), to walk; to live; to carry
5090 nâhag (1), to drive forth; to lead away
5095 nâhal (1), to flow; to conduct; to protect
71 agō (1), to lead; to bring, drive; to weigh
399 anaphĕrō (1), to take up; to lead up
520 apagō (2), to take away
1806 ĕxagō (1), to lead forth, escort
4863 sunagō (1), to gather together
5342 phĕrō (1), to bear or carry

LEAF
5929 'âleh (11), leaf; foliage

LEAGUE
1285 bᵉrîyth (17), compact, agreement
2266 châbar (1), to fascinate by spells
3772 kârath (1), to cut (off, down or asunder)

LEAH
3812 Lê'âh (29), weary

LEAH'S
3812 Lê'âh (5), weary

LEAN
1800 dal (1), weak, thin; humble, needy
5564 çâmak (2), to lean upon; take hold of
7329 râzâh (1), to make, become thin
7330 râzeh (2), thin, lean
7534 raq (1), emaciated, lank
8172 shâ'an (4), to support, rely on

LEANED
5564 çâmak (2), to lean upon; take hold of
8172 shâ'an (4), to support, rely on
377 anapiptō (1), lie down, lean back

LEANETH
2388 châzaq (1), to fasten upon; to seize
8127 shên (1), tooth; ivory; cliff

LEANFLESHED
1851+1320 daq (2), crushed; small or thin
7534 raq (1), emaciated, lank

LEANING
7514 râphaq (1), to recline
345 anakĕimai (1), to recline at a meal

LEANNESS
3585 kachash (1), emaciation; hypocrisy
7332 râzôwn (2), thinness
7334 râzîy (1), thinness

LEANNOTH
6030 'ânâh (1), to sing, shout

LEAP
1801 dâlag (2), to spring up, ascend
2178 zan (Ch.) (1), sort, kind
4422 mâlaţ (1), to escape as if by slipperiness
5425 nâthar (1), to jump; to be agitated
5927 'âlâh (1), to ascend, be high, mount
7520 râtsad (1), to look askant; to be jealous
7540 râqad (1), to spring about wildly or for joy
4640 skirtaō (1), to jump

LEAPED
1801 dâlag (2), to spring up, ascend
5927 'âlâh (1), to ascend, be high, mount
6452 pâçach (1), to hop, skip over; to limp
242 hallŏmai (1), to jump up; to gush up
2177 ĕphallŏmai (1), to spring upon, leap upon
4640 skirtaō (2), to jump

LEAPING
1801 dâlag (1), to spring up, ascend
6339 pâzaz (1), to solidify by refining; to spring
242 hallŏmai (1), to jump up; to gush up
1814 ĕxallŏmai (1), to spring forth

LEARN
502 'âlaph (1), to learn; to teach
3925 lâmad (17), to teach, train
3129 manthanō (13), to learn
3811 paidĕuō (1), to educate or discipline

LEARNED
3045+5612 yâda' (3), to know
3925 lâmad (5), to teach, train
3928 limmûwd (2), instructed one

5172 nâchash (1), to prognosticate
3129 manthanō (10), to learn
3811 paidĕuō (1), to educate or discipline

LEARNING
3948 leqach (4), instruction
5612 çêpher (2), writing
1121 gramma (1), writing; education
1319 didaskalia (1), instruction
3129 manthanō (1), to learn

LEASING
3577 kâzâb (2), falsehood; idol

LEAST
176 'ôw (1), or, whether; desire
389 'ak (1), surely; only, however
4591 mâ'aţ (1), to be, make small or few
6810 tsâ'îyr (4), little in number; few in age
6994 qâţôn (1), to be, make diminutive
6996 qâţân (10), small, least, youngest
7535 raq (1), merely; although
1646 ĕlachistŏs (9), least
1647 ĕlachistŏtĕrŏs (1), far less
1848 ĕxŏuthĕnĕō (1), to treat with contempt
2534 kaigĕ (1), and at least (or even, indeed)
2579 kan (1), and if
3398 mikrŏs (6), small, little

LEATHER
5785 'ôwr (1), skin, leather

LEATHERN
1193 dĕrmatinŏs (1), made of leather hide

LEAVE
2308 châdal (3), to desist, stop; be fat
3241 Yânîym (14), asleep
3322 yâtsag (1), to place
3498 yâthar (7), to remain or be left
3499 yether (1), remainder; small rope
5157 nâchal (1), to inherit
5203 nâţash (6), to disperse; to thrust off
5414 nâthan (2), to give
5800 'âzab (30), to loosen; relinquish
6168 'ârâh (1), to be, make bare; to empty
7503 râphâh (1), to slacken
7592 shâ'al (1), to ask
7604 shâ'ar (13), to leave, remain
7662 shᵉbaq (Ch.) (3), to allow to remain
8338 shâwshâw (1), (poss.) to annihilate

447 aniĕmi (1), to *desert, desist* from
657 apŏtassŏmai (2), to *say adieu;* to *renounce*
782 aspazŏmai (1), to *give salutation*
863 aphiĕmi (11), to *leave;* to *pardon, forgive*
1459 ĕgkatalĕipō (1), to *desert, abandon*
1544 ĕkballō (1), to *throw out*
2010 ĕpitrĕpō (2), *allow, permit*
2641 katalĕipō (6), to *abandon*

LEAVED
1817 deleth (1), *door; gate*

LEAVEN
2557 châmêts (5), *ferment, yeasted*
4682 matstsâh (1), *unfermented cake*
7603 se'ôr (4), yeast-cake for *fermentation*
2219 zumē (13), *ferment*

LEAVENED
2557 châmêts (11), *ferment, yeasted*
7603 se'ôr (1), yeast-cake for *fermentation*
2220 zumŏō (2), to *cause to ferment*

LEAVENETH
2220 zumŏō (2), to *cause to ferment*

LEAVES
1817 deleth (3), *door; gate*
2529 chem'âh (1), *curds, milk* or *cheese*
2964 ṭereph (1), *fresh torn prey*
6074 'ŏphîy (Ch.) (3), *foliage*
6763 tsêlâ' (1), *side*
7050 qela' (1), *slinging weapon; door screen*
5444 phullŏn (6), *leaf*

LEAVETH
5800 'âzab (2), to *loosen; relinquish; permit*
863 aphiĕmi (2), to *leave;* to *pardon, forgive*

LEAVING
863 aphiĕmi (3), to *leave;* to *pardon, forgive*
2641 katalĕipō (1), to *abandon*
5277 hupŏlimpanō (1), to *leave behind*

LEBANA
3848 le'bash (Ch.) (1), to *clothe*

LEBANAH
3848 le'bash (Ch.) (1), to *clothe*

LEBANON
3844 Le'bânôwn (71), *white snow* mountain

LEBAOTH
3822 Le'bâ'ôwth (1), *lionesses*

LEBBAEUS
3002 Lĕbbaiŏs (1), *Lebbæus*

LEBONAH
3829 Le'bôwnâh (1), *frankincense*

LECAH
3922 Lêkâh (1), *journey*

LED
833 'âshar (1), to *go forward; guide*
935 bôw' (2), to *go*
1869 dârak (2), to *tread, trample;* to *walk, lead*
2986 yâbal (1), to *bring*
3212 yâlak (13), to *walk;* to *live;* to *carry*
5090 nâhag (4), to *drive forth;* to *lead away*
5148 nâchâh (6), to *guide*
5437 çâbab (3), to *surround*
71 agō (11), to *lead;* to *bring, drive;* to *weigh*
162 aichmalōtĕuō (1), to *capture*
163 aichmalōtizō (1), to *make captive*
321 anagō (2), to *lead up;* to *bring out*
520 apagō (8), to *take away*
1521 ĕisagō (1), to *lead into*
1806 ĕxagō (3), to *lead forth, escort*
4879 sunapagō (1), to *take off together*
5496 chĕiragōgĕō (2), to *guide* a blind person

LEDDEST
3318 yâtsâ' (2), to *go, bring out*
5148 nâchâh (2), to *guide*
1806 ĕxagō (1), to *lead forth, escort*

LEDGES
3027 yâd (2), *hand; power*
7948 shâlâb (3), *interval*

LEEKS
2682 châtsîyr (1), *grass; leek* plant

LEES
8105 shemer (4), *settlings* of wine, *dregs*

LEFT
2308 châdal (7), to *desist, stop; be fat*
2790 chârash (1), to *be silent;* to *be deaf*
3240 yânach (8), to *allow to stay*
3241 Yânîym (3), *asleep*
3498 yâthar (47), to *remain* or *be left*
3499 yether (3), *remainder; small rope*
3615 kâlâh (3), to *cease, be finished, perish*
3885 lûwn (1), to *be obstinate with*
4672 mâtsâ' (2), to *find* or *acquire;* to *occur*
5203 nâṭash (1), to *disperse;* to *thrust off*
5414 nâthan (1), to *give*

5493 çûwr (1), to *turn* off
5800 'âzab (43), to *loosen; relinquish*
5975 'âmad (2), to *stand*
6275 'âthaq (1), to *remove;* to *grow old*
7604 shâ'ar (65), to *leave, remain*
7611 she'êrîyth (1), *remainder* or *residual*
7662 she'baq (Ch.) (1), to *allow to remain*
7673 shâbath (1), to *repose;* to *desist*
7971 shâlach (1), to *send away*
8040 se'mô'wl (55), *north; left* hand
8041 sâma'l (4), to *use* the *left* hand or go *left*
8042 se'mâ'lîy (9), on the *left* side; *northern*
8300 sârîyd (3), *survivor; remainder*
620 apŏlĕipō (3), to *leave* behind; to *forsake*
710 aristĕrŏs (3), *left* hand
863 aphiĕmi (36), to *leave;* to *pardon, forgive*
1439 ĕaō (1), to *let be,* i.e. *permit* or *leave* alone
1459 ĕgkatalĕipō (1), to *desert, abandon*
2176 ĕuōnumŏs (10), *left; at the left* hand; *south*
2641 katalĕipō (15), to *abandon*
3973 pauō (2), to *stop,* i.e. *restrain, quit*
4051 pĕrissĕuma (1), *superabundance*
4052 pĕrissĕuō (1), to *superabound*
5275 hupŏlĕipō (1), to *remain, survive*

LEFTEST
5800 'âzab (1), to *loosen; relinquish; permit*

LEFTHANDED
334+3027+3225 'iṭṭêr (2), *impeded* (as to the right hand), *left-handed*

LEG
7640 shôbel (1), lady's garment *train*

LEGION
3003 lĕgĕōn (3), *legion*

LEGIONS
3003 lĕgĕōn (1), *legion*

LEGS
3767 kârâ' (9), *leg*
6807 tse'âdâh (1), *march; ankle-chain*
7272 regel (1), *foot; step*
7785 shôwq (4), lower *leg*
8243 shâq (Ch.) (1), *shank,* or *whole leg*
4628 skĕlŏs (3), *leg*

LEHABIM
3853 Le'hâbîym (2), *flames*

LEHI
3896 Lechîy (3), *jaw*-bone

LEISURE
2119 ĕukairĕō (1), to *have leisure*

LEMUEL
3927 Le'mûw'êl (2), (belonging) *to God*

LEND
3867 lâvâh (4), to *unite;* to *remain;* to *lend*
5383 nâshâh (2), to *lend* or *borrow*
5391 nâshak (3), to *strike;* to *oppress*
5414 nâthan (1), to *give*
5670 'âbaṭ (2), to *pawn;* to *lend;* to *entangle*
1155 danĕizō (3), to *loan* on interest; to *borrow*
5531 chraō (1), to *loan, lend*

LENDER
3867 lâvâh (2), to *unite;* to *borrow;* to *lend*

LENDETH
3867 lâvâh (3), to *unite;* to *borrow;* to *lend*
5383 nâshâh (1), to *lend* or *borrow*

LENGTH
319 'achărîyth (1), *future; posterity*
753 'ôrek (70), *length*
3372 mēkŏs (3), *length*
4218 pŏtĕ (1), at *some time, ever*

LENGTHEN
748 'ârak (2), to *be, make long*

LENGTHENED
748 'ârak (1), to *be, make long*

LENGTHENING
754 'arkâ' (Ch.) (1), *length*

LENT
5383 nâshâh (2), to *lend* or *borrow*
5391 nâshak (1), to *strike;* to *oppress*
7592 shâ'al (4), to *ask*

LENTILES
5742 'âdâsh (4), *lentil* bean

LEOPARD
5245 ne'mar (Ch.) (1), *leopard*
5246 nâmêr (4), *leopard*
3917 pardalis (1), *leopard, panther*

LEOPARDS
5246 nâmêr (2), *leopard*

LEPER
6879 tsâra' (13), to *be stricken with leprosy*
3015 lĕprŏs (4), *leper*

LEPERS
6879 tsâra' (1), to *be stricken with leprosy*
3015 lĕprŏs (5), *leper*

LEPROSY
6883 tsâra'ath (35), *leprosy*
3014 lĕpra (4), *leprosy*

LEPROUS
6879 tsâra' (6), to *be stricken with leprosy*

L

LESHEM
3959 Leshem (2), *jacinth stone*

LESS
657 'epheç (1), *end; no further*
4295 maṭṭâh (1), *below or beneath*
4591 mâ'aṭ (4), *to be, make small or few*
6996 qâṭân (3), *small, least, youngest*
253 alupŏtĕrŏs (1), *more without grief*
820 atimŏs (1), *without honor*
1640 ĕlassŏn (1), *smaller*
1647 ĕlachistŏtĕrŏs (1), *far less*
2276 hēttŏn (1), *worse; less*
3398 mikrŏs (2), *small, little*

LESSER
6996 qâṭân (2), *small, least, youngest*
7716 seh (1), *sheep or goat*

LEST
1077 bal (1), *nothing; not at all; lest*
1115 biltîy (3), *not, except, without, unless*
3808 lô' (12), *no, not*
6435 pên (120), *lest, not*
3361 mē (13), *not; lest*
3379 mēpŏtĕ (20), *not ever; if, or lest ever*
3381 mēpōs (12), *lest somehow*

LET
3212 yâlak (1), *to walk; to live; to carry*
3240 yânach (3), *to allow to stay*
3381 yârad (7), *to descend*
5117 nûwach (1), *to rest; to settle down*
5186 nâṭâh (1), *to stretch or spread out*
5414 nâthan (3), *to give*
6544 pâra' (1), *to loosen*
7503 râphâh (2), *to slacken*
7725 shûwb (1), *to turn back; to return*
7971 shâlach (2), *to send away*
630 apŏluō (10), *to relieve, release*
863 aphiēmi (16), *to leave; to pardon, forgive*
1439 ĕaō (4), *to let be, i.e. permit or leave alone*
1554 ĕkdidōmi (4), *to lease, rent*
1832 ĕxĕsti (1), *it is right, it is proper*
1929 ĕpididōmi (1), *to give over*
2010 ĕpitrĕpō (1), *allow, permit*
2524 kathiēmi (1), *to lower, let down*
2722 katĕchō (1), *to hold down fast*
2967 kōluō (1), *to stop*

5465 chalaō (5), *to lower as into a void*

LETTER
104 'iggᵉrâ' (Ch.) (3), *epistle, letter*
107 'iggereth (4), *epistle, letter*
5406 nishtᵉvân (2), *written epistle*
5407 nishtᵉvân (Ch.) (3), *written epistle*
5612 çêpher (13), *writing*
6600 pithgâm (Ch.) (1), *decree; report*
1121 gramma (6), *writing; education*
1989 ĕpistĕllō (1), *to communicate by letter*
1992 ĕpistŏlē (3), *written message*

LETTERS
107 'iggereth (6), *epistle, letter*
5612 çêpher (16), *writing*
1121 gramma (3), *writing; education*
1992 ĕpistŏlē (6), *written message*

LETTEST
8257 shâqa' (1), *to be overflowed; to cease*
630 apŏluō (1), *to relieve, release*

LETTETH
6362 pâṭar (1), *to burst through; to emit*
2722 katĕchō (1), *to hold down fast*

LETUSHIM
3912 Lᵉṭûwshîm (1), *oppressed ones*

LEUMMIM
3817 Lᵉ'ummîym (1), *communities*

LEVI
3878 Lêvîy (64), *attached*
3017 Lĕuï (5), *attached*
3018 Lĕuïs (3), *attached*

LEVIATHAN
3882 livyâthân (5), *serpent (crocodile)*

LEVITE
3881 Lêvîyîy (26), *Levite*
3019 Lĕuïtēs (2), *descendants of Levi*

LEVITES
3878 Lêvîy (1), *attached*
3879 Lêvîy (Ch.) (4), *attached*
3881 Lêvîyîy (259), *Levite*
3019 Lĕuïtēs (1), *descendants of Levi*

LEVITICAL
3020 Lĕuïtikŏs (1), *relating to the Levites*

LEVY
4522 maç (4), *forced labor*
5927 'âlâh (1), *to ascend, be high, mount*
7311 rûwm (1), *to be high; to rise or raise*

LEWD
2154 zimmâh (2), *bad plan*

4190 pŏnērŏs (1), *malice, wicked, bad; crime*

LEWDLY
2154 zimmâh (1), *bad plan*

LEWDNESS
2154 zimmâh (14), *bad plan*
4209 mᵉzimmâh (1), *plan; sagacity*
5040 nablûwth (1), *female genitals*
4467 rhaₗdiŏurgēma (1), *crime, legal fraction*

LIAR
376+3576 'îysh (1), *man; male; someone*
391 'akzâb (1), *deceit; treachery*
3576 kâzab (2), *to lie, deceive*
8267 sheqer (1), *untruth; sham*
5583 psĕustēs (8), *falsifier*

LIARS
907 bad (2), *brag or lie; liar, boaster*
3576 kâzab (1), *to lie, deceive*
3584 kâchash (1), *to lie, disown; to disappoint*
5571 psĕudēs (2), *erroneous, deceitful*
5583 psĕustēs (2), *falsifier*

LIBERAL
1293 bᵉrâkâh (1), *benediction, blessing*
5081 nâdîyb (3), *generous*
572 haplŏtēs (1), *sincerity; generosity*

LIBERALITY
572 haplŏtēs (1), *sincerity; generosity*
5485 charis (1), *graciousness*

LIBERALLY
6059 'ânaq (1), *to collar; to fit out*
574 haplōs (1), *bountifully, generously*

LIBERTINES
3032 Libĕrtinŏs (1), *Freedman*

LIBERTY
1865 dᵉrôwr (7), *freedom; clear, pure*
2670 chophshîy (1), *exempt from bondage*
7342 râchâb (1), *roomy, spacious*
425 anĕsis (1), *relaxation; relief*
630 apŏluō (2), *to relieve, release; to pardon*
859 aphĕsis (1), *pardon, freedom*
1657 ĕlĕuthĕria (11), *freedom*
1658 ĕlĕuthĕrŏs (1), *unrestrained*
1849 ĕxŏusia (1), *authority, power, right*
2010 ĕpitrĕpō (1), *to allow*

LIBNAH
3841 Libnâh (18), *storax-tree*

LIBNI
3845 Libnîy (5), *white*

LIBNITES
3864 Lûwbîy (2), *dry region*

LIBYA
6316 Pûwṭ (2), *Put, person*
3033 Libuē (1), *south region*

LIBYANS
3864 Lûwbîy (1), *dry region*
6316 Pûwṭ (1), *Put, person*

LICE
3654 kên (6), *stinging bug*

LICENCE
2010 ĕpitrĕpō (1), *allow, permit*
5117 tŏpŏs (1), *place*

LICK
3897 lâchak (4), *to lick*
3952 lâqaq (1), *to lick*

LICKED
3897 lâchak (1), *to lick*
3952 lâqaq (2), *to lick*
621 apŏlĕichō (1), *to lick off clean*

LICKETH
3897 lâchak (1), *to lick*

LID
1817 deleth (1), *door; gate*

LIE
391 'akzâb (1), *deceit; treachery*
693 'ârab (2), *to ambush, lie in wait*
2583 chânâh (2), *to encamp*
3576 kâzab (12), *to lie, deceive*
3584 kâchash (1), *to lie, disown; to disappoint*
3885 lûwn (2), *to be obstinate*
4769 marbêts (1), *reclining or resting place*
5203 nâṭash (1), *to disperse; to abandon*
5307 nâphal (1), *to fall*
5414+7903 nâthan (3), *to give*
6658 tsâdâh (1), *to desolate*
7250 râba' (2), *to lay down; have sex*
7257 râbats (15), *to recline, repose, brood*
7258 rebets (1), *place of repose*
7693 shâgal (1), *to copulate*
7901 shâkab (59), *to lie down*
8266 shâqar (5), *to cheat, i.e. be untrue in words*
8267 sheqer (8), *untruth; sham*
893 apsĕudēs (1), *veracious, free of deceit*
2621 katakĕimai (1), *to lie down; to recline*

LIED

2749 *kĕimai* (1), to *lie outstretched*
3180 *mĕthŏdĕia* (1), *trickery, scheming*
3582 *xĕstēs* (1), *vessel*
5574 *psĕudŏmai* (11), to *utter an untruth*
5579 *psĕudŏs* (7), *falsehood*

LIED

3576 *kâzab* (2), to *lie, deceive*
3584 *kâchash* (1), to *lie, disown;* to *disappoint*
5574 *psĕudŏmai* (1), to *utter an untruth*

LIEN

7693 *shâgal* (1), to *copulate* with
7901 *shâkab* (2), to *lie down*

LIES

907 *bad* (3), *brag or lie; liar, boaster*
1697+3576 *dâbâr* (1), *word; matter; thing*
1697+8267 *dâbâr* (1), *word; matter; thing*
3576 *kâzab* (22), to *lie, deceive*
3585 *kachash* (4), *emaciation; hypocrisy*
7723 *shâv'* (1), *ruin; guile; idolatry*
8267 *sheqer* (17), *untruth; sham*
8383 *teʾûn* (1), *toil*
5573 *psĕudŏlŏgŏs* (1), *promulgating erroneous doctrine*

LIEST

5307 *nâphal* (1), to *fall*
7901 *shâkab* (4), to *lie down*

LIETH

3318 *yâtsâ'* (3), to *go, bring out*
3584 *kâchash* (1), to *lie, disown;* to *disappoint*
4904 *mishkâb* (1), *bed; sleep; intercourse*
5564 *çâmak* (1), to *lean* upon; *take hold of*
6437 *pânâh* (1), to *turn,* to *face*
7257 *râbats* (2), to *recline, repose, brood*
7901 *shâkab* (20), to *lie down*
8172 *shâ'an* (1), to *support, rely on*
906 *ballō* (1), to *throw*
991 *blĕpō* (1), to *look at*
2192 *ĕchō* (1), to *have; hold; keep*
2749 *kĕimai* (2), to *lie outstretched*

LIEUTENANTS

323 *'ăchashdarpan* (4), *satrap*

LIFE

2416 *chay* (143), *alive; raw; fresh; life*
2417 *chay* (Ch.) (1), *alive; life*
2421 *châyâh* (10), to *live;* to *revive*

2425 *châyay* (1), to *live;* to *revive*
3117 *yôwm* (3), *day; time period*
3117+5921 *yôwm* (1), *day; time period*
5315 *nephesh* (90), *life; breath; soul; wind*
6106 *'etsem* (1), *bone; body; substance*
72 *agōgē* (1), *mode of living, way of life*
895 *apsuchŏs* (1), *lifeless,* i.e. *inanimate*
979 *biŏs* (5), *present state of existence*
981 *biŏsis* (1), mode of *living*
982 *biŏtikŏs* (3), *relating* to the present *existence*
2198 *zaō* (1), to *live*
2222 *zōē* (132), *life*
2227 *zōŏpŏiĕō* (2), to (re-)*vitalize, give life*
4151 *pnĕuma* (1), *spirit*
5590 *psuchē* (36), *soul, vitality; heart, mind*

LIFETIME

2416 *chay* (1), *alive; raw; fresh; life*
2198 *zaō* (1), to *live*
2222 *zōē* (1), *life*

LIFT

5127 *nûwç* (1), to *vanish away, flee*
5130 *nûwph* (3), to *quiver, vibrate, rock*
5375 *nâsâ'* (66), to *lift up*
5414 *nâthan* (1), to *give*
6030 *'ânâh* (1), to *respond, answer*
6670 *tsâhal* (1), to be *cheerful;* to *sound*
6965 *qûwm* (3), to *rise*
7311 *rûwm* (18), to be *high;* to *rise or raise*
352 *anakuptō* (1), to *straighten up*
461 *anŏrthŏō* (1), to *straighten up*
1458 *ĕgkalĕō* (1), to *charge, criminate*
1869 *ĕpairō* (4), to *raise up, look up*
5312 *hupsŏō* (1), to *elevate;* to *exalt*

LIFTED

935 *bôw'* (1), to *go or come*
1361 *gâbahh* (7), to be *lofty;* to be *haughty*
1431 *gâdal* (1), to be *great, make great*
1802 *dâlâh* (1), to *draw out water);* to *deliver*
5130 *nûwph* (1), to *quiver, vibrate, rock*
5191 *neʿṭal* (Ch.) (2), to *raise;* to *repent*
5264 *nâçaç* (1), to *gleam;* to *flutter a flag*
5375 *nâsâ'* (92), to *lift up*
5423 *nâthaq* (1), to *tear off*
5782 *'ûwr* (3), to *awake*
5927 *'âlâh* (1), to *ascend, be high, mount*

6075 *'âphal* (1), to *swell;* be *elated*
7213 *râ'am* (1), to *rise*
7311 *rûwm* (15), to be *high;* to *rise or raise*
7313 *rûwm* (Ch.) (2), *elation, arrogance*
7426 *râmam* (2), to *rise*
142 *airō* (4), to *lift,* to *take up*
352 *anakuptō* (2), to *straighten up*
450 *anistēmi* (1), to *stand up;* to *come back to life*
1453 *ĕgĕirō* (3), to *waken,* i.e. *rouse*
1869 *ĕpairō* (10), to *raise up, look up*
5188 *tuphō* (1), to *make a smoke*
5312 *hupsŏō* (5), to *elevate;* to *exalt*

LIFTER

7311 *rûwm* (1), to be *high;* to *rise or raise*

LIFTEST

5375 *nâsâ'* (1), to *lift up*
5414 *nâthan* (1), to *give*
7311 *rûwm* (2), to be *high;* to *rise or raise*

LIFTETH

4754 *mârâ'* (1), to *rebel;* to *lash with whip; flap*
5375 *nâsâ'* (2), to *lift up*
5749 *'ûwd* (1), to *duplicate or repeat*
5927 *'âlâh* (2), to *ascend, be high, mount*
7311 *rûwm* (4), to be *high;* to *rise or raise*

LIFTING

1348 *gê'ûwth* (1), *ascending; majesty*
1466 *gêvâh* (1), *exaltation; arrogance*
4607 *mŏ'al* (1), *raising of the hands*
4864 *mas'êth* (1), *raising; beacon; present*
5375 *nâsâ'* (1), to *lift up*
5782 *'ûwr* (1), to *awake*
7311 *rûwm* (1), to be *high;* to *rise or raise*
7427 *rômêmûth* (1), *exaltation*
1869 *ĕpairō* (1), to *raise up, look up*

LIGHT

215 *'ôwr* (1), to be *luminous*
216 *'ôwr* (126), *luminary; lightning; happiness*
217 *'ûwr* (1), *flame; East*
219 *'ôwrâh* (2), *luminousness, light*
3313 *yâpha'* (1), to *shine*
3974 *mâ'ôwr* (15), *luminary, light source*
4237 *mechĕzâh* (2), *window*
5051 *nôgahh* (1), *brilliancy*
5094 *neʿhîyr* (Ch.) (3), *illumination*
5105 *neʿhârâh* (1), *daylight*

5117 *nûwach* (1), to *rest;* to *settle* down
5216 *nîyr* (4), *lamp; lamplight*
5927 *'âlâh* (2), to *ascend, be high, mount*
6348 *pâchaz* (2), to be *unimportant*
7031 *qal* (1), *rapid, swift*
7034 *qâlâh* (1), to be *light*
7043 *qâlal* (7), to be, *make light*
7052 *qeʿlôqêl* (1), *insubstantial food*
7136 *qârâh* (1), to *bring about;* to *impose*
7837 *shachar* (1), *dawn*
272 *amĕlĕō* (1), to be *careless of, neglect*
681 *haptō* (1), to *set on fire*
1645 *ĕlaphrŏs* (2), *light,* i.e. *easy*
2014 *ĕpiphainō* (1), to *become visible*
2017 *ĕpiphauō* (1), to *illuminate, shine on*
2545 *kaiō* (1), to *set on fire*
2989 *lampō* (1), to *radiate brilliancy*
3088 *luchnŏs* (5), lamp or other *illuminator*
4098 *piptō* (1), to *fall*
5338 *phĕggŏs* (3), *brilliancy, radiance*
5457 *phōs* (65), *luminousness, light*
5458 *phōstēr* (1), celestial *luminary*
5460 *phōtĕinŏs* (4), *well-illuminated*
5461 *phōtizō* (4), to *shine* or to *brighten* up
5462 *phōtismŏs* (2), *light; illumination*

LIGHTED

3381 *yârad* (2), to *descend*
4672 *mâtsâ'* (1), to *find* or *acquire;* to *occur*
5307 *nâphal* (3), to *fall*
5927 *'âlâh* (2), to *ascend, be high, mount*
6293 *pâga'* (1), to *impinge*
6795 *tsânach* (2), to *descend,* i.e. *drive* down
681 *haptō* (2), to *set on fire*

LIGHTEN

215 *'ôwr* (2), to be *luminous*
5050 *nâgahh* (1), to *illuminate*
7043 *qâlal* (2), to be, *make light*
602 *apŏkalupsis* (1), *disclosure, revelation*
5461 *phōtizō* (1), to *shine* or to *brighten* up

LIGHTENED

215 *'ôwr* (1), to be *luminous*
5102 *nâhar* (1), to *sparkle;* to be *cheerful*
1546+4160 *ĕkbŏlē* (1), *jettison of cargo*

L

2893 kŏuphizō (1), to
unload, make lighter
5461 phōtizō (1), to shine
or to brighten up
LIGHTENETH
215 'ôwr (1), to be
luminous
797 astraptō (1), to flash
as lightning
LIGHTER
7043 qâlal (4), to be,
make light
LIGHTEST
5927 'âlâh (1), to ascend,
be high, mount
LIGHTETH
4672 mâtsâ' (1), to find
or acquire; to occur
5927 'âlâh (1), to ascend,
be high, mount
5461 phōtizō (1), to shine
or to brighten up
LIGHTING
5183 nachath (1),
descent; quiet
2064 ĕrchŏmai (1), to go
or come
LIGHTLY
4592 mᵉ'aṭ (1), little or
few
5034 nâbêl (1), to wilt; to
fall away; to be foolish
7034 qâlâh (1), to be light
7043 qâlal (3), to be,
make light
5035 tachu (1), without
delay, soon, suddenly
LIGHTNESS
6350 pachăzûwth (1),
frivolity
6963 qôwl (1), voice or
sound
1644 ĕlaphria (1),
fickleness
LIGHTNING
216 'ôwr (1), luminary;
lightning; happiness
965 bâzâq (1), flash of
lightning
1300 bârâq (5), lightning;
flash of lightning
2385 chăzîyz (2), flash of
lightning
796 astrapē (4),
lightning; light's glare
LIGHTNINGS
1300 bârâq (9), lightning;
flash of lightning
3940 lappîyd (1), flaming
torch, lamp or flame
796 astrapē (4),
lightning; light's glare
LIGHTS
216 'ôwr (1), luminary;
lightning; happiness
3974 mâ'ôwr (1),
luminary, light source
8261 shâqûph (1),
opening
2985 lampas (1), lamp,
lantern, torch
3088 luchnŏs (1), lamp
or other illuminator
5457 phōs (1),
luminousness, light

5458 phōstēr (1),
celestial luminary
LIGURE
3958 leshem (2), (poss.)
jacinth
LIKE
251 'âch (1), brother;
relative; member
1571 gam (2), also; even
1819 dâmâh (16), to
resemble, liken
1821 dᵉmâh (Ch.) (2), to
resemble; be like
1823 dᵉmûwth (2),
resemblance, likeness
1825 dimyôwn (1),
resemblance, likeness
1922 hădar (Ch.) (1), to
magnify, glorify
2088 zeh (1), this or that
2421 châyâh (1), to live;
to revive
2654 châphêts (2), to be
pleased with, desire
2803 châshab (1), to
think, regard; to value
3541 kôh (1), thus
3644 kᵉmôw (61), like,
as; for; with
3651 kên (7), just; right,
correct
4711 mâtsats (1), to suck
4911 mâshal (5), to use
figurative language
4915 môshel (1), empire;
parallel
5973 'îm (2), with
5974 'îm (Ch.) (1), with
7737 shâvâh (2), to
resemble; to adjust
407 andrizŏmai (1), to
act manly
499 antitupŏn (1),
representative
871 aphŏmŏiŏō (1), to be
like
1381 dŏkimazō (1), to
test; to approve
1503 ĕikō (1), to
resemble, be like
2470 isŏs (1), similar
2472 isŏtimŏs (1), of
equal value or honor
2504 kagō (1), and also
2532 kai (1), and; or
3663 hŏmŏiŏpathēs (2),
similarly affected
3664 hŏmŏiŏs (47),
similar
3665 hŏmŏiŏtēs (1),
resemblance, similarity
3666 hŏmŏiŏō (4), to
become like
3667 hŏmŏiōma (1),
form; resemblance
3779 hŏutō (2), in this
way; likewise
3945 parŏmŏiazō (2), to
resemble, be like
3946 parŏmŏiŏs (2),
similar, like
4832 summŏrphŏs (1),
similar, conformed to
5024 tauta (2), in the
same way
5108 tŏiŏutŏs (1), truly
this, i.e. of this sort
5613 hōs (10), which,
how, i.e. in that manner

5615 hōsautōs (2), in the
same way
5616 hōsĕi (6), as if
5618 hōspĕr (1), exactly
like
LIKED
7521 râtsâh (1), to be
pleased with; to satisfy
LIKEMINDED
2473 isŏpsuchŏs (1), of
similar spirit
3588+846+5426 hŏ (2),
"the," definite article
LIKEN
1819 dâmâh (4), to
resemble, liken
3666 hŏmŏiŏō (5), to
become like
LIKENED
1819 dâmâh (2), to
resemble, liken
3666 hŏmŏiŏō (4), to
become like
LIKENESS
1823 dᵉmûwth (19),
resemblance, likeness
8403 tabnîyth (5),
resemblance
8544 tᵉmûwnâh (5),
something fashioned
3666 hŏmŏiŏō (1), to
become like
3667 hŏmŏiōma (3),
form; resemblance
LIKETH
157 'âhab (1), to have
affection, love
2896 ṭôwb (2), good; well
LIKEWISE
1571 gam (15), also;
even; yea; though
2063 zō'th (2), this
3162 yachad (1), unitedly
3651 kên (14), just; right
36 agĕnēs (1), ignoble,
lowly
437 anthŏmŏlŏgĕŏmai
(1), respond in praise
2532 kai (11), and; or
3668 hŏmŏiŏs (29), in the
same way
3779 hŏutō (5), in this
way; likewise
3898 paraplēsiōs (1), in a
manner near by
5615 hōsautōs (13), in
the same way
LIKHI
3949 Liqchîy (1), learned
LIKING
2492 châlam (1), to be,
make plump; to dream
LILIES
7799 shûwshan (8), white
lily; straight trumpet
2918 krinŏn (2), lily
LILY
7799 shûwshan (5), white
lily; straight trumpet
LIME
7875 sîyd (2), lime
LIMIT
1366 gᵉbûwl (1),
boundary, border

LIMITED
8428 tâvâh (1), to grieve,
bring pain
LIMITETH
3724 hŏrizō (1), to
appoint, decree, specify
LINE
2256 chebel (5),
company, band
2339 chûwṭ (1), string;
line
6616 pâthîyl (1), twine,
cord
6957 qav (14), rule;
musical string
8279 sered (1),
scribing-awl
8515 Tᵉla'ssar (1),
Telassar
8615 tiqvâh (1), cord;
expectancy
2583 kanōn (1), rule,
standard
LINEAGE
3965 patria (1), family,
group, race, i.e. nation
LINEN
906 bad (23), linen
garment
948 bûwts (9), Byssus,
(poss.) cotton
4723 miqveh (4),
confidence; collection
5466 çâdîyn (2), shirt
6593 pishteh (9), linen,
from carded thread
8162 sha'aṭnêz (1), linen
and woolen
8336 shêsh (37), white
linen; white marble
1039 bussinŏs (4), linen
1040 bussŏs (2), white
linen
3043 linŏn (1), flax linen
3608 ŏthŏniŏn (5), strips
of linen bandage
4616 sindōn (6), byssos,
i.e. bleached linen
LINES
2256 chebel (2),
company, band
LINGERED
4102 mâhahh (2), to be
reluctant
LINGERETH
691 argĕō (1), to delay,
grow weary
LINTEL
352 'ayîl (1), chief; ram;
oak tree
3730 kaphtôr (1), capital;
wreath-like button
4947 mashqôwph (2),
lintel
LINTELS
3730 kaphtôr (1), capital;
wreath-like button
LINUS
3044 Linŏs (1), (poss.)
flax linen
LION
738 'ărîy (56), lion
739 'ărîy'êl (2), Lion of
God

LION'S
3715 kᵉphîyr (16), walled
village; young lion
3833 lâbîy' (9), lion,
lioness
3918 layish (3), lion
7826 shachal (6), lion
3023 lĕôn (6), lion

LION'S
738 'ărîy (4), lion
3833 lâbîy' (1), lion,
lioness
7830 shachats (1),
haughtiness; dignity

LIONESS
3833 lâbîy' (1), lion,
lioness

LIONESSES
3833 lâbîy' (1), lion,
lioness

LIONLIKE
739 'ărîy'êl (2), Lion of
God

LIONS
738 'ărîy (17), lion
744 'aryêh (Ch.) (8), lion
3715 kᵉphîyr (14), walled
village; young lion
3833 lâbîy' (1), lion,
lioness
3023 lĕôn (3), lion

LIONS'
738 'ărîy (2), lion
744 'aryêh (Ch.) (1), lion

LIP
822 'eshnâb (1), latticed
window
8193 sâphâh (2), lip,
language, speech

LIPS
2193 zâ'ak (1), to
extinguish
8193 sâphâh (109), lip,
language, speech
8222 sâphâm (3), beard
5491 chĕîlŏs (6), lip

LIQUOR
4197 mezeg (1),
tempered wine
4952 mishrâh (1),
steeped juice

LIQUORS
1831 dema' (1), juice

LISTED
2309 thĕlō (2), to will; to
desire; to choose

LISTEN
8085 shâma' (1), to hear
intelligently

LISTETH
2309 thĕlō (1), to will; to
desire; to choose
3730+1014 hŏrmē (1),
impulse, i.e. onset

LITTERS
6632 tsâb (1), lizard;
covered cart

LITTLE
1851 daq (1), crushed;
small or thin
2191 zᵉ'êyr (3), small,
little
2192 zᵉ'êyr (Ch.) (1),
small, little

2835 châsîph (1), small
company, flock
2945 ṭaph (32), family of
children and women
3530 kibrâh (3), measure
of length
3563 kôwç (2), cup;
(poss.) owl
4591 mâ'aṭ (3), to be,
make small or few
4592 mᵉ'aṭ (52), little or
few
4704 mitstsᵉ'îyrâh (1),
diminutive
4705 mits'âr (3), little;
short time
5759 ăvîyl (1), infant,
young child
5768 'ôwlêl (1), suckling
child
6810 tsâ'îyr (4), little in
number; few in age
6819 tsâ'ar (1), to be
small; be trivial
6966 qûwm (Ch.) (1), to
rise
6995 qôṭen (2), little
finger
6996 qâṭân (20), small,
least, youngest
8102 shemets (2), inkling
8241 shetseph (1),
outburst of anger
8585 tᵉ'âlâh (1), channel;
bandage or plaster
974 bibliaridiŏn (4), little
scroll
1024 brachus (6), little,
short
1646 ĕlachistŏs (1), least
2365 thugatriŏn (1), little
daughter
2485 ichthudiŏn (1), little
fish
3357 mĕtriŏs (1),
moderately, i.e. slightly
3397 mikrŏn (14), small
space of time or degree
3398 mikrŏs (16), small,
little
3640 ŏligŏpistŏs (5), little
confidence
3641 ŏligŏs (9), puny,
small
3813 paidiŏn (12), child:
immature
4142 plŏiariŏn (2), small
boat
5040 tĕkniŏn (9), infant,
i.e. a darling Christian
5177 tugchanō (1), to
take part in; to obtain

LIVE
2414 châṭaph (3), to seize
as a prisoner
2416 chay (44), alive;
raw; fresh; life
2418 chăyâ' (Ch.) (2), to
live
2421 châyâh (110), to
live; to revive
2425 châyay (15), to live;
to revive
3117 yôwm (2), day; time
period
7531 ritspâh (1), hot
stone; pavement
390 anastrĕphō (2), to
remain, to live

980 biŏō (1), to live life
1514 ĕirēnĕuō (2), to be,
act peaceful
2068 ĕsthiō (1), to eat
2071+3118 ĕsŏmai (1),
will be
2198 zaō (53), to live
2225 zōŏgŏnĕō (1), to
rescue; be saved
4800 suzaō (3), to live in
common with
5225 huparchō (1), to
come into existence

LIVED
2416 chay (5), alive; raw;
fresh; life
2421 châyâh (39), to live;
to revive
2425 châyay (5), to live;
to revive
326 anazaō (1), to
recover life, live again
2198 zaō (4), to live
4176 pŏlitĕuŏmai (1), to
behave as a citizen
5171 truphaō (1), to live
indulgently

LIVELY
2416 chay (1), alive; raw;
fresh; life
2422 châyeh (1), vigorous
2198 zaō (3), to live

LIVER
3516 kâbêd (14), liver

LIVES
2416 chay (2), alive; raw;
fresh; life
2417 chay (Ch.) (1), alive;
life
2421 châyâh (2), to live;
to revive
5315 nephesh (18), life;
breath; soul; wind
5590 psuchē (5), soul,
vitality; heart, mind

LIVEST
2416 chay (1), alive; raw;
fresh; life
3117 yôwm (1), day; time
period
2198 zaō (2), to live

LIVETH
2416 chay (61), alive;
raw; fresh; life
2421 châyâh (1), to live;
to revive
2425 châyay (2), to live;
to revive
3117 yôwm (1), day; time
period
2198 zaō (24), to live

LIVING
2416 chay (98), alive;
raw; fresh; life
2417 chay (Ch.) (4), alive;
life
2424 chayûwth (1), life,
lifetime
979 biŏs (5), present
state of existence
1236 diagō (1), to pass
time or life
2198 zaō (34), to live

LIZARD
3911 lᵉṭâ'âh (1), kind of
lizard

LO
718 'ărûw (Ch.) (1), lo!,
behold!
1883 dethe' (Ch.) (1),
sprout; green grass
1888 hê' (Ch.) (1), Lo!,
Look!
2005 hên (13), lo!; if!
2009 hinnêh (103), lo!;
Look!
2114 zûwr (1), to be
foreign, strange
7200 râ'âh (3), to see
2395 iatrŏs (1), physician
2396 idĕ (2), surprise!,
lo!, look!
2400 idŏu (29), lo!, note!,
see!

LO-AMMI
3818 Lô' 'Ammîy (1), not
my people

LO-DEBAR
3810 Lô' Dᵉbar (3),
pastureless

LO-RUHAMAH
3819 Lô' Rûchâmâh (2),
not pitied

LOADEN
6006 'âmaç (1), to impose
a burden

LOADETH
6006 'âmaç (1), to impose
a burden

LOAF
3603 kikkâr (2), round
loaf; talent
740 artos (1), loaf of
bread

LOAN
7596 shᵉ'êlâh (1), petition

LOATHE
3988 mâ'aç (1), to spurn;
to disappear

LOATHETH
947 bûwç (1), to trample
down; oppress
6973 qûwts (1), to be,
make disgusted

LOATHSOME
887 bâ'ash (1), to be a
moral stench
2214 zârâ' (1),
disgusting, loathing
3988 mâ'aç (1), to spurn;
to disappear
7033 qâlâh (1), to toast,
scorch

LOAVES
3603 kikkâr (2), round
loaf; talent
3899 lechem (5), food,
bread
740 artos (22), loaf of
bread

LOCK
4514 man'ûwl (1), bolt on
door
6734 tsîytsîth (1),
fore-lock of hair; tassel

LOCKED
5274 nâ'al (2), to fasten
up, lock

LOCKS
4253 machlâphâh (2), *ringlet* or *braid*, of hair
4514 man'ûwl (5), *bolt* on door
6545 pera' (2), *hair* as *dishevelled*
6777 tsammâh (4), *veil*
6977 qᵉvutstsâh (2), *forelock* of hair

LOCUST
697 'arbeh (9), *locust*
5556 çol'âm (1), destructive *locust* kind
6767 tsᵉlâtsal (1), *cricket*

LOCUSTS
697 'arbeh (11), *locust*
1357 gêb (1), *locust* swarm
2284 châgâb (1), *locust*
200 akris (4), *locust*

LOD
3850 Lôd (4), *Lod*

LODGE
3885 lûwn (22), to *be obstinate*
4412 mᵉlûwnâh (1), *hut*
2647 kataluô (1), to *halt* for the night
2681 kataskēnŏō (2), to *remain, live*
3579 xĕnizō (1), to *be a host; to be a guest*

LODGED
3885 lûwn (12), to *be obstinate*
4411 mâlôwn (1), *lodging* for night
7901 shâkab (1), to *lie down*
835 aulizŏmai (1), to *pass the night*
2681 kataskēnŏō (1), to *remain, live*
3579 xĕnizō (4), to *be a host; to be a guest*
3580 xĕnŏdŏchĕō (1), to *be hospitable*

LODGEST
3885 lûwn (1), to *be obstinate*

LODGETH
3579 xĕnizō (1), to *be a host; to be a guest*

LODGING
3885 lûwn (1), to *be obstinate*
4411 mâlôwn (3), *lodgment* for night
3578 xĕnia (2), *place of entertainment*

LODGINGS
4411 mâlôwn (1), *lodgment* for night

LOFT
5944 'ǎlîyâh (1), *upper* things; *second-story*

LOFTILY
4791 mârôwm (1), *elevation; elation*

LOFTINESS
1363 gôbahh (1), *height; grandeur; arrogance*
1365 gabhûwth (1), *pride, arrogance*

LOFTY
1364 gâbôahh (2), *high; powerful; arrogant*
1365 gabhûwth (1), *pride, arrogance*
5375 nâsâ' (1), to *lift up*
7311 rûwm (3), to *be high; to rise or raise*
7682 sâgab (1), to *be, make lofty; be safe*

LOG
3849 lôg (5), liquid *measure*

LOINS
2504 châlâts (9), *loins, areas* of the *waist*
2788 chârêr (1), *arid, parched*
3409 yârêk (2), *leg* or *shank, flank; side*
3689 keçel (1), *loin; back; viscera*
4975 môthen (42), *loins*
3751 ŏsphus (8), *loin; belt*

LOIS
3090 Lŏïs (1), *Loïs*

LONG
748 'ârak (4), to *be, make long*
752 'ârôk (2), *long*
753 'ôrek (23), *length*
954 bûwsh (1), to *be delayed*
1419 gâdôwl (1), *great*
2442 châkâh (1), to *await; hope for*
3117 yôwm (16), *day; time period*
4101 mâh (Ch.) (1), *what?, how?, why?*
4900 mâshak (2), to *draw out; to be tall*
4970 mâthay (1), *when; when?, how long?*
5704 'ad (51), *as far (long) as; during*
5750 'ôwd (1), *again; repeatedly; still; more*
5769 'ôwlâm (3), *eternity; ancient; always*
5973 'îm (1), *with*
6256 'êth (1), *time*
6440 pânîym (1), *face; front*
7221 rî'shâh (1), *beginning*
7227 rab (11), *great*
7230 rôb (2), *abundance*
7235 râbâh (3), to *increase*
7350 râchôwq (3), *remote, far*
8615 tiqvâh (1), *cord; expectancy*
1909 ĕpi (1), *on, upon*
1909+4119 ĕpi (1), *on, upon*
1971 ĕpipŏthĕō (3), *intensely crave*
2118 ĕuthutēs (1), *rectitude, uprightness*
2193 hĕōs (7), *until*
2425 hikanŏs (6), *ample; fit*
2863 kŏmaō (2), to *wear long hair*
3114 makrŏthumĕō (3), to *be forbearing, patient*

3117 makrŏs (3), *long*, in place or time
3752 hŏtan (1), *inasmuch as, at once*
3756+3641 ŏu (1), *no or not*
3819 palai (1), *formerly; sometime since*
4183 pŏlus (4), *much, many*
4214 pŏsŏs (1), *how much?; how much!*
5118 tŏsŏutŏs (2), *such great*
5550 chrŏnŏs (4), *space of time, period*

LONGED
183 'âvâh (2), to *wish for, desire*
2968 yâ'ab (1), to *desire, long for*
3615 kâlâh (1), to *cease, be finished, perish*
8373 tâ'ab (2), to *desire*
1971 ĕpipŏthĕō (1), *intensely crave*
1973 ĕpipŏthētŏs (1), *yearned upon*

LONGEDST
3700 kâçaph (1), to *pine after; to fear*

LONGER
752 'ârôk (1), *long*
3254 yâçaph (1), to *add or augment*
5750 'ôwd (4), *again; repeatedly; still; more*
2089 ĕti (2), *yet, still*
3370 Mēdŏs (5), *inhabitant of Media*
4119 plĕiōn (1), *more*

LONGETH
183 'âvâh (1), to *wish for, desire*
2836 châshaq (1), to *join; to love, delight*
3642 kâmahh (1), to *pine after, long for*
3700 kâçaph (1), to *pine after; to fear*

LONGING
8264 shâqaq (1), to *seek greedily*
8375 ta'ăbâh (1), *desire*

LONGSUFFERING
750+639 'ârêk (4), *patient*
3114 makrŏthumĕō (1), to *be forbearing, patient*
3115 makrŏthumia (12), *forbearance; fortitude*

LONGWINGED
750+83 'ârêk (1), *patient*

LOOK
2342 chûwl (1), to *wait; to pervert*
2372 châzâh (3), to *gaze at; to perceive*
2376 chêzev (Ch.) (1), *sight, revelation*
4758 mar'eh (6), *appearance; vision*
5027 nâbaṭ (24), to *scan; to regard* with favor
5869 'ayin (3), *eye; sight*
6437 pânâh (13), to *turn, to face*

6440 pânîym (1), *face; front*
6485 pâqad (1), to *visit, care for, count*
6822 tsâphâh (2), to *peer into the distance*
6960 qâvâh (4), to *collect; to expect*
7200 râ'âh (53), to *see*
7210 rô'îy (1), *sight; spectacle*
7688 shâgach (1), to *glance sharply at*
7760 sûwm (2), to *put, place*
7789 shûwr (1), to *spy out, survey*
7896 shîyth (1), to *place, put*
8159 shâ'âh (4), to *inspect, consider*
8259 shâqaph (3), to *peep or gaze*
308 anablĕpō (1), to *look up; to recover sight*
352 anakuptō (1), to *straighten up*
553 apĕkdĕchŏmai (2), to *expect fully*
816 atĕnizō (2), to *gaze intently*
991 blĕpō (5), to *look at*
1492 ĕidō (1), to *know*
1551 ĕkdĕchŏmai (1), to *await, expect*
1914 ĕpiblĕpō (1), to *gaze at*
1980 ĕpiskĕptŏmai (1), to *inspect; to go to see*
2300 thĕaŏmai (1), to *look closely at*
3700 ŏptanŏmai (2), to *appear*
3706 hŏrasis (1), *vision*
3879 parakuptō (1), to *lean over to peer within*
4328 prŏsdŏkaō (5), to *anticipate; to await*
4648 skŏpĕō (2), to *watch out for, i.e. to regard*

LOOKED
5027 nâbaṭ (12), to *scan; to regard* with favor
6437 pânâh (18), to *turn, to face*
6440 pânîym (1), *face; front*
6960 qâvâh (8), to *collect; to expect*
6970 Qôwa' (1), *curtailment*
7200 râ'âh (55), to *see*
7805 shâzaph (1), to *scan*
8159 shâ'âh (1), to *inspect, consider*
8259 shâqaph (12), to *peep or gaze*
8559 Tâmâr (1), *palm tree*
308 anablĕpō (6), to *look up; to recover sight*
816 atĕnizō (4), to *gaze intently*
991 blĕpō (1), to *look at*
1492 ĕidō (7), to *know*
1551 ĕkdĕchŏmai (1), to *await, expect*
1689 ĕmblĕpō (2), to *observe; to discern*

1869 ĕpairō (1), to raise up, look up
2300 thĕaŏmai (1), to look closely at
4017 pĕriblĕpō (6), to look all around
4327 prŏsdĕchŏmai (1), to receive; to await for
4328 prŏsdŏkaō (2), to anticipate; to await

LOOKEST
5027 nâbaṭ (1), to scan; to regard with favor
8104 shâmar (1), to watch

LOOKETH
995 bîyn (1), to understand; discern
4758+5869 mar'eh (1), appearance; vision
5027 nâbaṭ (3), to scan; to regard with favor
6437 pânâh (8), to turn, to face
6440 pânîym (2), face; front
6822 tsâphâh (2), to peer into the distance
6960 qâvâh (1), to collect; to expect
7200 râ'âh (4), to see
7688 shâgach (2), to glance sharply at
7789 shûwr (1), to spy out, survey
8259 shâqaph (4), to peep or gaze
991 blĕpō (1), to look at
3879 parakuptō (1), to lean over to peer within
4328 prŏsdŏkaō (2), anticipate; to await

LOOKING
6437 pânâh (9), to turn, to face
7209 rᵉ'îy (1), mirror
8259 shâqaph (1), to peep or gaze
308 anablĕpō (3), to look up; to recover sight
816 atĕnizō (1), to gaze intently
872 aphŏraō (1), to consider attentively
991 blĕpō (1), to look at
1561 ĕkdŏchē (1), expectation
1689 ĕmblĕpō (2), to observe; to discern
1983 ĕpiskŏpĕō (1), to oversee; to beware
2334 thĕŏrĕō (1), to see; to discern
4017 pĕriblĕpō (1), to look all around
4327 prŏsdĕchŏmai (3), to receive; to await for
4328 prŏsdŏkaō (1), anticipate; to await
4329 prŏsdŏkia (1), apprehension of evil

LOOKINGGLASSES
4759 mar'âh (1), vision; mirror

LOOKS
5869 'ayin (3), eye; sight; fountain

6400 pelach (2), slice

LOOPS
3924 lûlâ'âh (13), curtain loop

LOOSE
2502 châlats (1), to pull off; to strip; to depart
5394 nâshal (1), to divest, eject, or drop
5425 nâthar (1), to terrify; shake off; untie
6605 pâthach (7), to open wide; to loosen, begin
7971 shâlach (3), to send away
8271 shᵉrê' (Ch.) (1), to free, separate; unravel
3089 luō (15), to loosen

LOOSED
2118 zâchach (2), to shove or displace
2502 châlats (1), to pull off; to strip; to depart
4549 mâçaç (1), to waste with disease; to faint
5203 nâṭash (1), to disperse; to thrust off
5425 nâthar (1), to terrify; shake off; untie
6605 pâthach (5), to open wide; to loosen, begin
7368 râchaq (1), to recede; remove
8271 shᵉrê' (Ch.) (1), to free, separate; unravel
321 anagō (2), to lead up; to bring out; to sail
447 aniēmi (2), to slacken, loosen
630 apŏluō (2), to relieve, release; to pardon
2673 katargĕō (1), to be, render entirely useless
3080 lusis (1), divorce
3089 luō (10), to loosen

LOOSETH
5425 nâthar (1), to terrify; shake off; untie
6605 pâthach (1), to open wide; to loosen, begin

LOOSING
142 airō (1), to lift, to take up
321 anagō (1), to lead up; to bring out; to sail
3089 luō (2), to loosen

LOP
5586 çâ'aph (1), to dis-branch a tree

LORD
113 'âdôwn (201), sovereign, i.e. controller
136 'Ădônây (430), the Lord
1376 gᵉbîyr (2), master
3050 Yâhh (50), Jehovah, self-Existent or Eternal
3068 Yᵉhôvâh (6394), Jehovah, self-Existent
4756 mârê' (Ch.) (4), master
7229 rab (Ch.) (1), great
7991 shâlîysh (3), officer; of the third rank
1203 dĕspŏtēs (4), absolute ruler

2961 kuriĕuō (1), to rule, be master of
2962 kuriŏs (694), supreme, controller, Mr.
4462 rhabbŏni (1), my master

LORD'S
113 'âdôwn (8), sovereign, i.e. controller
136 'Ădônây (1), the Lord
3068 Yᵉhôvâh (108), Jehovah, self-Existent
2960 kuriakŏs (2), belonging to the Lord
2962 kuriŏs (15), supreme, controller, Mr.

LORDLY
117 'addîyr (1), powerful; majestic

LORDS
113 'âdôwn (4), sovereign, i.e. controller
1167 ba'al (2), master; husband; owner; citizen
5633 çeren (21), axle; peer
7261 rabrᵉbân (Ch.) (6), magnate, noble
7300 rûwd (1), to ramble free or disconsolate
7991 shâlîysh (1), officer; of the third rank
8269 sar (1), head person, ruler
2634 katakuriĕuō (1), to control, subjugate, lord
2961 kuriĕuō (1), to rule, be master of
2962 kuriŏs (3), supreme, controller, Mr.
3175 mĕgistanĕs (1), great person

LORDSHIP
2634 katakuriĕuō (1), to subjugate, lord over
2961 kuriĕuō (1), to rule, be master of

LOSE
6 'âbad (1), perish; destroy
622 'âçaph (1), to gather, collect
3772 kârath (1), to cut (off, down or asunder)
5307 nâphal (1), to fall
7843 shâchath (1), to decay; to ruin
622 apŏllumi (17), to perish or lose
2210 zēmiŏō (2), to suffer loss

LOSETH
622 apŏllumi (1), to perish or lose

LOSS
2398 châṭâ' (1), to sin
7674 shebeth (1), rest, interruption, cessation
7921 shâkôl (2), to miscarry
580 apŏbŏlē (1), rejection, loss
2209 zēmia (3), detriment; loss
2210 zēmiŏō (2), to suffer loss

LOST
6 'âbad (9), to perish
9 'âbêdâh (4), destruction
5307 nâphal (2), to fall
7908 shᵉkôwl (1), bereavement
7923 shikkûlîym (1), childlessness
358+1096 analŏs (1), saltless, i.e. insipid
622 apŏllumi (13), to perish or lose
3471 mōrainō (2), to become insipid

LOT
1486 gôwrâl (60), lot, allotment
2256 chebel (3), company, band
3876 Lôwṭ (32), veil
2624 kataklērŏdŏtĕō (1), to apportion an estate
2819 klērŏs (2), lot, portion
2975 lagchanō (1), to determine by lot
3091 Lôt (3), veil

LOT'S
3876 Lôwṭ (1), veil

LOTAN
3877 Lôwṭân (5), covering

LOTAN'S
3877 Lôwṭân (2), covering

L

LOTHE
3811 lâ'âh (1), to tire; to be, make disgusted
6962 qûwṭ (3), to detest

LOTHED
1602 gâ'al (2), to detest; to reject; to fail
7114 qâtsar (1), to curtail, cut short

LOTHETH
1602 gâ'al (1), to detest; to reject; to fail

LOTHING
1604 gô'al (1), abhorrence

LOTS
1486 gôwrâl (16), lot, allotment
2819 klērŏs (6), lot, portion
2975 lagchanō (1), to determine by lot

LOUD
1419 gâdôwl (19), great
1993 hâmâh (1), to be in great commotion
2389 châzâq (1), strong; severe, hard, violent
5797 'ôz (1), strength
7311 rûwm (1), to be high; to rise or raise
8085 shâma' (2), to hear
3173 mĕgas (33), great, many

LOUDER
3966 mᵉôd (1), very, utterly

LOVE
157 'âhab (73), to have affection, love
160 'ahăbâh (34), affection, love

1730 dôwd (7), *beloved, friend; uncle, relative*
2836 châshaq (3), *to join; to love, delight*
5690 'egeb (1), *amative words, words of love*
5691 'ăgâbâh (1), *love, amorousness*
7355 râcham (1), *to be compassionate*
7474 ra'yâh (9), *female associate*
25 agapaō (70), *to love*
26 agapē (85), *love; love-feast*
2309 thĕlō (1), *to will; to desire; to choose*
5360 philadĕlphia (4), *fraternal affection*
5361 philadĕlphŏs (1), *fraternal*
5362 philandrŏs (1), *affectionate as a wife to her husband*
5363 philanthrōpia (1), *benevolence*
5365 philarguria (1), *avarice, greedy love of possessions*
5368 philĕō (10), *to be a friend, have affection*
5388 philŏtĕknŏs (1), *loving one's child*(ren)

LOVE'S
26 agapē (1), *love*

LOVED
157 'âhab (48), *to have affection, love*
160 'ahăbâh (7), *affection, love*
2245 châbab (1), *to cherish*
25 agapaō (37), *to love*
26 agapē (1), *love*
5368 philĕō (3), *to be a friend, have affection*

LOVEDST
157 'âhab (1), *to have affection, love*
25 agapaō (1), *to love*

LOVELY
157 'âhab (1), *to have affection, love*
4261 machmâd (1), *object of affection*
5690 'egeb (1), *amative words, words of love*
4375 prŏsphilēs (1), *acceptable, pleasing*

LOVER
157 'âhab (2), *to have affection, love*
5358 philagathŏs (1), *promoter of virtue*
5382 philŏxĕnŏs (1), *hospitable*

LOVERS
157 'âhab (17), *to have affection, love*
158 'ahab (1), *affection, love*
5689 'âgab (1), *to lust sensually*
7453 rêa' (1), *associate; one close*
5367 philautŏs (1), *selfish*

5369 philĕdŏnŏs (1), *loving pleasure*
5377 philŏthĕŏs (1), *pious, i.e. loving God*

LOVES
159 'ôhab (1), *affection, love*
1730 dôwd (1), *beloved, friend; uncle, relative*
3039 yᵉdîyd (1), *loved*

LOVEST
157 'âhab (7), *to have affection, love*
25 agapaō (2), *to love*
5368 philĕō (3), *to be a friend, have affection*

LOVETH
157 'âhab (37), *to have affection, love*
25 agapaō (19), *to love*
5368 philĕō (6), *to be a friend, have affection*
5383 philŏprōtĕuō (1), *loving to be first*

LOVING
157 'âhab (1), *to have affection, love*
158 'ahab (1), *affection, love*
2896 ṭôwb (1), *good; well*

LOVINGKINDNESS
2617 cheçed (26), *kindness, favor*

LOVINGKINDNESSES
2617 cheçed (4), *kindness, favor*

LOW
120 'âdâm (1), *human being; mankind*
1809 dâlal (3), *to slacken, dangle*
3665 kâna' (2), *to humiliate, subdue*
3766 kâra' (1), *to prostrate*
4295 maṭṭâh (1), *below or beneath*
4355 mâkak (2), *to tumble in ruins*
6030 'ânâh (1), *to respond, answer*
6819 tsâ'ar (1), *to be small; be trivial*
7817 shâchach (3), *to sink or depress*
8213 shâphêl (11), *to humiliate*
8216 shephel (1), *humble state or rank*
8217 shâphâl (5), *depressed, low*
8219 shᵉphêlâh (5), *lowland,*
8482 tachtîy (2), *lowermost; depths*
5011 tapĕinŏs (3), *humiliated, lowly*
5013 tapĕinŏō (1), *to depress; to humiliate*
5014 tapĕinōsis (1), *humbleness, lowliness*

LOWER
2637 châçêr (1), *to lack; to fail, want, make less*
8213 shâphêl (1), *humiliate*

8217 shâphâl (4), *depressed, low*
8481 tachtôwn (5), *bottommost*
8482 tachtîy (4), *lowermost; depths*
1642 ĕlattŏō (2), *to lessen*
2737 katōtĕrŏs (1), *inferior, lower*

LOWEST
7098 qâtsâh (3), *termination; fringe*
8481 tachtôwn (2), *bottommost*
8482 tachtîy (4), *lowermost; depths*
2078 ĕschatŏs (2), *farthest, final*

LOWETH
1600 gâ'âh (1), *to bellow, i.e. low of a cow*

LOWING
1600 gâ'âh (1), *to bellow, i.e. low of a cow*
6963 qôwl (1), *voice or sound*

LOWLINESS
5012 tapĕinŏphrŏsunē (2), *modesty, humility*

LOWLY
6041 'ânîy (3), *depressed*
6800 tsâna' (1), *to humiliate*
8217 shâphâl (1), *depressed, low*
5011 tapĕinŏs (1), *humiliated, lowly*

LOWRING
4768 stugnazō (1), *to be overcast, somber*

LUBIM
3864 Lûwbîy (2), *dry region*

LUBIMS
3864 Lûwbîy (1), *dry region*

LUCAS
3065 Lŏukas (2), *Lucanus*

LUCIFER
1966 hêylêl (1), *Venus (i.e. morning star)*

LUCIUS
3066 Lŏukiŏs (2), *illuminative*

LUCRE
1215 betsa' (1), *plunder; unjust gain*
146 aischrŏkĕrdēs (2), *shamefully greedy*
147 aischrŏkĕrdōs (1), *sordidly, greedily*
866 aphilargurŏs (1), *unavaricious*

LUCRE'S
2771 kĕrdŏs (1), *gain, profit*

LUD
3865 Lûwd (4), *Lud*

LUDIM
3866 Lûwdîy (2), *Ludite*

LUHITH
3872 Lûwchîyth (2), *floored*

LUKE
3065 Lŏukas (2), *Lucanus*

LUKEWARM
5513 chliarŏs (1), *tepid*

LUMP
1690 dᵉbêlâh (2), *cake of pressed figs*
5445 phurama (5), *lump of clay; mass of dough*

LUNATICK
4583 sĕlēniazŏmai (2), *to be moon-struck*

LURK
6845 tsâphan (2), *to hide; to hoard; to lurk*

LURKING
3427 yâshab (1), *to dwell, to remain; to settle*
3993 ma'ărâb (1), *ambuscade, ambush*
4224 machăbê' (1), *refuge, shelter*

LUST
2530 châmad (1), *to delight in; lust for*
5315 nephesh (1), *life; breath; soul; wind*
8307 shᵉrîyrûwth (1), *obstinacy*
8378 ta'ăvâh (1), *longing; delight*
1511+1938 ĕinai (1), *to exist*
1937 ĕpithumĕō (2), *to long for*
1939 ĕpithumia (9), *longing*
3715 ŏrĕxis (1), *longing after, lust, desire*
3806 pathŏs (1), *passion, especially concupiscence*

LUSTED
183 'âvâh (2), *to wish for, desire*
1937 ĕpithumĕō (2), *to long for*

LUSTETH
183 'âvâh (4), *to wish for, desire*
1937 ĕpithumĕō (1), *to long for*
1971 ĕpipŏthĕō (1), *intensely crave*

LUSTING
8378 ta'ăvâh (1), *longing; delight*

LUSTS
1939 ĕpithumia (22), *longing*
2237 hēdŏnē (2), *delight; desire*

LUSTY
8082 shâmên (1), *rich; fertile*

LUZ
3870 Lûwz (7), *Luz*

LYCAONIA
3071 Lukaŏnia (2), *Lycaonia*

LYCIA
3073 Lukia (1), *Lycia*

LYDDA
3069 Ludda (3), *Lod*

M

3421 mnēmŏněuō (1), to *exercise memory*
3447 mŏschŏpŏiěō (1), to *fabricate a bull image*
3471 mōrainō (1), to *become insipid*
3489 nauagěō (1), to be *shipwrecked*
3666 hŏmŏiŏō (2), to *become like*
3670 hŏmŏlŏgěō (1), to *acknowledge, agree*
3822 palaiŏō (1), to *make, become worn out*
3903 paraskěuazō (1), to *get ready, prepare*
3982 pěithō (1), to *pacify* or *conciliate*
4087 pikrainō (1), to *embitter, turn sour*
4147 plŏutěō (2), to be, *become wealthy*
4160 pŏiěō (51), to *make*
4161 pŏiēma (1), *what is made, product*
4198 pŏrěuŏmai (1), to *go, come; to travel*
4222 pŏtizō (2), to *furnish drink, irrigate*
4364 prŏspŏiěŏmai (1), to *pretend as if about to*
4483 rhěō (1), to *utter*, i.e. *speak* or *say*
4692 spěudō (1), to *urge*; to *await eagerly*
4732 stěrěŏō (1), to be, *become strong*
4776 sugkathizō (1), to *give, take a seat in company with*
4832 summŏrphŏs (1), *similar, conformed to*
4955 sustasiastēs (1), *fellow-insurgent*
4982 sōzō (9), to *deliver*; to *protect*
5014 tapěinōsis (1), *humbleness, lowliness*
5048 tělěiŏō (9), to *perfect, complete*
5055 tělěō (1), to *end*, i.e. *complete, execute*
5087 tithēmi (3), to *place*
5293 hupŏtassō (2), to *subordinate*; to *obey*
5319 phaněrŏō (13), to *render apparent*
5487 charitŏō (1), to *give special honor*
5499 chěirŏpŏiětŏs (6), of *human construction*

MADEST
3045 yâda' (1), to *know*
3772 kârath (1), to *cut* (off, down or asunder)
6213 'âsâh (1), to *make*
387 anastatŏō (1), to *disturb, cause trouble*
1642 ělattŏō (1), to *lessen*

MADIAN
3099 Madian (1), *contest* or *quarrel*

MADMANNAH
4089 Madmannâh (2), *dunghill*

MADMEN
4086 Madmên (1), *dunghill*

MADMENAH
4088 Madmênâh (1), *dunghill*

MADNESS
1947 hôwlêlâh (4), *folly, delusion*
1948 hôwlêlûwth (1), *folly, delusion*
7697 shiggâ'ôwn (2), *craziness*
454 anŏia (1), *stupidity; rage*
3913 paraphrŏnia (1), *foolhardiness, insanity*

MADON
4068 Mâdôwn (2), *height*

MAGBISH
4019 Magbîysh (1), *stiffening*

MAGDALA
3093 Magdala (1), *tower*

MAGDALENE
3094 Magdalēnē (12), of *Magdala*

MAGDIEL
4025 Magdîy'êl (2), *preciousness of God*

MAGICIAN
2749 charṭôm (Ch.) (1), *horoscopist, magician*

MAGICIANS
2748 charṭôm (11), *horoscopist, magician*
2749 charṭôm (Ch.) (4), *horoscopist, magician*

MAGISTRATE
3423+6114 yârash (1), to *inherit; to impoverish*
758 archōn (1), *first*

MAGISTRATES
8200 shᵉphaṭ (Ch.) (1), to *judge*
746 archē (1), *first in rank; first in time*
3980 pěitharchěō (1), to *submit to authority*
4755 stratēgŏs (5), *military governor*

MAGNIFICAL
1431 gâdal (1), to be *great, make great*

MAGNIFICENCE
3168 měgalěiŏtēs (1), *grandeur* or *splendor*

MAGNIFIED
1431 gâdal (17), to be *great, make great*
5375 nâsâ' (1), to *lift up*
3170 měgalunō (3), to *increase* or *extol*

MAGNIFY
1431 gâdal (15), to be *great, make great*
7679 sâgâ' (1), to *laud, extol*
1392 dŏxazō (1), to *render, esteem glorious*
3170 měgalunō (2), to *increase* or *extol*

MAGOG
4031 Mâgôwg (4), *Magog*
3098 Magōg (1), *Magog*

MAGOR-MISSABIB
4036 Mâgôwr miç-Çâbîyb (1), *affright from around*

MAGPIASH
4047 Magpiy'âsh (1), *exterminator of* (the) *moth*

MAHALAH
4244 Machlâh (1), *sickness*

MAHALALEEL
4111 Mahălal'êl (7), *praise of God*

MAHALATH
4257 Machălath (2), *sickness*
4258 Machălath (2), *sickness*

MAHALI
4249 Machlîy (1), *sick*

MAHANAIM
4266 Machănayim (13), *double camp*

MAHANEH-DAN
4265 Machănêh-Dân (1), *camp of Dan*

MAHARAI
4121 Mahăray (3), *hasty*

MAHATH
4287 Machath (3), *erasure*

MAHAVITE
4233 Machăvîym (1), *Machavite*

MAHAZIOTH
4238 Machăzîy'ôwth (2), *visions*

MAHER-SHALAL-HASH-BAZ
4122 Mahêr Shâlâl Châsh Baz (2), *hasting is he to the booty, swift to the prey*

MAHLAH
4244 Machlâh (4), *sickness*

MAHLI
4249 Machlîy (10), *sick*

MAHLITES
4250 Machlîy (2), *Machlite*

MAHLON
4248 Machlôwn (3), *sick*

MAHLON'S
4248 Machlôwn (1), *sick*

MAHOL
4235 Mâchôwl (1), (round) *dance*

MAID
519 'âmâh (5), *female servant* or *slave*
1330 bᵉthûwlâh (4), *virgin maiden*
1331 bᵉthûwlîym (2), *virginity*
5291 na'ărâh (4), *female child; servant*
5347 nᵉqêbâh (1), *female, woman*
5959 'almâh (2), *lass, young woman*

8198 shiphchâh (12), household *female slave*
2877 kŏrasiŏn (2), *little girl*
3814 paidiskē (2), *female slave* or *servant*
3816 pais (2), *child; slave* or *servant*

MAID'S
5291 na'ărâh (1), *female child; servant*

MAIDEN
1330 bᵉthûwlâh (2), *virgin maiden*
5291 na'ărâh (3), *female child; servant*
8198 shiphchâh (2), household *female slave*
3816 pais (1), *child; slave* or *servant*

MAIDENS
1330 bᵉthûwlâh (3), *virgin maiden*
5291 na'ărâh (13), *female child; servant*
8198 shiphchâh (1), household *female slave*
3814 paidiskē (1), *female slave* or *servant*

MAIDS
519 'âmâh (3), *female servant* or *slave*
1330 bᵉthûwlâh (3), *virgin maiden*
5291 na'ărâh (2), *female child; servant*
3814 paidiskē (1), *female slave* or *servant*

MAIDSERVANT
519 'âmâh (13), *female servant* or *slave*
8198 shiphchâh (3), household *female slave*

MAIDSERVANT'S
519 'âmâh (1), *female servant* or *slave*

MAIDSERVANTS
519 'âmâh (4), *female servant* or *slave*
8198 shiphchâh (5), household *female slave*

MAIDSERVANTS'
519 'âmâh (1), *female servant* or *slave*

MAIL
7193 qasqeseth (2), fish *scales; coat of mail*

MAIMED
2782 chârats (1), to be *alert, to decide*
376 anapěrŏs (2), *maimed; crippled*
2948 kullŏs (4), *crippled*, i.e. *maimed*

MAINSAIL
736 artěmōn (1), *foresail* or *jib*

MAINTAIN
2388 châzaq (1), to *bind, restrain, conquer*
3198 yâkach (1), to be *correct; to argue*
6213 'âsâh (6), to *do* or *make*

MAINTAINED
4291 prŏïstēmi (2), to preside; to practice

MAINTAINED
6213 'âsâh (1), to do or make

MAINTAINEST
8551 tâmak (1), to obtain, keep fast

MAINTENANCE
2416 chay (1), alive; raw; fresh; life
4415 mᵉlach (Ch.) (1), to eat salt

MAJESTY
1347 gâ'ôwn (7), ascending; majesty
1348 gê'ûwth (2), ascending; majesty
1420 gᵉdûwlâh (1), greatness, grandeur
1923 hâdar (Ch.) (1), magnificence, glory
1926 hâdâr (7), magnificence
1935 hôwd (4), grandeur, majesty
7238 rᵉbûw (Ch.) (3), increase
3168 mĕgălĕiŏtēs (1), grandeur or splendor
3172 mĕgalōsunē (3), divinity, majesty

MAKAZ
4739 Mâqats (1), end

MAKE
1124 bᵉnâ' (Ch.) (1), to build
1254 bârâ' (1), to create; fashion
1443 gâdar (2), to build a stone wall
2015 hâphak (1), to change, overturn
3331 yâtsa' (1), to strew as a surface
3335 yâtsar (1), to form; potter; to determine
3635 kᵉlal (Ch.) (2), to complete
3772 kârath (31), to cut (off, down or asunder)
3823 lâbab (1), transport with love; to stultify
5414 nâthan (64), to give
5674 'âbar (2), to cross over; to transition
6014 'âmar (1), to gather grain into sheaves
6213 'âsâh (238), to make
6381 pâlâ' (1), to be, make great, wonderful
7760 sûwm (65), to put, place
7761 sûwm (Ch.) (5), to put, place
7896 shîyth (9), to place
8074 shâmêm (1), to devastate; to stupefy
142 airō (1), to lift, to take up
347 anaklinō (2), to lean back, recline
805 asphalizō (1), to render secure
1107 gnōrizō (6), to make known, reveal

1303 diatithēmai (2), to put apart, i.e. dispose
1325 didōmi (2), to give
1510 ĕimi (1), I exist, I am
1519 ĕis (1), to or into
1659 ĕlĕuthĕrŏō (2), to exempt, liberate
1710 ĕmpŏrĕuŏmai (1), to trade, do business
1793 ĕntugchanō (1), to entreat, petition
2005 ĕpitĕlĕō (1), to terminate; to undergo
2090 hĕtŏimazō (6), to prepare
2116 ĕuthunō (1), to straighten or level
2146 ĕuprŏsōpĕō (1), to make a good display
2165 ĕuphrainō (3), to rejoice, be glad
2350 thŏrubĕō (1), to disturb; clamor
2433 hilaskŏmai (1), to conciliate, to atone for
2476 histēmi (1), to stand, establish
2511 katharizō (5), to cleanse
2525 kathistēmi (6), to designate, constitute
2625 kataklinō (1), to recline, take a place
2673 katargĕō (3), to be, render entirely useless
2675 katartizō (2), to repair; to prepare
2758 kĕnŏō (1), to make empty
2936 ktizō (1), to fabricate, create
3076 lupĕō (1), to distress; to be sad
3753 hŏtĕ (1), when; as
3856 paradĕigmatizō (1), to expose to infamy
3868 paraitĕŏmai (1), to deprecate, decline
4052 pĕrissĕuō (1), to superabound
4062 pĕritrĕpō (1), to drive crazy
4087 pikrainō (1), to embitter, turn sour
4115 platunō (1), to widen
4121 plĕŏnazō (1), to increase; superabound
4122 plĕŏnĕktĕō (2), to be covetous
4135 plērŏphŏrĕō (1), to fill completely; assure
4137 plērŏō (1), to fill, make complete
4160 pŏiĕō (48), to make
4170 pŏlĕmĕō (3), to battle, make war
4294 prŏkatartizō (1), to prepare in advance
4336 prŏsĕuchŏmai (3), to supplicate, pray
4400 prŏchĕirizŏmai (1), to purpose
4624 skandalizō (2), to entrap, i.e. trip up
4679 sŏphizō (1), to be cleverly invented
4692 spĕudō (2), to urge on

4766 strōnnumi (1), strew, i.e. spread
4820 sumballō (1), to aid; to join, attack
4921 sunistaō (1), to set together, to introduce
4931 suntĕlĕō (1), to complete entirely
5055 tĕlĕō (3), to end, i.e. complete, execute
5087 tithēmi (6), to place
5319 phanĕrŏō (2), to render apparent
5461 phōtizō (1), to shine or to brighten up

MAKER
3335 yâtsar (4), to form; potter; to determine
6213 'âsâh (13), to make
6466 pâ'al (1), to make
6467 pô'al (1), act or work, deed
1217 dēmiŏurgŏs (1), worker, mechanic

MAKERS
2796 chârâsh (1), skilled fabricator or worker

MAKEST
6213 'âsâh (6), to make
7760 sûwm (1), to place
7896 shîyth (1), to place
2744 kauchaŏmai (2), to glory in, rejoice in
4160 pŏiĕō (4), to make

MAKETH
3772 kârath (1), to cut (off, down or asunder)
5414 nâthan (2), to give
6213 'âsâh (23), to make
6466 pâ'al (1), to make
7706 Shadday (1), the Almighty God
7737 shâvâh (2), to level, i.e. equalize
7760 sûwm (6), to place
393 anatĕllō (1), to cause to arise
1252 diakrinō (1), to decide; to hesitate
1308 diaphĕrō (1), to bear, carry; to differ
1793 ĕntugchanō (3), to entreat, petition
2165 ĕuphrainō (1), to rejoice, be glad
2390 iaŏmai (1), to cure, heal
2525 kathistēmi (1), to designate, constitute
2617 kataischunō (1), to disgrace or shame
4160 pŏiĕō (6), to make
4977 schizō (1), to split or sever
5241 hupĕrĕntugchanō (1), to intercede in behalf of
5319 phanĕrŏō (1), to render apparent

MAKHELOTH
4721 maqhêl (2), assembly

MAKING
3772 kârath (1), to cut (off, down or asunder)
4639 ma'ăseh (2), action; labor

6213 'âsâh (1), to make
208 akurŏō (1), to invalidate, nullify
1189 dĕŏmai (1), to beg, petition, ask
1252 diakrinō (1), to decide; to hesitate
2350 thŏrubĕō (1), to disturb; clamor
4148 plŏutizō (1), to make wealthy
4160 pŏiĕō (7), to make
5567 psallō (1), to play a stringed instrument

MAKKEDAH
4719 Maqqêdâh (9), herding-fold

MAKTESH
4389 Maktêsh (1), dell

MALACHI
4401 Mal'âkîy (1), ministrative

MALCHAM
4445 Malkâm (2), Malcam or Milcom

MALCHI-SHUA
4444 Malkîyshûwa' (3), king of wealth

MALCHIAH
4441 Malkîyâh (9), appointed by Jehovah

MALCHIEL
4439 Malkîy'êl (3), appointed by God

MALCHIELITES
4440 Malkîy'êlîy (1), Malkiëlite

MALCHIJAH
4441 Malkîyâh (6), appointed by Jehovah

MALCHIRAM
4443 Malkîyrâm (1), king of a high one

MALCHUS
3124 Malchŏs (1), king

MALE
376 'îysh (2), man; male
2138 zâkûwr (1), male
2142 zâkar (1), to be male
2145 zâkâr (37), male
730 arrhēn (4), male

MALEFACTOR
2555 kakŏpŏiŏs (1), bad-doer; criminal

MALEFACTORS
2557 kakŏurgŏs (3), criminal, evildoer

MALELEEL
3121 Malĕlēĕl (1), praise of God

MALES
2138 zâkûwr (2), male
2145 zâkâr (30), male

MALICE
2549 kakia (6), depravity; malignity

MALICIOUS
4190 pŏnĕrŏs (1), malice, wicked, bad; crime

MALICIOUSNESS
2549 kakia (2), depravity; malignity

M

MALIGNITY
2550 kakŏĕthĕia (1),
mischievousness

MALLOTHI
4413 Mallôwthîy (2),
loquacious

MALLOWS
4408 mallûwach (1),
salt-purslain

MALLUCH
4409 Mallûwk (6),
regnant

MAMMON
3126 mammōnas (4),
wealth, riches

MAMRE
4471 Mamrê' (10), lusty

MAN
120 'âdâm (388), human
being; mankind
375 'êyphôh (1), where?;
when?; how?
376 'îysh (967), man;
male; someone
376+2145 'îysh (1), man;
male; someone
582 'ĕnôwsh (32), man;
person, human
606 'ĕnâsh (Ch.) (8), man
935 bôw' (1), to go, come
1121 bên (3), son,
descendant; people
1121+120 bên (1), son,
descendant; people
1167 ba'al (5), master;
husband; owner; citizen
1201 Ba'shâ' (1),
offensiveness
1396 gâbar (1), to be
strong; to prevail
1397 geber (54), person,
man
1400 gᵉbar (Ch.) (2),
person; someone
1538 gulgôleth (2), skull
2145 zâkâr (11), male
5315 nephesh (3), life;
breath; soul; wind
5958 'elem (1), lad,
young man
435 anĕr (75), man; male
442 anthrōpinŏs (2),
human
444 anthrōpŏs (347),
human being; mankind
730 arrhēn (2), male
1520 hĕis (3), one
1538 hĕkastŏs (1), each
or every
2478 ischurŏs (1),
forcible, powerful
3367 mĕdĕis (33), not
even one
3494 nĕanias (4), youth
3495 nĕaniskŏs (5), youth
3762 ŏudĕis (96), none,
nobody, nothing
3956 pas (3), all, any,
every, whole
5100 tis (40), some or any

MAN'S
120 'âdâm (17), human
being; mankind
312 'achêr (1), other,
another, different
376 'îysh (42), man;
male; someone

582 'ĕnôwsh (3), man;
person, human
606 'ĕnâsh (Ch.) (3), man
1167 ba'al (1), master;
husband; owner; citizen
1397 geber (2), person,
man
245 allŏtriŏs (4), not
one's own
435 anĕr (1), man; male
442 anthrōpinŏs (3),
human
444 anthrōpŏs (10),
human being; mankind
3494 nĕanias (1), youth
3762 ŏudĕis (1), none,
nobody, nothing
5100 tis (3), some or any

MANAEN
3127 Manaĕn (1),
Manaĕn

MANAHATH
4506 Mânachath (3), rest

MANAHETHITES
2679 Chătsîy
ham-Mᵉnûchôwth (1),
midst of the
resting-places
2680 Chătsîy
ham-Mᵉnachtîy (1),
Chatsi-ham-Menachtite

MANASSEH
4519 Mᵉnashsheh (141),
causing to forget
4520 Mᵉnashshîy (2),
Menashshite

MANASSEH'S
4519 Mᵉnashsheh (4),
causing to forget

MANASSES
3128 Manassēs (3),
causing to forget

MANASSITES
4519 Mᵉnashsheh (1),
causing to forget
4520 Mᵉnashshîy (2),
Menashshite

MANDRAKES
1736 dûwday (6),
mandrake

MANEH
4488 mâneh (1), weight

MANGER
5336 phatnē (3), crib;
stall

MANIFEST
1305 bârar (1), to
examine; select
852 aphanēs (1),
non-apparent, invisible
1212 dēlŏs (1), clear,
plain, evident
1552 ĕkdēlŏs (1), wholly
evident, clear
1717 ĕmphanēs (1),
apparent, seen, visible
1718 ĕmphanizō (2), to
show forth
4271 prŏdēlŏs (1),
obvious, evident
5318 phanĕrŏs (7),
apparent, visible, clear
5319 phanĕrŏō (23), to
render apparent

MANIFESTATION
602 apŏkalupsis (1),
disclosure, revelation
5321 phanĕrōsis (2),
manifestation

MANIFESTED
5319 phanĕrŏō (10), to
render apparent

MANIFESTLY
5319 phanĕrŏō (1), to
render apparent

MANIFOLD
7227 rab (3), great
7231 râbab (1), to
increase
4164 pŏikilŏs (2), various
4179 pŏllaplasiōn (1),
very much more
4182 pŏlupŏikilŏs (1),
multifarious

MANKIND
1320+376 bâsâr (1), flesh;
body; person
2145 zâkâr (2), male
733 arsĕnŏkŏitēs (2),
sodomite
5449+442 phusis (1),
genus or sort

MANNA
4478 mân (14), manna,
i.e. a "whatness?"
3131 manna (5), edible
gum-like food

MANNER
734 'ôrach (1), road;
manner of life
1571 gam (1), also; even;
yea; though
1697 dâbâr (15), word;
matter; thing
1699 dôber (1), grazing
pasture
1823 dᵉmûwth (1),
resemblance, likeness
1870 derek (8), road;
course of life
1881 dâth (1), royal edict
or statute
2177 zan (1), form or sort
3541 kôh (6), thus
3605 kôl (1), all, any or
every
3651 kên (3), just; right,
correct
3654 kên (1), stinging bug
4941 mishpât (36),
verdict; decree; justice
8452 tôwrâh (1), custom
72 agōgē (1), mode of
living, way of life
195 akribĕia (1),
thoroughness
442 anthrōpinŏs (1),
human
686 ara (3), then, so,
therefore
981 biōsis (1), mode of
living
1483 ĕthnikōs (1), as a
Gentile
1485 ĕthŏs (5), usage
prescribed
1486 ĕthō (1), to be used
by habit or convention
3592 hŏdĕ (1), this or
that; these or those

3634 hŏiŏs (2), such or
what sort of
3697 hŏpŏiŏs (2), what
kind of, what sort of
3779 hŏutō (5), in this
way; likewise
4012 pĕri (1), about;
around
4169 pŏiŏs (1), what sort
of?; which one?
4217 pŏtapŏs (6), of what
possible sort?
4458 -pōs (1), particle
used in composition
5158 trŏpŏs (2),
deportment, character
5179 tupŏs (1), shape,
resemblance; "type"
5615 hōsautōs (1), in the
same way

MANNERS
2708 chuqqâh (1), to
delineate
4941 mishpât (2), verdict;
formal decree; justice
2239 ēthŏs (1), usage, i.e.
moral habits
4187 pŏlutrŏpōs (1), in
many ways
5159 trŏpŏphŏrĕō (1), to
endure one's habits

MANOAH
4495 Mânôwach (18), rest

MANSERVANT
5650 'ebed (12), servant

MANSERVANT'S
5650 'ebed (1), servant

MANSERVANTS
5650 'ebed (1), servant

MANSIONS
3438 mŏnē (1), residence,
dwelling place

MANSLAYER
7523 râtsach (2), to
murder

MANSLAYERS
409 andrŏphŏnŏs (1),
murderer

MANTLE
155 'addereth (5), large;
splendid
4598 mᵉîyl (7), outer
garment or robe
8063 sᵉmîykâh (1), rug

MANTLES
4595 ma'ătâphâh (1),
cloak

MANY
1995 hâmôwn (3), noise,
tumult; many, crowd
3513 kâbad (2), to be
heavy, severe, dull
3605 kôl (1), all, any or
every
7227 rab (196), great
7230 rôb (4), abundance
7231 râbab (6), to
increase; to multiply
7233 rᵉbâbâh (1), myriad
7235 râbâh (27), to
increase
7690 saggîy' (Ch.) (2),
large
2425 hikanŏs (11),
ample; fit

3745 hŏsŏs (31), *as much
as*
4119 plĕiōn (14), *more*
4183 pŏlus (207), *much,
many*
4214 pŏsŏs (11), *how
much?; how much!*
5118 tŏsŏutŏs (6), *such
great*

MAOCH
4582 Mâ'ôwk (1),
oppressed

MAON
4584 Mâ'ôwn (7),
residence

MAONITES
4584 Mâ'ôwn (1),
residence

MAR
3510 kâ'ab (1), *to feel
pain; to grieve; to spoil*
5420 nâthaç (1), *to tear
up*
7843 shâchath (4), *to
decay; to ruin*

MARA
4755 Mârâ' (1), *bitter*

MARAH
4785 Mârâh (5), *bitter*

MARALAH
4831 Mar'ălâh (1), (poss.)
earthquake

MARANATHA
3134 maran atha (1),
Come, Lord!

MARBLE
7898 shayith (1), *wild
growth of weeds*
8336 shêsh (2), *white
linen; white marble*
8338 shâwshâw (1),
(poss.) *to annihilate*
3139 marmarŏs (1),
sparkling white marble

MARCH
1980 hâlak (1), *to walk;
live a certain way*
3212 yâlak (2), *to walk;
to live; to carry*
6805 tsâ'ad (2), *to pace,
step regularly*

MARCHED
5265 nâça' (1), *start on a
journey*

MARCHEDST
6805 tsâ'ad (1), *to pace,
step regularly*

MARCUS
3138 Markŏs (3), *Marcus*

MARESHAH
4762 Mar'êshâh (8),
summit

MARINERS
4419 mallâch (4),
salt-water sailor
7751 shûwţ (1), *to travel,
roam*

MARISHES
1360 gebe' (1), *reservoir;
marsh*

MARK
226 'ôwth (1), *signal, sign*

995 bîyn (1), *to
understand; discern*
3045 yâda' (3), *to know*
4307 maţţârâ' (3), *jail
(guard-*house*); aim*
4645 miphgâ' (1), *object
of attack, target*
6437 pânâh (1), *to turn,
to face*
7181 qâshab (1), *to prick
up the ears*
7200 râ'âh (1), *to see*
7760 sûwm (1), *to place*
7896 shîyth (1), *to place*
8104 shâmar (4), *to
watch*
8420 tâv (2), *mark;
signature*
3138 Markŏs (5), *Marcus*
4648 skŏpĕō (2), *to watch
out for, i.e. to regard*
4649 skŏpŏs (1), *goal*
5480 charagma (8),
mark, stamp

MARKED
2856 châtham (1), *to
close up; to affix a seal*
3799 kâtham (1), *to
inscribe indelibly*
7181 qâshab (1), *to prick
up the ears*
8104 shâmar (2), *to
watch*
1907 ĕpĕchō (1), *to pay
attention to*

MARKEST
8104 shâmar (1), *to
watch*

MARKET
4627 ma'ărâb (4),
mercantile goods
58 agŏra (2),
town-square, market

MARKETH
8104 shâmar (1), *to
watch*
8388 tâ'ar (2), *to
delineate; to extend*

MARKETPLACE
58 agŏra (5),
town-square, market

MARKETPLACES
58 agŏra (1),
town-square, market

MARKETS
58 agŏra (4),
town-square, market

MARKS
7085 qa'ăqa' (1), *incision
or gash*
4742 stigma (1), *mark,
scar of service*

MAROTH
4796 Mârôwth (1), *bitter
springs*

MARRED
4893 mishchâth (1),
disfigurement
7843 shâchath (3), *to
decay; to ruin*
622 apŏllumi (1), *to
destroy fully*

MARRIAGE
1984 hâlal (1), *to shine,
flash, radiate*

5772 'ôwnâh (1), *marital
cohabitation*
1061 gamiskō (1), *to
espouse*
1062 gamŏs (9), *nuptials*
1547 ĕkgamizō (3), *to
marry off a daughter*
1548 ĕkgamiskō (4), *to
marry off a daughter*

MARRIAGES
2859 châthan (3), *to be
related by marriage*

MARRIED
802 'ishshâh (3), *woman,
wife; women, wives*
1166 bâ'al (7), *to be
master; to marry*
1166+802 bâ'al (1), *to be
master; to marry*
3427 yâshab (1), *to dwell,
to remain; to settle*
3947 lâqach (4), *to take*
5375 nâsâ' (1), *to lift up*
1060 gamĕō (9), *to wed*
1096 ginŏmai (3), *to be,
become*

MARRIETH
1166 bâ'al (1), *to be
master; to marry*
1060 gamĕō (3), *to wed*

MARROW
2459 cheleb (1), *fat;
choice part*
4221 môach (1), *bone
marrow*
4229 mâchâh (1), *to
erase; to grease*
8250 shiqqûwy (1),
beverage; refreshment
3452 muĕlŏs (1), *marrow*

MARRY
802 'ishshâh (2), *woman,
wife; women, wives*
1166 bâ'al (1), *to be
master; to marry*
1961+376 hâyâh (1), *to
exist, i.e. be or become*
2992 yâbam (1), *to marry
a dead brother's widow*
1060 gamĕō (16), *to wed*
1918 ĕpigambrĕuō (1), *to
form an affinity with*

MARRYING
3427 yâshab (1), *to dwell,
to remain; to settle*
1060 gamĕō (1), *to wed*

MARS'
697 Arĕiŏs Pagŏs (1),
rock of Ares

MARSENA
4826 Marçenâ' (1),
Marsena

MART
5505 çâchar (1), *profit
from trade*

MARTHA
3136 Martha (12),
mistress, i.e. lady lord

MARTYR
3144 martus (2), *witness*

MARTYRS
3144 martus (1), *witness*

MARVEL
8539 tâmahh (1), *to be
astounded*

2296 thaumazō (9), *to
wonder; to admire*
2298 thaumastŏs (1),
wonderful, marvelous

MARVELLED
8539 tâmahh (2), *to be
astounded*
2296 thaumazō (21), *to
wonder; to admire*

MARVELLOUS
6381 pâlâ' (16), *to be,
make great, wonderful*
6382 pele' (1), *miracle*
6395 pâlâh (1), *to
distinguish*
2298 thaumastŏs (6),
wonderful, marvelous

MARVELLOUSLY
6381 pâlâ' (2), *to be,
make great, wonderful*
8539 tâmahh (1), *to be
astounded*

MARVELS
6381 pâlâ' (1), *to be,
make great, wonderful*

MARY
3137 Maria (54),
rebelliously

MASCHIL
4905 maskîyl (13),
instructional poem

MASH
4851 Mash (1), *Mash*

MASHAL
4913 Mâshâl (1), *request*

MASONS
1443 gâdar (2), *to build a
stone wall*
2672 châtsab (3), *to cut
stone or carve wood*

MASREKAH
4957 Masrêqâh (2),
vineyard

MASSA
4854 Massâ' (2), *burden*

MASSAH
4532 Maççâh (4), *testing*

MAST
2260 chibbêl (1), *ship's
mast*
8650 tôren (1), *mast ship
pole; flag-staff pole*

MASTER
113 'âdôwn (75),
sovereign, i.e. controller
729 'âraz (2), *of cedar*
1167 ba'al (3), *master;
husband; owner; citizen*
5782 'ûwr (1), *to awake*
7227 rab (1), *great*
8269 sar (1), *head
person, ruler*
1320 didaskalŏs (47),
instructor
1988 ĕpistatēs (6),
commander
2519 kathēgĕtēs (2),
teacher
2942 kubĕrnētēs (1),
helmsman, captain
2962 kuriŏs (4), *supreme,
controller, Mr.*
3617 ŏikŏdĕspŏtēs (2),
head of a family

M

4461 rhabbi (8), *my master*

MASTER'S
113 'âdôwn (22), *sovereign,* i.e. *controller*
1167 ba'al (1), *master; husband; owner; citizen*
1203 děspŏtēs (1), absolute *ruler*

MASTERBUILDER
753 architěktōn (1), *architect, expert builder*

MASTERS
113 'âdôwn (5), *sovereign,* i.e. *controller*
1167 ba'al (1), *master; husband; owner; citizen*
1203 děspŏtēs (4), absolute *ruler*
1320 didaskalŏs (1), *instructor*
2519 kathēgētēs (1), *teacher*
2962 kuriŏs (8), *supreme, controller, Mr.*

MASTERS'
113 'âdôwn (1), *sovereign,* i.e. *controller*
2962 kuriŏs (1), *supreme, controller, Mr.*

MASTERY
1369 gᵉbûwrâh (1), *force; valor; victory*
6981 Qôwrê' (1), *crier*

MASTS
8650 tôren (1), mast ship *pole;* flag-staff *pole*

MATE
7468 rᵉ'ûwth (2), *female associate*

MATHUSALA
3103 Mathŏusala (1), *man of a dart*

MATRED
4308 Maṭrêd (2), *propulsive*

MATRI
4309 Maṭriy (1), *rainy*

MATRIX
7358 rechem (5), *womb*

MATTAN
4977 Mattân (3), *present, gift*

MATTANAH
4980 Mattânâh (2), *present;* sacrificial *offering; bribe*

MATTANIAH
4983 Mattanyâh (16), *gift of Jehovah*

MATTATHA
3160 Mattatha (1), *gift of Jehovah*

MATTATHAH
4992 Mattattâh (1), *gift of Jehovah*

MATTATHIAS
3161 Mattathias (2), *gift of Jehovah*

MATTENAI
4982 Mattᵉnay (3), *liberal*

MATTER
1697 dâbâr (48), *word; matter; thing*
1836 dên (Ch.) (1), *this*
2659 châphêr (1), to *shame, reproach*
2941 ṭa'am (Ch.) (1), *sentence, command*
3602 kâkâh (1), *just so*
4405 millâh (1), *word; discourse; speech*
4406 millâh (Ch.) (4), *command, discourse*
6600 pithgâm (Ch.) (2), *decree; report*
1308 diaphěrō (1), to *bear, carry;* to *differ*
2596 kata (1), *down; according to*
3056 lŏgŏs (4), *word, matter, thing*
4229 pragma (3), *matter, deed, affair*
5208 hulē (1), *forest,* i.e. *wood fuel*

MATTERS
1419 gâdôwl (1), *great*
1697 dâbâr (15), *word; matter; thing*
4406 millâh (Ch.) (1), *word, command*

MATTHAN
3157 Matthan (2), *present, gift*

MATTHAT
3158 Matthat (2), *gift of Jehovah*

MATTHEW
3156 Matthaiŏs (5), *gift of Jehovah*

MATTHIAS
3159 Matthias (2), *gift of Jehovah*

MATTITHIAH
4993 Mattithyâh (8), *gift of Jehovah*

MATTOCK
4281 machărêshâh (1), (poss.) *pick-axe*
4576 ma'dêr (1), *hoe*

MATTOCKS
2719 chereb (1), *knife, sword*
4281 machărêshâh (1), (poss.) *pick-axe*

MAUL
4650 mêphîyts (1), *mallet-club*

MAW
6896 qêbâh (1), *paunch cavity; stomach*

MAY
194 'ûwlay (4), *if not; perhaps*
3201 yâkôl (11), *to be able*
1410 dunamai (9), *to be able or possible*
1832 ěxěsti (1), *it is right, it is proper*
2481 isŏs (1), *perhaps*

MAYEST
3201 yâkôl (5), *to be able*
1410 dunamai (2), *to be able or possible*

1832 ěxěsti (1), *it is right, it is proper*

MAZZAROTH
4216 Mazzârâh (1), *constellation*

ME-JARKON
4313 Mêy hay-Yarqôwn (1), *water of the yellowness*

MEADOW
260 'âchûw (2), *bulrush or any marshy grass*

MEADOWS
4629 ma'ăreh (1), *nude place,* i.e. *a common*

MEAH
3968 Mê'âh (2), *hundred*

MEAL
7058 qemach (9), *flour*
7058+5560 qemach (1), *flour*
224 alěurŏn (2), *flour*

MEALTIME
6256+400 'êth (1), *time*

MEAN
120 'âdâm (3), *human being; mankind*
2823 châshôk (1), *obscure*
5704+3541 'ad (1), *as far (long) as; during*
767 asēmŏs (1), *ignoble,* i.e. *ordinary*
1498 ěiēn (1), *might could, would*
2076 ěsti (1), *he (she or it) is; they are*
2309+1511 thělō (1), to *will;* to *desire;* to *choose*
3342 mětaxu (2), *betwixt; meanwhile*
4160 pŏiěō (1), *to make*

MEANETH
1819 dâmâh (1), to *resemble, liken*
2076 ěsti (2), *he (she or it) is; they are*
2309+1511 thělō (1), to *will;* to *desire;* to *choose*

MEANING
998 bîynâh (1), *understanding*
1411 dunamis (1), *force, power, miracle*
3195 měllō (1), *to intend,* i.e. *be about to*

MEANS
1157 bᵉ'ad (1), *at, beside, among, behind, for*
3027 yâd (4), *hand; power*
4284 machăshâbâh (1), *contrivance; plan*
6903 qᵉbêl (Ch.) (1), *on account of, so as, since*
1096 ginŏmai (1), *to be, become*
3361 mē (1), *not; lest*
3364 ŏu mē (1), *not at all, absolutely not*
3843 pantōs (2), *entirely; at all events*
4458 -pōs (9), *particle used in composition*
4459 pōs (2), *in what way?; how?; how much!*

1832 ěxěsti (1), *it is right, it is proper*

MAZZAROTH
4216 Mazzârâh (1), *constellation*

ME-JARKON
4313 Mêy hay-Yarqôwn (1), *water of the yellowness*

5158 trŏpŏs (2), *deportment, character*

MEANT
2803 châshab (1), to *think, regard;* to *value*
1498 ěiēn (2), *might could, would be*

MEARAH
4632 Mᵉ'ârâh (1), *cave*

MEASURE
374 'êyphâh (2), *dry grain measure*
520 'ammâh (1), *cubit*
2706 chôq (1), *appointment; allotment*
4055 mad (1), *vesture, garment; carpet*
4058 mâdad (7), to *measure*
4060 middâh (15), *measure; portion*
4884 mᵉsûwrâh (4), *liquid measure*
4941 mishpâṭ (2), *verdict; formal decree; justice*
4971 mathkôneth (1), *proportion*
5429 çᵉ'âh (3), *volume measure for grain*
5432 ça'çᵉ'âh (1), *moderation*
7991 shâlîysh (2), *three-fold measure*
8506 tôken (1), *fixed quantity*
280 amětrŏs (2), *immoderate*
3354 mětrěō (3), to *admeasure*
3358 mětrŏn (13), *what is apportioned*
4053 pěrissŏs (1), *superabundant*
4057 pěrissōs (1), *superabundantly*
5234 hupěrballŏntōs (1), *to a greater degree*
5236 hupěrbŏlē (2), *super-eminence*
5249 hupěrpěrissōs (1), *beyond all measure*
5518 chŏinix (1), *about a dry quart measure*

MEASURED
4058 mâdad (40), to *measure*
4128 mûwd (1), to *shake*
488 antimětrěō (2), to *measure in return*
3354 mětrěō (3), to *admeasure*

MEASURES
374 'êyphâh (2), *dry grain measure*
3734 kôr (8), *dry measure*
4055 mad (1), *vesture, garment; carpet*
4060 middâh (12), *measure; portion*
4461 mêmad (1), *measurement*
5429 çᵉ'âh (6), *volume measure for grain*
943 batôs (1), *measure for liquids*
2884 kŏrŏs (1), *dry bushel measure*

4568 satŏn (2), *measure of about 12 dry quarts*
5518 chŏinix (1), about *a dry quart measure*

MEASURING
4060 middâh (10), *measure; portion*
3354 mĕtrĕŏ (1), to *admeasure*

MEAT
396 'ăkîylâh (1), *food*
398 'âkal (5), to *eat*
400 'ôkel (18), *food*
402 'oklâh (8), *food*
1262 bârâh (1), to *feed*
1267 bârûwth (1), *food*
1279 biryâh (3), *food*
2964 ţereph (3), *fresh torn prey*
3899 lechem (18), *food, bread*
3978 ma'ăkâl (22), *food, something to eat*
4202 mâzôwn (1), *food, provisions*
4203 mâzôwn (Ch.) (2), *food, provisions*
6595 path (1), *bit, morsel*
6598 pathbag (6), *dainty food*
6720 tsêydâh (1), *food, supplies*
1033 brōma (10), *food*
1034 brōsimŏs (1), *eatable*
1035 brōsis (7), *food; rusting corrosion*
4371 prŏsphagiŏn (1), *little fish*
4620 sitŏmĕtrŏn (1), *allowance or ration*
5132 trapĕza (1), *four-legged table*
5160 trŏphē (13), *nourishment; rations*
5315 phagō (3), *outer garment, i.e. a mantle*

MEATS
1033 brōma (6), *food*

MEBUNNAI
4012 Mᵉbunnay (1), *built up*

MECHERATHITE
4382 Mᵉkêrâthîy (1), *Mekerathite*

MEDAD
4312 Mêydâd (2), *affectionate*

MEDAN
4091 Mᵉdân (2), *contest or quarrel*

MEDDLE
1624 gârâh (4), to *provoke to anger*
6148 'ârab (2), to *intermix*

MEDDLED
1566 gâla' (1), to *be obstinate; to burst forth*

MEDDLETH
5674 'âbar (1), to *cross over; to transition*

MEDDLING
1566 gâla' (1), to *be obstinate; to burst forth*

MEDE
4075 Mâday (1), *Madian*

MEDEBA
4311 Mêydᵉbâ' (5), *water of quiet*

MEDES
4074 Mâday (9), *Madai*
4076 Mâday (Ch.) (4), *Madai*
3370 Mēdŏs (1), *inhabitant of Media*

MEDIA
4074 Mâday (6), *Madai*

MEDIAN
4077 Mâday (Ch.) (1), *Madian*

MEDIATOR
3316 mĕsitēs (6), *reconciler, intercessor*

MEDICINE
1456 gêhâh (1), *medicinal cure*
8644 tᵉrûwphâh (1), *remedy, healing*

MEDICINES
7499 rᵉphû'âh (2), *medicament, healing*

MEDITATE
1897 hâgâh (6), to *murmur, ponder*
7742 sûwach (1), to *muse pensively*
7878 sîyach (5), to *ponder, muse aloud*
3191 mĕlĕtaō (1), to *plot, think about*
4304 prŏmĕlĕtaō (1), to *premeditate*

MEDITATION
1900 hâgûwth (1), *musing, meditation*
1901 hâgîyg (1), *complaint, sighing*
1902 higgâyôwn (1), *musical notation*
7879 sîyach (1), *uttered contemplation*
7881 sîychâh (2), *reflection; devotion*

MEEK
6035 'ânâv (13), *needy; oppressed*
4235 praιŏs (1), *gentle, i.e. humble*
4239 praüs (3), *mild, humble, gentle*

MEEKNESS
6037 'anvâh (1), *mildness; oppressed*
6038 'ănâvâh (1), *modesty, clemency*
4236 praιŏtēs (9), *gentleness, humility*
4240 praütēs (3), *humility, meekness*

MEET
749 'ărak (Ch.) (1), to *suit*
1121 bên (1), *son, descendant; people*
3259 yâ'ad (8), to *meet; to summon; to direct*
3474 yâshar (1), to *be straight; to make right*
3476 yôsher (1), *right*
3477 yâshâr (1), *straight*

3559 kûwn (1), to *set up: establish, fix, prepare*
4672 mâtsâ' (2), to *find or acquire; to occur*
5828 'êzer (2), *aid*
6213 'âsâh (2), to *make*
6293 pâga' (5), to *impinge*
6298 pâgash (6), to *come in contact with*
6440 pânîym (3), *face; front*
6743 tsâlach (1), to *push forward*
7125 qir'âh (70), to *encounter, to happen*
7136 qârâh (1), to *bring about; to impose*
7200 râ'âh (2), to *see*
514 axiŏs (4), *deserving, comparable or suitable*
528 apantaō (2), *encounter, meet*
529 apantēsis (4), *friendly encounter*
1163 dĕi (2), *it is (was) necessary*
1342 dikaiŏs (2), *equitable, holy*
2111 ĕuthĕtŏs (1), *appropriate, suitable*
2173 ĕuchrēstŏs (1), *useful, serviceable*
2425 hikanŏs (1), *ample; fit*
2427 hikanŏō (1), to *make competent*
2570 kalŏs (2), *good; beautiful; valuable*
4876 sunantaō (1), to *meet with; to occur*
4877 sunantēsis (1), *meeting with*
5222 hupantēsis (1), *encounter; concurrence*

MEETEST
3477 yâshâr (1), *straight*
6293 pâga' (1), to *impinge*

MEETETH
6293 pâga' (2), to *impinge*
6298 pâgash (1), to *come in contact with*

MEETING
6116 'ătsârâh (1), *assembly*
7125 qir'âh (1), to *encounter, to happen*

MEGIDDO
4023 Mᵉgiddôwn (11), *rendezvous*

MEGIDDON
4023 Mᵉgiddôwn (1), *rendezvous*

MEHETABEEL
4105 Mᵉhêyţab'êl (1), *bettered of God*

MEHETABEL
4105 Mᵉhêyţab'êl (2), *bettered of God*

MEHIDA
4240 Mᵉchîydâ' (2), *junction*

MEHIR
4243 Mᵉchîyr (1), *price*

MEHOLATHITE
4259 Mᵉchôlâthîy (2), *Mecholathite*

MEHUJAEL
4232 Mᵉchûwyâ'êl (2), *smitten of God*

MEHUMAN
4104 Mᵉhûwmân (1), *Mehuman*

MEHUNIM
4586 Mᵉ'ûwnîy (1), *Menite*

MEHUNIMS
4586 Mᵉ'ûwnîy (1), *Menite*

MEKONAH
4368 Mᵉkônâh (1), *base*

MELATIAH
4424 Mᵉlaţyâh (1), *Jehovah has delivered*

MELCHI
3197 Mĕlchi (2), *king*

MELCHI-SHUA
4444 Malkîyshûwa' (2), *king of wealth*

MELCHIAH
4441 Malkîyâh (1), *appointed by Jehovah*

MELCHISEDEC
3198 Mĕlchisĕdĕk (9), *king of right*

MELCHIZEDEK
4442 Malkîy-Tsedeq (2), *king of right*

MELEA
3190 Mĕlĕas (1), *Meleas*

MELECH
4429 Melek (2), *king*

MELICU
4409 Mallûwk (1), *regnant*

MELITA
3194 Mĕlitē (1), *Melita*

MELODY
2172 zimrâh (2), *song*
5059 nâgan (1), to *play; to make music*
5567 psallō (1), to *play a stringed instrument*

MELONS
20 'ăbaţţiyach (1), *melon*

MELT
3988 mâ'aç (1), to *spurn; to disappear*
4127 mûwg (4), to *soften, flow down, disappear*
4529 mâçâh (1), to *dissolve, melt*
4549 mâçaç (6), to *waste; to faint*
5413 nâthak (2), to *pour out; to liquefy, melt*
6884 tsâraph (1), to *fuse metal; to refine*
3089 luō (1), to *loosen*
5080 tēkō (1), to *liquefy, melt*

MELTED
2046 hittûwk (1), *melting*
4127 mûwg (3), to *soften, flow down, disappear*
4549 mâçaç (6), to *waste; to faint fear or grief*
5140 nâzal (1), to *drip, or shed by trickling*
5413 nâthak (2), to *pour out; to liquefy, melt*

MELTETH
1811 dâlaph (1), to *drip*
4549 mâçaç (3), to *waste*; to *faint*
5258 nâçak (1), to *pour a libation*
6884 tsâraph (1), to *fuse metal*; to *refine*
8557 temeç (1), *melting disappearance*

MELTING
2003 hâmâç (1), dry *twig* or *brushwood*

MELZAR
4453 Meltsâr (2), court *officer* (poss.) *butler*

MEMBER
3196 mĕlŏs (5), *limb* or part of the body

MEMBERS
3338 yâtsûr (1), *structure, human frame*
3196 mĕlŏs (29), *limb* or part of the body

MEMORIAL
234 'azkârâh (7), *remembrance-offering*
2143 zêker (5), *recollection; commemoration*
2146 zikrôwn (17), *commemoration*
3422 mnēmŏsunŏn (3), *memorandum*

MEMORY
2143 zêker (5), *commemoration*

MEMPHIS
4644 Môph (1), *Moph*

MEMUCAN
4462 Mᵉmûwkân (3), *Memucan* or *Momucan*

MEN
120 'âdâm (107), *human being; mankind*
376 'îysh (211), *man; male; someone*
582 'ĕnôwsh (491), *man; person, human*
606 'ĕnâsh (Ch.) (12), *man*
1121 bên (16), *son, descendant; people*
1167 ba'al (20), *master; husband; owner; citizen*
1368 gibbôwr (1), *powerful; great warrior*
1397 geber (6), *person, man*
1400 gᵉbar (Ch.) (18), *person; someone*
2145 zâkâr (1), *male*
2388 châzaq (1), to *be strong; courageous*
4962 math (14), *men*
4974 mᵉthôm (1), *completely*
407 andrizŏmai (1), to *act manly*
435 anēr (79), *man; male*
442 anthrōpinŏs (1), *human*
444 anthrōpŏs (192), *human being; mankind*
730 arrhēn (3), *male*
3495 nĕaniskŏs (5), *youth*

4753 stratĕuma (1), *body of troops*
5046 tĕlĕiŏs (1), *complete; mature*

MEN'S
120 'âdâm (10), *human being; mankind*
582 'ĕnôwsh (2), *man; person, human*
444 anthrōpŏs (4), *human being; mankind*
4283 prŏĕuaggĕlizŏmai (1), to *announce* glad news *in advance*

MENAHEM
4505 Mᵉnachêm (8), *comforter*

MENAN
3104 Maïnan (1), *Maïnan*

MEND
2388 châzaq (1), to *fasten* upon; to *bind*

MENDING
2675 katartizō (2), to *repair*; to *prepare*

MENE
4484 menê' (Ch.) (2), *numbered*

MENPLEASERS
441 anthrōparĕskŏs (2), *man-courting, fawning*

MENSERVANTS
5650 'ebed (9), *servant*
3816 pais (1), *child; slave* or *servant*

MENSTEALERS
405 andrapŏdistēs (1), *enslaver, kidnapper*

MENSTRUOUS
1739 dâveh (1), *menstrual; fainting*
5079 niddâh (2), *time of menstrual impurity*

MENTION
2142 zâkar (18), to *remember*; to *mention*
3417 mnēia (4), *recollection; recital*
3421 mnēmŏnĕuō (1), to *exercise memory*

MENTIONED
935 bôw' (1), to *go, come*
2142 zâkar (3), to *remember*; to *mention*
5927 'âlâh (1), to *ascend, be high, mount*
7121 qârâ' (1), to *call out*
8052 shᵉmûw'âh (1), *announcement*

MEONENIM
6049 'ânan (1), to *cover, becloud*; to *act covertly*

MEONOTHAI
4587 Mᵉ'ôwnôthay (1), *habitative*

MEPHAATH
4158 Môwpha'ath (4), *illuminative*

MEPHIBOSHETH
4648 Mᵉphîybôsheth (15), *dispeller of Shame*

MERAB
4764 Mêrâb (3), *increase*

MERAIAH
4811 Mᵉrâyâh (1), *rebellion*

MERAIOTH
4812 Mᵉrâyôwth (7), *rebellious*

MERARI
4847 Mᵉrârîy (39), *bitter*

MERARITES
4848 Mᵉrârîy (1), *Merarite*

MERATHAIM
4850 Mᵉrâthayim (1), *double bitterness*

MERCHANDISE
4267 machănaq (1), *choking, strangling*
4627 ma'ărâb (4), *mercantile goods*
4819 markôleth (1), *mart, market*
5504 çachar (4), *profit from trade*
5505 çachar (2), *profit from trade*
5506 çᵉchôrâh (1), *traffic*
6014 'âmar (2), to *gather grain into sheaves*
7404 rᵉkullâh (2), *peddled trade*
1117 gŏmŏs (2), *cargo, wares* or *freight*
1711 ĕmpŏria (1), *traffic, business trade*
1712 ĕmpŏriŏn (1), *emporium* marketplace

MERCHANT
3667 Kᵉna'an (3), *humiliated*
5503 çâchar (4), to *travel round*; to *palpitate*
7402 râkal (3), to *travel for trading*
1713 ĕmpŏrŏs (1), *tradesman, merchant*

MERCHANTMEN
5503 çâchar (1), to *travel round*; to *palpitate*
8446 tûwr (1), to *wander, meander* for trade

MERCHANTS
3669 Kᵉna'ănîy (1), *Kenaanite; merchant*
5503 çâchar (9), to *travel round*; to *palpitate*
7402 râkal (14), to *travel for trading*
1713 ĕmpŏrŏs (4), *tradesman, merchant*

MERCHANTS'
5503 çâchar (1), to *travel round*; to *palpitate*

MERCIES
2617 cheçed (9), *kindness, favor*
7356 racham (25), *compassion; womb*
7359 rᵉchêm (Ch.) (1), *pity*
3628 ŏiktirmŏs (4), *pity, compassion*
3741 hŏsiŏs (1), *hallowed, pious, sacred*

MERCIES'
2617 cheçed (3), *kindness, favor*
7356 racham (1), *compassion; womb*

MERCIFUL
2551 chemlâh (1), *commiseration, pity*
2603 chânan (11), to *implore*
2616 châçad (2), to *reprove, shame*
2617 cheçed (5), *kindness, favor*
2623 châçîyd (3), *religiously pious, godly*
3722 kâphar (2), to *cover; to expiate*
7349 rachûwm (8), *compassionate*
7355 râcham (1), to *be compassionate*
1655 ĕlĕēmŏn (2), *compassion*
2433 hilaskŏmai (1), to *conciliate, to atone for*
2436 hilĕŏs (1), God be *gracious!, far* be it!
3629 ŏiktirmŏn (2), *compassionate*

MERCURIUS
2060 Hĕrmēs (1), born of god Hermes

MERCY
2603 chânan (16), to *implore*
2604 chănan (Ch.) (1), to *favor*
2617 cheçed (137), *kindness, favor*
3727 kappôreth (27), *lid, cover*
7355 râcham (31), to *be compassionate*
7356 racham (4), *compassion; womb*
448 anilĕŏs (1), *inexorable, merciless*
1653 ĕlĕĕŏ (27), to *give out compassion*
1656 ĕlĕŏs (28), *compassion*
3628 ŏiktirmŏs (1), *pity, compassion*
3629 ŏiktirmŏn (1), *compassionate*

MERCYSEAT
2435 hilastēriŏn (1), *expiatory place*

MERED
4778 Mered (2), *rebellion*

MEREMOTH
4822 Mᵉrêmôwth (6), *heights*

MERES
4825 Mereç (1), *Meres*

MERIB-BAAL
4807 Mᵉrîyb Ba'al (3), *quarreller of Baal*
4810 Mᵉrîy Ba'al (1), *rebellion against Baal*

MERIBAH
4809 Mᵉrîybâh (6), *quarrel*

MERIBAH-KADESH
4809+6946 Mᵉrîybâh (1), *quarrel*

MERODACH
4781 Mᵉrôdâk (1), *Merodak*

MERODACH-BALADAN
4757 Mᵉrô'dak Bal'âdân (1), *Merodak-Baladan*

MEROM
4792 Mêrôwm (2), *height*

MERONOTHITE
4824 Mêrônôthîy (2), *Meronothite*

MEROZ
4789 Mêrôwz (1), *Meroz*

MERRILY
8056 sâmêach (1), *blithe or gleeful*

MERRY
1974 hillûwl (1), *harvest celebration*
2896 ţôwb (7), *good; well*
3190 yâţab (5), *to be, make well*
7832 sâchaq (2), *to laugh; to scorn; to play*
7937 shâkar (1), *to become tipsy, to satiate*
8055 sâmach (2), *to be, make gleesome*
8056 sâmêach (3), *blithe or gleeful*
2114 ĕuthumĕō (1), *to be cheerful; keep courage*
2165 ĕuphrainō (6), *to rejoice, be glad*

MERRYHEARTED
8056+3820 sâmêach (1), *blithe or gleeful*

MESECH
4902 Meshek (1), *Meshek*

MESHA
4331 Mêyshâ' (1), *departure*
4337 Mêyshâ' (1), *safety*
4338 Mêyshâ' (1), *safety*
4852 Mêshâ' (1), *Mesha*

MESHACH
4335 Mêyshak (1), *Meshak*
4336 Mêyshak (Ch.) (14), *Meshak*

MESHECH
4902 Meshek (8), *Meshek*

MESHELEMIAH
4920 Mᵉshelemyâh (4), *ally of Jehovah*

MESHEZABEEL
4898 Mᵉshêyzab'êl (3), *delivered of God*

MESHILLEMITH
4921 Mᵉshillêmîyth (1), *reconciliation*

MESHILLEMOTH
4919 Mᵉshillêmôwth (2), *reconciliations*

MESHOBAB
4877 Mᵉshôwbâb (1), *returned*

MESHULLAM
4918 Mᵉshullâm (25), *allied*

MESHULLEMETH
4922 Mᵉshullemeth (1), *Meshullemeth*

MESOBAITE
4677 Mᵉtsôbâyâh (1), *found of Jehovah*

MESOPOTAMIA
763 'Ăram Nahărayim (5), *Aram of* (the) *two rivers*
3318 Mĕsŏpŏtamia (2), *between the Rivers*

MESS
4864 mas'êth (2), *raising; beacon; present*

MESSAGE
1697 dâbâr (3), *word; matter; thing*
4400 mal'ăkûwth (1), *message*
31 aggĕlia (1), *message*
1860 ĕpaggĕlia (1), *divine assurance*
4242 prĕsbĕia (1), *delegates*

MESSENGER
1319 bâsar (1), *to announce* (good news)
4397 mal'âk (24), *messenger*
5046 nâgad (2), *to announce*
6680 tsâvâh (1), *to constitute, enjoin*
6735 tsîyr (1), *hinge; herald or errand-doer*
32 aggĕlŏs (4), *messenger; angel*
652 apŏstŏlŏs (1), *commissioner of Christ*

MESSENGERS
4397 mal'âk (74), *messenger*
6735 tsîyr (1), *hinge; herald or errand-doer*
32 aggĕlŏs (3), *messenger; angel*
652 apŏstŏlŏs (1), *commissioner of Christ*

MESSES
4864 mas'êth (1), *raising; beacon; present*

MESSIAH
4899 mâshîyach (2), *consecrated; Messiah*

MESSIAS
3323 Mĕssias (2), *consecrated*

MET
3259 yâ'ad (1), *to meet; to summon; to direct*
4672 mâtsâ' (3), *to occur, meet or be present*
6293 pâga' (1), *to impinge*
6298 pâgash (7), *to come in contact with*
6923 qâdam (2), *to anticipate, meet*
7122 qârâ' (2), *to encounter, to happen*
7125 qir'âh (3), *to encounter, to happen*
7135 qârâh (1), *coolness, cold*
7136 qârâh (4), *to bring about; to impose*

MESHULLEMETH
296 amphŏdŏn (1), *fork in the road*
528 apantaō (5), *encounter, meet*
3909 paratugchanō (1), *to chance near*
4820 sumballō (1), *to aid; to join, attack*
4876 sunantaō (4), *to meet with; to occur*
5221 hupantaō (5), *to meet, encounter*

METE
4058 mâdad (3), *to measure*
3354 mĕtrĕō (3), *to admeasure*

METED
6978 qav-qav (2), *stalwart*
8505 tâkan (1), *to balance, i.e. measure*

METEYARD
4060 middâh (1), *measure; portion*

METHEG-AMMAH
4965 Metheg hâ-'Ammâh (1), *bit of the metropolis*

METHUSAEL
4967 Mᵉthûwshâ'êl (2), *man who* (is) *of God*

METHUSELAH
4968 Mᵉthûwshelach (6), *man of a dart*

MEUNIM
4586 Mᵉ'ûwnîy (1), *Menite*

MEZAHAB
4314 Mêy Zâhâb (2), *water of gold*

MIAMIN
4326 Mîyâmin (2), *from* (the) *right hand*

MIBHAR
4006 Mibchâr (1), *select, i.e. best*

MIBSAM
4017 Mibsâm (3), *fragrant*

MIBZAR
4014 Mibtsâr (2), *fortification; defender*

MICAH
4316 Mîykâ' (1), *who* (is) *like Jehovah?*
4318 Mîykâh (22), *who* (is) *like Jehovah?*
4319 Mîykâhûw (4), *who* (is) *like Jehovah?*
4320 Mîykâyâh (1), *who* (is) *like Jehovah?*

MICAH'S
4318 Mîykâh (3), *who* (is) *like Jehovah?*

MICAIAH
4318 Mîykâh (1), *who* (is) *like Jehovah?*
4319 Mîykâhûw (1), *who* (is) *like Jehovah?*
4321 Mîykâyᵉhûw (16), *who* (is) *like Jehovah?*

MICE
5909 'akbâr (4), *mouse*

MICHA
4316 Mîykâ' (4), *who* (is) *like Jehovah?*

MICHAEL
4317 Mîykâ'êl (13), *who* (is) *like God?*
3413 Michaĕl (2), *who* (is) *like God?*

MICHAH
4318 Mîykâh (3), *who* (is) *like Jehovah?*

MICHAIAH
4320 Mîykâyâh (3), *who* (is) *like Jehovah?*
4321 Mîykâyᵉhûw (2), *who* (is) *like Jehovah?*
4322 Mîykâyâhûw (2), *who* (is) *like Jehovah?*

MICHAL
4324 Mîykâl (18), *rivulet*

MICHMAS
4363 Mikmâç (2), *hidden*

MICHMASH
4363 Mikmâç (9), *hidden*

MICHMETHAH
4366 Mikmᵉthâth (2), *concealment*

MICHRI
4381 Mikrîy (1), *salesman*

MICHTAM
4387 Miktâm (6), *poem*

MIDDAY
4276+3117 machătsîyth (1), *halving or middle*
6672 tsôhar (1), *window: noon time*
2250+3319 hĕmĕra (1), *day; period of time*

MIDDIN
4081 Middîyn (1), *contest or quarrel*

MIDDLE
2677 chêtsîy (1), *half or middle, midst*
2872 ţabbûwr (1), *summit*
8432 tâvek (6), *center, middle*
8484 tîykôwn (9), *central, middle*
3320 mĕsŏtŏichŏn (1), *partition wall*

MIDDLEMOST
8484 tîykôwn (2), *central, middle*

MIDIAN
4080 Midyân (39), *contest or quarrel*

MIDIANITE
4084 Midyânîy (1), *Midjanite*

MIDIANITES
4080 Midyân (20), *contest or quarrel*
4084 Midyânîy (3), *Midjanite*
4092 Mᵉdânîy (1), *Midjanite*

MIDIANITISH
4084 Midyânîy (3), *Midjanite*

MIDNIGHT
2676+3915 châtsôwth (3), *middle* of the night
2677+3915 chêtsîy (3), *half* or *middle*, *midst*
8432+3915 tâvek (1), *center*, *middle*
3317 mĕsŏnuktiŏn (4), *midnight* watch
3319+3571 mĕsŏs (2), *middle*

MIDST
1459 gav (Ch.) (10), *middle*
2436 chêyq (1), *bosom*, *heart*
2673 châtsâh (1), to *cut* or *split* in two; to *halve*
2677 chêtsîy (8), *half* or *middle*, *midst*
2686 châtsats (1), to *curtail*; to *distribute*
2872 ţabbûwr (1), *summit*
3820 lêb (12), *heart*
3824 lêbâb (1), *heart*
7130 qereb (73), *nearest* part, i.e. the *center*
8432 tâvek (209), *center*, *middle*
8484 tîykôwn (1), *central*, *middle*
3319 mĕsŏs (41), *middle*
3321 mĕsŏuranêma (3), *mid-sky*, *mid-heaven*
3322 mĕsŏŏ (1), to *be at midpoint*

MIDWIFE
3205 yâlad (3), to *bear young*; to *father a child*

MIDWIVES
3205 yâlad (7), to *bear young*; to *father a child*

MIGDAL-EL
4027 Migdal-'Êl (1), *tower of God*

MIGDAL-GAD
4028 Migdal-Gâd (1), *tower of Fortune*

MIGDOL
4024 Migdôwl (4), *tower*

MIGHT
202 'ôwn (2), *ability*, *power*; *wealth*
410 'êl (1), *mighty*; the *Almighty*
1369 gᵉbûwrâh (27), *force*; *valor*; *victory*
1370 gᵉbûwrâh (Ch.) (2), *power*, *strength*
2428 chayil (6), *army*; *wealth*; *virtue*; *strength*
3201 yâkôl (2), to *be able*
3581 kôach (7), *force*, *might*; *strength*
3966 mᵉ'ôd (2), *very*, *utterly*
5797 'ôz (2), *strength*
5807 'ĕzûwz (1), *forcibleness*
6108 'ôtsem (1), *power*; framework of the *body*
8632 tᵉqôph (Ch.) (1), *power*
1410 dunamai (6), to *be able* or *possible*
1411 dunamis (4), *force*, *power*, *miracle*

MIGHTIER
117 'addîyr (1), *powerful*; *majestic*
6099 'âtsûwm (7), *powerful*; *numerous*
6105 'âtsam (1), to *be*, *make powerful*
8623 taqqîyph (1), *powerful*
2478 ischurŏs (3), *forcible*, *powerful*

MIGHTIES
1368 gibbôwr (2), *powerful*; great *warrior*

MIGHTIEST
1368 gibbôwr (1), *powerful*; great *warrior*

MIGHTILY
2393 chezqâh (2), *prevailing power*
3966 mᵉ'ôd (2), *very*, *utterly*
1722+1411 ĕn (1), *in*; *during*; *because of*
1722+2479 ĕn (1), *in*; *during*; *because of*
2159 ĕutŏnōs (1), *intensely*, *cogently*
2596+2904 kata (1), *down*; *according to*

MIGHTY
46 'âbîyr (6), *mighty*
47 'abbîyr (4), *mighty*
117 'addîyr (5), *powerful*; *majestic*
193 'ûwl (1), *powerful*; *mighty*
352 'ayil (2), *chief*; *ram*; *oak* tree
376 'îysh (2), *man*; *male*; *someone*
386 'êythân (4), *never-failing*; *eternal*
410 'êl (5), *mighty*; the *Almighty*
430 'ĕlôhîym (2), the true *God*; great *ones*
533 'ammîyts (1), *strong*; *mighty*; *brave*
650 'âphîyq (1), *valley*; *stream*; *mighty*, *strong*
1121+410 bên (1), *son*, *descendant*; *people*
1219 bâtsar (1), to *be inaccessible*
1368 gibbôwr (135), *powerful*; great *warrior*
1369 gᵉbûwrâh (7), *force*; *valor*; *victory*
1396 gâbar (1), to *be strong*; to *prevail*
1397 geber (2), *person*, *man*
1401 gibbâr (Ch.) (1), *valiant man*, or *warrior*
1419 gâdôwl (7), *great*
2220 zᵉrôwa' (1), *arm*; *foreleg*; *force*, *power*
2388 châzaq (2), to *be strong*; *courageous*
2389 châzâq (20), *strong*; *severe*, *hard*, *violent*
2428 chayil (1), *army*; *wealth*; *virtue*; *strength*
3524 kabbîyr (5), *mighty*; *aged*; *mighty*
3966 mᵉ'ôd (1), *very*, *utterly*
5794 'az (3), *strong*, *vehement*, *harsh*
5797 'ôz (1), *strength*
5868 'ăyâm (1), (poss.) *strength*
6099 'âtsûwm (8), *powerful*; *numerous*
6105 'âtsam (4), to *be*, *make powerful*
6184 'ârîyts (1), *powerful* or *tyrannical*
6697 tsûwr (2), *rock*
7227 rab (5), *great*
7989 shallîyţ (1), *prince* or *warrior*
8624 taqqîyph (Ch.) (2), *powerful*
972 biaiŏs (1), *violent*
1411 dunamis (14), *force*, *power*, *miracle*
1413 dunastês (1), *ruler* or *officer*
1414 dunatĕŏ (1), to *be efficient*, *able*, *strong*
1415 dunatŏs (7), *powerful* or *capable*
1754 ĕnĕrgĕŏ (1), to *be active*, *efficient*, *work*
2478 ischurŏs (7), *forcible*, *powerful*
2479 ischus (1), *forcefulness*, *power*
2900 krataiŏs (1), *powerful*, *mighty*
3168 mĕgalĕiŏtēs (1), *grandeur* or *splendor*
3173 mĕgas (1), *great*, *many*
5082 tēlikŏutŏs (1), so *vast*

MIGRON
4051 Migrôwn (2), *precipice*

MIJAMIN
4326 Mîyâmîn (2), *from* (the) *right hand*

MIKLOTH
4732 Miqlôwth (4), *rods*

MIKNEIAH
4737 Miqnêyâhûw (2), *possession of Jehovah*

MILALAI
4450 Mîlălay (1), *talkative*

MILCAH
4435 Milkâh (11), *queen*

MILCH
3243 yânaq (1), to *suck*; to *give milk*
5763 'ûwl (2), to *suckle*, i.e. *give milk*

MILCOM
4445 Malkâm (3), *Malcam* or *Milcom*

MILDEW
3420 yêrâqôwn (5), *paleness*; *mildew*

MILE
3400 miliŏn (1), about 4,850 feet, Roman *mile*

MILETUM
3399 Milētŏs (1), *Miletus*

MILETUS
3399 Milētŏs (2), *Miletus*

MILK
2461 châlâb (42), *milk*
4711 mâtsats (1), to *suck*
1051 gala (5), *milk*

MILL
7347 rêcheh (1), *mill-stone*
3459 mulôn (1), *mill-house*

MILLET
1764 dôchan (1), *millet* cereal *grain*

MILLIONS
7233 rᵉbâbâh (1), *myriad* number

MILLO
4407 millôw' (10), *citadel*

MILLS
7347 rêcheh (1), *mill-stone*

MILLSTONE
7347 rêcheh (1), *mill-stone*
7393 rekeb (2), *upper millstone*
3037+3457 lithŏs (1), *stone*
3458 mulŏs (2), *grinder millstone*
3458+3684 mulŏs (2), *grinder millstone*

MILLSTONES
7347 rêcheh (2), *mill-stone*

MINCING
2952 ţâphaph (1), to *trip* or *step*

MIND
3336 yêtser (1), *form*
3820 lêb (12), *heart*
3824 lêbâb (4), *heart*
5315 nephesh (11), *life*; *breath*; *soul*; *wind*
5973 'îm (1), *with*
6310 peh (1), *mouth*; *opening*
7307 rûwach (6), *breath*; *wind*; *life*-spirit
363 anamimnēskō (1), to *remind*; to *recollect*
1106 gnōmē (2), *cognition*, *opinion*
1271 dianŏia (7), *mind* or *thought*
1771 ĕnnŏia (1), *moral understanding*
1878 ĕpanamimnēskō (1), to *remind again of*
3563 nŏus (15), *intellect*, *mind*; *understanding*
3661 hŏmŏthumadŏn (1), *unanimously*
3675 hŏmŏphrōn (1), *like-minded*
4288 prŏthumia (4), *alacrity*, *eagerness*
4290 prŏthumōs (1), *with alacrity*, *with eagerness*
4993 sōphrŏnĕŏ (2), to *be in a right state of mind*

MINDED

4995 sōphrŏnismŏs (1),
  self-discipline
5012 tapĕinŏphrŏsunē
  (1), *modesty, humility*
5279 hupŏmimnēskō (1),
  to *suggest to memory*
5426 phrŏněō (9), to *be*
  mentally *disposed*
5427 phrŏnēma (2),
  inclination or *purpose*
5590 psuchē (1), *soul,*
  vitality; heart, mind

MINDED

5973+3820 'îm (1), *with*
1011 bŏulĕuō (1), to
  deliberate; to *resolve*
1014 bŏulŏmai (3), to *be*
  willing, desire
1374 dipsuchŏs (2),
  vacillating
4993 sōphrŏnĕō (1), to *be*
  in a right state of mind
5426 phrŏněō (3), to *be*
  mentally *disposed*
5427 phrŏnēma (2),
  mental *inclination*

MINDFUL

2142 zākar (6), to
  remember; to *mention*
3403 mimnēskō (3), to
  remind or to *recall*
3421 mnēmŏněuō (1), to
  exercise memory

MINDING

3195 mēllō (1), to *intend,*
  i.e. *be about* to

MINDS

5315 nephesh (4), *life;*
  breath; soul; wind
1271 dianŏia (2), *mind*
  or *thought*
3540 nŏēma (4),
  perception, i.e. *purpose*
3563 nŏus (2), *intellect,*
  mind; understanding
5590 psuchē (2), *soul,*
  vitality; heart, mind

MINGLE

4537 mâçak (1), to *mix*
6151 'ărab (Ch.) (1), to
  co-mingle, mix

MINGLED

1101 bâlal (37), to *mix;*
  confuse; to *feed*
3610 kil'ayim (2), *two*
  different kinds of thing
3947 lâqach (1), to *take*
4537 mâçak (4), to *mix*
6148 'ârab (2), to *intermix*
6154 'êreb (4), *mixed* or
  woven things
3396 mignumi (4), to
  mix, mingle

MINIAMIN

4509 Minyâmîyn (3),
  from (the) *right hand*

MINISH

1639 gâra' (1), to *shave,*
  remove, lessen

MINISHED

4591 mâ'aṭ (1), to *be,*
  make small or *few*

MINISTER

1777 dîyn (1), to *judge;* to
  strive or *contend for*

8334 shârath (50), to
  attend as a menial
8335 shârêth (1), *service*
1247 diakŏněō (8), to *act*
  as a deacon
1248 diakŏnia (1),
  attendance, aid, service
1249 diakŏnŏs (14),
  waiter; deacon (-ess)
1325 didōmi (1), to *give*
2038 ĕrgazŏmai (1), to
  toil
3008 lěitŏurgěō (1), to
  perform religious or
  charitable *functions*
3011 lěitŏurgŏs (2),
  functionary in the
  Temple or Gospel
3930 parěchō (1), to *hold*
  near, i.e. to *present*
5256 hupěrětěō (1), to *be*
  a *subordinate*
5257 hupěrětēs (3),
  servant, attendant
5524 chŏrēgěō (1), to
  furnish, supply, provide

MINISTERED

8120 shemash (Ch.) (1),
  to *serve*
8334 shârath (15), to
  attend as a menial
1247 diakŏněō (14), to
  wait upon, serve
2023 ěpichŏrēgěō (2), to
  fully *supply;* to *aid*
3008 lěitŏurgěō (1), to
  perform religious or
  charitable *functions*
3011 lěitŏurgŏs (1),
  functionary in the
  Temple or Gospel
5256 hupěrětěō (1), to *be*
  a *subordinate*

MINISTERETH

2023 ěpichŏrēgěō (2), to
  fully *supply;* to *aid*

MINISTERING

5656 'ăbôdâh (1), *work* of
  any kind
8334 shârath (1), to
  attend as a menial
1247 diakŏněō (1), to
  wait upon, serve
1248 diakŏnia (3),
  attendance, aid, service
2418 hiěrŏurgěō (1),
  officiate as a priest
3008 lěitŏurgěō (1), to
  perform religious or
  charitable *functions*
3010 lěitŏurgikŏs (1),
  engaged in holy service

MINISTERS

6399 pelach (Ch.) (1), to
  serve or *worship*
8334 shârath (15), to
  attend as a menial
1249 diakŏnŏs (6),
  attendant, deacon
3011 lěitŏurgŏs (2),
  functionary in the
  Temple or Gospel
5257 hupěrětēs (2),
  servant, attendant

MINISTRATION

1248 diakŏnia (6),
  attendance, aid, service

3009 lěitŏurgia (1),
  service, ministry

MINISTRY

3027 yâd (2), *hand; power*
5656 'ăbôdâh (1), *work*
8335 shârêth (1), *service*
  in the Temple
1248 diakŏnia (16),
  attendance, aid, service
3009 lěitŏurgia (2),
  service, ministry

MINNI

4508 Minnîy (1), *Minni*

MINNITH

4511 Minnîyth (2),
  enumeration

MINSTREL

5059 nâgan (2), to *play;*
  to *make music*

MINSTRELS

834 aulētēs (1),
  flute-player

MINT

2238 hēduŏsmŏn (2),
  sweet-scented, mint

MIPHKAD

4663 Miphqâd (1),
  assignment

MIRACLE

4159 môwphêth (1),
  miracle; token or *omen*
1411 dunamis (1), *force,*
  power, miracle
4592 sēmĕiŏn (7),
  indication, sign, signal

MIRACLES

226 'ôwth (2), *signal, sign*
4159 môwphêth (1),
  miracle; token or *omen*
6381 pâlâ' (1), to *be,*
  make great, wonderful
1411 dunamis (8), *force,*
  power, miracle
4592 sēmĕiŏn (15),
  indication, sign, signal

MIRE

1206 bôts (1), *mud*
1207 bitstsâh (1), *swamp,*
  marsh
2563 chômer (2), *clay;*
  dry measure
2916 ṭîyṭ (8), *mud* or *clay*
3121 yâvên (1), *mud,*
  sediment
7516 rephesh (1), *mud* of
  the sea
1004 bŏrbŏrŏs (1), *mud*

MIRIAM

4813 Miryâm (15),
  rebelliously

MIRMA

4821 Mirmâh (1), *fraud*

MIRTH

4885 mâsôws (3), *delight*
7797 sûws (1), to *be*
  bright, i.e. *cheerful*
8057 simchâh (8),
  blithesomeness or *glee*
8342 sâsôwn (3),
  cheerfulness; welcome

MIRY

1207 bitstsâh (1), *swamp,*
  marsh

2917 ṭîyn (Ch.) (2), *wet*
  clay
3121 yâvên (1), *mud,*
  sediment

MISCARRYING

7921 shâkôl (1), to
  miscarry

MISCHIEF

205 'âven (4), *trouble,*
  vanity, wickedness
611 'âçôwn (5), *hurt,*
  injury
1943 hôvâh (2), *ruin,*
  disaster
2154 zimmâh (3), *bad*
  plan
4827 mêra' (1),
  wickedness
5771 'âvôn (1), *moral evil*
5999 'âmâl (9), *wearing*
  effort; worry
7451 ra' (19), *bad; evil*
7489 râ'a' (1), to *be good*
  for nothing
4468 rha₁diŏurgia (1),
  malignity, trickery

MISCHIEFS

1942 havvâh (1), *desire;*
  craving
7451 ra' (2), *bad; evil*

MISCHIEVOUS

1942 havvâh (2), *desire;*
  craving
4209 mezimmâh (2),
  plan; sagacity
7451 ra' (1), *bad; evil*

MISERABLE

5999 'âmâl (1), *wearing*
  effort; worry
1652 ělěěinŏs (2), *worthy*
  of mercy

MISERABLY

2560 kakŏs (1), *badly;*
  wrongly; ill

MISERIES

4788 mârûwd (1),
  outcast; destitution
5004 talaipŏria (1),
  calamity, distress

MISERY

4788 mârûwd (1),
  outcast; destitution
5999 'âmâl (3), *wearing*
  effort; worry
6001 'âmêl (1), *toiling;*
  laborer; sorrowful
7451 ra' (1), *bad; evil*
5004 talaipŏria (1),
  calamity, distress

MISGAB

4869 misgâb (1), *high*
  refuge

MISHAEL

4332 Mîyshâ'êl (8), *who*
  (is) *what God* (is)?

MISHAL

4861 Mish'âl (1), *request*

MISHAM

4936 Mish'âm (1),
  inspection

MISHEAL

4861 Mish'âl (1), *request*

MISHMA

4927 Mishmâ' (4), *report*

M

MISHMANNAH
4925 Mishmannâh (1), *fatness*

MISHRAITES
4954 Mishrâ'îy (1), *extension*

MISPERETH
4559 Miçpereth (1), *enumeration*

MISREPHOTH-MAIM
4956 Misr^ephôwth Mayim (2), *burnings of water*

MISS
2398 châṭâ' (1), to *sin*
6485 pâqad (1), to *visit, care for, count*

MISSED
6485 pâqad (3), to *visit, care for, count*

MISSING
6485 pâqad (2), to *visit, care for, count*

MIST
108 'êd (1), *fog*
887 achlus (1), *dimness of sight, i.e. cataract*
2217 zŏphŏs (1), *gloom*

MISTRESS
1172 ba'ălâh (2), *mistress; female owner*
1404 g^ebereth (7), *mistress, noblewoman*

MISUSED
8591 tâ'a' (1), to *cheat; to maltreat*

MITE
3016 lĕptŏn (1), small *coin*

MITES
3016 lĕptŏn (2), small *coin*

MITHCAH
4989 Mithqâh (2), *sweetness*

MITHNITE
4981 Mithnîy (1), *slenderness*

MITHREDATH
4990 Mithr^edâth (2), *Mithredath*

MITRE
4701 mitsnepheth (11), *royal/priestly turban*
6797 tsânîyph (2), *head-dress, turban*

MITYLENE
3412 Mitulēnē (1), *abounding in shell-fish*

MIXED
1101 bâlal (1), to *mix; confuse; to feed*
4107 mâhal (1), to *dilute a mixture*
4469 mamçâk (1), *mixed-wine*
6151 'ărab (Ch.) (3), to *co-mingle, mix*
6154 'êreb (2), *mixed or woven things*
4786 sugkĕrannumi (1), to *combine; assimilate*

MIXTURE
4538 meçek (1), *wine mixture with spices*
194 akratŏs (1), *undiluted*
3395 migma (1), *compound, mixture*

MIZAR
4706 Mits'âr (1), *little*

MIZPAH
4708 Mitspeh (5), *observatory*
4709 Mitspah (18), *observatory*

MIZPAR
4558 Miçpâr (1), *number*

MIZPEH
4708 Mitspeh (9), *observatory*
4709 Mitspah (14), *observatory*

MIZRAIM
4714 Mitsrayim (4), double *border*

MIZZAH
4199 Mizzâh (3), *terror*

MNASON
3416 Mnasōn (1), *Mnason*

MOAB
4124 Môw'âb (165), *from mother's father*
4125 Môw'âbîy (2), *Moäbite or Moäbitess*

MOABITE
4125 Môw'âbîy (3), *Moäbite or Moäbitess*

MOABITES
4124 Môw'âb (16), *from mother's father*
4125 Môw'âbîy (3), *Moäbite or Moäbitess*

MOABITESS
4125 Môw'âbîy (6), *Moäbite or Moäbitess*

MOABITISH
4125 Môw'âbîy (1), *Moäbite or Moäbitess*

MOADIAH
4153 Môw'adyâh (1), *assembly of Jehovah*

MOCK
2048 hâthal (1), to *deride, mock*
3887 lûwts (1), to *scoff; to interpret; to intercede*
3932 lâ'ag (2), to *deride; to speak unintelligibly*
5953 'âlal (1), to *glean; to overdo*
6711 tsâchaq (2), to *scorn; to make sport of*
7046 qâlaç (1), to *disparage, i.e. ridicule*
7832 sâchaq (1), to *laugh; to scorn; to play*
1702 ĕmpaizō (3), *deride, ridicule*

MOCKED
2048 hâthal (4), to *deride, mock*
3931 lâ'ab (1), to *deride, mock*
3932 lâ'ag (2), to *deride; to speak unintelligibly*

MOCKER
3887 lûwts (1), to *scoff; to interpret; to intercede*

MOCKERS
2049 hâthôl (1), *derision, mockery*
3887 lûwts (1), to *scoff; to interpret; to intercede*
3934 lâ'êg (1), *buffoon; foreigner*
7832 sâchaq (1), to *laugh; to scorn; to play*
1703 ĕmpaiktēs (1), *derider; false teacher*

MOCKEST
3932 lâ'ag (1), to *deride; to speak unintelligibly*

MOCKETH
2048 hâthal (1), to *deride, mock*
3932 lâ'ag (3), to *deride; to speak unintelligibly*
7832 sâchaq (1), to *laugh; to scorn; to play*

MOCKING
6711 tsâchaq (1), to *scorn; to make sport of*
7048 qallâçâh (1), *ridicule*
1702 ĕmpaizō (2), to *deride, ridicule*
5512 chlĕuazō (1), *jeer at, sneer at*

MOCKINGS
1701 ĕmpaigmŏs (1), *derision, jeering*

MODERATELY
6666 ts^edâqâh (1), *rightness*

MODERATION
1933 ĕpiĕikēs (1), *mild, gentle*

MODEST
2887 kŏsmiŏs (1), *orderly*

MOIST
3892 lach (1), *fresh cut, i.e. unused or undried*

MOISTENED
8248 shâqâh (1), to *quaff, i.e. to irrigate*

MOISTURE
3955 l^eshad (1), *juice; vigor; sweet or fat cake*
2429 hikmas (1), *dampness, dampness*

MOLADAH
4137 Môwlâdâh (4), *birth*

MOLE
8580 tanshemeth (1), (poss.) *tree-toad*

MOLECH
4432 Môlek (8), *king*

MOLES
2661 chăphôr (1), *hole, i.e. a burrowing rat*

MOLID
4140 Môwlîyd (1), *genitor*

MOLLIFIED
7401 râkak (1), to *soften*

MOLOCH
4432 Môlek (1), *king*
3434 Mŏlŏch (1), *king*

MOLTEN
3332 yâtsaq (6), to *pour out*
4541 maççêkâh (25), *cast image); libation*
4549 mâçaç (1), to *waste; to faint*
5258 nâçak (1), to *pour a libation*
5262 neçek (4), *libation; cast idol*
5413 nâthak (1), to *flow forth, pour out*
6694 tsûwq (1), to *pour out; melt*

MOMENT
7281 rega' (19), *very short space of time*
823 atŏmŏs (1), *indivisible unit of time*
3901 pararrhuĕō (1), to *flow by*
4743 stigmē (1), *point of time, i.e. an instant*

MONEY
3701 keçeph (112), *silver money*
3702 k^eçaph (Ch.) (1), *silver money*
7192 q^esîyṭah (2), *coin of unknown weight*
694 arguriŏn (11), *silver; silver money*
2772 kĕrma (1), *coin*
2773 kĕrmatistēs (1), *money-broker*
3546 nŏmisma (1), *coin*
4715 statēr (1), *coin worth four day's wage*
5365 philarguria (1), *avarice*
5475 chalkŏs (2), *copper*
5536 chrēma (4), *wealth, price*

MONEYCHANGERS
2855 kŏllubistēs (2), *coin-dealer*

MONSTERS
8577 tannîyn (1), *sea-serpent; jackal*

MONTH
2320 chôdesh (215), *new moon; month*
3391 yerach (6), *lunar month*
3393 y^erach (Ch.) (1), *lunar month*
3376 mēn (4), *month; month's time*

MONTHLY
2320 chôdesh (1), *new moon; month*

MONTHS
2320 chôdesh (37), *new moon; month*
3391 yerach (5), *lunar month*
3393 yᵉrach (Ch.) (1), *lunar month*
3376 mēn (14), *month; month's time*
5072 tĕtramēnŏn (1), *four months' time*
5150 trimēnŏn (1), *three months' space*

MONUMENTS
5341 nâtsar (1), *to guard, protect, maintain*

MOON
2320 chôdesh (9), *new moon; month*
3391 yerach (2), *lunar month*
3394 yârêach (26), *moon*
3842 lᵉbânâh (3), *white moon*
3561 nŏumēnia (1), *festival of new moon*
4582 sĕlēnē (9), *moon*

MOONS
2320 chôdesh (11), *new moon; month*

MORASTHITE
4183 Mowrashtiy (2), *Morashtite*

MORDECAI
4782 Mordᵉkay (58), *Mordecai*

MORDECAI'S
4782 Mordᵉkay (2), *Mordecai*

MORE
637 'aph (1), *also or yea; though*
1058 bâkâh (1), *to weep, moan*
1490 gizbâr (Ch.) (3), *treasurer*
1980 hâlak (1), *to walk; live a certain way*
2351 chûwts (1), *outside, outdoors; open market; countryside*
3148 yôwthêr (3), *moreover; rest; gain*
3254 yâçaph (59), *to add or augment*
3499 yether (1), *remainder; small rope*
3513 kâbad (1), *to be heavy, severe, dull*
3651 kên (2), *just; right, correct*
4480 min (4), *from, out of*
4481 min (Ch.) (1), *from or out of*
5674 'âbar (1), *to cross over; to transition*
5720 'Àdîyn (1), *voluptuous*
5736 'ádaph (1), *to be redundant, have surplus*
5750 'ôwd (196), *again; repeatedly; still; more*
5922 'al (Ch.) (1), *above, over, upon, or against*
5973 'îm (1), *with*

6105 'âtsam (2), *to be, make numerous*
6440 pânîym (1), *face; front*
7138 qârôwb (1), *near, close*
7227 rab (14), *great*
7230 rôb (1), *abundance*
7231 râbab (2), *to increase*
7235 râbâh (11), *to increase*
7608 sha'ărâh (1), *female kindred by blood*
7725 shûwb (1), *to turn back; to return*
8145 shênîy (3), *second; again*
197 akribĕstĕrŏn (4), *more exactly*
243 allŏs (1), *different, other*
316 anagkaiŏs (1), *necessary*
414 anĕktŏtĕrŏs (6), *more bearable*
1065 gĕ (1), *particle of emphasis*
1308 diaphĕrō (2), *to differ; to surpass*
1508 ĕi mē (1), *if not*
1617 ĕktĕnĕstĕrŏn (1), *more intently*
1833 ĕxĕtazō (1), *to ascertain or interrogate*
2001 ĕpischuō (7), *to insist stoutly*
2089 ĕti (1), *yet, still*
2115 ĕuthumŏs (1), *cheerful, encouraged*
3122 malista (1), *in the greatest degree*
3123 mallŏn (47), *in a greater degree*
3185 mĕizōn (1), *in greater degree*
3187 mĕizōn (1), *larger, greater*
3370 Mēdŏs (3), *inhabitant of Media*
3745 hŏsŏs (1), *as much as*
3761 ŏudĕ (1), *neither, nor, not even*
3765 ŏukĕti (17), *not yet, no longer*
3844 para (2), *from; with; besides; on account of*
4053 pĕrissŏs (2), *superabundant*
4054 pĕrissŏtĕrŏn (1), *more superabundant*
4055 pĕrissŏtĕrŏs (10), *more superabundant*
4056 pĕrissŏtĕrōs (10), *more superabundantly*
4057 pĕrissōs (1), *superabundantly*
4065 pĕriphrŏnĕō (1), *to depreciate, contemn*
4119 plĕiōn (25), *more*
4179 pŏllaplasiōn (1), *very much more*
4325 prŏsdapanaō (1), *to expend additionally*
4369 prŏstithēmi (2), *to lay beside, repeat*
4707 spŏudaiŏtĕrŏs (2), *more prompt*

5112 tŏlmĕrŏtĕrŏn (1), *more daringly*
5228 hupĕr (4), *over; above; beyond*
5245 hupĕrnikaō (1), *to gain a decisive victory*

MOREH
4176 Môwreh (3), *archer; teaching; early rain*

MOREOVER
518 'îm (1), *whether?; if, although; Oh that!*
637 'aph (2), *also or yea; though*
1571 gam (25), *also; even; yea; though*
3148 yôwthêr (1), *moreover; rest; gain*
3254 yâçaph (1), *to add or augment*
5750 'ôwd (6), *again; repeatedly; still; more*
1161 dĕ (12), *but, yet; and then*
2089 ĕti (1), *yet, still*
2532 kai (1), *and; or; even; also*

MORESHETH-GATH
4182 Môwresheth Gath (1), *possession of Gath*

MORIAH
4179 Môwrîyâh (2), *seen of Jehovah*

MORNING
216 'ôwr (1), *luminary; lightning; happiness*
1242 bôqer (187), *morning*
4891 mishchâr (1), *dawn*
5053 nôgahh (Ch.) (1), *dawn*
6843 tsᵉphîyrâh (2), *mishap*
7836 shâchar (1), *to search for*
7837 shachar (12), *dawn*
7904 shâkâh (1), *to roam because of lust*
7925 shâkam (1), *to start early in the morning*
3720 ŏrthrinŏs (1), *matutinal, i.e. early*
4404 prŏï (6), *at dawn; day-break watch*
4405 prōïa (3), *day-dawn, early morn*
4407 prōïnŏs (1), *matutinal, i.e. early*

MORROW
1242 bôqer (7), *morning*
4279 mâchar (45), *tomorrow; hereafter*
4283 mochŏrâth (28), *tomorrow, next day*
839 auriŏn (14), *to-morrow*
1836 hĕxēs (1), *successive, next*
1887 ĕpauriŏn (8), *to-morrow*

MORSEL
3603 kikkâr (1), *round loaf; talent*
6595 path (8), *bit, morsel*
1035 brōsis (1), *food; rusting corrosion*

MORSELS
6595 path (1), *bit, morsel*

MORTAL
582 'ĕnôwsh (1), *man; person, human*
2349 thnētŏs (5), *liable to die, i.e. mortal*

MORTALITY
2349 thnētŏs (1), *liable to die, i.e. mortal*

MORTALLY
5315 nephesh (1), *life; breath; soul; wind*

MORTAR
4085 mᵉdôkâh (1), *mortar for bricks*
4388 maktêsh (1), *mortar; socket*

MORTER
2563 chômer (4), *clay; dry measure*
6083 'âphâr (2), *dust, earth, mud; clay,*

MORTGAGED
6148 'ârab (1), *to intermix; to give or be security*

MORTIFY
2289 thanatŏō (1), *to kill*
3499 nĕkrŏō (1), *to deaden, i.e. to subdue*

MOSERA
4149 Môwçêrâh (1), *corrections*

MOSEROTH
4149 Môwçêrâh (2), *corrections*

MOSES
4872 Môsheh (749), *drawing out of the water*
4873 Môsheh (Ch.) (1), *drawing out of the water*
3475 Môsĕus (77), *drawing out of the water*

MOSES'
4872 Môsheh (16), *drawing out of the water*
3475 Môsĕus (3), *drawing out of the water*

MOST
2429 chayil (Ch.) (1), *army; strength*
2896 tôwb (1), *good; well*
3524 kabbîyr (1), *mighty; aged; mighty*
3800 kethem (1), *pure gold*
4581 mâ'ôwz (1), *fortified place; defense*
4971 mathkôneth (1), *proportion*
5920 'al (2), *the Highest God*
5943 'illay (Ch.) (9), *the supreme God*
5945 'elyôwn (25), *loftier, higher; Supreme God*
5946 'elyôwn (Ch.) (3), *the Supreme God*

M

6579 partam (1),
grandee, noble
6944 qôdesh (48), *sacred
place or thing*
7230 rôb (1), *abundance*
8077 sh°mâmâh (1),
devastation
8563 tamrûwr (1),
bitterness
40 hagiŏs (1), *sacred,
holy*
2236 hēdista (1), *with
great pleasure*
2903 kratistŏs (4), *very
honorable*
3122 malista (1), *in the
greatest degree*
4118 plēistŏs (1), *very
large,* i.e. *the most*
4119 plēiŏn (3), *more*
5310 hupsistŏs (5),
*highest; the Supreme
God*

MOTE
2595 karphŏs (6), *dry
twig or straw*

MOTH
6211 'âsh (7), *moth*
4597 sēs (3), *moth insect*

MOTHEATEN
4598 sētŏbrŏtŏs (1),
moth-eaten

MOTHER
517 'êm (143), *mother*
2545 chămôwth (11),
mother-in-law
2859 châthan (1), *to
become related* by
marriage,
282 amētōr (1), *of
unknown maternity*
3384 mētēr (76), *mother*
3994 pĕnthĕra (6), *wife's
mother*

MOTHER'S
517 'êm (67), *mother*
3384 mētēr (7), *mother*

MOTHERS
517 'êm (3), *mother*
3384 mētēr (2), *mother*
3389 mētralō̧as (1),
matricide

MOTHERS'
517 'êm (1), *mother*

MOTIONS
3804 pathēma (1),
passion; suffering

MOULDY
5350 niqqud (2), *crumb,
morsel; biscuit*

MOUNT
55 'âbak (1), *to coil
upward*
1361 gâbahh (1), *to be
lofty; to be haughty*
2022 har (222), *mountain
or range* of hills
2042 hârâr (1), *mountain*
4674 mutstsâb (1),
station, military *post*
5550 çôl°lâh (5), *military
siege mound, rampart*
5927 'âlâh (4), *to ascend,
be high, mount*
7311 rûwm (1), *to be
high; to rise or raise*

3735 ŏrŏs (21), *hill,
mountain*

MOUNTAIN
2022 har (104), *mountain
or range* of hills
2042 hârâr (2), *mountain*
2906 ţûwr (Ch.) (2), *rock
or hill*
3735 ŏrŏs (28), *hill,
mountain*

MOUNTAINS
2022 har (155), *mountain
or range* of hills
2042 hârâr (8), *mountain*
3735 ŏrŏs (13), *hill,
mountain*

MOUNTED
7426 râmam (1), *to rise*

MOUNTING
4608 ma'ăleh (1),
elevation; platform

MOUNTS
5550 çôl°lâh (3), *military
siege mound, rampart*

MOURN
56 'âbal (15), *to bewail*
57 'âbêl (3), *lamenting*
578 'ânâh (1), *to groan,
lament*
584 'ânach (1), *to sigh,
moan*
1897 hâgâh (4), *to
murmur, utter a sound*
5098 nâham (2), *to growl,
groan*
5110 nûwd (1), *to
deplore; to taunt*
5594 çâphad (9), *to tear
the hair, wail*
6937 qâdar (2), *to mourn
in dark garments*
7300 rûwd (1), *to ramble*
2875 kŏptō (1), *to beat
the breast*
3996 pĕnthĕō (5), *to
grieve*

MOURNED
56 'âbal (10), *to bewail*
1058 bâkâh (2), *to weep,
moan*
5594 çâphad (6), *to tear
the hair, wail*
2354 thrēnĕō (2), *to
bewail, lament*
3996 pĕnthĕō (2), *to
grieve*

MOURNER
56 'âbal (1), *to bewail*

MOURNERS
57 'âbêl (2), *lamenting*
205 'âven (1), *trouble,
vanity, wickedness*
5594 çâphad (1), *to tear
the hair, wail*

MOURNETH
56 'âbal (8), *to bewail*
57 'âbêl (1), *lamenting*
1669 dâ'ab (1), *to pine,
feel sorrow*
5594 çâphad (1), *to tear
the hair, wail*

MOURNFULLY
6941 q°dôrannîyth (1), *in
sackcloth*

MOURNING
56 'âbal (2), *to bewail*
57 'âbêl (1), *lamenting*
60 'êbel (24), *lamentation*
205 'âven (1), *trouble,
vanity, wickedness*
585 'ănâchâh (1),
sighing, moaning
1086 bâlâh (1), *to wear
out, decay; consume*
1899 hegeh (1),
muttering; mourning
1993 hâmâh (1), *to be in
great commotion*
3382 Yered (1), *descent*
4553 miçpêd (6),
lamentation, howling
4798 marzêach (1), *cry of
lamentation*
6937 qâdar (4), *to mourn
in dark garments*
6969 qûwn (1), *to chant
or wail at a funeral*
8386 ta'ănîyâh (1),
lamentation
3602 ŏdurmŏs (2),
lamentation
3997 pĕnthŏs (2), *grief,
mourning, sadness*

MOUSE
5909 'akbâr (2), *mouse*

MOUTH
1627 gârôwn (1), *throat*
2441 chêk (14), *area of
mouth*
5716 'ădîy (2), *finery;
outfit; headstall*
6310 peh (326), *mouth;
opening*
6433 pûm (Ch.) (5),
mouth
8651 t°ra' (Ch.) (1), *door;
palace*
3056 lŏgŏs (1), *word,
matter, thing*
4750 stŏma (69), *mouth;
edge*

MOUTHS
6310 peh (12), *mouth;
opening*
6433 pûm (Ch.) (1),
mouth
1993 ĕpistŏmizō (1), *to
silence*
4750 stŏma (4), *mouth;
edge*

MOVE
2782 chârats (1), *to be
alert, to decide*
5110 nûwd (1), *to waver;
to wander, flee*
5128 nûwa' (1), *to waver*
5130 nûwph (1), *to
quiver, vibrate, rock*
6328 pûwq (1), *to waver*
6470 pâ'am (1), *to tap; to
impel or agitate*
7264 râgaz (2), *to quiver*
8318 sherets (1), *swarm,
teeming mass*
2795 kinĕō (2), *to stir,
move, remove*
3056+4160 lŏgŏs (1),
word, matter, thing

MOVEABLE
5128 nûwa' (1), *to waver*

MOVED
1607 gâ'ash (3), *to
agitate violently, shake*
1949 hûwm (1), *to make
an uproar; agitate*
1993 hâmâh (1), *to be in
great commotion*
2111 zûwâ' (1), *to shake
with fear, tremble*
2782 chârats (1), *to be
alert, to decide*
4131 môwţ (19), *to slip,
shake, fall*
4132 môwţ (3), *pole; yoke*
5074 nâdad (1), *to rove,
flee; to drive away*
5120 nûwţ (1), *to quake*
5128 nûwa' (5), *to waver*
5425 nâthar (1), *to jump;
to be agitated*
5496 çûwth (4), *to
stimulate; to seduce*
5648 'âbad (Ch.) (1), *to
do, work, serve*
7043 qâlal (1), *to be,
make light, swift*
7264 râgaz (5), *to quiver*
7363 râchaph (1), *to
brood; to be relaxed*
7430 râmas (1), *to glide
swiftly, move, swarm*
7493 râ'ash (2), *to
undulate, quake*
23 aganaktĕō (1), *to be
indignant*
383 anasĕiō (1), *to
excite, stir up*
761 asalĕutŏs (1),
immovable, fixed
2125 ĕulabĕŏmai (1), *to
have reverence*
2206 zēlŏō (2), *to have
warmth of feeling for*
2795 kinĕō (2), *to stir,
move, remove*
3334 mĕtakinĕō (1), *to be
removed, shifted from*
4525 sainŏ (1), *to shake;
to disturb*
4531 salĕuō (1), *to waver,
i.e. agitate, rock, topple*
4579 sĕiō (1), *to vibrate;
to agitate*
4697 splagchnizŏmai (5),
to feel sympathy, to pity
5342 phĕrō (1), *to bear or
carry*

MOVEDST
5496 çûwth (1), *to
stimulate; to seduce*

MOVER
2795 kinĕō (1), *to stir,
move, remove*

MOVETH
1980 hâlak (1), *to walk;
live a certain way*
2654 châphêts (1), *to be
pleased with, desire*
7430 râmas (5), *to glide
swiftly,* i.e. *crawl,
move, swarm*
8317 shârats (1), *to
wriggle, swarm*

MOVING
5205 nîyd (1), *motion of
the lips in speech*
7169 qârats (1), *to bite
the lips, blink the eyes*

M

MUSICIANS
3451 mŏusikŏs (1), minstrel, musician

MUSICK
2170 zᵉmâr (Ch.) (4), instrumental music
4485 mangîynâh (1), satire, mocking
5058 nᵉgîynâh (1), stringed instrument
7892 shîyr (7), song; singing
4858 sumphōnia (1), concert of instruments

MUSING
1901 hâgîyg (1), complaint, sighing

MUST
318 anagkĕ (1), constraint; distress
1163 dĕi (63), it is (was) necessary
2192 ĕchō (1), to have; hold; keep
2443 hina (1), in order that
3784 ŏphĕilō (1), to owe; to be under obligation

MUSTARD
4615 sinapi (5), mustard

MUSTERED
6633 tsâbâ' (2), to mass an army or servants

MUSTERETH
6485 pâqad (1), to visit, care for, count

MUTH-LABBEN
4192 Mûwth (1), "To die for the son"

MUTTER
1897 hâgâh (1), to murmur, utter a sound

MUTTERED
1897 hâgâh (1), to murmur, utter a sound

MUTUAL
1722+240 ĕn (1), in; during; because of

MUZZLE
2629 châcam (1), to muzzle; block
5392 phimŏō (2), to muzzle; silence

MYRA
3460 Mura (1), Myra

MYRRH
3910 lôṭ (2), sticky gum resin (poss.) ladanum
4753 môr (12), myrrh
4666 smurna (2), myrrh
4669 smurnizō (1), to mix with myrrh

MYRTLE
1918 hădaç (6), myrtle

MYSIA
3463 muriŏi (2), ten thousand

MYSTERIES
3466 mustēriŏn (5), secret

MYSTERY
3466 mustēriŏn (22), secret

NAAM
5277 Na'am (1), pleasure

NAAMAH
5279 Na'âmâh (5), pleasantness

NAAMAN
5283 Na'ămân (15), pleasantness
3497 Nĕĕman (1), pleasantness

NAAMAN'S
5283 Na'ămân (1), pleasantness

NAAMATHITE
5284 Na'ămâthîy (4), Naamathite

NAAMITES
5280 Na'âmîy (1), Naamanite

NAARAH
5292 Na'ărâh (3), female child; servant

NAARAI
5293 Na'ăray (1), youthful

NAARAN
5295 Na'ărân (1), juvenile

NAARATH
5292 Na'ărâh (1), female child; servant

NAASHON
5177 Nachshôwn (1), enchanter

NAASSON
3476 Naassōn (3), enchanter

NABAL
5037 Nâbâl (18), dolt

NABAL'S
5037 Nâbâl (4), dolt

NABOTH
5022 Nâbôwth (22), fruits

NACHON'S
5225 Nâkôwn (1), prepared

NACHOR
5152 Nâchôwr (1), snorer
3493 Nachōr (1), snorer

NADAB
5070 Nâdâb (20), liberal

NAGGE
3477 Naggai (1), (poss.) brilliancy

NAHALAL
5096 Nahălâl (1), pasture

NAHALIEL
5160 Nachălîy'êl (2), valley of God

NAHALLAL
5096 Nahălâl (1), pasture

NAHALOL
5096 Nahălâl (1), pasture

NAHAM
5163 Nacham (1), consolation

NAHAMANI
5167 Nachămânîy (1), consolatory

NAHARAI
5171 Nachăray (1), snorer

NAHARI
5171 Nachăray (1), snorer

NAHASH
5176 Nâchâsh (9), snake

NAHATH
5184 Nachath (5), quiet

NAHBI
5147 Nachbîy (1), occult

NAHOR
5152 Nâchôwr (15), snorer

NAHOR'S
5152 Nâchôwr (2), snorer

NAHSHON
5177 Nachshôwn (9), enchanter

NAHUM
5151 Nachûwm (1), comfortable

NAIL
3489 yâthêd (8), tent peg

NAILING
4338 prŏsēlŏō (1), to nail to something

NAILS
2953 ṭᵉphar (Ch.) (2), finger-nail; claw
4548 maçmêr (4), peg
4930 masmᵉrâh (1), pin on the end of a goad
6856 tsippôren (1), nail; point of a pen
2247 hēlŏs (2), stud, i.e. spike or nail

NAIN
3484 Naïn (1), cf. a home, dwelling; pasture

NAIOTH
5121 Nâvîyth (6), residence

NAKED
4636 ma'ărôm (1), bare, stripped
5783 'ûwr (1), to (be) bare
5903 'êyrôm (9), naked; nudity
6168 'ârâh (1), to be, make bare; to empty
6174 'ârôwm (16), nude; partially stripped
6181 'eryâh (1), nudity
6544 pâra' (3), to loosen; to expose, dismiss
1130 gumnētĕuō (1), go poorly clad, be in rags
1131 gumnŏs (14), nude or poorly clothed

NAKEDNESS
4589 mâ'ôwr (1), nakedness; exposed
4626 ma'ar (1), bare place; nakedness
5903 'êyrôm (1), naked; nudity
6172 'ervâh (50), nudity; disgrace; blemish
1132 gumnŏtēs (3), nudity or poorly clothed

NAME
559 'âmar (2), to say
8034 shêm (735), appellation
8036 shum (Ch.) (8), name

NAHARI

NAME'S
8034 shêm (19), appellation, i.e. name
3686 ŏnŏma (11), name

NAMED
559 'âmar (1), to say
1696 dâbar (1), to speak, say; to subdue
5344 nâqab (1), to specify, designate, libel
7121 qârâ' (5), to call out
7121+8034 qârâ' (1), to call out
8034 shêm (4), appellation, i.e. name
8034+7121 shêm (1), appellation, i.e. name
8036 shum (Ch.) (1), name
2564 kalĕō (2), to call
3004 lĕgō (2), to say
3686 ŏnŏma (28), name
3687 ŏnŏmazō (7), to give a name

NAMELY
1722 ĕn (1), in; during; because of

NAMES
8034 shêm (82), appellation, i.e. name
8036 shum (Ch.) (3), name
3686 ŏnŏma (11), name

NAMETH
3687 ŏnŏmazō (1), to give a name

NAOMI
5281 No'ŏmîy (20), pleasant

NAOMI'S
5281 No'ŏmîy (1), pleasant

NAPHISH
5305 Nâphîysh (2), refreshed

NAPHTALI
5321 Naphtâlîy (49), my wrestling

NAPHTUHIM
5320 Naphtûchîym (1), Naphtuchim

NAPKIN
4676 sŏudariŏn (3), towel

NAPHTUHIM
5320 Naphtûchîym (1), Naphtuchim

NARCISSUS
3488 Narkissŏs (1), stupefaction

NARROW
213 'ûwts (1), to be close, hurry, withdraw
331 'âṭam (4), to close
3334 yâtsar (1), to be in distress
6862 tsar (2), trouble; opponent
2346 thlibō (1), to crowd, press, trouble

NARROWED
4052 miqrâ'âh (1), ledge or offset

NAAM
5277 Na'am (1), pleasure

NACHOR
5152 Nâchôwr (1), snorer

NAME
559 'âmar (2), to say
8034 shêm (735), appellation
8036 shum (Ch.) (8), name

NARROWER
6887 tsârar (1), to *cramp*

NARROWLY
8104 shâmar (1), to *watch*

NATHAN
5416 Nâthân (42), *given*
3481 Nathan (1), *given*

NATHAN-MELECH
5419 Nᵉthan-Melek (1), *given of* (the) *king*

NATHANAEL
3482 Nathanaël (6), *given of God*

NATION
249 'ezrâch (1), *native born*
524 'ummâh (Ch.) (1), *community, clan, tribe*
1471 gôwy (105), *foreign nation; Gentiles*
3816 lᵉ'ôm (1), *community, nation*
5971 'am (2), *people; tribe; troops*
246 allŏphulŏs (1), *Gentile, foreigner*
1074 gĕnĕa (1), *generation; age*
1085 gĕnŏs (2), *kin, offspring in kind*
1484 ĕthnŏs (24), *race; tribe; pagan*

NATIONS
523 'ummâh (1), *community, clan, tribe*
524 'ummâh (Ch.) (7), *community, clan, tribe*
776 'erets (1), *earth, land, soil; nation*
1471 gôwy (266), *foreign nation; Gentiles*
3816 lᵉ'ôm (9), *community, nation*
5971 'am (14), *people; tribe; troops*
1484 ĕthnŏs (37), *race; tribe; pagan*

NATIVE
4138 môwledeth (1), *lineage, native country*

NATIVITY
4138 môwledeth (6), *lineage, native country*
4351 mᵉkûwrâh (1), *origin*

NATURAL
3893 lêach (1), *fresh strength, vigor*
1083 gĕnnēsis (1), *nativity*
2596+6449 kata (2), *down; according to*
5446 phusikŏs (3), *instinctive, natural*
5591 psuchikŏs (4), *physical and brutish*

NATURALLY
1103 gnēsiŏs (1), *genuine, true*
5447 phusikŏs (1), *instinctively, naturally*

NATURE
1078 genesis (1), *nativity, nature*

NAUGHT
5449 phusis (10), *genus or sort; disposition*

NAUGHT
7451 ra' (2), *bad; evil*

NAUGHTINESS
1942 havvâh (1), *desire; craving*
7455 rôa' (1), *badness, evil*
2549 kakia (1), *depravity; malignity; trouble*

NAUGHTY
1100 bᵉlîya'al (1), *wickedness, trouble*
1942 havvâh (1), *desire; craving*
7451 ra' (1), *bad; evil*

NAUM
3486 Naŏum (1), *comfortable*

NAVEL
8270 shôr (2), umbilical *cord; strength*
8306 shârîyr (1), *sinew*
8326 shôrer (1), umbilical *cord*

NAVES
1354 gab (1), *mounded: top, rim; arch, bulwarks*

NAVY
590 'ŏnîy (6), *ship; fleet of ships*

NAY
408 'al (8), *not; nothing*
1571 gam (2), *also; even*
3808 lô' (17), *no, not*
6440 pânîym (1), *face; front*
235 alla (4), *but, yet*
3304 mĕnŏungĕ (1), *so then at least*
3756 ŏu (8), *no or not*
3780 ŏuchi (5), *not indeed*

NAZARENE
3480 Nazōraiŏs (1), *inhabitant of Nazareth*

NAZARENES
3480 Nazōraiŏs (1), *inhabitant of Nazareth*

NAZARETH
3478 Nazarĕth (29), *Nazareth or Nazaret*

NAZARITE
5139 nâzîyr (9), *prince; separated Nazirite*

NAZARITES
5139 nâzîyr (3), *prince; separated Nazirite*

NEAH
5269 Nê'âh (1), *motion*

NEAPOLIS
3496 Nĕapŏlis (1), *new town*

NEAR
413 'êl (1), *to, toward*
681 'êtsel (3), *side; near*
3027 yâd (3), *hand; power*
5060 nâga' (4), *to strike*
5066 nâgash (58), *to be, come, bring near*
5921 'al (1), *above, over, upon, or against*
5973 'îm (1), *with*

7126 qârab (54), *to approach, bring near*
7127 qᵉrêb (Ch.) (5), *to approach, bring near*
7131 qârêb (2), *near*
7132 qᵉrâbâh (1), *approach*
7138 qârôwb (42), *near, close*
7200 râ'âh (1), *to see*
7607 shᵉ'êr (4), *flesh, meat; kindred by blood*
7608 sha'ărâh (1), *female kindred by blood*
316 anagkaiŏs (1), *necessary*
1448 ĕggizō (10), *to approach*
1451 ĕggus (4), *near, close*
4139 plēsiŏn (1), *neighbor, fellow*
4317 prŏsagō (1), *to bring near*
4334 prŏsĕrchŏmai (3), *to come near, visit*

NEARER
7138 qârôwb (1), *near, close*
1452 ĕggutĕrŏn (1), *nearer, closer*

NEARIAH
5294 Nᵉ'aryâh (3), *servant of Jehovah*

NEBAI
5109 Nôwbay (1), *fruitful*

NEBAIOTH
5032 Nᵉbâyôwth (2), *fruitfulnesses*

NEBAJOTH
5032 Nᵉbâyôwth (3), *fruitfulnesses*

NEBALLAT
5041 Nᵉballâṭ (1), *foolish secrecy*

NEBAT
5028 Nᵉbâṭ (25), *regard*

NEBO
5015 Nᵉbôw (13), *Nebo*

NEBUCHADNEZZAR
5019 Nᵉbûwkadne'tstsar (29), *Nebukadnetstsar*
5020 Nᵉbûwkadnetstsar (Ch.) (31), *Nebukadnetstsar*

NEBUCHADREZZAR
5019 Nᵉbûwkadne'tstsar (31), *Nebukadnetstsar*

NEBUSHASBAN
5021 Nᵉbûwshazbân (1), *Nebushazban*

NEBUZAR-ADAN
5018 Nᵉbûwzar'ădân (15), *Nebuzaradan*

NECESSARY
2706 chôq (1), *appointment; allotment*
316 anagkaiŏs (5), *necessary*
318 anagkē (1), *constraint; distress*
1876 ĕpanagkĕs (1), *necessarily*
4314+3588+5532 prŏs (1), *for; on, at; to, toward*

NECESSITIES
318 anagkē (2), *constraint; distress*
5532 chrĕia (1), *demand, requirement*

NECESSITY
316 anagkaiŏs (1), *necessary*
318 anagkē (6), *constraint; distress*
2192+318 ĕchō (1), *to have; hold; keep*
5532 chrĕia (2), *demand, requirement*

NECHO
5224 Nᵉkôw (3), *Neko*

NECK
1621 gargᵉrôwth (4), *throat*
1627 gârôwn (1), *throat*
4665 miphreketh (1), *vertebra of the neck*
6202 'âraph (3), *to break the neck, to destroy*
6203 'ôreph (12), *nape or back of the neck*
6676 tsavva'r (Ch.) (5), *back of the neck*
6677 tsavvâ'r (30), back *of the neck*
5137 trachēlŏs (6), *throat or neck; life*

NECKS
1627 gârôwn (1), *throat*
6203 'ôreph (6), *nape or back of the neck*
6677 tsavvâ'r (10), back *of the neck*
5137 trachēlŏs (1), *throat or neck; life*

NECROMANCER
1875+4191 dârash (1), *to seek or ask; to worship*

NEDABIAH
5072 Nᵉdabyâh (1), *largess of Jehovah*

NEED
2637 châcêr (1), *to lack; to fail, want, make less*
2638 châcêr (1), *lacking*
2818 chăshach (Ch.) (1), *to need*
4270 machçôwr (1), *impoverishment*
6878 tsôrek (1), *need*
1163 dĕi (1), *it is (was) necessary*
2121 ĕukairŏs (1), *opportune, suitable*
2192+5532 ĕchō (8), *to have; hold; keep*
3784 ŏphĕilō (1), *to owe; to be under obligation*
5532 chrĕia (26), *demand, requirement*
5535 chrĕ̦zō (4), *to have necessity, be in want of*

NEEDED
2192+5532 ĕchō (1), *to have; hold; keep*
4326 prŏsdĕŏmai (1), *to require additionally*

NEEDEST
2192+5532 ĕchō (1), *to have; hold; keep*

NEEDETH
422 anĕpaischuntŏs (1), *unashamed*
2192+318 ĕchō (1), *to have; hold; keep*
2192+5532 ĕchō (1), *to have; hold; keep*
5532 chrĕia (1), *demand, requirement*
5535 chrḗizō (1), *to have necessity, be in want of*

NEEDFUL
2819 chashchûwth (1), *necessity*
316 anagkaiŏs (1), *necessary*
318 anagkē (1), *constraint; distress*
1163 dĕi (1), *it is (was) necessary*
2006 ĕpitēdĕiŏs (1), *requisite, needful*
5532 chrĕia (1), *demand, requirement*

NEEDLE
4476 rhaphis (2), *sewing needle*

NEEDLE'S
4476 rhaphis (1), *sewing needle*

NEEDLEWORK
4639+7551 ma'ăseh (1), *action; labor*
7551 râqam (5), *variegation; embroider*
7553 riqmâh (3), *variegation of color; embroidery*

NEEDS
318 anagkē (3), *constraint; distress*
3843 pantōs (1), *entirely; at all events*

NEEDY
34 'ebyôwn (35), *destitute; poor*
1800 dal (2), *weak, thin; humble, needy*
7326 rûwsh (1), *to be destitute*

NEESINGS
5846 'ătîyshâh (1), *sneezing*

NEGINAH
5058 nᵉgîynâh (1), *stringed instrument*

NEGINOTH
5058 nᵉgîynâh (6), *stringed instrument*

NEGLECT
272 amĕlĕō (2), *to be careless of, neglect*
3878 parakŏuō (2), *to disobey*

NEGLECTED
3865 parathĕōrĕō (1), *to overlook or disregard*

NEGLECTING
857 aphĕidia (1), *austerity, asceticism*

NEGLIGENT
7952 shâlâh (1), *to mislead*
272 amĕlĕō (1), *to be careless of, neglect*

NEHELAMITE
5161 Nechĕlâmîy (3), *dreamed*

NEHEMIAH
5166 Nᵉchemyâh (8), *consolation of Jehovah*

NEHILOTH
5155 Nᵉchîylâh (1), *flute*

NEHUM
5149 Nᵉchûwm (1), *comforted*

NEHUSHTA
5179 Nᵉchushtâ' (1), *copper*

NEHUSHTAN
5180 Nᵉchushtân (1), *copper serpent*

NEIEL
5272 Nᵉ'îy'êl (1), *moved of God*

NEIGHBOUR
5997 'âmîyth (7), *comrade or kindred*
7138 qârôwb (2), *near, close*
7453 rêa' (74), *associate; one close*
7468 rᵉ'ûwth (2), *female associate*
7934 shâkên (6), *resident; fellow-citizen*
4139 plēsiŏn (16), *neighbor, fellow*

NEIGHBOUR'S
5997 'âmîyth (2), *comrade or kindred*
7453 rêa' (26), *associate; one close*

NEIGHBOURS
7138 qârôwb (3), *near, close*
7453 rêa' (2), *associate; one close*
7934 shâkên (11), *resident; fellow-citizen*
1069 gĕitōn (4), *neighbour*
4040 pĕriŏikŏs (1), *neighbor*

NEIGHBOURS'
7453 rêa' (1), *associate; one close*

NEIGHED
6670 tsâhal (1), *to be cheerful; to sound*

NEIGHING
4684 matshâlâh (1), *whinnying*

NEIGHINGS
4684 matshâlâh (1), *whinnying*

NEITHER
369 'ayin (40), *there is no, i.e., not exist, none*
408 'al (66), *not; nothing*
518 'îm (5), *whether?; if, although; Oh that!*
1077 bal (3), *nothing; not at all; lest*
1115 biltîy (4), *not, except, without, unless*
1571 gam (5), *also; even*
3608 kele' (2), *prison*

3804 kether (1), *royal headdress*
3808 lô' (475), *no, not*
3809 lâ' (Ch.) (3), *as nothing*
4480 min (2), *from, out of*
2228 ē (4), *or; than*
3361 mē (5), *not; lest*
3366 mĕdĕ (34), *but not, not even; nor*
3383 mētĕ (19), *neither or nor; not even*
3756 ŏu (12), *no or not*
3761 ŏudĕ (67), *neither, nor, not even*
3763 ŏudĕpŏtĕ (1), *never at all*
3777 ŏutĕ (39), *not even*

NEKEB
5346 Neqeb (1), *dell*

NEKODA
5353 Nᵉqôwdâ' (4), *distinction*

NEMUEL
5241 Nᵉmûw'êl (3), *day of God*

NEMUELITES
5242 Nᵉmûw'êlîy (1), *Nemuelite*

NEPHEG
5298 Nepheg (4), *sprout*

NEPHEW
5220 neked (2), *offspring*

NEPHEWS
1121 bên (1), *son, descendant; people*
1549 ĕkgŏnŏn (1), *grandchild*

NEPHISH
5305 Nâphîysh (1), *refreshed*

NEPHISHESIM
5300 Nᵉphûwshᵉçîym (1), *expansions*

NEPHTHALIM
3508 Nĕphthalĕim (2), *my wrestling*

NEPHTOAH
5318 Nephtôwach (2), *spring*

NEPHUSIM
5304 Nᵉphîyçîym (1), *expansions*

NEPTHALIM
3508 Nĕphthalĕim (1), *my wrestling*

NER
5369 Nêr (16), *lamp*

NEREUS
3517 Nĕrĕus (1), *wet*

NERGAL
5370 Nêrgal (1), *Nergal*

NERGAL-SHAREZER
5371 Nêrgal Shar'etser (3), *Nergal-Sharetser*

NERI
3518 Nĕri (1), *light of Jehovah*

NERIAH
5374 Nêrîyâh (10), *light of Jehovah*

NERO
3505 Nĕrōn (1), *Nero*

NEST
7064 qên (12), *nest; nestlings; chamber*
7077 qânan (3), *to nestle*

NESTS
7077 qânan (2), *to nestle*
2682 kataskēnōsis (2), *perch or nest*

NET
2764 chêrem (5), *doomed object*
4364 makmâr (1), *hunter's snare-net*
4685 mâtsôwd (2), *net or snare; besieging tower*
4686 mâtsûwd (2), *net or capture; fastness*
7568 resheth (20), *hunting net; network*
293 amphiblēstrŏn (2), *fishing net which is cast*
1350 diktuŏn (6), *drag net*
4522 sagēnē (1), *seine*

NETHANEEL
5417 Nᵉthan'êl (14), *given of God*

NETHANIAH
5418 Nᵉthanyâh (20), *given of Jehovah*

NETHER
7347 rêcheh (1), *mill-stone*
8481 tachtôwn (5), *bottommost*
8482 tachtîy (9), *lowermost; depths*

NETHERMOST
8481 tachtôwn (1), *bottommost*

NETHINIMS
5411 Nâthîyn (17), *ones given to duty*
5412 Nᵉthîyn (Ch.) (1), *ones given to duty*

NETOPHAH
5199 Nᵉtôphâh (2), *distillation*

NETOPHATHI
5200 Nᵉtôphâthîy (1), *Netophathite*

NETOPHATHITE
5200 Nᵉtôphâthîy (8), *Netophathite*

NETOPHATHITES
5200 Nᵉtôphâthîy (2), *Netophathite*

NETS
2764 chêrem (4), *doomed object*
4364 makmâr (1), *hunter's snare-net*
4365 mikmereth (1), *fishing-net*
7638 sâbâk (1), *netting*
1350 diktuŏn (6), *drag net*

NETTLES
2738 chârûwl (3), *bramble, thorny weed*
7057 qimmôwsh (2), *prickly plant*

NETWORK
4640+7568 Ma'say (2), *operative*
7639 s^ebâkâh (5), *net-work balustrade*

NETWORKS
2355 chôwr (1), *white linen*
7639 s^ebâkâh (2), *net-work balustrade*

NEVER
369 'ayin (2), *there is no, i.e., not exist, none*
408 'al (1), *not; nothing*
1253 bôr (1), *vegetable lye as soap; flux*
1755 dôwr (1), *dwelling*
3808 lô' (17), *no, not*
165 aiōn (1), *perpetuity, ever; world*
3361 mē (1), *not; lest*
3364 ŏu mē (1), *not at all, absolutely not*
3368 mēdĕpŏtĕ (1), *not even ever*
3756 ŏu (5), *no or not*
3762 ŏudĕis (1), *none, nobody, nothing*
3763 ŏudĕpŏtĕ (14), *never at all*
3764 ŏudĕpō (2), *not even yet*

NEVERTHELESS
61 'âbâl (2), *truly, surely; yet, but*
389 'ak (11), *surely; only, however*
403 'âkên (1), *surely!, truly!; but*
657 'epheç (1), *end; no further*
1297 b^eram (Ch.) (1), *however, but*
1571 gam (3), *also; even*
3588 kîy (4), *for, that because*
7535 raq (5), *merely; although*
235 alla (10), *but, yet, except, instead*
1161 dĕ (11), *but, yet; and then*
2544 kaitŏigĕ (1), *although really*
3305 mĕntŏi (1), *however*
4133 plēn (8), *albeit, save that, rather, yet*

NEW
1069 bâkar (1), *bear the first born*
1278 b^erîy'âh (1), *creation*
2319 châdâsh (50), *new, recent*
2320 chôdesh (20), *new moon; month*
2323 chădath (Ch.) (1), *new*
2961 ṭârîy (1), *fresh*
8492 tîyrôwsh (11), *fresh squeezed grape-juice*
46 agnaphŏs (2), *new, unshrunk cloth*
1098 glĕukŏs (1), *sweet wine*
2537 kainŏs (44), *freshness, i.e. new*
3501 nĕŏs (11), *new*

3561 nŏumēnia (1), *festival of new moon*
4372 prŏsphatŏs (1), *lately made, i.e. new*

NEWBORN
738 artigĕnnētŏs (1), *new born; young convert*

NEWLY
6965 qûwm (1), *to rise*
7138 qârôwb (1), *near, close*

NEWNESS
2538 kainŏtēs (2), *renewal, newness*

NEWS
8052 sh^emûw'âh (1), *announcement*

NEXT
312 'achêr (2), *other, another, different; next*
4283 mochŏrâth (3), *tomorrow, next day*
4932 mishneh (7), *duplicate copy; double*
7138 qârôwb (5), *near, close*
839 auriŏn (1), *to-morrow*
1206 dĕutĕraiŏs (1), *on the second day*
1836 hĕxēs (2), *successive, next*
1887 ĕpauriŏn (7), *to-morrow*
1966 ĕpiŏusa (3), *ensuing*
2064 ĕrchŏmai (1), *to go or come*
2087 hĕtĕrŏs (2), *other or different*
2192 ĕchō (3), *to have; hold; keep*
3342 mĕtaxu (1), *betwixt; meanwhile*

NEZIAH
5335 N^etsîyach (2), *conspicuous*

NEZIB
5334 N^etsîyb (1), *station*

NIBHAZ
5026 Nibchaz (1), *Nibchaz*

NIBSHAN
5044 Nibshân (1), *Nibshan*

NICANOR
3527 Nikanōr (1), *victorious*

NICODEMUS
3530 Nikŏdēmŏs (5), *victorious among his people*

NICOLAITANES
3531 Nikŏlaïtēs (2), *adherent of Nicolaüs*

NICOLAS
3532 Nikŏlaŏs (1), *victorious over the people*

NICOPOLIS
3533 Nikŏpŏlis (2), *victorious city*

NIGER
3526 Nigĕr (1), *black*

NIGH
4952 mishrâh (1), *steeped juice*
5060 nâga' (3), *to strike*
5066 nâgash (12), *to be, come, bring near*
7126 qârab (32), *to approach, bring near*
7138 qârôwb (4), *near, close*
7607 sh^e'êr (1), *flesh, meat; kindred by blood*
7934 shâkên (1), *resident; fellow-citizen*
1448 ĕggizō (21), *to approach*
1451 ĕggus (18), *near, close*
3844 para (2), *from; with; besides; on account of*
3897 paraplēsiŏn (1), *almost*
4314 prŏs (1), *for; on, at; to, toward; against*

NIGHT
956 bûwth (Ch.) (1), *to lodge over night*
2822 chôshek (1), *darkness; misery*
3915 layil (208), *night; adversity*
3916 leyl^eyâ' (Ch.) (4), *night*
5399 nesheph (3), *dusk, dawn*
6153 'ereb (4), *dusk*
6916 qiddâh (1), *cassia bark*
8464 tachmâç (2), *unclean bird (poss.) owl*
1273 dianuktĕrĕuō (1), *to pass, spend the night*
3571 nux (60), *night*
3574 nuchthēmĕrŏn (1), *full day*

NIGHTS
3915 layil (15), *night; adversity*
3571 nux (3), *night*

NIMRAH
5247 Nimrâh (1), *clear water*

NIMRIM
5249 Nimrîym (2), *clear waters*

NIMROD
5248 Nimrôwd (4), *Nimrod*

NIMSHI
5250 Nimshîy (5), *extricated*

NINE
8672 têsha' (44), *nine; ninth*
1767 ĕnnĕa (1), *nine*
1768 ĕnnĕnēkŏntaĕnnĕa (4), *ninety-nine*

NINETEEN
8672+6240 têsha' (3), *nine; ninth*

NINETEENTH
8672+6240 têsha' (4), *nine; ninth*

NINETY
8673 tish'îym (20), *ninety*

1768 ĕnnĕnēkŏntaĕnnĕa (4), *ninety-nine*

NINEVE
3535 Ninĕuï (1), *Nineveh*

NINEVEH
5210 Nîyn^evêh (17), *Nineveh*
3536 Ninĕuïtēs (1), *inhabitant of Nineveh*

NINEVITES
3536 Ninĕuïtēs (1), *inhabitant of Nineveh*

NINTH
8671 t^eshîy'îy (18), *ninth*
8672 têsha' (6), *nine; ninth*
1766 ĕnnatŏs (10), *ninth*

NISAN
5212 Nîyçân (2), *Nisan*

NISROCH
5268 Niçrôk (2), *Nisrok*

NITRE
5427 nether (2), *mineral potash for washing*

NOADIAH
5129 Nôw'adyâh (2), *convened of Jehovah*

NOAH
5146 Nôach (44), *rest*
5270 Nô'âh (4), *movement*
3575 Nōĕ (3), *rest*

NOAH'S
5146 Nôach (2), *rest*

NOB
5011 Nôb (6), *fruit*

NOBAH
5025 Nôbach (3), *bark*

NOBLE
3358 yaqqîyr (Ch.) (1), *precious*
6579 partam (1), *grandee, noble*
2104 ĕugĕnēs (2), *high in rank; generous*
2908 krĕissŏn (2), *better, i.e. greater advantage*

NOBLEMAN
937 basilikŏs (2), *befitting the sovereign*
2104+444 ĕugĕnēs (1), *high in rank; generous*

NOBLES
117 'addîyr (7), *powerful; majestic*
678 'âtsîyl (1), *extremity; noble*
1281 bârîyach (1), *fleeing, gliding serpent*
1419 gâdôwl (1), *great*
2715 chôr (13), *noble, i.e. in high rank*
3513 kâbad (1), *to be rich, glorious*
5057 nâgîyd (1), *commander, official*
5081 nâdîyb (4), *magnanimous*
6579 partam (1), *grandee, noble*

NOD
5113 Nôwd (1), *vagrancy*

N

NODAB
5114 Nôwdâb (1), *noble*

NOE
3575 Nôĕ (5), *rest*

NOGAH
5052 Nôgahh (2), *brilliancy*

NOHAH
5119 Nôwchâh (1), *quietude*

NOISE
1949 hûwm (2), to *make an uproar; agitate*
1993 hâmâh (4), to *be in great commotion*
1995 hâmôwn (4), *noise, tumult; many, crowd*
1998 hemyâh (1), *sound, tone*
6476 pâtsach (1), to *break out in sound*
6963 qôwl (48), *voice or sound*
7267 rôgez (1), *disquiet; anger*
7452 rêa' (1), *crash; noise; shout*
7588 shâ'ôwn (8), *uproar; destruction*
8085 shâma' (2), to *hear intelligently*
8643 tᵉrûw'âh (1), *battle-cry; clangor*
8663 tᵉshû'âh (1), *crashing or clamor*
2350 thŏrubĕŏ (1), to *disturb; clamor*
4500 rhŏizĕdŏn (1), *with a crash, with a roar*
5456 phŏnĕ (1), *voice, sound*

NOISED
191 akŏuŏ (1), to *hear; obey*
1096+5408 ginŏmai (1), to *be, become*
1255 dialalĕŏ (1), to *converse, discuss*

NOISOME
1942 havvâh (1), *desire; craving*
7451 ra' (2), *bad; evil*
2556 kakŏs (1), *bad, evil, wrong*

NON
5126 Nûwn (1), *perpetuity*

NOON
6672 tsôhar (11), *window: noon time*
3314 mĕsĕmbria (1), *midday; south*

NOONDAY
6672 tsôhar (10), *window: noon time*

NOONTIDE
6256+6672 'êth (1), *time*

NOPH
5297 Nôph (7), *Noph*

NOPHAH
5302 Nôphach (1), *gust*

NORTH
4215 mᵉzâreh (1), *north wind*
6828 tsâphôwn (128), *north, northern*

1005 borrhas (2), *north*
5566 chôrŏs (66), *north-west* wind

NORTHERN
6828 tsâphôwn (1), *north, northern*
6830 tsᵉphôwnîy (1), *northern*

NORTHWARD
6828 tsâphôwn (24), *north, northern*

NOSE
639 'aph (11), *nose or nostril; face; person*
2763 charam (1), to *devote to destruction*

NOSES
639 'aph (1), *nose or nostril; face; person*

NOSTRILS
639 'aph (13), *nose or nostril; face; person*
5156 nᵉchîyr (1), pair of *nostrils*
5170 nachar (1), *snorting*

NOTABLE
2380 châzûwth (2), *striking appearance*
1110 gnôstŏs (1), *well-known*
1978 ĕpisēmŏs (1), *eminent, prominent*
2016 ĕpiphanēs (1), *conspicuous*

NOTE
2710 châqaq (1), to *engrave; to enact* laws
1978 ĕpisēmŏs (1), *eminent, prominent*
4593 sēmĕiŏŏ (1), to *mark for avoidance*

NOTED
7559 râsham (1), to *record*

NOTHING
369 'ayin (23), *there is no, i.e., not exist, none*
408 'al (3), *not; nothing*
657 'epheç (2), *end; no further*
1099 bᵉlîymâh (1), *nothing whatever*
1115 biltîy (3), *not, except, without, unless*
1697 dâbâr (2), *word; matter; thing*
2600 chinnâm (2), *gratis, free*
3605 kôl (1), *all, any or every*
3808 lô' (25), *no, not*
3809 lâ' (Ch.) (1), *as nothing*
4591 mâ'aṭ (1), to *be, make small or few*
7535 raq (1), *merely; although*
8414 tôhûw (1), *waste, desolation, formless*
114 athĕtĕŏ (1), to *disesteem, neutralize*
3361 mē (1), *not; lest*
3367 mēdĕis (27), *not even one*
3385 mēti (2), *whether at all*

3756 ŏu (4), *no or not*
3762 ŏudĕis (66), *none, nobody, nothing*
3777 ŏutĕ (1), *not even*

NOTICE
5234 nâkar (1), to *acknowledge*
4293 prŏkataggĕllŏ (1), to *predict, promise*

NOTWITHSTANDING
389 'ak (6), *surely; only, however*
657 'epheç (1), *end; no further*
7535 raq (2), *merely; although*
235 alla (1), *but, yet, except, instead*
4133 plēn (4), *albeit, save that, rather, yet*

NOUGHT
205 'âven (1), *trouble, vanity, wickedness*
369 'ayin (1), *there is no, i.e., not exist, none*
408+3972 'al (1), *not; nothing*
434 'ĕlûwl (1), *good for nothing*
656 'âphĕç (1), to *cease*
657 'epheç (1), *end; no further*
659 'êpha' (1), *nothing*
2600 chinnâm (6), *gratis, free*
3808 lô' (1), *no, not*
3808+1697 lô' (1), *no, not*
3808+1952 lô' (1), *no, not*
5034 nâbêl (1), to *wilt; to fall away; to be foolish*
6331 pûwr (1), to *crush*
6544 pâra' (1), to *loosen; to expose, dismiss*
6565 pârar (2), to *break up; to violate, frustrate*
8045 shâmad (1), to *desolate*
8414 tôhûw (2), *waste, desolation, formless*
557 apĕlĕgmŏs (1), *refutation, discrediting*
1432 dōrĕan (1), *gratuitously, freely*
1847 ĕxŏudĕnŏŏ (1), to *be treated with contempt*
1848 ĕxŏuthĕnĕŏ (3), to *treat with contempt*
2049 ĕrēmŏŏ (1), to *lay waste*
2647 kataluŏ (1), to *demolish*
2673 katargĕŏ (2), to *be, render entirely useless*
3762 ŏudĕis (1), *none, nobody, nothing*

NOURISH
1431 gâdal (2), to *be great, make great*
2421 châyâh (1), to *live; to revive*
3557 kûwl (2), to *keep in; to maintain*

NOURISHED
1431 gâdal (1), to *be great, make great*

2421 châyâh (1), to *live; to revive*
3557 kûwl (1), to *keep in; to measure*
7235 râbâh (1), to *increase*
397 anatrĕphō (2), to *rear, care for*
1789 ĕntrĕphō (1), to *educate; to be trained*
5142 trĕphō (3), to *nurse, feed, care for*

NOURISHER
3557 kûwl (1), to *keep in; to measure*

NOURISHETH
1625 ĕktrĕphō (1), to *cherish or train*

NOURISHING
1431 gâdal (1), to *be great, make great*

NOURISHMENT
2023 ĕpichŏrĕgĕŏ (1), to *fully supply; to aid*

NOVICE
3504 nĕŏphutŏs (1), *young convert*

NOW
116 'ĕdayin (Ch.) (2), *then*
227 'âz (1), *at that time or place; therefore*
645 'êphôw (10), *then*
1768 dîy (Ch.) (1), *that; of*
2008 hênnâh (1), *from here; from there*
2088 zeh (3), *this or that*
3117 yôwm (4), *day; time period*
3528 kᵉbâr (4), *long ago, formerly, hitherto*
3588 kîy (2), *for, that because*
3705 kᵉ'an (Ch.) (14), *now*
4994 nâ' (172), *I pray!, please!, I beg you!*
6254 'Ashtᵉrâthîy (1), *Ashterathite*
6258 'attâh (401), *at this time, now*
6288 pᵉ'ôrâh (3), *foliage, branches*
6471 pa'am (5), *time; step; occurence*
737 arti (25), just *now; at once*
1160 dapanē (2), *expense, cost*
1161 dĕ (160), *but, yet; and then*
1211 dĕ (1), *now, then; indeed, therefore*
2235 ēdē (3), *even now*
2236 hēdista (38), *with great pleasure*
2532 kai (5), *and; or; even; also*
3063 lŏipŏn (2), *remaining; finally*
3568 nun (127), *now; the present or immediate*
3570 nuni (20), just *now, indeed, in fact*
3765 ŏukĕti (5), *not yet, no longer*
3767 ŏun (12), *certainly; accordingly*

NUMBER
2714 chêqer (1), examination
3187 yâchas (1), to enroll by family list
4373 mikçâh (1), valuation of a thing
4487 mânâh (7), to allot; to enumerate or enroll
4507 Meniy (1), Apportioner, i.e. Fate
4510 minyân (Ch.) (1), enumeration, number
4557 miçpâr (108), number
4557+3187 miçpâr (1), number
4662 miphqâd (2), designated spot; census
5608 çâphar (10), to inscribe; to enumerate
5736 'âdaph (1), to be redundant
6485 pâqad (14), to visit, care for, count
705 arithmĕō (1), to enumerate or count
706 arithmŏs (18), reckoned number
1469 ĕgkrinō (1), to count among
2639 katalĕgō (1), to enroll, put on a list
3793 ŏchlŏs (2), throng

NUMBERED
4483 menâ' (Ch.) (1), to count, appoint
4487 mânâh (7), to allot; to enumerate or enroll
4557 miçpâr (1), number
5608 çâphar (11), to inscribe; to enumerate
6485 pâqad (102), to visit, care for, count
705 arithmĕō (2), to enumerate or count
2674 katarithmĕō (1), to be numbered among
3049 lŏgizŏmai (1), to credit; to think, regard
4785 sugkatapsēphizō (1), to number with

NUMBEREST
5608 çâphar (1), to inscribe; to enumerate
6485 pâqad (2), to visit, care for, count

NUMBERING
5608 çâphar (1), to inscribe; to enumerate
5610 çephâr (1), census

NUMBERS
4557 miçpâr (1), number
5615 çephôrâh (1), numeration
6486 pequddâh (1), visitation; punishment

NUN
5126 Nûwn (29), perpetuity

NURSE
539 'âman (2), to be firm, faithful, true; to trust
3243 yânaq (7), to suck; to give milk
5162 trŏphŏs (1), nurse-mother

NURSED
539 'âman (1), to be firm, faithful, true; to trust
5134 nûwq (1), to suckle

NURSING
539 'âman (2), to be firm, faithful, true; to trust
3243 yânaq (1), to suck; to give milk

NURTURE
3809 paidĕia (1), disciplinary correction

NUTS
93 'ĕgôwz (1), nut
992 bôṭen (1), pistachio

NYMPHAS
3564 Numphas (1), nymph-born

OAK
424 'êlâh (11), oak
427 'allâh (1), oak
437 'allôwn (3), oak

OAKS
352 'ayîl (1), chief; ram; oak tree
437 'allôwn (5), oak

OAR
4880 mâshôwṭ (1), oar

OARS
4880 mâshôwṭ (1), oar
7885 shayiṭ (1), oar

OATH
423 'âlâh (14), curse, oath
7621 shebûw'âh (26), sworn oath
7650 shâba' (7), to swear
332 anathĕmatizō (1), to declare or vow an oath
3727 hŏrkŏs (7), sacred restraint, i.e. an oath
3728 hŏrkōmŏsia (4), asseveration on oath

OATH'S
3727 hŏrkŏs (2), sacred restraint, i.e. an oath

OATHS
7621 shebûw'âh (2), sworn oath
3727 hŏrkŏs (1), sacred restraint, i.e. an oath

OBADIAH
5662 'Ôbadyâh (20), serving Jehovah

OBAL
5745 'Ôwbâl (1), Obal

OBED
5744 'Ôwbêd (9), serving
5601 Ŏbēd (3), serving

OBED-EDOM
5654 'Ôbêd 'Êdôwm (20), worker of Edom

OBEDIENCE
5218 hupakŏē (11), compliance, submission
5293 hupŏtassō (1), to subordinate; to obey

OBEDIENT
8085 shâma' (8), to hear intelligently
5218 hupakŏē (2), compliance, submission
5219 hupakŏuō (2), to heed or conform

5255 hupēkŏŏs (2), to listen attentively
5293 hupŏtassō (2), to subordinate; to obey

OBEISANCE
7812 shâchâh (9), to prostrate in homage

OBEY
3349 yiqqâhâh (1), obedience
4928 mishma'ath (1), obedience; royal subject
8085 shâma' (40), to hear intelligently
8086 shema' (Ch.) (1), to hear intelligently
544 apĕithĕō (3), to disbelieve
3980 pĕitharchĕō (3), to submit to authority
3982 pĕithō (5), to pacify or conciliate; to assent
5218 hupakŏē (1), compliance, submission
5219 hupakŏuō (13), to heed or conform
5255+1036 hupēkŏŏs (1), to listen attentively

OBEYED
8085 shâma' (34), to hear
3982 pĕithō (2), to pacify or conciliate; to assent
5219 hupakŏuō (5), to heed or conform

OBEYEDST
8085 shâma' (2), to hear

OBEYETH
8085 shâma' (3), to hear

OBEYING
8085 shâma' (2), to hear
5218 hupakŏē (1), compliance, submission

OBIL
179 'Ôwbîyl (1), mournful

OBJECT
2723 katēgŏrĕō (1), to bring a charge

OBLATION
4503 minchâh (5), tribute; offering
4541 maççêkâh (1), libation; woven coverlet
7133 qorbân (11), sacrificial present
8641 terûwmâh (17), sacrifice, tribute
8642 terûwmîyâh (1), sacrificial offering

OBLATIONS
4503 minchâh (1), sacrificial offering
4864 mas'êth (1), raising; beacon; present
7133 qorbân (1), sacrificial present
8641 terûwmâh (2), sacrifice, tribute

OBOTH
88 'Ôbôth (4), water-skins

OBSCURE
380 'îyshôwn (1), pupil; eyeball; middle

OBSCURITY
652 'ôphel (1), dusk, darkness
2822 chôshek (2), darkness; misery

OBSERVATION
3907 paratērēsis (1), careful observation

OBSERVE
5172 nâchash (1), to prognosticate
5341 nâtsar (1), to guard, protect, maintain
6049 'ânan (1), to cover, becloud; to act covertly
6213 'âsâh (3), to do or make
7789 shûwr (1), to spy out, survey
8104 shâmar (41), to watch
3906 paratērĕō (1), to note insidiously
4160 pŏiĕō (1), to make
5083 tērĕō (3), to keep, guard, obey
5442 phulassō (1), to watch, i.e. be on guard

OBSERVED
6049 'ânan (2), to cover, becloud; to act covertly
6213 'âsâh (1), to do or make
7789 shûwr (1), to spy out, survey
8104 shâmar (3), to watch
8107 shimmûr (2), observance
4933 suntērĕō (1), to preserve in memory
5442 phulassō (1), to watch, i.e. be on guard

OBSERVER
6049 'ânan (1), to cover, becloud; to act covertly

OBSERVERS
6049 'ânan (1), to cover, becloud; to act covertly

OBSERVEST
8104 shâmar (1), to watch

OBSERVETH
8104 shâmar (1), to watch

OBSTINATE
553 'âmats (1), to be strong; be courageous
7186 qâsheh (1), severe

OBTAIN
1129 bânâh (1), to build; to establish
2388 châzaq (1), to fasten upon; to seize
5381 nâsag (2), to reach
6329 pûwq (1), to issue; to furnish; to secure
1653 ĕlĕĕō (2), to give out compassion
2013 ĕpitugchanō (1), to attain, obtain
2638 katalambanō (1), to seize; to possess
2983 lambanō (2), to take, receive

O

4047 pĕripŏiēsis (1), acquisition
5177 tugchanŏ (3), to take part in; to obtain

OBTAINED
5375 nâsâ' (5), to lift up
7592 shâ'al (1), to ask
1653 ĕlĕĕŏ (6), to give out compassion
2013 ĕpitugchanō (4), to attain, obtain
2147 hĕuriskŏ (1), to find
2816 klĕrŏnŏmĕŏ (1), to be an heir to, inherit
2820 klĕrŏŏ (1), to allot
2902 kratĕŏ (1), to seize
2932 ktaŏmai (1), to get, i.e. acquire
2975 lagchanŏ (2), to determine by lot
3140 marturĕŏ (3), to testify; to commend
5177 tugchanŏ (2), to take part in; to obtain

OBTAINETH
6329 pûwq (2), to issue; to furnish; to secure

OBTAINING
4047 pĕripŏiēsis (1), acquisition

OCCASION
1556 gâlal (1), to roll; to commit
4672 mâtsâ' (2), to find or acquire; to occur
5308 nᵉphal (Ch.) (1), to fall
5931 'îllâh (Ch.) (3), pretext, legal grounds
8385 ta'ănâh (2), opportunity; purpose
874 aphŏrmē (6), opportunity, pretext
1223 dia (1), through, by means of; because of
4625 skandalŏn (2), snare

OCCASIONED
5437 çâbab (1), to surround

OCCASIONS
5949 'ălîylâh (2), opportunity, action
8569 tᵉnûw'âh (1), enmity

OCCUPATION
4399 mᵉlâ'kâh (1), work; property
4639 ma'ăseh (2), action; labor
5078 tĕchnē (1), trade, craft; skill

OCCUPIED
5414 nâthan (3), to give
5503 çâchar (1), to travel round; to palpitate
6213 'âsâh (1), to do or make
6213+4399 'âsâh (1), to do or make
4043 pĕripatĕŏ (1), to walk; to live a life

OCCUPIERS
6148 'ârab (1), to intermix

OCCUPIETH
378 anaplērŏŏ (1), to complete; to occupy

OCCUPY
6148 'ârab (1), to intermix
4231 pragmatĕuŏmai (1), to trade, do business

OCCURRENT
6294 pega' (1), casual impact

OCRAN
5918 'Okrân (5), muddler

ODD
5736 'âdaph (1), to be redundant

ODED
5752 'Ôwdêd (3), reiteration

ODIOUS
887 bâ'ash (1), to smell bad; be a moral stench
8130 sânê' (1), to hate

ODOUR
3744 ŏsmē (2), fragrance; odor

ODOURS
1314 besem (2), spice; fragrance; balsam
5207 nîchôwach (1), pleasant; delight
5208 nîychôwach (Ch.) (1), pleasure
2368 thumiama (2), incense offering

OFF
5921 'al (65), above, over, upon, or against
114 athĕtĕŏ (1), to neutralize or set aside
554 apĕkduŏmai (2), to divest wholly oneself
568 apĕchŏ (1), to be distant
575 apŏ (13), from, away
595 apŏthĕsis (1), laying aside
609 apŏkŏptŏ (8), mutilate the genitals
631 apŏmassŏmai (1), to scrape away, wipe off
659 apŏtithēmi (3), to put away; get rid of
660 apŏtinassō (1), to brush off, shake off
851 aphairĕŏ (2), to remove, cut off
1537 ĕk (1), out, out of
1562 ĕkduŏ (1), to divest
1575 ĕkklaŏ (4), to exscind, cut off
1581 ĕkkŏptŏ (4), to cut off; to frustrate
1601 ĕkpiptŏ (2), to drop away
1621 ĕktinassŏ (3), to shake violently
3089 luŏ (1), to loosen
3112 makran (1), at a distance, far away
4048 pĕrirrhēgnumi (1), to tear completely away
4496 rhiptŏ (1), to fling, toss; to lay out

OFFENCE
816 'âsham (1), to be guilty; to be punished
4383 mikshôwl (2), stumbling-block
266 hamartia (1), sin

677 aprŏskŏpŏs (3), faultless
3900 paraptōma (5), error; transgression
4348 prŏskŏmma (1), occasion of apostasy
4349 prŏskŏpē (1), occasion of sin
4625 skandalŏn (5), snare

OFFENCES
2399 chêṭ' (1), crime or its penalty
3900 paraptōma (2), error; transgression
4625 skandalŏn (4), snare

OFFEND
816 'âsham (4), to be guilty; to be punished
898 bâgad (1), to act treacherously
2254 châbal (1), to pervert, destroy
4383 mikshôwl (1), stumbling-block
4417 ptaiŏ (3), to trip up, stumble morally
4624 skandalizŏ (14), to entrap, i.e. trip up
4625 skandalŏn (1), snare

OFFENDED
816 'âsham (2), to be guilty; to be punished
819 'ashmâh (1), guiltiness
2398 châṭâ' (4), to sin
6586 pâsha' (1), to break away from authority
264 hamartanŏ (1), to miss the mark, to sin
4624 skandalizŏ (16), to entrap, i.e. trip up

OFFENDER
2398 châṭâ' (1), to sin
91 adikĕŏ (1), to do wrong

OFFENDERS
2400 chaṭṭâ' (1), criminal, guilty

OFFER
2076 zâbach (20), to (sacrificially) slaughter
2077 zebach (1), animal flesh; sacrifice
5066 nâgash (4), to be, come, bring near
5130 nûwph (3), to quiver, vibrate, rock
5186 nâṭâh (1), to stretch or spread out
5190 nâṭal (1), to lift; to impose
5258 nâçak (2), to pour a libation
5260 nᵉçak (Ch.) (1), to pour out a libation
5375 nâsâ' (1), to lift up
5414 nâthan (2), to give
5927 'âlâh (34), to ascend, be high, mount
6213 'âsâh (41), to do or make
6999 qâṭar (1), to turn into fragrance by fire

7126 qârab (79), to approach, bring near
7127 qᵉrêb (Ch.) (2), to approach, bring near
7311 rûwm (14), to be high; to rise or raise
7819 shâchaṭ (1), to slaughter; butcher
399 anaphĕrŏ (3), to lead up; to offer sacrifice
1325 didōmi (2), to give
1929 ĕpididōmi (1), to give over
3930 parĕchō (1), to hold near, i.e. to present
4374 prŏsphĕrŏ (10), to present to; to treat as

OFFERED
1684 dᵉbach (Ch.) (1), to sacrifice an animal
2076 zâbach (17), to (sacrificially) slaughter
2398 châṭâ' (1), to sin
4639 ma'ăseh (1), action; labor
5066 nâgash (2), to be, come, bring near
5068 nâdab (1), to volunteer; to present
5069 nᵉdab (Ch.) (1), be, give without coercion
5130 nûwph (2), to quiver, vibrate, rock
5927 'âlâh (38), to ascend, be high, mount
6213 'âsâh (6), to do or make
6999 qâṭar (2), to turn into fragrance by fire
7126 qârab (16), to approach, bring near
7127 qᵉrêb (Ch.) (1), to approach, bring near
7133 qorbân (1), sacrificial present
7311 rûwm (2), to be high; to rise or raise
8641 tᵉrûwmâh (1), sacrifice, tribute
321 anagŏ (1), to lead up; to bring out; to sail
399 anaphĕrŏ (1), to lead up; to offer sacrifice
1494 ĕidōlŏthutŏn (8), idolatrous offering
4374 prŏsphĕrŏ (14), present to; to treat as
4689 spĕndō (2), to pour out as a libation

OFFERETH
2076 zâbach (1), to (sacrificially) slaughter
2398 châṭâ' (1), to sin
5066 nâgash (1), to be, come, bring near
5926 'îllêg (1), stuttering, stammering
5927 'âlâh (2), to ascend, be high, mount
7126 qârab (9), to approach, bring near

OFFERING
817 'âshâm (1), guilt; fault; sin-offering
2076 zâbach (1), to (sacrificially) slaughter
4503 minchâh (147), tribute; offering

OFFERINGS

5927 'âlâh (9), to *ascend, be high, mount*
5930 'ôlâh (1), *sacrifice wholly consumed in fire*
6213 'âsâh (2), to *make*
7126 qârab (1), to *approach, bring near*
7133 qorbân (66), *sacrificial present*
8573 tᵉnûwphâh (6), *undulation of offerings*
8641 tᵉrûwmâh (40), *sacrifice, tribute*
4374 prŏsphĕrō (2), to *present to; to treat as*
4376 prŏsphŏra (8), *presentation; oblation*

OFFERINGS

1890 habhâb (1), *gift given as a sacrifice*
2077 zebach (5), *animal flesh; sacrifice*
4503 minchâh (16), *tribute; offering*
5262 neçek (1), *libation; cast idol*
7133 qorbân (1), *sacrificial present*
8641 tᵉrûwmâh (10), *sacrifice, tribute*
1435 dôrŏn (1), *sacrificial present*
3646 hŏlŏkautōma (3), *wholly-consumed sacrifice*
4376 prŏsphŏra (1), *presentation; oblation*

OFFICE

3653 kên (1), *pedestal or station of a basin*
4612 ma'ămâd (1), *position; attendant*
5656 'ăbôdâh (1), *work*
6486 pᵉquddâh (3), *visitation; punishment*
1247 diakŏnĕō (2), to *wait upon, serve*
1248 diakŏnia (2), *attendance, aid, service*
1984 ĕpiskŏpē (1), *episcopate*
2405 hiĕratĕia (2), *priestly office*
2407 hiĕratĕuō (1), to *be a priest*
4234 praxis (1), *act; function*

OFFICER

5324 nâtsab (1), to *station*
5333 nᵉtsîyb (1), *military post; statue*
5631 çârîyç (5), *eunuch; official of state*
6496 pâqîyd (2), *superintendent, officer*
4233 praktōr (2), *official collector*
5257 hupĕrĕtēs (1), *servant, attendant*

OFFICERS

5324 nâtsab (6), to *station*
5631 çârîyç (7), *eunuch; official of state*
6213 'âsâh (1), to *do*
6485 pâqad (3), to *visit, care for, count*
6486 pᵉquddâh (3), *visitation; punishment*

6496 pâqîyd (3), *superintendent, officer*
7227 rab (1), *great*
7860 shôṭêr (23), to *write; official who is a scribe*
5257 hupĕrĕtēs (10), *servant, attendant*

OFFICES

4929 mishmâr (1), *guard; deposit; usage; example*
4931 mishmereth (1), *watch, sentry, post*
6486 pᵉquddâh (2), *visitation; punishment*

OFFSCOURING

5501 çᵉchîy (1), *refuse*
4067 pĕripsōma (1), *scum, garbage*

OFFSPRING

6631 tse'ĕtsâ' (9), *produce, children*
1085 gĕnŏs (3), *kin*

OFT

1767 day (1), *enough, sufficient*
3740 hŏsakis (1), *as often as, when*
4178 pŏllakis (5), *many times, i.e. frequently*
4183 pŏlus (1), *much, many*
4212 pŏsakis (1), *how many times*
4435 pugmē (1), *with the fist*

OFTEN

3740 hŏsakis (6), *as often as, when*
4178 pŏllakis (3), *many times, i.e. frequently*
4212 pŏsakis (2), *how many times*
4437 puknŏs (2), *frequent; frequently*

OFTENER

4437 puknŏs (2), *frequent; frequently*

OFTENTIMES

6471+7227 pa'am (1), *time; step; occurence*
6471+7969 pa'am (1), *time; step; occurence*
4178 pŏllakis (3), *many times, i.e. frequently*
4183+5550 pŏlus (1), *much, many*

OFTTIMES

4178 pŏllakis (3), *many times, i.e. frequently*

OG

5747 'Ôwg (22), *round*

OH

518 'îm (1), *whether?; if, although; Oh that!*
577 'ânnâ' (1), *oh now!, I ask you!*
994 bîy (7), *Oh that!*
3863 lûw' (2), *if; would that!*
4994 nâ' (6), *I pray!, please!, I beg you!*

OHAD

161 'Ôhad (2), *unity*

OHEL

169 'Ôhel (1), *Ohel*

OIL

3323 yitshâr (21), *olive oil; anointing*
4887 mᵉshach (Ch.) (2), *olive oil*
6671 tsâhar (1), to *press out olive oil*
8081 shemen (163), *olive oil, wood, lotions*
1637 ĕlaiŏn (11), *olive oil*

OILED

8081 shemen (2), *olive oil, wood, lotions*

OINTMENT

4841 merqâchâh (1), *unguent-kettle*
4842 mirqachath (1), *aromatic unguent*
4888 mishchâh (1), *unction; gift*
7545 rôqach (1), *aromatic; fragrance*
8081 shemen (11), *olive oil, wood, lotions*
3464 murŏn (12), *perfumed oil*

OINTMENTS

8081 shemen (3), *olive oil, wood, lotions*
3464 murŏn (2), *perfumed oil*

OLD

227 'âz (2), *at that time or place; therefore*
865 'ethmôwl (1), *heretofore, formerly*
1086 bâlâh (11), to *wear out, decay; consume*
1087 bâleh (5), *worn out*
1094 bᵉlôw' (3), *rags, worn out fabric*
1121 bên (132), *son, descendant; people*
1247 bar (Ch.) (1), *son, child; descendant*
1323 bath (1), *daughter, descendant, woman*
2204 zâqên (26), to *be old, venerated*
2205 zâqên (41), *old, venerated*
2208 zâqûn (4), *old age*
2209 ziqnâh (6), *old age*
2416 chay (1), *alive; raw; fresh; life*
3117 yôwm (1), *day; time period*
3117+8140+3117 yôwm (1), *day; time period*
3453 yâshîysh (1), *old man*
3462 yâshên (2), to *sleep; to grow old, stale*
3465 yâshân (7), *old*
3833 lâbîy' (1), *lion, lioness*
3918 layish (1), *lion*
5288 na'ar (1), *male child; servant*
5669 'âbûwr (2), *kept over; stored grain*
5703 'ad (1), *perpetuity; ancient*
5769 'ôwlâm (26), *eternity; ancient*
5957 'âlam (Ch.) (2), *forever*

6275 'âthaq (2), to *remove; to grow old*
6440 pânîym (3), *face; front*
6924 qedem (17), *East, eastern; antiquity*
6927 qadmâh (1), *priority in time; before; past*
6931 qadmôwnîy (2), *anterior time; oriental*
7223 rî'shôwn (2), *first*
7350 râchôwq (2), *remote, far*
7872 sêybâh (6), *old age*
7992 shᵉlîyshîy (2), *third*
8027 shâlash (3), to *be, triplicate*
744 archaiŏs (11), *original or primeval*
1088 gĕrōn (1), *aged, old person*
1094 gĕras (1), *senility, old age*
1095 gĕraskō (2), to *be senescent, grow old*
1126 graŏdēs (1), *old lady-like, i.e. silly*
1332 diĕtēs (1), *of two years in age*
1541 hĕkatŏntaĕtēs (1), *centenarian*
1597 ĕkpalai (1), *long ago, for a long while*
3819 palai (2), *formerly; sometime since*
3820 palaiŏs (19), *not recent, worn out, old*
3822 palaiŏō (3), to *become worn out*
4218 pŏtĕ (2), *at some time, ever*
4245 prĕsbutĕrŏs (1), *elderly; older; presbyter*
4246 prĕsbutēs (1), *old man*
5550 chrŏnŏs (1), *space of time, period*

OLDNESS

3821 palaiŏtēs (1), *antiquatedness*

OLIVE

2132 zayith (27), *olive*
8081 shemen (4), *olive oil, wood, lotions*
65 agriĕlaiŏs (2), *wild olive tree*
1636 ĕlaia (4), *olive*
2565 kalliĕlaiŏs (1), *cultivated olive*

OLIVES

2132 zayith (4), *olive*
1636 ĕlaia (11), *olive*

OLIVET

2132 zayith (1), *olive*
1638 ĕlaiŏn (1), *Mt. of Olives*

OLIVEYARD

2132 zayith (1), *olive*

OLIVEYARDS

2132 zayith (5), *olive*

OLYMPAS

3632 ŏinŏphlugia (1), *drunkenness*

OMAR

201 'Ôwmâr (3), *talkative*

OMEGA
5598 Ō (4), last letter of the Greek alphabet

OMER
6016 'ômer (5), sheaf of grain; dry measure

OMERS
6016 'ômer (1), sheaf of grain; dry measure

OMITTED
863 aphiēmi (1), to leave; to pardon, forgive

OMNIPOTENT
3841 pantŏkratōr (1), Absolute sovereign

OMRI
6018 'Omrîy (18), heaping

ONAM
208 'Ôwnâm (4), strong

ONAN
209 'Ôwnân (8), strong

ONCE
227 'âz (1), at that time or place; therefore
259 'echâd (15), first
996 bêyn (1), between; "either...or"
3162 yachad (1), unitedly
4118 mahêr (1), in a hurry
5750 'ôwd (1), again; repeatedly; still; more
6471 pa'am (10), time; step; occurence
6471+259 pa'am (1), time; step; occurence
530 hapax (15), once for all
2178 ĕphapax (5), upon one occasion
3366 mēdĕ (1), but not, not even; nor
3826 pamplēthĕi (1), in full multitude
4218 pŏtĕ (2), at some time, ever

ONE
259 'echâd (658), first
376 'îysh (173), man; male; someone
428 'êl-leh (2), these or those
492 'almônîy (1), certain so and so, whoever
802 'ishshâh (8), woman, wife; women, wives
1397 geber (1), person, man
1571 gam (1), also; even
1668 dâ' (Ch.) (2), this
1836 dên (Ch.) (1), this
2063 zô'th (1), this
2088 zeh (10), this or that
2297 chad (1), one
2298 chad (Ch.) (5), one; single; first; at once
3605 kôl (1), all, any
3627 kᵉlîy (1), implement, thing
3671 kânâph (1), edge or extremity; wing
5315 nephesh (1), life; breath; soul; wind
6918 qâdôwsh (2), sacred
240 allēlōn (77), one another

243 allŏs (4), different, other
1438 hĕautŏu (6), himself, herself, itself
1515 ĕirēnē (1), peace; health; prosperity
1520 hĕis (231), one
2087 hĕtĕrŏs (1), other or different
3303 mĕn (2), not translated
3391 mia (56), one or first
3442 mŏnŏphthalmŏs (2), one-eyed
3661 hŏmŏthumadŏn (12), unanimously
3675 hŏmŏphrōn (1), like-minded
3739 hŏs (1), who, which, what, that
3956 pas (2), all, any, every, whole
4861 sumpsuchŏs (1), similar in sentiment
5100 tis (35), some or any person or object
5129 tŏutŏi (1), in this person or thing

ONES
1121 bên (1), son, descendant; people

ONESIMUS
3682 Ŏnēsimŏs (4), profitable

ONESIPHORUS
3683 Ŏnēsiphŏrŏs (2), profit-bearer

ONIONS
1211 betsel (1), onion

ONLY
259 'echâd (2), first
389 'ak (33), surely; only, however
905 bad (35), apart, only, besides
910 bâdâd (1), separate, alone
2108 zûwlâh (1), except; apart from; besides
3162 yachad (1), unitedly
3173 yâchîyd (7), only son; alone; beloved
3535 kibsâh (1), ewe sheep
3697 kâçam (1), to shear, clip
7535 raq (52), merely; although
1520 hĕis (1), one
3439 mŏnŏgĕnēs (9), sole, one and only
3440 mŏnŏn (62), merely, just
3441 mŏnŏs (24), single, only; by oneself

ONO
207 'Ôwnôw (5), strong

ONYCHA
7827 shᵉchêleth (1), scale or shell, mussel

ONYX
7718 shôham (11), (poss.) pale green beryl stone

OPEN
1540 gâlâh (6), to denude; uncover

3605 kôl (1), all, any or every
4725 mâqôwm (1), general locality, place
5869 'ayin (1), eye; sight; fountain
6358 pâṭûwr (4), opened; bud
6363 peṭer (1), firstling, first born
6440 pânîym (13), face; front
6475 pâtsâh (3), to rend, i.e. open
6491 pâqach (10), to open the eyes
6555 pârats (1), to break out
6566 pâras (1), to break apart, disperse, scatter
6605 pâthach (49), to open wide; to loosen
6606 pᵉthach (Ch.) (1), to open
6610 pithchôwn (1), act of opening the mouth
8365 shâtham (2), to unveil, i.e. open
71 agō (1), to lead; to bring, drive; to weigh
343 anakaluptō (1), to unveil
455 anŏigō (21), to open up
1722+457 ĕn (1), in; during; because of
3856 paradĕigmatizō (1), to expose to infamy
4271 prŏdēlŏs (1), obvious, evident

OPENED
1540 gâlâh (3), to denude; uncover
3738 kârâh (1), to dig; to plot; to bore, hew
6473 pâ'ar (3), to open wide
6475 pâtsâh (7), to rend, i.e. open
6491 pâqach (7), to open the eyes
6589 pâsaq (1), to dispart, i.e., spread
6605 pâthach (51), to open wide; to loosen
6606 pᵉthach (Ch.) (1), to open
380 anaptussō (1), to unroll a scroll
455 anŏigō (53), to open up
1272 dianŏigō (6), to open thoroughly
4977 schizō (1), to split or sever
5136 trachēlizō (1), to lay bare

OPENEST
6605 pâthach (2), to open wide; to loosen, begin

OPENETH
1540 gâlâh (3), to denude; uncover
6363 peṭer (7), firstling, first born
6491 pâqach (2), to open the eyes

6589 pâsaq (1), to dispart, i.e., spread
6605 pâthach (4), to open wide; to loosen, begin
455 anŏigō (3), to open up
1272 dianŏigō (1), to open thoroughly

OPENING
4668 maphtêach (1), opening; key
4669 miphtâch (1), utterance of lips
6491 pâqach (1), to open the eyes
6495 pᵉqach-qôwach (1), jail-delivery; salvation
6605 pâthach (1), to open wide; to loosen, begin
6610 pithchôwn (1), act of opening the mouth
1272 dianŏigō (1), to open thoroughly

OPENINGS
6607 pethach (1), opening; door, entrance

OPENLY
5879 'Êynayim (1), double fountain
1219 dēmŏsiŏs (1), public; in public
1717 ĕmphanēs (1), apparent in self, seen
1722+3588+5318 ĕn (3), in; during; because of
1722+3954 ĕn (2), in; during; because of
3954 parrhēsia (4), frankness, boldness
5320 phanĕrōs (2), plainly, i.e. clearly

OPERATION
4639 ma'âseh (2), action; labor
1753 ĕnĕrgĕia (1), efficiency, energy

OPERATIONS
1755 ĕnĕrgēma (1), effect, activity

OPHEL
6077 'Ôphel (5), fortress

OPHIR
211 'Ôwphîyr (13), Ophir

OPHNI
6078 'Ophnîy (1), Ophnite

OPHRAH
6084 'Ophrâh (8), female fawn

OPINION
1843 dêa' (3), knowledge

OPINIONS
5587 çâ'îph (1), divided in mind; sentiment

OPPORTUNITY
170 akairĕŏmai (1), to fail of a proper occasion
2120 ĕukairia (2), favorable occasion
2540 kairŏs (2), occasion, set time

OPPOSE
475 antidiatithĕmai (1), be disputatious

OPPOSED
498 antitassŏmai (1), *oppose, resist*

OPPOSEST
7852 sâṭam (1), to *persecute*

OPPOSETH
480 antikĕimai (1), to be an *opponent*

OPPOSITIONS
477 antithĕsis (1), *opposition*

OPPRESS
1792 dâkâ' (1), to *pulverize; be contrite*
3238 yânâh (5), to *suppress; to maltreat*
3905 lâchats (5), to *press; to distress*
6206 'ârats (1), to *awe; to dread; to harass*
6231 'âshaq (9), to *oppress; to defraud*
7703 shâdad (1), to *ravage*
2616 katadunastĕuō (1), to *oppress, exploit*

OPPRESSED
1790 dak (3), *injured, oppressed*
2541 châmôwts (1), *violent*
3238 yânâh (3), to *suppress; to maltreat*
3905 lâchats (7), to *press; to distress*
5065 nâgas (2), to *exploit; to tax, harass*
6217 'âshûwq (1), used *tyranny*
6231 'âshaq (11), to *oppress; to defraud*
6234 'oshqâh (1), *anguish, trouble*
7533 râtsats (6), to *crack in pieces, smash*
2616 katadunastĕuō (1), to *oppress, exploit*
2669 katapŏnĕō (1), to *harass, oppress*

OPPRESSETH
3905 lâchats (1), to *press; to distress*
6231 'âshaq (3), to *oppress; to defraud*
6887 tsârar (1), to *cramp*

OPPRESSING
3238 yânâh (3), to *suppress; to maltreat*

OPPRESSION
3238 yânâh (1), to *suppress; to maltreat*
3906 lachats (7), *distress*
4939 mispâch (1), *slaughter*
6115 'ôtser (1), *closure; constraint*
6125 'âqâh (1), *constraint*
6233 'ôsheq (12), *injury; fraud; distress*
7701 shôd (1), *violence, ravage, destruction*

OPPRESSIONS
4642 ma'ăshaqqâh (1), *oppression*

OPPOSED *(col. 2)*
6217 'âshûwq (2), used *tyranny*

OPPRESSOR
376+2555 'îysh (1), *man; male; someone*
3238 yânâh (1), to *suppress; to maltreat*
4642 ma'ăshaqqâh (1), *oppression*
5065 nâgas (5), to *exploit; to tax, harass*
6184 'ârîyts (1), *powerful or tyrannical*
6216 'âshôwq (1), *tyrant*
6231 'âshaq (2), to *oppress; to defraud*
6693 tsûwq (2), to *oppress, distress*

OPPRESSORS
3905 lâchats (1), to *press; to distress*
5065 nâgas (2), to *exploit; to tax, harass*
6184 'ârîyts (2), *powerful or tyrannical*
6231 'âshaq (2), to *oppress; to defraud*
7429 râmaç (1), to *tread upon*

ORACLE
1687 dᵉbîyr (16), *inmost part of the sanctuary*
1697 dâbâr (1), *word; matter; thing*

ORACLES
3051 lŏgiŏn (4), *utterance of God*

ORATION
1215 dēmēgŏrĕō (1), to *address an assembly*

ORATOR
3908 lachash (1), *incantation; amulet*
4489 rhētōr (1), *legal advocate*

ORCHARD
6508 pardêç (1), *park, cultivated garden area*

ORCHARDS
6508 pardêç (1), *park, cultivated garden area*

ORDAIN
3245 yâçad (1), *settle, establish a foundation*
7760 sûwm (1), to *put, place*
8239 shâphath (1), to *place or put*
1299 diatassō (1), to *institute, prescribe*
2525 kathistēmi (1), to *designate, constitute*

ORDAINED
3245 yâçad (1), *settle, establish a foundation*
3559 kûwn (1), to *set up: establish, fix, prepare*
4483 mᵉnâ' (Ch.) (1), to *count, appoint*
5414 nâthan (2), to *give*
5975 'âmad (1), to *stand*
6186 'ârak (2), to *set in a row, i.e. arrange,*
6213 'âsâh (3), to *do or make*
6965 qûwm (1), to *rise*

OPPOSED *(col. 3)*
7760 sûwm (2), to *put, place*
1096 ginŏmai (1), to *be, become*
1299 diatassō (2), to *institute, prescribe*
2525 kathistēmi (2), to *designate, constitute*
2680 kataskĕuazō (1), to *prepare thoroughly*
2919 krinō (1), to *decide; to try, condemn, punish*
3724 hŏrizō (2), to *appoint, decree, specify*
4160 pŏiĕō (1), to *make or do*
4270 prŏgraphō (1), to *announce, prescribe*
4282 prŏĕtŏimazō (1), to *fit up in advance*
4304 prŏmĕlĕtaō (1), to *premeditate*
5021 tassō (2), to *arrange, assign*
5087 tithēmi (2), to *place*
5500 chĕirŏtŏnĕō (3), to *select or appoint*

ORDAINETH
6466 pâ'al (1), to *do, make or practice*

ORDER
631 'âçar (1), to *fasten; to join battle*
1700 dibrâh (1), *reason, suit or style; because*
3027 yâd (2), *hand; power*
3559 kûwn (3), to *set up: establish, fix, prepare*
4634 ma'ărâkâh (1), *arrangement, row; pile*
4941 mishpâṭ (5), *verdict; formal decree; justice*
5468 çeder (1), to *arrange, order*
6186 'ârak (19), to *set in a row, i.e. arrange,*
6187 'êrek (1), *pile, equipment, estimate*
6471 pa'am (1), *time; step; occurence*
6680 tsâvâh (3), to *constitute, enjoin*
7947 shâlab (1), to *make equidistant*
8626 tâqan (1), to *straighten; to compose*
1299 diatassō (3), to *institute, prescribe*
1930 ĕpidiŏrthŏō (1), to *arrange additionally*
2517 kathĕxēs (3), in a *sequence, subsequent*
5001 tagma (1), *series or succession*
5010 taxis (10), *succession; kind*

ORDERED
3559 kûwn (1), to *set up: establish, fix, prepare*
4634 ma'ărâkâh (1), *arrangement, row; pile*
6186 'ârak (2), to *set in a row, i.e. arrange,*

ORDERETH
7760 sûwm (1), to *put, place*

ORDERINGS
6486 pᵉquddâh (1), *visitation; punishment*

ORDERLY
4748 stŏichĕō (1), to *follow, walk; to conform*

ORDINANCE
2706 chôq (6), *appointment; allotment*
2708 chuqqâh (12), to *delineate*
3027 yâd (1), *hand; power*
4931 mishmereth (3), *watch, sentry, post*
4941 mishpâṭ (5), *verdict; formal decree; justice*
1296 diatagē (1), *institution*
2937 ktisis (1), *formation*

ORDINANCES
2706 chôq (3), *appointment; allotment*
2708 chuqqâh (10), to *delineate*
4687 mitsvâh (1), *command*
4941 mishpâṭ (6), *verdict; formal decree; justice*
1345 dikaiōma (3), *statute or decision*
1378 dŏgma (2), *law*
1379 dŏgmatizō (1), to *submit to a certain rule*
3862 paradŏsis (1), *precept; tradition*

ORDINARY
2706 chôq (1), *appointment; allotment*

OREB
6157 'ârôb (6), *swarming mosquitoes*

OREN
767 'Ôren (1), *ash tree*

ORGAN
5748 'ûwgâb (3), *reed-instrument*

ORGANS
5748 'ûwgâb (1), *reed-instrument*

ORION
3685 Kᵉçîyl (3), *constellation Orion*

ORNAMENT
642 'êphuddâh (1), *plating*
2481 châlîy (1), *polished trinket, ornament*
3880 livyâh (2), *wreath*
5716 'ădîy (2), *finery; outfit; headstall*

ORNAMENTS
5716 'ădîy (9), *finery; outfit; headstall*
5914 'ekeç (1), *anklet, bangle*
6287 pᵉ'êr (1), *fancy head-dress*
6807 tsᵉ'âdâh (1), *march; ankle-chain*
7720 sahărôn (2), *round pendant or crescent*

ORNAN
771 'Ornân (11), *strong*

ORPAH
6204 'Orpâh (2), *mane*

ORPHANS
3490 yâthôwm (1), child
alone, fatherless child

OSEE
5617 Hōsēĕ (1), deliverer

OSHEA
1954 Hôwshêä' (2),
deliverer

OSPRAY
5822 'oznîyâh (2), (poss.)
sea-eagle

OSSIFRAGE
6538 pereç (2), kind of
eagle

OSTRICH
5133 nôwtsâh (1),
plumage

OSTRICHES
3283 yâ'ên (1), ostrich

OTHER
251 'âch (1), brother;
relative; member
259 'echâd (32), first
269 'achôwth (1), sister
312 'achêr (99), other,
another, different; next,
more
317 'ochŏrîy (Ch.) (1),
other, another
321 'ochŏrân (Ch.) (3),
other, another
428 'êl-leh (3), these or
those
2063 zô'th (2), this
2088 zeh (16), this or that
3541 kôh (1), thus
3671 kânâph (1), edge or
extremity; wing
5048 neged (2), over
against or before
5676 'êber (25), opposite
side; east
6311 pôh (5), here or
hence
7453 rêa' (2), associate;
one close
7605 she'âr (1),
remainder
8145 shênîy (36), second;
again
237 allachŏthĕn (1), from
elsewhere
240 allēlōn (5), one
another
243 allŏs (51), different,
other
244 allotriĕpiskŏpŏs (1),
meddler, busybody
245 allŏtriŏs (2), not
one's own
492 antiparĕrchŏmai (2),
to go along opposite
846 autŏs (1), he, she, it
1520 hĕis (7), one
1565 ĕkĕinŏs (2), that one
1622 ĕktŏs (1), aside
from, besides; except
2084 hĕtĕrŏglōssŏs (1),
foreigner
2085 hĕtĕrŏdidaskalĕō
(1), to instruct
differently
2087 hĕtĕrŏs (34), other
or different
2548 kakĕinŏs (2),
likewise that or those

3062 lŏipŏi (16),
remaining ones
3739 hŏs (2), who, which,
what, that
4008 pĕran (12), across,
beyond

OTHERS
312 'achêr (9), other,
another, different; next
428 'êl-leh (1), these
243 allŏs (29), different,
other
245 allŏtriŏs (1), not
one's own
2087 hĕtĕrŏs (11), other
or different
3062 lŏipŏi (9),
remaining ones
3588 hŏ (2), "the," i.e. the
definite article
3739 hŏs (1), who, which

OTHERWISE
176 'ôw (1), or, whether
3808 lô' (1), no, not
243 allŏs (1), different,
other
247 allŏs (1), differently
1490 ĕi dĕ mĕ(gĕ) (3), but
if not
1893 ĕpĕi (4), since
2085 hĕtĕrŏdidaskalĕō
(1), to instruct
differently
2088 hĕtĕrŏs (1),
differently, otherly

OTHNI
6273 'Otnîy (1), forcible

OTHNIEL
6274 'Othnîy'êl (7), force
of God

OUCHES
4865 mishbᵉtsâh (8),
reticulated setting

OUGHT
1697 dâbâr (2), word;
matter; thing
3972 mᵉ'ûwmâh (6),
something; anything
4465 mimkâr (1),
merchandise
1163 dĕi (29), it is (was)
necessary
3762 ŏudĕis (1), none,
nobody, nothing
3784 ŏphĕilō (15), to owe;
to be under obligation
5100 tis (8), some or any
5534 chrē (1), it needs
(must or should) be

OUGHTEST
1163 dĕi (3), it is (was)
necessary

OUTCAST
5080 nâdach (1), to push
off, scattered

OUTCASTS
1760 dâchâh (3), to push
down; to totter
5080 nâdach (4), to push
off, scattered

OUTER
2435 chîytsôwn (1), outer
wall side; exterior;
secular
1857 ĕxōtĕrŏs (3),
exterior, outer

OUTGOINGS
4161 môwtsâ' (1), going
forth
8444 tôwtsâ'âh (7), exit,
boundary; deliverance

OUTLANDISH
5237 nokrîy (1), foreign;
non-relative

OUTLIVED
748+3117+310 'ârak (1),
to be, make long

OUTMOST
7020 qîytsôwn (1),
terminal, end
7097 qâtseh (2), extremity

OUTRAGEOUS
7858 shetseph (1), deluge,
torrent

OUTRUN
4370+5032 prŏstrĕchō (1),
to hasten by running

OUTSIDE
2351 chûwts (2), outside,
outdoors; open market
7097 qâtseh (3), extremity
1623 hĕktŏs (1), sixth
1855 ĕxōthĕn (2),
outside, external (-ly)

OUTSTRETCHED
5186 nâţâh (3), to stretch
or spread out

OUTWARD
2435 chîytsôwn (8), outer
wall side; exterior
5869 'ayin (1), eye; sight;
fountain
1722+3588+5318 ĕn (1),
in; during; because of
1854 ĕxō (1), out, outside
1855 ĕxōthĕn (2),
outside, external (-ly)
4383 prŏsōpŏn (1), face,
presence

OUTWARDLY
1722+5318 ĕn (1), in;
during; because of
1855 ĕxōthĕn (1),
outside, external (-ly)

OUTWENT
4281 prŏĕrchŏmai (1), to
go onward, precede

OVEN
8574 tannûwr (10),
fire-pot
2823 klibanŏs (2),
earthen pot

OVENS
8574 tannûwr (1), fire-pot

OVER
413 'êl (19), to, toward
1157 bᵉ'ad (1), up to or
over against
1541 gᵉlâh (Ch.) (1), to
reveal mysteries
1591 gᵉnêbâh (1),
something stolen
1869 dârak (1), to tread,
trample; to walk, lead
2498 châlaph (1), to
hasten away; to pass on
3148 yôwthêr (1),
moreover; rest; gain
4136 mûwl (14), in front
of, opposite
4480 min (1), from, out of

4605 ma'al (3), upward,
above, overhead
5048 neged (27), over
against or before
5226 nêkach (1), opposite
5227 nôkach (9),
opposite, in front of
5414 nâthan (1), to give
5462 çâgar (2), to shut
up; to surrender
5534 çâkar (1), to shut
up; to surrender
5674 'âbar (171), to cross
over; to transition
5736 'âdaph (3), to have
surplus
5764 'ûwl (2), nursing
babe
5848 'âţaph (1), to
shroud, i.e. clothe
5921 'al (406), above,
over, upon, or against
5922 'al (Ch.) (12), above,
over, upon, or against
5924 'êllâ' (Ch.) (1), above
5927 'âlâh (1), to ascend,
be high, mount
5975 'âmad (1), to stand
5980 'ummâh (23), near,
beside, along with
6440 pânîym (2), face;
front
6743 tsâlach (1), to push
forward
6903 qᵉbêl (Ch.) (1), in
front of, before
7235 râbâh (1), to
increase
481 antikru (1), opposite
of
495 antipĕran (1), on the
opposite side
561 apĕnanti (2),
opposite, before
1224 diabainō (1), to
pass by, over, across
1276 diapĕraō (5), to
cross over
1277 diaplĕō (1), to sail
through, across
1330 diĕrchŏmai (4), to
traverse, travel through
1537 ĕk (3), out, out of
1608 ĕkpŏrnĕuō (1), to be
utterly unchaste
1722 ĕn (1), in; during;
because of
1883 ĕpanō (6), over or on
1909 ĕpi (49), on, upon
1924 ĕpigraphō (1), to
inscribe, write upon
2596 kata (2), down;
according to
2634 katakuriĕuō (1), to
control, lord over
2713 katĕnanti (4),
directly opposite
3346 mĕtatithēmi (1), to
transport; to exchange
3860 paradidōmi (2), to
hand over
3928 parĕrchŏmai (1), to
go by; to perish
4008 pĕran (3), across,
beyond
4012 pĕri (2), about;
around
4052 pĕrissĕuō (1), to
superabound

1438 hĕautŏu (24), *himself, herself, itself*
1683 ĕmautŏu (2), *myself*
1699 ĕmŏs (2), *my*
2398 idiŏs (76), *private or separate*
2596 kata (1), *down; according to*
4572 sĕautŏu (2), *of yourself*

OWNER
113 'âdôwn (1), *sovereign, i.e. controller*
1167 ba'al (10), *master; husband; owner; citizen*
7069 qânâh (1), *to create; to procure*
3490 nauklĕrŏs (1), ship *captain*

OWNERS
1167 ba'al (4), *master; husband; owner; citizen*
2962 kuriŏs (1), *supreme, controller, Mr.*

OWNETH
2076 ĕsti (1), he (she or it) *is; they are*

OX
441 'allûwph (1), *friend, one familiar; chieftain, leader*
1241 bâqâr (3), *plowing ox; herd*
7794 shôwr (53), *bullock*
8377 tᵉ'ôw (1), *antelope*
1016 bŏus (4), *ox, cattle*

OXEN
441 'allûwph (1), *friend, one familiar; chieftain*
504 'eleph (2), *ox; cow or cattle*
1241 bâqâr (74), *plowing ox; herd*
5091 nâhâh (1), *to bewail; to assemble*
6499 par (2), *bullock*
7794 shôwr (8), *bullock*
8450 tôwr (Ch.) (4), *bull*
1016 bŏus (4), *ox, cattle*
5022 taurŏs (2), *bullock, ox*

OZEM
684 'Ôtsem (2), *strong*

OZIAS
3604 Ŏzias (2), *strength of Jehovah*

OZNI
244 'Oznîy (1), *having (quick) ears*

OZNITES
244 'Oznîy (1), *having (quick) ears*

PAARAI
6474 Pa'ăray (1), *yawning*

PACATIANA
3818 Pakatianē (1), *Pacatianian*

PACES
6806 tsa'ad (1), *pace or regular step*

PACIFIED
3722 kâphar (1), *to placate or cancel*
7918 shâkak (1), *to lay a trap; to allay*

PACIFIETH
3240 yânach (1), *to allow to stay*
3711 kâphâh (1), *to tame or subdue*

PACIFY
3722 kâphar (1), *to cover; to placate*

PADAN
6307 Paddân (1), *table-land of Aram*

PADAN-ARAM
6307 Paddân (10), *table-land of Aram*

PADDLE
3489 yâthêd (1), tent *peg*

PADON
6303 Pâdôwn (2), *ransom*

PAGIEL
6295 Pag'îy'êl (5), *accident of God*

PAHATH-MOAB
6355 Pachath Môw'âb (6), *pit of Moâb*

PAI
6464 Pâ'ûw (1), *screaming*

PAID
3052 yᵉhab (Ch.) (1), *to give*
5414 nâthan (1), *to give*
591 apŏdidōmi (2), *to give away*

PAIN
2256 chebel (1), *company, band*
2342 chûwl (6), *to dance, whirl; to writhe in pain*
2427 chîyl (3), *throe of painful childbirth*
2470 châlâh (1), *to be weak, sick, afflicted*
2479 chalchâlâh (4), *writhing in childbirth*
3510 kâ'ab (1), *to feel pain; to grieve; to spoil*
3511 kᵉ'êb (1), *suffering; adversity*
4341 mak'ôb (2), *anguish; affliction*
5999 'âmâl (1), *wearing effort; worry*
4192 pŏnŏs (2), *toil, i.e. anguish*

PAINED
2342 chûwl (3), *to dance, whirl; to writhe in pain*
3176 yâchal (1), *to wait; to be patient, hope*
928 basanizō (1), *to torture, torment*

PAINFUL
5999 'âmâl (1), *wearing effort; worry*

PAINFULNESS
3449 mŏchthŏs (1), *sadness*

PAINS
4712 mêtsar (1), *trouble*
6735 tsîyr (1), *hinge; trouble*
4192 pŏnŏs (1), *toil, i.e. anguish*

PAINTED
4886 mâshach (1), *to rub or smear with oil*
7760+6320 sûwm (1), *to put, place*

PAINTEDST
3583 kâchal (1), *to paint the eyes with stibnite*

PAINTING
6320 pûwk (1), *stibium*

PAIR
2201 zĕugŏs (1), *team, pair*
2218 zugŏs (1), *coupling, yoke*

PALACE
643 'appeden (1), *pavilion or palace-tent*
759 'armôwn (4), *citadel, high fortress*
1002 bîyrâh (17), *palace, citadel*
1004 bayith (1), *house; temple; family, tribe*
1055 bîythân (3), *large house*
1964 hêykâl (8), *palace; temple; hall*
1965 hêykal (Ch.) (4), *palace; temple*
2038 harmôwn (1), *high castle or fortress*
2918 tîyrâh (1), *fortress; hamlet*
833 aulē (7), *palace; house; courtyard*
4232 praitōriŏn (1), *court-room or palace*

PALACES
759 'armôwn (27), *citadel, high fortress*
1964 hêykâl (3), *palace; temple; hall*
2918 tîyrâh (1), *fortress; hamlet*

PALAL
6420 Pâlâl (1), *judge*

PALE
2357 châvar (1), *to blanch with shame*
5515 chlōrŏs (1), *greenish, verdant*

PALENESS
3420 yêrâqôwn (1), *paleness; mildew*

PALESTINA
6429 Pᵉlesheth (3), *migratory*

PALESTINE
6429 Pᵉlesheth (1), *migratory*

PALLU
6396 Pallûw' (4), *distinguished*

PALLUITES
6384 Pallû'îy (1), *Palluite*

PALM
3709 kaph (2), hollow of *hand; paw; sole of foot*
8558 tâmâr (12), *palm tree*

PALM
8560 tômer (2), *palm trunk*
8561 timmôr (17), *palm-like pilaster*
4475 rhapisma (1), *slap, strike*
5404 phŏinix (1), *palm-tree*

PALMERWORM
1501 gâzâm (3), kind of *locust*

PALMS
3709 kaph (4), hollow of *hand; paw; sole of foot*
4474 rhapizō (1), *to slap, rap, strike*
4475 rhapisma (1), *slap, strike*
5404 phŏinix (1), *palm-tree*

PALSIES
3886 paraluō (1), *to be paralyzed or enfeebled*

PALSY
3885 paralutikŏs (10), *lame person*
3886 paraluō (3), *to be paralyzed or enfeebled*

PALTI
6406 Palţîy (1), *delivered*

PALTIEL
6409 Palţîy'êl (1), *deliverance of God*

PALTITE
6407 Palţîy (1), *Paltite*

PAMPHYLIA
3828 Pamphulia (5), *every-tribal, i.e. heterogeneous*

PAN
3595 kîyôwr (1), *caldron; washbowl*
4227 machăbath (6), metal *pan for baking in*
4958 masrêth (1), *pan*

PANGS
2256 chebel (2), *company, band*
2427 chîyl (2), *throe of painful childbirth*
6735 tsîyr (3), *hinge; herald, trouble*
6887 tsârar (2), *to cramp*

PANNAG
6436 Pannag (1), *food, (poss.) pastry*

PANS
2281 châbêth (1), *griddle-cake*
5518 çîyr (1), *thorn; hook*
6517 pârûwr (1), *skillet*
6745 tsêlâchâh (1), *flattened out platter*

PANT
7602 shâ'aph (1), *to be angry; to hasten*

PANTED
7602 shâ'aph (1), *to be angry; to hasten*
8582 tâ'âh (1), *to vacillate, i.e. reel*

PANTETH
5503 çâchar (1), *to travel round; to palpitate*

PAPER
6165 'ârag (2), to *long for, pant for*

PAPER
6169 'ârâh (1), *bulrushes, reeds*
5489 chartês (1), *sheet of papyrus paper*

PAPHOS
3974 Paphŏs (2), *Paphus*

PAPS
7699 shad (1), *female breast*
3149 mastŏs (3), *female breast; chest area*

PARABLE
4912 mâshâl (17), *pithy maxim; taunt*
3850 parabŏlē (31), *fictitious narrative*
3942 parŏimia (1), *illustration; adage*

PARABLES
4912 mâshâl (1), *pithy maxim; taunt*
3850 parabŏlē (15), *fictitious narrative*

PARADISE
3857 paradĕisŏs (3), *park*

PARAH
6511 Pârâh (1), *heifer*

PARAMOURS
6370 pîylegesh (1), *concubine; paramour*

PARAN
6290 Pâ'rân (11), *ornamental*

PARBAR
6503 Parbâr (2), *Parbar or Parvar*

PARCEL
2513 chelqâh (5), *allotment*
5564 chŏriŏn (1), *spot or plot of ground*

PARCHED
2788 chârêr (1), *arid, parched*
7039 qâlîy (6), *roasted ears of cereal grain*
8273 shârâb (1), *glow of the hot air; mirage*

PARCHMENTS
3200 mĕmbrana (1), *sheep-skin for writing*

PARDON
3722 kâphar (1), to *cover; to expiate*
5375 nâsâ' (3), to *lift up*
5545 çâlach (11), to *forgive*
5547 çᵉlîychâh (1), *pardon*

PARDONED
5545 çâlach (2), to *forgive*
7521 râtsâh (1), to *be pleased with; to satisfy*

PARDONETH
5375 nâsâ' (1), to *lift up*

PARE
6213 'âsâh (1), to *do or make*

PARENTS
1118 gŏnĕus (19), *parents*

3962 patêr (1), *father*
4269 prŏgŏnŏs (1), *ancestor*

PARLOUR
3957 lishkâh (1), *room*
5944 'ălîyâh (4), *upper things; second-story*

PARLOURS
2315 cheder (1), *apartment, chamber*

PARMASHTA
6534 Parmashtâ' (1), *Parmashta*

PARMENAS
3937 Parmĕnas (1), *constant*

PARNACH
6535 Parnak (1), *Parnak*

PAROSH
6551 Par'ôsh (5), *flea*

PARSHANDATHA
6577 Parshandâthâ' (1), *Parshandatha*

PART
2505 châlaq (3), to *be smooth; be slippery*
2506 chêleq (19), *allotment*
2513 chelqâh (1), *flattery; allotment*
2673 châtsâh (1), to *cut or split in two; to halve*
2677 chêtsîy (3), *half or middle, midst*
4481 min (Ch.) (5), *from or out of*
4490 mânâh (1), *ration; lot or portion*
4940 mishpâchâh (2), *family, clan, people*
5337 nâtsal (1), to *deliver; snatched away*
6418 pelek (7), *spindle-whorl; crutch*
6447 paç (Ch.) (2), *palm of the hand*
6504 pârad (1), to *spread or separate*
6626 pâthath (1), to *break, crumble*
7117 qᵉtsâth (1), *termination; portion*
2819 klērŏs (2), *lot, portion*
3307 mĕrizŏ (1), to *apportion, share*
3310 mĕris (5), *portion, share, participation*
3313 mĕrŏs (17), *division or share*
3348 mĕtĕchŏ (1), to *share or participate*
4119 plĕiŏn (1), *more*
4403 prumna (1), *stern of a ship*

PARTAKER
2506 chêleq (1), *smoothness; allotment*
2841 kŏinŏnĕŏ (2), to *share or participate*
2844 kŏinŏnŏs (1), *associate, partner*
3335 mĕtalambanō (1), to *participate*
3348 mĕtĕchŏ (2), to *share or participate*

4777 sugkakŏpathĕŏ (1), to *suffer hardship with*
4791 sugkŏinŏnŏs (1), *co-participant*

PARTAKERS
482 antilambanŏmai (1), to *succor; aid*
2841 kŏinŏnĕŏ (3), to *share or participate*
2844 kŏinŏnŏs (4), *associate, partner*
3310 mĕris (1), *portion, share, participation*
3335 mĕtalambanō (1), to *participate*
3348 mĕtĕchŏ (3), to *share or participate*
3353 mĕtŏchŏs (4), *sharer, associate*
4790 sugkŏinŏnĕŏ (1), to *co-participate in*
4791 sugkŏinŏnŏs (1), *co-participant*
4829 summĕrizŏmai (1), to *share jointly*
4830 summĕtŏchŏs (2), *co-participant*

PARTAKEST
1096+4791 Bĕlᵗᵉsha'tstsar (Ch.) (1), *Belteshatstsar*

PARTED
2505 châlaq (2), to *be smooth; be slippery*
2673 châtsâh (1), to *cut or split in two; to halve*
6504 pârad (2), to *spread or separate*
1266 diamĕrizō (6), to *have dissension*
1339 diïstēmi (1), to *remove, intervene*

PARTETH
6504 pârad (1), to *spread or separate*
6536 pâraç (2), to *break in pieces; to split*

PARTHIANS
3934 Parthŏs (1), *inhabitant of Parthia*

PARTIAL
5375+6440 nâsâ' (1), to *lift up*
1252 diakrinō (1), to *decide; to hesitate*

PARTIALITY
87 adiakritŏs (1), *impartial*
4346 prŏsklisis (1), *favoritism*

PARTICULAR
3313 mĕrŏs (1), *division or share*
3588+1520 hŏ (1), *"the," i.e. the definite article*

PARTICULARLY
1520+1538+2596 hĕis (1), *one*
2596+3313 kata (1), *down; according to*

PARTING
517 'êm (1), *mother*

PARTITION
5674 'âbar (1), to *cross over; to transition*

5418 phragmŏs (1), *fence or enclosing barrier*

PARTLY
7118 qᵉtsâth (Ch.) (1), *termination; portion*
1161 dĕ (1), *but, yet*
3313+5100 mĕrŏs (1), *division or share*
5124+3303 tŏutŏ (1), *that thing*

PARTNER
2505 châlaq (1), to *be smooth; be slippery*
2844 kŏinŏnŏs (2), *associate, partner*

PARTNERS
2844 kŏinŏnŏs (1), *associate, partner*
3353 mĕtŏchŏs (1), *sharer, associate*

PARTRIDGE
7124 qôrê' (2), *calling partridge*

PARTS
905 bad (1), *limb, member; bar*
1335 bether (2), *section, piece*
1506 gezer (1), *portion, piece*
1697 dâbâr (1), *word; matter; thing*
2506 chêleq (6), *smoothness; allotment*
2677 chêtsîy (1), *half or middle, midst*
3027 yâd (3), *hand; power*
3411 yᵉrêkâh (2), *recesses, far places*
5409 nêthach (1), *fragment*
6310 peh (1), *mouth; opening*
7098 qâtsâh (1), *termination; fringe*
2825 klinē (1), *couch*
3313 mĕrŏs (6), *division or share*

PARUAH
6515 Pârûwach (1), *blossomed*

PARVAIM
6516 Parvayim (1), *Parvaim*

PAS-DAMMIM
6450 Paç Dammîym (1), *dell of bloodshed*

PASACH
6457 Pâçak (1), *divider*

PASEAH
6454 Pâçêach (3), *limping*

PASHUR
6583 Pashchûwr (14), *liberation*

PASS
935 bôw' (3), to *go or come*
1980 hâlak (1), to *walk; live a certain way*
2498 châlaph (2), to *hasten away; to pass on*
2499 chălaph (Ch.) (4), to *have time pass by*
3615 kâlâh (1), to *cease, be finished, perish*

P

PASSAGE

4569 ma'ăbâr (1), crossing-place
5674 'âbar (153), to cross over; to transition
5709 'ădâ' (Ch.) (1), to pass on or continue
6213 'âsâh (5), to do or make
6452 pâçach (2), to hop, skip over; to hesitate
390 anastrĕphō (1), to remain, to live
1224 diabainō (1), to pass by, over, across
1276 diaperaō (1), to cross over
1279 diaporĕuŏmai (1), to travel through
1330 diĕrchŏmai (7), to traverse, travel through
3928 parĕrchŏmai (19), to go by; to perish
5230 hupĕrakmŏs (1), past the bloom of youth

PASSAGE

1552 gᵉlîylâh (1), circuit or region
4569 ma'ăbâr (2), crossing-place
5674 'âbar (1), to cross over; to transition

PASSAGES

4569 ma'ăbâr (4), crossing-place
5676 'êber (1), opposite side; east

PASSED

1431 gâdal (1), to be great, make great
2498 châlaph (2), to hasten away; to pass on
5674 'âbar (117), to cross over; to transition
5709 'ădâ' (Ch.) (1), to pass on or continue
5710 'ădâh (1), to pass on or continue; to remove
6437 pânâh (1), to turn, to face
6452 pâçach (1), to hop, skip over; to hesitate
492 antiparĕrchŏmai (2), to go along opposite
565 apĕrchŏmai (1), to go off, i.e. depart
1224 diabainō (1), to pass by, over, across
1276 diaperaō (3), to cross over
1330 diĕrchŏmai (11), to traverse, travel through
1353 diŏdĕuō (1), to travel through
3327 mĕtabainō (2), to depart, move from
3855 paragō (6), to go along or away
3899 parapŏĕruŏmai (4), to travel near
3928 parĕrchŏmai (3), to go by; to perish, neglect
4281 prŏĕrchŏmai (1), to go onward, precede

PASSEDST

5674 'âbar (1), to cross over; to transition

PASSENGERS

5674 'âbar (4), to cross over; to transition
5674+1870 'âbar (1), to cross over; to transition

PASSEST

5674 'âbar (5), to cross over; to transition

PASSETH

1980 hâlak (4), to walk; live a certain way
2498 châlaph (1), to hasten away; to pass on
5674 'âbar (28), to cross over; to transition
3855 paragō (2), to go along or away
3928 parĕrchŏmai (1), to go by; to perish
5235 hupĕrballō (1), to surpass
5242 hupĕrĕchō (1), to excel; superior

PASSING

5674 'âbar (7), to cross over; to transition
1330 diĕrchŏmai (2), to traverse, travel through
2064 ĕrchŏmai (1), to go, come
3881 paralĕgŏmai (1), to sail past
3928 parĕrchŏmai (1), to go by; to perish

PASSION

3958 paschō (1), to experience pain

PASSIONS

3663 hŏmŏiŏpathēs (2), similarly affected

PASSOVER

6453 Peçach (48), Passover
3957 pascha (28), Passover events

PASSOVERS

6453 Peçach (1), Passover

PAST

369 'ayin (1), there is no, i.e., not exist, none
5493 çûwr (2), to turn off
5674 'âbar (8), to cross over; to transition
6924 qedem (1), eastern; antiquity; before
7223 ri'shôwn (1), first
7291 râdaph (1), to run after with hostility
7725 shûwb (1), to turn back; to return
8032 shilshôwm (9), day before yesterday
421 anĕxichniastŏs (1), untraceable
524 apalgĕō (1), become apathetic
565 apĕrchŏmai (2), to go off, i.e. depart
1096 ginŏmai (2), to be, become
1230 diaginŏmai (1), to have time elapse
1330 diĕrchŏmai (1), to traverse, travel through
3819 palai (1), formerly; sometime since

3844 para (1), from; with; besides; on account of
3855 paragō (1), to go along or away
3928 parĕrchŏmai (3), to go by; to perish
3944 parŏichŏmai (1), to escape along
4266 prŏginŏmai (1), to have previously transpired
4302 prŏlĕgō (1), to predict, forewarn

PASTOR

7462 râ'âh (1), to tend a flock, i.e. pasture it

PASTORS

7462 râ'âh (7), to tend a flock, i.e. pasture it
4166 pŏimēn (1), shepherd

PASTURE

4829 mir'eh (11), pasture; haunt
4830 mir'îyth (8), pasturage; flock
3542 nŏmē (1), pasture, i.e. the act of feeding

PASTURES

3733 kar (2), ram sheep
4829 mir'eh (2), pasture; haunt
4830 mir'îyth (1), pasturage; flock
4945 mashqeh (1), butler; drink; well-watered
4999 nâ'âh (5), home, dwelling; pasture
7471 rᵉ'îy (1), pasture

PATARA

3959 Patara (1), Patara

PATE

6936 qodqôd (1), crown of the head

PATH

734 'ôrach (9), road; manner of life
4546 mᵉçillâh (1), main thoroughfare; viaduct
4570 ma'gâl (3), circular track or camp rampart
4934 mish'ôwl (1), narrow passage
5410 nâthîyb (8), (beaten) track, path
7635 shâbîyl (1), track or passage-way

PATHROS

6624 Pathrôwç (5), Pathros

PATHRUSIM

6625 Pathrûçîy (2), Pathrusite

PATHS

734 'ôrach (16), road; manner of life
4546 mᵉçillâh (1), main thoroughfare; viaduct
4570 ma'gâl (6), circular track or camp rampart
5410 nâthîyb (8), (beaten) track, path
7635 shâbîyl (1), track or passage-way
5147 tribŏs (3), rut, or worn track

5163 trŏchia (1), course of conduct, path of life

PATHWAY

1870+5410 derek (1), road; course of life

PATIENCE

3114 makrŏthumĕō (3), to be forbearing, patient
3115 makrŏthumia (2), forbearance; fortitude
5281 hupŏmŏnē (29), endurance, constancy

PATIENT

750 'ârêk (1), patient
420 anĕxikakŏs (1), forbearing
1933 ĕpiĕikēs (1), mild, gentle
3114 makrŏthumĕō (3), to be forbearing, patient
5278 hupŏmĕnō (1), to undergo, bear (trials)
5281 hupŏmŏnē (2), perseverence

PATIENTLY

2342 chûwl (1), to dance, whirl; to wait; to pervert
6960 qâvâh (1), to collect; to expect
3114 makrŏthumĕō (1), to be forbearing, patient
3116 makrŏthumōs (1), with long, enduring temper, i.e. leniently
5278 hupŏmĕnō (2), to undergo, bear (trials)

PATMOS

3963 Patmŏs (1), Patmus

PATRIARCH

3966 patriarchēs (2), progenitor or patriarch

PATRIARCHS

3966 patriarchēs (2), progenitor or patriarch

PATRIMONY

1+5921 'âb (1), father

PATROBAS

3969 Patrŏbas (1), father's life

PATTERN

4758 mar'eh (1), appearance; vision
8403 tabnîyth (9), structure; model
8508 toknîyth (1), admeasurement
5179 tupŏs (2), shape, resemblance; "type"
5296 hupŏtupōsis (1), example, pattern

PATTERNS

5262 hupŏdĕigma (1), exhibit; specimen

PAU

6464 Pâ'ûw (1), screaming

PAUL

3972 Paulŏs (157), little

PAUL'S

3972 Paulŏs (6), little

PAULUS

3972 Paulŏs (1), little

PAVED
3840 libnâh (1),
transparency
7528 râtsaph (1), to
tessellate, embroider

PAVEMENT
4837 martsepheth (1),
pavement, stone base
7531 ritspâh (7), hot
stone; pavement
3037 lithŏs (1), stone

PAVILION
5520 çôk (1), hut of
entwined boughs
5521 çukkâh (2),
tabernacle; shelter
8237 shaphrûwr (1),
tapestry or canopy

PAVILIONS
5521 çukkâh (3),
tabernacle; shelter

PAW
3027 yâd (2), hand; power

PAWETH
2658 châphar (1), to
delve, to explore

PAWS
3709 kaph (1), hollow of
hand; paw; sole of foot

PAY
5414 nâthan (2), to give
5414+4377 nâthan (1), to
give
5415 nethan (Ch.) (1), to
give
5927 'âlâh (1), to ascend,
be high, mount
7725 shûwb (1), to turn
back; to return
7999 shâlam (19), to be
safe; be, make complete
8254 shâqal (4), to
suspend in trade
586 apŏdĕkatŏŏ (1), to
tithe, give a tenth
591 apŏdidōmi (7), to
give away
5055 tĕlĕŏ (2), to end,
discharge (a debt)

PAYED
7999 shâlam (1), to be
safe; be, make complete
1183 dĕkatŏŏ (1), to give
or take a tenth

PAYETH
7999 shâlam (1), to be
safe; be, make complete

PAYMENT
591 apŏdidōmi (1), to
give away

PEACE
1826 dâmam (1), to be
silent; to be astonished
2013 hâçâh (2), to hush,
be quiet
2790 chârash (26), to be
silent; to be deaf
2814 châshâh (9), to
hush or keep quiet
6963 qôwl (1), voice or
sound
7962 shalvâh (1),
security, ease
7965 shâlôwm (169),
safe; well; health, peace

PEELED
7999 shâlam (11), to be
safe; be, make complete
8001 shelâm (Ch.) (4),
prosperity
8002 shelem (87), thank
offering
1515 ĕirēnē (87), peace;
health; prosperity
1517 ĕirēnŏpŏiĕŏ (1), to
harmonize, make peace
1518 ĕirēnŏpŏiŏs (3),
peaceable
2270 hēsuchazō (2), to
refrain
4263 prŏbatŏn (1), sheep
4601 sigaŏ (4), to keep
silent
4623 siōpaŏ (9), to be
quiet
5392 phimŏŏ (2), to
muzzle; restrain to
silence

PEACEABLE
7961 shâlêv (1), careless,
carefree; security
7965 shâlôwm (2), safe;
well; health, peace
7999 shâlam (1), to be
safe; be, make complete
8003 shâlêm (1),
complete; friendly; safe
1516 ĕirēnikŏs (2),
pacific, peaceful
2272 hēsuchiŏs (1), still,
undisturbed

PEACEABLY
7962 shalvâh (2),
security, ease
7965 shâlôwm (9), safe;
well; health, peace
1518 ĕirēnŏpŏiŏs (1),
peaceable

PEACEMAKERS
1518 ĕirēnŏpŏiŏs (1),
peaceable

PEACOCKS
7443 renen (1), female
ostrich
8500 tukkîy (2), (poss.)
peacock

PEARL
3135 margaritēs (2), pearl

PEARLS
1378 gâbîysh (1), crystal
3135 margaritēs (7), pearl

PECULIAR
5459 çegullâh (5), wealth
1519+4047 ĕis (1), to or
into
4041 pĕriŏusiŏs (1),
special, one's very own

PEDAHEL
6300 Pedah'êl (1), God
has ransomed

PEDAHZUR
6301 Pedâhtsûwr (5),
Rock has ransomed

PEDAIAH
6305 Pedâyâh (8),
Jehovah has ransomed

PEDIGREES
3205 yâlad (1), to bear
young; to father a child

PEELED
4178 môwrâṭ (2),
obstinate, independent
4803 mâraṭ (1), to polish;
to make bald

PEEP
6850 tsâphaph (1), to coo
or chirp as a bird

PEEPED
6850 tsâphaph (1), to coo
or chirp as a bird

PEKAH
6492 Peqach (11), watch

PEKAHIAH
6494 Peqachyâh (3),
Jehovah has observed

PEKOD
6489 Peqôwd (2),
punishment

PELAIAH
6411 Pelâyâh (3),
Jehovah has
distinguished

PELALIAH
6421 Pelalyâh (1),
Jehovah has judged

PELATIAH
6410 Pelaṭyâh (5),
Jehovah has delivered

PELEG
6389 Peleg (7),
earthquake

PELET
6404 Peleṭ (2), escape

PELETH
6431 Peleth (2), swiftness

PELETHITES
6432 Pelêthîy (7), courier
or official messenger

PELICAN
6893 qâ'ath (3), pelican

PELONITE
6397 Pelôwnîy (3),
separate

PEN
2747 cheret (1), chisel;
style for writing
5842 'êṭ (4), stylus; reed
pen
7626 shêbeṭ (1), stick;
clan, family
2563 kalamŏs (1), reed;
pen

PENCE
1220 dēnariŏn (5),
denarius

PENIEL
6439 Penûw'êl (1), face of
God

PENINNAH
6444 Peninnâh (3), round
pearl

PENKNIFE
8593 ta'ar (1), knife;
razor; scabbard

PENNY
1220 dēnariŏn (9),
denarius

PENNYWORTH
1220 dēnariŏn (2),
denarius

PENTECOST
4005 pĕntēkŏstē (3), the
festival of Pentecost

PENUEL
6439 Penûw'êl (7), face of
God

PENURY
4270 machçôwr (1),
impoverishment
5303 hustĕrēma (1),
deficit; poverty; lacking

PEOPLE
376 'îysh (1), man; male;
someone
523 'ummâh (1),
community, clan, tribe
528 'Âmôwn (1), Amon
582 'ĕnôwsh (1), man;
person, human
1121 bên (1), son,
descendant; people
1471 gôwy (11), foreign
nation; Gentiles
3816 le'ôm (24),
community, nation
5712 'êdâh (1),
assemblage; family
5971 'am (1827), people;
tribe; troops
5972 'am (Ch.) (15),
people, nation
1218 dēmŏs (4), public,
crowd
1484 ĕthnŏs (2), race;
tribe; pagan
2992 laŏs (138), people;
public
3793 ŏchlŏs (83), throng

PEOPLE'S
5971 'am (2), people;
tribe; troops
2992 laŏs (2), people;
public

PEOPLES
2992 laŏs (2), people;
public

PEOR
6465 Pe'ôwr (4), gap

PEOR'S
6465 Pe'ôwr (1), gap

PERADVENTURE
194 'ûwlay (23), if not;
perhaps
3863 lûw' (1), if; would
that!
6435 pên (1), lest, not
3379 mēpŏtĕ (1), not
ever; if, or lest ever
5029 tacha (1), shortly,
i.e. possibly

PERAZIM
6559 Perâtsîym (1),
breaks

PERCEIVE
995 bîyn (1), to
understand; discern
3045 yâda' (7), to know
7200 râ'âh (1), to see
8085 shâma' (1), to hear
intelligently
991 blĕpŏ (1), to look at
1097 ginŏskŏ (2), to know
1492 ĕidō (3), to know
2334 thĕōrĕō (4), to see;
to discern

2638 katalambanō (1), to seize; to possess
3539 nŏiĕŏ (2), to exercise the mind
3708 hŏraŏ (1), to stare, see clearly; to discern

PERCEIVED
238 'ăzan (1), to listen
995 bîyn (3), to understand; discern
3045 yâda' (11), to know
5234 nâkar (1), to acknowledge
7200 râ'âh (4), to see
8085 shâma' (1), to hear intelligently
143 aisthanŏmai (1), to apprehend
1097 ginōskō (7), to know
1921 ĕpiginōskō (3), to become fully acquainted with
2147 hĕuriskō (1), to find
2638 katalambanō (1), to possess; to understand
2657 katanŏĕō (1), to observe fully

PERCEIVEST
3045 yâda' (1), to know
2657 katanŏĕō (1), to observe fully

PERCEIVETH
995 bîyn (1), to understand; discern
2938 ţâ'am (1), to taste; to perceive, experience
7789 shûwr (1), to spy out, survey

PERCEIVING
1492 ĕidō (3), to know

PERDITION
684 apŏlĕia (8), ruin or loss

PERES
6537 pᵉraç (Ch.) (1), to split up

PERESH
6570 Peresh (1), excrement

PEREZ
6557 Perets (3), breech

PEREZ-UZZA
6560 Perets 'Uzzâ' (1), break of Uzza

PEREZ-UZZAH
6560 Perets 'Uzzâ' (1), break of Uzza

PERFECT
1584 gâmar (1), to end; to complete; to fail
1585 gᵉmar (Ch.) (1), complete
3559 kûwn (1), to render sure, proper
3632 kâlîyl (3), whole, entire; complete; whole
3634 kâlal (1), to complete
4357 miklâh (1), wholly, solidly
7999 shâlam (1), to be safe; be, make complete
8003 shâlêm (15), complete; friendly; safe

8503 taklîyth (1), extremity
8535 tâm (9), morally pious; gentle, dear
8537 tôm (1), prosperity
8549 tâmîym (18), entire, complete; integrity
8552 tâmam (2), to complete, finish
195 akribĕia (1), exactness
197 akribĕstĕrŏn (1), more exactly
199 akribōs (1), exactly, carefully
739 artiŏs (1), complete, thorough, capable
2005 ĕpitĕlĕō (1), to terminate; to undergo
2675 katartizō (1), to repair; to prepare
3647 hŏlŏklēria (1), wholeness
4137 plērŏō (1), to fill, make complete
5046 tĕlĕiŏs (17), complete; mature
5048 tĕlĕiŏō (13), to perfect, complete

PERFECTED
3634 kâlal (1), to complete
5927+724 'âlâh (1), to ascend, be high, mount
8003 shâlêm (1), complete; friendly; safe
2675 katartizō (1), to repair; to prepare
5048 tĕlĕiŏō (4), to perfect, complete

PERFECTING
2005 ĕpitĕlĕō (1), to terminate; to undergo
2677 katartismŏs (1), complete furnishing

PERFECTION
3632 kâlîyl (1), whole, entire; complete; whole
4359 miklâl (1), perfection of beauty
4512 minleh (1), wealth
8502 tiklâh (1), completeness
8503 taklîyth (2), extremity
8537 tôm (1), completeness
2676 katartisis (1), thorough equipment
5050 tĕlĕiōsis (1), completion; verification
5051 tĕlĕiŏtēs (1), consummator, perfecter
5052 tĕlĕsphŏrĕō (1), to ripen fruit

PERFECTLY
998 bîynâh (1), discernment
197 akribĕstĕrŏn (3), more exactly
199 akribōs (1), exactly, carefully
1295 diasōzō (1), to cure, preserve, rescue
2675 katartizō (1), to repair; to prepare

PERFECTNESS
5047 tĕlĕiōtēs (1), completeness; maturity

PERFORM
5414 nâthan (1), to give
6213 'âsâh (12), to do or make
6633 tsâbâ' (1), to mass an army or servants
6965 qûwm (13), to rise
7999 shâlam (4), to be safe; be, make complete
591 apŏdidōmi (1), to give away
2005 ĕpitĕlĕō (2), to terminate; to undergo
2716 katĕrgazŏmai (1), to finish; to accomplish
4160 pŏiĕō (2), to do

PERFORMANCE
2005 ĕpitĕlĕō (1), to terminate; to undergo
5050 tĕlĕiōsis (1), completion; verification

PERFORMED
1214 bâtsa' (1), to plunder; to finish
6213 'âsâh (5), to do or make
6965 qûwm (11), to rise
7999 shâlam (1), to be safe; be, make complete
1096 ginŏmai (1), to be, become
2005 ĕpitĕlĕō (1), to terminate; to undergo
5055 tĕlĕō (1), to end, i.e. complete, execute

PERFORMETH
1584 gâmar (1), to end; to complete; to fail
6965 qûwm (1), to rise
7999 shâlam (2), to be safe; be, make complete

PERFORMING
6381 pâlâ' (2), to be, make great, wonderful

PERFUME
7004 qᵉţôreth (3), fumigation

PERFUMED
5130 nûwph (1), to quiver, vibrate, rock
6999 qâţar (1), to turn into fragrance by fire

PERFUMES
7547 raqqûach (1), scented ointment

PERGA
4011 Pĕrgē (3), tower

PERGAMOS
4010 Pĕrgamŏs (2), fortified

PERHAPS
686 ara (1), then, so, therefore
3381 mēpŏs (1), lest somehow
5029 tacha (1), shortly, i.e. possibly

PERIDA
6514 Pᵉrûwdâ' (1), dispersion

PERIL
2794 kindunŏs (1), danger, risk

PERILOUS
5467 chalĕpŏs (1), difficult, i.e. dangerous

PERILS
2794 kindunŏs (8), danger, risk

PERISH
6 'âbad (73), perish; destroy
7 'âbad (Ch.) (2), perish; destroy
8 'ôbêd (2), wretched; destruction
1478 gâva' (1), to expire, die
1820 dâmâh (2), to be silent; to fail, cease
3772 kârath (1), to cut (off, down or asunder)
5307 nâphal (1), to fall
5486 çûwph (1), to terminate
5595 çâphâh (2), to scrape; to remove
5674 'âbar (1), to cross over; to transition
6544 pâra' (1), to loosen; to expose, dismiss
7843 shâchath (1), to decay; to ruin
622 apŏllumi (25), to destroy fully; to perish
853 aphanizō (1), to disappear, be destroyed
1311 diaphthĕirō (1), to ruin, to decay
1510+1519+604 ĕimi (1), I exist, I am
2704 kataphthĕirō (1), to spoil entirely
5356 phthŏra (1), ruin; depravity, corruption

PERISHED
6 'âbad (17), perish; destroy
1478 gâva' (1), to expire, die
8045 shâmad (1), to desolate
599 apŏthnĕskō (1), to die off
622 apŏllumi (5), to destroy fully; to perish
4881 sunapŏllumi (1), to destroy, be slain with

PERISHETH
6 'âbad (6), perish; destroy
622 apŏllumi (3), to destroy fully; to perish

PERISHING
5674 'âbar (1), to cross over; to transition

PERIZZITE
6522 Pᵉrîzzîy (5), of the open country

PERIZZITES
6522 Pᵉrîzzîy (18), of the open country

PERJURED
1965 ĕpiŏrkŏs (1), forswearer, perjurer

PERMISSION
4774 suggnōmē (1), concession

PERMIT
2010 ĕpitrĕpō (2), allow, permit

PERMITTED
2010 ĕpitrĕpō (2), allow, permit

PERNICIOUS
684 apŏlĕia (1), ruin or loss

PERPETUAL
5331 netsach (4), splendor; lasting
5769 'ôwlâm (22), eternity; always
8548 tâmîyd (2), constantly, regularly

PERPETUALLY
3605+3711 kôl (2), all, any or every
5703 'ad (1), perpetuity

PERPLEXED
943 bûwk (2), to be confused
639 apŏrĕō (1), be at a mental loss, be puzzled
1280 diapŏrĕō (2), to be thoroughly puzzled

PERPLEXITY
3998 mᵉbûwkâh (2), perplexity, confusion
640 apŏria (1), state of quandary, perplexity

PERSECUTE
1814 dâlaq (1), to flame; to pursue
7291 râdaph (14), to run after with hostility
7921+310 shâkôl (1), to miscarry
1377 diōkō (8), to pursue; to persecute
1559 ĕkdiōkō (1), to expel or persecute

PERSECUTED
4783 murdâph (1), persecuted
7291 râdaph (5), to run after with hostility
1377 diōkō (13), to pursue; to persecute
1559 ĕkdiōkō (1), to expel or persecute

PERSECUTEST
1377 diōkō (6), to pursue; to persecute

PERSECUTING
1377 diōkō (1), to pursue; to persecute

PERSECUTION
7291 râdaph (1), to run after with hostility
1375 diōgmŏs (5), persecution
1377 diōkō (3), to pursue; to persecute
2347 thlipsis (1), pressure, trouble

PERSECUTIONS
1375 diōgmŏs (5), persecution

PERSECUTOR
1376 diōktēs (1), persecutor

PERSECUTORS
1814 dâlaq (1), to flame; to pursue
7291 râdaph (7), to run after with hostility

PERSEVERANCE
4343 prŏskartĕrēsis (1), perseverance

PERSIA
6539 Pârâç (27), Paras
6540 Pârâç (Ch.) (2), Paras

PERSIAN
6523 parzel (Ch.) (1), iron
6542 Parçîy (1), Parsite

PERSIANS
6539 Pârâç (1), Paras
6540 Pârâç (Ch.) (4), Paras

PERSIS
4069 Pĕrsis (1), Persis

PERSON
120 'âdâm (2), human being; mankind
376 'îysh (3), man; male; someone
376+120 'îysh (1), man; male; someone
1167 ba'al (1), master; husband; owner; citizen
5315 nephesh (14), life; breath; soul; wind
6440 pânîym (10), face; front
4383 prŏsōpŏn (5), face, presence
5287 hupŏstasis (1), essence; assurance

PERSONS
120 'âdâm (3), human being; mankind
376 'îysh (8), man; male; someone
582 'ĕnôwsh (2), man; person, human
4962 math (1), men
5315 nephesh (12), life; breath; soul; wind
5315+120 nephesh (4), life; breath; soul; wind
6440 pânîym (11), face; front
678 aprŏsōpŏlēptŏs (2), without prejudice
4380 prŏsōpŏlēptĕō (1), to show partiality
4381 prŏsōpŏlēptēs (1), exhibiting partiality
4382 prŏsōpŏlēpsia (4), favoritism
4383 prŏsōpŏn (2), face, presence

PERSUADE
5496 çûwth (3), to stimulate; to seduce
6601 pâthâh (3), to be, make simple; to delude
3982 pĕithō (3), to assent to evidence

PERSUADED
5496 çûwth (1), to stimulate; to seduce

6601 pâthâh (1), to be, make simple; to delude
3982 pĕithō (16), to assent to evidence
4135 plērŏphŏrĕō (2), to assure or convince

PERSUADEST
3982 pĕithō (1), to assent to evidence

PERSUADETH
5496 çûwth (1), to stimulate; to seduce
374 anapĕithō (1), to incite, persuade

PERSUADING
3982 pĕithō (2), to assent to evidence

PERSUASION
3988 pĕismŏnē (1), persuadableness

PERTAINED
1961 hâyâh (1), to exist

PERTAINETH
1961 hâyâh (1), to exist
3627 kᵉlîy (1), implement, thing
3348 mĕtĕchō (1), to share or participate

PERTAINING
4012 pĕri (1), about

PERUDA
6514 Pᵉrûwdâ' (1), dispersion

PERVERSE
1942 havvâh (1), desire; craving
2015 hâphak (1), to change, pervert
3399 yâraṭ (1), to be rash
3868 lûwz (1), to depart; to be perverse
3891 lᵉzûwth (1), perverseness
5753 'âvâh (2), to be crooked
5773 'av'eh (1), perversity
6140 'âqash (2), to knot or distort; to pervert
6141 'iqqêsh (4), distorted, warped, false
8419 tahpûkâh (1), perversity or fraud
1294 diastrĕphō (4), to be morally corrupt
3859 paradiatribē (1), meddlesomeness

PERVERSELY
5753 'âvâh (2), to be crooked
5791 'âvath (1), to wrest, twist

PERVERSENESS
3868 lûwz (1), to depart; to be perverse
4297 muṭṭeh (1), distortion; iniquity
5558 çeleph (2), distortion; viciousness
5766 'evel (1), moral evil
5999 'âmâl (1), wearing effort; worry

PERVERT
5186 nâṭâh (2), to stretch or spread out

PERVERTED
2015 hâphak (1), to change, pervert
5186 nâṭâh (1), to stretch or spread out
5753 'âvâh (2), to be crooked
7725 shûwb (1), to turn back; to return

PERVERTETH
5186 nâṭâh (1), to stretch or spread out
5557 çâlaph (2), to wrench; to subvert
6140 'âqash (1), to knot or distort; to pervert
654 apŏstrĕphō (1), to turn away or back

PERVERTING
1294 diastrĕphō (1), to be morally corrupt

PESTILENCE
1698 deber (47), pestilence, plague

PESTILENCES
3061 lŏimŏs (2), plague; disease; pest

PESTILENT
3061 lŏimŏs (1), plague; disease; pest

PESTLE
5940 'ĕlîy (1), mortar pestle

PETER
4074 Pĕtrŏs (157), piece of rock

PETER'S
4074 Pĕtrŏs (4), piece of rock

PETHAHIAH
6611 Pᵉthachyâh (4), Jehovah has opened

PETHOR
6604 Pᵉthôwr (2), Pethor

PETHUEL
6602 Pᵉthûw'êl (1), enlarged of God

PETITION
1159 bâ'ûw (Ch.) (2), request; prayer
7596 shᵉ'êlâh (10), petition

PETITIONS
4862 mish'âlâh (1), request
155 aitēma (1), thing asked, request

PEULTHAI
6469 Pᵉ'ull'thay (1), laborious

P

PHALEC
5317 *Phalĕk* (1),
earthquake

PHALLU
6396 *Pallûw'* (1),
distinguished

PHALTI
6406 *Palţîy* (1), *delivered*

PHALTIEL
6409 *Palţîy'êl* (1),
deliverance of God

PHANUEL
5323 *Phanŏuēl* (1), *face
of God*

PHARAOH
6547 *Par'ôh* (221), *Paroh*
5328 *Pharaō* (3), *Pharaoh*

PHARAOH'S
6547 *Par'ôh* (46), *Paroh*
5328 *Pharaō* (2), *Pharaoh*

PHARAOH-HOPHRA
6548 *Par'ôh Chophra'*
(1), *Paroh-Chophra*

PHARAOH-NECHO
6549 *Par'ôh Nᵉkôh* (1),
Paroh-Nekoh (or -Neko)

PHARAOH-NECHOH
6549 *Par'ôh Nᵉkôh* (4),
Paroh-Nekoh (or -Neko)

PHARES
5329 *Pharĕs* (3), *breech*

PHAREZ
6557 *Perets* (12), *breech*

PHARISEE
5330 *Pharisaiŏs* (10),
separatist

PHARISEE'S
5330 *Pharisaiŏs* (2),
separatist

PHARISEES
5330 *Pharisaiŏs* (86),
separatist

PHARISEES'
5330 *Pharisaiŏs* (1),
separatist

PHAROSH
6551 *Par'ôsh* (1), *flea*

PHARPAR
6554 *Parpar* (1), *rapid*

PHARZITES
6558 *Partsîy* (1), *Partsite*

PHASEAH
6454 *Pâçêach* (1), *limping*

PHEBE
5402 *Phŏibē* (2), *bright*

PHENICE
5403 *Phŏinikē* (2),
palm-country
5405 *Phŏinix* (1),
palm-tree

PHENICIA
5403 *Phŏinikē* (1),
palm-country

PHICHOL
6369 *Pîykôl* (3), *mouth of
all*

PHILADELPHIA
5359 *Philadĕlphĕia* (2),
fraternal

PHILEMON
5371 *Philēmōn* (2),
friendly

PHILETUS
5372 *Philētŏs* (1), *amiable*

PHILIP
5376 *Philippŏs* (33), *fond
of horses*

PHILIP'S
5376 *Philippŏs* (3), *fond
of horses*

PHILIPPI
5375 *Philippŏi* (8),
Philippi

PHILIPPIANS
5374 *Philippēsiŏs* (1),
native of Philippi

PHILISTIA
6429 *Pᵉlesheth* (3),
migratory

PHILISTIM
6430 *Pᵉlishtîy* (1),
Pelishtite

PHILISTINE
6430 *Pᵉlishtîy* (33),
Pelishtite

PHILISTINES
6430 *Pᵉlishtîy* (250),
Pelishtite

PHILISTINES'
6430 *Pᵉlishtîy* (4),
Pelishtite

PHILOLOGUS
5378 *Philŏlŏgŏs* (1),
argumentative, learned

PHILOSOPHERS
5386 *philŏsŏphŏs* (1), *one
fond of wise things,* i.e.
philosopher

PHILOSOPHY
5385 *philŏsŏphia* (1),
wise things

PHINEHAS
6372 *Pîynᵉchâç* (24),
mouth of a serpent

PHINEHAS'
6372 *Pîynᵉchâç* (1),
mouth of a serpent

PHLEGON
5393 *Phlĕgōn* (1), *blazing*

PHRYGIA
5435 *Phrugia* (4), *Phrygia*

PHURAH
6513 *Pûrâh* (2), *foliage*

PHUT
6316 *Pûwţ* (2), *Put*

PHUVAH
6312 *Pûw'âh* (1), *blast*

PHYGELLUS
5436 *Phugĕllŏs* (1),
fugitive

PHYLACTERIES
5440 *phulaktēriŏn* (1),
guard-case

PHYSICIAN
7495 *râphâ'* (1), to *cure,
heal*
2395 *iatrŏs* (5), *physician*

PHYSICIANS
7495 *râphâ'* (4), to *cure,
heal*

2395 *iatrŏs* (2), *physician*

PI-BESETH
6364 *Pîy-Beçeth* (1),
Pi-Beseth

PI-HAHIROTH
6367 *Piy ha-Chîrôth* (4),
mouth of the gorges

PICK
5365 *nâqar* (1), to *bore;*
to *gouge*

PICTURES
4906 *maskîyth* (2),
carved figure
7914 *sᵉkîyâh* (1),
conspicuous object

PIECE
95 *'ăgôwrâh* (1), *coin*
829 *'eshpâr* (2), *portion*
915 *bâdâl* (1), *part*
1335 *bether* (1), *piece*
2513 *chelqâh* (3),
flattery; allotment
3603 *kikkâr* (2), *round
loaf; talent*
4060 *middâh* (7),
measure; portion
4749 *miqshâh* (1), *work
molded by hammering*
5409 *nêthach* (2),
fragment
6400 *peiach* (6), *slice*
6595 *path* (2), *bit, morsel*
1406 *drachmē* (2), *coin*
1915 *ĕpiblēma* (4), *patch*
3313 *mĕrŏs* (1), *division
or share*
4138 *plērōma* (1), *what
fills; what is filled*

PIECES
1506 *gezer* (1), *portion,
piece*
1917 *haddâm* (Ch.) (2),
bit, piece
5409 *nêthach* (9),
fragment
6595 *path* (3), *bit, morsel*
7168 *qera'* (3), *rag, torn
pieces*
7518 *rats* (1), *fragment*
1288 *diaspaō* (1), to *sever
or dismember*
1406 *drachmē* (1), *coin*

PIERCE
4272 *mâchats* (1), to
crush; to *subdue*
5344 *nâqab* (1), to
puncture, perforate
1330 *dierchŏmai* (1), to
traverse, travel through

PIERCED
738 *'ărîy* (1), *lion*
1856 *dâqar* (1), to *stab,
pierce*
4272 *mâchats* (1), to
crush; to *subdue*
5365 *nâqar* (1), to *bore;*
to *gouge*
1574 *ĕkkĕntĕō* (2), to
pierce or impale
3572 *nussō* (1), to *pierce,
stab*
4044 *pĕripĕirō* (1), to
penetrate entirely

PIERCETH
5344 *nâqab* (1), to
puncture, perforate

PIERCING
1281 *bârîyach* (1),
fleeing, gliding serpent
1338 *diïknĕŏmai* (1),
penetrate, pierce

PIERCINGS
4094 *madqârâh* (1),
wound

PIETY
2151 *ĕusĕbĕō* (1), to *put
show piety toward*

PIGEON
1469 *gôwzâl* (1), *young of
a bird*
3123 *yôwnâh* (1), *dove*

PIGEONS
3123 *yôwnâh* (9), *dove*
4058 *peristĕra* (1),
pigeon, dove

PILATE
4091 *Pilatŏs* (55), *firm*

PILDASH
6394 *Pildâsh* (1), *Pildash*

PILE
4071 *mᵉdûwrâh* (2), *pile*

PILEHA
6401 *Pilchâ'* (1), *slicing*

PILGRIMAGE
4033 *mâgûwr* (4), *abode*

PILGRIMS
3927 *parepidēmŏs* (2),
resident foreigner

PILLAR
4676 *matstsêbâh* (10),
column or stone
4678 *matstsebeth* (4),
stock of a tree
5324 *nâtsab* (1), to *station*
5333 *nᵉtsîyb* (1), *military
post; statue*
5982 *'ammûwd* (29),
column, pillar
4769 *stulŏs* (2),
supporting pillar; leader

PILLARS
547 *'ômᵉnâh* (1), *column*
4552 *miç'âd* (1),
balustrade for stairs
4676 *matstsêbâh* (2),
column or stone
4690 *mâtsûwq* (1),
column; hilltop
5982 *'ammûwd* (79),
column, pillar
8490 *tîymârâh* (2),
column, i.e. *cloud*
4769 *stulŏs* (2),
supporting pillar; leader

PILLED
6478 *pâtsal* (2), to *peel*

PILLOW
3523 *kᵉbîyr* (2), *matrass,
quilt of animal hair*
4344 *prŏskĕphalaiŏn* (1),
cushion pillow

PILLOWS
3704 *keçeth* (2), *cushion
or pillow*
4763 *mᵉra'ăshâh* (2),
headpiece; head-rest

PILOTS
2259 *chôbêl* (4), *sailor*

PILTAI
6408 Piltay (1), *Piltai*

PIN
3489 yâthêd (3), tent *peg*

PINE
2100 zûwb (1), to *waste
away*
4743 mâqaq (4), to *melt;
to flow, dwindle, vanish*
6086+8081 'êts (1), *wood*
8410 tidhâr (2), *lasting
tree* (poss.) *oak*

PINETH
3583 xěrainō (1), to
shrivel, to *mature*

PINING
1803 dallâh (1), *loose
hair; indigent, needy*

PINNACLE
4419 ptěrugiŏn (2),
winglet, i.e. *extremity*

PINON
6373 Pîynôn (2), *Pinon*

PINS
3489 yâthêd (10), tent *peg*

PIPE
2485 châlîyl (3), *flute*
836 aulŏs (1), *flute*

PIPED
2490 châlal (1), to *play
the flute*
832 aulĕō (3), to *play the
flute*

PIPERS
834 aulētēs (1),
flute-player

PIPES
2485 châlîyl (3), *flute
instrument*
4166 mûwtsâqâh (1), *tube*
5345 neqeb (1), *bezel,
gem mounting*
6804 tsantârâh (1), *tube,
pipe*

PIRAM
6502 Pir'âm (1), *wildly*

PIRATHON
6552 Pir'âthôwn (1),
chieftaincy

PIRATHONITE
6553 Pir'âthôwnîy (5),
Pirathonite

PISGAH
6449 Piçgâh (5), *cleft*

PISIDIA
4099 Pisidia (2), *Pisidia*

PISON
6376 Pîyshôwn (1),
dispersive

PISPAH
6462 Piçpâh (1),
dispersion

PISS
7890 shayin (2), *urine*

PISSETH
8366 shâthan (6), to
urinate as a male

PIT
875 be'êr (3), *well, cistern*
953 bôwr (41), *pit hole,
cistern, well; prison*
1360 gebe' (1), *reservoir*

1475 gûwmmâts (1), *pit*
6354 pachath (8), *pit* for
catching animals
7585 she'ôwl (3), *abode
of the dead*
7743+7882 shûwach (1),
to *sink*
7745 shûwchâh (2),
chasm
7816 she'chûwth (1), *pit*
7845 shachath (14), *pit;
destruction*
7882 shîychâh (1), *pit*-fall
999 bŏthunŏs (1), *cistern,
pit-hole*
5421 phrěar (5), *cistern*
or water *well; abyss*

PITCH
167 'âhal (1), to *pitch a
tent*
2203 zepheth (3), *asphalt*
2583 chânâh (11), to
encamp
3724 kôpher (1), *village;
bitumen; henna*
6965 qùwm (1), to *rise*
8628 tâqa' (1), to *clatter,
slap, drive, clasp*

PITCHED
167 'âhal (1), to *pitch a
tent*
2583 chânâh (70), to
encamp
5186 nâṭâh (8), to *stretch
or spread out*
8628 tâqa' (2), to *clatter,
slap, drive, clasp*
4078 pēgnumi (1), to *set
up* a tent

PITCHER
3537 kad (10), *jar, pitcher*
2765 kěramiŏn (2),
earthenware vessel

PITCHERS
3537 kad (4), *jar, pitcher*
5035 nebel (1), skin-*bag*
for liquids; *vase; lyre*

PITHOM
6619 Pîthôm (1), *Pithom*

PITHON
6377 Pîythôwn (2),
expansive

PITIED
2347 chûwç (1), to be
compassionate
2550 châmal (4), to
spare, have pity on
7356 racham (1),
compassion; womb

PITIETH
4263 machmâl (1),
delight
7355 râcham (2), to be
compassionate

PITIFUL
7362 rachmânîy (1),
compassionate
2155 ĕusplagchnŏs (1),
compassionate
4184 pŏlusplagchnŏs (1),
*extremely
compassionate*

PITS
953 bôwr (2), *pit hole,
cistern, well; prison*

1356 gêb (1), *well,
cistern; pit*
7745 shûwchâh (1),
chasm
7825 she'chîyth (1), *pit*-fall
7882 shîychâh (1), *pit*-fall

PITY
2347 chûwç (6), to be
compassionate
2550 châmal (14), to
spare, have pity on
2551 chemlâh (1),
commiseration, pity
2603 chânan (3), to
implore
2617 cheçed (1),
kindness, favor
5110 nûwd (1), to
*console, deplore; to
taunt*
7355 râcham (1), to *be
compassionate*
7356 racham (1),
compassion; womb
1653 ělěŏ (1), to *give out
compassion*

PLACE
870 'âthar (Ch.) (5), *after*
1004 bayith (7), *house;
temple; family, tribe*
1367 ge'bûwlâh (1), *region*
3027 yâd (7), *hand; power*
3241 Yânîym (1), *asleep*
3427 yâshab (2), to *dwell,
to remain; to settle*
3653 kên (1), *pedestal* or
station of a basin
4349 mâkôwn (11), *basis;
place*
4612 ma'ămâd (1),
position; attendant
4634 ma'ărâkâh (1),
arrangement, row; pile
4724 miqvâh (1), *water
reservoir*
4725 mâqôwm (373),
general *locality, place*
4800 merchâb (1), *open
space; liberty*
5182 ne'chath (Ch.) (1), to
descend; to depose
5414 nâthan (3), to *give*
5977 'ômed (6), fixed *spot*
6607 pethach (1),
opening; door
7675 shebeth (1), *abode
or locality*
7760 sûwm (1), to *place*
7931 shâkan (5), to *reside*
8414 tôhûw (1), *waste,
desolation, formless*
8478 tachath (17),
bottom; underneath
201 akrŏatēriŏn (1),
audience-room
402 anachōrĕō (1), to
retire, withdraw
1502 ĕikō (1), to be *weak,*
i.e. *yield*
1564 ĕkĕithěn (1), *from
there*
1786 ĕntŏpiŏs (1), local
resident
3692 ŏpē (1), *hole,* i.e.
cavern; spring of water
3699 hŏpŏu (1), *at
whichever* spot
4042 pěriŏchē (1),
passage of Scripture

5117 tŏpŏs (74), *place*
5562 chōrĕō (1), to *pass,
enter; to hold, admit*
5564 chōriŏn (2), *spot* or
plot of ground
5602 hōdĕ (2), *here*

PLACED
776 'erets (1), *earth,
land, soil; country*
3240 yânach (2), to *allow
to stay*
3427 yâshab (5), to *dwell,
to remain; to settle*
3947 lâqach (1), to *take*
5414 nâthan (1), to *give*
5975 'âmad (1), to *stand*
7760 sûwm (1), to *place*
7931 shâkan (2), to *reside*

PLACES
168 'ôhel (1), *tent*
1004 bayith (9), *house;
temple; family, tribe*
2723 chorbâh (1),
desolation, dry desert
3027 yâd (1), *hand; power*
4585 me'ôwnâh (1), *abode*
4725 mâqôwm (20),
general *locality, place*
5439 çâbîyb (1), *circle;
environs; around*
8478 tachath (1), *bottom;
underneath;* in *lieu of*
3837 pantachŏu (1),
universally, everywhere
5117 tŏpŏs (7), *place*

PLAGUE
4046 maggêphâh (20),
pestilence; defeat
4347 makkâh (2), *blow;
wound; pestilence*
5061 nega' (64),
*infliction, affliction;
leprous spot*
5063 negeph (7),
infliction of disease
3148 mastix (2), *flogging
device*
4127 plēgē (2), *stroke;
wound; calamity*

PLAGUED
4046 maggêphâh (1),
pestilence; defeat
5060 nâga' (3), to *strike*
5062 nâgaph (2), to
inflict a disease

PLAGUES
1698 deber (1),
pestilence, plague
4046 maggêphâh (1),
pestilence; defeat
4347 makkâh (8), *blow;
wound; pestilence*
5061 nega' (1), *infliction,
affliction; leprous spot*
3148 mastix (2), *flogging
device*
4127 plēgē (10), *stroke;
wound; calamity*

PLAIN
58 'âbêl (1), *meadow*
436 'êlôwn (7), *oak*
874 bâ'ar (1), to *explain*
1236 biq'â (Ch.) (1), wide
level *valley*
1237 biq'âh (7), wide
level *valley*

P

3603 kikkâr (13), *tract or region; round loaf*
4334 mîyshôwr (14), *plain; justice*
5228 nâkôach (1), *equitable, correct*
5549 çâlal (1), to *mound up; to exalt; to oppose*
6160 'ărâbâh (22), *desert, wasteland*
7737 shâvâh (1), to *level,* i.e. *equalize*
8219 sheᵉphêlâh (3), *lowland,*
8535 tâm (1), morally *pious; gentle, dear*
3723 ŏrthōs (1), *correctly, rightly*
5117+3977 tŏpŏs (1), *place*

PLAINLY
559 'âmar (1), to *say*
874 bâ'ar (1), to *explain*
1540 gâlâh (1), to *denude; uncover*
5046 nâgad (1), to *announce*
6568 peᵉrash (Ch.) (1), to *specify, translate*
6703 tsach (1), *dazzling,* i.e. *sunny, bright*
1718 ĕmphanizō (1), to *show forth*
3954 parrhēsia (4), *frankness, boldness*

PLAINNESS
3954 parrhēsia (1), *frankness, boldness*

PLAINS
436 'êlôwn (2), *oak*
4334 mîyshôwr (1), *plain; justice*
6160 'ărâbâh (20), *desert, wasteland*
8219 sheᵉphêlâh (2), *lowland,*

PLAISTER
1528 gîyr (Ch.) (1), *lime for plaster*
2902 tûwach (1), to *whitewash*
4799 mârach (1), to *apply by rubbing*
7874 sîyd (2), to *plaster, whitewash with lime*

PLAISTERED
2902 tûwach (2), to *whitewash*

PLAITING
1708 ĕmplŏkē (1), *braiding* of the hair

PLANES
4741 maqtsû'âh (1), wood-carving *chisel*

PLANETS
4208 mazzâlâh (1), *constellations*

PLANKS
5646 'âb (1), *architrave*
6086 'êts (1), *wood, things made of wood*
6763 tsêlâ' (1), *side*

PLANT
4302 maţţâ' (1), something *planted*
5193 nâţa' (31), to *plant*

5194 neţa' (3), *plant; plantation; planting*
5414 nâthan (1), to *give*
7880 sîyach (1), *shrubbery*
8362 shâthal (2), to *transplant*
5451 phuţêia (1), *shrub or vegetable*

PLANTATION
4302 maţţâ' (1), something *planted*

PLANTED
5193 nâţa' (21), to *plant*
8362 shâthal (8), to *transplant*
4854 sumphutŏs (1), closely *united* to
5452 phuţeuō (8), to *implant,* i.e. to *instill* doctrine

PLANTEDST
5193 nâţa' (2), to *plant*

PLANTERS
5193 nâţa' (1), to *plant*

PLANTETH
5192 nêţel (2), *burden*
5452 phuţeuō (3), to *implant,* i.e. to *instill*

PLANTING
4302 maţţâ' (2), something *planted*

PLANTINGS
4302 maţţâ' (1), something *planted*

PLANTS
4302 maţţâ' (1), something *planted*
5189 neᵉţîyshâh (1), *tendril* plant shoot
5194 neţa' (2), *plant; plantation; planting*
5195 nâţîya' (1), *plant*
7973 shelach (1), *spear; shoot* of growth
8291 sarûwq (1), choice *grapevine*
8363 sheᵉthîyl (1), *sucker* plant

PLAT
2513 chelqâh (2), *smoothness; flattery*

PLATE
6731 tsîyts (3), burnished *plate;* bright *flower*

PLATES
3871 lûwach (1), *tablet*
5633 çeren (1), *axle; peer*
6341 pach (2), thin metallic *sheet; net*

PLATTED
4120 plĕkō (3), to *twine* or *braid*

PLATTER
3953 parŏpsis (2), *side-dish receptacle*
4094 pinax (1), *plate, platter, dish*

PLAY
5059 nâgan (4), to *play;* to *make music*
6711 tsâchaq (1), to *laugh;* to *make sport* of

7832 sâchaq (5), to *laugh;* to *scorn;* to *play*
8173 shâ'a' (1), to *fondle, please* or *amuse* (self)
3815 paizō (1), to *indulge in (sexual) revelry*

PLAYED
5059 nâgan (4), to *play;* to *make music*
7832 sâchaq (3), to *laugh;* to *scorn;* to *play*

PLAYER
5059 nâgan (1), to *play;* to *make music*

PLAYERS
2490 châlal (1), to *play* the flute
5059 nâgan (1), to *play;* to *make music*

PLAYING
5059 nâgan (1), to *play;* to *make music*
7832 sâchaq (2), to *laugh;* to *scorn;* to *play*

PLEA
1779 dîyn (1), *judge; judgment; law suit*

PLEAD
1777 dîyn (2), to *judge;* to *strive or contend for*
3198 yâkach (3), to *be correct;* to *argue*
7378 rîyb (23), to *hold a controversy;* to *defend*
8199 shâphaţ (9), to *judge*

PLEADED
7378 rîyb (2), to *hold a controversy;* to *defend*
8199 shâphaţ (1), to *judge*

PLEADETH
7378 rîyb (1), to *hold a controversy;* to *defend*
8199 shâphaţ (1), to *judge*

PLEADINGS
7379 rîyb (1), *contest, personal or legal*

PLEASANT
2530 châmad (3), to *delight* in; *lust for*
2531 chemed (2), *delight*
2532 chemdâh (11), *delight*
2580 chên (1), *graciousness; beauty*
2656 chêphets (1), *pleasure; desire*
2896 ţôwb (2), *good; well*
3303 yâpheh (1), *beautiful; handsome*
4022 meged (3), *valuable*
4261 machmâd (5), *delightful*
4262 machmûd (3), *desired; valuable*
4999 nâ'âh (1), *home, dwelling; pasture*
5116 nâveh (1), *at home; lovely; home*
5273 nâ'îym (8), *delightful; sweet*
5276 nâ'êm (5), to be *agreeable*
5278 no'am (2), *agreeableness, delight*
6027 'ôneg (1), *luxury*
6148 'ârab (1), to *intermix*

6643 tseᵉbîy (1), *conspicuous* splendor
8191 sha'shûa' (2), *enjoyment*
8378 ta'ăvâh (1), *longing; delight*
8588 ta'ănûwg (1), *luxury; delight*

PLEASANTNESS
5278 no'am (1), *agreeableness*

PLEASE
2654 châphêts (5), to be *pleased* with, *desire*
2655 châphêts (1), *pleased* with
2894 ţûw' (3), to *sweep away*
2895 ţowb (6), to be *good*
2896 ţôwb (2), *good; well*
3190 yâţab (2), to *be, make well*
3477+5869 yâshâr (1), *straight*
5606 çâphaq (1), to be *enough;* to *vomit*
7451+5869 ra' (1), *bad; evil*
7521 râtsâh (3), to be *pleased with;* to *satisfy*
700 arĕskō (11), to *seek to please*
701 arĕstŏs (1), *agreeable; desirable; fit*
2001+1511 ĕpischuō (1), to *insist stoutly*
2100 ĕuarĕstĕō (1), to *gratify entirely, please*

PLEASED
2654 châphêts (8), to be *pleased* with, *desire*
2895 ţowb (1), to be *good*
2896+5869 ţôwb (1), *good; well*
2974 yâ'al (1), to *assent;* to *undertake, begin*
3190 yâţab (2), to *be, make well*
3190+5869 yâţab (10), to *be, make well*
3477+5869 yâshâr (7), *straight*
7451+5869 ra' (1), *bad; evil*
7521 râtsâh (4), to be *pleased with;* to *satisfy*
8232 sheᵉphar (Ch.) (1), to *be beautiful*
700 arĕskō (5), to *seek to please*
701 arĕstŏs (1), *agreeable; desirable; fit*
1380 dŏkĕō (2), to *think, regard, seem good*
2100 ĕuarĕstĕō (2), to *gratify entirely, please*
2106 ĕudŏkĕō (12), to *think well,* i.e. *approve*
2309 thĕlō (2), to *will;* to *desire;* to *choose*
4909 sunĕudŏkĕō (2), to *assent* to, *feel gratified*

PLEASETH
2654 châphêts (1), to be *pleased* with, *desire*
2896+5869 ţôwb (2), *good; well*

2896+6440 ṭôwb (1),
good; well
3190+5869 yâṭab (1), to
be, make well
3477+5869 yâshâr (1),
straight

PLEASING
2896 ṭôwb (1), *good; well*
6148 'ârab (1), to *give* or
be security
699 arĕskĕia (1),
complaisance, amiable
700 arĕskō (2), to *seek to
please*
701 arĕstŏs (1),
agreeable; desirable; fit

PLEASURE
185+5315 'avvâh (1),
longing
2654 châphêts (3), to *be
pleased* with, *desire*
2655 châphêts (2),
pleased with
2656 chêphets (16),
pleasure; desire
2837 chêsheq (1),
delight, desired thing
2896 ṭôwb (2), *good; well*
5315 nephesh (3), *life;
breath; soul; wind*
5730 'êden (1), *pleasure*
6148 'ârab (1), to *give* or
be security
7470 rᵉ'ûwth (Ch.) (1),
desire
7521 râtsâh (6), to *be
pleased with; to satisfy
a debt*
7522 râtsôwn (5), *delight*
8057 simchâh (1),
blithesomeness or *glee*
2106 ĕudŏkĕō (6), to
think well, i.e. *approve*
2107 ĕudŏkia (4),
delight, kindness, wish
2237 hēdŏnē (1), *delight;
desire*
2307 thĕlēma (1), *decree;
inclination*
3588+1380 hŏ (1), *"the,"*
i.e. the definite article
4684 spatalaō (1), to *live
in luxury*
4909 sunĕudŏkĕō (1), to
assent to, feel gratified
5171 truphaō (1), to
indulge in luxury
5485 charis (2),
gratitude; benefit given

PLEASURES
5273 nâ'îym (2),
delightful; sweet
5719 'âdîyn (1),
voluptuous
5730 'êden (1), *pleasure*
2237 hēdŏnē (2), *delight;
desire*
5569 psĕudadĕlphŏs (1),
pretended associate

PLEDGE
2254 châbal (10), to *bind
by a pledge; to pervert*
2258 châbôl (4), *pawn,
pledge* as security
5667 'âbôwṭ (4), *pledged
item*
6161 'ărubbâh (1), as
security; bondsman

6162 'ărâbôwn (3), *pawn,
security pledge*

PLEDGES
6148 'ârab (2), to *give* or
be security

PLEIADES
3598 Kîymâh (2), *cluster*
of stars, *Pleiades*

PLENTEOUS
1277 bârîy' (1), *fatted* or
plump; healthy
3498 yâthar (2), to
remain or *be left*
7227 rab (3), *great*
7235 râbâh (1), to
increase
7647 sâbâ' (2),
copiousness
8082 shâmên (1), *rich;
fertile*
4180 pŏlulŏgia (1),
prolixity, wordiness

PLENTEOUSNESS
4195 môwthar (1), *gain;
superiority*
7647 sâbâ' (1),
copiousness

PLENTIFUL
3759 karmel (3), planted
field; garden *produce*
5071 nᵉdâbâh (1),
abundant gift

PLENTIFULLY
3499 yether (1),
remainder; small rope
7230 rôb (3), *abundance*
2164 ĕuphŏrĕō (1), to *be
fertile, produce a crop*

PLENTY
398 'âkal (1), to *eat*
4723 miqveh (1),
confidence; collection
7230 rôb (3), *abundance*
7235 râbâh (1), to
increase
7646 sâba' (2), *fill to
satiety*
7647 sâbâ' (4),
copiousness
8443 tôw'âphâh (1),
treasure; speed

PLOTTETH
2161 zâmam (1), to *plan*

PLOUGH
723 arŏtrŏn (1), *plow*

PLOW
2790 chârash (6), to
engrave; to *plow*
722 arŏtriŏō (1), to
plough, make furrows

PLOWED
2790 chârash (5), to
engrave; to *plow*

PLOWERS
2790 chârash (1), to
engrave; to *plow*

PLOWETH
722 arŏtriŏō (1), to
plough, make furrows

PLOWING
2790 chârash (2), to
engrave; to *plow*
5215 nîyr (1), *freshly
plowed* land

722 arŏtriŏō (1), to
plough, make furrows

PLOWMAN
2790 chârash (2), to
engrave; to *plow*

PLOWMEN
406 'ikkâr (2), *farmer*

PLOWSHARES
855 'êth (3), *digging
implement*

PLUCK
717 'ârâh (1), to *pluck,
pick fruit*
1497 gâzal (2), to *rob*
3318 yâtsâ' (1), to *go,
bring out*
3615 kâlâh (1), to *cease,
be finished, perish*
5255 nâçach (1), to *tear
away*
5375 nâsâ' (1), to *lift up*
5423 nâthaq (2), to *tear
off*
5428 nâthash (10), to
tear away, be uprooted
5493 çûwr (1), to *turn off*
6131 'âqar (1), to *pluck
up roots; to hamstring*
6998 qâṭaph (1), to *strip
off, pick off*
8045 shâmad (1), to
desolate
726 harpazō (2), to *seize*
1544 ĕkballō (1), to
throw out
1807 ĕxairĕō (1), to *tear
out; to select; to release*
1808 ĕxairō (1), to
remove, drive away
5089 tillō (2), to *pull off*
grain heads

PLUCKED
1497 gâzal (2), to *rob*
3318 yâtsâ' (1), to *go,
bring out*
4803 mâraṭ (3), to *polish;
to make bald*
4804 mᵉraṭ (Ch.) (1), to
pull off, tear off
5255 nâçach (1), to *tear
away*
5337 nâtsal (2), to *be
snatched away*
5423 nâthaq (1), to *tear
off*
5428 nâthash (4), to *tear
away, be uprooted*
6132 'ăqar (Ch.) (1), to
pluck up roots
7993 shâlak (1), to *throw
out, down* or *away*
8025 shâlaph (1), to *pull
out, up or off*
1288 diaspaō (1), to *sever
or dismember*
1610 ĕkrizŏō (2), to
uproot
1846 ĕxŏrussō (1), to *dig
out*
5089 tillō (1), to *pull off*
grain heads

PLUCKETH
2040 hâraç (1), to *pull
down; break, destroy*

PLUCKT
2965 ṭârâph (1), *freshly
picked vegetation*

722 arŏtriŏō (1), to
plough, make furrows

PLOWMAN
2790 chârash (2), to
engrave; to *plow*

PLUMBLINE
594 'ănâk (4),
plumb-line, plummet

PLUMMET
68+913 'eben (1), *stone*
4949 mishqeleth (2),
plummet weight

PLUNGE
2881 ṭâbal (1), to *dip*

POCHERETH
6380 Pôkereth
Tsᵉbâyîym (2), *trap of
gazelles*

POETS
4163 pŏiētēs (1),
performer; poet

POINT
19 'ibchâh (1),
brandishing of a sword
184 'âvâh (1), to *extend
or mark out*
1980 hâlak (1), to *walk;
live a certain way*
6856 tsippôren (1), *nail;
point* of a style or pen
8376 tâ'âh (2), to *mark
off,* i.e. *designate*
2079 ĕschatŏs (1), *finally,*
i.e. *at the extremity*
3195 mĕllō (1), to *intend,*
i.e. *be about to*

POINTED
2742 chârûwts (1),
threshing-sledge

POINTS
5980 'ummâh (1), *near,
beside, along with*

POISON
2534 chêmâh (5), *heat;
anger; poison*
7219 rô'sh (1), poisonous
plant; poison
2447 iŏs (2), *corrosion;
venom*

POLE
5251 nêç (2), *flag; signal;
token*

POLICY
7922 sekel (1),
intelligence; success

POLISHED
1305 bârar (1), to
brighten; purify
2404 châṭab (1), to *chop
or carve* wood
7044 qâlâl (1),
brightened, polished

POLISHING
1508 gizrâh (1), *figure,
appearance; enclosure*

POLL
1494 gâzaz (1), to *shear;
shave; destroy*
1538 gulgôleth (1), *skull*
3697 kâçam (1), to *shear,
clip*

POLLED
1548 gâlach (3), to *shave;
to lay waste*

POLLS
1538 gulgôleth (6), *skull*

POLLUTE
2490 châlal (8), to
profane, defile

P

POLLUTED
2610 chânêph (1), to *soil, be defiled*
2930 tâmê' (2), to *be morally contaminated*

POLLUTED
947 bûwç (2), to *trample down; oppress*
1351 gâ'al (7), to *soil, stain; desecrate*
2490 châlal (13), to *profane, defile*
2610 chânêph (3), to *soil, be defiled*
2930 tâmê' (12), to *be morally contaminated*
2931 tâmê' (1), *foul; ceremonially impure*
6121 'âqôb (1), *fraudulent; tracked*
2840 kôinôô (1), to *make profane*

POLLUTING
2490 châlal (2), to *profane, defile*

POLLUTION
2931 tâmê' (1), *foul; ceremonially impure*

POLLUTIONS
234 alisgĕma (1), *ceremonially polluted*
3393 miasma (1), *foulness, corruption*

POLLUX
1359 Diŏskŏurŏi (1), *twins of Zeus*

POMEGRANATE
7416 rimmôwn (10), *pomegranate*

POMEGRANATES
7416 rimmôwn (22), *pomegranate*

POMMELS
1543 gullâh (3), *fountain; bowl or globe*

POMP
1347 gâ'ôwn (5), *ascending; majesty*
7588 shâ'ôwn (1), *uproar; destruction*
5325 phantasia (1), *vain show, i.e. pomp*

PONDER
6424 pâlaç (2), to *weigh mentally*

PONDERED
4820 sumballō (1), to *consider; to aid; to join, attack*

PONDERETH
6424 pâlaç (1), to *weigh mentally*
8505 tâkan (2), to *balance, i.e. measure*

PONDS
98 'âgam (2), *marsh; pond; pool*
99 'âgêm (1), *sad*

PONTIUS
4194 Pŏntiŏs (4), *bridged*

PONTUS
4195 Pŏntŏs (3), *sea*

POOL
98 'âgam (2), *marsh; pond; pool*

1295 bᵉrêkâh (15), *reservoir, pool*
2861 kŏlumbēthra (5), *pond*

POOLS
98 'âgam (2), *marsh; pond; pool*
1293 bᵉrâkâh (1), *benediction, blessing*
1295 bᵉrêkâh (1), *reservoir, pool*
4723 miqveh (1), *confidence; collection*

POOR
34 'ebyôwn (25), *destitute; poor*
1800 dal (44), *weak, thin; humble, needy*
1803 dallâh (4), *indigent, needy*
2489 chêlᵉkâ' (3), *unhappy wretch*
3423 yârash (2), to *impoverish; to ruin*
4134 mûwk (4), to *be impoverished*
4270 machçôwr (1), *impoverishment*
4542 miçkên (4), *indigent, needy*
6033 'ănâh (Ch.) (1), to *afflict, be afflicted*
6035 'ânâv (1), *needy; oppressed*
6035+6041 'ânâv (3), *needy; oppressed*
6041 'ânîy (56), *depressed*
7326 rûwsh (21), to *be destitute*
3993 pĕnēs (1), *poor*
3998 pĕnichrŏs (1), *needy, impoverished*
4433 ptōchĕuō (1), to *become indigent, poor*
4434 ptōchŏs (31), *pauper, beggar*

POORER
4134 mûwk (1), to *be impoverished*

POOREST
1803 dallâh (1), *indigent, needy*

POPLAR
3839 libneh (1), *whitish tree, (poss.) storax*

POPLARS
3839 libneh (1), *whitish tree, (poss.) storax*

POPULOUS
527 'âmôwn (1), *crowd*
7227 rab (1), *great*

PORATHA
6334 Pôwrâthâ' (1), *Poratha*

PORCH
197 'ûwlâm (33), *vestibule, portico*
4528 miçdᵉrôwn (1), *colonnade or portico*
4259 prŏauliŏn (1), *vestibule, i.e. alley-way*
4440 pulōn (1), *gate-way, door-way*
4745 stŏa (3), *colonnade or interior piazza*

PORCHES
197 'ûwlâm (1), *vestibule, portico*
4745 stŏa (1), *colonnade or interior piazza*

PORCIUS
4201 Pŏrkiŏs (1), *swinish*

PORT
8179 sha'ar (1), *opening, i.e. door or gate*

PORTER
7778 shôw'êr (4), *janitor, door-keeper*
2377 thurōrŏs (2), *gate-warden, doorkeeper*

PORTERS
7778 shôw'êr (31), *janitor, door-keeper*
8179 sha'ar (1), *opening, i.e. door or gate*
8652 târâ' (Ch.) (1), *doorkeeper*

PORTION
270 'âchaz (2), to *seize, grasp; possess*
1697 dâbâr (4), *word; matter; thing*
2256 chebel (2), *company, band*
2505 châlaq (1), to *be smooth; be slippery*
2506 chêleq (36), *allotment*
2508 chălâq (Ch.) (3), *part, portion*
2513 chelqâh (6), *allotment*
2706 chôq (3), *appointment; allotment*
4490 mânâh (4), *ration; lot or portion*
4521 mᵉnâth (4), *allotment*
6310 peh (2), *mouth; opening*
6598 pathbag (5), *dainty food*
7926 shᵉkem (1), *neck; spur of a hill*
3313 mĕrŏs (3), *division or share*
4620 sitŏmĕtrŏn (1), *allowance or ration*

PORTIONS
2256 chebel (2), *company, band*
2506 chêleq (4), *allotment*
4256 machălôqeth (1), *section or division*
4490 mânâh (6), *ration; lot or portion*
4521 mᵉnâth (3), *allotment*

POSSESS
423 'âlâh (2), *public agreement*
2631 chăçan (Ch.) (1), to *take possession*
3423 yârash (93), to *inherit; to impoverish*
5157 nâchal (5), to *inherit*
2932 ktaŏmai (3), to *get*

POSSESSED
270 'âchaz (1), to *seize, grasp; possess*

2631 chăçan (Ch.) (1), to *take possession*
3423 yârash (19), to *inherit; to impoverish*
7069 qânâh (3), to *create; to procure*
1139 daimŏnizŏmai (11), to *be demon-possessed*
2192 ĕchō (2), to *have; hold; keep*
2722 katĕchō (1), to *hold down fast*
5224 huparchŏnta (1), *property or possessions*

POSSESSEST
3423 yârash (1), to *inherit; to impoverish*

POSSESSETH
3423 yârash (1), to *inherit; to impoverish*
5224 huparchŏnta (1), *property or possessions*

POSSESSING
2722 katĕchō (1), to *hold down fast*

POSSESSION
270 'âchaz (1), to *seize, grasp; possess*
272 'ăchuzzâh (64), *possession*
3423 yârash (6), to *inherit; to impoverish*
3424 yᵉrêshâh (2), *occupancy*
3425 yᵉrushâh (11), *conquest*
4180 môwrâsh (1), *possession*
4181 môwrâshâh (6), *possession*
4735 miqneh (3), *live-stock*
4736 miqnâh (1), *acquisition*
5157 nâchal (1), to *inherit*
5159 nachălâh (1), *occupancy*
7272 regel (1), *foot; step*
2697 kataschĕsis (2), *occupancy, possession*
2933 ktēma (1), *estate; wealth, possessions*
4047 pĕripŏiēsis (1), *acquisition*

POSSESSIONS
270 'âchaz (3), to *seize, grasp; possess*
272 'ăchuzzâh (2), *possession*
4180 môwrâsh (1), *possession*
4639 ma'ăseh (1), *action; labor*
4735 miqneh (2), *live-stock*
2933 ktēma (3), *estate; wealth, possessions*
5564 chōriŏn (1), *spot or plot of ground*

POSSESSOR
7069 qânâh (2), to *create; to procure*

POSSESSORS
7069 qânâh (1), to *create; to procure*
2935 ktētōr (1), *land owner*

POSSIBLE
102 adunatŏs (1), *weak; impossible*
1410 dunamai (1), *to be able or possible*
1415 dunatŏs (13), *capable; possible*

POST
352 'ayîl (4), *chief; ram; oak tree*
4201 mᵉzûwzâh (4), *door-post*
4947 mashqôwph (1), *lintel*
7323 rûwts (2), to *run*

POSTERITY
310 'achar (4), *after*
319 'achărîyth (3), *future; posterity*
1755 dôwr (1), *dwelling*
7611 shᵉ'êrîyth (1), *remainder or residual*

POSTS
352 'ayîl (17), *chief; ram; oak tree*
520 'ammâh (1), *cubit*
4201 mᵉzûwzâh (15), *door-post*
5592 çaph (3), *dish*
7323 rûwts (6), to *run*

POT
610 'âçûwk (1), *oil-flask*
1731 dûwd (1), *pot, kettle; basket*
3627 kᵉlîy (1), *implement, thing*
4715 mitsrêph (2), *crucible*
5518 çîyr (12), *thorn; hook*
6517 pârûwr (2), *skillet*
6803 tsintseneth (1), *vase, receptacle*
4713 stamnŏs (1), *jar or earthen tank*

POTENTATE
1413 dunastēs (1), *ruler or officer*

POTI-PHERAH
6319 Pôwṭîy Phera' (3), *Poti-Phera*

POTIPHAR
6318 Pôwṭîyphar (2), *Potiphar*

POTS
1375 gᵉbîya' (1), *goblet; bowl*
1731 dûwd (1), *pot, kettle; basket*
5518 çîyr (9), *thorn; hook*
8240 shâphâth (1), *hook; hearth*
3582 xěstēs (2), *vessel; measure*

POTSHERD
2789 cheres (4), *piece of earthenware pottery*

POTSHERDS
2789 cheres (1), *piece of earthenware pottery*

POTTAGE
5138 nâzîyd (6), *boiled soup or stew*

POTTER
3335 yâtsar (8), to *form; potter; to determine*
2763 kěraměus (1), *potter*
2764 kěramikŏs (1), *made of clay*

POTTER'S
3335 yâtsar (7), to *form; potter; to determine*
2763 kěraměus (2), *potter*

POTTERS
3335 yâtsar (1), to *form; potter; to determine*

POTTERS'
3335 yâtsar (1), to *form; potter; to determine*
6353 pechâr (Ch.) (1), *potter*

POUND
4488 mâneh (2), *fixed weight*
3046 litra (2), 12 *oz. measure, i.e. a pound*
3414 mna (4), *certain weight*

POUNDS
4488 mâneh (2), *fixed weight*
3414 mna (5), *certain weight*

POUR
2212 zâqaq (1), to *strain, refine; extract, clarify*
3332 yâtsaq (13), to *pour out*
5042 nâba' (1), to *gush forth; to utter*
5064 nâgar (2), to *pour out; to deliver over*
5140 nâzal (2), to *drip, or shed by trickling*
5258 nâçak (6), to *pour a libation; to anoint*
5414 nâthan (1), to *give*
7324 rûwq (1), to *pour out, i.e. empty*
8210 shâphak (33), to *spill forth; to expend*
1632 ěkchěŏ (3), to *pour forth; to bestow*

POURED
2229 zâram (1), to *gush water, pour forth*
3251 yâçak (1), to *pour*
3332 yâtsaq (13), to *pour*
5064 nâgar (1), to *pour out; to deliver over*
5258 nâçak (10), to *pour a libation; to anoint*
5413 nâthak (13), to *flow forth, pour out*
6168 'ârâh (2), to *empty, pour out; demolish*
6694 tsûwq (2), to *pour out; melt*
7324 rûwq (1), to *pour out, i.e. empty*
8210 shâphak (25), to *spill forth*
8211 shephek (2), *ash-heap, dump*
906 ballō (1), to *throw*
1632 ěkchěŏ (9), to *pour forth; to bestow*
2708 katachěŏ (2), to *pour down or out*

POUREDST
8210 shâphak (1), to *spill forth; to expend*

POURETH
1811 dâlaph (1), to *drip*
5042 nâba' (2), to *gush forth; to utter*
5064 nâgar (1), to *pour out; to deliver over*
8210 shâphak (6), to *spill forth; to expend*
906 ballō (1), to *throw*

POURING
8210 shâphak (1), to *spill forth; to expend*

POURTRAY
2710 châqaq (1), to *engrave; to enact laws*

POURTRAYED
2707 châqah (2), to *carve; to delineate*
2710 châqaq (1), to *engrave; to enact laws*

POVERTY
2639 cheçer (1), *lack; destitution*
3423 yârash (3), to *impoverish; to ruin*
4270 machçôwr (1), *impoverishment*
7389 rêysh (7), *poverty*
4432 ptōchěia (3), *indigence, poverty*

POWDER
80 'âbâq (1), *fine dust; cosmetic powder*
1854 dâqaq (2), to *crush; crumble*
6083 'âphâr (3), *dust, earth, mud; clay,*
3039 likmaŏ (2), to *grind to powder*

POWDERS
81 'ăbâqâh (1), *cosmetic powder*

POWER
410 'êl (3), *mighty; the Almighty*
1369 gᵉbûwrâh (9), *force; valor; victory*
2220 zᵉrôwa' (3), *arm; foreleg; force, power*
2428 chayil (9), *army; wealth; virtue; strength*
2429 chayil (Ch.) (1), *army; strength; loud sound*
2632 chêçen (Ch.) (2), *strength, powerful rule*
3027 yâd (13), *hand; power*
3028 yad (Ch.) (1), *hand; power*
3201 yâkôl (1), to *be able*
3581 kôach (47), *force, might; strength*
3709 kaph (1), *hollow of hand; paw; sole of foot*
4475 memshâlâh (1), *rule; realm or a ruler*
4910 mâshal (2), to *rule*
5794 'az (1), *strong, vehement, harsh*
5797 'ôz (11), *strength*
5808 'izzûwz (1), *forcible; army*
6184 'ârîyts (1), *powerful or tyrannical*
7786 sûwr (1), to *rule, crown*
7980 shâlaṭ (3), to *dominate, i.e. govern*
7981 shᵉlêṭ (Ch.) (1), to *dominate, i.e. govern*
7983 shilṭôwn (2), *potentate*
7989 shallîyṭ (1), *prince or warrior*
8280 sârâh (2), to *prevail, contend*
8592 ta'ătsûmâh (1), *might*
8617 tᵉqûwmâh (1), *resistfulness*
8633 tôqeph (1), *might*
746 archē (1), *first in rank; first in time*
1325 didōmi (2), to *give*
1410 dunamai (1), to *be able or possible*
1411 dunamis (71), *force, power, miracle*
1415 dunatŏs (1), *powerful or capable; possible*
1849 ěxŏusia (61), *authority, power, right*
1850 ěxŏusiazŏ (3), to *control, master another*
2479 ischus (2), *forcefulness, power*
2904 kratŏs (6), *vigor, strength*
3168 měgalěiŏtēs (1), *grandeur or splendor*

POWERFUL
3581 kôach (1), *force, might; strength*
1756 ěněrgēs (1), *active, operative*
2478 ischurŏs (1), *forcible, powerful*

POWERS
1411 dunamis (6), *force, power, miracle*
1849 ěxŏusia (8), *authority, power, right*

PRACTISE
5953 'âlal (1), to *glean; to overdo*
6213 'âsâh (3), to *do or make*

PRACTISED
2790 chârash (1), to *engrave; to plow*
6213 'âsâh (1), to *do*

PRAETORIUM
4232 praitōriŏn (1), *governor's court-room*

PRAISE
1288 bârak (1), to *bless*
1974 hillûwl (1), *harvest celebration*
1984 hâlal (92), to *praise; thank; boast*
2167 zâmar (4), to *play music*
3034 yâdâh (52), to *revere or worship*
4110 mahălâl (1), *fame, good reputation*

P

7623 shâbach (4), to address; to pacify
7624 sheʰbach (Ch.) (2), to adulate, i.e. adore
8416 teʰhillâh (52), laudation; hymn
8426 tôwdâh (5), expressions of thanks
133 ainĕsis (1), thank-offering. praise
134 ainĕō (3), to praise
136 ainŏs (2), praise
1391 dŏxa (4), glory; brilliance
1867 ĕpainĕō (3), to applaud, commend
1868 ĕpainŏs (12), laudation
5214 humnĕō (1), to celebrate in song

PRAISED
1288 bârak (1), to bless
1984 hâlal (19), to praise; thank; boast
3034 yâdâh (1), to throw; to revere or worship
7623 shâbach (1), to address
7624 sheʰbach (Ch.) (3), to adulate, i.e. adore
2127 ĕulŏgĕō (1), to invoke a benediction

PRAISES
1984 hâlal (1), to praise; thank; boast
8416 teʰhillâh (5), laudation; hymn
8426 tôwdâh (1), expressions of thanks
703 arĕtē (1), excellence, virtue

PRAISETH
1984 hâlal (1), to praise; thank; boast

PRAISING
1984 hâlal (4), to praise; thank; boast
134 ainĕō (6), to praise

PRANSING
1725 dâhar (1), to prance

PRANSINGS
1726 dahăhar (2), gallop

PRATING
8193 sâphâh (2), lip, language, speech
5396 phluarĕō (1), to berate

PRAY
577 'ánnâ' (2), oh now!, I ask you!
2470 châlâh (3), to be weak, sick, afflicted
2603 chânan (1), to implore
3863 lûw' (1), if; would that!
4994 nâ' (195), I pray!, please!, I beg you!
6279 'âthar (1), intercede
6293 pâga' (1), to impinge
6419 pâlal (34), to intercede, pray
6739 tseʰlâ' (Ch.) (1), pray
7592 shâ'al (1), to ask
7878 sîyach (1), to ponder, muse aloud

1189 dĕŏmai (7), to beg, petition, ask
2065 ĕrōtaō (10), to interrogate; to request
2172 ĕuchŏmai (2), to wish for; to pray
3870 parakalĕō (4), to call, invite
4336 prŏsĕuchŏmai (42), to supplicate, pray

PRAYED
6419 pâlal (30), to intercede, pray
6739 tseʰlâ' (Ch.) (1), pray
1189 dĕŏmai (3), to beg, petition, ask
2065 ĕrōtaō (4), to interrogate; to request
3870 parakalĕō (2), to call, invite
4336 prŏsĕuchŏmai (25), to supplicate, pray

PRAYER
2470 châlâh (1), to be weak, sick, afflicted
3908 lachash (1), incantation; amulet
6279 'âthar (1), intercede in prayer
6419 pâlal (2), to intercede, pray
7878 sîyach (1), to ponder, muse aloud
7879 sîyach (1), uttered contemplation
8605 teʰphillâh (75), intercession
1162 dĕĕsis (7), petition, request
1783 ĕntĕuxis (1), intercession
2171 ĕuchē (1), wish, petition
4335 prŏsĕuchē (21), prayer; prayer chapel
4336 prŏsĕuchŏmai (1), to supplicate, pray

PRAYERS
8605 teʰphillâh (2), intercession
1162 dĕĕsis (5), petition, request
4335 prŏsĕuchē (15), prayer; prayer chapel
4336 prŏsĕuchŏmai (2), to supplicate, pray

PRAYEST
4336 prŏsĕuchŏmai (2), to supplicate, pray

PRAYETH
6419 pâlal (4), to intercede, pray
4336 prŏsĕuchŏmai (3), to supplicate, pray

PRAYING
1156 beʰ'â' (Ch.) (1), to seek or ask
6419 pâlal (5), to intercede, pray
1189 dĕŏmai (2), to beg, petition, ask
4336 prŏsĕuchŏmai (12), to supplicate, pray

PREACH
1319 bâsar (1), to announce (good news)
7121 qârâ' (2), to call out

1229 diaggĕllō (1), to herald thoroughly
2097 ĕuaggĕlizō (18), to announce good news
2605 kataggĕllō (4), to proclaim, promulgate
2784 kĕrussō (22), to herald
2980 lalĕō (1), to talk

PREACHED
1319 bâsar (1), to announce (good news)
189 akŏĕ (1), hearing; thing heard
1256 dialĕgŏmai (1), to discuss
2097 ĕuaggĕlizō (22), to announce good news
2605 kataggĕllō (6), to proclaim, promulgate
2784 kĕrussō (20), to herald
2907 krĕas (1), meat
2980 lalĕō (4), to talk
3954 parrhēsia (1), frankness, boldness
4137 plĕrŏō (1), to fill, make complete
4283 prŏĕuaggĕlizŏmai (1), to announce glad news in advance
4296 prŏkĕrussō (2), to proclaim in advance

PREACHER
6953 qôheleth (7), assembler i.e. lecturer
2783 kĕrux (3), herald
2784 kĕrussō (1), to herald

PREACHEST
2784 kĕrussō (1), to herald

PREACHETH
2097 ĕuaggĕlizō (1), to announce good news
2784 kĕrussō (2), to herald

PREACHING
7150 qeʰrîy'âh (1), proclamation
1256 dialĕgŏmai (1), to discuss
2097 ĕuaggĕlizō (6), to announce good news
2782 kĕrugma (8), proclamation
2784 kĕrussō (8), to herald
2980 lalĕō (1), to talk
3056 lŏgŏs (1), word, matter, thing; Word

PRECEPT
4687 mitsvâh (1), command
6673 tsav (4), injunction
1785 ĕntŏlē (2), prescription, regulation

PRECEPTS
4687 mitsvâh (3), command
6490 piqqûwd (21), mandate of God, Law

PRECIOUS
2530 châmad (3), to delight in; lust for

2532 chemdâh (1), delight
2580 chên (1), graciousness; beauty
2667 chôphesh (1), carpet
2896 tôwb (4), good; well
3365 yâqar (8), to be valuable; to make rare
3366 yeʰqâr (4), wealth; costliness; dignity
3368 yâqâr (25), valuable
4022 meged (5), valuable
4030 migdânâh (3), preciousness, i.e. a gem
4901 meshek (1), sowing; possession
5238 neʰkôth (1), valuables
927 barutimŏs (1), highly valuable
1784 ĕntimŏs (2), valued, considered precious
2472 isŏtimŏs (1), of equal value or honor
4185 pŏlutĕlēs (1), extremely expensive
5092 timē (1), esteem; nobility; money
5093 timiŏs (11), costly; honored, esteemed

PREDESTINATE
4309 prŏŏrizō (2), to predetermine

PREDESTINATED
4309 prŏŏrizō (2), to predetermine

PREEMINENCE
4195 môwthar (1), gain; superiority
4409 prōtĕuō (1), to be first
5383 philŏprōtĕuō (1), loving to be first

PREFER
5927 'âlâh (1), to ascend, be high, mount

PREFERRED
5330 neʰtsach (Ch.) (1), to become chief
8138 shânâh (1), to fold, to transmute
1096 ginŏmai (3), to be, become

PREFERRING
4285 prŏĕgĕŏmai (1), to show deference
4299 prŏkrima (1), prejudgment, partiality

PREMEDITATE
3191 mĕlĕtaō (1), to plot, think about

PREPARATION
3559 kûwn (2), to set up: establish, fix, prepare
2091 hĕtŏimasia (1), preparation
3904 paraskĕuē (6), readiness

PREPARATIONS
4633 ma'ărâk (1), mental disposition, plan

PREPARE
631 'âçar (1), to fasten; to join battle
3559 kûwn (41), to set up: establish, fix, prepare

PREPARED
4487 mânâh (1), to *allot; to enumerate* or enroll
6186 'ârak (2), to set in a row, i.e. *arrange*,
6213 'âsâh (9), to *do* or *make*
6437 pânâh (4), to *turn*, to *face*
6942 qâdâsh (7), to *be, make clean*
2090 hĕtŏimazō (11), to *prepare*
2680 kataskĕuazō (3), to *prepare thoroughly*
3903 paraskĕuazō (1), to *get ready, prepare*

PREPARED
2164 zᵉman (Ch.) (1), to *agree, conspire*
2502 châlats (2), to *deliver, equip*
3559 kûwn (53), to *set up: establish, fix, prepare*
3739 kârâh (1), to *purchase* by bargaining
4487 mânâh (4), to *allot; to enumerate* or enroll
6186 'ârak (2), to set in a row, i.e. *arrange*,
6213 'âsâh (13), to *do* or *make*
6437 pânâh (1), to *turn*, to *face*
7543 râqach (1), to *perfume, blend spice*
2090 hĕtŏimazō (18), to *prepare*
2092 hĕtŏimŏs (1), *ready, prepared*
2675 katartizō (1), to *repair; to prepare*
2680 kataskĕuazō (2), to *prepare thoroughly*
4282 prŏĕtŏimazō (1), to *fit up in advance*

PREPAREDST
6437 pânâh (1), to *turn*, to *face*

PREPAREST
3559 kûwn (1), to *set up: establish, fix, prepare*
6186 'ârak (1), to set in a row, i.e. *arrange*,
6213 'âsâh (1), to *do* or *make*

PREPARETH
3559 kûwn (3), to *set up: establish, fix, prepare*

PREPARING
6213 'âsâh (1), to *do* or *make*
2680 kataskĕuazō (1), to *prepare thoroughly*

PRESBYTERY
4244 prĕsbutĕriŏn (1), *order of elders*

PRESCRIBED
3789 kâthab (1), to *write*

PRESCRIBING
3792 kᵉthâb (Ch.) (1), *writing, record* or *book*

PRESENCE
5048 neged (8), *over against* or *before*
5869 'ayin (9), *eye; sight; fountain*
5921 'al (1), *above, over, upon,* or *against*
6440 pânîym (76), *face; front*
6925 qŏdâm (Ch.) (1), *before*
561 apĕnanti (1), *before* or *against*
1715 ĕmprŏsthĕn (1), *in front of*
1799 ĕnōpiŏn (9), *in the face of, before*
2714 katĕnōpiŏn (1), *directly in front of*
3952 parŏusia (2), *coming; presence*
4383 prŏsōpŏn (7), *face, presence*

PRESENT
814 'eshkâr (1), *gratuity, gift; payment*
1293 bᵉrâkâh (3), *benediction, blessing*
3320 yâtsab (5), to *station, offer, continue*
3557 kûwl (1), to *keep in; to measure*
4503 minchâh (22), *tribute; offering*
4672 mâtsâ' (17), to *find* or *acquire; to occur*
5307 nâphal (3), to *fall*
5324 nâtsab (1), to *station*
5975 'âmad (6), to *stand*
7810 shachad (2), to *bribe; gift*
7862 shay (1), *gift*
7964 shillûwach (1), daughter's *dower*
8670 tᵉshûwrâh (1), *gift*
737 arti (2), *just now; at once*
1736 ĕndēmĕō (2), to be *at home*
1764 ĕnistēmi (5), to be *present*
2186 ĕphistēmi (1), to be *present; to approach*
2476 histēmi (1), to *stand, establish*
3306 mĕnō (1), to *stay, remain*
3568 nun (4), *now; the present* or *immediate*
3854 paraginōmai (1), to *arrive; to appear*
3873 parakĕimai (2), to be *at hand*
3918 parĕimi (14), to be *present; to have come*
3936 paristēmi (7), to *stand beside, present*
4840 sumparĕimi (1), to *be now present*

PRESENTED
3320 yâtsab (4), to *station, offer, continue*
3322 yâtsag (1), to *place*
4672 mâtsâ' (3), to *find meet* or *be present*
5066 nâgash (1), to *be, come, bring near*
5307 nâphal (1), to *fall*
5414 nâthan (1), to *give*
5975 'âmad (1), to *stand*
7126 qârab (2), to *approach, bring near*
7200 râ'âh (1), to *see*

PRESENTING
5307 nâphal (1), to *fall*

PRESENTLY
3117 yôwm (2), *day; time period*
1824 ĕxautēs (1), *instantly, at once*
3916 parachrēma (1), *instantly, immediately*
3936 paristēmi (1), to *stand beside, present*

PRESENTS
4030 migdânâh (1), *preciousness,* i.e. *a gem*
4503 minchâh (6), *tribute; offering*
7862 shay (2), *gift*
7964 shillûwach (1), daughter's *dower*

PRESERVE
2421 châyâh (4), to *live; to revive*
3498 yâthar (1), to *remain* or *be left*
4241 michyâh (1), *preservation of life*
4422 mâlaṭ (1), to *escape* as if by *slipperiness*
5341 nâtsar (11), to *guard, protect*
7760 sûwm (1), to *put*
8104 shâmar (9), to *watch*
2225 zōŏgŏnĕō (1), to *rescue; be saved*
4982 sōzō (1), to *deliver; to protect*

PRESERVED
3467 yâsha' (4), to *make safe, free*
5336 nâtsîyr (1), *delivered*
5337 nâtsal (1), to *deliver; to be snatched*
8104 shâmar (6), to *watch*
4933 suntērĕō (2), to *preserve in memory*
5083 tērĕō (2), to *keep, guard, obey*

PRESERVER
5314 nâphash (1), to be *refreshed*

PRESERVEST
2421 châyâh (1), to *live; to revive*
3467 yâsha' (1), to *make safe, free*

PRESERVETH
2421 châyâh (1), to *live; to revive*
5341 nâtsar (1), to *guard, protect, maintain*
8104 shâmar (6), to *watch*

PRESIDENTS
5632 çârêk (Ch.) (5), *emir, high official*

PRESS
1660 gath (1), wine-*press* or *vat*
6333 pûwrâh (1), *wine-press* trough

598 apŏthlibō (1), to *crowd, press up* against
1377 diōkō (1), to *pursue; to persecute*
3793 ŏchlŏs (5), *throng,* i.e. *crowd or mob*

PRESSED
1765 dâchaph (1), to *urge; to hasten*
4600 mâ'ak (1), to *press*
5781 'ûwq (2), to *pack, be pressed*
6484 pâtsar (2), to *stun* or *dull*
6555 pârats (2), to *break out*
6693 tsûwq (1), to *oppress, distress*
7818 sâchaṭ (1), to *tread out,* i.e. *squeeze grapes*
916 barĕō (1), to *weigh down, cause pressure*
1945 ĕpikĕimai (1), to *rest upon; press upon*
1968 ĕpipiptō (1), to *embrace; to seize*
4085 piĕzō (1), to *pack down firm*
4912 sunĕchō (1), to *hold together, compress*

PRESSES
3342 yeqeb (2), wine-*vat,* wine-*press*

PRESSETH
5181 nâchath (1), to *sink, descend; to press* down
971 biazō (1), to *crowd oneself* into

PRESSFAT
3342 yeqeb (1), wine-*vat,* wine-*press*

PRESUME
2102 zûwd (1), to be *insolent*
4390 mâlê' (1), to *fill; be full*

PRESUMED
6075 'âphal (1), to *swell; be elated*

PRESUMPTUOUS
2086 zêd (1), *arrogant, proud*
5113 tŏlmētēs (1), *daring (audacious)* man

PRESUMPTUOUSLY
2087 zâdôwn (2), *arrogance, pride*
2102 zûwd (3), to be *insolent*
3027 yâd (1), *hand; power*

PRETENCE
4392 prŏphasis (3), *pretext, excuse*

PREVAIL
1396 gâbar (5), to *act insolently*
2388 châzaq (2), to *bind, restrain, conquer*
3201 yâkôl (13), to be *able*
3898 lâcham (1), to *fight a battle*
5810 'âzaz (1), to be *stout; be bold*
6113 'âtsar (1), to *hold back; to maintain, rule*

P

6206 'ărats (1), to awe; to dread; to harass
8630 tâqaph (2), to overpower
2729 katischuō (1), to overpower, prevail
5623 ōphĕlĕō (2), to benefit, be of use

PREVAILED
553 'âmats (1), to be strong; be courageous
1396 gâbar (9), to be strong; to prevail
2388 châzaq (8), to bind, restrain, conquer
3201 yâkôl (9), to be able
3202 yᵉkêl (Ch.) (1), to be able
3513 kâbad (1), to be heavy, severe, dull
5810 'âzaz (2), to be stout; be bold
7186 qâsheh (1), severe
2480 ischuō (3), to have or exercise force
2729 katischuō (1), to overpower, prevail
3528 nikaō (1), to subdue, conquer

PREVAILEST
8630 tâqaph (1), to overpower

PREVAILETH
7287 râdâh (1), to subjugate; to crumble

PREVENT
6923 qâdam (6), to anticipate, hasten
5348 phthanō (1), to anticipate or precede

PREVENTED
6923 qâdam (8), to anticipate, hasten
4399 prŏphthanō (1), to anticipate

PREVENTEST
6923 qâdam (1), to anticipate, hasten

PREY
400 'ôkel (2), food
957 baz (17), plunder, loot
961 bizzâh (4), booty, plunder
962 bâzaz (9), to plunder, take booty
2863 chetheph (1), robber or robbery
2963 ţâraph (1), to pluck off or pull to pieces
2964 ţereph (18), fresh torn prey
4455 malqôwach (6), spoil, plunder
5706 'ad (3), booty
7997 shâlal (1), to drop or strip; to plunder
7998 shâlâl (11), booty

PRICE
3365 yâqar (1), to be valuable; to make rare
3701 keçeph (3), silver money
4242 mᵉchîyr (11), price, payment, wages
4377 meker (1), merchandise; value

4736 miqnâh (2), acquisition
4901 meshek (1), sowing; possession
6187 'êrek (1), pile, equipment, estimate
7939 sâkâr (2), payment, salary; compensation
4185 pŏlutĕlēs (1), extremely expensive
4186 pŏlutimŏs (1), extremely valuable
5092 timē (7), esteem; nobility; money

PRICES
5092 timē (1), esteem; nobility; money

PRICKED
3513 kâbad (1), to be heavy, severe, dull
8150 shânan (1), to pierce; to inculcate
2669 katapŏnĕō (1), to harass, oppress

PRICKING
3992 mâ'ar (1), to be painful; destructive

PRICKS
7899 sêk (1), brier of a hedge
2759 kĕntrŏn (2), sting; goad

PRIDE
1344 gê'âh (1), arrogance, pride
1346 ga'ăvâh (9), arrogance; majesty
1347 gâ'ôwn (20), ascending; majesty
1348 gê'ûwth (2), ascending; majesty
1363 gôbahh (2), height; grandeur; arrogance
1466 gêvâh (3), arrogance, pride
2087 zâdôwn (6), arrogance, pride
2103 zûwd (Ch.) (1), to be proud
7407 rôkeç (1), snare as of tied meshes
7830 shachats (1), haughtiness; dignity
212 alazŏnĕia (1), boasting
5187 tuphŏō (1), to inflate with self-conceit
5243 hupĕrēphania (1), haughtiness, arrogance

PRIEST
3547 kâhan (2), to officiate as a priest
3548 kôhên (423), one officiating as a priest
3549 kâhên (Ch.) (1), one officiating as a priest
748 archiĕratikŏs (1), high-priestly
749 archiĕrĕus (53), high-priest, chief priest
2409 hiĕrĕus (16), priest

PRIEST'S
3547 kâhan (20), to officiate as a priest
3548 kôhên (17), one officiating as a priest
3550 kᵉhunnâh (4), priesthood

749 archiĕrĕus (4), high-priest, chief priest
2405 hiĕratĕia (1), priestly office
2407 hiĕratĕuō (1), to be a priest

PRIESTHOOD
3550 kᵉhunnâh (9), priesthood
2405 hiĕratĕia (1), priestly office
2406 hiĕratĕuma (2), priestly order
2420 hiĕrōsunē (4), priestly office

PRIESTS
3548 kôhên (300), one officiating as a priest
3549 kâhên (Ch.) (6), one officiating as a priest
3649 kâmâr (1), pagan priest
749 archiĕrĕus (67), high-priest, chief priest
2409 hiĕrĕus (15), priest

PRIESTS'
3548 kôhên (8), one officiating as a priest

PRINCE
5057 nâgîyd (8), commander, official
5081 nâdîyb (4), grandee or tyrant
5387 nâsîy' (56), leader; rising mist, fog
7101 qâtsîyn (2), magistrate; leader
7333 râzôwn (1), dignitary
8269 sar (19), head person, ruler
8323 sârar (1), to have, exercise, get dominion
747 archēgŏs (2), chief leader; founder
758 archōn (8), first

PRINCE'S
5081 nâdîyb (1), grandee or tyrant
5387 nâsîy' (2), leader; rising mist, fog

PRINCES
324 ăchashdarpan (Ch.) (9), satrap
2831 chashmân (1), (poss.) wealthy
3548 kôhên (1), one officiating as a priest
5057 nâgîyd (1), commander, official
5081 nâdîyb (10), grandee or tyrant
5257 nᵉçîyk (3), libation; molten image; prince
5387 nâsîy' (40), leader; rising mist, fog
5461 çâgân (1), prfect of a province
6579 partam (1), grandee, noble
7101 qâtsîyn (2), magistrate; leader
7227 rab (2), great
7261 rabrᵉbân (Ch.) (2), magnate, noble
7336 râzan (5), honorable

7991 shâlîysh (1), officer; of the third rank
8269 sar (190), head person, ruler
758 archōn (3), first
2232 hēgĕmōn (1), chief

PRINCESS
8282 sârâh (1), female noble

PRINCESSES
8282 sârâh (1), female noble

PRINCIPAL
1 'âb (1), father
117 'addîyr (3), powerful; majestic
3548 kôhên (1), one officiating as a priest
5257 nᵉçîyk (1), libation; molten image; prince
7218 rô'sh (5), head
7225 rê'shîyth (1), first
7795 sôwrâh (1), row
8269 sar (2), head person, ruler
8291 sarûwq (1), choice grapevine

PRINCIPALITIES
4761 mar'âshâh (1), headship, dominion
746 archē (6), first in rank; first in time

PRINCIPALITY
746 archē (2), first in rank; first in time

PRINCIPLES
746 archē (1), first in rank; first in time
4747 stŏichĕiŏn (1), basic principles

PRINT
2707 châqah (1), to carve; to delineate
5414 nâthan (1), to give
5179 tupŏs (2), shape, resemblance; "type"

PRINTED
2710 châqaq (1), to engrave; to enact laws

PRISCA
4251 Priska (1), ancient

PRISCILLA
4252 Priskilla (5), little Prisca

PRISED
3365 yâqar (1), to be valuable; to make rare

PRISON
631 'âçar (2), to fasten; to join battle
1004+612 bayith (3), house; temple; family
1004+3608 bayith (7), house; temple; family
1004+5470 bayith (8), house; temple; family
1004+6486 bayith (1), house; temple; family
3608 kele' (4), prison
4115 mahpeketh (2), stocks for punishment
4307 maţţârâ' (13), jail (guard-house); aim
4525 maçgêr (3), prison; craftsman

4929 mishmâr (1), *guard; deposit; usage; example*
6115 'ôtser (1), *closure; constraint*
6495 pᵉqach-qôwach (1), *jail-delivery; salvation*
1200 dĕsmŏphulax (2), *jailer*
1201 dĕsmōtĕriŏn (4), *dungeon, jail*
3612 ŏikēma (1), *jail cell*
3860 paradidōmi (2), *to hand over*
5084 tērēsis (1), *observance; prison*
5438 phulakē (33), *night watch; prison; haunt*

PRISONER
615 'âçîyr (1), *captive, prisoner*
616 'açĉiyr (1), *captive, prisoner*
1198 dĕsmiŏs (11), bound *captive; one arrested*

PRISONERS
615 'âçîyr (8), *captive, prisoner*
616 'açĉiyr (3), *captive, prisoner*
631 'âçar (2), to *fasten*; to *join* battle
7628 shᵉbîy (2), *exile; booty*
1198 dĕsmiŏs (3), bound *captive; one arrested*
1202 dĕsmōtēs (2), *captive*

PRISONS
5438 phulakē (3), *night watch; prison; haunt*

PRIVATE
2398 idiŏs (1), *private or separate*

PRIVATELY
2596+2398 kata (8), *down; according to*

PRIVILY
652 'ôphel (1), *dusk, darkness*
2934 tâman (3), to *hide*
3909 lât (1), *incantation; secrecy; covertly*
5643 çêther (1), *cover, shelter*
6845 tsâphan (1), to *hide; to protect; to lurk*
8649 tormâh (1), *fraud*
2977 lathra (3), *privately, secretly*
3918 parĕimi (1), to be *present; to have come*
3922 parĕisĕrchŏmai (1), to *supervene stealthily*

PRIVY
2314 châdar (1), to *enclose; to beset*
3045 yâda' (1), to *know*
8212 shophkâh (1), *penis*
4894 sunĕidō (1), to *understand*

PRIZE
1017 brabĕiŏn (2), *prize in the public games*

PROCEED
3254 yâçaph (2), to *add or augment*

3318 yâtsâ' (8), to *go, bring out*
1607 ĕkpŏrĕuŏmai (3), to *proceed, project*
1831 ĕxĕrchŏmai (1), to *issue; to leave*
4298 prŏkŏptō (1), to *go ahead, advance*

PROCEEDED
3254 yâçaph (1), to *add or augment*
3318 yâtsâ' (2), to *go, bring out*
4161 môwtsâ' (1), *going forth*
1607 ĕkpŏrĕuŏmai (3), to *proceed, project*
1831 ĕxĕrchŏmai (1), to *issue; to leave*
4369 prŏstithēmi (1), to *annex, repeat*

PROCEEDETH
3318 yâtsâ' (6), to *go, bring out*
4161 môwtsâ' (1), *going forth*
1607 ĕkpŏrĕuŏmai (3), to *proceed, project*
1831 ĕxĕrchŏmai (1), to *issue; to leave*

PROCEEDING
1607 ĕkpŏrĕuŏmai (1), to *proceed, project*

PROCESS
7093 qêts (1), *extremity; after*
7227 rab (1), *great*
7235 râbâh (1), to *increase*

PROCHORUS
4402 Prŏchŏrŏs (1), *before the dance*

PROCLAIM
5674 'âbar (1), to *cross over; to transition*
6942 qâdâsh (1), to *be, make clean*
7121 qârâ' (21), to *call out*

PROCLAIMED
2199 zâ'aq (1), to *call out, announce*
5674 'âbar (1), to *cross over; to transition*
7121 qârâ' (11), to *call out*
8085 shâma' (1), to *hear*
2784 kērussō (1), to *herald*

PROCLAIMETH
7121 qârâ' (1), to *call out*

PROCLAIMING
7121 qârâ' (2), to *call out*
2784 kērussō (1), to *herald*

PROCLAMATION
3745 kᵉraz (Ch.) (1), to *proclaim*
5674+6963 'âbar (4), to *cross over; to transition*
6963 qôwl (1), *voice or sound*
7121 qârâ' (1), to *call out*
7440 rinnâh (1), *shout*
8085 shâma' (1), to *hear*

PROCURE
6213 'âsâh (2), to *make*

PROCURED
6213 'âsâh (2), to *make*

PROCURETH
1245 bâqash (1), to *search out*

PRODUCE
7126 qârab (1), to *approach, bring near*

PROFANE
2455 chôl (4), *profane, common, not holy*
2490 châlal (18), to *profane, defile*
2491 châlâl (3), *pierced to death, one slain*
2610 chânêph (1), to *soil, be defiled*
952 bĕbēlŏs (5), *irreligious, profane*
953 bĕbēlŏō (2), to *desecrate, profane*

PROFANED
2490 châlal (15), to *profane, defile*

PROFANENESS
2613 chănûphâh (1), *impiety, ungodliness*

PROFANETH
2490 châlal (1), to *profane, defile*

PROFANING
2490 châlal (2), to *profane, defile*

PROFESS
5046 nâgad (1), to *announce*
3670 hŏmŏlŏgĕō (2), to *acknowledge, declare*

PROFESSED
3670 hŏmŏlŏgĕō (1), to *acknowledge, declare*
3671 hŏmŏlŏgia (1), *acknowledgment*

PROFESSING
1861 ĕpaggĕllō (2), to *assert*
5335 phaskō (1), to *assert a claim*

PROFESSION
3671 hŏmŏlŏgia (4), *acknowledgment*

PROFIT
1215 betsa' (3), *plunder; unjust gain*
3148 yôwthêr (1), *moreover; rest; gain*
3276 yâ'al (18), to be *valuable*
3504 yithrôwn (5), *preeminence, gain*
4195 môwthar (1), *gain; superiority*
7737 shâvâh (1), to *resemble; to adjust*
3786 ŏphĕlŏs (2), *accumulate or benefit*
4851 sumphĕrō (4), to *collect; advantage*
5539 chrēsimŏs (1), *useful, valued*
5622 ŏphĕlĕia (1), *value, advantage*

5623 ŏphĕlĕō (4), to *benefit, be of use*

PROFITABLE
3276 yâ'al (1), to be *valuable*
3504 yithrôwn (1), *preeminence, gain*
5532 çâkan (2), to be *serviceable to*
6743 tsâlach (1), to *push forward*
2173 ĕuchrēstŏs (2), *useful, serviceable*
4851 sumphĕrō (3), to *conduce; advantage*
5624 ŏphĕlimŏs (3), *advantageous, useful*

PROFITED
7737 shâvâh (1), to *resemble; to adjust*
4298 prŏkŏptō (1), to *go ahead, advance*
5623 ŏphĕlĕō (4), to *benefit, be of use*

PROFITETH
3276 yâ'al (1), to be *valuable*
5532 çâkan (1), to be *serviceable to*
5623 ŏphĕlĕō (3), to *benefit, be of use*
5624+2076 ŏphĕlimŏs (1), *useful, valuable*

PROFITING
4297 prŏkŏpē (1), *progress, advancement*

PROFOUND
6009 'âmaq (1), to *be, make deep*

PROGENITORS
2029 hârâh (1), to *conceive, be pregnant*

PROGNOSTICATORS
3045 yâda' (1), to *know*

PROLONG
748 'ârak (12), to *be, make long*
3254 yâçaph (1), to *add or augment*
5186 nâṭah (1), to *stretch or spread out*

PROLONGED
748 'ârak (5), to *be, make long*
754+3052 'arkâ' (Ch.) (1), *length*
4900 mâshak (3), to *draw out; to be tall*

PROLONGETH
748 'ârak (1), to *be, make long*
3254 yâçaph (1), to *add or augment*

PROMISE
562 'ômer (1), *something said*
1697 dâbâr (6), *word; matter; thing*
1860 ĕpaggĕlia (40), *divine assurance*
1861 ĕpaggĕllō (3), to *assert*
1862 ĕpaggĕlma (1), *self-committal*

PROMISED
559 'âmar (5), to *say*
1696 dâbar (29), to
speak, say; to *subdue*
1843 ĕxŏmŏlŏgĕō (1), to
acknowledge or *agree*
1861 ĕpaggĕllō (10), to
assert
3670 hŏmŏlŏgĕō (1), to
acknowledge, agree
4279 prŏĕpaggĕllŏmai
(1), to *promise before*

PROMISEDST
559 'âmar (1), to *say*
1696 dâbar (2), to *speak*

PROMISES
1860 ĕpaggĕlia (12),
divine *assurance*
1862 ĕpaggĕlma (1),
self-committal

PROMISING
2421 châyâh (1), to *live*;
to *revive*

PROMOTE
1431 gâdal (1), to *make
great, enlarge*
3513 kâbad (3), to *be
rich, glorious*
7311 rûwm (1), to *be
high*; to *rise* or *raise*

PROMOTED
1431 gâdal (1), to *make
great, enlarge*
5128 nûwa' (3), to *waver*
6744 tsᵉlach (Ch.) (1), to
advance; promote

PROMOTION
7311 rûwm (2), to *be
high*; to *rise* or *raise*

PRONOUNCE
981 bâṭâ' (1), to *babble,
speak rashly*
1696 dâbar (1), to *speak*

PRONOUNCED
1691 Diblayim (2), *two
cakes*
1696 dâbar (11), to *speak*
7126 qârab (1), to
approach, bring near

PRONOUNCING
981 bâṭâ' (1), to *babble,
speak rashly*

PROOF
1382 dŏkimē (3), *test*, i.e.
trustiness
1732 ĕndĕixis (1),
demonstration
4135 plērŏphŏrĕō (1), to
assure or *convince*

PROOFS
5039 tĕkmēriŏn (1),
criterion of certainty

PROPER
5459 çᵉgullâh (1), *wealth*
791 astĕiŏs (1),
handsome
2398 idiŏs (2), *private* or
separate

PROPHECIES
4394 prŏphētĕia (2),
prediction

PROPHECY
4853 massâ' (2), *burden,
utterance*

5016 nᵉbûw'âh (3),
prediction
5030 nâbîy' (1), *prophet;
inspired* man
4394 prŏphētĕia (14),
prediction
4397 prŏphētikŏs (1),
prophetic

PROPHESIED
5012 nâbâ' (40), to speak
as a *prophet*
5013 nᵉbâ' (Ch.) (1), to
speak as a *prophet*
4395 prŏphētĕuō (9), to
foretell events, *divine*

PROPHESIETH
5012 nâbâ' (3), to speak
as a *prophet*
4395 prŏphētĕuō (4), to
foretell events, *divine*

PROPHESY
2372 châzâh (2), to *gaze
at*; *have a vision*
5012 nâbâ' (66), to speak
as a *prophet*
5197 nâṭaph (5), to *speak*
by inspiration
4395 prŏphētĕuō (14), to
foretell events, *divine*

PROPHESYING
5012 nâbâ' (2), to speak
as a *prophet*
5017 nᵉbûw'âh (Ch.) (1),
inspired *teaching*
4394 prŏphētĕia (2),
prediction
4395 prŏphētĕuō (1), to
foretell events, *divine*

PROPHESYINGS
4394 prŏphētĕia (1),
prediction

PROPHET
5012 nâbâ' (2), to speak
as a *prophet*
5029 nᵉbîy' (Ch.) (2),
prophet
5030 nâbîy' (164),
prophet; inspired man
5197 nâṭaph (1), to *speak*
by inspiration
4396 prŏphētēs (67),
foreteller
5578 psĕudŏprŏphētēs
(4), *pretended foreteller*

PROPHET'S
5030 nâbîy' (1), *prophet;
inspired* man
4396 prŏphētēs (1),
foreteller

PROPHETESS
5031 nᵉbîy'âh (6),
prophetess
4398 prŏphētis (2),
female foreteller

PROPHETS
2374 chôzeh (1),
beholder in vision
5029 nᵉbîy' (Ch.) (2),
prophet
5030 nâbîy' (147),
prophet; inspired man
4396 prŏphētēs (80),
foreteller
4397 prŏphētikŏs (1),
prophetic

5578 psĕudŏprŏphētēs
(7), *pretended foreteller*

PROPITIATION
2434 hilasmŏs (2),
atonement
2435 hilastēriŏn (1),
expiatory place

PROPORTION
4626 ma'ar (1), vacant
space
6187 'êrek (1), *pile,
equipment, estimate*
356 analŏgia (1),
proportion

PROSELYTE
4339 prŏsēlutŏs (2),
convert, i.e. *proselyte*

PROSELYTES
4339 prŏsēlutŏs (2),
convert, i.e. *proselyte*

PROSPECT
6440 pânîym (6), *face;
front*

PROSPER
3787 kâshêr (1), to *be
straight* or *right*
6743 tsâlach (37), to *push
forward*
7919 sâkal (7), to *be* or
act circumspect
7951 shâlâh (3), to *be
secure* or *successful*
2137 ĕuŏdŏō (1), to
succeed in business

PROSPERED
1980 hâlak (1), to *walk;
live a certain way*
6743 tsâlach (6), to *push
forward*
6744 tsᵉlach (Ch.) (2), to
advance; promote
7919 sâkal (1), to *be* or
act circumspect
7965 shâlôwm (1), *safe;
well; health, prosperity*
7999 shâlam (1), to *be
safe; be, make complete*
2137 ĕuŏdŏō (1), to
succeed in business

PROSPERETH
6743 tsâlach (1), to *push
forward*
6744 tsᵉlach (Ch.) (1), to
advance; promote
7919 sâkal (1), to *be* or
act circumspect
2137 ĕuŏdŏō (1), to
succeed in business

PROSPERITY
2896 ṭôwb (6), *good; well*
6743 tsâlach (1), to *push
forward*
7961 shâlêv (2), *careless,
carefree; security*
7962 shalvâh (3),
security, ease
7965 shâlôwm (4), *safe;
well; health, prosperity*

PROSPEROUS
6743 tsâlach (5), to *push
forward*
7965 shâlôwm (1), *safe;
well; health, prosperity*
7999 shâlam (1), to *be
safe; be, make complete*

2137 ĕuŏdŏō (1), to
succeed in business

PROSPEROUSLY
6743 tsâlach (2), to *push
forward*

PROSTITUTE
2490 châlal (1), to
profane, defile

PROTECTION
5643 çêther (1), *cover,
shelter*

PROTEST
5749 'ûwd (2), to *protest*
3513 nê (1), *as sure as*

PROTESTED
5749 'ûwd (3), to *protest*

PROTESTING
5749 'ûwd (1), to *protest*

PROUD
1341 gê' (2), *haughty,
proud*
1343 gê'eh (8), *arrogant,
haughty*
1346 ga'ăvâh (1),
arrogance; majesty
1347 gâ'ôwn (1),
ascending; majesty
1349 ga'ăyôwn (1),
haughty, arrogant
1362 gâbâhh (2), *high;
lofty*
1364 gâbôahh (1), *high;
powerful; arrogant*
1419 gâdôwl (1), *great*
2086 zêd (12), *arrogant,
proud*
2087 zâdôwn (3),
arrogance, pride
2102 zûwd (1), to *seethe,
to be insolent*
2121 zêydôwn (1),
boiling, raging wave
3093 yâhîyr (1), *arrogant*
7293 rahab (2), *bluster*
7295 râhâb (1), *insolent*
7311 rûwm (1), to *be
high*; to *rise* or *raise*
7342 râchâb (3), *roomy,
spacious*
5187 tuphŏō (1), to
inflate with self-conceit
5244 hupĕrēphanŏs (5),
haughty, arrogant

PROUDLY
1346 ga'ăvâh (1),
arrogance; majesty
1348 gê'ûwth (1),
ascending; majesty
1364 gâbôahh (1), *high;
powerful; arrogant*
1431 gâdal (1), to *be
great, make great*
2102 zûwd (4), to *seethe;
to be insolent*
7292 râhab (1), to *urge,
embolden*

PROVE
974 bâchan (1), to *test*; to
investigate
5254 nâçâh (14), to *test,
attempt*
584 apŏdĕiknumi (1), to
demonstrate
1381 dŏkimazō (6), to
test; to *approve*

PROVED

3936 paristēmi (1), to
stand beside, present
3985 pĕirazō (1), to
endeavor, scrutinize

PROVED
974 bắchan (6), to *test;* to
investigate
5254 nắçâh (5), to *test,*
attempt
1381 dŏkimazō (3), to
test; to approve
4256 prŏaitiaŏmai (1), to
previously charge

PROVENDER
1098 bᵉlîyl (1), *feed,*
fodder
1101 bâlal (1), to *mix;*
confuse; to feed
4554 miçpôw' (5), *fodder,*
animal feed

PROVERB
2420 chîydâh (1), *puzzle;*
conundrum; maxim
4911 mâshal (4), to *use*
figurative language
4912 mâshâl (12), pithy
maxim; taunt
3850 parabŏlē (1),
fictitious narrative
3942 parŏimia (2),
illustration; adage

PROVERBS
4911 mâshal (2), to *use*
figurative language
4912 mâshâl (5), pithy
maxim; taunt
3942 parŏimia (2),
illustration; adage

PROVETH
5254 nắçâh (1), to *test,*
attempt

PROVIDE
2372 châzâh (1), to *gaze*
at; to perceive
3559 kûwn (2), to *set up:*
establish, fix, prepare
6213 'âsâh (1), to *do*
7200 râ'âh (2), to *see*
2532 kai (1), *and; or*
3936 paristēmi (1), to
stand beside, present
4160 pŏiĕō (1), to *do*
4306 prŏnŏĕō (2), to *look*
out for beforehand

PROVIDED
3559 kûwn (1), to *set up:*
establish, fix, prepare
6213 'âsâh (1), to *do*
7200 râ'âh (2), to *see*
2090 hĕtŏimazō (1), to
prepare
4265 prŏblĕpō (1), to
furnish in advance

PROVIDENCE
4307 prŏnŏia (1),
provident care, supply

PROVIDETH
3559 kûwn (2), to *set up:*
establish, fix, prepare

PROVIDING
4306 prŏnŏĕō (1), to *look*
out for beforehand

PROVINCE
4082 mᵉdîynâh (20),
governmental region

4083 mᵉdîynâh (Ch.) (5),
governmental region
1885 ĕparchia (2),
Roman præfecture

PROVINCES
4082 mᵉdîynâh (29),
governmental region
4083 mᵉdîynâh (Ch.) (1),
governmental region

PROVING
1381 dŏkimazō (1), to
test; to approve
4822 sumbibazō (1), to
infer, show, teach

PROVISION
1697 dâbâr (1), *word;*
matter; thing
3557 kûwl (1), to
measure; to maintain
3559 kûwn (1), to *set up:*
establish, fix, prepare
3740 kêrâh (1), *purchase*
3899 lechem (1), *food,*
bread
6679 tsûwd (1), to *lie in*
wait; to catch
6718 tsayid (1), hunting
game; lunch, food
6720 tsêydâh (2), *food,*
supplies
4307 prŏnŏia (1),
provident care, supply

PROVOCATION
3708 ka'aç (4), *vexation,*
grief
4784 mârâh (1), to *rebel*
or resist; to provoke
4808 mᵉrîybâh (1),
quarrel
3894 parapikrasmŏs (2),
irritation

PROVOCATIONS
3708 ka'aç (1), *vexation,*
grief
5007 nᵉâtsâh (2), *scorn;*
to bloom

PROVOKE
4784 mârâh (2), to *rebel*
or resist; to provoke
4843 mârar (1), to *be,*
make bitter
5006 nâ'ats (2), to *scorn*
7264 râgaz (1), to *quiver*
653 apŏstŏmatizō (1), to
question carefully
2042 ĕrĕthizō (1), to
stimulate, provoke
3863 parazēlŏō (4), to
excite to rivalry
3893 parapikrainō (1), to
embitter alongside
3948 parŏxusmŏs (1),
incitement to good
3949 parŏrgizō (1), to
enrage, exasperate

PROVOKED
3707 kâ'aç (4), to *grieve,*
rage, be indignant
4784 mârâh (4), to *rebel*
or resist; to provoke
5006 nâ'ats (3), to *scorn*
5496 çûwth (1), to
stimulate; to seduce
7265 rᵉgaz (Ch.) (1), to
quiver
2042 ĕrĕthizō (1), to
stimulate, provoke

3947 parŏxunō (1), to
exasperate

PROVOKETH
5674 'âbar (1), to *cross*
over; to transition

PROVOKING
3707 kâ'aç (1), to *grieve,*
rage, be indignant
4784 mârâh (1), to *rebel*
or resist; to provoke
4292 prŏkalĕŏmai (1), to
irritate

PRUDENCE
6195 'ormâh (1), *trickery;*
discretion
7922 sekel (1),
intelligence; success
5428 phrŏnēsis (1), moral
insight, understanding

PRUDENT
995 bîyn (8), to
understand; discern
6175 'ârûwm (8),
cunning; clever
6191 'âram (1), to *be*
cunning; be prudent
7080 qâçam (1), to *divine*
magic
7919 sâkal (2), to *be* or
act circumspect
4908 sunĕtŏs (4),
sagacious, learned

PRUDENTLY
7919 sâkal (1), to *be* or
act circumspect

PRUNE
2168 zâmar (2), to *trim*
or a vine

PRUNED
2167 zâmar (1), to *play*
music

PRUNINGHOOKS
4211 mazmêrâh (4),
pruning-knife

PSALM
2172 zimrâh (2), *song*
4210 mizmôwr (58),
poem set to music
5568 psalmŏs (2), *psalm;*
book of the Psalms

PSALMIST
2158 zâmîyr (1), *song*

PSALMS
2158 zâmîyr (1), *song*
2167 zâmar (2), to *play*
music
5567 psallō (1), to *play* a
stringed instrument
5568 psalmŏs (5), *psalm;*
book of the Psalms

PSALTERIES
3627 kᵉlîy (1),
implement, thing
5035 nebel (13), skin-bag
for liquids; vase; lyre

PSALTERY
3627 kᵉlîy (1),
implement, thing
5035 nebel (8), skin-bag
for liquids; vase; lyre
6460 pᵉçanṭêrîyn (Ch.)
(4), lyre instrument

PTOLEMAIS
4424 Ptŏlĕmaïs (1), of
Ptolemy

PUA
6312 Pûw'âh (1), *blast*

PUAH
6312 Pûw'âh (2), *blast*
6326 Pûw'âh (1),
brilliancy

PUBLICAN
5057 tĕlōnēs (6),
collector of revenue

PUBLICANS
754 architĕlōnēs (1),
chief tax-gatherer
5057 tĕlōnēs (16),
collector of revenue

PUBLICK
3856 paradĕigmatizō (1),
to expose to infamy

PUBLICKLY
1219 dēmŏsiŏs (2),
public; in public

PUBLISH
1319 bâsar (2), to
announce (good news)
7121 qârâ' (1), to *call* out
8085 shâma' (11), to *hear*
2784 kērussō (2), to
herald

PUBLISHED
559 'âmar (1), to *say*
1319 bâsar (1), to
announce (good news)
1540 gâlâh (2), to *reveal*
1696 dâbar (1), to *speak*
8085 shâma' (1), to *hear*
1096 ginŏmai (1), to *be,*
become
1308 diaphĕrō (1), to
bear, carry; to differ
2784 kērussō (3), to
herald

PUBLISHETH
8085 shâma' (4), to *hear*

PUBLIUS
4196 Pŏpliŏs (2), popular

PUDENS
4227 Pŏudēs (1), modest

PUFFED
5448 phusiŏō (6), to
inflate, i.e. make proud

PUFFETH
6315 pûwach (2), to *blow,*
to fan, kindle; to utter
5448 phusiŏō (1), to
inflate, i.e. make proud

PUHITES
6336 Pûwthîy (1), *hinge*

PUL
6322 Pûwl (4), *Pul,* i.e. a
person or tribe

PULL
2040 hâraç (3), to *pull*
down; break, destroy
3318 yâtsâ' (1), to *go,*
bring out
5422 nâthats (2), to *tear*
down
5423 nâthaq (2), to *tear*
off
6584 pâshaṭ (1), to *strip,*
i.e. unclothe, plunder

P

7725 shûwb (1), to *turn* back; to *return*
385 anaspaō (1), to *take up* or *extricate*
1544 ĕkballō (3), to *throw out*
2507 kathairĕō (1), to *lower*, or *demolish*

PULLED
935 bôw' (1), to *go, come*
4026 migdâl (1), *tower; rostrum*
5256 nᵉçach (Ch.) (1), to *tear away*
5414 nâthan (1), to *give*
5428 nâthash (1), to *tear away, be uprooted*
6582 pâshach (1), to *tear in pieces*
1288 diaspaō (1), to *sever* or *dismember*

PULLING
726 harpazō (1), to *seize*
2506 kathairĕsis (1), *demolition*

PULPIT
4026 migdâl (1), *tower; rostrum*

PULSE
2235 zêrôa' (2), *vegetable*

PUNISH
3256 yâçar (1), to *chastise; to instruct*
5221 nâkâh (1), to *strike, kill*
6064 'ânash (1), to *inflict a penalty, to fine*
6485 pâqad (27), to *visit, care for, count*
7489 râ'a' (1), to *break to pieces*
2849 kŏlazō (1), to *chastise, punish*

PUNISHED
2820 châsak (1), to *restrain* or *refrain*
5358 nâqam (2), to *avenge* or *punish*
6064 'ânash (4), to *inflict a penalty, to fine*
6485 pâqad (4), to *visit, care for, count*
1349+5099 dikē (1), *justice*
2849 kŏlazō (1), to *chastise, punish*
5097 timōrĕō (2), to *avenge*

PUNISHMENT
2399 chêṭ' (1), *crime or its penalty*
2403 chaṭṭâ'âh (3), *offence; sin offering*
5771 'âvôn (9), moral *evil*
6066 'ônesh (1), *fine*
1557 ĕkdikĕsis (1), *retaliation, punishment*
2009 ĕpitimia (1), *penalty*
2851 kŏlasis (1), *infliction, punishment*
5098 timōria (1), *penalty, punishment*

PUNISHMENTS
5771 'âvôn (2), moral *evil*

PUNITES
6324 Pûwnîy (1), *turn*

PUNON
6325 Pûwnôn (2), *perplexity*

PUR
6332 Pûwr (3), *lot* cast

PURCHASE
1350 gâ'al (1), to *redeem; to be the next of kin*
4736 miqnâh (6), *acquisition*
4046 pĕripŏiĕŏmai (1), to *acquire; to gain*

PURCHASED
7069 qânâh (5), to *create; to procure*
2932 ktaŏmai (2), to *get,* i.e. *acquire*
4046 pĕripŏiĕŏmai (1), to *acquire; to gain*
4047 pĕripŏiĕsis (1), *acquisition*

PURE
1249 bar (2), *beloved; pure; empty*
1305 bârar (3), to *brighten; purify*
1865 dᵉrôwr (1), *freedom; clear, pure*
2134 zak (9), *pure; clear*
2135 zâkâh (1), to *be innocent*
2141 zâkak (1), to *be transparent; clean, pure*
2561 chemer (1), *fermenting wine*
2888 Ṭabbath (2), *Tabbath*
2889 ṭâhôwr (40), *pure, clean, flawless*
2891 ṭâhêr (2), to *be pure, unadulterated*
3795 kâthîyth (1), pure *oil from beaten olives*
5343 nᵉqê' (Ch.) (1), *clean, pure*
5462 çâgar (8), to *shut up; to surrender*
6337 pâz (1), *pure gold*
6884 tsâraph (2), to *fuse metal; to refine*
53 hagnŏs (4), *innocent, modest, perfect, pure*
1506 ĕilikrinĕs (1), *tested as genuine,* i.e. *pure*
2513 katharŏs (16), *clean, pure*

PURELY
1252 bôr (1), *purity, cleanness*

PURENESS
1252 bôr (1), *purity, cleanness*
2890 ṭᵉhôwr (1), *purity*
54 hagnŏtēs (1), *blamelessness, purity*

PURER
2141 zâkak (1), to *be transparent; clean, pure*
2889 ṭâhôwr (1), *pure, clean, flawless*

PURGE
1305 bârar (2), to *brighten; purify*
2212 zâqaq (1), to *strain, refine; extract, clarify*
2398 châṭâ' (1), to *sin*

2891 ṭâhêr (1), to *be pure, unadulterated*
3722 kâphar (4), to *cover; to expiate*
6884 tsâraph (1), to *fuse metal; to refine*
1245 diakatharizō (2), to *cleanse perfectly*
1571 ĕkkathairō (2), to *cleanse thoroughly*
2511 katharizō (1), to *cleanse*

PURGED
1740 dûwach (1), to *rinse clean, wash*
2891 ṭâhêr (4), to *be pure, unadulterated*
3722 kâphar (5), to *cover; to expiate*
2508 kathairō (1), to *prune dead wood*
2511 katharizō (1), to *cleanse*
2512 katharismŏs (1), *ablution; expiation*
4160+2512 pŏiĕō (1), to *make or do*

PURGETH
2508 kathairō (1), to *prune dead wood*

PURGING
2511 katharizō (1), to *cleanse*

PURIFICATION
2403 chaṭṭâ'âh (2), *offence; sin offering*
2893 ṭohŏrâh (2), *ceremonial purification*
8562 tamrûwq (2), *scouring, perfumery*
49 hagnismŏs (1), *purification*
2512 katharismŏs (1), *ablution; expiation*

PURIFICATIONS
4795 mârûwq (1), *rubbing*

PURIFIED
1305 bârar (1), to *brighten; purify*
2212 zâqaq (1), to *strain, refine; extract, clarify*
2398 châṭâ' (3), to *sin*
2891 ṭâhêr (3), to *be pure, unadulterated*
6942 qâdâsh (1), to *be, make clean*
48 hagnizō (2), *sanctify; to cleanse in ritual*
2511 katharizō (1), to *cleanse*

PURIFIER
2891 ṭâhêr (1), to *be pure, unadulterated*

PURIFIETH
2398 châṭâ' (1), to *sin*
48 hagnizō (1), *sanctify; to cleanse in ritual*

PURIFY
2398 châṭâ' (7), to *sin*
2891 ṭâhêr (3), to *be pure, unadulterated*
48 hagnizō (3), *sanctify; to cleanse in ritual*
2511 katharizō (1), to *cleanse*

PURIFYING
2403 chaṭṭâ'âh (1), *offence; sin offering*
2892 ṭôhar (2), *ceremonial purification*
2893 ṭohŏrâh (3), *ceremonial purification*
8562 tamrûwq (1), *scouring, perfumery*
48 hagnizō (1), *sanctify; to cleanse in ritual*
2511 katharizō (1), to *cleanse*
2512 katharismŏs (2), *ablution; expiation*
2514 katharŏtēs (1), *cleanness*

PURIM
6332 Pûwr (5), *lot* cast

PURITY
47 hagnĕia (2), moral *chastity, purity*

PURLOINING
3557 nŏsphizŏmai (1), to *embezzle*

PURPLE
710 'argᵉvân (1), *purple*
713 'argâmân (38), *purple*
4209 pŏrphura (5), *red-blue color*
4210 pŏrphurŏus (3), *bluish-red*
4211 pŏrphurŏpōlis (1), *trader in bluish-red cloth*

PURPOSE
559 'âmar (2), to *say*
1697 dâbâr (1), *word; matter; thing*
2656 chêphets (3), *pleasure; desire*
2803 châshab (2), to *plot; to think, regard*
4284 machăshâbâh (3), *contrivance; plan*
4639 ma'ăseh (1), *action; labor*
6098 'êtsâh (2), *advice; plan; prudence*
6640 tsᵉbûw (Ch.) (1), *determination*
7385 rîyq (1), *emptiness; worthless thing; in vain*
7997 shâlal (1), to *drop or strip; to plunder*
1011 bŏulĕuō (2), to *deliberate; to resolve*
1013 bŏulēma (1), *resolve, willful choice*
4286 prŏthĕsis (8), *setting forth*

PURPOSED
2161 zâmam (2), to *plan*
2803 châshab (4), to *plot; to think, regard*
3289 yâ'ats (5), to *advise*
3335 yâtsar (1), to *form; potter; to determine*
6440 pânîym (1), *face; front*
7760 sûwm (1), to *put, place*
1096+1106 ginŏmai (1), to *be, become*
4160 pŏiĕō (1), to *do*
4388 prŏtithĕmai (2), to *propose, determine*

5087 tithēmi (1), to *place*

PURPOSES
2154 zimmâh (1), *plan*
4284 machăshâbâh (3), *contrivance; plan*
8356 shâthâh (1), *basis*

PURPOSETH
4255 prŏairĕŏmai (1), to *propose, intend, decide*

PURSE
3599 kîyç (1), *cup;* utility *bag*
905 balantiŏn (3), money *pouch*
2223 zōnē (1), *belt, sash*

PURSES
2223 zōnē (1), *belt, sash*

PURSUE
3212 yâlak (1), to *walk;* to *live;* to *carry*
7291 râdaph (28), to *run after* with hostility

PURSUED
1692 dâbaq (1), to *cling* or *adhere;* to *catch*
1814 dâlaq (2), to *flame;* to *pursue*
7291 râdaph (35), to *run after* with hostility

PURSUER
7291 râdaph (1), to *run after* with hostility

PURSUERS
7291 râdaph (5), to *run after* with hostility

PURSUETH
7291 râdaph (7), to *run after* with hostility

PURSUING
310 'achar (2), *after*
7291 râdaph (4), to *run after* with hostility
7873 sîyg (1), *withdrawal* into a private place

PURTENANCE
7130 qereb (1), *nearest* part, i.e. the *center*

PUSH
5055 nâgach (6), to *butt*
5056 naggâch (2), act of *butting*
7971 shâlach (1), to *send* away

PUSHED
5055 nâgach (1), to *butt*

PUSHING
5055 nâgach (1), to *butt*

PUT
622 'âçaph (2), to *gather, collect*
935 bôw' (10), to *go, come*
1197 bâ'ar (13), to *be brutish, be senseless*
1396 gâbar (1), to *be strong; to prevail*
1644 gârash (2), to *drive out; to divorce*
1645 geresh (1), *produce, yield*
1846 dâ'ak (6), to *be extinguished; to expire*
1911 hâdâh (1), to *stretch forth* the hand

1921 hâdar (1), to *favor* or *honor;* to *be high*
2026 hârag (1), to *kill, slaughter*
2280 châbash (2), to *wrap* firmly, *bind*
2296 châgar (1), to *gird* on a belt; *put on* armor
2330 chûwd (4), to *propound* a riddle
2502 châlats (1), to *pull off;* to *strip;* to *depart*
3240 yânach (5), to *allow to stay*
3254 yâçaph (5), to *add* or *augment*
3318 yâtsâ' (2), to *go, bring out*
3322 yâtsag (2), to *place*
3381 yârad (2), to *descend*
3455 yâsam (1), to *put*
3518 kâbâh (3), to *extinguish*
3637 kâlam (1), to *taunt* or *insult*
3722 kâphar (1), to *cover; to expiate*
3847 lâbash (41), to *clothe*
3947 lâqach (1), to *take*
4191 mûwth (3), to *die;* to *kill*
4229 mâchâh (3), to *touch,* i.e. reach to
4916 mishlôwach (1), *sending* out
5056 naggâch (1), act of *butting*
5079 niddâh (2), time of menstrual *impurity*
5114 Nôwdâb (3), *noble*
5148 nâchâh (1), to *guide*
5186 nâṭâh (1), to *stretch* or *spread out*
5365 nâqar (2), to *bore; to gouge*
5381 nâsag (1), to *reach*
5394 nâshal (2), to *divest, eject,* or *drop*
5411 Nâthîyn (1), ones *given* to duty
5414 nâthan (187), to *give*
5493 çûwr (19), to *turn* off
5564 çâmak (5), to *lean* upon; *take hold* of
5595 çâphâh (1), to *scrape; to remove*
5596 çâphach (1), to *associate; be united*
5674 'âbar (4), to *cross over; to transition*
5786 'âvar (3), to *blind*
5927 'âlâh (3), to *ascend, be high, mount*
6006 'âmaç (1), to *impose* a burden
6186 'ârak (1), to *set in a row,* i.e. *arrange,*
6213 'âsâh (1), to *do*
6316 Pûwṭ (2), *Put*
6319 Pôwṭîy Phera' (2), *Poti-Phera*
6584 pâshaṭ (6), to *strip,* i.e. *unclothe, plunder*
6605 pâthach (1), to *open* wide; to *loosen, begin*
6695 tsôwq (1), *distress*

7368 râchaq (4), to *recede; remove*
7392 râkab (2), to *ride*
7673 shâbath (2), to *repose; to desist*
7725 shûwb (7), to *turn* back; to *return*
7760 sûwm (150), to *put*
7896 shîyth (11), to *put*
7971 shâlach (45), to *send away*
7972 sheʻlach (Ch.) (1), to *send away*
7973 shelach (1), *spear; shoot* of growth
8214 sheᵉphal (Ch.) (1), to *humiliate*
115 athĕtēsis (1), *cancellation*
142 airō (1), to *lift,* to *take up*
337 anairĕō (2), to *take away,* i.e. *abolish*
363 anamimnḗskō (1), to *remind; to recollect*
506 anupŏtaktŏs (1), *independent*
520 apagō (1), to *take away*
554 apĕkduŏmai (1), to *divest wholly* oneself
595 apŏthĕsis (1), *laying aside*
615 apŏktĕinō (6), to *kill* outright; to *destroy*
630 apŏluō (13), to *relieve, release*
654 apŏstrĕphō (1), to *turn away* or *back*
659 apŏtithēmi (2), to *put away; get rid of*
683 apōthĕŏmai (2), to *push off; to reject*
863 aphiēmi (2), to *leave; to pardon, forgive*
906 ballō (14), to *throw*
1096 ginŏmai (1), to *be, become*
1252 diakrinō (1), to *decide; to hesitate*
1325 didōmi (5), to *give*
1544 ĕkballō (4), to *throw out*
1614 ĕktĕinō (3), to *stretch*
1677 ĕllŏgĕō (1), *attribute*
1688 ĕmbibazō (1), to *transfer*
1746 ĕnduō (16), to *dress*
1749 ĕnĕdrŏn (1), *ambush*
1808 ĕxairō (1), to *remove, drive away*
1911 ĕpiballō (1), to *throw upon*
2007 ĕpitithēmi (9), to *impose*
2289 thanatŏō (7), to *kill*
2507 kathairĕō (2), to *lower, or demolish*
2673 katargĕō (2), to *be, render entirely useless*
3004 lĕgō (1), to *say*
3089 luō (5), to *loosen*
3179 mĕthistēmi (1), to *move*
3856 paradĕigmatizō (1), to *expose to infamy*

3860 paradidōmi (1), to *hand over*
3908 paratithēmi (2), to *present*
3982 pĕithō (1), to *pacify* or *conciliate*
4016 pĕriballō (1), to *wrap around, clothe*
4060 pĕritithēmi (5), to *present*
4160 pŏiĕō (3), to *do*
4374 prŏsphĕrō (1), to *present to; to treat as*
5087 tithēmi (15), to *place, put*
5279 hupŏmimnēskō (4), to *suggest to memory*
5293 hupŏtassō (9), to *subordinate; to obey*
5294 hupŏtithēmi (1), to *hazard; to suggest*
5392 phimŏō (1), to *restrain to silence*
5562 chōrĕō (2), to *pass, enter; to hold, admit*

PUTEOLI
4223 Pŏtiŏlŏi (1), little *wells*

PUTIEL
6317 Pûwṭîy'êl (1), *contempt of God*

PUTRIFYING
2961 ṭârîy (1), *fresh*

PUTTEST
4916 mishlôwach (2), *presentation; seizure*
5414 nâthan (1), to *give*
5596 çâphach (1), to *associate; be united*
7673 shâbath (1), to *repose; to desist*
7760 sûwm (2), to *put, place*

PUTTETH
2590 chânaṭ (1), to *embalm; to ripen*
5414 nâthan (4), to *give*
5844 'âṭâh (1), to *wrap,* i.e. *cover, veil, clothe*
6605 pâthach (1), to *open* wide; to *loosen, begin*
7760 sûwm (5), to *put*
7971 shâlach (2), to *send away*
8213 shâphêl (1), to *humiliate*
630 apŏluō (1), to *relieve, release; divorce*
649 apŏstĕllō (1), to *send out* on a mission
906 ballō (2), to *throw*
1544 ĕkballō (1), to *throw out*
1631 ĕkphuō (2), to *sprout up, put forth*
1911 ĕpiballō (2), to *throw upon*
5087 tithēmi (2), to *place, put*

PUTTING
5414 nâthan (1), to *give*
7760 sûwm (1), to *put, place*
7971 shâlach (2), to *send away*
555 apĕkdusis (1), *divestment, removal*

P

595 apŏthĕsis (1), *laying aside*
659 apŏtithēmi (1), *to put away; get rid of*
1745 ĕndusis (1), *investment*
1746 ĕnduō (1), *to dress*
1878 ĕpanamimnĕskō (1), *to remind again of*
1936 ĕpithĕsis (1), *imposition*
2007 ĕpitithēmi (2), *to impose*
4261 prŏballō (1), *to push to the front, germinate*
5087 tithēmi (1), *to place, put*
5279 hupŏmimnĕskō (1), *to suggest to memory*

PYGARG
1787 Dîyshôwn, (1), *antelope*

QUAILS
7958 sᵉlâv (4), *quail* bird

QUAKE
7264 râgaz (1), *to quiver*
7493 râ'ash (1), *to undulate, quake*
1790 ĕntrŏmŏs (1), *terrified*
4579 sĕiō (1), *to vibrate; to agitate*

QUAKED
2729 chârad (1), *to shudder*
7264 râgaz (1), *to quiver*

QUAKING
2731 chărâdâh (1), *fear, anxiety*
7494 ra'ash (1), *vibration, uproar*

QUARREL
579 'ânâh (1), *to meet, to happen*
5359 nâqâm (1), *revenge*
1758 ĕnĕchō (1), *to keep a grudge*
3437 mŏmphē (1), *blame*

QUARRIES
6456 pᵉçîyl (2), *idol*

QUARTER
5676 'ēber (1), *opposite side; east*
6285 pē'âh (4), *region; extremity*
7098 qâtsâh (2), *termination; fringe*
3836 pantachŏthĕn (1), *from all directions*

QUARTERS
1366 gᵉbûwl (1), *boundary, border*
3411 yᵉrêkâh (1), *far away places*
3671 kânâph (1), *edge or extremity; wing*
7098 qâtsâh (2), *termination; fringe*
7307 rûwach (1), *breath; wind; life-spirit*
1137 gōnia (1), *angle; cornerstone*
5117 tŏpŏs (2), *place*

QUARTUS
2890 Kŏuartŏs (1), *fourth*

QUATERNIONS
5069 tĕtradiŏn (1), *squad of four Roman soldiers*

QUEEN
1377 gᵉbîyrâh (6), *mistress*
4427 mâlak (2), *to reign as king*
4433 malkâ' (Ch.) (2), *queen*
4436 malkâh (33), *queen*
4446 mᵉleketh (5), *queen*
7694 shêgâl (2), *queen*
938 basilissa (4), *queen*

QUEENS
4436 malkâh (2), *queen*
8282 sârâh (1), *female noble*

QUENCH
3518 kâbâh (8), *to extinguish*
7665 shâbar (1), *to burst*
4570 sbĕnnumi (3), *to extinguish, snuff out*

QUENCHED
1846 dâ'ak (1), *to be extinguished; to expire*
3518 kâbâh (9), *to extinguish*
8257 shâqa' (1), *to be overflowed; to cease*
762 asbĕstŏs (2), *not extinguished*
4570 sbĕnnumi (4), *to extinguish, snuff out*

QUESTION
1458 ĕgkalĕō (1), *to bring crimination*
2213 zētēma (2), *debate, dispute*
2214 zētēsis (1), *dispute or its theme*
2919 krinō (2), *to decide; to try, condemn, punish*
3056 lŏgŏs (1), *word, matter, thing; Word*
4802 suzētĕō (2), *to discuss, controvert*

QUESTIONED
1875 dârash (1), *to seek or ask; to worship*
1905 ĕpĕrōtaō (1), *to inquire, seek*
4802 suzētĕō (1), *to discuss, controvert*

QUESTIONING
4802 suzētĕō (2), *to discuss, controvert*

QUESTIONS
1697 dâbâr (2), *word; matter; thing*
2420 chîydâh (2), *puzzle; conundrum; maxim*
1905 ĕpĕrōtaō (1), *to inquire, seek*
2213 zētēma (3), *debate, dispute*
2214 zētēsis (5), *dispute*

QUICK
2416 chay (3), *alive; raw; fresh; life*
4241 michyâh (2), *preservation of life*
2198 zaō (4), *to live*

QUICKEN
2421 châyâh (12), *to live*

2227 zōŏpŏiĕō (1), *to (re-) vitalize, give life*

QUICKENED
2421 châyâh (2), *to live*
2227 zōŏpŏiĕō (2), *to (re-) vitalize, give life*
4806 suzōŏpŏiĕō (2), *to reanimate conjointly*

QUICKENETH
2227 zōŏpŏiĕō (5), *to (re-) vitalize, give life*

QUICKENING
2227 zōŏpŏiĕō (1), *to (re-) vitalize, give life*

QUICKLY
3966 mᵉ'ôd (1), *very*
4116 mâhar (3), *to hurry*
4118 mahêr (8), *in a hurry*
4120 mᵉhêrâh (10), *hurry; promptly*
1722+5034 ĕn (2), *in; during; because of*
5030 tachĕŏs (2), *speedily, rapidly*
5032 tachiŏn (1), *more rapidly, more speedily*
5035 tachu (12), *without delay, soon, suddenly*

QUICKSANDS
4950 surtis (1), *sand drawn by the waves*

QUIET
2790 chârash (1), *to be silent; to be deaf*
4496 mᵉnûwchâh (1), *peacefully; consolation*
5117 nûwach (1), *to rest; to settle down*
5183 nachath (1), *descent; quiet*
7282 râgêa' (1), *restful, i.e. peaceable*
7599 shâ'an (2), *to loll, i.e. be peaceful*
7600 sha'ănân (2), *secure; haughty*
7961 shâlêv (1), *carefree; security, at ease*
8003 shâlêm (1), *complete; friendly; safe*
8252 shâqat (15), *to repose*
8367 shâthaq (1), *to subside*
2263 ērĕmŏs (1), *tranquil, peaceful*
2270 hēsuchazō (1), *to refrain*
2272 hēsuchiŏs (1), *still, undisturbed*
2687 katastĕllō (1), *to quell, quiet*

QUIETED
1826 dâmam (1), *to be silent; to stop, cease*
5117 nûwach (1), *to rest; to settle down*

QUIETETH
8252 shâqat (1), *to repose*

QUIETLY
7987 shᵉlîy (1), *privacy*

QUIETNESS
5183 nachath (1), *quiet*
7961 shâlêv (1), *carefree; security, at ease*

7962 shalvâh (1), *security, ease*
8252 shâqat (4), *to repose*
8253 sheqet (1), *tranquillity*
1515 ĕirēnē (1), *peace; health; prosperity*
2271 hēsuchia (1), *stillness*

QUIT
1961 hâyâh (1), *to exist, i.e. be or become*
5352 nâqâh (1), *to be bare, i.e. extirpated*
5355 nâqîy (2), *innocent*
407 andrizŏmai (1), *to act manly*

QUITE
3615 kâlâh (1), *to cease, be finished, perish*
5080 nâdach (1), *to push off, scattered*
6181 'eryâh (1), *nudity*

QUIVER
827 'ashpâh (6), *quiver*
8522 tᵉlîy (1), *quiver*

QUIVERED
6750 tsâlal (1), *to tinkle, to rattle together*

RAAMAH
7484 Ra'mâh (5), *horse's mane*

RAAMIAH
7485 Ra'amyâh (1), *Jehovah has shaken*

RAAMSES
7486 Ra'mᵉçêç (1), *Rameses or Raamses*

RAB-MAG
7248 Rab-Mâg (2), *chief Magian*

RAB-SARIS
7249 Rab-Çârîyç (3), *chief chamberlain*

RAB-SHAKEH
7262 Rabshâqêh (8), *chief butler*

RABBAH
7237 Rabbâh (13), *great*

RABBATH
7237 Rabbâh (2), *great*

RABBI
4461 rhabbi (7), *my master*

RABBITH
7245 Rabbîyth (1), *multitude*

RABBONI
4462 rhabbŏni (1), *my master*

RABSHAKEH
7262 Rabshâqêh (8), *chief butler*

RACA
4469 rhaka (1), *O empty one, i.e. worthless*

RACE
734 'ôrach (1), *road; manner of life*
4793 mêrôwts (1), *running foot-race*
73 agōn (1), *contest, struggle*

4712 stadiŏn (1), *length of about 200 yards*

RACHAB
4477 Rhachab (1), *proud*

RACHAL
7403 Râkâl (1), *merchant*

RACHEL
7354 Râchêl (41), *ewe*
4478 Rhachêl (1), *ewe*

RACHEL'S
7354 Râchêl (5), *ewe*

RADDAI
7288 Radday (1), *domineering*

RAFTERS
7351 rᵉchîyṭ (1), *panel*

RAGAU
4466 Rhagau (1), *friend*

RAGE
1984 hâlal (2), *to boast*
2195 za'am (1), *fury*
2197 za'aph (2), *anger*
2534 chêmâh (2), *heat; anger; poison*
5678 'ebrâh (2), *outburst*
7264 râgaz (5), *to quiver*
7266 rᵉgaz (Ch.) (1), *violent anger*
7267 rôgez (1), *disquiet; anger*
7283 râgash (1), *to be tumultuous*
5433 phruassō (1), *to make a tumult*

RAGED
1993 hâmâh (1), *to be in great commotion*

RAGETH
5674 'âbar (1), *to cross over; to transition*

RAGING
1348 gê'ûwth (1), *ascending; majesty*
1993 hâmâh (1), *to be in great commotion*
2197 za'aph (1), *anger, rage*
66 agriŏs (1), *wild (country)*
2830 kludōn (1), *surge, raging*

RAGS
899 beged (1), *clothing; treachery or pillage*
4418 mâlâch (2), *rag or old garment*
7168 qera' (1), *rag, torn pieces*

RAGUEL
7467 Rᵉ'ûw'êl (1), *friend of God*

RAHAB
7294 Rahab (3), *boaster*
7343 Râchâb (5), *proud*
4460 Rhaab (2), *proud*

RAHAM
7357 Racham (1), *pity*

RAHEL
7354 Râchêl (1), *ewe*

RAIL
2778 châraph (1), *to spend the winter*

RAILED
5860 'îyṭ (1), *to swoop down upon; to insult*
987 blasphēmĕō (2), *to speak impiously*

RAILER
3060 lŏidŏrŏs (1), *verbal abuser*

RAILING
988 blasphēmia (1), *impious speech*
989 blasphēmŏs (1), *slanderous*
3059 lŏidŏria (1), *slander*

RAILINGS
988 blasphēmia (1), *impious speech*

RAIMENT
899 beged (12), *clothing; treachery or pillage*
3682 kᵉçûwth (1), *cover; veiling*
3830 lᵉbûwsh (1), *garment; wife*
4055 mad (1), *vesture, garment; carpet*
4254 machălâtsâh (1), *mantle, garment*
4403 malbûwsh (3), *garment, clothing*
7553 riqmâh (1), *variegation of color*
8008 salmâh (5), *clothing*
8071 simlâh (11), *dress*
1742 ĕnduma (5), *apparel, outer robe*
2066 ĕsthēs (2), *to clothe*
2440 himatiŏn (12), *to put on clothes*
2441 himatismŏs (2), *clothing*
4629 skĕpasma (1), *clothing; covering*

RAIN
1653 geshem (30), *rain*
3138 yôwreh (1), *autumn rain showers*
3384 yârâh (2), *to throw, shoot an arrow*
4175 môwreh (3), *archer; teaching; early rain*
4305 mâṭar (11), *to rain*
4306 mâṭâr (37), *rain, shower of rain*
4456 malqôwsh (6), *spring rain*
8164 sâ'îyr (1), *shower*
1026 brĕchō (2), *to make wet; to rain*
1026+5205 brĕchō (1), *to make wet; to rain*
1028 brŏchē (2), *rain*
5205 huĕtŏs (5), *rain; rain shower*

RAINBOW
2463 iris (2), *rainbow*

RAINED
1656 gôshem (1), *rain downpour*
4305 mâṭar (6), *to rain*
1026 brĕchō (2), *to make wet; to rain*

RAINY
5464 çagrîyd (1), *pouring rain*

RAISE
5375 nâsâ' (2), *to lift up*
5549 çâlal (2), *to mound up; to exalt*
5782 'ûwr (6), *to awake*
6965 qûwm (30), *to rise*
450 anistēmi (8), *to rise; to come to life*
1453 ĕgĕirō (8), *to waken, i.e. rouse*
1817 ĕxanistēmi (2), *to beget, raise up*
1825 ĕxĕgĕirō (1), *to resuscitate; release*

RAISED
1361 gâbahh (1), *to be lofty; to be haughty*
5782 'ûwr (12), *to awake*
5927 'âlâh (3), *to ascend, be high, mount*
5975 'âmad (1), *to stand*
6209 'ârar (1), *to bare; to demolish*
6965 qûwm (10), *to rise*
6966 qûwm (Ch.) (1), *to rise*
386 anastasis (1), *resurrection from death*
450 anistēmi (6), *to rise; to come to life*
1326 diĕgĕirō (1), *to arouse, stimulate*
1453 ĕgĕirō (45), *to waken, i.e. rouse*
1825 ĕxĕgĕirō (1), *to resuscitate; release*
1892 ĕpĕgĕirō (1), *to excite against, stir up*
4891 sunĕgĕirō (1), *to raise up with*

RAISER
5674 'âbar (1), *to cross over; to transition*

RAISETH
2210 zâqaph (2), *to lift up, comfort*
5975 'âmad (1), *to stand*
6965 qûwm (2), *to rise*
7613 sᵉ'êth (1), *elevation; swelling leprous scab*
1453 ĕgĕirō (1), *to waken, i.e. rouse*

RAISING
5872 'Êyn Gedîy (1), *fountain of a kid*
4160+1999 pŏiĕō (1), *to do*

RAISINS
6778 tsammûwq (4), *lump of dried grapes*

RAKEM
7552 Reqem (1), *versi-color*

RAKKATH
7557 Raqqath (1), *beach (as expanded shingle)*

RAKKON
7542 Raqqôwn (1), *thinness*

RAM
352 'ayîl (89), *chief; ram*
7410 Râm (7), *high*

RAM'S
3104 yôwbêl (1), *blast of a ram's horn*

RAMA
4471 Rhama (1), *height*

RAMAH
7414 Râmâh (36), *height*

RAMATH
7418 Râmôwth-Negeb (1), *heights of* (the) *South*

RAMATH-LEHI
7437 Râmath Lechîy (1), *height of* (a) *jaw-bone*

RAMATH-MIZPEH
7434 Râmath ham-Mitspeh (1), *height of the watch-tower*

RAMATHAIM-ZOPHIM
7436 Râmâthayim Tsôwphîym (1), *double height of watchers*

RAMATHITE
7435 Râmâthîy (1), *Ramathite*

RAMESES
7486 Ra'mᵉçêç (4), *Rameses or Raamses*

RAMIAH
7422 Ramyâh (1), *Jehovah has raised*

RAMOTH
3406 Yᵉrîymôwth (1), *elevations*
7216 Râ'môwth (6), *heights*
7418 Râmôwth-Negeb (1), *heights of* (the) *South*

RAMOTH-GILEAD
7433 Râmôth Gil'âd (19), *heights of Gilad*

RAMPART
2426 chêyl (2), *rampart, battlement*

RAMS
352 'ayîl (61), *chief; ram*
1798 dᵉkar (Ch.) (3), *male sheep*
3733 kar (2), *ram sheep; battering ram*
6260 'attûwd (2), *he-goats; leaders*

RAMS'
352 'ayîl (5), *chief; ram*
3104 yôwbêl (4), *blast of a ram's horn*

RAN
1272 bârach (1), *to flee suddenly*
1980 hâlak (2), *to walk; live a certain way*
3331 yâtsa' (1), *to strew as a surface*
3332 yâtsaq (1), *to pour out*
5064 nâgar (1), *to pour out; to deliver over*
6379 pâkâh (1), *to pour, trickle*
6584 pâshaṭ (1), *to strip, i.e. unclothe, plunder*
7323 rûwts (30), *to run*
7519 râtsâ' (1), *to run; to delight in*
7857 shâṭaph (1), *to gush; to inundate*

R

1530 ĕispēdaō (1), to *rush in*

1532 ĕistrĕchō (1), to *hasten inward*

1632 ĕkchĕō (1), to *pour forth; to bestow*

2027 ĕpŏkĕllō (1), to *beach a ship vessel*

2701 katatrĕchō (1), to *hasten, run*

3729 hŏrmaō (4), to *dash or plunge, stampede*

4063 pĕritrĕchō (1), to *traverse, run about*

4370 prŏstrĕchō (1), to *hasten by running*

4390 prŏtrĕchō (1), to *run ahead, i.e. to precede*

4890 sundrŏmĕ (1), (riotous) *concourse*

4936 suntrĕchō (2), to *rush together*

5143 trĕchō (6), to *run or walk hastily; to strive*

RANG

1949 hûwm (2), to *make an uproar; agitate*

RANGE

3491 yâthûwr (1), *gleaning*

RANGES

3600 kîyr (1), portable cooking *range*

7713 sᵉdêrâh (3), *row, i.e. rank of soldiers; story*

RANGING

8264 shâqaq (1), to *seek*

RANK

1277 bârîy' (2), *fatted or plump; healthy*

4634 ma'ărâkâh (1), *row; pile; military array*

5737 'âdar (1), to *arrange; hoe a vineyard*

RANKS

734 'ôrach (1), *road; manner of life*

6471 pa'am (2), *time; step; occurence*

4237 prasia (1), arranged *group*

RANSOM

3724 kôpher (8), *village; redemption*-price

6299 pâdâh (1), to *ransom; to release*

6306 pidyôwm (1), *ransom; payment*

487 antilutrŏn (1), *redemption*-price

3083 lutrŏn (2), *redemption*-price

RANSOMED

1350 gâ'al (2), to *redeem; to be the next of kin*

6299 pâdâh (1), to *ransom; to release*

RAPHA

7498 Râphâ' (2), *giant*

RAPHU

7505 Râphûw' (1), *cured*

RARE

3358 yaqqîyr (Ch.) (1), *precious*

RASE

6168 'ârâh (1), to *be, make bare; demolish*

RASH

926 bâhal (1), to *tremble; hasten, hurry anxiously*

4116 mâhar (1), to *hurry; promptly*

RASHLY

4312 prŏpĕtēs (1), falling forward *headlong*

RASOR

8593 ta'ar (1), *knife; razor; scabbard*

RATE

1697 dâbâr (5), *word; matter; thing*

RATHER

408 'al (2), *not; nothing*

977 bâchar (1), *select, chose, prefer*

2228 ē (3), *or; than*

2309 thĕlō (1), to *will; to desire; to choose*

3123 mallŏn (34), *in a greater degree*

3304 mĕnŏungĕ (1), *so then at least*

4056 pĕrissŏtĕrōs (1), *more superabundantly*

4133 plēn (2), *rather, yet*

RATTLETH

7439 rânâh (1), to *whiz, rattle*

RATTLING

7494 ra'ash (1), *vibration, bounding*

RAVEN

6158 'ôrêb (6), *dusky-hue raven*

RAVENING

2963 țâraph (3), to *pluck off or pull to pieces*

724 harpagē (1), *pillage; greediness; robbery*

727 harpax (1), *rapacious; robbing*

RAVENOUS

5861 'ayiţ (2), bird of prey (poss.) *hawk*

6530 pᵉrîyts (1), *violent*

RAVENS

6158 'ôrêb (4), *dusky-hue raven*

2876 kŏrax (1), *crow or raven*

RAVIN

2963 țâraph (1), to *pluck off or pull to pieces*

2966 țᵉrêphâh (1), *torn prey*

RAVISHED

3823 lâbab (2), *transport with love; to stultify*

6031 'ânâh (1), to *afflict, be afflicted*

7686 shâgâh (2), to *stray, wander; to transgress*

7693 shâgal (2), to *copulate with*

RAW

2416 chay (6), *alive; raw; fresh; life*

4995 nâ' (1), *uncooked*

RAZOR

4177 môwrâh (3), *razor*

8593 ta'ar (2), *knife; razor; scabbard*

REACH

1272 bârach (1), to *flee suddenly*

1961 hâyâh (1), to *exist, i.e. be or become*

4229 mâchâh (1), to *touch, i.e. reach to*

5060 nâga' (5), to *strike*

5381 nâsag (2), to *reach*

2185 ĕphiknĕŏmai (1), to *extend to, reach to*

5342 phĕrō (2), to *bear or carry*

REACHED

4291 mᵉțâ' (Ch.) (2), to *arrive, to extend*

5060 nâga' (1), to *strike*

6293 pâga' (1), to *impinge*

6642 tsâbaț (1), to *hand out food*

190 akŏlŏuthĕō (1), to *accompany, follow*

2185 ĕphiknĕŏmai (1), to *extend to, reach to*

REACHETH

4291 mᵉțâ' (Ch.) (1), to *arrive, to extend*

5060 nâga' (4), to *strike*

6293 pâga' (1), to *impinge*

7971 shâlach (1), to *send away*

REACHING

5060 nâga' (3), to *strike*

1901 ĕpĕktĕinŏmai (1), to *stretch oneself forward*

READ

7121 qârâ' (35), to *call out*

7123 qᵉrâ' (Ch.) (7), to *call out*

314 anaginŏskō (28), to *read aloud in public*

READEST

314 anaginŏskō (2), to *read aloud in public*

READETH

7121 qârâ' (1), to *call out*

314 anaginŏskō (3), to *read aloud in public*

READINESS

2092 hĕtŏimŏs (1), *ready, prepared*

4288 prŏthumia (2), *alacrity, eagerness*

READING

4744 miqrâ' (1), *public meeting*

7121 qârâ' (2), to *call out*

320 anagnōsis (3), act of public *reading*

READY

631 'âçar (4), to *fasten; to join battle*

1951 hûwn (1), to *be, act light*

2363 chûwsh (1), to *hurry; to be eager*

2896 țôwb (1), *good; well*

3559 kûwn (17), to *set up: establish, fix, prepare*

4106 mâhîyr (2), *skillful*

4116 mâhar (2), to *hurry; promptly*

4131 môwț (1), to *slip, shake, fall*

4672 mâtsâ' (1), to *find or acquire; to occur*

5750 'ôwd (1), *again; repeatedly; still; more*

6257 'âthad (1), to *prepare*

6263 'ăthîyd (Ch.) (1), *prepared*

6264 'âthîyd (4), *prepared; treasure*

7126 qârab (1), to *approach, bring near*

7138 qârôwb (1), *near, close*

8003 shâlêm (1), *complete; friendly; safe*

1451 ĕggus (1), *near, close*

2090 hĕtŏimazō (10), to *prepare*

2092 hĕtŏimŏs (15), *ready, prepared*

2093 hĕtŏimōs (3), *in readiness*

2130 ĕumĕtadŏtŏs (1), *liberal, generous*

3195 mĕllō (4), to *intend, i.e. be about to*

3903 paraskĕuazō (3), to *get ready, prepare*

4288 prŏthumia (1), *alacrity, eagerness*

4289 prŏthumŏs (3), *alacrity, eagerness*

4689 spĕndō (1), to *pour out as a libation*

REAIA

7211 Rᵉ'âyâh (1), *Jehovah has seen*

REAIAH

7211 Rᵉ'âyâh (3), *Jehovah has seen*

REALM

4437 malkûw (Ch.) (3), *dominion*

4438 malkûwth (4), *rule; dominion*

REAP

7114 qâtsar (18), to *curtail, cut short*

2325 thĕrizō (13), to *harvest, reap a crop*

REAPED

7114 qâtsar (1), to *curtail, cut short*

270 amaō (1), *reap, mow down grain*

2325 thĕrizō (2), to *harvest, reap a crop*

REAPER

7114 qâtsar (1), to *curtail, cut short*

REAPERS

7114 qâtsar (7), to *curtail, cut short*

2327 thĕristēs (2), *harvester, reaper*

REAPEST

7114 qâtsar (1), to *curtail, cut short*

2325 thĕrizō (1), to *harvest, reap a crop*

REAPETH
7114 qâtsar (1), to *curtail, cut short*
2325 *thĕrizō* (3), to *harvest, reap a crop*

REAPING
7114 qâtsar (1), to *curtail, cut short*
2325 *thĕrizō* (2), to *harvest, reap a crop*

REAR
6965 qûwm (3), to *rise*
1453 *ĕgĕirō* (1), to *waken, i.e. rouse*

REARED
5324 nâtsab (1), to *station*
6965 qûwm (9), to *rise*

REASON
413 'êl (1), *to, toward*
1697 dâbâr (1), *word; matter; thing*
2808 cheshbôwn (1), *intelligent plan*
2940 ţa'am (1), *taste; intelligence; mandate*
3198 yâkach (3), to *be correct; to argue*
4480 min (5), *from, out of*
4486 manda' (Ch.) (1), *wisdom or intelligence*
5921 'al (2), *above, over, upon, or against*
5973 'îm (1), *with*
6440 pânîym (9), *face; front*
6903 qᵉbêl (Ch.) (1), *on account of, so as, since*
8199 shâphaţ (1), to *judge*
701 arĕstŏs (1), *agreeable; desirable; fit*
1223 dia (5), *through*, by means of; *because* of
1260 dialŏgizŏmai (5), to *deliberate*
1537 ĕk (3), *out, out of*
1752 hĕnĕka (1), *on account of*
3056 lŏgŏs (2), *word, matter, thing; Word*

REASONABLE
3050 lŏgikŏs (1), *rational, logical*

REASONED
1256 dialĕgŏmai (4), to *discuss*
1260 dialŏgizŏmai (5), to *deliberate*
3049 lŏgizŏmai (1), to *credit; to think, regard*
4802 suzĕtĕō (1), to *discuss, controvert*
4817 sullŏgizŏmai (1), to *reckon together*

REASONING
8433 tôwkêchâh (1), *correction, refutation*
1260 dialŏgizŏmai (1), to *deliberate*
1261 dialŏgismŏs (1), *consideration; debate*
4802 suzĕtĕō (1), to *discuss, controvert*
4803 suzĕtĕsis (1), *discussion, dispute*

REASONS
8394 tâbûwn (1), *intelligence; argument*

REBA
7254 Reba' (2), *fourth*

REBECCA
4479 Rhĕbĕkka (1), *fettering* (by beauty)

REBEKAH
7259 Ribqâh (28), *fettering* (by beauty)

REBEKAH'S
7259 Ribqâh (2), *fettering* (by beauty)

REBEL
4775 mârad (9), to *rebel*
4784 mârâh (4), to *rebel* or *resist; to provoke*
5493 çûwr (1), to *turn off*

REBELLED
4775 mârad (12), to *rebel*
4784 mârâh (16), to *rebel* or *resist; to provoke*
6586 pâsha' (5), to *break away from authority*
6856 tsippôren (1), *nail; point* of a style or pen

REBELLEST
4775 mârad (2), to *rebel*

REBELLION
4776 mᵉrad (Ch.) (1), *rebellion*
4779 mârâd (Ch.) (1), *rebellious*
4805 mᵉrîy (4), *rebellion, rebellious*
5627 çârâh (2), *apostasy; crime; remission*
6588 pesha' (1), *revolt*

REBELLIOUS
4775 mârad (1), to *rebel*
4779 mârâd (Ch.) (2), *rebellious*
4780 mardûwth (1), *rebelliousness*
4784 mârâh (9), to *rebel* or *resist; to provoke*
4805 mᵉrîy (17), *rebellion, rebellious*
5637 çârar (6), to *be refractory, stubborn*

REBELS
4775 mârad (1), to *rebel*
4784 mârâh (1), to *rebel* or *resist; to provoke*
4805 mᵉrîy (1), *rebellion, rebellious*

REBUKE
1605 gâ'ar (7), to *chide, reprimand*
1606 gᵉ'ârâh (12), *chiding, rebuke*
2781 cherpâh (2), *contumely, disgrace*
3198 yâkach (8), to *be correct; to argue*
4045 mig'ereth (1), *reproof* (i.e. a curse)
8433 tôwkêchâh (4), *refutation, proof*
298 amōmĕtŏs (1), *unblemished*
1651 ĕlĕgchō (4), to *admonish, rebuke*

REASONS — continued listing
1969 ĕpiplēssō (1), to *upbraid, rebuke*
2008 ĕpitimaō (6), to *rebuke, warn, forbid*

REBUKED
1605 gâ'ar (4), to *chide, reprimand*
3198 yâkach (1), to *be correct; to argue*
7378 rîyb (1), to *hold a controversy; to defend*
1651 ĕlĕgchō (1), to *admonish, rebuke*
2008 ĕpitimaō (17), to *rebuke, warn, forbid*
2192+1649 ĕchō (1), to *have; hold; keep*

REBUKER
4148 mûwçâr (1), *reproof, warning*

REBUKES
8433 tôwkêchâh (3), *correction, refutation*

REBUKETH
1605 gâ'ar (1), to *chide, reprimand*
3198 yâkach (3), to *be correct; to argue*

REBUKING
1606 gᵉ'ârâh (1), *chiding, rebuke*
2008 ĕpitimaō (1), to *rebuke, warn, forbid*

RECALL
7725 shûwb (1), to *turn back; to return*

RECEIPT
5058 tĕlōniŏn (3), *tax-gatherer's booth*

RECEIVE
1878 dâshên (1), to *fatten; to satisfy*
3557 kûwl (2), to *keep in; to measure*
3947 lâqach (35), to *take*
5162 nâcham (1), to *be sorry; to pity, console*
5375 nâsâ' (3), to *lift up*
6901 qâbal (3), to *admit; to take*
6902 qᵉbal (Ch.) (1), to *acquire*
8254 shâqal (1), to *suspend* in trade
308 anablĕpō (7), to *look up; to recover sight*
568 apĕchō (1), to *be distant*
588 apŏdĕchŏmai (1), to *welcome; approve*
618 apŏlambanō (8), to *receive; be repaid*
1209 dĕchŏmai (24), to *receive, welcome*
1325 didōmi (1), to *give*
1523 ĕisdĕchŏmai (1), to *take into one's favor*
1926 ĕpidĕchŏmai (1), to *admit, welcome*
2210 zēmiŏō (1), to *experience detriment*
2865 kŏmizō (6), to *provide* for
2983 lambanō (61), to *take, receive*

RECEIVED
622 'âçaph (1), to *gather, collect*
1961 hâyâh (2), to *exist, i.e. be or become*
2388 châzaq (1), to *fasten upon; to seize*
2505 châlaq (1), to *be smooth; be slippery*
3947 lâqach (22), to *take*
4672 mâtsâ' (1), to *find* or *acquire; to occur*
6901 qâbal (3), to *admit; to take*
308 anablĕpō (8), to *look up; to recover sight*
324 anadĕchŏmai (2), to *entertain* as a guest
353 analambanō (3), to *take up, bring up*
354 analēpsis (1), *ascension*
568 apĕchō (1), to *be distant*
588 apŏdĕchŏmai (4), to *welcome; approve*
618 apŏlambanō (1), to *receive; be repaid*
1183 dĕkatŏō (1), to *give* or *take a tenth*
1209 dĕchŏmai (16), to *receive, welcome*
1653 ĕlĕĕō (1), to *give out compassion*
2865 kŏmizō (3), to *provide for, to carry off*
2983 lambanō (56), to *take, receive*
3336 mĕtalēmpsis (1), *participation, sharing*
3549 nŏmŏthĕtĕō (1), to *be given law*
3880 paralambanō (13), to *assume* an office
4355 prŏslambanō (3), to *welcome, receive*
4687 spĕirō (4), to *scatter, i.e. sow seed*
4732 stĕrĕŏō (1), to *be, become strong*
5264 hupŏdĕchŏmai (4), to *entertain hospitably*
5274 hupŏlambanō (1), to *take up, i.e. continue*

RECEIVEDST
618 apŏlambanō (1), to *receive; be repaid*

RECEIVER
8254 shâqal (1), to *suspend* in trade

RECEIVETH
622 'âçaph (1), to *gather, collect*
3947 lâqach (4), to *take*
1209 dĕchŏmai (8), to *receive, welcome*
1926 ĕpidĕchŏmai (1), to *admit, welcome*

R

RECEIVING

2983 lambanō (14), to take, receive
3335 mĕtalambanō (1), to *participate*
3858 paradĕchŏmai (1), to *accept, receive*
4327 prŏsdĕchŏmai (1), to *receive;* to *await* for

RECEIVING

3947 lâqach (1), to *take*
618 apŏlambanō (1), to *receive; be repaid*
2865 kŏmizŏ (1), to *provide* for, to *carry* off
2983 lambanō (1), to take, receive
3028 lēmpsis (1), act of receipt
3880 paralambanō (1), to *assume* an office
4356 prŏslēpsis (1), *admission, acceptance*

RECHAB

7394 Rêkâb (13), *rider*

RECHABITES

7397 Rêkâh (4), *softness*

RECHAH

7397 Rêkâh (1), *softness*

RECKON

2803 châshab (3), to *think, regard;* to *value*
5608 çâphar (1), to *inscribe;* to *enumerate*
6485 pâqad (1), to *visit, care for, count*
3049 lŏgizŏmai (2), to *credit;* to *think, regard*
4868 sunairō (1), to *compute* an account

RECKONED

2803 châshab (4), to *think, regard;* to *value*
3187 yâchas (12), to *enroll by family list*
7737 shâvâh (1), to *resemble;* to *adjust*
3049 lŏgizŏmai (4), to *credit;* to *think, regard*

RECKONETH

4868+3056 sunairō (1), to *compute* an account

RECKONING

2803 châshab (1), to *think, regard;* to *value*
6486 pᵉquddâh (1), *visitation; punishment*

RECOMMENDED

3860 paradidōmi (2), to *hand over*

RECOMPENCE

1576 gᵉmûwl (9), *act; reward, recompense*
7966 shillûwm (1), *requital; retribution; fee*
8005 shillêm (1), *requital*
8545 tᵉmûwrâh (1), *barter, compensation*
468 antapŏdŏma (2), *requital, recompense*
489 antimisthia (2), *correspondence*
3405 misthapŏdŏsia (3), *requital, good or bad*

RECOMPENCES

1578 gᵉmûwlâh (1), *act; reward, recompense*
7966 shillûwm (1), *requital; retribution; fee*

RECOMPENSE

1580 gâmal (2), to *benefit* or *requite;* to *wean*
5414 nâthan (9), to *give*
7725 shûwb (3), to *return* or restore
7999 shâlam (7), to *be safe;* to *reciprocate*
467 antapŏdidōmi (3), to *requite* good or evil
591 apŏdidōmi (1), to *give away*

RECOMPENSED

5414 nâthan (1), to *give*
7725 shûwb (5), to *return* or restore
7999 shâlam (2), to *be safe;* to *reciprocate*
467 antapŏdidōmi (2), to *requite* good or evil

RECOMPENSEST

7999 shâlam (1), to *be safe;* to *reciprocate*

RECOMPENSING

5414 nâthan (1), to *give*

RECONCILE

3722 kâphar (2), to *placate* or *cancel*
7521 râtsâh (1), to *be pleased with;* to *satisfy*
604 apŏkatallassŏ (2), to *reconcile fully, reunite*

RECONCILED

604 apŏkatallassŏ (1), to *reconcile fully, reunite*
1259 diallassŏ (1), to *be reconciled*
2644 katallassŏ (5), to *change mutually*

RECONCILIATION

2398 châṭâ' (1), to *sin*
3722 kâphar (4), to *placate* or *cancel*
2433 hilaskŏmai (1), to *conciliate,* to *atone* for
2643 katallagē (2), *restoration*

RECONCILING

3722 kâphar (1), to *cover;* to *expiate*
2643 katallagē (1), *restoration*
2644 katallassŏ (1), to *change mutually*

RECORD

1799 dikrôwn (Ch.) (1), official *register*
2142 zâkar (2), to *remember;* to *mention*
5749 'ûwd (3), to *duplicate* or *repeat*
7717 sâhêd (1), *witness*
3140 marturĕŏ (13), to *testify;* to *commend*
3141 marturia (7), *evidence given*
3143 marturŏmai (1), to *witness*
3144 martus (2), *witness*

RECORDED

3789 kâthab (1), to *write*

RECORDER

2142 zâkar (9), to *remember;* to *mention*

RECORDS

1799 dikrôwn (Ch.) (2), official *register*
2146 zikrôwn (1), *commemoration*

RECOUNT

2142 zâkar (1), to *remember;* to *mention*

RECOVER

622 'âçaph (4), to *gather, collect*
1082 bâlag (1), to *be comforted*
2421 châyâh (6), to *live;* to *revive*
2492 châlam (1), to *be, make plump;* to *dream*
4241 michyâh (1), *preservation of life; sustenance*
5337 nâtsal (3), to *deliver;* to *be snatched*
6113 'âtsar (1), to *hold back;* to *maintain, rule*
7069 qânâh (1), to *create;* to *procure*
7725 shûwb (1), to *turn back;* to *return*
366 ananēphŏ (1), to *regain* one's senses
2192+2573 ĕchŏ (1), to *have; hold; keep*

RECOVERED

2388 châzaq (1), to *fasten* upon; to *seize*
2421 châyâh (2), to *live;* to *revive*
5337 nâtsal (2), to *deliver;* to *be snatched*
5927 'âlâh (1), to *ascend, be high, mount*
7725 shûwb (5), to *turn back;* to *return*

RECOVERING

309 anablĕpsis (1), *restoration of sight*

RED

119 'âdam (9), to *be red in the face*
122 'âdôm (7), *rosy, red*
132 'admônîy (1), *reddish, ruddy*
923 bahaṭ (1), *white marble*
2447 chaklîyl (1), *darkly flashing eyes; brilliant*
2560 châmar (1), to *ferment, foam;* to *glow*
2561 chemer (1), *fermenting wine*
5488 çûwph (24), *papyrus reed; reed*
5489 Çûwph (1), *reed*
5492 çûwphâh (1), *hurricane* wind
2281 thalassa (2), *sea* or *lake*
4449 purrhazŏ (2), to *redden*
4450 purrhŏs (2), *fire-like, flame-colored*

REDDISH

125 'ădamdâm (6), *reddish*

REDEEM

1350 gâ'al (23), to *redeem; be next of kin*
1353 gᵉullâh (5), *redemption*
6299 pâdâh (24), to *ransom;* to *release*
6304 pᵉdûwth (1), *distinction; deliverance*
1805 ĕxagŏrazŏ (1), to *buy up, ransom*
3084 lutrŏŏ (1), to *free by paying a ransom*

REDEEMED

1350 gâ'al (24), to *redeem; be next of kin*
1353 gᵉullâh (2), *redemption*
6299 pâdâh (23), to *ransom;* to *release*
6302 pâdûwy (2), *ransom*
6306 pidyôwm (2), *ransom payment*
6561 pâraq (1), to *break off* or *crunch;* to *deliver*
7069 qânâh (1), to *create;* to *procure*
59 agŏrazŏ (3), to *purchase;* to *redeem*
1805 ĕxagŏrazŏ (1), to *buy up, ransom*
3084 lutrŏŏ (2), to *free by paying a ransom*
4160+3085 pŏiĕŏ (1), to *make* or *do*

REDEEMEDST

6299 pâdâh (1), to *ransom;* to *release*

REDEEMER

1350 gâ'al (18), to *redeem; be next of kin*

REDEEMETH

1350 gâ'al (1), to *redeem;* to *be the next of kin*
6299 pâdâh (1), to *ransom;* to *release*

REDEEMING

1353 gᵉullâh (1), *redemption*
1805 ĕxagŏrazŏ (2), to *buy up, ransom*

REDEMPTION

1353 gᵉullâh (5), *redemption*
6304 pᵉdûwth (2), *distinction; deliverance*
6306 pidyôwm (2), *ransom payment*
629 apŏlutrŏsis (9), *ransom in full*
3085 lutrŏsis (2), *ransoming*

REDNESS

2498 châlaph (1), to *hasten* away; to *pass on*

REDOUND

4052 pĕrissĕuŏ (1), to *superabound*

REED

7070 qâneh (21), *reed*
2563 kalamŏs (11), *reed*

REEDS

98 'ăgam (1), *marsh; pond; pool*
7070 qâneh (6), *reed*

R

REIGNING
4427 mâlak (1), to *reign as king*

REINS
2504 châlâts (1), *loins, areas of the waist*
3629 kilyâh (13), *kidney; mind, heart, spirit*
3510 něphrŏs (1), *inmost mind*

REJECT
3988 mâ'aç (1), to *spurn; to disappear*
114 athětěō (2), to *disesteem, neutralize*
3868 paraitěŏmai (1), to *deprecate, decline*

REJECTED
2310 châdêl (1), *ceasing or destitute*
3988 mâ'aç (17), to *spurn; to disappear*
96 adŏkimŏs (1), *failing the test, worthless*
114 athětěō (1), to *disesteem, neutralize*
593 apŏdŏkimazō (7), to *repudiate, reject*
1609 ěkptuō (1), to *spurn, scorn*

REJECTETH
14 agathŏěrgěō (1), to do *good work*

REJOICE
1523 gîyl (23), *rejoice*
1524 gîyl (2), *age, stage in life*
4885 mâsôws (1), *delight*
5937 'âlaz (8), to *jump for joy*
5947 'allîyz (3), *exultant; reveling*
5965 'âlaç (1), to *leap for joy, i.e. exult, wave*
5970 'âlats (4), to *jump for joy*
7442 rânan (11), to *shout for joy*
7797 sûws (14), to *be bright, i.e. cheerful*
7832 sâchaq (1), to *laugh; to scorn; to play*
8055 sâmach (70), to *be, make gleesome*
8056 sâmêach (5), *blithe or gleeful*
8057 simchâh (4), *blithesomeness or glee*
21 agalliaō (4), to *exult*
2165 ěuphrainō (5), to *rejoice, be glad*
2744 kauchaŏmai (4), to *glory in, rejoice in*
2745 kauchēma (1), *boast; brag*
4796 sugchairō (5), to *sympathize in gladness*
5463 chairō (24), to be *cheerful*

REJOICED
1523 gîyl (2), *rejoice*
2302 châdâh (1), to *rejoice, be glad*
5937 'âlaz (1), to *jump for joy*
6670 tsâhal (1), to *be cheerful*

REGION
7797 sûws (3), to *be bright, i.e. cheerful*
8055 sâmach (20), to *be, make gleesome*
8056 sâmêach (3), *blithe or gleeful*
8057 simchâh (1), *blithesomeness or glee*
21 agalliaō (4), to *exult*
2165 ěuphrainō (1), to *rejoice, be glad*
4796 sugchairō (1), to *sympathize in gladness*
5463 chairō (8), to be *cheerful*

REJOICEST
5937 'âlaz (1), to *jump for joy*

REJOICETH
1523 gîyl (1), *rejoice*
4885 mâsôws (1), *delight*
5937 'âlaz (1), to *jump for joy*
5938 'âlêz (1), *exultant*
5970 'âlats (2), to *jump for joy*
7797 sûws (3), to *be bright, i.e. cheerful*
8055 sâmach (4), to *be, make gleesome*
2620 katakauchaŏmai (1), to *exult over*
4796 sugchairō (1), to *sympathize in gladness*
5463 chairō (3), to be *cheerful*

REJOICING
1524 gîyl (1), *age, stage in life*
1525 gîylâh (1), *joy, delight*
5947 'allîyz (1), *exultant; reveling*
5951 'ălîytsûwth (1), *exultation*
7440 rinnâh (3), *shout*
7832 sâchaq (2), to *laugh; to scorn; to play*
8055 sâmach (1), to *be, make gleesome*
8056 sâmêach (1), *blithe or gleeful*
8057 simchâh (2), *blithesomeness or glee*
8342 sâsôwn (1), *cheerfulness; welcome*
8643 tᵉrûw'âh (1), *battle-cry; clangor*
2745 kauchēma (4), *boast; brag*
2746 kauchēsis (4), *boasting; bragging*
5463 chairō (5), to be *cheerful*

REKEM
7552 Reqem (5), *versi-color*

RELEASE
2010 hănâchâh (1), *quiet*
8058 shâmaṭ (2), to *let alone, desist, remit*
8059 shᵉmiṭṭâh (5), *remission of debt*
630 apŏluō (13), to *relieve, release*

RELEASED
630 apŏluō (4), to *relieve, release; to divorce*

RELIED
8172 shâ'an (3), to *support, rely on*

RELIEF
1248 diakŏnia (1), *attendance, aid, service*

RELIEVE
833 'âshar (1), to *go forward; guide; prosper*
2388 châzaq (1), to *bind, restrain, conquer*
7725 shûwb (3), to *turn back; to return*
1884 ěparkěō (2), to *help*

RELIEVED
1884 ěparkěō (1), to *help*

RELIEVETH
5749 'ûwd (1), to *protest, testify; to restore*

RELIGION
2356 thrēskěia (3), *observance, religion*
2454 Iŏudaismŏs (2), *Jewish faith*

RELIGIOUS
2357 thrēskŏs (1), *ceremonious, pious*
4576 sěbŏmai (1), to *revere, i.e. adore*

RELY
8172 shâ'an (1), to *support, rely on*

REMAIN
1481 gûwr (1), to *sojourn, live as an alien*
1961 hâyâh (1), to *exist, i.e. be or become*
3241 Yânîym (1), *asleep*
3427 yâshab (11), to *dwell, to remain*
3498 yâthar (13), to *remain or be left*
3885 lûwn (5), to *be obstinate with*
5117 nûwach (1), to *rest; to settle down*
5975 'âmad (3), to *stand*
6965 qûwm (1), to *rise*
7604 shâ'ar (15), to *leave, remain*
7611 shᵉ'êrîyth (1), *remainder or residual*
7931 shâkan (3), to *reside*
8245 shâqad (1), to *be alert, i.e. sleepless*
8300 sârîyd (8), *survivor; remainder*
3062 lŏipŏi (1), *remaining ones*
3306 měnō (8), to *remain*
4035 pěrilěipō (2), to *survive, be left, remain*
4052 pěrissěuō (1), to *superabound*

REMAINDER
3498 yâthar (4), to *remain or be left*
7611 shᵉ'êrîyth (2), *remainder or residual*

REMAINED
1961 hâyâh (1), to *exist, i.e. be or become*

REIGNING
3427 yâshab (10), to *dwell, to remain*
3462 yâshên (1), to *sleep; to grow old, stale*
3498 yâthar (5), to *remain or be left*
5975 'âmad (4), to *stand*
7604 shâ'ar (23), to *leave, remain*
8277 sârad (1), to *escape or survive*
8300 sârîyd (1), *survivor; remainder*
1265 diaměnō (1), to *stay constantly*
3306 měnō (3), to *remain*
4052 pěrissěuō (3), to *superabound*

REMAINEST
3427 yâshab (1), to *dwell, to remain; to settle*
1265 diaměnō (1), to *stay constantly*

REMAINETH
3117 yôwm (1), *day; time period*
3427 yâshab (1), to *dwell, to remain; to settle*
3498 yâthar (4), to *remain or be left*
3885 lûwn (2), to *be obstinate with*
5736 'âdaph (4), to *be redundant*
5975 'âmad (1), to *stand*
7604 shâ'ar (8), to *leave, remain*
7931 shâkan (1), to *reside*
8300 sârîyd (3), *survivor; remainder*
620 apŏlěipō (3), to *leave behind; to forsake*
3306 měnō (5), to *stay, remain*
3588+3063 hŏ (1), "*the,*" i.e. the definite article

REMAINING
3320 yâtsab (1), to *station, offer, continue*
3498 yâthar (1), to *remain or be left*
7931 shâkan (1), to *reside*
8300 sârîyd (9), *survivor; remainder*
3306 měnō (1), to *remain*

REMALIAH
7425 Rᵉmalyâhûw (11), *Jehovah has bedecked*

REMALIAH'S
7425 Rᵉmalyâhûw (2), *Jehovah has bedecked*

REMEDY
4832 marpê' (3), *cure; deliverance; placidity*

REMEMBER
2142 zâkar (120), to *remember; to mention*
6485 pâqad (1), to *visit, care for, count*
3403 mimnēskō (1), to *remind or to recall*
3415 mnaŏmai (9), to *bear in mind*
3421 mněmŏněuō (16), to *exercise memory*
5279 hupŏmimnēskō (1), to *suggest to memory*

REMEMBERED
2142 zâkar (48), to *remember; to mention*
2143 zêker (1), *commemoration*
3415 mnaŏmai (6), to *recollect*
3421 mnēmŏnĕuō (1), to *recall*
5279 hupŏmimnēskō (1), to *remind oneself*

REMEMBEREST
2142 zâkar (1), to *remember; to mention*
3415 mnaŏmai (1), to *recollect*

REMEMBERETH
2142 zâkar (3), to *remember; to mention*
363 anamimnēskō (1), to *remind; to recollect*
3421 mnēmŏnĕuō (1), to *recall*

REMEMBERING
2142 zâkar (1), to *remember; to mention*
3421 mnēmŏnĕuō (1), to *recall*

REMEMBRANCE
2142 zâkar (13), to *remember; to mention*
2143 zêker (11), *recollection*
2146 zikrôwn (5), *commemoration*
6485 pâqad (1), to *visit, care for, count*
363 anamimnēskō (3), to *remind; to recollect*
364 anamnēsis (5), *recollection*
3415 mnaŏmai (3), to *recollect*
3417 mnĕia (3), *recollection; recital*
3418 mnēma (1), *sepulchral monument*
5179 tupŏs (2), *shape, resemblance; "type"*
5279 hupŏmimnēskō (2), to *remind oneself*
5280 hupŏmnēsis (3), *reminding*
5294 hupŏtithēmi (1), to *hazard; to suggest*

REMEMBRANCES
2146 zikrôwn (1), *commemoration*

REMETH
7432 Remeth (1), *height*

REMISSION
859 aphĕsis (9), *pardon, freedom*
3929 parĕsis (1), *toleration, passing over*

REMIT
863 aphiēmi (1), to *leave; to pardon, forgive*

REMITTED
863 aphiēmi (1), to *leave; to pardon, forgive*

REMMON
7417 Rimmôwn (1), *pomegranate*

REMMON-METHOAR
7417 Rimmôwn (1), *pomegranate*

REMNANT
310 'achar (1), *after*
319 'achărîyth (1), *future; posterity*
3498 yâthar (4), to *remain or be left*
3499 yether (14), *remainder; small rope*
5629 çerach (1), *redundancy*
6413 pᵉlêyţâh (1), *escaped portion*
7604 shâ'ar (4), to *leave, remain*
7605 shᵉ'âr (11), *remainder*
7611 shᵉ'êrîyth (44), *remainder or residual*
8293 shêrûwth (1), *freedom*
8300 sârîyd (2), *survivor; remainder*
2640 katalĕimma (1), *few, remnant*
3005 lĕimma (1), *remainder, remnant*
3062 lŏipŏi (4), *remaining ones*

REMOVE
1540 gâlâh (2), to *denude; uncover*
1556 gâlal (1), to *roll; to commit*
4185 mûwsh (4), to *withdraw*
5110 nûwd (4), to *waver; to wander, flee*
5253 nâçag (4), to *retreat*
5265 nâça' (1), *start*
5437 çâbab (2), to *surround*
5472 çûwg (1), to *go back, to retreat*
5493 çûwr (15), to *turn off*
7368 râchaq (5), to *recede; remove*
7493 râ'ash (1), to *undulate, quake*
2795 kinĕō (1), to *stir, move, remove*
3179 mĕthistēmi (1), to *move*
3327 mĕtabainō (2), to *depart, move from*
3911 paraphĕrō (1), to *carry off; to avert*

REMOVED
167 'âhal (1), to *pitch a tent*
1540 gâlâh (3), to *denude; uncover*
1556 gâlal (1), to *roll; to commit*
2186 zânach (1), to *reject, forsake, fail*
2189 za'ăvâh (6), *agitation, maltreatment*
3014 yâgâh (1), to *push away, be removed*
3670 kânaph (1), to *withdraw*
4131 môwţ (5), to *slip, shake, fall*

REMMON
7417 Rimmôwn (1), *pomegranate*

4171 mûwr (1), to *alter; to barter, to dispose of*
4185 mûwsh (2), to *withdraw*
5074 nâdad (1), to *rove, flee; to drive away*
5079 niddâh (2), time of *menstrual impurity*
5110 nûwd (1), to *waver; to wander, flee*
5128 nûwa' (1), to *waver*
5206 nîydâh (1), *removal*
5265 nâça' (26), *start*
5437 çâbab (1), to *surround*
5493 çûwr (21), to *turn off*
5674 'âbar (1), to *cross over; to transition*
6275 'âthaq (4), to *remove*
7368 râchaq (4), to *recede*
142 airō (2), to *lift, to take up*
3179 mĕthistēmi (1), to *move*
3346 mĕtatithēmi (1), to *transport; to exchange*
3351 mĕtŏikizō (1), to *transfer as a settler*

REMOVETH
5253 nâçag (1), to *retreat*
5265 nâça' (1), *start*
5493 çûwr (1), to *turn off*
5709 'ădâ' (Ch.) (1), to *pass on or continue*
6275 'âthaq (1), to *remove*

REMOVING
1473 gôwlâh (2), *exile; captive*
5493 çûwr (2), to *turn off*
3331 mĕtathĕsis (1), *transferral to heaven*

REMPHAN
4481 Rhĕmphan (1), *Kijun (a pagan god)*

REND
1234 bâqa' (3), to *cleave, break, tear open*
6533 pâram (2), to *tear, be torn*
7167 qâra' (11), to *rend*
4486 rhēgnumi (1), to *tear to pieces*
4977 schizō (1), to *split or sever*

RENDER
5415 nᵉthan (Ch.) (1), to *give*
7725 shûwb (16), to *turn back; to return*
7999 shâlam (7), to *be safe; be, make complete*
467 antapŏdidōmi (1), to *requite good or evil*
591 apŏdidōmi (8), to *give away*

RENDERED
7725 shûwb (4), to *turn back; to return*

RENDEREST
7999 shâlam (1), to *be safe; be, make complete*

RENDERETH
7999 shâlam (1), to *be safe; be, make complete*

RENDERING
591 apŏdidōmi (1), to *give away*

RENDING
6561 pâraq (1), to *break off or crunch; to deliver*

RENEW
2318 châdash (3), to *be new, renew; to rebuild*
2498 châlaph (2), to *spring up; to change*
340 anakainizō (1), to *restore, bring back*

RENEWED
2318 châdash (2), to *be new, renew; to rebuild*
2498 châlaph (1), to *spring up; to change*
341 anakainŏō (2), to *renovate, renew*
365 ananĕŏō (1), to *renovate, i.e. reform*

RENEWEST
2318 châdash (2), to *be new, renew; to rebuild*

RENEWING
342 anakainōsis (2), *renovation, renewal*

RENOUNCED
550 apĕipŏmēn (1), to *disown*

RENOWN
8034 shêm (7), *name, appellation*

RENOWNED
1984 hâlal (1), to *boast*
7121 qârâ' (3), to *call out*

RENT
1234 bâqa' (5), to *cleave, break, tear open*
2963 ţâraph (1), to *pluck off or pull to pieces*
5364 niqpâh (1), *rope*
6533 pâram (1), to *tear, be torn*
6561 pâraq (1), to *break off or crunch; to deliver*
7167 qârâ' (43), to *rend*
8156 shâça' (2), to *split or tear; to upbraid*
1284 diarrhēssō (3), to *tear asunder*
4048 pĕrirrhēgnumi (1), to *tear all around*
4682 sparassō (1), to *convulse with epilepsy*
4977 schizō (5), to *split or sever*
4978 schisma (2), *divisive dissension*

RENTEST
7167 qârâ' (1), to *rend*

REPAID
7999 shâlam (1), to *be safe; to reciprocate*

REPAIR
918 bâdaq (1), to *mend a breach*
2318 châdash (3), to *be new, renew; to rebuild*
2388 châzaq (8), to *fasten upon; to seize*
2393 chezqâh (1), *prevailing power*
5975 'âmad (1), to *stand*

R

REPAIRED
1129 bânâh (2), to *build*;
to *establish*
2388 châzaq (39), to
fasten upon; to *seize*
2421 châyâh (1), to *live*;
to *revive*
5462 çâgar (1), to *shut*
up; to *surrender*
7495 râphâ' (1), to *cure*,
heal

REPAIRER
1443 gâdar (1), to *build a*
stone wall

REPAIRING
3247 yᵉçôwd (1),
foundation

REPAY
7999 shâlam (5), to *be*
complete; to *reciprocate*
457 anŏixis (1), act of
opening
591 apŏdidōmi (1), to
give away
661 apŏtinō (1), to *pay* in
full, *make restitution*

REPAYETH
7999 shâlam (1), to *be*
complete; to *reciprocate*

REPEATETH
8138 shânâh (1), to *fold*,
i.e. *duplicate*

REPENT
5162 nâcham (19), to *be*
sorry; to *pity, rue*
7725 shûwb (3), to *turn*
back; to *return*
3338 mĕtamĕllŏmai (2),
to *regret*
3340 mĕtanŏĕō (21), to
reconsider

REPENTANCE
5164 nôcham (1),
ruefulness
278 amĕtamĕlētŏs (1),
irrevocable
3341 mĕtanŏia (24),
reversal

REPENTED
5162 nâcham (17), to *be*
sorry; to *pity, rue*
278 amĕtamĕlētŏs (1),
irrevocable
3338 mĕtamĕllŏmai (3),
to *regret*
3340 mĕtanŏĕō (11), to
reconsider

REPENTEST
5162 nâcham (1), to *be*
sorry; to *pity, rue*

REPENTETH
5162 nâcham (3), to *be*
sorry; to *pity, rue*
3340 mĕtanŏĕō (2), to
reconsider

REPENTING
5162 nâcham (1), to *be*
sorry; to *pity, rue*

REPENTINGS
5150 nichûwm (1),
consoled; solace

REPETITIONS
945 battŏlŏgĕō (1), to
prate tediously, *babble*

REPHAEL
7501 Rᵉphâ'êl (1), *God*
has cured

REPHAH
7506 Rephach (1),
support

REPHAIAH
7509 Rᵉphâyâh (5),
Jehovah has cured

REPHAIM
7497 râphâ' (6), *giant*

REPHAIMS
7497 râphâ' (2), *giant*

REPHIDIM
7508 Rᵉphîydîym (5),
balusters

REPLENISH
4390 mâlê' (2), to *fill; be*
full

REPLENISHED
4390 mâlê' (5), to *fill; be*
full

REPLIEST
470 antapŏkrinŏmai (1),
to *contradict* or *dispute*

REPORT
1681 dibbâh (3), *slander,*
bad report
1697 dâbâr (2), *word;*
matter; thing
5046 nâgad (1), to
announce
8034 shêm (1), *name,*
appellation
8052 shᵉmûw'âh (4),
announcement
8088 shêma' (5),
something heard
189 akŏē (2), *hearing;*
thing heard
518 apaggĕllō (1), to
announce, proclaim
1426 dusphēmia (1),
defamation, slander
2162 ĕuphēmia (1), good
repute
2163 ĕuphēmŏs (1),
reputable
3140 marturĕō (6), to
testify; to commend
3141 marturia (1),
evidence given

REPORTED
559 'âmar (2), to *say*
7725 shûwb (1), to *turn*
back; to *return*
8085 shâma' (2), to *hear*
191 akŏuō (1), to *hear*
312 anaggĕllō (1), to
announce, report
518 apaggĕllō (1), to
announce, proclaim
987 blasphēmĕō (1), to
speak impiously
1310 diaphēmizō (1), to
spread news
3140 marturĕō (2), to
testify; to commend

REPROACH
2617 cheçed (1),
kindness, favor
2659 châphêr (1), to
shame, reproach
2778 châraph (10), to
spend the winter

2781 cherpâh (65),
contumely, disgrace
3637 kâlam (1), to *taunt*
or *insult*
3639 kᵉlimmâh (1),
disgrace, scorn
7036 qâlôwn (1), *disgrace*
819 atimia (1), *disgrace*
3679 ŏnĕidizō (2), to *rail*
at, *chide, taunt*
3680 ŏnĕidismŏs (3),
with insult
3681 ŏnĕidŏs (1),
notoriety, i.e. a taunt

REPROACHED
2778 châraph (12), to
spend the winter
3637 kâlam (1), to *taunt*
or *insult*
3679 ŏnĕidizō (2), to *rail*
at, *chide, taunt*

REPROACHES
1421 giddûwph (1),
vilification, scorn
2781 cherpâh (1),
contumely, disgrace
3679 ŏnĕidizō (1), to *rail*
at, *chide, taunt*
3680 ŏnĕidismŏs (1),
with insult
5196 hubris (1), *insult*

REPROACHEST
5195 hubrizō (1), to
exercise violence, abuse

REPROACHETH
1442 gâdaph (1), to
revile, blaspheme
2778 châraph (5), to
spend the winter
2781 cherpâh (1),
contumely, disgrace

REPROACHFULLY
2781 cherpâh (1),
contumely, disgrace
5484+3059 charin (1), on
account of, because of

REPROBATE
3988 mâ'aç (1), to *spurn;*
to *disappear*
96 adŏkimŏs (3), *failing*
the test, worthless

REPROBATES
96 adŏkimŏs (3), *failing*
the test, worthless

REPROOF
1606 gᵉ'ârâh (2), *chiding,*
rebuke
8433 tôwkêchâh (12),
correction, refutation
1650 ĕlĕgchŏs (1), *proof,*
conviction

REPROOFS
8433 tôwkêchâh (2),
correction, refutation

REPROVE
3198 yâkach (16), to *be*
correct; to argue
1651 ĕlĕgchō (3), to
confute, admonish

REPROVED
1605 gâ'ar (1), to *chide,*
reprimand
3198 yâkach (4), to *be*
correct; to argue

8433 tôwkêchâh (2),
correction, refutation
1651 ĕlĕgchō (3), to
confute, admonish

REPROVER
3198 yâkach (2), to *be*
correct; to argue

REPROVETH
3198 yâkach (3), to *be*
correct; to argue
3256 yâçar (1), to
chastise; to instruct

REPUTATION
3368 yâqâr (1), *valuable*
1380 dŏkĕō (1), to *think,*
regard, seem good
1784 ĕntimŏs (1), *valued,*
considered precious
2758 kĕnŏō (1), to *make*
empty
5093 timiŏs (1), *costly;*
honored, esteemed

REPUTED
2804 châshab (Ch.) (2), to
regard

REQUEST
782 'âresheth (1),
longing for
1245 bâqash (3), to
search; to strive after
1246 baqqâshâh (8),
petition, request
1697 dâbâr (2), *word;*
matter; thing
7596 shᵉ'êlâh (3), *petition*
1162 dĕēsis (1), *petition,*
request
1189 dĕŏmai (1), to *beg,*
petition, ask

REQUESTED
1156 bᵉ'â' (Ch.) (1), to
seek or ask
1245 bâqash (1), to
search; to strive after
7592 shâ'al (3), to *ask*

REQUESTS
155 aitēma (1), *thing*
asked, request

REQUIRE
977 bâchar (1), *select,*
chose, prefer
1245 bâqash (10), to
search; to strive after
1875 dârash (11), to
pursue or search
3117 yôwm (1), *day; time*
period
7592 shâ'al (3), to *ask*
7593 shᵉ'êl (Ch.) (1), to
ask
154 aitĕō (1), to *ask* for
1096 ginŏmai (1), to *be,*
become

REQUIRED
1245 bâqash (3), to
search; to strive after
1875 dârash (2), to
pursue or search
1961 hâyâh (1), to *exist,*
i.e. *be or become*
3117 yôwm (3), *day; time*
period
7592 shâ'al (4), to *ask*
155 aitēma (1), *thing*
asked, request

523 apaitĕō (1), to
demand back
1567 ĕkzētĕō (2), to seek
out
2212 zētĕō (2), to seek
4238 prassō (1), to
execute, accomplish

REQUIREST
559 'âmar (1), to say

REQUIRETH
1245 bâqash (1), to
search; to strive after
7593 sheʾêl (Ch.) (1), to
ask

REQUIRING
154 aitĕō (1), to ask for

REQUITE
1580 gâmal (1), to benefit
or requite; to wean
5414 nâthan (1), to give
6213 'âsâh (1), to do or
make
7725 shûwb (2), to turn
back; to return
7999 shâlam (3), to be
safe; to reciprocate
287+591 amŏibē (1),
requital, recompense

REQUITED
7725 shûwb (1), to turn
back; to return
7999 shâlam (1), to be
safe; to reciprocate

REQUITING
7725 shûwb (1), to turn
back; to return

REREWARD
314 'achărôwn (1), late
or last; behind; western
622 'âçaph (5), to gather,
collect

RESCUE
3467 yâsha' (1), to make
safe, free
5337 nâtsal (1), to
deliver; to be snatched
7725 shûwb (1), to turn
back; to return

RESCUED
5337 nâtsal (1), to
deliver; to be snatched
6299 pâdâh (1), to
ransom; to release
1807 ĕxairĕō (1), to tear
out; to select; to release

RESCUETH
5338 neʾtsal (Ch.) (1), to
extricate, deliver

RESEMBLANCE
5869 'ayin (1), eye; sight;
fountain

RESEMBLE
3666 hŏmŏiŏō (1), to
become similar

RESEMBLED
8389 tô'ar (1), outline,
figure or appearance

RESEN
7449 Reçen (1), bridle

RESERVE
5201 nâṭar (1), to guard;
to cherish anger
7604 shâ'ar (1), to be,
make redundant

5083 tērĕō (1), to keep,
guard, obey

RESERVED
680 'âtsal (1), to select;
refuse; narrow
2820 châsak (2), to
restrain or refrain
3498 yâthar (3), to
remain or be left
3947 lâqach (1), to take
2641 katalĕipō (1), to
have remaining
5083 tērĕō (7), to keep,
guard, obey

RESERVETH
5201 nâṭar (1), to guard;
to cherish anger
8104 shâmar (1), to
watch

RESHEPH
7566 Resheph (1), flame

RESIDUE
319 'achărîyth (1), future;
posterity
3498 yâthar (3), to
remain or be left
3499 yether (8),
remainder; small rope
7605 sheʾâr (4),
remainder
7606 sheʾâr (Ch.) (2),
remainder
7611 sheʾêrîyth (13),
remainder or residual
2645 katalŏipŏs (1),
remaining; rest
3062 lŏipŏi (1),
remaining ones

RESIST
7853 sâṭan (1), to attack
by accusation
436 anthistēmi (7),
oppose, rebel
496 antipiptō (1), to
oppose, resist
498 antitassŏmai (1),
oppose, resist

RESISTED
436 anthistēmi (1),
oppose, rebel
478 antikathistēmi (1),
withstand, contest

RESISTETH
436 anthistēmi (1),
oppose, rebel
498 antitassŏmai (3),
oppose, resist

RESOLVED
1097 ginōskō (1), to know

RESORT
935 bôw' (1), to go, come
6908 qâbats (1), to
collect, assemble
4848 sumpŏrĕuŏmai (1),
to journey together
4905 sunĕrchŏmai (1), to
gather together

RESORTED
3320 yâtsab (1), to
station, offer, continue
2064 ĕrchŏmai (2), to go
4863 sunagō (1), to
gather together
4905 sunĕrchŏmai (1), to
gather together

RESPECT
3045 yâda' (1), to know
4856 massô' (1), partiality
5027 nâbaṭ (3), to scan;
to regard with favor
5234 nâkar (3), to
respect, revere
5375 nâsâ' (2), to lift up
6437 pânâh (6), to turn,
to face
7200 râ'âh (4), to see
8159 shâ'âh (3), to
inspect, consider
578 apŏblĕpō (1),
intently regard, pay
attention
678 aprŏsōpŏlēptōs (1),
without prejudice
1914 ĕpiblĕpō (1), to gaze
at
2596 kata (1), down;
according to
3313 mĕrŏs (2), division
or share
3382 mĕrŏs (1), thigh
4380 prŏsōpŏlēptĕō (1),
to show partiality
4382 prŏsōpŏlēpsia (3),
favoritism

RESPECTED
5375 nâsâ' (1), to lift up

RESPECTER
4381 prŏsōpŏlēptēs (1),
exhibiting partiality

RESPECTETH
6437 pânâh (1), to turn,
to face
7200 râ'âh (1), to see

RESPITE
7309 reʾvâchâh (1), relief
7503 râphâh (1), to
slacken

REST
1824 deʾmîy (1), quiet,
peacefulness
1826 dâmam (1), to be
silent; to be astonished;
to stop, cease; to perish
2308 châdal (1), to desist,
stop; be fat
2342 chûwl (1), to wait;
to pervert
2790 chârash (1), to be
silent; to be deaf
3498 yâthar (12), to
remain or be left
3499 yether (65),
remainder; small rope
4494 mânôwach (6),
quiet spot, home
4496 meʾnûwchâh (16),
peacefully; consolation
4771 margôwa' (1),
resting place
5117 nûwach (44), to
rest; to settle down
5118 nûwach (2), quiet
5183 nachath (4),
descent; quiet
6314 pûwgâh (1),
intermission, relief
7257 râbats (1), to
recline, repose, brood
7280 râga' (5), to settle,
i.e. quiet; to wink
7599 shâ'an (1), to loll,
i.e. be peaceful

7604 shâ'ar (2), to be,
make redundant
7605 sheʾâr (10),
remainder
7606 sheʾâr (Ch.) (9),
remainder
7611 sheʾêrîyth (3),
remainder or residual
7673 shâbath (7), to
repose; to desist
7677 shabbâthôwn (8),
special holiday
7901 shâkab (2), to lie
down
7931 shâkan (2), to reside
7954 sheʾlâh (Ch.) (1), to
be secure, at rest
7965 shâlôwm (1), safe;
well; health, prosperity
8058 shâmaṭ (1), to let
alone, desist, remit
8172 shâ'an (2), to
support, rely on
8252 shâqaṭ (15), to
repose
8300 sârîyd (1), survivor;
remainder
372 anapausis (4),
recreation, rest
373 anapauō (6), to
repose; to refresh
425 anĕsis (3),
relaxation; relief
1515 ĕirēnē (1), peace;
health; prosperity
1879 ĕpanapauŏmai (1),
to settle on, rely on
1954 ĕpilŏipŏs (1),
remaining, rest
1981 ĕpiskēnŏō (1), to
abide with
2192+372 ĕchō (1), to
have; hold; keep
2663 katapausis (9),
abode for resting
2664 katapauō (2), to
settle down
2681 kataskēnŏō (1), to
remain, live
3062 lŏipŏi (13),
remaining ones
4520 sabbatismŏs (1),
sabbatism

RESTED
270 'âchaz (1), to seize,
grasp; possess
1826 dâmam (1), to stop,
cease; to perish
2583 chânâh (2), to
encamp
5117 nûwach (7), to rest;
to settle down
5118 nûwach (2), quiet
5564 çâmak (1), to lean
upon; take hold of
7673 shâbath (4), to
repose; to desist
7931 shâkan (1), to reside
8252 shâqaṭ (1), to repose
2270 hēsuchazō (1), to
refrain

RESTEST
1879 ĕpanapauŏmai (1),
to settle on, rely on

RESTETH
5117 nûwach (2), to rest
8172 shâ'an (1), to
support, rely on

R

373 anapauō (1), to *repose*; to *refresh*

RESTING
4496 m^enûwchâh (2), *peacefully; consolation*
5118 nûwach (1), *quiet*
7258 rebets (1), place of *repose*

RESTINGPLACE
7258 rebets (1), place of *repose*

RESTITUTION
7999 shâlam (4), to *make complete; to reciprocate*
8545 t^emûwrâh (1), *barter, compensation*
605 *apŏkatastasis* (1), *reconstitution*

RESTORE
5927 'âlâh (1), to *ascend, be high, mount*
7725 shûwb (27), to *return* or restore
7999 shâlam (8), to *make complete; to reciprocate*
591 *apŏdidōmi* (1), to *give away*
600 *apŏkathistēmi* (2), to *reconstitute*
2675 *katartizō* (1), to *repair; to prepare*

RESTORED
2421 châyâh (4), to *live; to revive*
5414 nâthan (1), to *give*
7725 shûwb (16), to *return* or restore
8421 tûwb (Ch.) (1), to *come back with answer*
600 *apŏkathistēmi* (5), to *reconstitute*

RESTORER
7725 shûwb (2), to *return* or restore

RESTORETH
7725 shûwb (1), to *return* or restore
600 *apŏkathistēmi* (1), to *reconstitute*

RESTRAIN
1639 gâra' (1), to *shave, remove, lessen*
2296 châgar (1), to *gird on a belt; put on armor*

RESTRAINED
662 'âphaq (1), to *abstain*
1219 bâtsar (1), to *be inaccessible*
3543 kâhâh (1), to *grow dull, fade; to be faint*
3607 kâlâ' (2), to *hold back or in; to prohibit*
4513 mâna' (1), to *deny, refuse*
6113 'âtsar (1), to *hold back; to maintain, rule*
2664 *katapauō* (1), to *cause to desist*

RESTRAINEST
1639 gâra' (1), to *remove, lessen, or withhold*

RESTRAINT
4622 ma'tsôwr (1), *hindrance*

RESURRECTION
386 *anastasis* (39), *resurrection from death*
1454 *ĕgĕrsis* (1), *resurgence from death*
1815 *ĕxanastasis* (1), *rising from death*

RETAIN
2388 châzaq (1), to *fasten upon; to seize*
3607 kâlâ' (1), to *hold back or in; to prohibit*
6113 'âtsar (1), to *hold back; to maintain, rule*
8551 tâmak (2), to *obtain, keep fast*
2192 *ĕchō* (1), to *have; hold; keep*
2902 *kratĕō* (1), to *seize*

RETAINED
2388 châzaq (2), to *fasten upon; to seize*
6113 'âtsar (2), to *hold back; to maintain, rule*
2722 *katĕchō* (1), to *hold down fast*
2902 *kratĕō* (1), to *seize*

RETAINETH
2388 châzaq (1), to *fasten upon; to seize*
8551 tâmak (2), to *obtain, keep fast*

RETIRE
5756 'ûwz (1), to *strengthen; to save*
7725 shûwb (1), to *return* or restore

RETIRED
2015 hâphak (1), to *return, pervert*
6327 pûwts (1), to *dash in pieces; to disperse*

RETURN
3427 yâshab (1), to *dwell, to remain; to settle*
6437 pânâh (1), to *turn, to face*
7725 shûwb (242), to *turn back; to return*
8666 t^eshûwb (3), *recurrence; reply*
344 *anakamptō* (1), to *turn back, come back*
360 *analuō* (1), to *depart*
390 *anastrĕphō* (1), to *remain; to return*
844 *autŏmatŏs* (1), *spontaneous, by itself*
1994 *ĕpistrĕphō* (4), to *revert, turn back to*
5290 *hupŏstrĕphō* (5), to *turn under, to return*

RETURNED
5437 çâbab (2), to *surround*
7725 shûwb (151), to *turn back; to return*
8421 tûwb (Ch.) (2), to *reply*
344 *anakamptō* (1), to *turn back, come back*
390 *anastrĕphō* (1) to *remain, to return*
1877 *ĕpanagō* (1), to *put out to sea; to return*
1880 *ĕpanĕrchŏmai* (1), *return home*

RETURNETH
1994 *ĕpistrĕphō* (2), to *revert, turn back to*
5290 *hupŏstrĕphō* (24), to *turn under, to return*

RETURNETH
7725 shûwb (6), to *turn back; to return*
8138 shânâh (1), to *fold, to transmute*

RETURNING
7729 shûwbâh (1), *return, i.e. repentance*
5290 *hupŏstrĕphō* (3), to *turn under, to return*

REU
7466 R^e'ûw (5), *friend*

REUBEN
7205 R^e'ûwbên (72), *see ye a son*
7206 R^e'ûwbênîy (1), *Rebenite*
4502 *Rhŏubēn* (1), see ye a son

REUBENITE
7206 R^e'ûwbênîy (1), *Rebenite*

REUBENITES
7206 R^e'ûwbênîy (16), *Rebenite*

REUEL
7467 R^e'ûw'êl (10), *friend of God*

REUMAH
7208 R^e'ûwmâh (1), *raised*

REVEAL
1540 gâlâh (2), to *denude; to reveal*
1541 g^elâh (Ch.) (1), to *reveal mysteries*
601 *apŏkaluptō* (4), *disclose, reveal*

REVEALED
1540 gâlâh (11), to *denude; to reveal*
1541 g^elâh (Ch.) (2), to *reveal mysteries*
601 *apŏkaluptō* (22), *disclose, reveal*
602 *apŏkalupsis* (2), *disclosure, revelation*
5537 *chrēmatizō* (1), to *utter an oracle*

REVEALER
1541 g^elâh (Ch.) (1), to *reveal mysteries*

REVEALETH
1540 gâlâh (3), to *denude; to reveal*
1541 g^elâh (Ch.) (3), to *reveal mysteries*

REVELATION
602 *apŏkalupsis* (10), *disclosure, revelation*

REVELATIONS
602 *apŏkalupsis* (2), *disclosure, revelation*

REVELLINGS
2970 *kōmŏs* (2), *carousal, reveling, orgy*

REVENGE
5358 nâqam (1), to *avenge or punish*

REVENGE
5360 n^eqâmâh (2), *avengement*
1556 *ĕkdikĕō* (1), to *vindicate; retaliate*
1557 *ĕkdikēsis* (1), *vindication; retaliation*

REVENGED
5358 nâqam (1), to *avenge or punish*

REVENGER
1350 gâ'al (6), to *redeem; to be the next of kin*
1558 *ĕkdikŏs* (1), *punisher, avenger*

REVENGERS
1350 gâ'al (1), to *redeem; to be the next of kin*

REVENGES
6546 par'âh (1), *leadership*

REVENGETH
5358 nâqam (2), to *avenge or punish*

REVENGING
5360 n^eqâmâh (1), *avengement*

REVENUE
674 'app^ethôm (Ch.) (1), *revenue*
8393 t^ebûw'âh (2), *income, i.e. produce*

REVENUES
8393 t^ebûw'âh (3), *income, i.e. produce*

REVERENCE
3372 yârê' (2), to *fear; to revere*
7812 shâchâh (5), to *prostrate in homage*
127 *aidōs* (1), *modesty; awe*
1788 *ĕntrĕpō* (4), to *respect; to confound*
5399 *phŏbĕō* (1), to *be in awe of, i.e. revere*

REVERENCED
7812 shâchâh (1), to *prostrate in homage*

REVEREND
3372 yârê' (1), to *fear; to revere*

REVERSE
7725 shûwb (3), to *turn back; to return*

REVILE
7043 qâlal (1), to *be easy, trifling, vile*
3679 *ŏnĕidizō* (1), to *rail at, chide, taunt*

REVILED
486 *antilŏidŏrĕō* (1), to *rail in reply, retaliate*
937 *basilikŏs* (1), *befitting the sovereign*
3058 *lŏidŏrĕō* (2), *vilify, insult*
3679 *ŏnĕidizō* (1), to *rail at, chide, taunt*

REVILERS
3060 *lŏidŏrŏs* (1), verbal *abuser*

REVILEST
3058 *lŏidŏrĕō* (1), *vilify, insult*

REVILINGS
1421 giddûwph (2), *vilification, scorn*

REVIVE
2421 châyâh (8), to *live; to revive*

REVIVED
2421 châyâh (4), to *live; to revive*
326 anazaō (2), to *recover life, live again*

REVIVING
4241 michyâh (2), *preservation of life*

REVOLT
5627 çârâh (2), *apostasy; crime; remission*
6586 pâsha' (1), to *break away from authority*

REVOLTED
5498 çâchab (1), to *trail along*
5627 çârâh (1), *apostasy; crime; remission*
6586 pâsha' (5), to *break away from authority*

REVOLTERS
5637 çârar (2), to *be refractory, stubborn*
7846 sêṭ (1), *departure*

REVOLTING
5637 çârar (1), to *be refractory, stubborn*

REWARD
319 'achăriyth (2), *future; posterity*
868 'ethnan (3), *gift price of harlotry*
1309 bᵉsôwrâh (1), glad *tidings, good news*
1576 gᵉmûwl (3), *reward, recompense*
1578 gᵉmûwlâh (1), *reward, recompense*
1580 gâmal (1), to *benefit or requite; to wean*
4864 mas'êth (1), *tribute; reproach*
4909 maskôreth (1), *wages; reward*
4991 mattâth (1), *present*
6118 'êqeb (3), unto the *end; for ever*
6468 pᵉ'ullâh (1), *work, deed*
6529 pᵉriy (1), *fruit*
7725 shûwb (2), to *turn back; to return*
7809 shâchad (1), to *bribe; gift*
7810 shachad (7), to *bribe; gift*
7938 seker (1), *wages, reward*
7939 sâkâr (5), *payment, salary; compensation*
7966 shillûwm (1), *requital; retribution; fee*
7999 shâlam (6), to *make complete; to reciprocate*
8011 shillumâh (1), *retribution*
469 antapŏdŏsis (1), *requital, reward*
514 axiŏs (1), *deserving, comparable or suitable*

591 apŏdidōmi (6), to *give away*
2603 katabrabĕuō (1), to *award the price*
3405 misthapŏdŏsia (3), *requital, good or bad*
3408 misthŏs (24), *pay*

REWARDED
1580 gâmal (7), to *benefit or requite; to wean*
7760 sûwm (1), to *place*
7939 sâkâr (2), *payment, salary; compensation*
7999 shâlam (3), to *make complete; to reciprocate*
591 apŏdidōmi (1), to *give away*

REWARDER
3406 misthapŏdŏtēs (1), *rewarder*

REWARDETH
7725 shûwb (1), to *turn back; to return*
7936 sâkar (2), to *hire*
7999 shâlam (3), to *make complete; to reciprocate*

REWARDS
866 'êthnâh (1), *gift price of harlotry*
5023 nᵉbizbâh (Ch.) (2), *largess, gift*
8021 shalmôn (1), *bribe; gift*

REZEPH
7530 Retseph (2), hot *stone for baking*

REZIA
7525 Ritsyâ' (1), *delight*

REZIN
7526 Rᵉtsîyn (10), *delight*

REZON
7331 Rᵉzôwn (1), *prince*

RHEGIUM
4484 Rhēgiŏn (1), *Rhegium*

RHESA
4488 Rhēsa (1), (poss.) *Jehovah has cured*

RHODA
4498 Rhŏdē (1), *rose*

RHODES
4499 Rhŏdŏs (1), *rose*

RIB
6763 tsêlâ' (1), *side*

RIBAI
7380 Rîybay (2), *contentious*

RIBBAND
6616 pâthîyl (1), *twine, cord*

RIBLAH
7247 Riblâh (11), *fertile*

RIBS
6763 tsêlâ' (2), *side*

RICH
1952 hôwn (1), *wealth*
3513 kâbad (1), to *be rich, glorious*
5381 nâsag (1), to *reach*
6223 'âshîyr (23), *rich; rich person*
6238 'âshar (13), to *grow, make rich*

7771 shôwa' (1), *noble, i.e. liberal; opulent*
4145 plŏusiŏs (28), *wealthy; abounding*
4147 plŏutĕō (11), to *be, become wealthy*
4148 plŏutizō (1), to *make wealthy*

RICHER
6238 'âshar (1), to *grow, make rich*

RICHES
1952 hôwn (9), *wealth*
1995 hâmôwn (1), *noise, tumult; many, crowd*
2428 chayil (11), *army; wealth; virtue; valor*
2633 chôçen (1), *wealth, stored riches*
3502 yithrâh (1), *wealth, abundance*
4301 maṭmôwn (1), *secret storehouse*
5233 nekeç (1), *treasure*
6239 'ôsher (37), *wealth*
7075 qinyân (1), *purchase, wealth*
7399 rᵉkûwsh (5), *property*
7769 shûwa' (1), *call*
4149 plŏutŏs (22), *abundant riches*
5536 chrēma (3), *wealth*

RICHLY
4146 plŏusiŏs (2), *copiously, abundantly*

RID
5337 nâtsal (3), to *deliver; to be snatched*
6475 pâtsâh (2), to *rend*
7673 shâbath (1), to *repose; to desist*

RIDDANCE
3615 kâlâh (1), to *cease, be finished, perish*
3617 kâlâh (1), *complete destruction*

RIDDEN
7392 râkab (1), to *ride*

RIDDLE
2420 chîydâh (9), *puzzle; conundrum; maxim*

RIDE
7392 râkab (20), to *ride*

RIDER
7392 râkab (7), to *ride*

RIDERS
7392 râkab (5), to *ride*

RIDETH
7392 râkab (7), to *ride*

RIDGES
8525 telem (1), *bank or terrace*

RIDING
7392 râkab (10), to *ride*

RIE
3698 kuççemeth (2), *spelt*

RIFLED
8155 shâçaç (1), to *plunder, ransack*

RIGHT
541 'âman (1), to take *the right hand road*

571 'emeth (3), *certainty, truth, trustworthiness*
1353 gᵉullâh (1), *blood relationship*
3225 yâmîyn (136), *right; south*
3227 yᵉmîynîy (1), *right*
3231 yâman (4), to *be right-handed*
3233 yᵉmânîy (31), *right*
3474 yâshar (2), to *be straight; to make right*
3476 yôsher (2), *right*
3477 yâshâr (52), *straight*
3559 kûwn (4), to *render sure, proper*
3651 kên (3), *just; right*
3787 kâshêr (1), to *be straight or right*
3788 kishrôwn (1), *success; advantage*
4334 mîyshôwr (1), *plain; justice*
4339 mêyshâr (3), *straightness; rectitude*
4941 mishpâṭ (19), *verdict; decree; justice*
5227 nôkach (2), *forward, in behalf of*
5228 nâkôach (1), *equitable, correct*
5229 nᵉkôchâh (2), *integrity; truth*
6227 'âshân (1), *smoke*
6437 pânâh (1), to *turn, to face*
6440 pânîym (1), *face; front*
6664 tsedeq (3), *right*
6666 tsᵉdâqâh (9), *rightness*
1188 dĕxiŏs (53), *right*
1342 dikaiŏs (5), *equitable, holy*
1849 ĕxŏusia (2), *authority, power, right*
2117 ĕuthus (3), *at once, immediately*
3723 ŏrthōs (1), *rightly*
4993 sōphrŏnĕō (2), to *be in a right state of mind*

RIGHTEOUS
3477 yâshâr (8), *straight*
6662 tsaddîyq (166), *just*
6663 tsâdaq (8), to *be, make right*
6664 tsedeq (9), *right*
6666 tsᵉdâqâh (3), *rightness*
1341 dikaiŏkrisia (1), *proper judgment*
1342 dikaiŏs (39), *equitable, holy*
1343 dikaiŏsunē (1), *equity, justification*

RIGHTEOUSLY
4334 mîyshôwr (1), *plain; justice*
4339 mêyshâr (1), *straightness; rectitude*
6664 tsedeq (3), *right*
6666 tsᵉdâqâh (1), *rightness*
1346 dikaiŏs (2), *equitably*

RIGHTEOUSNESS
6663 tsâdaq (1), to *be, make right*

R

6664 tsedeq (78), *right*
6665 tsidqâh (Ch.) (1),
beneficence
6666 ts⁰dâqâh (124),
rightness
1343 dikaiŏsunē (91),
equity, justification
1345 dikaiōma (4),
equitable deed; statute
1346 dikaiōs (1),
equitably
2118 ĕuthutēs (1),
rectitude, uprightness

RIGHTEOUSNESS'
6664 tsedeq (1), *right*
6666 ts⁰dâqâh (1),
rightness
1343 dikaiŏsunē (2),
equity, justification

RIGHTEOUSNESSES
6666 ts⁰dâqâh (3),
rightness

RIGHTLY
3588 kîy (1), *for, that
because*
3723 ŏrthōs (3), *rightly*

RIGOUR
6531 perek (5), *severity*

RIMMON
7417 Rimmôwn (14),
pomegranate

RIMMON-PAREZ
7428 Rimmôn Perets (2),
pomegranate of (the)
breach

RING
2885 ṭabba'ath (9), *ring;
signet ring* for sealing
1146 daktuliŏs (1),
finger-ring
5554 chrusŏdaktuliŏs
(1), *gold-ringed*

RINGLEADER
4414 prŏtŏstatēs (1),
leader, ring leader

RINGS
1354 gab (2), *mounded
or rounded: top or rim*
1550 gâlîyl (2), *curtain
ring*
2885 ṭabba'ath (39), *ring;
signet ring* for sealing

RINGSTRAKED
6124 'âqôd (7), *striped,
streaked animals*

RINNAH
7441 Rinnâh (1), *shout*

RINSED
7857 shâṭaph (3), *to
inundate, cleanse*

RIOT
810 asōtia (2), *profligacy,
debauchery*
5172 truphē (1), *luxury
or debauchery*

RIOTING
2970 kōmŏs (1),
carousal, reveling, orgy

RIOTOUS
2151 zâlal (2), *to be loose
morally, worthless*
811 asōtōs (1), *with
debauchery*

RIP
1234 bâqa' (1), *to cleave,
break, tear open*

RIPE
1310 bâshal (2), *to boil
up, cook; to ripen*
187 akmazō (1), *to be
mature, be ripe*
3583 xērainō (1), *to
shrivel, to mature*

RIPENING
1580 gâmal (1), *to benefit
or require; to wean*

RIPHATH
7384 Rîyphath (2),
Riphath

RIPPED
1234 bâqa' (3), *to cleave,
break, tear open*

RISE
2224 zârach (1), *to rise;
to be bright*
5927 'âlâh (6), *to ascend,
be high, mount*
6965 qûwm (76), *to rise*
6966 qûwm (Ch.) (1), *to
rise*
7925 shâkam (5), *to load
up,* i.e. *to start early*
8618 t⁰qôwmêm (1),
opponent
305 anabainō (1), *to go
up, rise*
386 anastasis (1),
resurrection from death
393 anatĕllō (2), *to cause
to arise*
450 anistēmi (23), *to rise;
to come back to life*
1453 ĕgeirō (23), *to
waken,* i.e. *rouse*
1881 ĕpanistamai (2), *to
stand up on*

RISEN
1342 gâ'âh (1), *to rise; to
grow tall; be majestic*
2224 zârach (2), *to rise;
to be bright*
3318 yâtsâ' (1), *to go,
bring out*
6965 qûwm (16), *to rise*
393 anatĕllō (1), *to cause
to arise*
450 anistēmi (6), *to rise;
to come back to life*
1453 ĕgeirō (22), *to
waken,* i.e. *rouse*
4891 sunĕgeirō (2), *to
raise up with*

RISEST
6965 qûwm (2), *to rise*

RISETH
2224 zârach (2), *to rise;
to be bright*
5927 'âlâh (1), *to ascend,
be high, mount*
6965 qûwm (9), *to rise*
7837 shachar (1), *dawn*
1453 ĕgeirō (1), *to
waken,* i.e. *rouse*

RISING
510 'alqûwm (1),
resistlessness
2225 zerach (1), *rising* of
light, *dawning*

4217 mizrâch (8), *place
of sunrise; east*
5927 'âlâh (1), *to ascend,
be high, mount*
6965 qûwm (1), *to rise*
7012 qîymâh (1), *arising*
7613 s⁰'êth (7), *elevation;
swelling*
7836 shâchar (1), *to
search for*
7925 shâkam (14), *to
load up, to start early*
305 anabainō (1), *to rise*
386 anastasis (1),
resurrection from death
393 anatĕllō (1), *to cause
to arise*
450 anistēmi (1), *to rise;
to come back to life*

RISSAH
7446 Riççâh (2), *ruin*

RITES
2708 chuqqâh (1), *to
delineate*

RITHMAH
7575 Rithmâh (2), *broom
tree*

RIVER
180 'ûwbâl (3), *stream*
2975 y⁰'ôr (35), Nile
River; Tigris *River*
3105 yûwbal (1), *stream*
5103 n⁰har (Ch.) (14),
river; Euphrates *River*
5104 nâhâr (66), *stream;
Nile;* Euphrates; Tigris
5158 nachal (46), *valley*
4215 pŏtamŏs (6),
current, brook

RIVER'S
2975 y⁰'ôr (3), Nile *River;*
Tigris *River*
5104 nâhâr (1), *stream;
Nile;* Euphrates; Tigris

RIVERS
650 'âphîyq (10), *valley;
stream; mighty, strong*
2975 y⁰'ôr (15), Nile
River; Tigris *River*
5103 n⁰har (Ch.) (9),
river; Euphrates *River*
5104 nâhâr (22), *stream;
Nile;* Euphrates; Tigris
5158 nachal (8), *valley*
6388 peleg (8), *small
irrigation channel*
6390 p⁰laggâh (1), *gully*
8585 t⁰'âlâh (1),
irrigation channel
4215 pŏtamŏs (3),
current, brook

RIZPAH
7532 Ritspâh (4), *hot
stone; pavement*

ROAD
6584 pâshaṭ (1), *to strip,*
i.e. *unclothe, plunder*

ROAR
1993 hâmâh (6), *to be in
great commotion*
5098 nâham (2), *to growl,
groan*
6873 tsârach (1), *to
whoop*
7481 râ'am (2), *to crash
thunder; to irritate*

7580 shâ'ag (12), *to
rumble* or *moan*

ROARED
1993 hâmâh (1), *to be in
great commotion*
7580 shâ'ag (4), *to
rumble* or *moan*

ROARETH
1993 hâmâh (1), *to be in
great commotion*
7580 shâ'ag (1), *to
rumble* or *moan*
3455 mukaŏmai (1), *to
roar*

ROARING
1897 hâgâh (1), *to
murmur, utter a sound*
5098 nâham (1), *to growl,
groan*
5099 naham (2), *snarl,
growl*
5100 n⁰hâmâh (1),
snarling, growling
7580 shâ'ag (2), *to
rumble* or *moan*
7581 sh⁰'âgâh (6),
rumbling or *moan*
2278 ĕchĕŏ (1), *to
reverberate, ring out*
5612 ŏruŏmai (1), *to roar*

ROARINGS
7581 sh⁰'âgâh (1),
rumbling or *moan*

ROAST
1310 bâshal (1), *to boil
up, cook; to ripen*
6740 tsâlâh (1), *to roast*
6748 tsâlîy (3), *roasted*

ROASTED
1310 bâshal (1), *to boil
up, cook; to ripen*
6740 tsâlâh (1), *to roast*
7033 qâlâh (1), *to toast*

ROASTETH
740 'Ărî'êl (1), *Lion of
God*
2760 chârak (1), *to catch*

ROB
962 bâzaz (3), *to plunder,
take booty*
1497 gâzal (2), *to rob*
6906 qâba' (1), *to
defraud, rob*
7921 shâkôl (1), *to
miscarry*
8154 shâçah (1), *to
plunder*

ROBBED
962 bâzaz (4), *to plunder,
take booty*
1497 gâzal (1), *to rob*
5100 n⁰hâmâh (1),
snarling, growling
5749 'ûwd (1), *to
encompass, restore*
6906 qâba' (2), *to
defraud, rob*
7909 shakkuwl (2),
bereaved
8154 shâçah (1), *to
plunder*
4813 sulaō (1), *to despoil,
rob*

ROBBER
6530 p⁰rîyts (1), *violent*

ROBBERS
6782 tsammîym (2), *noose, snare*
3027 lē₁stēs (2), *brigand*

ROBBERS
962 bâzaz (1), *to plunder, take booty*
6530 perîyts (3), *violent*
7703 shâdad (2), *to ravage*
2417 hiĕrŏsulŏs (1), *temple-despoiler*
3027 lē₁stēs (2), *brigand*

ROBBERY
1498 gâzêl (3), *robbery, stealing*
6503 Parbâr (1), *Parbar or Parvar*
7701 shôd (2), *violence, ravage, destruction*
725 harpagmŏs (1), *plunder*

ROBBETH
1497 gâzal (1), *to rob*

ROBE
145 'eder (1), *mantle; splendor*
155 'addereth (1), *large; splendid*
3301 Yiphdeyâh (1), *Jehovah will liberate*
4598 meʻîyl (17), *outer garment or robe*
2066 ĕsthēs (1), *to clothe*
2440 himatiŏn (2), *to put on clothes*
4749 stŏlē (1), *long-fitting gown*
5511 chlamus (2), *military cloak*

ROBES
899 beged (4), *clothing; treachery or pillage*
4598 meʻîyl (2), *outer garment or robe*
4749 stŏlē (5), *long-fitting gown*

ROBOAM
4497 Rhŏbŏam (2), *people has enlarged*

ROCK
2496 challâmîysh (1), *flint, flinty rock*
4581 mâʻôwz (1), *fortified place; defense*
5553 çela' (44), *craggy rock; fortress*
5558 çeleph (2), *distortion; viciousness*
6697 tsûwr (56), *rock*
4073 pĕtra (13), *mass of rock*

ROCKS
3710 kêph (2), *hollow rock*
5553 çela' (10), *craggy rock; fortress*
6697 tsûwr (7), *rock*
4073 pĕtra (3), *mass of rock*
5138+5117 trachus (1), *uneven, jagged, rocky*

ROD
2415 chôṭer (2), *twig; shoot of a plant*
4294 maṭṭeh (42), *tribe; rod, scepter; club*

4731 maqqêl (2), *shoot; stick; staff*
7626 shêbeṭ (34), *stick; clan, family*
4464 rhabdŏs (6), *stick, rod*

RODE
7392 râkab (15), *to ride*

RODS
4294 maṭṭeh (8), *tribe; rod, scepter; club*
4731 maqqêl (6), *shoot; stick; staff*
4463 rhabdizŏ (1), *to strike with a stick*

ROE
3280 ya'ălâh (1), *ibex*
6643 tsebîy (6), *gazelle*

ROEBUCK
6643 tsebîy (4), *gazelle*

ROEBUCKS
6643 tsebîy (1), *gazelle*

ROES
6643 tsebîy (3), *gazelle*
6646 tsebîyâh (2), *gazelle*

ROGELIM
7274 Rŏgelîym (2), *fullers as tramping the cloth*

ROHGAH
7303 Rôwhăgâh (1), *outcry*

ROLL
1549 gillâyôwn (1), *tablet for writing; mirror*
1556 gâlal (4), *to roll; to commit*
4039 megillâh (14), *roll, scroll*
4040 megillâh (Ch.) (7), *roll, scroll*
6428 pâlash (1), *to roll in dust*
617 apŏkuliŏ (1), *to roll away, roll back*

ROLLED
1556 gâlal (6), *to roll; to commit*
617 apŏkuliŏ (3), *to roll away, roll back*
1507 hĕlissŏ (1), *to roll, coil or wrap*
4351 prŏskuliŏ (2), *to roll towards*

ROLLER
2848 chittûwl (1), *bandage for a wound*

ROLLETH
1556 gâlal (1), *to roll*

ROLLING
1534 galgal (1), *wheel; something round*

ROLLS
5609 çephar (Ch.) (1), *book*

ROMAMTI-EZER
7320 Rôwmamtîy 'Ezer (2), *I have raised up a help*

ROMAN
4514 Rhŏmaiŏs (5), *Roman; of Rome*

ROMANS
4514 Rhŏmaiŏs (7), *Roman; of Rome*

ROME
4516 Rhŏmē (15), *strength*

ROOF
1406 gâg (11), *roof; top*
2441 chêk (5), *area of mouth*
6982 qôwrâh (1), *rafter; roof*
4721 stĕgē (3), *roof*

ROOFS
1406 gâg (2), *roof; top*

ROOM
4725 mâqôwm (3), *general locality, place*
4800 merchâb (1), *open space; liberty*
7337 râchab (2), *to broaden*
8478 tachath (11), *bottom; underneath*
473 anti (1), *instead of, because of*
508 anŏgĕŏn (1), *dome or a balcony*
1240 diadŏchŏs (1), *successor in office*
4411 prŏtŏklisia (1), *pre-eminence at meals*
5117 tŏpŏs (5), *place*
5253 hupĕrŏ₁ŏn (1), *upper room*
5362 philandrŏs (1), *affectionate as a wife to her husband*

ROOMS
7064 qên (1), *nest; nestlings; chamber*
8478 tachath (2), *bottom; underneath; in lieu of*
4411 prŏtŏklisia (4), *pre-eminence at meals*

ROOT
5428 nâthash (2), *to tear away, be uprooted*
8327 shârash (7), *to root, insert; to uproot*
8328 sheresh (17), *root*
1610 ĕkrizŏŏ (2), *to uproot*
4491 rhiza (15), *root*

ROOTED
5255 nâçach (1), *to tear away*
5423 nâthaq (1), *to tear off*
5428 nâthash (1), *to tear away, be uprooted*
6131 'âqar (1), *to pluck up roots; to hamstring*
8327 shârash (1), *to root, insert; to uproot*
1610 ĕkrizŏŏ (1), *to uproot*
4492 rhizŏŏ (2), *to root; to become stable*

ROOTS
5428 nâthash (1), *to tear away, be uprooted*
6132 'âqar (Ch.) (1), *to pluck up roots*
8328 sheresh (13), *root*

8330 shôresh (Ch.) (3), *root*
1610 ĕkrizŏŏ (1), *to uproot*
4491 rhiza (1), *root*

ROPE
5688 'ăbôth (1), *entwined things: a string, wreath*

ROPES
2256 chebel (3), *band*
5688 'ăbôth (2), *entwined things: a string, wreath*
4979 schŏiniŏn (1), *withe or tie or rope*

ROSE
2224 zârach (3), *to rise; to be bright*
2261 chăbatstseleth (2), *meadow-saffron*
5927 'âlâh (2), *to ascend, be high, mount*
6965 qûwm (71), *to rise*
7925 shâkam (29), *to load up, to start early*
305 anabainŏ (1), *to go up, rise*
450 anistēmi (18), *to rise; to come back to life*
1453 ĕgĕirŏ (3), *to waken, i.e. rouse*
1817 ĕxanistēmi (1), *to beget, raise up*
4911 sunĕphistēmi (1), *to resist or assault jointly*

ROSH
7220 Rô'sh (1), *head*

ROT
5307 nâphal (3), *to fall*
7537 râqab (2), *to decay by worm-eating*

ROTTEN
4418 mâlâch (2), *rag or old garment*
5685 'âbash (1), *to dry up*
7538 râqâb (1), *decay by caries*
7539 riqqâbôwn (1), *decay by caries*

ROTTENNESS
4716 maq (1), *putridity, stench*
7538 râqâb (4), *decay by caries*

ROUGH
386 'êythân (1), *never-failing; eternal*
5569 çâmâr (1), *shaggy*
7186 qâsheh (1), *severe*
7406 rekeç (1), *ridge*
8163 sâ'îyr (1), *shaggy; he-goat; goat idol*
8181 sê'âr (1), *tossed hair*
5138 trachus (1), *uneven, jagged, rocky, reefy*

ROUGHLY
5794 'az (1), *strong, vehement, harsh*
7186 qâsheh (5), *severe*

ROUND
1754 dûwr (1), *circle; ball; pile*
2636 chaçpaç (1), *to peel; to be scale-like*
3803 kâthar (2), *to enclose, besiege; to wait*

4524 mêçab (3), *divan couch; around*
5362 nâqaph (4), *to strike; to surround*
5437 çâbab (7), *to surround*
5439 çâbîyb (254), *circle; environs; around*
5469 çahar (1), *roundness*
5696 'âgôl (6), *circular*
5921 'al (2), *above, over*
7720 sahârôn (1), round *pendant or crescent*
2943 kuklôthên (10), *from the circle*
2944 kuklôō (2), *to surround, encircle*
3840 pantôthên (1), *from, on all sides*
4015 pĕriastraptō (2), *to shine around*
4017 pĕriblĕpō (5), *to look all around*
4026 pĕriistēmi (1), *to stand around; to avoid*
4033 pĕrikuklôō (1), *to blockade completely*
4034 pĕrilampō (2), *to shine all around*
4038 pĕrix (1), all *around*
4039 pĕriŏikĕō (1), *to be a neighbor*
4066 pĕrichōrŏs (9), *surrounding country*

ROUSE
6965 qûwm (1), *to rise*

ROW
2905 tûwr (14), *row, course built into a wall*
4635 ma'ăreketh (2), *pile of loaves, arrangement*
5073 nidbâk (Ch.) (1), *layer, row*

ROWED
2864 châthar (1), *to row*
1643 ĕlaunō (1), *to push*

ROWERS
7751 shûwṭ (1), *to travel, roam*

ROWING
1643 ĕlaunō (1), *to push*

ROWS
2905 tûwr (12), *row, course built into a wall*
2918 tîyrâh (1), *fortress; hamlet*
4634 ma'ărâkâh (1), *arrangement, row; pile*
5073 nidbâk (Ch.) (1), *layer, row*
8447 tôwr (1), *succession*

ROYAL
4410 mᵉlûwkâh (4), *realm, rulership*
4428 melek (2), *king*
4430 melek (Ch.) (1), *king*
4438 malkûwth (13), *rule; dominion*
4467 mamlâkâh (4), *royal dominion*
8237 shaphrûwr (1), *tapestry or canopy*
934 basilĕiŏs (1), *royal, kingly* in nature
937 basilikŏs (2), *befitting the sovereign*

RUBBING
5597 psōchō (1), *to rub out grain kernels*

RUBBISH
6083 'âphâr (2), *dust, earth, mud; clay,*

RUBIES
6443 pânîyn (6), (poss.) *round pearl*

RUDDER
4079 pēdaliŏn (1), *blade*

RUDDY
119 'âdam (1), *to red in the face*
132 'admônîy (3), *reddish, ruddy*

RUDE
2399 idiōtēs (1), *not initiated; untrained*

RUDIMENTS
4747 stŏichĕiŏn (2), *elementary truths*

RUE
4076 pēganŏn (1), *rue*

RUFUS
4504 Rhŏuphŏs (2), *red*

RUHAMAH
7355 râcham (1), *to be compassionate*

RUIN
4072 midcheh (1), *overthrow, downfall*
4288 mᵉchittâh (1), *ruin; consternation*
4383 mikshôwl (1), *obstacle; enticement*
4384 makshêlâh (1), *enticement*
4654 mappâlâh (2), *ruin*
4658 mappeleth (2), *down-fall; ruin; carcase*
6365 pîyd (1), *misfortune*
4485 rhēgma (1), *ruin*

RUINED
2040 hâraç (2), *to pull down; break, destroy*
3782 kâshal (1), *to totter, waver; to falter*

RUINOUS
4654 mappâlâh (1), *ruin*
5327 nâtsâh (2), *to be desolate, to lay waste*

RUINS
2034 hărîyçâh (1), *demolished, ruins*
4383 mikshôwl (1), *obstacle; enticement*
2679 kataskaptō (1), *to destroy, be ruined*

RULE
4427 mâlak (1), *to reign as king*
4475 memshâlâh (4), *rule; realm or a ruler*
4623 ma'tsâr (1), *self-control*
4910 mâshal (25), *to rule*
7287 râdâh (10), *to subjugate; to crumble*
7980 shâlaṭ (3), *to dominate, i.e. govern*
7981 shᵉlêṭ (Ch.) (1), *to dominate, i.e. govern*

7990 shallîyṭ (Ch.) (1), *premier, sovereign*
8323 sârar (3), *to have, exercise, get dominion*
746 archē (1), *first*
757 archō (1), *to rule, be first in rank*
1018 brabĕuō (1), *to govern; to prevail*
2233 hēgĕŏmai (3), *to lead, i.e. command*
2583 kanōn (4), *rule, standard*
4165 pŏimainō (4), *to tend as a shepherd*
4291 prŏïstēmi (2), *to preside; to practice*

RULED
4474 mimshâl (1), *ruler; dominion, rule*
4910 mâshal (5), *to rule*
5401 nâshaq (1), *to kiss; to equip with weapons*
7287 râdâh (3), *to subjugate; to crumble*
7990 shallîyṭ (Ch.) (2), *premier, sovereign*
8199 shâphaṭ (1), *to judge*

RULER
834+5921 'ăsher (1), *who, which, what, that*
4910 mâshal (13), *to rule*
5057 nâgîyd (19), *commander, official*
5387 nâsîy' (3), *leader; rising mist, fog*
6485 pâqad (2), *to visit, care for, count*
7101 qâtsîyn (2), *magistrate; leader*
7287 râdâh (1), *to subjugate; to crumble*
7860 shôṭêr (1), *to write; official who is a scribe*
7981 shᵉlêṭ (Ch.) (4), *to dominate, i.e. govern*
7989 shallîyṭ (1), *prince or warrior*
7990 shallîyṭ (Ch.) (2), *premier, sovereign*
8269 sar (10), *head person, ruler*
752 archisunagōgŏs (6), *director of the synagogue services*
755 architriklinŏs (1), *director of the entertainment*
758 archōn (9), *first*
2525 kathistēmi (6), *to designate, constitute*

RULER'S
4910 mâshal (1), *to rule*
758 archōn (1), *first*

RULERS
4043 mâgên (1), small *shield (buckler)*
4910 mâshal (4), *to rule*
5057 nâgîyd (1), *commander, official*
5387 nâsîy' (3), *leader; rising mist, fog*
5461 çâgân (16), *prefect*
6485 pâqad (1), *to visit, care for, count*
7101 qâtsîyn (1), *magistrate; leader*
7218 rô'sh (2), *head*

7336 râzan (1), *honorable*
7984 shilṭôwn (Ch.) (2), *official*
8269 sar (21), *ruler*
752 archisunagōgŏs (2), *director of the synagogue services*
758 archōn (14), *first*
2232 hēgĕmōn (2), *chief*
2888 kŏsmŏkratōr (1), *world-ruler*
4178 pŏllakis (2), *many times,* i.e. *frequently*

RULEST
4910 mâshal (2), *to rule*

RULETH
4910 mâshal (7), *to rule*
7300 rûwd (1), *to ramble*
7980 shâlaṭ (4), *to dominate,* i.e. *govern*
4291 prŏïstēmi (2), *to preside; to practice*

RULING
4910 mâshal (2), *to rule*
4291 prŏïstēmi (1), *to preside; to practice*

RUMAH
7316 Rûwmâh (1), *height*

RUMBLING
1995 hâmôwn (1), *noise, tumult; many, crowd*

RUMOUR
8052 shᵉmûw'âh (8), *announcement*
3056 lŏgŏs (1), *word, matter, thing*

RUMOURS
189 akŏē (2), *hearing; thing heard*

RUMP
451 'alyâh (5), fat *tail*

RUN
935 bôw' (1), *to go, come*
1556 gâlal (1), *to roll; to commit*
1980 hâlak (3), *to walk; live a certain way*
2100 zûwb (1), *to flow freely, gush*
3212 yâlak (1), *to walk; to live; to carry*
3381 yârad (6), *to descend*
6293 pâga' (1), *to impinge*
6805 tsâ'ad (1), *to pace*
7323 rûwts (36), *to run*
7325 rûwr (1), *to emit a fluid*
7751 shûwṭ (6), *to travel, roam*
8264 shâqaq (2), *to seek*
4936 suntrĕchō (1), *to rush together*
5143 trĕchō (8), *to run or walk hastily; to strive*

RUNNEST
7323 rûwts (1), *to run*

RUNNETH
935 bôw' (1), *to go, come*
3381 yârad (2), *to descend*
7310 rᵉvâyâh (1), *satisfaction*
7323 rûwts (4), *to run*

S

SAINTS'
40 hagiŏs (1), *holy*

SAITH
559 'âmar (581), to *say*
1696 dâbar (7), to *speak*
5001 nâ'am (10), to *utter* as an oracle
5002 nᵉ'ûm (353), *oracle*
6310 peh (1), *mouth*
2036 ĕpō (1), to *speak*
2980 laléō (2), to *talk*
3004 lĕgō (297), to *say*
5346 phēmi (5), to *make known* one's thoughts

SAKE
182 'ôwdôwth (1), on *account of; because*
1558 gâlâl (3), on *account of, because of*
1697 dâbâr (2), *word; matter; thing*
4616 ma'an (45), *on account of*
5668 'âbûwr (15), on *account of*
7068 qin'âh (1), *jealousy*
7945 shel (1), on *account of; whatsoever*
8478 tachath (2), *bottom; underneath; in lieu of*
1722 ĕn (1), *because of*
1752 hĕnĕka (14), *on account of*

SAKES
1558 gâlâl (1), on *account of, because of*
1697 dâbâr (1), *matter*
1701 dibrâh (Ch.) (1), *because, on account of*
5668 'âbûwr (1), on *account of*
5921 'al (3), *above, over*
6616 pâthîyl (6), *twine*

SALA
4527 Sala (1), *spear*

SALAH
7974 Shelach (6), *spear*

SALAMIS
4529 Salamis (1), *surge*

SALATHIEL
7597 Shᵉ'altîy'êl (1), *I have asked God*
4528 Salathiĕl (3), *I have asked God*

SALCAH
5548 Çalkâh (2), *walking*

SALCHAH
5548 Çalkâh (2), *walking*

SALE
4465 mimkâr (3), *merchandise*

SALEM
8004 Shâlêm (2), *peaceful*
4532 Salêm (2), *peaceful*

SALIM
4530 Salĕim (1), (poss.) *waver*

SALLAI
5543 Çallûw (2), *weighed*

SALLU
5543 Çallûw (3), *weighed*

SALMA
8007 Salmâ' (4), *clothing*

SALMON
6756 Tsalmôwn (1), *shady*
8009 Salmâh (1), *clothing*
8012 Salmôwn (1), *investiture*
4533 Salmōn (3), *investiture*

SALMONE
4534 Salmōnē (1), (poss.) *surge on the shore*

SALOME
4539 Salōmē (2), *peace*

SALT
4416 mᵉlach (Ch.) (2), *salt*
4417 melach (27), *salt*
4420 mᵉlêchâh (1), *salted* land, i.e. a *desert*
5898 'Îyr ham-Melach (1), *city of* (the) *salt*
217 halas (8), *salt*
251 hals (1), *salt*
252 halukŏs (1), *salty*

SALTED
4414 mâlach (1), to *salt*
233 halizō (3), to *salt*

SALTNESS
1096+358 ginŏmai (1), to *be, become*

SALTPITS
4417 melach (1), *salt*

SALU
5543 Çallûw (1), *weighed*

SALUTATION
783 aspasmŏs (6), *greeting*

SALUTATIONS
783 aspasmŏs (1), *greeting*

SALUTE
1288 bârak (4), to *bless*
7592+7965 shâ'al (1), to *ask*
7965 shâlôwm (2), *safe; well; health, prosperity*
782 aspazŏmai (32), to *give salutation*

SALUTED
1288 bârak (1), to *bless*
7592+7965 shâ'al (3), to *ask*
782 aspazŏmai (5), to *give salutation*

SALUTETH
782 aspazŏmai (5), to *give salutation*

SALVATION
3444 yᵉshûw'âh (65), *deliverance; aid*
3467 yâsha' (3), to make *safe, free*
3468 yesha' (32), *liberty, deliverance, prosperity*
4190 môwshâ'âh (1), *deliverance*
8668 tᵉshûw'âh (17), *rescue, deliverance*
4991 sōtēria (40), *rescue*
4992 sōtēriŏn (1), *defender* or *defence*

SAMARIA
8111 Shômᵉrown (109), *watch-station*

8115 Shomrayin (Ch.) (2), *watch-station*
4540 Samarĕia (13), *watch-station*

SAMARITAN
4541 Samarĕitēs (3), *inhabitant of Samaria*

SAMARITANS
8118 Shômᵉrônîy (1), *Shomeronite*
4541 Samarĕitēs (6), *inhabitant of Samaria*

SAME
428 'êl-leh (1), *these*
1459 gav (Ch.) (1), *middle*
1791 dêk (Ch.) (1), *this*
1797 dikkên (Ch.) (1), *this*
1931 hûw' (73), *this*
1933 hâvâ' (1), to *be*
1992 hêm (4), *they*
2063 zô'th (1), *this*
2088 zeh (9), *this* or *that*
6106 'etsem (6), *selfsame*
8478 tachath (1), *bottom*
846 autŏs (87), *he, she, it*
1565 ĕkĕinŏs (24), *that*
2532 kai (1), *even; also*
3673 hŏmŏtĕchnŏs (1), *of the same trade*
3748 hŏstis (1), *whoever*
3761 ŏudĕ (1), *neither*
3778 hŏutŏs (37), *this*
4954 sussōmŏs (1), *fellow-member*
5023 tauta (2), *these*
5026 tautȩ̄ (5), (*toward* or *of*) *this*
5126 tŏuton (2), to *this*
5129 tŏutō̧ (1), in *this*
5615 hōsautōs (1), *in the same way*

SAMGAR-NEBO
5562 Çamgar Nᵉbôw (1), *Samgar-Nebo*

SAMLAH
8072 Samlâh (4), *mantle*

SAMOS
4544 Samŏs (1), *Samus*

SAMOTHRACIA
4543 Samōthra̧kē (1), *Samos of Thrace*

SAMSON
8123 Shimshôwn (35), *sunlight*
4546 Sampsōn (1), *sunlight*

SAMSON'S
8123 Shimshôwn (3), *sunlight*

SAMUEL
8050 Shᵉmûw'êl (135), *heard of God*
4545 Samŏuēl (3), *heard of God*

SANBALLAT
5571 Çanballaṭ (10), *Sanballat*

SANCTIFICATION
38 hagiasmŏs (5), state of *purity*

SANCTIFIED
6942 qâdâsh (46), to *be, make clean*
37 hagiazō (16), to *purify*

SANCTIFIETH
37 hagiazō (4), to *purify*

SANCTIFY
6942 qâdâsh (63), to *be, make clean*
37 hagiazō (6), to *purify*

SANCTUARIES
4720 miqdâsh (5), *sanctuary of deity*

SANCTUARY
4720 miqdâsh (64), *sanctuary of deity*
6944 qôdesh (68), *sacred*
39 hagiŏn (4), *sacred*

SAND
2344 chôwl (23), *sand*
285 ammŏs (5), *sand*

SANDALS
4547 sandaliŏn (2), *sandal*

SANG
6030 'ânâh (2), to *sing*
7442 rânan (1), to *shout* for joy
7891 shîyr (7), to *sing*
5214 humnĕō (2), to *celebrate* God in song

SANK
3381 yârad (1), to *descend*
6749 tsâlal (1), to *settle*

SANSANNAH
5578 Çançannâh (1), *bough*

SAPH
5593 Çaph (1), *dish*

SAPHIR
8208 Shâphîyr (1), *beautiful*

SAPPHIRA
4551 Sapphĕirē (1), *sapphire or lapis-lazuli*

SAPPHIRE
5601 çappîyr (8), *sapphire*
4552 sapphĕirŏs (1), *sapphire or lapis-lazuli*

SAPPHIRES
5601 çappîyr (3), *sapphire*

SARA
4564 Sarrha (1), *princess*

SARAH
8283 Sârâh (36), *princess*
8294 Serach (1), *superfluity*
4564 Sarrha (2), *princess*

SARAH'S
8283 Sârâh (2), *princess*
4564 Sarrha (1), *princess*

SARAI
8297 Sâray (16), *dominative*

SARAI'S
8297 Sâray (1), *dominative*

SARAPH
8315 Sâraph (1), *burning one, serpent*

SARDINE
4555 sardinŏs (1), *sard*

SARDIS
4554 Sardĕis (3), Sardis

SARDITES
5625 Çardîy (1), Seredite

SARDIUS
124 'ôdem (3), ruby
4556 sardiŏs (1), sardian

SARDONYX
4557 sardŏnux (1), sard-onyx

SAREPTA
4558 Sarĕpta (1), refinement

SARGON
5623 Çargôwn (1), Sargon

SARID
8301 Sârîyd (2), survivor

SARON
4565 Sarŏn (1), plain

SARSECHIM
8310 Sarçᵉkîym (1), Sarsekim

SARUCH
4562 Sarŏuch (1), tendril

SAT
3427 yâshab (94), to dwell
8497 tâkâh (1), to camp
339 anakathizō (2), to sit up
345 anakĕimai (6), to recline at a meal
347 anaklinō (1), to lean back, recline
377 anapiptō (4), lie down, lean back
2516 kathĕzŏmai (4), to sit down, be seated
2521 kathēmai (43), to sit down; to remain
2523 kathizō (21), to seat down, dwell
2621 katakĕimai (3), to lie down; recline
2625 kataklinō (1), to recline, take a place
3869 parakathizō (1), to sit down near, beside
4775 sugkathēmai (2), to seat oneself with
4873 sunanakĕimai (8), to recline with

SATAN
7854 sâṭân (18), opponent
4567 Satanas (34), accuser, i.e. the Devil

SATAN'S
4567 Satanas (1), accuser, i.e. the Devil

SATEST
3427 yâshab (2), to settle

SATIATE
7301 râvâh (1), to slake
7646 sâba' (1), to fill

SATIATED
7301 râvâh (1), to slake

SATISFACTION
3724 kôpher (2), redemption-price

SATISFIED
4390 mâlê' (1), to fill
7301 râvâh (1), to slake
7646 sâba' (36), fill

SATISFIEST
7646 sâba' (1), to fill

SATISFIETH
7646 sâba' (2), to fill
7654 sob'âh (1), satiety

SATISFY
4390 mâlê' (1), to fill
7301 râvâh (1), to slake
7646 sâba' (7), to fill
5526 chŏrtazō (1), to supply food

SATISFYING
7648 sôba' (1), satisfaction
4140 plēsmŏnĕ (1), gratification

SATISIFED
7649 sâbêa' (1), satiated

SATYR
8163 sâ'îyr (1), shaggy; he-goat; goat idol

SATYRS
8163 sâ'îyr (1), shaggy; he-goat; goat idol

SAUL
7586 Shâ'ûwl (367), asked
4569 Saulŏs (23), asked

SAUL'S
7586 Shâ'ûwl (31), asked

SAVE
389 'ak (1), surely; only
518 'îm (1), Oh that!
657 'epheç (1), end; no further
1107 bil'ădêy (4), except
1115 biltîy (2), except
1115+518 biltîy (1), not, except, without, unless
2108 zûwlâh (6), except
2421 châyâh (21), to live; to revive
2425 châyay (1), to live; to revive
3444 yᵉshûw'âh (1), deliverance; aid
3467 yâsha' (106), to make safe, free
3588+518 kîy (12), for, that because
3861 lâhên (Ch.) (2), therefore; except
4422 mâlaṭ (4), to escape
7535 raq (1), although
8104 shâmar (1), to watch
235 alla (2), except
1295 diasōzō (1), to cure, preserve, rescue
1508 ěi mē (18), if not
2228 ē (1), or; than
3844 para (1), besides
4133 plēn (1), save that
4982 sōzō (41), to deliver

SAVED
2421 châyâh (8), to live; to revive
3467 yâsha' (35), to make safe, free
4422 mâlaṭ (1), to escape
5337 nâtsal (1), to deliver
8104 shâmar (1), to watch
1295 diasōzō (1), to cure, preserve, rescue

SATISFIED
7649 sâbêa' (3), satiated

SATISFIEST

SAVEST
3467 yâsha' (3), to make safe, free

SAVETH
3467 yâsha' (7), to make safe, free

SAVING
518 'îm (1), Oh that!
657 'epheç (1), end; no further
2421 châyâh (1), to live; to revive
3444 yᵉshûw'âh (2), deliverance; aid
3468 yesha' (1), liberty, deliverance, prosperity
1508 ěi mē (2), if not
3924 parěktŏs (1), besides
4047 pĕripŏiēsis (1), preservation
4991 sōtēria (1), rescue

SAVIOUR
3467 yâsha' (13), to make safe, free
4990 sōtēr (24), Deliverer

SAVIOURS
3467 yâsha' (2), to make safe, free

SAVOUR
6709 tsachănâh (1), stench
7381 rêyach (46), odor
2175 ĕuōdia (1), aroma
3471 mōrainō (2), to become insipid
3744 ŏsmē (4), fragrance

SAVOUREST
5426 phrŏnĕō (2), to be mentally disposed

SAVOURS
5208 nîychôwach (Ch.) (1), pleasure

SAVOURY
4303 maṭ'am (6), delicacy

SAW
2370 chăzâ' (Ch.) (9), to gaze upon; to dream
2372 châzâh (8), to gaze at; to perceive
4883 massôwr (1), saw
7200 râ'âh (306), to see
7805 shâzaph (1), to scan
991 blěpō (9), to look at
1492 ěidō (188), to know
1689 ěmblěpō (1), to observe; to discern
2147 hěuriskō (1), to find
2300 thěaŏmai (8), to look closely at
2334 thěōrěō (9), to see
3708 hŏraō (4), to stare, see clearly; to discern

SAWED
1641 gârar (1), to saw

SAWEST
2370 chăzâ' (Ch.) (7), to gaze upon; to dream
2372 châzâh (1), to gaze at; to perceive
7200 râ'âh (6), to see
1492 ěidō (7), to know

SAWN
4249 prizō (1), to saw in two

SAWS
4050 mᵉgêrâh (3), saw

SAY
559 'âmar (573), to say
560 'ămar (Ch.) (2), to say
1696 dâbar (28), to speak
1697 dâbâr (1), word
4405 millâh (2), word
471 antěpō (1), to refute
2036 ěpō (66), to speak
2046 ěrěō (39), to utter
2980 lalěō (6), to talk
3004 lěgō (293), to say
3056 lŏgŏs (1), word
5335 phaskō (1), to assert a claim
5346 phēmi (6), to make known one's thoughts

SAYEST
559 'âmar (18), to say
2036 ěpō (1), to speak
3004 lěgō (20), to say

SAYING
559 'âmar (916), to say
560 'ămar (Ch.) (2), to say
1697 dâbâr (20), word
2420 chîydâh (1), puzzle; conundrum; maxim
2036 ěpō (18), to speak
2981 lalia (1), talk
3004 lěgō (380), to say
3007 lěipō (5), to fail
3056 lŏgŏs (33), word
3058 lŏidŏrěō (1), to vilify, insult
4487 rhēma (6), utterance; matter
5335 phaskō (1), to assert

SAYINGS
561 'êmer (2), saying
1697 dâbâr (5), word
2420 chîydâh (2), puzzle; conundrum; maxim
6310 peh (1), mouth
3004 lěgō (1), to say
3056 lŏgŏs (16), word
4487 rhēma (3), utterance; matter

SCAB
1618 gârâb (1), itching
4556 miçpachath (3), scurf, rash
5597 çappachath (3), skin mange

SCABBARD
8593 ta'ar (1), scabbard

SCABBED
3217 yallepheth (2), scurf

SCAFFOLD
3595 kîyôwr (1), caldron

SCALES
650+4043 'âphîyq (1), valley; stream; mighty
6425 peleç (1), balance
7193 qasqeseth (7), fish scales; coat of mail
3013 lěpis (1), flake, scale

SCALETH
5927 'âlâh (1), to ascend, be high, mount

SCALL
5424 netheq (14), scurf

S

SCALP
6936 qodqôd (1), *crown* of the head

SCANT
7332 râzôwn (1), *thinness*

SCAPEGOAT
5799 'ăză'zêl (4), *goat of departure; scapegoat*

SCARCE
3433 *môlis* (2), *with difficulty*

SCARCELY
3433 *môlis* (2), *with difficulty*

SCARCENESS
4544 miçkênûth (1), *indigence, poverty*

SCAREST
2865 châthath (1), *to break* down

SCARLET
711 'arg^{e}vân (Ch.) (3), *purple*
8144 shânîy (9), *crimson*
8144+8438 shânîy (33), *crimson* dyed stuffs
8529 tâla' (1), *to dye crimson*
2847 kŏkkinŏs (6), *crimson*

SCATTER
921 b^{e}dar (Ch.) (1), *to scatter*
967 bâzar (2), *to scatter*
2210 zâqaph (1), *to lift up*
2219 zârâh (11), *to diffuse*
2236 zâraq (2), *to sprinkle, scatter*
5128 nûwa' (1), *to waver*
5310 nâphats (1), *to dash*
6284 pâ'âh (1), *to blow away*
6327 pùwts (18), *to dash*

SCATTERED
2219 zârâh (6), *to diffuse*
4900 mâshak (2), *to draw out; to be tall*
5310 nâphats (2), *to dash*
6327 pùwts (34), *to dash*
6340 pâzar (7), *to scatter*
6504 pârad (2), *to spread*
6555 pârats (1), *to break out*
6566 pâras (3), *to scatter*
1262 dialuō (1), *to break up*
1287 diaskŏrpizō (4), *to scatter; to squander*
1289 diaspĕirō (3), *to scatter like seed*
1290 diaspŏra (1), *dispersion*
4496 rhiptō (1), *to fling*
4650 skŏrpizō (1), *to dissipate*

SCATTERETH
2219 zârâh (2), *to diffuse*
6327 pùwts (3), *to dash* in pieces; *to disperse*
6340 pâzar (2), *to scatter*
4650 skŏrpizō (3), *to dissipate*

SCATTERING
5311 nephets (1), *storm* which disperses

SCENT
2143 zêker (1), *commemoration*
7381 rêyach (2), *odor*

SCEPTRE
7626 shêbeţ (9), *stick*
8275 sharbîyţ (4), *ruler's rod*
4464 rhabdŏs (2), *stick*

SCEPTRES
7626 shêbeţ (1), *stick*

SCEVA
4630 Skĕuas (1), *left-handed*

SCHISM
4978 schisma (1), *divisive dissension*

SCHOLAR
6030 'ânâh (1), *to respond*
8527 talmîyd (1), *pupil*

SCHOOL
4981 schŏlē (1), *lecture hall, i.e. school*

SCHOOLMASTER
3807 paidagōgŏs (2), *tutor, cf. pedagogue*

SCIENCE
4093 maddâ' (1), *intelligence*
1108 gnōsis (1), *knowledge*

SCOFF
7046 qâlaç (1), *to disparage, i.e. ridicule*

SCOFFERS
1703 ĕmpaiktēs (1), *derider; false teacher*

SCORCH
2739 kaumatizō (1), *to burn, scorch, sear*

SCORCHED
2739 kaumatizō (3), *to burn, scorch, sear*

SCORN
959 bâzâh (1), *to scorn*
3887 lûwts (1), *to scoff*
3933 la'ag (2), *scoffing*
4890 mischâq (1), *laughing-stock*
2606 katagĕlaō (3), *to laugh down, i.e. deride*

SCORNER
3887 lûwts (11), *to scoff*

SCORNERS
3887 lûwts (3), *to scoff*
3945 lâtsats (1), *to scoff*

SCORNEST
3887 lûwts (1), *to scoff*
7046 qâlaç (1), *to disparage, i.e. ridicule*

SCORNETH
3887 lûwts (2), *to scoff; to interpret; to intercede*
7832 sâchaq (2), *to scorn*

SCORNFUL
3887 lûwts (1), *to scoff*
3944 lâtsôwn (2), *scoffing*

SCORNING
3933 la'ag (2), *scoffing*
3944 lâtsôwn (1), *scoffing*

SCORPION
4651 skŏrpiŏs (2), *scorpion*

SCORPIONS
6137 'aqrâb (6), *scorpion*
4651 skŏrpiŏs (3), *scorpion*

SCOURED
4838 mâraq (1), *to polish*

SCOURGE
7752 shôwţ (4), *lash*
7885 shayiţ (1), *oar*
3147 mastizō (1), *to whip*
3164 machŏmai (5), *to war, i.e. to quarrel*
5416 phragĕlliŏn (1), *lash*

SCOURGED
1244 biqqôreth (1), *due punishment*
3146 mastigŏō (1), *to punish by flogging*
5417 phragĕllŏō (2), *to whip, i.e. to lash*

SCOURGES
7850 shôţêţ (1), *goad, flogging* device

SCOURGETH
3146 mastigŏō (1), *to punish by flogging*

SCOURGING
3148 mastix (1), *flogging* device

SCOURGINGS
3148 mastix (1), *flogging* device

SCRABBLED
8427 tâvâh (1), *to mark*

SCRAPE
1623 gârad (1), *to rub off*
5500 çâchâh (1), *to sweep away*
7096 qâtsâh (1), *to cut off*

SCRAPED
7096 qâtsâh (1), *to cut off*
7106 qâtsa' (1), *to scrape*

SCREECH
3917 lîylîyth (1), *night spectre (spirit)*

SCRIBE
5608 çâphar (42), *to inscribe; to enumerate*
5613 çâphêr (Ch.) (6), *scribe, recorder*
1122 grammatĕus (4), *secretary, scholar*

SCRIBE'S
5608 çâphar (2), *to inscribe; to enumerate*

SCRIBES
5608 çâphar (6), *to inscribe; to enumerate*
1122 grammatĕus (62), *secretary, scholar*

SCRIP
3219 yalqûwţ (1), *pouch*
4082 pēra (6), *wallet*

SCRIPTURE
3791 kâthâb (1), *writing*
1124 graphē (31), *document, i.e. holy Writ*

SCRIPTURES
1121 gramma (1), *writing*

1124 graphē (20), *document, i.e. holy Writ*

SCROLL
5612 çêpher (1), *writing*
975 bibliŏn (1), *scroll*

SCUM
2457 chel'âh (5), *rust*

SCURVY
1618 gârâb (2), *itching*

SCYTHIAN
4658 Skuthēs (1), *Scythene*

SEA
3220 yâm (291), *sea*
3221 yâm (Ch.) (2), *sea*
1724 ĕnaliŏs (1), *marine*
2281 thalassa (93), *sea*
3864 parathalassiŏs (1), *by the lake*
3882 paraliŏs (1), *maritime; seacoast*
3989 pĕlagŏs (1), *open sea*

SEAFARING
3220 yâm (1), *sea; basin*

SEAL
2368 chôwthâm (5), *seal*
2856 châtham (6), *to close up; to affix a seal*
4972 sphragizō (4), *to stamp with a signet*
4973 sphragis (11), *stamp impressed*

SEALED
2856 châtham (14), *to close up; to affix a seal*
2857 chătham (Ch.) (1), *to affix a seal*
2696 katasphragizō (1), *to seal closely*
4972 sphragizō (20), *to stamp with a signet*

SEALEST
2856 châtham (1), *to close up; to affix a seal*

SEALETH
2856 châtham (3), *to close up; to affix a seal*

SEALING
4972 sphragizō (1), *to stamp with a signet*

SEALS
4973 sphragis (5), *stamp*

SEAM
729 arrhaphŏs (1), *without seam*

SEARCH
1239 bâqar (1), *to inspect, admire*
1240 b^{e}qar (Ch.) (4), *to inspect, admire*
1875 dârash (4), *to pursue or search*
2658 châphar (3), *to delve, to explore*
2664 châphas (8), *to seek; to let be sought*
2665 chêphes (1), *secret trick, plot*
2713 châqar (11), *to examine, search*
2714 chêqer (3), *examination*

4290 machtereth (1),
burglary
8446 tûwr (9), to *meander*
1833 ĕxĕtazō (1), to
ascertain or *interrogate*
2045 ĕrĕunaō (2), to
seek, i.e. to *investigate*

SEARCHED
2664 châphas (3), to *seek*
2713 châqar (7), to
examine intimately
2714 chêqer (1),
examination
4959 mâshash (2), to *feel*
7270 râgal (1), to
reconnoiter; to slander
8446 tûwr (4), to *meander*
350 anakrinō (1), to
interrogate, determine
1830 ĕxĕrĕunaō (1), to
explore

SEARCHEST
1875 dârash (1), to *search*
2664 châphas (1), to *seek*

SEARCHETH
1875 dârash (2), to *search*
2713 châqar (3), to *search*
2045 ĕrĕunaō (3), to *seek*

SEARCHING
2664 châphas (1), to *seek*
2714 chêqer (2),
examination
8446 tûwr (1), to *meander*
2045 ĕrĕunaō (1), to *seek*

SEARCHINGS
2714 chêqer (1),
examination

SEARED
2743 kautĕriazō (1), to
brand or *cauterize*

SEAS
3220 yâm (24), *sea*
1337 dithalassŏs (1),
having two seas

SEASON
2165 zᵉmân (1), *time*
2166 zᵉmân (Ch.) (1),
time, appointed
3117 yôwm (3), *day; time*
4150 môw'êd (10), *place
of meeting*
4414 mâlach (1), to
disappear as dust
6256 'êth (14), *time*
171 akairōs (1),
inopportunely
741 artuō (1), to *spice*
2121 ĕukairŏs (1),
opportune, suitable
2540 kairŏs (11), *set or
proper* time
3641 ŏligŏs (1), *puny*
4340 prŏskairŏs (1),
temporary
5550 chrŏnŏs (3), *time*
5610 hōra (3), *hour*

SEASONED
741 artuō (2), to *spice*

SEASONS
2166 zᵉmân (Ch.) (1),
time, appointed
4150 môw'êd (3), *place of
meeting; assembly*
6256 'êth (2), *time*
2540 kairŏs (4), *set or
proper* time

5550 chrŏnŏs (1), *time*

SEAT
3678 kiççê' (7), *throne*
4186 môwshâb (7), *seat*
7674 shebeth (1), *rest*
7675 shebeth (2), *abode*
8499 tᵉkûwnâh (1),
something arranged
968 bēma (10), *tribunal
platform; judging place*
2362 thrŏnŏs (3), *throne*
2515 kathĕdra (1), *bench*

SEATED
5603 çâphan (1), to *roof*

SEATS
2362 thrŏnŏs (4), *throne*
2515 kathĕdra (2), *bench*
4410 prŏtŏkathĕdria (4),
pre-eminence in council

SEBA
5434 Çᵉbâ' (4), *Seba*

SEBAT
7627 Shᵉbâṭ (1), *Shebat*

SECACAH
5527 Çᵉkâkâh (1),
enclosure

SECHU
7906 Sêkûw (1), *Seku*

SECOND
4932 mishneh (12),
double; second
8138 shânâh (3), to *fold,
i.e. duplicate*
8145 shênîy (99), *second*
8147 shᵉnayim (10),
two-fold
8578 tinyân (Ch.) (1),
second
8648 tᵉrêyn (Ch.) (1), *two*
1207 dĕutĕrŏprŏtŏs (1),
second-first
1208 dĕutĕrŏs (42),
second; secondly

SECONDARILY
1208 dĕutĕrŏs (1),
second; secondly

SECRET
328 'aṭ (1), *gently, softly*
2934 ṭâman (1), to *hide*
4565 miçtâr (8), *covert
hiding place*
5475 çôwd (8), *secret*
5640 çâtham (1), to
repair; to keep secret
5641 çâthar (4), to *hide*
5642 çᵉthar (Ch.) (1), to
demolish
5643 çêther (15), *cover*
5956 'âlam (2), to *conceal*
6383 pil'îy (1),
remarkable
6596 pôth (1), *hole; hinge*
6845 tsâphan (2), to *hide*
7328 râz (Ch.) (6),
mystery
8368 sâthar (1), to *break
out as an eruption*
614 apŏkruphŏs (1),
secret, hidden things
2926 kruptē (1), *hidden*
2927 kruptŏs (10), *private*
2928 kruptō (1), to
conceal
2931 kruphē (1), *in secret*
4601 sigaō (1), to *keep
silent*

5009 tamĕïŏn (1), *room*

SECRETLY
1589 gânab (1), to *deceive*
2244 châbâ' (1), to *secrete*
2644 châphâ' (1), to *act
covertly*
2790 chârash (1), to
engrave; to plow
2791 cheresh (1),
magical craft; silence
3909 lâṭ (1), *secrecy*
4565 miçtâr (2), *covert
hiding place*
5643 çêther (9), *cover*
6845 tsâphan (1), to *hide*
2928 kruptō (1), to
conceal
2977 lathra (1), *secretly*

SECRETS
4016 mâbûsh (1), *male
genitals*
5475 çôwd (2), *secret*
7328 râz (Ch.) (3),
mystery
8587 ta'ălummâh (2),
secret
2927 kruptŏs (2), *private*

SECT
139 hairĕsis (5), *sect*

SECUNDUS
4580 Sĕkŏundŏs (1),
second

SECURE
982 bâṭach (4), to *trust*
983 beṭach (1), *security*
987 baṭṭûchôwth (1),
security
4160+275 mûwts (1), to
oppress

SECURELY
983 beṭach (2), *safety,
security, trust*

SECURITY
2425 hikanŏs (1), *ample*

SEDITION
849 'eshtaddûwr (Ch.)
(2), *rebellion*
4714 stasis (3), one
leading an uprising

SEDITIONS
1370 dichŏstasia (1),
dissension

SEDUCE
635 apŏplanaō (1), to
lead astray; to wander
4105 planaō (2), to
deceive

SEDUCED
2937 tâ'âh (1), to *lead
astray*
8582 tâ'âh (2), to *stray*

SEDUCERS
1114 gŏēs (1), *imposter*

SEDUCETH
8582 tâ'âh (1), to *stray*

SEDUCING
4108 planŏs (1), *roving*

SEE
2009 hinnêh (2), *Look!*
2370 chăzâ' (Ch.) (4), to
gaze upon; to dream
2372 châzâh (15), to *gaze
at; to perceive*

2374 chôzeh (2),
beholder in vision
4758 mar'eh (1),
appearance; vision
5027 nâbaṭ (4), to *scan;
to regard* with favor
7200 râ'âh (346), to *see*
7789 shûwr (4), to *spy
out, survey*
308 anablĕpō (1), to *look
up; to recover sight*
542 apĕidō (1), to *see
fully*
991 blĕpō (46), to *look at*
1227 diablĕpō (2), to *see
clearly, recover vision*
1492 ĕidō (79), to *know*
1689 ĕmblĕpō (1), to
observe; to discern
2300 thĕaŏmai (4), to
look closely at
2334 thĕōrĕō (17), to *see*
2396 idĕ (1), *lo!, look!*
2400 idŏu (3), *lo!, see!*
2477 histŏrĕō (1), to *visit*
3467 muōpazō (1), to *see
indistinctly, be myopic*
3700 ŏptanŏmai (29), to
appear
3708 hŏraō (11), to *stare,
see clearly; to discern*
5461 phōtizō (1), to *shine
or to brighten* up

SEED
2233 zera' (218), *seed*
2234 zᵉra' (Ch.) (1),
posterity, progeny
6507 pᵉrûdâh (1), *kernel*
4687 spĕirō (4), to
scatter, i.e. *sow* seed
4690 spĕrma (41), *seed*
4701 spŏra (1), *sowing*
4703 spŏrŏs (5), *seed*

SEED'S
2233 zera' (1), *seed; fruit*

SEEDS
4690 spĕrma (3), *seed*

SEEDTIME
2233 zera' (1), *seed; fruit*

SEEING
310 'achar (1), *after*
518 'îm (1), *whether?; if*
1768 dîy (Ch.) (1), *that; of*
3282 ya'an (1), *because*
3588 kiy (9), *for, that*
6493 piqqêach (1),
clear-sighted
7200 râ'âh (16), to *see*
990 blemma (1), *vision*
991 blĕpō (8), to *look at*
1063 gar (1), *for, indeed,
but, because*
1492 ĕidō (8), to *know*
1512 ĕi pĕr (1), *if perhaps*
1893 ĕpĕi (4), *since*
1894 ĕpĕidē (2), *whereas*
1897 ĕpĕipĕr (1), *since*
2334 thĕōrĕō (1), to *see*
3708 hŏraō (1), to *stare,
see clearly; to discern*
3754 hŏti (1), *that; since*
4275 prŏĕidō (1), to
foresee

SEEK
1239 bâqar (3), to
inspect, admire

1245 bâqash (112), to
search out; to strive
1556 gâlal (1), to roll
1875 dârash (56), to seek
2713 châqar (1), to search
7125 qîr'âh (1), to
encounter, to happen
7836 shâchar (8), to
search for
8446 tûwr (1), to wander
327 anazētĕō (1), to
search out
1567 ĕkzētĕō (2), to seek
out
1934 ĕpizētĕō (6), to
search (inquire) for
2212 zētĕō (48), to seek

SEEKEST
1245 bâqash (7), to
search out; to strive
2212 zētĕō (2), to seek

SEEKETH
579 'ânâh (1), to meet
1243 baqqârâh (1),
looking after
1245 bâqash (19), to
search out; to strive
1875 dârash (6), to seek
2658 châphar (1), to delve
7836 shâchar (1), to
search for
1567 ĕkzētĕō (1), to seek
out
1934 ĕpizētĕō (3), to
search (inquire) for
2212 zētĕō (9), to seek

SEEKING
1875 dârash (2), to seek
2212 zētĕō (12), to seek

SEEM
3191 yᵉṭab (Ch.) (1), to
be, make well
4591 mâ'aṭ (1), to be,
make small or few
4758 mar'eh (1),
appearance; vision
5869 'ayin (2), eye; sight
7034 qâlâh (1), to be light
7185 qâshâh (1), to be
tough or severe
1380 dŏkĕō (5), to seem

SEEMED
5869 'ayin (4), eye; sight
1380 dŏkĕō (6), to think,
regard, seem good
5316 phainō (1), to
lighten; to appear

SEEMETH
5869 'ayin (18), eye; sight
6440 pânîym (2), face
7200 râ'âh (1), to see
1380 dŏkĕō (5), to seem

SEEMLY
5000 nâ'veh (2), suitable

SEEN
2370 chăzâ' (Ch.) (3), to
gaze upon; to dream
2372 châzâh (9), to gaze
at; to perceive
7200 râ'âh (162), to see
7210 rô'îy (2), sight
7805 shâzaph (1), to scan
991 blĕpō (9), to look at
1492 ĕidō (33), to know
2300 thĕaŏmai (8), to
look closely at

2334 thĕōrĕō (2), to see
2529 kathŏraō (1), to see
clearly
3700 ŏptanŏmai (8), to
appear
3708 hŏraō (32), to stare,
see clearly; to discern
3780 ŏuchi (1), not indeed
4308 prŏŏraō (1), to
notice previously
5316 phainō (2), to
lighten; be visible

SEER
2374 chôzeh (11),
beholder in vision
7200 râ'âh (10), to see

SEER'S
7200 râ'âh (1), to see

SEERS
2374 chôzeh (5),
beholder in vision
7200 râ'âh (1), to see

SEEST
2372 châzâh (2), to gaze
at; to perceive
7200 râ'âh (27), to see
7210 rô'îy (1), sight;
spectacle
991 blĕpō (5), to look at
2334 thĕōrĕō (1), to see

SEETH
2372 châzâh (3), to gaze
at; to perceive
7200 râ'âh (27), to see
7210 rô'îy (1), sight;
spectacle
991 blĕpō (11), to look at
2334 thĕōrĕō (9), to see
3708 hŏraō (1), to stare

SEETHE
1310 bâshal (8), to boil

SEETHING
1310 bâshal (1), to boil
5301 nâphach (2), to
inflate, blow, kindle

SEGUB
7687 Sᵉgûwb (3), aloft

SEIR
8165 Sê'îyr (39), rough

SEIRATH
8167 Sᵉ'îyrâh (1),
roughness

SEIZE
3423 yârash (1), to
inherit; to impoverish
3451 yᵉshîymâh (1),
desolation
3947 lâqach (1), to take
2722 katĕchō (1), to hold
down fast

SEIZED
2388 châzaq (1), to seize

SELA
5554 Çela' (1), craggy
rock; fortress

SELA-HAMMAHLEKOTH
5555 Çela' ham-
machlᵉqôwth (1), rock
of the divisions

SELAH
5542 Çelâh (74),
suspension of music
5554 Çela' (1), craggy
rock; fortress

SELED
5540 Çeled (1),
exultation

SELEUCIA
4581 Sĕlĕukĕia (1), of
Seleucus

SELFWILL
7522 râtsôwn (1), delight

SELFWILLED
829 authadēs (2),
self-pleasing, arrogant

SELL
4376 mâkar (24), to sell
7666 shâbar (3), to deal
1710 ĕmpŏrĕuŏmai (1),
to trade, do business
4453 pōlĕō (7), to barter

SELLER
4376 mâkar (3), to sell
4211 pŏrphurŏpōlis (1),
female trader in
bluish-red cloth

SELLERS
4376 mâkar (1), to sell

SELLEST
4376 mâkar (1), to sell

SELLETH
4376 mâkar (5), to sell
7666 shâbar (1), to deal
4453 pōlĕō (1), to barter

SELVEDGE
7098 qâtsâh (2),
termination; fringe

SEM
4590 Sēm (1), name

SEMACHIAH
5565 Çᵉmakyâhûw (1),
supported of Jehovah

SEMEI
4584 Sĕmĕï (1), famous

SENAAH
5570 Çᵉnâ'âh (2), thorny

SENATE
1087 gĕrŏusia (1), Jewish
Sanhedrin

SENATORS
2205 zâqên (1), old,
venerated

SEND
935 bôw' (1), to go, come
5042 nâba' (1), to gush
5130 nûwph (1), to rock
5414 nâthan (6), to give
7136 qârâh (1), to bring
about; to impose
7971 shâlach (157), to
send away
7972 shᵉlach (Ch.) (1), to
send away
630 apŏluō (6), to relieve,
release; divorce
649 apŏstĕllō (23), to
send out on a mission
906 ballō (3), to throw
1032 bruō (1), to gush
1544 ĕkballō (3), to
throw out
1821 ĕxapŏstĕllō (1), to
despatch, or to dismiss
3343 mĕtapĕmpō (2), to
summon or invite
3992 pĕmpō (25), to send

SENDEST
7971 shâlach (6), to send
away

SENDETH
5414 nâthan (2), to give
7971 shâlach (8), to send
away
649 apŏstĕllō (4), to send
out on a mission
1026 brĕchō (1), to make
wet; to rain

SENDING
4916 mishlôwach (3),
sending out
4917 mishlachath (1),
mission; release; army
7971 shâlach (9), to send
away
3992 pĕmpō (1), to send

SENEH
5573 Çeneh (1), thorn

SENIR
8149 Shᵉnîyr (2), peak

SENNACHERIB
5576 Çanchêrîyb (13),
Sancherib

SENSE
7922 sekel (1),
intelligence; success

SENSES
145 aisthētēriŏn (1),
judgment, sense

SENSUAL
5591 psuchikŏs (2),
physical and brutish

SENT
1980 hâlak (1), to walk
2904 ṭûwl (1), to cast
down or out, hurl
3947 lâqach (1), to take
5414 nâthan (5), to give
5674 'âbar (2), to cross
over; to transition
6680 tsâvâh (1), to
constitute, enjoin
7725 shûwb (1), to return
7964 shillûwach (1),
divorce; dower
7971 shâlach (459), to
send away
7972 shᵉlach (Ch.) (12),
to send away
375 anapĕmpō (4), to
send up or back
628 apŏlŏuō (2), to wash
fully
630 apŏluō (6), to
release; divorce
640 apŏria (1), state of
quandary, perplexity
649 apŏstĕllō (104), to
send out on a mission
652 apŏstŏlŏs (2),
commissioner of Christ
657 apŏtassŏmai (1), to
say adieu; to renounce
863 aphiēmi (2), to leave
1524 ĕisĕimi (1), to enter
1544 ĕkballō (1), to
throw out
1599 ĕkpĕmpō (2), to
despatch, send out
1821 ĕxapŏstĕllō (10), to
despatch, or to dismiss
3343 mĕtapĕmpō (4), to
summon or invite

SENTENCE
3992 pĕmpō (49), to send
4842 sumpĕmpō (2), to
  dispatch with
4882 sunapŏstĕllō (1), to
  despatch with

SENTENCE
1697 dâbâr (3), word
4941 mishpâṭ (2), verdict;
  formal decree; justice
6310 peh (1), mouth
6599 pithgâm (1),
  judicial sentence; edict
7081 qeçem (1),
  divination
610 apŏkrima (1),
  decision or sentence
1948 ĕpikrinō (1), to
  adjudge, decide
2919 krinō (1), to decide

SENTENCES
280 'ăchîydâh (Ch.) (1),
  enigma
2420 chîydâh (1), puzzle

SENTEST
7971 shâlach (4), to send
  away

SENUAH
5574 Çᵉnûw'âh (1),
  pointed

SEORIM
8188 Sᵉ'ôrîym (1), barley

SEPARATE
914 bâdal (7), to divide
1508 gizrâh (7), figure,
  appearance; enclosure
2505 châlaq (1), to be
  smooth; be slippery
3995 mibdâlâh (1),
  separation; separate
5139 nâzîyr (1), prince;
  separated Nazirite
5144 nâzar (4), to set
  apart, devote
6381 pâlâ' (1), to be,
  make great, difficult
6504 pârad (2), to spread
873 aphŏrizō (5), to limit,
  exclude, appoint
5562 chōrĕō (3), to pass,
  enter; to hold, admit

SEPARATED
914 bâdal (17), to divide
5139 nâzîyr (1), prince;
  separated Nazirite
5144 nâzar (1), to set
  apart, devote
6395 pâlâh (2), to
  distinguish
6504 pârad (8), to spread
873 aphŏrizō (4), to limit,
  exclude, appoint

SEPARATETH
5144 nâzar (3), to set
  apart, devote
6504 pârad (2), to spread

SEPARATING
5144 nâzar (1), to set
  apart, devote

SEPARATION
914 bâdal (1), to divide
5079 niddâh (14), time of
  menstrual impurity
5145 nezer (11), set
  apart; dedication

SEPHAR
5611 Çᵉphâr (1), census

SEPHARAD
5614 Çᵉphârâd (1),
  Sepharad

SEPHARVAIM
5617 Çᵉpharvayim (6),
  Sepharvajim

SEPHARVITES
5616 Çᵉpharvîy (1),
  Sepharvite

SEPULCHRE
6900 qᵉbûwrâh (5),
  sepulchre
6913 qeber (14),
  sepulchre
3418 mnēma (4),
  sepulchral monument
3419 mnēmĕiŏn (26),
  place of interment
5028 taphŏs (5), grave

SEPULCHRES
6913 qeber (12),
  sepulchre
3419 mnēmĕiŏn (3),
  place of interment
5028 taphŏs (1), grave

SERAH
8294 Serach (2),
  superfluity

SERAIAH
8304 Sᵉrâyâh (20),
  Jehovah has prevailed

SERAPHIMS
8314 sârâph (2), saraph

SERED
5624 Çered (2), trembling

SERGIUS
4588 Sĕrgiŏs (1), Sergius

SERJEANTS
4465 rhabdŏuchŏs (2),
  constable

SERPENT
5175 nâchâsh (25), snake
8314 sârâph (3),
  poisonous serpent
8577 tannîyn (2),
  sea-serpent; jackal
3789 ŏphis (8), snake

SERPENT'S
5175 nâchâsh (2), snake

SERPENTS
2119 zâchal (1), to crawl
5175 nâchâsh (4), snake
8577 tannîyn (1),
  sea-serpent; jackal
2062 hĕrpĕtŏn (1), reptile
3789 ŏphis (6), snake

SERUG
8286 Sᵉrûwg (5), tendril

SERVANT
5288 na'ar (30), servant
5647 'âbad (1), to serve
5649 'ăbad (Ch.) (1),
  servant
5650 'ebed (363), servant
7916 sâkîyr (8), man at
  wages, hired hand
8334 shârath (4), to
  attend
1248 diakŏnia (2),
  attendance, aid, service
1249 diakŏnŏs (3),
  attendant, deacon

1401 dŏulŏs (66), servant
1402 dŏulŏō (1), to
  enslave
2324 thĕrapōn (1),
  menial attendant
3610 ŏikĕtēs (3), menial
  domestic servant
3816 pais (8), servant

SERVANT'S
5650 'ebed (8), servant
1401 dŏulŏs (1), servant

SERVANTS
582 'ĕnôwsh (1), man
5288 na'ar (21), servant
5647 'âbad (4), to serve
5649 'ăbad (Ch.) (6),
  servant
5650 'ebed (367), servant
5657 'ăbuddâh (1),
  service
8334 shârath (1), to
  attend as a menial
341 anakainŏō (1), to
  renovate, renew
1249 diakŏnŏs (2),
  attendant, deacon
1401 dŏulŏs (55), servant
1402 dŏulŏō (2), to
  enslave
3407 misthiŏs (2),
  hired-worker
3610 ŏikĕtēs (1), menial
  domestic servant
3816 pais (1), servant
5257 hupērĕtēs (4),
  servant, attendant

SERVANTS'
5650 'ebed (4), servant

SERVE
5647 'âbad (162), to serve
5656 'ăbôdâh (1), work
5975+6440 'âmad (1), to
  stand
6399 pᵉlach (Ch.) (7), to
  serve or worship
8334 shârath (4), to
  attend as a menial
1247 diakŏnĕō (7), to
  wait upon, serve
1398 dŏulĕuō (13), to
  serve as a slave
3000 latrĕuō (13), to
  minister to God

SERVED
1580 gâmal (1), to benefit
  or requite; to wean
5647 'âbad (61), to serve
5975+6440 'âmad (1), to
  stand
6213 'âsâh (1), to do
8334 shârath (4), to
  attend as a menial
1247 diakŏnĕō (1), to
  wait upon, serve
1398 dŏulĕuō (1), to
  serve as a slave
3000 latrĕuō (2), to
  minister to God
5256 hupērĕtĕō (1), to be
  a subordinate

SERVEDST
5647 'âbad (1), to serve

SERVEST
6399 pᵉlach (Ch.) (2), to
  serve or worship

SERVETH
5647 'âbad (2), to serve
5656 'ăbôdâh (1), work
1247 diakŏnĕō (2), to
  wait upon, serve
1398 dŏulĕuō (1), to
  serve as a slave

SERVICE
3027 yâd (2), hand; power
5647 'âbad (4), to serve
5656 'ăbôdâh (98), work
5673 'ăbîydâh (Ch.) (1),
  labor or business
6402 polchân (Ch.) (1),
  worship
6635 tsâbâ' (4), army,
  military host
8278 sᵉrâd (4), stitching
8334 shârath (3), to
  attend as a menial
1248 diakŏnia (3),
  attendance, aid, service
1398 dŏulĕuō (3), to
  serve as a slave
2999 latrĕia (5), worship,
  ministry service
3000 latrĕuō (1), to
  minister to God
3009 lĕitŏurgia (3),
  service, ministry

SERVILE
5656 'ăbôdâh (12), work

SERVING
5647 'âbad (2), to serve
1248 diakŏnia (1),
  attendance, aid, service
1398 dŏulĕuō (3), to
  serve as a slave
3000 latrĕuō (1), to
  minister to God

SERVITOR
8334 shârath (1), to
  attend as a menial

SERVITUDE
5656 'ăbôdâh (2), work

SET
530 'ĕmûwnâh (5),
  fidelity; steadiness
631 'âçar (1), to fasten
935 bôw' (1), to go, come
1129 bânâh (2), to build
1197 bâ'ar (1), to be
  brutish, be senseless
1379 gâbal (1), to set a
  boundary line, limit
1431 gâdal (1), to be
  great, make great
2211 zᵉqaph (Ch.) (1), to
  impale by hanging
2232 zâra' (1), to sow
  seed; to disseminate
2706 chôq (1),
  appointment; allotment
2710 châqaq (1), to
  engrave; to enact laws
3051 yâhab (1), to give
3240 yânach (8), to allow
  to stay
3245 yâçad (1), settle,
  consult, establish
3259 yâ'ad (3), to meet;
  to summon; to direct
3320 yâtsab (5), to
  station, offer, continue
3322 yâtsag (8), to place
3332 yâtsaq (1), to pour
  out

S

3335 yâtsar (1), to *form*
3341 yâtsath (1), to *burn*
3427 yâshab (13), to *settle*
3488 yᵉthîb (Ch.) (2), to *sit*
3559 kûwn (6), to *set up*
3635 kᵉlal (Ch.) (4), to *complete*
3966 mᵉʼôd (2), *very*
4142 mûwçabbâh (1), *backside; fold*
4150 môwʼêd (10), *place of meeting*
4390 mâlê' (5), to *fill*
4394 millû' (4), *fulfilling; setting; consecration*
4427 mâlak (1), to *reign as king*
4483 mᵉnâ' (Ch.) (3), to *count, appoint*
4487 mânâh (1), to *allot*
4853 massâ' (1), *burden*
5079 niddâh (1), time of menstrual *impurity*
5117 nûwach (2), to *rest; to settle* down
5128 nûwa' (1), to *waver*
5183 nachath (1), *descent; quiet*
5258 nâçak (2), to *pour*
5265 nâça' (16), *start*
5324 nâtsab (18), to *station*
5329 nâtsach (4), to *be eminent*
5375 nâsâ' (9), to *lift up*
5414 nâthan (103), to *give*
5473 çûwg (1), to *hem* in
5496 çûwth (1), to *stimulate; to seduce*
5526 çâkak (1), to *entwine; to fence* in
5564 çâmak (1), to *lean* upon; *take hold* of
5774 'ûwph (1), to *cover,* to *fly; to faint*
5927 'âlâh (2), to *ascend, be high, mount*
5975 'âmad (44), to *stand*
6186 'ârak (1), to set in a row, i.e. *arrange,*
6187 'êrek (1), *pile, equipment, estimate*
6213 'âsâh (3), to *do*
6395 pâlâh (1), to *distinguish*
6485 pâqad (7), to *care*
6496 pâqîyd (1), *superintendent, officer*
6584 pâshaṭ (1), to *strip*
6605 pâthach (1), to *open*
6845 tsâphan (1), to *hide*
6965 qûwm (28), to *rise*
6966 qûwm (Ch.) (11), to *rise*
7311 rûwm (7), to *rise*
7313 rûwm (Ch.) (1), *elation, arrogance*
7392 râkab (2), to *ride*
7660 shâbats (1), to *interweave*
7682 sâgab (1), to *be, make lofty; be safe*
7725 shûwb (1), to *return*
7737 shâvâh (1), to *level*
7760 sûwm (129), to *put*
7761 sûwm (Ch.) (2), to *put, place*
7896 shîyth (22), to *place*
7931 shâkan (3), to *reside*

7947 shâlab (1), to *make equidistant*
7971 shâlach (5), to *send away*
8239 shâphath (2), to *put*
8371 shâthath (1), to *place,* i.e. *array; to lie*
8427 tâvâh (1), to *mark out; imprint*
321 anagō (1), to *lead up; to bring out*
345 anakĕimai (1), to *recline* at a meal
377 anapiptō (1), *lie down, lean back*
392 anatassŏmai (1), to *arrange*
461 anŏrthŏō (1), to *strengthen, build*
584 apŏdĕiknumi (1), to *demonstrate*
630 apŏluŏ (2), to *relieve, release; divorce*
649 apŏstĕllō (1), to *send out* on a mission
816 atĕnizō (1), to *gaze*
968 bēma (1), *tribunal platform; judging place*
1299 diatassŏ (1), to *institute, prescribe*
1325 didōmi (1), to *give*
1369 dichazō (1), to *sunder,* i.e. *alienate*
1416 dunŏ (1), to *have the sun set*
1847 ĕxŏudĕnŏō (1), to *be treated with contempt*
1848 ĕxŏuthĕnĕō (3), to *treat with contempt*
1913 ĕpibibazŏ (3), to *cause to mount*
1930 ĕpidiŏrthŏō (1), to *set in order*
1940 ĕpikathizō (1), to *seat upon*
2007 ĕpitithēmi (3), to *impose*
2064 ĕrchŏmai (1), to *go*
2350 thŏrubĕō (1), to *clamor; start a riot*
2476 histēmi (11), to *stand, establish*
2521 kathēmai (1), to *sit down; to remain, reside*
2523 kathizō (6), to *seat down, dwell*
2525 kathistēmi (1), to *designate, constitute*
2749 kĕimai (6), to *lie outstretched*
3908 paratithēmi (9), to *present something*
4060 pĕritithēmi (1), to *present*
4270 prŏgraphō (1), to *announce, prescribe*
4295 prŏkĕimai (4), to *be present to the mind*
4388 prŏtithēmai (2), to *place before*
4741 stērizō (1), to *turn resolutely; to confirm*
4776 sugkathizō (1), to *give, take a seat with*
4900 sunĕlaunŏ (1), to *drive together*
4972 sphragizō (2), to *stamp* with a signet

5002 taktŏs (1), *appointed* or *stated*
5021 tassŏ (1), to *arrange, assign*
5087 tithēmi (5), to *place*
5394 phlŏgizō (1), to *cause a blaze, ignite*
5426 phrŏnĕō (1), to *be mentally disposed*

SETH
8352 Shêth (7), *put*
4589 Sēth (1), *put*

SETHUR
5639 Çᵉthûwr (1), *hidden*

SETTER
2604 kataggĕlĕus (1), *proclaimer*

SETTEST
4916 mishlôwach (3), *sending out*
5324 nâtsab (1), to *station*
7760 sûwm (1), to *put*
7896 shîyth (1), to *place*

SETTETH
3320 yâtsab (1), to *station, offer, continue*
3427 yâshab (1), to *dwell, to remain; to settle*
3559 kûwn (1), to *set up: establish, fix, prepare*
3857 lâhaṭ (1), to *blaze*
5265 nâça' (2), *start*
5375 nâsâ' (1), to *lift up*
5496 çûwth (1), to *stimulate; to seduce*
5927 'âlâh (2), to *ascend, be high, mount*
5975 'âmad (2), to *stand*
6966 qûwm (Ch.) (2), to *rise*
7034 qâlâh (1), to *be light*
7311 rûwm (1), to *raise*
7760 sûwm (1), to *put*
7918 shâkak (1), to *lay a trap; to allay*
2007 ĕpitithēmi (1), to *impose*
2476 histēmi (1), to *stand*
5394 phlŏgizō (1), to *cause a blaze,* i.e. *ignite*

SETTING
5414 nâthan (1), to *give*
1416 dunŏ (1), to *have the sun set*
3326 mĕta (1), *with*

SETTINGS
4396 millû'âh (1), *setting*

SETTLE
3427 yâshab (1), to *settle*
5835 'ăzârâh (6), *enclosure; border*
5975 'âmad (1), to *stand*
2311 thĕmĕliŏō (1), to *erect; to consolidate*
5087 tithēmi (1), to *place*

SETTLED
2883 ṭâba' (1), to *sink*
4349 mâkôwn (1), *place*
5324 nâtsab (1), to *station*
5975 'âmad (1), to *stand*
7087 qâphâ' (1), to *thicken, congeal*
8252 shâqaṭ (1), to *repose*
1476 hĕdraiŏs (1), *immovable; steadfast*

SETTLEST
5181 nâchath (1), to *sink*

SEVEN
3598 Kîymâh (1), *cluster of stars, the Pleiades*
7651 sheba' (346), *seven*
7655 shib'âh (Ch.) (6), *satiety*
7658 shib'ânâh (1), *seven*
7659 shib'âthayim (1), *seven-fold*
2033 hĕpta (80), *seven*
2034 hĕptakis (4), *seven times*
2035 hĕptakischiliŏi (1), *seven times a thousand*

SEVENFOLD
7659 shib'âthayim (6), *seven-fold*

SEVENS
7651 sheba' (2), *seven*

SEVENTEEN
7651+6240 sheba' (9), *seven*
7657+7651 shib'îym (1), *seventy*

SEVENTEENTH
7651+6240 sheba' (6), *seven*

SEVENTH
7637 shᵉbîy'îy (96), *seventh*
7651 sheba' (13), *seven*
1442 hĕbdŏmŏs (9), *seventh*
2035 hĕptakischiliŏi (1), *seven times a thousand*

SEVENTY
7657 shib'îym (58), *seventy*
1440 hĕbdŏmēkŏnta (2), *seventy*
1441 hĕbdŏmēkŏntakis (1), *seventy times*

SEVER
914 bâdal (1), to *divide, separate, distinguish*
6395 pâlâh (2), to *distinguish*
873 aphŏrizō (1), to *limit, exclude, appoint*

SEVERAL
2669 chôphshûwth (2), *prostration by sickness*
2398 idiŏs (1), *private*

SEVERALLY
2398 idiŏs (1), *private*

SEVERED
914 bâdal (2), to *divide*
6504 pârad (1), to *spread*

SEVERITY
663 apŏtŏmia (2), *rigor, severity*

SEW
8609 tâphar (2), to *sew*

SEWED
8609 tâphar (2), to *sew*

SEWEST
2950 ṭâphal (1), to *impute* falsely

SEWETH
1976 ĕpirrhaptō (1), to *stitch upon*

SHAALABBIN
8169 Sha'albîym (1),
fox-holes

SHAALBIM
8169 Sha'albîym (2),
fox-holes

SHAALBONITE
8170 Sha'albônîy (2),
Shaalbonite

SHAAPH
8174 Sha'aph (2),
fluctuation

SHAARAIM
8189 Sha'ărayim (2),
double gates

SHAASHGAZ
8190 Sha'ashgaz (1),
Shaashgaz

SHABBETHAI
7678 Shabbᵉthay (3),
restful

SHACHIA
7634 Shobyâh (1),
captivation

SHADE
6783 tsᵉmîythûth (1),
perpetually

SHADOW
2927 ṭᵉlal (Ch.) (1), to
cover with shade
6738 tsêl (47), *shade*
6752 tsêlel (1), *shade*
6757 tsalmâveth (16),
shade of death
644 apŏskiasma (1),
shading off
4639 skia (7), *shade*

SHADOWING
6751 tsâlal (1), to *shade*;
to *grow dark*
6767 tsᵉlâtsal (1),
whirring of wings
2683 kataskiazō (1), to
cover, overshadow

SHADOWS
6752 tsêlel (3), *shade*

SHADRACH
7714 Shadrak (1),
Shadrak
7715 Shadrak (Ch.) (14),
Shadrak

SHADY
6628 tse'el (2), *lotus* tree

SHAFT
2671 chêts (1), *shaft*
3409 yârêk (3), *shank*

SHAGE
7681 Shâgê' (1), *erring*

SHAHAR
7837 shachar (1), *dawn*

SHAHARAIM
7842 Shachărayim (1),
double dawn

SHAHAZIMAH
7831 Shachatsôwm (1),
proudly

SHAKE
2554 châmaç (1), to *be
violent*; to *maltreat*
4571 mâ'ad (1), to *waver*
5128 nûwa' (2), to *waver*
5130 nûwph (5), to
quiver, vibrate, rock

5287 nâ'ar (4), to *tumble*
5426 nᵉthar (Ch.) (1), to
tear off; to *shake off*
6206 'ârats (2), to *dread*
6342 pâchad (1), to *fear*
7264 râgaz (1), to *quiver*
7363 râchaph (1), to
brood; to *be relaxed*
7493 râ'ash (14), to *quake*
660 apŏtinassō (1), to
brush off, shake off
1621 ĕktinassō (2), to
shake violently
4531 salĕuō (1), to *waver*
4579 sĕiō (2), to *agitate*

SHAKED
5128 nûwa' (1), to *waver*

SHAKEN
1607 gâ'ash (1), to *agitate*
5086 nâdaph (1), to
disperse, be windblown
5110 nûwd (1), to *waver*
5128 nûwa' (3), to *waver*
5287 nâ'ar (2), to *tumble*
6327 pûwts (1), to *dash*
7477 râ'al (1), to *reel*
4531 salĕuō (11), to *waver*
4579 sĕiō (2), to *agitate*

SHAKETH
2342 chûwl (2), to *writhe*
4131 môwṭ (1), to *shake*
5130 nûwph (2), to *rock*
5287 nâ'ar (1), to *tumble*
7264 râgaz (1), to *quiver*

SHAKING
4493 mânôwd (1), *nod*
5363 nôqeph (2),
threshing of olives
7494 ra'ash (3),
vibration, bounding
8573 tᵉnûwphâh (2),
undulation of offerings

SHALEM
8003 shâlêm (1),
complete; friendly; safe

SHALIM
8171 Sha'ălîym (1), *foxes*

SHALISHA
8031 Shâlîshâh (1),
trebled land

SHALLECHETH
7996 Shalleketh (1),
felling of trees

SHALLUM
7967 Shallûwm (27),
retribution

SHALLUN
7968 Shallûwn (1),
retribution

SHALMAI
8014 Salmay (1), *clothed*
8073 Shamlay (1), *clothed*

SHALMAN
8020 Shalman (1),
Shalman

SHALMANESER
8022 Shalman'eçer (2),
Shalmaneser

SHAMA
8091 Shâmâ' (1), *obedient*

SHAMBLES
3111 makĕllŏn (1),
butcher's stall

SHAME
954 bûwsh (9), be
ashamed
955 bûwshâh (4), *shame*
1317 boshnâh (1),
shamefulness
1322 bôsheth (20), *shame*
2616 châçad (1), to
reprove, shame
2659 châphêr (4), to *be
ashamed*
2781 cherpâh (3),
contumely, disgrace
3637 kâlam (6), to *taunt*
3639 kᵉlimmâh (20),
disgrace, scorn
3640 kᵉlimmûwth (1),
disgrace, scorn
6172 'ervâh (1), *disgrace*
7036 qâlôwn (13),
disgrace
8103 shimtsâh (1),
scornful whispering
149 aischrŏn (3),
shameful thing
152 aischunē (5), *shame*
808 aschēmŏsunē (1),
indecency; shame
818 atimazō (1), to
maltreat, dishonor
819 atimia (1), *disgrace*
1788 ĕntrĕpō (1), to
respect; to confound
1791 ĕntrŏpē (2), *shame*
2617 kataischunō (1), to
disgrace or shame
3856 paradĕigmatizō (1),
to *expose to infamy*

SHAMED
937 bûwz (1), *disrespect*
954 bûwsh (1), to be
ashamed
3001 yâbêsh (1), to *dry
up*; to *wither*
8106 Shemer (1),
settlings of wine, *dregs*

SHAMEFACEDNESS
127 aidōs (1), *modesty*

SHAMEFUL
1322 bôsheth (1), *shame*
7022 qîyqâlôwn (1),
disgrace

SHAMEFULLY
3001 yâbêsh (1), to *dry
up*; to *wither*
818 atimazō (1), to
maltreat, dishonor
821 atimŏō (1), to
maltreat, disgrace
5195 hubrizō (1), to
exercise violence, abuse

SHAMELESSLY
1540 gâlâh (1), to *denude*

SHAMER
8106 Shemer (2),
settlings of wine, *dregs*

SHAMETH
3637 kâlam (1), to *taunt*

SHAMGAR
8044 Shamgar (2),
Shamgar

SHAMHUTH
8049 Shamhûwth (1),
desolation

SHAMIR
8053 Shâmûwr (1),
observed
8069 Shâmîyr (3), *thorn*
or (poss.) *diamond*

SHAMMA
8037 Shammâ' (1),
desolation

SHAMMAH
8048 Shammâh (8),
desolation

SHAMMAI
8060 Shammay (6),
destructive

SHAMMOTH
8054 Shammôwth (1),
ruins

SHAMMUA
8051 Shammûwa' (4),
renowned

SHAMMUAH
8051 Shammûwa' (1),
renowned

SHAMSHERAI
8125 Shamshᵉray (1),
sun-like

SHAPE
1491 ĕidŏs (2), *form,
appearance, sight*

SHAPEN
2342 chûwl (1), to *dance,
whirl*; to *writhe* in pain

SHAPES
3667 hŏmŏiōma (1), *form*

SHAPHAM
8223 Shâphâm (1), *baldly*

SHAPHAN
8227 shâphân (30), *hyrax*

SHAPHAT
8202 Shâphâṭ (8), *judge*

SHAPHER
8234 Shepher (2), *beauty*

SHARAI
8298 Shâray (1), *hostile*

SHARAIM
8189 Sha'ărayim (1),
double gates

SHARAR
8325 Shârâr (1), *hostile*

SHARE
4282 machăresheth (1),
(poss.) *hoe*

SHAREZER
8272 Shar'etser (2),
Sharetser

SHARON
8289 Shârôwn (6), *plain*

SHARONITE
8290 Shârôwnîy (1),
Sharonite

SHARP
2299 chad (4), *sharp*
sword
2303 chaddûwd (1),
pointed, jagged
2742 chârûwts (2),
threshing-sledge
3913 lâṭash (1), to
sharpen; to *pierce*
6697 tsûwr (2), *rock*
6864 tsôr (1), *flint-stone*
knife

S

8127 shên (2), *tooth*
8150 shânan (4), to *pierce*
3691 ŏxus (7), *sharp*

SHARPEN
3913 lâṭash (1), to
sharpen; to pierce
5324 nâtsab (1), to *station*

SHARPENED
2300 châdad (3), to *be,
make sharp; severe*
8150 shânan (1), to
pierce; to inculcate

SHARPENETH
2300 châdad (2), to *be,
make sharp; severe*
3913 lâṭash (1), to
sharpen; to pierce

SHARPER
5114 tŏmôtĕrŏs (1), *more
keen*

SHARPLY
2394 chozqâh (1),
vehemence, harshness
664 apŏtŏmōs (1),
abruptly, peremptorily

SHARPNESS
664 apŏtŏmōs (1),
abruptly, peremptorily

SHARUHEN
8287 Shârûwchen (1),
abode of pleasure

SHASHAI
8343 Shâshay (1), *whitish*

SHASHAK
8349 Shâshaq (2),
pedestrian

SHAUL
7586 Shâ'ûwl (7), *asked*

SHAULITES
7587 Shâ'ûwlîy (1),
Shalite

SHAVE
1548 gâlach (12), to *shave*
5674+8593 'âbar (1), to
cross over; to transition
3587 xuraō (1), to *shave*

SHAVED
1494 gâzaz (1), to *shave*
1548 gâlach (3), to *shave*

SHAVEH
7740 Shâvêh (1), *plain*
7741 Shâvêh
Qiryâthayim (1), *plain
of a double city*

SHAVEN
1548 gâlach (5), to *shave*
3587 xuraō (2), to *shave*

SHAVSHA
7798 Shavshâ' (1), *joyful*

SHEAF
485 'âlummâh (2), *sheaf*
5995 'âmîyr (1), *bunch*
6016 'ômer (6), *measure*

SHEAL
7594 She'âl (1), *request*

SHEALTIEL
7597 She'altîy'êl (9), *I
have asked God*

SHEAR
1494 gâzaz (4), to *shear*

SHEAR-JASHUB
7610 She'âr Yâshûwb (1),
remnant will return

SHEARER
2751 kĕirō (1), to *shear*

SHEARERS
1494 gâzaz (3), to *shear*

SHEARIAH
8187 She'aryâh (2),
Jehovah has stormed

SHEARING
1044 Bêyth 'Êqed (1),
house of (the) *binding*
1044+7462 Bêyth 'Êqed
(1), *house of* (the)
binding
1494 gâzaz (1), to *shear*

SHEATH
5084 nâdân (1), *sheath*
8593 ta'ar (6), *scabbard*
2336 thēkē (1), *scabbard*

SHEAVES
485 'âlummâh (3), *sheaf*
5995 'âmîyr (2), *bunch*
6016 'ômer (2), *measure*
6194 'ârêm (1), *sheaf*

SHEBA
7614 Sheba' (22), *Sheba*
7652 Sheba' (10), *seven*

SHEBAH
7656 Shib'âh (1), *seventh*

SHEBAM
7643 Sebâm (1), *spice*

SHEBANIAH
7645 Shebanyâh (7),
Jehovah has prospered

SHEBARIM
7671 Shebârîym (1), *ruins*

SHEBER
7669 Sheber (1), *crushing*

SHEBNA
7644 Shebnâ' (9), *growth*

SHEBUEL
7619 Shebûw'êl (3),
captive (or *returned*) of
God

SHECANIAH
7935 Shekanyâh (2),
Jehovah has dwelt

SHECHANIAH
7935 Shekanyâh (8),
Jehovah has dwelt

SHECHEM
7927 Shekem (45), *ridge*
7928 Shekem (17),
shoulder

SHECHEM'S
7927 Shekem (2), *ridge*

SHECHEMITES
7930 Shikmîy (1),
Shikmite

SHED
5064 nâgar (1), to *pour*
7760 sûwm (1), to *put*
8210 shâphak (35), to
spill forth; to expend;
1632 ĕkchĕō (11), to *pour*

SHEDDER
8210 shâphak (1), to *spill
forth; to expend*

SHEDDETH
8210 shâphak (2), to *spill*

SHEDDING
130 haimatĕkchusia (1),
pouring of blood

SHEDEUR
7707 Shedêy'ûwr (5),
spreader of light

SHEEP
3532 kebes (2), *young
ram*
3775 keseb (9), *young
ram sheep*
6629 tsô'n (111), *flock of
sheep or goats*
6792 tsônê' (2), *flock*
7353 râchêl (2), *ewe*
7716 seh (16), *sheep*
4262 prŏbatikŏs (1),
Sheep Gate
4263 prŏbatŏn (39), *sheep*

SHEEP'S
4263 prŏbatŏn (1), *sheep*

SHEEPCOTE
5116 nâveh (2), *at home;
lovely; home*

SHEEPCOTES
1448+6629 gedêrâh (1),
enclosure for flocks

SHEEPFOLD
833+4263 aulē (1), *house;
courtyard; sheepfold*

SHEEPFOLDS
1488+6629 gêz (1), *shorn
fleece; mown grass*
4356+6629 miklâ'âh (1),
sheep or goat pen
4942 mishpâth (1), *pair
of stalls for cattle*

SHEEPMASTER
5349 nôqêd (1), *owner or
tender of sheep*

SHEEPSHEARERS
1494 gâzaz (2), to *shear;
shave; destroy*
1494+6629 gâzaz (1), to
shear; shave; destroy

SHEEPSKINS
3374 mēlōtē (1),
sheep-skin

SHEET
3607 ŏthŏnē (2), *linen
sail cloth*

SHEETS
5466 çâdîyn (2), *shirt*

SHEHARIAH
7841 Shecharyâh (1),
Jehovah has sought

SHEKEL
1235 beqa' (1), *half
shekel*
8255 sheqel (41),
standard weight

SHEKELS
8255 sheqel (45),
standard weight

SHELAH
7956 Shêlâh (10), *request*
7974 Shelach (1), *spear*

SHELANITES
8024 Shêlânîy (1),
Shelanite

SHELEMIAH
8018 Shelemyâh (10),
*thank-offering of
Jehovah*

SHELEPH
8026 Sheleph (2), *extract*

SHELESH
8028 Shelesh (1), *triplet*

SHELOMI
8015 Shelômîy (1),
peaceable

SHELOMITH
8013 Shelômôwth (4),
pacifications
8019 Shelômîyth (5),
peaceableness

SHELOMOTH
8013 Shelômôwth (1),
pacifications

SHELTER
4268 machçeh (2),
shelter; refuge

SHELUMIEL
8017 Shelûmîy'êl (5),
peace of God

SHEM
8035 Shêm (17), *name*

SHEMA
8087 Shema' (6), *heard*

SHEMAAH
8094 Shemâ'âh (1),
annunciation

SHEMAIAH
8098 Shema'yâh (40),
Jehovah has heard

SHEMARIAH
8114 Shemaryâh (4),
Jehovah has guarded

SHEMEBER
8038 Shem'êber (1),
illustrious

SHEMER
8106 Shemer (2),
settlings of wine, dregs

SHEMIDA
8061 Shemîydâ' (2),
name of knowing

SHEMIDAH
8061 Shemîydâ' (1),
name of knowing

SHEMIDAITES
8062 Shemîydâ'îy (1),
Shemidaite

SHEMINITH
8067 shemîynîyth (3),
(poss.) *eight-stringed
lyre*

SHEMIRAMOTH
8070 Shemîyrâmôwth
(4), *name of heights*

SHEMUEL
8050 Shemûw'êl (3),
heard of God

SHEN
8129 Shên (1), *crag*

SHENAZAR
8137 Shen'atstsar (1),
Shenatstsar

SHENIR
8149 Shenîyr (2), *peak*

SHEPHAM

English Word Index

SHILONI   231

SHEPHAM
8221 Shephâm (2), *bare*

SHEPHATIAH
8203 Shephaṭyâh (13),
Jehovah has judged

SHEPHERD
7462 râ'âh (27), to *tend* a
flock, i.e. *pasture* it
7462+6629 râ'âh (1), to
tend a flock
7473 rô'îy (1), *shepherd*
750 archipŏimēn (1),
head shepherd
4166 pŏimēn (13),
shepherd

SHEPHERD'S
7462 râ'âh (1), to *tend* a
flock, i.e. *pasture* it
7473 rô'îy (1), *shepherd*

SHEPHERDS
7462 râ'âh (31), to *tend* a
flock, i.e. *pasture* it
7462+6629 râ'âh (2), to
tend a flock
4166 pŏimēn (4),
shepherd

SHEPHERDS'
7462 râ'âh (1), to *tend* a
flock, i.e. *pasture* it

SHEPHI
8195 Shephôw (1),
baldness

SHEPHO
8195 Shephôw (1),
baldness

SHEPHUPHAN
8197 Shephûwphâm (1),
serpent-like

SHERAH
7609 She'ĕrâh (1),
kindred by blood

SHERD
2789 cheres (1), *pottery*

SHERDS
2789 cheres (1), *pottery*

SHEREBIAH
8274 Shêrêbyâh (8),
Jehovah has brought heat

SHERESH
8329 Sheresh (1), *root*

SHEREZER
8272 Shar'etser (1),
Sharetser

SHERIFFS
8614 tiphtay (Ch.) (2),
lawyer, officer

SHESHACH
8347 Shêshak (2),
Sheshak

SHESHAI
8344 Shêshay (3), *whitish*

SHESHAN
8348 Shêshân (4), *lily*

SHESHBAZZAR
8339 Shêshbatstsar (4),
Sheshbatstsar

SHETH
8352 Shêth (2), *put*, i.e.
substituted

SHETHAR
8369 Shêthâr (1), *Shethar*

SHETHAR-BOZNAI
8370 Shethar Bôwzenay
(4), *Shethar-Bozenai*

SHEVA
7724 Shevâ' (2), *false*

SHEW
1319 bâsar (3), to
announce (good news)
1540 gâlâh (5), to *reveal*
1971 hakkârâh (1),
respect, i.e. partiality
2324 chăvâ' (Ch.) (13), to
show
2331 châvâh (5), to *show*
3045 yâda' (12), to *know*
3313 yâpha' (1), to *shine*
5046 nâgad (37), to
announce
5414 nâthan (5), to *give*
5608 çâphar (5), to
inscribe; to enumerate
6213 'âsâh (21), to *do*
6754 tselem (1),
phantom; idol
7200 râ'âh (27), to *see*
7760 sûwm (1), to *put*
7896 shîyth (1), to *place*
8085 shâma' (3), to *hear*
312 anaggĕllō (4), to
announce in detail
322 anadĕiknumi (1), to
indicate, appoint
518 apaggĕllō (5), to
announce, proclaim
1165 dĕigmatizō (1), to
exhibit, expose
1166 dĕiknuō (20), to
show, make known
1325 didōmi (3), to *give*
1334 diēgĕŏmai (1), to
relate fully, describe
1731 ĕndĕiknumi (7), to
show, display
1754 ĕnĕrgĕō (2), to be
active, efficient, work
1804 ĕxaggĕllō (1), to
declare, proclaim
1925 ĕpidĕiknumi (6), to
exhibit, call attention to
2097 ĕuaggĕlizō (1), to
announce good news
2146 ĕuprŏsōpĕō (1), to
make a good display
2151 ĕusĕbĕō (1), to *put*
religion into practice
2605 kataggĕllō (3), to
proclaim, promulgate
2698 katatithēmi (1), to
place down, to deposit
3004 lĕgō (1), to *say*
3056 lŏgŏs (1), *word,
matter, thing; Word*
3377 mēnuō (1), to
report, declare
3936 paristēmi (1), to
stand beside, present
4392 prŏphasis (1),
pretext, excuse
5263 hupŏdĕiknumi (2),
to *exemplify*
5319 phanĕrŏō (1), to
render apparent

SHEWBREAD
3899+4635 lechem (4),
food, bread
3899+6440 lechem (6),
food, bread

4635 ma'ăreketh (3), *pile*
of loaves, *arrangement*
6440 pânîym (1), *face*
740+4286 artos (3), *loaf
of bread*
4286+740 prŏthĕsis (1),
setting forth

SHEWED
1540 gâlâh (2), to *reveal*
3045 yâda' (5), to *know*
3190 yâṭab (1), to *be,
make well*
3384 yârâh (1), to *throw*
5046 nâgad (18), to
announce
5186 nâṭah (1), to *stretch*
5414 nâthan (1), to *give*
6213 'âsâh (17), to *do*
6567 pârash (1), to
separate; to disperse
7200 râ'âh (37), to *see*
7760 sûwm (1), to *put*
8085 shâma' (4), to *hear*
312 anaggĕllō (2), to
announce in detail
518 apaggĕllō (6), to
announce, proclaim
1096 ginŏmai (1), to *be*
1166 dĕiknuō (8), to
show, make known
1213 dēlŏō (1), to *make
plain by words*
1325+1717+1096 didōmi
(1), to *give*
1718 ĕmphanizō (1), to
show forth
1731 ĕndĕiknumi (1), to
show, display
1925 ĕpidĕiknumi (1), to
exhibit, call attention to
3170 mĕgalunō (1), to
increase or extol
3377 mēnuō (2), to
report, declare
3700 ŏptanŏmai (1), to
appear
3930 parĕchō (1), to *hold
near*, i.e. to *present*
3936 paristēmi (1), to
stand beside, present
4160 pŏiĕō (1), to *make*
4293 prŏkataggĕllō (2),
to *predict, promise*
5268 hupŏzugiŏn (1),
donkey
5319 phanĕrŏō (4), to
render apparent

SHEWEDST
5414 nâthan (1), to *give*
7200 râ'âh (1), to *see*

SHEWEST
6213 'âsâh (1), to *do*
1166 dĕiknuō (1), to *show*
4160 pŏiĕō (1), to *make*

SHEWETH
1540+241 gâlâh (2), to
denude; uncover
2331 châvâh (1), to *show*
5046 nâgad (6), to
announce
6213 'âsâh (2), to *do*
7200 râ'âh (3), to *see*
1166 dĕiknuō (2), to *show*
1658 ĕlĕuthĕrŏs (2),
unrestrained

SHEWING
263 'achăvâh (Ch.) (1),
solution
5608 çâphar (1), to
inscribe; to enumerate
6213 'âsâh (2), to *do*
6692 tsûwts (1), to
twinkle, i.e. *glance*
323 anadĕixis (1), act of
public *exhibition*
584 apŏdĕiknumi (1), to
demonstrate
1731 ĕndĕiknumi (2), to
show, display
1925 ĕpidĕiknumi (2), to
exhibit, call attention to
3930 parĕchō (1), to *hold
near*, i.e. to *present*

SHIBBOLETH
7641 shibbôl (1), *stream;
ear* of grain

SHIBMAH
7643 Sebâm (1), *spice*

SHICRON
7942 Shikkerôwn (1),
drunkenness

SHIELD
3591 kîydôwn (2), *dart*
4043 mâgên (33), small
shield (buckler)
6793 tsinnâh (9), large
shield; piercing cold
2375 thurĕŏs (1), large
door-shaped *shield*

SHIELDS
4043 mâgên (15), small
shield (buckler)
6793 tsinnâh (1), large
shield; piercing cold
7982 sheleṭ (7), *shield*

SHIGGAION
7692 Shiggâyôwn (1),
dithyramb or poem

SHIGIONOTH
7692 Shiggâyôwn (1),
dithyramb or poem

SHIHON
7866 Shî'yôwn (1), *ruin*

SHIHOR
7883 Shîychôwr (1),
dark, i.e. *turbid*

SHIHOR-LIBNATH
7884 Shîychôwr Libnâth
(1), *darkish whiteness*

SHILHI
7977 Shilchîy (2), *armed*

SHILHIM
7978 Shilchîym (1),
javelins or sprouts

SHILLEM
8006 Shillêm (2), *requital*

SHILLEMITES
8016 Shillêmîy (1),
Shilemite

SHILOAH
7975 Shilôach (1), *small
stream*

SHILOH
7886 Shîylôh (1), *tranquil*
7887 Shîylôh (32),
tranquil

SHILONI
8023 Shîlônîy (1), *Shiloni*

S

SHILONITE
7888 Shiylôwnîy (5), *Shilonite*

SHILONITES
7888 Shiylôwnîy (1), *Shilonite*

SHILSHAH
8030 Shilshâh (1), *triplication*

SHIMEA
8092 Shim'â' (4), *annunciation*

SHIMEAH
8039 Shim'âh (1), *obedient*
8092 Shim'â' (1), *annunciation*
8093 Shim'âh (2), *annunciation*

SHIMEAM
8043 Shim'âm (1), *obedient*

SHIMEATH
8100 Shim'âth (2), *annunciation*

SHIMEATHITES
8101 Shim'âthiy (1), *Shimathite*

SHIMEI
8096 Shim'iy (41), *famous*
8097 Shim'iy (1), *Shimite*

SHIMEON
8095 Shim'ôwn (1), *hearing*

SHIMHI
8096 Shim'iy (1), *famous*

SHIMI
8096 Shim'iy (1), *famous*

SHIMITES
8097 Shim'iy (1), *Shimite*

SHIMMA
8092 Shim'â' (1), *annunciation*

SHIMON
7889 Shîymôwn (1), *desert*

SHIMRATH
8119 Shimrâth (1), *guardship*

SHIMRI
8113 Shimriy (3), *watchful*

SHIMRITH
8116 Shimrîyth (1), *female guard*

SHIMROM
8110 Shimrôwn (1), *guardianship*

SHIMRON
8110 Shimrôwn (4), *guardianship*

SHIMRON-MERON
8112 Shimrôwn Mᵉr'ôwn (1), *guard of lashing*

SHIMRONITES
8117 Shimrônîy (1), *Shimronite*

SHIMSHAI
8124 Shimshay (Ch.) (4), *sunny*

SHINAB
8134 Shin'âb (1), *father has turned*

SHINAR
8152 Shin'âr (7), *Shinar*

SHINE
215 'ôwr (11), to *be luminous*
1984 hâlal (1), to *shine*
2094 zâhar (1), to *enlighten*
3313 yâpha' (4), to *shine*
5050 nâgahh (3), to *illuminate*
5774 'ûwph (1), to *cover*
6245 'âshath (1), to *be sleek; to excogitate*
6670 tsâhal (1), to *be cheerful; to sound*
826 augazō (1), to *beam forth*
1584 ĕklampō (1), to *be resplendent, shine*
2989 lampō (3), to *radiate brilliancy*
5316 phainō (3), to *shine*

SHINED
215 'ôwr (1), to *be luminous*
1984 hâlal (2), to *shine*
3313 yâpha' (2), to *shine*
5050 nâgahh (1), to *illuminate*
2989 lampō (2), to *radiate brilliancy*
4015 pĕriastraptō (1), to *envelop in light, shine*

SHINETH
166 'âhal (1), to *be bright*
215 'ôwr (2), to *be luminous*
2989 lampō (1), to *radiate*
5316 phainō (5), to *shine*

SHINING
5051 nôgahh (6), *brilliancy*
796 astrapē (1), *lightning; light's glare*
797 astraptō (1), to *flash*
4034 pĕrilampō (1), to *shine all around*
4744 stilbō (1), to *gleam*
5316 phainō (1), to *shine*

SHIP
591 'ŏnîyâh (4), *ship*
5600 çᵉphîynâh (1), *sea-going vessel*
6716 tsîy (1), *ship*
3490 nauklērŏs (1), *ship captain*
3491 naus (1), *boat*
4142 plŏiariŏn (2), *small boat*
4143 plŏiŏn (58), *ship*

SHIPHI
8230 Shiph'îy (1), *copious*

SHIPHMITE
8225 Shiphmîy (1), *Shiphmite*

SHIPHRAH
8236 Shiphrâh (1), *brightness of skies*

SHIPHTAN
8204 Shiphţân (1), *judge-like*

SHIPMASTER
7227+2259 rab (1), *great*
2942 kubĕrnētēs (1), *helmsman, captain*

SHIPMEN
582+591 'ĕnôwsh (1), *man; person, human*
3492 nautēs (2), *sailor*

SHIPPING
4143 plŏiŏn (1), *ship*

SHIPS
591 'ŏnîyâh (26), *ship*
6716 tsîy (3), *ship*
4142 plŏiariŏn (1), *small boat*
4143 plŏiŏn (8), *boat*

SHIPWRECK
3489 nauagĕō (2), to *be shipwrecked*

SHISHA
7894 Shîyshâ' (1), *whiteness*

SHISHAK
7895 Shîyshaq (7), *Shishak*

SHITRAI
7861 Shiţray (1), *magisterial*

SHITTAH
7848 shiţţâh (1), *acacia*

SHITTIM
7848 shiţţâh (27), *acacia*
7851 Shiţţîym (5), *acacia*

SHIVERS
4937 suntribō (1), to *crush completely*

SHIZA
7877 Shîyzâ' (1), *Shiza*

SHOA
7772 Shôwa' (1), *rich*

SHOBAB
7727 Shôwbâb (4), *rebellious*

SHOBACH
7731 Shôwbâk (2), (poss.) *thicket*

SHOBAI
7630 Shôbay (2), *captor*

SHOBAL
7732 Shôwbâl (9), *overflowing*

SHOBEK
7733 Shôwbêq (1), *forsaking*

SHOBI
7629 Shôbîy (1), *captor*

SHOCHO
7755 Sôwkôh (1), *hedged*

SHOCHOH
7755 Sôwkôh (2), *hedged*

SHOCK
1430 gâdîysh (1), *stack of sheaves, shock of grain*

SHOCKS
1430 gâdîysh (1), *stack of sheaves, shock of grain*

SHOCO
7755 Sôwkôh (1), *hedged*

SHOD
5274 nâ'al (2), to *fasten up, to put on sandals*

5265 hupŏdĕō (2), to *put on shoes or sandals*

SHOE
5275 na'al (9), *sandal*

SHOE'S
5266 hupŏdēma (1), *sandal*

SHOELATCHET
8288+5275 sᵉrôwk (1), *sandal thong*

SHOES
4515 man'âl (1), *bolt on gate*
5275 na'al (11), *sandal*
5266 hupŏdēma (9), *sandal*

SHOHAM
7719 Shôham (1), *beryl*

SHOMER
7763 Shôwmêr (2), *keeper*

SHONE
2224 zârach (1), to *rise; to be bright*
7160 qâran (3), to *shine*
4015 pĕriastraptō (1), to *envelop in light, shine*
4034 pĕrilampō (1), to *shine all around*
5316 phainō (1), to *shine*

SHOOK
1607 gâ'ash (3), to *agitate violently, shake*
5287 nâ'ar (1), to *tumble*
7264 râgaz (1), to *quiver*
7493 râ'ash (2), to *quake*
8058 shâmaţ (1), to *jostle*
660 apŏtinassō (1), to *brush off, shake off*
1621 ĕktinassō (2), to *shake violently*
4531 salĕuō (1), to *waver*

SHOOT
1272 bârach (1), to *flee*
1869 dârak (1), to *tread; to string a bow*
3034 yâdâh (1), to *throw*
3384 yârâh (10), to *throw, shoot an arrow*
5414 nâthan (2), to *give*
6362 pâţar (1), to *burst through; to emit*
7971 shâlach (1), to *send away*
4261 prŏballō (1), to *push to the front, germinate*

SHOOTERS
3384 yârâh (1), to *throw, shoot an arrow*

SHOOTETH
3318 yâtsâ' (1), to *go, bring out*
7971 shâlach (1), to *send away*
4160 pŏiĕō (1), to *do*

SHOOTING
5927 'âlâh (1), to *ascend, be high, mount*

SHOPHACH
7780 Shôwphâk (2), *poured*

S

1407 drĕpanŏn (8), gathering *hook*

SICKLY
732 arrhôstŏs (1), infirmed, *ill*

SICKNESS
1739 dâveh (1), menstrual; *fainting*
2483 chŏlîy (11), *malady*
4245 machăleh (3), *sickness*
769 asthĕnĕia (1), feebleness of body
3554 nŏsŏs (3), *malady*

SICKNESSES
2483 chŏlîy (1), *malady*
8463 tachălûw' (1), malady, *disease*
3554 nŏsŏs (2), *malady*

SIDDIM
7708 Siddîym (3), *flats*

SIDE
2296 châgar (1), to *gird*
2348 chôwph (1), *cove*
3027 yâd (5), *hand; power*
3225 yâmîyn (4), *right*
3409 yârêk (7), *side*
3411 yᵉrêkâh (2), *far away places*
3541 kôh (2), *thus*
3802 kâthêph (29), *side-piece*
4217 mizrâch (2), *east*
4975 môthen (4), *loins*
5048 neged (2), *beside*
5437 çâbab (1), to *surround*
5439 çâbîyb (26), *circle*
5675 'ăbar (Ch.) (7), region *across*
5676 'êber (56), *opposite*
6285 pê'âh (50), *direction*
6311 pôh (2), *here*
6654 tsad (20), *side*
6753 Tsᵉlelpôwnîy (2), *shade-facing*
6763 tsêlâ' (22), *side*
6921 qâdîym (1), *East; eastward; east wind*
6924 qedem (3), *East, eastern; antiquity*
6954 Qᵉhêlâthâh (1), *convocation*
7023 qîyr (2), *side-wall*
7097 qâtseh (1), *extremity*
7307 rûwach (5), *breath; wind; life-spirit*
7859 sᵉṭar (Ch.) (1), *side*
8040 sᵉmô'wl (1), *left*
8193 sâphâh (3), *edge*
492 antiparĕrchŏmai (2), to go along *opposite*
1188 dĕxiŏs (2), *right*
1782 ĕntĕuthen (2), on *both sides*
3313 mĕros (1), *division*
3840 pantŏthĕn (1), *from, on all sides*
3844 para (15), *besides*
4008 pĕran (13), *across*
4125 plĕura (5), *side*

SIDES
3411 yᵉrêkâh (19), *far away places*
3802 kâthêph (4), *shoulder-piece; wall*
5676 'êber (4), *opposite*

6285 pê'âh (1), *direction*
6654 tsad (9), *side*
6763 tsêlâ' (4), *side*
7023 qîyr (2), *side-wall*
7253 reba' (3), *fourth*
7307 rûwach (1), *breath; wind; life-spirit*

SIDON
6721 Tsîydôwn (2), *fishery*
4605 Sidōn (12), *fishery*

SIDONIANS
6722 Tsîydônîy (5), *Tsidonian*

SIEGE
4692 mâtsôwr (13), siege-*mound; distress*
6696 tsûwr (1), to *cramp*

SIEVE
3531 kᵉbârâh (1), *sieve*
5299 nâphâh (1), *sieve*

SIFT
5128 nûwa' (1), to *waver*
5130 nûwph (1), to *quiver, vibrate, rock*
4617 siniazō (1), to *shake in a sieve*

SIFTED
5128 nûwa' (1), to *waver*

SIGH
584 'ânach (7), to *sigh*

SIGHED
584 'ânach (1), to *sigh*
389 anastĕnazō (1), to *sigh deeply*
4727 stĕnazō (1), to *sigh*

SIGHEST
584 'ânach (1), to *sigh*

SIGHETH
584 'ânach (1), to *sigh*

SIGHING
585 'ănâchâh (5), *sighing*
603 'ănâqâh (2), *shrieking, groaning*

SIGHS
585 'ănâchâh (1), *sighing*

SIGHT
2379 chăzôwth (Ch.) (2), *view, visible sight*
4758 mar'eh (18), *appearance; vision*
5048 neged (2), *before*
5869 'ayin (218), *sight*
6440 pânîym (39), *face*
7200 râ'âh (1), to *see*
308 anablĕpō (15), to look up; to recover *sight*
309 anablĕpsis (1), restoration of *sight*
991 blĕpō (2), to *look at*
1491 ĕidŏs (1), *sight*
1715 ĕmprŏsthĕn (3), *in front of*
1726 ĕnantiŏn (1), *in the presence of*
1799 ĕnôpiŏn (21), *before*
2335 thĕōria (1), *sight*
2714 katĕnôpiŏn (2), *directly in front of*
3705 hŏrama (1), supernatural *spectacle*
3706 hŏrasis (1), *appearance, vision*
3788 ŏphthalmŏs (1), *eye*
3844 para (1), *from; with; besides; on account of*

5324 phantazō (1), to appear; spectacle, *sight*

SIGHTS
5400 phŏbĕtrŏn (1), *frightening* thing

SIGN
226 'ôwth (33), *sign*
4159 môwphêth (8), *miracle; token or omen*
4864 mas'êth (1), *beacon*
5251 nêç (1), *flag; signal*
6725 tsîyûwn (1), *guiding pillar, monument*
7560 rᵉsham (Ch.) (1), to *record*
3902 parasēmŏs (1), *labeled, marked*
4592 sēmĕiŏn (29), *sign*

SIGNED
7560 rᵉsham (Ch.) (4), to *record*

SIGNET
2368 chôwthâm (8), signature-ring, *seal*
2858 chôthemeth (1), signet ring *seal*
5824 'izqâ' (Ch.) (2), signet or signet-*ring*

SIGNETS
2368 chôwthâm (1), signature-ring, *seal*

SIGNIFICATION
880 aphōnŏs (1), *mute, silent; unmeaning*

SIGNIFIED
4591 sēmainō (2), to *indicate, make known*

SIGNIFIETH
1213 dēlŏō (1), to *make plain by words*

SIGNIFY
1213 dēlŏō (1), to *make plain by words*
1229 diaggĕllō (1), to *herald thoroughly*
1718 ĕmphanizō (1), to *show forth*
4591 sēmainō (1), to *indicate, make known*

SIGNIFYING
1213 dēlŏō (1), to *make plain by words*
4591 sēmainō (3), to *indicate, make known*

SIGNS
226 'ôwth (27), *sign*
852 'âth (Ch.) (3), *sign*
1770 ĕnnĕuŏ (1), to *signal*
4591 sēmainō (17), to *indicate, make known*
4592 sēmĕiŏn (5), *sign*

SIHON
5511 Çîychôwn (37), *tempestuous*

SIHOR
7883 Shîychôwr (3), *dark*, i.e. *turbid*

SILAS
4609 Silas (13), *sylvan*

SILENCE
481 'âlam (1), to *be silent*
1745 dûwmâh (2), *silence*
1747 dûwmîyâh (1), *silently; quiet, trust*

1820 dâmâh (1), to *be silent; to fail, cease*
1824 dᵉmîy (2), *quiet*
1826 dâmam (6), to be *silent; to be astonished*
1827 dᵉmâmâh (1), *quiet*
2013 hâçâh (3), to *hush*
2790 chârash (5), to be *silent; to be deaf*
2814 châshâh (2), to *hush*
2271 hēsuchia (3), *stillness*
4601 sigaō (3), to *keep silent*
4602 sigē (2), *silence*
5392 phimŏō (2), to *restrain to silence*

SILENT
1748 dûwmâm (1), *silently*
1826 dâmam (4), to be *silent; to be astonished*
1947 hôwlêlâh (1), *folly*
2013 hâçâh (1), to *hush*
2790 chârash (2), to be *silent; to be deaf*

SILK
4897 meshîy (2), *silk*
8336 shêsh (1), *white linen; white marble*
2596 kata (1), *down; according to*

SILLA
5538 Çillâ' (1), *embankment*

SILLY
6601 pâthâh (2), to be, *make simple; to delude*
1133 gunaikariŏn (1), *little*, i.e. *foolish woman*

SILOAH
7975 Shilôach (1), *rill*

SILOAM
4611 Silōam (3), *rill*

SILVANUS
4610 Silŏuanŏs (4), *sylvan*

SILVER
3701 keçeph (280), *silver*
3702 kᵉçaph (Ch.) (12), *silver money*
7192 qᵉsîyṭah (1), *coin*
693 argurĕŏs (3), *made of silver*
694 arguriŏn (9), *silver*
696 argurŏs (5), *silver*
1406 drachmē (1), *silver coin*

SILVERLINGS
3701 keçeph (1), *silver*

SILVERSMITH
695 argurŏkŏpŏs (1), *worker of silver*

SIMEON
8095 Shim'ôwn (43), *hearing*
8099 Shim'ônîy (1), *Shimonite*
4826 Sumĕōn (6), *hearing*

SIMEONITES
8099 Shim'ônîy (3), *Shimonite*

SIMILITUDE
1823 dᵉmûwth (2), *resemblance, likeness*

SIMILITUDES
8403 tabnîyth (2), *model, resemblance*
8544 tᵉmûwnâh (4), *something fashioned*
3665 hŏmŏiŏtēs (1), *resemblance, similarity*
3667 hŏmŏiōma (1), *form; resemblance*
3669 hŏmŏiōsis (1), *resemblance, likeness*

SIMILITUDES
1819 dâmâh (1), to *liken*

SIMON
4613 Simōn (67), *hearing*

SIMON'S
4613 Simōn (7), *hearing*

SIMPLE
6612 pᵉthîy (17), *silly*
6615 pᵉthayûwth (1), *silliness, i.e. seducible*
172 akakŏs (1), *innocent*
185 akĕraiŏs (1), *innocent*

SIMPLICITY
6612 pᵉthîy (1), *silly*
8537 tôm (1), *innocence*
572 haplŏtēs (3), *sincerity*

SIMRI
8113 Shimriy (1), *watchful*

SIN
817 'âshâm (3), *guilt*
819 'ashmâh (2), *guiltiness*
2398 châṭâ' (68), to *sin*
2399 chêṭ' (22), *crime*
2401 châṭâ'âh (8), *offence*
2402 chaṭṭâ'âh (Ch.) (2), *offence, and penalty*
2403 chaṭṭâ'âh (215), *offence; sin offering*
2409 chaṭṭâyâ' (Ch.) (1), *expiation, sin offering*
5512 Çîyn (6), *Sin*
5771 'âvôn (1), *moral evil*
6588 pesha' (1), *revolt*
7686 shâgâh (1), to *stray*
264 hamartanō (15), to *miss the mark, to err*
265 hamartēma (1), *sin*
266 hamartia (91), *sin*
361 anamartētŏs (1), *sinless*

SINA
4614 Sina (2), *Sinai*

SINAI
5514 Çîynay (35), *Sinai*
4614 Sina (2), *Sinai*

SINCE
227 'âz (3), *therefore*
310 'achar (2), *after*
518 'îm (1), *whether?; if, although; Oh that!*
1767 day (3), *enough, sufficient*
2008 hênnâh (1), *from here; from there*
3588 kîy (3), *for, that*
4480 min (12), *from*
4480+227 min (1), *from*
4481 min (Ch.) (1), *from*
5750 'ôwd (2), *more*
575 apŏ (9), *from, away*
575+3739 apŏ (3), *from*
1537 ĕk (1), *out, out of*
1893 ĕpĕi (1), *since*

1894 ĕpĕidē (1), *when*
3326 mĕta (1), *after, later*
5613 hōs (1), *which, how*

SINCERE
97 adŏlŏs (1), *pure*
1506 ĕilikrinēs (1), *pure*

SINCERELY
8549 tâmîym (2), *entire*
55 hagnōs (1), *purely*

SINCERITY
8549 tâmîym (1), *integrity*
861 aphtharsia (2), *genuineness*
1103 gnēsiŏs (1), *genuine*
1505 ĕilikrinĕia (3), *purity, sincerity*

SINEW
1517 gîyd (3), *tendon*

SINEWS
1517 gîyd (4), *tendon*
6207 'âraq (1), to *gnaw*

SINFUL
2398 châṭâ' (1), to *sin*
2400 chaṭṭâ' (1), *guilty*
2401 châṭâ'âh (1), *offence or sacrifice*
266 hamartia (1), *sin*
268 hamartōlŏs (4), *sinner; sinful*

SING
1984 hâlal (2), to *speak praise; thank*
2167 zâmar (33), to *play music*
5414+6963 nâthan (1), to *give*
6030 'ânâh (4), to *sing*
6031 'ânâh (2), to *afflict*
7440 rinnâh (1), to *shout*
7442 rânan (25), to *shout*
7788 shûwr (1), to *travel*
7891 shîyr (32), to *sing*
7892 shîyr (1), *singing*
103 a₁dō (1), to *sing*
5214 humnĕō (1), to *celebrate God in song*
5567 psallō (4), to *play a stringed instrument*

SINGED
2761 chărak (Ch.) (1), to *scorch, singe*

SINGER
5329 nâtsach (1), i.e. to *be eminent*
7891 shîyr (1), to *sing*

SINGERS
2171 zammâr (Ch.) (1), *musician*
7891 shîyr (35), to *sing*
7892 shîyr (1), *singing*

SINGETH
7891 shîyr (1), to *sing*

SINGING
2158 zâmîyr (1), *song*
7440 rinnâh (9), *shout*
7442 rânan (2), to *shout for joy*
7445 rᵉnânâh (1), *shout for joy*
7891 shîyr (5), to *sing*
7892 shîyr (4), *singing*
103 a₁dō (2), to *sing*

SINGLE
573 haplŏus (2), *single*

SINGLENESS
572 haplŏtēs (2), *sincerity*
858 aphĕlŏtēs (1), *simplicity; sincerity*

SINGULAR
6381 pâlâ' (1), to *be, make great, difficult*

SINIM
5515 Çîynîym (1), *Sinim*

SINITE
5513 Çîynîy (2), *Sinite*

SINK
2883 ṭâba' (2), to *sink*
8257 shâqa' (1), to *be overflowed; to abate*
1036 buthizō (1), to *sink*
2670 katapŏntizō (1), to *submerge, be drowned*
5087 tithēmi (1), to *place*

SINNED
2398 châṭâ' (102), to *sin*
264 hamartanō (15), to *miss the mark, to sin*
4258 prŏamartanō (2), to *sin previously*

SINNER
2398 châṭâ' (8), to *sin*
2403 chaṭṭâ'âh (1), *offence; sin offering*
268 hamartōlŏs (12), *sinner; sinful*

SINNERS
2400 chaṭṭâ' (16), *guilty*
268 hamartōlŏs (30), *sinner; sinful*
3781 ŏphĕilĕtēs (1), *person indebted*

SINNEST
2398 châṭâ' (1), to *sin*

SINNETH
2398 châṭâ' (13), to *sin*
6213 'âsâh (1), to *do*
7683 shâgag (1), to *sin*
264 hamartanō (7), to *sin*

SINNING
2398 châṭâ' (1), to *sin*

SINS
819 'ashmâh (2), *guiltiness*
2399 chêṭ' (8), *crime*
2403 chaṭṭâ'âh (71), *offence; sin offering*
2408 chăṭîy (Ch.) (1), *sin*
6588 pesha' (2), *revolt*
265 hamartēma (3), *sin*
266 hamartia (78), *sin*
3900 paraptōma (3), *error; transgression*

SION
6726 Tsîyôwn (1), *capital*
7865 Sîy'ôn (1), *peak*
4622 Siōn (7), *capital*

SIPHMOTH
8224 Siphmôwth (1), *Siphmoth*

SIPPAI
5598 Çippay (1), *bason-like*

SIR
113 'âdôwn (1), *sovereign, i.e. controller*
2962 kuriŏs (11), *supreme, controller, Mr.*

SIRAH
5626 Çîrâh (1), *departure*

SIRION
8304 Sᵉrâyâh (2), *Jehovah has prevailed*

SIRS
435 anēr (6), *man; male*
2962 kuriŏs (1), *supreme, controller, Mr.*

SISAMAI
5581 Çiçmay (2), *Sismai*

SISERA
5516 Çîyçᵉrâ' (21), *Sisera*

SISTER
269 'achôwth (91), *sister*
1733 dôwdâh (1), *aunt*
2994 yᵉbêmeth (2), *sister-in-law*
79 adĕlphē (15), *sister*

SISTER'S
269 'achôwth (5), *sister*
79 adĕlphē (1), *sister*
431 anĕpsiŏs (1), *cousin*

SISTERS
269 'achôwth (11), *sister*
79 adĕlphē (8), *sister*

SIT
3427 yâshab (65), to *dwell, to settle*
3488 yᵉthîb (Ch.) (2), to *sit*
5414 nâthan (1), to *give*
5437 çâbab (1), to *surround*
7674 shebeth (1), *rest*
347 anaklinō (6), to *recline*
377 anapiptō (5), *lie down, lean back*
2521 kathēmai (12), to *sit down; to remain*
2523 kathizō (15), to *seat down, dwell*
2621 katakĕimai (1), to *lie down*
2625 kataklinō (2), to *recline, take a place*
4776 sugkathizō (1), to *give, take a seat with*
4873 sunanakĕimai (1), to *recline with at meal*

SITH
518 'îm (1), *whether?; if, although; Oh that!*

SITNAH
7856 Siṭnâh (1), *opposition*

SITTEST
3427 yâshab (6), to *settle*
2521 kathēmai (1), to *sit*

SITTETH
1716 dâgar (1), to *brood over; to care for young*
3427 yâshab (25), to *settle*
345 anakĕimai (2), to *recline at a meal*
2521 kathēmai (10), to *sit down; to reside*
2523 kathizō (3), to *seat down, dwell*

SITTING
3427 yâshab (15), to *settle*
4186 môwshâb (2), *seat*
7257 râbats (1), to *recline*
1910 ĕpibainō (1), to *mount, ascend*

S

2516 kathĕzŏmai (2), to
  sit down, be seated
2521 kathēmai (21), to
  sit down; to reside
2523 kathizō (1), to *seat
  down, dwell*

SITUATE
3427 yâshab (2), to *settle*
4690 mâtsûwq (1),
  column; hilltop

SITUATION
4186 môwshâb (1), *site*
5131 nôwph (1), *elevation*

SIVAN
5510 Çîyvân (1), *Sivan*

SIX
8337 shêsh (185), *six;
  sixth*
8353 shêth (Ch.) (1), *six;
  sixth*
1803 hĕx (11), *six*
1812 hĕxakŏsioi (1), *six
  hundred*
5516 chi xi stigma (1), 666

SIXSCORE
3967+6242 mê'âh (1),
  hundred
8147+6240+7239
  sh^enayim (1), *two*-fold

SIXTEEN
8337+6240 shêsh (22),
  six; sixth
1440+1803
  hĕbdŏmēkŏnta (1),
  seventy

SIXTEENTH
8337+6240 shêsh (3), *six;
  sixth*

SIXTH
8337 shêsh (2), *six; sixth*
8338 shâwshâw (1),
  (poss.) to *annihilate*
8341 shâshâh (1), to
  divide into sixths
8345 shishshîy (26), *sixth*
8353 shêth (Ch.) (1), *six;
  sixth*
1623 hĕktŏs (14), *sixth*

SIXTY
8346 shishshîym (11),
  sixty
1835 hĕxēkŏnta (3), *sixty*

SIXTYFOLD
1835 hĕxēkŏnta (1), *sixty*

SIZE
4060 middâh (3),
  measure; portion
7095 qetseb (2), *shape*

SKIES
7834 shachaq (5), *clouds*

SKILFUL
995 bîyn (1), to *discern*
2451 chokmáh (1),
  wisdom
2796 chârâsh (1), skilled
  fabricator or worker
3045 yâda' (2), to *know*
3925 lâmad (1), to *teach*
7919 sâkal (1), to *be* or
  act circumspect

SKILFULLY
3190 yâṭab (1), to *be,
  make well*

SKILFULNESS
8394 tâbûwn (1),
  intelligence; argument

SKILL
995 bîyn (1), to *discern*
3045 yâda' (4), to *know*
7919 sâkal (2), to *be* or
  act circumspect

SKIN
1320 bâsâr (1), *flesh*
1539 geled (1), *skin*
5785 'ôwr (71), *skin*
1193 dĕrmatinŏs (1),
  made of leather *hide*

SKINS
5785 'ôwr (20), *skin*

SKIP
7540 râqad (1), to *spring*

SKIPPED
7540 râqad (2), to *spring*

SKIPPEDST
5110 nûwd (1), to *waver*

SKIPPING
7092 qâphats (1), to *leap*

SKIRT
3671 kânâph (12), *wing*

SKIRTS
3671 kânâph (2), *wing*
6310 peh (1), *mouth*
7757 shûwl (4), *skirt*

SKULL
1538 gulgôleth (2), *skull*
2898 kraniŏn (3), *skull*

SKY
7834 shachaq (2), *clouds*
3772 ŏuranŏs (5), *sky*

SLACK
309 'âchar (2), to *delay*
6113 'âtsar (1), to *hold
  back; to maintain, rule*
7423 r^emîyâh (1),
  remissness; treachery
7503 râphâh (3), to
  slacken
1019 bradunō (1), to
  delay, hesitate

SLACKED
6313 pûwg (1), to *be
  sluggish; be numb*

SLACKNESS
1022 bradutēs (1),
  tardiness, slowness

SLAIN
2026 hârag (31), to *kill*
2027 hereg (1), *kill*
2076 zâbach (2), to
  (sacrificially) *slaughter*
2490 châlal (1), to
  profane, defile
2491 châlâl (75), *slain*
2717 chârab (1), to
  desolate, destroy
2873 ṭâbach (1), to *kill*
4191 mûwth (18), to *kill*
5062 nâgaph (2), to *strike*
5221 nâkâh (20), to *kill*
6992 q^eṭal (Ch.) (4), to *kill*
7523 râtsach (3), to
  murder
7819 shâchaṭ (5), to
  slaughter; butcher
337 anairĕō (3), to *take
  away, murder*
615 apŏktĕinō (7), to *kill*

1722+5408+599 ĕn (1), *in;
  during; because of*
4968 sphagiŏn (1),
  offering for slaughter
4969 sphazō (6), to
  slaughter or to *maim*

SLANDER
1681 dibbâh (3), *slander*

SLANDERED
7270 râgal (1), to *slander*

SLANDERERS
1228 diabŏlŏs (1),
  traducer, i.e. *Satan*

SLANDEREST
5414+1848 nâthan (1), to
  give

SLANDERETH
3960 lâshan (1), to
  calumniate, malign

SLANDEROUSLY
987 blasphēmĕō (1), to
  speak impiously

SLANDERS
7400 râkîyl (2),
  scandal-monger

SLANG
7049 qâla' (1), to *sling*

SLAUGHTER
2027 hereg (4), *kill*
2028 hărêgâh (5), *kill*
2873 ṭâbach (5), to *kill*
2875 Ṭebach (9),
  massacre
2878 ṭibehâh (1),
  butchery
4046 maggêphâh (3),
  pestilence; defeat
4293 maṭbêach (1),
  slaughter place
4347 makkâh (14), *blow;
  wound; pestilence*
4660 mappâts (1),
  striking to pieces
5221 nâkâh (5), to *kill*
6993 qeṭel (1), *death*
7524 retsach (1),
  crushing; murder-cry
7819 shâchaṭ (1), to
  slaughter; butcher
2871 kŏpē (1), *carnage*
4967 sphagē (3), *butchery*
5408 phŏnŏs (1), *slaying*

SLAVES
4983 sōma (1), *body*

SLAY
1194 B^e'ôn (1), *Beon*
2026 hârag (38), to *kill*
2717 chârab (1), to
  desolate, destroy
2763 charam (1), to
  devote to destruction
2873 ṭâbach (1), to *kill,
  butcher*
2875 Ṭebach (1),
  massacre
4191 mûwth (43), to *kill*
5221 nâkâh (15), to *kill*
5221+5315 nâkâh (1), to
  strike, kill
6991 qâṭal (2), to *put to
  death*
6992 q^eṭal (Ch.) (1), to *kill*
7819 shâchaṭ (9), to
  slaughter; butcher

337 anairĕō (2), to *take
  away, murder*
615 apŏktĕinō (3), to *kill*
2380 thuō (1), to *kill*
2695 katasphattō (1), to
  slaughter, strike down

SLAYER
2026 hârag (1), to *kill*
5221 nâkâh (1), to *kill*
7523 râtsach (17), to
  murder

SLAYETH
2026 hârag (2), to *kill*
2490 châlal (1), to
  profane, defile
4191 mûwth (1), to *kill*
7523+5315 râtsach (1), to
  murder

SLAYING
2026 hârag (3), to *kill*
4191 mûwth (1), to *kill*
5221 nâkâh (2), to *kill*
7819 shâchaṭ (1), to
  slaughter; butcher

SLEEP
3462 yâshên (11), to
  sleep; to grow old
3463 yâshên (4), *sleepy*
7290 râdam (3), to
  stupefy
7901 shâkab (11), to *lie*
8139 sh^enâh (Ch.) (1),
  sleep
8142 shênâh (24), *sleep*
8639 tardêmâh (4),
  trance, deep sleep
1852 ĕxupnizō (1), to
  waken, rouse
1853 ĕxupnŏs (1), *awake*
2518 kathĕudō (7), to *fall
  asleep*
2837 kŏimaō (5), to
  slumber; to decease
5258 hupnŏs (6), *sleep*

SLEEPER
7290 râdam (1), to
  stupefy

SLEEPEST
3462 yâshên (1), to *sleep*
7901 shâkab (1), to *lie*
2518 kathĕudō (2), to *fall
  asleep*

SLEEPETH
3463 yâshên (2), *sleepy*
7290 râdam (1), to
  stupefy
2518 kathĕudō (3), to *fall
  asleep*
2837 kŏimaō (1), to
  slumber; to decease

SLEEPING
1957 hâzâh (1), to *dream*
3463 yâshên (1), *sleepy*
2518 kathĕudō (2), to *fall
  asleep*
2837 kŏimaō (2), to
  slumber; to decease

SLEIGHT
2940 kubĕia (1), *artifice*
  or *fraud, deceit*

SLEPT
3462 yâshên (5), to *sleep*
3463 yâshên (1), *sleepy*
5123 nûwm (1), to
  slumber
7901 shâkab (37), to *lie*

SLEW
2518 kathĕudō (2), to *fall asleep*
2837 kŏimaō (3), to *slumber; to decease*

SLEW
2026 hârag (55), to *kill*
2076 zâbach (3), to (sacrificially) *slaughter*
2126 Zîynâ' (1), well-*fed*
2490 châlal (1), to *profane, defile*
2491 châlâl (3), *slain*
4191 mûwth (40), to *kill*
5221 nâkâh (57), to *kill*
5307 nâphal (1), to *fall*
6992 qᵉṭal (Ch.) (2), to *kill*
7819 shâchaṭ (21), to *slaughter; butcher*
337 anairĕō (3), to *take away, murder*
615 apŏktĕinō (4), to *kill*
1315 diachĕirizŏmai (1), to *lay hands upon*
4969 sphazō (2), to *slaughter or to maim*
5407 phŏnĕuō (1), to *commit murder*

SLEWEST
5221 nâkâh (1), to *kill*

SLIDDEN
7725 shûwb (1), to *return*

SLIDE
4131 môwṭ (1), to *slip*
4571 mâ'ad (2), to *waver*

SLIDETH
5637 çârar (1), to be *refractory, stubborn*

SLIGHTLY
7043 qâlal (2), to *be, make light*

SLIME
2564 chêmâr (2), *bitumen*

SLIMEPITS
2564 chêmâr (1), *bitumen*

SLING
4773 margêmâh (1), sling for *stones*
7049 qâla' (3), to *sling*
7050 qela' (4), *sling*

SLINGERS
7051 qallâ' (1), *slinger*

SLINGS
7050 qela' (1), *sling*

SLINGSTONES
68+7050 'eben (1), *stone*

SLIP
4131 môwṭ (1), to *slip*
4571 mâ'ad (3), to *waver*
3901 pararrhuĕō (1), to *flow by, to pass (miss)*

SLIPPED
6362 pâṭar (1), to *burst through; to emit*
8210 shâphak (1), to *spill forth; to expend*

SLIPPERY
2513 chelqâh (1), *smoothness; flattery*
2519 châlaqlaqqâh (2), *smooth; treacherous*

SLIPPETH
4131 môwṭ (2), to *slip*
5394 nâshal (1), to *drop*

SLIPS
2156 zᵉmôwrâh (1), *twig, vine branch*

SLOTHFUL
6101 'âtsal (1), to be *slack*
6102 'âtsêl (8), *indolent*
7423 rᵉmîyâh (2), *remissness; treachery*
7503 râphâh (1), to *slacken*
3576 nōthrŏs (1), *lazy*
3636 ŏknērŏs (2), *lazy*

SLOTHFULNESS
6103 'atslâh (2), *indolence*

SLOW
750 'ârêk (10), *patient*
3515 kâbêd (1), *stupid*
692 argŏs (1), *lazy*
1021 bradus (2), *slow*

SLOWLY
1020 braduplŏĕō (1), to *sail slowly*

SLUGGARD
6102 'âtsêl (6), *indolent*

SLUICES
7938 seker (1), *wages*

SLUMBER
5123 nûwm (5), to *slumber*
8572 tᵉnûwmâh (4), *drowsiness, i.e. sleep*
2659 katanuxis (1), *stupor, bewilderment*

SLUMBERED
3573 nustazō (1), to *fall asleep; to delay*

SLUMBERETH
3573 nustazō (1), to *fall asleep; to delay*

SLUMBERINGS
8572 tᵉnûwmâh (1), *drowsiness, i.e. sleep*

SMALL
1571 gam (1), *also; even*
1639 gâra' (1), to *lessen*
1851 daq (5), *small*
1854 dâqaq (5), to *crush*
3190 yâṭab (1), to be, *make well*
4213 miz'âr (1), *fewness*
4592 mᵉ'aṭ (9), *little*
4705 mits'âr (2), *little; short time*
4962 math (1), *men*
6694 tsûwq (1), to *pour out; melt*
6810 tsâ'îyr (2), *small*
6819 tsâ'ar (1), to be *small; be trivial*
6862 tsar (1), *trouble; opponent*
6994 qâṭôn (2), to be, *make diminutive*
6996 qâṭân (34), *small*
7116 qâtsêr (2), *short*
1646 ĕlachistŏs (2), *least*
2485 ichthudiŏn (1), *little fish*
3398 mikrŏs (6), *small*
3641 ŏligŏs (5), *small*
3795 ŏpsariŏn (1), *small fish*
4142 plŏiariŏn (1), small *boat*

4979 schŏiniŏn (1), *rope*

SMALLEST
6996 qâṭân (1), *small*
1646 ĕlachistŏs (1), *least*

SMART
7321+7451 rûwa' (1), to *shout for alarm or joy*

SMELL
1314 besem (1), *spice*
7306 rûwach (5), to *smell*
7381 rêyach (10), *odor*
7382 rêyach (Ch.) (1), *odor*
2175 ĕuōdia (1), *fragrance, aroma*

SMELLED
7306 rûwach (2), to *smell*

SMELLETH
7306 rûwach (1), to *smell*

SMELLING
5674 'âbar (2), to *cross over; to transition*
3750 ŏsphrēsis (1), *smell*

SMITE
1986 hâlam (1), to *strike*
3807 kâthath (1), to *strike*
4272 mâchats (2), to *crush; to subdue*
5062 nâgaph (9), to *strike*
5221 nâkâh (94), to *strike*
5307 nâphal (1), to *fall*
5596 çâphach (1), to *associate; be united*
5606 çâphaq (1), to *clap*
6221 'Äsîy'êl (2), *made of God*
6375 pîyq (1), *tottering*
1194 dĕrō (1), to *flay*
3960 patassō (5), to *strike*
4474 rhapizō (1), to *slap*
5180 tuptō (3), to *strike*

SMITERS
5221 nâkâh (1), to *strike*

SMITEST
5221 nâkâh (1), to *strike*
1194 dĕrō (1), to *flay*

SMITETH
4272 mâchats (1), to *crush; to subdue*
5221 nâkâh (11), to *strike*
5180 tuptō (1), to *strike*

SMITH
2796 chârâsh (2), skilled *fabricator or worker*
2796+1270 chârâsh (1), skilled *fabricator*

SMITHS
4525 maçgêr (4), *prison; craftsman*

SMITING
5221 nâkâh (5), to *strike*

SMITTEN
1792 dâkâ' (1), to *pulverize; be contrite*
3807 kâthath (1), to *strike*
5060 nâga' (1), to *strike*
5062 nâgaph (15), to *inflict; to strike*
5221 nâkâh (43), to *strike*
4141 plēssō (1), to *pound*
5180 tuptō (1), to *strike*

SMOKE
6225 'âshan (5), to *envelope in smoke*

6227 'âshân (24), *smoke*
7008 qîyṭôwr (3), *fume*
2586 kapnŏs (13), *smoke*

SMOKING
3544 kêheh (1), *feeble; obscure*
6226 'âshên (2), *smoky*
6227 'âshân (1), *smoke*
5187 tuphŏō (1), to *inflate with self-conceit*

SMOOTH
2509 châlâq (1), *smooth*
2511 challâq (1), *smooth*
2512 challûq (1), *smooth*
2513 chelqâh (2), *smoothness; flattery*
3006 lĕiŏs (1), *smooth*

SMOOTHER
2505 châlaq (1), to be *smooth; be slippery*
2513 chelqâh (1), *smoothness; flattery*

SMOOTHETH
2505 châlaq (1), to be *smooth; be slippery*

SMOTE
1986 hâlam (2), to *strike*
3766 kâra' (1), to *prostrate*
4223 mᵉchâ' (Ch.) (2), to *strike; to impale*
4277 mâchaq (1), to *crush*
4347 makkâh (1), *blow*
5060 nâga' (2), to *strike*
5062 nâgaph (6), to *strike*
5221 nâkâh (194), to *strike*
5368 nᵉqash (Ch.) (1), to *knock; to be frightened*
5606 çâphaq (2), to *clap*
8628 tâqa' (1), to *slap*
851 aphairĕō (1), to *remove, cut off*
1194 dĕrō (1), to *flay, i.e. to scourge or thrash*
1325+4475 didōmi (1), to *give*
3817 paiō (4), to *hit*
3960 patassō (4), to *strike*
4474 rhapizō (1), to *strike*
5180 tuptō (4), to *strike*

SMOTEST
5221 nâkâh (1), to *strike*

SMYRNA
4667 Smurna (1), *myrrh*
4668 Smurnaiŏs (1), *inhabitant of Smyrna*

SNAIL
2546 chômeṭ (1), *lizard*
7642 shablûwl (1), *snail*

SNARE
2256 chebel (1), *band*
3369 yâqôsh (1), to *trap*
4170 môwqêsh (14), *noose*
4686 mâtsûwd (2), *net*
5367 nâqash (1), to *entrap with a noose*
6315 pûwach (1), to *blow, to fan, kindle; to utter*
6341 pach (17), *net*
6354 pachath (1), *pit for catching animals*
6983 qôwsh (1), to *set a trap*
7639 sᵉbâkâh (1), *snare*

S

1029 brŏchŏs (1), *noose*
3803 pagis (5), *trap; trick*

SNARED
3369 yâqôsh (5), *to trap*
4170 môwqêsh (1), *noose*
5367 nâqash (2), *to entrap* with a noose
6351 pâchach (1), *to spread a net*

SNARES
3353 yâqûwsh (1), *snarer*
4170 môwqêsh (6), *noose*
4685 mâtsôwd (1), *snare*
5367 nâqash (1), *to entrap* with a noose
6341 pach (6), *net*

SNATCH
1504 gâzar (1), *to destroy*

SNEEZED
2237 zârar (1), *to sneeze*

SNORTING
5170 nachar (1), *snorting*

SNOUT
639 'aph (1), *nose, nostril*

SNOW
7949 shâlag (1), *to be snow-white*
7950 sheleg (19), *white snow*
8517 t^elag (Ch.) (1), *snow*
5510 chiŏn (3), *snow*

SNOWY
7950 sheleg (1), *white snow*

SNUFFDISHES
4289 machtâh (3), *pan for live coals*

SNUFFED
5301 nâphach (1), *to inflate, blow, expire*
7602 shâ'aph (1), *to be angry; to hasten*

SNUFFERS
4212 m^ezamm^erâh (5), *tweezer, trimmer*
4457 melqâch (1), *pair of tweezers or tongs*

SNUFFETH
7602 shâ'aph (1), *to be angry; to hasten*

SOAKED
7301 râvâh (1), *to slake*

SOBER
3524 nêphalĕŏs (2), *circumspect, temperate*
3525 nêphō (4), *to abstain from wine*
4993 sōphrŏnĕō (3), *to be in a right state of mind*
4994 sōphrŏnizō (1), *to discipline or correct*
4998 sōphrōn (2), *self-controlled*

SOBERLY
1519+4993 ĕis (1), *to*
4996 sōphrŏnōs (1), *with sound mind*

SOBERNESS
4997 sōphrŏsunē (1), *self-control, propriety*

SOBRIETY
4997 sōphrŏsunē (2), *self-control, propriety*

SOCHO
7755 Sôwkôh (1), *hedged*

SOCHOH
7755 Sôwkôh (1), *hedged*

SOCKET
134 'eden (1), *footing*

SOCKETS
134 'eden (52), *footing*

SOCOH
7755 Sôwkôh (2), *hedged*

SOD
1310 bâshal (1), *to boil*
2102 zûwd (1), *to seethe*

SODDEN
1310 bâshal (5), *to boil*
1311 bâshêl (1), *boiled*

SODERING
1694 debeq (1), *solder*

SODI
5476 Çôwdîy (1), *confidant*

SODOM
5467 Ç^edôm (39), *volcanic or bituminous*
4670 Sŏdŏma (9), *volcanic or bituminous*

SODOMA
4670 Sŏdŏma (1), *volcanic or bituminous*

SODOMITE
6945 qâdêsh (1), *sacred male prostitute*

SODOMITES
6945 qâdêsh (3), *sacred male prostitute*

SOFT
4127 mûwg (1), *to soften*
7390 rak (3), *tender*
7401 râkak (1), *to soften*
3120 malakŏs (3), *soft*

SOFTER
7401 râkak (1), *to soften*

SOFTLY
328 'aṭ (3), *gently, softly*
3814 lâ'ṭ (1), *silently*
3909 lâṭ (1), *covertly*
5285 hupŏpnĕō (1), *to breathe gently*

SOIL
7704 sâdeh (1), *field*

SOJOURN
1481 gûwr (30), *to sojourn*
4033 mâgûwr (1), *abode*
1510+3941 ĕimi (1), I *exist, I am*

SOJOURNED
1481 gûwr (11), *to sojourn*
3939 parŏikĕō (1), *to reside as a foreigner*

SOJOURNER
1616 gêr (1), *foreigner*
8453 tôwshâb (7), *temporary dweller*

SOJOURNERS
1481 gûwr (1), *to sojourn*
8453 tôwshâb (2), *temporary dweller*

SOJOURNETH
1481 gûwr (15), *to sojourn*

SOJOURNING
1481 gûwr (1), *to sojourn*
4186 môwshâb (1), *seat*

3940 parŏikia (1), *foreign residence*

SOLACE
5965 'âlaç (1), *to leap for joy, i.e. exult, wave*

SOLD
935+4242 bôw' (1), *to go*
4376 mâkar (45), *to sell*
4465 mimkâr (5), *merchandise*
7666 shâbar (2), *to deal*
591 apŏdidōmi (3), *to give away*
4097 pipraskō (9), *to sell*
4453 pōlĕō (14), *to barter*

SOLDIER
4757 stratiōtēs (4), common *warrior*
4758 stratŏlŏgĕō (1), *to enlist* in the army

SOLDIERS
1121 bên (1), *son, descendant; people*
2428 chayil (1), *army*
2502 châlats (1), *to equip*
6635 tsâbâ' (1), *army*
4753 stratĕuma (1), body of *troops*
4754 stratĕuŏmai (1), *to serve* in military
4757 stratiōtēs (21), common *warrior*

SOLDIERS'
4757 stratiōtēs (1), common *warrior*

SOLE
3709 kaph (12), *sole*

SOLEMN
2282 chag (3), solemn *festival*
2287 châgag (1), *to observe* a festival
4150 môw'êd (14), *assembly*
6116 'atsârâh (10), *assembly*

SOLEMNITIES
4150 môw'êd (3), *assembly*

SOLEMNITY
2282 chag (1), solemn *festival*
4150 môw'êd (1), *assembly*

SOLEMNLY
5749 'ûwd (2), *to protest, testify; to encompass*

SOLES
3709 kaph (7), *sole of foot*

SOLITARILY
910 bâdâd (1), *separate*

SOLITARY
910 bâdâd (1), *separate*
1565 galmûwd (2), *sterile, barren, desolate*
3173 yâchîyd (1), *only son*
3452 y^eshîymôwn (1), *desolation*
6723 tsîyâh (1), desert
2048 ĕrēmŏs (1), *remote place, deserted place*

SOLOMON
8010 Sh^elômôh (271), *peaceful*

4672 Sŏlŏmōn (9), *peaceful*

SOLOMON'S
8010 Sh^elômôh (22), *peaceful*
4672 Sŏlŏmōn (3), *peaceful*

SOME
259 'echâd (7), *first*
428 'êl-leh (3), *these*
582 'ĕnôwsh (3), *person*
1697 dâbâr (1), *thing*
4592 m^e'aṭ (2), *little*
7097 qâtseh (2), *extremity*
243 allôs (9), *other*
1520 hĕis (2), *one*
2087 hĕtĕrŏs (2), *other*
3381 mēpōs (1), *lest somehow*
3588 hŏ (7), *"the," i.e. the definite article*
4218 pŏtĕ (1), *some time*
5100 tis (79), *some*

SOMEBODY
5100 tis (2), *some or any*

SOMETHING
4745 miqreh (1), *accident or fortune*
5100 tis (5), *some or any*

SOMETIME
4218 pŏtĕ (2), *some time*

SOMETIMES
4218 pŏtĕ (3), *some time*

SOMEWHAT
3544 kêheh (5), *feeble*
3972 m^e'ûwmâh (1), *something; anything*
3313 mĕrŏs (1), *division*
5100 tis (6), *some or any*

SON
1121 bên (1798), *son, descendant; people*
1125 Ben-'Ăbîynâdâb (1), (the) *son of Abinadab*
1127 Ben-Geber (1), *son of* (the) *hero*
1128 Ben-Deqer (1), *son of piercing*
1133 Ben-Chûwr (1), *son of Chur*
1136 Ben-Checed (1), *son of kindness*
1247 bar (Ch.) (7), *son*
1248 bar (4), *son, heir*
2859 châthan (5), *to become related*
2860 châthân (7), *relative; bridegroom*
3025 yâgôr (1), *to fear*
3173 yâchîyd (1), *only son*
4497 mânôwn (1), *heir*
5209 nîyn (2), *progeny*
5220 neked (1), *offspring*
431 anĕpsiŏs (1), *cousin*
3816 pais (3), *child; slave*
5043 tĕknŏn (14), *child*
5048 tĕlĕiŏō (1), *to perfect, complete*
5207 huiŏs (304), *son*

SON'S
1121 bên (21), *son*
5220 neked (1), *offspring*

SONG
2176 zimrâth (3), *song*
4853 massâ' (3), *burden, utterance*

5058 nᵉgîynâh (4),
instrument, poem
7892 shîyr (62), *song*
*5603 ō₁dē (5), religious
chant or ode*

SONGS
2158 zâmîyr (3), *song*
5058 nᵉgîynâh (1),
instrument; poem
7438 rôn (1), *shout of
deliverance*
7440 rinnâh (1), *shout*
7892 shîyr (12), *song*
*5603 ō₁dē (2), religious
chant or ode*

SONS
1121 bên (1024), *son*
1123 bên (Ch.) (3), *son*
2860 châthân (2),
relative; bridegroom
3206 yeled (3), *young
male*
3211 yâlîyd (2), *born;
descendants*
5043 tĕknŏn (6), child
*5206 huiŏthĕsia (1),
placing as a son*
5207 huiŏs (24), son

SONS'
1121 bên (26), *son*

SOON
834 'âsher (6), *because,
in order that*
1571 gam (1), *also; even*
2440 chîysh (1), *hurry*
4116 mâhar (3), to *hurry*
4120 mᵉhêrâh (1), *hurry*
4592 mᵉ'aṭ (2), *little*
4758 mar'eh (1),
appearance; vision
7116 qâtsêr (1), *short*
7323 rûwts (1), to *run*
1096 ginŏmai (1), to be
2112 ĕuthĕŏs (2), soon
*3711 ŏrgilŏs (1),
irascible, hot-tempered*
*3752 hŏtan (2),
inasmuch as, at once*
3753 hŏtĕ (2), when; as
*3916 parachrēma (1),
instantly, immediately*
*5030 tachĕŏs (2),
speedily, rapidly*

SOONER
*5032 tachiŏn (1), more
rapidly, more speedily*

SOOTHSAYER
7080 qâçam (1), to *divine
magic*

SOOTHSAYERS
1505 gᵉzar (Ch.) (4), to
determine by divination
6049 'ânan (2), to *cover,
becloud; to act covertly*

SOOTHSAYING
*3132 mantĕuŏmai (1), to
utter spells, fortune-tell*

SOP
5596 psōmiŏn (4), morsel

SOPATER
*4986 Sōpatrŏs (1), of a
safe father*

SOPE
1287 bôrîyth (2), *alkali
soap*

SOPHERETH
5618 Çôphereth (2),
female scribe

SORCERER
*3097 magŏs (2), Oriental
scientist, i.e. magician*

SORCERERS
3784 kâshaph (3), to
enchant
3786 kashshâph (1),
magician, sorcerer
*5332 pharmakĕus (1),
magician, sorcerer*
*5333 pharmakŏs (1),
magician, sorcerer*

SORCERESS
6049 'ânan (1), to *cover,
becloud; to act covertly*

SORCERIES
3785 kesheph (2), *sorcery*
3095 magĕia (1), sorcery
*5331 pharmakĕia (1),
magic, witchcraft*

SORCERY
*3096 magĕuō (1), to
practice magic, sorcery*

SORE
1419 gâdôwl (3), *great*
2388 châzaq (4), to
fasten upon; to seize
2389 châzâq (3), *severe*
2470 châlâh (2), to *be
weak, sick, afflicted*
3027 yâd (1), *hand; power*
3510 kâ'ab (2), to *feel
pain; to grieve; to spoil*
3513 kâbad (3), to *be
heavy, severe, dull*
3515 kâbêd (4), *severe*
3708 ka'aç (1), *vexation*
3966 mᵉ'ôd (22), *very*
4834 mârats (1), to *be
pungent or vehement*
5061 nega' (5), *infliction,
affliction; leprous spot*
*5704+3966 'ad (1), as far
(long) as; during*
7185 qâshâh (1), to *be
tough or severe*
7186 qâsheh (1), *severe*
7188 qâshach (1), to *be,
make unfeeling*
7235 râbâh (1), to
increase
7451 ra' (9), *bad; evil*
7690 saggîy' (Ch.) (1),
large
8178 sa'ar (1), *tempest;
terror*
*23 aganaktĕō (1), to be
indignant*
*1568 ĕkthambĕō (1), to
astonish utterly*
*1630 ĕkphŏbŏs (1),
frightened out*
1668 hĕlkŏs (1), sore
2425 hikanŏs (1), ample
*2560 kakŏs (1), badly;
wrongly; ill*
3029 lian (1), very much
3173 mĕgas (1), great
4183 pŏlus (1), much
4970 sphŏdra (1), much

SOREK
7796 Sôwrêq (1), *vine*

SORELY
4843 mârar (1), to
embitter

SORER
*5501 chĕirōn (1), more
evil or aggravated*

SORES
4347 makkâh (1), *wound*
1668 hĕlkŏs (2), sore
*1669 hĕlkŏō (1), to be
ulcerous*

SORROW
17 'ăbôwy (1), *want*
205 'âven (1), *trouble,
vanity, wickedness*
592 'ănîyâh (1), *groaning*
1669 dâ'ab (1), to *pine*
1670 dᵉ'âbâh (1), *pining*
1671 dᵉ'âbôwn (1), *pining*
1674 dᵉ'âgâh (1), *anxiety*
1727 dûwb (1), to *pine*
2342 chûwl (1), to *dance,
whirl; to writhe in pain*
2427 chîyl (2), *throe*
2490 châlal (1), to
profane, defile
3015 yâgôwn (12), *sorrow*
3511 kᵉ'êb (3), *suffering*
3708 ka'aç (4), *vexation*
4044 mᵉginnâh (1),
covering, veil
4341 mak'ôb (6), *anguish*
4620 ma'ătsêbâh (1),
anguish place
5999 'âmâl (2), *worry*
6089 'etseb (2), *painful
toil; mental pang*
6090 'ôtseb (2), *pain*
6093 'itstsâbôwn (2),
labor or pain
6094 'atstsebeth (2), *pain
or wound, sorrow*
6862 tsar (1), *trouble;
opponent*
7451 ra' (1), *bad; evil*
7455 rôa' (1), *badness*
8424 tûwgâh (1), *grief*
3076 lupĕō (1), to be sad
3077 lupē (10), sadness
3601 ŏdunē (1), grief
3997 pĕnthŏs (3), grief

SORROWED
3076 lupĕō (2), to be sad

SORROWETH
1672 dâ'ag (1), *be
anxious, be afraid*

SORROWFUL
1669 dâ'ab (1), to *pine*
1741 dᵉvay (1), *sickness*
2342 chûwl (1), to *dance,
whirl; to writhe in pain*
3013 yâgâh (1), to *grieve*
3510 kâ'ab (2), to *feel
pain; to grieve; to spoil*
7186 qâsheh (1), *severe*
*253 alupŏtĕrŏs (1), more
without grief*
3076 lupĕō (6), to be sad
*4036 pĕrilupŏs (4),
intensely sad*

SORROWING
3600 ŏdunaō (2), to grieve

SORROWS
2256 chebel (10),
company, band
4341 mak'ôb (5), *anguish*

SORELY *(continued)*
6089 'etseb (1), *pang*
6094 'atstsebeth (2), *pain*
6735 tsîyr (1), *trouble*
3601 ŏdunē (1), grief
5604 ōdin (2), pang

SORRY
1672 dâ'ag (1), *be
anxious, be afraid*
2470 châlâh (1), to *be
weak, sick, afflicted*
5110 nûwd (1), to *console*
6087 'âtsab (1), to *worry*
3076 lupĕō (9), to be sad
4036 pĕrilupŏs (1),
intensely sad

SORT
1524 gîyl (1), *age, stage*
1697 dâbâr (1), *thing*
3660 kᵉnêmâ' (Ch.) (1),
so or thus
3671 kânâph (2), *edge*
516 axiōs (1), *suitable*
3313 mĕrŏs (1), *division*
3697 hŏpŏiŏs (1), *what
kind of, what sort of*

SORTS
4358 miklôwl (1),
perfection; splendidly
4360 miklûl (1), *perfectly
splendid garment*

SOSIPATER
*4989 Sōsipatrŏs (1), of a
safe father*

SOSTHENES
*4988 Sōsthĕnēs (2), of
safe strength*

SOTAI
5479 Çôwṭay (2), *roving*

SOTTISH
5530 çâkâl (1), *silly*

SOUGHT
1156 bᵉ'â' (Ch.) (1), to
seek or ask
1158 bâ'âh (3), to *ask*
1245 bâqash (55), to
search; to strive after
1875 dârash (25), to *seek
or ask; to worship*
2713 châqar (1), to
examine, search
8446 tûwr (1), to *wander*
*327 anazētĕō (1), to
search out*
1567 ĕkzētĕō (1), to seek
*1934 ĕpizētĕō (1), to
search (inquire) for*
2212 zētĕō (36), to seek

SOUL
5082 nᵉdîybâh (1),
nobility, i.e. reputation
5315 nephesh (416), *soul*
5590 psuchē (39), soul

SOUL'S
5315 nephesh (1), *soul*

SOULS
5315 nephesh (58), *soul*
5397 nᵉshâmâh (1),
breath, life
5590 psuchē (19), soul

SOUND
1899 hegeh (1),
muttering; rumbling
1902 higgâyôwn (1),
musical notation

1993 hâmâh (3), to *be in great commotion*
4832 marpê' (1), *cure; deliverance; placidity*
5674 'âbar (2), to *cross over; to transition*
6310 peh (1), *mouth*
6963 qôwl (39), *sound*
7032 qâl (Ch.) (4), *sound*
7321 rûwa' (2), to *shout*
8085 shâma' (3), to *hear*
8454 tûwshîyâh (3), *ability, help*
8549 tâmîym (1), *entire, complete; integrity*
8629 têqa' (1), *blast* of a *trumpet*
8643 t⁰rûw'âh (1), *battle-cry; clangor*
2279 ēchŏs (2), *roar*
4537 salpizō (5), to *sound a trumpet blast*
4995 sōphrŏnismŏs (1), *self-control*
5198 hugiainō (8), to *have sound health*
5199 hugiēs (1), *well*
5353 phthŏggŏs (1), *utterance; musical*
5456 phōnē (8), *sound*

SOUNDED
2690 châtsar (3), to blow the *trumpet*
2713 châqar (1), to *search*
8628 tâqa' (2), to *clatter, slap, drive, clasp*
1001 bŏlizō (2), to *heave* a *weight*
1096 ginŏmai (1), to *be*
1837 ĕxēchĕŏmai (1), to *echo forth*, i.e. *resound*
4537 salpizō (7), to *sound a trumpet blast*

SOUNDING
1906 hêd (1), *shout of joy*
1995 hâmôwn (1), *noise*
2690 châtsar (1), to blow the *trumpet*
8085 shâma' (1), to *hear*
8643 t⁰rûw'âh (2), *battle-cry; clangor*
2278 ēchĕō (1), to *reverberate, ring out*

SOUNDNESS
4974 m⁰thôm (3), *wholesomeness*
3647 hŏlŏklēria (1), *wholeness*

SOUNDS
5353 phthŏggŏs (1), *utterance; musical*

SOUR
1155 bôçer (4), *immature, sour grapes*
5493 çûwr (1), to *turn off*

SOUTH
1864 dârôwm (17), *south; south wind*
2315 cheder (1), *apartment, chamber*
3220 yâm (1), *sea; west*
3225 yâmîyn (3), *south*
4057 midbâr (1), *desert*
5045 negeb (97), *South*
8486 têymân (14), *south; southward; south* wind
3047 lips (1), *southwest*

3314 mĕsēmbria (1), *midday; south*
3558 nŏtŏs (7), *south*

SOUTHWARD
5045 negeb (17), *south*
8486 têymân (7), *south*

SOW
2232 zâra' (28), to *sow seed; to disseminate*
4687 spĕirō (8), to *scatter*, i.e. *sow* seed
5300 hus (1), *swine*

SOWED
2232 zâra' (2), to *sow seed; to disseminate*
4687 spĕirō (8), to *scatter*, i.e. *sow* seed

SOWEDST
2232 zâra' (1), to *sow seed; to disseminate*

SOWER
2232 zâra' (2), to *sow seed; to disseminate*
4687 spĕirō (6), to *scatter*, i.e. *sow* seed

SOWEST
4687 spĕirō (3), to *scatter*, i.e. *sow* seed

SOWETH
2232 zâra' (2), to *sow seed; to disseminate*
4900 mâshak (1), to *draw out; to be tall*
7971 shâlach (3), to *send away*
4687 spĕirō (9), to *scatter*, i.e. *sow* seed

SOWING
2221 zêrûwa' (1), *plant*
2233 zera' (1), *seed; fruit, plant, sowing-time*

SOWN
2221 zêrûwa' (1), *plant*
2232 zâra' (14), to *sow seed; to disseminate*
4218 mizrâ' (1), *planted field*
4687 spĕirō (15), to *scatter*, i.e. *sow* seed

SPACE
1366 g⁰bûwl (2), *border*
3117 yôwm (3), *day; time*
4390 mâlê' (1), to *fill*
4725 mâqôwm (1), *place*
5750 'ôwd (1), *again*
7281 rega' (1), very *short space* of time
7305 revach (1), *room*
7350 râchôwq (1), *remote*
575 apŏ (1), *from, away*
1024 brachus (1), *short*
1292 diastēma (1), *interval* of time
1339 diïstēmi (1), to *remove, intervene*
1909 ĕpi (3), *on, upon*
4158 pŏdērēs (1), robe reaching the *ankles*
5550 chrŏnŏs (2), *space* of *time, period*

SPAIN
4681 Spania (2), *Spania*

SPAKE
559 'âmar (109), to *say*
560 'ămar (Ch.) (1), to *say*

981 bâţâ' (1), to *babble*
1696 dâbar (318), to *say*
4449 m⁰lal (Ch.) (2), to *speak, say*
5002 n⁰'ûm (1), *oracle*
6030 'ânâh (3), to *respond*
6032 'ănâh (Ch.) (14), to *respond, answer*
400 anaphōnĕō (1), to *exclaim*
483 antilĕgō (2), to *dispute, refuse*
626 apŏlŏgĕŏmai (1), to *give an account*
2036 ĕpō (30), to *speak*
2046 ĕrĕō (3), to *utter*
2551 kakŏlŏgĕō (1), to *revile, curse*
2980 lalĕō (72), to *talk*
3004 lĕgō (17), to *say*
4227 Pŏudēs (1), *modest*
4377 prŏsphōnĕō (3), to *address, exclaim*
4814 sullalĕō (1), to *talk together*, i.e. *converse*
5537 chrēmatizō (1), to *utter an oracle*

SPAKEST
559 'âmar (1), to *say*
1696 dâbar (8), to *speak*
1697 dâbâr (1), *word*

SPAN
2239 zereth (7), *span*
2949 ţippûch (1), *nursing, caring for*

SPANNED
2946 ţâphach (1), to *extend, spread out*

SPARE
2347 chûwç (14), to be *compassionate*
2550 châmal (13), to *spare, have pity on*
2820 châsak (3), to *refuse, spare, preserve*
5375 nâsâ' (3), to *lift up*
5545 çâlach (1), to *forgive*
8159 shâ'âh (1), to *inspect, consider*
4052 pĕrissĕuō (1), to *superabound*
5339 phĕidŏmai (4), to *treat leniently*

SPARED
2347 chûwç (2), to be *compassionate*
2550 châmal (4), to *spare, have pity on*
2820 châsak (2), to *refuse, spare, preserve*
5339 phĕidŏmai (4), to *treat leniently*

SPARETH
2550 châmal (1), to *spare, have pity on*
2820 châsak (3), to *refuse, spare, preserve*

SPARING
5339 phĕidŏmai (1), to *treat leniently*

SPARINGLY
5340 phĕidŏmĕnōs (2), *stingily, sparingly*

SPARK
5213 nîytsôwts (1), *spark*
7632 shâbîyb (1), *flame*

SPARKLED
5340 nâtsats (1), to *be bright*-colored

SPARKS
1121+7565 bên (1), *son, descendant; people*
2131 zîyqâh (2), *flash*
3590 kîydôwd (1), *spark*

SPARROW
6833 tsippôwr (2), little *hopping bird*

SPARROWS
4765 strŏuthiŏn (4), *little sparrow*

SPAT
4429 ptuō (1), to *spit*

SPEAK
559 'âmar (47), to *say*
560 'ămar (Ch.) (2), to *say*
1680 dâbab (1), to *move slowly*, i.e. *glide*
1696 dâbar (276), to *speak*
1897 hâgâh (3), to *murmur, utter a sound*
2790 chârash (1), to *engrave; to plow*
4405 millâh (1), *word; discourse; speech*
4448 mâlal (1), to *speak*
4449 m⁰lal (Ch.) (1), to *speak, say*
4911 mâshal (2), to *use figurative language*
5608 çâphar (2), to *recount* an event
5790 'ûwth (1), to *succor*
6030 'ânâh (5), to *answer*
6315 pûwach (1), to *utter*
7878 sîyach (4), to *ponder, muse aloud*
653 apŏstŏmatizō (1), to *question carefully*
669 apŏphthĕggŏmai (1), *declare, address*
987 blasphēmĕō (5), to *speak impiously*
1097 ginōskō (1), to *know*
2036 ĕpō (6), to *speak*
2046 ĕrĕō (2), to *utter*
2551 kakŏlŏgĕō (1), to *revile, curse*
2635 katalalĕō (3), to *speak slander*
2980 lalĕō (101), to *talk*
3004 lĕgō (30), to *say*
4354 prŏslalĕō (1), to *converse with*
5350 phthĕggŏmai (2), to *utter* a *clear sound*

SPEAKER
376+3956 'îysh (1), *man*
3056 lŏgŏs (1), *word*

SPEAKEST
1696 dâbar (11), to *speak*
2980 lalĕō (4), to *talk*
3004 lĕgō (2), to *say*

SPEAKETH
559 'âmar (7), to *say*
981 bâţâ' (1), to *babble*
1696 dâbar (22), to *say*
1897 hâgâh (1), to *murmur, utter a sound*
4448 mâlal (2), to *speak*
5046 nâgad (1), to *announce*

SPEAKING

6315 pûwach (5), to utter
6963 qôwl (1), voice
483 antilĕgō (1), to dispute, refuse
1256 dialĕgŏmai (1), to discuss
2036 ĕpō (2), to speak
2635 katalalĕō (2), to speak slander
2980 lalĕō (22), to talk
3004 lĕgō (4), to say

SPEAKING

1696 dâbar (37), to speak
2790 chârash (1), to engrave; to plow
4405 millâh (2), word; discourse; speech
4449 mᵉlal (Ch.) (1), to speak, say
226 alēthĕuō (1), to be true
987 blasphēmĕō (1), to speak impiously
988 blasphēmia (1), impious speech
2980 lalĕō (11), to talk
3004 lĕgō (1), to say
4180 pŏlulŏgia (1), prolixity, wordiness
4354 prŏslalĕō (1), to converse with
5350 phthĕggŏmai (1), to utter a clear sound
5573 psĕudŏlŏgŏs (1), promulgating erroneous doctrine

SPEAKINGS

2636 katalalia (1), defamation, slander

SPEAR

2595 chănîyth (34), lance, spear
3591 kîydôwn (5), dart, javelin
7013 qayin (1), lance
7420 rômach (3), iron pointed spear
3057 lŏgchē (1), lance, spear

SPEAR'S

2595 chănîyth (1), lance, spear

SPEARMEN

7070 qâneh (1), reed
1187 dĕxiŏlabŏs (1), guardsman

SPEARS

2595 chănîyth (6), lance, spear
6767 tsᵉlâtsal (1), whirring of wings
7420 rômach (9), iron pointed spear

SPECIAL

5459 çᵉgullâh (1), wealth
3756+3858+5177 ŏu (1), no or not

SPECIALLY

3122 malista (5), particularly

SPECKLED

5348 nâqŏd (9), spotted
6641 tsâbûwa' (1), hyena
8320 sâruq (1), bright red, bay colored

SPECTACLE

2302 thĕatrŏn (1), audience-room

SPED

4672 mâtsâ' (1), to find or acquire; to occur

SPEECH

562 'ômer (2), something said
565 'imrâh (7), something said
1697 dâbâr (7), word
1999 hămullâh (1), sound, roar, noise
3066 Yᵉhûwdîyth (2), in the Jewish language
3948 leqach (1), instruction
4057 midbâr (1), desert; also speech; mouth
4405 millâh (4), word; discourse; speech
6310 peh (1), mouth; opening
8088 shêma' (1), something heard
8193 sâphâh (6), lip, language, speech
2981 lalia (3), talk, speech
3056 lŏgŏs (8), word
3072 Lukaŏnisti (1), in Lycaonian language
3424 mŏgilalŏs (1), hardly talking

SPEECHES

561 'êmer (2), something said
2420 chîydâh (1), puzzle; conundrum; maxim
4405 millâh (2), word; discourse; speech
2129 ĕulŏgia (1), benediction

SPEECHLESS

1769 ĕnnĕŏs (1), speechless, silent
2974 kōphŏs (1), silent
5392 phimŏō (1), to restrain to silence

SPEED

553 'âmats (2), to be strong; be courageous
629 'oçparnâ' (Ch.) (1), with diligence
4116 mâhar (2), to hurry
4120 mᵉhêrâh (2), hurry
7136 qârâh (1), to bring about; to impose
5463 chairō (2), salutation, "be well"
5613+5033 hōs (1), which, how, i.e. in that manner

SPEEDILY

629 'oçparnâ' (Ch.) (4), with diligence
926 bâhal (1), to hasten, hurry anxiously
1980 hâlak (1), to walk; live a certain way
4116 mâhar (1), to hurry; promptly
4118 mahêr (4), in a hurry
4120 mᵉhêrâh (4), hurry; promptly

SPEEDY

926 bâhal (1), to hasten, hurry anxiously

SPEND

3615 kâlâh (4), to cease, be finished, perish
8254 shâqal (1), to suspend in trade
1159 dapanaō (1), to incur cost; to waste
5551 chrŏnŏtribĕō (1), to procrastinate, linger

SPENDEST

4325 prŏsdapanaō (1), to expend additionally

SPENDETH

6 'âbad (1), perish; destroy
1104 bâla' (1), to swallow; to destroy
6213 'âsâh (1), to do

SPENT

235 'âzal (1), to disappear
3615 kâlâh (4), to complete, consume
7286 râdad (1), to conquer; to overlay
8552 tâmam (3), to complete, finish
1159 dapanaō (2), to incur cost; to waste
1230 diaginŏmai (1), to have time elapse
1550 ĕkdapanaō (1), to exhaust, be exhausted
2119 ĕukairĕō (1), to have opportunity
2827 klinō (1), to slant
4160 pŏiĕō (1), to do
4298 prŏkŏptō (1), to go ahead, advance
4321 prŏsanaliskō (1), to expend further

SPEWING

7022 qîyqâlôwn (1), disgrace

SPICE

1313 bâsâm (1), balsam
1314 besem (2), spice; fragrance; balsam
7402 râkal (1), to travel
7543 râqach (1), to perfume, blend spice

SPICED

7544 reqach (1), spice

SPICERY

5219 nᵉkô'th (1), gum, (poss.) styrax

SPICES

1314 besem (22), spice; fragrance; balsam
5219 nᵉkô'th (1), gum, (poss.) styrax
5561 çam (3), aroma
759 arōma (4), scented oils, perfumes, spices

SPIDER

8079 sᵉmâmîyth (1), lizard

SPIDER'S

5908 'akkâbîysh (2), web-making spider

SPIED

7200 râ'âh (5), to see
7270 râgal (1), to reconnoiter; to slander

SPIES

871 'Athârîym (1), places to step
7270 râgal (10), to reconnoiter; to slander
8104 shâmar (1), to watch
1455 ĕgkathĕtŏs (1), spy
2685 kataskŏpŏs (1), reconnoiterer, i.e. a spy

SPIKENARD

5373 nêrd (3), nard
3487+4101 nardŏs (2), oil from spike-nard root

SPILLED

7843 shâchath (1), to decay; to ruin
1632 ĕkchĕō (2), to pour forth; to bestow

SPILT

5064 nâgar (1), to pour out; to deliver over

SPIN

2901 țâvâh (1), to spin yarn
3514 nēthō (2), to spin yarn

SPINDLE

3601 kîyshôwr (1), spindle or shank

SPIRIT

178 'ôwb (7), wineskin; necromancer, medium
5397 nᵉshâmâh (2), breath, life
7307 rûwach (226), breath; wind; life-spirit
7308 rûwach (Ch.) (8), breath; wind; life-spirit
4151 pnĕuma (255), spirit
5326 phantasma (2), spectre, apparition

SPIRITS

178 'ôwb (9), wineskin; necromancer, medium
7307 rûwach (5), breath; wind; life-spirit
4151 pnĕuma (32), spirit

SPIRITUAL

7307 rûwach (1), breath; wind; life-spirit
4151 pnĕuma (3), spirit
4152 pnĕumatikŏs (25), spiritual

SPIRITUALLY

3588+4151 hŏ (1), "the," i.e. the definite article
4153 pnĕumatikōs (2), non-physical

SPIT

3417 yâraq (2), to spit
7536 rôq (1), spittle, saliva
7556 râqaq (1), to spit
1716 ĕmptuō (5), to spit at
4429 ptuō (2), to spit

SPITE
3708 ka'aç (1), *vexation*

SPITEFULLY
5195 hubrizō (2), to *exercise violence, abuse*

SPITTED
1716 ĕmptuō (1), to *spit at*

SPITTING
7536 rôq (1), *spittle*

SPITTLE
7388 rîyr (1), *saliva; broth*
7536 rôq (1), *spittle*
4427 ptusma (1), *saliva*

SPOIL
957 baz (4), *plunder, loot*
961 bizzâh (6), *plunder*
962 bâzaz (8), to *plunder*
1500 gᵉzêlâh (1), *robbery, stealing; things stolen*
2254 châbal (1), to *pervert, destroy*
2488 chălîytsâh (1), *spoil, booty* of the dead
2964 ṭereph (1), *fresh torn prey*
4882 mᵉshûwçâh (1), *spoilation, loot*
4933 mᵉshiççâh (3), *plunder*
5337 nâtsal (1), to *deliver; to be snatched*
6584 pâshaṭ (1), to *strip*
6906 qâba' (1), to *defraud, rob*
7701 shôd (5), *violence, ravage, destruction*
7703 shâdad (8), to *ravage*
7921 shâkôl (1), to *miscarry*
7997 shâlal (4), to *drop or strip; to plunder*
7998 shâlâl (62), *booty*
8154 shâçâh (3), to *plunder*
8155 shâçaç (1), to *plunder, ransack*
1283 diarpazō (4), *plunder, rob*
4812 sulagōgĕō (1), to *take captive as booty*

SPOILED
957 baz (2), *plunder, loot*
958 bâzâ' (2), to *divide*
962 bâzaz (6), to *plunder*
1497 gâzal (7), to *rob*
5337 nâtsal (1), to *deliver; to be snatched*
6906 qâba' (1), to *defraud*
7701 shôd (3), *violence, ravage, destruction*
7703 shâdad (20), to *ravage*
7758 shôwlâl (2), *stripped; captive*
7997 shâlal (4), to *drop or strip; to plunder*
8154 shâçâh (3), to *plunder*
8155 shâçaç (3), to *plunder, ransack*
554 apĕkduŏmai (1), to *despoil*

SPOILER
7701 shôd (1), *violence, ravage, destruction*

SPOILERS
7703 shâdad (3), to *ravage*
7843 shâchath (2), to *decay; to ruin*
8154 shâçâh (2), to *plunder*

SPOILEST
7703 shâdad (1), to *ravage*

SPOILETH
1497 gâzal (1), to *rob*
6584 pâshaṭ (2), to *strip*
7703 shâdad (1), to *ravage*

SPOILING
7701 shôd (3), *violence, ravage, destruction*
7908 shᵉkôwl (1), *bereavement*
724 harpagē (1), *pillage*

SPOILS
698 'orŏbâh (1), *ambuscades*
7998 shâlâl (2), *booty*
205 akrŏthiniŏn (1), *best of the booty*
4661 skulŏn (1), *plunder*

SPOKEN
559 'âmar (15), to *say*
560 'ămar (Ch.) (1), to *say*
1696 dâbar (174), to *speak, say*
1697 dâbâr (2), *word*
6310 peh (1), *mouth*
312 anaggĕllō (1), to *announce, report*
369 anantirrhētōs (1), *without objection*
483 antilĕgō (2), to *dispute, refuse*
987 blasphēmĕō (5), to *speak impiously*
2036 ĕpō (19), to *speak*
2046 ĕrĕō (4), to *utter*
2605 kataggĕllō (1), to *proclaim, promulgate*
2980 lalĕō (33), to *talk*
3004 lĕgō (7), to *say*
4280 prŏĕrĕō (2), to *say already, predict*
4369 prŏstithēmi (1), to *repeat*
4483 rhĕō (15), to *utter*

SPOKES
2840 chishshûr (1), *hub*

SPOKESMAN
1696 dâbar (1), to *speak*

SPOON
3709 kaph (12), *bowl; handle*

SPOONS
3709 kaph (12), *bowl; handle*

SPORT
6026 'ânag (1), to *be soft or pliable*
6711 tsâchaq (1), to *laugh; to make sport of*
7814 sᵉchôwq (1), *laughter; scorn*
7832 sâchaq (3), to *laugh; to scorn; to play*

SPORTING
6711 tsâchaq (1), to *laugh; to make sport of*
1792 ĕntruphaō (1), to *revel in, carouse*

SPOT
933 bôhaq (1), *white scurf, rash*
934 bôhereth (9), *whitish, bright spot*
3971 m'ûwm (3), *blemish; fault*
8549 tâmîym (6), *entire, complete; integrity*
299 amômŏs (1), *unblemished, blameless*
784 aspilŏs (3), *unblemished*
4696 spilŏs (1), *stain or blemish, i.e. defect*

SPOTS
934 bôhereth (2), *whitish, bright spot*
2272 chăbarbûrâh (1), *streak, stripe*
4694 spilas (1), *ledge or reef* of rock in the sea
4696 spilŏs (1), *stain or blemish, i.e. defect*

SPOTTED
2921 ṭâlâ' (6), to *be spotted or variegated*
4695 spilŏō (1), to *soil*

SPOUSE
3618 kallâh (6), *bride; son's wife*

SPOUSES
3618 kallâh (2), *bride; son's wife*

SPRANG
305 anabainō (1), to *go up, rise*
393 anatĕllō (1), to *cause to arise*
1080 gĕnnaō (1), to *procreate, regenerate*
1530 ĕispēdaō (1), to *rush in*
1816 ĕxanatĕllō (1), to *germinate, spring forth*
4855 sumphuō (1), to *grow jointly*
5453 phuō (1), to *germinate or grow*

SPREAD
2219 zârâh (2), to *toss about; to diffuse*
3212 yâlak (2), to *walk; to live; to carry*
3318 yâtsâ' (1), to *go, bring out*
3331 yâtsa' (2), to *strew*
4894 mishtôwach (2), *spreading*-place
5186 nâṭâh (6), to *stretch or spread out*
5203 nâṭash (4), to *disperse; to thrust off*
5259 nâçak (1), to *interweave*
6327 pûwts (2), to *dash in pieces; to disperse*
6335 pûwsh (1), to *spread; to act proudly*
6555 pârats (1), to *break out*
6566 pâras (49), to *break apart, disperse, scatter*
6581 pâsâh (17), to *spread*
6584 pâshaṭ (2), to *strip*
6605 pâthach (1), to *open wide; to loosen, begin*
7286 râdad (1), to *conquer; to overlay*
7554 râqa' (4), to *pound*
7849 shâṭach (3), to *expand*
1268 dianĕmō (1), to *spread information*
1310 diaphēmizō (1), to *spread news*
1831 ĕxĕrchŏmai (2), to *issue; to leave*
4766 strōnnumi (3), *strew, i.e. spread*
5291 hupŏstrōnnumi (1), to *strew underneath*

SPREADEST
4666 miphrâs (1), *expansion*

SPREADETH
4969 mâthach (1), to *stretch out*
5186 nâṭâh (1), to *stretch or spread out*
6566 pâras (6), to *break apart, disperse, scatter*
6576 parshêz (1), to *expand*
6581 pâsâh (1), to *spread*
7502 râphad (1), to *spread a bed; to refresh*
7554 râqa' (2), to *pound*
7971 shâlach (1), to *send away*

SPREADING
4894 mishtôwach (1), *spreading*-place
5628 çârach (1), to *extend even to excess*
6168 'ârâh (1), to *pour out; demolish*
6524 pârach (1), to *break forth; to bloom; to fly*

SPREADINGS
4666 miphrâs (1), *expansion*

SPRIGS
2150 zalzal (1), *twig, shoot*
6288 pᵉ'ôrâh (1), *foliage, branches*

SPRING
1530 gal (1), *heap; ruins*
1876 dâshâ' (1), to *sprout new plants*
3318 yâtsâ' (1), to *go, bring out*
4161 môwtsâ' (2), *going forth*
4726 mâqôwr (2), *flow of liquids, or ideas*
5927 'âlâh (3), to *ascend, be high, mount*
6524 pârach (1), to *break forth; to bloom; to fly*
6779 tsâmach (10), to *sprout*
6780 tsemach (1), *sprout, branch*
985 blastanō (1), to *yield fruit*

SPRINGETH
3318 yâtsâ' (1), to *go, bring out*
6524 pârach (1), to *break forth; to bloom; to fly*
7823 shâchîyç (2), *after-growth*

SPRINGING
2416 chay (1), *alive; raw; fresh; life*
6780 tsemach (1), *sprout, branch*
242 hallŏmai (1), to *jump up; to gush up*
5453 phuŏ (1), to *germinate or grow*

SPRINGS
794 'ăshêdâh (3), *ravine*
1543 gullâh (4), *fountain; bowl or globe*
4002 mabbûwa' (2), *fountain, water spring*
4161 môwtsâ' (1), *going forth*
4599 ma'yân (2), *fountain; source*
4726 mâqôwr (1), *flow*
5033 nêbek (1), *fountain*

SPRINKLE
2236 zâraq (14), to *sprinkle, scatter*
5137 nâzâh (17), to *splash or sprinkle*

SPRINKLED
2236 zâraq (16), to *sprinkle, scatter*
5137 nâzâh (6), to *splash or sprinkle*
4472 rhantizō (3), to *asperse, sprinkle*

SPRINKLETH
2236 zâraq (1), to *sprinkle, scatter*
5137 nâzâh (1), to *splash or sprinkle*

SPRINKLING
4378 prŏschusis (1), *affusion, sprinkling*
4472 rhantizō (1), to *asperse, sprinkle*
4473 rhantismŏs (2), *aspersion, sprinkling*

SPROUT
2498 châlaph (1), to *spring up; to pierce*

SPRUNG
6524 pârach (1), to *break forth; to bloom; to fly*
6779 tsâmach (2), to *sprout*
305 anabainō (1), to *go up, rise*
393 anatĕllō (1), to *cause to arise*
985 blastanō (1), to *yield fruit*
1816 ĕxanatĕllō (1), to *germinate, spring forth*
5453 phuŏ (1), to *germinate or grow*

SPUE
6958 qôw' (2), to *vomit*
7006 qâyâh (1), to *vomit*
1692 ĕmĕō (1), to *vomit*

SPUED
6958 qôw' (1), to *vomit*

SPUN
2901 ṭâvâh (1), to *spin yarn*
4299 maṭveh (1), *something spun*

SPUNGE
4699 spŏggŏs (3), *sponge*

SPY
7200 râ'âh (2), to *see*
7270 râgal (7), to *reconnoiter; to slander*
8446 tûwr (2), to *wander, meander*
2684 kataskŏpĕō (1), to *inspect, spy on*

SQUARE
7251 râba' (3), to *be four sided, to be quadrate*

SQUARED
7251 râba' (1), to *be four sided, to be quadrate*

SQUARES
7253 reba' (2), *fourth*

STABILITY
530 'ĕmûwnâh (1), *fidelity; steadiness*

STABLE
3559 kûwn (1), to *set up: establish, fix, prepare*
5116 nâveh (1), *at home; lovely; home*

STABLISH
3559 kûwn (2), to *set up: establish, fix, prepare*
5324 nâtsab (1), to *station*
6965 qûwm (3), to *rise*
4741 stērizō (6), to *confirm*

STABLISHED
3559 kûwn (2), to *set up: establish, fix, prepare*
5975 'âmad (1), to *stand*
950 bĕbaiŏō (1), to *stabilitate, keep strong*

STABLISHETH
3559 kûwn (1), to *set up: establish, fix, prepare*
950 bĕbaiŏō (1), to *stabilitate, keep strong*

STACHYS
4720 Stachus (1), *head of grain*

STACKS
1430 gâdîysh (1), *stack of sheaves, shock of grain*

STACTE
5198 nâṭâph (1), *drop; aromatic gum resin*

STAFF
2671 chêts (1), *arrow; shaft of a spear*
4132 môwṭ (1), *pole; yoke*
4294 maṭṭeh (15), *tribe; rod, scepter; club*
4731 maqqêl (7), *shoot; stick; staff*
4938 mish'ênâh (11), *walking-stick*
6086 'êts (3), *wood*
6418 pelek (1), *spindle-whorl; crutch*
7626 shêbeṭ (2), *stick*
4464 rhabdŏs (2), *stick, rod*

STAGGER
5128 nûwa' (2), to *waver*
8582 tâ'âh (1), to *vacillate, i.e. reel*

STAGGERED
1252 diakrinō (1), to *decide; to hesitate*

STAGGERETH
8582 tâ'âh (1), to *vacillate, i.e. reel*

STAIN
1350 gâ'al (1), to *redeem; to be the next of kin*
1351 gâ'al (1), to *soil, stain; desecrate*
2490 châlal (1), to *profane, defile*

STAIRS
3883 lûwl (1), *spiral step*
4095 madrêgâh (1), *steep or inaccessible place*
4608 ma'ăleh (1), *platform; stairs*
4609 ma'ălâh (5), *thought arising*
304 anabathmŏs (2), *stairway step*

STAKES
3489 yâthêd (2), *tent peg*

STALK
7054 qâmâh (1), *stalk of grain*
7070 qâneh (2), *reed*

STALKS
6086 'êts (1), *wood*

STALL
4770 marbêq (2), *stall*
5336 phatnē (1), *stall*

STALLED
75 'âbac (1), to *feed*

STALLS
723 'urvâh (3), *herding-place*
7517 repheth (1), *stall for cattle*

STAMMERERS
5926 'illêg (1), *stuttering, stammering*

STAMMERING
3932 lâ'ag (1), to *deride; to speak unintelligibly*
3934 lâ'êg (1), *buffoon; foreigner*

STAMP
1854 dâqaq (1), to *crush*
7554 râqa' (1), to *pound*

STAMPED
1854 dâqaq (3), to *crush*
3807 kâthath (1), to *bruise, strike, beat*
7429 râmaç (2), to *tread*
7512 rᵉphaç (Ch.) (2), to *trample; to ruin*
7554 râqa' (1), to *pound*

STAMPING
8161 sha'ăṭâh (1), *clatter of hoofs*

STANCHED
2476 histēmi (1), to *stand, establish*

STAND
539 'âman (1), to *be firm, faithful, true; to trust*

STANDING
1481 gûwr (1), to *sojourn*
1826 dâmam (1), to *stop, cease; to perish*
3318 yâtsâ' (1), to *go, bring out*
3320 yâtsab (22), to *station, offer, continue*
5066 nâgash (1), to *be, come, bring near*
5324 nâtsab (9), to *station*
5564 çâmak (1), to *lean upon; take hold of*
5749 'ûwd (1), to *protest, testify; to restore*
5975 'âmad (144), to *stand*
5976 'âmad (1), to *shake*
6965 qûwm (31), to *rise*
6966 qûwm (Ch.) (2), to *rise*
7126 qârab (1), to *approach, bring near*
8617 tᵉqûwmâh (1), *resistfulness*
450 anistēmi (2), to *rise; to come back to life*
639 apŏrĕō (1), *be at a mental loss, be puzzled*
1453 ĕgĕirō (1), to *waken, i.e. rouse*
1510 ĕimi (1), *I exist, I am*
2476 histēmi (36), to *stand, establish*
3306 mĕnō (1), to *stay*
3936 paristēmi (3), to *stand beside, present*
4026 pĕriistēmi (1), to *stand around; to avoid*
4739 stēkō (7), to *persevere, be steadfast*

STANDARD
1714 degel (10), *flag, standard, banner*
5127 nûwç (1), to *vanish*
5251 nêç (7), *flag; signal*

STANDARD-BEARER
5264 nâçaç (1), to *gleam; to flutter a flag*

STANDARDS
1714 degel (3), *flag, standard, banner*

STANDEST
5975 'âmad (4), to *stand*
2476 histēmi (2), to *stand*

STANDETH
3559 kûwn (1), to *set up*
5324 nâtsab (4), to *station*
5975 'âmad (14), to *stand*
2476 histēmi (8), to *stand*
4739 stēkō (1), to *persevere, be steadfast*

STANDING
98 'ăgam (2), *marsh; pond; pool*
3320 yâtsab (1), to *station, offer, continue*
4613 mo'ŏmâd (1), *foothold*
4676 matstsêbâh (2), *column or stone*
5324 nâtsab (1), to *station*
5975 'âmad (12), to *stand*
5979 'emdâh (1), *station*
7054 qâmâh (5), *stalk*
2186 ĕphistēmi (1), to *be present; to approach*

S

2192+4174 ĕchō (1), *to have; hold; keep*
2476 histēmi (23), *to stand, establish*
3936 paristēmi (1), *to stand beside, present*
4921 sunistaō (1), *to set together; to stand near*

STANK
887 bâ'ash (4), *to smell bad*

STAR
3556 kôwkâb (2), *star*
792 astēr (11), *star*
798 astrŏn (1), *constellation; star*
5459 phōsphŏrŏs (1), *morning-star*

STARE
7200 râ'âh (1), *to see*

STARGAZERS
2374+3556 chôzeh (1), *beholder* in vision

STARS
3556 kôwkâb (34), *star*
3598 Kîymâh (1), *cluster* of stars, the *Pleiades*
792 astēr (13), *star*
798 astrŏn (3), *constellation; star*

STATE
3027 yâd (2), *hand; power*
3651 kên (1), *just; right, correct*
4612 ma'ămâd (1), *position; attendant*
4971 mathkôneth (1), *proportion*
5324 nâtsab (1), *to station*
6440 pânîym (1), *face; front*
3588+2596 hŏ (1), *"the,"* i.e. the definite article
3588+4012 hŏ (2), *"the,"* i.e. the definite article

STATELY
3520 kᵉbûwddâh (1), *magnificence, wealth*

STATION
4673 matstsâb (1), *fixed spot; office; post*

STATURE
4055 mad (1), *vesture, garment; carpet*
4060 middâh (4), *measure; portion*
6967 qôwmâh (7), *height*
2244 hēlikia (5), *maturity*

STATUTE
2706 chôq (13), *appointment; allotment*
2708 chuqqâh (20), *to delineate*
7010 qᵉyâm (Ch.) (2), *edict arising* in law

STATUTES
2706 chôq (73), *appointment; allotment*
2708 chuqqâh (58), *to delineate*
6490 piqqûwd (1), *mandate* of God, *Law*

STAVES
905 bad (37), *limb, member; bar; chief*

4133 môwṭâh (1), *pole; ox-bow; yoke*
4294 maṭṭeh (1), *tribe; rod, scepter; club*
4731 maqqêl (2), *shoot; stick; staff*
4938 mish'ênâh (1), *walking-stick*
3586 xulŏn (5), *timber,* i.e. a *stick, club*
4464 rhabdŏs (2), *stick, rod*

STAY
4102 mâhahh (1), *to be reluctant*
4223 mᵉchâ' (Ch.) (1), *to strike; to arrest*
4937 mish'ên (5), *support; protector*
5564 çâmak (2), *to lean upon; take hold* of
5702 'âgan (1), *to debar, withdraw*
5975 'âmad (10), *to stand*
6117 'âqab (1), *to seize by the heel; to circumvent*
6438 pinnâh (1), *pinnacle; chieftain*
7503 râphâh (3), *to slacken*
7901 shâkab (1), *to lie down*
8172 shâ'an (5), *to support, rely on*
8551 tâmak (1), *to obtain, keep fast*

STAYED
309 'âchar (1), *to remain*
2342 chûwl (2), *to wait; to pervert*
3176 yâchal (1), *to wait; to be patient, hope*
3322 yâtsag (1), *to place*
3607 kâlâ' (3), *to hold back or in; to prohibit*
5564 çâmak (1), *to lean upon; take hold* of
5975 'âmad (9), *to stand*
6113 'âtsar (7), *to hold back; to maintain*
7896 shîyth (1), *to place*
8156 shâça' (1), *to split or tear; to upbraid*
8551 tâmak (1), *to obtain, keep fast*
1907 ĕpĕchō (1), *to retain; to detain*
2722 katĕchō (1), *to hold down fast*

STAYETH
1898 hâgâh (1), *to remove*

STAYS
3027 yâd (4), *hand; power*

STEAD
8478 tachath (91), in *lieu* of
5228 hupĕr (2), in *behalf* of

STEADS
8478 tachath (1), in *lieu* of

STEADY
530 'ĕmûwnâh (1), *fidelity; steadiness*

STEAL
1589 gânab (11), *to thieve; to deceive*
2813 klĕptō (10), *to steal*

STEALETH
1589 gânab (3), *to thieve*

STEALING
1589 gânab (2), *to thieve*

STEALTH
1589 gânab (1), *to thieve*

STEDFAST
539 'âman (2), *to be firm, faithful, true; to trust*
3332 yâtsaq (1), *to pour out*
7011 qayâm (Ch.) (1), *permanent*
949 bĕbaiŏs (4), *stable, certain, binding*
1476 hĕdraiŏs (2), *immovable; steadfast*
4731 stĕrĕŏs (1), *solid, stable*

STEDFASTLY
553 'âmats (1), *to be strong; be courageous*
7760 sûwm (1), *to put*
816 atĕnizō (6), *to gaze intently*
4342 prŏskartĕrĕō (1), *to be constantly diligent*
4741 stĕrizō (1), *to turn resolutely; to confirm*

STEDFASTNESS
4733 stĕrĕōma (1), *stability, firmness*
4740 stĕrigmŏs (1), *stability; firmness*

STEEL
5154 nᵉchûwshâh (3), *copper; bronze*
5178 nᵉchôsheth (1), *copper; bronze*

STEEP
4095 madrêgâh (1), *steep or inaccessible* place
4174 môwrâd (1), *descent, slope*
2911 krēmnŏs (3), *precipice, steep cliff*

STEM
1503 geza' (1), *stump*

STEP
838 'âshshûwr (1), *step*
6587 pesa' (1), *stride, step*

STEPHANAS
4734 Stĕphanas (3), *crowned*

STEPHANUS
4734 Stĕphanas (1), *crowned*

STEPHEN
4736 Stĕphanŏs (7), *wreath*

STEPPED
1684 ĕmbainō (1), *to embark; to reach*

STEPPETH
2597 katabainō (1), *to descend*

STEPS
838 'âshshûwr (5), *step*
1978 hâlîyk (1), *step*

4609 ma'ălâh (11), *thought* arising
4703 mits'âd (2), *step*
6119 'âqêb (1), *track, footprint; rear* position
6471 pa'am (4), *step*
6806 tsa'ad (11), *step*
2487 ichnŏs (3), *track*

STERN
4403 prumna (1), *stern*

STEWARD
376+834+5921 'îysh (1), *man; male; someone*
834+5921 'âsher (3), *who*
1121+4943 bên (1), *son, descendant; people*
2012 ĕpitrŏpŏs (2), *manager, guardian*
3621 ŏikŏnŏmĕō (1), *to manage a household*
3622 ŏikŏnŏmia (3), *administration*
3623 ŏikŏnŏmŏs (2), *overseer, manager*

STEWARDS
8269 sar (1), *head, ruler*
3623 ŏikŏnŏmŏs (3), *overseer, manager*

STEWARDSHIP
3622 ŏikŏnŏmia (3), *administration*

STICK
1692 dâbaq (2), *to cling or adhere; to catch*
3920 lâkad (1), *to catch; to capture*
5181 nâchath (1), *to sink, descend; to press down*
6086 'êts (9), *wood*
8205 shᵉphîy (1), *bare hill or plain*

STICKETH
1695 dâbêq (1), *adhering, sticking to*

STICKS
6086 'êts (5), *wood*
5484 charin (1), *on account of, because of*

STIFF
6277 'âthâq (1), *impudent*
7185 qâshâh (1), *to be tough or severe*
7186 qâsheh (1), *severe*

STIFFENED
7185 qâshâh (1), *to be tough or severe*

STIFFHEARTED
2389+3820 châzâq (1), *strong; severe, hard*

STIFFNECKED
7185+6203 qâshâh (2), *to be tough or severe*
7186+6203 qâsheh (6), *severe*
4644 sklērŏtrachēlŏs (1), *obstinate*

STILL
1826 dâmam (6), *to be silent; to be astonished*
1827 dᵉmâmâh (1), *quiet*
2790 chârash (1), *to be silent; to be deaf*
2814 châshâh (2), *to hush or keep quiet*

4496 mᵉnûwchâh (1), *peacefully; consolation*
5265 nâça' (1), to *start*
5750 'ôwd (19), *still; more*
5975 'âmad (3), to *stand*
7503 râphâh (1), to *slacken*
7673 shâbath (2), to *repose; to desist*
8252 shâqaṭ (2), to *repose*
2089 ĕti (4), *yet, still*
2476 histēmi (4), to *stand, establish*
4357 prŏsmĕnō (1), to *remain* in a place
5392 phimŏō (1), to *restrain to silence*

STILLED
2013 hâçâh (1), to *hush*
2814 châshâh (1), to *hush* or *keep quiet*

STILLEST
7623 shâbach (1), to *pacify*

STILLETH
7623 shâbach (1), to *pacify*

STING
2759 kĕntrŏn (2), *sting*

STINGETH
6567 pârash (1), to *wound*

STINGS
2759 kĕntrŏn (1), *sting*

STINK
887 bâ'ash (4), to *smell bad*
889 bᵉ'ôsh (3), *stench*
4716 maq (1), *putridity, stench*

STINKETH
887 bâ'ash (1), to *smell bad*
3605 ŏzō (1), to *stink*

STINKING
887 bâ'ash (1), to *smell bad*

STIR
5782 'ûwr (13), to *awake*
5927 'âlâh (1), to *ascend, be high, mount*
6965 qûwm (1), to *rise*
329 anazōpurĕō (1), to *re-enkindle, fan a flame*
1326 diĕgĕirō (2), to *arouse, stimulate*
5017 tarachŏs (2), *disturbance, tumult*

STIRRED
1624 gârâh (3), to *provoke to anger*
5375 nâsâ' (3), to *lift up*
5496 çûwth (2), to *stimulate; to seduce*
5782 'ûwr (5), to *awake*
5916 'âkar (1), to *disturb* or *afflict*
6965 qûwm (3), to *rise*
1892 ĕpĕgĕirō (1), to *excite against, stir up*
3947 parŏxunō (1), to *exasperate*
3951 parŏtrunō (1), to *stimulate* to hostility

4531 salĕuō (1), to *waver*, i.e. *agitate, rock, topple*
4787 sugkinĕō (1), to *excite* to sedition
4797 sugchĕō (1), to *throw into disorder*

STIRRETH
1624 gârâh (3), to *provoke to anger*
5782 'ûwr (4), to *awake*
383 anasĕiō (1), to *excite, stir up*

STIRS
8663 tᵉshû'âh (1), *crashing* or *clamor*

STOCK
944 bûwl (1), *produce*
1503 geza' (2), *stump*
6086 'êts (2), *wood*
6133 'êqer (1), *naturalized* citizen
1085 gĕnŏs (2), *kin*

STOCKS
4115 mahpeketh (2), *stocks* for punishment
5465 çad (2), *stocks*
5914 'ekeç (1), *anklet*
6086 'êts (2), (of) *wood*
6729 tsîynôq (1), *pillory*
3586 xulŏn (1), (of) *timber*

STOICKS
4770 Stŏïkŏs (1), *porch*

STOLE
1589 gânab (4), to *thieve*
2813 klĕptō (2), to *steal*

STOLEN
1589 gânab (14), to *thieve*

STOMACH'S
4751 stŏmachŏs (1), *stomach*

STOMACHER
6614 pᵉthîygîyl (1), fine *mantle* for holidays

STONE
68 'eben (104), *stone*
69 'eben (Ch.) (6), *stone*
1496 gâzîyth (3), *dressed* stone
5619 çâqal (7), to *throw large stones*
6697 tsûwr (1), *rock*
6872 tsᵉrôwr (1), *parcel, kernel* or *particle*
7275 râgam (10), to *cast stones*
8068 shâmîyr (1), *thorn*; (poss.) *diamond*
2642 katalithazō (1), to *stone to death*
2991 laxĕutŏs (1), *rock-quarried*
3034 lithazō (4), to *lapidate, to stone*
3035 lithinŏs (3), made of *stone*
3036 lithŏbŏlĕō (1), to *throw stones*
3037 lithŏs (36), *stone*
4074 Pĕtrŏs (1), piece of *rock*
5586 psēphŏs (2), pebble *stone*

STONE'S
3037 lithŏs (1), *stone*

STONED
5619 çâqal (8), to *throw large stones*
7275 râgam (5), to *cast stones*
3034 lithazō (4), to *lapidate, to stone*
3036 lithŏbŏlĕō (5), to *throw stones*

STONES
68 'eben (136), *stone*
69 'eben (Ch.) (2), *stone*
810 'eshek (1), *testicle*
1496 gâzîyth (4), *dressed* stone
2106 zâvîyth (1), *angle, corner* (as *projecting*)
2687 châtsâts (1), *gravel*
2789 cheres (1), piece of earthenware *pottery*
5553 çela' (1), *craggy rock; fortress*
5619 çâqal (1), to *throw large stones*
6344 pachad (1), *male testicle*
6697 tsûwr (1), *rock*
3036 lithŏbŏlĕō (1), to *throw stones*
3037 lithŏs (16), *stone*

STONESQUARERS
1382 Gibliy (1), *Gebalite*

STONEST
3036 lithŏbŏlĕō (2), to *throw stones*

STONING
5619 çâqal (1), to *throw large stones*

STONY
68 'eben (2), *stone*
5553 çela' (1), *craggy rock; fortress*
4075 pĕtrŏdēs (4), *rocky*

STOOD
1826 dâmam (1), to *stop, cease; to perish*
3320 yâtsab (7), to *station, offer, continue*
3559 kûwn (1), to *set up*
4673 matstsâb (2), fixed *spot; office; post*
5324 nâtsab (19), to *station*
5568 çâmar (1), to *bristle*
5975 'âmad (189), to *stand*
5977 'ômed (1), fixed *spot*
6965 qûwm (15), to *rise*
6966 qûwm (Ch.) (4), to *rise*
450 anistēmi (7), to *rise; to come back to life*
2186 ĕphistēmi (5), to *be present; to approach*
2476 histēmi (60), to *stand, establish*
2944 kuklŏō (1), to *surround, encircle*
3936 paristēmi (14), to *stand beside, present*
4026 pĕriistēmi (1), to *stand around; to avoid*
4836 sumparaginŏmai (1), to *convene; to appear in aid*
4921 sunistaō (1), to *set together*

STOODEST
5324 nâtsab (1), to *station*
5975 'âmad (2), to *stand*

STOOL
3678 kiççê' (1), *throne*

STOOLS
70 'ôben (1), potter's *wheel*; midwife's *stool*

STOOP
7164 qâraç (1), to *hunch*
7812 shâchâh (1), to *prostrate* in homage
7817 shâchach (1), to *sink* or *depress*
2955 kuptō (1), to *bend forward, stoop down*

STOOPED
3486 yâshêsh (1), *gray-haired, aged*
3766 kâra' (1), to *prostrate*
6915 qâdad (2), to *bend*
2955 kuptō (2), to *bend forward, stoop down*
3879 parakuptō (1), to *lean over to peer within*

STOOPETH
7164 qâraç (1), to *hunch*

STOOPING
3879 parakuptō (2), to *lean over to peer within*

STOP
2629 châçam (1), to *muzzle; block*
5462 çâgar (1), to *shut up*
5640 çâtham (2), to *stop up; to repair*
6113 'âtsar (1), to *hold back; to maintain, rule*
7092 qâphats (1), to *draw together, to leap; to die*
5420 phrassō (1), to *fence or enclose, to block up*

STOPPED
2856 châtham (1), to *close up; to affix a seal*
3513 kâbad (1), to *be heavy, severe, dull*
5534 çâkar (2), to *shut up*
5640 çâtham (6), to *stop up; to repair*
8610 tâphas (1), to *manipulate*, i.e. *seize*
1998 ĕpisuntrĕchō (1), to *hasten together upon*
4912 sunĕchō (1), to *hold together*
5420 phrassō (2), to *fence or enclose, to block up*

STOPPETH
331 'âṭam (3), to *close*
7092 qâphats (1), to *draw together, to leap; to die*

STORE
214 'ôwtsâr (1), *depository*
686 'âtsar (3), to *store* up
1995 hâmôwn (2), *noise, tumult; many, crowd*
3462 yâshên (1), to *sleep; to grow old, stale*
4543 miçkᵉnâh (5), *storage-magazine*
4863 mish'ereth (2), *kneading-trough*

6487 piqqâdôwn (1), *deposit*
7235 râbâh (1), to *increase*
8498 t°kûwnâh (1), *structure; equipage*
597 apŏthēsaurizō (1), to store *treasure away*
2343 thēsaurizō (2), to *amass, reserve, store up*

STOREHOUSE
214 'ôwtsâr (1), *depository*
5009 tamĕiŏn (1), *room*

STOREHOUSES
214 'ôwtsâr (2), *depository*
618 'âçâm (1), *storehouse, barn*
834 'âsher (1), *who, which, what, that*
3965 ma'ăbûwç (1), *granary, barn*
4543 miçk°nâh (1), storage-*magazine*

STORIES
4609 ma'ălâh (1), *thought* arising

STORK
2624 chăçîydâh (5), *stork*

STORM
2230 zerem (3), *flood*
5492 çûwphâh (3), *hurricane* wind
5584 çâ'âh (1), to *rush*
5591 ça'ar (1), *hurricane*
7722 shôw' (1), *tempest; devastation*
8178 sa'ar (1), *tempest*
8183 s°'ârâh (1), *hurricane* wind
2978 lailaps (2), *whirlwind; hurricane*

STORMY
5591 ça'ar (4), *hurricane*

STORY
4097 midrâsh (2), *treatise*

STOUT
1433 gôdel (1), *magnitude, majesty*
2388 châzaq (1), to be *strong; courageous*
7229 rab (Ch.) (1), *great*

STOUTHEARTED
47+3820 'abbîyr (2), *mighty*

STOUTNESS
1433 gôdel (1), *magnitude, majesty*

STRAIGHT
3474 yâshar (9), to be *straight; to make right*
4334 mîyshôwr (2), *plain; justice*
5676 'êber (3), *opposite*
8626 tâqan (2), to *straighten; to compose*
461 anŏrthŏō (1), to *straighten up*
2113 ĕuthudrŏmĕō (2), to *sail direct*
2116 ĕuthunō (1), to *straighten or level*
2117 ĕuthus (5), *at once, immediately*

3717 ŏrthŏs (1), *straight*

STRAIGHTWAY
3651 kên (1), *just; right*
4116 mâhar (1), to *hurry*
6258 'attâh (1), *now*
6597 pith'ôwm (1), *instantly, suddenly*
1824 ĕxautēs (1), *instantly, at once*
2112 ĕuthĕōs (32), *at once or soon*
2117 ĕuthus (2), *at once*
3916 parachrēma (3), *instantly, immediately*

STRAIN
1368 diulizō (1), to *strain out*

STRAIT
6862 tsar (3), *trouble*
6887 tsârar (3), to *cramp*
4728 stĕnŏs (3), *narrow*
4912 sunĕchō (1), to *hold together*

STRAITEN
6693 tsûwq (1), to *oppress*

STRAITENED
680 'âtsal (1), to *select; refuse; narrow*
3334 yâtsar (2), to be in *distress*
4164 mûwtsaq (1), *distress*
7114 qâtsar (1), to *curtail, cut short*
4729 stĕnŏchōrĕō (2), to *hem in* closely
4912 sunĕchō (1), to *hold together*

STRAITENETH
5148 nâchâh (1), to *guide*

STRAITEST
196 akribĕstatŏs (1), *most exact, very strict*

STRAITLY
547 apĕilē (1), *menace, threat*
4183 pŏlus (2), *much*

STRAITNESS
4164 mûwtsaq (1), *distress*
4689 mâtsôwq (4), *confinement; disability*

STRAITS
3334 yâtsar (1), to be in *distress*
4712 mêtsar (1), *trouble*

STRAKE
5465 chalaō (1), to *lower* as into a *void*

STRAKES
6479 p°tsâlâh (1), *peeling*
8258 sh°qa'rûwrâh (1), *depression*

STRANGE
312 'achêr (1), *different*
1970 hâkar (1), (poss.) to *injure*
2114 zûwr (22), to be *foreign, strange*
3937 lâ'az (1), to *speak in a foreign tongue*
5234 nâkar (1), to *treat as a foreigner*
5235 neker (1), *calamity*

5236 nêkâr (16), *foreigner; heathendom*
5237 nokrîy (20), *foreign; non-relative; different*
6012 'âmêq (2), *obscure*
245 allŏtriŏs (2), *not one's own*
1854 ĕxō (1), *out, outside*
2087 hĕtĕrŏs (1), *different*
3579 xĕnizō (3), to be a *guest; to be strange*
3581 xĕnŏs (3), *alien*
3861 paradŏxŏs (1), *extraordinary*

STRANGELY
5234 nâkar (1), to *treat as a foreigner*

STRANGER
376+1616 'îysh (1), *man; male; someone*
376+2114 'îysh (3), *man; male; someone*
376+5237 'îysh (2), *man; male; someone*
1121+5235 bên (3), *son, descendant; people*
1121+5236 bên (2), *son, descendant; people*
1616 gêr (69), *foreigner*
2114 zûwr (18), to be *foreign, strange*
4033 mâgûwr (3), *abode*
5235 neker (1), *calamity*
5236 nêkâr (3), *foreigner*
5237 nokrîy (14), *foreign*
8453 tôwshâb (2), *temporary dweller*
241 allŏgĕnēs (1), *foreign,* i.e. not a Jew
245 allŏtriŏs (1), *not one's own*
3581 xĕnŏs (4), *alien*
3939 parŏikĕō (1), to *reside* as a *foreigner*
3941 parŏikŏs (1), *strange; stranger*

STRANGER'S
1121+5236 bên (1), *son, descendant; people*
1616 gêr (1), *foreigner*

STRANGERS
582+1616 'ĕnôwsh (1), *man; person, human*
1121+5236 bên (6), *son, descendant; people*
1481 gûwr (6), to *sojourn*
1616 gêr (18), *stranger*
2114 zûwr (26), to be *foreign, strange*
4033 mâgûwr (1), *abode*
5236 nêkâr (3), *foreigner*
5237 nokrîy (2), *foreign*
8453 tôwshâb (1), *temporary dweller*
245 allŏtriŏs (3), *not one's own*
1722+3940 ĕn (1), *in; during; because of*
1927 ĕpidēmĕō (1), to *make oneself at home*
3580 xĕnŏdŏchĕō (1), to *be hospitable*
3581 xĕnŏs (6), *alien*
3927 parepidēmŏs (1), *resident foreigner*
3941 parŏikŏs (1), *strange; stranger*

5381 philŏnĕxia (1), *hospitableness to strangers*

STRANGERS'
2114 zûwr (1), to be *foreign, strange*

STRANGLED
2614 chânaq (1), to *choke*
4156 pniktŏs (3), animal *choked to death*

STRANGLING
4267 machănaq (1), *choking, strangling*

STRAW
4963 mathbên (1), *straw*
8401 teben (15), *threshed stalks* of grain

STRAWED
2219 zârâh (1), to *toss about; to winnow*
1287 diaskŏrpizō (2), to *scatter; to squander*
4766 strŏnnumi (2), *strew,* i.e. *spread*

STREAM
650 'âphîyq (1), *valley; stream; mighty, strong*
793 'eshed (1), *stream*
5103 n°har (Ch.) (1), *river;* Euphrates *River*
5158 nachal (7), *valley*
4215 pŏtamŏs (2), *current, brook*

STREAMS
650 'âphîyq (1), *valley; stream; mighty, strong*
2975 y°'ôr (1), Nile *River;* Tigris *River*
2988 yâbâl (1), *stream*
5104 nâhâr (2), *stream*
5140 nâzal (2), to *drip*
5158 nachal (4), *valley*
6388 peleg (1), *small irrigation channel*

STREET
2351 chûwts (8), *outside, outdoors; open market*
2351+6440 chûwts (1), *outside, outdoors*
7339 r°chôb (22), *myriad*
7784 shûwq (1), *street*
4113 platĕia (3), *wide, open square*
4505 rhumē (2), *alley* or crowded *avenue*

STREETS
2351 chûwts (34), *outside, outdoors*
7339 r°chôb (19), *myriad*
7784 shûwq (3), *street*
58 agŏra (1), *town-square, market*
4113 platĕia (6), *wide, open square*
4505 rhumē (1), *alley* or crowded *avenue*

STRENGTH
193 'ûwl (1), *powerful; mighty*
202 'ôwn (7), *ability, power; wealth*
353 'ĕyâl (1), *strength*
360 'ĕyâlûwth (1), *power*
386 'êythân (2), *never-failing; eternal*

S

2051 ĕrizō (1), to *wrangle, quarrel*
3054 lŏgŏmachĕō (1), to *be disputatious*
3164 machŏmai (1), to *quarrel, dispute*
4865 sunagōnizŏmai (1), to *struggle with*

STRIVED
5389 philŏtimĕŏmai (1), *eager or earnest to do*

STRIVEN
1624 gârâh (1), to *provoke to anger*

STRIVETH
7378 rîyb (1), to *hold a controversy; to defend*
75 agōnizŏmai (1), to *struggle; to contend*

STRIVING
75 agōnizŏmai (1), to *struggle; to contend*
464 antagōnizŏmai (1), to *struggle against*
4866 sunathlĕō (1), to *wrestle with*

STRIVINGS
7379 rîyb (2), *contest*
3163 machĕ (1), *controversy, conflict*

STROKE
3027 yâd (1), *hand; power*
4046 maggêphâh (1), *pestilence; defeat*
4273 machats (1), *contusion*
4347 makkâh (2), *blow; wound; pestilence*
5061 nega' (3), *infliction, affliction; leprous spot*
5607 çêpheq (1), *satiety*

STROKES
4112 mahălummâh (1), *blow*

STRONG
47 'abbîyr (3), *mighty*
386 'êythân (5), *never-failing; eternal*
410 'êl (1), *mighty*
533 'ammîyts (4), *strong; mighty; brave*
553 'âmats (4), to *be strong; be courageous*
559 'âmar (1), to *say*
650 'âphîyq (1), *valley; stream; mighty, strong*
1219 bâtsar (1), to *be inaccessible*
1225 bitstsârôwn (1), *fortress*
1368 gibbôwr (5), *powerful; great warrior*
1634 gerem (1), *bone; self*
2364 Chûwshâh (1), *haste*
2388 châzaq (47), to *be strong; courageous*
2389 châzâq (26), *strong; severe, hard, violent*
2393 chezqâh (1), *power*
2394 chozqâh (1), *vehemence, harshness*
2428 chayil (5), *army; wealth; virtue; strength*
2626 chăçîyn (1), *mighty*
2634 châçôn (1), *strong*

3524 kabbîyr (1), *mighty; aged; mighty*
4013 mibtsâr (14), *fortification; defender*
4581 mâ'ôwz (5), *fortified place; defense*
4679 mᵉtsad (5), *stronghold*
4686 mâtsûwd (2), *net or capture; fastness*
4692 mâtsôwr (3), *siege-mound; distress*
4694 mᵉtsûwrâh (1), *rampart, fortification*
5553 çela' (1), *craggy rock; fortress*
5794 'az (12), *strong, vehement, harsh*
5797 'ôz (17), *strength*
5808 'izzûwz (1), *forcible; army*
5810 'âzaz (1), to *be stout; be bold*
6076 'ôphel (1), *tumor; fortress*
6099 'âtsûwm (13), *powerful; numerous*
6105 'âtsam (4), to *be, make powerful*
6108 'ôtsem (1), *power; framework of the body*
6110 'atstsûmâh (1), *defensive argument*
6184 'ârîyts (1), *powerful or tyrannical*
6339 pâzaz (1), to *solidify by refining; to spring*
6697 tsûwr (1), *rock*
7682 sâgab (1), to *be safe, strong*
7941 shêkâr (1), *liquor*
8624 taqqîyph (Ch.) (3), *powerful*
8631 tᵉqêph (Ch.) (3), to *become, make mighty*
1415 dunatŏs (3), *powerful or capable*
1743 ĕndunamŏō (4), to *empower, strengthen*
1753 ĕnĕrgĕia (1), *energy, power*
2478 ischurŏs (11), *forcible, powerful*
2901 krataiŏō (3), *increase in vigor*
3173 mĕgas (1), *great*
3794 ŏchurōma (1), *fortress, stronghold*
4608 sikĕra (1), *intoxicant*
4731 stĕrĕŏs (2), *solid*
4732 stĕrĕŏō (1), to *be, become strong*

STRONGER
553 'âmats (2), to *be strong; be courageous*
555 'ômets (1), *strength*
1396 gâbar (1), to *be strong; to prevail*
2388 châzaq (6), to *be strong; courageous*
2389 châzâq (1), *strong*
2390 châzêq (1), *powerful; loud*
5794 'az (1), *strong*
6105 'âtsam (1), to *be, make powerful*
7194 qâshar (2), to *tie, bind*

2478 ischurŏs (3), *forcible, powerful*

STRONGEST
1368 gibbôwr (1), *powerful; great warrior*

STROVE
1519 gîyach (Ch.) (1), to *rush forth*
5327 nâtsâh (6), to *quarrel, fight*
6229 'âsaq (1), to *quarrel*
7378 rîyb (3), to *hold a controversy; to defend*
1264 diamachŏmai (1), to *fight fiercely*
3164 machŏmai (2), to *war, quarrel, dispute*

STROWED
2236 zâraq (1), to *scatter*

STRUCK
5062 nâgaph (2), to *inflict a disease; strike*
5221 nâkâh (1), to *strike*
8138 shânâh (1), to *fold*
1325+4475 didōmi (1), to *give*
3960 patassō (1), to *strike*
5180 tuptō (1), to *strike*

STRUGGLED
7533 râtsats (1), to *crack in pieces, smash*

STUBBLE
7179 qash (16), *dry straw*
8401 teben (1), *threshed stalks of grain*
2562 kalamē (1), *stubble*

STUBBORN
5637 çârar (4), to *be refractory, stubborn*
7186 qâsheh (1), *severe*

STUBBORNNESS
6484 pâtsar (1), to *stun or dull*
7190 qᵉshîy (1), *obstinacy*

STUCK
1692 dâbaq (1), to *cling or adhere; to catch*
4600 mâ'ak (1), to *press*
2043 ĕrĕidō (1), to *make immovable*

STUDIETH
1897 hâgâh (2), to *murmur, ponder*

STUDS
5351 nᵉquddâh (1), *ornamental boss*

STUDY
3854 lahag (1), *mental application*
4704 spŏudazō (1), to *make effort*
5389 philŏtimĕŏmai (1), *eager or earnest to do*

STUFF
3627 kᵉlîy (14), *thing*
4399 mᵉlâ'kâh (1), *work*
4632 skĕuŏs (1), *vessel*

STUMBLE
3782 kâshal (15), to *stumble*
5062 nâgaph (2), to *inflict a disease; strike*
6328 pûwq (1), to *waver*

4350 prŏskŏptō (1), to *trip up; to strike*

STUMBLED
3782 kâshal (3), to *totter*
8058 shâmaṭ (1), to *jostle; to let alone*
4350 prŏskŏptō (1), to *trip up; to strike*
4417 ptaiō (1), to *trip up*

STUMBLETH
3782 kâshal (1), to *totter*
4350 prŏskŏptō (3), to *trip up; to strike*

STUMBLING
5063 negeph (1), *trip*
4625 skandalŏn (1), *snare*

STUMBLINGBLOCK
4383 mikshôwl (7), *stumbling-block*
4348 prŏskŏmma (2), *occasion of apostasy*
4625 skandalŏn (3), *snare*

STUMBLINGBLOCKS
4383 mikshôwl (1), *stumbling-block*
4384 makshêlâh (1), *stumbling-block*

STUMBLINGSTONE
3037+4348 lithŏs (2), *stone*

STUMP
6136 'iqqar (Ch.) (3), *stock*

SUAH
5477 Çûwach (1), *sweeping*

SUBDUE
1696 dâbar (1), to *subdue*
3533 kâbash (3), to *conquer, subjugate*
3665 kâna' (1), to *humiliate, subdue*
7286 râdad (1), to *conquer; to overlay*
8214 shᵉphal (Ch.) (1), to *humiliate*
5293 hupŏtassō (1), to *subordinate; to obey*

SUBDUED
3381 yârad (1), to *descend*
3533 kâbash (5), to *conquer, subjugate*
3665 kâna' (9), to *humiliate, subdue*
3766 kâra' (2), to *prostrate*
2610 katagōnizŏmai (1), to *overcome, defeat*
5293 hupŏtassō (1), to *subordinate; to obey*

SUBDUEDST
3665 kâna' (1), to *humiliate, subdue*

SUBDUETH
1696 dâbar (1), to *subdue*
2827 chăshal (Ch.) (1), to *crush, pulverize*
7286 râdad (1), to *conquer; to overlay*

SUBJECT
1379 dŏgmatizō (1), to *submit to a certain rule*

1777 ĕnŏchŏs (1), *liable*
3663 hŏmŏiŏpathēs (1), *similarly affected*
5293 hupŏtassō (14), to *subordinate; to obey*

SUBJECTED
5293 hupŏtassō (1), to *subordinate; to obey*

SUBJECTION
3533 kâbash (2), to *conquer, subjugate*
3665 kâna' (1), to *humiliate, subdue*
1396 dŏulagōgĕō (1), to *enslave, subdue*
5292 hupŏtagē (4), *subordination*
5293 hupŏtassō (6), to *subordinate; to obey*

SUBMIT
3584 kâchash (3), to *lie, disown; to cringe*
6031 'ânâh (1), to *afflict, be afflicted*
7511 râphaç (1), to *trample; to prostrate*
5226 hupĕikō (1), to *surrender, yield*
5293 hupŏtassō (6), to *subordinate; to obey*

SUBMITTED
3584 kâchash (1), to *lie, disown; to cringe*
5414+3027 nâthan (1), to *give*
5293 hupŏtassō (1), to *subordinate; to obey*

SUBMITTING
5293 hupŏtassō (1), to *subordinate; to obey*

SUBORNED
5260 hupŏballō (1), to *throw in stealthily*

SUBSCRIBE
3789 kâthab (2), to *write*

SUBSCRIBED
3789 kâthab (2), to *write*

SUBSTANCE
202 'ôwn (1), *ability, power; wealth*
1564 gôlem (1), *embryo*
1942 havvâh (1), *desire; craving*
1952 hôwn (7), *wealth*
2428 chayil (7), *wealth; virtue; valor; strength*
3351 yᵉqûwm (1), *living thing*
3426 yêsh (1), there *is*
3428 Yesheb'âb (1), *seat of* (his) *father*
3581 kôach (1), *force, might; strength*
4678 matstsebeth (2), *stock of a tree*
4735 miqneh (2), *stock*
6108 'ôtsem (1), *power; framework of the body*
7009 qîym (1), *opponent*
7075 qinyân (4), *acquisition, purchase*
7399 rᵉkûwsh (11), *property*
7738 shâvâh (1), to *destroy*

3776 ŏusia (1), *wealth, property, possessions*
5223 huparxis (1), *property, possessions*
5224 huparchŏnta (1), *property or possessions*
5287 hupŏstasis (1), *essence; assurance*

SUBTIL
2450 châkâm (1), *wise, intelligent, skillful*
5341 nâtsar (1), to *conceal, hide*
6175 'ârûwm (1), *cunning; clever*

SUBTILLY
5230 nâkal (1), to *act treacherously*
6191 'âram (1), to *be cunning; be prudent*
2686 katasŏphizŏmai (1), to *be crafty against*

SUBTILTY
4820 mirmâh (1), *fraud*
6122 'oqbâh (1), *trickery*
6195 'ormâh (1), *trickery; discretion*
1388 dŏlŏs (2), *wile, deceit, trickery*
3834 panŏurgia (1), *trickery or sophistry*

SUBURBS
4054 migrâsh (110), *open country*
6503 Parbâr (1), *Parbar*

SUBVERT
5791 'âvath (1), to *wrest, twist*
396 anatrĕpō (1), to *overturn, destroy*

SUBVERTED
1612 ĕkstrĕphō (1), to *pervert, be warped*

SUBVERTING
384 anaskĕuazō (1), to *upset, trouble*
2692 katastrŏphē (1), *catastrophical ruin*

SUCCEED
6965 qûwm (1), to *rise*

SUCCEEDED
3423 yârash (3), to *impoverish; to ruin*

SUCCEEDEST
3423 yârash (2), to *impoverish; to ruin*

SUCCESS
7919 sâkal (1), to *be or act circumspect*

SUCCOTH
5523 Çukkôwth (18), *booths*

SUCCOTH-BENOTH
5524 Çukkôwth Bᵉnôwth (1), *brothels*

SUCCOUR
5826 'âzar (2), to *aid*
997 bŏēthĕō (1), to *aid*

SUCCOURED
5826 'âzar (1), to *aid*
997 bŏēthĕō (1), to *aid*

SUCCOURER
4368 prŏstatis (1), *assistant, helper*

SUCHATHITES
7756 Sûwkâthîy (1), *Sukathite*

SUCK
3243 yânaq (13), to *suck*
4680 mâtsâh (1), to *drain; to squeeze out*
5966 'âla' (1), to *sip up*
2337 thēlazō (4), to *suck*

SUCKED
3243 yânaq (1), to *suck*
2337 thēlazō (1), to *suck*

SUCKING
2461 châlâb (1), *milk*
3243 yânaq (3), to *suck*
5764 'ûwl (1), *babe*

SUCKLING
3243 yânaq (1), to *suck*

SUCKLINGS
3243 yânaq (3), to *suck*
2337 thēlazō (1), to *suck*

SUDDEN
6597 pith'ôwm (2), *instantly, suddenly*
160 aiphnidiŏs (1), *suddenly*

SUDDENLY
4116 mâhar (1), to *hurry*
4118 mahêr (1), *in a hurry*
6597 pith'ôwm (22), *instantly, suddenly*
6621 petha' (4), *wink, i.e. moment; quickly*
7280 râga' (2), to *settle, i.e. quiet; to wink*
7281 rega' (1), *very short space* of time
869 aphnō (3), *suddenly*
1810 ĕxaiphnēs (5), *suddenly, unexpectedly*
1819 ĕxapina (1), *unexpectedly*
5030 tachĕōs (1), *rapidly*

SUE
2919 krinō (1), to *decide; to try, condemn, punish*

SUFFER
3201 yâkôl (1), to *be able*
3240 yânach (3), to *allow to stay*
3803 kâthar (1), to *enclose, besiege; to wait*
5375 nâsâ' (5), to *lift up*
5414 nâthan (11), to *give up* with, *endure*
430 anĕchŏmai (7), to *put up* with, *endure*
818 atimazō (1), to *maltreat, dishonor*
863 aphiēmi (8), to *leave; to pardon, forgive*
1325 didōmi (2), to *give*
1377 diōkō (3), to *pursue; to persecute*
1439 ĕaō (2), to *let be, i.e. permit or leave alone*
2010 ĕpitrĕpō (6), *allow*
2210 zēmiŏō (1), to *experience detriment*
2553 kakŏpathĕō (1), to *undergo suffering*
2558 kakŏuchĕō (1), to *maltreat; to torment*
3805 pathētŏs (1), *doomed to pain*

3958 paschō (20), to *experience pain*
4722 stĕgō (1), to *endure patiently*
4778 sugkakŏuchĕō (1), to *endure persecution*
4841 sumpaschō (2), to *experience pain jointly*
5278 hupŏmĕnō (1), to *undergo,* bear (trials)
5302 hustĕrĕō (1), to *be inferior; to fall short*

SUFFERED
3240 yânach (2), to *allow to stay*
5203 nâṭash (1), to *disperse; to thrust off*
5375 nâsâ' (1), to *lift up*
5414 nâthan (7), to *give*
863 aphiēmi (6), to *leave; to pardon, forgive*
1439 ĕaō (5), to *let be, i.e. permit or leave alone*
2010 ĕpitrĕpō (4), *allow*
2210 zēmiŏō (1), to *suffer loss*
2967 kōluō (1), to *stop*
3958 paschō (17), to *experience pain*
4310 prŏpaschō (1), to *undergo hardship*
5159 trŏpŏphŏrĕō (1), to *endure one's habits*

SUFFEREST
1439 ĕaō (1), to *let be*

SUFFERETH
5414 nâthan (1), to *give*
971 biazō (1), to *crowd oneself into*
1439 ĕaō (1), to *let be*
3114 makrŏthumĕō (1), to *be forbearing, patient*

SUFFERING
2552 kakŏpathĕia (1), *hardship, suffering*
3804 pathēma (1), *passion; suffering*
3958 paschō (1), to *experience pain*
4330 prŏsĕaō (1), to *permit further progress*
5254 hupĕchō (1), to *endure with patience*

SUFFERINGS
3804 pathēma (10), *passion; suffering*

SUFFICE
4672 mâtsâ' (2), to *find or acquire; to occur*
5606 çâphaq (1), to *be enough; to vomit*
7227 rab (3), *great*
713 arkĕtŏs (1), *enough*

SUFFICED
4672 mâtsâ' (1), to *find or acquire; to occur*
7646 sâba' (1), *fill to satiety*
7648 sôba' (1), *satisfaction*

SUFFICETH
714 arkĕō (1), to *avail; be satisfactory*

SUFFICIENCY
5607 çêpheq (1), *satiety*

S

841 autarkeia (1),
contentedness
2426 hikanŏtēs (1),
ability, competence

SUFFICIENT
1767 day (5), enough
7227 rab (1), great
713 arkĕtŏs (1), enough
714 arkĕŏ (2), to avail; be
satisfactory
2425 hikanŏs (3), ample

SUFFICIENTLY
4078 madday (1),
sufficiently
7654 sob'âh (1), satiety

SUIT
2470 châlâh (1), to be
weak, sick, afflicted
6187 'êrek (1), pile,
equipment, estimate
7379 rîyb (1), contest

SUKKIIMS
5525 Çukkîy (1),
hut-dwellers

SUM
3724 kôpher (1),
redemption-price
4557 miçpâr (2), number
6485 pâqad (1), to visit,
care for, count
6575 pârâshâh (1),
exposition
7217 rê'sh (Ch.) (1), head
7218 rô'sh (9), head
8508 toknîyth (1),
consummation
8552 tâmam (1), to
complete, finish
2774 kĕphalaiŏn (2),
principal; amount
5092 timē (1), esteem;
nobility; money

SUMMER
4747 mᵉqêrâh (2),
cooling off, coolness
6972 qûwts (1), to spend
the harvest season
7007 qâyit (Ch.) (1),
harvest season
7019 qayits (20), harvest
2330 thĕrŏs (3), summer

SUMPTUOUSLY
2983 lambanŏ (1), to
take, receive

SUN
216 'ôwr (1), luminary
2535 chammâh (4), heat
of sun
2775 chereç (3), itch; sun
8121 shemesh (120), sun
8122 shemesh (Ch.) (1),
sun
2246 hēliŏs (30), sun

SUNDERED
6504 pârad (1), to spread
or separate

SUNDRY
4181 pŏlumĕrōs (1), in
many portions

SUNG
7891 shîyr (1), to sing
103 aₐdō (2), to sing
5214 humnĕŏ (2), to
celebrate God in song

SUNK
2883 tâba' (5), to sink
3766 kâra' (1), to
prostrate
2702 kataphĕrō (1), to
bear down

SUNRISING
4217 mizrâch (1), place
of sunrise; east
4217+8121 mizrâch (9),
place of sunrise; east

SUP
4041 mᵉgammâh (1),
accumulation
1172 dĕipnĕŏ (2), to eat
the principal meal

SUPERFLUITY
4050 pĕrissĕia (1),
superabundance

SUPERFLUOUS
8311 sâra' (2), to be
deformed
4053 pĕrissŏs (1),
superabundant

SUPERSCRIPTION
1923 ĕpigraphē (5),
superscription

SUPERSTITION
1175 dĕisidaimŏnia (1),
religion

SUPERSTITIOUS
1174 dĕisidaimŏnĕstĕrŏs
(1), more religious

SUPPED
1172 dĕipnĕŏ (1), to eat
the principal meal

SUPPER
1172 dĕipnĕŏ (1), to eat
the principal meal
1173 dĕipnŏn (13),
principal meal

SUPPLANT
6117 'âqab (1), to seize by
the heel; to circumvent

SUPPLANTED
6117 'âqab (1), to seize by
the heel; to circumvent

SUPPLE
4935 mish'îy (1),
inspection

SUPPLIANTS
6282 'âthâr (1), incense;
worshipper

SUPPLICATION
2420 chîydâh (1), puzzle;
conundrum; maxim
2603 chânan (10), to
implore
2604 chănan (Ch.) (1), to
favor
6419 pâlal (1), to
intercede, pray
8467 tᵉchinnâh (22),
supplication
1162 dĕēsis (4), petition

SUPPLICATIONS
8467 tᵉchinnâh (1),
supplication
8469 tachănûwn (17),
earnest prayer, plea
1162 dĕēsis (2), petition
2428 hikĕtēria (1),
entreaty, supplication

SUPPLIED
378 anaplērŏŏ (1), to
complete; to supply
4322 prŏsanaplērŏŏ (1),
to furnish fully

SUPPLIETH
2024 ĕpichŏrēgia (1),
contribution, aid
4322 prŏsanaplērŏŏ (1),
to furnish fully

SUPPLY
378 anaplērŏŏ (1), to
complete; to supply
2024 ĕpichŏrēgia (1),
contribution, aid
4137 plērŏŏ (1), to fill,
make complete

SUPPORT
472 antĕchŏmai (1), to
adhere to; to care for
482 antilambanŏmai (1),
to succor; aid

SUPPOSE
559 'âmar (1), to say
1380 dŏkĕŏ (3), to think,
regard, seem good
3049 lŏgizŏmai (2), to
credit; to think, regard
3543 nŏmizō (1), to deem
3633 ŏiŏmai (1), to
imagine, opine
5274 hupŏlambanō (2),
to assume, presume

SUPPOSED
1380 dŏkĕŏ (2), to think
2233 hēgĕŏmai (1), to
deem, i.e. consider
3543 nŏmizō (4), to deem
5282 hupŏnŏĕŏ (1), to
think; to expect

SUPPOSING
1380 dŏkĕŏ (2), to think
3543 nŏmizō (4), to deem
3633 ŏiŏmai (1), to
imagine, opine

SUPREME
5242 hupĕrĕchō (1), to
excel; be superior

SUR
5495 Çûwr (1),
deteriorated

SURE
539 'âman (11), to be
firm, faithful, true
546 'omnâh (1), surely
548 'ămânâh (1),
covenant
571 'emeth (1), certainty,
truth, trustworthiness
982 bâtach (1), to trust,
be confident or sure
2388 châzaq (1), to bind
3045 yâda' (4), to know
3245 yâçad (1), settle,
consult, establish
4009 mibtâch (1),
security; assurance
6965 qûwm (2), to rise
7011 qayâm (Ch.) (1),
permanent
*7292 râhab (1), to urge,
embolden, capture*
8104 shâmar (1), to
watch
804 asphalēs (1), secure

805 asphalizō (3), to
render secure
949 bĕbaiŏs (3), stable,
certain, binding
1097 ginōskŏ (2), to know
1492 ĕidō (3), to know
4103 pistŏs (1),
trustworthy; reliable
4731 stĕrĕŏs (1), solid

SURETIES
6148 'ârab (1), to give or
be security

SURETISHIP
8628 tâqa' (1), to clatter,
slap, drive, clasp

SURETY
389 'ak (1), surely
552 'umnâm (1), verily
3045 yâda' (1), to know
6148 'ârab (8), to give or
be security
6161 'ărubbâh (1), as
security; bondsman
230 alēthōs (1), surely
1450 ĕgguŏs (1),
bondsman, guarantor

SURFEITING
2897 kraipalē (1),
debauch

SURMISINGS
5283 hupŏnŏia (1),
suspicion

SURNAME
3655 kânâh (1), to
address, give title
1941 ĕpikalĕŏmai (6), to
invoke
2564 kalĕŏ (1), to call

SURNAMED
3655 kânâh (1), to
address, give title
1941 ĕpikalĕŏmai (5), to
invoke
2007+3686 ĕpitithēmi (2),
to impose

SURPRISED
270 'âchaz (1), to seize
8610 tâphas (2), to seize*

SUSANCHITES
7801 Shûwshankîy (Ch.)
(1), Shushankite

SUSANNA
4677 Sŏusanna (1), lily

SUSI
5485 Çûwçîy (1),
horse-like

SUSTAIN
3557 kûwl (4), to
maintain

SUSTAINED
5564 çâmak (3), to lean
upon; take hold of

SUSTENANCE
3557 kûwl (1), to
maintain
4241 michyâh (1),
sustenance
5527 chŏrtasma (1), food

SWADDLED
2853 châthal (1), to
swathe, wrap in cloth
2946 tâphach (1), to
nurse

SWADDLING
4683 sparganŏŏ (2), to *wrap with cloth*

SWADDLINGBAND
2854 chăthulláh (1), *swathing cloth to wrap*

SWALLOW
1104 bâla' (13), to *swallow; to destroy*
1866 dᵉrôwr (2), *swallow*
3886 lûwa' (1), to *be rash*
5693 'âgûwr (2), *swallow*
7602 shâ'aph (4), to *be angry; to hasten*
2666 katapinŏ (1), to *devour by swallowing*

SWALLOWED
1104 bâla' (19), to *swallow; to destroy*
1105 bela'(1), *gulp*
3886 lûwa' (1), to *be rash*
7602 shâ'aph (1), to *be angry; to hasten*
2666 katapinŏ (4), to *devour by swallowing*

SWALLOWETH
1572 gâmâ' (1), to *swallow*
7602 shâ'aph (1), to *be angry; to hasten*

SWAN
8580 tanshemeth (2), *(poss.) water-hen*

SWARE
5375 nâsâ' (1), to *lift up*
7650 shâba' (70), to *swear*
3660 ŏmnuŏ (7), to *swear, declare on oath*

SWAREST
7650 shâba' (5), to *swear*

SWARM
5712 'êdâh (1), *assemblage; family*
6157 'ârôb (2), swarming *mosquitoes*

SWARMS
6157 'ârôb (5), swarming *mosquitoes*

SWEAR
422 'âlâh (2), *imprecate, utter a curse*
5375 nâsâ' (2), to *lift up*
7650 shâba' (43), to *swear*
3660 ŏmnuŏ (13), to *swear, declare on oath*

SWEARERS
7650 shâba' (1), to *swear*

SWEARETH
7650 shâba' (7), to *swear*
3660 ŏmnuŏ (4), to *swear, declare on oath*

SWEARING
422 'âlâh (2), *imprecate, utter a curse*
423 'âlâh (2), *imprecation: curse*

SWEAT
2188 zê'âh (1), *sweat*
3154 yeza' (1), *sweat*
2402 hidrōs (1), *sweat*

SWEEP
2894 ṭûw' (1), to *sweep away*

3261 yâ'âh (1), to *brush aside*
4563 sarŏŏ (1), to *sweep clean*

SWEEPING
5502 çâchaph (1), to *scrape off, sweep off*

SWEET
1314 besem (5), *spice; fragrance; balsam*
2896 ṭôwb (1), *good; well*
3190 yâṭab (1), to *be, make well*
4452 mâlats (1), to *be smooth; to be pleasant*
4477 mamtaq (2), *sweet*
4575 ma'ădannâh (1), *bond, i.e. group*
4840 merqâch (1), *spicy*
4966 mâthôwq (7), *sweet*
4985 mâthaq (5), to *relish; to be sweet*
5207 nîchôwach (43), *pleasant; delight*
5208 nîychôwach (Ch.) (2), *pleasure*
5273 nâ'îym (2), *delightful; sweet*
5276 nâ'êm (1), to *be agreeable*
5561 çam (16), *aroma*
5674 'âbar (2), to *cross over; to transition*
6071 'âçîyç (2), *expressed fresh grape-juice*
6148 'ârab (5), to *intermix*
6149 'ârêb (2), *agreeable*
8492 tîyrôwsh (1), *wine; squeezed grape-juice*
1099 glukus (3), *sweet*
2175 ĕuŏdia (2), *fragrance, aroma*

SWEETER
4966 mâthôwq (2), *sweet*

SWEETLY
4339 mêyshâr (1), *straightness; rectitude*
4988 mâthâq (1), sweet *food*

SWEETNESS
4966 mâthôwq (2), *sweet*
4986 metheq (2), *pleasantness*
4987 môtheq (1), *sweetness*

SWEETSMELLING
2175 ĕuŏdia (1), *fragrance, aroma*

SWELL
1216 bâtsêq (1), to *blister*
6638 tsâbâh (2), to *array an army against*
6639 tsâbeh (1), *swollen*

SWELLED
1216 bâtsêq (1), to *blister*

SWELLING
1158 bâ'âh (1), to *ask; be bulging, swelling*
1346 ga'ăvâh (1), *arrogance; majesty*
1347 gâ'ôwn (3), *ascending; majesty*
5246 hupĕrŏgkŏs (2), *insolent, boastful*

SWELLINGS
5450 phusiŏsis (1), *haughtiness, arrogance*

SWEPT
1640 gâraph (1), to *sweep away*
5502 çâchaph (1), to *scrape off, sweep off*
4563 sarŏŏ (2), to *sweep clean*

SWERVED
795 astŏchĕŏ (1), *deviate*

SWIFT
16 'êbeh (1), *papyrus*
3753 karkârâh (1), *cow-camel*
4116 mâhar (3), to *hurry*
7031 qal (9), *rapid, swift*
7043 qâlal (1), to *be, make light (swift)*
7409 rekesh (1), *relay*
3691 ŏxus (1), *rapid, fast*
5031 tachinŏs (1), *soon, immanent*
5036 tachus (1), *prompt*

SWIFTER
7031 qal (1), *rapid, swift*
7043 qâlal (5), to *be, make light (swift)*

SWIFTLY
3288 yᵉ'âph (1), utterly *exhausted*
4120 mᵉhêrâh (1), *hurry*
7031 qal (2), *rapid, swift*

SWIM
6687 tsûwph (1), to *overflow*
7811 sâchâh (2), to *swim*
7813 sâchûw (1), *pond for swimming*
1579 ĕkkŏlumbaō (1), to *escape by swimming*
2860 kŏlumbaō (1), to *plunge into water*

SWIMMEST
6824 tsâphâh (1), *inundation*

SWIMMETH
7811 sâchâh (1), to *swim*

SWINE
2386 chăzîyr (2), *hog*
5519 chŏirŏs (14), *pig*

SWINE'S
2386 chăzîyr (4), *hog*

SWOLLEN
4092 pimprēmi (1), to *become inflamed*

SWOON
5848 'âṭaph (1), to *languish*

SWOONED
5848 'âṭaph (1), to *languish*

SWORD
1300 bârâq (1), *lightning; flash of lightning*
2719 chereb (380), *sword*
7524 retsach (1), *crushing; murder-cry*
7973 shelach (3), *spear*
3162 machaira (22), *short sword*
4501 rhŏmphaia (7), *sabre, cutlass*

SWORDS
2719 chereb (17), *sword*
6609 pᵉthîchâh (1), *drawn sword*
3162 machaira (6), *short sword*

SWORN
1167+7621 ba'al (1), *master; husband*
3027+5920+3676 yâd (1), *hand; power*
5375 nâsâ' (1), to *lift up*
7650 shâba' (42), to *swear*
3660 ŏmnuŏ (3), to *swear*

SYCAMINE
4807 sukaminŏs (1), *sycamore-fig tree*

SYCHAR
4965 Suchar (1), *liquor*

SYCHEM
4966 Suchĕm (2), *ridge*

SYCOMORE
8256 shâqâm (6), *sycamore tree*
4809 sukŏmōraia (1), *sycamore-fig tree*

SYCOMORES
8256 shâqâm (1), *sycamore tree*

SYENE
5482 Çᵉvênêh (2), the local *Seven*

SYNAGOGUE
656 apŏsunagŏgŏs (2), *excommunicated*
752 archisunagōgŏs (7), *director of the synagogue services*
4864 sunagōgē (34), *assemblage*

SYNAGOGUE'S
752 archisunagōgŏs (2), *director of the synagogue services*

SYNAGOGUES
4150 môw'êd (1), *place of meeting; congregation*
656 apŏsunagōgŏs (1), *excommunicated*
4864 sunagōgē (22), *assemblage*

SYNTYCHE
4941 Suntuchē (1), *accident*

SYRACUSE
4946 Surakŏusai (1), *Syracuse*

SYRIA
758 'Arâm (66), *highland*
4947 Suria (8), (poss.) *rock*

SYRIA-DAMASCUS
758+1834 'Arâm (1), *highland*

SYRIA-MAACHAH
758 'Arâm (1), *highland*

SYRIACK
762 'Arâmîyth (1), *in Araman*

SYRIAN
761 'Ărammîy (7), *Aramite*

S

762 'Ărâmîyth (4), *in Araman*

4948 Surŏs (1), *native of Syria*

SYRIANS
758 'Ărâm (57), *highland*
761 'Ărammîy (4), *Aramite*

SYROPHENICIAN
4949 Surŏphŏinissa (1), *native of Phœnicia*

TAANACH
8590 Ta'ănâk (6), *Taanak or Tanak*

TAANATH-SHILOH
8387 Ta'ănath Shîlôh (1), *approach of Shiloh*

TABBAOTH
2884 Ṭabbâ'ôwth (2), *rings*

TABBATH
2888 Ṭabbath (1), *Tabbath*

TABEAL
2870 Ṭâbᵉ'êl (1), *pleasing* (to) *God*

TABEEL
2870 Ṭâbᵉ'êl (1), *pleasing* (to) *God*

TABERAH
8404 Tab'êrâh (2), *burning*

TABERING
8608 tâphaph (1), to *drum* on a tambourine

TABERNACLE
168 'ôhel (187), *tent*
4908 mishkân (114), *residence*
5520 çôk (1), *hut* of *entwined* boughs
5521 çukkâh (3), *tabernacle; shelter*
5522 çikkûwth (1), idolatrous *booth*
7900 sôk (1), *booth*
4633 skēnē (15), *tent*
4636 skēnŏs (2), *tent*
4638 skēnōma (3), *dwelling*: the *Temple*

TABERNACLES
168 'ôhel (11), *tent*
4908 mishkân (5), *residence*
5521 çukkâh (9), *tabernacle; shelter*
4633 skēnē (4), *tent*
4634 skēnŏpēgia (1), *tabernacles, i.e. booths*

TABITHA
5000 Tabitha (2), *gazelle*

TABLE
3871 lûwach (4), *tablet*
4524 mêçab (1), *divan couch; around*
7979 shulchân (56), *table*
345 anakĕimai (1), to *recline at a meal*
4093 pinakidiŏn (1), wooden writing *tablet*
5132 trapĕza (9), four-legged *table or stool*

TABLES
3871 lûwach (34), *tablet*

7979 shulchân (14), *table*
2825 klinē (1), *couch*
4109 plax (3), *tablet*
5132 trapĕza (4), four-legged *table or stool*

TABLETS
1004+5315 bayith (1), *house; temple; family*
3558 kûwmâz (2), *jewel*

TABOR
8396 Tâbôwr (10), *broken*

TABRET
8596 tôph (3), *tambourine*
8611 tôpheth (1), *smiting*

TABRETS
8596 tôph (5), *tambourine*

TABRIMON
2886 Ṭabrimmôwn (1), *pleasing* (to) *Rimmon*

TACHES
7165 qereç (10), *knob*

TACHMONITE
8461 Tachkᵉmônîy (1), *sagacious*

TACKLING
4631 skĕuē (1), *tackle*

TACKLINGS
2256 chebel (1), *company*

TADMOR
8412 Tadmôr (2), *palm*

TAHAN
8465 Tachan (2), *station*

TAHANITES
8470 Tachănîy (1), *Tachanite*

TAHAPANES
8471 Tachpanchêç (1), *Tachpanches*

TAHATH
8480 Tachath (6), *bottom*

TAHPANHES
8471 Tachpanchêç (5), *Tachpanches*

TAHPENES
8472 Tachpᵉnêyç (3), *Tachpenes*

TAHREA
8475 Tachrêa' (1), (poss.) *earth, ground; low*

TAHTIM-HODSHI
8483 Tachtîym Chodshîy (1), *lower* (ones) *monthly*

TAIL
2180 zânâb (8), *tail*
3769 ŏura (1), *tail*

TAILS
2180 zânâb (2), *tail*
3769 ŏura (4), *tail*

TAKE
6 'âbad (1), to *perish*
270 'âchaz (12), to *seize*
622 'âçaph (3), to *gather*
680 'âtsal (1), to *select*
935 bôw' (1), to *go, come*
962 bâzaz (9), to *plunder*
1197 bâ'ar (4), to *be brutish, be senseless*
1497 gâzal (3), to *rob*

1692 dâbaq (1), to *cling* or *adhere*; to *catch*
1898 hâgâh (2), to *remove, expel*
1961 hâyâh (1), to *exist*
2095 zᵉhar (Ch.) (1), *be admonished, be careful*
2254 châbal (7), to *bind by a pledge*; to *pervert*
2388 châzaq (9), to *fasten* upon; to *seize*
2502 châlats (1), to *present, strengthen*
2834 châsaph (1), to *drain* away or *bail* up
2846 châthâh (3), to *lay hold* of; to *take away*
3051 yâhab (1), to *give*
3212 yâlak (1), to *carry*
3318 yâtsâ' (2), to *go, bring out*
3381 yârad (3), to *descend*
3423 yârash (3), to *inherit*
3615 kâlâh (1), to *complete, prepare*
3920 lâkad (19), to *catch*
3947 lâqach (367), to *take*
5253 nâçag (2), to *retreat*
5267 nᵉçaq (Ch.) (1), to *go up*
5312 nᵉphaq (Ch.) (1), to *issue forth; to bring out*
5337 nâtsal (1), to *deliver; to be snatched*
5375 nâsâ' (60), to *lift up*
5376 nᵉsâ' (Ch.) (1), to *lift up*
5381 nâsag (5), to *reach*
5414 nâthan (1), to *give*
5493 çûwr (45), to *turn off*
5496 çûwth (1), to *stimulate; to seduce*
5535 çâkath (1), to *be silent; to observe*
5674 'âbar (2), to *cross over; to transition*
5709 'ădâ' (Ch.) (1), to *pass* on or *continue*
5749 'ûwd (2), to *encompass, restore*
5927 'âlâh (4), to *ascend*
5978 'immâd (1), *with*
6213 'âsâh (1), to *do*
6331 pûwr (1), to *crush*
6679 tsûwd (1), to *catch*
6901 qâbal (1), to *admit*
6902 qᵉbal (Ch.) (1), to *acquire*
7061 qâmats (3), to *grasp*
7126 qârab (1), to *approach, bring near*
7200 râ'âh (2), to *see*
7311 rûwm (11), to *be high; to rise or raise*
7760 sûwm (2), to *put*
7896 shîyth (1), to *place*
7901 shâkab (2), to *lie*
7997 shâlal (4), to *drop* or *strip*; to *plunder*
8175 sâ'ar (1), to *storm; to shiver, i.e. fear*
8551 tâmak (2), to *obtain*
8610 tâphas (10), to *manipulate, i.e. seize*
142 airō (35), to *lift up*
353 analambanō (3), to *take up, bring up*
726 harpazō (3), to *seize*

851 aphairĕō (5), to *remove, cut off*
1209 dĕchŏmai (3), to *receive, accept*
1949 ĕpilambanŏmai (2), to *seize*
2507 kathairĕō (1), to *lower, or demolish*
2722 katĕchō (1), to *hold down fast*
2902 kratĕō (4), to *seize*
2983 lambanō (31), to *take, receive*
3335 mĕtalambanō (1), to *accept and use*
3880 paralambanō (5), to *associate with oneself*
3911 paraphĕrō (1), to *carry off; to avert*
4014 pĕriairĕō (1), to *unveil; to cast off*
4084 piazō (4), to *seize*
4355 prŏslambanō (1), to *take along, receive*
4648 skŏpĕō (1), to *watch out for, i.e. to regard*
4815 sullambanō (3), to *seize (arrest, capture)*
4838 sumparalambanō (2), to *take along*
4868 sunairō (1), to *compute an account*

TAKEN
247 'âzar (1), to *belt*
270 'âchaz (7), to *seize*
622 'âçaph (7), to *gather*
935 bôw' (1), to *go, come*
1197 bâ'ar (2), to *be brutish, be senseless*
1497 gâzal (5), to *rob*
1639 gâra' (4), to *remove, lessen, or withhold*
2254 châbal (1), to *bind by a pledge; to pervert*
2388 châzaq (5), to *fasten* upon; to *seize*
2502 châlats (1), to *pull off; to strip; to depart*
2974 yâ'al (2), to *assent; to undertake, begin*
3289 yâ'ats (2), to *advise*
3381 yârad (1), to *descend*
3427 yâshab (5), to *dwell*
3885 lûwn (1), to *be obstinate with*
3920 lâkad (42), to *catch*
3921 leked (1), *noose*
3947 lâqach (84), to *take*
4672 mâtsâ' (1), to *find*
5267 nᵉçaq (Ch.) (1), to *go up*
5312 nᵉphaq (Ch.) (2), to *issue forth; to bring out*
5337 nâtsal (3), to *deliver; to be snatched*
5375 nâsâ' (10), to *lift up*
5381 nâsag (1), to *reach*
5414 nâthan (1), to *give*
5493 çûwr (19), to *turn off*
5674 'âbar (1), to *cross over; to transition*
5709 'ădâ' (Ch.) (1), to *remove; to bedeck*
5927 'âlâh (9), to *ascend*
6001 'âmêl (1), *laborer*
6213 'âsâh (1), to *make*
6679 tsûwd (1), to *catch*
6813 tsâ'an (1), to *load*

7092 qâphats (1), to *draw together*, to *leap*; to *die*
7287 râdâh (1), to *subjugate*; to *crumble*
7311 rûwm (4), to *be high*; to *rise* or *raise*
7628 shebîy (2), *booty*
7725 shûwb (1), to *turn back*; to *return*
8610 tâphas (12), to *manipulate*, i.e. *seize*
142 airō (16), to *lift up*
259 halōsis (1), *capture*
353 analambanō (3), to *take up, bring up*
522 apairō (3), to *remove, take away*
642 apórphanizō (1), to *separate*
782 aspazŏmai (1), to *give salutation*
851 aphaireō (1), to *remove*
1096 ginŏmai (1), to *be*
1723 ĕnagkalizŏmai (1), *take into one's arms*
1808 ĕxairō (1), to *remove, drive away*
1869 ĕpairō (1), to *raise*
2021 ĕpichĕirĕō (1), to *undertake, try*
2221 zōgrĕō (1), to *capture or ensnare*
2638 katalambanō (2), to *seize*; to *possess*
2639 katalĕgō (1), to *enroll, put on a list*
2983 lambanō (12), to *take, receive*
3880 paralambanō (5), to *associate with* oneself
4014 pĕriairĕō (3), to *unveil*; to *cast off*
4084 piazō (2), to *seize*
4355 prŏslambanō (1), to *take along; receive*
4815 sullambanō (2), to *seize (arrest, capture)*
4912 sunĕchō (3), to *hold together*

TAKEST
622 'âçaph (1), to *gather*
1980 hâlak (1), to *walk*
3947 lâqach (2), to *take*
5375 nâsâ' (1), to *lift up*
6001 'âmêl (1), *laborer*
8104 shâmar (1), to *watch*
142 airō (1), to *lift up*

TAKETH
270 'âchaz (2), to *seize*
1197 bâ'ar (1), to *be brutish, be senseless*
2254 châbal (1), to *bind by a pledge; to pervert*
2388 châzaq (4), to *fasten upon; to seize*
2862 châthaph (1), to *clutch, snatch*
3920 lâkad (5), to *catch*
3947 lâqach (11), to *take*
5190 nâṭal (1), to *lift*; to *impose*
5337 nâtsal (1), to *deliver; to be snatched*
5375 nâsâ' (3), to *lift up*
5493 çûwr (2), to *turn off*
5710 'âdâh (1), to *pass on or continue*; to *remove*

5998 'âmal (2), to *work severely, put forth effort*
6908 qâbats (1), to *collect, assemble*
7953 shâlah (1), to *draw out or off*, i.e. *remove*
8610 tâphas (1), to *manipulate*, i.e. *seize*
142 airō (11), to *lift up*
337 anairĕō (1), to *take away*, i.e. *abolish*
851 aphairĕō (1), to *remove, cut off*
1405 drassŏmai (1), to *grasp*, i.e. *entrap*
2018 ĕpiphĕrō (1), to *inflict, bring upon*
2638 katalambanō (1), to *seize; to possess*
2983 lambanō (4), to *take, receive*
3880 paralambanō (8), to *associate with* oneself
4301 prŏlambanō (1), to *take before; be caught*

TAKING
3947 lâqach (1), to *take*
4727 miqqâch (1), *reception*
8610 tâphas (1), to *manipulate*, i.e. *seize*
142 airō (1), to *lift up*
321 anagō (1), to *lead up; to bring out*
353 analambanō (1), to *take up, bring up*
1325 didŏmi (1), to *give*
2983 lambanō (4), to *take*

TALE
1899 hegeh (1), *muttering*
4557 miçpâr (1), *number*
4971 mathkôneth (1), *proportion*
8506 tôken (1), *quantity*

TALEBEARER
1980+7400 hâlak (1), to *walk; live a certain way*
5372 nirgân (2), *slanderer*
7400 râkîyl (2), *scandal-monger*

TALENT
3603 kikkâr (10), *talent*
5006 talantiaiŏs (1), *weight* of 57-80 lbs.
5007 talantŏn (3), *weight*

TALENTS
3603 kikkâr (38), *talent*
3604 kikkêr (Ch.) (1), *talent weight*
5007 talantŏn (12), *weight* of 57-80 lbs.

TALES
7400 râkîyl (1), *scandal-monger*
3026 lērŏs (1), *twaddle*

TALITHA
5008 talitha (1), *young girl*

TALK
1696 dâbar (11), to *speak*
1697 dâbâr (2), *word*
1897 hâgâh (1), to *murmur, utter a sound*
5608 çâphar (1), to *recount an event*
6310 peh (1), *mouth*

7878 sîyach (5), to *ponder, muse aloud*
8193 sâphâh (1), *lip, language, speech*
2980 lalĕō (1), to *talk*
3056 lŏgŏs (1), *word, matter, thing*

TALKED
559 'âmar (1), to *say*
1696 dâbar (29), to *speak*
2980 lalĕō (8), to *talk*
3656 hŏmilĕō (2), to *talk*
4814 sullalĕō (1), to *talk*
4926 sunŏmilĕō (1), to *converse* mutually

TALKERS
3956 lâshôwn (1), *tongue*
3151 mataiŏlŏgŏs (1), *senseless talker*

TALKEST
1696 dâbar (2), to *speak*
2980 lalĕō (1), to *talk*

TALKETH
1696 dâbar (1), to *speak*
2980 lalĕō (1), to *talk*

TALKING
1696 dâbar (3), to *speak*
4405 millâh (1), *word; discourse; speech*
7879 sîyach (1), *uttered contemplation*
2980 lalĕō (1), to *talk*
3473 mŏrŏlŏgia (1), *buffoonery, foolish talk*
4814 sullalĕō (2), to *talk together*, i.e. *converse*

TALL
6967 qôwmâh (2), *height*
7311 rûwm (3), to *be high*

TALLER
7311 rûwm (1), to *be high*

TALMAI
8526 Talmay (6), *ridged*

TALMON
2929 Ṭalmôwn (5), *oppressive*

TAMAH
8547 Temach (1), *Temach*

TAMAR
8559 Tâmâr (24), *palm*

TAME
1150 damazō (2), to *tame*

TAMED
1150 damazō (2), to *tame*

TAMMUZ
8542 Tammûwz (1), *Tammuz*

TANACH
8590 Ta'ănâk (1), *Taanak or Tanak*

TANHUMETH
8576 Tanchûmeth (2), *compassion, solace*

TANNER
1033 brŏma (3), *food*

TAPHATH
2955 Ṭâphath (1), *dropping (of ointment)*

TAPPUAH
8599 Tappûwach (6), *apple*

TARAH
8646 Terach (2), *Terach*

TARALAH
8634 Tar'ălâh (1), *reeling*

TARE
1234 bâqa' (1), to *cleave, break, tear open*
7167 qâra' (1), to *rend*
4682 sparassō (1), to *convulse with epilepsy*
4952 susparassō (1), to *convulse* violently

TAREA
8390 Ta'ărêa' (1), (poss.) *earth, ground; low*

TARES
2215 zizaniŏn (8), *darnel*

TARGET
3591 kîydôwn (1), *dart*
6793 tsinnâh (2), *large shield; piercing cold*

TARGETS
6793 tsinnâh (3), *large shield; piercing cold*

TARPELITES
2967 Ṭarpelay (Ch.) (1), *Tarpelite*

TARRIED
748 'ârak (2), to *be long*
2342 chûwl (1), to *wait*
3176 yâchal (1), to *wait*
3186 yâchar (1), to *delay*
3427 yâshab (6), to *dwell, to remain; to settle*
3885 lûwn (3), to *be obstinate with*
4102 mâhahh (2), to *be reluctant*
5116 nâveh (1), *at home*
5975 'âmad (1), to *stand*
1304 diatribō (2), to *stay*
1961 ĕpimĕnō (3), to *remain; to persevere*
3306 mĕnō (3), to *stay*
4160 pŏiĕō (1), to *do*
4328 prŏsdŏkaō (1), to *anticipate; to await*
4357 prŏsmĕnō (1), to *remain in a place*
5278 hupŏmĕnō (1), to *undergo, (trials)*
5549 chrŏnizō (2), to *take time*, i.e. *linger*

TARRIEST
3195 mĕllō (1), to *intend*, i.e. *be about to*

TARRIETH
3427 yâshab (1), to *dwell, to remain; to settle*
6960 qâvâh (1), to *expect*

TARRY
309 'âchar (4), to *remain; to delay*
1826 dâmam (1), to *stop, cease; to perish*
2442 châkâh (2), to *await; hope for*
3176 yâchal (2), to *wait*
3427 yâshab (13), to *dwell, to remain*
3559 kûwn (1), to *set up: establish, fix, prepare*
3885 lûwn (7), to *be obstinate with*

T

4102 mâhahh (3), *to be reluctant*
5975 'âmad (1), *to stand*
7663 sâbar (1), *to scrutinize; to expect*
1019 bradunō (1), *to delay, hesitate*
1551 ĕkdĕchŏmai (1), *to await, expect*
1961 ĕpimĕnō (4), *to remain; to persevere*
2523 kathizō (1), *to seat down, dwell*
3306 mĕnō (7), *to stay*
5549 chrŏnizō (1), *to take time, i.e. linger*

TARRYING
309 'âchar (2), *to remain*

TARSHISH
8659 Tarshîysh (24), *merchant vessel*

TARSUS
5018 Tarsĕus (2), *native of Tarsus*
5019 Tarsŏs (3), *flat*

TARTAK
8662 Tartâq (1), *Tartak*

TARTAN
8661 Tartân (2), *Tartan*

TASK
1697 dâbar (1), *word; matter; thing*
2706 chôq (1), *appointment; allotment*

TASKMASTERS
5065 nâgas (5), *to exploit; to tax, harass*

TASKS
1697 dâbar (1), *word; matter; thing*

TASTE
2441 chêk (4), *area of mouth*
2938 ţâ'am (6), *to taste*
2940 ţa'am (5), *taste*
1089 gĕuŏmai (7), *to taste*

TASTED
2938 ţâ'am (2), *to taste*
2942 ţe'êm (Ch.) (1), *judgment; account*
1089 gĕuŏmai (5), *to taste; to eat*

TASTETH
2938 ţâ'am (1), *to taste*

TATNAI
8674 Tattenay (4), *Tattenai*

TATTLERS
5397 phluarŏs (1), *pratery*

TAUGHT
995 bîyn (1), *to understand; discern*
1696 dâbar (2), *to speak*
3045 yâda' (3), *to know*
3256 yâçar (2), *to instruct*
3384 yârâh (5), *to teach*
3925 lâmad (17), *to teach*
3928 limmûwd (1), *instructed one*
4000 mâbôwn (1), *instructing*
7919 sâkal (1), *to be or act circumspect*

8637 tirgal (1), *to cause to walk*
1318 didaktŏs (1), *instructed, taught*
1321 didaskō (36), *to teach*
1322 didachē (1), *instruction*
2258+1321 ēn (4), *I was*
2312 thĕŏdidaktŏs (1), *divinely instructed*
2727 katēchĕō (1), *to indoctrinate*
3100 mathētĕuō (1), *to become a student*
3811 paidĕuō (1), *to educate or discipline*

TAUNT
1422 gedûwphâh (1), *revilement, taunt*
8148 sheniynâh (1), *gibe, verbal taunt*

TAUNTING
4426 meliytsâh (1), *aphorism, saying*

TAVERNS
4999 Tabĕrnai (1), *huts*

TAXATION
6187 'êrek (1), *estimate*

TAXED
6186 'ârak (1), *to arrange*
582 apŏgraphē (3), *census registration*

TAXES
5065 nâgas (1), *to exploit; to tax, harass*

TAXING
583 apŏgraphō (2), *enroll, take a census*

TEACH
502 'âlaph (1), *to teach*
2094 zâhar (1), *to enlighten*
3045 yâda' (5), *to know*
3046 yeda' (Ch.) (1), *to know*
3384 yârâh (33), *to teach*
3925 lâmad (32), *to teach*
8150 shânan (1), *to pierce; to inculcate*
1317 didaktikŏs (2), *instructive*
1321 didaskō (26), *to teach*
2085 hĕtĕrŏdidaskalĕō (2), *to instruct differently*
2605 kataggĕllō (1), *to proclaim, promulgate*
2727 katēchĕō (1), *to indoctrinate*
3100 mathētĕuō (1), *to become a student*
4994 sōphrŏnizō (1), *to train up*

TEACHER
995 bîyn (1), *to understand; discern*
3384 yârâh (1), *to teach*
1320 didaskalŏs (4), *instructor*

TEACHERS
3384 yârâh (3), *to teach*
3887 lûwts (1), *to scoff; to interpret; to intercede*
3925 lâmad (1), *to teach*

1320 didaskalŏs (6), *instructor*
2567 kalŏdidaskalŏs (1), *teacher of the right*
3547 nŏmŏdidaskalŏs (1), *Rabbi*
5572 psĕudŏdidaskalŏs (1), *propagator of erroneous doctrine*

TEACHEST
3925 lâmad (1), *to teach*
1321 didaskō (7), *to teach*

TEACHETH
502 'âlaph (1), *to teach*
3384 yârâh (3), *to teach*
3925 lâmad (5), *to teach*
7919 sâkal (1), *to be or act circumspect*
1318 didaktŏs (2), *taught*
1321 didaskō (3), *to teach*
2727 katēchĕō (1), *to indoctrinate*

TEACHING
3384 yârâh (1), *to teach*
3925 lâmad (1), *to teach*
1319 didaskalia (1), *instruction*
1321 didaskō (21), *to teach*
3811 paidĕuō (1), *to educate or discipline*

TEAR
1234 bâqa' (1), *to cleave, break, tear open*
1758 dûwsh (1), *to trample or thresh*
2963 ţâraph (5), *to pluck off or pull to pieces*
5498 çâchab (1), *to trail along*
6536 pâraç (1), *to break in pieces; to split*
6561 pâraq (1), *to break off or crunch; to deliver*
7167 qâra' (3), *to rend*

TEARETH
2963 ţâraph (4), *to pluck off or pull to pieces*
4486 rhēgnumi (1), *to tear to pieces*
4682 sparassō (1), *to convulse with epilepsy*

TEARS
1058 bâkâh (1), *to weep*
1832 dim'âh (23), *tears*
1144 dakru (11), *teardrop*

TEATS
1717 dad (2), *female breast or bosom*
7699 shad (1), *breast*

TEBAH
2875 Ţebach (1), *massacre*

TEBALIAH
2882 Ţebalyâhûw (1), *Jehovah has dipped*

TEBETH
2887 Ţêbeth (1), *a month*

TEDIOUS
1465 ĕgkŏptō (1), *to impede, detain*

TEETH
4973 methalle'âh (3), *tooth*
6374 pîyphîyâh (1), *tooth*

8127 shên (31), *tooth*
8128 shên (Ch.) (3), *tooth*
3599 ŏdŏus (10), *tooth*
3679 ŏnĕidizō (1), *to rail at, chide, taunt*

TEHAPHNEHES
8471 Tachpanchêç (1), *Tachpanches*

TEHINNAH
8468 Techinnâh (1), *supplication*

TEIL
424 'êlâh (1), *oak*

TEKEL
8625 teqal (Ch.) (2), *to weigh in a scale*

TEKOA
8620 Teqôwa' (6), *trumpet*

TEKOAH
8620 Teqôwa' (1), *trumpet*
8621 Teqôw'îy (2), *Tekoite*

TEKOITE
8621 Teqôw'îy (3), *Tekoite*

TEKOITES
8621 Teqôw'îy (2), *Tekoite*

TEL-ABIB
8512 Têl 'Âbîyb (1), *mound of green growth*

TEL-HARESHA
8521 Têl Charshâ' (1), *mound of workmanship*

TEL-HARSA
8521 Têl Charshâ' (1), *mound of workmanship*

TEL-MELAH
8528 Têl Melach (2), *mound of salt*

TELAH
8520 Telach (1), *breach*

TELAIM
2923 Ţelâ'îym (1), *lambs*

TELASSAR
8515 Tela'ssar (1), *Telassar*

TELEM
2928 Ţelem (2), *oppression*

TELL
559 'âmar (29), *to say*
560 'ămar (Ch.) (5), *to say*
1696 dâbar (7), *to speak*
3045 yâda' (7), *to know*
5046 nâgad (69), *to announce*
5608 çâphar (12), *to recount an event*
8085 shâma' (2), *to hear*
226 alēthĕuō (1), *to be true*
312 anaggĕllō (2), *to announce, report*
518 apaggĕllō (6), *to announce, proclaim*
1334 diēgĕŏmai (2), *to relate fully, describe*
1492 ĕidō (9), *to know*
1583 ĕklalĕō (1), *to tell*
1650 ĕlĕgchŏs (1), *proof*
2036 ĕpō (28), *to speak*
2046 ĕrĕō (3), *to utter*
2980 lalĕō (2), *to talk*
3004 lĕgō (28), *to say*

4302 prŏlĕgō (1), to
predict, forewarn

TELLEST
5608 çâphar (1), to
recount an event

TELLETH
1696 dâbar (2), to speak
4487 mânâh (2), to allot;
to enumerate or enroll
5046 nâgad (2), to
announce
3004 lĕgō (1), to say

TELLING
1696 dâbar (1), to speak
4557 miçpâr (1), number
5608 çâphar (1), to
recount an event

TEMA
8485 Têymâ' (5), Tema

TEMAN
8487 Têymân (11), south

TEMANI
8489 Têymânîy (1),
Temanite

TEMANITE
8489 Têymânîy (6),
Temanite

TEMANITES
8489 Têymânîy (1),
Temanite

TEMENI
8488 Têymᵉnîy (1),
Temeni

TEMPER
7450 râçaç (1), to
moisten with drops

TEMPERANCE
1466 ĕgkratĕia (4),
self-control

TEMPERATE
1467 ĕgkratĕuŏmai (1),
to exercise self-restraint
1468 ĕgkratēs (1),
self-controlled
4998 sōphrŏn (1),
self-controlled

TEMPERED
1101 bâlal (1), to mix
4414 mâlach (1), to salt
4786 sugkĕrannumi (1),
to combine, assimilate

TEMPEST
2230 zerem (3), flood
5492 çûwphâh (1),
hurricane wind
5590 çâ'ar (1), to rush
upon; to toss about
5591 ça'ar (4), hurricane
7307 rûwach (1), breath;
wind; life-spirit
8183 sᵉ'ârâh (1),
hurricane wind
2366 thuĕlla (1), blowing
2978 lailaps (1),
whirlwind; hurricane
4578 sĕismŏs (1), gale
storm; earthquake
5492 chĕimazō (1), to be
battered in a storm
5494 chĕimōn (1), winter
season; stormy weather

TEMPESTUOUS
5490 çôwph (2),
termination; end

8175 sâ'ar (1), to storm
5189 tuphōnikŏs (1),
stormy

TEMPLE
1004 bayith (11), house;
temple; family, tribe
1964 hêykâl (68), temple
1965 hêykâl (Ch.) (8),
palace; temple
2411 hiĕrŏn (71), sacred
place; sanctuary
3485 naŏs (43), temple
3624 ŏikŏs (1), dwelling

TEMPLES
1964 hêykâl (2), temple
7451 ra' (5), bad; evil
3485 naŏs (2), temple

TEMPORAL
4340 prŏskairŏs (1),
temporary

TEMPT
974 bâchan (1), to test
5254 nâçâh (4), to test
1598 ĕkpĕirazō (3), to
test thoroughly
3985 pĕirazō (6), to
endeavor, scrutinize

TEMPTATION
4531 maççâh (1), testing
3986 pĕirasmŏs (15), test

TEMPTATIONS
4531 maççâh (3), testing
3986 pĕirasmŏs (5), test

TEMPTED
5254 nâçâh (8), to test
551 apĕirastŏs (1), not
temptable
1598 ĕkpĕirazō (1), to
test thoroughly
3985 pĕirazō (14), to
endeavor, scrutinize

TEMPTER
3985 pĕirazō (2), to
endeavor, scrutinize

TEMPTETH
3985 pĕirazō (1), to
endeavor, scrutinize

TEMPTING
3985 pĕirazō (7), to
endeavor, scrutinize

TEN
6218 'âsôwr (4), ten
6235 'eser (164), ten
6236 'ăsar (Ch.) (4), ten
7231 râbab (1), to
multiply by the myriad
7233 rᵉbâbâh (13),
myriad
7239 ribbôw (2), myriad
7240 ribbôw (Ch.) (2),
myriad
1176 dĕka (24), ten
3461 murias (3), ten
thousand
3463 muriŏi (3), ten
thousand; innumerably

TEN'S
6235 'eser (1), ten

TENDER
3126 yôwnêq (1), sucker
plant; nursing infant
3127 yôwneqeth (1),
sprout, new shoot
7390 rak (10), tender
7401 râkak (2), to soften

527 hapalŏs (2), tender
3629 ŏiktirmōn (1),
compassionate
4698 splagchnŏn (1),
intestine; affection, pity

TENDERHEARTED
7390+3824 rak (1),
tender; weak
2155 ĕusplagchnŏs (1),
compassionate

TENDERNESS
7391 rôk (1), softness

TENONS
3027 yâd (6), hand; power

TENOR
6310 peh (2), mouth

TENS
6235 'eser (3), ten

TENT
167 'âhal (3), to pitch a
tent
168 'ôhel (89), tent
6898 qubbâh (1), pavilion

TENTH
4643 ma'ăsêr (4), tithe,
one-tenth
6218 'âsôwr (13), ten
6224 'ăsîyrîy (26), tenth
6237 'âsar (3), to tithe
6241 'issârôwn (28), tenth
1181 dĕkatē (2), tenth
1182 dĕkatŏs (3), tenth

TENTMAKERS
4635 skēnŏpŏiŏs (1),
manufacturer of tents

TENTS
168 'ôhel (50), tent
2583 chânâh (1), to
encamp
4264 machăneh (5),
encampment
4908 mishkân (1),
residence
5521 çukkâh (1),
tabernacle; shelter

TERAH
8646 Terach (11), Terach

TERAPHIM
8655 tᵉrâphîym (6),
healer

TERESH
8657 Teresh (2), Teresh

TERMED
559 'âmar (2), to say

TERRACES
4546 mᵉçillâh (1),
viaduct; staircase

TERRESTRIAL
1919 ĕpigĕiŏs (2),
worldly, earthly

TERRIBLE
366 'âyôm (3), frightful
367 'êymâh (2), fright
574 'emtânîy (Ch.) (1),
burly or mighty
1763 dᵉchal (Ch.) (1), to
fear; be formidable
2152 zal'âphâh (1), glow
3372 yârê' (30), to fear
6184 'ârîyts (13),
powerful or tyrannical
5398 phŏbĕrŏs (1),
frightful, i.e. formidable

TERRIBLENESS
3372 yârê' (1), to fear
4172 môwrâ' (1), fearful
8606 tiphletseth (1),
fearfulness

TERRIBLY
6206 'ârats (2), to dread

TERRIFIED
6206 'ârats (1), to dread
4422 ptŏĕō (2), to be
scared
4426 pturō (1), to be
frightened

TERRIFIEST
1204 bâ'ath (1), to fear

TERRIFY
1204 bâ'ath (2), to fear
2865 châthath (1), to
break down
1629 ĕkphŏbĕō (1), to
frighten utterly

TERROR
367 'êymâh (4), fright
928 behâlâh (1), sudden
panic, destruction
1091 ballâhâh (3),
sudden destruction
2283 châgâ' (1), terror
2847 chittâh (1), terror
2851 chittîyth (8), terror
4032 mâgôwr (1), fright
4172 môwrâ' (2), fearful
4288 mᵉchittâh (2), ruin;
consternation
4637 ma'ărâtsâh (1),
terrifying violent power
6343 pachad (2), fear
5401 phŏbŏs (3), alarm,
or fright; reverence

TERRORS
367 'êymâh (3), fright
928 behâlâh (1), sudden
panic, destruction
1091 ballâhâh (6),
sudden destruction
1161 bî'ûwthîym (2),
alarms, startling things
4032 mâgôwr (1), fright
4048 mâgar (1), to yield
up, be thrown
4172 môwrâ' (1), fearful

TERTIUS
5060 Tĕrtiŏs (1), third

TERTULLUS
5061 Tĕrtullŏs (2),
Tertullus

TESTAMENT
1242 diathēkē (11),
contract; devisory will
1248 diakŏnia (2),
attendance, aid, service

TESTATOR
1303 diatithĕmai (2), to
put apart, i.e. dispose

TESTIFIED
5749 'ûwd (7), to protest,
testify; to encompass
6030 'ânâh (3), to
respond, answer
1263 diamarturŏmai (6),
to attest earnestly
3140 marturĕō (6), to
testify; to commend
3142 marturiŏn (1),
something evidential

4303 prŏmarturŏmai (1), to *predict beforehand*

TESTIFIEDST
5749 'ûwd (2), to *protest, testify;* to *encompass*

TESTIFIETH
6030 'ânâh (1), to *respond, answer*
3140 marturĕō (4), to *testify;* to *commend*

TESTIFY
5749 'ûwd (6), to *protest, testify;* to *encompass*
6030 'ânâh (8), to *respond, answer*
1263 diamarturŏmai (4), to *attest earnestly*
3140 marturĕō (8), to *testify;* to *commend*
3143 marturŏmai (2), to *be witness,* i.e. to *obtest*
4828 summarturĕō (1), to *testify jointly*

TESTIFYING
1263 diamarturŏmai (1), to *attest earnestly*
1957 ĕpimarturĕō (1), to *corroborate*
3140 marturĕō (1), to *testify;* to *commend*

TESTIMONIES
5713 'êdâh (21), *testimony*
5715 'êdûwth (15), *testimony*

TESTIMONY
5713 'êdâh (1), *testimony*
5715 'êdûwth (40), *testimony*
8584 tᵉ'ûwdâh (3), *attestation, precept*
3140 marturĕō (3), to *testify;* to *commend*
3141 marturia (14), *evidence given*
3142 marturiŏn (15), *something evidential*

TETRARCH
5075 tĕtrarchĕō (3), to *be a tetrarch*
5076 tĕtrarchēs (4), *ruler of a fourth* part

THADDAEUS
2280 Thaddaiŏs (2), *Thaddæus*

THAHASH
8477 Tachash (1), (poss.) *antelope*

THAMAH
8547 Temach (1), *Temach*

THAMAR
2283 Thamar (1), *palm*

THANK
2192+5485 zᵉ'êyr (Ch.) (3), *small, little*
3029 yᵉdâ' (Ch.) (1), to *praise*
3034 yâdâh (4), to *throw;* to *revere or worship*
8426 tôwdâh (3), *thanks*
1843 ĕxŏmŏlŏgĕō (2), to *acknowledge*
2168 ĕucharistĕō (11), to *express gratitude*

5485 charis (3), *gratitude; benefit given*

THANKED
1288 bârak (1), to *bless*
2168 ĕucharistĕō (1), to *express gratitude*
5485 charis (1), *gratitude; benefit given*

THANKFUL
3034 yâdâh (1), to *throw;* to *revere or worship*
2168 ĕucharistĕō (1), to *express gratitude*
2170 ĕucharistŏs (1), *grateful, thankful*

THANKFULNESS
2169 ĕucharistia (1), *gratitude*

THANKING
3034 yâdâh (1), to *throw;* to *revere or worship*

THANKS
3029 yᵉdâ' (Ch.) (1), to *praise*
3034 yâdâh (32), to *throw;* to *revere, worship*
8426 tôwdâh (3), *thanks*
437 anthŏmŏlŏgĕŏmai (1), to *give thanks*
2168 ĕucharistĕō (26), to *express gratitude*
2169 ĕucharistia (5), *gratitude*
3670 hŏmŏlŏgĕō (1), to *acknowledge, agree*
5485 charis (4), *gratitude; benefit given*

THANKSGIVING
1960 huyᵉdâh (1), *choir*
3034 yâdâh (2), to *throw;* to *revere or worship*
8426 tôwdâh (16), *thanks*
2169 ĕucharistia (8), *gratitude; grateful*

THANKSGIVINGS
8426 tôwdâh (1), *thanks*
2169 ĕucharistia (1), *gratitude; grateful*

THANKWORTHY
5485 charis (1), *gratitude; benefit given*

THARA
2291 Thara (1), *Thara*

THARSHISH
8659 Tarshîysh (4), *merchant vessel*

THEATRE
2302 thĕatrŏn (2), *audience-room; show*

THEBEZ
8405 Têbêts (3), *whiteness*

THEFT
1591 gᵉnêbâh (2), *something stolen*

THEFTS
2804 Klaudiŏs (1), *Claudius*
2829 klŏpē (2), *theft*

THELASAR
8515 Tᵉla'ssar (1), *Telassar*

THEOPHILUS
2321 Thĕŏphilŏs (2), *friend of God*

THERE
2008 hênnâh (1), *from here; from there*
8033 shâm (440), *there*
8536 tâm (Ch.) (2), *there*
847 autŏu (3), *in this*
1563 ĕkĕi (98), *there*
1564 ĕkĕithĕn (1), *from there*
1566 ĕkĕisĕ (2), *there*
1759 ĕnthadĕ (1), *here*
1927 ĕpidēmĕō (1), to *make oneself at home*
5602 hŏdĕ (1), *here*

THEREABOUT
4012+5127 pĕri (1), *about*

THEREAT
1223+846 dia (1), *through, by means of*

THEREBY
2004 hên (2), *they*
5921 'al (2), *above, over*

THEREFORE
1571 gam (5), *also; even*
2006 hên (Ch.) (2), *lo; therefore, unless*
2063 zô'th (1), *this*
3588 kîy (2), *for, that*
3651 kên (170), *just; right, correct*
235 alla (3), *but, yet*
686 ara (6), *therefore*
1063 gar (1), *for, indeed*
1160 dapanē (1), *expense, cost*
1211 dē (1), *therefore*
1352 diŏ (9), *therefore*
1360 diŏti (1), *inasmuch as*
2532 kai (1), *and; or*
3747 ŏstĕŏn (1), *bone*
3757 hŏu (1), *at which*
3767 ŏun (255), *certainly*
5105 tŏigarŏun (1), *then*
5106 tŏinun (3), *then*
5124 tŏutŏ (1), *that thing*
5620 hōstĕ (9), *thus*

THEREIN
413 'êl (2), *to, toward*
1459 gav (Ch.) (1), *middle*
2004 hên (4), *they*
2007 hênnâh (1), *themselves*
4393 mᵉlô' (7), *fulness*
5921 'al (9), *above, over*
7130 qereb (1), *nearest*
8033 shâm (10), *there*
8432 tâvek (3), *center*
5125 tŏutŏis (1), *in these*

THEREINTO
1519+846 ĕis (1), *to*

THEREOF
8033 shâm (1), *there*
846 autŏs (26), *he, she, it*

THEREON
5921 'al (48), *above, over*
846 autŏs (2), *he, she, it*
1911 ĕpiballō (1), to *throw upon*
1913 ĕpibibazō (1), to *cause to mount*
1924 ĕpigraphō (1), to *inscribe, write upon*

1945 ĕpikĕimai (1), to *rest upon; press upon*
2026 ĕpŏikŏdŏmĕō (1), to *rear up, build up*

THEREOUT
8033 shâm (1), *where, there*

THERETO
5921 'al (8), *above, over*
1928 ĕpidiatassŏmai (1), to *appoint besides*

THEREUNTO
1519+846+5124 ĕis (1), *to*
1519+5124 ĕis (2), *to*
4334 prŏsĕrchŏmai (1), to *come near, visit*

THEREUPON
2026 ĕpŏikŏdŏmĕō (2), to *rear up, build up*

THEREWITH
854 'êth (1), *with; by; at*
5921 'al (2), *above, over*
1722+846 ĕn (2), *in*
1909+5125 ĕpi (1), *on*
5125 tŏutŏis (1), *in these*

THESSALONIANS
2331 Thĕssalŏnikĕus (5), *of Thessalonice*

THESSALONICA
2331 Thĕssalŏnikĕus (1), *of Thessalonice*
2332 Thĕssalŏnikē (5), *Thessalonice*

THEUDAS
2333 Thĕudas (1), *Theudas*

THICK
653 'ăphêlâh (1), *duskiness, darkness*
3515 kâbêd (1), *numerous; severe*
5441 çôbek (1), *thicket*
5645 'âb (2), *thick clouds*
5666 'âbâh (1), to *be dense*
5672 'ăbîy (2), *density*
5687 'âbôth (4), *dense*
5688 'ăbôth (4), *entwined*
6282 'âthâr (1), *incense; worshipper*
7341 rôchab (1), *width*

THICKER
5666 'âbâh (2), to *be dense*

THICKET
5441 çôbek (1), *thicket*
5442 çᵉbâk (1), *thicket*

THICKETS
2337 châvâch (1), *dell or crevice of rock*
5442 çᵉbâk (2), *thicket*
5645 'âb (1), *thick clouds; thicket*

THICKNESS
5672 'ăbîy (2), *density*
7341 rôchab (2), *width*

THIEF
1590 gannâb (13), *stealer*
2812 klĕptēs (12), *stealer*
3027 lēᵢstēs (3), *brigand*

THIEVES
1590 gannâb (4), *stealer*
2812 klĕptēs (4), *stealer*
3027 lēᵢstēs (8), *brigand*

THIGH
3409 yârêk (19), leg or
  shank, flank; side
7785 shôwq (1), lower leg
3382 mêrôs (1), thigh

THIGHS
3409 yârêk (2), leg or
  shank, flank; side
3410 yarkâ' (Ch.) (1),
  thigh

THIMNATHAH
8553 Timnâh (1), portion

THIN
1809 dâlal (1), to
  slacken, dangle
1851 daq (5), thin
4174 môwrâd (1),
  descent, slope
7534 raq (1), emaciated

THING
562 'ômer (1), something
  said
1697 dâbâr (182), thing
3627 kᵉlîy (11), thing
3651 kên (2), just; right
3972 mᵉ'ûwmâh (3),
  something; anything
4399 mᵉlâ'kâh (2), work;
  property
4406 millâh (Ch.) (9),
  word, command
4859 mashshâ'âh (1),
  secured loan
5315 nephesh (2), life;
  breath; soul; wind
1520 hêis (1), one
3056 lŏgŏs (2), word,
  matter, thing
4110 plasma (1), molded
4229 pragma (2), matter
4487 rhêma (1), matter
5313 hupsōma (1), barrier

THINGS
1697 dâbâr (47), thing
4406 millâh (Ch.) (1),
  word or subject
18 agathŏs (1), good
846 autŏs (1), he, she, it
3056 lŏgŏs (3), thing
4229 pragma (4), matter
4487 rhêma (2), thing
5023 tauta (1), these

THINK
559 'âmar (3), to say
995 bîyn (1), to
  understand; discern
1819 dâmâh (1), to
  consider, think
2142 zâkar (3), to
  remember; to mention
2803 châshab (6), to
  think, regard; to value
5452 çᵉbar (Ch.) (1), to
  bear in mind, i.e. hope
5869 'ayin (1), eye; sight
6245 'âshath (1), to be
  sleek; to excogitate
1380 dŏkĕō (22), to think
1760 ĕnthumĕŏmai (1),
  ponder, reflect on
2233 hēgĕŏmai (2), to
  deem, i.e. consider
3049 lŏgizŏmai (7), to
  credit; to think, regard
3539 nŏiĕō (1), to
  exercise the mind

3543 nŏmizō (4), to deem
  or regard
3633 ŏiŏmai (1), to
  imagine, opine
5252 hupĕrphrŏnĕō (1),
  to esteem oneself
5282 hupŏnŏĕō (1), to
  think; to expect
5316 phainō (1), to
  lighten (shine)
5426 phrŏnĕō (4), to be
  mentally disposed

THINKEST
2803 châshab (1), to
  think, regard; to value
5869 'ayin (2), eye; sight
1380 dŏkĕō (4), to think
3049 lŏgizŏmai (1), to
  think, regard
5426 phrŏnĕō (1), to be
  mentally disposed

THINKETH
2803 châshab (1), to
  think, regard; to value
7200 râ'âh (1), to see
8176 shâ'ar (3), to
  estimate
1380 dŏkĕō (2), to think
3049 lŏgizŏmai (1), to
  think, regard

THINKING
559 'âmar (1), to say
1931+1961 hûw' (1), this

THIRD
7969 shâlôwsh (9), three;
  third; thrice
7992 shᵉlîyshîy (104),
  third
8027 shâlash (2), to be
  triplicate
8029 shillêsh (5), great
  grandchild
8523 tᵉlîythay (Ch.) (2),
  third
8531 tᵉlath (Ch.) (3),
  tertiary, i.e. third rank
5152 tristĕgŏn (1), third
  story place
5154 tritŏs (56), third
  part; third time, thirdly

THIRDLY
5154 tritŏs (1), third part

THIRST
6770 tsâmê' (2), to thirst
6771 tsâmê' (1), thirsty
6772 tsâmâ' (16), thirst
6773 tsim'âh (1), thirst
1372 dipsaō (10), to thirst
1373 dipsŏs (1), thirst

THIRSTED
6770 tsâmê' (2), to thirst

THIRSTETH
6770 tsâmê' (2), to thirst
6771 tsâmê' (1), thirsty

THIRSTY
6770 tsâmê' (2), to thirst
6771 tsâmê' (7), thirsty
6772 tsâmâ' (1), thirst
6774 tsimmâ'ôwn (1),
  desert
1372 dipsaō (3), to thirst

THIRTEEN
7969 shâlôwsh (2), three
7969+6240 shâlôwsh (13),
  three; third; thrice

THIRTEENTH
7969+6240 shâlôwsh (11),
  three; third; thrice

THIRTIETH
7970 shᵉlôwshîym (9),
  thirty; thirtieth

THIRTY
7970 shᵉlôwshîym (161),
  thirty; thirtieth
8533 tᵉlâthîyn (Ch.) (2),
  thirty
5144 triakŏnta (9), thirty

THIRTYFOLD
5144 triakŏnta (2), thirty

THISTLE
1863 dardar (1), thorn
2336 chôwach (4), thorn

THISTLES
1863 dardar (1), thorn
2336 chôwach (1), thorn
5146 tribŏlŏs (1), thorny
  caltrop plant

THITHER
1988 hălôm (1), hither
2008 hênnâh (3), from
  here; from there
5704 'ad (1), until
8033 shâm (63), there
1563 ĕkĕi (8), thither
1904 ĕpĕrchŏmai (1), to
  supervene
3854 paraginŏmai (1), to
  arrive; to appear
4370 prŏstrĕchō (1), to
  hasten by running

THITHERWARD
2008 hênnâh (1), from
  here; from there
8033 shâm (1), there
1563 ĕkĕi (1), thither

THOMAS
2381 Thōmas (12), twin

THONGS
2438 himas (1), strap

THORN
2336 chôwach (2), thorn
4534 mᵉçûwkâh (1),
  thorn-hedge
5285 na'ătsûwts (1),
  brier; thicket
6975 qôwts (2), thorns
4647 skŏlŏps (1), thorn

THORNS
329 'âṭâd (1), buckthorn
2312 chêdeq (1), prickly
2336 chôwach (3), thorn
5285 na'ătsûwts (1),
  brier; thicket
5518 çîyr (4), thorn; hook
5544 çillôwn (1), prickle
6791 tsên (2), thorn
6975 qôwts (12), thorns
7063 qimmâshôwn (1),
  prickly plant
7898 shayith (7), wild
  growth of briers
173 akantha (14), thorn
174 akanthinŏs (2),
  thorny

THOROUGHLY
3190 yâṭab (1), to be,
  make well
7495 râphâ' (1), to cure

THOUGHT
559 'âmar (9), to say

1672 dâ'ag (1), be
  anxious, be afraid
1696 dâbar (1), to speak
1697 dâbâr (1), word;
  matter; thing
1819 dâmâh (4), to think
2154 zimmâh (1), plan
2161 zâmam (5), to plan
2803 châshab (10), to
  think, regard; to value
4093 maddâ' (1),
  intelligence
4209 mᵉzimmâh (1), plan
4284 machăshâbâh (1),
  contrivance; plan
5869 'ayin (3), eye; sight
6246 'ăshîth (Ch.) (1), to
  purpose, plan
6248 'ashtûwth (1),
  cogitation, thinking
6419 pâlal (1), to
  intercede, pray
7454 rêa' (1), thought
7807 shach (1), sunk
8232+6925 shᵉphar (Ch.)
  (1), to be beautiful
1260 dialŏgizŏmai (1), to
  deliberate
1261 dialŏgismŏs (1),
  consideration; debate
1380 dŏkĕō (5), to think
1760 ĕnthumĕŏmai (2),
  ponder, reflect on
1911 ĕpiballō (1), to
  throw upon
1963 ĕpinŏia (1),
  thought, intention
2106 ĕudŏkĕō (1), to
  think well, i.e. approve
2233 hēgĕŏmai (2), to
  deem, i.e. consider
2919 krinō (1), to decide;
  to try, condemn, punish
3049 lŏgizŏmai (1), to
  credit; to think, regard
3309 mĕrimnaō (11), to
  be anxious about
3540 nŏēma (1),
  perception, i.e. purpose
3543 nŏmizō (1), to deem
4305 prŏmĕrimnaō (1), to
  care in advance

THOUGHTEST
1819 dâmâh (1), to
  consider, think

THOUGHTS
2031 harhôr (Ch.) (1),
  mental conception
2711 chêqeq (1),
  enactment, resolution
4180 môwrâsh (1),
  possession
4209 mᵉzimmâh (2),
  plan; sagacity
4284 machăshâbâh (24),
  contrivance; plan
5587 çâ'îph (2), divided
  in mind; sentiment
5588 çê'êph (1), divided
  in mind; skeptic
6250 'eshtônâh (1),
  thinking
7454 rêa' (1), thought
7476 ra'yôwn (Ch.) (5),
  mental conception
8312 sar'aph (2),
  cogitation
1261 dialŏgismŏs (8),
  consideration; debate

1270 dianŏēma (1), *sentiment, thought*
1761 ĕnthumēsis (3), *deliberation; idea*
3053 lŏgismŏs (1), *reasoning; conscience*

THOUSAND
505 'eleph (436), *thousand*
506 'ălaph (Ch.) (3), *thousand*
7233 r^{e}bâbâh (4), *myriad*
7239 ribbôw (5), *myriad*
7239+505 ribbôw (1), *myriad, large number*
7240 ribbôw (Ch.) (1), *myriad, large number*
1367 dischiliŏi (1), *two thousand*
2035 hĕptakischiliŏi (1), *seven times a thousand*
3461 murias (3), *ten thousand*
3463 muriŏi (3), *ten thousand*
4000 pĕntakischiliŏi (6), *five times a thousand*
5070 tĕtrakischiliŏi (5), *four times a thousand*
5153 trischiliŏi (1), *three times a thousand*
5505 chilias (21), *one thousand*
5507 chiliŏi (11), *thousand*

THOUSANDS
503 'ălaph (1), *increase by thousands*
505 'eleph (46), *thousand*
506 'ălaph (Ch.) (1), *thousand*
7232 râbab (1), *to shoot*
7233 r^{e}bâbâh (7), *myriad*
7239 ribbôw (1), *myriad*
3461 murias (2), *ten thousand*
5505 chilias (1), *one thousand*

THREAD
2339 chûwṭ (4), *string*
6616 pâthîyl (1), *twine*

THREATEN
546 apĕilĕō (1), *to menace; to forbid*

THREATENED
546 apĕilĕō (1), *to menace; to forbid*
4324 prŏsapĕilĕō (1), *to menace additionally*

THREATENING
547 apĕilē (1), *menace*

THREATENINGS
547 apĕilē (2), *menace*

THREE
7969 shâlôwsh (377), *three; third; thrice*
7991 shâlîysh (1), *triangle, three*
7992 sh^{e}lîyshîy (4), *third*
8027 shâlash (6), *to be triplicate*
8032 shilshôwm (1), *day before yesterday*
8532 t^{e}lâth (Ch.) (10), *three or third*
5140 trĕis (69), *three*

5145 triakŏsiŏi (2), *three hundred*
5148 triĕtia (1), *three years' period*
5150 trimēnŏn (1), *three months' space*
5151 tris (1), *three times*
5153 trischiliŏi (1), *three times a thousand*

THREEFOLD
8027 shâlash (1), *to be triplicate*

THREESCORE
7239 ribbôw (1), *myriad*
7657 shib'îym (38), *seventy*
8346 shishshîym (42), *sixty*
8361 shittîyn (Ch.) (4), *sixty*
1440 hĕbdŏmēkŏnta (3), *seventy*
1835 hĕxēkŏnta (4), *sixty*
5516 chi xi stigma (1), 666

THRESH
1758 dûwsh (3), *to thresh*
1869 dârak (1), *to tread*

THRESHED
1758 dûwsh (2), *to thresh*
2251 châbaṭ (1), *to thresh*

THRESHETH
248 alŏaō (1), *to tread*

THRESHING
1758 dûwsh (3), *to thresh*
1786 dayîsh (1), *threshing-time*
2742 chârûwts (2), *threshing-sledge*
4098 m^{e}dushshâh (1), *down-trodden people*
4173 môwrag (3), *threshing sledge*

THRESHINGFLOOR
1637 gôren (17), *open area*

THRESHINGFLOORS
147 'iddar (Ch.) (1), *threshing-floor*
1637 gôren (1), *open area*

THRESHINGPLACE
1637 gôren (1), *open area*

THRESHOLD
4670 miphtân (8), *sill*
5592 çaph (6), *dish*

THRESHOLDS
624 'âçûph (1), *collection, stores*
5592 çaph (2), *dish*

THREW
5422 nâthats (1), *to tear down*
5619 çâqal (1), *to throw large stones*
8058 shâmaṭ (1), *to jostle*
906 ballō (2), *to throw*
4952 susparassō (1), *to convulse violently*

THREWEST
7993 shâlak (1), *to throw*

THRICE
7969+6471 shâlôwsh (4), *three; third; thrice*
5151 tris (11), *three times*

THROAT
1627 gârôwn (4), *throat*
3930 lôa' (1), *throat*
2995 larugx (1), *throat*
4155 pnigō (1), *to throttle*

THRONE
3678 kiççê' (120), *throne*
3764 korçê' (Ch.) (2), *throne*
968 bēma (1), *tribunal platform; judging place*
2362 thrŏnŏs (50), *throne*

THRONES
3678 kiççê' (4), *throne*
3764 korçê' (Ch.) (1), *throne*
2362 thrŏnŏs (4), *throne*

THRONG
2346 thlibō (1), *to crowd*
4912 sunĕchō (1), *to hold together*

THRONGED
4846 sumpnigō (1), *to drown; to crowd*
4918 sunthlibō (1), *to compress, i.e. to crowd*

THRONGING
4918 sunthlibō (1), *to compress, i.e. to crowd*

THROUGH
413 'êl (2), *to, toward*
1119 b^{e}môw (1), *in, with*
1157 b^e'ad (5), *through*
1234 bâqa' (3), *to cleave*
1811 dâlaph (1), *to drip*
1856 dâqar (2), *to pierce*
1870 derek (1), *road*
2864 châthar (1), *to break or dig into*
2944 ṭâ'an (1), *to stab*
3027 yâd (1), *hand; power*
4480 min (2), *from, out of*
5674 'âbar (10), *to cross*
5921 'al (5), *over, upon*
6440 pânîym (1), *face*
7130 qereb (2), *nearest part, i.e. the center*
7751 shûwṭ (1), *to travel*
8432 tâvek (7), *center*
303 ana (1), *through*
1223 dia (93), *through*
1224 diabainō (1), *to pass by, over, across*
1279 diapŏrĕuŏmai (1), *to travel through*
1330 diĕrchŏmai (8), *to traverse, travel through*
1350 diktuŏn (1), *drag net*
1358 diŏrussō (3), *to penetrate burglariously*
1537 ĕk (3), *out, out of*
1653 ĕlĕĕō (1), *to give out compassion*
1722 ĕn (37), *in; during*
1909 ĕpi (2), *on, upon*
2569 kalŏpŏiĕō (1), *to do well*
2596 kata (4), *down; according to*
2700 katatŏxĕuō (1), *to shoot down*
4044 pĕripĕirō (1), *to penetrate entirely*
4063 pĕritrĕchō (1), *traverse, run about*

THROUGHLY
7235 râbâh (1), *to increase*
1245 diakatharizō (2), *to cleanse perfectly*
1722+3956 ĕn (1), *in*
1822 ĕxartizō (1), *to finish out; to equip fully*

THROUGHOUT
5921 'al (2), *above, over*
1223 dia (3), *through*
1330 diĕrchŏmai (2), *to traverse, travel through*
1519 ĕis (6), *to or into*
1722 ĕn (5), *in; during*
1909 ĕpi (2), *on, upon*
2596 kata (8), *down; according to*

THROW
2040 hâraç (6), *to pull down; break, destroy*
5307 nâphal (1), *to fall*
5422 nâthats (1), *to tear down*
8058 shâmaṭ (1), *to jostle*

THROWING
3027 yâd (1), *hand; power*

THROWN
2040 hâraç (7), *to pull down; break, destroy*
5422 nâthats (3), *to tear down*
7411 râmâh (1), *to hurl*
7993 shâlak (1), *to throw*
906 ballō (1), *to throw*
2647 kataluō (3), *to demolish; to halt*
4496 rhiptō (1), *to toss*

THRUST
926 bâhal (1), *to be, make agitated; hasten*
1333 bâthaq (1), *to cut in pieces, hack up*
1644 gârash (6), *to drive out; to expatriate*
1760 dâchâh (1), *to push down; to totter*
1766 dâchaq (1), *to oppress*
1856 dâqar (8), *to stab*
1920 hâdaph (4), *to push away or down; drive out*
2115 zûwr (1), *to press*
2944 ṭâ'an (1), *to stab*
3238 yânâh (1), *to suppress; to maltreat*
3905 lâchats (1), *to press*
5074 nâdad (1), *to rove, flee; to drive away*
5080 nâdach (2), *to push off, scattered*
5365 nâqar (1), *to bore*
5414 nâthan (1), *to give*
8628 tâqa' (2), *to clatter, slap, drive, clasp*
683 apōthĕŏmai (2), *push off; to reject*
906 ballō (5), *to throw*
1544 ĕkballō (3), *to throw out*
1856 ĕxōthĕō (1), *to expel; to propel*
1877 ĕpanagō (1), *to put out to sea; to return*
2601 katabibazō (1), *cause to bring down*

THRUSTETH
2700 katatŏxĕuō (1), to shoot down
3992 pĕmpō (2), to send

THRUSTETH
5086 nâdaph (1), to disperse, be windblown

THUMB
931 bôhen (6), thumb

THUMBS
931 bôhen (1), thumb
931+3027 bôhen (2), thumb; big toe

THUMMIM
8550 Tummîym (5), perfections

THUNDER
6963 qôwl (7), sound
7481 râ'am (2), to crash thunder; to irritate
7482 ra'am (6), peal of thunder
7483 ra'mâh (1), horse's mane
1027 brŏntē (3), thunder

THUNDERBOLTS
7565 resheph (1), flame

THUNDERED
7481 râ'am (3), to crash thunder; to irritate
1027+1096 brŏntē (1), thunder

THUNDERETH
7481 râ'am (3), to crash thunder; to irritate

THUNDERINGS
6963 qôwl (2), sound
1027 brŏntē (4), thunder

THUNDERS
6963 qôwl (3), sound
1027 brŏntē (4), thunder

THYATIRA
2363 Thuatĕira (4), Thyatira

THYINE
2367 thuïnŏs (1), of citron

TIBERIAS
5085 Tibĕrias (3), Tiberius

TIBERIUS
5086 Tibĕriŏs (1), (poss.) pertaining to the river Tiberis or Tiber

TIBHATH
2880 Ṭibchath (1), slaughter

TIBNI
8402 Tibnîy (3), strawy

TIDAL
8413 Tid'âl (2), fearfulness

TIDINGS
1309 bᵉsôwrâh (6), glad tidings, good news
1319 bâsar (16), to announce (good news)
1697 dâbâr (4), word
8052 shᵉmûw'âh (8), announcement
8088 shêma' (2), something heard
2097 ĕuaggĕlizō (6), to announce good news
3056 lŏgŏs (1), word
5334 phasis (1), news

TIE
631 'âçar (1), to fasten
6029 'ânad (1), to bind

TIED
631 'âçar (3), to fasten
5414 nâthan (1), to give
1210 dĕō (4), to bind

TIGLATH-PILESER
8407 Tiglath Pil'eçer (3), Tiglath-Pileser

TIKVAH
8616 Tiqvâh (2), hope

TIKVATH
8616 Tiqvâh (1), hope

TILE
3843 lᵉbênâh (1), brick

TILGATH-PILNESER
8407 Tiglath Pil'eçer (3), Tiglath-Pileser

TILING
2766 kĕramŏs (1), clay roof tile

TILL
5647 'âbad (4), to work
5704 'ad (90), until
5705 'ad (Ch.) (1), until
6440 pânîym (1), face; front
891 achri (5), until, up to
1519 ĕis (1), to or into
2193 hĕōs (41), until
3360 mĕchri (2), until

TILLAGE
5215 nîyr (1), plowed land
5656 'ăbôdâh (2), work

TILLED
5647 'âbad (2), to work

TILLER
5647 'âbad (1), to work

TILLEST
5647 'âbad (1), to work

TILLETH
5647 'âbad (2), to work

TILON
8436 Tûwlôn (1), suspension

TIMAEUS
5090 Timaiŏs (1), (poss.) foul; impure

TIMBER
636 'â' (Ch.) (3), wood
6086 'êts (23), wood

TIMBREL
8596 tôph (5), tambourine

TIMBRELS
8596 tôph (4), tambourine
8608 tâphaph (1), to drum on a tambourine

TIME
116 'ĕdayin (Ch.) (1), then
227 'âz (5), at that time
268 'âchôwr (1), behind, backward; west
570 'emesh (1), yesterday evening
1767 day (1), enough
2165 zᵉmân (2), time
2166 zᵉmân (Ch.) (6), time, appointed
3117 yôwm (55), day
3118 yôwm (Ch.) (2), day

TIMES
2165 zᵉmân (1), time
2166 zᵉmân (Ch.) (3), time, appointed
3027 yâd (1), hand; power
3117 yôwm (5), day; time
4150 môw'êd (1), assembly
4151 môw'âd (1), troop
4489 môneh (2), instance
5732 'iddân (Ch.) (6), set time; year
6256 'êth (22), time
6471 pa'am (42), time
8543 tᵉmôwl (2), yesterday
1074 gĕnĕa (1), age
1441 hĕbdŏmēkŏntakis (1), seventy times
2034 hĕptakis (4), seven times
2540 kairŏs (8), set time
3999 pĕntakis (1), five times
4218 pŏtĕ (3), ever
5151 tris (1), three times
5550 chrŏnŏs (8), time

TIMNA
8555 Timnâ' (4), restraint

TIMNAH
8553 Timnâh (3), portion
8555 Timnâ' (2), restraint

TIMNATH
8553 Timnâh (8), portion

TIMNATH-HERES
8556 Timnath Chereç (1), portion of (the) sun

TIMNATH-SERAH
8556 Timnath Chereç (2), portion of (the) sun

TIMNITE
8554 Timnîy (1), Timnite

TIMON
5096 Timōn (1), valuable

TIMOTHEOUS
5095 Timŏthĕŏs (1), dear to God

TIMOTHEUS
5095 Timŏthĕŏs (18), dear to God

TIMOTHY
5095 Timŏthĕŏs (9), dear to God

TIN
913 bᵉdîyl (5), tin

TINGLE
6750 tsâlal (3), to tinkle

TINKLING
5913 'âkaç (1), to put on anklets
214 alalazō (1), to clang

TIP
8571 tᵉnûwk (8), pinnacle, i.e. extremity
206 akrŏn (1), extremity

TIPHSAH
8607 Tiphçach (2), ford

TIRAS
8493 Tîyrᵉyâ' (2), fearful

TIRATHITES
8654 Tir'âthîy (1), gate

TIRE
6287 pᵉ'êr (1), head-dress

TIRED
3190 yâṭab (1), to be, make well; successful

TIRES
6287 pᵉ'êr (1), fancy head-dress
7720 sahărôn (1), round pendant or crescent

TIRHAKAH
8640 Tirhâqâh (2), Tirhakah

TIRHANAH
8647 Tirchănâh (1), Tirchanah

TIRIA
8493 Tîyrᵉyâ' (1), fearful

TIRSHATHA
8660 Tirshâthâ' (5), deputy or governor

TIRZAH
8656 Tirtsâh (18), delightsomeness

TISHBITE
8664 Tishbîy (6), Tishbite

TITHE
4643 ma'ăsêr (11), tithe
6237 'âsar (1), to tithe

T

586 apŏdĕkatŏō (2), to *tithe*

TITHES
4643 ma'ăsêr (16), *tithe*
6237 'âsar (2), to *tithe*
586 apŏdĕkatŏō (2), to *tithe, give a tenth*
1181 *dĕkatē* (1), *tithe*
1183 *dĕkatŏō* (3), to *give* or *take a tenth*

TITHING
4643 ma'ăsêr (1), *tithe*
6237 'âsar (1), to *tithe*

TITLE
6725 tsîyûwn (1), *guiding pillar, monument*
5102 *titlŏs* (2), *title*

TITTLE
2762 kĕraia (2), *horn-like*

TITUS
5103 Tĭtŏs (15), *Titus*

TIZITE
8491 Tîytsîy (1), *Titsite*

TOAH
8430 Tôwach (1), *humble*

TOB
2897 Tôwb (2), *good*

TOB-ADONIJAH
2899 Tôwb Ădônîyâhûw (1), *pleasing* (to) *Adonijah*

TOBIAH
2900 Tôwbîyâh (15), *goodness of Jehovah*

TOBIJAH
2900 Tôwbîyâh (3), *goodness of Jehovah*

TOCHEN
8507 Tôken (1), *quantity*

TOE
931 bôhen (6), *big toe*

TOES
676 'etsba' (2), *finger; toe*
677 'etsba' (Ch.) (2), *toe*
931 bôhen (1), *big toe*
931+7272 bôhen (2), *thumb; big toe*

TOGARMAH
8425 Tôwgarmâh (4), *Togarmah*

TOGETHER
259 'echâd (5), *first*
2298 chad (Ch.) (1), *one*
3162 yachad (125), *unitedly*
6776 tsemed (1), *yoke*
240 allēlōn (1), *one another*
260 hama (3), *together*
346 anakĕphalaiŏmai (1), to *sum up*
1794 *ĕntulissō* (1), *wind up in, enwrap*
1865 *ĕpathrŏizō* (1), to *accumulate, increase*
1996 *ĕpisunagō* (6), to *collect upon*
1997 *ĕpisunagōgē* (2), *meeting, gathering*
1998 *ĕpisuntrĕchō* (1), to *hasten together upon*
2086 *hĕtĕrŏzugĕō* (1), to *associate discordantly*

2675 katartizō (1), to *prepare, equip*
3674 *hŏmŏu* (3), *at the same place or time*
4776 *sugkathizō* (2), to *give, take a seat with*
4779 *sugkalĕō* (8), to *convoke, call together*
4786 *sugkĕrannumi* (1), to *combine, assimilate*
4789 *sugklērŏnŏmŏs* (1), *participant in common*
4794 *sugkuptō* (1), to *be completely overcome*
4801 *suzĕugnumi* (2), to *conjoin* in marriage
4802 *suzētĕō* (1), to *discuss, controvert*
4806 *suzŏŏpŏiĕō* (2), to *reanimate conjointly*
4811 *sukŏphantĕō* (1), to *defraud*, i.e. *exact*
4816 *sullĕgō* (1), to *gather*
4822 *sumbibazō* (2), to *drive together, unite*
4831 *summimētēs* (1), *co-imitator*
4836 *sumparaginŏmai* (1), to *convene*
4837 *sumparakalĕō* (1), to *console jointly*
4851 *sumphĕrō* (1), to *collect; to conduce*
4853 *sumphulĕtēs* (1), *native of the same country*
4854 *sumphutŏs* (1), *closely united* to
4856 *sumphōnĕō* (1), to *be harmonious*
4863 *sunagō* (31), to *gather together*
4865 *sunagōnizŏmai* (1), to *struggle with*
4866 *sunathlĕō* (1), to *wrestle with*
4867 *sunathrŏizō* (3), to *convene*
4873 *sunanakĕimai* (1), to *recline with*
4883 *sunarmŏlŏgĕō* (2), to *render close-jointed*
4886 *sundĕsmŏs* (1), *ligament; uniting*
4888 *sundŏxazō* (1), to *share glory with*
4890 *sundrŏmē* (1), (riotous) *concourse*
4891 *sunĕgĕirō* (1), to *raise up with*
4896 *sunĕimi* (1), to *assemble, gather*
4897 *sunĕisĕrchŏmai* (1), to *enter with*
4899 *sunĕklĕktŏs* (1), *chosen together with*
4903 *sunĕrgĕō* (2), to *be a fellow-worker*
4904 *sunĕrgŏs* (1), *fellow-worker*
4905 *sunĕrchŏmai* (16), to *gather together*
4911 *sunĕphistēmi* (1), to *resist or assault jointly*
4925 *sunŏikŏdŏmĕō* (1), to *construct*
4943 *sunupŏurgĕō* (1), to *assist, join to help*

4944 sunōdinō (1), to *sympathize*

TOHU
8459 Tôchûw (1), *abasement*

TOI
8583 Tô'ûw (3), *error*

TOIL
5999 'âmâl (1), *effort*
6093 'itstsâbôwn (1), *labor or pain*
2872 kŏpiaō (2), to *feel fatigue; to work hard*

TOILED
2872 kŏpiaō (1), to *feel fatigue; to work hard*

TOILING
928 basanizō (1), to *torture, torment*

TOKEN
226 'ôwth (10), *sign*
1730 *ĕndĕigma* (1), *plain indication*
1732 *ĕndĕixis* (1), *indication*
4592 *sēmĕiŏn* (1), *sign*
4953 *sussēmŏn* (1), *sign in common*

TOKENS
226 'ôwth (4), *signal, sign*

TOLA
8439 Tôwlâ' (6), *worm*

TOLAD
8434 Tôwlâd (1), *posterity*

TOLAITES
8440 Tôwlâ'îy (1), *Tolaite*

TOLD
559 'âmar (13), to *say*
560 'ămar (Ch.) (5), to *say*
1540 gâlâh (2), to *reveal*
1696 dâbar (15), to *speak*
4487 mânâh (1), to *allot; to enumerate or enroll*
5046 nâgad (152), to *announce*
5608 çâphar (27), to *recount an event*
8085 shâma' (2), to *hear*
8505 tâkan (1), to *balance*, i.e. *measure*
312 anaggĕllō (4), to *announce, report*
513 axinē (3), *axe*
518 apaggĕllō (17), to *announce, proclaim*
1285 diasaphĕō (1), to *declare, tell*
1334 diĕgĕŏmai (2), to *relate fully, describe*
1834 *ĕxēgĕŏmai* (1), to *tell, relate again*
2036 *ĕpō* (13), to *speak*
2046 *ĕrĕō* (1), to *utter*
2980 lalĕō (10), to *talk*
3004 lĕgō (4), to *say*
3377 mēnuō (1), to *report*
4277 prŏĕpō (1), to *say already, to predict*
4280 prŏĕrĕō (2), to *say already, predict*
4302 prŏlĕgō (1), to *predict, forewarn*

TOLERABLE
414 anĕktŏtĕrŏs (6), *more endurable*

TOLL
4061 middâh (Ch.) (3), *tribute, tax money*

TOMB
1430 gâdîysh (1), *stack*
3419 mnēmĕiŏn (2), *place of interment*

TOMBS
3418 mnēma (3), *monument*
3419 mnēmĕiŏn (3), *place of interment*
5028 taphŏs (1), *grave*

TONGS
4457 melqâch (5), *tongs*
4621 ma'ătsâd (1), *axe*

TONGUE
762 'Ărâmîyth (2), *in Aramean*
2013 hâçâh (1), to *hush*
2790 chârash (4), to *be silent; to be deaf*
3956 lâshôwn (89), *tongue; tongue-shaped*
1100 glōssa (24), *tongue*
1258 dialĕktŏs (5), *language*
1447 Hĕbraïsti (3), *in the Jewish language*

TONGUES
3956 lâshôwn (9), *tongue*
1100 glōssa (26), *tongue*
2084 hĕtĕrŏglōssŏs (1), *foreigner*

TOOK
270 'âchaz (6), to *seize*
622 'âçaph (2), to *gather*
680 'âtsal (1), to *select*
935 bôw' (1), to *go, come*
1197 bâ'ar (1), to *be brutish, be senseless*
1491 gâzâh (1), to *cut off*
1497 gâzal (1), to *rob*
1518 gîyach (1), to *issue forth; to burst forth*
2388 châzaq (4), to *fasten upon; to seize*
3318 yâtsâ' (1), to *bring out*
3381 yârad (4), to *descend*
3920 lâkad (43), to *catch*
3947 lâqach (359), to *take*
4185 mûwsh (1), to *withdraw*
5265 nâça' (2), to *start*
5267 n°çaq (Ch.) (1), to *go up*
5312 n°phaq (Ch.) (2), to *issue forth; to bring out*
5375 nâsâ' (45), to *lift up*
5384 nâsheh (1), *rheumatic or crippled*
5414 nâthan (1), to *give*
5493 çûwr (11), to *turn off*
5674 'âbar (2), to *cross over; to transition*
5709 'ădâ' (Ch.) (1), to *remove*
5927 'âlâh (3), to *ascend*
6901 qâbal (3), to *take*
6902 q°bal (Ch.) (1), to *acquire*
7287 râdâh (1), to *subjugate; to crumble*
7311 rûwm (2), to *be high; to rise or raise*

7673 shâbath (1), *to
repose; to desist*
7760 sûwm (1), *to put*
8610 tâphas (18), *to
manipulate*, i.e. *seize*
142 airō (18), *to take up*
337 anairēō (1), *to take
away*, i.e. *abolish*
353 analambanō (3), *to
take up, bring up*
520 apagō (1), *to take
away*
589 apŏdēmĕō (2), *visit a
foreign land*
618 apŏlambanō (1), *to
receive; be repaid*
643 apŏskĕuazō (1), *to
pack up baggage*
657 apŏtassŏmai (1), *to
say adieu; to renounce*
941 bastazō (1), *to lift*
1011 bŏulĕuō (1), *to
deliberate; to resolve*
1209 dĕchŏmai (2), *to
receive, welcome*
1453 ĕgĕirō (1), *to waken*
1544 ĕkballō (1), *to
throw out*
1562 ĕkduō (2), *to divest*
1723 ĕnagkalizŏmai (1),
take into one's arms
1921 ĕpiginōskō (1), *to
acknowledge*
1949 ĕpilambanŏmai
(12), *to seize*
1959 ĕpimĕlĕŏmai (1), *to
care for*
2021 ĕpichĕirĕō (1), *to
undertake, try*
2192 ĕchō (1), *to have*
2507 kathairĕō (3), *to
lower, or demolish*
2902 kratĕō (11), *to seize*
2983 lambanō (57), *to
take, receive*
3348 mĕtĕchō (1), *to
share or participate*
3830 pandŏchĕus (1),
innkeeper
3880 paralambanō (16),
to associate with
4084 piazō (1), *to seize*
4160 pŏiĕō (1), *to make*
4327 prŏsdĕchŏmai (1),
to receive; to await for
4355 prŏslambanō (5), *to
take along*
4815 sullambanō (3), *to
seize (arrest, capture)*
4823 sumbŏulĕuō (1), *to
recommend, deliberate*
4838 sumparalambanō
(2), *to take along with*
4863 sunagō (3), *to
gather together*

TOOKEST
3947 lâqach (1), *to take*

TOOL
2719 chereb (1), *knife*
3627 kᵉliy (1), *thing*

TOOTH
8127 shên (6), *tooth*
3599 ŏdŏus (1), *tooth*

TOOTH'S
8127 shên (1), *tooth*

TOP
1406 gâg (8), *roof; top*

1634 gerem (1), *bone; self*
5585 çâ'îyph (2), *bough*
6706 tsᵉchîyach (4),
exposed to the sun
6788 tsammereth (3),
foliage
6936 qodqôd (2), *crown*
7218 rô'sh (67), *head*
206 akrŏn (1), *extremity*
509 anōthĕn (3), *from
above; from the first*

TOPAZ
6357 piṭdâh (4), *topaz*
5116 tŏpaziŏn (1), *topaz*

TOPHEL
8603 Tôphel (1),
quagmire

TOPHET
8612 Tôpheth (8), *smiting*
8613 Tophteh (1), *place
of cremation*

TOPHETH
8612 Tôpheth (1), *smiting*

TOPS
1406 gâg (2), *roof; top*
5585 çâ'îyph (1), *bough*
7218 rô'sh (8), *head*

TORCH
3940 lappîyd (1), *torch*

TORCHES
3940 lappîyd (1), *torch*
6393 pᵉlâdâh (1), iron
armature
2985 lampas (1), *torch*

TORMENT
928 basanizō (3), *to
torture, torment*
929 basanismŏs (6),
torture, agony
931 basanŏs (1), *torture*
2851 kŏlasis (1),
infliction, punishment

TORMENTED
928 basanizō (5), *to
torture, torment*
2558 kakŏuchĕō (1), *to
maltreat; to torment*
3600 ŏdunaō (2), *to grieve*

TORMENTORS
930 basanistēs (1),
torturer

TORMENTS
931 basanŏs (2), *torture*

TORN
1497 gâzal (1), *to rob*
2963 ṭâraph (4), *to pluck*
2966 ṭᵉrêphâh (8), *torn
prey*
5478 çûwchâh (1), *filth*
7665 shâbar (2), *to burst*
4682 sparassō (1), *to
convulse* with epilepsy

TORTOISE
6632 tsâb (1), *lizard*

TORTURED
5178 tumpanizō (1), *to
beat* to death

TOSS
1607 gâ'ash (1), *to
agitate violently, shake*
6802 tsᵉnêphâh (1), *ball*

TOSSED
5086 nâdaph (1), *to
disperse, be windblown*

5287 nâ'ar (1), *to tumble*
928 basanizō (1), *to
torture, torment*
2831 kludōnizŏmai (1),
to fluctuate on waves
4494 rhipizō (1), *to be
tossed about*
5492 chĕimazō (1), *to be
battered in a storm*

TOSSINGS
5076 nâdûd (1), *tossing
and rolling* on the bed

TOTTERING
1760 dâchâh (1), *to totter*

TOU
8583 Tô'ûw (2), *error*

TOUCH
5060 nâga' (31), *to strike*
680 haptŏmai (13), *to
touch*
2345 thigganō (2), *to
touch*
4379 prŏspsauō (1), *to
lay a finger on*

TOUCHED
5060 nâga' (24), *to strike*
5401 nâshaq (1), *to touch*
680 haptŏmai (21), *to
touch*
2609 katagō (1), *to lead
down; to moor a vessel*
4834 sumpathĕō (1), *to
commiserate*
5584 psēlaphaō (1), *to
manipulate*

TOUCHETH
5060 nâga' (37), *to strike*
7306 rûwach (1), *to smell*
680 haptŏmai (2), *to
touch*

TOUCHING
413 'êl (3), *to, toward*
5921 'al (1), *against*
1909 ĕpi (2), *on, upon*
2596 kata (3), *down;
according to*
4012 pĕri (11), *about*

TOW
5296 nᵉ'ôreth (2), *tow*
6594 pishtâh (1), *flax*

TOWEL
3012 lĕntiŏn (2), *linen*

TOWER
969 bâchôwn (1), *assayer*
1431 gâdal (1), *to be
great, make great*
4024 Migdôwl (2), *tower*
4026 migdâl (34), *tower*
4692 mâtsôwr (1),
siege-mound; distress
4869 misgâb (3), *refuge*
6076 'ôphel (1), *fortress*
4444 purgŏs (4), *tower*

TOWERS
971 bachîyn (1),
siege-tower
975 bachan (1),
watch-tower
4026 migdâl (13), *tower*
6438 pinnâh (2), *pinnacle*

TOWN
5892 'îyr (3), *city, town*
7023 qîyr (2), *wall*
2968 kōmē (8), *town*

TOWNCLERK
1122 grammatĕus (1),
secretary, scholar

TOWNS
1323 bath (27), *outlying
village*
2333 chavvâh (4), *village*
2691 châtsêr (1), *village*
5892 'îyr (3), *city, town*
6519 pᵉrâzâh (1), *rural*
2968 kōmē (3), town
2969 kōmŏpŏlis (1),
unwalled city

TRACHONITIS
5139 Trachōnitis (1),
rough district

TRADE
582 'ĕnôwsh (2), *man;
person, human*
5503 çâchar (2), *to travel*
2038 ĕrgazŏmai (1), *to
toil*

TRADED
5414 nâthan (4), *to give*
2038 ĕrgazŏmai (1), *to
toil*

TRADING
1281 diapragmatĕuŏmai
(1), *to earn, make gain*

TRADITION
3862 paradŏsis (11),
Jewish *traditional law*

TRADITIONS
3862 paradŏsis (2),
Jewish *traditional law*

TRAFFICK
3667 Kᵉna'an (1),
humiliated
4536 miçchâr (1), *trade*
5503 çâchar (1), *to travel
round; to palpitate*
7404 rᵉkullâh (2),
peddled trade

TRAFFICKERS
3669 Kᵉna'ănîy (1),
Kenaanite; pedlar

TRAIN
2428 chayil (1), *army;
wealth; virtue; valor*
2596 chânak (1), *to
initiate or discipline*
7757 shûwl (1), *skirt*

TRAINED
2593 chânîyk (1), *trained*

TRAITOR
4273 prŏdŏtēs (1),
betraying

TRAITORS
4273 prŏdŏtēs (1),
betraying

TRAMPLE
7429 râmaç (2), *to tread*
2662 katapatĕō (1), *to
trample down; to reject*

TRANCE
1611 ĕkstasis (3),
bewilderment, ecstasy

TRANQUILITY
7963 shᵉlêvâh (Ch.) (1),
safety

TRANSFERRED
3345 mĕtaschēmatizō
(1), *to transfigure*

TRANSFIGURED
3339 mĕtamŏrphŏō (2), to *transform*

TRANSFORMED
3339 mĕtamŏrphŏō (1), to *transform*
3345 mĕtaschēmatizō (2), to *transfigure*

TRANSFORMING
3345 mĕtaschēmatizō (1), to *transfigure*

TRANSGRESS
898 bâgad (1), to *act treacherously*
4603 mâ'al (2), to *act treacherously*
5647 'âbad (1), to *do*
5674 'âbar (4), to *cross*
6586 pâsha' (3), to *break away from authority*
3845 parabainō (2), to *violate a command*
3848 parabatēs (1), *violator, lawbreaker*

TRANSGRESSED
898 bâgad (1), to *act treacherously*
4603 mâ'al (7), to *act treacherously*
5674 'âbar (12), to *cross*
6586 pâsha' (13), to *break from authority*
3928 parĕrchŏmai (1), to *go by; to perish*

TRANSGRESSEST
5674 'âbar (1), to *cross*

TRANSGRESSETH
898 bâgad (1), to *act treacherously*
4603 mâ'al (1), to *act treacherously*
458+4160 anŏmia (1), *violation of law*
3845 parabainō (1), to *violate a command*

TRANSGRESSING
5674 'âbar (1), to *cross*
6586 pâsha' (1), to *break away from authority*

TRANSGRESSION
4604 ma'al (6), *treachery*
6586 pâsha' (1), to *break away from authority*
6588 pesha' (38), *revolt*
458 anŏmia (1), *violation of law, wickedness*
3845 parabainō (1), to *violate a command*
3847 parabasis (4), *violation, breaking*

TRANSGRESSIONS
6588 pesha' (46), *revolt*
3847 parabasis (2), *violation, breaking*

TRANSGRESSOR
898 bâgad (2), to *act treacherously*
6586 pâsha' (1), to *break away from authority*
3848 parabatēs (2), *violator, lawbreaker*

TRANSGRESSORS
898 bâgad (8), to *act treacherously*
5674 'âbar (1), to *cross*

6586 pâsha' (8), to *break away from authority*
459 anŏmŏs (2), *without Jewish law*
3848 parabatēs (1), *violator, lawbreaker*

TRANSLATE
5674 'âbar (1), to *cross*

TRANSLATED
3179 mĕthistēmi (1), to *move*
3346 mĕtatithēmi (2), to *transport; to exchange*

TRANSLATION
3331 mĕtathĕsis (1), *transferral* to heaven

TRANSPARENT
1307 diaphanēs (1), *appearing through*

TRAP
4170 môwqêsh (1), *noose*
4434 malkôdeth (1), *snare*
4889 mashchîyth (1), *bird snare; corruption*
2339 thēra (1), *hunting*

TRAPS
4170 môwqêsh (1), *noose*

TRAVAIL
2342 chûwl (2), to *dance, whirl; to writhe* in pain
2470 châlâh (1), to *be weak, sick, afflicted*
3205 yâlad (11), to *bear young; to father a child*
5999 'âmâl (3), *worry*
6045 'inyân (6), *labor; affair, care*
8513 t'elâ'âh (1), *distress*
3449 mŏchthŏs (2), *sadness*
5088 tiktō (1), to *produce from seed*
5604 ōdin (1), *pang*
5605 ōdinō (1), to *experience labor pains*

TRAVAILED
2342 chûwl (2), to *dance, whirl; to writhe* in pain
3205 yâlad (3), to *bear young; to father a child*

TRAVAILEST
5605 ōdinō (1), to *experience labor pains*

TRAVAILETH
2254 châbal (1), to *writhe* in labor pain
2342 chûwl (1), to *writhe* in pain; to *wait*
3205 yâlad (4), to *bear young; to father a child*
4944 sunōdinō (1), to *sympathize*

TRAVAILING
3205 yâlad (2), to *bear young; to father a child*
5605 ōdinō (1), to *experience labor pains*

TRAVEL
8513 t'elâ'âh (2), *distress*
4898 sunĕkdēmŏs (2), *fellow-traveller*

TRAVELERS
1980+5410 hâlak (1), to *walk*

TRAVELLED
1330 diĕrchŏmai (1), to *traverse, travel through*

TRAVELLER
734 'ôrach (1), *road*
1982 hêlek (1), *wayfarer*

TRAVELLETH
1980 hâlak (2), to *walk*

TRAVELLING
736 'ôr'echâh (1), *caravan*
6808 tsâ'âh (1), to *tip over; to depopulate*
589 apŏdēmĕō (1), *visit a foreign land*

TRAVERSING
8308 sârak (1), to *interlace*

TREACHEROUS
898 bâgad (6), to *act treacherously*
900 bôg'edôwth (1), *treachery*
901 bâgôwd (2), *treacherous*

TREACHEROUSLY
898 bâgad (23), to *act treacherously*

TREACHERY
4820 mirmâh (1), *fraud*

TREAD
947 bûwç (6), to *trample*
1758 dûwsh (1), to *trample or thresh*
1759 dûwsh (Ch.) (1), to *trample; destroy*
1869 dârak (14), to *tread*
1915 hâdak (1), to *crush*
6072 'âçaç (1), to *trample*
7429 râmaç (6), to *tread*
7760+4823 sûwm (1), to *put, place*
3961 patĕō (2), to *trample*

TREADER
1869 dârak (1), to *tread*

TREADERS
1869 dârak (1), to *tread*

TREADETH
1758 dûwsh (1), to *trample or thresh*
1869 dârak (4), to *tread*
7429 râmaç (2), to *tread*
248 alŏaō (2), to *tread out grain*
3961 patĕō (1), to *trample*

TREADING
1318 bâshaç (1), to *trample down*
1869 dârak (1), to *tread*
4001 m'ebûwçâh (1), *trampling, oppression*
4823 mirmâç (1), *abasement*

TREASON
7195 qesher (5), *unlawful alliance*

TREASURE
214 'ôwtsâr (11), *depository*
1596 g'enaz (Ch.) (2), *treasury storeroom*
2633 chôçen (2), *wealth*
4301 maṭmôwn (1), *secret storehouse*

4543 miçk'enâh (1), *storage-magazine*
1047 gaza (1), *treasure*
2343 thēsaurizō (2), to *amass or reserve*
2344 thēsaurŏs (13), *wealth*, what is *stored*

TREASURED
686 'âtsar (1), to *store up*

TREASURER
1489 gizbâr (1), *treasurer*
5532 çâkan (1), to *minister to*

TREASURERS
686 'âtsar (1), to *store up*
1411 g'edâbâr (Ch.) (2), *treasurer*
1490 gizbâr (Ch.) (1), *treasurer*

TREASURES
214 'ôwtsâr (50), *depository*
1596 g'enaz (Ch.) (1), *treasury storeroom*
4301 maṭmôwn (3), *secret storehouse*
4362 mikman (1), *hidden-treasure*
6259 'âthûwd (1), *prepared*
8226 sâphan (1), to *conceal*
2344 thēsaurŏs (5), *wealth*, what is *stored*

TREASUREST
2343 thēsaurizō (1), to *amass or reserve*

TREASURIES
214 'ôwtsâr (7), *depository*
1595 genez (2), *treasury coffer*
1597 ginzak (1), *treasury storeroom*

TREASURY
214 'ôwtsâr (3), *depository*
1049 gazŏphulakiŏn (5), *treasure-house*
2878 kŏrban (1), *votive offering or gift*

TREATISE
3056 lŏgŏs (1), *word*

TREE
363 'îylân (Ch.) (6), *tree*
815 'êshel (2), *tamarisk*
6086 'êts (88), *wood*
65 agriĕlaiŏs (2), *wild olive* tree
1186 dĕndrŏn (17), *tree*
2565 kalliĕlaiŏs (1), *cultivated olive*
3586 xulŏn (10), *timber*
4808 sukē (16), *fig-tree*
4809 sukŏmŏraia (1), *sycamore-fig* tree

TREES
352 'ayîl (2), *oak* tree
6086 'êts (77), *wood*
6097 'êtsâh (1), *timber*
1186 dĕndrŏn (9), *tree*

TREMBLE
2111 zûwâ' (1), to *tremble*
2112 zûwa' (Ch.) (1), to *shake* with fear

2342 chûwl (2), to *writhe*
2648 châphaz (1), to
hasten away, to *fear*
2729 chârad (6), to
shudder with terror
2730 chârêd (2), *fearful*
6426 pâlats (1), to *quiver*
7264 râgaz (9), to *quiver*
7322 rûwph (1), to *quake*
7493 râ'ash (4), to *quake*
5425 phrissō (1), to
shudder in *fear*

TREMBLED
2112 zûwa' (Ch.) (1), to
shake with fear
2342 chûwl (2), to *writhe*
2729 chârad (5), to
shudder with terror
2730 chârêd (2), *fearful*
7264 râgaz (2), to *quiver*
7364 râchats (1), to *bathe*
7493 râ'ash (5), to *quake*
1719+1096 ĕmphŏbŏs (1),
alarmed, terrified
1790+1096 ĕntrŏmŏs (1),
terrified
2192+5156 ĕchō (1), to
have; hold; keep

TREMBLETH
2729 chârad (1), to
shudder with terror
2730 chârêd (1), *fearful*
5568 çâmar (1), to *bristle*
7460 râ'ad (1), to *shudder*

TREMBLING
2729 chârad (1), to
shudder with terror
2731 chârâdâh (4), *fear*
6427 pallâtsûwth (1),
trembling fear
7268 raggâz (1), *timid*
7269 rogzâh (1),
trepidation
7460 râ'ad (6), to
shudder violently
7478 ra'al (1), *reeling*
7578 rᵉthêth (1), *terror*
8653 tar'êlâh (2), *reeling*
1096+1790 ginŏmai (1),
to *be, become*
5141 trĕmō (3), to *tremble*
5156 trŏmŏs (4), quaking
with *fear*

TRENCH
2426 chêyl (1),
entrenchment
4570 ma'gâl (3), circular
track or camp *rampart*
8565 tan (2), *jackal*
8585 tᵉ'âlâh (1),
irrigation *channel*
5482 charax (1), *rampart*

TRESPASS
816 'âsham (2), to *be
guilty; to be punished*
817 'âsham (41), *guilt*
819 'ashmâh (11),
guiltiness
2398 châṭâ' (1), to *sin*
4603 mâ'al (1), to *act
treacherously*
4604 ma'al (18), sinful
treachery
6588 pesha' (5), *revolt*
264 hamartanō (3), to *sin*

TRESPASSED
816 'âsham (2), to *be
guilty; to be punished*
819 'ashmâh (1),
guiltiness
4603 mâ'al (8), to *act
treacherously*
4604 ma'al (3), sinful
treachery

TRESPASSES
817 'âsham (1), *guilt*
819 'ashmâh (1),
guiltiness
4604 ma'al (1), sinful
treachery
3900 paraptōma (9),
error; transgression

TRESPASSING
819 'ashmâh (1),
guiltiness
4603 mâ'al (1), to *act
treacherously*

TRIAL
974 bâchan (1), to *test*
4531 maççâh (1), *testing*
1382 dŏkimē (1), *test*
1383 dŏkimiŏn (1),
testing; trustworthiness
3984 pĕira (1), *attempt*

TRIBE
4294 maṭṭeh (160), *tribe*
7626 shêbeṭ (57), *clan*
5443 phulē (19), *clan*

TRIBES
4294 maṭṭeh (20), *tribe*
7625 shᵉbaṭ (Ch.) (1), *clan*
7626 shêbeṭ (84), *clan*
1429 dōdĕkaphulŏn (1),
twelve tribes
5443 phulē (6), *clan*

TRIBULATION
6862 tsar (1), *trouble*
6869 tsârâh (2), *trouble*
2346 thlibō (1), to *trouble*
2347 thlipsis (18), *trouble*

TRIBULATIONS
6869 tsârâh (1), *trouble*
2347 thlipsis (3), *trouble*

TRIBUTARIES
4522 maç (4), *labor*

TRIBUTARY
4522 maç (1), *labor*

TRIBUTE
1093 bᵉlôw (Ch.) (3), *tax*
4060 middâh (1), *tribute*
4061 middâh (Ch.) (1),
tribute
4371 mekeç (6),
assessment, census-tax
4522 maç (12), *labor*
4530 miççâh (1), *liberally*
4853 massâ' (1), *burden*
6066 'ônesh (1), *fine*
1323 didrachmŏn (2),
double drachma
2778 kēnsŏs (4),
enrollment
5411 phŏrŏs (4), *tax, toll*

TRICKLETH
5064 nâgar (1), to *pour*
out; to *deliver* over

TRIED
974 bâchan (4), to *test; to
investigate*
976 bôchan (1), *trial*

6884 tsâraph (7), to *refine*
1381 dŏkimazō (1), to
test; to approve
1384 dŏkimŏs (1),
acceptable, approved
3985 pĕirazō (3), to
endeavor, scrutinize
4448 purŏō (1), to *be
ignited, glow*

TRIEST
974 bâchan (3), to *test*

TRIETH
974 bâchan (4), to *test; to
investigate*
1381 dŏkimazō (1), to
test; to approve

TRIMMED
6213 'âsâh (1), to *do*
2885 kŏsmeō (1), to *snuff*

TRIMMEST
3190 yâṭab (1), to *be,
make well*

TRIUMPH
5937 'âlaz (2), to *jump* for
joy
5970 'âlats (1), to *jump*
for *joy*
7321 rûwa' (3), to *shout*
7440 rinnâh (1), *shout*
7442 rânan (2), to *shout*
for *joy*
7623 shâbach (1), to
address in a loud tone;
to *pacify*
2358 thriambĕuō (1), to
*give victory, lead in
triumphal procession*

TRIUMPHED
1342 gâ'âh (2), to *be
exalted*

TRIUMPHING
7445 rᵉnânâh (1), *shout*
for *joy*
2358 thriambĕuō (1), to
*give victory, lead in
triumphal procession*

TROAS
5174 Trōas (6), *plain of
Troy*

TRODDEN
947 bûwç (3), to *trample*
1758 dûwsh (2), to
trample or *thresh*
1869 dârak (7), to *tread*
4001 mᵉbûwçâh (2),
trampling, oppression
4823 mirmâç (4),
abasement
5541 çâlâh (2), to
contemn, reject
7429 râmaç (2), to *tread*
2662 katapatĕō (3), to
trample down; to reject
3961 patĕō (1), to *trample*

TRODE
1869 dârak (2), to *tread*
7429 râmaç (5), to *tread*
2662 katapatĕō (1), to
trample down; to reject

TROGYLLIUM
5175 Trŏgulliŏn (1),
Trogyllium

TROOP
92 'ăguddâh (2), *band*
1409 gâd (2), *fortune*

1416 gᵉdûwd (7), *band*
2416 chay (2), *alive; raw*

TROOPS
734 'ôrach (1), *road*
1416 gᵉdûwd (3), *band*

TROPHIMUS
5161 Trŏphimŏs (3),
nutritive

TROUBLE
926 bâhal (2), to *tremble*
927 bᵉhal (Ch.) (2), to
terrify; hasten
928 behâlâh (2), *sudden
panic, destruction*
1091 ballâhâh (1),
sudden *destruction*
1205 bᵉ'âthâh (2), *fear*
1804 dâlach (1), to *roil*
water, *churn up*
2189 za'ăvâh (1),
agitation
2960 ṭôrach (1), *burden*
4103 mᵉhûwmâh (4),
confusion or uproar
5916 'âkar (4), to *disturb*
5999 'âmâl (3), *worry*
6040 'ŏnîy (3), *misery*
6862 tsar (17), *trouble*
6869 tsârâh (34), *trouble*
6887 tsârar (2), to *cramp*
7186+3117 qâsheh (1),
severe
7267 rôgez (2), *disquiet*
7451 ra' (9), *bad; evil*
7561 râsha' (1), to *be, do,
declare wrong*
8513 tᵉlâ'âh (1), *distress*
387 anastatŏō (1), to
disturb, cause trouble
1613 ĕktarassō (1), to
disturb wholly
1776 ĕnŏchleō (1), to
annoy, cause trouble
2346 thlibō (1), to *trouble*
2347 thlipsis (3), *trouble*
2350 thŏrubĕō (1), to
disturb; clamor
2553 kakŏpathĕō (1), to
undergo hardship
2873 kŏpŏs (1), *toil; pains*
2873+3930 kŏpŏs (2), *toil*
3926 parĕnŏchleō (1), to
annoy, make trouble
3930 parĕchō (1), to *hold
near*, i.e. to *present*
4660 skullō (2), to *harass*
5015 tarassō (1), to
trouble, disturb

TROUBLED
926 bâhal (12), to *tremble*
927 bᵉhal (Ch.) (6), to
terrify; hasten
1089 bâlahh (1), to *terrify*
1204 bâ'ath (1), to *fear,
be afraid*
1607 gâ'ash (1), to
agitate violently, *shake*
1644 gârash (1), to *drive*
out; to *divorce*
1993 hâmâh (2), to *be in
great commotion*
2000 hâmam (1), to *put
in commotion*
2560 châmar (3), to
ferment, foam
5590 çâ'ar (1), to *rush*
upon; to *toss about*

5753 'âvâh (1), to be crooked
5916 'âkar (4), to disturb
6031 'ânâh (1), to afflict
6470 pâ'am (4), to impel or agitate
7114 qâtsar (1), to curtail, cut short
7264 râgaz (3), to quiver
7481 râ'am (1), to crash thunder; to irritate
7515 râphas (1), to trample, i.e. roil water
1298 diatarassō (1), to disturb wholly
2346 thlibō (3), to crowd, press, trouble
2360 thrŏĕō (3), to frighten, be alarmed
5015 tarassō (14), to trouble, disturb
5015+1438 tarassō (1), to trouble, disturb
5182 turbazō (1), to make turbid

TROUBLEDST
1804 dâlach (1), to roil water, churn up

TROUBLER
5916 'âkar (1), to disturb or afflict

TROUBLES
6869 tsârâh (10), trouble
7451 ra' (1), bad; evil
5016 tarachē (1), mob disturbance; roiling

TROUBLEST
4660 skullō (1), to harass

TROUBLETH
598 ănaç (Ch.) (1), to distress
926 bâhal (2), to tremble
1204 bâ'ath (1), to fear, be afraid
5916 'âkar (4), to disturb
3930+2873 parĕchō (1), to hold near
5015 tarassō (1), to trouble, disturb

TROUBLING
7267 rôgez (1), disquiet; anger
5015 tarassō (1), to trouble, disturb

TROUBLOUS
5916 'âkar (1), to disturb or afflict

TROUGH
8268 shôqeth (1), watering-trough

TROUGHS
7298 rahaṭ (1), ringlet of hair
8268 shôqeth (1), watering-trough

TROW
1380 dŏkĕō (1), to think, regard, seem good

TRUCEBREAKERS
786 aspŏndŏs (1), not reconcilable

TRUE
551 'omnâm (1), verily, indeed, truly

571 'emeth (18), truth, trustworthiness
3330 yatstsîyb (Ch.) (2), fixed, sure
3651 kên (5), just; right
6656 tsᵉdâ' (Ch.) (1), (sinister) design
227 alēthēs (22), true; genuine
228 alēthinŏs (27), truthful
1103 gnēsiŏs (1), genuine, true
2227 zōŏpŏiĕō (1), to (re-) vitalize, give life
3588+225 hŏ (1), "the," i.e. the definite article
4103 pistŏs (2), trustworthy; reliable

TRULY
199 'ûwlâm (4), however
389 'ak (3), surely; only
403 'âkên (2), truly!
530 'ĕmûwnâh (1), fidelity; steadiness
551 'omnâm (1), truly
571 'emeth (8), certainty, truth, trustworthiness
577 'ânnâ' (1), oh now!
3588 kîy (1), for, that
227 alēthēs (1), true
230 alēthōs (2), truly
686 ara (1), then, so
1161 dĕ (1), but, yet
1909+225 ĕpi (1), on, upon
3303 mĕn (12), truly

TRUMP
2689 chătsôtsᵉrâh (1), trumpet
7782 shôwphâr (1), curved ram's horn
4536 salpigx (2), trumpet

TRUMPET
3104 yôwbêl (1), blast of a ram's horn
7782 shôwphâr (47), curved ram's horn
8628 tâqa' (1), to clatter, slap, drive, clasp
4536 salpigx (7), trumpet
4537 salpizō (1), to sound a trumpet blast

TRUMPETERS
2689 chătsôtsᵉrâh (2), trumpet
2690 châtsar (1), to blow the trumpet
4538 salpistēs (1), trumpeter

TRUMPETS
2689 chătsôtsᵉrâh (24), trumpet
7782 shôwphâr (20), curved ram's horn
4536 salpigx (2), trumpet

TRUST
539 'âman (4), to be firm, faithful, true; to trust
982 bâṭach (61), to trust, be confident or sure
2342 chûwl (1), to wait; to pervert
2620 châçâh (32), to confide in
2622 châçûwth (1), confidence

3176 yâchal (2), to wait; to be patient, hope
4004 mibchôwr (1), select, i.e. well fortified
4009 mibṭâch (3), security; assurance
4268 machăçeh (1), shelter; refuge
1679 ĕlpizō (15), to confide, hope for
3892 paranŏmia (1), wrongdoing
3982 pĕithō (6), to rely by inward certainty
4006 pĕpŏithēsis (1), reliance, trust
4100 pistĕuō (3), to have faith, credit; to entrust

TRUSTED
539 'âman (1), to trust, to be permanent
982 bâṭach (18), to trust, be confident or sure
1556 gâlal (1), to roll; to commit
2620 châçâh (1), to confide in
7365 rᵉchats (Ch.) (1), to attend upon, trust
1679 ĕlpizō (2), to expect or confide, hope for
3982 pĕithō (3), to rely by inward certainty
4276 prŏĕlpizō (1), to hope in advance

TRUSTEDST
982 bâṭach (3), to trust, be confident or sure

TRUSTEST
982 bâṭach (6), to trust, be confident or sure

TRUSTETH
982 bâṭach (14), to trust, be confident or sure
2620 châçâh (2), to confide in
1679 ĕlpizō (1), to expect or confide, hope for

TRUSTING
982 bâṭach (1), to trust, be confident or sure

TRUSTY
539 'âman (1), to be firm, faithful, true; to trust

TRUTH
518+3808 'îm (1), if, although; Oh that!
529 'ĕmûwn (1), trustworthiness; faithful
530 'ĕmûwnâh (13), fidelity; steadiness
544 'ômen (1), verity, faithfulness
548 'ămânâh (2), covenant
551 'omnâm (3), verily, indeed, truly
571 'emeth (90), certainty, truth
3321 yᵉtsêb (Ch.) (1), to speak surely
3330 yatstsîyb (Ch.) (1), fixed, sure
3588+518 kîy (1), for, that because
7187 qᵉshôwṭ (Ch.) (2), fidelity, truth

7189 qôsheṭ (1), reality
225 alēthĕia (99), truth, truthfulness
226 alēthĕuō (8), to be true
227 alēthēs (1), true; genuine
230 alēthōs (7), truly, surely
3483 nai (1), yes
3689 ŏntōs (1), really, certainly

TRUTH'S
571 'emeth (1), certainty, truth, trustworthiness
225 alēthĕia (1), truth, truthfulness

TRY
974 bâchan (8), to test; to investigate
2713 châqar (1), to examine, search
5254 nâçâh (1), to test, attempt
6884 tsâraph (3), to fuse metal; to refine
1381 dŏkimazō (2), to test; to approve
3985 pĕirazō (1), to endeavor, scrutinize
4314+3986 prŏs (1), to, toward; against

TRYING
1383 dŏkimiŏn (1), testing; trustworthiness

TRYPHENA
5170 Truphaina (1), luxurious

TRYPHOSA
5173 Truphōsa (1), luxuriating

TUBAL
8422 Tûwbal (8), Tubal

TUBAL-CAIN
8423 Tûwbal Qayin (2), offspring of Cain

TUMBLED
2015 hâphak (1), to change, overturn

TUMULT
1993 hâmâh (1), to be in great commotion
1995 hâmôwn (4), noise, tumult; many, crowd
1999 hămullâh (1), sound, roar, noise
4103 mᵉhûwmâh (1), confusion or uproar
7588 shâ'ôwn (3), uproar; destruction
7600 sha'ănân (2), secure; haughty
2351 thŏrubŏs (4), disturbance

TUMULTS
4103 mᵉhûwmâh (1), confusion or uproar
181 akatastasia (2), disorder, riot

TUMULTUOUS
1121+7588 bên (1), son, descendant; people
1993 hâmâh (1), to be in great commotion

U

3920 parĕisaktŏs (1), smuggled in, infiltrated
3921 parĕisdunŏ (1), to slip in secretly

UNBELIEF
543 apĕithĕia (4), disbelief
570 apistia (12), disbelief; disobedience

UNBELIEVERS
571 apistŏs (4), without faith; untrustworthy

UNBELIEVING
544 apĕithĕŏ (1), to disbelieve
571 apistŏs (5), without faith; untrustworthy

UNBLAMEABLE
299 amŏmŏs (2), unblemished, blameless

UNBLAMEABLY
274 amĕmptŏs (1), faultlessly

UNCERTAIN
82 adĕlŏs (1), indistinct, not clear
83 adēlŏtēs (1), uncertainty

UNCERTAINLY
82 adēlŏs (1), indistinct, not clear

UNCHANGEABLE
531 aparabatŏs (1), untransferable

UNCIRCUMCISED
6189 'ârêl (34), to be uncircumcised
6190 'orlâh (2), prepuce or penile foreskin
203+2192 akrŏbustia (1), uncircumcised
564 apĕritmētŏs (1), uncircumcised
1722+3588+203 ĕn (2), in; during; because of
1986 ĕpispaŏmai (1), to efface the mark of circumcision

UNCIRCUMCISION
203 akrŏbustia (16), uncircumcised

UNCLE
1730 dôwd (10), beloved, friend; uncle, cousin

UNCLE'S
1730 dôwd (1), beloved, friend; uncle, cousin
1733 dôwdâh (6), aunt

UNCLEAN
2930 tâmê' (74), to be morally contaminated
2931 tâmê' (78), foul; ceremonially impure
2932 tum'âh (4), ceremonial impurity
5079 niddâh (2), time of menstrual impurity
6172 'ervâh (1), nudity; disgrace; blemish
6945 qâdêsh (1), sacred male prostitute
169 akathartŏs (28), impure; evil
2839 kŏinŏs (3), common, i.e. profane

2840 kŏinŏŏ (1), to make profane

UNCLEANNESS
2930 tâmê' (1), to be morally contaminated
2932 tum'âh (25), ceremonial impurity
5079 niddâh (1), time of menstrual impurity
6172 'ervâh (1), nudity; disgrace; blemish
7137 qâreh (1), accidental occurrence
167 akatharsia (10), quality of impurity
3394 miasmŏs (1), act of moral contamination

UNCLEANNESSES
2932 tum'âh (1), ceremonial impurity

UNCLOTHED
1562 ĕkduŏ (1), to divest

UNCOMELY
807 aschēmŏnĕŏ (1), to be, act unbecoming
809 aschēmōn (1), inelegant, indecent

UNCONDEMNED
178 akatakritŏs (2), without legal trial

UNCORRUPTIBLE
862 aphthartŏs (1), undecaying, immortal

UNCORRUPTNESS
90 adiaphthŏria (1), purity of doctrine

UNCOVER
1540 gâlâh (22), to denude; uncover
6168 'ârâh (1), to be, make bare; to empty
6544 pâra' (3), to loosen; to expose, dismiss

UNCOVERED
1540 gâlâh (10), to denude; uncover
2834 châsaph (2), to drain away or bail up
6168 'ârâh (1), to be, make bare; to empty
177 akatakaluptŏs (2), unveiled
648 apŏstĕgazŏ (1), to unroof, make a hole in a roof

UNCOVERETH
1540 gâlâh (2), to denude; uncover
6168 'ârâh (1), to be, make bare; to empty

UNCTION
5545 chrisma (1), special endowment of the Holy Spirit

UNDEFILED
8535 tâm (2), morally pious; gentle, dear
8549 tâmîym (1), entire, complete; integrity
283 amiantŏs (4), pure

UNDER
413 'êl (2), to, toward
4295 mattâh (1), below or beneath

5921 'al (9), above, over, upon, or against
8460 t^e chôwth (Ch.) (4), beneath, under
8478 tachath (231), bottom; underneath
332 anathĕmatizŏ (2), to declare or vow an oath
506 anupŏtaktŏs (1), independent
1640 ĕlassŏn (1), smaller
1722 ĕn (2), in; during; because of
1772 ĕnnŏmŏs (1), legal, or subject to law
1909 ĕpi (3), on, upon
2662 katapatĕŏ (2), to trample down; to reject
2709 katachthŏniŏs (1), infernal
2736 katŏ (1), downwards
5259 hupŏ (47), under; by means of; at
5270 hupŏkatŏ (8), down under, i.e. beneath
5273 hupŏkritēs (1), dissembler, hypocrite
5284 hupŏplĕŏ (2), to sail under the lee of
5293 hupŏtassŏ (4), to subordinate; to obey
5295 hupŏtrĕchŏ (1), to run under
5299 hupŏpiazŏ (1), to beat up; to wear out

UNDERGIRDING
5269 hupŏzŏnnumi (1), to gird under

UNDERNEATH
4295 mattâh (2), below or beneath
8478 tachath (1), bottom; underneath; in lieu of

UNDERSETTERS
3802 kâthêph (4), shoulder-piece; wall

UNDERSTAND
995 bîyn (44), to understand; discern
998 bîynâh (1), understanding
3045 yâda' (3), to know
7919 sâkal (9), to be or act circumspect
8085 shâma' (6), to hear intelligently
50 agnŏĕŏ (1), to not know; not understand
1097 ginŏskŏ (3), to know
1107 gnŏrizŏ (1), to make known, reveal
1492 ĕidŏ (1), to know
1987 ĕpistamai (1), to comprehend
3539 nŏiĕŏ (8), to exercise the mind
4920 suniĕmi (13), to comprehend

UNDERSTANDEST
995 bîyn (2), to understand; discern
8085 shâma' (1), to hear intelligently
1097 ginŏskŏ (1), to know

UNDERSTANDETH
995 bîyn (5), to understand; discern

5921 'al (9), above, over,

UNDERSTANDING
995 bîyn (33), to understand; discern
998 bîynâh (32), understanding
999 bîynâh (Ch.) (1), understanding
2940 ta'am (1), taste; intelligence; mandate
3820 lêb (10), heart
3824 lêbâb (3), heart
4486 manda' (Ch.) (1), wisdom or intelligence
7306 rûwach (1), to smell or perceive
7919 sâkal (5), to be or act circumspect
7922 sekel (7), intelligence; success
7924 sokl^e thânûw (Ch.) (3), intelligence
8085 shâma' (1), to hear intelligently
8394 tâbûwn (38), intelligence; argument
801 asunĕtŏs (3), senseless, dull; wicked
1271 dianŏia (3), mind or thought
3563 nŏus (7), intellect, mind; understanding
3877 parakŏlŏuthĕŏ (1), to attend; trace out
4907 sunĕsis (6), understanding
4920 suniĕmi (2), to understand
5424 phrēn (2), mind or cognitive faculties

UNDERSTOOD
995 bîyn (11), to understand; discern
3045 yâda' (4), to know
7919 sâkal (2), to be or act circumspect
8085 shâma' (1), to hear intelligently
50 agnŏĕŏ (2), to not know; not understand
1097 ginŏskŏ (4), to know
1425 dusnŏētŏs (1), difficult of perception
2154 ĕusēmŏs (1), significant
3129 manthanŏ (1), to learn
3539 nŏiĕŏ (1), to exercise the mind
4441 punthanŏmai (1), to ask for information
4920 suniĕmi (7), to understand
5426 phrŏnĕŏ (1), to be mentally disposed

UNDERTAKE
6148 'ârab (1), to intermix; to give or be security

UNDERTOOK
6901 qâbal (1), to admit; to take

UNDO
5425 nâthar (1), to
terrify; shake off; untie
6213 'âsâh (1), to do or
make

UNDONE
6 'âbad (1), to perish;
destroy
1820 dâmâh (1), to be
silent; to fail, cease
5493 çûwr (1), to turn off

UNDRESSED
5139 nâzîyr (2), prince;
separated Nazirite

UNEQUAL
3808+8505 lô' (2), no, not

UNEQUALLY
2086 hĕtĕrŏzugĕō (1), to
associate discordantly

UNFAITHFUL
898 bâgad (1), to act
treacherously

UNFAITHFULLY
898 bâgad (1), to act
treacherously

UNFEIGNED
505 anupŏkritŏs (4),
sincere, genuine

UNFRUITFUL
175 akarpŏs (6), barren,
unfruitful

UNGIRDED
6605 pâthach (1), to open
wide; to loosen, begin

UNGODLINESS
763 asĕbĕia (4),
wickedness, impiety

UNGODLY
1100 bᵉlîya'al (4),
wickedness, trouble
3808+2623 lô' (1), no, not
5760 'ăvîyl (1), morally
perverse
7563 râshâ' (8), morally
wrong; bad person
763 asĕbĕia (3),
wickedness, impiety
764 asĕbĕō (2), to be, act
impious or wicked
765 asĕbēs (8), impious
or wicked

UNHOLY
2455 chôl (1), profane,
common, not holy
462 anŏsiŏs (2), wicked,
unholy
2839 kŏinŏs (1),
common, i.e. profane

UNICORN
7214 rᵉ'êm (6), wild bull

UNICORNS
7214 rᵉ'êm (3), wild bull

UNITE
3161 yâchad (1), to be,
become one

UNITED
3161 yâchad (1), to be,
become one

UNITY
3162 yachad (1), unitedly
1775 hĕnŏtēs (2),
unanimity, unity

UNJUST
205 'âven (1), trouble,
vanity, wickedness
5766 'evel (2), moral evil
5767 'avvâl (1), morally
evil
8636 tarbîyth (1),
percentage or bonus
91 adikĕō (1), to do
wrong
93 adikia (2),
wrongfulness
94 adikŏs (8), unjust,
wicked

UNJUSTLY
5765 'âval (1), to morally
distort
5766 'evel (1), moral evil

UNKNOWN
50 agnŏĕō (2), to not
know; not understand
57 agnōstŏs (1), unknown

UNLADE
670 apŏphŏrtizŏmai (1),
to unload

UNLAWFUL
111 athĕmitŏs (1),
illegal; detestable
459 anŏmŏs (1), without
Jewish law

UNLEARNED
62 agrammatŏs (1),
illiterate, unschooled
261 amathēs (1),
ignorant
521 apaidĕutŏs (1),
stupid, uneducated
2399 idiōtēs (3), not
initiated; untrained

UNLEAVENED
4682 matstsâh (51),
unfermented cake
106 azumŏs (9), made
without yeast; Passover

UNLESS
194 'ûwlay (1), if not;
perhaps
3884 lûwlê' (3), if not

UNLOOSE
3089 luō (3), to loosen

UNMARRIED
22 agamŏs (4),
unmarried

UNMERCIFUL
415 anĕlĕēmōn (1),
merciless, ruthless

UNMINDFUL
7876 shâyâh (1), to keep
in memory

UNMOVABLE
277 amĕtakinētŏs (1),
immovable

UNMOVEABLE
761 asalĕutŏs (1),
immovable, fixed

UNNI
6042 'Unnîy (3), afflicted

UNOCCUPIED
2308 châdal (1), to desist,
stop; be fat

UNPREPARED
532 aparaskĕuastŏs (1),
unready

UNPROFITABLE
5532 çâkan (1), to be
serviceable to
255 alusitĕlēs (1),
gainless, pernicious
512 anōphĕlēs (1), useless
888 achrĕiŏs (2), useless,
i.e. unmeritorious
889 achrĕiŏō (1), render
useless, i.e. spoil
890 achrēstŏs (1),
inefficient, detrimental

UNPROFITABLENESS
512 anōphĕlēs (1), useless

UNPUNISHED
5352 nâqâh (11), to be,
make clean; to be bare

UNQUENCHABLE
762 asbĕstŏs (2), not
extinguished

UNREASONABLE
249 alŏgŏs (1), irrational,
not reasonable
824 atŏpŏs (1), improper;
injurious; wicked

UNREBUKEABLE
423 anĕpilēptŏs (1), not
open to blame

UNREPROVEABLE
410 anĕgklētŏs (1),
irreproachable

UNRIGHTEOUS
205 'âven (2), trouble,
vanity, wickedness
2555 châmâç (2),
violence; malice
5765 'âval (1), to morally
distort
5767 'avvâl (1), morally
evil
94 adikŏs (4), unjust,
wicked

UNRIGHTEOUSLY
5766 'evel (1), moral evil

UNRIGHTEOUSNESS
3808+6664 lô' (1), no, not
5766 'evel (1), moral evil
93 adikia (16),
wrongfulness
458 anŏmia (1), violation
of law, wickedness

UNRIPE
1154 beçer (1),
immature, sour grapes

UNRULY
183 akataschĕtŏs (1),
unrestrainable
506 anupŏtaktŏs (2),
insubordinate
813 ataktŏs (1),
insubordinate

UNSATIABLE
1115+7654 biltîy (1), not,
except, without, unless

UNSAVOURY
6617 pâthal (1), to
struggle; to be tortuous
8602 tâphêl (1), to
plaster; be tasteless

UNSEARCHABLE
369+2714 'ayin (3), there
is no, i.e., not exist
419 anĕxĕrĕunētŏs (1),
inscrutable

421 anĕxichniastŏs (1),
unsearchable

UNSEEMLY
808 aschēmŏsunē (1),
indecency; shame

UNSHOD
3182 mĕthuskō (1), to
intoxicate, become
drunk

UNSKILFUL
552 apĕirŏs (1), ignorant,
not acquainted with

UNSPEAKABLE
411 anĕkdiēgētŏs (1),
indescribable
412 anĕklalētŏs (1),
unutterable
731 arrhētŏs (1),
inexpressible

UNSPOTTED
784 aspilŏs (1),
unblemished

UNSTABLE
6349 pachaz (1),
ebullition, turbulence
182 akatastatŏs (1),
inconstant, restless
793 astēriktŏs (2),
vacillating, unstable

UNSTOPPED
6605 pâthach (1), to open
wide; to loosen, begin

UNTAKEN
3361+348 mē (1), not; lest

UNTEMPERED
8602 tâphêl (5), to be
tasteless; frivolity

UNTHANKFUL
884 acharistŏs (2),
ungrateful

UNTIL
5704 'ad (288), as far
(long) as; during; until
891 achri (16), until or
up to
1519 ĕis (1), to or into
2193 hĕōs (35), until
3360 mĕchri (7), until, to
the point of

UNTIMELY
5309 nephel (3), abortive
miscarriage
3653 ŏlunthŏs (1), unripe
fig

UNTOWARD
4646 skŏliŏs (1), crooked;
perverse

UNWALLED
6519 pᵉrâzâh (1), rural,
open country
6521 pᵉrâzîy (1), rustic

UNWASHEN
449 aniptŏs (3), without
ablution, unwashed

UNWISE
3808+2450 lô' (2), no, not
453 anŏētŏs (1),
unintelligent, senseless
878 aphrōn (1), ignorant;
egotistic; unbelieving

UNWITTINGLY
1097+1847 bᵉlîy (2),
without, not yet

U

7684 shᵉgâgâh (1), *mistake*, inadvertent *transgression*

UNWORTHILY
371 anaxiŏs (2), in a manner *unworthy*

UNWORTHY
370 anaxiŏs (1), *unfit, unworthy*
3756+514 ŏu (1), *no or not*

UPBRAID
2778 châraph (1), to spend the *winter*
3679 ŏnĕidizō (1), to *rail at, chide, taunt*

UPBRAIDED
3679 ŏnĕidizō (1), to *rail at, chide, taunt*

UPBRAIDETH
3679 ŏnĕidizō (1), to *rail at, chide, taunt*

UPHARSIN
6537 pᵉraç (Ch.) (1), to *split* up

UPHAZ
210 'Ûwphâz (2), *Uphaz*

UPHELD
5564 çâmak (1), to *lean* upon; *take hold* of

UPHOLD
5564 çâmak (5), to *lean* upon; *take hold* of
8551 tâmak (3), to *obtain, keep fast*

UPHOLDEN
5582 çâ'ad (1), to *support*
6965 qûwm (1), to *rise*

UPHOLDEST
8551 tâmak (1), to *obtain, keep fast*

UPHOLDETH
5564 çâmak (3), to *lean* upon; *take hold* of
8551 tâmak (1), to *obtain, keep fast*

UPHOLDING
5342 phĕrō (1), to *bear* or *carry*

UPPER
3730 kaphtôr (1), *capital; wreath-like button*
4947 mashqôwph (1), *lintel*
5942 'illîy (2), *higher*
5944 'ăliyâh (4), *upper things; second-story*
5945 'elyôwn (8), *loftier, higher; Supreme* God
7393 rekeb (1), *upper millstone*
8222 sâphâm (1), *beard*
508 anōgĕŏn (2), *dome* or a *balcony*
510 anōtĕrikŏs (1), *more remote regions*
5250 hupĕrplĕŏnazō (1), to *superabound*
5253 hupĕrō̧ŏn (3), *room in the third story*

UPPERMOST
5945 'elyôwn (1), *loftier, higher; Supreme* God
4410 prōtŏkathĕdria (1), *pre-eminence in council*

4411 prōtŏklisia (2), *pre-eminence at meals*

UPRIGHT
3474 yâshar (1), to be *straight;* to *make right*
3476 yôsher (1), *right*
3477 yâshâr (43), *straight*
4339 mêyshâr (1), *straightness; rectitude*
4749 miqshâh (1), work *molded by hammering*
5977 'ōmed (2), fixed *spot*
6968 qôwmᵉmîyûwth (1), *erectly, with head high*
8535 tâm (1), *morally pious; gentle, dear*
8537 tôm (2), *prosperity; innocence*
8549 tâmîym (8), *entire, complete; integrity*
8549+8552 tâmîym (1), *complete; integrity*
8552 tâmam (2), to *complete, finish*
3717 ŏrthŏs (1), *straight, level*

UPRIGHTLY
3474 yâshar (1), to be *straight;* to *make right*
3477 yâshâr (1), *straight*
4339 mêyshâr (3), *straightness; rectitude*
8537 tôm (2), *prosperity; innocence*
8549 tâmîym (4), *entire, complete; integrity*
3716 ŏrthŏpŏdĕō (1), to *act rightly*

UPRIGHTNESS
3476 yôsher (9), *right*
3477 yâshâr (1), *straight*
3483 yishrâh (1), *moral integrity*
4334 mîyshôwr (1), *plain; justice*
4339 mêyshâr (3), *straightness; rectitude*
5228 nâkôach (1), *equitable, correct*
5229 nᵉkôchâh (1), *integrity; truth*
8537 tôm (2), *prosperity; innocence*

UPRISING
6965 qûwm (1), to *rise*

UPROAR
1993 hâmâh (1), to *be in great commotion*
387 anastatŏō (1), to *disturb, cause trouble*
2350 thŏrubĕō (1), to *clamor; start a riot*
2351 thŏrubŏs (3), *commotion*
4714 stasis (1), one *leading an uprising*
4797 sugchĕō (1), to *throw into disorder*

UPSIDE
5921+6440 'al (2), *above, over, upon, or against*
389 anastĕnazō (1), to *sigh deeply*

UPWARD
1361 gâbahh (1), to *be lofty;* to *be haughty*

4605 ma'al (59), *upward, above, overhead*
4791 mârôwm (1), *elevation; elation*

UR
218 'Ûwr (5), *Ur*

URBANE
3779 hŏutō (1), *in this way; likewise*

URGE
1758 ĕnĕchō (1), to *keep a grudge*

URGED
509 'âlats (1), to *press, urge*
6484 pâtsar (4), to *stun or dull*
6555 pârats (1), to *break out*

URGENT
2388 châzaq (1), to *fasten* upon; to *seize*
2685 chătsaph (Ch.) (1), to *be severe*

URI
221 'Ûwrîy (8), *fiery*

URIAH
223 'Ûwrîyâh (27), *flame of Jehovah*

URIAH'S
223 'Ûwrîyâh (1), *flame of Jehovah*

URIAS
3774 Ŏurias (1), *flame of Jehovah*

URIEL
222 'Ûwrîy'êl (4), *flame of God*

URIJAH
223 'Ûwrîyâh (11), *flame of Jehovah*

URIM
224 'Ûwrîym (7), *lights*

US-WARD
413 'êl (1), *to, toward*
1519+2248 ĕis (2), *to or into*

USE
559 'âmar (1), to *say*
3231 yâman (1), to *be right-handed*
3947 lâqach (1), to *take*
4399 mᵉlâ'kâh (1), *work; property*
4911 mâshal (3), to *use figurative language*
4912 mâshâl (1), *pithy maxim; taunt*
5172 nâchash (1), to *prognosticate*
5656 'ăbôdâh (1), *work*
7080 qâçam (1), to *divine magic*
1838 hĕxis (1), *practice, constant use*
1908 ĕpĕrĕazō (2), to *insult with threats*
5195 hubrizō (1), to *exercise violence, abuse*
5382 philŏxĕnŏs (1), *hospitable*
5530 chraŏmai (7), to *furnish* what is needed

5532 chrĕia (1), *affair; occasion, demand*
5540 chrēsis (2), *employment*

USED
3928 limmûwd (1), *instructed one*
6213 'âsâh (2), to *do or make*
390 anastrĕphō (1), to *remain, to live*
1247 diakŏnĕō (1), to *wait upon, serve*
1387 dŏliŏō (1), to *practice deceit*
1510 ĕimi (1), I *exist, I am*
3096 magĕuō (1), to *practice magic, sorcery*
4238 prassō (1), to *execute, accomplish*
5530 chraŏmai (3), to *furnish* what is needed

USES
5532 chrĕia (1), *affair; occasion, demand*

USEST
4941 mishpâṭ (1), *verdict; formal decree; justice*

USETH
1696 dâbar (1), to *speak, say;* to *subdue*
3348 mĕtĕchō (1), to *share or participate*

USING
671 apŏchrēsis (1), *consumption, using up*
2192 ĕchō (1), to *have; hold; keep*

USURER
5383 nâshâh (1), to *lend or borrow*

USURP
831 authĕntĕō (1), to *dominate*

USURY
5378 nâshâ' (1), to *lend on interest*
5383 nâshâh (5), to *lend or borrow*
5391 nâshak (4), to *oppress* through *finance*
5392 neshek (11), *interest*
5110 tŏkŏs (2), *interest* on money loaned

UTHAI
5793 'Ûwthay (2), *succoring*

UTMOST
314 'achărôwn (2), *late or last; behind; western*
7093 qêts (1), *extremity; after*
7097 qâtseh (3), *extremity*
7112 qâtsats (3), to *chop off;* to *separate*
4009 pĕras (1), *extremity, end, limit*

UTTER
1696 dâbar (5), to *speak, say;* to *subdue*
1897 hâgâh (1), to *murmur, utter a sound; ponder*

UTTERANCE

2435 chîytsôwn (12), outer *wall side; exterior*
2531 chemed (1), *delight*
3318 yâtsâ' (3), to *go, bring out*
3617 kâlâh (2), *complete destruction*
4448 mâlal (2), to *speak, say*
4911 mâshal (1), to *use figurative language*
5042 nâba' (4), to *gush forth; to utter*
5046 nâgad (3), to *announce*
5414 nâthan (4), to *give*
6030 'ânâh (1), to *respond, answer*
6315 pûwach (1), to *blow, to fan, kindle; to utter*
1325 didōmi (1), to *give*
2044 ĕrĕugŏmai (1), to *speak out*
2980 laleō (1), to *talk*

UTTERANCE

669 apŏphthĕggŏmai (1), *declare, address*
3056 lŏgŏs (4), *word, matter, thing*

UTTERED

1696 dâbar (1), to *speak, say; to subdue*
3318 yâtsâ' (1), to *go, bring out*
4008 mibţâ' (2), rash *utterance*
5046 nâgad (2), to *announce*
5414 nâthan (5), to *give*
6475 pâtsâh (1), to *rend, i.e. open*
215 alalētŏs (1), *unspeakable*
2980 laleō (3), to *talk*
3004 lĕgō (1), to *say*

UTTERETH

502 'âlaph (1), to *learn; to teach*
559 'âmar (1), to *say*
1696 dâbar (1), to *speak, say; to subdue*
3318 yâtsâ' (2), to *go, bring out*
5042 nâba' (1), to *gush forth; to utter*
5414 nâthan (3), to *give*

UTTERING

1897 hâgâh (1), to *murmur, utter a sound*

UTTERLY

3605 kôl (1), *all, any or every*
3615 kâlâh (1), to *complete, prepare*
3632 kâlîyl (1), *whole, entire; complete; whole*
3966 mᵉ'ôd (2), *very, utterly*
7703 shâdad (1), to *ravage*
2618 katakaiō (1), to *consume wholly by burning*
2704 kataphthĕirō (1), to *spoil entirely*
3654 hŏlōs (1), *completely, altogether*

UTTERMOST

314 'achârôwn (1), *late or last; behind; western*
319 'achărîyth (1), *future; posterity*
657 'epheç (1), *end; no further*
3671 kânâph (1), *edge or extremity; wing*
7020 qîytsôwn (3), *terminal, end*
7097 qâtseh (10), *extremity*
7098 qâtsâh (3), *termination; fringe*
206 akrŏn (2), *extremity: end; top*
1231 diaginōskō (1), *ascertain exactly*
2078 ĕschatŏs (2), *farthest, final*
3838 pantĕlēs (1), *entire; completion*
4009 pĕras (1), *extremity, end, limit*
5056 tĕlŏs (1), *conclusion*

UZ

5780 'Ûwts (7), *consultation*

UZAI

186 'Ûwzay (1), *Uzai*

UZAL

187 'Ûwzâl (2), *Uzal*

UZZA

5798 'Uzzâ' (10), *strength*

UZZAH

5798 'Uzzâ' (4), *strength*

UZZEN-SHERAH

242 'Uzzên She'ĕrâh (1), *land of Sheerah*

UZZI

5813 'Uzzîy (11), *forceful*

UZZIA

5814 'Uzzîyâ' (1), *strength of Jehovah*

UZZIAH

5818 'Uzzîyâh (27), *strength of Jehovah*

UZZIEL

5816 'Uzzîy'êl (16), *strength of God*

UZZIELITES

5817 'Ozzîy'êlîy (2), *Uzziëlite*

VAGABOND

5110 nûwd (2), to *waver; to wander, flee*
4022 pĕriĕrchŏmai (1), to *stroll, vacillate, veer*

VAGABONDS

5128 nûwa' (1), to *waver*

VAIL

4304 miṭpachath (1), *cloak, woman's shawl*
4533 maçveh (1), *veil, cover*
4541 maççêkâh (1), *woven coverlet*
6532 pôreketh (25), *sacred screen, curtain*
6809 tsâ'îyph (3), *veil*
2571 kaluma (4), *veil, covering*

VAILS

7289 râdîyd (1), *veil*

VAIN

205 'âven (1), *trouble, vanity, wickedness*
1891 hâbal (5), to *be vain, be worthless*
1892 hebel (11), *emptiness or vanity*
2600 chinnâm (2), *gratis, free*
3576 kâzab (1), to *lie, deceive*
5014 nâbab (1), to *be hollow; be foolish*
7307 rûwach (2), *breath; wind; life-spirit*
7385 rîyq (8), *emptiness; worthless thing; in vain*
7386 rêyq (7), *empty; worthless*
7387 rêyqâm (1), *emptily; ineffectually*
7723 shâv' (22), *ruin; guile; idolatry*
8193 sâphâh (2), *lip, language, speech*
8267 sheqer (6), *untruth; sham*
8414 tôhûw (4), *waste, formless; in vain*
1432 dōrĕan (1), *gratuitously, freely*
1500 ĕikē (5), *idly, i.e. without reason or effect*
2755 kĕnŏdŏxŏs (1), *self-conceited*
2756 kĕnŏs (14), *empty; vain; useless*
2757 kĕnŏphōnia (2), *fruitless discussion*
2761 kĕnŏs (2), *vainly, i.e. to no purpose*
3150 mataiŏlŏgia (1), *meaningless talk*
3151 mataiŏlŏgŏs (1), *mischievous talker*
3152 mataiŏs (5), *profitless, futile; idol*
3154 mataiŏō (1), *wicked; idolatrous*
3155 matēn (2), *to no purpose, in vain*

VAINGLORY

2754 kĕnŏdŏxia (1), *self-conceit, vanity*

VAINLY

1500 ĕikē (1), *idly, i.e. without reason or effect*

VAJEZATHA

2055 Vayᵉzâthâ' (1), *Vajezatha*

VALE

6010 'êmeq (4), broad *depression or valley*
8219 shᵉphêlâh (5), *lowland,*

VALIANT

47 'abbîyr (1), *mighty*
691 'er'êl (1), *hero, brave person*
1121+2428 bên (4), *son, descendant; people*
1368 gibbôwr (6), *powerful; great warrior*
1396 gâbar (1), to *be strong; to prevail*

VANISHED

2428 chayil (16), *army; wealth; virtue; valor*
3524 kabbîyr (1), *mighty; aged; mighty*
2478 ischurŏs (1), *forcible, powerful*

VALIANTEST

1121+2428 bên (1), *son, descendant; people*

VALIANTLY

2388 châzaq (1), to *be strong; courageous*
2428 chayil (5), *army; wealth; virtue; valor*

VALLEY

1237 biq'âh (9), *wide level valley*
1516 gay' (52), *gorge, valley*
5158 nachal (18), *valley, ravine; mine shaft*
6010 'êmeq (54), broad *depression or valley*
8219 shᵉphêlâh (6), *lowland,*
5327 pharagx (1), *wadi ravine; valley*

VALLEYS

1237 biq'âh (4), *wide level valley*
1516 gay' (8), *gorge, valley*
5158 nachal (5), *valley, ravine; mine shaft*
6010 'êmeq (9), broad *depression or valley*
8219 shᵉphêlâh (2), *lowland,*

VALOUR

2428 chayil (37), *army; wealth; virtue; valor*

VALUE

457 'ĕlîyl (1), *vain idol*
6186 'ârak (3), to *set in a row, i.e. arrange,*
1308 diaphĕrō (2), to *bear, carry; to differ*
5091 timaō (1), to *revere, honor, show respect*

VALUED

5541 çâlâh (2), to *contemn, reject*
5091 timaō (1), to *revere, honor, show respect*

VALUEST

6187 'êrek (1), *pile, equipment, estimate*

VANIAH

2057 Vanyâh (1), *Vanjah*

VANISH

4414 mâlach (1), to *disappear as dust*
6789 tsâmath (1), to *extirpate, root out*
854 aphanismŏs (1), *disappearance*
2673 katargĕō (1), to *be, render entirely useless*

VANISHED

5628 çârach (1), to *extend even to excess*
1096+855 ginŏmai (1), to *be, become*

VANISHETH
3212 yâlak (1), to *walk*;
to *live*; to *carry*
853 aphanizō (1), to
disappear, be destroyed

VANITIES
1892 hebel (12),
emptiness or *vanity*
3152 mataiŏs (1),
profitless, futile; idol

VANITY
205 'âven (6), *trouble,
vanity, wickedness*
1892 hebel (49),
emptiness or *vanity*
7385 rîyq (2), *emptiness;
worthless* thing; *in vain*
7723 shâv' (22), *ruin;
guile; idolatry*
8414 tôhûw (4), *waste,
formless; in vain*
3153 mataiŏtēs (3),
transientness; depravity

VAPORS
5387 nâsîy' (2), *leader;
rising mist, fog*

VAPOUR
108 'êd (1), *fog*
5927 'âlâh (1), to *ascend,
be high, mount*
822 atmis (2), *mist,
vapor; billows of smoke*

VAPOURS
5387 nâsîy' (1), *leader;
rising mist, fog*
7008 qîytôwr (1), *fume,*
i.e. *smoke cloud*

VARIABLENESS
3883 parallagē (1),
change or variation

VARIANCE
1369 dichazō (1), to
sunder, i.e. *alienate*
2054 ĕris (1), *quarrel,* i.e.
wrangling

VASHNI
2059 Vashnîy (1), *weak*

VASHTI
2060 Vashtîy (10), *Vashti*

VAUNT
6286 pâ'ar (1), to *shake a
tree*

VAUNTETH
4068 pĕrpĕrĕuŏmai (1),
to *boast, brag*

VEHEMENT
2759 chârîyshîy (1),
sultry, searing
3050 Yâhh (1), *Jehovah,*
(the) self-*Existent or
Eternal One*
1972 ĕpipŏthēsis (1),
longing for

VEHEMENTLY
1171 dĕinōs (1), *terribly,*
i.e. *excessively, fiercely*
1722+4 ĕn (1), *in; during;
because of*
2159 ĕutŏnōs (1),
intensely, cogently
4366 prŏsrēgnumi (2), to
burst upon

VEIL
7289 râdîyd (1), *veil*

VANISHETH
2665 katapĕtasma (6),
door screen

VEIN
4161 môwtsâ' (1), *going
forth*

VENGEANCE
5358 nâqam (4), to
avenge or punish
5359 nâqâm (15), *revenge*
5360 nᵉqâmâh (19),
avengement
1349 dikē (2), *justice*
1557 ĕkdikēsis (4),
retaliation, punishment
3709 ŏrgē (1), *ire;
punishment*

VENISON
6718 tsayid (7), *hunting
game; lunch, food*
6720 tsêydâh (1), *food,
supplies*

VENOM
7219 rô'sh (1), *poisonous
plant; poison*

VENT
6605 pâthach (1), to *open
wide; to loosen, begin*

VENTURE
8537 tôm (2), *prosperity;
innocence*

VERIFIED
539 'âman (3), to *be firm,
faithful, true; to trust*

VERILY
61 'ăbâl (3), *truly, surely;
yet, but*
389 'ak (6), *surely; only,
however*
403 'âkên (2), *surely!,
truly!; but*
518 'îm (1), *whether?; if,
although; Oh that!*
518+3808 'îm (1), *Oh that!*
530 'ĕmûwnâh (1),
fidelity; steadiness
559 'âmar (1), to *say*
7069 qânâh (1), to *create;
to procure*
230 alēthōs (1), *truly,
surely*
281 amēn (76), *surely; so
be it*
1063 gar (2), *for, indeed,
but, because*
1222 dēpŏu (1), *indeed
doubtless*
2532 kai (2), *and; or;
even; also*
3303 mĕn (13), *verily*
3303+3767 mĕn (1), *verily*
3304 mĕnŏungĕ (1), *so
then at least*
3483 nai (1), *yes*
3689 ŏntōs (1), *really,
certainly*

VERITY
571 'emeth (1), *certainty,
truth, trustworthiness*
225 alēthĕia (1), *truth,
truthfulness*

VERMILION
8350 shâshar (2), *red*

VERY
199 'ûwlâm (2), *however
or on the contrary*

430 'ĕlôhîym (1), the true
God; great ones
552 'umnâm (1), *verily,
indeed, truly*
651 'âphêl (1), *dusky,
dark*
898 bâgad (1), to *act
covertly*
899 beged (2), *clothing;
treachery or pillage*
1419 gâdôwl (1), *great*
1767 day (2), *enough,
sufficient*
1851 daq (1), *crushed;
small or thin*
1854 dâqaq (1), to *crush;
crumble*
1942 havvâh (1), *desire;
craving*
2088 zeh (2), *this* or *that*
3190 yâṭab (2), to *be,
make well; be
successful*
3304 yᵉphêh-phîyâh (1),
very beautiful
3453 yâshîysh (2), *old
man*
3559 kûwn (1), to *render
sure, proper*
3966 mᵉ'ôd (136), *very,
utterly*
4213 miz'âr (3), *fewness,
smallness*
4295 maṭṭâh (1), *below
or beneath*
4592 mᵉ'aṭ (1), *little or
few*
4605 ma'al (2), *upward,
above, overhead*
4801 merchâq (1),
distant place; from afar
5464 çagrîyd (1), *pouring
rain*
5690 'egeb (1), *amative
words, words of love*
5704 'ad (2), *as far (long)
as; during; while; until*
6106 'etsem (2), *bone;
substance; selfsame*
6621 petha' (1), *wink,* i.e.
moment; quickly
6985 qaṭ (1), *little,* i.e.
merely
7023 qîyr (1), *wall,
side-wall*
7230 rôb (1), *abundance*
7260 rabrab (Ch.) (1),
huge, domineering
7690 saggîy' (Ch.) (1),
large
85 adēmŏnĕŏ (2), to *be in
mental distress*
230 alēthōs (1), *truly,
surely*
662 apŏtŏlmaŏ (1), to
venture plainly
846 autŏs (5), *he, she, it*
927 barutimŏs (1), *highly
valuable*
957 bĕltiŏn (1), *better*
1565 ĕkĕinŏs (2), *that one*
1582 ĕkkrĕmamai (1), to
listen closely
1646 ĕlachistŏs (3), *least*
1888 ĕpautŏphōrŏi (1), *in
actual crime*
2236 hēdista (1), *with
great pleasure*

2532 kai (4), *and; or;
even; also*
2566 kalliŏn (1), *better*
2735 katŏrthōma (1),
made fully upright
3029 lian (2), *very much*
3827 pampŏlus (1), *full
many,* i.e. *immense*
4036 pĕrilupŏs (1),
intensely sad
4118 plĕistŏs (1), *very
large,* i.e. *the most*
4119 plĕiŏn (1), *more*
4184 pŏlusplagchnŏs (1),
*extremely
compassionate*
4185 pŏlutĕlēs (1),
extremely expensive
4186 pŏlutimŏs (1),
extremely valuable
4361 prŏspĕinŏs (1),
intensely hungry
4708 spŏudaiŏtĕrŏs (1),
more speedily
4970 sphŏdra (4), *high
degree, much*
5228 hupĕr (2), *over;
above; beyond*

VESSEL
3627 kᵉlîy (33),
implement, thing
5035 nebel (1), *skin-bag
for liquids; vase; lyre*
4632 skĕuŏs (11), *vessel,
implement, equipment*

VESSELS
3627 kᵉlîy (129),
implement, thing
3984 mâ'n (Ch.) (7),
utensil, vessel
30 aggĕiŏn (2),
receptacle, vessel
4632 skĕuŏs (8), *vessel,
implement, equipment*

VESTMENTS
3830 lᵉbûwsh (1),
garment; wife
4403 malbûwsh (1),
garment, clothing

VESTRY
4458 meltâchâh (1),
wardrobe

VESTURE
3682 kᵉçûwth (1), *cover;
veiling*
3830 lᵉbûwsh (2),
garment; wife
2440 himatiŏn (2), to *put
on clothes*
2441 himatismŏs (2),
clothing
4018 pĕribŏlaiŏn (1),
thrown around

VESTURES
899 beged (1), *clothing;
treachery or pillage*

VEX
926 bâhal (1), to *tremble;
be, make agitated*
2000 hâmam (1), to *put
in commotion*
2111 zûwâ' (1), to *shake
with fear, tremble*
3013 yâgâh (1), to *grieve;
to torment*
3238 yânâh (2), to *rage
or be violent*

VEXATION

3707 kâ'aç (1), to *grieve, rage, be indignant*
6213+7451 'âsâh (1), to *do* or *make*
6887 tsârar (5), to *cramp*
6973 qûwts (1), to *be, make anxious*
2559 kakôŏ (1), to *injure; to oppress; to embitter*

VEXATION

2113 zᵉvâ'âh (1), *agitation, fear*
4103 mᵉhûwmâh (1), *confusion* or *uproar*
4164 mûwtsaq (1), *distress*
7469 rᵉ'ûwth (7), *grasping* after
7475 ra'yôwn (3), *desire, chasing after*
7667 sheber (1), *fracture; ruin*

VEXATIONS

4103 mᵉhûwmâh (1), *confusion* or *uproar*

VEXED

926 bâhal (3), to *tremble; be, make agitated*
1766 dâchaq (1), to *oppress*
3238 yânâh (2), to *rage* or *be violent*
3334 yâtsar (1), to *be in distress*
4103 mᵉhûwmâh (1), *confusion* or *uproar*
4843 mârar (2), to *be, make bitter*
6087 'âtsab (1), to *worry, have pain* or *anger*
6887 tsârar (1), to *cramp*
7114 qâtsar (1), to *curtail, cut short*
7489 râ'a' (1), to *be good for nothing*
7492 râ'ats (1), to *break in pieces; to harass*
7561 râsha' (1), to *be, do, declare wrong*
928 basanizō (1), to *torture, torment*
1139 daimŏnizŏmai (1), to *be exercised by a demon*
2669 katapŏnéŏ (1), to *harass, oppress*
3791 ŏchléŏ (2), to *harass, be tormented*
3958 paschō (1), to *experience* pain

VIAL

6378 pak (1), *flask, small jug*
5357 phialē (7), broad shallow *cup*, i.e. a *phial*

VIALS

5357 phialē (5), broad shallow *cup*, i.e. a *phial*

VICTORY

3467 yâsha' (1), to make *safe, free*
5331 netsach (2), *splendor; lasting*
8668 tᵉshûw'âh (3), *rescue, deliverance*
3528 nikaō (1), to *subdue, conquer*
3529 nikē (1), *conquest, victory, success*
3534 nikŏs (4), *triumph, victory*

VICTUAL

3557 kûwl (1), to *measure; to maintain*
3978 ma'ăkâl (1), *food, something to eat*
4202 mâzôwn (1), *food, provisions*
6720 tsêydâh (2), *food, supplies*

VICTUALS

400 'ôkel (3), *food*
737 'ărûchâh (1), *ration, portion* of food
3557 kûwl (1), to *measure; to maintain*
3899 lechem (2), *food, bread*
4241 michyâh (1), *sustenance; quick*
6718 tsayid (2), *hunting game; lunch, food*
6720 tsêydâh (4), *food, supplies*
7668 sheber (1), *grain*
1033 brōma (1), *food*
1979 ἐpisitismŏs (1), *food*

VIEW

5048 neged (2), *in front of*
7200 râ'âh (1), to *see*
7270 râgal (1), to *reconnoiter; to slander*

VIEWED

995 bîyn (1), to *understand; discern*
7370 râchash (1), to *gush*
7663 sâbar (2), to *scrutinize; to expect*

VIGILANT

1127 grēgŏrĕuō (1), to *watch, guard*
3524 nēphalĕŏs (1), *circumspect, temperate*

VILE

959 bâzâh (2), to *disesteem, ridicule*
2151 zâlal (2), to *be loose* morally, *worthless*
2933 ṭâmâh (1), to *be ceremonially impure*
5034 nâbêl (1), to *wilt; to fall away; to be foolish*
5036 nâbâl (2), *stupid; impious*
5039 nᵉbâlâh (1), moral *wickedness; crime*
5240 nᵉmibzeh (1), *despised*
7034 qâlâh (1), to *be, hold in contempt*
7043 qâlal (4), to *be easy, trifling, vile*
8182 shô'âr (1), *harsh* or *horrid*, i.e. *offensive*
819 atimia (1), *disgrace*
4508 rhuparŏs (1), *shabby, dirty; wicked*
5014 tapĕinōsis (1), *humbleness, lowliness*

VILELY

1602 gâ'al (1), to *detest; to reject; to fail*

VILER

5217 nâkâ' (1), to *smite*, i.e. *drive away*

VILEST

2149 zullûwth (1), (poss.) *tempest*

VILLAGE

2968 kômē (10), *hamlet, town*

VILLAGES

1323 bath (12), *daughter, outlying village*
2691 châtsêr (47), *yard; walled village*
3715 kᵉphîyr (1), walled *village; young lion*
3723 kâphâr (2), walled *village*
3724 kôpher (1), *village; bitumen; henna*
6518 pârâz (1), *chieftain*
6519 pᵉrâzâh (1), *rural, open country*
6520 pᵉrâzôwn (2), *magistracy, leadership*
6521 pᵉrâzîy (1), *rustic*
2968 kômē (7), *hamlet, town*

VILLANY

5039 nᵉbâlâh (2), moral *wickedness; crime*

VINE

1612 gephen (44), grape *vine*
2156 zᵉmôwrâh (1), *pruned twig, branch*
3196 yayin (1), *wine; intoxication*
3755 kôrêm (1), *vinedresser*
5139 nâzîyr (2), *prince; unpruned vine*
8321 sôrêq (3), *choice vine stock*
288 ampĕlŏs (9), grape *vine*

VINEDRESSERS

3755 kôrêm (4), *vinedresser*

VINEGAR

2558 chômets (6), *vinegar*
3690 ŏxŏs (7), *sour* wine

VINES

1612 gephen (9), grape *vine*
3754 kerem (3), *garden* or *vineyard*

VINEYARD

3657 kannâh (1), *plant*
3754 kerem (44), *garden* or *vineyard*
289 ampĕlŏurgŏs (1), *vineyard caretaker*
290 ampĕlōn (23), *vineyard*

VINEYARDS

3754 kerem (45), *garden* or *vineyard*

VINTAGE

1208 bâtsôwr (1), *inaccessible*
1210 bâtsîyr (7), *grape crop, harvest*
3754 kerem (1), *garden* or *vineyard*

VIOL

5035 nebel (2), skin-*bag* for liquids; *vase; lyre*

VIOLATED

2554 châmaç (1), to *be violent; to maltreat*

VIOLENCE

1497 gâzal (1), to *rob*
1498 gâzêl (1), *robbery, stealing*
1499 gêzel (1), *violence*
1500 gᵉzêlâh (3), *robbery, stealing; things stolen*
2554 châmaç (2), to *be violent; to maltreat*
2555 châmâç (39), *violence; malice*
4835 mᵉrûtsâh (1), *oppression*
6231 'âshaq (1), to *violate; to overflow*
970 bia (4), *force, pounding violence*
971 biazō (1), to *crowd oneself into*
1286 diasĕiō (1), to *intimidate, extort*
1411 dunamis (1), *force, power, miracle*
3731 hŏrmēma (1), *sudden attack*

VIOLENT

1499 gêzel (1), *violence*
2555 châmâç (7), *violence; malice*
6184 'ârîyts (1), *powerful* or *tyrannical*
973 biastēs (1), *energetic, forceful one*

VIOLENTLY

1497 gâzal (4), to *rob*
1500 gᵉzêlâh (1), *robbery, stealing; things stolen*
2554 châmaç (1), to *be violent; to maltreat*

VIOLS

5035 nebel (2), skin-*bag* for liquids; *vase; lyre*

VIPER

660 'eph'eh (2), *asp*
2191 ĕchidna (1), *adder*

VIPER'S

660 'eph'eh (1), *asp*

VIPERS

2191 ĕchidna (4), *adder*

VIRGIN

1330 bᵉthûwlâh (24), *virgin*
5959 'almâh (2), *lass, young woman*
3933 parthĕnŏs (7), *virgin*

VIRGIN'S

3933 parthĕnŏs (1), *virgin*

VIRGINITY

1331 bᵉthûwlîym (8), *virginity; proof of female virginity*
3932 parthĕnia (1), *maidenhood, virginity*

VIRGINS

1330 bᵉthûwlâh (14), *virgin*
5959 'almâh (2), *lass, young woman*
3933 parthĕnŏs (6), *virgin*

V

VIRTUE
703 *arĕtē* (4), *excellence, virtue*
1411 *dunamis* (3), *force, power, miracle*

VIRTUOUS
2428 chayil (3), *army; wealth; virtue; valor*

VIRTUOUSLY
2428 chayil (1), *army; wealth; virtue; valor*

VISAGE
600 'ănaph (Ch.) (1), *face*
4758 mar'eh (1), *appearance; vision*
8389 tô'ar (1), *outline, appearance*

VISIBLE
3707 *hŏratŏs* (1), *capable of being seen*

VISION
2376 chêzev (Ch.) (2), *sight, revelation*
2377 châzôwn (32), *sight; revelation*
2380 châzûwth (2), *striking appearance*
2384 chizzâyôwn (6), *dream; vision*
4236 machăzeh (4), *vision*
4758 mar'eh (14), *appearance; vision*
4759 mar'âh (3), *vision; mirror*
7203 rô'eh (1), *seer; vision*
3701 *ŏptasia* (2), *supernatural vision*
3705 *hŏrama* (12), *supernatural spectacle*
3706 *hŏrasis* (1), *appearance, vision*

VISIONS
2376 chêzev (Ch.) (9), *sight, revelation*
2377 châzôwn (3), *sight; revelation*
2378 châzôwth (1), *revelation*
2384 chizzâyôwn (3), *dream; vision*
4759 mar'âh (5), *vision; mirror*
7200 râ'âh (1), to *see*
3701 *ŏptasia* (1), *supernatural vision*
3706 *hŏrasis* (1), *appearance, vision*

VISIT
6485 pâqad (33), to *visit, care for, count*
1980 *ĕpiskĕptŏmai* (4), to *inspect, to go to see*

VISITATION
6486 p^equddâh (13), *visitation; punishment*
1984 *ĕpiskŏpē* (2), *episcopate*

VISITED
6485 pâqad (18), to *visit, care for, count*
1980 *ĕpiskĕptŏmai* (5), to *inspect; to go to see*

VISITEST
6485 pâqad (2), to *visit, care for, count*
1980 *ĕpiskĕptŏmai* (1), to *inspect; to go to see*

VISITETH
6485 pâqad (1), to *visit, care for, count*

VISITING
6485 pâqad (4), to *visit, care for, count*

VOCATION
2821 *klēsis* (1), *invitation; station in life*

VOICE
6963 qôwl (379), *voice or sound*
7032 qâl (Ch.) (3), *sound, music*
5456 *phōnē* (116), *voice, sound*
5586 *psēphŏs* (1), *pebble stone*

VOICES
6963 qôwl (2), *voice or sound*
5456 *phōnē* (15), *voice, sound*

VOID
6 'âbad (1), *perish; destroy*
922 bôhûw (2), *ruin, desolation*
1238 bâqaq (1), to *depopulate, ruin*
1637 gôren (2), open *area*
2638 châçêr (6), *lacking*
4003 m^ebûwqâh (1), *emptiness, devastation*
5010 nâ'ar (1), to *reject*
6565 pârar (5), to *break up; to violate, frustrate*
7387 rêyqâm (1), *emptily; ineffectually*
677 aprŏskŏpŏs (1), *not led into sin*
2673 katargĕō (1), to *be, render entirely useless*
2758 kĕnŏō (2), to *make empty*

VOLUME
4039 m^egillâh (1), *roll, scroll*
2777 kĕphalis (1), *roll, scroll*

VOLUNTARILY
5071 n^edâbâh (1), *abundant gift*

VOLUNTARY
5071 n^edâbâh (2), *abundant gift*
7522 râtsôwn (1), *delight*
2309 *thĕlō* (1), to *will; to desire; to choose*

VOMIT
6892 qê' (4), *vomit*
6958 qôw' (3), to *vomit*
1829 *ĕxĕrama* (1), *vomit*

VOMITED
6958 qôw' (1), to *vomit*

VOMITETH
6958 qôw' (1), to *vomit*

VOPHSI
2058 Vophçîy (1), *additional*

VOW
5087 nâdar (9), to *promise, vow*
5088 neder (30), *promise to God; thing promised*
2171 *ĕuchē* (2), *wish, petition*

VOWED
5087 nâdar (16), to *promise, vow*
5088 neder (2), *promise to God; thing promised*

VOWEDST
5087 nâdar (1), to *promise, vow*

VOWEST
5087 nâdar (2), to *promise, vow*

VOWETH
5087 nâdar (1), to *promise, vow*

VOWS
5088 neder (30), *promise to God; thing promised*

VOYAGE
4144 *plŏŏs* (1), *navigation, voyage*

VULTURE
1676 dâ'âh (1), *kite*
1772 dayâh (1), *falcon*

VULTURE'S
344 'ayâh (1), *hawk*

VULTURES
1772 dayâh (1), *falcon*

WAFER
7550 râqîyq (3), *thin cake, wafer*

WAFERS
6838 tsappîychîth (1), *flat thin cake*
7550 râqîyq (4), *thin cake, wafer*

WAG
5110 nûwd (1), to *waver; to wander, flee*
5128 nûwa' (2), to *waver*

WAGES
2600 chinnâm (1), *gratis, free*
4909 maskôreth (3), *wages; reward*
6468 p^e'ullâh (1), *work, deed*
7936 sâkar (1), to *hire*
7939 sâkâr (6), *payment, salary; compensation*
3408 misthŏs (2), *pay for services, good or bad*
3800 ŏpsōniŏn (3), *rations, stipend or pay*

WAGGING
2795 kinĕō (2), to *stir, move, remove*

WAGON
5699 'ăgâlâh (1), *wheeled vehicle*

WAGONS
5699 'ăgâlâh (8), *wheeled vehicle*
7393 rekeb (1), *vehicle for riding*

WAIL
5091 nâhâh (1), to *bewail; to assemble*
5594 çâphad (1), to *tear the hair, wail*
2875 kŏptō (1), to *beat the breast*

WAILED
214 alalazō (1), to *wail; to clang*

WAILING
4553 miçpêd (6), *lamentation, howling*
5089 nôahh (1), *lamentation*
5092 n^ehîy (4), *elegy*
5204 nîy (1), *lamentation*
2805 klauthmŏs (2), *lamentation, weeping*
3996 pĕnthĕō (2), to *grieve*

WAIT
693 'ârab (34), to *ambush, lie in wait*
695 'ereb (1), *hiding place; lair*
696 'ôreb (1), *hiding place; lair*
1748 dûwmâm (1), *silently*
1826 dâmam (1), to *stop, cease; to perish*
2342 chûwl (1), to *wait; to pervert*
2442 châkâh (6), to *await; hope for*
3027 yâd (1), *hand; power*
3176 yâchal (5), to *wait; to be patient, hope*
3993 ma'ărâb (1), *ambuscade, ambush*
6119 'âqêb (1), *track, footprint; rear position*
6633 tsâbâ' (1), to *mass an army or servants*
6658 tsâdâh (1), to *desolate*
6660 ts^edîyâh (2), *design, lying in wait*
6960 qâvâh (22), to *collect; to expect*
7663 sâbar (2), to *scrutinize; to expect*
7789 shûwr (1), to *spy out, survey*
8104 shâmar (4), to *watch*
362 anamĕnō (1), to *await in expectation*
553 apĕkdĕchŏmai (2), to *expect fully, await*
1096+1917 ginŏmai (1), to *be, become*
1747 ĕnĕdra (1), *ambush*
1748 ĕnĕdrĕuō (2), to *lurk*
1917 ĕpibŏulē (2), *plot, plan*
3180 mĕthŏdĕia (1), *trickery, scheming*
4037 pĕrimĕnō (1), to *await*
4160+1747 pŏiĕō (1), to *make or do*
4327 prŏsdĕchŏmai (1), to *receive; to await for*
4332 prŏsĕdrĕuō (1), to *attend as a servant*

4342 prŏskartĕrĕŏ (1), to
persevere

WAITED
1961+6440 hâyâh (1), to
exist, i.e. *be* or *become*
2342 chûwl (1), to *wait;*
to *pervert*
2442 châkâh (2), to
await; hope for
3176 yâchal (6), to *wait;*
to *be patient, hope*
5975 'âmad (5), to *stand*
6822 tsâphâh (1), to
observe, await
6960 qâvâh (8), to *collect;*
to *expect*
8104 shâmar (1), to
watch
8334 shârath (1), to
attend as a menial
1551 ĕkdĕchŏmai (2), to
await, expect
4327 prŏsdĕchŏmai (2),
to *receive;* to *await for*
4328 prŏsdŏkaō (2), to
anticipate; to *await*
4342 prŏskartĕrĕŏ (1), to
persevere, be constant

WAITETH
1747 dûwmîyâh (2),
silently; quiet, trust
2442 châkâh (3), to
await; hope for
3176 yâchal (1), to *wait;*
to *be patient, hope*
8104 shâmar (2), to
watch
553 apĕkdĕchŏmai (1),
to *expect fully, await*
1551 ĕkdĕchŏmai (1), to
await, expect

WAITING
6635 tsâbâ' (1), *army,
military host*
8104 shâmar (1), to
watch
553 apĕkdĕchŏmai (2),
to *expect fully, await*
1551 ĕkdĕchŏmai (1), to
await, expect
4327 prŏsdĕchŏmai (1),
to *receive;* to *await for*
4328 prŏsdŏkaō (1), to
anticipate; to *await*

WAKE
5782 'ûwr (1), to *awake*
6974 qûwts (2), to *awake*
1127 grĕgŏrĕuŏ (1), to
watch, guard

WAKED
5782 'ûwr (1), to *awake*

WAKENED
5782 'ûwr (1), to *awake*

WAKENETH
5782 'ûwr (2), to *awake*

WAKETH
5782 'ûwr (1), to *awake*
8245 shâqad (1), to *be
alert,* i.e. *sleepless*

WAKING
8109 shᵉmûrâh (1),
eye-lid

WALK
1869 dârak (2), to *tread,
trample;* to *walk*

1979 hălîykâh (1),
walking; procession
1980 hâlak (61), to *walk;
live a certain way*
1981 hălak (Ch.) (1), to
walk; live a certain way
3212 yâlak (79), to *walk;*
to *live;* to *carry*
4108 mahlêk (1), *access;
journey*
4109 mahălâk (1),
passage or a *distance*
5437 çâbab (1), to
surround
1704 ĕmpĕripatĕŏ (1), to
be occupied among
4043 pĕripatĕŏ (55), to
walk; to *live a life*
4198 pŏrĕuŏmai (4), to
go, come; to *travel*
4748 stŏichĕŏ (4), to
follow, walk; to *conform*

WALKED
1980 hâlak (67), to *walk;
live a certain way*
1981 hălak (Ch.) (1), to
walk; live a certain way
3212 yâlak (32), to *walk;*
to *live;* to *carry*
3716 ŏrthŏpŏdĕŏ (1), to
act rightly
4043 pĕripatĕŏ (19), to
walk; to *live a life*
4198 pŏrĕuŏmai (1), to
go, come; to *travel*

WALKEDST
4043 pĕripatĕŏ (1), to
walk; to *live a life*

WALKEST
1980 hâlak (1), to *walk;
live a certain way*
3212 yâlak (3), to *walk;*
to *live;* to *carry*
4043 pĕripatĕŏ (2), to
walk; to *live a life*
4748 stŏichĕŏ (1), to
follow, walk; to *conform*

WALKETH
1980 hâlak (31), to *walk;
live a certain way*
3212 yâlak (2), to *walk;*
to *live;* to *carry*
1330 diĕrchŏmai (2), to
traverse, travel through
4043 pĕripatĕŏ (5), to
walk; to *live a life*

WALKING
1980 hâlak (10), to *walk;
live a certain way*
1981 hălak (Ch.) (1), to
walk; live a certain way
3212 yâlak (3), to *walk;*
to *live;* to *carry*
4043 pĕripatĕŏ (12), to
walk; to *live a life*
4198 pŏrĕuŏmai (4), to
go, come; to *travel*

WALL
846 'ushsharnâ' (Ch.) (1),
wall
1444 geder (2), *wall* or
fence
1447 gâdêr (5),
enclosure, i.e. *wall*
1448 gᵉdêrâh (1),
enclosure for flocks
2346 chôwmâh (92), *wall*

2426 chêyl (1),
entrenchment
2434 chayits (1), *wall*
2742 chârûwts (1),
mined gold; trench
3796 kôthel (1), *house
wall*
3797 kᵉthal (Ch.) (1),
house wall
7023 qîyr (50), *wall,
side-wall*
7791 shûwr (3), *wall*
7794 shôwr (1), *bullock*
5038 tĕichŏs (8), *house
wall*
5109 tŏichŏs (1), *wall*

WALLED
1219 bâtsar (2), to *be
inaccessible*
2346 chôwmâh (2), *wall*

WALLOW
5606 çâphaq (1), to *be
enough;* to *vomit*
6428 pâlash (3), to *roll* in
dust

WALLOWED
1556 gâlal (1), to *roll;* to
commit
2947 kuliŏŏ (1), to *roll
about*

WALLOWING
2946 kulisma (1),
wallowing in filth

WALLS
846 'ushsharnâ' (Ch.) (1),
wall
1447 gâdêr (1),
enclosure, i.e. *wall*
2346 chôwmâh (39), *wall*
2426 chêyl (1), *rampart,
battlement*
3797 kᵉthal (Ch.) (1),
house wall
7023 qîyr (16), *wall,
side-wall*
7791 shûwr (4), *wall*
8284 shârâh (1),
fortification
5038 tĕichŏs (1), *house
wall*

WANDER
5074 nâdad (1), to *rove,
flee;* to *drive away*
5128 nûwa' (4), to *waver*
6808 tsâ'âh (1), to *tip
over;* to *depopulate*
7462 râ'âh (1), to *tend* a
flock, i.e. *pasture* it
7686 shâgâh (2), to *stray,
wander;* to *transgress*
8582 tâ'âh (5), to
vacillate, i.e. *reel, stray*

WANDERED
1980 hâlak (1), to *walk;
live a certain way*
5128 nûwa' (3), to *waver*
7686 shâgâh (1), to *stray,
wander;* to *transgress*
8582 tâ'âh (3), to
vacillate, i.e. *reel, stray*
4022 pĕriĕrchŏmai (1), to
stroll, vacillate, veer
4105 planaō (1), to *roam,
wander* from safety

WANDERERS
5074 nâdad (1), to *rove,
flee;* to *drive* away
6808 tsâ'âh (1), to *tip
over;* to *depopulate*

WANDEREST
6808 tsâ'âh (1), to *tip
over;* to *depopulate;* to
imprison; to *lay down*

WANDERETH
5074 nâdad (5), to *rove,
flee;* to *drive* away
8582 tâ'âh (1), to
vacillate, i.e. *reel, stray*

WANDERING
1981 hălak (Ch.) (1), to
walk; live a certain way
5074 nâdad (1), to *rove,
flee;* to *drive* away
5110 nûwd (1), to *waver;*
to *wander, flee*
8582 tâ'âh (1), to
vacillate, i.e. *reel, stray*
4022 pĕriĕrchŏmai (1), to
stroll, vacillate, veer
4107 planĕtĕs (1), *roving,
erratic* teacher

WANDERINGS
5112 nôwd (1), *exile*

WANT
657 'epheç (1), *end; no
further*
1097 bᵉlîy (2), *without,
not yet; lacking*
2637 châçêr (4), to *lack;*
to *fail, want, make less*
2638 châçêr (1), *lacking*
2639 cheçer (1), *lack;
destitution*
2640 chôçer (3), *poverty*
3772 kârath (3), to *cut*
(off, down or asunder)
3808 lô' (1), *no, not*
4270 machçôwr (7),
impoverishment
6485 pâqad (1), to *visit,
care for, count*
5302 hustĕrĕŏ (1), to *be
inferior;* to *fall short* (be
deficient)
5303 hustĕrēma (3),
deficit; poverty; lacking
5304 hustĕrēsis (2),
penury, lack, need

WANTED
2637 châçêr (1), to *lack;*
to *fail, want, make less*
5302 hustĕrĕŏ (2), to *be
inferior;* to *fall short*

WANTETH
2308 châdal (1), to *desist,
stop; be fat*
2637 châçêr (2), to *lack;*
to *fail, want, make less*
2638 châçêr (4), *lacking*

WANTING
2627 chaççîyr (Ch.) (1),
deficient, wanting
2642 cheçrôwn (1),
deficiency
3808 lô' (1), *no, not*
6485 pâqad (2), to *visit,
care for, count*
3007 lĕipŏ (3), to *fail* or
be absent

W

WANTON
8265 sâqar (1), to *ogle*,
i.e. *blink* coquettishly
2691 *katastrēniaō* (1), to
be voluptuous against
4684 *spatalaō* (1), to *live
in luxury*

WANTONNESS
766 *asĕlgĕia* (2),
debauchery, lewdness

WANTS
4270 machçôwr (1),
impoverishment
5532 chrĕia (1), *affair;
requirement*

WAR
2428 chayil (1), *army;
wealth; virtue; valor*
2438 Chîyrâm (1), *noble*
3898 lâcham (9), to *fight
a battle*
3901 lâchem (1), *battle,
war*
4421 milchâmâh (151),
battle; war; fighting
4421+7128 milchâmâh
(1), *battle; war; fighting*
6635 tsâbâ' (41), *army,
military host*
6904 qôbel (1),
battering-ram
7128 qᵉrâb (3), *hostile
encounter*
7129 qᵉrâb (Ch.) (1),
hostile encounter
4170 pŏlĕmĕō (4), to
battle, make war
4171 pŏlĕmŏs (6),
warfare; battle; fight
4753 stratĕuma (1), *body
of troops*
4754 stratĕuŏmai (4), to
serve in military

WARD
4929 mishmâr (11),
guard; deposit; usage
4931 mishmereth (6),
watch, sentry, post
5474 çûwgar (1), *animal
cage*
6488 pᵉqîdûth (1),
supervision
5438 phulakē (1),
guarding or guard

WARDROBE
899 beged (2), *clothing;
treachery or pillage*

WARDS
4931 mishmereth (3),
watch, sentry, post

WARE
4377 meker (1),
merchandise; value
4465 mimkâr (1),
merchandise
4728 maqqâchâh (1),
merchandise, wares
1737 ĕndiduskō (1), to
clothe
4894 sunĕidō (1), to
understand or be aware
5442 phulassō (1), to
watch, i.e. *be on guard*

WARES
3627 kᵉlîy (1),
implement, thing

WARM
3666 kin'âh (1), *package,
bundle*
4639 ma'ăseh (2), *action;
labor*
5801 'izzâbôwn (1),
trade, merchandise

WARFARE
6635 tsâbâ' (2), *army,
military host*
4752 stratĕia (2),
warfare; fight
4754 stratĕuŏmai (1), to
serve in military

WARM
2215 zârab (1), to *flow
away, be dry*
2525 châm (1), *hot,
sweltering*
2527 chôm (1), *heat*
2552 châmam (4), to *be
hot;* to *be in a rage*
3179 yâcham (1), to
conceive

WARMED
2552 châmam (1), to *be
hot;* to *be in a rage*
2328 thĕrmainō (5), to
heat oneself

WARMETH
2552 châmam (2), to *be
hot;* to *be in a rage*

WARMING
2328 thĕrmainō (1), to
heat oneself

WARN
2094 zâhar (8), to
enlighten
3560 nŏuthĕtĕō (3), to
caution or reprove

WARNED
2094 zâhar (4), to
enlighten
5263 hupŏdĕiknumi (2),
to *exemplify*
5537 chrēmatizō (4), to
utter an oracle

WARNING
2094 zâhar (6), to
enlighten
5749 'ûwd (1), to
duplicate or repeat
3560 nŏuthĕtĕō (1), to
caution or reprove

WARP
8359 shᵉthîy (9), *warp in
weaving*

WARRED
3898 lâcham (7), to *fight
a battle*
6633 tsâbâ' (2), to *mass
an army or servants*

WARRETH
4754 stratĕuŏmai (1), to
serve in military

WARRING
3898 lâcham (2), to *fight
a battle*
497 antistratĕuŏmai (1),
destroy, wage war

WARRIOR
5431 çâ'an (1), *soldier
wearing boots*

WARRIORS
6213+4421 'âsâh (2), to
do or make

WARS
4421 milchâmâh (9),
battle; war; fighting
4171 pŏlĕmŏs (4),
warfare; battle; fight

WASH
3526 kâbaç (39), to *wash*
7364 râchats (36), to
lave, bathe
628 apŏlŏuō (1), to *wash
fully*
907 baptizō (1), *baptize*
1026 brĕchō (1), to *make
wet;* to *rain*
3538 niptō (11), to *wash,
bathe*

WASHED
1740 dûwach (2), to *rinse
clean, wash*
3526 kâbaç (7), to *wash*
7364 râchats (17), to
lave, bathe
7857 shâṭaph (2), to
inundate, cleanse
628 apŏlŏuō (1), to *wash
fully*
633 apŏniptō (1), to *wash
off* hands
907 baptizō (1), *baptize*
1026 brĕchō (1), to *make
wet;* to *rain*
3068 lŏuō (6), to *bathe;* to
wash
3538 niptō (6), to *wash,
bathe*
4150 plunō (1), to *wash
or launder* clothing

WASHEST
7857 shâṭaph (1), to
inundate, cleanse

WASHING
3526 kâbaç (1), to *wash*
4325 mayim (1), *water*
7364 râchats (1), to *lave,
bathe*
7367 rachtsâh (2),
bathing place
637 apŏplunō (1), to
rinse off, wash out
909 baptismŏs (2),
baptism
3067 lŏutrŏn (2),
washing, baptism

WASHINGS
909 baptismŏs (1),
baptism

WASHPOT
5518+7366 çîyr (2), *thorn;
hook*

WAST
1961 hâyâh (13), to *exist,*
i.e. *be or become*
2258 ēn (5), I *was*
5607 ôn (1), *being,
existence*

WASTE
1086 bâlâh (1), to *wear
out, decay; consume*
1110 bâlaq (2), to
annihilate, devastate
1326 bâthâh (1), *area of
desolation*

WATCH
2717 chârab (13), to
desolate, destroy
2720 chârêb (6), *ruined;
desolate*
2721 chôreb (2),
parched; ruined
2723 chorbâh (14),
desolation, dry desert
3615 kâlâh (1), to
complete, prepare
3765 kirçem (1), to *lay
waste, ravage*
4875 mᵉshôw'âh (2), *ruin*
5327 nâtsâh (1), to *be
desolate, to lay waste*
7489 râ'a' (1), to *be good
for nothing*
7582 shâ'âh (2), to *moan;
to desolate*
7703 shâdad (5), to
ravage
8047 shammâh (3), *ruin;
consternation*
8074 shâmêm (5), to
devastate; to stupefy
8077 shᵉmâmâh (1),
devastation
8414 tôhûw (1), *waste,
desolation, formless*
684 apŏlĕia (2), *ruin or
loss*

WASTED
1197 bâ'ar (1), to *be
brutish, be senseless*
2717 chârab (3), to
parch; desolate, destroy
2723 chorbâh (1),
desolation, dry desert
3615 kâlâh (1), to
complete, consume
7582 shâ'âh (1), to *moan;
to desolate*
7703 shâdad (2), to
ravage
7843 shâchath (1), to
decay; to *ruin*
8437 tôlâl (1), *oppressor*
8552 tâmam (2), to
complete, finish
1287 diaskŏrpizō (2), to
scatter; to *squander*
4199 pŏrthĕō (1), to
ravage, pillage

WASTENESS
7722 shôw' (1), *tempest;
devastation*

WASTER
7843 shâchath (2), to
decay; to *ruin*

WASTES
2723 chorbâh (7),
desolation, dry desert

WASTETH
2522 châlash (1), to
prostrate, lay low
7703 shâdad (1), to
ravage
7736 shûwd (1), to
devastate

WASTING
7701 shôd (2), *violence,
ravage, destruction*

WATCH
821 'ashmûrâh (4), *night
watch*
4707 mitspeh (1),
military observatory

WATCHED
4929 mishmâr (4), *guard; deposit; usage; example*
4931 mishmereth (5), *watch, sentry, post*
6822 tsâphâh (5), to *observe, await*
8104 shâmar (5), to *watch*
8108 shomrâh (1), *watchfulness*
8245 shâqad (6), to *be on the lookout*
69 agrupněō (3), to *be sleepless, keep awake*
1127 grěgŏrěuŏ (16), to *watch, guard*
2892 kŏustōdia (3), *sentry*
3525 něphō (2), to *abstain from wine*
5438 phulakē (6), *night watch; prison; haunt*

WATCHED
6822 tsâphâh (1), to *observe, await*
8104 shâmar (2), to *watch*
8245 shâqad (2), to *be on the lookout*
1127 grěgŏrěuŏ (2), to *watch, guard*
3906 paratěrěō (5), to *note insidiously*
5083 těrěō (1), to *keep, guard, obey*

WATCHER
5894 'îyr (Ch.) (2), *watcher-angel*

WATCHERS
5341 nâtsar (1), to *guard, protect, maintain*
5894 'îyr (Ch.) (1), *watcher-angel*

WATCHES
821 'ashmûrâh (3), *night watch*
4931 mishmereth (2), *watch, sentry, post*

WATCHETH
6822 tsâphâh (1), to *observe, await*
6974 qûwts (1), to *awake*
1127 grěgŏrěuŏ (1), to *watch, guard*

WATCHFUL
1127 grěgŏrěuŏ (1), to *watch, guard*

WATCHING
6822 tsâphâh (2), to *observe, await*
8245 shâqad (1), to *be on the lookout*
69 agrupněō (1), to *be sleepless, keep awake*
1127 grěgŏrěuŏ (1), to *watch, guard*
5083 těrěō (1), to *keep, guard, obey*

WATCHINGS
70 agrupnia (2), *keeping awake*

WATCHMAN
6822 tsâphâh (14), to *peer into the distance*
8104 shâmar (4), to *watch*

WATCHMAN'S
6822 tsâphâh (1), to *peer into the distance*

WATCHMEN
5341 nâtsar (3), to *guard, protect, maintain*
6822 tsâphâh (5), to *peer into the distance*
8104 shâmar (4), to *watch*

WATCHTOWER
4707 mitspeh (1), *military observatory*
6844 tsâphîyth (1), *sentry*

WATER
1119 bᵉmôw (1), *in, with, by*
2222 zarzîyph (1), *pouring rain*
4325 mayim (308), *water*
4529 mâçâh (1), to *dissolve, melt*
7301 râvâh (1), to *slake thirst or appetites*
8248 shâqah (9), to *quaff, i.e. to irrigate*
504 anudrŏs (2), *dry, arid*
5202 hudrŏpŏtěō (1), to *drink water exclusively*
5204 hudōr (62), *water*

WATERCOURSE
4161+4325 môwtsâ' (1), *going forth*
8585 tᵉ'âlâh (1), *irrigation channel*

WATERED
3384 yârâh (1), to *point; to teach*
4945 mashqeh (1), *butler; drink; well-watered*
7302 râveh (2), *sated, full with drink*
8248 shâqah (6), to *quaff, i.e. to irrigate*
4222 pŏtizō (1), to *furnish drink, irrigate*

WATEREDST
8248 shâqah (1), to *quaff, i.e. to irrigate*

WATEREST
7301 râvâh (1), to *slake thirst or appetites*
7783 shûwq (1), to *overflow*

WATERETH
7301 râvâh (2), to *slake thirst or appetites*
8248 shâqah (1), to *quaff, i.e. to irrigate*
4222 pŏtizō (2), to *furnish drink, irrigate*

WATERFLOOD
7641+4325 shibbôl (1), *stream; ear of grain*

WATERING
4325 mayim (1), *water*
7377 rîy (1), *irrigation*
4222 pŏtizō (2), to *furnish drink, irrigate*

WATERPOT
5201 hudria (1), *water jar, i.e. receptacle*

WATERPOTS
5201 hudria (2), *water jar, i.e. receptacle*

WATERS
4325 mayim (265), *water*
4215 pŏtamŏs (1), *current, brook, running water*
5204 hudōr (15), *water*

WATERSPOUTS
6794 tsinnûwr (1), *culvert, water-shaft*

WATERSPRINGS
4161+4325 môwtsâ' (2), *going forth*

WAVE
5130 nûwph (11), to *quiver, vibrate, rock*
8573 tᵉnûwphâh (19), *official undulation of sacrificial offerings*
2830 kludōn (1), *surge, raging*

WAVED
5130 nûwph (5), to *quiver, vibrate, rock*
8573 tᵉnûwphâh (1), *official undulation of sacrificial offerings*

WAVERETH
1252 diakrinō (1), to *decide; to hesitate*

WAVERING
186 aklinēs (1), *firm, unswerving*
1252 diakrinō (1), to *decide; to hesitate*

WAVES
1116 bâmâh (1), *elevation, high place*
1530 gal (14), *heap; ruins*
1796 dŏkîy (1), *dashing, pounding of surf*
4867 mishbâr (4), *breaker sea-waves*
2949 kuma (5), *bursting or toppling*
4535 salŏs (1), *billow, i.e. rolling motion of waves*

WAX
1749 dôwnag (4), *bees-wax*
2691 katastrēniaō (1), to *be voluptuous against*
3822 palaiŏō (2), to *make, become worn out*
4298 prŏkŏptō (1), to *go ahead, advance*
5594 psuchō (1), to *chill, grow cold*

WAXED
1980 hâlak (5), to *walk; live a certain way*
1096 ginŏmai (2), to *be, become*
2901 krataiŏō (2), to *increase in vigor*
3955 parrhēsiazŏmai (1), to *be frank in utterance*
3975 pachunō (2), to *fatten; to render callous*
4147 plŏutěō (1), to *be, become wealthy*

WAXETH
1095 gēraskō (1), to *be senescent, grow old*

WAXING
3982 pěithō (1), to *pacify or conciliate; to assent*

WAY
734 'ôrach (18), *road; manner of life*
776 'erets (3), *earth, land, soil; country*
935 bôw' (1), to *go, come*
1870 derek (466), *road; course of life; mode*
2008 hênnâh (1), *from here; from there*
2088 zeh (1), *this or that*
3212 yâlak (6), to *walk; to live; to carry*
3541 kôh (1), *thus*
4498 mânôwç (1), *fleeing; place of refuge*
5265 nâça' (1), *start on a journey*
5410 nâthîyb (2), *(beaten) track, path*
7125 qîr'âh (1), to *encounter; to happen*
7971 shâlach (1), to *send away*
8582 tâ'âh (2), to *vacillate, i.e. reel*
1545 ěkbasis (1), *exit, way out*
1624 ěktrěpō (1), to *turn away*
1722 ěn (1), *in; during; because of*
3112 makran (2), *at a distance, far away*
3319 měsŏs (2), *middle*
3598 hŏdŏs (81), *road*
3938 parŏdŏs (1), *by-road, i.e. a route*
4105 planaō (1), to *roam, wander from safety*
4206 pŏrrhō (1), *forwards*
4311 prŏpěmpō (5), to *send forward*
5158 trŏpŏs (2), *deportment, character*

WAYFARING
732 'ârach (4), to *travel, wander*
1980+1870 hâlak (1), to *walk; live a certain way*
5674+734 'âbar (1), to *cross over; to transition*

WAYMARKS
6725 tsîyûwn (1), *guiding pillar, monument*

WAYS
734 'ôrach (8), *road; manner of life*
735 'ôrach (Ch.) (2), *road*
1870 derek (161), *road; course of life; mode of action*
1979 hălîykâh (2), *walking; procession or march; caravan*
4546 mᵉçillâh (1), *main thoroughfare; viaduct*
4570 ma'gâl (1), *circular track or camp rampart*
7339 rᵉchôb (1), *myriad*
296 amphŏdŏn (1), *fork in the road*
684 apŏlěia (1), *ruin or loss*
3598 hŏdŏs (11), *road*

W

4197 pŏrĕia (1), *journey; life's daily conduct*

WAYSIDE
3027+4570 yâd (1), *hand; power*
3197+1870 yak (1), *hand or side*

WEAK
535 'âmal (1), *to be weak; to be sick*
536 'umlal (1), *sick, faint*
2470 châlâh (4), *to be weak, sick, afflicted*
2523 challâsh (1), *frail, weak*
3212 yâlak (2), *to walk; to live; to carry*
3782 kâshal (1), *to totter, waver; to falter*
7390 rak (1), *tender; weak*
7503 râphâh (1), *to slacken*
7504 râpheh (4), *slack*
102 adunatŏs (1), *weak; impossible*
770 asthĕnĕō (19), *to be feeble*
772 asthĕnēs (8), *strengthless, weak*

WEAKEN
2522 châlash (1), *to prostrate, lay low*

WEAKENED
6031 'ânâh (1), *to afflict, be afflicted*
7503 râphâh (2), *to slacken*

WEAKENETH
7503 râphâh (2), *to slacken*

WEAKER
1800 dal (1), *weak, thin; humble, needy*
772 asthĕnēs (1), *strengthless, weak*

WEAKNESS
769 asthĕnĕia (5), *feebleness; frailty*
772 asthĕnēs (2), *strengthless, weak*

WEALTH
1952 hôwn (5), *wealth*
2428 chayil (10), *army; wealth; virtue; valor*
2896 tôwb (3), *good; well*
3581 kôach (1), *force, might; strength*
5233 nekeç (4), *treasure, riches*
2142 ĕupŏria (1), *resources, prosperity*

WEALTHY
7310 rᵉvâyâh (1), *satisfaction*
7961 shâlêv (1), *careless, carefree; security*

WEANED
1580 gâmal (12), *to benefit or requite*

WEAPON
240 'âzên (1), *spade; paddle*
3627 kᵉlîy (4), *implement, thing*

5402 nesheq (1), *military arms, arsenal*
7973 shelach (2), *spear; shoot of growth*

WEAPONS
3627 kᵉlîy (17), *implement, thing*
5402 nesheq (2), *military arms, arsenal*
3696 hŏplŏn (2), *implement, or utensil*

WEAR
1080 bᵉlâ' (Ch.) (1), *to afflict, torment*
1961 hâyâh (1), *to exist, i.e. be or become*
3847 lâbash (4), *to clothe*
5034 nâbêl (1), *to wilt; to fall away; to be foolish*
5375 nâsâ' (2), *to lift up*
7833 shâchaq (1), *to grind or wear away*
2827 klinō (1), *to slant or slope*
5409 phŏrĕō (1), *to wear*

WEARETH
5409 phŏrĕō (1), *to wear*

WEARIED
3021 yâga' (5), *to be exhausted, to tire,*
3811 lâ'âh (5), *to tire; to be, make disgusted*
5888 'âyêph (1), *to languish*
2577 kamnō (1), *to tire; to faint, sicken*
2872 kŏpiaō (1), *to feel fatigue; to work hard*

WEARIETH
2959 țârach (1), *to overburden*
3021 yâga' (1), *to be exhausted, to tire,*

WEARINESS
3024 yᵉgî'âh (1), *fatigue*
4972 mattᵉlâ'âh (1), *what a trouble!*
2873 kŏpŏs (1), *toil; pains*

WEARING
5375 nâsâ' (1), *to lift up*
4025 pĕrithĕsis (1), *putting all around, i.e. decorating oneself with*
5409 phŏrĕō (1), *to wear*

WEARISOME
5999 'âmâl (1), *wearing effort; worry*

WEARY
3019 yâgîya' (1), *tired, exhausted*
3021 yâga' (7), *to be exhausted, to tire,*
3023 yâgêa' (2), *tiresome*
3286 yâ'aph (5), *to tire*
3287 yâ'êph (1), *exhausted*
3811 lâ'âh (10), *to tire; to be, make disgusted*
5354 nâqaț (1), *to loathe*
5774 'ûwph (1), *to cover, to fly; to faint*
5889 'âyêph (8), *languid*
6973 qûwts (2), *to be, make disgusted*
7646 sâba' (1), *fill to satiety*

1573 ĕkkakĕō (2), *to be weak, fail*
5299 hupōpiazō (1), *to beat up; to wear out*

WEASEL
2467 chôled (1), *weasel*

WEATHER
2091 zâhâb (1), *gold, piece of gold*
3117 yôwm (1), *day; time period*
2105 ĕudia (1), *clear sky, i.e. fine weather*
5494 chĕimôn (1), *winter season; stormy weather*

WEAVE
707 'ârag (2), *to plait or weave*

WEAVER
707 'ârag (2), *to plait or weave*

WEAVER'S
707 'ârag (4), *to plait or weave*

WEAVEST
707 'ârag (1), *to plait or weave*

WEB
1004 bayith (1), *house; temple; family, tribe*
4545 maççeketh (2), *length-wise threads*
6980 qûwr (1), *spider web*

WEBS
6980 qûwr (1), *spider web*

WEDDING
1062 gamŏs (7), *nuptials*

WEDGE
3956 lâshôwn (2), *tongue; tongue-shaped*

WEDLOCK
5003 nâ'aph (1), *to commit adultery*

WEEDS
5488 çûwph (1), *papyrus reed; reed*

WEEK
7620 shâbûwa' (4), *seven-day week*
4521 sabbatŏn (9), *day of weekly repose*

WEEKS
7620 shâbûwa' (15), *seven-day week*

WEEP
1058 bâkâh (29), *to weep, moan*
1065 bᵉkîy (2), *weeping*
1830 dâma' (1), *to weep*
2799 klaiō (15), *to sob, wail*

WEEPEST
1058 bâkâh (1), *to weep, moan*
2799 klaiō (2), *to sob, wail*

WEEPETH
1058 bâkâh (4), *to weep, moan*

WEEPING
1058 bâkâh (8), *to weep, moan*
1065 bᵉkîy (21), *weeping*

2799 klaiō (9), *to sob, wail*
2805 klauthmŏs (6), *lamentation, weeping*

WEIGH
4948 mishqâl (2), *weight, weighing*
6424 pâlaç (2), *to weigh mentally*
8254 shâqal (2), *to suspend in trade*

WEIGHED
8254 shâqal (12), *to suspend in trade*
8505 tâkan (1), *to balance, i.e. measure*
8625 tᵉqal (Ch.) (1), *to weigh in a balance*

WEIGHETH
8505 tâkan (2), *to balance, i.e. measure*

WEIGHT
68 'eben (4), *stone*
4946 mishqôwl (1), *weight*
4948 mishqâl (44), *weight, weighing*
6425 peleç (1), *balance, scale*
922 barŏs (1), *load, abundance, authority*
3591 ŏgkŏs (1), *burden, hindrance*
5006 talantiaiŏs (1), *weight of 57-80 lbs.*

WEIGHTIER
926 barus (1), *weighty*

WEIGHTS
68 'eben (6), *stone*

WEIGHTY
5192 nêțel (1), *burden*
926 barus (1), *weighty*

WELFARE
2896 țôwb (1), *good; well*
3444 yᵉshûw'âh (1), *victory; prosperity*
7965 shâlôwm (5), *safe; well; health, prosperity*

WELL
71 'Äbânâh (1), *stony*
369 'ayin (1), *there is no, i.e., not exist, none*
375 'êyphôh (2), *where?; when?; how?*
875 bᵉ'êr (21), *well, cistern*
883 Bᵉ'êr la-Chay Rô'îy (1), *well of a living (One) my seer*
953 bôwr (6), *pit hole, cistern, well; prison*
995 bîyn (1), *to understand; discern*
2090 zôh (1), *this or that*
2654 châphêts (1), *to be pleased with, desire*
2895 țowb (9), *to be good*
2896 țôwb (20), *good; well*
2898 țûwb (9), *good; goodness; beauty, gladness, welfare*
3190 yâțab (35), *to be, make well*
3303 yâpheh (5), *beautiful; handsome*

W

1535 galgal (Ch.) (1), *wheel*
6471 pa'am (1), *time; step; occurence*

WHELP
1482 gûwr (3), *cub*

WHELPS
1121 bên (2), *son, descendant; people*
1482 gûwr (3), *cub*
1484 gôwr (2), *lion cub*

WHEN
310 'achar (1), *after*
518 'îm (19), *whether?*
834 'ăsher (83), *who, what, that; when*
1767 day (3), *enough, sufficient*
1768 dîy (Ch.) (4), *that; of*
1961 hâyâh (4), *to exist*
3117 yôwm (7), *day; time*
3588 kîy (280), *for, that*
3644 kᵉmôw (1), *like, as*
4970 mâthay (14), *when; when?, how long?*
5704 'ad (3), *as far (long) as; during; while; until*
5750 'ôwd (2), *again; repeatedly; still; more*
5921 'al (1), *above, over, upon, or against*
6256 'êth (7), *time*
6310 peh (2), *mouth; opening*
1437 ĕan (2), *indefiniteness*
1875 ĕpan (3), *whenever*
1893 ĕpĕi (1), *since*
2259 hĕnika (2), *at which time, whenever*
2531 kathōs (1), *just or inasmuch as, that*
3326 mĕta (2), *with, among; after, later*
3698 hŏpŏtĕ (1), *as soon as, when*
3704 hŏpōs (1), *in the manner that*
3752 hŏtan (123), *inasmuch as, at once*
3753 hŏtĕ (99), *when; as*
3756 ŏu (1), *no or not*
4218 pŏtĕ (13), *at some time, ever*
5613 hōs (40), *which, how, i.e. in that manner*
5618 hōspĕr (2), *exactly like*

WHENCE
335 'ay (1), *where?*
370 'ayin (19), *where from?, whence?*
1992 hêm (1), *they*
3606 hŏthĕn (4), *from which place or source*
3739 hŏs (2), *who, which, what, that*
4159 pŏthĕn (28), *from which; what*

WHENSOEVER
3605 kôl (1), *all, any or every*
3752 hŏtan (1), *inasmuch as, at once*
5613+1437 hōs (1), *which, how, i.e. in that manner*

WHERE
335 'ay (16), *where?*
346 'ayêh (45), *where?*
349 'êyk (1), *where?*
351 'êykôh (1), *where*
370 'ayin (2), *where from?, whence?*
375 'êyphôh (9), *where?*
413 'êl (2), *to, toward*
575 'ân (2), *where from?*
645 'êphôw (5), *then*
657 'epheç (1), *end; no further*
834 'ăsher (58), *where*
1768 dîy (Ch.) (1), *that; of*
3027 yâd (1), *hand; power*
5921 'al (2), *above, over, upon, or against*
8033 shâm (20), *where*
8478 tachath (1), *bottom; underneath; in lieu of*
8536 tâm (Ch.) (1), *there*
296 amphŏdŏn (1), *fork in the road*
1330 dierchŏmai (1), *to traverse, travel through*
1337 dithalassŏs (1), *having two seas*
2596 kata (1), *down; according to*
3606 hŏthĕn (2), *from which place or source*
3699 hŏpŏu (58), *at whichever spot*
3757 hŏu (21), *at which place, i.e. where*
3837 pantachŏu (5), *universally, everywhere*
3838 pantĕlēs (1), *entire; completion*
4226 pŏu (37), *at what locality?*
5101 tis (1), *who?, which? or what?*

WHEREABOUT
834 'ăsher (1), *where, how, because*

WHEREAS
518 'îm (1), *whether?; if, although; Oh that!*
834 'ăsher (2), *because, in order that*
1768 dîy (Ch.) (4), *that; of*
3588 kîy (5), *for, that because*
6258 'attâh (2), *at this time, now*
8478 tachath (1), *bottom; underneath; in lieu of*
3699 hŏpŏu (2), *at whichever spot*
3748 hŏstis (1), *whoever*

WHEREBY
834 'ăsher (17), *because, in order that*
4100 mâh (1), *whatever; that which*
4482 mên (1), *part; musical chord*
3588 hŏ (1), *"the," i.e. the definite article*
3739 hŏs (3), *who, which, what, that*

WHEREFORE
199 'ûwlâm (1), *however or on the contrary*
3651 kên (18), *just; right, correct*

3861 lâhên (Ch.) (1), *therefore; except*
4069 maddûwa' (28), *why?, what?*
4100 mâh (86), *what?, how?, why?, when?*
686 ara (1), *therefore*
1161 dĕ (2), *but, yet*
1302 diati (4), *why?*
1352 diŏ (41), *consequently, therefore*
1355 diŏpĕr (3), *on which very account*
3606 hŏthĕn (4), *from which place or source*
3767 ŏun (7), *certainly; accordingly*
5101 tis (3), *who?, which? or what?*
5105 tŏigarŏun (1), *consequently, then*
5620 hōstĕ (17), *thus, therefore*

WHEREIN
834 'ăsher (70), *when, where, how, because*
1459 gav (Ch.) (1), *middle*
2098 zûw (2), *this or that*
4100 mâh (15), *what?, how?, why?, when?*
8033 shâm (1), *where*
3739 hŏs (1), *what, that*
3757 hŏu (3), *where*

WHEREINSOEVER
1722+3739+302 ĕn (1), *in; during; because of*

WHEREINTO
824+8432 'Esh'ân (1), *support*
834+413+8432 'ăsher (1), *when, where, how*
1519+3739 ĕis (1), *to or into*

WHEREOF
834 'ăsher (24), *where*
3739 hŏs (11), *who, which, what, that*

WHEREON
834 'ăsher (2), *where, how, because*
834+5921 'ăsher (13), *where, how, because*
5921 'al (2), *above, over, upon, or against*
5921+4100 'al (1), *above, over, upon, or against*
1909+3739 ĕpi (4), *on, upon*
3739 hŏs (1), *who, which, what, that*

WHERESOEVER
834 'ăsher (1), *where, how, because*
3605 kôl (1), *all, any*
3699 hŏpŏu (1), *at whichever spot*

WHERETO
834 'ăsher (1), *where, how, because*
4100 mâh (1), *what?, how?, why?, when?*
1519+3739 ĕis (1), *to or into*

WHEREUNTO
834 'ăsher (6), *where, how, because*

3739 hŏs (6), *who, which, what, that*
5101 tis (7), *who?, which? or what?*

WHEREUPON
413 'êl (2), *to, toward*
5921 'al (1), *above, over, upon, or against*
3606 hŏthĕn (3), *from which place or source*

WHEREWITH
834 'ăsher (68), *when, where, how, because*
1697 dâbâr (1), *word; matter; thing*
4100 mâh (9), *what?, how?, why?, when?*
1722+3739 ĕn (2), *in; during; because of*
1722+5101 ĕn (3), *in; during; because of*
3739 hŏs (9), *who, which*
3745 hŏsŏs (1), *as much as*
5101 tis (1), *who?, which? or what?*

WHEREWITHAL
5101 tis (1), *who?, which? or what?*

WHET
3913 lâṭash (1), *to sharpen; to pierce*
7043 qâlal (1), *to be, make light (sharp)*
8150 shânan (2), *to pierce; to inculcate*

WHETHER
176 'ôw (8), *or, whether*
335 'ay (1), *where?*
518 'îm (27), *whether?*
996 bêyn (4), *"either...or"*
2006 hên (Ch.) (2), *whether, but, if*
3588 kîy (1), *for, that because*
4100 mâh (1), *what?, how?, why?, when?*
4480 min (3), *from, out of*
5704 'ad (1), *as far (long) as; during; while; until*
5750 'ôwd (2), *again; repeatedly; still; more*
1487 ĕi (22), *if, whether*
1535 ĕitĕ (31), *if too*
2273 ĕtŏi (1), *either...or*
3379 mēpŏtĕ (1), *not ever; if, or lest ever*
4220 pŏtĕrŏn (1), *which*
5037 tĕ (1), *both or also*
5101 tis (8), *who?, which? or what?*

WHILE
518 'îm (1), *whether?; if, although; Oh that!*
834 'ăsher (1), *when, where, how, because*
3117 yôwm (7), *day; time*
3541 kôh (1), *thus*
3588 kîy (3), *for, that because*
4705 mits'âr (1), *little; short time*
5704 'ad (9), *during; while*
5750 'ôwd (7), *again; repeatedly; still; more*
5751 'ôwd (Ch.) (1), *again; repeatedly; still*

7350 râchôwq (1), *remote, far*
2193 hêŏs (8), *until*
2250 hēmĕra (2), *day; period of time*
2540 kairŏs (1), *occasion, i.e. set time*
3153 mataiŏtēs (1), *transientness; depravity*
3397 mikrŏn (2), *small space of time or degree*
3641 ŏligŏs (2), *puny, small*
3752 hŏtan (1), *inasmuch as, at once*
3753 hŏtĕ (1), *when; as*
3819 palai (1), *formerly; sometime since*
4340 prŏskairŏs (1), *temporary*
5550 chrŏnŏs (3), *time*
5613 hōs (4), *which, how, i.e. in that manner*

WHILES
5750 'ôwd (1), *again; repeatedly; still; more*
2193+3755 hĕŏs (1), *until*

WHILST
834 'ăsher (1), *when, where, how, because*
5704 'ad (4), *as far (long) as; during; while; until*

WHIP
7752 shôwṭ (2), *lash*

WHIPS
7752 shôwṭ (4), *lash*

WHIRLETH
1980 hâlak (1), *to walk; live a certain way*

WHIRLWIND
5492 çûwphâh (10), *hurricane wind*
5590 çâ'ar (3), *to rush upon; to toss about*
5591 ça'ar (11), *hurricane wind*
7307+5591 rûwach (1), *breath; wind; life-spirit*
8175 sâ'ar (2), *to storm; to shiver, i.e. fear*

WHIRLWINDS
5492 çûwphâh (1), *hurricane wind*
5591 ça'ar (1), *hurricane*

WHISPER
3907 lâchash (1), *to whisper a magic spell*
6850 tsâphaph (1), *to coo or chirp as a bird*

WHISPERED
3907 lâchash (1), *to whisper a magic spell*

WHISPERER
5372 nirgân (1), *slanderer, gossip*

WHISPERERS
5588 psithuristēs (1), *maligning gossip*

WHISPERINGS
5587 psithurismŏs (1), *whispering, detraction*

WHIT
1697 dâbâr (1), *word; matter; thing*

3632 kâliyl (1), *whole, entire; complete; whole*
3367 mĕdĕis (1), *not even*
3650 hŏlŏs (2), *whole or all, i.e. complete*

WHITE
1858 dar (1), *mother-of-pearl or alabaster*
2353 chûwr (2), *white linen*
2751 chôrîy (1), *white bread*
3835 lâban (4), *to be, become white*
3836 lâbân (29), *white*
6703 tsach (1), *dazzling*
6713 tsachar (1), *whiteness*
6715 tsâchôr (1), *white*
7388 rîyr (1), *saliva; broth*
2986 lamprŏs (2), *radiant; clear*
3021 lĕukainō (2), *to whiten*
3022 lĕukŏs (24), *bright white*

WHITED
2867 kŏniaō (2), *to whitewash*

WHITER
3835 lâban (1), *to be, become white*
6705 tsâchach (1), *to be dazzling white*

WHITHER
413 'êl (2), *to, toward*
575 'ân (20), *where from?, when?*
834 'ăsher (6), *when, where, how, because*
8033 shâm (3), *where*
3699 hŏpŏu (9), *at whichever spot*
3757 hŏu (2), *where*
4226 pŏu (10), *at what?*

WHITHERSOEVER
413+3605+834 'êl (1), *to, toward*
413+3605+834+8033 'êl (1), *to, toward*
575 'ân (1), *where from?*
834 'ăsher (2), *where, how, because*
1870+834 derek (1), *road; course of life*
3605+834 kôl (13), *all, any or every*
3605+834+8033 kôl (1), *all, any or every*
4725+834 mâqôwm (1), *general locality, place*
5921+834+8033 'al (1), *above, over, upon*
5921+3605+834 'al (1), *above, over, upon*
3699+302 hŏpŏu (4), *at whichever spot*
3699+1437 hŏpŏu (1), *at whichever spot*
3757+1437 hŏu (1), *at which place, i.e. where*

WHOLE
854+3605 'êth (13), *with; by; at; among*
2421 châyâh (1), *to live; to revive*

3117 yôwm (4), *day; time*
3605 kôl (115), *all, any*
3606 kôl (Ch.) (6), *all, any*
3632 kâliyl (2), *whole*
4749 miqshâh (1), *work molded by hammering*
7495 râphâ' (2), *to heal*
8003 shâlêm (4), *complete; friendly; safe*
8549 tâmîym (4), *entire*
8552 tâmam (1), *to complete, finish*
537 hapas (3), *whole*
1295 diasōzō (1), *to cure*
2390 iaŏmai (1), *to heal*
2480 ischuō (2), *to have or exercise force*
3390 mētrŏpŏlis (1), *main city, metropolis*
3646 hŏlŏkautōma (1), *wholly-consumed*
3648 hŏlŏklērŏs (1), *sound in the entire body*
3650 hŏlŏs (43), *whole*
3956 pas (10), *all, any*
3958 paschō (2), *experience pain*
4982 sōzō (11), *to deliver; to protect*
5198 hugiainō (2), *to have sound health*
5199 hugiēs (13), *well, healthy; true*

WHOLESOME
4832 marpê' (1), *cure; deliverance; placidity*
5198 hugiainō (1), *to have sound health*

WHOLLY
3605 kôl (9), *all, any*
3615 kâlâh (1), *to complete, prepare*
3632 kâliyl (4), *whole*
4390 mâlê' (6), *to fill*
5352 nâqâh (1), *to be, make clean; to be bare*
6942 qâdâsh (1), *to be, make clean*
7760 sûwm (1), *to put*
7965 shâlôwm (1), *safe; well; health, prosperity*
1510+1722 ĕimi (1), *I exist, I am*
3651 hŏlŏtĕlēs (1), *absolutely perfect*

WHORE
2181 zânâh (9), *to commit adultery*
6948 qᵉdêshâh (1), *sacred female prostitute*
4204 pŏrnē (4), *prostitute*

WHORE'S
2181 zânâh (1), *to commit adultery*

WHOREDOM
2181 zânâh (11), *to commit adultery*
2183 zânûwn (1), *adultery; idolatry*
2184 zᵉnûwth (7), *adultery, infidelity*
8457 taznûwth (3), *harlotry*

WHOREDOMS
2181 zânâh (2), *to commit adultery*
2183 zânûwn (11), *adultery; idolatry*
2184 zᵉnûwth (2), *adultery, infidelity*
8457 taznûwth (15), *harlotry, physical or spiritual*

WHOREMONGER
4205 pŏrnŏs (1), *debauchee, immoral*

WHOREMONGERS
4205 pŏrnŏs (4), *debauchee, immoral*

WHORES
2181 zânâh (2), *to commit adultery*

WHORING
2181 zânâh (19), *to commit adultery*

WHORISH
2181 zânâh (3), *to commit adultery*

WHY
4060 middah (1), *measure*
4069 maddûwa' (41), *why?, what?*
4100 mâh (119), *what?, how?, why?, when?*
4101 mâh (Ch.) (2), *what?, how?, why?*
1063 gar (4), *for, indeed, but, because*
1302 diati (23), *why?*
2444 hinati (4), *why?*
3754 hŏti (2), *that; because; since*
5101 tis (66), *who?, which? or what?*

WICKED
205 'âven (6), *trouble, vanity, wickedness*
605 'ânash (1), *to be frail, feeble*
1100 bᵉlîya'al (5), *wickedness, trouble*
2154 zimmâh (2), *bad plan*
2162 zâmâm (1), *plot*
2617 cheçed (1), *kindness, favor*
4209 mᵉzimmâh (3), *plan; sagacity*
4849 mirsha'ath (1), *female wicked-doer*
5766 'evel (1), *evil*
5767 'avvâl (3), *evil*
6001 'âmêl (1), *toiling; laborer; sorrowful*
6090 'ôtseb (1), *idol; pain*
7451 ra' (26), *bad; evil*
7489 râ'a' (5), *to be good for nothing*
7561 râsha' (4), *to be, do, declare wrong*
7562 resha' (4), *wrong*
7563 râshâ' (252), *wrong; bad person*
113 athĕsmŏs (2), *criminal*
459 anŏmŏs (2), *without Jewish law*
2556 kakŏs (1), *wrong*

4190 pŏnērŏs (17), malice, wicked, bad
4191 pŏnērŏtĕrŏs (2), more evil

WICKEDLY
4209 mᵉzimmâh (1), plan; sagacity
5753 'âvâh (1), to be crooked
5766 'evel (1), moral evil
7451 ra' (1), bad; evil
7489 râ'a' (5), to be good for nothing
7561 râsha' (13), to be, do, declare wrong
7564 rish'âh (1), moral wrong

WICKEDNESS
205 'âven (2), trouble, vanity, wickedness
1942 havvâh (3), desire; craving
2154 zimmâh (4), bad plan
5766 'evel (7), moral evil
5999 'âmâl (1), wearing effort; worry
7451 ra' (59), bad; evil
7455 rôa' (3), badness
7561 râsha' (1), to be, do, declare wrong
7562 resha' (25), wrong
7564 rish'âh (13), wrong
2549 kakia (1), depravity; malignity; trouble
4189 pŏnēria (6), malice, evil, wickedness
4190 pŏnērŏs (1), malice, wicked, bad; crime
5129+824 tŏutŏᵢ (1), in this person or thing

WIDE
2267 cheber (2), society, group; magic spell;
4060 middâh (1), measure; portion
6605 pâthach (3), to open wide; to loosen, begin
7337 râchab (3), to broaden
7342 râchâb (1), roomy
7342+3027 râchâb (2), roomy, spacious
4116 platus (1), wide

WIDENESS
7341 rôchab (1), width

WIDOW
490 'almânâh (37), widow
5503 chēra (13), widow

WIDOW'S
490 'almânâh (4), widow
491 'almânûwth (1), widow; widowhood

WIDOWHOOD
489 'almôn (1), widowhood
491 'almânûwth (3), widow; widowhood

WIDOWS
490 'almânâh (12), widow
5503 chēra (10), widow

WIDOWS'
5503 chēra (3), widow

WIFE
802 'ishshâh (301), woman, wife
1166 bâ'al (1), to be master; to marry
1753 dûwr (Ch.) (1), to reside, live in
2994 yᵉbêmeth (3), sister-in-law
1134 gunaikĕiŏs (1), feminine
1135 gunē (80), wife

WIFE'S
802 'ishshâh (8), woman, wife; women, wives
3994 pĕnthēra (3), wife's mother

WILD
338 'îy (3), solitary wild creature that howls
689 'aqqôw (1), ibex
891 bᵉ'ûshîym (2), rotten fruit
2123 zîyz (2), fulness
2416 chay (1), alive; raw
3277 yâ'êl (3), ibex
6167 'ărâd (Ch.) (1), onager or wild donkey
6171 'ârôwd (1), onager or wild donkey
6501 pere' (10), onager, wild donkey
6728 tsîyîy (3), wild beast
7704 sâdeh (8), field
8377 tᵉ'ôw (2), antelope
65 agriĕlaiŏs (2), wild olive tree
66 agriŏs (2), wild
2342 thēriŏn (3), dangerous animal

WILDERNESS
3452 yᵉshîymôwn (2), desolation
4057 midbâr (255), desert; also speech
6160 'ărâbâh (4), desert, wasteland
6166 'Ărâd (1), fugitive
6723 tsîyâh (2), desert
6728 tsîyîy (3), wild beast
8414 tôhûw (2), waste, desolation, formless
2047 ĕrēmia (3), place of solitude, remoteness
2048 ĕrēmŏs (32), remote place, deserted place

WILES
5231 nêkel (1), deceit
3180 mĕthŏdĕia (1), trickery; scheming

WILFULLY
1596 hĕkŏusiŏs (1), voluntarily, willingly

WILILY
6195 'ormâh (1), trickery; discretion

WILL
14 'âbâh (5), to be acquiescent
165 'ĕhîy (3), Where?
2654 châphêts (2), to be pleased with, desire
3045 yâda' (1), to know
5314 nâphash (1), to be refreshed
5315 nephesh (3), life; breath; soul; wind

6634 tsᵉbâ' (Ch.) (5), to please
7470 rᵉ'ûwth (Ch.) (1), desire
7522 râtsôwn (15), delight
210 akŏn (1), unwilling
1012 bŏulē (1), purpose, plan, decision
1013 bŏulēma (1), resolve, willful choice
1014 bŏulŏmai (12), to be willing, desire
1106 gnōmē (1), opinion, resolve
1479 ĕthĕlŏthrēskĕia (1), voluntary piety
2107 ĕudŏkia (2), delight, kindness, wish
2133 ĕunŏïa (1), eagerly, with a whole heart
2307 thĕlēma (62), purpose; decree
2308 thĕlēsis (1), determination
2309 thĕlō (70), to will; to desire; to choose
3195 mĕllō (6), to intend, i.e. be about to

WILLETH
2309 thĕlō (1), to will; to desire; to choose

WILLING
14 'âbâh (4), to be acquiescent
2655 châphêts (1), pleased with
5068 nâdab (3), to volunteer
5071 nᵉdâbâh (2), spontaneous gift
5081 nâdîyb (3), magnanimous
830 authairĕtŏs (1), self-chosen,voluntary
1014 bŏulŏmai (5), to be willing, desire
2106 ĕudŏkĕō (2), to think well, i.e. approve
2309 thĕlō (5), to will; to desire; to choose
2843 kŏinōnikŏs (1), liberal
4288 prŏthumia (1), alacrity, eagerness
4289 prŏthumŏs (1), alacrity, eagerness

WILLINGLY
2656 chêphets (1), pleasure; desire
2974 yâ'al (1), to assent; to undertake, begin
3820 lêb (1), heart
5068 nâdab (13), to volunteer
5071 nᵉdâbâh (1), spontaneous gift
5414 nâthan (1), to give
1596 hĕkŏusiŏs (1), voluntarily, willingly
1635 hĕkōn (2), voluntary
2309 thĕlō (2), to will

WILLOW
6851 tsaphtsâphâh (1), willow tree

WILLOWS
6155 'ârâb (5), willow

WILT
2309 thĕlō (21), to will

WIMPLES
4304 miṭpachath (1), cloak, shawl

WIN
1234 bâqa' (1), to cleave
2770 kĕrdainō (1), to gain; to spare

WIND
7307 rûwach (82), breath; wind; life-spirit
7308 rûwach (Ch.) (1), breath; wind; life-spirit
416 anemizō (1), to toss with the wind
417 anĕmŏs (20), wind
4151 pneuma (1), spirit
4154 pnĕō (1), to breeze
4157 pnŏē (1), breeze; breath

WINDING
3583 kâchal (1), to paint
4141 mûwçâb (1), circuit
5437 çâbab (1), to surround

WINDOW
2474 challôwn (13), window; opening
6672 tsôhar (1), window
2376 thuris (2), window

WINDOWS
699 'ărubbâh (8), window; chimney
2474 challôwn (18), window; opening
3551 kav (Ch.) (1), window
8121 shemesh (1), sun
8260 sheqeph (1), loophole
8261 shâqûph (1), opening

WINDS
7307 rûwach (11), breath; wind; life-spirit
7308 rûwach (Ch.) (1), breath; wind; life-spirit
417 anĕmŏs (11), wind

WINDY
7307 rûwach (1), breath; wind; life-spirit

WINE
2561 chemer (1), fermenting wine
2562 châmar (Ch.) (6), wine
3196 yayin (135), wine
3342 yeqeb (1), wine-vat
4469 mamçâk (1), mixed-wine
5435 çôbe' (1), wine
6025 ênâb (1), grape
6071 'âçîyç (4), expressed fresh grape-juice
7491 râ'aph (1), to drip
8492 tîyrôwsh (40), wine, squeezed grape-juice
1098 glĕukŏs (1), sweet wine
3631 ŏinŏs (32), wine
3632 ŏinŏphlugia (1), drunkenness
3943 parŏinŏs (2), tippling

WINEBIBBER
3630 ŏinŏpŏtēs (1), tippler

WINEBIBBERS
5433+3196 çâbâ' (1), to become tipsy

WINEFAT
1660 gath (1), wine-press or vat
5276 hupŏlēniŏn (1), lower wine vat

WINEPRESS
1660 gath (2), wine-press or vat
3342 yeqeb (7), wine-vat, wine-press
6333 pûwrâh (1), wine-press trough
3025 lēnŏs (4), trough, i.e. wine-vat
3025+3631 lēnŏs (1), trough, i.e. wine-vat

WINEPRESSES
1660 gath (1), wine-press
3342 yeqeb (3), wine-press

WINES
8105 shemer (2), settlings of wine, dregs

WING
3671 kânâph (13), edge or extremity; wing

WINGED
3671 kânâph (2), edge or extremity; wing

WINGS
34 'ebyôwn (1), destitute; poor
83 'êber (2), pinion
84 'ebrâh (1), pinion
1611 gaph (Ch.) (3), wing
3671 kânâph (60), edge or extremity; wing
6731 tsîyts (1), wing
4420 ptĕrux (5), wing

WINK
7169 qârats (1), to blink
7335 râzam (1), to twinkle the eye

WINKED
5237 hupĕrĕidō (1), to not punish

WINKETH
7169 qârats (2), to blink

WINNETH
3947 lâqach (1), to take

WINNOWED
2219 zârâh (1), to winnow

WINNOWETH
2219 zârâh (1), to winnow

WINTER
2778 châraph (2), to spend the winter
2779 chôreph (3), autumn, ripeness of age
5638 çᵉthâv (1), winter
3914 parachĕimazō (3), to spend the winter
3915 parachĕimasia (1), wintering over
5494 chĕimōn (4), winter

WINTERED
3916 parachrēma (1), instantly, immediately

WINTERHOUSE
2779 chôreph (1), autumn (and winter)

WIPE
4229 mâchâh (3), to erase; to grease
631 apŏmassŏmai (1), to scrape away, wipe off
1591 ĕkmassō (2), to wipe dry
1813 ĕxalĕiphō (2), to obliterate

WIPED
4229 mâchâh (1), to erase; to grease
1591 ĕkmassō (3), to wipe dry

WIPETH
4229 mâchâh (2), to erase; to grease

WIPING
4229 mâchâh (1), to erase; to grease

WIRES
6616 pâthîyl (1), twine, cord

WISDOM
998 bîynâh (2), understanding
2449 châkam (1), to be wise
2451 chokmâh (144), wisdom
2452 chokmâh (Ch.) (8), wisdom
2454 chokmôwth (4), wisdom
2942 ţᵉˈêm (Ch.) (1), judgment; account
3820 lêb (6), heart
6195 'ormâh (1), trickery; discretion
7919 sâkal (2), to be or act circumspect
7922 sekel (3), intelligence; success
8394 tâbûwn (1), intelligence; argument
8454 tûwshîyâh (7), undertaking
4678 sŏphia (51), wisdom
5428 phrŏnēsis (1), moral insight, understanding

WISE
995 bîyn (3), to understand; discern
2445 chakkîym (Ch.) (14), wise one
2449 châkam (19), to be wise
2450 châkâm (122), wise, intelligent, skillful
2454 chokmôwth (1), wisdom
3198 yâkach (1), to be correct; to argue
3823 lâbab (1), transport with love; to stultify
6031 'ânâh (1), to afflict, be afflicted
6493 piqqêach (1), clear-sighted
7919 sâkal (12), to be or act circumspect
7922 sekel (1), intelligence; success

3097 magŏs (4), Oriental scientist, i.e. magician
3364 ŏu mē (1), not at all, absolutely not
3588+3838 hŏ (1), "the," i.e. the definite article
3779 hŏutō (6), in this way; likewise
3843 pantōs (1), entirely; at all events
4679 sŏphizō (1), to make wise
4680 sŏphŏs (21), wise
4920 suniēmi (1), to comprehend
5429 phrŏnimŏs (13), sagacious or discreet

WISELY
995 bîyn (1), to understand; discern
2449 châkam (2), to be wise
2451 chokmâh (2), wisdom
7919 sâkal (8), to be or act circumspect
5430 phrŏnimōs (1), prudently, shrewdly

WISER
2449 châkam (4), to be wise
2450 châkâm (2), wise, intelligent, skillful
4680 sŏphŏs (1), wise
5429 phrŏnimŏs (1), sagacious or discreet

WISH
2655 châphêts (1), pleased with
4906 maskîyth (1), carved figure
6310 peh (1), mouth
2172 ĕuchŏmai (3), to wish for; to pray

WISHED
7592 shâ'al (1), to ask
2172 ĕuchŏmai (1), to wish for; to pray

WISHING
7592 shâ'al (1), to ask

WIST
3045 yâda' (7), to know
1492 ĕidō (6), to know

WIT
3045 yâda' (2), to know
1107 gnōrizō (1), to make known, reveal
5613 hōs (1), which, how

WIT'S
2451 chokmâh (1), wisdom

WITCH
3784 kâshaph (2), to enchant

WITCHCRAFT
3784 kâshaph (1), to enchant
7081 qeçem (1), divination
5331 pharmakĕia (1), magic, witchcraft

WITCHCRAFTS
3785 kesheph (4), magic, sorcery

WITHAL
834+3605 'âsher (1), who, which, what, that
1992 hêm (1), they
2004 hên (3), they
3162 yachad (2), unitedly
5973 'îm (1), with
260 hama (3), at the same time, together

WITHDRAW
622 'âçaph (4), to gather, collect
3240 yânach (1), to allow to stay
3365 yâqar (1), to be valuable; to make rare
5493 çûwr (1), to turn off
7368 râchaq (1), to recede
7725 shûwb (1), to turn back; to return
868 aphistēmi (1), to desist, desert
4724 stĕllō (1), to repress

WITHDRAWEST
7725 shûwb (1), to turn back; to return

WITHDRAWETH
1639 gâra' (1), to shave, remove, lessen

WITHDRAWN
2502 châlats (1), to pull off; to strip; to depart
2559 châmaq (1), to depart, i.e. turn about
5080 nâdach (1), to push off, scattered
7725 shûwb (2), to turn back; to return
645 apŏspaŏ (1), withdraw with force

WITHDREW
5414+5437 nâthan (1), to give
7725 shûwb (1), to turn back; to return
402 anachōrĕŏ (2), to retire, withdraw
5288 hupŏstĕllō (1), to cower or shrink
5298 hupŏchōrĕō (1), to vacate down, i.e. retire

WITHER
3001 yâbêsh (8), to wither
5034 nâbêl (2), to wilt
7060 qâmal (1), to wither

WITHERED
3001 yâbêsh (11), to wither
6798 tsânam (1), to blast
3583 xērainō (9), to shrivel, to mature
3584 xērŏs (4), withered

WITHERETH
3001 yâbêsh (5), to wither
3583 xērainō (2), to shrivel, to mature
5352 phthinŏpōrinŏs (1), autumnal

WITHHELD
2820 châsak (3), to restrain or refrain
4513 mâna' (3), to deny, refuse

WITHHELDEST
4513 mâna' (1), to deny, refuse

W

WITHHOLD
3240 yânach (1), to *allow to stay*
3607 kâlâ' (2), to *hold*
4513 mâna' (5), to *deny*
6113 'âtsar (1), to *hold*

WITHHOLDEN
1219 bâtsar (1), to *be inaccessible*
2254 châbal (1), to *bind by a pledge; to pervert*
4513 mâna' (8), to *deny, refuse*

WITHHOLDETH
2820 châsak (1), to *restrain or refrain*
4513 mâna' (1), to *deny, refuse*
6113 'âtsar (1), to *hold back; to maintain*
2722 katĕchō (1), to *hold down fast*

WITHIN
413 'êl (2), *to, toward*
990 beṭen (2), *belly; womb; body*
996 bêyn (1), *between*
1004 bayith (23), *house; temple; family, tribe*
1157 bᵉ'ad (3), *up to or over against*
2315 cheder (1), *apartment, chamber*
2436 chêyq (1), *bosom, heart*
4481 min (Ch.) (1), *from or out of*
5704 'ad (2), *as far (long) as; during; while; until*
5705 'ad (Ch.) (1), *as far (long) as; during*
5750 'ôwd (4), *again; repeatedly; still; more*
5921 'al (8), *above, over, upon, or against*
5978 'immâd (1), *along with*
6440 pânîym (1), *face; front*
6441 pᵉnîymâh (10), *indoors, inside*
6442 pᵉnîymîy (1), *interior, inner*
7130 qereb (26), *nearest part, i.e. the center*
7146 qârachath (1), *bald spot; threadbare spot*
8432 tâvek (20), *center, middle*
8537 tôm (1), *completeness*
1223 dia (1), *through, by means of; because of*
1722 ĕn (13), *in; during; because of*
1737 ĕndiduskō (1), to *clothe*
1787 ĕntŏs (1), *inside, within*
2080 ĕsō (3), *inside, inner, in*
2081 ĕsōthĕn (10), *from inside; inside*
2082 ĕsōtĕrŏs (1), *interior, inner*
4314 prŏs (1), *for; on, at; to, toward; against*

WITHOUT
268 'âchôwr (1), *behind, backward; west*
369 'ayin (42), *there is no, i.e., not exist, none*
657 'epheç (3), *end; no further*
1097 bᵉlîy (16), *without, not yet; lacking;*
1107 bil'ădêy (4), *except, without, besides*
1115 biltîy (4), *not, except, without, unless*
1372 gabbachath (1), *baldness on forehead*
2351 chûwts (71), *outside, outdoors*
2435 chîytsôwn (5), *outer wall side; exterior*
2600 chinnâm (17), *gratis, free*
2963 ṭâraph (1), to *pluck off or pull to pieces*
3808 lô' (29), *no, not*
3809 lâ' (Ch.) (1), *as nothing*
4682 matstsâh (1), *unfermented cake*
5493 çûwr (1), to *turn off*
7387 rêyqâm (2), *emptily; ineffectually*
8267 sheqer (1), *untruth; sham*
8414 tôhûw (2), *waste, desolation, formless*
8549 tâmîym (50), *entire, complete; integrity*
35 agĕnĕalŏgĕtŏs (1), *unregistered as to birth*
77 adapanŏs (1), *free of charge*
87 adiakritŏs (1), *impartial*
88 adialĕiptŏs (1), *permanent, constant*
89 adialĕiptŏs (4), *without omission*
112 athĕŏs (1), *godless*
175 akarpŏs (1), *barren, unfruitful*
186 aklinēs (1), *firm, unswerving*
194 akratŏs (1), *undiluted*
267 amarturŏs (1), *without witness*
275 amĕrimnŏs (1), *not anxious, free of care*
278 amĕtamĕlētŏs (1), *irrevocable*
280 amĕtrŏs (2), *immoderate*
282 amētōr (1), *of unknown maternity*
298 amōmētŏs (1), *unblemished*
299 amōmŏs (5), *unblemished, blameless*
361 anamartētŏs (1), *sinless*
369 anantirrhētŏs (1), *without raising objection*
379 anapŏlŏgētŏs (1), *without excuse*
427 anĕu (3), *without, apart from*
448 anilĕōs (1), *inexorable, merciless*
459 anŏmŏs (4), *without Jewish law*
460 anŏmŏs (2), *lawlessly, i.e. apart from Jewish Law*
504 anudrŏs (2), *dry, arid*
505 anupŏkritŏs (2), *sincere, genuine*
540 apatōr (1), *of unrecorded paternity*
563 apĕrispastŏs (1), *undistractedly*
677 aprŏskŏpŏs (1), *faultless*
678 aprŏsōpŏlēptŏs (1), *without prejudice*
729 arrhaphŏs (1), *of a single piece, without seam*
772 asthĕnēs (1), *strengthless, weak*
784 aspilŏs (1), *unblemished*
794 astŏrgŏs (2), *hard-hearted*
801 asunĕtŏs (3), *senseless, dull; wicked*
815 atĕknŏs (2), *childless*
817 atĕr (1), *apart from, without*
820 atimŏs (2), *without honor*
866 aphilargurŏs (1), *not greedy*
870 aphŏbŏs (4), *fearlessly*
880 aphōnŏs (1), *mute, silent; unmeaning*
886 achĕirŏpŏiētŏs (2), *unmanufactured*
895 apsuchŏs (1), *lifeless, i.e. inanimate*
1432 dōrĕan (1), *gratuitously, freely*
1500 ĕikē (1), *idly, i.e. without reason or effect*
1618 ĕktĕnēs (1), *intent, earnest*
1622 ĕktŏs (1), *aside from, besides; except*
1854 ĕxō (23), *out, outside*
1855 ĕxōthĕn (6), *outside, external (-ly)*
2673 katargĕō (1), to *be, render entirely useless*
3361 mē (1), *not; lest*
3672 hŏmŏlŏgŏumĕnōs (1), *confessedly*
3924 parĕktŏs (1), *besides; apart from*
5565 chōris (36), *at a space, i.e. separately*

WITHS
3499 yether (3), *remainder; small rope*

WITHSTAND
2388 châzaq (2), to *bind, restrain, conquer*
3320 yâtsab (1), to *station, offer, continue*
5975 'âmad (4), to *stand*
7854 sâṭân (1), *opponent*
436 anthistēmi (1), *oppose, rebel*
2967 kōluō (1), to *stop*

WITHSTOOD
5975 'âmad (2), to *stand*

436 anthistēmi (4), *oppose, rebel*

WITNESS
5707 'êd (45), *witness; testimony*
5711 'Ădâh (1), *ornament*
5713 'êdâh (3), *testimony*
5715 'êdûwth (4), *testimony*
5749 'ûwd (5), to *protest, testify; to encompass*
6030 'ânâh (2), to *respond, answer*
8085 shâma' (1), to *hear intelligently*
267 amarturŏs (1), *without witness*
2649 katamarturĕō (4), to *testify against*
3140 marturĕō (28), to *testify; to commend*
3141 marturia (15), *evidence given*
3142 marturiŏn (4), *something evidential; the Decalogue*
3144 martus (8), *witness*
4828 summarturĕō (3), to *testify jointly*
4901 sunĕpimarturĕō (1), to *testify further jointly*
5576 psĕudŏmarturĕō (6), to *be an untrue testifier*
5577 psĕudŏmarturia (2), *untrue testimony*

WITNESSED
5749 'ûwd (1), to *protest, testify; to encompass*
3140 marturĕō (3), to *testify; to commend*

WITNESSES
5707 'êd (23), *witness; testimony*
3140 marturĕō (1), to *testify; to commend*
3144 martus (21), *witness*
5575 psĕudŏmartur (3), *bearer of untrue testimony*

WITNESSETH
1263 diamarturŏmai (1), to *attest or protest*
3140 marturĕō (1), to *testify; to commend*

WITNESSING
3140 marturĕō (1), to *testify; to commend*

WITTINGLY
7919 sâkal (1), to *be or act circumspect*

WIVES
802 'ishshâh (115), *woman, wife*
5389 nâshîyn (Ch.) (1), *women, wives*
7695 shêgâl (Ch.) (3), *queen*
1135 gunē (12), *woman; wife*

WIVES'
1126 graŏdēs (1), *old lady-like, i.e. silly*

WIZARD
3049 yiddᵉ'ônîy (2), *conjurer; ghost*

WIZARDS
3049 yiddeʻônîy (9), conjurer; ghost

WOE
188 ʼôwy (22), Oh!, Woe!
190 ʼôwyâh (1), Oh!, Woe!
337 ʼîy (2), alas!
480 ʼalʻlay (2), alas!; woe!
1929 hâhh (1), ah!; woe!
1945 hôwy (36), oh!, woe!
1958 hîy (1), lamentation, woe
3759 ŏuai (39), woe!; woe

WOEFUL
605 ʼânash (1), to be frail, feeble

WOES
3759 ŏuai (1), woe!; woe

WOLF
2061 zeʻêb (4), wolf
3074 lukŏs (2), wolf

WOLVES
2061 zeʻêb (3), wolf
3074 lukŏs (4), wolf

WOMAN
802 ʼishshâh (211), woman, wife
5291 naʻărâh (1), female child; servant
5347 neqêbâh (2), female, woman
1135 gunē (96), woman; wife
1658 ĕlĕuthĕrŏs (1), not a slave
2338 thēlus (1), female

WOMAN'S
802 ʼishshâh (7), woman

WOMANKIND
802 ʼishshâh (1), woman, wife; women, wives

WOMB
990 beṭen (31), belly; womb; body
4578 mêʻâh (1), viscera; anguish, tenderness
7356 racham (4), compassion; womb
7358 rechem (20), womb
1064 gastēr (1), stomach; womb; gourmand
2836 kŏilia (11), abdomen, womb, heart
3388 mētra (2), womb

WOMBS
7358 rechem (1), womb
2836 kŏilia (1), abdomen, womb, heart

WOMEN
802 ʼishshâh (104), woman, wife
5347 neqêbâh (1), female
1133 gunaikariŏn (1), little woman
1135 gunē (33), woman
2338 thēlus (1), female
4247 prĕsbutis (1), old woman

WOMEN'S
802 ʼishshâh (1), woman

WOMENSERVANTS
8198 shiphchâh (3), household female slave

WON
2770 kĕrdainō (1), to gain; to spare

WONDER
4159 môwphêth (6), miracle; token or omen
6382 pele' (1), miracle
8539 tâmahh (3), to be astounded
2285 thambŏs (1), astonishment
2296 thaumazō (2), to wonder; to admire
4592 sēmĕiŏn (2), indication, sign, signal

WONDERED
4159 môwphêth (1), miracle; token or omen
8074 shâmêm (2), to devastate; to stupefy
1839 ĕxistēmi (1), to astound
2296 thaumazō (11), to wonder; to admire

WONDERFUL
6381 pâlâ' (13), to be, make great
6382 pele' (3), miracle
6383 pilʼîy (1), remarkable
8047 shammâh (1), ruin, consternation
1411 dunamis (1), force, power, miracle
2297 thaumasiŏs (1), miracle, wondrous act
3167 mĕgalĕiŏs (1), great things, wonderful works

WONDERFULLY
5953 ʻâlal (1), to glean; to overdo
6381 pâlâ' (1), to be, make wonderful
6382 pele' (1), miracle
6395 pâlâh (1), to distinguish

WONDERING
7583 shâʼâh (1), to be astonished
1569 ĕkthambŏs (1), utterly astounded
2296 thaumazō (1), to wonder; to admire

WONDEROUSLY
6381 pâlâ' (1), to be, make wonderful

WONDERS
4159 môwphêth (19), miracle; token or omen
6381 pâlâ' (9), to be, make wonderful
6382 pele' (7), miracle
8540 temahh (Ch.) (3), miracle
4592 sēmĕiŏn (1), indication, sign, signal
5059 tĕras (16), omen or miracle sign

WONDROUS
4652 miphlâʼâh (1), miracle
6381 pâlâ' (14), to be, make wonderful

WONDROUSLY
6381 pâlâ' (1), to be, make wonderful

WONT
1696 dâbar (1), to speak, say; to subdue
1980 hâlak (1), to walk; live a certain way
2370 chăzăʼ (Ch.) (1), to gaze upon; to dream
5056 naggâch (1), act of butting
5532 çâkan (1), to be serviceable to
1486 ĕthō (2), to be used by habit
2596+1485 kata (1), down; according to
3543 nŏmizō (1), to deem

WOOD
636 ʼâ (Ch.) (2), tree; wood; plank
2793 chôresh (4), wooded forest
3293 yaʻar (18), honey in the comb
6086 ʻêts (106), wood
3585 xulinŏs (2), made of wood
3586 xulŏn (3), timber and its products

WOODS
3264 yâʼôwr (1), forest

WOOF
6154 ʻêreb (9), mixed or woven things

WOOL
6015 ʻămar (Ch.) (1), wool
6785 tsemer (11), wool
2053 ĕriŏn (2), wool

WOOLLEN
6785 tsemer (5), wool
8162 shaʼaṭnêz (1), linen and woolen

WORD
562 ʼômer (2), something said
565 ʼimrâh (26), something said
1697 dâbâr (433), word; matter; thing
1699 dôber (2), grazing pasture
3983 mêʼmar (Ch.) (1), edict, command
4405 millâh (2), word; discourse; speech
4406 millâh (Ch.) (2), word, command
6310 peh (15), mouth; opening
6600 pithgâm (Ch.) (1), decree; report
518 apaggĕllō (2), to announce, proclaim
2036 ĕpō (1), to speak
3050 lŏgikŏs (1), rational, logical
3056 lŏgŏs (173), word, matter, thing; Word
4487 rhēma (28), utterance; matter

WORD'S
1697 dâbâr (1), word; matter; thing
3056 lŏgŏs (1), word, matter, thing; Word

WORDS
561 ʼêmer (42), something said
565 ʼimrâh (3), something said
1697 dâbâr (373), word; matter; thing
1703 dabbârâh (1), word, instruction
4405 millâh (21), word; discourse; speech
4406 millâh (Ch.) (5), word, command
3054 lŏgŏmachĕō (1), to be disputatious
3055 lŏgŏmachia (1), disputation
3056 lŏgŏs (48), word, matter, thing; Word
4086 pithanŏlŏgia (1), persuasive language
4487 rhēma (31), utterance; matter
5542 chrēstŏlŏgia (1), fair speech

WORK
731 ʼarzâh (1), cedar paneling
1697 dâbâr (1), word; matter; thing
3018 yeĝîyaʼ (1), toil, work; produce, property
3027 yâd (1), hand; power
3336 yêtser (1), form
4399 melâʼkâh (125), work; property
4639 maʻăseh (113), action; labor
4640 Maʻsay (1), operative
4649 Muppîym (1), wavings
4749 miqshâh (5), work molded by hammering
5627 çârâh (1), apostasy; crime; remission
5647 ʻâbad (4), to do, work, serve
5656 ʻăbôdâh (10), work
5673 ʻăbîydâh (Ch.) (3), labor or business
5950 ʻălîylîyâh (2), execution, deed
6213 ʻâsâh (23), to do
6381 pâlâ' (2), to be, make wonderful
6466 pâʻal (5), to do, make or practice
6467 pôʻal (28), act or work, deed
6468 peʻullâh (8), work
6603 pittûwach (1), sculpture; engraving
7553 riqmâh (5), variegation of color
7639 sebâkâh (2), reticulated ornament
1411 dunamis (1), force, power, miracle
1754 ĕnĕrgĕō (2), to be active, efficient, work
2038 ĕrgazŏmai (12), to toil
2039 ĕrgasia (1), occupation; profit
2040 ĕrgatēs (1), toiler, worker
2041 ĕrgŏn (45), work

W

2716 katĕrgazŏmai (1),
to finish; to accomplish
3056 lŏgŏs (2), word,
matter, thing; Word
3433+2480 mŏlis (1), with
difficulty
4229 pragma (1), matter,
deed, affair
4903 sunĕrgĕō (1), to be
a fellow-worker

WORK'S
2041 ĕrgŏn (1), work

WORKER
2790 chârash (1), to
engrave; to plow

WORKERS
2796 chârâsh (1), skilled
fabricator or worker
6213 'âsâh (1), to do
6466 pâ'al (19), to do,
make or practice
1411 dunamis (1), force,
power, miracle
2040 ĕrgatēs (3), toiler,
worker
4903 sunĕrgĕō (1), to be
a fellow-worker

WORKETH
5648 'ăbad (Ch.) (1), to
work, serve
6213 'âsâh (6), to do or
make
6466 pâ'al (4), to do,
make or practice
1754 ĕnĕrgĕō (11), to be
active, efficient, work
2038 ĕrgazŏmai (7), to
toil
2716 katĕrgazŏmai (7),
to finish; to accomplish
4160 pŏiĕō (1), to make
or do

WORKFELLOW
4904 sunĕrgŏs (1),
fellow-worker

WORKING
4639 ma'ăseh (1), action;
labor
6213 'âsâh (1), to do or
make
6466 pâ'al (1), to do,
make or practice
8454 tûwshîyâh (1),
ability, i.e. direct help
1753 ĕnĕrgĕia (6),
efficiency, energy
1755 ĕnĕrgēma (1),
effect, activity
2038 ĕrgazŏmai (4), to
toil
2716 katĕrgazŏmai (2),
to finish; to accomplish
4160 pŏiĕō (2), to make
or do
4903 sunĕrgĕō (1), to be
a fellow-worker

WORKMAN
542 'âmân (1), expert
artisan, craftsman
2796 chârâsh (5), skilled
fabricator or worker
2803 châshab (2), to
weave, fabricate
2040 ĕrgatēs (2), toiler,
worker

WORKMANSHIP
4399 mᵉlâ'kâh (5), work;
property
4639 ma'ăseh (1), action;
labor
4161 pŏiēma (1), what is
made, product

WORKMEN
582+4399 'ĕnôwsh (1),
man; person, human
2796 chârâsh (1), skilled
fabricator or worker
6213+4399 'âsâh (7), to
do or make
2040 ĕrgatēs (1), toiler,
worker

WORKMEN'S
6001 'âmêl (1), toiling;
laborer; sorrowful

WORKS
1697 dâbâr (1), word;
matter; thing
4399 mᵉlâ'kâh (3), work;
property
4566 ma'bâd (1), act,
deed
4567 ma'bâd (Ch.) (1),
act, deed
4611 ma'ălâl (3), act,
deed
4639 ma'ăseh (70),
action; labor
4640 Ma'say (2),
operative
4659 miph'âl (3),
performance, deed
5652 'ăbâd (1), deed
5949 'ălîylâh (3),
opportunity, action
6467 pô'al (2), act or
work, deed
6468 pᵉ'ullâh (1), work,
deed
2041 ĕrgŏn (104), work
4234 praxis (1), act;
function

WORKS'
2041 ĕrgŏn (1), work

WORLD
776 'erets (4), earth,
land, soil; country
2309 chedel (1), state of
the dead, deceased
2465 cheled (2), fleeting
time; this world
5769 'ôwlâm (4), eternity;
ancient; always
8398 têbêl (35), earth;
world; inhabitants
165 aiōn (37), perpetuity,
ever; world
166 aiōniŏs (3),
perpetual, long ago
1093 gē (1), soil, region,
whole earth
2889 kŏsmŏs (183), world
3625 ŏikŏumĕnē (14),
Roman empire

WORLD'S
2889 kŏsmŏs (1), world

WORLDLY
2886 kŏsmikŏs (2),
earthly, worldly

WORLDS
165 aiōn (2), perpetuity,
ever; world

WORM
5580 çâç (1), garment
moth
7415 rimmâh (5), maggot
8438 tôwlâ' (5), maggot
worm; crimson-grub
4663 skōlēx (3), grub,
maggot or earth-worm

WORMS
2119 zâchal (1), to crawl;
glide
7415 rimmâh (2), maggot
8438 tôwlâ' (3), maggot
worm; crimson-grub
4662 skōlēkŏbrōtŏs (1),
diseased with maggots

WORMWOOD
3939 la'ănâh (7),
poisonous wormwood
894 apsinthŏs (2),
wormwood, bitterness

WORSE
2196 zâ'aph (1), to be
angry
5062 nâgaph (5), to
inflict a disease
7451 ra' (1), bad; evil
7489 râ'a' (5), to be good
for nothing
1640 ĕlassōn (1), smaller
2276 hēttōn (1), worse
5302 hustĕrĕō (1), to be
inferior; to fall short
5501 chĕirōn (10), more
evil or aggravated

WORSHIP
5457 çᵉgîd (Ch.) (8), to
prostrate oneself
6087 'âtsab (1), to
fabricate or fashion
7812 shâchâh (54), to
prostrate in homage
1391 dŏxa (1), glory;
brilliance
1479 ĕthĕlŏthrēskĕia (1),
voluntary piety
2151 ĕusĕbĕō (1), to put
religion into practice
3000 latrĕuō (3), to
minister to God
4352 prŏskunĕō (34), to
prostrate oneself
4352+1799 prŏskunĕō (1),
to prostrate oneself
4576 sĕbŏmai (3), to
revere, i.e. adore

WORSHIPPED
5457 çᵉgîd (Ch.) (2), to
prostrate oneself
7812 shâchâh (39), to
prostrate in homage
2323 thĕrapĕuō (1), to
adore God
4352 prŏskunĕō (24), to
prostrate oneself
4573 sĕbazŏmai (1), to
venerate, worship
4574 sĕbasma (1), object
of worship
4576 sĕbŏmai (2), to
revere, i.e. adore

WORSHIPPER
2318 thĕŏsĕbēs (1), pious,
devout, God-fearing
3511 nĕōkŏrŏs (1),
temple servant

WORSHIPPERS
5647 'âbad (5), to serve
3000 latrĕuō (1), to
minister to God
4353 prŏskunētēs (1),
adorer

WORSHIPPETH
5457 çᵉgîd (Ch.) (2), to
prostrate oneself
7812 shâchâh (3), to
prostrate in homage
4576 sĕbŏmai (1), to
revere, i.e. adore

WORSHIPPING
7812 shâchâh (3), to
prostrate in homage
2356 thrēskĕia (1),
observance, religion
4352 prŏskunĕō (1), to
prostrate oneself

WORST
7451 ra' (1), bad; evil

WORTH
3644 kᵉmôw (1), like, as;
for; with
4242 mᵉchîyr (1), price,
payment, wages
4373 mikçâh (1),
valuation of a thing
4392 mâlê' (1), full;
filling; fulness; fully
7939 sâkâr (1), payment,
salary; compensation

WORTHIES
117 'addîyr (1), powerful;
majestic

WORTHILY
2428 chayil (1), army;
wealth; virtue; valor

WORTHY
376 'îysh (1), man; male;
someone
639 'aph (1), nose or
nostril; face; person
1121 bên (2), son,
descendant; people
2428 chayil (1), army;
wealth; virtue; valor
6994 qâṭôn (1), to be,
make diminutive
514 axiŏs (35), deserving,
comparable or suitable
515 axiŏō (5), to deem
entitled or fit, worthy
516 axiōs (3),
appropriately, suitable
2425 hikanŏs (5), ample;
fit
2570 kalŏs (1), good;
beautiful; valuable
2661 kataxiŏō (4), to
deem entirely deserving
2735 katŏrthōma (1),
made fully upright

WOT
3045 yâda' (6), to know
1107 gnōrizō (1), to
make known, reveal
1492 ĕidō (3), to know

WOTTETH
3045 yâda' (1), to know

WOULD
14 'âbâh (41), to be
acquiescent
305 'achălay (1), would
that!, Oh that!, If Only!

2654 châphêts (1), to *be pleased* with, *desire*
2655 châphêts (1), *pleased* with
2974 yâ'al (3), to *assent; to undertake, begin*
3863 lûw' (6), *would that!*
5315 nephesh (1), *life; breath; soul; wind*
6634 tsᵉbâ' (Ch.) (5), to *please*
1096 ginŏmai (1), to *be, become*
2172 ĕuchŏmai (1), to *wish for; to pray*
2309 thĕlō (73), to *will; to desire; to choose*
3195 mĕllō (9), to *intend,* i.e. *be about to*
3785 ŏphĕlŏn (4), *I wish*

WOULDEST
3426 yêsh (1), there *is*
2309 thĕlō (4), to *will; to desire; to choose*

WOUND
2671 chêts (1), *arrow; wound;* thunder-*bolt*
4204 mâzŏwr (1), *ambush*
4205 mâzŏwr (2), *sore*
4272 mâchats (3), to *crush; to subdue*
4347 makkâh (8), *blow; wound; pestilence*
5061 nega' (1), *infliction, affliction; leprous spot*
6482 petsa' (2), *wound*
1210 dĕō (1), to *bind*
4127 plēgē (3), *stroke; wound; calamity*
4958 sustĕllō (1), to *draw together,* i.e. *enwrap or enshroud a corpse*
5180 tuptō (1), to *strike, beat, wound*

WOUNDED
1214 bâtsa' (1), to *plunder; to finish*
1795 dakkâh (1), *mutilated by crushing*
1856 dâqar (1), to *stab, pierce; to starve*
2342 chûwl (2), to *dance, whirl; to writhe in pain*
2470 châlâh (3), to *be weak, sick, afflicted*
2490 châlal (3), to *profane, defile*
2491 châlâl (10), *pierced to death, one slain*
4272 mâchats (2), to *crush; to subdue*
4347 makkâh (1), *blow; wound; pestilence*
5218 nâkê' (1), *smitten; afflicted*
5221 nâkâh (3), to *strike, kill*
6481 pâtsa' (2), to *wound*
4127+2007 plēgē (1), *stroke; wound*
4969 sphazō (1), to *slaughter or to maim*
5135 traumatizō (2), to *inflict a wound*

WOUNDEDST
4272 mâchats (1), to *crush; to subdue*

WOUNDETH
4272 mâchats (1), to *crush; to subdue*

WOUNDING
6482 petsa' (1), *wound*

WOUNDS
2250 chabbûwrâh (1), *weal, bruise*
3859 lâham (2), to *rankle*
4347 makkâh (6), *blow; wound; pestilence*
6094 'atstsebeth (1), *pain or wound, sorrow*
6482 petsa' (4), *wound*
5134 trauma (1), *wound*

WOVE
707 'ârag (1), to *plait or weave*

WOVEN
707 'ârag (3), to *plait or weave*
5307 huphantŏs (1), *knitted, woven*

WRAP
3664 kânaç (1), to *collect; to enfold*
5686 'âbath (1), to *pervert*

WRAPPED
1563 gâlam (1), to *fold*
2280 châbash (1), to *wrap firmly, bind*
3874 lûwṭ (2), to *wrap* up
4593 mâ'ŏṭ (1), *sharp, thin-edged*
5440 çâbak (1), to *entwine*
5968 'âlaph (1), to *be languid, faint*
8276 sârag (1), to *entwine*
1750 ĕnĕilĕō (1), to *enwrap*
1794 ĕntulissō (3), *wind* up in, *enwrap*
4683 sparganŏō (2), to *strap or wrap*

WRATH
639 'aph (42), *nose or nostril; face; person*
2197 za'aph (1), *anger, rage*
2534 chêmâh (34), *heat; anger; poison*
2740 chârôwn (6), *burning* of anger
3707 kâ'aç (1), to *grieve, rage, be indignant*
3708 ka'aç (4), *vexation, grief*
5678 'ebrâh (31), *outburst* of passion
7107 qâtsaph (5), to *burst out in rage*
7109 qᵉtsaph (Ch.) (1), *rage*
7110 qetseph (23), *rage or strife*
7265 rᵉgaz (Ch.) (1), to *quiver*
7267 rôgez (1), *disquiet; anger*
2372 thumŏs (14), *passion, anger*
3709 ŏrgē (31), *ire; punishment*
3949 parŏrgizō (1), to *enrage, exasperate*

3950 parŏrgismŏs (1), *rage*

WRATHFUL
2534 chêmâh (1), *heat; anger; poison*
2740 chârôwn (1), *burning* of anger

WRATHS
2372 thumŏs (1), *passion, anger*

WREATH
7639 sᵉbâkâh (1), *reticulated* ornament

WREATHED
8276 sârag (1), to *entwine*

WREATHEN
5688 'ăbôth (8), *entwined* things: a *string, wreath*
7639 sᵉbâkâh (2), *reticulated* ornament

WREATHS
1434 gᵉdîl (1), *tassel; festoon*
7639 sᵉbâkâh (2), *reticulated* ornament

WREST
5186 nâṭâh (3), to *stretch* or spread out
6087 'âtsab (1), to *fabricate or fashion*
4761 strĕblŏō (1), to *pervert, twist*

WRESTLE
2076+3823 ĕsti (1), he (she or it) *is;* they *are*

WRESTLED
79 'âbaq (2), *grapple, wrestle*
6617 pâthal (1), to *struggle; to be tortuous*

WRESTLINGS
5319 naphtûwl (1), *struggle*

WRETCHED
5005 talaipōrŏs (2), *miserable, wretched*

WRETCHEDNESS
7451 ra' (1), *bad; evil*

WRING
4454 mâlaq (2), to *wring* a bird's neck
4680 mâtsâh (1), to *drain; to squeeze* out

WRINGED
4680 mâtsâh (1), to *drain; to squeeze* out

WRINGING
4330 mîyts (1), *pressure*

WRINKLE
4512 rhutis (1), face *wrinkle*

WRINKLES
7059 qâmaṭ (1), to *pluck,* i.e. *destroy*

WRITE
3789 kâthab (35), to *write*
3790 kᵉthab (Ch.) (1), to *write*
1125 graphō (50), to *write*
1924 ĕpigraphō (2), to *inscribe, write upon*
1989 ĕpistĕllō (1), to *communicate by letter*

WRITER
5608 çâphar (2), to *inscribe; to enumerate*

WRITER'S
5608 çâphar (2), to *inscribe; to enumerate*

WRITEST
3789 kâthab (2), to *write*

WRITETH
3789 kâthab (1), to *write*

WRITING
3789 kâthab (1), to *write*
3791 kâthâb (14), *writing, record or book*
3792 kᵉthâb (Ch.) (10), *writing, record or book*
4385 miktâb (8), *written thing*
975 bibliŏn (1), *scroll; certificate*
1125 graphō (1), to *write*
4093 pinakidiŏn (1), *wooden writing tablet*

WRITINGS
1121 gramma (1), *writing; education*

WRITTEN
3789 kâthab (138), to *write*
3790 kᵉthab (Ch.) (2), to *write*
3792 kᵉthâb (Ch.) (1), *writing, record or book*
7560 rᵉsham (Ch.) (2), to *record*
583 apŏgraphō (1), *enroll, take a census*
1123 graptŏs (1), *inscribed, written*
1125 graphō (134), to *write*
1449 ĕggraphō (2), *inscribe, write*
1722+1121 ĕn (1), *in; during; because of*
1924 ĕpigraphō (2), to *inscribe, write upon*
1989 ĕpistĕllō (2), to *communicate by letter*
4270 prŏgraphō (2), to *write previously; to announce, prescribe*

WRONG
2555 châmâç (3), *violence; malice*
3238 yânâh (1), to *suppress; to maltreat*
3808+4941 lô' (1), no, *not*
5627 çârâh (1), *apostasy; crime; remission*
5753 'âvâh (1), to *be crooked*
5792 'avvâthâh (1), *oppression*
6127 'âqal (1), to *wrest, be crooked*
6231 'âshaq (2), to *violate; to overflow*
7451 ra' (1), *bad; evil*
7563 râshâ' (1), morally *wrong; bad* person
91 adikĕō (11), to *do wrong*
92 adikēma (1), *wrong*
93 adikia (1), *wrongfulness*

W

WRONGED
91 adikéō (2), *to do wrong*

WRONGETH
2554 châmaç (1), *to be violent; to maltreat*

WRONGFULLY
2554 châmaç (1), *to be violent; to maltreat*
3808+4941 lō' (1), *no, not*
8267 sheqer (4), *untruth; sham*
95 adikōs (1), *unjustly*

WROTE
3789 kâthab (34), *to write*
3790 kᵉthab (Ch.) (5), *to write*
1125 graphō (21), *to write*
4270 prōgraphō (1), *to write previously; to announce, prescribe*

WROTH
2196 zâ'aph (2), *to be angry*
2534 chêmâh (1), *heat; anger; poison*
2734 chârâh (13), *to blaze up*
3707 kâ'aç (1), *to grieve, rage, be indignant*
5674 'âbar (5), *to cross over; to transition*
7107 qâtsaph (22), *to burst out in rage*
7264 râgaz (1), *to quiver*
2373 thumŏō (1), *to enrage*
3710 ŏrgizō (3), *to become exasperated*

WROUGHT
1496 gâzîyth (1), *dressed stone*
1980 hâlak (2), *to walk; live a certain way*
2790 chârash (1), *to engrave; to plow*
4639 ma'ăseh (3), *action; labor*
4865 mishbᵉtsâh (1), *reticulated setting*
5647 'âbad (1), *to do, work, serve*
5648 'âbad (Ch.) (1), *to work, serve*
5656 'ăbôdâh (1), *work*
5927 'âlâh (1), *to ascend, be high, mount*
5953 'âlal (2), *to glean; to overdo*
6213 'âsâh (52), *to do*
6466 pâ'al (7), *to do, make or practice*
7194 qâshar (1), *to tie, bind*
7551 râqam (1), *variegation; embroider*
7760 sûwm (1), *to put, place*
1096 ginŏmai (2), *to be, become*
1754 ĕnĕrgéō (2), *to be active, efficient, work*
2038 ĕrgazŏmai (7), *to toil*
2716 katĕrgazŏmai (6), *to finish; to accomplish*

4160 pŏiĕō (5), *to make or do*
4903 sunĕrgĕō (1), *to be a fellow-worker*

WROUGHTEST
6213 'âsâh (1), *to make*

WRUNG
4680 mâtsâh (4), *to drain; to squeeze out*

YARN
4723 miqveh (4), *confidence; collection*

YEA
432 'illûw (1), *if*
637 'aph (39), *also or yea; though*
834 'ăsher (1), *who, which, what, that*
1571 gam (66), *also; even; yea; though*
3588 kîy (7), *for, that because*
235 alla (15), *but, yet, except, instead*
1161 dĕ (13), *but, yet; and then*
2089 ĕti (1), *yet, still*
2228 ē (1), *or; than*
2532 kai (5), *and; or; even; also*
3304 mĕnŏungĕ (1), *so then at least*
3483 nai (22), *yes*

YEAR
3117 yôwm (6), *day; time period*
8140 shᵉnâh (Ch.) (5), *year*
8141 shâneh (323), *year*
1763 ĕniautŏs (13), *year*
2094 ĕtŏs (46), *year*
4070 pĕrusi (2), *last year; from last year*

YEAR'S
3117 yôwm (1), *day; time period*
8141 shâneh (1), *year*

YEARLY
3117 yôwm (6), *day; time period*
8141 shâneh (3), *year*

YEARN
3648 kâmar (1), *to shrivel with heat*

YEARNED
3648 kâmar (1), *to shrivel with heat*

YEARS
3027 yâd (1), *hand; power*
3117 yôwm (3), *day; time period*
8027 shâlash (2), *to be, triplicate*
8140 shᵉnâh (Ch.) (2), *year*
8141 shâneh (466), *year*
1096+3173 ginŏmai (1), *to be, become*
1332 diĕtēs (1), *of two years in age*
1333 diĕtia (2), *interval of two years*
1541 hĕkatŏntaĕtēs (1), *centenarian*
1763 ĕniautŏs (2), *year*
2094 ĕtŏs (46), *year*

2250 hēmĕra (2), *day; period of time*
5063 tĕssarakŏntaĕtēs (2), *of forty years* of age
5148 triĕtia (1), *triennium, three years*

YEARS'
8141 shâneh (2), *year*

YELL
5286 nâ'ar (1), *to growl*

YELLED
5414+6963 nâthan (1), *to give*

YELLOW
3422 yᵉraqraq (1), *yellowishness*
6669 tsâhôb (3), *golden in color*

YES
3304 mĕnŏungĕ (1), *so then at least*
3483 nai (3), *yes*

YESTERDAY
570 'emesh (1), *yesterday evening*
865 'ethmôwl (1), *heretofore, formerly*
8543 tᵉmôwl (4), *yesterday*
5504 chthĕs (3), *yesterday; in time past*

YESTERNIGHT
570 'emesh (3), *yesterday evening*

YET
227 'âz (1), *at that time or place; therefore*
389 'ak (13), *surely; only, however*
559 'âmar (1), *to say*
637 'aph (1), *also or yea*
1297 bᵉram (Ch.) (2), *however, but*
1571 gam (14), *also; even; yea; though*
2962 ṭerem (4), *not yet or before*
3588 kîy (14), *for, that because*
5704 'ad (4), *as far (long) as; during; while; until*
5728 'ăden (2), *till now, yet*
5750 'ôwd (142), *again; repeatedly; still; more*
7535 raq (2), *merely; although*
188 akmēn (1), *just now, still*
235 alla (11), *but, yet, except, instead*
1063 gar (3), *for, indeed, but, because*
1065 gĕ (2), *particle of emphasis*
1161 dĕ (19), *but, yet; and then*
2089 ĕti (54), *yet, still*
2236 hēdista (2), *with great pleasure*
2532 kai (7), *and; or; even; also*
2539 kaipĕr (1), *nevertheless*
2579 kan (1), *and (or even) if*

2596 kata (2), *down; according to*
3195 mĕllō (1), *to intend, i.e. be about to*
3305 mĕntŏi (2), *however*
3364 ŏu mē (1), *not at all, absolutely not*
3369 mĕdĕpō (1), *not even yet*
3380 mēpō (1), *not yet*
3764 ŏudĕpō (4), *not even yet*
3765 ŏukĕti (3), *not yet, no longer*
3768 ŏupō (21), *not yet*

YIELD
3254 yâçaph (1), *to add or augment*
5186 nâṭâh (1), *to stretch or spread out*
5375 nâsâ' (1), *to lift up*
5414 nâthan (13), *to give*
5414+3027 nâthan (1), *to give*
6213 'âsâh (6), *to do or make*
1325 didōmi (1), *to give*
3936 paristēmi (4), *to stand beside, present*
3982 pĕithō (1), *to assent to authority*
4160 pŏiĕō (1), *to make or do*

YIELDED
1478 gâva' (1), *to expire, die*
1580 gâmal (1), *to benefit or requite; to wean*
3052 yᵉhab (Ch.) (1), *to give*
591 apŏdidōmi (1), *to give away*
863 aphiēmi (1), *to leave; to pardon, forgive*
1325 didōmi (1), *to give*
1634 ĕkpsuchō (1), *to expire, die*
3936 paristēmi (1), *to stand beside, present*

YIELDETH
5414 nâthan (1), *to give*
7235 râbâh (1), *to increase*
591 apŏdidōmi (1), *to give away*

YIELDING
2232 zâra' (3), *to sow seed; to disseminate*
4832 marpê' (1), *cure; deliverance; placidity*
6213 'âsâh (3), *to do or make*

YOKE
4132 môwṭ (1), *pole; yoke*
4133 môwṭâh (4), *pole; ox-bow; yoke*
5923 'ôl (39), *neck yoke*
6776 tsemed (7), *paired yoke*
2201 zĕugŏs (1), *team*
2218 zugŏs (5), *coupling, yoke*

YOKED
2086 hĕtĕrŏzugĕō (1), *to associate discordantly*

YOKEFELLOW
4805 suzugŏs (1), colleague

YOKES
4133 môwṭâh (4), pole; ox-bow; yoke

YONDER
1973 hâlᵉâh (1), far away; thus far
3541 kôh (2), thus
5676 'êber (1), opposite side; east
5704+3541 'ad (1), as far (long) as; during; while; until
1563 ĕkĕi (2), there, thither

YOUNG
667 'ephrôach (4), brood of a bird
970 bâchûwr (42), male youth; bridegroom
979 bᵉchûrôwth (1), youth
1121 bên (20), son, descendant; people
1121+1241 bên (34), son, descendant; people
1123 bên (Ch.) (1), son
1241 bâqâr (1), plowing ox; herd
1469 gôwzâl (2), young of a bird
1482 gûwr (1), cub
3127 yôwneqeth (1), sprout, new shoot
3206 yeled (10), young male
3242 yᵉnîqâh (1), sucker or sapling
3715 kᵉphîyr (25), walled village; young lion
3833 lâbîy' (1), lion, lioness
5288 na'ar (92), male child; servant
5288+970 na'ar (1), male child; servant
5291 na'ărâh (6), female child; servant
5763 'ûwl (3), to suckle, i.e. give milk
5958 'elem (1), lad, young man
6082 'ôpher (5), dusty-colored fawn
6499 par (1), bullock
6810+3117 tsâ'îyr (1), young in value
6996 qâṭân (1), small, least, youngest
7988 shilyâh (1), fetus or infant baby
1025 brĕphŏs (1), infant
2365 thugatriŏn (1), little daughter
3494 nĕanias (5), youth, up to about forty years
3495 nĕaniskŏs (10), youth under forty
3501 nĕŏs (4), new
3502 nĕŏssŏs (1), young
3678 ŏnariŏn (1), little donkey
3813 paidiŏn (10), child; immature
3816 pais (1), child; slave or servant

YOUNGER
6810 tsâ'îyr (7), little, young
6810+3117 tsâ'îyr (1), little, young
6996 qâṭân (14), small, least, youngest
1640 ĕlassŏn (1), smaller
3501 nĕŏs (8), new

YOUNGEST
6810 tsâ'îyr (3), little, young
6996 qâṭân (15), small, least, youngest

YOUTH
979 bᵉchûrôwth (2), youth
2779 chôreph (1), autumn (and winter)
3208 yaldûwth (2), boyhood or girlhood
5271 nâ'ûwr (46), youth; juvenility; young people
5288 na'ar (5), male child; servant
5290 nô'ar (2), boyhood
5934 'âlûwm (4), adolescence; vigor
6526 pirchach (1), progeny, i.e. a brood
6812 tsᵉ'îyrâh (1), juvenility
7839 shachărûwth (1), juvenescence, youth
3503 nĕŏtēs (5), youthfulness

YOUTHFUL
3512 nĕŏtĕrikŏs (1), juvenile, youthful

YOUTHS
1121 bên (1), son, descendant; people
5288 na'ar (1), male child; servant

ZAANAIM
6815 Tsa'ănannîym (1), removals

ZAANAN
6630 Tsa'ănân (1), sheep pasture

ZAANANNIM
6815 Tsa'ănannîym (1), removals

ZAAVAN
2190 Za'ăvân (1), disquiet

ZABAD
2066 Zâbâd (8), giver

ZABBAI
2079 Zabbay (2), Zabbai

ZABBUD
2072 Zabbûwd (1), given

ZABDI
2067 Zabdîy (6), giving

ZABDIEL
2068 Zabdîy'êl (2), gift of God

ZABUD
2071 Zâbûwd (1), given

ZABULON
2194 Zaboŭlôn (3), habitation

ZACCAI
2140 Zakkay (2), pure

ZACCHAEUS
2195 Zakchaiŏs (3), Zacchæus

ZACCHUR
2139 Zakkûwr (1), mindful

ZACCUR
2139 Zakkûwr (8), mindful

ZACHARIAH
2148 Zᵉkaryâh (4), Jehovah has remembered

ZACHARIAS
2197 Zacharias (11), Jehovah has remembered

ZACHER
2144 Zeker (1), recollection; commemoration

ZADOK
6659 Tsâdôwq (52), just

ZADOK'S
6659 Tsâdôwq (1), just

ZAHAM
2093 Zaham (1), loathing

ZAIR
6811 Tsâ'îyr (1), little

ZALAPH
6764 Tsâlâph (1), Tsalaph

ZALMON
6756 Tsalmôwn (2), shady

ZALMONAH
6758 Tsalmônâh (2), shadiness

ZALMUNNA
6759 Tsalmunnâ' (12), shade has been denied

ZAMZUMMIMS
2157 Zamzôm (1), intriguing

ZANOAH
2182 Zânôwach (5), rejected

ZAPHNATH-PAANEAH
6847 Tsophnath Pa'nêach (1), Tsophnath-Paneäch

ZAPHON
6829 Tsâphôwn (1), boreal, northern

ZARA
2196 Zara (1), rising of light, dawning

ZARAH
2226 Zerach (2), rising of light, dawning

ZAREAH
6881 Tsor'âh (1), stinging wasp

ZAREATHITES
6882 Tsor'îy (1), Tsorite or Tsorathite

ZARED
2218 Zered (1), lined with shrubbery

ZAREPHATH
6886 Tsârᵉphath (3), refinement

ZARETAN
6891 Tsârᵉthân (1), Tsarethan

ZARETH-SHAHAR
6890 Tsereth hash-Shachar (1), splendor of the dawn

ZARHITES
2227 Zarchîy (6), Zarchite

ZARTANAH
6891 Tsârᵉthân (1), Tsarethan

ZARTHAN
6891 Tsârᵉthân (1), Tsarethan

ZATTHU
2240 Zattûw' (1), Zattu

ZATTU
2240 Zattûw' (3), Zattu

ZAVAN
2190 Za'ăvân (1), disquiet

ZAZA
2117 Zâzâ' (1), prominent

ZEAL
7065 qânâ' (1), to be, make zealous, jealous or envious
7068 qin'âh (9), jealousy or envy
2205 zēlŏs (6), zeal, ardor; jealousy, malice

ZEALOUS
7065 qânâ' (2), to be, make zealous
2206 zēlŏŏ (1), to have warmth of feeling for
2207 zēlōtēs (5), zealot

ZEALOUSLY
2206 zēlŏŏ (2), to have warmth of feeling for

ZEBADIAH
2069 Zᵉbadyâh (9), Jehovah has given

ZEBAH
2078 Zebach (12), sacrifice

ZEBAIM
6380 Pôkereth Tsᵉbâyîym (2), trap of gazelles

ZEBEDEE
2199 Zĕbĕdaiŏs (10), Zebedæus

ZEBEDEE'S
2199 Zĕbĕdaiŏs (2), Zebedæus

ZEBINA
2081 Zᵉbîynâ' (1), gainfulness

ZEBOIIM
6636 Tsᵉbô'iym (2), gazelles

ZEBOIM
6636 Tsᵉbô'iym (3), gazelles
6650 Tsᵉbô'îym (2), hyenas

ZEBUDAH
2081 Zᵉbîynâ' (1), gainfulness

ZEBUL
2083 Zᵉbûl (6), dwelling

Z

ZEBULONITE
2075 Z^{e}bûwlôniy (2), *Zebulonite*

ZEBULUN
2074 Z^{e}bûwlûwn (44), *habitation*

ZEBULUNITES
2075 Z^{e}bûwlôniy (1), *Zebulonite*

ZECHARIAH
2148 Z^{e}karyâh (39), *Jehovah has remembered*

ZEDAD
6657 Ts^{e}dâd (2), *siding*

ZEDEKIAH
6667 Tsidqîyâh (61), *right of Jehovah*

ZEDEKIAH'S
6667 Tsidqîyâh (1), *right of Jehovah*

ZEEB
2062 Z^e'êb (6), *wolf*

ZELAH
6762 Tsela' (2), *limping*

ZELEK
6768 Tseleq (2), *fissure*

ZELOPHEHAD
6765 Ts^{e}lophchâd (11), *Tselophchad*

ZELOTES
2208 Zēlōtēs (2), *Zealot, partisan*

ZELZAH
6766 Tseltsach (1), *clear shade*

ZEMARAIM
6787 Ts^{e}mârayim (2), *double fleece*

ZEMARITE
6786 Ts^{e}mâriy (2), *Tsemarite*

ZEMIRA
2160 Z^{e}mîyrâh (1), *song*

ZENAN
6799 Ts^{e}nân (1), *Tsenan*

ZENAS
2211 Zēnas (1), *Jove-given*

ZEPHANIAH
6846 Ts^{e}phanyâh (10), *Jehovah has secreted*

ZEPHATH
6857 Ts^{e}phath (1), *watch-tower*

ZEPHATHAH
6859 Ts^{e}phâthâh (1), *watch-tower*

ZEPHI
6825 Ts^{e}phôw (1), *observant*

ZEPHO
6825 Ts^{e}phôw (2), *observant*

ZEPHON
6827 Ts^{e}phôwn (1), *watch-tower*

ZEPHONITES
6831 Ts^{e}phôwniy (1), *Tsephonite*

ZER
6863 Tsêr (1), *rock*

ZERAH
2226 Zerach (19), *rising of light, dawning*

ZERAHIAH
2228 Z^{e}rachyâh (5), *Jehovah has risen*

ZERED
2218 Zered (3), lined with *shrubbery*

ZEREDA
6868 Ts^{e}rêdâh (1), *puncture*

ZEREDATHAH
6868 Ts^{e}rêdâh (1), *puncture*

ZERERATH
6888 Ts^{e}rêrâh (1), *puncture*

ZERESH
2238 Zeresh (4), *Zeresh*

ZERETH
6889 Tsereth (1), *splendor*

ZERI
6874 Ts^{e}rîy (1), *balsam*

ZEROR
6872 ts^{e}rôwr (1), *parcel; kernel* or *particle*

ZERUAH
6871 Ts^{e}rûw'âh (1), *leprous*

ZERUBBABEL
2216 Z^{e}rubbâbel (21), *from Babylon*
2217 Z^{e}rubbâbel (Ch.) (1), *from Babylon*

ZERUIAH
6870 Ts^{e}rûwyâh (26), *wounded*

ZETHAM
2241 Zêthâm (2), *seed*

ZETHAN
2133 Zêythân (1), *olive grove*

ZETHAR
2242 Zêthar (1), *Zethar*

ZIA
2127 Zîya' (1), *agitation*

ZIBA
6717 Tsîybâ' (16), *station*

ZIBEON
6649 Tsib'ôwn (8), *variegated*

ZIBIA
6644 Tsibyâ' (1), *female gazelle*

ZIBIAH
6645 Tsibyâh (2), *female gazelle*

ZICHRI
2147 Zikrîy (12), *memorable*

ZIDDIM
6661 Tsiddîym (1), *sides*

ZIDKIJAH
6667 Tsidqîyâh (1), *right of Jehovah*

ZIDON
6721 Tsîydôwn (20), *fishery*
6722 Tsîydôniy (1), *Tsidonian*

ZIDONIANS
6722 Tsîydôniy (10), *Tsidonian*

ZIF
2099 Zîv (2), *flowers*

ZIHA
6727 Tsîychâ' (3), *drought*

ZIKLAG
6860 Tsiqlâg (14), *Tsiklag* or *Tsikelag*

ZILLAH
6741 Tsillâh (3), *Tsillah*

ZILPAH
2153 Zilpâh (7), fragrant *dropping* as myrrh

ZILTHAI
6769 Tsill^{e}thay (2), *shady*

ZIMMAH
2155 Zimmâh (3), bad *plan*

ZIMRAN
2175 Zimrân (2), *musical*

ZIMRI
2174 Zimrîy (15), *musical*

ZIN
6790 Tsîn (10), *crag*

ZINA
2126 Zîynâ' (1), well-*fed*

ZION
6726 Tsîyôwn (152), permanent *capital* or *monument*

ZION'S
6726 Tsîyôwn (1), permanent *capital* or *monument*

ZIOR
6730 Tsîy'ôr (1), *small*

ZIPH
2128 Zîyph (10), *flowing*

ZIPHAH
2129 Zîyphâh (1), *flowing*

ZIPHIMS
2130 Zîyphîy (1), *Ziphite*

ZIPHION
6837 Tsiphyôwn (1), *watch-tower*

ZIPHITES
2130 Zîyphîy (2), *Ziphite*

ZIPHRON
2202 Ziphrôn (1), *fragrant*

ZIPPOR
6834 Tsippôwr (7), little *hopping bird*

ZIPPORAH
6855 Tsippôrâh (3), *bird*

ZITHRI
5644 Çithrîy (1), *protective*

ZIZ
6732 Tsîyts (1), *bloom*

ZIZA
2124 Zîyzâ' (2), *prominence*

ZIZAH
2125 Zîyzâh (1), *prominence*

ZOAN
6814 Tsô'an (7), *Tsoän*

ZOAR
6820 Tsô'ar (10), *little*

ZOBA
6678 Tsôwbâ' (2), *station*

ZOBAH
6678 Tsôwbâ' (11), *station*

ZOBEBAH
6637 Tsôbêbâh (1), *canopier*

ZOHAR
6714 Tsôchar (4), *whiteness*

ZOHELETH
2120 Zôcheleth (1), *serpent*

ZOHETH
2105 Zôwchêth (1), *Zocheth*

ZOPHAH
6690 Tsôwphach (2), *breath*

ZOPHAI
6689 Tsûwph (1), *honey-comb*

ZOPHAR
6691 Tsôwphar (4), *departing*

ZOPHIM
6839 Tsôphîym (1), *watchers*

ZORAH
6681 tsâvach (8), to *screech* exultingly

ZORATHITES
6882 Tsor'îy (1), *Tsorite* or *Tsorathite*

ZOREAH
6881 Tsor'âh (1), *stinging wasp*

ZORITES
6882 Tsor'îy (1), *Tsorite* or *Tsorathite*

ZOROBABEL
2216 Zŏrŏbabĕl (3), *from Babylon*

ZUAR
6686 Tsûw'âr (5), *small*

ZUPH
6689 Tsûwph (3), *honey-comb*

ZUR
6698 Tsûwr (5), *rock*

ZURIEL
6700 Tsûwrîy'êl (1), *rock of God*

ZURISHADDAI
6701 Tsûwrîyshadday (5), *rock of* (the) *Almighty*

ZUZIMS
2104 Zûwzîym (1), *prominent*

The Strong's Family of Products

CONCORDANCES

1. Classic Edition
Our Flagship volume, this edition sets the standard for all other concordances. Our number one best-selling reference book. This edition is truly exhaustive, with *Strong's* numbering system, easy-to-read modern type, a 200-page topical index, the famous Greek and Hebrew dictionaries, pronunciation guides, words of Christ highlighted, and Nelson's Fan-Tab Thumb Index system.
Hardcover / 1,824 pages / 0-7852-6750-1

2. Comfort Print Edition
Our Comfort Print Edition is the only truly enlarged-type exhaustive edition available! Newly typeset and updated, with corrected text throughout, this volume is a sight for sore eyes. Includes the famous Greek and Hebrew dictionaries, and Fan-Tab reference system.
Hardcover / 1,968 pages / 0-7852-2072-6

3. Portable/Super Value Edition
Same contents as our Comfort Print Edition, only in a smaller more portable size! Perfect for the classroom, Bible study group, or just to keep around the house, this edition has everything you want in a *Strong's Concordance,* in an easy-to-carry size!
Hardcover / 1,920 pages / 0-7852-1155-1

4. Concise Edition
A slightly trimmed-down version of the Classic Edition, both in size and content. It contains most of the word entries from the full-size edition, without the Greek and Hebrew dictionaries and *Strong's* numbering system. It does include Fan-Tab Thumb index reference system, easy-to-read typeface, and brief definitions and pronunciation guides for all proper names.
Paperback / 768 pages / 0-7852-1166-7

WORD STUDIES

5. Complete Dictionary of Bible Words
The famous *Strong's* dictionaries are now available in a fully corrected, updated version as a separate volume, in an enlarged, easy-to-read format. Includes a completely new and exclusive

English word index showing which Greek and Hebrew words are translated into specific English words, how often each translation occurs, and brief definitions.
Hardcover / 736 pages / 0-7852-1147-0

6. New Strong's Guide to Bible Words

Helps you get the full benefit of your current Bible study resources. This exclusive guide gives quick access to over 14,000 biblical words, showing Hebrew and Greek words that lie behind each English word, along with the number of times each occurs, Strong's numbers, and brief definitions. It belongs in the library of every owner of a *Strong's Exhaustive Concordance*.
Hardcover / 292 pages / 0-7852-1197-7

The Vine's Family of Products

Collected Writings of W. E. Vine—5-vol. set

All of W. E. Vine's writings are available in this 5-volume set. His writings on biblical studies and theology, his commentaries on selected Bible books and other topics, and his self-study Greek grammar are all here. Also available as individual volumes.

5-volume hardcover set / 0-7852-1159-4

Vine's Complete Expository Dictionary

This classic edition combines *Vine's Expository Dictionary of New Testament Words* with the *Expository Dictionary of the Old Testament* by M. F. Unger and W. White. Entries are coded to *Strong's Concordance,* to the *B-D-B Hebrew Lexicon* and the *Bauer-Arndt-Gingrich Greek Lexicon.*

Hardcover / 1,128 pages / 0-7852-7559-8

Vine's Complete Expository Dictionary with Topical Index

In addition to the features of the classic edition, above, a new Topical Index has been created to aid Bible study. It is organized so it can become at once a dictionary, a commentary, and a concordance.

Hardcover / 1,184 pages / 0-7852-1160-8

Vine's Expository Dictionary of Old and New Testament Words—Super Value Edition

This Super Value Edition offers the combination of Vine's *original* Old Testament dictionary and his New Testament dictionary. This is the most affordable edition of the famous dictionaries.

Hardcover / 912 pages / 0-7852-1181-0

Vine's Expository Commentary on Galatians
Vine's Expository Commentary on 1 & 2 Thessalonians

These small but thorough commentaries use an approach that takes into consideration every reference to particular words in the Bible—and their uses in ancient Greek—the language of the New Testament. The verse-by-verse word studies are in-depth commentaries on Galatians and the two epistles to the Thessalonians.

Hardcover / 224 pages / 0-7852-1172-1 (Galatians)
0-7852-1171-3 (1 & 2 Thessalonians)

Vine's Learn New Testament Greek

Designed especially for the layperson, this book is an easy "teach yourself" course for those who have no previous knowledge of Greek. Start by learning the Greek alphabet and by the third

lesson read directly from the Greek New Testament. Includes grammar, lessons, charts, tables, and diagrams—all created for self-study.
Paperback / 128 pages / 0-7852-1232-9

NQR Vine's Dictionary of Bible Words

Covers both Old and New Testament words in one easy-to-use A—Z listing, this compact size *Vine's* has the most-theologically significant and most-often consulted entries in the ultimate quick-reference resource. Keyed to *Strong's* reference numbers, each entry includes how the word is used, key Bible occurrences, English transliteration, and definitions. An exceptional value for studying the meaning of biblical words.
Paperback / 800 pages / 0-7852-1169-1